R. L. WILSON

THE OFFICIAL® PRICE GUIDE TO

GUN COLLECTING

R. L. WILSON

THE OFFICIAL® PRICE GUIDE TO

GUN COLLECTING

FIRST EDITION

HOUSE OF COLLECTIBLES
The Ballantine Publishing Group • New York

Important Notice. All of the information, including valuations, in this book has been compiled from the most reliable sources, and every effort has been made to eliminate errors and questionable data. Nevertheless, the possibility of error, in a work of such immense scope, always exists. The publisher will not be held responsible for losses that may occur in the purchase, sale, or other transaction of items because of information contained herein. Readers who feel they have discovered errors are invited to *write* and inform us, so they may be corrected in subsequent editions. Those seeking further information on the topics covered in this book are advised to refer to the complete line of *Official Price Guides* published by the House of Collectibles.

Published by: House of Collectibles
The Ballantine Publishing Group
201 East 50th Street
New York, NY 10022

Distributed by The Ballantine Publishing Group, a division of Random House, Inc., New York, and simultaneously in Canada by Random House of Canada Limited, Toronto.

http://www.randomhouse.com

Manufactured in the United States of America

ISSN: 1096-3960

ISBN: 0-676-60122-7

Text design by Holly Johnson
Cover design by Kristine V. Mills-Noble

First Edition: January 1998

10 9 8 7 6 5 4 3 2 1

Dedicated with Respect and Affection
to
William B. Ruger Sr.
Chairman of the Board and Founder
Sturm, Ruger & Co., Inc.
Inventor, Gun Designer, Gunmaker,
and Arms Collector

For the Pleasure He Has Brought
to
Millions of Sportsmen, Target and Recreational Shooters,
and Gun Collectors
Through His Unique Line
of
Fine Guns
and Advocacy of the Shooting and Outdoor Life

Contents

Acknowledgments

The author gratefully acknowledges the cooperation of the many who have helped make this publication possible:

To the staff at House of Collectibles, The Ballantine Publishing Group (a division of Random House), particularly Tim Kochuba, vice president; Simon Vukelj, marketing director; Randy Ladenheim-Gil, editor; Alex Klapwald, senior production manager; Cindy Berman, associate managing editor; and Roger Sperberg, database coordinator.

To Wm. "Pete" Harvey, dealer and auction house owner, for the benefit of his years of experience and knowledge of the immense field of firearms, of all periods and types, and of their values. His help in arriving at prices has proven of particular importance and is greatly appreciated.

To Martin J. Lane, for innumerable favors and assistance, for several crucial insights into his own experience in the firearms field, for assistance in collecting photographs, and for numerous assists over the years on this book and other projects. And to his staff at United Protective Security Systems and his Martin Lane Historical Americana Gallery, New York City, particularly Dominick Cervone, Mary Campion, Phil Kolman, Jim Judge, Joseph and Pearl Lane, and Susan Wisner.

To my gifted and innovative agent, Peter Riva, and his wife and colleague, Sandy, for their mastery of the publishing world, and for guiding the author's career to publishers the likes of Ballantine, Random House, Simon & Schuster, and Abbeville Press.

To Stephen Fjestad, Bill Rooney, and John Allen of Blue Book Publishing, for their role in the author's series of columns developed for *Gun Journal*, and for permission to draw on some of this material for the present volume.

To Robert M. Lee, founder and president, Hunting World, Inc., for his inspiration, cooperation, and assistance. His dedicated connoisseurship continues to play a vital role in setting a new standard of excellence in the arms field. To Anne Brockinton, Scott Bergan, and the Hunting World and Deeside Trading Co. staffs, for their help, support, and interest.

To the late George A. Strichman, chairman of the board, Colt Industries, for his unstinting support of the author's studies over the years.

To Alvin A. White for his ongoing education of the author (from 1961) in the rarefied realm of the arms engraver, and of—as he so uniquely knows—the world of the all-around craftsman in decorative arts. And to Andrew Bourbon, Daniel Cullity, Denise Thirion, and John Adams Sr. and John Adams Jr., for the insights on the gunmaking arts they have shared with the author.

To William B. Ruger Sr. and the talented staff at Sturm, Ruger & Co., Inc., for the wisdom unique to their firm, which has impacted significantly all the writer's work during and following completion of *Ruger & His Guns*.

To John R. Woods Jr., NRA Foundation president, and H. Wayne Sheets, executive director, and to Wilson Phillips, treasurer, National Rifle Association of America, for their dedication to public education on firearms subjects, for their support of the author's projects over the years, and for their roles in creating the R. L. Wilson Educational Endowment of the NRA Foundation.

To Greg and Petra Martin, and Greta, for their cordiality during the author's period of being sequestered in San Francisco while completing this tome.

To Peter Buxtun, not only for his hospitality while the author was escaping from his office in Connecticut in order to complete the manuscript for this book, but for his own insights and extensive files shedding light on the captivating universe of firearms.

To Gene and Jackie Autry, Monte and Joanne Hale, and James and Mary Ellen Hennessey Nottage, and to the staff of the Autry Museum of Western Heritage, for their devoted and imaginative presentation of historic firearms, including the George and Sandi Strichman Colt Collection.

To Guy Wilson, director of the Royal Armouries Museum (Leeds) and Master of the Armouries, H.M. Tower of London, and to Graeme Rimer, Keeper of Weapons, for their continued support of the concept of "The Art of American Arms" and "The Arms of Tiffany" traveling loan exhibitions. And to Paul Rovetti, director emeritus, the William Benton Museum of Art, University of Connecticut, and to Larry Doherty, president, Fine Arts Express, and to Peter Tillou of Peter Tillou Fine Arts, for their efforts on behalf of those projects.

Special appreciation to the following officials of Colt Industries, Colt Firearms Division, and to the present Colt's Mfg. Co., Inc.: Donald Zilkha, chairman of the board; Ronald L. Stewart, president; former presidents Gary W. French and C. E. Warner; Al DeJohn; Jackie Frascarelli; Kathleen Hoyt (Historian); R. H. Wagner; M. S. Huber; Beverly Jean Rhodes; Monika E. C. Uber; and Edie Ocampo, and to former Colt Industries, New York, executives Guy C. Shafer, John F. Campbell, and Peter C. Williamson, and to George A. Strichman's secretary, Virginia Macho.

To Peter Hawkins, David Williams, Christopher Austyn, and Natasha Hanscomb of Christie's Arms and Armour and Gun departments, in both London and New York, over the years.

To Gary Reynolds, whose Hamburg Cove emporium has served as a point of rejuvenation and inspiration for the author, for his assistance in collecting firearms and illustrations.

To the many additional collectors, dealers, museum curators, engravers, and others who have generously supplied the author with literally thousands of photographs and reams of information on American and European arms.

To a myriad of dealers and collectors, all friends of the author, some dating back to the 1950s: Robert E. Petersen, Herb Glass and Herb Glass Jr., John Gangel, Fred Sweeney, George S. Lewis Jr., Michael Zomber, David Condon, Richard Ellis, Mike Clark, Ronald A. Ogan, Tom Wibberley, Bernard Braverman, Norm Flayderman, Jack Malloy, Monte Whitley, John Jones (CIA Investments), Buck Stevens, Richard P. Mellon, Walter B. Ford III, Mrs. John B. Solley III, Jerry D. Berger, David S. Woloch, Rene Delcour, John Amicucci, John Hovaness Hintlian, Howard L. Blackmore, Claude Blair, William Reid, Donald Stika, Buddy Hackett, Michael V. Korda, Don Wilkerson, Albert and Paula Brichaux, James U. Blanchard III, James B. Smith, Richard Ulbrich, William Guthman, Tony Lamb, Harry H. Sefried II, Reggie Pearce and Mardel Lyon, Dr. Paul R. McCombs, A. T. Seymour III, Horace Greeley IV, R. B. Berryman, Conor Fitzgerald, Charles Ruger, Alexander Vogel, Carolyn R. Vogel, Craddock Goins, William E. Simon, John G. Hamilton, George L. Deal Sr. and George L. Deal Jr., Dr. Chester P. Bonoff, Roy G. Jinks, Mrs. James E. Serven, Mrs. L. C. Jackson, Thomas Haas, Jonathan M. Peck, John S. duMont, Lynton S. M. McKenzie, David Winks, Dr. R. L. Moore Jr., William H. Myers, N. Brigham and Louise Pemberton, Glode M. Requa, Joseph G. Rosa, Charles Schreiner III, Larry Sheerin, Andrew Singer, G. Maxwell Longfield, M.D., George Taylor, Dennis Levette, Chris deGuigne IV, Ira Weinstein, William Hosley, Karen Blanchfield, Bernard Osher and John Gallo of Butterfield & Butterfield, and that master finder of fine guns and fellow vintage automobile racer *extraordinaire*, Hans W. Schemke.

A special tribute to the memory of the following, now deceased, who played a role in the evolution of the author's gun-collecting career over the years: Hans Barthel, Johnie Bassett, Charles L. Bricker, Arnold M. Chernoff, Dr. Robert G. Cox, C. C. Cunningham, Gaines deGraffenried, Stanley Diefenthal, Jack Dutton, Hugh J. Fitzgerald, Gerald G. Fox, Glenn Gierhart, William H. Goldbach, Karl Glahn, Stephen V. Grancsay, Barry Gray, Herbert E. Green, Robert E. Hable, Jim Hoiby, Benjamin F. Hubbell, Lew Hutcheson, L. C. Jackson, Harry C. Knode, Merrill K. Lindsay, John Jarvis, Mr. and Mrs. William M. Locke, Dr. Richard C. Marohn, Miss E. B. McCormick, A. I. McCroskie, Mrs. William D. Maver, Henry P. Maynard, John E. Parsons, Harold L. Peterson, Philip R. Phillips, H. A. Redfield, Fred A. Roff Jr., James E. Serven, Clare F. Short, Samuel E. Smith, John B. Solley III, William Otis Sweet, Dr. Leonid Tarassuk, Thomas A. Thornber, Arno Werner, Hermann Warner Williams Jr., and Dr. John M. Wilson Sr.

With thanks to the following photographers, and a salute to their artistry, imagination, patience, and skills:

Peter Beard, Tom Beiswenger, E. Irving Blomstrann, G. Alan Brown, Susan Einstein, Richard Ellis, Roger Fuhr (Roland Design), Harrington-Olson, Gus Johnson, Sid Latham, Meyers Studio, Inc., Rick Oltmans, Louise Pemberton, Bruce Pendleton, Beau Pierce, Ed Prentiss, Douglas Sandberg, Phil Spangenberger, S. P. Stevens, David Wesbrook, and Christopher T. Wilson.

To Mark K. Benenson and the members of the board of the National Foundation for Firearms Education, headquartered in New York City, for their role in public education on firearms matters.

To Richard M. O'Neill, Judi Glover, and staff at MBI, Inc., for the opportunity to research and write the "America's Greatest Firearms Patches" Program, in conjunction with the NRA's 125th Anniversary year. And for permission to draw on this material within the present volume.

To marketing whiz Jeffrey Starr and his energetic and perceptive wife, Carolyn, for their encouragement of the author over the years, and for inspired insights on the fine art of selling books and other products.

To Barbara Cromeenes, the author's longtime secretary and assistant, who patiently deals with countless details, deadlines, double- and triple-checking, follow-ups, emergencies, the seemingly endless wrapping and shipping of books by the ton, and making sure nothing goes undone.

And finally, with special thanks to the author's loyal and patient family: Heidi and Neal, Heather and Peter (and their new baby), Christopher and Stephen, all of them keen on firearms, and each knowing the joy of a day in the field or at the range, or hours at home, in museums and in art and auction galleries, admiring the creations of the dedicated craftsmen who have made—and are making—the firearms we all enjoy.

—R. L. Wilson
Castle View
Hadlyme, Connecticut
May 1, 1997

Preface

In the multifaceted world of collecting, there are endless themes for the enthusiast to pursue: paintings, drawings, prints, and other two-dimensional art and artifacts, and the vast domain of the three-dimensional: sculpture, decorative arts, the world of "kitsch," matchbooks, ashtrays, *ad infinitum*. Devoted to these specialties are collectors' clubs, buy-sell-trade meets and shows, magazines, newspapers, and even TV shows (like the *Antiques Road Show* on PBS), mail-order companies, and the relatively new medium available to millions: the Internet. When a mainstream magazine like *Forbes* has its own collectors' column, and when *Time* magazine gives the collecting world cover stories, then you know this extraordinary universe has truly arrived.

It is this author's contention that the realm of the arms collector easily ranks at or certainly near the pinnacle of the most fascinating of all fields of collecting. We arms enthusiasts cover the complete history of man, from the beginning. Weapons were crucial for survival in the Stone Age, and although not universally essential for survival in modern times, they bring immense pleasure to countless millions. Going beyond the world of the arms collector, firearms also encompass satellite interests, as expressed in the author's dedication to the NRA Foundation in the book *Steel Canvas*:

> Collectors, curators, historians, antiquarians, sport-, target-, and silhouette-handgun shooters, local club marksmen through Olympic-level international competitors, gunsmiths, engravers, trap-, skeet-, and sporting clay-shotgun shooters, historical reenactors, muzzle loading devotees, air-gun and pellet shooters, handloaders and cartridge enthusiasts

And any person from those satellites might experience the transition to becoming a collector, loosely translated as one who accumulates with a purpose, and—usually—a passion.

An arms collector is usually born, that is, he started by collecting something; in the author's case, it was coins, accumulated at first from payments collected from customers on his *Minneapolis Star and Tribune* paper route. Somehow that collecting instinct led to firearms.

The collecting appeal of firearms objects is multifaceted, more so than any other field of collecting: It encompasses art and craftsmanship, history, mechanics, performance, and romance. As an indication of this deep and abiding interest, consider the fact that as of this date the existing literature on firearms numbers approximately 10,000 books and countless issues of magazines—with more coming out on a regular basis.

Still another factor to consider: the scale of guns. Unlike cars or many other collector passions, a gun is generally of a size that allows handling, transporting, taking apart, and otherwise enjoying. Unlike a car, which requires a garage or, for a large collection, a warehouse, a large gun collection can be kept in a safe, in a closet, or under a bed!

THE MAKING OF AN ARMS COLLECTOR

Many times a collector has come from the ranks of active shooters, such as hunters. One member of the Mellon banking family became a keen arms collector, but his first interest was sparked by hunting. Young Mellon was led to the antiquarian world under the astute guidance of legendary shotgun-shooting champion Rudy Etchen and pistol-shooting champion and antique-arms dealer Herb Glass.

As the collector becomes increasingly consumed by his fascination with firearms, he begins to branch out. Needing to research a particular item, he often becomes a bibliophile. Documenting an arm means poring not only through books, but often through the world of photographs, and sometimes paintings, drawings, or other artwork. To learn about a particular historical figure may require investigating genealogies and other unpublished sources. If the historical figure was involved in the Revolutionary War, the Mountain Man period, or the Wild West of Jesse James, Wyatt Earp, and Doc Holliday, or in any number of other eras, themes, or events, the collector soon becomes knowledgeable in those subjects as well.

Perhaps due to a special exhibit at his or her home or office, the collector will become familiar with methods of displaying artifacts, with lighting, with fabrics, with design and presentation. Sometimes collectors are more up-to-date with advanced techniques, like fiber optics, than are professionals in the museum field. The exhibit or research trail may well lead to the world of autograph collecting, to the history of photography, to the circus and Wild West shows (e.g., Buffalo Bill and Annie Oakley), to memorabilia, costumes, badges, and any number of other interests. In the author's own research for special exhibitions, books, detailed research on particular arms, and so forth, there is barely a field of collectibles that he has not examined. In fact, he enjoys attending a book fair, or visiting an autograph dealer, or attending a general antiques fair, even touring a country house, almost as much as one of his favorite enthusiasms: attending a show dedicated to arms collecting.

The author's pathway through the universe of art and antiques always returns to his pivotal dedication to the world of firearms. Janet Zapata, formerly Archivist at Tiffany & Co., and an expert in the associated world of silver, has said that of all the different types of collectors she has met over the years, the arms collectors have been consistently the most interesting—and more likely to be able to speak with authority on a broader range of subjects than collectors from any other specialty. My old friend Norm Flayderman, a dealer in arms for nearly fifty years, is probably as knowledgeable on any subject as any person one could meet in a lifetime. His primary consuming passion, of course, is firearms. And when Norm suffered from a brain tumor in his sixties, his love of life and of his collecting passions were instrumental in his complete recovery!

Thus, the firearms field is not only totally captivating, but it is invigorating and stimulating. Having made a comfortable living from a dedication to the field of arms collecting for nearly forty years, the author can honestly say that he feels he has never "worked" a day in his life—it's been fun all the way, and he wouldn't trade places with anyone on earth. He has no intention of ever retiring, and likes to quote gunmaker, inventor, designer, and arms, art, and automobile collector William B. Ruger: "When you rest, you rust."

CELEBRITY ARMS ENTHUSIASTS

Far more people are keen on firearms and their responsible uses than is generally thought, even by analysts in the arms field. This immense fraternity of men and women comes from all walks of life, and from virtually every sphere of human interest and lifestyle. From bankers, lawyers, doctors, and politicians to film, TV, and rock stars, to priests and other clerics, to secretaries and insurance salesmen—from the lowliest of voters and nonvoters to (sometimes, but sadly *not* just now) presidents of the United States—and from the most leftwing of liberals to the most rightwing of conservatives, *ad infinitum*. Gun collectors may be screaming leftwing liberals, moderates, or rightwingers, but what they generally are not is of the socialist bent—capitalism is definitely the drumbeat to which nearly all arms collectors march.

Consider this list of enthusiasts, some shooters, some collectors, some hunters, some just plinkers, some keen on the craftsmanship or the mechanics or the artistry, or the performance, or even the precise discipline of hand loading or target shooting: Ronald Lauder (younger son of cosmetics tycoon Estée Lauder), John Entwhistle (bass guitarist of The Who), actresses Cybill Shepherd and Sharon Stone, financier Henry Kravis, Arnold Schwarzenegger, Sylvester Stallone, the British royal family, race driver Jackie Stewart, Frank Sinatra, Jerry Lewis, Dan Aykroyd, *ad infinitum*. For still more names, see the chapter titled "A Noble Tradition: A History of Arms Collecting," page 11.

Gun collecting is a crucial element in the seemingly endless battle against those who dismiss all guns as simply "made to kill" and "without socially redeeming value." Gun collectors represent a relatively small group in number, but form potentially the most powerful of all firearms groups in terms of access and influence where it counts. Further, gun collectors present the reality of scholarship, of careful, dedicated, and enthusiastic studies of the art and craftsmanship, history, mechanics, and romance of fine guns.

"PETE" HARVEY AND THE VALUES IN THIS BOOK

One of the best-known figures in firearms, William "Pete" Harvey has been active in the field since 1944, first as a collector and later as a collector/dealer, and then as president of one of the world's leading auction houses specializing in all types of firearms. A member of numerous arms collectors' organizations, Pete was instrumental in setting up the auction for the first NRA Gun Collectors Show and Conference, in Nashville, 1996. Operation of the Wm. "Pete"

Author, left, *with Wm. "Pete" Harvey, whose assistance helped in determining values in the* Price Guide.

Harvey Auction Service, Inc., began full-time in 1993. Prior to that Pete had been in partnership with another New England auction house since 1987, and had worked with the Richard Bourne Co., auctioneers, from the mid-1970s.

An experienced sportsman, collector, and widely recognized expert, having handled virtually every type of firearm known to collectors, shooters, and enthusiasts in general, Pete is uniquely qualified to play a key role in corroboration of the values presented in the *Price Guide*, and will continue to do so as the book continues to be refined in future editions.

The author has known Pete since the early 1960s, and when taking on the contract to do the *Price Guide*, immediately thought of calling on his expertise. Certainly an important part of the pleasure of doing this complex project has been to work with a professional of the stature of Pete Harvey.

A WONDERFUL OPPORTUNITY

The Official Price Guide to Gun Collecting has offered a wonderful opportunity to the writer. Because the work not only provides values and identifications for a broad range of firearms, it is also designed to introduce readers to the incredible world of guns. And it's designed to do so in a way that will appeal, we fervently hope, not only to novices, but to the old-timers who think that, perhaps, they've "been there and done that" in this field.

This book will be in a state of evolution throughout its lifetime. The subject of collectors firearms is too vast for the work to evolve in any other way. Each year's edition, therefore, will present a fresh "The Year in Review" section. Each edition will have additional information in a variety of sections and on a variety of subjects, as dealers, collector/dealers, and collectors help with more material, and as the author continues his never-ending quest for fresh data and illustrations. Updated values, of course, will continue to be a paramount feature of each of these new editions.

So, look for the 1999 edition to appear in the fall of 1998, with more than enough new facts and observations, and illustrations, to satisfy the most demanding of gun devotees.

The author looks upon each new *Official Price Guide to Gun Collecting* as if it were a totally new book—and will be striving to make each and every edition full of surprises, and the most exciting and informative new book in the world of gun collecting every year. We feel strongly that a first-class basic firearms library, for any collector, dealer, collector/dealer, historian, gun crank, or whatever, should contain, at the least, *Flayderman's Guide to Antique American Firearms and their Values*, S. P. Fjestad's *Blue Book of Gun Values*, Stoeger's *The Shooter's Bible*, Ken Warner's *The Gun Digest*, and (of course) the author's *Price Guide to Gun Collecting*. To go beyond these basic titles, the author's further suggestions are in the detailed bibliography on pages 425–434.

As a freelance writer and antiquarian, and one fortunate enough to travel extensively, I've had the opportunity to meet tens of thousands of people from a great many different spheres of influence. It is no understatement that in virtually every such sphere there are persons keen on firearms. One thing a professional in the arms-collecting world quickly realizes nearly every day is that this business is so vast that no one knows it all, or has done it all! And that's part of the excitement, adventure, and appeal. I cannot wait to get started every day, and all-night sessions on a manuscript or other project are not unusual—sometimes it's hard to put on the brakes and stop for some rest!

I am honored to be a part of this international fraternity of dedicated enthusiasts. In every single article and book ever written in my forty-seven years in this field (the first piece was on King Henry VIII's "gonne shields" in the National Muzzle Loading Rifle Association's *Muzzle Blasts* magazine), my excitement for this incredible subject has remained keen.

Good collecting, and remember, you can never have too many good guns!

Note: The author is continually collecting photographs and information on the subject of collectors firearms, and the history and art of collecting. For anyone wishing to share pictures or information, the author can be contacted at P.O. Box 430, Hadlyme, Connecticut 06439. As a professional in the field, he also evaluates firearms and collections on a fee basis. His specialties include rare American arms, guns of the West, and engraving.

Introduction:
The Season in Review, 1996–97

For someone lucky enough to be able to work full time in the incredible world of guns and gun collecting, 1996–97 proved an extraordinary period to digest. Gun auctions and gun shows continued to evolve and were in a constant state of refinement, publications continued to flow, prices and values continued generally to escalate, the availability of many collectors' arms continued to increase in scarcity (and thus in desirability), and there were more and more collectors seeking pieces than there were pieces to buy.

On the other hand, the modern gun business (with a few exceptions, like best-quality custom guns) took a nosedive following the tragic event in Oklahoma City, when a federal office building was blown up by a terrorist truck-bomb attack. Although no firearms were involved in this calamity, somehow the gun lobby was tainted by the deed, partly due to the fact that the perpetrator had been known to frequent gun shows. The good news is that Charlton Heston was elected First Vice President of the NRA, a moderating factor that should prove crucial in improving the public image of the organization.

POST–WORLD WAR II DAYS OF GUN COLLECTING

The author can remember the 1950s and 1960s, when it seemed that important collectors firearms would turn up at nearly every gun show, and that his own "finds" would occur a half dozen or more times per year. Today, collectors and dealers are finding it increasingly difficult to get fresh material; good "stock" is harder and harder to locate. The author jokingly refers to his own role as an amateur of arms as one who plays the "gunstock market," rather than the stock market. But unlike in the stock market, there is often no gun stock to buy! Give a dealer $1,000,000 and ask him to find one of the "superguns," like a rare presentation deluxe Colt percussion revolver with gold inlaid decoration, and the chances are a million to one against his being able to do it. Even lesser rarities, from many sub-specialties within arms collecting, are simply not findable. For the really good material, today is truly a seller's market.

COMPETITION BETWEEN AUCTION HOUSES AND DEALERS

Gun shows are still very active, though in some instances the material offered is recycled from an auction, having been freshly purchased by a dealer—who may have difficulty obtaining stock through conventional means.

The resulting competition among dealers and auction houses has enlivened the business, helping to make firearms among the hottest collectibles of the 1990s. Many of the new auction houses in the arms field are actually the result of dealers realizing that auctions are presently dominating the field—and that starting their own galleries was one way to deal with the phenomenon.

Two dealers who publish some of the most handsome and comprehensive catalogues are Walt Moreau and Norm Flayderman; each publication is available at a reasonable fee. Moreau is also represented in the world of cyberspace, with his America Online site (wmoreau130@aol.com) and his Internet domain (moreau.com). He also serves as editor of *The Rampant Colt*, the quarterly publication of the Colt Collectors Association. Flayderman, widely known in the antique arms and collectibles field and publisher of numerous uniquely learned catalogues, had yet another edition, his 118th, appearing in the late spring of 1997. Flayderman's *Guide to American Antique Firearms and Their Values* continues to be one of the most useful and detailed antique arms books ever published, and in 1998 will enter its seventh edition.

Just judging from the author's ever-increasing collection of catalogues by auctioneers and dealers, as well as advertisements in numerous publications, and the consistent increase in prices and values, the field of collectors firearms has never been healthier than at present.

BUTTERFIELD & BUTTERFIELD LEADS THE WAY

There is no denying that in the United States at present Butterfield & Butterfield occupies the dominant position in arms collectors' auctions. Directed by Greg Martin, who is generally recognized as the leading auction figure and dealer in the arms business today (and one of the top collectors as well), the San Francisco–based firm has captured such prime business as the Charles Bremner Hogg Jackson Collection (consigned by the Smithsonian Institution's National Museum of American History), the Dr. Richard C. Marohn Collection of Colt Lightning Revolvers and John Wesley Hardin guns and memorabilia, the George R. Repaire Colt Collection, the John K. Watson Jr. U.S. Martial Collection, and the Lowenstein Colt Collection. In 1996 alone, Butterfield sold more than $20 million in collectors firearms, making that the largest-grossing and the most profitable of the firm's departments.

In the spring of 1997, Butterfield's captured an amazing amount of publicity from the sale of the bullet-riddled shirt of the notorious Depression-era folk figure and bandit Clyde Barrow, consigned by his younger sister. Approximately 400 newspapers around the United States and Canada carried the story of how such artifacts as the shirt, guns, and a watch grossed more money than the outlaw, with his girlfriend Bonnie Parker, had managed to steal in all their bank jobs and other stickups!

COMPETITORS TO BUTTERFIELD & BUTTERFIELD

Other auction houses, however, were holding their own: Little John's (John Gangel) held several sales, as did Brad Witherell's Americana Auctions, Jeff Faintich, Rock Island Auction Co., Jim Supica, and the Eastern contingent of David Condon, Inc., J. C. Devine, Inc., Wm. "Pete" Harvey, and James D. Julia, Inc.—to name but a few of the most active. The point is: There has been plenty of business for everyone.

A new auction house has just been established by Martin Lane (one of the leading antique arms dealers and collectors in the field today): Bannerman's. Located in New York City, this new organization has revived the historic name of a firm that was the leading source of fine guns and militaria for generations of collectors. A legend in the arms field, the original Bannerman's operated on a worldwide basis for approximately a century, established in the Civil War era by a wily Scotsman (who had a castle, now a landmark ruin, built on his own island in the Hudson River). Martin Lane's plan is to revive and energize the grand traditions of the old company. Appropriately, the new Bannerman's is located only blocks away from the site of the original, at 589 Broadway.

EUROPEAN AND BRITISH AUCTION HOUSES AND DEALERS

Meanwhile, in England, Sotheby's, Christie's, Wallis & Wallis, and Weller & Dufty carried on with their own departments in antique arms and armor, and in vintage and modern sporting arms. The future of gun collecting in Great Britain, however, is presently very much in doubt. That sad and illogical state of affairs is due to the hysterical reaction by the press and the public in the wake of the "Dunblaine Massacre," in which a mentally deranged man murdered several schoolchildren and their teacher in Scotland. Rather than accepting the report of a special commission that recommended a reasonable response to the tragedy, socialist politicians (with little resistance from the Tories) used the issue as a political football. Those same socialists wrested control from the conservatives, and the victory might well spell the doom for *all* guns in the U.K. Time alone will tell.

At the least, one would hope that this negative state of affairs would not affect the collecting of antique and obsolete arms. The colorful illustrated catalogues of Peter Finer, spectacular, scholarly, and brimming with rarities spanning several centuries, rival or surpass the vast majority of heavily illustrated books on collectors firearms. The published collection is offered for sale. Clients can contact Finer via e-mail, and can view his arms and armor on his Internet web page (http://www.peterfiner.com). The third edition of this handsome series of books was published in the summer of 1997.

One of the auction houses visited by the author in 1996 was that of Fischer, in Lucerne, Switzerland. The high level of interest was clearly evident by the packed salesroom, like a veritable United Nations of collectors and dealers. The material was accurately described, and featured not only what one would expect in Europe—European arms and armor—but quite a bit of Americana. There I met the proud owner of one of the greatest rarities in American Western collectibles—a Single Action Army known to have been carried by one of Custer's command at the Battle of the Little Big Horn! The auctioneer and the audience's dedication and knowledge at this sale were an indication of the ever-growing worldwide community of arms collectors.

DEALERS REMAIN ACTIVE

As also reflected by lists of auction houses, the list of dealers presented in Appendix 4 is a reflection of the fact that there remains plenty of business for those who wish to work at the collectible firearms business. Any one of these professionals can attest to the fact that the business is healthier now than it has ever been. Although good guns are increasingly hard to find, nevertheless the number of keen collectors continues to increase, and there will always be the turnover of collectors whose estates need to be settled through sales, or whose guns are to be sold due to divorce, debt, or simply the movement to another subject of collecting (recycling, as it were).

Among the extraordinary pieces sold through dealers in this past season were a gold-inlaid and engraved Colt Single Action Army (by Helfricht), a cased Second Model Dragoon in near-new condition, a Winchester Model 1873 Serial No. 3 (Nimschke engraved, and finished in a combination of nickel-, silver-, and gold-plating, bluing, and case-hardening), the magnificent and historic Colt Lightning .22 rifle presented to Dr. Longstreet by the Kickapoo Medicine encampment, an exquisite pair of deluxe embellished (including enameled) Colt No. 3 derringer pistols, a cased Texas Paterson Colt revolver with extra twelve-inch barrel—and a limited number of the finest in Kentucky Rifles, a few great Kentucky pistols, and not a few European wheelock and flintlock firearms.

PRE-1934 SMOOTHBORE PISTOLS COMING INTO THEIR OWN

Smoothbore pistols that were commercially manufactured in or before 1934 have come into their own as unique historical artifacts. For many years, confusion and controversy have surrounded the ownership of these guns.

Eric M. Larson's special piece on these arms will be found on pages 56–59. Firearms researcher Larson summarizes the history of how these unusual firearms came to be manufactured, largely as sporting firearms, and then inappropriately regulated as "gangster weapons" under the National Firearms Act of 1934.

It appears that there may be a resolution in sight regarding the problems collectors have experienced in legally owning these guns. Watch for the 1998 edition of the *Price Guide*, as well as the writings of Eric Larson in various publications, for updates on this issue.

RUSSIA AND THE EASTERN BLOC COUNTRIES

It is still too early to come to any conclusions about the future of firearms, whether collecting, hunting, or any of the many other facets of the industry and business, in the former Eastern Bloc. Suffice it to say, however, that their totalitarian traditions might preclude general and reasonably supervised private ownership of firearms, as in the U.S. However, since our view is that freedom is a prerequisite to gun ownership, and vice versa, one is hopeful that these countries will institute reasonable government supervision of gun ownership, unlike the severe restrictions that were among the instruments relied upon by the Soviets to remain in power.

Navy Arms founder Val Forgett has already established an office in Moscow, working with a former highly placed government official. Considering the vast quantities of firearms shipped into Russia in Czarist days by such firms as Colt, Smith & Wesson, Winchester, and Remington, there are tons of guns in Russia, and certainly no small number in other Eastern Bloc countries. It was in fact Czechoslovakia in which Dr. Nolfo diCarpegna discovered, in 1961, an original gold-inlaid Colt Model 1849 Pocket revolver, evidently shipped for display in Europe as a sample of Colt's gunmaking expertise. Some of the finest American presentation arms went to European rulers and other dignitaries. Where is, for example, the exquisitely decorated Smith & Wesson Russian Model revolver given by the factory to the Grand Duke Alexis in Springfield, Massachusetts, in December 1871, on his tour of the U.S.? The revolver cost the factory $400—a small fortune in those days. According to a local press report at the time, the "elegant pistol, inlaid with gold [by Gustave Young, had a] pearl butt upon which were the coat of arms of America and Russia and [enclosed] into a rosewood case, bearing the inscription 'From S & W to A.A.' " His Grace died in Paris in the 1890s; what lucky collector might find this extraordinary rarity—one of the finest handguns ever made!

GEORGE AND BUTONNE REPAIRE DONATE THE SULTAN OF TURKEY COLT DRAGOON CASED SET TO THE METROPOLITAN MUSEUM OF ART

In the world of fine arts, a truly important painting is recognized by a nickname, like da Vinci's "The Last Supper" and Gainsborough's "The Blue Boy." For truly distinguished specimens in the firearms field, the same practice applies. And such is the case with the magnificent "Sultan of Turkey Dragoon." This exquisite cased revolver, bearing serial number 12406, was originally the mate to number 12407, the former a presentation to the Sultan of Turkey, the latter to the Russian Czar Nicholas I.

Both the "Sultan of Turkey" and the "Czar Nicholas" revolvers were richly engraved and inlaid with gold. Colonel Samuel Colt's gift to the Sultan of Turkey was presented c. 1854. Long after the presentation, the cased set was discovered in Istanbul c. 1967 by a British arms collector, Robin Braid-Taylor. The saga of the Sultan was the subject of articles by the author in the "Gun of the Month" feature of the July 1997 issue of *Gun Journal*, as well as the Spring 1997 issue of *The Rampant Colt* (journal of the Colt Collectors Association).

To paraphrase briefly from the former article, from

George and Butonne Repaire, at the first gun show held at the Danville Hotel, East Bay, near San Francisco, c. 1964. The Repaires' donation of the Sultan of Turkey Colt Third Model Dragoon to the Metropolitan Museum of Art, in 1995, was a landmark event in the history of arms collecting. Photograph by Peter Buxtun.

time to time the author had the opportunity to discuss the future of the Sultan of Turkey with the Repaires, owners since 1973, and to encourage their interest in the Metropolitan Museum of Art becoming recipient of the set.

A Quiet Offer, and Finally, the Gift

A prominent collector visited the Repaires' California residence in an attempt to purchase the outfit. Despite an offer that stunned the couple, they steadfastly refused to consider the revolver's sale.

The urging of Butonne Repaire continued, along with my reminder to George that the Metropolitan would never lose its keen desire to own the Sultan's treasure. I remember telling him that curator Stuart Pyhrr wanted the set more than anything and that its addition to the museum's collections would be a triumph for the Arms and Armor Department, and especially for the newly endowed Robert M. Lee Gallery of American Arms.

Like a thunderbolt, Stuart received his wish: Out of the blue, George called to advise that the Repaires had decided to *donate* the Sultan of Turkey Dragoon to the Metropolitan, at no charge whatsoever. Stuart was thrilled, and when he called to tell me the grand news it was clearly evident that this was one of the most exciting moments in the history of the collecting of fine guns in our own experience.

The first public display of the new donation also coincided with the release of the writer's book, *Steel Canvas: The Art of American Arms*. How appropriate that this magnificent revolver, featured significantly in that volume, was placed on permanent display at the Metropolitan (in the Robert M. Lee Gallery) on the same day as the book signing party in December 1995 (at Bob Lee's New York Hunting World store).

It was equally exciting to call the Repaires and congratulate them for their extraordinary generosity. George explained that they had decided the Sultan was too important to remain in private hands, that the Metropolitan was not only the ideal home for the set but the *only home*, that curator Stuart Pyhrr and the museum staff would display and care for the treasure as it deserved, and that the money from a sale was not as important to them as the pleasure of doing the right thing.

Interestingly, George also indicated that some of their relatives in Ohio had failed to understand the merit of the Repaires' gun-collecting interests. The donation of the Sultan to the world's greatest art museum finally impressed upon them the significance of the Repaire Collection.

As donors of the Sultan—unquestionably the crown jewel in the museum's collection of American arms—the Repaires' names are chiseled in marble in the grand staircase leading up to the main galleries, joining such luminaries as J. P. Morgan, the Havemeyers, the Vanderbilts, Walter Annenberg, and Henry Kravis.

The 1996 edition of the Metropolitan's *Journal* featured an essay by Stuart Pyhrr on the Sultan of Turkey's artistic merits, and pictured the revolver in brilliant color.

The Sultan of Turkey Colt Dragoon is also highly significant in being the mate to the Czar Nicholas I revolver, arguably the finest American firearm in any of the European national, imperial, or private collections. Great guns like these stand as convincing evidence in support of the increasingly widespread view that fine guns rival masterworks in any field of decorative arts.

QUEEN ELIZABETH II OPENS THE ROYAL ARMOURIES MUSEUM IN LEEDS, YORKSHIRE, ENGLAND

Eight years and $75 million in the making, the Royal Armouries Museum was opened by Queen Elizabeth II on March 15, 1996, with pageantry and pomp unequaled in the opening of any arms-related museum in history. Immediately, the institution established itself as the premier arms and armor museum in the world.

The Royal Armouries, for centuries headquartered at the Tower of London, had long been squeezed for exhibition space, and was drawing no income from the millions of paying visitors to the Tower. With a priceless collection of over 15,000 guns and a total of over 50,000 objects (only 10 percent of which were ever on public view), Master of the Armouries Guy Wilson and his trustees and staff were faced with a dilemma: find a new site in the U.K., and fund this in a significant way with private-sector money.

The historic and ancient city of Leeds is but a quick flight from London and only two hours by train, and the new museum is a ten-minute cab ride from the Leeds station. On a thirteen-acre site, the 14,399.5-square-meter, six-floor-high complex will not only thrill the most traveled of arms and armor enthusiasts, it is a presentation on a scale and with such merit that visitors need not even have an interest in the subject to be totally captivated. The building itself, by world-renowned architect Derek Walker, has been hailed by *The Times* of London as a "landmark building" in which "history had to live as well as entertain. . . . [and] the plan of these galleries should give coherence to the display by showing how arms have evolved down the centuries, from the bows and arrows of 1066 to the nuclear bomb."

The Royal Armouries Museum presents exhibits of centuries of weaponry and armor, audiovisual wizardry, live demonstrations of theatrical quality, and more, to give the place star quality as part museum, part theater, and part interactive technology—all of it absolute magic. Interactive technology is highlighted, with touch-screen computers and more than forty specially commissioned films and computer programs. Live demonstrations offer gunmaking and shooting demonstrations, sword duels, falconry, and military processions, as well as armored knights battling on foot and jousting on horseback. Visitors can shoot crossbows and longbows, and fire rifles geared to hit their targets electronically. A menagerie presents falcons, hawks, dogs, and horses that are worked in traditional fashion in the outdoor Tiltyard.

The displays and the live and computer action are divided into galleries of war, the tournament, hunting, self-defense, and Oriental arms, as well as themes including education, crafts, media treatment of arms-related subjects ("The Newsroom"), animals in the world of arms, and a unique six-story "Hall of Steel" with a myriad of guns, swords, armor, and other instruments.

In her inaugural speech, Queen Elizabeth II recognized the art of the gunmaker and all the elements of craftsmanship, history, mechanics, performance, glamour, pageantry, and romance associated with arms. To quote from her address, a ringing endorsement of the new concepts: "I believe it is right that there should be a museum such as this, designed to entertain and to educate, dedicated to the history of armor and weapons, where young and old can admire the craftsman's work of yesterday and the technology of today."

A highlight of the opening ceremony was the Royal Masque, a pageant worthy of a Broadway show, presenting Yeoman Warders of the Tower, military and police bands, a choral group, dancers, reenactment specialists in costumes from medieval times to today, and renowned performers such as Robert Hardy (portraying a most realistic Winston Churchill, who was a firearms enthusiast and experienced big-game hunter).

Although there remains a presence of the Royal Armouries at the Tower of London, as well as at the Fort Nelson Artillery Museum (Portsmouth), the Leeds facility is now the world headquarters of the Armouries.

Having completed this stunning presentation, the next major project for the museum is to open a facility in America, probably on the East Coast, which would complement the NRA Museum, now in the final stages of planning and funding. Designed to present highlights from the Armouries' collections to American audiences, the new facility would also bring the prestige of aristocratic fascination with hunting and shooting to the United States, a message that would help to awaken the awareness of an ofttimes hostile press on the fascination of arms and armor, and their innumerable roles in history and culture.

HOLLAND & HOLLAND'S NEW YORK STORE

New York City can boast the finest museums, restaurants, clubs, architecture, entertainment, and any number of other "bests." But due to draconian laws, designed to stifle private firearms ownership, the "Big Apple" has had a dearth of best-quality arms-related stores since the passage of the Sullivan Law some eighty-five years ago. Of first-rate firearms stores, only Griffin & Howe (est. 1923) and Beretta (est. 1995) existed, accompanied by a handful of more conventional gun stores, in this highly restricted climate.

But as of May 1996, New York City can rightfully claim the finest emporium of firearms, sporting clothing, and accessories in the Western Hemisphere: Holland & Holland's new store at 50 East 57th Street. At this high-end address, just off Park Avenue and two blocks from Tiffany & Co., Holland & Holland is equal to the exquisite Madison Avenue shop of renowned retailer and trendsetter Ralph Lauren, but goes one step further: You'll find *shotguns and rifles* at Holland & Holland.

These are not just any shotguns and rifles, but sporting arms of the most exquisite style and quality, often beautifully engraved, and of such distinction that they are under the royal warrant of the Duke of Edinburgh and of the Prince of Wales. But the fifth-floor firearms showroom not only offers the superb artistry of Holland & Holland: as in their stores in London and Paris, the company sells antique and modern fine arms by a myriad of makers. Ironically, the first sale on the very first day of opening, May 13, was a Colt double-barrel shotgun, the Model of 1878 Hammer gun.

Founded in 1835, and now owned by the legendary luxury-goods giant Chanel, Inc., Holland & Holland has created a bastion of taste and fashion that makes a powerful statement to anyone who walks through the firm's luxurious doors: Hunting and shooting are legitimate sports with a time-honored tradition, and with clothing, accessories, firearms, and accouterments that speak of beauty, artistry, craftsmanship, quality, travel, treasured memories, and adventure. Accompanying the fifth-floor showroom is a museum, known as the "Brevis Room,"* where guns and other objects that represent the history and traditions of Holland & Holland are exhibited in a relaxed atmosphere.

The New York showrooms of Holland & Holland make a statement that cannot be ignored by the gun-haters and the animal-rights fanatics: Guns and shooting, and the responsible pursuit thereof, are here to stay and cannot be summarily dismissed as the interests of criminals or nuts.

The East 57th Street store combines the best qualities of an elegant sporting-oriented townhouse with the finest in refined British and continental taste in sporting art, best-quality firearms, and accouterments, illustrating the passionate worldwide pursuit of the shooting sports. One can walk into this magnificent emporium as a misguided anti-gun and anti-hunting city person, and walk out a dedicated shooter and sportsman or sportswoman.

This store can serve to convert a citified nonsportsman or -woman into a dedicated hunter, and is among the most important pro-gun and pro-hunting establishments, indeed institutions, in the world today.

*The "Short Room," a play on the stately "Long Room" of Purdey's South Audley Street, London, showrooms.

PUBLICATION OF RUGER & HIS GUNS: THE NATURE OF THE MAN, AND OF THE BOOK

In the fall of 1996, the author's *Ruger & His Guns* was published by Simon & Schuster, under the editorship of Michael Korda and Paul McCarthy. The book is about the life and work of the ultimate achiever in the history of gunmaking—and how a boyhood fascination with the art and craftsmanship, history, mechanics, performance, and romance of guns led a boy from New York City to found, in 1949, what would become the all-around achiever among history's gunmakers: Sturm, Ruger & Co., Inc.

William B. Ruger himself stands as one of the most remarkable personalities in the history of firearms, and one of the most exemplary figures in the annals of manufacturing and gunmaking.

Arms collector, designer, inventor, shooter, hunter, outdoorsman, sportsman, manufacturer, entrepreneur, connoisseur, explorer, and conqueror of the unknown, Bill Ruger is a creative artist whose functional sculptures are unprecedented originals that have brought and continue to bring countless hours of pleasure to millions who share his lifelong love of firearms and the shooting sports.

The author with William B. Ruger and editor Paul McCarthy at the publication party sponsored by Holland & Holland, Ltd., New York, for the release of Ruger & His Guns *in November 1996. Only 200 copies of the book were signed by the author and the subject for that event. A leatherbound limited edition was published by the NRA Modern Firearms Library, with all 1,000 copies signed by the author, but only numbers 1 to 25 signed by Mr. Ruger.*

Not since Samuel Colt himself has there been a figure in the arms field who is heralded with such admiration, respect, and affection. When the firearms industry needs a spokesman, the universal choice among those who know is William B. Ruger. His brilliance is more than a match for the doyens of TV and the print media, who have never met his kind before, and find his innate charm and his charismatic presence, eloquence, knowledge, and piercing logic quite irresistible.

The first advance copy of the book was presented to Mr. Ruger for his eightieth birthday, on June 21, 1996. He was pleased.

THE STORY OF THE GUN, PARTS I AND II: THE A&E SPECIAL, FIRST BROADCAST JULY 21, 1996

The A&E television special *The Story of the Gun*, parts I and II, was warmly received by firearms enthusiasts, and emerged as a tribute to the remarkable appeal of firearms. For once, a program on guns was not cheapened by politics—the sad fate of a decidedly biased program on The Discovery Channel only weeks before (*Gunpower*, riddled with the tired old clichés, a veritable cacophony of cheap shots at guns and gun owners).

Narrated by Cliff Robertson, *The Story of the Gun* was commissioned by A&E from Greystone Productions. Part I was written and directed by Yann Debonne, with Part II ably done by Rob Lahoni. Hopefully, the success of this show will lead to more television programming based on the broad-based appeal of firearms.

The Story of the Gun presented a panoramic history, from the beginnings up through the end of the 20th century, all done with honesty, integrity, accuracy, insight, and creative artistry. This landmark production deserves to be rebroadcast for years to come, and should also be staple programming for schools, colleges, and universities.

The only shortcoming of the production was that the first two hours were more comprehensive than the second two hours, to the extent that the latter gave the impression that the story of firearms in the 20th century was one of armies shooting at armies. Part II did not deal with the sporting and target use of arms, or their collecting, handloading, or any number of other pursuits. Accordingly, the comments presented here are primarily directed at the contents of Part I.

The relationship of firearms to history was interwoven superbly, and the cultural significance of guns was evident throughout. The objects themselves emerge as works of art as well as instruments of historical and technological importance. The role of the gun in various cultures emerges through this multi-century spectrum of powerful images. Presentation of the rich heritage of firearms using works by major artists served to weave the seemingly divergent universes of the gun and the culture together. Clearly, the much-maligned firearm has been a pivotal object historically for over 600 years. Cars and airplanes, both themes of considerable international fascination, are Johnny-come-latelies in comparison to the gun.

The full spectrum of gun usage through 1900 was covered: warfare, hunting, self-defense, target shooting, and even collecting. The role of firearms in art, in industry, and in the evolution of technology was also clearly portrayed. Fittingly, William B. Ruger himself comments on how gunmaking pioneered mass production and parts interchangeability—the ultimate evolutionary perfection of which is evident in his own brilliantly run factories.

Clearly presented was the close relationship of firearms evolution and proliferation with the dawn of freedom and liberty.

This visual feast featured numerous period images of firearms-related paintings, prints, drawings, illuminated manuscripts, and photographs. Great art and music is part of the story of the gun, and those cultural connections were given due recognition. Leonardo da Vinci's design for a wheelock was but one of several seldom seen or previously unbroadcast images. Rubens, Catlin, and Remington are among the artists represented.

A hefty array of historical quotations serves to edify and to further weave the narrative and images within the context of history. The first of these is Oliver Winchester's definition of a gun as "a machine for throwing balls." Beautifully rendered diagrams and guns being fired reveal their mechanics and physics, even showing a revolving-cylinder firearm surviving a multiple discharge.

America's vital leadership role in firearms history is revealed through the Kentucky Rifle, the Springfield Armory, and the evolution of the American system of manufacture. The contributions of gunmaking pioneers such as Colt, Smith & Wesson, Remington, and Winchester, and inventors like Thomas Blanchard, are all respectfully noted. Appropriately, the promotional trailer for the four-hour production recognizes William B. Ruger's dominant role as well.

In addition to appearances by Ruger, on-screen specialists who help tell the story are Whit Collins (chief consultant to the program), Garry James, Ian Hogg, Sarah Ritgers (Smithsonian Institution), Steve Beatty (Springfield Armory), Roy Jinks, James Nottage (Autry Museum of Western Heritage), and the present writer.* Among those listed in Part I's end-screen credits are Val Forgett, Michael Zomber, Steve Sanetti, Robert Stutler, and Margaret Sheldon (Sturm, Ruger & Co.), Jay Hansen and Ken Levin (Hansen & Co.), and New York's Martin Lane Historical Americana gallery.

*Film director John Milius is among those appearing in Part II (covering the late 19th and 20th centuries), accompanied by actual film footage of such dominant figures as John Browning, John T. Thompson, John Garand, and "Carbine" Williams.

Entertaining, educating, movingly and dramatically written and filmed, rife with memorable images, *The Story of the Gun,* Part I, is a feast for the senses—even the sound effects of gunshots are stirring and authentic. The magical world of the history of firearms has finally been captured visually, as never before.

The Story of the Gun will give the public an opportunity to appreciate the complexities of firearms, and the evolution from hand cannon through matchlock, wheelock, flintlock, and percussion to the metallic cartridge. The handsome and fast-moving presentation will appeal to the uninitiated and the most seasoned expert alike. A companion book by Ian Hogg has been marketed aggressively, as has been the videocassette.

Perhaps the success of this program, which has been rebroadcast on several occasions, will be the beginning of further documentary programming on the myriad facets of the history of firearms. Congratulations to Yann Debonne, to Rob Lahoni, to Greystone Productions, and to A&E for a job truly well done.

"SAM AND ELIZABETH": A MAJOR EVENT FOR FIREARMS AND HISTORY

Two courageous museologists, curator William Hosley and associate curator Karen Blanchfield of the American Decorative Arts Department of the Wadsworth Atheneum, Hartford, Connecticut, created a landmark, milestone, blockbuster exhibition and book on Colonel and Mrs. Samuel Colt and their extraordinary impact on Hartford, on Connecticut, on America, and on the world.

Opening September 8, 1996, and running for six months, "Sam and Elizabeth: Legend and Legacy of Colt's Empire" was linked together by numerous exquisite firearms—many from the Colts' own collection and some from high-profile collectors like Robert E. Petersen and distinguished institutions such as the Smithsonian's National Museum of American History. "Sam and Elizabeth" revealed the surprisingly comprehensive influence of the Colts on manufacturing, business entrepreneurship, the art of public relations, the arts and art collecting (and the *art* of collecting), philanthropy, gardening, and architecture—and, in the broadest possible sense, the Colt impact on American civilization and culture.

Enlisting the skills of designer Lucian Leone, "Sam and Elizabeth" recreated the Colt Cabinet of Arms and Cabinet of Memorials, and the Paintings Gallery—all displays organized by Mrs. Colt in their Italianate mansion, Armsmear ("Meadow of Arms"). One of the first private museums in America, Armsmear was a property so celebrated that it received more attention in the book *Homes of America* (1876) than did the White House! "Sam and Elizabeth" powerfully captured the vision the Colts had for America. To quote Curator Hosley's advance statement of purpose:

The exhibition will feature over three hundred objects, period images and quotations arranged in six thematic sections totaling 5000 square feet. A 256-page book, published by The University of Massachusetts Press, will accompany the show, and Connecticut Public Television is producing a complementary program about Colt for its award-winning "Connecticut Experience" series. Never before has such a comprehensive interpretation of the Colt enterprise been undertaken.

In 1905, Elizabeth Hart Jarvis Colt, Sam Colt's widow, bequeathed over one thousand items to the Wadsworth Atheneum, forming the museum's Colt collection. Highlights of this legacy include Samuel Colt's personal firearms collection, Elizabeth Colt's American and European paintings collection, furnishings from the Colts' home, gifts from foreign heads of state, photographs and documentary materials, all of which will be part of the exhibition.

A landmark exhibition in every respect, "Sam and Elizabeth" was worth coming from anywhere in the world to see, and dwarfed this writer's own efforts of some thirty-five years ago: "Samuel Colt Presents." That exhibition's catalogue sold for $6, and is now worth about $125. The same will happen with William Hosley's excellent book, *Colt: The Making of an American Legend.*

THREE AMAZING GUN SHOWS

For a sportsman, gun enthusiast, collector, shooter, or any other person dedicated to the vast spectrum of firearms-related hobbies and businesses, the January 1997 trade and collector shows in Las Vegas were quite literally "the greatest shows on earth"! First came the SHOT Show extravaganza, bigger and better than ever, with over 25,000 in attendance, and representing virtually all the companies and individuals who make the contemporary firearms, ammunition, and accessory industry a truly exciting and vibrant entity. The SHOT Show was at the Las Vegas Convention Center, within walking distance from the Las Vegas Hilton.

The convention area of the Sands was the site of Safari Club International's annual show and meetings—this too was "bigger and better," complete with U.S. senators and congressmen, former president George Bush, general Schwarzkopf, and former vice president Dan Quayle. There were several hundred exhibitors, including professional hunters from around the world and gunmakers like J. Purdey & Sons, Holland & Holland, Ltd., J. Rigby & Co., Ltd., Westley Richards, Sturm, Ruger & Co. (showing in its booth a rare video of Bill Ruger and Pete Kuhlhoff hunting in Uganda in 1961, edited by Kevin James), plus sporting apparel and luggage firms like Hunting World, Inc., and Euro Chasse, and great taxidermists like Michael Boyce's Animal Artistry, numerous talented wildlife artists, and thousands of dedicated hunter-conservationists.

Finally, oriented more toward the collector of antique, vintage, and contemporary firearms was Wallace Beinfeld's Sahara Antique Arms Show, at the Hotel Sahara for the last time; hereafter this three-times-a-year event will be held in the spacious and elegant ballroom of the Hotel Riviera. With the likes of Greg Martin, Butterfield & Butterfield, Norm Flayderman, Jack Malloy, C. W. Slagle, Ron Ogan, Martin Lane Historical Americana, Pete Harvey, Jeff Faintich, Richard Ellis, Jim Supica, John Gangel, Michael Zomber, Mike Clark's Collectors' Firearms gallery, Jaqua's, Griffin & Howe, Jim Austen's New England Arms, Herschel Chadick, Tony Galazan and Connecticut Shotgun Mfg. Co., and many, many more, this show was, on average, the most successful it has ever been in the event's thirty-five-year history. Wally Beinfeld himself was on the loudspeaker at show's end to congratulate everyone in attendance.

IWA—1997, THE SHOT SHOW OF EUROPE

Known as IWA, the International Trade Fair for Hunting and Sporting Arms, Outdoor Articles and Accessories is the most comprehensive firearms-related annual event held in Europe. This show was the twenty-fourth in its annual cycle, and was held at the Messezentrum complex in Nuremberg, Germany. Regularly scheduled for the second weekend of March, IWA again lived up to its reputation as the European equivalent of the SHOT Show.

IWA boasts over 740 exhibitors from thirty-six countries, and upwards of 15,000 visitors, in its four-day run from Friday through Monday. The organizers encourage public visitors on Sunday, for a fee paid at the door (or complimentary from exhibitors).

The site of IWA for many years, the Messezentrum is a cleverly designed multi-building exhibition center, easily accessible from hotels by taxi or via a tram, with a station only a few hundred yards from the main entrance. Shipping facilities, banking, import/export services, and so forth are all part of the complex. The Messezentrum offers thirteen interconnected exhibition buildings; the present IWA format uses buildings A, B, C, D and L.

In this uniquely European charm and ambiance, visitors can see the firearms, ammunition, and hunting and shooting world presented with the finest possible imaging. Many elegantly dressed, beautiful, and charming women have roles in running the exhibits, or attend as keenly interested visitors. Generally all participants and visitors are well dressed, friendly, polite, and dedicated to the subjects presented. Some even attend accompanied by a favorite hunting dog.

The arrangement of many of the exhibits by nationality, and the frequent presence of participants dressed in national costumes, add to the unique appeal of this outstanding event. For the citizens of Nuremberg, which had been bombed to rubble in World War II, IWA offers an opportunity to attract visitors from around the world, and to bring commerce to its ancient and proud city.

The handsome and detailed guidebook—an impressive 500 pages—is primarily in English, but presents a noteworthy amount of material in German, French, Italian, and Spanish. The guide is mainly an alphabetical compilation of participants, with separate listings of trademarks, exhibitors by country, products, and catalogue advertisers. Fax and phone information is presented, as well as quite a bit of advertising. Welcoming messages from the president of the German Hunting Association, from the chairman of the Association of Manufacturers of Hunting and Sporting Arms and Ammunition (equivalent of our National Shooting Sports Foundation), and much more are included. The page size is smaller, but the IWA guidebook is actually fifty pages longer than that of the SHOT Show.

With impressive marketing and inimitable European sophistication, IWA is one of those events in the firearms world that everyone who has ever attended looks forward to with no little anticipation and enthusiasm.

This was the writer's fifth IWA since first attending the event in the late 1980s. This year I was again impressed by the strength and variety of the American exhibitors, many of whom were together in building C, with American flag motifs defining their nationality. Since this show is a plum for any attendee, many of the firms and organizations have their top executives or officials on hand. Since the arms field is under siege from a large segment of the mainstream press—on an international basis—IWA presents a unique global opportunity for an inter-industry exchange of views on how best to deal with common problems and challenges.

Despite the length of the show, it is difficult to cover everything, and the temptation is to collect vast amounts of literature—all of it handsomely designed and printed—to absorb in the comfort of home or office. One of the displays that particularly impressed this writer was that of Hunting World, now celebrating its thirtieth anniversary. Bob Lee's company has more than eighty stores worldwide, and in some markets is bigger than Gucci. The firm's elegantly appointed flagship store in New York City presents its complete line of merchandise, an extraordinary and broad range of luggage, clothing, sport watches, ties, scarves, accessories, and books. Further, the firm's promotional themes incorporate conservation, exploration, and education, and its distinctive logo is a handsome elephant motif. The exquisite design and quality of the firm's products and the company's widespread advertising in mainstream publications are dynamic forces in educating the public about the vital role hunting plays in wildlife and habitat conservation. The fields of firearms and hunting owe Bob Lee a major debt of gratitude for the powerful and convincing positive pro-gun and pro-hunting public relations he and Hunting World have consistently and effectively broadcast worldwide over the years. The Hunting World display at IWA was one of the most striking at the fair.

A highlight of the European exhibitors was the announcement and press party for the spectacular new book *Walther Eine Deutsche Legende*, by Manfred Kersten, published by Verlag Weispfennig. Although this official Walther history is presently available only in German, at a price of about $80, plans are under way for an English edition—probably not available until the fall of 1998.

Although not visible to the attendees, an important international firearms industry meeting was held prior to IWA, for the exchange of ideas in the seemingly unending battle against press, public, and political misinformation and (all too often) hysteria on firearms and hunting issues. Among those attending the session were representatives of the NRA, the National Shooting Sports Council, and other pro-active organizations and companies.

Clearly IWA is one of the world's premier firearm and hunting events, and everyone who was present is already looking forward eagerly to next year's fair. For those wishing to attend the 1998 IWA, the dates are March 13 to 16. For further information, contact NurnbergMesse GmbH, Messenzentrum, D-90471 Nurnberg, Germany. Telephone (direct dial from the U.S.) 01149 911 86 06 0; fax 01149 911 86 06 228; e-mail compuserve 100763.260, or http://www.nuernbergmesse.de.

CHARLTON HESTON AND THE NRA

The election of Charlton Heston as first vice president of the National Rifle Association at the annual meetings early in May 1997 augurs well for this historic organization. Heston, age seventy-two, one of Hollywood's most respected and renowned superstars, will serve in that capacity for another year, and then is eligible for election as NRA president, a position currently held by Marion Hammer. The president may serve for two one-year terms. Mrs. Hammer's leadership has been distinguished by several favorable interviews in the press, not the least of which was a feature piece in *George* magazine, published by none other than John F. Kennedy Jr.

As the first female president of the NRA, Marion Hammer has been able to focus public and media attention on the important role women have played in the field of firearms, from pioneer times through the stardom of Annie Oakley, and up to today, when the hottest market in firearms is the substantial block of women gun owners and gun buyers.

Known as a conservative politically, Heston had been romanced by both Democrats and Republicans over the years, and the NRA position is his first acceptance of any major elective office outside the sphere of show business.

REMINGTON ARMS EXHIBITION AT BUFFALO BILL HISTORICAL CENTER'S CODY FIREARMS MUSEUM, AND THE ANNUAL NRA SHOW AND GUN COLLECTORS CONFERENCE

As one of the world's foremost arms collections, the Cody Firearms Museum has mounted still another major special exhibition: "It Never Failed Me: The Arms and Art of the Remington Arms Company." This loan showing of Remington arms and history, sponsored by the Remington Arms Company with support of the Remington Society of America, opened with fanfare on May 17, 1997, on the heels of Charlton Heston's election as vice president of the NRA. This mammoth undertaking is the most ambitious showing of Remington arms ever held.

The name of the show was taken from Buffalo Bill's presentation letter to cowboy Charles Trego, on the gift of an ivory-gripped New Model Army Remington revolver, which Cody described as his trusty frontier companion: "It never failed me!" That revolver, featured in the author's *The Peacemakers: Arms and Adventure in the American West*, was one of over 750 selected arms from all periods of Remington production. About fifty of these arms were lent by the company, with the balance from Society members, and a few from the Cody Firearms Museum.

A catalogue based on the collection was written by museum curator Howard Madaus and members of the Remington Society of America, with fresh photography by Paul Goodwin, adding significantly to the relatively limited literature on Remington firearms and the company's long and significant history.

Other major projects from the 1996–97 season were the first and second annual NRA shows and Gun Collector Conferences. The first was held in Nashville, Tennessee, in mid-September 1996. Organized jointly by Wallace Beinfeld of the NRA staff and members of the NRA Gun Collecting Committee, the event featured a top-quality show for collectors of several kinds of firearms, speeches by leading specialists on a variety of collecting themes, awards for displays, and a super-charged fund-raising auction to help underwrite the National Firearms Museum. The sum raised was matched by a private donor, so that the total added to the museum fund was $270,000.

The 1997 event, held in Pittsburgh, Pennsylvania, and also organized and run by Beinfeld, NRA staff, and the NRA Gun Collecting Committee, repeated the success of the previous year. Donations to future auctions should be made by contacting Cliff Burgess, NFM Charity Auction, 11250 Waples Mill Road, Fairfax, Virginia 22030; phone (800) 672-4521, or fax (703) 267-3986. Support of the museum is crucial in fulfilling the educational goals of the National Rifle Association, and of the NRA Foundation.

CONCLUSION

In 1971 the author had the pleasure of editing the *Antique Arms Annual*, published in a Texas-size paperback by the Texas Gun Collectors Association. This 264-page publication was as comprehensive as it could be at the time, and those who were involved in its production were hopeful of doing the tome on an annual basis. However, at that time the complexity of completing such a challenging project, year-in and year-out, proved impossible.

Thanks largely to the magic of computer technology, to twenty-five years of added experience in the world of fine guns, and to the opportunity to present to the firearms community, on an annual basis, the *Official Price Guide to Gun Collecting*, that wish from 1971 has finally become a reality.

A Noble Tradition: A History of Arms Collecting[1]

Due to their history, artistry, craftsmanship, mechanics, romance, and performance, arms and related collectibles have been coveted for centuries. Never a dull or uninteresting pursuit, the passion for these objects is as old as civilization. With the cultural explosion that was a hallmark of the European Renaissance, the collecting of arms became a popular pastime of royalty. No royal house or aristocratic family in Europe lacked a treasury made up of art, artifacts, and arms and armor. Some of these were objects in use; others were ancestral, preserved as trophies or as pieces used in historic events, booty of war, and so forth.

EARLY RULERS AND FINE GUNS

Among the earliest houses actively conserving arms and armor was that of the German Emperor Frederick III (ruled 1440–93),[2] and his son and successor Maximilian (1493–1519). Maximilian was a keen admirer of the art of the armorer and gave these craftsmen privileged positions in his vast domains, as well as enriching the Hapsburg arms collections with a great many striking masterpieces. Both of Maximilian's grandsons and heirs, Charles V and Ferdinand, followed his lead, each in his own way. The dukes of Brabant, in Brussels, made up still another royal house amassing a major armory.

While the period of c. 1400 through 1550 was one of major achievement in the production of armor, hand-held firearms remained relatively unsophisticated implements, used mainly by foot soldiers. Among the several inventors attempting to replace primitive matchlocks with improved systems of ignition was the artistic and scientific genius Leonardo da Vinci (1452–1519). An enthusiast of firearms, he designed (in the *Codex Atlanticus*) a wheelock, the earliest mechanism of automatic ignition.

By 1550, practical application of this revolutionary invention had dramatically advanced the role of hand firearms in military, political, economic, and social evolution. The wheelock made it possible to introduce pistols and light arquebuses for cavalry. It gave birth to superior guns and to combination devices requiring instant automatic ignition, and was further responsible for the rapidly expanding role of firearms for hunting.

From clumsy tools of the infantry, guns quickly developed into expensive weapons of princes and select military units. And since the privileged and wealthy appreciated firearms and proved to be generous patrons of gunmakers, engravers, and stockmakers, every care was taken to produce weapons that were looked upon both as mechanical marvels and as works of art, worthy of being treasured and collected by the elite.

A successor to arms connoisseur Maximilian I was Charles V (1519–58), German emperor and Spanish king, in whose personal armories were several dozen elaborately decorated wheelock pistols and carbines. Many of these firearms have been preserved at the Royal Armory established in Madrid by Charles' son, King Philip II of Spain (1556–98), and a few pieces can be seen in other famous arms collections, among them the magnificent holdings of the Metropolitan Museum of Art, New York.

Maximilian's second grandson, Ferdinand (1558–64), Archduke of Austria, who became king of Bohemia and Hungary, and finally German emperor, was particularly fond of collecting historic armor, weapons, and militaria. He and his son, the archduke of Tyrol, made valuable additions to the Hapsburg hereditary armories by creating a Hall of Heroes with a splendid array of arms and armor that had belonged to the dynasty's members and to famous military leaders. Regarded by many as the greatest arms and armor collection in the world, these magnificent works of artistry, craftsmanship, and mechanical ingenuity are housed at the Kunsthistorisches Museum, Vienna.

KING HENRY VIII

A renowned contemporary and ally of these German rulers, King Henry VIII of England (1509–47) had several personal armories in royal palaces and paid special attention to such novelties of his time as wheelocks, breechloaders, and combination weapons. The King's armories were later assembled at the Tower of London, which still houses portions of one of the world's premier arms collections (most of the balance redisplayed in 1996 at the Royal Armouries Museum, Leeds).

SAXON RULERS

Prince-Elector August of Saxony (1553–86) was a connoisseur fortunate to have inherited large family collections of artistic and historic treasures. He took care to separate from

[1]This chapter was adapted and revised from articles by Dr. Leonid Tarassuk and the author for *Man at Arms* and *American Rifleman* magazines.
[2]Except where stated otherwise, dates for royalty indicate period of rule.

them all militaria, actually establishing Saxony's historic collection of arms and armor in special galleries with their own attendants. His successors, Christian I (1586–91) and Christian II (1591–1611), great patrons of armorers and artists, erected a new armory building and generously expanded the hereditary treasures with a number of pieces of exquisite artistic and technical quality. Another powerful prince of the time, Duke Julius of Brunswick (1568–89), had a predilection for spectacularly decorated all-metal wheelock firearms, which he collected in considerable numbers in his armory.

FIREARMS IMPROVEMENTS AND LOUIS XIII

By the 1630s, new and significant improvements in hand firearms appeared in Europe. More and more smoothbore longarms, rifles, pistols, and even revolvers were being provided with flintlocks of different construction, which gradually superseded the complicated and expensive wheelock. The most efficient design of flintlock, to be used for over two hundred years, was introduced in France, whose King Louis XIII (1610–43) enjoyed a well-deserved reputation as a connoisseur of firearms and shooting.

Starting at the age of ten, the king soon assembled an important arms collection, his famous *Cabinet d'armes*. Some of His Majesty's striking array of deluxe and military firearms were specifically rendered in a remarkable portrait by an artist from the school of Rubens. The king was so fond of his collection that he would spend long hours in the privacy of his *Cabinet*, dismounting, cleaning, assembling, and admiring his favorite pieces. A contemporary expert claimed that the king's knowledge and skills could even allow him to make firearms with his own hands. From over 650 weapons and armors collected by Louis XIII, nearly 500 were firearms, both contemporary and antique. Louis XIV being the Sun King, his father Louis XIII could be termed the "Gun King."[3]

Louis XIII of France, the "Gun King," with selected pieces from his exquisite arms and armor collection, begun when he was a boy. (School of Rubens, reproduced by permission of The Royal Armouries Museum)

RUSSIAN IMPERIAL COLLECTORS

Far away from France, another passionate lover of firearms and shooting came to supreme power soon after Louis XIII's death. Alexy Mikhailovich, Czar of Muscovy (1645–76), was a somewhat unusual figure among Russian rulers of the period. Keen on knowledge, he was dedicated to the arts, theater, heraldry, fine arms, and the chase. From his predecessors he inherited the Kremlin Armories with vast stores and workshops employing many first-class craftsmen and artists, both Russian and foreign. During his long reign, Czar Alexy ordered hundreds of guns of various designs for his private use and for his collection, which has remained nearly intact in the museums of Moscow.

His son, Peter the Great (1682–1725), also favored firearms and was responsible for establishing a new imperial factory, in Tula, which soon gained world renown. Peter was a gifted craftsman of no little talent.

In addition to the Kremlin Armories, another distinguished Russian family, that of Sheremetev (later counts), had traditionally deposited personal weapons and armors at their ancestral armory, formed before the 18th century. This custom was carried on throughout the centuries. Still another collection, that of the Boyars, numbered some 1,400 items (including approximately 600 antique firearms). The 1917 Revolution led to confiscation by the Soviets of all private arms collections in Russia and in other lands under Communist domination, and some museum-held cartridge firearms were drilled through the breech to prevent their being fired by enemies of the state!

POLISH COLLECTORS

Russia's neighbors and rivals also demonstrated a keen enthusiasm for arms collecting. The Polish-Lithuanian princes Czartoryski and Radziwill established family armories, with the earliest pieces dating back to the 16th century. August the Strong (1694–1733), King of Poland and Prince Elector of Saxony, especially favored luxurious

[3]The renowned royal property of Versailles was originally built as a hunting estate.

hunting firearms and added a sumptuous "Gun Gallery" to the Saxon hereditary armory in Dresden. His successor, August III (1733–63), augmented the gallery with splendid pieces he collected for pleasure, and for his elaborate hunting parties. Despite unfortunate losses over the years, the Saxon arms collection still boasts over 10,000 pieces, about a third of them deluxe firearms.

SCANDINAVIAN COLLECTIONS

A small but precious historic arms collection was founded by King Frederick III of Denmark (1648–70) at Rosenborg Castle, where he assembled armor, weapons, costumes, and regalia of Danish rulers. Another treasury of antique weapons in Scandinavia was put together at Skokloster Castle, Sweden, by the great collector Field Marshal Count Carl Gustaf Wrangel (1613–76). Through the marriage of his daughter, the Wrangel Armory fortunately came into possession of the arms and armor of the Counts Brahe, who were passionate and active arms collectors themselves. Both armories at Skokloster eventually became a public museum.

King Charles XV of Sweden and Norway was still another dedicated collector. His holdings were handsomely enriched by regally embellished and cased gifts from President Abraham Lincoln and Samuel Remington. Many of Charles' arms are on view at the Royal Armory, Stockholm. But his magnificent cased pair of Colt Model 1860 Army revolvers, gold inlaid and engraved by Gustave Young, and presented by Lincoln, were stolen in the 1960s and have yet to be recovered.

ARTISTS AS ARMS COLLECTORS

Many great artists were lovers of fine arms. Among them, Rembrandt van Rijn (1606–69) had an arms collection, some of which he used in his paintings. Flemish painter David Teniers Jr. (1610–90) showed his profound knowledge of weapons, especially firearms, in several canvases showing military scenes. A number of pieces were painted with almost photographic accuracy.

NOBLE RUSSIAN LADIES, AND GRANDSONS

Nor were some noble ladies strangers to the related passions of hunting and arms collecting. Peter the Great's daughter Empress Elizabeth of Russia (1741–62) earnestly patronized the Tula gunmakers, who produced for her hunting pavilions dozens of magnificent garnitures of fowling pieces, rifles, and paired pistols. Empress Catherine the Great (1762–96) followed suit, adding still more fine firearms to the imperial gun rooms. To please her beloved grandsons, Grand Princes Alexander and Constantine, the empress presented them working miniatures of pistols, revolvers, and longarms made to her order by Tula's finest armorers and artists. Ironically, not these boys but their two brothers, born shortly after their grandmother's death, were to become especially active arms collectors.

RUSSIAN CZARIST COLLECTORS

Grand Prince Nicholas (b. 1796, d. 1855) started collecting arms and armor, as well as militaria, while still a boy. By the date of his accession to the Russian throne (1825) he had already assembled so many items that they required special premises for proper display. To accommodate this collection, a new palace, known as Tsarskoseliskii Arsenal, was built near the capital city of St. Petersburg. As czar, Nicholas I had many opportunities to enlarge his collection.

Antique and rare arms and armor were brought in from old state armories and imperial palaces, acquired abroad and at home, seized at captured armories during foreign wars, and donated by relatives and others. Firearms were often presented to the czar by gunmakers and manufacturers. The most prominent of these foreign donors was Colonel Samuel Colt, who personally presented Nicholas I a spectacular set of three gold-inlaid percussion revolvers. The fact that Nicholas was an arms collector undoubtedly served to encourage Colt's own collecting interests.

The czar's youngest brother, Grand Prince Michael (1798–1849), shared this love for fine weapons and patiently put together his own impressive arms collection, which he bequeathed to Nicholas. The next Russian ruler, Alexander II (1855–81), was a dedicated hunter with a special passion for collecting contemporary high-quality firearms. He too received a splendid set of rifles and revolvers from Colonel Colt. Alexander II significantly enlarged the imperial arms collection, which is now preserved at the Hermitage Museum in St. Petersburg. The Grand Duke Alexis, on a visit to the United States in 1871–72, was presented a gold-inlaid and engraved revolver by Smith & Wesson, which His Highness proceeded to use while buffalo hunting on the plains. His enthusiastic guides were Lieutenant Colonel George Armstrong Custer and William F. "Buffalo Bill" Cody. Alexis' buffalo hunts were the highlight of his extended visit to the New World. The whereabouts of the grand duke's elaborate revolver is unknown at this writing—a treasure perhaps awaiting a lucky collector or dealer at some future date.

NAPOLEON BONAPARTE, IMPERIAL COLLECTOR

To Napoleon, Emperor of France (1801–14), arms collectors owe the existence of some of the finest firearms produced in the 19th century. A patron and protector of all the arts, Napoleon particularly favored gunmakers and arms decorators. Their choice pieces came into the emperor's personal possession or were reserved by him for presentation to dignitaries and for awards honoring distinguished military service.

His nephew, Emperor Napoleon III (1852–70), also patronized producers of deluxe firearms and proved to be an eager collector of arms and armor, as well as an active hunter—and a remarkably talented shot. Displayed in the formidable medieval castle of Pierrofonds, the imperial collection later joined the Musée de l'Armée in Paris, which also preserves certain key segments of the arms collections assembled by King Louis XIII, the princes de Conde, and the dukes de Bouillon. Count de Nieuwerkerke, Superintendent of Fine Arms and Director of the Louvre Museum, and the French architect and antiquarian Viollet-le-Duc were two other distinguished French connoisseurs.

BRITISH ARISTOCRATIC ENTHUSIASTS

Among the most prominent connoisseurs and collectors of firearms in the 19th century, mention should be made of the Prince Regent, who became King George IV (1811–30), as well as Prince Albert (b. 1819, d. 1861; consort to Queen Victoria) and King George V (1910–36). The British public was favored by a generous bequest, in 1897, of art collections formed by the Wallace family. Included were about 2,400 pieces of armor and weapons, with many beautiful and fine antique firearms. Most important in this group were items assembled by Sir Richard Wallace, who had been lucky enough to acquire the distinguished collections of arms and armor of Sir Samuel Rush Meyrick and Count de Nieuwerkerke. Today the Wallace Collection is displayed in the family's London mansion, known as Hertford House.

A fascinating series of historical connections began with the arms and armor gallery at British author Horace Walpole's Strawberry Hill estate. Walpole's armory served as the inspirational setting for the first of the "gothic" novels, his *Castle of Otranto* (1764). Early-19th-century author Sir Walter Scott is considered to have patterned his own country house and armory, Abbotsford, on the model of Walpole's. And Sir Samuel Rush Meyrick (1783–1848), a contemporary of Scott, became the first serious scholar in the study of arms and armor. Scott's novels, especially *Ivanhoe* and *The Tales of the Crusaders*, had a profound influence on the interests of British antiquarians and collectors.

Scott's romantic period novels and Meyrick's studies reflected an interest that became almost a Victorian epidemic—armories or, at the least, arms and armor displays in the grand mansions of aristocrats and the new rich. When the Meyrick-Wallace collection opened as a British national museum in June 1900, the ceremonies were distinguished by the presence of an avid shooter and gun enthusiast, Edward, Prince of Wales (later King Edward VII).

For many years, the largest and most fascinating private collection of quality arms extant was that of the English connoisseur and author W. Keith Neal. These amazing treasures were preserved for years in a special building on the Neal estate on the Island of Guernsey. The Neal Collection was reminiscent of princely ancestral armories, and his reputation as an arms specialist was of regal proportions. Much of the collection remains intact, in the hands of his heirs.

In the Soviet Union of 1917 to 1991, arms collecting was not specifically prohibited by law, but the keeping by private citizens of firearms and edged weapons of any kind and of any date was punishable by confiscation of such property and mandatory imprisonment of the owner. Exempt from these prohibitions were members of state-controlled hunting clubs (allowed to have registered shotguns only) and professional hunters catering to state trade institutions (who could own licensed rifles and ammunition). Certainly there were a few passionate lovers of antique weapons in Russia who attempted to collect despite the risk of heavy civil penalties. Understandably, they tried to keep their collections secret—as far as possible.

Since the collapse of the Soviet Union, another problem exists for contemporary collectors in Russia: the fear of theft in the present crime wave, resulting from the chaos of a country emerging from centuries of czars and dictators. One thing is certain: There are collectors in Russia, and always will be.

Among those with the privilege to collect firearms in Soviet times, and who could afford to do so—modern guns included—was the late Field Marshal G. Zhukov (1896–1974). His was the largest private collection of firearms in the U.S.S.R., composed of about 1,000 pieces, mostly "war trophies" from private mansions and castles (taken during World War II). After Zhukov's death, the collection quietly passed into the hands of the state, with a number of his firearms going to Moscow's state museums.

Another important collection of firearms, mainly modern deluxe presentations, was owned by the secretary general of the Soviet Union's Communist Party, Leonid Brezhnev, who was also the U.S.S.R.'s commander in chief. The secretary's favorite hobbies were, reportedly, the collecting of firearms and exotic foreign cars.

RENOWNED ENGLISH, AMERICAN, AND CONTINENTAL COLLECTORS

The Wallace Collection was a vital link in the evolution of arms and armor as a fashionable hobby, and Sir Richard's collection set the fashion of private art galleries for American collectors in the late 19th and early 20th centuries. Among the prominent U.S. patrons of the arts who were influenced were J. Pierpont Morgan, Clarence H. Mackay, and William Randolph Hearst. And among the Europeans who became dedicated collectors were Baron Ferdinand de Rothschild, Sir Ralph Payne-Gallwey, and Henry H. Harrod (of the London department-store family).

In Italy, by the late 19th century, Prince Ladislas

Odescalchi had collected some 1,200 items of fine arms, which were later acquired by the state and established as a national arms museum in Rome. Another connoisseur of art, Federigo Stibbert, put together extensive collections, strong in European and Oriental arms and armor. In 1908, the Stibbert collections were willed to the city of Florence, and are now on display in his richly appointed villa.

MEXICAN AND SOUTH AMERICAN DEVOTEES

Surely one of the keenest arms collectors in history was Porfirio Diaz, president of Mexico for most of the years 1877 to 1911. Although he was a dictator who ruled with an iron hand, Diaz took the time to not only assemble a remarkable collection, but to have custom-made arms built—sometimes to his own order. These pieces are primarily at the Royal Military College Museum, Kingston, Ontario, Canada, and are so extraordinary that the author has traveled to Kingston specifically to admire them.

Peru boasts the phenomenal collection of Miguel Musica Gallo, one of the most impressive groups of arms assembled privately in the history of the Western Hemisphere. Gallo, better known for his museum of gold, built his varied arms group at his home base of Lima, but enjoyed hunting to the extent that his display of animal heads and horns is one of the finest privately owned. A monograph was published on the Gallo collection, revealing a great many rare, embellished, and historic pieces.

Judging from the numbers of exquisite arms sold to clients south of the border, there are numbers of wealthy families in Mexico and in Central and South America who have been keenly interested in possessing fine arms. However, most of these would be regarded not so much as collectors, but as enthusiasts of high-grade arms, many of them used for hunting.

CONTEMPORARY COLLECTORS IN EUROPE

The ranks of contemporary collectors of arms in Europe no longer include many of the ancestral estates, due to the ravages of war and taxation. The majority of treasured family collections have been split up under the auctioneer's hammer, while others have gone directly into public museums. In any case, it seems a higher proportion of arms and armor collectors can remain anonymous, because the best-quality of objects seldom are publicly sold—and the relatively small scale of firearms makes them less a challenge (and less costly) to move from place to place.

The number of arms auctions of quality pieces are relatively few in comparison to fine furniture, silver, or even Impressionist paintings. And even private sales are few and far between, so much of the exceptional specimens of armor having long been in public collections, and the same becoming increasingly so with arms. The sale by Christie's in London, November 18, 1981, set what was then the all-time record price at auction for an object of arms and armor when the duke of Brunswick suit of Greenwich armor went for $790,000. However, just a few years later Sotheby's sold a suit of armor of the French King Francis I at $3.5 million! Today both armors are worth noticeably more.

Major firms like Holland & Holland, Ltd., based in London, are promoting arms collecting, with exquisitely appointed shops in Paris and New York and elegantly designed advertising in fashionable publications, and by catering to extremely wealthy clients. Firms like Holland & Holland and J. Purdey & Sons are instrumental in promoting arms collecting as a fashionable, indeed chic, collecting pursuit.

Despite the trend toward privacy in modern circles of arms and armor collectors of distinction, the identities of a few individuals are known. It appears that among them, and certainly the most distinguished, is H.R.H. Prince Philip, the Duke of Edinburgh. The degree of dedication of His Grace to arms collecting is not publicly known, but at the least it is enough to find him appearing on television discussing arms subjects with obvious knowledge, relish, and insight, and to have been the honored guest at the dedication of the new firearms galleries at The Armouries, H.M. Tower of London, in 1974.

Prince Philip is also quite knowledgeable on the subject of modern gunmaking, and his patronage of such firms as Holland & Holland and Purdey is well known. Aristotle Onassis, though he was not an arms collector *per se*, did enjoy shotgun shooting and appreciated the craftsmanship of fine arms. A photograph of Onassis in quarters aboard his yacht *Christina* reveals a deluxe pair of Napoleonic-period flintlock pistols displayed on the wall in the background.

MIDDLE EASTERN OIL POTENTATES AND CONTINENTAL COLLECTORS

Now residing in Paris is an Iranian prince, half brother to the late shah, who is an active sportsman and prizes quality rifles and shotguns: Prince Abdolrezza. Several prominent industrialists in Switzerland, Holland, Italy, France, and Germany are keen arms collectors, among them Ugo Gussalli Beretta, patriarch of the world-famous gunmakers.

But these fanciers of fine arms are faced with increasing competition from Middle Eastern sheiks and princes, whose oil wealth allows an indulgence on a scale that harks back to the grand aristocrats of the 17th and 18th centuries and the age of Napoleon. And according to an article in *The New Yorker* magazine, the world's richest man, the sultan of Brunei, is a collector of fine Colt revolvers.

Generally leaning toward large quantities of shooting guns, Middle Eastern collectors have a special affection for deluxe gold-mounted and inlaid modern arms. The best known of arms enthusiasts from that part of the world is

King Hussein I of Jordan. Several members of the Saudi Arabian royal family are known to be keen collectors. An entire new special category in rare arms has been created by Swiss jeweler and watchmaker Ives St. Blaize, whose line of deluxe modern arms features diamond-encrusted grips of 18-karat gold and other exotica. Considering the international fascination with the American West, it would not be surprising to see a craving develop among the Middle Eastern collecting fraternity for Americana, especially Colts and Winchesters.

Jewelers the likes of Asprey & Co., Ltd, in London and New York–based Tiffany & Co. have made some of the most deluxe firearms in history, the former even setting up its own gunmaking operation. Tiffany's creations in this challenging area began in the 1850s, and today the firm concentrates on exquisite Colt and S&W revolvers, wholly designed to exclusive custom orders.

Although the stately collectors merit envy in their private possessions, a tradition has been established since the French Revolution (and particularly strong in the 20th century) of the very finest specimens of antique arms gradually going into museums. Already much of the best of European arms and armor has gone into public hands, with the result that these exquisite objects are available for the public to see and appreciate. With the passage of time the same pattern is evolving in America, aided by beneficial circumstances of tax laws and an increasing public awareness of museums and their prominent role in American culture.

AMERICAN COLLECTORS

The American experience with firearms is unique. British historian Thomas Carlyle classified the "three great elements of modern civilization" as "gunpowder, printing, and the Protestant religion." In no nation have these elements proven to be of such profound significance as in our own. Without firearms, our pioneer civilization would never have survived, and in our nearly 500-year history, no object has played a more vital role.

America does indeed have a "gun culture," and one in which we can take considerable and justifiable pride. Our myriad of gun-related businesses, hobbies, and sports, including the collecting of arms, are wholly understandable.

The origins of arms collecting in America are somewhat akin to those of Europe. The "ruling families" in the New World, like their European counterparts, assembled ancestral arms holdings, accumulated over years of shooting and hunting. Families here did not have the opportunities or wealth for large collections on the European scale, at least not until the late 19th and early 20th centuries. But by American standards, fine early collections were formed, one of which was that of the "father of his country," George Washington.

GEORGE WASHINGTON, A KEEN COLLECTOR

Writer Ashley Halsey's research on Washington's favorite guns (*American Rifleman*, February 1968) documented that the first president "may have owned 50 firearms," of which about ten are known to collectors and museums today. Private diary entries and other sources show that Washington appreciated firearms for their artistic, mechanical, and functional excellence, and that he had a predilection for English-made flintlock pistols and fowling pieces of quality. As an active and enthusiastic shooter, Washington appreciated the importance of fine design and craftsmanship, and to quote Halsey, he was "a sportsman hunter of the first rank."

In common with many an American "aristocrat," Washington frequently rode to the hounds on fox hunts and went afield with gun in hand after duck, hare, deer, and other game. Halsey proves that Washington was not only an avid sportsman, but one who knew guns and had great affection for them. Evidence of his appreciation of quality is found in such arms as his silver-mounted pair of gentleman's pistols from Hawkins, London.

That his contemporaries shared a similar appreciation for guns and shooting is shown by Washington's gifts of firearms to relatives, friends, and fellow soldiers, not the least of whom was General the Marquis de Lafayette. Our first president also received gifts of arms, and among those of record were two pairs of flintlock pistols that he described in letters to the donors as "very elegant." Unfortunately, the Washington collection was split up over the years, and thus the few pieces known today are as far afield as the Mount Vernon historic site, near Alexandria, Virginia, and a private collection in the western United States.

THOMAS JEFFERSON—ARMS COLLECTOR AND INNOVATOR

Surely the most enlightened gun and shooting enthusiast in the early years of arms collecting in America was Thomas Jefferson. His brilliant mind and cultured, artistic eye attracted Jefferson to a wide range of interests, indeed passions, encompassing art and architecture, music, literature, science, guns and shooting, the world of ideas, and affairs of state. It was Jefferson who wrote some time-honored advice to his nephew, Peter Carr:

> A strong body makes the mind strong. As to the species of exercise, I advise the gun. While this gives a moderate exercise to the body, it gives boldness, enterprise, and independence to the mind. . . . Let your gun therefore be the constant companion of your walks.

Jefferson was recognized as an aristocrat but also a man of freedom, and a liberal in the classic sense. His views on gun use and ownership ring true today. In 1776, in a draft for the constitution of Virginia, he wrote: "No freeman shall ever be debarred the use of arms." He also wrote to George Washington that "one loves to possess arms." Ashley Halsey's article "Jefferson's Beloved Guns" (*American Rifleman*, November 1969) concludes, "To this cultural genius . . . few things surpassed the delight that he derived from shooting."

As with Washington, Jefferson's account books and other papers bear frequent reference to the purchase, repair, and even restocking of pistols, fowling pieces, and muskets. However, only two pistols have survived that can be accepted as his; they are a pair of brass screw-barrel flintlocks by Dealtry, London, on display at Monticello.

Jefferson's main love for guns was for field shooting, but one of the most significant results of his knowledge and experience with arms was in introducing the idea of parts interchangeability to U.S. industry. While ambassador to France, Jefferson had been introduced to the pioneering work of Blanc in producing gun locks on a theory of parts interchangeability. Jefferson saw the potential in Blanc's work and wrote of it in some detail to American officials. Although that correspondence served to introduce the concept to American industry, it remained for Eli Whitney and, more important, such creative industrialists as Simeon North and Robbins & Lawrence to make practical application of these ideas in the United States.

OTHER DEVOTEES OF ARMS

Washington and Jefferson shared their love for guns and shooting with the majority of their male contemporaries. America has been a virtual paradise for the gun enthusiast and shooter since the arrival of the original colonists and explorers. A relatively limited body of information has been ferreted out by researchers on the degree of private enjoyment of gun ownership by the better-known of our pioneer citizen-shooters. This is inevitable, since when a scholar pursues the likes of the governing class, he is generally in pursuit of information specific to subjects for which the individuals are best known.

But to consider only U.S. presidents prior to 1900, those who had gun and shooting interests far outnumber those likely to have had no practical experience or interest. In the former category, standouts would be, in addition to Washington and Jefferson, James Madison, Andrew Jackson, William Henry Harrison, James K. Polk, Zachary Taylor, Franklin Pierce, Abraham Lincoln, Ulysses S. Grant, and Grover Cleveland (an active bird shooter).

In a modern sense we would not term these gentlemen pure collectors; rather, they were shooters who enjoyed guns. However, as in the cases of Washington and Jefferson, who both had quite a few arms during their lifespans, at least one could use the terminology "informed accumulator."

Washington even owned trophies of war, such as a pair of flintlock pistols believed to have been presented to him by Lafayette and carried by him in the Revolutionary War; another pistol is traditionally considered to have been a gift from General Edward Braddock, who had carried it during the French and Indian War.

Relics or trophies of war have spawned many an arms collection over the years. And it is safe to say that such was the origin of most pioneer U.S. arms collections of the 19th century. But the two most important private arms groups of the pre–1900 period in America originated from quite another inspiration—the Industrial Revolution.

SAMUEL COLT AND OLIVER WINCHESTER

Both Samuel Colt and Oliver Winchester were able to deduce to some extent their historic impact on industry, technology, contemporary history, and the field of gun making. As early as 1853, Colt's collecting intent was implied in a letter that announced to the gunmaker that a shipment of curious guns representative of the Turkish empire had been dispatched to him. In 1856 Commodore Matthew Perry wrote that he understood Colt had already assembled a "number of . . . arms" and would "establish a museum of arms well worthy of the commendable object he had in mind." And a Colt journal of 1861 records the existence of a museum room, with its contents valued at $3,245.75.

Colt collected arms because he had a genuine passion for them, but also in order to provide reference specimens for design work, to dramatize his own role in firearms history, and to keep abreast of his own production and that of rivals. That he had a good working knowledge of the evolution of repeating firearms is apparent from the paper he delivered to the Institution of Civil Engineers, London, in 1851. The plates in the article and Colt's published expertise lead one to believe that his serious collecting began at least as early as 1850.

On the colonel's death in 1862, the collection was divided into two sections, with about 100 pieces at his home, Armsmear, and several hundred at the factory. The Armsmear group was bequeathed by his widow to the Wadsworth Atheneum, Hartford, in 1905, and the factory collection was generously presented to the State of Connecticut by the Colt firm in 1957. Sharing a known origin estimated at least as early as 1850, these two arms groups represent, to the author's knowledge, the oldest formal American arms collection privately assembled and still existing.

Oliver Winchester was a manufacturer, not a keen gun fancier, who created in the Winchester Repeating Arms Co. one of the giant private armories of the 19th century. His industrial background had been as a shirtmaker in New Haven. But it would appear that Winchester became quite infatuated with firearms and was very much aware of the contributions of his firm to American industry and our emergence as a world power. A letter from Winchester to manufacturer B. S. Lawrence documents that Winchester had an arms collection by 1871; he was delighted to have acquired from Lawrence a Jennings rifle, which he correctly termed "a connecting link in the history of our gun."

The Winchester factory collection was a gift to the Buffalo Bill Historical Center, Cody, Wyoming, in 1975, and is displayed in one of the most impressive installations of any of the world's arms museums. The collection today is in its own specially constructed wing of the Historical Center, and is termed the Cody Firearms Museum.

OTHER U.S. GUNMAKERS

Other U.S. gunmakers also put together collections, and among the earliest were Remington and Smith & Wesson. The Remington firm was founded in 1816, but no records exist that date the arms collection exactly. An estimate of its likely origins can be gleaned from specimen guns. By the mid- to late 1860s, the firm was on a course that called for maintaining a display collection of experimental and production models. The Remington Gun Museum in Ilion, New York, was reopened to the public in August 1980, after an ambitious program of development and fresh displays.

Smith & Wesson's collection can also be dated by study of surviving specimens and by considering the firm's antiquity. Founded in 1852, the company was producing its first Model .22 rimfire revolver by 1860. S&W Volcanic lever-action pistols in the factory museum suggest that the owners were gun collectors before 1860.

It is important for every firearms manufacturer to have reference collections, and one of the most modern of the former, Sturm, Ruger & Co., has its own impressive holdings. William B. Ruger himself launched the firm's collecting, which is devoted to as wide a spread of makes and types as are relevant to the broad range of Ruger's own product interests and that of the company. Bill Ruger's outlook on a company collection and mastery of gun knowledge (historical and otherwise) closely parallels the approach of Sam Colt.

Surely rivaling Ruger in gun savvy and experience, and akin to Colonel Colt, is Samuel Cummings, the American munitions magnate whose firm, Interarms, is headquartered in Europe. As founder and president, Cummings established major offices around the world. His gun enthusiasms, and those of Interarms, are broad, covering the complete history of firearms, and particularly the military armaments of the 20th century. The collection is housed in Manchester, England, but, like that of Sturm, Ruger & Co., it is not on public display.

Other major U.S. gun manufacturers with important collections include Browning in Morgan, Utah, and Navy Arms in Ridgefield, New Jersey.

Older than all of the collections, even that of Colt, is the Springfield Armory Museum. Established by Congress in 1795, the Armory began accumulating guns immediately, and its formal collecting may well have predated 1850. This public assemblage numbering into the thousands of small arms is now maintained by the National Park Service on the original site in Springfield, Massachusetts.

FAMILY AND PRIVATE COLLECTIONS

As one might expect, the collections of the manufacturers have a continuity lacking in the American collections of private individuals or families, in contrast to the great ancestral holdings of the royal houses and private estates of Europe.

Since collecting in many fields of antiquities, firearms included, has often been done quietly, the author has no doubt that at least a few old-time, pre-1900 arms groups are still together at this writing. Some of the prominent private U.S. collections from before 1900 that survived into the 20th century should be noted.

Though not well known himself, A. E. Brooks of Hartford began as a collector in the post–Civil War period. His was a large and general collection of antiques, featuring U.S. arms, and concentrating on Colts more than any other maker. At about the turn of the century the U.S. Cartridge Co. bought the Brooks Collection, and then published the items in book form. Brooks himself had published his own *Illustrated Catalogue of The A.E. Brooks Collection* (1899). Brooks–U.S. Cartridge Co. pieces are of special appeal to modern-day collectors, and specimens are usually marked with catalogue reference numbers. In the mid-1940s Robbins Ritter of East Hartford, Connecticut, sold the Brooks–U.S. Cartridge collection.

A contemporary of Brooks who was a celebrity in his day and a keen Colt enthusiast was Major John R. Hegeman Jr., scion of an old Massachusetts and New York family. Son of the first president of the Metropolitan Life Insurance Company, Hegeman was a friend of William F. "Buffalo Bill" Cody and General Nelson A. Miles. Thanks partly to close connections with the Colt company, Hegeman was able to put together an exceptional array of specimens, from the Paterson up to semi-automatic pistols; more than half a dozen of the latter bore serial number 1. The Hegeman collection was broken up around 1947, sold largely by the old-time arms dealership of W.G.C. Kimball, Woburn, Massachusetts.

GUN COLLECTING INTO THE 20TH CENTURY

Brooks and Hegeman are representative of pioneer private arms collectors. Their interest in guns paralleled that of collectors in other fields, a serious pursuit largely limited to persons with both money and time. Collecting art and antiques had been a tradition among the wealthy in Europe since the Renaissance. But in America, the passion did not become infectious until toward the end of the 19th century.

Our public museums blossomed as the nation's wealth, leisure time, and national and local consciousness and pride rapidly developed—aided in the 20th century by laws covering tax-deductible donations. Wealthy Americans on the "Grand Tour" of Europe often purchased liberally of art and antiques, seeming to be acquiring status and culture in the process. Observing the magnificent European collections in public and private hands powerfully influenced the evolution of collecting in America.

Samuel Colt was one of the first Americans to frequent Europe, and the influence of the regal wealth he saw there is evident in his lavish estate, Armsmear. The mansion house was an Italianate villa, the centerpiece of a massive landscaped park along the lines of fashionable English country estates. A Cabinet of Memorials, featuring guns, paintings, and sundry antiquities and sculpture, was displayed in an upper gallery of substantial proportions. The gallery was developed mainly by Mrs. Colt as tribute to her late husband's genius. Also part of establishing a respectable position among the wealthy, the arms collection, documents, and memorabilia would be bequeathed to Hartford museums on Mrs. Colt's death.

Large estates with mansion houses, like Colt's Armsmear, were springing up almost like mushrooms in Victorian America. As a shooter's paradise, the great West drew like a magnet not a few scions of wealthy Eastern families. At the same time, the South was returning to a position of power, and pockets of wealth in real estate, minerals, ranching, oil, industry, and finance were rapidly developing in the West and the Midwest. America discovered it was truly rich. And the leisure time that sometimes accompanies fortune coincided with an ever-growing interest in and appreciation of collecting.

William F. "Buffalo Bill" Cody, gun collector, holding one of his favorites, the Winchester Model 1873 Sporting Rifle.

The welcome new epidemic offered a variety of specialties—paintings, bronzes, antiques, decorative art—and, of the latter, arms and armor had a definite, and very native, appeal. Buffalo Bill's Wild West show and its successors traveled America and Europe from 1883 until 1916. Not only was Cody himself a crack shot and dedicated hunter, but he had an arms collection made up of several types and makes of guns. John R. Hegeman's gun interest was partially sparked by his friendship with Buffalo Bill. Furthermore, millions of Americans and Europeans saw firearms in romantic settings, as they enjoyed the extravaganzas of Buffalo Bill and his troupe.

Theodore Roosevelt, whose social and political credentials were impeccable, was a lover of fine arms and of hunting, and was already a regular customer of outfitter-dealer Schuyler, Hartley and Graham, and of Winchester, by the mid-1880s. More than fifty guns belonging to Roosevelt have been identified, and TR was the most gun-oriented and knowledgeable president since Thomas Jefferson. Roosevelt had a keen love of custom-made Winchesters, and two of his Colts were deluxe engraved and plated Single Action Armies. No president before or since contributed more to wildlife and habitat conservation and to a national appreciation of marksmanship and gun sports.

DISTINGUISHED COLLECTORS AND MUSEUMS

Hegeman and Brooks were contemporaries of TR, and among other active arms collectors of the Victorian period were the Nash and Williams families of Boston, the Bryants of central Connecticut, Lieutenant Colonel George Armstrong Custer, Annie Oakley, Doc Carver, and, as noted, Buffalo Bill himself. Cody was also a collector of art and patronized contemporaries the likes of Frederic Remington, Rosa Bonheur, and Charles Schreyvogel. A corporate collector of note, whose museum was begun by an officer in the 1920s, is the Wells Fargo Bank of San Francisco. Its arms collection rates high marks for color and history.

A most fascinating development in arms collecting in the U.S. took place under the inspiration of the first Curator of Arms and Armor at the Metropolitan Museum of Art in New York City, Dr. Bashford Dean. Dean was Curator of Reptiles and Fish at the American Museum of Natural History when the Metropolitan Museum acquired the splendid collection of the Duke de Dino in 1904. The purchase immediately established the Metropolitan as the major institution with arms and armor holdings in the United States. Dean was pressed into service to set up the collection, simultaneously continuing his duties at the Museum of Natural History.

In 1912 Dean was appointed Curator of Arms and Armor at the Metropolitan. From the early 20th century until his death in 1928, this scholarly and innovative gentleman was the central figure in a circle of enthusiastic collectors, which at times numbered financier J. Pierpont Morgan, banker William H. Riggs, social scion Rutherford Stuyvesant, silver heir Clarence H. Mackay (Irving Berlin was his son-in-law), financier Edward Hubbard Litchfield, Francis P. Garvan (a generous benefactor of Yale University), Howard Mansfield (a lawyer friend of artist James Abbott McNeill Whistler), George Cameron Stone (friend of Rudyard Kipling and a prominent metallurgist), C. O. von Kienbusch (tobacco merchant of note who gave his armory to the Philadelphia Museum of Art), Alexander McMillan Welch (N.Y.C. architect who married Bashford Dean's sister), George F. Harding (Chicago realtor who set up a museum by bequest, later absorbed by the Art Institute of Chicago), John Woodman Higgins (who founded Worcester Pressed Steel and established a museum at the company site), John Long Severance (a benefactor of the Cleveland Museum of Art), and George A. Douglass (whose wife was an heiress to the Helm tobacco fortune). Most of the above were members of the Armor and Arms Club of New York. Founded in 1921, it was the first organization of its kind in America. Its president was, of course, Bashford Dean.

Early arms collector Albert Foster Jr., who had the enviable position of manager of Colt's New York sales office, which undoubtedly offered him many opportunities for acquiring fine guns. He holds a decorated wheelock; several Colts and Kentucky Rifles can be seen in the background of his New Jersey gun room. This photo was used by James E. Serven in his landmark catalogue of the Foster collection, some of the photographs from which are presented in this book, the author having acquired the negatives, along with thousands of other images, from Mrs. Serven.

WILLIAM RANDOLPH HEARST AND OTHERS

A friend of Dean's and a most active arms and armor collector was publishing giant William Randolph Hearst. But so distinguished and exclusive was the New York Club that Hearst was never allowed membership! He nevertheless maintained an acquaintance with Dr. Dean and lived in baronial style at residences like the fabulous San Simeon and, though he spent relatively little time there, St. Donat's Castle in Wales. European arms and armor were among the favorites in Hearst's broad collecting interests. Among other celebrity arms collectors contemporary with Hearst were Henry Ford, Tom Mix, William S. Hart, Josiah K. Lilly, William K. Vanderbilt II, Stephen Van Rensselaer, Henry du Pont, and distinguished artist Maxfield Parrish (also a dedicated machinist, with a first-rate machine shop).

A later member of the Armor and Arms Club was John E. Parsons: Yale graduate, law clerk to U.S. Supreme Court Chief Justice William Howard Taft (1928–29), Wall Street lawyer, author, trustee of the New-York Historical Society, and active Colt collector and authority. Parsons almost single-handedly created a reference library on American arms collecting in the 1950s, doing books and articles on Colt, Winchester, Smith & Wesson, and derringers. He was a fly-fishing friend of Nelson Rockefeller's, and it was through Rockefeller that Parsons met Colt aficionado Philip R. Phillips of the prominent Oklahoma oil family. Parsons' death in 1976 signaled the end of an era in American arms collecting.

A NEW ERA OF ARMS COLLECTING IN AMERICA

In the 1950s and '60s, as the airplane made gun-collecting shows more accessible and gun values were skyrocketing, some of the moneyed-celebrity collectors slowed down or eliminated their attendance at collector meetings. The rapid pace of modern life has also led some enthusiasts to forgo the gun-show circuit, preferring instead to enjoy their firearms in the privacy of home or apartment, or by occasional private visits to bank vaults or museums where their pieces are on loan display.

The Armor and Arms Club of New York is still active. Among its post-1950 members were *The New Yorker* cartoonist Charles Addams, Dr. John Lattimer (author of a celebrated book on the Lincoln and Kennedy assassinations), Richard H. Randall Jr. (for many years director of the Walters Art Gallery, Baltimore), P. R. Phillips (father and uncle founded Phillips 66), Clay P. Bedford (president of Kaiser Aerospace & Electronics, and builder of the Hoover Dam), and Russell B. Aitken (one of the world's most experienced big-game hunters and bird shots). With the threat of crime in New York City, and the city's long-term negative attitude toward firearms, attendance at club meetings is not what one would wish it to be, but the historic arms and armor organization is still active.

JOHN B. SOLLEY AND TODAY'S COLLECTING FRATERNITY

A New Yorker who never belonged to the Armor and Arms Club and who had no interest in attending shows or belonging to any gun organization (except the National Rifle Association) was the late John B. Solley III. A grandson of Evan Lilly and an heir to the Lilly pharmaceutical fortune, Solley launched his collection when he was four years old and a family friend gave him a flintlock pistol. At his death in 1979, John Solley had, gun for gun, the finest collection of American antique arms in the world. His favorites were Colts, and he had the Serial No. 1 pre-Paterson Colt revolver, a pair of Lieutenant Colonel Custer's Navy Colts, five pairs of Dragoon Colts, *the* cased Walker Colt, *the* cased pair of Texas Patersons, several presentations from Colonel Colt (one of them to President Franklin Pierce), and the sensational forty-six-gun display board of Colt jobbers and New York dealers Hartley & Graham. The entire Solley collection was sold in 1979, and some of the most important pieces became part of the Colt Collection of the Raymond Baldwin Museum of Connecticut History. John Solley represented a modern species of collector to whom privacy is paramount.

In terms of numbers of collectors, values, and demand, the period since World War II has seen a rapidly expanding boom for arms collecting in America. Among the better-known collectors active in that period: members of the Ford, Mellon, Lilly, du Pont, Phillips, Olin, Donnolley, Woolworth, and Tufts families; entertainers Buddy Hackett, John Wayne, Johnny Cash, Hank Williams Jr., Mel Torme, Steve Cropper (of Booker T and the MGs), John Entwhistle (of The Who), Sammy Davis Jr., Clark Gable, Elvis Presley, Robert Conrad, Robert Fuller, Erik Estrada, Charlie Callas, Johnny Depp, Steve McQueen, Steven Seagal, Sylvester Stallone, Ernie Kovacs, Ted Nugent, and Jerry Lewis. Others include author and editor Michael V. Korda, New York radio commentator Barry Gray (originator of the talk-show format), novelist-screenwriter-playwright Dan Greenburg, screenwriter-playwright David Mamet, Calhoun Norton (whose father endowed the Norton Gallery of Art, Palm Beach, Florida), film producer-director Blake Edwards, director-writer John Milius, oilmen Jay P. Altmayer and John Mecom, athlete Kareem Abdul Jabbar, YO Ranch owner and developer Charles Schreiner III, magazine publisher Robert E. Petersen, George Strichman (for over twenty years chairman of the board of Colt Industries), and several very, very prominent giants of American contemporary business who would prefer to remain anonymous—among them the president of a major philanthropic and educational organization; the founder and president of a luxury luggage, clothing, and accessories company; and an heir to a major cosmetics concern.

From Henry VIII to the Fords and Mellons, what a rich heritage arms collectors share—both in the objects collected and in the pedigrees of past and present collectors of note. All have found captivating the unique attraction of arms, their history, mechanics, artistry, and function. What other collectibles can equal this rich and fascinating heritage, and what objects can boast of a more significant role in history's past 500 years?

How to Find Guns and Buy Them

Bearing in mind that injudicious advertising might invite a thief to your home or place of business, there are many ways to find collectors firearms. Basically these divide up into the following sources, all of which require hard work and developing a network of contacts.

THE GUN-SHOW CIRCUIT, LETTERHEADS, AND CARDS

A great deal will be said about gun shows in the present discourse; suffice it to say that much of the trading, buying, and selling in arms takes place at these events. This is the arena in which the skills of the trader come out, and there is a show ethic that must be observed: e.g., if you are scouting the show looking for treasures, and you see someone else already negotiating for a particular item, it is considered unethical to barge in and try to buy the item(s) out from under the person already trying to make a deal. However, having observed that a sale or trade did not take place, you may well wish to approach the seller, and inquire if the object still remains available.

If you know certain dealers and collectors are the source of the kinds of guns you seek, there is nothing wrong with advising them of your interest. A sample card that could solicit pieces is as follows:

J. D. Jones
Collector-Dealer
Seeking Fine Derringer Pistols
1100 Main Street
Any Town, CT 06999 U.S.A.
(860) 666-6666
Fax: (860) 666-6667

An appropriate letterhead could also be designed. In the author's case he has a half dozen different letterheads, some that are more personal and have nothing commercial on them whatever, and others that are quite commercial.

Cards and letterheads show that one is serious and active in a field, and not a tire-kicker, who could turn into a "time-sponge" and end up wasting time and energy on the part of those who are contacted.

The writer began collecting business cards when in his early twenties, and now has in excess of 5,000 of them. One thing that is clearly evident in this mass of material is that some cards are rather elegant, while others are on the cheap side—most are somewhat average. Any and all, however, are clear declarations that the party is serious about his gun collecting, and is willing to pay to purchase in the field of his desires.

GUN SHOPS

Every gun shop has potential as a source of items for the collector. And many such shops already carry in stock pieces that are more suited for the collector than for the shooter. Granted most of these are secondhand guns, but all the guns we collect were once "secondhand." If you are a traveler, like most Americans, and you find out the locations of gun shops that might have the goods, it might pay to call on them. On the other hand, most such shops already have someone, usually local, who is seeking objects, and might very well give that regular client first refusal on the good stuff. Being aware that many shops already have a loyalty to a dealer or friendly collector, sometimes it is not worth the effort to call on gun shops at all.

AUCTIONS

The business of collectors firearms seems to run in cycles. In the pioneering days of arms collecting, auction houses and dealers were an important source of material, with the dealers doing a lot of the action. These were such pre–World War II operations as the American Art Association, which later became Parke-Bernet (still later bought out by Sotheby's); one of the old-time dealers was Stephen Van Rensselaer, and still another was Sumner Healey. In the early days of collecting in New York City, Bashford Dean, first Curator of Arms and Armor for the Metropolitan Museum of Art, was a key source of fine items to the upper crust of collectors. Today, of course, that kind of commercialism would not be permitted by museum officials.

In the post–World War II era, much of the business in the United States was among dealers and collectors who were part-time dealers ("collector/dealers"). But in the 1980s the auction houses really came on with a vengeance, particularly Christie's and Sotheby's, and for several years Richard Bourne Co.; next, in a very big way (and still dominating the field), arose Butterfield & Butterfield. There are presently several other very active firms handling quite a bit of merchandise. Names and addresses of the leading auctioneers now presenting arms auctions are listed in Appendix 3.

Buying at auctions allows the client the opportunity to examine his purchases, or at the least to discuss the items beforehand with the experts who handle the material and operate the sales. Viewing days preceding the sales present the objects under ideal conditions. The client should handle whatever is of interest, and decide on a limit to which he or she will bid for each piece. Though this requires a good deal of willpower, it is best to establish limits, thus avoiding the inevitable urge to keep on bidding and sometimes ending up paying more than the object might be worth.

You will also see other experts, besides those employed by the auction house, to whom queries can be addressed. It is, of course, up to you to decide whose opinion you will accept, bearing in mind that sometimes advice is worth what it costs (usually nothing).

If you are uncertain about any aspect of an auction, be sure to read the exposition published in the preface material to the catalogue. If you have any questions, be sure to ask and get the answers.

When it is sale time, you have to be alert, since the auctioneers often go at a rapid pace. There is not a lot of time in which to dwell on whether or not you want to go another notch up in the bidding. There again, having set a limit and standing by it is important—preventing one from going out of control.

Another advantage of auction buying is the educational value: Often the tremendous variety at these sales allows the collector and collector/dealer the chance to see a great deal of material and to quickly learn about values, about different types of guns, about what collectors want, and countless other things one should know.

The sale also presents an opportunity to meet a number of people in the gun business: fellow collectors, fellow dealers, journalists, photographers, and more.

Although it is possible for good clients to get some time from most auction houses in which to pay for purchases, most will charge a penalty, storage charges, and interest for objects not paid for within the prescribed time period.

It is illegal in many states and municipalities for "shills" to run up prices at auctions, or for the consigners themselves to arrange to have prices artificially run up. Also illegal is the often-discussed practice of an auctioneer taking a price off a chandelier, or "off the wall." However, for auction houses that have reserve figures on lots, the auctioneer has the right to bid on behalf of the owner until that protective figure is reached.

A ring of collaborators, in which persons agree not to bid on certain items or to allow an agreed-upon bidder to buy something without competition, is also illegal.

Popular antique-arms specialist and New York gallery owner Martin Lane (at right), with his friend Nick Fallana. They are holding the Colt Texas Paterson revolver donated by entertainer Johnny Cash to the Metropolitan Museum of Art for the 1985 benefit auction at Christie's, New York. The guitar was part of the sale lot, and was signed by Johnny—who also made an unusual appearance as a guest auctioneer, assisted by Brian Cole, one of America's foremost auctioneers (later appointed director of Butterfield & Butterfield's galleries in Los Angeles).

ANTIQUE SHOPS

Although antiques dealers often have broad general knowledge, many know just enough to price their material. And sometimes not enough to realize when they are really trying to get too much—and you are simply not willing to pay more than a fair figure. Thinking back over the years, the author can recollect only a few instances in which the countless hours he has spent in antiques shops paid off in finding a good gun. In most instances he enjoyed the visits, and may have found some other object of antiquity to purchase, thus at least getting his reward from that aspect of the visit.

Often the antiques dealer already has a client in mind, who will see any and all guns that come into the store or gallery. But if you do call on antiques shops, be sure to have a business card, or a want list, or some other means of leaving an impression.

YARD OR GARAGE SALES

Such informal sales are highly unlikely to be productive. But it is still a good idea to have that business card or other giveaway that could eventually turn up a treasure from new contacts. I have never found a firearms-related object in a yard or garage sale. On the other hand, there are a few collectors and dealers who have. Gerald Fox, one of the old-time collectors, bought a rare and original Walker Colt revolver brought to him by a mother whose lucky son found the gun in a garbage can on his way home from school. Imagine finding a Walker model, one of the great prizes of arms collecting, in an ash can!

ADVERTISING IN TRADE PUBLICATIONS AND ELSEWHERE

Judging from the number of dealers and collector/dealers who run advertisements in trade magazines and other likely venues, there must be something to the exposure and the costs. Such advertising might often seem more like the "institutional" kind, for image and prestige purposes. But in the early days of collecting the effort often paid off. With the diminishing number of guns coming out of private homes and other non-gun-collector sources, a respectful person with a dedicated interest in firearms might actually be lucky with those sources—despite the costs involved.

Try a display ad in a publication like *The Gun Report* or *Man at Arms*, or even the more expensive *Outdoor Life*, and see what happens. But be certain to weigh the advantages and the disadvantages. William M. Locke, for decades the acknowledged dean of arms collectors, occasionally ran small display advertisements. But it was his network of contacts and friends, which he had developed since he was in his twenties, that led to many of the guns he was able to locate. Further, actively attending gun shows and, in those days, an occasional auction, as well as an unending correspondence and telephone follow-ups, were all good reasons for his dominant role in arms collecting for over forty years.

Running an advertisement, however, requires responsibility. If people respond to your ads, and you don't in turn respond to them, they will soon become discouraged. The author virtually never advertises, although, in a way, each of his books is like a business card. That follow-up is crucial, and is simply a part of being efficient and professional, and successful.

FIREARMS INDUSTRY AND COLLECTOR/DEALER SHOWS

For the gun enthusiast, whether collector, shooter, or any other person keen on the considerable variety of firearms-related hobbies and vocations, there are three major trade and collector shows, often held in Las Vegas, Nevada, which are comparable to "the greatest shows on earth." Conveniently, the dates for these three most significant of all U.S. arms shows are within a week's time of each other, in late January and early February.

The first of these three mega-events is SHOT Show, a true extravaganza, with over 25,000 persons in attendance, representing virtually all the companies and individuals who make contemporary firearms, ammunition, and accessories.

The second of these events is the annual meeting and show of Safari Club International, complete with U.S. senators and congressmen, and, at the 1997 show, former president George Bush, General Norman D. Schwarzkopf, and former vice president Dan Quayle. There were several hundred exhibitors, among them professional hunters from around the world and gunmakers like J. Purdey & Sons, Holland & Holland, Ltd., J. Rigby & Co., Ltd., Westley Richards, and Sturm, Ruger & Co., as well as sporting-apparel firms the likes of Hunting World, Inc., and Euro Chasse, and great taxidermists, numerous talented wildlife artists, and thousands of dedicated hunter-conservationists.

Finally, oriented more for the collector of antique, vintage, and contemporary firearms—and therefore most important for readers of this book—is Wallace Beinfeld's Antique Arms Show, held for approximately thirty-five years at the Hotel Sahara in Las Vegas. Beginning in the summer of 1997, this three-times-a-year event was held at the spacious and elegant ballroom of the Hotel Riviera. With the likes of most of the top dealers, many leading collectors, and a throng of visiting collectors and the public, this show is truly "world-class."

These quite extraordinary events reflect the tremendous numbers of persons who share a devotion and a dedication to firearms. There are two additional major events, each in their own time slots, the first of which is the American Firearms Industry annual trade show in Atlantic City, New Jersey, held in May. For details contact the American Firearms Industry, 2455 E. Sunrise Boulevard, Suite 916, Ft. Lauderdale, Florida 33304.

The National Rifle Association Annual Meetings, which usually take place in late April or early May at various large cities around the country, have been premier shows for decades. Further, in 1996 the annual meeting was joined by a separate show, recognizing the importance of arms collecting to the future of gun ownership in America: the NRA Gun Collectors Show and Conference held at Opryland in Nashville, Tennessee, in mid-September. The 1997 show was scheduled for mid-August, in Pittsburgh, Pennsylvania.

WRITING ARTICLES AND BOOKS, I.E., ESTABLISHING EXPERT CREDENTIALS

Although he never had the above-noted goal in mind, the author's writings, and his dedication to the world of firearms, have inevitably led to an avalanche of phone calls, e-mail, snail-mail (regular mail via post office), media notices of interest, and word-of-mouth leads. Further, on publication of each book, the author's appearance in promotions at gun shows, on radio and TV interviews, and at press parties in New York City and elsewhere, all precipitate even more leads and inquiries.

The results have been satisfying and rewarding, though they have meant sixteen- and eighteen-hour days along the way, working at that backbreaking pace virtually nonstop for decades.

However, no one in the field of arms collecting is not pleased to be busy. This is like being paid for pursuing one's hobby, a dream job to virtually everyone who makes a living in the arms-collecting arena.

TRAVELING AND FIREARMS

For up-to-date information on what travelers need to know about firearms, the NRA-ILA publishes a brochure entitled *Guide to the Interstate Transportation of Firearms*.* To quote from this publication,

> Federal law prohibits the carrying of any firearm, concealed or unconcealed, on or about the person or in carry-on baggage while aboard an aircraft. Unloaded firearms not accessible to the passenger while aboard the aircraft are permitted when:
>
> 1. The passenger has notifed the airline when checking the baggage that the firearm is in the baggage and that it is unloaded.
> 2. The baggage in which the firearm is carried is locked, and only the passenger checking the baggage retains a key.
> 3. The baggage is carried in an area, other than the flight crew compartment, that is inaccessible to passengers. . . .

The brochure states further, regarding other carriers:

> Any passenger who owns or legally possesses a firearm being transported aboard any common or contract carrier for movement with the passenger in interstate or foreign commerce must deliver the unloaded firearm into the custody of the pilot, captain, conductor, or operator of such common or contract carrier for the duration of the trip. Check with each carrier before your trip to avoid problems.
>
> Bus companies usually refuse to transport firearms. Trains usually allow the transportation of encased long guns, if they are dissassembled or the bolt is removed.

The brochure also explains the ins and outs of transporting firearms interstate in your automobile, something particularly important to dealers, collector/dealers, and collectors when traveling to and from gun shows.

*Available from the NRA-ILA Grassroots, 11250 Waples Mill Road, Fairfax, VA 22030-9400; (800) 392-8683.

THE ETIQUETTE AND TECHNIQUE OF BUYING GUNS

A lot of what follows is simply common sense, but it reflects the particular mores of the arms-collecting fraternity. This is a world virtually devoid of lawyers, other than those who are collectors themselves. Rarely is there a lawsuit brought against anyone in the arms-collecting field. This gentlemanly conduct is one of the reasons collectors derive such joy and pleasure from arms collecting. The greed of some lawyers (we all agree there are *too many* lawyers) has been instrumental in creating the current atmosphere of litigation madness. But this is not so in the world of arms collecting.

There are several reasons for the insignificance of lawyers in the field. First, a handshake is enough to seal a deal, even if you change your mind. Sometimes a collector or dealer may feel the next day that perhaps he paid too much, or acted impulsively, in making a purchase. Too bad; a deal is a deal.

Generally speaking, the only exceptions that would allow a buyer to back out are if he has discovered, and can prove, that the gun has been misrepresented—or if both he and the seller wish to back out of a deal.

In making an offer on a gun, the buyer has made, in effect, a verbal commitment to purchase. Should the seller agree to those points, you have a deal.

In these days of long-winded contracts on such purchases as real estate, cars, or other expensive merchandise, it may be a surprise to the novice to learn that a deal on a costly firearm could be a simple exchange of payment, or trade, with a simple bill of sale. The author has sold firearms for over $400,000, for which he received a check and the buyer received a one-page bill of sale. Generally, however, a valuable antique of that distinction will also be accompanied by papers and documents, a pedigree, and possibly even copies of photographs, articles, and books relevant to the item's history and other merits.

Dealers normally give a three-day inspection privilege for merchandise that has been sold through the mail, by fax, over the phone, or over the Internet.

If the buyer feels he should have an expert look at the piece, he should bloody well be sure that the "expert" really is qualified. Nothing is more annoying to a dealer who sells a piece in good faith than to find that the collector wants to return the item because "someone" feels the item has been refinished, or is otherwise not as represented. The author more than once has had to assure collectors that a Paterson Colt does indeed have its original finish—although few can tell for sure, since these arms are often misleading: high polishes brought about high-gloss blues, but sometimes the factory workmen leaned hard on the polishing wheel, thereby overpolishing, and sometimes leaving the genuine markings weak.

Another common failing is for collectors to question the finish on mint Colts from the Hartford period. The author remembers his amusement when one well-meaning writer remarked how disappointed he was in the quality of the Samuel Colt Collection at the Wadsworth Atheneum: "Too bad most of the guns were refinished." Fact is, nearly all the Colts at the Atheneum are in perfect, unfired condition, including the world's finest Paterson Colt revolver. The exceptions are two revolvers (a Navy with a reblued barrel and a Belt Model Paterson refinished overall, undoubtedly by the Colt factory in the 19th century).

PRICES QUOTED

Bear in mind that at gun shows, and even in dealers' lists, the buyer is permitted to try to haggle, up to a point. Some dealers will not back off a dime. At gun shows, the sticker price is often considered the price at which negotiations begin. The author likes to state simply, "What's your best price on this piece?" But other techniques include: "How about a clergyman's discount?" and "I'm interested in this piece, at a price of $XXX." Another means is simply to offer some items in trade. Once you offer a trade or a specified price, you are committed to follow through if the seller agrees to your offer.

It is not unusual for the quoted or list price of a piece to be as much as 10 to 15 percent above what the seller will actually take. One collector, known for his sense of humor, says that he takes the quoted price, divides that by four, and then offers half of that.

Although the arms-collecting field truly does not have a ticker-tape type source of values for collectors firearms, used guns are another matter. These are easier to figure, since most are still in production, and therefore readily available through publications like *Gun List*, *Shotgun News*, and *Gun Journal*. Further, many are in gun shops and sporting-goods stores around the country. And manufacturers publish catalogues and lists, which help to provide guidance.

Antique and obsolete firearms for the collector are, however, another matter entirely. Some of these pieces are so rare that many collectors will never see an example in their lifetime. At the same time, the buyer has to be able to judge which of these are going to appreciate, and which are, perhaps, extremely rare, but not necessarily wanted by most collectors.

Thus it is easier for a Colt or Winchester collector, because there are more collectors keen on owning these pieces, and therefore more willing to spend top dollar. The market is stronger for them, because more people want to own examples. And there is more reference material that can provide guidance to the keen buyer. *Flayderman's Guide to Historical American Arms and Their Values* is an important source, specific to a great many variations, some of which do not appear in this price guide, since this volume also includes a great many modern arms, and European ones as well.

A collector should not be flip in trying to buy something he wants, making an outrageously low offer. On the other hand, he can get a feel for how determined the seller is to realize a particular price—and might well enjoy the sales pitch the dealer or dealer/collector will present. After a while the buyer can recognize B.S. as opposed to solid expertise, experience, and sincerity.

MAKING AN OFFER

The fact that most gun shows are only two-day affairs does not allow a lot of time for one to make a decision. Further, in that arena, there are a great many experienced and knowledgeable individuals who are capable of making a decision quickly. You may well find some great piece, a "sleeper" that no one else has spotted. You have to act fast, or that item is gone. When the author was doing about thirty gun shows a year, he would prowl about as the show opened, looking for treasures. He saw others doing the same, some of them quite aggressively, to the point that they might help the seller unwrap his wares! You may not have the opportunity to make a phone call (though that's much easier now, with cellular phones), and someone else may be looking over your shoulder ready to pounce.

Asking a dealer or other seller to hold something at a gun show is unfair unless your decision will come quickly. Sometimes the shows settle down after the first couple of hours, and if you have tied up a piece and then decide not to take it, that could damage the item, killing its sale to others.

KILLING A GUN

A collector or dealer has "killed" a gun when he has "bad-mouthed" it with comments detrimental to the future sale of that piece. Killing can happen through some irresponsible person who claims the gun is refinished or otherwise altered, or that it has been faked or is otherwise not as represented. A few dealers and collectors have the reputation for "bad-mouthing" or "poison-gassing" guns. Dealing with irresponsible assaults on the integrity of firearms is part of the education of the serious arms collector. The big-mouth who "bad-mouths" a good gun is likely also to be the kind of boor who will do the same to the reputation of someone who often does not deserve that kind of treatment.

The author has written approximately 1,000 letters of documentation on collectors firearms. Many of these are on perfectly authentic pieces that did not have the advantage of "factory" letters. Or the letters were needed because some supposed expert had claimed the gun had serious defects.

FACTORY LETTERS

Colt's Manufacturing Co., Smith & Wesson, the Marlin Firearms Co., and Ruger are four major firms that maintain records, which can be accessed by collectors, sometimes on a fee basis, sometimes for free. The records of Winchester were transferred to the Buffalo Bill Historical Center, Cody, Wyoming, and are available for a fee.

Factory letters tell you only what the original ledger books state about a firearm. These are not to be construed, necessarily, as "letters of authenticity." Sometimes a gun has been faked and sold with a letter stating the features present on the original gun. An example is a fake Buntline Special Colt revolver that was accompanied by a letter stating the features of an original revolver bearing the same serial number.

A factory letter is important to have with a gun—but it's not always absolutely crucial. The author has written many a letter on a perfectly authentic Single Action Army or percussion Colt for which the factory clerk somehow failed to note certain important facts; usually that omitted detail was the simple word *engraved*. Or perhaps the fact that the grips were relief carved, or that the revolver was gold inlaid, was not noted.

Fortunately, as noted in the section on fakes, doing a truly creative job in faking an antique firearm is not easily accomplished. With experience and education, and seeing lots of original specimens, the collector will soon pick up the ability to spot most miscreants. Factory letters are, in most instances, entirely accurate, and will prove to be useful.

PAYMENT

Until a collector has established a reputation, he may encounter some difficulty in getting sellers to accept checks. Occasionally a bad-check expert will do a tap dance on a gun show, but that is extremely rare. Although there are risks in carrying around cash for acquisitions, there are some who find that the best means of closing a deal quickly. Writing a check for cash and cashing it at your bank before leaving for a show can eliminate the possible problems of dealing with sellers who won't take a check or credit cards. Increasingly sellers are accepting credit cards, and traveler's checks are another alternative.

Many dealers also offer variations of a "lay-away" plan, allowing purchase of a piece over a period of months. Usually the object remains in the possession of the seller until fully paid for.

Trading is also a viable means of closing a deal. Trade and cash immediately, trades and cash over time, or variations on the theme are all acceptable. The most creative trader of all was Johnie Bassett, who could make a down payment of $1,000 on a $40,000 sale, then give any number of postdated checks, and trade sculpture and paintings, furniture, silver, porcelains, and even guns! Johnie spoke and carried on like a good old boy, but he once confided to the author that he felt no one could out-trade him—and nobody ever did. Because of his skills, and his nerve, he owned many of the finest Colts and Winchesters in existence during his lifetime of collecting.

A final note: Collectors who become friendly with a particular dealer can often call on that dealer's connections and expertise to close a deal. Make no mistake about it, no great collector was able to put together his collection without relying in some way on the expertise and experience of a top dealer.

How to Sell Guns

Commerce in the domain of collectors firearms is a combination of selling through gun stores, through gun shows, through auction houses, through friends and acquaintances, through mail order, and, lately, through the Internet.

DIRECTLY TO COLLECTORS AND TO DEALERS

When Norm Flayderman speaks of the marketing of collectors firearms, he likes to use the term "the last frontier." Most of those in the business are self-employed; most of them are free to travel and find that they do so perhaps all too often. One never knows for sure where he or she might end up in a particular week, or month, or year. It is possible to schedule shows that are worth attending. But learning of a collection that you can buy, or take on consignment, or whatever your *modus operandi* is, may suddenly change your plans completely. In fact, while completing the manuscript for this book, the author was interrupted on three occasions by gun collections that suddenly became available, by an urgent appraisal involved in a contentious divorce case, and by the opportunity to get a rare Colt revolver he had first seen in 1962(!), still in the hands of the same owner.

A typical year for the author: besides commitments for writing articles and books and a regular column for *Gun Journal*, duties include researching and writing letters of documentation for collectors and dealers specific to important guns, assisting a museum in identifying or selling a piece or a collection, identifying guns for the public, assisting Christie's with evaluations and identifications and sometimes specifically with items for auction (the author has been associated with that august firm since 1981), writing to old-time collector/dealer contacts to locate fresh guns, searching through over thirty-five years of correspondence for leads, and even occasionally dealing with the media when their interest is piqued by some timely event (such as the promotion attendant to a new collectors firearms book, or perhaps an item being sold in a public auction).

Thus, although the writer tries to plan an entire year of activity, he (like all his colleagues in the field) has to remain flexible—a distinct advantage of being self-employed. On the other hand, it has often been observed that making a living in this business is a matter of feast or famine. And with the increasing competition at finding good guns to sell, the famine part often overtakes the feast.

In order to plan out a year, my own method of operation is to try to have a new book appear each fall, which will allow for worthwhile action at a show—since many visitors to those events are desirous of keeping their libraries up to date. And while attending the shows, the opportunities are good for finding guns for collector clients—and for including some pieces on my sales table that might appeal to other collectors and dealers.

Particularly when planning to visit a European show, your schedule and plans need to be set up months in advance, since one way to get the word out that you will be at a particular event is to contact a foreign magazine—for me, luckily, my German publisher, Motorbuch Verlag—to see whether room is available for a special promotion in its booth.

One of the old-time gun dealers, now retired, used to be proud of his ability to come to a gun show with a few hundred dollars in his pocket, to buy or get some pieces "on the arm" (on consignment), and work the show so effectively that by the time Sunday afternoon rolled around, he had made a few thousand dollars! He was consistently good at this, and was able to do so because he knew guns, what they were worth, and what customers wanted. Also, it was helpful that people at the shows knew him, and expected him to come up with good material.

But what about the novice, who has to start from scratch? This is not an easy world to break into, and the novice finds out rather quickly the quality of his or her buying, trading, and selling skills.

OVEREXPOSING A GOOD GUN

The seller who may have a fine gun should be aware that if he does not go about selling it in an intelligent manner, he may very well overexpose it, and find that the best client for the piece doesn't want to buy it, sometimes at any price.

Here's what happened in a famous case from the 1980s, when a new collector located a rare and beautiful Single Action Army Colt from the mid-1870s. The revolver was richly engraved and in extraordinary condition. Not wanting to keep the piece for himself, he shopped it around trying to squeeze out the last dime by working one collector and dealer against the other. Finally, everyone who might have been interested would no longer tolerate the way the seller was marketing the gun. Further, the market took an unexpected dive, since the top collectors who might have been interested either died, changed interests, or were fed up with the squeeze tactics of the owner. Instead of being able to

HADLYME CONNECTICUT 06439
FAX 860 526-9514

R. L. Wilson

HISTORICAL CONSULTANT
COLT FIREARMS, HARTFORD
AND TO
"IN THE BLOOD"—FILM & VIDEO
"THE ART OF AMERICAN ARMS"
—MUSEUM LOAN EXHIBITION
"SON OF A GUN"—BBC-TV
"COLT FIREARMS LEGENDS" —SONY
AND
"WINCHESTER FIREARMS LEGENDS"
CHAIRMAN
ANTIQUE ARMS COMMITTEE
U.S. SOCIETY OF ARMS & ARMOUR

SAMUEL COLT PRESENTS (1961)
ARMS COLLECTION OF COLONEL COLT (1963)
L. D. NIMSCHKE, FIREARMS ENGRAVER (1965)
THE EVOLUTION OF THE COLT (1967)
THE RAMPANT COLT (1969)
COLT COMMEMORATIVE FIREARMS (1969 & 1974)
THEODORE ROOSEVELT – OUTDOORSMAN (1970)
THE BOOK OF COLT FIREARMS (1971 & 1993)
THE BOOK OF COLT ENGRAVING (1974)
THE BOOK OF WINCHESTER ENGRAVING (1975)
ANTIQUE ARMS ANNUAL (EDITOR)
COLT PISTOLS (1976) (WITH R. E. HABLE)
PATERSON COLT PISTOL VARIATIONS (1979) (WITH P. R. PHILLIPS)
THE COLT HERITAGE (1979)
THE "RUSSIAN" COLTS (1979)
COLT ENGRAVING (1982)
COLT HANDGUNS (JAPANESE, 1980)
RARE AND HISTORIC FIREARMS (1981)
WINCHESTER: THE GOLDEN AGE (1983)
COLT'S DATES OF MANUFACTURE 1837 - 1978 (1984)
THE DERINGER IN AMERICA (1985 & 1993) (WITH L. D. EBERHART)
COLT: AN AMERICAN LEGEND (1985)
RARE FIREARMS – A BENEFIT AUCTION (1985)
COLT UNA LEGGENDA AMERICANA (1987)
COLT UNE LEGENDE AMERICAINE (1988)
WINCHESTER ENGRAVING (1989)
COLT EINE AMERIKANISCHE LEGENDE (1989)
WINCHESTER AN AMERICAN LEGEND (1991)
THE PEACEMAKERS (1992)
STEEL CANVAS (1995)
RUGER (1996)

**THE L.D. NIMSCHKE
COLT THIRD MODEL DRAGOON REVOLVER
1 of 50
As Featured in
The Metropolitan Museum of Art-Christie's Benefit Auction
for the Museum's Department of Arms and Armor
October 8th 1985
Original Design by Alvin A. White
for The Heritage Guild, Trumbull, Connecticut
Revolvers Purchased in the White
from the Colt Factory
and Built by American Master Engravers
for The Heritage Guild, 1985-86
Serial Number 24549**

The Colt-L.D. Nimschke Third Model Dragoon 1 of 50 special series of revolvers was made in 1985 and 1986, with the original design by Alvin A. White, and the production exclusively for The Heritage Guild.

Enclosed is a copy of the advertising brochure issued in 1985, as well as a copy of relevant material from the catalogue of The Metropolitan Museum of Art, Department of Arms and Armor Benefit Auction, held by Christie's, October 8th 1985. The original brochure advertised the revolver at $3,790. The revolver donated to The Metropolitan Museum auction brought $4,180.

These revolvers were supplied by the Colt factory, "in the white", at the very end of the company's production of blackpowder revolvers, in 1985. The author was involved in the manufacture of the special Heritage Guild series, and will be featuring the issue in the forthcoming book, *The Modern Colt Blackpowder Revolver*, a joint project with co-author Thomas A. Conroy. The revolvers will also be featured in the forthcoming edition, *The Colt Engraving Book*, in the chapter on Alvin A. White.

This important limited edition series of cased, deluxe-engraved, gold- and silver-plated, and carved ivory-gripped Colt revolvers is worthy of the finest private or museum arms collection. Serial number **24549** is a superb example of this unique tribute to the legendary L.D. Nimschke, Master Firearms Engraver.

RLWilson

realize a fair price, the collector had no buyers, and eventually sold the revolver for about 40 percent less than the best offer he had received before the sudden changes! Overexposure and greed had "killed" what otherwise would have been a good sale.

Bearing that in mind, anyone who wishes to dispose of a privately owned firearm, and wants to sell to or otherwise work through a dealer, would be well advised to consider any of the professionals in Appendix 4, all of whom make their living in the business; the majority are from the U.S.A., with a few from outside the country.*

CONSIGNMENTS

Sometimes an object's purchase would require such a sum that many in the business might not be able to come up with the necessary cash. Or sometimes a collector or other owner recognizes the sale might realize more by consignment of the item to a broker, dealer, or another collector who would be willing to work for a lesser profit. Most consigners will take on the sale of an item at a commission of anywhere from 10 to 20 percent. For the agreed-upon figure, the dealer or broker is normally expected to assume all the time and effort, and costs, of marketing the piece.

Consignments call for a clear understanding between parties, and, in many instances, the seller should make clear to the consigner that the object might sell in a few days or weeks, or it might require up to as much as six months, and maybe even more. Some crucial and rare pieces demand a very careful orchestration. The following is a checklist for any consignment transaction.

- Draw up a consignment document, spelling out all terms.
- Write a document or letter on the item(s), to facilitate presenting same for sale. This could well be along the lines of the documenting sample letter illustrated here.
- Think through the best way to market the item: gun shows, a personal call to the potential buyer, putting the piece on the Internet, advertising in a magazine, and so forth.
- Actually acting on the above might mean awaiting a particular gun show, the proper timing to see the scoped-out buyer, perhaps arranging for a friend to advise the potential buyer of this new item (recommending it as just right for his or her collection), and so forth.
- As in selling any item, think out carefully just the way to present it. At many gun shows, the best pieces are

*This list concentrates on professionals in the field, many of them known to the author. Should any dealer's name be omitted, kindly contact the writer for inclusion in future editions.

kept under the seller's table, being held until that right moment to show it off ("timing is everything"). Sometimes that moment is not even during the show, but perhaps with some ceremony in the privacy of a hotel or motel room.

- Once a deal is made, the seller needs to be careful that he pays off the consigner as quickly as the funds have cleared. One must not fall into the trap of delaying payment, and later finding that the client's money vanished into some other use.

Many dealers do not want to take on consignments, preferring to own objects outright. But today it is not unusual for an owner to want a greater involvement in the sale process, hoping also to receive a better price for his material.

ADVANTAGES OF SELLING AN ITEM OR A COLLECTION THROUGH AN AUCTION HOUSE

There are several advantages of selling through an auction house.

- Wide exposure for the object(s), permitting more potential buyers to be aware of its availability, and therefore, hopefully, more competition in the bidding.
- Reasonable costs, varying from 10 to 15 percent (on average), plus possible costs for photography, insurance, shipping, and other expenses. Generally there is a 10 percent premium paid by the buyer, which goes entirely to the auction house.
- Expert assistance for proper cataloguing, scheduling of the sale, advertising and promotion, and related details. An endorsement by qualified experts can be crucial in gaining the confidence of bidders.
- A qualified auction house will provide expert descriptions and produce a handsome catalogue that will encourage bidders.

If the collection or object is valuable enough, it is possible with some auction companies for the seller to obtain an advance against estimated realized prices. This amount could be as much as 50 percent of value, and possibly more. Some houses will even buy your collection outright, although this practice is not the usual *modus operandi* of auctioneers.

Some auction-house staff can even provide guidance on tax liability and other questions. And giving estimates of prices objects should realize is free of charge. On the other hand, if an appraisal is needed, or certain other services are not part of the auction *per se*, the house would normally charge a per diem fee.

Finally, when someone has put together an impressive collection, he or she might very well like to have the material covered in a book. Collections like those of Richard C. Marohn, M.D., Carl Press, Robert Howard, Charles L. Bricker, Karl Moldenhauer, Keith Neal, George Repaire, and many others have been immortalized by the handsome catalogues of their collections. The importance of this is evident by reference to the bibliography accompanying this *Price Guide*—in which several private-collection auction catalogues are noted.

A note on scheduling: tying dates between gun shows or in conjunction with special events (like the annual NRA Gun Collectors Show and Conference), and avoiding holidays and potential bad weather, are among several factors to be considered. Further, it is important to avoid offering too much of the same type of material at any one time. Some collections, like the historic Press sales held by Butterfield & Butterfield, work better when spread out over a period of years.

DISADVANTAGES OF AUCTION-HOUSE SALE

Between the date of consignment and the date of actual sale there might be five to six months. Unless you are satisfied with possible partial advance payments, or can wait the approximate half year, other avenues for sale should be pursued.

- A public auction leaves no opportunity for trading an item, which some collectors prefer from time to time, as opposed to an outright sale.
- There may be some family or other professional or personal embarrassment attached to selling items at auction—a public venue open to considerable scrutiny.
- The protection price (the "reserve"), which establishes the lowest sum at which a consigner will sell an object, may be misjudged, and could be too high. As a consequence, the item might not sell. The best advice here is simply this: Do not set the protective figure so high that it will discourage bidders. The buyer does not mind bidding against another legitimate bidder, but he does not want to bid against the owner, or the owner's set restrictive figure.

  One can determine the reserve figure simply by looking at the estimates. This protective figure can never be higher than the upper end of the estimate range.

  Some sales do not reach their hoped-for figures, and it is worth contacting the auction house after a sale, in the event an item you want to buy went unsold. That might prove to be the most judicious time to make your purchase. However, it is risky to take the chance that something you want might remain unsold. If it does sell, and you still want it, try to keep track of who the purchaser was, and see if something might be arranged following the sale. If any object fails to sell, particularly if the object is an important one, it will be tainted, and might not be salable on the market again for several

BILL OF SALE FOR COLLECTOR FIREARM

(Please type or print)

RECEIVED OF ...., residing at ....

........................, the sum of .... dollars ($........................) and

.... in trade in full payment of the following described firearm:

Maker's Name ....

Maker's Address ....

Country and Date of Manufacture ....

Model .... Serial Number(s) ....

Condition (See other side for NRA Condition Standards) ....

Ignition System ....

Barrel(s) .... Barrel(s) Length ....

Caliber(s) or Gauge(s) ....

Over-all Length .... Weight ....

Accessories Included ....

Markings, Engravings and Inscriptions (Describe) ....

....

....

....

....

Stock or Grips (Describe) ....

....

Repairs, Alterations and Replacements (Describe) ....

....

....

....

....

....

The term "Firearm" used in this Bill of Sale is employed in the general sense and not in reference to any legal definition which might appear in published statutes.

(over)

Historical Claims (Authenticity and Origin of Arm and/or Inscriptions, etc.) ....

....

....

....

....

....

....

Name and Address of Previous Owner ....

....

I certify that the information in this Bill of Sale is true and complete, and that I have the right to sell and give possession of the firearm described.

SIGNED AND SEALED this .... day of ...., 19........

....
(Name of Seller)

Received the firearm described in the foregoing Bill of Sale:

....
(Signature of Seller)

....
(Street Address of Seller)

....
(City & State of Seller)

IMPORTANT INFORMATION FOR COLLECTOR FIREARMS BUYERS

This form should be filled in and signed by the seller of the firearm, and carefully read by the buyer before accepting the firearm and paying for it.

There are many spurious firearms in circulation and some are passed along in good faith as genuine, while others are misrepresented by the seller.

There is no simple way in which a collector can 'protect' himself against buying a spurious gun. But the following rules, if heeded, will reduce the risk to a minimum.

(1) Deal with a reputable dealer or individual.
(2) If you are not sure about a gun's authenticity, have it checked by a recognized authority.
(3) Above all demand a bill of sale that is signed by the seller and includes the name and address of the seller and a full description of the gun, as represented.

If the seller will not put down in writing, above his signature, what he represents the gun to be, then don't buy the gun.

NRA CONDITION STANDARDS FOR ANTIQUE FIREARMS

FACTORY NEW—all original parts; 100% original finish; in perfect condition in every respect, inside and out.

EXCELLENT—all original parts; over 80% original finish; sharp lettering, numerals and design on metal and wood; unmarred wood; fine bore.

FINE—all original parts; over 30% original finish; sharp lettering, numerals and design on metal and wood; minor marks in wood; good bore.

VERY GOOD—all original parts; none to 30% original finish; original metal surfaces smooth with all edges sharp; clear lettering, numerals and design on metal; wood slightly scratched or bruised; bore disregarded for collectors firearms.

GOOD—some minor replacement parts; metal smoothly rusted or lightly pitted in places, cleaned or reblued; principal lettering, numerals and design on metal legible; wood refinished, scratched, bruised or minor cracks repaired; in good working order.

FAIR—some major parts replaced; minor replacement parts may be required; metal rusted, may be lightly pitted all over, vigorously cleaned or reblued; rounded edges of metal and wood; principal lettering, numerals and design on metal partly obliterated; wood scratched, bruised, cracked or repaired where broken; in fair working order or can be easily repaired and placed in working order.

POOR—major and minor parts replaced; major replacement parts required and extensive restoration needed; metal deeply pitted; principal lettering, numerals and design obliterated; wood badly scratched, bruised, cracked or broken; mechanically inoperative; generally undesirable as a collectors firearm.

Form designed by the National Rifle Association of America.

This form may be reproduced in its entirety.

years. Therefore, if one is offering items for sale by auction, do all that is possible, and legal, to make sure it will not remain unsold on sale day.

- Selling your collection might well spell the end of your collecting activity and presence: Seeing that you have disposed of your treasures, old contacts might figure you are now entirely out of the arms field. If this is not the case, then make sure they understand that fact clearly. Normally, an auction of a person's collection represents the end of his days in the field.
- Tax complications: It is possible that a private sale might have offered a means of marketing the item(s) without the public exposure an auction presents. However, one must be careful to remain within the law. For example, an object or collection sold privately could be paid for over a period of time, which could be of benefit from a tax standpoint. Such arrangements are much easier done privately than with an auction house—although evidently some houses are much more flexible than others.

Also bear in mind that you will need to prepare for the tax liability from a bulk sale; this includes figuring capital gains on objects that might well have cost relatively little when purchased years before.

The Gun-Show Arena

The gun-show circuit has become, for some, a way of life. If one wanted to do so, he or she could be at a gun show virtually every weekend of the year. Texas alone probably has over 250 gun shows in a single year, and California perhaps even more! There are some regional shows that are not even published in such periodicals as *Gun Journal*, *Gun List*, or *Shotgun News*. For example, the author belongs to the Antique Arms Collectors Association of Connecticut; there are only fifteen active members, about a half dozen non-active, and an even smaller number honorary; we meet monthly (except for June, July, and August), in the homes of members, and have an annual shoot and picnic. Each host member is expected to give a brief talk about a gun in his collection, or some other relevant subject, and members sometimes bring guns to the meeting to share with others; guests are also welcome. Although the club is small, the group has provided some of the most fun this writer has had in his entire career in collecting.

In the late 1960s and early 1970s, the author attended as many as thirty gun shows per year. In those days the NRA's annual meetings and shows were crucial for any collector, and top dealers like Herb Glass and Jack Malloy put on impressive displays, saving some of their best guns for unveiling at the event. Collectors groups would put on lavish exhibits, and the exclusive American Society of Arms Collectors even timed one of their semi-annual meetings to coincide with that of the NRA. However, things change, and although the NRA show is still an important event to attend, sales on the showroom floor are not permitted (except by the NRA itself), and therefore no collectors' arms dealers exhibit at all. However, the tradition of gun-collector associations displaying continues, and that remains one of the event's highlights.

Although auctions have taken away some of the luster of gun shows in recent years, these meets still have their distinct merits. Most shows are at least two-day weekends, and sometimes are of three days' duration; a few are even four days long. The shows allow for dealers and collectors and others to have the opportunity to see, and generally handle, an array of firearms, accouterments, books and other literature, and memorabilia of an often substantial mix. Although some few shows are quite restricted in what is exhibited, most are generalized. Thus, the Beinfeld Las Vegas events have antique arms and armor, but also have high-grade modern sporting arms, and for the winter show, might have contingents from the S&W, Remington, Marlin, and other collector organizations holding special meetings. For some collectors and dealers, the winter Las Vegas show can be the most important event of the year.

The shows also offer an opportunity for the enthusiast who is not an exhibitor to meet the experts, although often one is so busy that there is very little free time. At a recent show the author spent the first day entirely on his feet, not sitting down once, and never left his table to look around the show at all. Too often an exhibitor who is doing the show on his own will not find the time to leave his table to see what others have brought to the event. However, when one has a reputation as an authority, generally things are brought for that person to see anyway.

Above all, gun shows are important for anyone who wishes to remain "current" in his or her field. Since attending his first gun show as a twelve-year-old in Minnesota—that of the Minnesota Weapons Collectors Association, at the Stagecoach Museum, Shakopee—the author has attended anywhere from half a dozen shows a year up to as many as thirty. The number of collectors and dealers one meets, the amount of information absorbed, the array of guns and other material handled and seen, and the experience garnered have an incalculable impact on any gun enthusiast. The legendary antique-arms collector William M. Locke used to have a selection of show badges in his suitcase, so that he was ready at any time for all of the events he regularly attended. Show exhibits he used to set up from his own collection were absolutely mind-boggling: gold-inlaid guns, shoulder-stocked Colts, derringers, U.S. martial pistols, historical arms—and more. It was worthwhile going to shows just to see Bill Locke and his almost always present wife, Elsa, and their fascinating arsenal.

A PARTIAL LISTING OF SHOWS

To investigate the world of gun shows, check magazines like *Gun List*, *Shotgun News*, *Man at Arms*, *Gun Journal*, and *The Gun Report* that publish timely information far enough in advance to allow for careful scheduling by would-be attendees. For some events you will *not* get a table without planning well beforehand. At this writing the major gun shows include the following:

- Any show put on by Wallace Beinfeld, including the winter, summer, and fall Las Vegas events at the Riviera Hotel and the Nashville, Tennessee, show in the spring (April).

Two legendary figures from the annals of American arms collecting. Seated, Arnold Marcus Chernoff, self-titled "biggest man in his field," who, despite the handicap of weighing around 700 pounds, was one of the most active and successful of antique arms dealers and collectors. Standing is Harry Mann, the founder of the Las Vegas Antique Arms Show (the greatest of them all), which has been managed by Wallace Beinfeld since the 1970s.

- The annual NRA Gun Collectors Show, in August or September, held to date in Nashville and Pittsburgh (managed by Wallace Beinfeld for the NRA).
- The Maryland Arms Collectors Show, generally held the second weekend in March, near Baltimore.
- The Texas Gun Collectors Show (a closed event, for members only), usually held in early May and early November; sometimes in Dallas, sometimes in San Antonio.
- The Houston Gun Collectors Show, held at the Astrohall, three times a year.
- The Great Western Arms Show, the biggest gun show in the world, by far—held at the California State Fairgrounds, Pomona, the first weekend in May and the first weekend in November, with a Christmas show the third weekend in December.
- National Gun Day, at Louisville, Kentucky, in June, organized by Ron Dickson.
- The Georgia Arms Collectors show, held near Atlanta.
- The Tulsa, Oklahoma, shows put on by Wanenmacher Productions, held approximately a half dozen times a year.
- The CADA shows, put on by the Collectors Arms Dealers Association, and held in places like Florida, Colorado, and Illinois.
- The Winchester Club of America annual show, held in Cody, Wyoming, in late June or early July.
- The Winchester Arms Collectors Association annual show, held the weekend before or the weekend after the above meet.
- The Colorado Gun Collectors Association Show, held in Denver at the Merchandise Mart, generally early in May.
- The Empire State Arms Collectors, held near Rochester, New York.
- The New York State Arms Collectors Syracuse Gun Show.
- The Ohio Gun Collectors Association, generally held near Cleveland and Canton.
- The Dallas Arms Collectors Show, held in Dallas a few times yearly.
- The Palm Beach (Florida) Gun Collectors, held in the Palm Beach area.
- The Weapons Collectors Society of Montana, in Missoula, generally late May or early June.
- Jackson Hole Gun Show, Wyoming, generally held early in July.
- The Pottstown Gun Shows of the Pennsylvania Antique Gun Collectors Association.
- The Minnesota Weapons Collectors Association at the Civic Center Arena, St. Paul.

Who might one meet at a gun show? Besides dealers and collectors, persons often attend the shows because they have a family heirloom, or a gun or gun-related object that they've inherited, found in the attic, or whatever. In other words, the shows also present the opportunity to buy something that might be a rather exciting "find." Some exhibitors have a sign making it quite clear that they are looking for things to buy. The author used to wear a belt that had written on the back serial numbers of as-yet-unfound rare Colts, such as revolvers known to have been shipped to W. B. "Bat" Masterson, W. F. Cody, and others. Although I never found one of these guns by that means, I did occasionally find rarities that I knew of previously through research in the Colt factory ledgers: e.g., presentations from Colonel Colt and from the company. Knowing that certain pieces were documented gave me an edge, since one needs to exercise caution, in the event some clever faker has had an inscription engraved on what is otherwise a legitimate firearm.

The novice should be aware that if he expects to buy at a show, he needs to be alert and knowledgeable. At some shows fakes will be offered for sale. Although certain shows (generally the so-called "closed" ones, open to members and guests only) police what is on view, most do not. It is therefore the responsibility of the attendee to be careful, and not be taken in by something "bad." The novice should look to a friend, generally an experienced collector or dealer, who can offer guidance. The learning curve can be fairly accelerated, depending on how much time the novice can spend at shows or other opportunities. Every collector has to go through that phase of his development, and gun shows offer this opportunity better than any other venue.

HERB GLASS—MASTER OF THE GUN SHOW

The art of selling guns at gun shows is one that has been fully mastered by some of the top dealers. How one of the masters has done it for some fifty years will reveal some of the secrets of the trade.

Herb Glass began dealing in collectors firearms after his military service in World War II. By the early 1950s, he was one of the top antique-arms dealers in the world. With the retirement of James E. Serven, Glass became number one, and remained so until the 1980s.

I had the privilege of attending a great many gun shows with Glass, and seeing him in action was the equivalent of receiving a Ph.D. in marketing. First, Herb was always appropriately attired for the occasion, some shows being more formal than others. At an NRA Annual Meeting and Show he was bedecked in sports jacket and tie, but at a Texas Gun Collectors Show, he was more likely to be in Western attire, wearing his expensive Lucchese boots or jodhpurs.

From right, legendary dealer Herb Glass Sr., renowned collector Richard P. Mellon, and (representing the new generation of dealer/collectors) Herb Glass Jr., at the 15th Annual Mid-Winter Antique Arms Show in Las Vegas, February 1977. Note the array of Colt revolvers, among them two Walkers, two Dragoons, and a Belt Model No. 2 Paterson. Photo by John Battaglia, who has chronicled more gun shows than any other photographer in the history of collecting.

He always made certain that his name tag was placed high enough on his person so the uninformed could easily read his name. Table locations were always critical, and he scoped those out, making every effort to be well placed. Carefully orchestrating displays of merchandise at shows, he also tailored the material so that guns, knives, etc., were saved for particular shows.

For the NRA and/or Las Vegas events, he might even have a special display cabinet built to feature some treasure, such as rare Colts like the Sultan of Turkey Dragoon or the E. K. Root Dragoon. For the Theodore Roosevelt Single Action Army Colt, Glass commissioned the writer to do a handsomely illustrated, detailed four-page brochure, and to build a special exhibition cabinet. The revolver and accouterments soon rested in the collection of one of his top customers and, some years later, ended up in the Autry Museum of Western Heritage.

Herb was fastidious about his table covers, about where he placed his briefcase, about the number and placement of chairs (for himself, any associate, guests, and customers). He had a handsome name plate displayed on his table, and used exhibition aids, like glass or wooden rods through trigger guards, to prop up certain pieces for emphasis. Documenting letters were a crucial part of his *modus operandi*, and over the years the author did at least 400 of these just for Herb Glass. Some of these were prepared in leather-bound books, with backup material, the covers embossed in gold leaf with such fancy titles as:

**FROM COL. SAMUEL COLT
TO E. K. ROOT
THE FINEST COLT DRAGOON
PRESENTATION CASED SET
IN EXISTENCE
SERIAL No. 16461**

Herb Glass could spot a prospective buyer from across a room, and had a way of giving that person his complete attention while working on a deal. He swept away any possible distractions and, if necessary, would arrange to meet the client privately, over drinks or dinner. The writer was present at some social and business events where Herb was entertaining members of the Mellon and Ford families, and everyone had a truly wonderful time.

Getting back to the gun shows: Herb was always ready to accommodate his clients with shipping arrangements or even personal delivery. Often, after he sold something important, he would arrange to exhibit the piece for the rest of the show, making delivery afterward. Wives and girlfriends were always encouraged to be present at the shows, and Glass's charm in dealing with them was certainly a part of his immense success.

Being punctual and staying at the show for the duration was also crucial. He never arrived late, was always businesslike, and did not encourage hangers-on to sponge up time with idle chatter.

Although he did not like to devote time to the politics of gun collecting, he always made his points of view known to show organizers. One reason the Las Vegas shows became so successful was his own input, advice, and encouragement to Wallace Beinfeld. Before Wally, Herb had worked closely with Harry Mann, the originator of the Hotel Sahara show concept.

Occasionally Herb would allow me a corner of his table to market a new book title. He advised on the making of signs (make them big enough to be read from a distance, make them brief and to the point, and be sure to have a front-cover dust-jacket image on the sign; then be sure to have a big enough stack of books so that you were ready for the hoped-for onslaught). The first such event for me was the NRA Show of 1962, in which I was marketing *Samuel Colt Presents*, just published the previous fall by the Wadsworth Atheneum. Herb even arranged for this shy young author to meet such luminaries as Roy Weatherby, Elmer Keith, Warren Page, and Bob Brownell—in each case encouraging their assistance in the promotion and sale of the book. When I returned to the Atheneum, all the books that had been taken to the Washington, D.C., event had been sold!

Herb also made it clear that there were certain supplies that had to be available for each show; thus the checklist published below. And finally, he pointed out the importance of making a gun show a buying event, as much as it was a selling and trading event. Some sound advice from that venue: There are always too many temptations to buy, while selling is equally crucial; one has to balance the urge to possess with the hard business reality of marketing and selling, and not let the buying get ahead of the selling, thus interfering with that crucial element in any business: cash flow.

SCHEDULING AND PREPARATION

The author has a checklist that is run through at least three weeks before a show date. This serves as a reminder of anything that needs to be done in advance, such as having a sign or two made up, or getting special-rate airplane tickets, hotel reservations, and so forth. As an idea of what's involved in preparation, see the following:

- Arrange for table space well in advance (at some shows, a year in advance is appropriate, and necessary)
- Pre-advertise (in show program or magazine, or in an arms publication, indicating that you will be exhibiting at such and such a show)
- Table sign
- Name plate (often supplied by show organizer)
- Pre-ticketing at hotels and airlines (discounting possible with many airlines; accumulated miles will also allow free tickets for later trips)
- Ship display materials (screwdrivers, gun sacks for purchases, oil, tool kit, display stands for guns, price tags or stickers, business cards, packing tape, credit-card machine and forms, etc.); ship guns in advance whenever possible
- Be sure to have table covers, not only for the table top, but for covering display and sale material, etc., when the show is closed
- Credit cards, cash, checks, and the usual needs for traveling
- Hire temporary help if needed; some shows will arrange for this, or can advise how to do so
- Pocket magnifying glass (some prefer the kind with a small light for better illumination)

Some subtleties which a lot of gun-show attendees have never figured out include the following:

- Check the show schedule so you are aware of set-up time; some shows are scheduled to begin on a Friday, but allow for set-up beginning at noon or in the afternoon or evening the day before. It is at set-up time that much of the good material comes out. Many who attend shows do not go to sell, but are there to buy.
- Usually seniority is crucial in getting a good position at shows—the best location usually being near the main entrance. For either buying or selling, your table locale is important. At the foremost gun collector shows in the world—those of Wallace Beinfeld at Las Vegas—one might have to wait for someone to retire, or even die, to move up to a prime spot, or even to get any show tables. The author was able to garner one of the best spots in that premier event because he heard of the unfortunate passing of a leading dealer, and called Wally Beinfeld before even he was aware of the death.
- Wear your name badge high on your chest, so it can be read easily; if the one supplied by the show is not legible, make one that is (some shows do not supply a badge; in that case, bring your own).
- If the floor is concrete, bring a small carpet for comfort.
- For further comfort, you might even wish to bring your own chair(s); those supplied at most shows are not particularly comfortable.
- Bring bottled water along, and snacks if you wish.
- Try to have another person with you, to allow yourself the opportunity to walk around the show while your table is attended.
- Bring a portable telephone.
- Be sure to ship in advance any supplies you cannot bring to the show; this is particularly important if you are traveling by air. Save the cardboard shipping boxes, since you may need to ship something back.
- Be alert to other show attendees, in case you need to send something on to the next show. Some exhibitors actually share the services of a truck, which brings merchandise and equipment to the show and takes it back to their home or shop again.

Enjoying Your Treasures

Enjoying your treasures, and keeping good records, are crucial to any collector or dealer. Not only are there practical considerations—estate planning, profit (and loss) and taxes, and reminders for when the memory starts to go—but maintaining good files is part of the fun, almost like writing your own book! Not a few collectors, and all dealers, will end up having owned such an array of firearms that it is not only good organization to have written up this "collection," but good business as well.

In the 1960s, when doing quite a bit of research and cataloguing work for dealer Herb Glass, the author devised catalogue formats for 3×5 and 4×6 file cards, as well as for $8^1/_2 \times 11$ file forms. Some of these we printed up professionally, with data on the front that could be xeroxed and sent to an author and researcher, while the back had the private history of cost and value, and other data that the owner might not want to share in a public way.

Item ____________ Catalog No. ____________
Make ____________ Serial No. ____________
From whom bought ____________
Price ____________ Date ____________
Condition ____________
Ref. Data ____________

Sold to ____________ Date ____________ Price ____________

Time passes by so quickly, especially as one advances in years, that these cards and forms became a ready and useful reference for each and every collector for whom the forms were developed. In my own instance, like the proverbial shoemaker's children having no shoes, my file records are spotty—I'm just too busy to sit down and complete the forms.

However, for virtually every important arm I've owned, some time was devoted to writing up a documenting letter. Initially under the guidance of the pioneering brilliance of Herb Glass, I developed my own letterhead and a format for such letters, which has its own characteristics. A sample letter appears on page 29. Note the following: The letter is not addressed to a particular person, so it can travel with the gun from owner to owner. The heading is designed to capture the essence of the firearm, while the body of the text logically presents the item's history and merits. If there is a relevant quotation from a book, that is presented as well—generally in the first part of the letter. Such headings as markings, a history of the original owner(s), pedigree, and a conclusion are standard features. The letters are generally kept as short as possible, but sometimes run to forty or fifty pages.

The author has actually done "books" on a collection by doing letters on each gun and then binding the results in leather. This was done for the renowned Larry Sheerin Collection, when he decided the market had peaked, had the letters prepared, and then used the letters in the sale of the collection. The leather-bound book was nearly an inch thick, and two copies were "published"—one for Larry Sheerin and the other for myself.

Over thirty-five years after first doing these letters, I have a reference collection of over 1,000, done not only on fine Colts and Winchesters, but on a variety of other makes of American arms and not a few distinguished European pieces as well. I am now trying to enter them all into my computer, although regrettably the majority were done in my B.C. period (before computer).

Printed on a copperplate-engraved letterhead and high-quality second sheets, the letters are then placed in plastilene holders, and are retained by collectors, and sometimes displayed with guns (on exhibit, or offered for sale) to the public.

Some of these letters have been mounted in leather-bound books, used in an appraisal format on some of the world's most important firearms, adapted into articles in a variety of magazines, and so forth. The author's "Gun of the Month" series for *Gun Journal* is based entirely on these letters, each revised for the magazine's own format. In many instances, color pictures of the subject guns are the featured cover art for the issue in which each article appears.

Researching each piece, and preparing the letters, has become such a pleasure that today I go virtually everywhere with a Macintosh laptop computer and can capture the essence of a gun on the spot, even sometimes doing this at night during gun shows, thus allowing the owner to keep his gun, and I have the chance to finish the letter in the privacy of my home office. The fee for these letters usually begins at $500, and I will do a letter only on a gun that warrants the time and effort, for both myself and the client.

PHOTOGRAPHY

Photographing your guns can be an extension of your hobby. Photography can be fun too—but the author has found that for him, at least, the picture-taking should be left to the professionals. When beginning my career at the Corcoran Gallery of Art and the Wadsworth Atheneum, I experimented with Nikons and Olympuses, all the while working with professionals like Eliot Elisofon of *Life* magazine and E. Irving Blomstrann (the Atheneum's photographer, who mainly concentrated on decorative art and paintings).

It soon became obvious that if I was to have first-class pictures for research and publication, the photography should be left to the professionals. Taking gun pictures is not easy; in fact, it is much more difficult than photographing virtually any other collectible: difficult angles, a combination of materials, varied finishes, challenging contrasts between such finishes as bluing, case-hardening, silver-plating, ivory, or pearl—all in one picture.

The author has worked with more than 100 photographers over the years, and has examined literally over 200,000 photographs, taken by hundreds and hundreds of photographers, most of them amateurs, but quite a few by professionals. One out of 100 of these pictures is good enough to reproduce, and acceptable for publication. The point is that gun photography is extremely difficult, and there are far fewer photographers capable of taking first-rate gun pictures than there are who can take high-quality photographs of people, or cars, or paintings, or silver, or any number of other subjects.

Having stated all of the above, for those who wish to attempt taking their own gun pictures, consider the fact that new photographic technology has led to the wonders of digital pictures, and developments in flash-assisted pictures have helped to eliminate the problems of lighting. The tips that follow from one of the best firearms photographers in the world, David Wesbrook, will help those who want to pursue their own picture-taking. A list of several of the best photographers is presented in the acknowledgments on page x, each of them freelance and capable of pictures good enough for the most demanding of publishers.

Considered by many as at the top of his art and craft, David Wesbrook studied under Frederick Sommer (a fine-arts photographer in the same league as Ansel Adams, and an innovator of the fine-arts photography movement of the 1950s). Dave has worked for some of today's most discriminating clients in the art and arms fields.

The writer used Wesbrook photographs exclusively for the dust jacket of *The Colt Engraving Book*, and sees in his pictures an artist who not only has mastered the difficult art of lighting, but understands firearms, and therefore is a master at selecting the proper angle for the best results. The material below, taken from the author's discussion with Wesbrook, is intended to guide the amateur and the professional in tackling the challenging task of taking fine-quality firearms photographs. Reviewing this material can also be helpful in the reader's decision as to whether he or she wants to take the pictures, or leave the work to a professional.

"The ideal firearms photograph shows superb detail throughout, including the shadow and highlight areas, is distortion-free with perfect focus, and is taken from the same viewpoint or aspect from which the gun would normally be viewed.

"To achieve this requires, first, a thorough knowledge and understanding of what you are photographing and how it should appear on film. Look, a gun is a piece of functional sculpture, often quite stunning in its own right. As with other forms of sculpture, there are certain angles that show and complement the line, form, and flow of shape to their best advantage. In my over twenty years at the bench as a custom gunmaker/stockmaker, first with muzzle-loaders and later with modern stocks, I've formed some definite opinions on which angles look best for the different period stylings and types of firearms being photographed. In addition, I have been privileged to study, handle, and photograph work from contemporary master gunmakers such as Monte Mandarino, Stephen Alexander, and John Bivins, as well as historic masters like Boutet and the Mantons, and exquisite 19th-century Colts and Winchesters. This knowledge of line and form is what I believe separates my work from the other firearm photographers."

VIDEOTAPING YOUR GUNS

Still another means of documenting your firearms is the use of videotape. Video equipment is available to everyone, and requires very little skill to use. As long as commentary accompanies the footage, the record presented is clear and useful. As many copies as needed can be made of the material.

Professional videos can be made for inventory and cataloguing purposes, but a written listing should accompany any tapes. Clearly this technology is not commonly used, but its potential has been realized by such auction houses as Butterfield & Butterfield, Little John's, and other firms. These companies employ video aids in promoting objects for sale, and Butterfield's cooperated with a San Francisco firm in creating a video production on presentation and engraved Colt percussion firearms.

Whether videotape or computer printouts, still photographs or handwritten notes, documentation of your guns can be vital. For insurance purposes, loss claims, eventual publication, or just plain nostalgia, keeping a record of your guns can give you some of the most valuable and rewarding time you will spend with your inventory or collection.

DISPLAYS AT HOME, OFFICE, OR GUN SHOWS

For a period of approximately twenty years (from the 1960s into the 1980s), displays at gun shows were popular, so much so that cash awards were presented, as well as trophies or other prizes that were truly worth all the time, effort, and cost of competition. The best of such shows were the Las Vegas events of Wallace Beinfeld, the Baltimore Gun Collectors, and a number of other state organizations.

However, for a variety of reasons, the number of shows that continue this tradition, and the number of collectors and dealers willing to go to the trouble, have diminished. The reasons are obvious: the increased value of the objects themselves, restrictions on traveling with some types of guns, concern over damage to the objects, and—not the least—the time, energy, and money that a fine display costs the collector or dealer.

Shows that have continued the tradition are specialty collector clubs like the Colt Collectors Association, the Smith & Wesson Collectors Association, the Winchester Club of America and the Winchester Collectors Association, the Ruger Collectors Association, the Remington Society of America, the Bowie Knife Association, the American Society of Arms Collectors, and the Colorado Arms Collectors Association. Most important, the National Rifle Association continues to encourage displays, awards the finest trophies for merit, and presents ten beautiful and highly prized sterling silver medals annually for the finest guns at the annual meetings, as well as ten medals for the finest miniatures. Further, at the newly inaugurated (as of 1996) annual NRA Gun Collectors Show and Conference, special awards are also given.

Judging of these displays is voluntary, and usually the panel is composed of three experts. I have judged many such events, and like nearly all judges, I dread the responsibility. Competition can get rather fierce, and some exhibitors simply do not understand that there was a good reason they did not win the grand prize. Although from time to time politics may have had a role in a decision, this is quite rare. The judges take their responsibility quite seriously, and know that these competitions are part of the culture of arms collecting. No one wants to discourage any collector from going to the tremendous effort required to do a successful display.

The late Dr. Richard Marohn, expert and keen collector in the realm of the Colt Lightning revolver, put on some of the finest displays ever seen at any gun show. His exhibits were thoroughly researched, finely and artistically presented, and captivating for the viewer, including the general public. Think about any historical or art museum you have visited, and try to remember the displays that were of the greatest interest and provided the most pleasure. Dick Marohn's exhibits could very easily have been moved from the gun show (usually Wallace Beinfeld's Las Vegas extravaganza) and set up in most any fine museum—all that would have been necessary was to put the display behind glass.

Today, with the wizardry available through computer technology, and perhaps through the assistance of a consultant (who might be the collector's wife or girlfriend or secretary), some assistance by a talented photographer, and a knowledge of display techniques, a collector can put something together that would not only be captivating in his home gun room or library, but would be a winner at an NRA event, at Las Vegas or Denver, or at the Texas Gun Collectors Association's semi-annual shows.

Once the author worked with collector Jerry Berger of Kansas City in preparing a display on the engraving of percussion Colt firearms. This exhibit won the grand prize at a Las Vegas show, and had such a beautifully designed format (by one of Jerry's employees in his Topsy's Popcorn company) that the writer to this day has part of the presentation on display in his office complex in Hadlyme. Some of the illustrations were used in *The Colt Engraving Book* and elsewhere.

Some collectors have even had a guest book as part of the display, allowing viewers to share their comments. Sometimes a brochure was printed up to give to the public. For the late R. Q. Sutherland, the author wrote an 84-page monogram, *The Evolution of the Colt*, which was sold in conjunction with an elaborate display that won the collector the grand prize at the spring 1967 Las Vegas Sahara Antique Arms Show. To date, that monograph has been the ultimate accompaniment to a gun-show exhibition in the writer's memory!

Due to widespread distrust of journalists, most gun shows do not permit the presence of the media. Photography is generally not allowed at these events, including videotaping. However, there are times when shows or auctions present the opportunity of interfacing with the press. When that happens, the author suggests that the collector or dealer consider carefully whether he should try to become a spokesperson for guns. Sometimes our friends inadvertently turn out to be our worst enemies. People who crusade against guns (and not a few of these impact negatively the world of collectors' guns) have made their crusade into a business. Often uninformed people from the press are used to create programming or interviews that are undeservedly harsh on the world of collecting.

Some collectors and dealers are just not cut out for mainstream media interviews. They should take a long, hard look at their abilities, and make sure their interview doesn't backfire. On the other hand, experts like Greg Martin are perfectly suited for press interviews, and present an excellent image for the world of arms collecting.

Factors and Fine Points of Collecting

Most collectors not only develop their own special sphere of interest, but devise their own means of chasing after arms that appeal to them. As a general rule of thumb, in order to avoid frustration and financial disaster, the collector should set his sights on objects within a specific budget. The collector needs to establish standards of condition, originality, historical merit, and other specifics, and the lengths to which he or she will go in pursuit of goals.

What follows are the areas demanding special attention.

CONDITION, CONDITION, CONDITION

The pursuit of mint unfired guns can be quite costly, particularly if one's interest is the blue chips of gun collecting: Colts and Winchesters. Not that much less costly are Sharps rifles in perfect condition, or the best in Remington, Smith & Wessons, derringers, Marlins, fine English sporting rifles and shotguns, and so forth. In some instances, like the Colt Walker and Dragoon revolvers, there may be no mint examples available to the collector, or so few that the value is substantial.

On the other hand, the obtaining of mint examples of U.S. military metallic cartridge arms is a more realizable goal. M1 Carbines, M1 Garand rifles, Colt Model 1911 Automatic pistols, and such arms as Colt New Service .45 caliber revolvers, still are available in pristine condition. But then one must consider the laws governing such usable guns in the collectors' state and locality of residence.

Mint condition also requires careful storage of arms, and making sure that unwelcome hands do not handle the objects, leaving rust marks or working the mechanisms (causing scratches and marks). Proper care of these rarities means the use of proper oils, storage in a controlled environment, and preventing damage of any kind. Keeping the pieces for long periods in a bank vault, for example, might actually be detrimental to their finish.

HISTORY

The collector keen on history usually is not a stickler for fine condition. He understands that when Indians were pounding on some settler's door, the latter was hardly concerned about conserving for some future collector the condition of the gun he was about to shoot in self-defense! Historical guns are the ones that "speak" the most to the collector. The writer was once with Monte Hale and Gene Autry and their wives when the Autry Museum was considering purchase of some rare Theodore Roosevelt firearms and related artifacts from TR's ranching days in the Dakotas. Monte remarked about how thrilled he was with holding TR's Single Action Army and Winchester, and that "these wonderful guns are speaking to us!" He was right—and many a time one is transfixed when thinking of the many stories these fabulous rarities could tell, "if only they could talk." The author has actually had the thrill of firing TR's Single Action Army no. 92248 (now in the Autry Museum), Bat Masterson's Single Action Army no. 112737, Jesse James' S&W Schofield no. 366, and TR's double-barreled Holland & Holland elephant rifle no. 19109. He still has the cartridge casings from firing these remarkable guns, and considers those experiences among the highlights of his arms-collecting career.

ROMANCE

The craze for TV and movie Westerns in the 1950s and 1960s almost certainly influenced two generations of arms collectors, this writer among them. The author's old friend and Hollywood shooting coach Arvo Ojala met many a star, some of whom were enamored of guns. Among that group were Steve McQueen, Frank Sinatra, Sammy Davis Jr., Jerry Lewis, and Dean Martin. A prized picture in the author's collection is one showing Arvo with Marilyn Monroe, signed "Larry, my friend wish you could have been here."

Movies starring actors the likes of Steve McQueen, Arnold Schwarzenegger, Charles Bronson, Clint Eastwood, Sylvester Stallone, Steven Seagal, and Wesley Snipes have been instrumental in encouraging a cult of collectors who are more interested in modern military arms. The author believes that more than 75 percent of arms collectors are primarily keen on 20th-century firearms. Films like *Shane*, *Dirty Harry*, *The Getaway*, and *The Wild Bunch* have all influenced directions taken by gun collectors. One of the writers of some of these films, and the director of *The Wind and the Lion*, *Red Dawn*, and other action thrillers, is John Milius, not only a keen arms collector, but a member of the board of directors of the National Rifle Association!

MECHANICS

Many times the author has been visiting with an arms collector and finds that his home includes a machine shop.

Recently a former top executive with Allied Signal, Tony Lamb, showed me his quite respectable home workshop, and told me of having bought a somewhat rusty S&W Schofield revolver, which he cleaned with stainless-steel wool and found that under the surface rust was quite a bit of original blue finish! The artist Maxfield Parrish was both a master machinist and a dedicated collector of 19th-century U.S. martial firearms. The former chief financial officer of the Timken corporation has shown me his collection of guns and Wells Fargo items, and he too had a fine collection of machine tools.

Rare was the collectors firearm that this author and his brother Jack didn't take apart, immediately after purchase. I can still remember taking down our first antique gun purchase, serial no. 7 Manhattan .31 caliber pocket model revolver, and giving it a total cleaning (too much, in retrospect). The revolver had an engraved frame, no doubt by L. D. Nimschke, and walnut grips. But something was wrong with the mainspring, and some truly amateur home gunsmithing made it work again.

During the author's internship at the Tower of London, Norris Kennard, the Deputy Master of the Armouries, was renowned for spending part of his day in the workshops, taking apart some of the collection's rare guns. This he did with the able assistance of the master gunsmiths, since some of the pieces were complex and not easy to reassemble.

And it was the mechanics of firearms that intrigued young Samuel Colt. According to *Armsmear*, the first Colt book (1866):

> Among the traditions of his boyhood, one is given by a neighbor . . . showing at how early an age his attention was directed toward the arm with which his name was to be so intimately connected, all the world over. When about seven years of age, he one day was for some time missing, and when at last discovered, he was sitting under a tree in the field, with a pistol taken entirely to pieces, the different parts carefully arranged around him, and which he was beginning to reconstruct. He soon, to his great delight, accomplished this feat.

When the wheelock was invented, the locks were actually built by lockmakers. And manufacture of best-quality firearms commonly called upon the skills of lockmakers, stockmakers, and barrel makers. The mechanics of firearms are so fascinating that a great many collectors seek variations, most of which are identifiable based on mechanical features: squareback triggerguards, V-main springs, oval cylinder stop slots, and horizontal or vertical loading lever latches are part of the lexicon, for example, of Colt percussion firearms.

A word of caution is in order, however. Care should be taken in stripping down any gun, and for good reason: A mistake with a screwdriver can scratch a "mint" gun, botch screw heads, and otherwise damage a treasured piece. Further, grips and stocks that have never been removed may chip or lose their "seal" from metal parts, and sometimes should never be removed. Trying to punch out a barrel wedge may actually break off the wedge screw (they should always be loosened or removed before you try to tap out a wedge, particularly when all parts are tight-fitting).

Trying to remove the barrel from a fine-condition Kentucky or Plains rifle might well lead to wedges driving out keyplates, or damage to stocks. Removing some locks may chip out surrounding wood, and pulling barrel tangs might do the same.

Even working the actions on some firearms might lead to disaster: snapping hammers, breaking weakened springs, causing drag marks from the cylinder stop on cylinder surfaces, and so forth. Better to work the action or strip down a gun that has already seen a lot of takedown in its life.

ART AND CRAFTSMANSHIP

Although there are machinists and gunmakers today who can equal the skills of the old masters, the fact remains that one must truly marvel at the sheer artistry and craftsmanship exhibited by the gunmakers of past centuries. These remarkably talented craftsmen were expected to ply their craft at high standard. They could count on enthusiastic patronage from the wealthy, from governments, and later from such clients as ranchers and cowboys, Wells Fargo and other express agents, the military (both official and unofficial), hunters, sportsmen, professional marksmen and -women, and any number of others. Many of these products were not only skillfully made but quite beautiful, often elegant.

There are compelling reasons why major international museums of art exhibit fine firearms. Anyone who appreciates art, in all its forms, cannot help but be impressed by the remarkable work of the skilled gunmakers, as displayed at such institutions as the Metropolitan Museum of Art, the Art Institute of Chicago, the Buffalo Bill Historical Center, and the Autry Museum of Western Heritage.

Commemorative, Replica, and Special-Issue Firearms, and More

The tradition of special-production firearms for collectors in the modern sense was begun by Robert E. P. Cherry, of Cherry's Sporting Goods, founded in 1929. Bob Cherry, in order to celebrate the anniversary of the city of Geneseo, Illinois, ordered one hundred .22 caliber Fourth Model Colt derringer pistols with special markings from the factory (1960), and that issue began a whole new category of collectible firearms. Today his son Kevin carries on the family tradition, and is now issuing special commemorative arms, some quite elaborately engraved, under the Cherrys' trademark.

At this writing, literally hundreds of different issues have been produced since that 1960 beginning, mainly Colts and Winchesters, but the number also includes Brownings, Smith & Wessons, Marlins, Remingtons, Rugers, Lugers, and many, many more. Although the practice of issuing commemorative firearms peaked when Winchester made approximately 120,000 Buffalo Bill Model 1894s, there remains an active group of collectors keen on purchasing these modern tributes to a variety of themes. As detailed in the author's own *Colt Commemorative Firearms* books, the commemoratives generally salute a town, city, state, territorial, or national anniversary, or historical events, historical forts, historical trails, a battle or other historic event, a famous person, or a company, organization, or corporation.

This sphere of collecting offers the opportunity to purchase pieces that are in perfect, brand-new, mint condition. The guns are often quite handsomely built, sometimes richly engraved, and popular for display purposes—rarely being shot or the actions worked in any way.

When the author was employed at the Colt factory in Hartford, Connecticut, in 1964 and 1965, he was responsible for much of the design of the Colonel Samuel Colt Sesquicentennial Single Action Army revolver and the Bat Masterson Single Action Army "Lawman" commemorative .45 and .22 revolvers. Every effort was made to be as authentic as possible with these issues, and for a number of years the Colt company maintained an advisory committee made up of authorities qualified to assist in creating responsible and logical commemorative issues. The Winchester company also relied to some extent on expert advice. One of the most respected advisors for these committees was Robert E. P. Cherry himself; another was antique-arms dealer Herb Glass.

In the 1950s and 1960s, replica firearms became a valued addition to the arms market, spurred by Civil War and frontier reenactments and by the upward-spiraling value of genuine antiques. Among the leaders in this new market were Val Forgett, founder and president, Navy Arms Co., and *Guns* magazine editor William B. Edwards. Created at about the same time was the U.S. Historical Society, which quickly became the leading issuing body of best-quality special-issue firearms. The Society's first issue was the George Washington silver-mounted pistols, replicating the pair in the West Point Museum of the U.S. military academy. Later issues included such rarities as the Burr-Hamilton Wogdon flintlock dueling pistols (in cooperation with the Chase Manhattan Bank, owner of the originals), Thomas Jefferson's screwbarrel flintlock pistols (from Monticello), Carbine Williams' deluxe Single Action Army, a miniature series of Colt percussion and cartridge revolvers, and a book-cased pair of derringer percussion pistols authorized by descendants of Henry Deringer. Early in the 1990s the Society underwent a name change, to the United States Society of Arms and Armour, a.k.a. America Remembers, under the leadership of Paul Warden, president. Recent issues have included the Ruger & His Guns Tribute Vaquero revolvers, the miniature Wyatt Earp Buntline Special, and special-issue Single Action Armies honoring Richard Petty and Gene Autry.

Another organization that has issued several commemorative firearms is the American Historical Foundation. Among their special issues, dating back to the 1970s, are the General Patton Single Action Army, the Vietnam Tribute M14 rifle, the World War II Colt .45 M1911A1, and the Beretta Golden Centurion .40 Caliber Model 96D pistol. The founder and president of the Foundation is Robert Buerlein.

Still another firm issuing special limited editions is Colt Blackpowder, authorized maker of Colt percussion firearms, under exclusive license from Colt's Manufacturing Co. The owners of Colt Blackpowder are Louis and Anthony Imperata, and their factory complex is in Brooklyn, New York—returning a gunmaking tradition that dates back to Colonial times in that noble city.

Guns Disappearing Off the Market

A fact of life is that fine guns are disappearing off the market. Considering the magic realm of Colt firearms, with the deaths of P. R. Phillips, George A. Strichman, and other top collectors, and the vacuuming up of great guns by collectors like Robert E. Petersen and similar multi-millionaires, very few fine pieces remain among the public. Donations to museums like the Metropolitan, which received some fine Colts from Jerry D. Berger and the late John E. Parsons, as well as the Sultan of Turkey Dragoon from George and Butonne Repaire, have taken these objects out of the marketplace forever. Phil Phillips's legendary Colt collection was donated in perpetuity to the Woolaroc Museum, Raymond Wielgus donated several of his exquisite engraved and gold-inlaid arms to the Art Institute of Chicago, and collector Ed Bitters' martial pieces went to the National Museum of American History. Furthermore, the Smith & Wesson factory donated most of its extraordinary archives and arms collection to the Springfield

From the private collection of William O. Sweet, one of the most successful of American arms collectors. Many of his best pieces are now in museums. His eclectic interests ranged from Colts and Winchesters to Indian weapons to Kentucky Rifles, Mountain Man rifles, and Bowie knives. Most of his purchases came from Herb Glass.

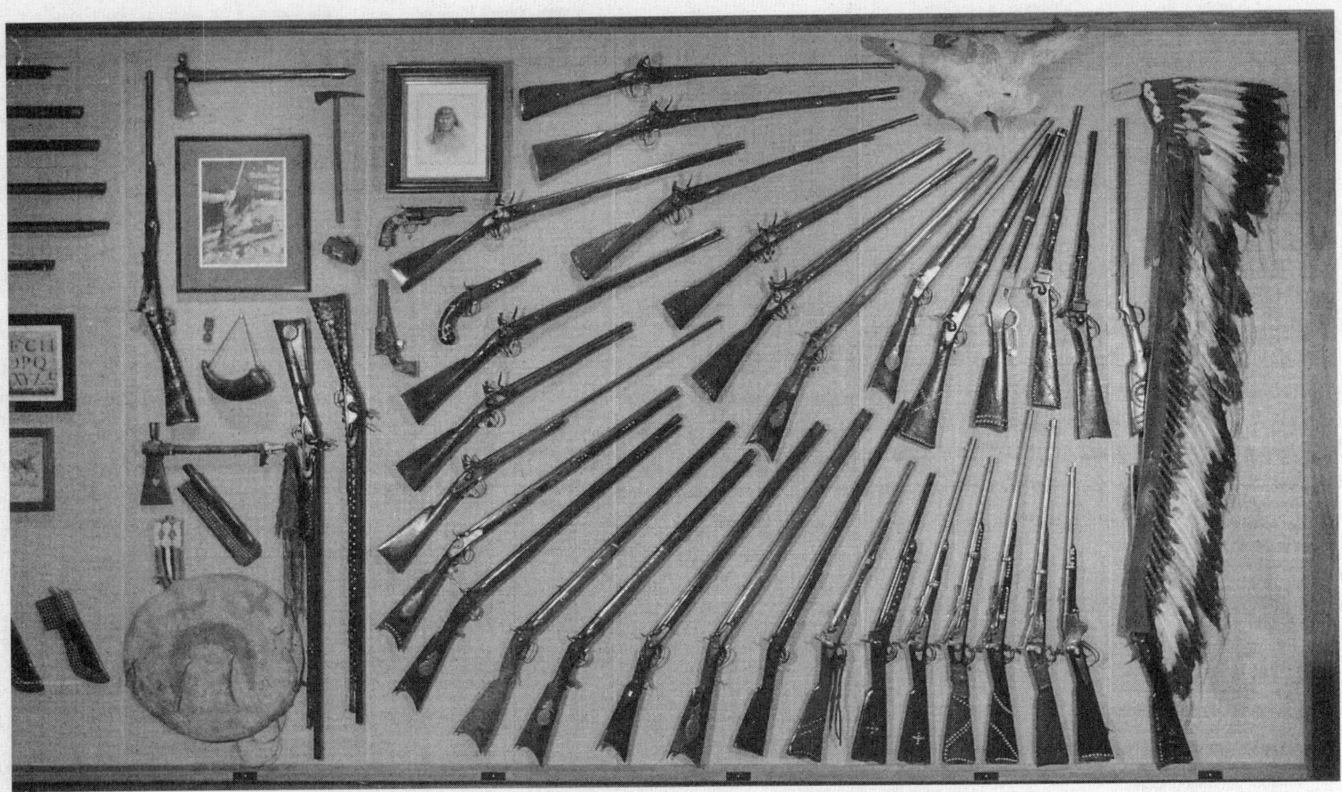

Museum, and over 3,000 guns of various types have been donated by members to the National Firearms Museum (a branch institution of the N.R.A.).

One astute collector asked me to estimate how many super Colts and super Winchesters from the 19th century had survived to date. My answer was quite a shocker, considering estimates of how many collectors are competing actively for the very best: My belief is that about 300 exceptional engraved Colt guns are known, and about that same number in Winchester lever-actions. No one will ever own these, and one can rest assured that new collectors are coming into the field on a regular basis. Sometimes the high demand within certain arenas of collecting can be truly discouraging.

Government-required Recordkeeping and Some BATF Rulings and Regulations

The antique-arms collector has virtually no legal problem with his arms, although muzzle-loading guns are considered illegal in certain jurisdictions, once they have been loaded and primed. On the other hand, collectors of metallic-cartridge firearms need to be aware that in some cities, such as New York, firearms that predate the federal cut-off date of 1898 may be subject to local law if they can accept cartridges that are readily available in present commerce: Thus, a Model 1873 Single Action Army and a Model 1873 Winchester, chambered for .45 Colt or .44-40 cartridges, are restricted—being considered the same as a modern gun taking the same ammunition.

Fortunately the Bureau of Alcohol, Tobacco, and Firearms issues copies of ordinances and regulations free of charge; they are regularly mailed to federal firearms license holders and to any of the public who request them. Since the number of gun laws is substantial—estimated at more than 20,000—it is a good idea for collectors interested in guns that might be subject to these regulations to be certain they have copies of these publications. Write to the BATF national headquarters at Bureau of Alcohol, Tobacco, and Firearms, Washington D.C. 20226.

For state and local laws, queries should be made of the state or local police (or both). All state police have a division devoted to firearms regulations. Eternal vigilance being the price of liberty, collectors should be aware of developments in some jurisdictions. The capricious New York City Council, after promising owners of so-called "assault rifles" that their firearms would never be confiscated, passed an ordinance requiring all registered assault rifles to be turned in to the authorities without compensation! Politicians are always trying to get votes, and no doubt somebody got reelected with that unproductive and truly outrageous ploy.

Nassau County, New York, tried to force owners of percussion revolvers to register their guns, just like metallic cartridge handguns, claiming that since a thug had held up a gas station with a Ruger Old Model Army, these guns should be restricted. No matter that once a gun like that is loaded, it is already covered by the same ordinance as a metallic-cartridge handgun. The author was the lead witness in a suit brought against Nassau County on this matter, before Supreme Court Justice Steven B. Derounian. The suit was filed by the Long Island Antique Gun Collectors Association Inc., the Nassau County Fish and Game Association, and others (1978). Of course, we won the case hands down.

For collectors interested in full automatic weapons, the author recommends subscribing to one of the finest magazines published on firearms: *Machine Gun News*. The address and relevant information appears in the bibliography (page 425), along with such generally better-known publications as *American Rifleman*, *American Hunter*, *Guns*, *Guns & Ammo*, *Gun Journal*, and *Man at Arms*. Collecting full automatic arms requires a particular diligence in recordkeeping; certain states, like California, do not permit ownership by private citizens. The author is fortunate in living in Connecticut, which has a quite reasonable law on these arms, and he has under federal and state permits a Colt-made Thompson Submachine Gun (formerly property of the New Orleans Police Department), a Colt M16A2 Carbine with suppresser, and a Sterling 9mm submachine gun (presented to the author by the Colt company, and the only non-Colt firearm ever presented by the company). None other than famed actress Sharon Stone has been quoted in *Vanity Fair* magazine on the thrill she received when firing a Colt AR-15, accompanied by her gun-enthusiast father.

SOME BATF DEFINITIONS AND RULINGS

The BATF definition of an antique firearm is as follows*:

Under section 921(a)(16) of the Gun Control Act, the term *antique firearm* means:

> (A) Any firearm (including any firearm with a matchlock, flintlock, percussion cap, or similar type of ignition system) manufactured in or before 1898; and
>
> (B) Any replica of any firearm described in subparagraph (A) if such replica—
>
> (i) is not designed or redesigned for using rimfire or conventional centerfire fixed ammunition, or
>
> (ii) uses rimfire or conventional centerfire fixed ammunition which is no longer manufactured

*These quotations are from the BATF *Federal Firearms Regulations Reference Guide*, formerly known as *Your Guide to Federal Firearms Regulations*. The booklet is identified by federal government publication code ATF P 5300.4 (10-95), totaling 114 pages, in an $8^1/_2 \times 11$ format.

> in the United States and which is not readily available in the ordinary channels of commercial trade.

Under section 5845(g) of the National Firearms Act, *antique firearm* means:

> . . . Any firearm not designed or redesigned for using rim fire or conventional center fire ignition with fixed ammunition and manufactured in or before 1898 (including any matchlock, flintlock, percussion cap, or similar type of ignition system or replica thereof, whether actually manufactured before or after 1898) and also any firearm using fixed ammunition manufactured in or before 1898, for which ammunition is no longer manufactured in the United States and is not readily available in the ordinary channels of commercial trade.

To illustrate the distinction between the two definitions of antique firearm under the GCA and NFA, a rifle manufactured in or before 1898 would not come under the provisions of the GCA, even though it uses conventional ammunition. However, if the rifle has a barrel of less than sixteen inches in length *and* uses conventional fixed ammunition that is available in the ordinary channels of commercial trade, it would still be a *firearm* subject to the provisions of the NFA.

An antique firearm as defined in *both* the GCA and NFA is exempt from all of the provisions and restrictions contained in both laws. Consequently, such an antique firearm may be bought, sold, transported, shipped, etc., without regard to the requirements of these laws.

Under the Arms Export Control Act, certain "antique firearms" are not subject to the import controls. These "antique firearms" are substantially the same as those exempted under the GCA, except that replicas of firearms manufactured after 1898 are exempt from the Arms Export Control Act only if they have a matchlock, flintlock, percussion cap, or similar type of ignition system. No all-inclusive list of antique firearms is published by BATF.

CURIOS AND RELICS

Quoting from the *Federal Firearms Regulations Reference Guide*, the BATF definition of this category of collectors firearm is as follows:

> As set out in the regulations (27 CFR 178.11), curios or relics include firearms which have special value to collectors because they possess some qualities not ordinarily associated with firearms intended for sporting use or as offensive or defensive weapons.
>
> Please note that ammunition is no longer classified as curios or relics since the Congress in 1986 removed the interstate controls over ammunition under the GCA.
>
> To be recognized as curios or relics, firearms must:
>
> 1. Have been manufactured at least 50 years prior to the current date, but not including replicas thereof; or
> 2. Be certified by the curator of a municipal, State or Federal museum which exhibits firearms to be curios or relics of museum interest; or
> 3. Derive a substantial part of their monetary value from the fact that they are novel, rare, or bizarre, or from the fact of their association with some historical figure, period, or event.
>
> Collectors wishing to obtain a determination whether a particular firearm qualifies for classification as a curio or relic in accordance with 27 CFR 178.26 should submit a written request for a ruling. The letter should include:
>
> (1) A complete physical description of the item.
>
> (2) Reasons the collector believes the item merits the classification.
>
> (3) Data concerning the history of the item, including production figures, if available, and market value.
>
> In some cases, actual submission of the firearm may be required prior to a determination being made. Requests should be sent to the Bureau of ATF, Firearms Technology Branch, Washington, DC 20226.
>
> ATF's classifications of curios or relics are published in ATF P 5300.12, Firearms Curios or Relics List. Curios or relics are listed in the publication under the following headings:
>
> Section I. Ammunition Classified as Curios or Relics. . . .
>
> Section II. Firearms Classified as Curios or Relics under the GCA. . . .
>
> Section III. NFA Firearms Removed From the NFA as Collectors' Items and Classified as Curios or Relics Under the GCA. . . .
>
> Section IV. NFA Firearms Classified as Curios or Relics Under the GCA. . . .

SOME OTHER DEFINITIONS

In addition to the BATF classifications of Antique and Curios and Relics, the reader should be aware of the following definitions:

Modern: Firearms manufactured post-1898, with the exception of replicas of antiques. There are special regulations dealing with Class III arms, as noted below. Various sources list serial number details that will assist in determination of the 1898 cut-off date. The author's own works are helpful with Colts; for a detailed reference on a wide variety of makes, see recent editions of Steven Fjestad's *Blue Book of Gun Values*, which is the most complete published source.

Class III Firearms: Machine guns, silencers, short-barrel shotguns (less than 18-inch barrel length), short-barrel rifles (less than 16-inch barrel length), modern-made smoothbore handguns, and firearms of modern manufacture having a rifled bore diameter in excess of .50 caliber.

National Rifle Association of America

The first thing any serious enthusiast of firearms and the shooting sports should do to show his or her dedication to the vast arena of firearms-related pursuits is to *join the National Rifle Association of America*. The address for this unique and unsurpassed-in-significance organization is as follows:

11250 Waples Hill Road
Fairfax VA 22030
(703) 267-1000
fax (703) 267-3913 (specifically for the Gun Collecting Program and the National Firearms Museum)
NRA-ILA Grassroots (800) 392-8683
e-mail: nra-contact@nra.org
web site for NRA: http://www.nra.org

At present, the award-winning NRA web site averages about 2,000 visits a day! The NRA-ILA home page on the World Wide Web provides the following services, as noted in a recent release from the NRA:

> allows you to search and retrieve the latest press releases, legislative alerts, state firearm law brochures, speeches by NRA officials, graphics files, fact sheets, and information on NRA programs from the Eddie Eagle Gun Safety Program . . . to Law Enforcement Training to competitive shooting events nationwide [as well as information on the NRA Museum and Gun Collector Programs]

A vital service of the NRA is the Publications division, which provides members with the choice of subscription to *The American Rifleman*, *The American Hunter*, or *The Guardian* magazines.

Annual NRA membership, as of 1997, costs $35; the fee to become a Life Member is $750. For other membership categories and general information, contact via the Internet: nra-services@nra.org.

THE PRESS AND THE NRA

Although the mainstream media has been generally unfair toward the organization for the past several years, that is to some extent simply due to the frustration many feel in dealing with firearms-related criminal behavior, and due to the naïveté of the media in believing the rubbish that is spewed out by the anti-gun and anti-hunting organizations.

If the media tackled the gun situation with an open mind and did its research thoroughly and responsibly, the result would be derision of the antis, and wholesale admiration for the NRA.

All that one asks is that the media examine what the anti-gun and anti-hunting groups present as their rhetoric with the same intensity and scrutiny as is customarily devoted to the NRA and its agenda.

Someday a responsible investigative journalist will do a study on the NRA. The NRA has over three million members—none of whom is a criminal, and all of whom are intent on helping to straighten out the crime problems and gun-abuse problems that have plagued America for generations.

THE NRA AND ARMS COLLECTING

Programs directed at assisting and encouraging arms collecting include development of the National Firearms Museum, the NRA Gun Collectors Committee, and the NRA Gun Collectors Division, all of which are involved with promoting gun shows, encouraging ethics in arms collecting, and support of the annual NRA Gun Collectors Show and Conference.

The NRA Gun Collectors Code of Ethics is indicative of the high standards in collecting that the NRA promotes.

Among the NRA staff actively working toward fostering public understanding of arms collecting, and working with collectors to promote the hobby, are Whit Fentem, director of the National Firearms Museum; Doug Wicklund, curator; and Phil Schreier, manager of the NRA Gun Collector Program.

For free brochures and information on the NRA, contact the organization at the address and numbers presented above.

THE NRA FOUNDATION

Still another organization deserves the full support of gun enthusiasts nationwide: The NRA Foundation.

The author's own support for the foundation has taken several turns. First, he has broadcast his dedication to furtherance of the goals of the institution verbally and in print. Second, in 1995 and 1996 he made direct gifts of cash, as

The author with Philip Schreier, manager of the NRA Gun Collecting Program; we are holding Captain Samuel H. Walker's own Walker Colt revolvers, serial numbers 1009 and 1010, as sent from the inventor/designer and gunmaker for Mexican War service just prior to Walker's death in 1847. This photo was taken at the NRA Annual Meeting and Show in 1995, on the occasion of Schreier's lecture recounting his detailed documentation of Walker's Walkers.

described in the following excerpt from the Foundation's 1996 Annual Report:

> ... Mr. Wilson has established the R. L. Wilson Educational Endowment through the NRA Foundation to fund an awareness of the positive values of firearms throughout history. . . .[his] commitment to The NRA Foundation is defined in the dedication of his 1995 book *Steel Canvas*:
>
> Education is the key to understanding firearms, their value and significance—historic, artistic and technical. All my adult life I have enjoyed firearms: researching and writing about them, placing them in museums and collections and (not least) using them. . . .There is a nonprofit foundation that is single-mindedly dedicated to education on firearms safety. More than that, this group supports an educational understanding of the appreciation of firearms—something close to my heart. . . . So I am dedicating this work to that organization, for its promotion of correct values in the magical world of firearms: To the NRA Foundation, a nonprofit institution dedicated to education in firearms safety, an understanding of the appreciation of firearms, and their responsible ownership and use.

As of this writing, the sum the author has donated to that endowment is $17,500. The minimum amount I intend to add to that figure is $10,000 annually. Use of the proceeds, administered by the NRA Foundation, is to the furtherance of education about firearms, particularly through the hobby of arms collecting.

Among the most generous donors to the NRA Foundation have been Dr. and Mrs. William L. Roberts. The couple donated the "Artistry in Arms" and the "American Liberty" collections to the National Firearms Museum, a total of 346 firearms and related material. Their gifts also established the William L. and Collette N. Roberts Endowment.

The NRA Foundation, whose hard-working, imaginative, and highly effective executive director is H. Wayne Sheets, can be reached at the same address as the NRA, and the phone and fax numbers are (703) 267-1121 and (703) 267-3986, respectively.

THE ILA

Still another organization affiliated with the National Rifle Association is the Institute of Legislative Action. Executive director of the ILA/Administration is Tanya Metaksa, often seen on television and frequently seen in print. Although some elements of the press try to claim that the NRA and ILA have been losing their influence with the public and legislators, those views are open to interpretation. On the whole, the ILA is highly effective, and without its hard work, and that of the NRA *per se*, the gun-haters and the hunting-haters might well have already wiped out private gun ownership and the sport of hunting, and in the process generations of immense good works in wildlife and habitat conservation.

To contact the ILA, call (703) 267-1140; fax (703) 267-3973. See also the NRA web site, reachable via nra.org or simply by the search engine nra.

With its size and comprehensive organization, and now with the potency of Charlton Heston joining the fray, the NRA offers the best united front against those who do not understand guns, and who do not understand hunting.

Commemoratives

BY KEVIN P. CHERRY

In an as yet unpublished article written for *The American Rifleman*, Larry Wilson considered the impact of commemorative firearms on the collecting world. The gist of this story is that these arms, besides offering the opportunity to collect beautiful pieces in perfect condition with strong investment potential, are an important magnet to attract many new enthusiasts to gun collecting. And in the R. L. Wilson book, *Colt Commemorative Firearms,* published by my father in 1974, James E. Serven noted:

> I have been a student of Colt firearms for many years and find nothing very unusual in the zeal of a collector who seeks factory-made Colt commemorative firearms with varied markings, different finishes, and interesting historical associations; that process has been going on among collectors for years. One veteran Oklahoma collector has twenty-one different variations of the rare Colt folding-trigger pistols made at Paterson. One could have perhaps fifty or more Colt cap-lock Navy model pistols with variations in markings, structural design, and other features.
>
> Collecting the early Colt models today, however, is not a field for one on a tight budget; many models are almost impossible to find. Where, then, do the increasing numbers of arms collectors turn? While certainly not an inexpensive pursuit, commemorative arms do open a field where there is generally a reasonable current availability of collectible items. . . .
>
> While some of the purists in Colt collecting remain critical of the commemorative pieces, it seems fair to assume that the field is wide enough to accommodate all shades of thought, and I am confident that this book will help to bring about a better understanding and a greater rapport among all who collect arms which bear the name of Colt.

These remarks also easily transfer to the subject of Winchester, Smith & Wesson, Remington, Marlin, and other marquees.

Commemorative firearms on the following list fulfill these criteria:

1. The series has a stated production limit.
2. Each series has its own serial number range.
3. The production has an endorsement by the manufacturer.
4. Distribution is generally through normal channels.

The majority of these arms are classified by the BATF as curios and relics.

Among the exceptions to the above criteria are special-issue guns, such as those pieces made for "The Friends of the NRA" banquet auctions or raffles, for Ducks Unlimited dinner fund-raisers, for fish and game clubs, and so forth. These are not guns bearing endorsements by the manufacturers, nor are they distributed in the normal manner of bona fide commemorative issues.

The 1985 edition of Larry Wilson's *Colt: An American Legend* contains a list of commemorative models (pages 388–89), and a separate list of Special Editions: Hand Engraved or Etched (pages 390–91). Comparison of the two, and consideration of the above-noted criteria, make clear the commemorative nature of the former and the non-commemorative nature of the latter.

I am proud of the role my father played in establishing this major specialty in the world of arms collecting.

The course of action taken by the Colt and Winchester (U.S. Repeating Arms) firms, which adversely affected the commemorative market, should be considered here. Mistakes were made by these two major companies, which proved to be temporary setbacks. Both companies made too many models and too many examples of these models, and the issues were generally overpriced. From the early 1980s until the end of that decade, the market was idle.

But beginning about 1989, the market had absorbed the excess commemoratives, and with increased pricings of standard production, the commemorative issues regained their appeal. Prices have been returning, and the larger-caliber Colt and Winchester lever-action carbines and rifles have proven particularly attractive.

Prices in the listing that follows apply to mint guns, with their original accessories, casings, and packaging. Commemoratives that have seen use, including being shot, generally have a value equal to the same model of standard production.

Books on commemorative firearms are listed in the bibliography, in Appendix 1. Additionally, commemorative Colts and Winchesters are featured in Larry Wilson's *Colt: An American Legend* and *Winchester: An American Legend*, each of which is the official history of these prime firms in the commemorative market.

All in all, for a significant block of firearms enthusiasts, commemoratives are an important segment of the collector market, and are definitely here to stay.

Year	Description	Production	Original Retail	Current Retail
1961	Colt Genseso, Illinois, 125th Anniversary Derringer	104	$27.50	$650.00
1961	Colt Sheriff's Model, Blue & Case Hardened	478	129.95	1995.00
1961	Colt Sheriff's Model, Nickel	25	139.95	5000.00
1961	Colt 125th Anniversary Model SAA	7390	150.00	995.00
1961	Colt Kansas Statehood Scout	6197	75.00	350.00
1961	Colt Pony Express Centennial Scout	1007	80.00	450.00
1961	Colt Civil War Centennial Pistol	24114	32.50	175.00
1961	Marlin 90th Anniversary 39A Rifle & Carbine	1000	100.00	995.00
1962	Colt Rock Island Arsenal Centennial Pistol	550	38.50	250.00
1962	Colt Columbus, Ohio Sesquicentennial Scout	200	100.00	550.00
1962	Colt Fort Findlay, Ohio Sesquicentennial Scout	110	89.50	650.00
1962	Colt Fort Findlay, Ohio Cased Pair, 22LR/22Mag	20	185.00	2500.00
1962	Colt New Mexico Golden Anniversary Scout	1000	79.95	375.00
1962	Colt Fort McPherson, Nebraska Centennial Derringer	300	28.95	395.00
1962	Colt West Virginia Statehood Centennial Scout	3451	75.00	375.00
1963	Colt West Virginia Statehood, Centennial SAA .45	600	150.00	1095.00
1963	Colt Arizona Territory Centennial Scout	5355	75.00	375.00
1963	Colt Arizona Territory Centennial SAA .45	1264	150.00	1095.00
1963	Colt Carolina Charter Tercentenary Scout	550	75.00	395.00
1963	Colt Carolina Charter Tercentenary .22/.45 Combo	250	240.00	1495.00
1963	Colt H. Cook "1 of 100" .22/.45 Combo	100	275.00	1695.00
1963	Colt Fort Stephenson, Ohio Sesq. Scout	200	75.00	550.00
1963	Colt Battle of Gettysburg Centennial Scout	1019	89.95	375.00
1963	Colt Idaho Territory Centennial Scout	902	75.00	375.00
1963	Colt Gen. John Hunt Morgan, Indiana Raid Scout	100	74.50	650.00
1964	Colt Cherry's 35th Anniversary .22/.45 Combo	100	275.00	1695.00
1964	Colt Nevada Statehood Centennial Scout	3981	75.00	375.00
1964	Colt Nevada Statehood Centennial SAA .45	1684	$150.00	$1095.00
1964	Colt Nevada Statehood Centennial .22/.45 Combo	189	240.00	1495.00
1964	Colt Nevada State, Combo w/Extra Engraved Cylinders	577	350.00	1595.00
1964	Colt Nevada "Battle Born" Scout	981	85.00	375.00
1964	Colt Nevada "Battle Born" SAA .45	80	175.00	1395.00
1964	Colt Nevada "Battle Born" SAA .22/.45 Combo	20	265.00	2595.00
1964	Colt Montana Territorial Centennial Scout	2296	75.00	375.00
1964	Colt Montana Territorial Centennial SAA .45	850	150.00	1095.00
1964	Colt Wyoming Diamond Jubilee Scout	2356	75.00	375.00
1964	Winchester Wyoming Diamond Jubilee Mdl. 94 Carbine	1500	99.95	1295.00
1964	Remington Montana Territorial Centennial 600 Rifle	1005	124.95	495.00
1964	Colt General Hood Centennial Scout	1502	75.00	375.00
1964	Colt New Jersey Tercentenary Scout	1000	75.00	375.00
1964	Colt New Jersey Tercentenary SAA .45	249	150.00	1095.00
1964	Colt St. Louis Bicentennial Scout	801	75.00	375.00
1964	Colt St. Louis Bicentennial SAA .45	199	150.00	1095.00
1964	Colt St. Louis Bicentennial .22/.45 Combo	250	240.00	1495.00
1964	Ithaca St. Louis Bicentennial Model 49 .22 Rifle	200	34.95	195.00
1964	Colt California Gold Rush Scout	500	79.50	375.00
1964	Colt Pony Express Presentation SAA .45	1004	250.00	1395.00
1964	Colt Chamizal Treaty Scout	450	85.00	395.00
1964	Colt Chamizal Treaty SAA .45	50	170.00	1295.00
1964	Colt Chamizal Treaty .22/.45 Combo	50	280.00	1995.00
1964	Colt Col. Sam Colt Sesquicentennial Presentation SAA .45	4750	225.00	1095.00
1964	Colt Col. Sam Colt Sesquicentennial Deluxe Presentation SAA .45	200	500.00	1950.00
1964	Colt Col. Sam Colt Sesquicentennial Special Dlx. Presentation SAA .45	50	1000.00	2950.00
1964	Colt Wyatt Earp Buntline SAA .45	150	250.00	1995.00

Year	Description	Production	Original Retail	Current Retail
1965	Colt Oregon Trail Scout	1995	$75.00	$375.00
1965	Colt Joaquin Murietta .22/.45 Combo	100	350.00	1695.00
1965	Colt Forty-Niner Miner Scout	500	85.00	375.00
1965	Colt Old Fort Des Moines, Reconstruction Scout	700	89.95	375.00
1965	Colt Old Fort Des Moines, Reconstruction SAA .45	100	169.95	1095.00
1965	Colt Old Fort Des Moines, Reconstruction .22/.45 Combo	100	289.95	1695.00
1965	Colt Appomattox Centennial Scout	1001	75.00	375.00
1965	Colt Appomattox Centennial SAA .45	250	150.00	1095.00
1965	Colt Appomattox Centennial .22/.45 Combo	250	240.00	1495.00
1965	Colt General Meade Campaign Scout	1197	75.00	350.00
1965	Colt Saint Augustine Quadricentennial Scout	500	85.00	375.00
1965	Colt Kansas Cowtown Series, Wichita Scout	500	85.00	350.00
1966	Colt Kansas Cowtown Series, Dodge City Scout	500	85.00	350.00
1966	Colt Colorado Gold Rush Scout	1350	85.00	375.00
1966	Colt Oklahoma Territory Scout	1343	85.00	375.00
1966	Colt Dakota Territory Scout	1000	85.00	375.00
1966	Winchester Centennial '66 Rifle	102309	125.00	450.00
1966	Winchester Centennial '66 Carbine	102309	125.00	425.00
1966	Colt General Meade SAA .45	197	165.00	1095.00
1966	Colt Abercrombie & Fitch "Trailblazer" New York	200	275.00	1095.00
1966	Colt Kansas Cowtown Series, Abilene Scout	500	95.00	350.00
1966	Colt Indiana Sesquicentennial Scout	1745	85.00	375.00
1966	Winchester Nebraska Centennial 94 Rifle	2500	125.00	1195.00
1966	Colt Pony Express SAA .45 "4-Square"		1400.00	5995.00
1966	Colt California Gold Rush SAA .45	130	175.00	1295.00
1966	Colt Abercrombie & Fitch "Trailblazer" Chicago	100	275.00	1095.00
1966	Colt Abercrombie & Fitch "Trailblazer" San Francisco	100	275.00	1095.00
1967	Remington Canadian Centennial 742 Rifle	1000	199.95	395.00
1967	Ruger Canadian Centennial 10/22 Rifle	2000	99.95	325.00
1967	Ruger Canadian Centennial, Matched #3 Set	1900	319.00	650.00
1967	Ruger Canadian Centennial, Matched #2 Set	70	$450.00	$850.00
1967	Ruger Canadian Centennial, Matched #1 Special Deluxe Set	30	600.00	1050.00
1967	Colt Lawman Series, Bat Masterson Scout	3000	90.00	375.00
1967	Colt Lawman Series, Bat Masterson SAA .45	500	180.00	1295.00
1967	Colt Alamo Scout	4239	85.00	350.00
1967	Colt Alamo SAA .45	750	165.00	1095.00
1967	Colt Alamo .22/.45 Combo	250	265.00	1495.00
1967	Colt Kansas Cowtown Series, Coffeyville Scout	500	95.00	350.00
1967	Winchester Canadian '67 Centennial Rifle	90301	125.00	450.00
1967	Winchester Canadian '67 Centennial Carbine	90301	125.00	425.00
1967	Winchester Alaskan Purchase Centennial Carbine	1500	125.00	1495.00
1967	Colt Kansas Trail Series, Chisholm Trail Scout	500	100.00	350.00
1967	Colt WWI Series, Chateau Thierry .45 Auto	7400	200.00	695.00
1967	Colt WWI Series, Chateau Thierry Deluxe .45 Auto	75	500.00	1350.00
1967	Colt WWI Series, Chateau Thierry Special Deluxe .45 Auto	25	1000.00	2750.00
1967	H&R "Abilene Anniversary" .22 Revolver	300	83.50	150.00
1968	Colt Nebraska Centennial Scout	6999	100.00	350.00
1968	Colt Kansas Trail Series, Pawnee Trail Scout	500	110.00	350.00
1968	Winchester Illinois Sesquicentennial, 94 Carbine	37648	110.00	350.00
1968	Winchester Buffalo Bill Rifle "1 of 300"	300	1000.00	2500.00
1968	Winchester Buffalo Bill Rifle	112923	129.95	450.00
1968	Winchester Buffalo Bill Carbine	112923	129.95	425.00
1968	Colt WWI Series, Belleau Wood .45 Auto	7400	200.00	695.00
1968	Colt WWI Series, Belleau Wood Deluxe .45 Auto	75	500.00	1350.00
1968	Colt WWI Series, Belleau Wood Special Deluxe .45 Auto	25	1000.00	2750.00
1968	Colt Lawman Series, Pat Garrett Scout	2966	110.00	375.00
1968	Colt Lawman Series, Pat Garrett SAA .45	500	220.00	1095.00
1969	Colt General Nathan Bedford Forest Scout	2996	110.00	350.00
1969	Colt Kansas Trail Series, Santa Fe Trail Scout	500	120.00	350.00

Year	Description	Production	Original Retail	Current Retail
1969	Colt WWI Series, Battle of 2nd Marne, .45 Auto	7400	$220.00	$695.00
1969	Colt WWI Series, Battle of 2nd Marne, Deluxe .45 Auto	75	500.00	1350.00
1969	Colt WWI Series, Battle of 2nd Marne, Special Deluxe .45 Auto	25	1000.00	2750.00
1969	Colt Alabama Sesquicentennial Scout	2998	110.00	350.00
1969	Colt Alabama Sesquicentennial SAA .45	1	N/A	15000.00
1969	Winchester Golden Spike Carbine	69996	119.95	350.00
1969	Winchester Theodore Roosevelt Carbine	52386	134.95	425.00
1969	Winchester Theodore Roosevelt Rifle	52386	134.95	450.00
1969	Colt Golden Spike Scout	10965	135.00	375.00
1969	Colt Kansas Trail Series, Shawnee Trail Scout	500	120.00	350.00
1969	Colt WWI Series, Meuse-Argonne .45 Auto	7400	220.00	695.00
1969	Colt WWI Series, Meuse-Argonne Deluxe .45 Auto	75	550.00	1350.00
1969	Colt WWI Series, Meuse-Argonne Special Deluxe .45 Auto	25	1000.00	2750.00
1969	Colt Arkansas Territory Sesquicentennial Scout	3487	110.00	350.00
1969	Colt Lawman Series, Wild Bill Hickock SAA	500	220.00	1095.00
1969	Colt Lawman Series, Wild Bill Hickock Scout	2984	116.00	375.00
1969	Colt California Bicentennial Scout	4997	135.00	350.00
1970	Colt Kansas Fort Series, Fort Larned Scout	500	120.00	350.00
1970	Colt WWII Series, European Theater	9767	250.00	695.00
1970	Colt WWII Series, Pacific Theater	9886	250.00	695.00
1970	Winchester Northwest Territories	2500	149.95	850.00
1970	Winchester Northwest Territories, Deluxe	500	249.95	1100.00
1970	Winchester Northwest Territories, Donation	10	N/A	N/A
1970	Winchester Cowboy Commemorative Carbine	27549	125.00	450.00
1970	Winchester Cowboy Commemorative Carbine "1 of 300"	300	1000.00	2500.00
1970	Winchester Lone Star Carbine	38385	140.00	425.00
1970	Winchester Lone Star Rifle	38385	140.00	450.00
1970	Colt Texas Ranger SAA .45	1000	650.00	2250.00
1970	Colt Texas Ranger SAA .45, Grade II	N/A	$2250.00	$4500.00
1970	Colt Texas Ranger SAA .45, Grade III	N/A	2950.00	5000.00
1970	Savage 75th Anniversary Model 99 Rifle	9999	195.00	495.00
1970	Colt Kansas Fort Series, Fort Hayes Scout	500	130.00	350.00
1970	Colt Maine Sesquicentennial Scout	2987	120.00	350.00
1970	Colt Missouri Sesquicentennial Scout	2975	125.00	350.00
1970	Colt Missouri Sesquicentennial SAA .45	888	220.00	995.00
1970	Colt Kansas Fort Series, Fort Riley	500	130.00	350.00
1970	Colt Lawman Series, Wyatt Earp Scout	2968	125.00	450.00
1970	Colt Lawman Series, Wyatt Earp SAA .45	500	395.00	2250.00
1971	Winchester NRA Centennial Musket	23400	149.95	425.00
1971	Winchester NRA Centennial Rifle	21000	149.95	425.00
1971	Winchester Yellow Boy	4903	149.95	1150.00
1971	Winchester R.C.M.P.	9500	189.95	795.00
1971	Winchester R.C.M.P. Members Issue	4850	189.95	795.00
1971	Winchester R.C.M.P. Presentation	10	N/A	9995.00
1971	Winchester MPX	32	78.00	6995.00
1971	Colt NRA Centennial SAA .45	3475	250.00	1095.00
1971	Colt NRA Centennial SAA .357	3475	250.00	850.00
1971	Colt NRA Centennial Gold Cup .45	2478	250.00	850.00
1971	Colt 1851 Navy, U.S. Grant	4140	250.00	595.00
1971	Colt 1851 Navy, Robert E. Lee	4645	250.00	595.00
1971	Colt 1851 Navy, Lee-Grant Set	250	500.00	1350.00
1971	Colt Kansas Fort Series, Fort Scott Scout	500	130.00	350.00
1971	H&R Officer's Model .45–70	10000	250.00	495.00
1971	Marlin Zane Grey .30–30 Carbine	N/A	150.00	350.00
1971	Stevens Favorite '71 .22 Single Shot	1000	75.00	250.00
1971	Marlin 336–39A Engraved Cased Pair	1000	750.00	995.00
1972	H&R Little Big Horn, .45–70	N/A	220.00	495.00
1972	Colt Florida Sesquicentennial Scout	1996	125.00	375.00
1972	Colt Arizona Ranger Scout	3000	135.00	375.00
1972	High Standard Olympic .22 Auto	N/A	550.00	1500.00

Year	Description	Production	Original Retail	Current Retail
1973	H&R 1873 Springfield	N/A	$250.00	$495.00
1973	Smith & Wesson Texas Ranger w/Knife	10000	250.00	595.00
1973	Smith & Wesson Texas Ranger	N/A	195.00	475.00
1973	H&R Custer Memorial, Officer's Model	25	3000.00	3995.00
1973	H&R Custer Memorial, Enlisted Man's Model	243	2000.00	1995.00
1974	High Standard Griswold & Gunnison	500	175.00	250.00
1974	High Standard Presidential Derringer	N/A	150.00	250.00
1974	High Standard Leech & Rigdon	500	175.00	250.00
1974	Winchester Texas Ranger Carbine	4850	129.95	695.00
1974	Winchester Texas Ranger Presentation	150	1000.00	2500.00
1974	Winchester Apache	8600	149.95	795.00
1974	Winchester Klondike Gold Rush	10200	229.95	795.00
1974	Winchester Klondike Dawson City	25	N/A	8500.00
1974	Winchester Comanche	11511	229.95	795.00
1975	Colt Peacemaker Centennial .45	1500	300.00	1395.00
1975	Colt Peacemaker Centennial .44–40	1500	300.00	1395.00
1975	Colt Peacemaker Centennial Pair	500	625.00	2895.00
1975	High Standard Schneider & Glassick	1000	325.00	325.00
1976	Ruger Colorado Centennial Single Six	N/A	250.00	325.00
1976	Colt U.S. Bicentennial Set	1776	1695.00	1895.00
1976	Winchester U.S. Bicentennial Carbine	19999	325.00	595.00
1976	Browning Bicentennial '78 .45/70 Rifle	1000	150.00	1850.00
1976	Winchester Sioux	12000	279.95	795.00
1976	Winchester Little Big Horn	11000	229.95	795.00
1977	Colt 2nd Amendment .22	3020	194.95	350.00
1977	Winchester Wells Fargo	19999	350.00	495.00
1977	S&W 125th Anniversary Model 125	10000	350.00	495.00
1977	Winchester Cheyenne .44/40	11225	300.00	795.00
1977	Winchester Cheyenne .22	5000	319.95	695.00
1977	Colt U.S. Calvary 200th Anniversary Set	2974	995.00	1250.00
1977	Winchester "Limited Edition I"	1500	1500.00	1395.00
1977	Winchester Cherokee .30–30	9000	384.95	795.00
1977	Winchester Cherokee .22	3950	348.95	695.00
1977	Winchester Legendary Lawman	19999	375.00	495.00

Year	Description	Production	Original Retail	Current Retail
1978	Browning Centennial Superposed Rifle-Shotgun	500	$7000.00	$5000.00
1978	Browning Centennial M92 .44 Magnum	6000	219.95	495.00
1978	Browning Centennial Hi-Power 9mm	3500	495.00	650.00
1978	Jonathan Browning Mountain Rifle	1000	650.00	650.00
1978	Winchester Antlered Game Carbine	19999	375.00	495.00
1978	Colt Statehood 3rd Model Dragoon	52	12500.00	6995.00
1979	Winchester Legendary Frontiersman Rifle	19999	425.00	495.00
1979	Winchester Bat Masterson	8000	650.00	795.00
1979	Winchester "Limited Edition II"	1500	1750.00	1395.00
1979	Colt Ned Buntline Single Action Army .45	2973	895.00	895.00
1980	Colt Heritage-Walker .44 Percussion	1850	1475.00	950.00
1980	Winchester Matched Set of 1000	1000	3000.00	2250.00
1980	Winchester Alberta Diamond Jubilee	2700	650.00	795.00
1980	Winchester Alberta Diamond Jubilee Deluxe	300	1900.00	1495.00
1980	Winchester Saskatchewan Diamond Jubilee	2700	695.00	795.00
1980	Winchester Saskatchewan Diamond Jubilee Deluxe	300	1695.00	1495.00
1980	Winchester Calgary Stampede	1000	2200.00	1250.00
1980	Winchester Canadian Pacific	2700	800.00	550.00
1980	Winchester Canadian Pacific, Employee Edition	2000	800.00	550.00
1980	Winchester Canadian Pacific, Presentation	300	2200.00	1100.00
1980	Winchester "Oliver Winchester"	19999	519.60	695.00
1981	Colt "John M. Browning" .45 Automatic	2986	1099.95	895.00
1981	Winchester John Wayne	50000	600.00	895.00
1981	Winchester Canadian John Wayne	999	600.00	1095.00
1981	Winchester "Duke"	1000	2250.00	2950.00
1981	Browning "American Waterfowl" Superposed	500	7000.00	3995.00
1981	Winchester U.S. Border Patrol, Members	800	950.00	595.00
1981	Winchester U.S. Border Patrol	1000	950.00	595.00
1981	Winchester John Wayne "1 of 300" Set	300	8500.00	6500.00
1981	Winchester Great Western Artists I	999	2500.00	1195.00

Year	Description	Production	Original Retail	Current Retail
1981	Winchester Great Western Artists II	999	$2500.00	$1195.00
1982	Colt John Wayne, Standard	3100	2995.00	1995.00
1982	Colt John Wayne, Deluxe	500	10000.00	7500.00
1982	Colt John Wayne, Presentation	100	20000.00	12000.00
1982	Winchester Annie Oakley .22	6000	699.00	695.00
1982	Winchester Oklahoma Diamond Jubilee	1000	2200.00	1395.00
1982	Winchester Bald Eagle, Silver	2800	895.00	595.00
1982	Winchester Bald Eagle, Gold	200	2950.00	2500.00
1983	Winchester Chief Crazy Horse	19999	600.00	495.00
1983	Colt Buffalo Bill Wild West Show Centennial SAA .45	283	1349.95	1350.00
1984	Winchester Colt	3250	3995.00	2250.00
1984	Colt "USA Edition" SAA .44–40	100	4995.00	3500.00
1984	Colt Kit Carson .22 New Frontier	951	549.95	395.00
1984	Colt Theodore Roosevelt .44/40	500	1695.00	1695.00
1984	Winchester Boy Scout 75th Anniversary 9422	15000	495.00	495.00
1984	Winchester Eagle Scout 75th Anniversary 9422	1000	1710.00	2500.00
1984	Browning A-5 "Classic" Semi-Auto Shotgun	5000	1260.00	950.00
1984	Browning Hi-Power "Classic" 9mm	5000	1000.00	850.00
1984	Browning Hi-Power "Gold Classic" 9mm	500	2000.00	1800.00
1985	Colt Texas Sesquicentennial SAA .45, Standard	1000	1836.00	1095.00
1985	Colt Texas Sesquicentennial SAA .45, Premier	75	7995.00	5000.00
1985	Winchester Texas Sesquicentennial Carbine	15000	695.00	695.00
1985	Winchester Texas Sesquicentennial, Rifle & Bowie Knife	1500	2995.00	2400.00
1985	Winchester Texas Sesquicentennial, Rifle, Carbine, & Bowie Knife Set	150	7995.00	6250.00
1986	Colt 150th Anniversary SAA .45	1000	$1595.00	$1595.00
1986	Winchester 120th Anniversary .44/40	1000	995.00	895.00
1986	Browning A-5 "Gold Classic" Shotgun	500	6500.00	3500.00
1986	Browning Superposed "Classic"	2500	2000.00	1750.00
1986	Browning Superposed "Gold Classic" Shotgun	350	6000.00	4750.00
1987	Winchester U.S. Constitution 200th Anniversary .44/40	17	12000.00	13000.00
1990	Winchester Wyoming Centennial .30–30	500	895.00	1095.00
1991	Winchester 125th Anniversary .30–30	61	4995.00	5250.00
1992	Winchester Arapaho .30–30	500	895.00	1095.00
1992	Winchester Ontario Conservation .30–30	400	1195.00	1195.00
1992	Winchester Kentucky Bicentennial .30–30	500	995.00	995.00
1993	Winchester Nez Perce .30–30	600	950.00	995.00
1994	Uberti Nimschke 1866 Rifle, .44/40	150	1495.00	1495.00
1994	Marlin "Century Limited" 94 Rifle, .44/40	2500	1087.90	925.00
1994	Pedersoli Creedmoor Rifle, 45/70	250	1495.00	1495.00
1995	Winchester Florida Sesquicentennial Carbine, 30/30	500	1195.00	1195.00
1995	Marlin 1895 125th Anniversary	350	1195.00	1195.00
1996	Winchester "Wild Bill Hickok" Model 94 .30/30	350	1195.00	1195.00
1996	Pedersoli Sharps Creedmoor .45/70	300	1995.00	1995.00
1997	Uberti Gustave Young Model 1866	300	1895.00	1895.00

Note: The author is grateful to Kevin Cherry for his detailed text on this increasingly complex subject. For further information, Mr. Cherry can be contacted c/o Cherry's, 3402-A Wendover Avenue, Greensboro NC 27407; telephone (910) 854-4182.

Smoothbore Pistols Firing Shotgun Shells

BY ERIC M. LARSON

As rare American cultural artifacts, certain smoothbore pistols originally manufactured in the United States in or before 1934 occupy a unique niche in U.S. firearms history and genealogy. They are highly prized by collectors, yet still inappropriately regulated strictly as machine guns by the Bureau of Alcohol, Tobacco and Firearms (ATF).

These guns were made when no federal laws (and relatively few state laws) affected firearms design. While it is rare, the most commonly encountered example is the 12¼"-barrel H&R Handy-Gun, designed to fire the 2½" .410 shotgun shell. It is one of several smoothbore pistols that competed with Marble's Game Getter Gun, a .22/.44 or .410 combination firearm with a folding shoulder stock that was first manufactured in 1908. A few smoothbore pistols (such as the 20-gauge Ithaca Auto & Burglar Gun) were marketed as defensive weapons, but most were relatively low-powered small-game guns.

Smoothbore pistols like the H&R Handy-Gun are currently regulated by the National Firearms Act (NFA) of 1934. The NFA is designed to control firearms thought to be mainly used by criminals by requiring registration of the firearms, and using prohibitive taxes to reduce their manufacture, distribution, and ownership. It is a harsh federal law to discourage illegally manufacturing, selling, or possessing hand grenades, machine guns, and similar weapons, and the cutting down of conventional shotguns or rifles (regardless of their caliber) to make concealable firearms.

Curiously, as passed in 1934, the NFA specifically excluded "a pistol or revolver," and still does today. As originally enacted, the NFA defined a "firearm" as:

> A shotgun or rifle having a barrel of less than eighteen inches in length, or any other weapon, except a pistol or revolver, from which a shot is discharged by an explosive if such weapon is capable of being concealed on the person, or a machine gun, and includes a muffler or silencer for any firearm whether or not such firearm is included within the foregoing definition.

But several original versions of the bill that eventually was enacted as the NFA included "a pistol, revolver . . . or any other firearm capable of being concealed on the person" within the definition of an NFA "firearm." Under the NFA as originally proposed, pistols and revolvers would have been regulated as strictly as machine guns.

After debate, the bill was amended to remove pistols and revolvers, but not other concealable firearms. Thus, small firearms not readily classifiable as traditional pistols or revolvers (such as cane-guns, knife-pistols, and so forth) had to be registered. But Congress did not define the terms "pistol," "revolver," "rifle," "shotgun," or "any other weapon" under the original NFA in 1934. Consequently, ATF applied the NFA using administrative regulations.

When the original NFA became effective on July 26, 1934, *all* items defined as "firearms" had to be registered, and there was a $200 tax on each transfer of ownership. The $200 rate, set to equal the cost (in 1934) of a new .45 caliber Thompson Submachine gun, was designed to be prohibitive.

Why were smoothbore pistols, which were clearly designed as handguns, deemed not to be pistols? In 1926, the Bureau of Internal Revenue determined that the H&R Handy-Gun was "not a pistol or revolver within the meaning . . . and is not, therefore, subject to tax" under the Internal Revenue Act of 1926. The 1926 Act had exempted rifles, shotguns, and ammunition from a 10 percent firearms excise tax enacted in 1918, but, because of anti-handgun politics, retained it for pistols and revolvers (the .410 Stevens Off-Hand Shot Gun, another smoothbore pistol, also was exempted).

The 1926 ruling resulted from an agitation by the H&R and Stevens manufacturers, who argued that these firearms were useful to trappers, farmers, hunters, lumberjacks, and others who worked outdoors, being relatively compact and less bulky than a firearm intended to be fired from the shoulder.

A circa 1928 H&R advertisement states: "The 'Handy-Gun' is classified by the U.S. Government as a shotgun." Other documentation of the H&R Handy-Gun's classification as a "shotgun" has not been located. Interestingly, H&R catalogues from that era state that under the laws of some states, any firearm with a barrel less than 12 inches in length was defined as a pistol; consequently, the 12¼-inch barrel caused the H&R Handy-Gun to avoid being regulated in those states as a pistol.

ATF determined that "since the manufacturer had argued successfully his point in 1926 that the H&R Handy-Gun was not a pistol, it was very easy for the Bureau in 1934 to point out . . . that the weapon could not be excepted from the definition of a firearm as defined in . . . the National Firearms Act . . . as being a pistol." "Therefore," ATF concluded, "it was easy" to place the H&R Handy-Gun within the term "firearm" as being "any other weapon" capable of being concealed on the person. ATF used this interpretation to classify all smoothbore pistols as "any other weapon" under two different rulings, each dated August 6, 1934. Ruling S.T. 772 applies to "a so-called shotgun with a pistol grip, which fires a shot shell," and Ruling S.T. 779 to a firearm that is "a single shot, single trigger, and single hammer gun with a pistol grip, and is chambered for shot loads." The test, S.T. 779 states, "is not the length of the barrel, but whether the weapon is capable of being concealed upon the person."

Because the $200 transfer tax vastly exceeded their value as firearms, no smoothbore pistol that was manufactured in 1934 was ever regularly, commercially manufactured again. Recognizing that some of these firearms have "legitimate uses," Congress reduced the $200 tax to $1 in 1938 for Marble's Game Getter Gun. The Congress declared: "The weapon to which the legislation refers may be utilized either as a shotgun or as a rifle and has legitimate uses." ATF administratively removed the 18-inch barrel variation from the NFA in 1939 because, "after reconsideration," it was not deemed concealable on the person.

In 1945, the Congress extended the $1 tax reduction to a single-shot smoothbore pistol with a barrel at least 12 inches in length. This reduction applied to the .410 and 28 gauge H&R Handy-Gun, .410 Stevens, and .410 Crescent Certified Shotgun, among others. Again Congress spoke definitively, and determined that these firearms "are particularly useful on farms and elsewhere for extermination of vermin and predatory animals, and in hunting and trapping activities where quick firing at close range is essential." The prohibitively high manufacturer, dealer, and transfer taxes, Congress found, work "an injustice both against those who need such low-powered, so-called small-game guns, and against those who make and deal in them."

In 1960, Congress changed the transfer tax to $5 for all NFA firearms classified as "any other weapon" (which included all smoothbore pistols), recognizing that they were mainly of interest to collectors and not likely to be used as weapons.

Under the Gun Control Act of 1968, Congress provided that ATF could administratively remove any firearm (except a machine gun or destructive device, such as a land mine or hand grenade) from the NFA if it determined that the firearm is primarily a collector's item and is not likely to be used as a weapon. Since 1968, it appears that ATF may have removed 50,000 to 100,000, or more, firearms from the NFA as collectors' items; and that the vast majority of these firearms were shoulder-stocked pistols of the Mauser and Luger variety. Fewer than 10,000 smoothbore pistols manufactured in or before 1934 are estimated to have survived until 1997, out of an original production of less than 100,000 (see table). While Marble's Game Getter Gun is not a smoothbore pistol, it is included in the table because of its historical relevance.

Modern rifled-barrel pistols that are designed to fire

Estimated Total Production of Smoothbore Pistols and Marble's Game Getter Gun Originally Commercially Manufactured in the United States in or Before 1934 by Years of Production, and the Estimated Number That Have Survived Until 1997, Still Under Purview of the National Firearms Act of 1934, as Amended

Name or type of firearm and years of manufacture	*Estimated original production*	*Estimated number that have survived until 1997*
Smoothbore Pistols		
.410 bore H&R Handy-Gun (1921–1934)	48,600	4,860
28 gauge H&R Handy-Gun (1921–1934)	5,400	540
.410 Crescent Certified Shotgun (1932–1934)	4,000	400
.410 Stevens "Auto Shot" and "Off Hand" pistol (1923–1934)	25,000	2,500
20 gauge Defiance Anti-Bandit Gun (1926–1927)	300	30
20 gauge Ithaca Auto & Burglar Gun, Model A (1922–1926)	2,500	250
20 gauge Ithaca Auto & Burglar Gun, Model B (1925–1934)	2,000	200
All other smoothbore pistols (circa 1867–1934)*	3,000	300
SUBTOTAL	90,800	9,080
Marble's Game Getter Gun		
.22/.44 smoothbore, Model 1908 (1908–1914)	10,000	1,000
.22/.410 smoothbore Model 1921 (1921–1942)	10,000	1,000
TOTAL	110,800	11,080

*These include the 20-gauge Remington Combination Pistol-Shotgun, .410 Victor Ejector Pistol, 20-gauge Knickerbocker Pistol, .410 or 20-gauge New Empire Auto & Burglar Gun, Marble's Game Getter .22/.44 Pistol, and others that are uncataloged and unknown at this time because of their extreme rarity (only a few, if any, may still exist). These do not include smoothbore pistols removed from the National Firearms Act of 1934, as amended, by the Bureau of Alcohol, Tobacco and Firearms (ATF) as collectors' items under the Gun Control Act of 1968.

shotgun shells are *not* subject to the NFA, that is, no federal registration with ATF or tax payment is required. The reason is that the Congress specifically exempted any pistol with a *rifled* barrel from the NFA in 1968. The pistols discussed in this research were originally manufactured with *smoothbore* barrels.

All of the smoothbore pistols and other firearms listed below are *Class III* firearms unless specifically noted. If they are not currently registered with ATF, their sale, transfer, or possession is illegal. Moreover, it is also illegal for any person to borrow or otherwise possess any NFA firearm that is registered to another person, even if the registered owner is present.

Because smoothbore pistols are not frequently bought or sold, establishing reliable values can be difficult. The values listed here are approximate, and may vary significantly according to local supply and demand. If ATF removed these rare firearms from NFA controls, as it has for 50,000 to 100,000 or more short-barreled Winchester and Marlin "trapper carbines" and various Luger, Mauser, and other shoulder-stocked pistols and other rare firearms, their values would probably increase substantially.

V.G. *Exc.*

CALIFORNIA ARMS CO.

San Jose, California, distributed circa 1926 to 1930, but manufactured by The American Machine Company in 1926–27; 2½" shotgun or tear-gas shells only; total production was probably fewer than 300. Model A has 12½" barrels and a checkered forearm; Model B has 12¼" barrels and a smooth forearm; Model C has 12" barrels and a smooth forearm.

Defiance Anti-Bandit Gun, 20 gauge, 12¼" or 12½" double barrels,
Class III, Curio .... RARE

CRESCENT FIRE ARMS CO.

Norwich, Connecticut: Knickerbocker Pistol, circa 1900s; total production unknown, nickel-plated barrels, receiver is case-hardened, right side marked AMERICAN GUN CO./NEW YORK U S A, left side marked KNICKERBOCKER, fitted with checkered pistol grip resembling that of the Model 1 and Model 2 smoothbore H&R Handy-Gun; Victor Ejector, circa 1928–30, total production unknown, left side of receiver marked Victor Ejector/ Crescent Fire Arms Co./Norwich, Conn. U.S.A., .410 on top left of receiver near breech, blued barrel marked GENUINE ARMORY STEEL, 2½" shells only; and New Empire, circa 1932, blued barrels, left side of case-colored receiver marked Crescent Fire Arms Co./Norwich, Conn. U.S.A., right side marked New Empire, probably fewer than 50 manufactured, four known specimens bear serial numbers S–1, S–13, S–18 and S–19; referred to as "Crescent Auto & Burglar Gun" in a 1932 advertisement in *Hunter Trapper Trader.*

Knickerbocker Pistol, 20 gauge, 14" double barrels,
Class III, Curio .... RARE

Victor Ejector Pistol, .410 bore, 12" single barrel,
Class III, Curio .... RARE

V.G. *Exc.*

New Empire, .410 bore or 20 gauge, 12¼" double barrels,
Class III, Curio $700 $900

CRESCENT-DAVIS ARMS CORP.

Norwich, Connecticut, circa 1930–32; production was probably fewer than 4,000; receiver may be blued, tiger-stripe or color case-hardened, left side marked Crescent Certified Shotgun/Crescent-Davis Arms Corp./Norwich, Conn. U.S.A.

Crescent Certified Shotgun, .410 bore, 12¼" single barrel,
Class III, Curio 650 800

Add $200 to $500 for original cardboard box.

HARRINGTON & RICHARDSON ARMS CO.

Worcester, Massachusetts, 1921–34; total production about 54,000; 8" or 12¼" .410 or 28-gauge single barrel; more than 50 variations exist; values below assume choked .410 or unchoked 28-gauge with 12¼" barrel, case-hardened receiver marked H.&R. HANDY-GUN, spur grip and plain trigger guard; early models have blued receivers and/or unchoked barrels, late models have choked barrels and/or hook on trigger guard. Other values may be estimated according to scarcity in serial number table, which is a work in progress. Private-branded or trade-branded (e.g., marked ESSEX GUN WORKS or HIBBARD MODEL W. H.) variations exist; all have nickel-plated receivers and blued barrels.

Variation	*Estimated year(s) of manufacture*	*Observed serial number ranges .410 bore*	*28 gauge*
MODEL 1			
Type I	1921–22	167 to 4981	5 to 4527
Type II	1922–23	5052 to 6588	5554 to 6274
Type III	1923–24	unknown to 6817	6973 to 7067
MODEL 2			
Type I	1924–25	8276 to 14660	10539 to 29731
Type II	1925–27	15159 to 38761	none observed
Type III	1927–30	39060 to 47528	44228 to 44247
MODEL 3			
Type I	1931	47642 to 48218	unknown to 48566
Type II	1932–33	48819 to 51655	none observed
Type III	1933–34	51920 to 53691	none observed

H&R Handy-Gun, .410 bore, 12¼" choked single barrel,
Class III, Curio ....

H&R Handy-Gun, 28 gauge, 12¼" unchoked single barrel,
Class III, Curio ....

Rare variations command premiums: 8" barrel, 25% to 50%; 18" barrel, 200% to 400%; unchoked .410, 20% to 50%; 28 gauge or Model 3 (only) with factory-equipped original detachable shoulder

	V.G.	Exc.

stock, 150% or more; holster, $75–$200; serial matching box, $150–$400; early boxes are extremely rare.

ITHACA GUN CO.

Ithaca, New York, 1922–34; Model A (spur on grip), $2^1/_2$" shells only, about 2,500 manufactured, 1922–26; Model B (no spur), 2" shells, about 2,000 manufactured; variations exist; values below assume 20-gauge, 10" double barrels.

	V.G.	Exc.
Auto & Burglar Gun, Model A, *Class III, Curio*	$1,110	$1,500
Auto & Burglar Gun, Model B, *Class III, Curio*	600	900

Only 11 special order or nonstandard (.410 bore, 28 gauge, and 16 gauge, with barrels from 10" to 26" in length) Auto & Burglar Guns have been documented. All are extremely rare, and command premiums of 100% or more; professional authentication is highly recommended. Original holsters (marked AUTO AND BURGLAR GUN/MADE BY/ITHACA GUN CO./ITHACA, N.Y.) are rare and worth $300–$500.

J. STEVENS ARMS CO.

Chicopee Falls, Massachusetts, Off-Hand from 1923–29, exact total production unknown, but probably about 23,000; Auto-Shot from 1929–34, about 2,000 manufactured.

	V.G.	Exc.
Off-Hand Shot Gun No. 35, .410 bore, 8" or $12^1/_4$" single barrel, *Class III, Curio*	200	300
Auto-Shot No. 35, .410 bore, 8" or $12^1/_4$" single barrel, *Class III, Curio*	250	350

MARBLE ARMS & MFG. CO.

Gladstone, Michigan, successor in 1911 to Marble Safety Axe Co. First model from 1908–14, second model from 1921–42 (total production was about 10,000 for each model). The 18" barrel variations are exempt from the NFA only if an original shoulder stock is attached. In 1961, ATF ruled that if the shoulder stock is removed from any Game Getter, regardless of its barrel length, it becomes "a firearm made from a shotgun" requiring registration as a short-barreled shotgun with a $200 transfer tax rate.

	V.G.	Exc.
Marble's Game Getter Gun, Model 1908		
12" or 15" barrels, with shoulder stock attached, *Class III, Curio*	900	1,500
18" barrels, with shoulder stock attached, *Curio, Exempt from NFA*	$1,000	$1,800
Marble's Game Getter Gun, Model 1921		
12" or 15" barrels, with shoulder stock attached, *Class III, Curio*	650	850
18" barrels, with shoulder stock attached, *Curio, Exempt from NFA*	900	1,000

Boxed guns with accessories, nonstandard calibers (.25–20, .32–20, .38–40, etc.) command premiums of 50% to 200% or more; add $75–$150 for original shoulder holster. An extremely small number of Model 1908 Game Getters were originally manufactured as over-and-under double rifles, with rifled barrels. ATF requires these firearms to be registered as short-barreled rifles, with a $200 transfer tax rate, if the barrels are less than 16" in length and originally manufactured with a shoulder stock. If the shoulder stock is removed, ATF has ruled it to be a "firearm made from a rifle," also requiring registration and a $200 transfer tax.

	V.G.	Exc.
Marble's Game Getter Pistol, Model 1908 9" barrels, .22/.44 smooth bore, *Class III, Curio*		RARE

In approximately 1913, Marble manufactured an extremely small number of pistols with barrels ranging from 9" to 18" as experimental and special-order guns, using the Model 1908 receiver. These firearms are currently defined as "any other weapon" and must be registered; the transfer tax is $5. These firearms may be reliably identified by the lack of an inlet in the receiver to attach a shoulder stock. One known specimen bears serial number 3837.

REMINGTON ARMS CO.

Ilion, New York, c. 1867–75; 20 gauge, singleshot with rolling block action; may be used as a pistol or shotgun; usually encountered with a detachable shoulder stock and classified as a "short-barreled shotgun" by ATF ($200 transfer tax) in that configuration. Whether it qualifies for the $5 transfer tax if unaccompanied by a shoulder stock is unclear. It cannot be classified as a *Curio* because it is an *Antique* firearm manufactured before 1899; it is also a *Class III* NFA firearm because it fires fixed (cartridge) ammunition that is currently available in ordinary commerce.

	V.G.	Exc.
Remington Combination Pistol-Shotgun, 11" single barrel, *Class III*		RARE

Note: The author wishes to thank Mr. Larson for his contribution of the text in this section. For more information on smoothbore pistols, Mr. Larson may be contacted at P.O. Box 5497, Takoma Park MD 20913; telephone (301) 270-3450.

Using This Price Guide

Given the difficulty of establishing precise values, the enclosed figures provide a general indication of value. That is to say, until the object is bought or sold, the price indicated is an estimate. However, this estimate is based on the facts that the appraiser is active in the field, has professional standards to maintain, and keeps up-to-date with changes in his field. Since we list three figures, one can determine intermediates relatively easily by noting the condition range priced. However, the most exact appraisal will come when the object is actually sold.

Factors that are not detailed in the present guide are the precise impact of such variables as engraving, any particular or unusual history (like a famous owner), out-of-the-ordinary condition, and what may be the spirited response of a client who might go overboard for a particular variation or for other sometimes hard-to-understand motivations.

Another arms-collecting legend from a distinguished family of antiquarians, Norm Flayderman holds a giant shoulder-stocked English double-action revolver. Norm's specialty of arms and militaria is highlighted by his renowned Flayderman's Guide, *a run of well over 100 highly detailed sales catalogues, and a career including big-game hunting, bird shooting, and travels worldwide.*

For assistance in determining more precise figures, the author recommends consulting other price guides, particularly *Flayderman's Guide to Antique American Firearms and Their Values* and Steven Fjestad's *Blue Book of Gun Values*. And if necessary, one can also contact any of the listed dealers and auction houses for a specific appraisal, at a pre-quoted fee. An informal appraised valuation is the usual practice of auction houses, but formal ones (for insurance, estate purposes, etc.) are generally done on a fee basis.

Of course, some arms will change hands at a less-than-appraised figure: Dealers buying are not about to pay full retail. (Although some dealers pride themselves on "paying more than guns are worth." That was, in fact, the motto of Herb Glass: "Glass pays more than guns are worth!") Also, some dealers have collector clients who, in order to obtain the best, realize that as difficult as it is to get fine guns today, they had best pay a premium and hope time will catch up to that value, or they might miss some great items.

GENERAL GUIDELINES TO DETERMINING VALUE

In considering antique firearms, when in condition of excellent to new or "mint," a range of from 50 percent to 200 percent, sometimes more and sometimes less, can be added to the given figure, determined by scarcity, demand, history, maker, and possibly other factors. To estimate value for arms in good condition, approximately 25 to 35 percent could be deducted from the very good listing. For poor condition, the deduction might be 50 percent, and possibly more. Poor-condition guns are often termed "wall hangers" in the collecting field. An exception can be "dug-up" firearms, such as a Dragoon or Walker Colt, or even a Paterson, in which the item might have a surprising worth in spite of the badly rusted condition. An intriguing dug-up Belt Model Paterson Colt is a featured display item at the Woolaroc Museum, Bartlesville, Oklahoma, and was featured in the book *Paterson Colt Pistol Variations* as the only known example of a particular variation of the Belt Model series!

For modern firearms values, for good condition, deduct approximately 25 to 35 percent from the very good listing. For fair condition, deduct approximately 40 to 60 percent. For poor, the range may well be 60 to 80 percent. Firearms in perfect or factory-new condition could have a value ranging from 30 to 70 percent above excellent, and possibly more, again determined by factors of demand, scarcity, history, maker, and so forth.

Engraved Firearms

Estimating values in this area is often particularly difficult. Not a few flintlock and early percussion arms, and even some cartridge antique arms, as well as some modern, had engraving as a standard production feature. In that case, the figures presented herewith need no adjustments. But for specially engraved or otherwise non-production embellishments, consideration must be given to added values for the decorations. The following guidelines are general; expert counsel should be consulted to be more precise.

Engraving that is lacking in quality (rough or ragged scrolls, primitive and inaccurate game or other scenes, overall crudity) could add somewhere around 25 percent for moderate amounts of decoration; if about medium, approximately 40 to 80 percent; if maximum decoration, 100 to 200 percent.

When the quality is evidently fine and factory original, the price increase range may be from 50 to 200 percent, and sometimes more, for moderate amounts; add 200 to 300 percent for medium; and perhaps as much as 300 percent, or more, for maximum coverage.

For engraving added at a later date, and not of the period, the value may actually be less. As a specific example, the Henry Rifle has been decorated by 20th-century craftsmen to the extent that perhaps half of the antique Henrys have non-original decoration! No matter how fancy this 20th-century work may be, it is detrimental to the actual value of the item.

The ultimate decoration is gold inlaying, usually accompanied by rather fine and rich engraving. The presence of such desirable decor could well increase the value of a piece 400 to 500 percent, and quite likely even more. Here, particularly, the services of a specialist are in order.

Generally less desirable (sometimes by far) than gold inlaying is gold damascening, in which the gold was added by cross-hatching the metal (generally steel) and hammering the gold into position, and sometimes engraving the precious metal once attached. These patterns can range from relatively plain on up to profuse, as seen on rare examples of Colt Model 1851 Navy revolvers, usually decorated in India. The increase in value may be as little as 25 to 50 percent, and could be as much as 200 percent, and perhaps more. Condition is especially important with such arms, since they may be rather unsightly if gold is missing and the patina is poor.

Deluxe Stock Work

The collector needs to determine whether or not the stock embellishments are standard production fare, or special. As with engraving, generalizing here is difficult: consulting an expert is generally wise. Quality of craftsmanship is also a crucial determining factor.

For relief carving, such as scrollwork, leaves, wildlife motifs, and so forth, add approximately 25 percent for minimal amounts, 25 to 50 percent for moderate, and 50 to 200 percent for profuse carvings.

For inlaying, most desirable is silver and gold wire, or plaques, sometimes with wildlife or other motifs. These too are hard to determine, but as a general rule may add 35 percent for minimal inlays, 35 to 60 percent for moderate, and 60 percent on up for profuse or particularly distinguished motifs.

As with other special decorations, checkering can add to value. Crude work can be detrimental, although one should be aware of the difference between "crude" and "folk art," as in the case of Kentucky Rifles. As a general rule, checkering (unless a standard feature) can add 10 percent on up to about 30 percent.

Ivory or mother-of-pearl grips may add 15 percent to 50 percent in value, and if carved, the amount might increase by as much as 100 percent, perhaps even more. However, quality again will be crucially important. In some cases exotic wood, such as ebony, will spiral value upward. Again, consult an expert!

Specially Marked Firearms

Consideration needs to be given to firearms with unusual markings, such as Wells Fargo & Co. or other express, mining, or other special inscriptions, police or law enforcement legends, a variety of historical inscriptions, presentation dedications, and so forth. As with engraved arms, it is impossible to generalize accurately, and sometimes the marking accounts for most of the value. As with engraving, consult a professional for specifics. In these cases condition will not be that much greater a factor in value, and often pieces are only good to very good—after all, the wear and tear shows the piece actually was used.

Express agency markings add 25 to 50 percent, perhaps more.

Police and other law enforcement markings add 25 to 50 percent, again, perhaps more.

Military markings add 25 to 75 percent; some countries, like Great Britain or Germany, will be more desirable than others.

Inscriptions or other markings of organizations or firms with romantic and adventurous associations, particularly British colonial sites, like India or Africa, could add 25 to 75 percent, and sometimes more.

Presentation inscriptions are a special category, and will often depend on the historical significance reflected in the inscription. The range here can be substantial, from an added 25 percent on up. Condition, again, may not be a critical factor, since use by the original owner can be part of the value.

Factory Mistakes in Markings

While by no means commanding astronomical prices, factory errors are intriguing to many collectors. These are not, however, comparable to upside-down airplanes on postage stamps! The increase in value may well be from 25 percent up to 100 percent, and perhaps more in very rare instances.

Special Features

When factories have modified production arms in special ways, there may be a premium for these features. The most obvious example is the Colt Buntline Special, in which the original models numbered not more than about thirty! These prizes are particularly in demand, especially since some specimens had barrels cut down (claimed for the piece traditionally ascribed as given to Bat Masterson) or were reportedly lost (the gun some say belonged to Wyatt Earp was supposedly lost by him in Alaska, dropped overboard from a river vessel).

Special barrel lengths might add from 20 to 40 percent, and possibly more. Special sights add 10 to 20 percent; special finishes, 10 to 30 percent (particularly attractive, gold or silver plating, but also extreme rarities like copper plating). Select woods, such as in Winchester, Marlin, Remington, Sharps, and Colt longarms, add from 15 to 35 percent.

A

A & R SALES

South El Monte, Calif. Current.

	Fair	V. Good	Excellent
HANDGUN, SEMI-AUTOMATIC			
Government, .45 ACP, Lightweight, Patterned After Colt Govt. Model, *Modern*	$125	$175	$300
RIFLE, SEMI-AUTOMATIC			
Mark IV Sporter, .308 Win., Clip Fed, Version of M-14, Adjustable Sights, *Modern*	155	225	350

ABBEY, GEORGE T.

Chicago, Ill. 1858-1875.

	Fair	V. Good	Excellent
RIFLE, PERCUSSION			
.44, Double Barrel, Over-Under, Brass Furniture, *Antique*	350	700	1350
.44, Octagon Barrel, Brass Furniture, *Antique*	225	400	750

ABBEY, J.F. & CO.

Chicago, Ill. 1858–1875. Also made by Abbey & Foster.

	Fair	V. Good	Excellent
RIFLE, PERCUSSION			
Various Calibers, *Antique*	150	300	600
SHOTGUN, PERCUSSION			
Various Gauges, *Antique*	200	350	600

ABILENNE

See Mossberg.

ACHA

Domingo Acha y Cia., Ermua, Spain 1927-1937.

	Fair	V. Good	Excellent
HANDGUN, SEMI-AUTOMATIC			
Ruby M1916, 7.65mm, Clip Fed, *Curio*	100	150	200

ACME

Made by Hopkins & Allen, Sold by Merwin & Hulbert, c. 1880.

	Fair	V. Good	Excellent
HANDGUN, REVOLVER			
.22 Short R.F., 7 Shot, Spur Trigger, Solid Frame, Single Action, *Antique*	$50	$95	$150
.32 Short R.F., 5 Shot, Spur Trigger, Solid Frame, Single Action, *Antique*	50	95	165

ACME ARMS

Sold by J. Stevens Arms Co. and Cornwall Hardware Co., c. 1880.

	Fair	V. Good	Excellent
HANDGUN, REVOLVER			
.22 Short R.F., 7 Shot, Spur Trigger, Solid Frame, Single Action, *Antique*	150	200	300
.32 Short R.F., 5 Shot, Spur Trigger, Solid Frame, Single Action, *Antique*	175	225	300
SHOTGUN, DOUBLE BARREL, SIDE-BY-SIDE			
12 Gauge, Damascus Barrel, *Antique*	125	175	300

ACME HAMMERLESS

Made by Hopkins & Allen for Hulbert Bros. 1893.

	Fair	V. Good	Excellent
HANDGUN, REVOLVER			
.32 S & W, 5 Shot, Top Break, Hammerless, Double Action, 2½" barrel, *Antique*	50	100	150
.38 S & W, 5 Shot, Top Break, Hammerless, Double Action, 3" Barrel, *Antique*	50	100	150

ACRA

Tradename used by Reinhard Fajen of Warsaw, Mo., c. 1970.

	Fair	V. Good	Excellent
RIFLE, BOLT ACTION			
M18, Various Calibers, Santa Barbara Barreled Action, Mannlicher Checkered Stock, *Modern*	75	175	275
RA, Various Calibers, Santa Barbara Barreled Action, Checkered Stock, *Modern*	65	125	250
S24, Various Calibers, Santa Barbara Barreled Action, Fancy Checkering, *Modern*	75	150	250

ACTION

Modesto Santos; Eibar, Spain.

HANDGUN, SEMI-AUTOMATIC

	Fair	V. Good	Excellent
#2, 7.65mm, Clip Fed, *Curio*	$50	$125	$225
Model 1920, .25 ACP, Clip Fed, *Curio*	35	75	150

ADAMS

Made by Deane, Adams, & Deane, London, England. British revolvers, particularly the percussion, but also early cartridge, are part of the warp and woof of the British Empire–on which "the sun never set." One of the most colorful periods in world history, the exquisite quality and beauty of these fine British arms symbolize the Empire, in a different way than fine British double rifles (especially those made for big game shooting in Africa and India), or best quality British shotguns (usually termed "game guns"). British (particularly English) gunmakers produced arms of such quality and distinction that even today, they are often considered the standard by which fine arms are measured. Many of these arms bore hand engraving as a customary feature of their craftsmanship. British percussion and early cartridge revolvers remain an area of collecting in which a lot of quality, history, mechanics and romance can be purchased, for a reasonable cost. Watch for these guns to move upward in price, at an increasing rate. Even Lt. Col. George Armstrong Custer had a keen affection for British revolvers, and had two bulldog types in his hands as he fell at the Little Big Horn. Some Confederate troops, particularly the cavalry, and several officers, also respected and used British revolvers.

HANDGUN, PERCUSSION

	Fair	V. Good	Excellent
12.4mm Beaumont-Adams, Revolver, Double Action, 7½" Barrel, *Antique*	500	1200	2000
12.4mm Beaumont-Adams, Revolver, Double Action, 7½" Barrel, *Antique*	500	1200	2000
12.4mm M1851, Revolver, Double Action, 7½" Barrel, *Antique*	400	800	1200
12.4mm M1851, Revolver, Double Action, 7½" Barrel, Cased with Accessories, *Antique*	500	1700	2600
8.1mm Pocket, Revolver, Double Action, 4½" Barrel, *Antique*	500	1000	2000
8.1mm, Revolver, Double Action, 4½" Barrel, Cased with Accessories, *Antique*	500	1500	2500

ADAMS, JOSEPH

Birmingham, England 1767–1813.

RIFLE, FLINTLOCK

	Fair	V. Good	Excellent
.65 Officers Model Brown Bess, Musket, Military, *Antique*	500	1750	2750

ADAMY GEBRUDER

Suhl, Germany 1921–1939.

SHOTGUN, DOUBLE BARREL, OVER-UNDER

	Fair	V. Good	Excellent
12 and 16 Ga., Automatic Ejector, Double Trigger, Engraved, Cased, *Curio*	$500	$1000	$1500

ADIRONDACK ARMS CO.

Plattsburg, N.Y. 1870–1874. Purchased by Winchester 1874.

RIFLE, LEVER ACTION

	Fair	V. Good	Excellent
Robinson 1875 Patent, First Model, Various Rimfires, Octagon Barrel, Open Rear Sight, *Antique*	850	1500	2500
Robinson Patent, Second Model, Various Calibers, Octagon Barrel, *Antique*	850	1500	2500

ADLER

Engelbrecht & Wolff; Zella St. Blasii, Germany 1905–1906.

HANDGUN, SEMI-AUTOMATIC

	Fair	V. Good	Excellent
7.25 Adler, Clip Fed, *Curio*	900	2250	3500

AERTS, JAN

Maastricht, Holland, c. 1650.

HANDGUN, FLINTLOCK

	Fair	V. Good	Excellent
Ornate Pair, Very Long Ebony Full Stock, Silver Inlay, High Quality, *Antique*			Rare

AETNA

Made by Harrington & Richardson, c. 1870–1890.

HANDGUN, REVOLVER

	Fair	V. Good	Excellent
.22 Short R.F., 7 Shot, Spur Trigger, Solid Frame, Single Action, *Antique*	100	200	300
Aetna 2½, .32 Short R.F., 5 Shot, Spur Trigger, Solid Frame, Single Action, *Antique*	125	225	300
Aetna 2, .32 Short R.F., 5 Shot, Spur Trigger, Solid Frame, Single Action, *Antique*	125	225	300

AETNA ARMS CO.

New York City, c. 1880.

HANDGUN, REVOLVER

	Fair	V. Good	Excellent
.22 Short R.F., 7 Shot, Spur Trigger, Tip-Up Barrel, *Antique*	100	225	350
.32 Short R.F., 5 Shot, Spur Trigger, Tip-Up Barrel, *Antique*	125	250	375

	Fair	V. Good	Excellent

AFFERBACH, WILLIAM
Philadelphia, Pa. 1860-1866.

HANDGUN, PERCUSSION

	Fair	V. Good	Excellent
.41 Derringer, Full Stock, *Antique*	$250	$650	$1250

AGAWAM ARMS
Agawam, Mass., c. 1970.

RIFLE, SINGLESHOT

	Fair	V. Good	Excellent
Model M-68, .22 L.R.R.F., Lever Action, Open Sights, *Modern*	20	35	65
Model M-68M, .22 W.M.R., Lever Action, Open Sights, *Modern*	25	45	75

AJAX ARMY
Maker Unknown, Sold by E. C. Meacham Co., c. 1880.

HANDGUN, REVOLVER

	Fair	V. Good	Excellent
.44 R.F., 5 Shot, 7" Barrel, Spur Trigger, Solid Frame, Single Action, *Antique*	150	350	600

AKRILL, E.
Probably St. Etienne, France, c. 1810.

RIFLE, FLINTLOCK

	Fair	V. Good	Excellent
.69, Smoothbore, Octagon Barrel, Damascus Barrel, Breech Loader, Plain, *Antique*	400	1000	2500

ALAMO
Tradename used by Stoeger Arms, c. 1958.

HANDGUN, REVOLVER

	Fair	V. Good	Excellent
Alamo, .22 L.R.R.F., Double Action, Ribbed Barrel, *Modern*	25	50	125

ALASKA
Made by Hood Firearms, Sold by E. C. Meacham Co. 1873-1882.

HANDGUN, REVOLVER

	Fair	V. Good	Excellent
.22 Short R.F., 7 Shot, Spur Trigger, Solid Frame, Single Action, *Antique*	50	125	175

ALASKAN
Skinner's Sportsman's Supply, Juneau, Alaska, c. 1970.

RIFLE, BOLT ACTION

	Fair	V. Good	Excellent
Carbine, Various Calibers, Checkered Stock, Sling Swivels, *Modern*	100	225	300
Magnum, Various Calibers, Checkered Stock, Recoil Pad, Sling Swivels, *Modern*	100	225	300
Standard, Various Calibers, Checkered Stock, Sling Swivels, *Modern*	$100	$195	$295

ALBRECHT, ANDREW
Lancaster, Pa. 1779-1782. See Kentucky Rifles and Pistols.

ALBRIGHT, HENRY
Lancaster, Pa. 1740-1745. See Kentucky Rifles and Pistols.

ALDENDERFER, M.
Lancaster, Pa. 1763-1784. See Kentucky Rifles and Pistols.

ALERT
Made by Hood Firearms Co., c. 1874.

HANDGUN, REVOLVER

	Fair	V. Good	Excellent
.22 Short R.F., 7 Shot, Spur Trigger, Solid Frame, Single Action, *Antique*	75	150	200

ALEXIA
Made by Hopkins & Allen, c. 1880.

HANDGUN, REVOLVER

	Fair	V. Good	Excellent
.22 Short R.F., 7 Shot, Spur Trigger, Solid Frame, Single Action, *Antique*	75	125	175
.32 Short R.F., 5 Shot, Spur Trigger, Solid Frame, Single Action, *Antique*	75	125	175
.38 Short R.F., 5 Shot, Spur Trigger, Solid Frame, Single Action, *Antique*	75	125	175
.41 Short R.F., 5 Shot, Spur Trigger, Solid Frame, Single Action, *Antique*	75	125	225

ALEXIS
Made by Hood Firearms Co., Sold by Turner & Ross Co. Boston, Mass.

HANDGUN, REVOLVER

	Fair	V. Good	Excellent
.22 Short R.F., 7 Shot, Spur Trigger, Solid Frame, Single Action, *Antique*	65	100	175

ALFA
Adolf Frank, Hamburg, Germany, c. 1900.

HANDGUN, MANUAL REPEATER

	Fair	V. Good	Excellent
"Reform" Type, .230 C.F., Four-barreled Repeater, Engraved, *Curio*	75	150	250

HANDGUN, SEMI-AUTOMATIC

	Fair	V. Good	Excellent
Pocket, 6.35mm, Clip Fed, Blue, *Curio*	50	100	150

RIFLE, PERCUSSION

	Fair	V. Good	Excellent
Back-lock, Various Calibers, Carved, Inlaid Stock, Imitation Damascus Barrel, *Antique*	$50	$95	$150
Back-lock, Various Calibers, Imitation Damascus Barrel, *Antique*	40	75	100

SHOTGUN, PERCUSSION

	Fair	V. Good	Excellent
Double Barrel, Various Gauges, Back-lock, Double Triggers, Damascus Barrels, *Antique*	40	75	125
Double Barrel, Various Gauges, Back-lock, Double Triggers, Damascus Barrels, Carved Stock, Engraved, *Antique*	65	125	175

SHOTGUN, DOUBLE BARREL, SIDE-BY-SIDE

	Fair	V. Good	Excellent
Greener Boxlock, Various Gauges, Checkered Stock, Double Triggers, *Curio*	75	125	200
Greener Boxlock, Various Gauges, Checkered Stock, Double Triggers, Engraved, *Curio*	85	175	265

SHOTGUN, SINGLESHOT

	Fair	V. Good	Excellent
Nuss Underlever, Various Gauges, Tip-Down Barrel, No Forestock, *Curio*	25	50	75
Roux Underlever, Various Gauges, Tip-Down Barrel, No Forestock, *Curio*	25	50	75
Sidebutton, Various Gauges, Tip-Down Barrel, No Forestock, *Curio*	25	50	75

ALFA

Armero Especialistas Reunidas, Eibar, Spain, c. 1920.

HANDGUN, REVOLVER

	Fair	V. Good	Excellent
Colt Police Positive Type, .38, Double Action, Blue, *Curio*	50	100	150
S. & W. #2 Type, *Curio*	65	125	175
S. & W. M & P Type, .38, Double Action, 6 Shot, Blue, *Curio*	50	100	150

ALKARTASUNA

Spain. Made by Alkartasuna Fabrica De Armas 1910–1922.

HANDGUN, SEMI-AUTOMATIC

	Fair	V. Good	Excellent
Alkar 1924, 6.35mm, Cartridge Counter, Grips, Clip Fed, *Curio*	100	225	350
Pocket, 7.65mm, Clip Fed, Long Grip, *Curio*	65	125	200
Pocket, 7.65mm, Clip Fed, Short Grip, *Curio*	65	125	200
Vest Pocket, 6.35mm, Clip Fed, *Modern*	50	95	175
Vest Pocket, 6.35mm, Clip Fed, Cartridge Counter, *Modern*	50	125	200

ALL RIGHT FIREARMS CO.

Lawrence, Mass., c. 1876.

HANDGUN, REVOLVER

	Fair	V. Good	Excellent
Little All Right Palm Pistol, .22 Short R.F., Squeeze Trigger, 5 Shot, *Antique*	$300	$500	$850

ALLEGHENY WORKS

Allegheny, Pa. 1836–1875. See Kentucky Rifles and Pistols.

ALLEN

Made by Hopkins & Allen, c. 1880.

HANDGUN, REVOLVER

	Fair	V. Good	Excellent
22 Short R.F., 7 Shot, Spur Trigger, Solid Frame, Single Action, *Antique*	35	75	165

ALLEN

Tradename used by McKeown's Guns of Pekin, Ill., c. 1970.

SHOTGUN, DOUBLE BARREL, OVER-UNDER

	Fair	V. Good	Excellent
MCK 68, 12 Ga., Vent Rib, Double Triggers, Plain, *Modern*	75	175	275
Olympic 68, 12 Ga., Vent Rib, Single Selective Trigger, Automatic Ejectors, Checkered Stock, Engraved, *Modern*	100	250	425
S201 Deluxe, Various Gauges, Vent Rib, Single Trigger, Automatic Ejectors, Checkered Stock, Engraved, *Modern*	125	300	450
S201, Various Gauges, Vent Rib, Double Triggers, Checkered Stock, Light Engraving, *Modern*	100	225	375

ALLEN & THURBER

Grafton, Mass. 1837–1842, Norwich, Conn. 1842–1847. One of the most distinguished names in 19th-century American gunmaking, the products of Ethan Allen, and the several other firms with the Allen connection, continue slowly but surely to develop a dedicated following, but have yet to reach their deserved potential as collectors' items. At least for awhile, Ethan Allen rivaled Samuel Colt as a prominent gunmaker, creating a variety of guns, of solid design and quality, with production based on the American system of manufacture. Allen's history is complex, and the number of companies that included his name is profuse: E. Allen (Grafton, 1831–37) Allen & Thurber (Grafton, 1837–42; Norwich, 1842–47; Worcester, Massachusetts, 1847–54) Allen Thurber & Co. (Worcester, 1854–56) Allen & Wheelock (Worcester, 1856–65) E. Allen & Company (Worcester, 1865–71). First of Allen's firearms was a cane gun (1836); next was an underhammer pocket rifle; followed by a tube hammer pocket pistol; next was the pepperbox, the product that, more than any other, made his reputation. In time brother-in-law Charles Thurber joined as the company expanded to meet increasing demands for pepperboxes and single-shot pistols, sporting and target rifles and shotguns, and even whaling guns. In 1871 Allen died, and the company carried on as Forehand & Wadsworth. The intriguing generic name, and the multi-shot nature, with a rather forbidding six charges pointed at one's adversary, meant that the pepperbox was destined to become symbolic of adventure in the Old West. The field of pepperbox arms is worthy of a solid historical treatment, and at present only rather introductory texts exist. Allen pepperboxes were the first American double-action revolving production firearms; their mechanisms were covered by two patents. First of these was that of November 11, 1837, covering the double-action system of cocking and firing by squeezing the trigger. The second patent was issued April 16, 1845, covering a design in which the revolver was cocked and fired by the trigger manually. The latter patent also simplified the mechanism of the 1837 patent. Determining the difference between an Allen pepperbox made with the 1837 patent features, or those of 1845, is the way to identify these guns: the former was built with a straight-style mainspring of one piece, within a clip at the grip frame's base. To adjust the spring's tension a screw was located on the lower front of the gripstrap. Post-1845 era guns feature a U-shaped mainspring, in which the adjustment screw appears in the center of the gripstrap at the front. The Allen and companies pepperbox line breaks down into categories based initially on the site of manufacture: Grafton, Norwich, Worcester. Further subdivision is based on size: pocket (Grafton only), medium or standard, and the rather hefty dragoon. Further classification is based on features determined by the firm's master patents, whether in 1837 (Grafton and Norwich) or 1845 (Norwich and Worcester). The pocket pepperbox calibers were .28, the medium or standard were .31, and the dragoon was .36. Since pepperboxes were manufactured in batch groupings, serial numbers were not sequential; numbers are therefore low, and of a few digits only. Still another classification by collectors is based on grip profiles: the quick drop (sharp, near right angle to frame; on Grafton and Norwich pistols of early date), slow drop (sharp angle to frame, slightly more curved than quick drop), dog leg grip, semi-dog leg grip (long shape; accompanied by German silver grip escutcheons), and late-rounded grip (majority of Worcester pistols). A standard feature was the open, relatively primitive scroll style on frames, accompanied customarily with etched scrollwork on the nipple shields (pioneer example of acid-etched embellishments on American firearms). Inscribed or cased dragoon pepperboxes are quite rare, and will command a premium. Many of the arms of Ethan Allen and the Allen companies—in addition to pepperboxes—still have a way to go to reach their deserved potential on the marketplace.

HANDGUN, PERCUSSION

	Fair	V. Good	Excellent
.28 (Grafton) Pepperbox, 6 Shot, 3" Barrel, *Antique*	$900	$1750	$2000
.28 (Norwich) Pepperbox, 6 Shot, Bar Hammer, 3" Barrel, *Antique*	300	600	675
.28 (Norwich) Pepperbox, 6 Shot, Hammerless, 3" Barrel, *Antique*	500	1250	1500
.28, Singleshot, Bar Hammer, Various Barrel Lengths, Half-Octagon Barrel, *Antique*	300	600	650
.31 (Grafton) Pepperbox, 6 Shot, 3" Barrel, *Antique*	500	1000	1250
.31 (Norwich) Pepperbox, 6 Shot, Bar Hammer, 3" Barrel, *Antique*	150	295	650
.31 (Norwich) Pepperbox, 6 Shot, Hammerless, 3" Barrel, *Antique*	300	600	675
.31, "In-Line" Singleshot, Center Hammer, Various Barrel Lengths, Half-Octagon Barrel, *Antique*	$250	$450	$400
.31, Singleshot, Tube Hammer, Various Barrel Lengths, Half-Octagon Barrel, *Antique*	500	1000	1250
.31, Singleshot, Under Hammer, Various Barrel Lengths, Half-Octagon Barrel, *Antique*	400	750	850
.31, Singleshot, Under Hammer, Various Barrel Lengths, Saw-Handle Grip, Half-Octagon Barrel, *Antique*	400	800	900
.34, Singleshot, Side Hammer, Various Barrel Lengths, Half-Octagon Barrel, *Antique*	300	600	700
.36 (Grafton) Pepperbox, 6" Barrel, *Antique*	1000	1250	1500
.36 (Norwich) Pepperbox, 6 Shot, Bar Hammer, 6" Barrel, *Antique*	700	850	1000
.36 (Norwich) Pepperbox, 6 Shot, Ring Trigger, 6" Barrel, *Antique*	1000	1250	1500
.36, Singleshot, Bar Hammer, Various Barrel Lengths, Half-Octagon Barrel, *Antique*	550	600	650
.36, Singleshot, Center Hammer, Various Barrel Lengths, Half-Octagon Barrel, *Antique*	75	150	300
.41, Singleshot, Side Hammer, Various Barrel Lengths, Half-Octagon Barrel, *Antique*	550	625	700

ALLEN & THURBER

Worcester, Mass. 1855–1856.

COMBINATION WEAPON, PERCUSSION

	Fair	V. Good	Excellent
Over-Under, Various Calibers, Rifle and Shotgun Barrels, *Antique*	1500	1750	2000

HANDGUN, PERCUSSION

	Fair	V. Good	Excellent
.28, Pepperbox, Bar Hammer, Various Barrel Lengths, 5 Shot, *Antique*	400	450	500
.31, Pepperbox, Bar Hammer, 5 Shot, Various Barrel Lengths, *Antique*	350	400	450
.31, Pepperbox, Ring Hammerless, 6 Shot, *Antique*	750	1000	1250
.31, Pepperbox, Thumb Hammer, 5 Shot, Various Barrel Lengths, *Antique*	750	850	950
.34, Pepperbox, Bar Hammer, Various Barrel Lengths, 4 Shot, *Antique*	125	250	550
.36, Target Pistol, 12" Octagon Barrel, Adjustable Sights, Detachable Shoulder Stock, *Antique*	2000	2500	3000

RIFLE, PERCUSSION

	Fair	V. Good	Excellent
.43, Singleshot, Sporting Rifle, *Antique*	$237	$475	$725

ALLEN & WHEELOCK

Worcester, Mass. 1856–1865. Mechanically the Allen & Wheelock revolvers are fascinating since the intriguing design called for the cylinders to move back, and then move forward, in order to overlap the barrel breech with the front end of the cylinder. This allowed for a seal that prevented the easily observable (and somewhat intimidating) flash of fire escaping between cylinder and barrel on firing. In the process, the Allen & Wheelock revolvers were also more energy efficient, since the majority of the force of propulsion went out of the front of the barrel, behind the projectile. The seal of the charge on the Allen & Wheelock revolvers also helped significantly to avoid chain fires, in which the flame from a firing chamber would reflect back into adjacent chambers, and set off neighboring charges inadvertently. Having experienced chain firing, the frightening consequences, much less the loss of precious fired charges, was something to seriously consider. Still another revolving arm that had the feature of the cylinder overlapping a projection from the barrel breech was the Collier flintlock and percussion revolver.

HANDGUN, PERCUSSION

	Fair	V. Good	Excellent
.25, Pepperbox, 4" Barrel, 5 Shot, *Antique*	300	475	550
.28, Revolver, Side Hammer, Octagon Barrel, 3" Barrel, 5 Shot, *Antique*	300	500	600
.31, Revolver, Bar Hammer, Octagon Barrel, 2¼" Barrel, 5 Shot, *Antique*	125	300	400
.31, Revolver, Side Hammer, Octagon Barrel, 3" Barrel, 5 Shot, *Antique*	125	300	400
.34, Revolver, Bar Hammer, Octagon Barrel, 4" Barrel, 5 Shot, *Antique*	125	300	400
.34, Revolver, Bar Hammer, Octagon Barrel, 4" Barrel, 5 Shot, *Antique*	125	225	400
.36, Pepperbox, 6" Barrel, 6 Shot, *Antique*	750	1000	1250
.36, Revolver, Center Hammer, Octagon Barrel, 5" Barrel, 6 Shot, Spur Trigger, *Antique*	225	450	1450
.36, Revolver, Center Hammer, Octagon Barrel, 7½" Barrel, 6 Shot, *Antique*	300	600	1200
.36, Revolver, Side Hammer, Octagon Barrel, 6" Barrel, 6 Shot, *Antique*	300	600	1750
.44, Revolver, Center Hammer, Half-Octagon Barrel, 7½" Barrel, 6 Shot, *Antique*	350	700	2000

HANDGUN, REVOLVER

	Fair	V. Good	Excellent
.22 Short R.F., 7 Shot, Side Hammer, Solid Frame, *Antique*	65	125	275
.25 L.F., 7 Shot, Side Hammer, Solid Frame, *Antique*	450	500	550
.32 L.F., 6 Shot Side Hammer, Solid Frame, *Antique*	600	675	750
.32 Short R.F., 6 Shot, Side Hammer, Solid Frame, *Antique*	$250	$300	$350
.36 L.F., 6 Shot, Side Hammer, Solid Frame, *Antique*	750	1000	1250
.38 Short R.F., 6 Shot, Side Hammer, Solid Frame, *Antique*	1000	1250	1500
.44 L.F., 6 Shot, Side Hammer, Solid Frame, *Antique*	1250	1500	1750
.44 Short R.F., 6 Shot, Side Hammer, Solid Frame, *Antique*	1500	2000	2500

HANDGUN, SINGLESHOT

	Fair	V. Good	Excellent
.22 Short R.F., Derringer, Spur Trigger, *Antique*	300	325	350
.22 Short R.F., Large Frame, Spur Trigger, *Antique*	75	150	250
.32 Short R.F., Derringer, Spur Trigger, *Antique*	250	300	350
.32 Short R.F., Large Frame, Spur Trigger, *Antique*	250	275	300
.41 Short R.F., Derringer, Spur Trigger, *Antique*	700	850	1000

RIFLE, PERCUSSION

	Fair	V. Good	Excellent
.36 Allen Patent, Carbine, Drop Breech Loader, *Antique*	650	750	850
.36 Allen Patent, Drop Breech Loader, Sporting Rifle, *Antique*	550	650	750
.38 Sidehammer, Plains Rifle, Iron Mounted, Walnut Stock, *Antique*	800	1250	1500
.44 Center Hammer, Octagon Barrel, Iron Frame, *Antique*	600	750	850
.44 Revolver, Carbine, 6 Shot, *Antique*	7500	10000	12500

RIFLE, REVOLVING

	Fair	V. Good	Excellent
.44 L.F., Walnut Stock, 6 Shot, *Antique*	7000	8500	10000

RIFLE, SINGLESHOT

	Fair	V. Good	Excellent
.22 R.F., Falling Block, Sporting Rifle, *Antique*	150	300	500
.38 R.F., Falling Block, Sporting Rifle, *Antique*	170	285	400
.62 Allen R.F., Falling Block, Sporting Rifle, *Antique*	135	275	450
.64 Allen R.F., Falling Block, Sporting Rifle, *Antique*	135	275	450

SHOTGUN, PERCUSSION

	Fair	V. Good	Excellent
12 Ga. Double, Hammers, Light Engraving, *Antique*	450	525	600

SHOTGUN, DOUBLE BARREL, SIDE-BY-SIDE

	Fair	V. Good	Excellent
12 Ga., Checkered Stock, Hammers, Double Triggers, *Antique*	450	525	600

	Fair	V. Good	Excellent

ALLEN, C. B.

Springfield, Mass. 1836–1841. See U.S. Military, Elgin. The turret-style percussion guns were at first thought to pose a truly competitive threat to the revolvers of Samuel Colt. However, Colt himself ridiculed these guns, and said that the firer thereof was under as much or more risk as the intended target. In Colt's own collection he had examples of turret-style firearms. The size of the turret itself was detrimental to the future of these guns. But most of all, the thought of having chambers of the turret aimed in the shooter's direction was intimidating, and truly dangerous. These arms played an intriguing role in the evolution of firepower, and were a challenging configuration mechanically to manufacture.

HANDGUN, PERCUSSION

	Fair	V. Good	Excellent
.36 Cochran Turret, 7 Shot, 4 3/4" Barrel, *Antique*	$5000	$7500	$10000
.40 Cochran Turret, 7 Shot, 5" Barrel, *Antique*	8000	10000	12000

RIFLE, PERCUSSION

	Fair	V. Good	Excellent
.40 Cochran Turret, 7 Shot, Octagon Barrel, *Antique*	3000	5500	8000
.40 Cochran Turret, 9 Shot, Octagon Barrel, *Antique*	3600	5800	8000

ALLEN, ETHAN

Grafton, Mass. 1835–1837, E. Allen & Co. Worcester, Mass. 1865–1871. Became Forehand & Wadsworth.

HANDGUN, PERCUSSION

	Fair	V. Good	Excellent
.31, Pepperbox, 6 Shot, 3" Barrel, *Antique*	550	650	750
.36, Pepperbox, 6 Shot, 5" Barrel, *Antique*	750	1000	1250
First Model Pocket "Rifle" Various Calibers, Various Barrel Lengths, Under Hammer, Singleshot, Saw Handle Grip, *Antique*	550	650	750
Second Model Pocket "Rifle" .31, Singleshot, Under Hammer, Half-Octagon Barrel, *Antique*	650	750	850

HANDGUN, REVOLVER

	Fair	V. Good	Excellent
.22 Short R.F., 7 Shot, Side Hammer, Sheath Trigger, *Antique*	225	300	375
.32 Short R.F., 6 Shot, Side Hammer, Sheath Trigger, *Antique*	225	275	325

HANDGUN, SINGLESHOT

	Fair	V. Good	Excellent
Derringer, .32 Short R.F., Side-Swing Barrel, Half-Octagon Barrel, *Antique*	250	300	350
Derringer, .32 Short R.F., Side-Swing Barrel, Octagon Barrel, *Antique*	200	250	300
Derringer, .41 Short R.F., Side-Swing Barrel, Round Barrel, *Antique*	700	800	900
Derringer, .41 Short R.F., Side-Swing Barrel, Half-Octagon Barrel, *Antique*	650	750	850
Derringer, .41 Short R.F., Side-Swing Barrel, Octagon Barrel, *Antique*	750	850	950

RIFLE, SINGLESHOT

	Fair	V. Good	Excellent
Sidehammer Muzzleloader, .38 Caliber, Sporting Rifle, *Antique*	$750	$1000	$1250

ALLEN, SILAS

Shrewsbury, Mass. 1796–1843. See Kentucky Rifles and Pistols.

ALLIES

Berasaluze Areitio-Arutena y Cia., Eibar, Spain, c. 1920.

HANDGUN, SEMI-AUTOMATIC

	Fair	V. Good	Excellent
Model 1924, .25 ACP, Clip Fed, *Curio*	35	75	175
Pocket, .32 ACP, Clip Fed, *Curio*	35	75	175
Vest Pocket, .25 ACP, Clip Fed, *Curio*	35	75	150
Vest Pocket, .32 ACP, Clip Fed, Short Grip, *Curio*	35	75	150

ALPINE INDUSTRIES

Los Angeles, Calif. 1962–1965.

RIFLE, SEMI-AUTOMATIC

	Fair	V. Good	Excellent
M-1 Carbine, .30 Carbine, Clip Fed, Military Style, *Modern*	75	150	250

ALSOP, C.R.

Middleton, Conn. 1858–1866 The author had the pleasure of acquiring an Alsop .36 caliber pocket revolver, with ivory grips, which had belonged to C.R. Alsop himself. The item, acquired from a member of the Alsop family, had only traveled about thirty miles from its original place of manufacture in over 140 years. Alsop was attempting to capitalize on the expiration of Samuel Colt's master patent on the revolver, as were Manhattan, Remington, and a number of other makers. Alsop's attempt at competing with Colt received some encouragement due to the Civil War, but in the shakeout in the arms business following the war, it was impossible for his firm to survive. These arms should increase in value as more collectors become enamored of the Civil War era, and find that the escalating prices in Colts force them to other makes, not as blue chip, but nevertheless attractive, including for their design, quality and relative scarcity.

HANDGUN, PERCUSSION

	Fair	V. Good	Excellent
.36 Navy, 5 Shot, Octagon Barrel, Spur Trigger, Top Hammer, Safety, *Antique*	750	1500	2500
.36 Navy, 5 Shot, Octagon Barrel, Spur Trigger, Top Hammer, No Safety, *Antique*	1000	1500	2000
.36 Pocket, 5 Shot, Octagon Barrel, Spur Trigger, *Antique*	285	575	900

	Fair	V. Good	Excellent

AMERICA
Made by Bliss & Goodyear, c. 1878.

HANDGUN, REVOLVER

	Fair	V. Good	Excellent
.22 Short R.F., 7 Shot, Spur Trigger, Solid Frame, Single Action, *Antique*	$65	$125	$250

AMERICA
Made by Norwich Falls Pistol Co., c. 1880.

HANDGUN, REVOLVER

	Fair	V. Good	Excellent
.32 Long R.F., Double Action, Solid Frame, *Antique*	35	75	125

AMERICAN ARMS & AMMUNITION CO.
Miami, Florida, c. 1979. Successors to North Armament Corp. (Norarmco).

HANDGUN, SEMI-AUTOMATIC

	Fair	V. Good	Excellent
TP-70, .22 L.R.R.F., Double Action, Stainless, Clip Fed, *Modern*	85	175	275
TP-70, .25 ACP, Double Action, Stainless, Clip Fed, *Modern*	75	150	250

AMERICAN ARMS CO.
Boston, Mass. 1861–1897, Milwaukee, Wisc. 1897–1901. Purchased by Marlin 1901.

HANDGUN, DOUBLE BARREL, OVER-UNDER

	Fair	V. Good	Excellent
Wheeler Pat, .22 Short R.F., 32 Short R.F., Brass Frame, Spur Trigger, *Antique*	350	425	500
Wheeler Pat, .32 Short R.F., Brass Frame, Spur Trigger, *Antique*	400	450	500
Wheeler Pat, .41 Short R.F., Brass Frame, Spur Trigger, *Antique*	550	600	650

HANDGUN, REVOLVER

	Fair	V. Good	Excellent
.32 S & W, 5 Shot, Double Action, Top Break, *Antique*	75	125	175
.32 S & W, 5 Shot, Double Action, Top Break, Hammerless, *Antique* ..	125	175	225
.32 S & W, 5 Shot, Single Action, Top Break, Spur Trigger, *Antique* .	100	150	200

SHOTGUN, DOUBLE BARREL, SIDE-BY-SIDE

	Fair	V. Good	Excellent
12 Ga., Semi-Hammerless, Checkered Stock, *Antique*	500	550	600
Whitmore Patent, 10 Ga., 27/8", Hammerless, Checkered Stock, *Antique*	475	550	625
Whitmore Patent, 12 Ga., Hammerless, Checkered Stock, *Antique*	225	450	675

SHOTGUN, SINGLESHOT

	Fair	V. Good	Excellent
12 Ga., Semi-Hammerless, Checkered Stock, *Antique*	$150	$200	$250

AMERICAN ARMS INTERNATIONAL
Salt Lake City, Utah. Current.

RIFLE, SEMI-AUTOMATIC

	Fair	V. Good	Excellent
American 180, .22 L.R.R.F., 177 Round Drum Magazine, Peep Sights, *Modern*	400	500	600
Extra Magazine, Add $50-$75			
Laser-Lok, Sight System, Add $350-$450			

AMERICAN BARLOCK WONDER
Made by Crescent for Sears-Roebuck & Co. See Crescent Fire Arms Co., Shotgun, Double Barrel, Side-by-Side; Shotgun, Single Shot.

AMERICAN BOY
Made by Bliss & Goodyear for Townley Hdw. Co.

HANDGUN, REVOLVER

	Fair	V. Good	Excellent
.32 Short R.F., Single Action, Solid Frame, Spur Trigger, 7 Shot, *Antique*	65	125	250

AMERICAN BULLDOG
Made by Johnson, Bye & Co., Worcester, Mass. 1882–1900.

HANDGUN, REVOLVER

	Fair	V. Good	Excellent
.22 Short R.F., 7 Shot, Spur Trigger, Solid Frame, Single Action, *Antique*	50	100	175
.32 S & W, 5 Shot, Spur Trigger, Solid Frame, Single Action, *Curio*	50	100	150
.32 S & W, 5 Shot, Spur Trigger, Solid Frame, Single Action, *Curio*	50	100	150
.32 Short R.F., 5 Shot, Spur Trigger, Solid Frame, Single Action, *Antique*	50	100	175
.38 Short R.F., 5 Shot, Spur Trigger, Solid Frame, Single Action, *Antique*	50	100	175
.41 Short C.F., 5 Shot, Spur Trigger, Solid Frame, Single Action, *Antique*	50	100	200

AMERICAN CHAMPION

SHOTGUN, SINGLESHOT

	Fair	V. Good	Excellent
M1899, 12 Gauge, Plain, *Modern* .	50	75	100

AMERICAN DERRINGER CORP.
Waco, Texas 1979 to date.

HANDGUN, DOUBLE BARREL, OVER-UNDER

	Fair	V. Good	Excellent
Model AD, .32 S & W Long, Remington Style Derringer, Stainless Steel, Spur Trigger, Hammer, *Modern*	125	150	175

	Fair	V. Good	Excellent
Model AD, .357 Mag., Remington Style Derringer, Stainless Steel, Spur Trigger, Hammer, *Modern*	$125	$150	$175
Model AD, .38 Spec., Remington Style Derringer, Stainless Steel, Spur Trigger, Hammer, *Modern*	125	150	175
Model AD, .41 Mag., Remington Style Derringer, Stainless Steel, Spur Trigger, Hammer, *Modern*	87	175	275
Model AD, .44 Mag., Remington Style Derringer, Stainless Steel, Spur Trigger, Hammer, *Modern*	125	200	275
Model AD, .45 ACP., Remington Style Derringer, Stainless Steel, Spur Trigger, Hammer, *Modern*	100	150	200
Model AD, .45 Win Mag., Remington Style Derringer, Stainless Steel, Spur Trigger, Hammer, *Modern*	115	225	350
Model ADL, Various Calibers, Remington Style Derringer, Stainless Steel, Lightweight, Spur Trigger, Hammer, *Modern*	100	125	150

HANDGUN, SEMI-AUTOMATIC

	Fair	V. Good	Excellent
Model ADBS, .25 ACP, Clip Fed, Blue, *Modern*	25	50	75
Model ADM, .250 Mag., Clip Fed, Stainless Steel, *Modern*	35	75	125
Model ADMB, .250 Mag., Clip Fed, Blue, *Modern*	25	50	75
Model ADSS, .25 ACP, Clip Fed, Stainless Steel, *Modern*	25	50	75

American Derringer ADSS, .25 Auto

HANDGUN, SINGLESHOT

	Fair	V. Good	Excellent
Model ADS, Various Calibers, Remington Style Derringer, Stainless Steel, Spur Trigger, Hammer, *Modern*	100	125	150

AMERICAN EAGLE

Made by Hopkins & Allen 1870–1898.

HANDGUN, REVOLVER

	Fair	V. Good	Excellent
.22 Short R.F., 7 Shot, Spur Trigger, Solid Frame, Single Action, *Antique*	$75	$125	$175
.32 Short R.F., 5 Shot, Spur Trigger, Solid Frame, Single Action, *Antique*	100	150	200

AMERICAN FIREARMS CO.

San Antonio, Texas 1966–1974.

HANDGUN, SEMI-AUTOMATIC

	Fair	V. Good	Excellent
.22 L.R.R.F., Clip Fed, Stainless Steel, *Modern*	35	75	150
.25 ACP, Clip Fed, Blue, *Modern*	100	125	150
.25 ACP, Clip Fed, Stainless Steel, *Modern*	125	150	175
.380 ACP, Clip Fed, Stainless Steel, *Modern*	400	500	600

AMERICAN GUN CO.

Made by Crescent Fire Arms Co. Sold By H. & D. Folsom Co. See Crescent Fire Arms Co. for shotguns.

HANDGUN, REVOLVER

	Fair	V. Good	Excellent
.32 S & W, 5 Shot, Double Action, Top Break, *Curio*	125	150	175

AMERICAN STANDARD TOOL CO.

Newark, N.J. 1865–1870, Successor to Manhattan Firearms Co.

HANDGUN, PERCUSSION

	Fair	V. Good	Excellent
Hero, .34, Screw Barrel, Center Hammer, Spur Trigger, *Antique*	50	100	200

HANDGUN, REVOLVER

	Fair	V. Good	Excellent
.22 Short R.F., 7 Shot, Spur Trigger, Tip-Up, *Antique*	125	250	375

AMERICUS

Made by Hopkins & Allen 1870–1900.

HANDGUN, REVOLVER

	Fair	V. Good	Excellent
.22 Short R.F., 7 Shot, Spur Trigger, Solid Frame, Single Action, *Antique*	50	100	150
.32 Short R.F., 5 Shot, Spur Trigger, Solid Frame, Single Action, *Antique*	50	100	175

AMSDEN, B.W.

Saratoga Springs, N.Y. 1852.

COMBINATION WEAPON, PERCUSSION

	Fair	V. Good	Excellent
.40-16 Ga., Double Barrel, Rifled, *Antique*	400	650	900

	Fair	V. Good	Excellent
RIFLE, PERCUSSION			
.40, Octagon Barrel, Set Trigger, Rifled, *Antique*	$200	$400	$600

AMT

Arcadia Machine & Tool, since 1976 in Arcadia, Calif. See Auto Mag.

	Fair	V. Good	Excellent
HANDGUN, SEMI-AUTOMATIC			
Back Up, .22 L.R.R.F., Stainless Steel, Clip Fed, *Modern*	200	225	250
Back Up, .380 ACP, AMT, Stainless Steel, Clip Fed, *Modern*	200	225	250
Back Up, .380 ACP, OMC, Stainless Steel, Clip Fed, *Modern*	125	150	175
Back Up, .380 ACP, TDE, Stainless Steel, Clip Fed, *Modern*	100	175	250
Combat Skipper, .45 ACP, Stainless Steel, Clip Fed, Fixed Sights, *Modern*	275	325	375
Government, .45 ACP, Stainless Steel, Clip Fed, Fixed Sights, *Modern*	200	300	400
Hardballer, .45 ACP, Stainless Steel, Clip Fed, Adjustable Sights, *Modern*	225	325	425
Lightning, .22 L.R., Stainless Steel, 5" Bull Barrel, Adjustable Sights, As Above, Fixed Sights, As Above, 6 1/2" Bull Barrel, Adjustable Sights, As Above, Fixed Sights	200	225	250
Lightning, .22 L.R., Stainless Steel, 6 1/2" Tapered Barrel, Adjustable Sights, As Above, Fixed Sights	150	200	250
Longslide, .45 ACP, Stainless Steel, Clip Fed, Adjustable Sights, *Modern*	300	400	500
Skipper, .45 ACP, Stainless Steel, Clip Fed, Adjustable Sights, *Modern*	200	300	400

AMT Skipper

ANDRUS & OSBORNE

Canton, Conn. 1847–1850, moved to Southbridge, Mass. 1850–1851.

	Fair	V. Good	Excellent
HANDGUN, PERCUSSION			
.36 Underhammer, Boot Pistol, Half-Octagon Barrel, *Antique*	$200	$300	$400

ANGSTADT, A. & J.

Berks County, Pa. 1792–1808. See Kentucky Rifles and U.S. Military.

ANGSTADT, PETER

Lancaster County, Pa. 1770–1777. See Kentucky Rifles and Pistols.

ANGUSH, JAMES

Lancaster, Pa. 1771. See Kentucky Rifles and Pistols.

ANNELY, L.

London, England 1650–1700.

	Fair	V. Good	Excellent
HANDGUN, FLINTLOCK			
.62, Holster Pistol, Brass Mounting, *Antique*	225	450	950

ANSCHUTZ

Zella Mehlis, Germany 1922–1938, 1945 to date in Ulm, West Germany. Also see Savage Arms Co. for rifle listings.

	Fair	V. Good	Excellent
HANDGUN, REVOLVER			
J.G.A., 7mm C.F., Folding Trigger, Pocket Revolver, *Curio*	65	125	200

Anschutz J. G. Revolver

ANSCHUTZ, E.

Philadelphia, Pa., c. 1860.

	Fair	V. Good	Excellent
RIFLE, PERCUSSION			
.36 Schutzen Rifle, Octagon Barrel, Target, *Antique*	625	1250	2000

ANSCHUTZ, UDO

Zella Mehlis, Germany 1927–1939.

HANDGUN, SINGLESHOT

	Fair	V. Good	Excellent
Record-Match M1933, .22 L.R.R.F., Free Pistol, Martini Action, Fancy Stocks, Target Sights, *Curio*	$250	$450	$650
Record-Match M210, .22 L.R.R.F., Free Pistol, Martini Action, Fancy Stocks, Target Sights, Light Engraving, *Curio*	650	750	850

ANSTADT, JACOB

Kutztown, Pa. 1815–1817. See Kentucky Rifles and Pistols.

APACHE

Fab. de Armas Garantazadas, Spain, c. 1920.

HANDGUN, REVOLVER

	Fair	V. Good	Excellent
Colt Police Positive Type, .38 Double Action, 6 Shots, *Curio*	35	75	125

APACHE

Made by Ojanguren y Vidosa; Eibar, Spain.

HANDGUN, SEMI-AUTOMATIC

	Fair	V. Good	Excellent
.25 ACP, Clip Fed, *Modern*	125	150	175

APAOLOZO HERMANOS

Zumorraga, Spain, c. 1925.

HANDGUN, REVOLVER

	Fair	V. Good	Excellent
Colt Police Positive Type, .38 Spec., Double Action, *Curio*	35	75	125

APEX RIFLE CO.

Sun Valley, Calif., c. 1952.

RIFLE, BOLT ACTION

	Fair	V. Good	Excellent
Apex Eight, Various Calibers, 8 Lbs., Monte Kennedy Stock, Standard Grade, No Sights, *Modern*	100	200	350
Bantam Light Sporter, Various Calibers, 7 Lbs., Monte Kennedy Stock, Standard Grade, No Sights, *Modern*	125	250	400
Bench Rester, Various Calibers, Monte Kennedy Laminated Stock with Rails, Bull Barrel, Canjar Trigger, *Modern*	125	250	475
Reliable Nine, Various Calibers, 9 Lbs., Monte Kennedy Stock, Standard Grade, No Sights, *Modern*	100	200	350
Varmint & Target, Various Calibers, Monte Kennedy Target Stock, Heavy Barrel, No Sights, *Modern*	$125	$250	$425

ARAMBERRI

Spain.

SHOTGUN, DOUBLE BARREL, SIDE-BY-SIDE

	Fair	V. Good	Excellent
Boxlock, 12 Gauge, Single Trigger, Checkered Stock, Vent Rib, *Modern*	100	125	150

ARGENTINE MILITARY

Aramberri.

HANDGUN, REVOLVER

	Fair	V. Good	Excellent
Colt M 1892, Double Action Trigger, Solid Frame, Swing-Out Cylinder, Military, *Curio*	250	300	350

HANDGUN, SEMI-AUTOMATIC

	Fair	V. Good	Excellent
Ballester-Molina, .45 ACP, Clip Fed, *Curio*	300	350	400
Ballester-Rigaud, .45 ACP, Clip Fed, *Curio*	350	400	450
Modelo 1916 (Colt 1911), 11.25mm, Clip Fed, *Curio*	450	550	650
Modelo 1927 (Colt 1911A1), .45 ACP, Clip Fed, *Curio*	550	650	750
Steyr M1905, 7.63 Mannlicher, *Curio*	225	275	325

RIFLE, BOLT ACTION

	Fair	V. Good	Excellent
M 1891, 7.65 Argentine, Carbine, Open Rear Sight, Full Stocked Military, *Curio*	200	250	300
M 1891, 7.65 Argentine, Rifle, Full Stocked Military, *Curio*	175	225	275
M 1909, 7.65 Argentine, Carbine, Open Rear Sight, Full-Stocked Military, *Modern*	175	225	275
M 1909, 7.65 Argentine, Rifle, Full Stocked Military, *Curio*	150	225	300

RIFLE, SINGLESHOT

	Fair	V. Good	Excellent
M 1879, .43 Mauser, Rolling Block, *Antique*	300	350	400

ARISTOCRAT

Made by Hopkins & Allen for Suplee Biddle Hardware 1870–1900.

HANDGUN, REVOLVER

	Fair	V. Good	Excellent
.22 Short R.F., 7 Shot, Spur Trigger, Solid Frame, Single Action, *Antique*	35	75	150
.32 Short R.F., 5 Shot, Spur Trigger, Solid Frame, Single Action, *Antique*	35	75	175

ARISTOCRAT

Made by Stevens Arms.

SHOTGUN, DOUBLE BARREL, SIDE-BY-SIDE

	Fair	V. Good	Excellent
M 315, Various Gauges, Hammerless, Steel Barrel, *Modern*	$35	$75	$150

ARIZAGA, GASPAR

Eibar, Spain.

HANDGUN, SEMI-AUTOMATIC

	Fair	V. Good	Excellent
.32 ACP, Clip Fed, *Modern*	50	100	150

ARMALITE

Costa Mesa, Calif. The author had the pleasure of being on a partridge shoot in Spain with the inventor of some of the Armalite products, the creator of the basis for the AR-15 and M16 series and a number of other .223-based firearms, Gene Stoner. It was a pleasure listening to this giant in contemporary firearms design and entrepreneurship sharing his extraordinary experiences. Some of those achievements and adventures were included in Edward Ezell's excellent work, *The Black Rifle.* The fascinating high-tech nature of the Armalite arms, and other .223-based firearms, are popular with a significant number of arms collectors. Following the market for this type of arm has proven that sometimes the type draws extremely well in sales figures.

RIFLE, SEMI-AUTOMATIC

	Fair	V. Good	Excellent
AR-180.223 Rem., Clip Fed, Folding Stock, *Modern*	625	750	875
AR-7 Explorer, .22 L.R.R.F., Clip Fed, *Modern*	50	75	100
AR-7 Explorer Custom, .22 L.R.R.F., Checkered Stock, Clip Fed, *Modern*	50	100	150

SHOTGUN, SEMI-AUTOMATIC

	Fair	V. Good	Excellent
AR-17, 12 Ga. Lightweight, *Modern*	375	475	575

ARMI JAGER

Turin, Italy. Imported by E.M.F.

HANDGUN, REVOLVER

	Fair	V. Good	Excellent
Dakota Sheriff, Various Calibers, Single Action, Western Style, 3½" Barrel, *Modern*	65	125	200
Dakota Target, Various Calibers, Single Action, Western Style, Adjustable Sights, Various Barrel Lengths, *Modern*	100	150	200
Dakota, .22 L.R.R.F. and .22 W.M.R., Single Action, Western Style, Various Barrel Lengths, *Modern*	75	125	175
Dakota, .22 L.R.R.F., Single Action, Western Style, Various Barrel Lengths, *Modern*	50	100	150
Dakota, Various Calibers, Single Action, Western Style, Various Barrel Lengths, *Modern*	$75	$125	$175
Dakota, Various Calibers, Single Action, Western Style, Buntline Barrel Lengths, *Modern*	75	125	175
Dakota, Various Calibers, Single Action, Western Style, Engraved Barrel Lengths, *Modern*	125	225	325

RIFLE, SEMI-AUTOMATIC

	Fair	V. Good	Excellent
AP-74, .22 L.R.R.F., Military Stock, Wood Stock, *Modern*	50	75	100
AP-74, .31 ACP, Military Style, Wood Stock, *Modern*	35	75	125
AP-74 Commando, .22 L.R.R.F., Military Style, Wood Stock, *Modern*	35	75	125
AP-74 Standard, .22 L.R.R.F., Military Style, Plastic Stock, *Modern*	25	50	100
AP-74 Standard, .32 ACP, Military Style, Plastic Stock, *Modern*	35	75	125

ARMINEX LTD.

Scottsdale, Ariz. since 1982–1985.

HANDGUN, SEMI-AUTOMATIC

	Fair	V. Good	Excellent
Trifire, .45 A.C.P., 9 mm Luger, or .38 Super, Blue or Nickel, Clip Fed, Hammer, Adjustable Sights, *Modern*	250	350	450

Arminex Trifire Standard

	Fair	V. Good	Excellent
Trifire Presentation, .45 A.C.P., 9 mm Luger, or .38 Super, Cased, Blue or Nickel, Clip Fed, Hammer, Adjustable Sights, *Modern*	300	400	500

ARMINIUS

Friedrich Pickert, Zella-Mehlis, Germany 1922–1939.

Arminex Trifire Target

	Fair	V. Good	Excellent
HANDGUN, REVOLVER			
Model 1, .22 L.R.R.F., Hammerless, *Curio*	$150	$200	$250
Model 2, .22 L.R.R.F., Hammer, *Curio*	200	250	300
Model 3, .25 ACP, Hammerless, Folding Trigger, *Curio*	75	125	175
Model 4, 5.5 Velo Dog, Hammerless, Folding Trigger, *Curio*	35	75	150
Model 5/1, 7.5mm Swiss, Hammer, *Curio*	50	100	175
Model 5/2, 7.62 Nagant, Hammer, *Curio*	50	100	175
Model 7, .320 Revolver, Hammer, *Curio*	35	75	125
Model 8, .320 Revolver, Hammerless, Folding Trigger, *Curio*	100	125	150
Model 9, .32 ACP, Hammer, *Curio*	75	125	175
Model 10, .32 ACP, Hammerless, Folding Trigger, *Curio*	50	100	150
Model 13, .380 Revolver, Hammer, *Curio*	50	100	150
Model 14, .380 Revolver, Hammerless, *Curio*	50	100	150
HANDGUN, SINGLESHOT			
TP 1, .22 L.R.R.F., Target Pistol, Hammer, *Modern*	150	200	250
TP 2, .22 L.R.R.F., Hammerless, Set Triggers, *Modern*	175	225	275

ARMINIUS

Herman Weihrauch Sportwaffenfabrik, Mellrichstadt/Bayern, West Germany before 1968; for current models, See F.I.E.

	Fair	V. Good	Excellent
HANDGUN, REVOLVER			
HW-3, .22 L.R.R.F., *Modern*	25	50	75
HW-3, .32 S & W Long, *Modern*	25	50	75
HW-5, .22 L.R.R.F., *Modern*	25	50	75
HW-5, .32 S & W Long, *Modern*	25	50	75
HW-7, .22 L.R.R.F., *Modern*	25	50	75
HW-9, .22 L.R.R.F., Adjustable Sights, *Modern*	25	50	75

ARMSPORT

Importers discontinued 1993, Miami, Fla.

	Fair	V. Good	Excellent
HANDGUN, FLINTLOCK			
Kentucky, .45, Reproduction	$25	$50	$85
HANDGUN, PERCUSSION			
1847 Colt Walker, .44, Reproduction, *Antique*	35	75	125
1851 Colt Navy, .36, Brass Frame, Reproduction	25	50	75
1851 Colt Navy, .36, Steel Frame, Reproduction	25	50	100
1851 Colt Navy, .44, Brass Frame, Reproduction	25	50	75
1851 Colt Navy, .44, Steel Frame, Reproduction	25	50	100
1860 Colt Army, .44, Brass Frame, Reproduction	25	50	75
1860 Colt Army, .44, Steel Frame, Reproduction	25	50	100
Corsair, .44, Double Barrel, Reproduction	25	50	75
Kentucky, .45 or .50, Reproduction	25	50	75
New Hartford Police, .36, Reproduction	25	50	100
New Remington Army, .44, Blue, Brass Trigger Guard, Reproduction	50	75	100
New Remington Army, .44, Stainless Steel, Brass Trigger Guard, Reproduction	35	75	125
Patriot, .45, Target Sights, Set Triggers, Reproduction	50	75	100
Spiller & Burr, .36, Solid Frame, Brass Frame, Reproduction	25	50	75
Whitney, .36, Solid Frame, Brass Trigger Guard, Reproduction	50	75	100
RIFLE, BOLT ACTION			
Tikka, Various Calibers, Open Sights, Checkered Stock, Clip Fed, *Modern*	350	500	650
RIFLE, LEVER ACTION			
Premier 1873 Winchester, Various Calibers, Carbine, Engraved, Reproduction, *Modern*	450	650	850
Premier 1873 Winchester, Various Calibers, Rifle, Engraved, Reproduction, *Modern*	500	750	1000
RIFLE, FLINTLOCK			
Deluxe Hawkin, .50, Reproduction	75	125	175
Deluxe Kentucky, .45, Reproduction	100	150	200
Hawkin, .45, Reproduction	75	125	175
Kentucky, .45, Reproduction	100	125	150
RIFLE, PERCUSSION			
Deluxe Hawkin, Various Calibers, Reproduction	125	150	175
Deluxe Kentucky, .45, Reproduction	100	150	200

	Fair	V. Good	Excellent
Hawkin, Various Calibers, Reproduction	$100	$125	$150
Kentucky, .45 or .50, Reproduction	50	100	150

COMBINATION WEAPON, OVER-UNDER

Tikka Turkey Gun, 12 Ga. and .222 Rem., Vent Rib, Sling Swivels, Muzzle Break, Checkered Stock, *Modern*	275	450	625

RIFLE, DOUBLE BARREL, SIDE-BY-SIDE

Emperor, Various Calibers, Holland and Holland Type Sidelock, Engraved, Checkered Stock, Extra Barrels, Cased, *Modern*	8200	12225	16250
Emperor Deluxe, Various Calibers, Holland and Holland Sidelock, Fancy Engraving, Checkered Stock, Extra Barrels, *Modern*	15000	20000	25000

RIFLE, DOUBLE BARREL, OVER-UNDER

Emperor, Various Calibers, Checkered Stock, Engraved, Extra Barrels, Cased, *Modern*	9000	12000	15000
Express, Various Calibers, Checkered Stock, Engraved, *Modern*	2500	3000	3500

SHOTGUN, PERCUSSION

Hook Breech, Double Barrel, Side-by-Side, 10 and 12 Gauges, Reproduction	100	175	250

SHOTGUN, DOUBLE BARREL, OVER-UNDER

Model 2500, 12 and 20 Ga., Checkered Stock, Adjustable Choke, Single Selective Trigger, *Modern*	250	450	650
Premier, 12 Ga., Skeet Grade, Checkered Stock, Engraved, *Modern*	600	900	1200

SHOTGUN, DOUBLE BARREL, SIDE-BY-SIDE

Express, 12 and 20 Gauges, Holland and Holland Type Sidelock, Engraved, Checkered Stock, *Modern*	2500	3000	3500
Goose Gun, 10 Ga. 3½" Mag., Checkered Stock, *Modern*	275	375	475
Side-by-Side, 12 and 20 Gauges, Checkered Stock, *Modern*	225	325	425
Western Double, 12 Ga. Mag. 3", Outside Hammers Double Trigger, *Modern*	200	300	400

SHOTGUN, SINGLESHOT

Monotrap, 12 Ga., Checkered Stock, *Modern*	850	1200	1550
Monotrap, 12 Ga., Two Barrel Set, Checkered Stock, *Modern*	900	1600	2300

ARMSTRONG, JOHN

Gettysburg, Pa. 1813–1817. Also See Kentucky Rifles and Pistols. Having owned some truly handsome, and sometimes quite striking, John Armstrong pieces, the author regards these fine guns as among the most artistic and appealing of American firearms, and at the front rank of Kentucky Rifles. This quality and style of rifle belongs in any American museum of art that purports to document and celebrate native achievements in decorative arts. One of America's indigenous art forms, a Kentucky Rifle by an artisan like John Armstrong is a true icon of American creativity and ingenuity. Armstrong excelled at gunmaking pure and simple, but his rifles also represented elegance, a mastery of the use of steel, silver and brass, beauty of design, and a lovely hand at rococo relief carving. An example of Armstrong's work should be displayed in the collection of American decorative arts at the White House–and surely that will happen. Watch for the Kentucky Rifle to become one of the darlings of the American antiques world, and continue to escalate in demand, and in price.

ARRIOLA HERMANOS

Eibar, Spain, c. 1930.

HANDGUN, REVOLVER

	Fair	V. Good	Excellent
Colt Police Positive Copy, .38 Spec., Double Action, *Curio*	$25	$50	$100

ARRIZABALAGA, HILOS DE CALIXTO

Eibar, Spain, c. 1915.

HANDGUN, SEMI-AUTOMATIC

Ruby Type, .32 ACP, Clip Fed, Blue, *Curio*	100	125	150

ASCASO, FRANCISCO

Tarassa, Spain, c. 1937.

HANDGUN, SEMI-AUTOMATIC

Astra 400 Copy, 9mm, Clip Fed, Military Type, *Curio*	800	900	1000

ASHEVILLE ARMORY

Asheville, N.C. 1861–1864.

RIFLE, PERCUSSION

.58 Enfield Type, Rifled, Brass Furniture, Military, *Antique*	2500	3500	4500

ASTRA

Founded in 1908 as Unceta y Esperanza in Eibar, Spain. In 1913 moved to Guernica, Spain, and the name was reversed to Esperanza y Unceta; name changed again in 1926 to Unceta y Cia.; named changed again in 1953 to Astra-Unceta y Cia.

	Fair	V. Good	Excellent
HANDGUN, REVOLVER			
250, .22 L.R.R.F., Double Action, Small Frame, *Modern*	$50	$100	$150
250, .22 W.M.R., Double Action, Small Frame, *Modern*	50	100	150
250, .32 S & W Long, Double Action, Small Frame, *Modern*	50	100	150
250, .38 Special, Double Action, Small Frame, *Modern*	75	125	175
357 Magnum, .357 Magnum, Double Action, Adjustable Sights, *Modern*	125	200	275
357 Magnum, .357 Magnum, Double Action, Adjustable Sights, Stainless Steel, *Modern*	200	250	300
44 Magnum, .44 Magnum, Double Action, Adjustable Sights, *Modern*	250	300	350

Astra .44 Magnum

	Fair	V. Good	Excellent
960, .38 Special, Double Action, Adjustable Sights, *Modern*	50	100	175
Cadix, .22 L.R.R.F., Double Action, Adjustable Sights, *Modern*	35	75	150
Cadix, .22 W.M.R., Double Action, Adjustable Sights, *Modern*	50	100	150
Cadix, .32 S & W Long, Double Action, Adjustable Sights, *Modern*	50	100	150
Cadix, .38 Special, Double Action, Adjustable Sights, *Modern*	125	150	175
Inox, .38 Special, Stainless Steel, Double Action, Small Frame, *Modern*	100	150	200
Match, .38 Special, Double Action, Adjustable Sights, *Modern*	50	100	175
Model 41, .41 Magnum, Blue, *Modern*	225	250	275
Model 45, .45 Colt, Blue, *Modern*	250	300	350

HANDGUN, SEMI-AUTOMATIC

Chrome Plating, Add $25.00-$45.00

Light Engraving, Add $60.00-$110.00

	Fair	V. Good	Excellent
A-50, Various Calibers, Blue, Single Action, *Modern*	75	150	225
A-80, Various Calibers, Double Action, Blue, Large Magazine, *Modern*	225	300	375
A-80, Various Calibers, Double Action, Chrome, Large Magazine, *Modern*	$200	$300	$400
Constable, Various Calibers, Blue, *Modern*	200	250	300

Astra Constable

	Fair	V. Good	Excellent
Constable Pocket, Various Calibers, Blue, *Modern*	200	250	300
Constable Sport, Various Calibers, Blue, *Modern*	200	250	300
Constable Target, .22 L.R.R.F., Blue, *Modern*	250	300	350
Model 100, .32 ACP, *Curio*	175	225	275
Model 100 Special, .32 ACP, 9 Shot, *Curio*	200	250	300
Model 1000, .23 ACP, 12 Shot, *Modern*	300	400	500
Model 1911, .32 ACP, *Curio*	200	250	300

Astra M1911 .32

	Fair	V. Good	Excellent
Model 1915, .32 ACP, *Curio*	125	200	275
Model 1916, .32 ACP, *Curio*	100	200	300

	Fair	V. Good	Excellent
Model 1924, .25 ACP, *Curio*	$125	$175	$225
Model 200 Firecat, .25 ACP, Early Model, Concave Indicator Cut, *Modern*	150	200	250
Model 200 Firecat, .25 ACP, Late Model, Long Clip, *Modern*	75	125	175

Astra Model 200 with Long Clip

	Fair	V. Good	Excellent
Model 200 Firecat, .25 ACP, Late Model, Rear Indicator, *Modern*	50	100	150
Model 2000 Camper or Cub, Conversion Kit Only,	50	75	100
Model 2000 Camper, .22 Short R.F., *Modern*	200	250	300
Model 2000 Cub, .22 Short R.F., *Modern*	125	150	175

Astra Cub

	Fair	V. Good	Excellent
Model 2000 Cub, .25 ACP, *Modern*	$125	$150	$175
Model 300, .32 ACP, Clip Fed, *Modern*	100	200	300
Model 300, .32 ACP, Nazi-Proofed, Clip Fed, *Curio*	275	375	475
Model 300, .380 ACP, Clip Fed, *Modern*	125	225	325
Model 300, .380 ACP, Nazi-Proofed, Clip Fed, *Curio*	300	400	500
Model 3000 (Late), .380 ACP, Clip Fed, *Modern*	150	200	250
Model 400, .32 ACP, *Modern*	400	500	600
Model 400, 9mm Bayard Long, *Modern*	225	300	375
Model 400, 9mm Bayard Long, Nazi-Proofed, Clip Fed, *Curio*	650	700	750
Model 4000 Falcon, .22 L.R.R.F., Clip Fed, *Modern*	300	400	500
Model 4000 Falcon, .32 ACP, Clip Fed, *Modern*	200	250	300
Model 4000 Falcon, .380 ACP, Clip Fed, *Modern*	200	250	300
Model 4000 Falcon, Conversion Kit Only	50	75	100
Model 5000 Sport (Constable), .22 L.R.R.F., Target Pistol, Clip Fed, *Modern*	200	250	300
Model 600, .32 ACP, Clip Fed, *Modern*	100	200	300
Model 600, 9mm Luger, Clip Fed, *Modern*	100	200	300
Model 600, 9mm Luger, Nazi-Proofed, Clip Fed, *Curio*	300	400	500
Model 700 Special, .32 ACP, 12 Shots, Clip Fed, *Modern*	400	500	600
Model 700, .32 ACP, Clip Fed, *Curio*	400	450	500
Model 7000, .22 L.R.R.F., Clip Fed, *Modern*	75	125	175
Model 800 Condor, .380 ACP, Clip Fed, *Modern*	700	850	1000
Model 900, 7.63 Mauser, Holster Stock, *Modern*	1000	1750	2500

Astra Model 900

	Fair	V. Good	Excellent
Model TS-22, .22 L.R.R.F., Target Pistol, Single Action, Clip Fed, *Modern*	$125	$225	$325

Astra TS-22

RIFLE, SEMI-AUTOMATIC

	Fair	V. Good	Excellent
Model 1000, .32 ACP, Clip Fed, *Modern*	200	325	450
Model 3000 (Early), .32 ACP, *Modern*	75	125	175
Model 3000 (Late), .22 L.R.R.F., *Modern*	50	100	150
Model 3000 (Late), .32 ACP, *Modern*	50	100	175
Model 800 Condor, 9mm Luger, *Curio*	250	450	650
Model 902, 7.63 Mauser, *Modern*	500	1000	1600

SHOTGUN, DOUBLE BARREL, OVER-UNDER

	Fair	V. Good	Excellent
Model 650, 12 Gauge, Checkered Stock, Double Triggers, Vent Rib, *Modern*	125	200	275
Model 650E, 12 Gauge, Checkered Stock, Double Triggers, Vent Rib, Selective Ejectors, *Modern*	112	225	375
Model 750 Skeet, 12 Gauge, Checkered Stock, Single Trigger, Vent Rib, Selective Ejectors, *Modern*	200	350	500
Model 750 Trap, 12 Gauge, Checkered Stock, Single Trigger, Vent Rib, Selective Ejectors, *Modern*	200	350	500
Model 750, 12 Gauge, Checkered Stock, Double Trigger, Vent Rib, *Modern*	112	225	375
Model 750E, 12 Gauge, Checkered Stock, Single Trigger, Vent Rib, Selective Ejectors, *Modern*	175	350	525
Model ID-13, 12 Gauge, Checkered Stock, Single Trigger, Selective Ejectors, Vent Rib, *Modern*	175	325	475

SHOTGUN, DOUBLE BARREL, SIDE-BY-SIDE

	Fair	V. Good	Excellent
Model 805, Various Gauges, Checkered Stock, Double Triggers, *Modern*	75	150	250
Model 811, 10 Gauge Magnum, Checkered Stock, Double Triggers, *Modern*	$115	$195	$275

SHOTGUN, SINGLESHOT

	Fair	V. Good	Excellent
Cyclops, Various Gauges, Checkered Stock, *Modern*	50	75	100

ATIS

Ponte S. Marco, Italy.

SHOTGUN, SEMI-AUTOMATIC

	Fair	V. Good	Excellent
12 Ga., Lightweight, Vent Rib, *Modern*	75	150	225
12 Ga., Lightweight, Vent Rib, Left-Hand, *Modern*	125	200	275

ATKIN, HENRY E. & CO.

London, England 1874–1900. This distinguished gunmaker has a history tied to that of J. Purdey & Sons. Atkin's own mechanical innovations influenced the work of Purdey, and the reader should consult the Hon. Richard Beaumont's landmark work on J. Purdey & Sons, to appreciate that connection.

SHOTGUN, DOUBLE BARREL, SIDE-BY-SIDE

	Fair	V. Good	Excellent
Raleigh, 12 Gauge, Sidelock, Double Triggers, Checkered Stock, Engraved, Automatic Ejectors, "Purdey" Barrels, *Curio*	5500	7000	8500

ATLAS

Domingo Acha y Cia., Ermua, Spain, c. 1920.

HANDGUN, SEMI-AUTOMATIC

	Fair	V. Good	Excellent
Vest Pocket, .25 ACP, Clip Fed, *Curio*	75	100	125

ATLAS ARMS

Chicago, Ill. from about 1962 to 1972.

HANDGUN, DOUBLE BARREL, OVER-UNDER

	Fair	V. Good	Excellent
Derringer, .22 L.R.R.F., Remington Style, *Modern*	25	50	75
Derringer, .38 Spec., Remington Style, *Modern*	25	50	75

SHOTGUN, DOUBLE BARREL, OVER-UNDER

	Fair	V. Good	Excellent
Grand Prix, 12 or 20 Gauge, Merkel Type Sidelock, Single Selective Trigger, Fancy Engraving, Automatic Ejectors, *Modern*	500	850	1200
Model 65, Various Gauges, Boxlock, Double Trigger, Vent Rib, *Modern*	150	250	350
Model 65-ST, Various Gauges, Boxlock, Single Trigger, Vent Rib, *Modern*	125	250	400

	Fair	V. Good	Excellent
Model 87, Various Gauges, Merkel Type Sidelock, Single Trigger, Vent Rib, Engraved, *Modern*	$250	$350	$450
Model 150, Various Gauges, Boxlock, Single Trigger, Vent Rib, *Modern*	125	250	400
Model 150, Various Gauges, Boxlock, Single Trigger, Vent Rib, Automatic Ejectors, *Modern*	175	300	425
Model 160, Various Gauges, Boxlock, Single Trigger, Vent Rib, Automatic Ejectors, *Modern*	250	350	450
Model 180, Various Gauges, Boxlock, Single Trigger, Vent Rib, Automatic Ejectors, Light Engraving, *Modern*	250	375	500
Model 750, Various Gauges, Merkel Type Sidelock, Single Trigger, Vent Rib, Engraved, *Modern*	250	350	450
Model 750, Various Gauges, Merkel Type Sidelock, Single Trigger, Vent Rib, Engraved, Automatic Ejectors, *Modern*	200	375	550

SHOTGUN, DOUBLE BARREL, SIDE-BY-SIDE

	Fair	V. Good	Excellent
Model 145, Various Gauges, Boxlock, Vent Rib, Engraved, Hammerless, Checkered Stock, *Modern*	175	300	425
Model 200, Various Gauges, Boxlock, Double Triggers, Hammerless, Checkered Stock, *Modern*	87	175	275
Model 204, Various Gauges, Boxlock, Single Trigger, Hammerless, Checkered Stock, *Modern*	175	225	275
Model 206, Various Gauges, Boxlock, Single Trigger, Automatic Ejector, Hammerless, Checkered Stock, *Modern*	200	275	350
Model 208, Various Gauges, Boxlock, Double Triggers, Vent Rib, Recoil Pad, *Modern*	175	250	325
Model 500, Various Gauges, Boxlock, Double Triggers, Vent Rib, Recoil Pad, *Modern*	175	250	325

SHOTGUN, SINGLESHOT

	Fair	V. Good	Excellent
Insuperable 101, Various Gauges, Vent Rib, Engraved, Checkered Stock, *Modern*	50	75	100
Trap Gun, 12 Gauge, Automatic Ejector, Engraved, Checkered Stock, *Modern*	325	425	525

AUBREY

Made by Meriden Arms Co., sold by Sears, Roebuck 1900–1930.

HANDGUN, REVOLVER

	Fair	V. Good	Excellent
.32 S & W, 5 Shot, Double Action, Top Break, *Modern*	55	75	95
.38 S & W, 5 Shot, Double Action, Top Break, *Modern*	55	75	95

AUDAX

Trade name of Manufacture d'Armes Des Pyrenees, Hendaye, France, marketed by La Cartoucherie Francaise, Paris 1931–1939.

HANDGUN, SEMI-AUTOMATIC

	Fair	V. Good	Excellent
.25 ACP, Clip Fed, Magazine Disconnect, Grip Safety, *Curio*	$55	$75	$95
.32 ACP, Clip Fed, Magazine Disconnect, Blue, *Curio*	55	75	95

AUSTRALIAN MILITARY

RIFLE, BOLT ACTION

	Fair	V. Good	Excellent
Mk. III, .303 British, Clip Fed, WW I Issue, *Curio*	175	225	275
Mk. III, .303 British, Clip Fed, WW II Issue, *Curio*	150	200	250

RIFLE, SINGLESHOT

	Fair	V. Good	Excellent
Martini, .310 Greener, Small Action, *Curio*	225	275	325

AUSTRIAN MILITARY

HANDGUN, PERCUSSION

	Fair	V. Good	Excellent
.54 Dragoon, with Shoulder Stock, Singleshot, *Antique*	225	450	750

HANDGUN, REVOLVER

	Fair	V. Good	Excellent
M1898 Rast & Gasser, 8mm Rast & Gasser, *Curio*	225	250	275

HANDGUN, SEMI-AUTOMATIC

	Fair	V. Good	Excellent
M1907 Roth Steyr, 8mm Roth-Steyr, *Curio*	350	400	450
M1908 Steyr, 8mm Roth-Steyr, *Curio*	300	350	400
M1911 Steyr Hahn, 9mm Steyr, *Curio*	275	325	375
M1912 Steyr Hahn, 9mm Steyr, *Curio*	200	250	300
Mannlicher 1901, 7.63 Mannlicher, *Curio*	1500	2000	2500
Mannlicher 1905, 7.63 Mannlicher, *Curio*	300	350	400

HANDGUN, SINGLESHOT

	Fair	V. Good	Excellent
Werder Lightning, 11mm, *Antique*	550	650	750

HANDGUN, TUBELOCK

	Fair	V. Good	Excellent
.69 Dragoon, with Shoulder Stock, Singleshot, *Antique*	300	350	400

RIFLE, BOLT ACTION

	Fair	V. Good	Excellent
M1883 Schulhof, 11.15 × 58R Werndl, 8 Shot, *Antique*	185	375	575
M1885 Steyr, 11.15 × 58R Werndl, Straight-Pull, *Antique*	300	375	450
M1886 Steyr, 11.15 × 58R Werndl, Straight-Pull Bolt, *Antique*	125	150	175
M1888, 8 × 50R Mannlicher, *Antique*	125	150	175

	Fair	V. Good	Excellent
M1888/90, 8 × 50R Mannlicher, *Antique*	$125	$150	$175
M1890, 8 × 50R Mannlicher, Carbine, *Antique*	125	150	175
M1895, 8 × 50R Mannlicher, *Curio*	75	100	125
M1895, 8 × 50R Mannlicher, Carbine, *Modern*	50	100	250
M1895 Stutzen, 8 × 50R Mannlicher, *Curio*	65	125	250

AUTO MAG

Started at Pasadena, Calif. in 1968, and moved to North Hollywood, Calif. when purchased by TDE in 1971. Marketed by TDE, Jurras Associates, and High Standard. See A M T. Without question these arms are in demand partly because of their popularity in Hollywood shoot-em-ups. This is a handful of gun to shoot, but will knock bowling pins down one after another, and has a strong following among sport and recreation shooters.

HANDGUN, SEMI-AUTOMATIC

	Fair	V. Good	Excellent
Alaskan Model, .44 AMP, Clip Fed, Stainless Steel, Hammer, Adjustable Sights, Cased, *Modern*	1250	1600	1950
First Model (Pasadena), .44 AMP, Clip Fed, Stainless Steel, Hammer, Adjustable Sights, Cased, *Modern*	1500	1750	2000
High Standard, .44 AMP, Clip Fed, Stainless Steel, Hammer, Adjustable Sights, Cased, *Modern*	1200	1500	1800
Jurras Custom Model 200, .44 AMP, Clip Fed, Stainless Steel, Hammer, Adjustable Sights, Cased, *Modern*	2200	2350	2500
Model 160, .357 AMP, Clip Fed, Stainless Steel, Hammer, Adjustable Sights, Cased, *Modern*	1600	1700	1800
Model 170, .41 JMP, Clip Fed, Stainless Steel, Hammer, Adjustable Sights, Cased, *Modern*	1300	1400	1500
Model 180, .44 AMP, Clip Fed, Stainless Steel, Hammer, Adjustable Sights, Cased, *Modern*	1650	1750	1850

Auto Mag Model 180

	Fair	V. Good	Excellent
Model 260, .357 AMP, Clip Fed, Stainless Steel, Hammer, Adjustable Sights, Cased, *Modern*	1150	1250	1350
Model 280, .44 AMP, Clip Fed, Stainless Steel, Hammer, Adjustable Sights, Cased, *Modern*	$1000	$1100	$1200

AUTOMATIC

Made by Hopkins & Allen, c. 1900.

HANDGUN, REVOLVER

	Fair	V. Good	Excellent
.32 S & W, 5 Shot, Top Break, Hammerless, Double Action, *Curio*	65	125	200
.38 S & W, 5 Shot, Top Break, Hammerless, Double Action, *Curio*	65	125	200

AUTOMATIC HAMMERLESS

Made by Iver Johnson, c. 1900.

HANDGUN, REVOLVER

	Fair	V. Good	Excellent
.22 L.R.R.F., 7 Shot, Double Action, Top Break, Hammerless, *Curio*	50	100	150
.32 S & W, 5 Shot, Top Break, Hammerless, Double Action, *Curio*	35	75	125
.38 S & W, 5 Shot, Top Break, Hammerless, Double Action, *Curio*	35	75	125

AUTOMATIC PISTOL

Spain.

HANDGUN, SEMI-AUTOMATIC

	Fair	V. Good	Excellent
Pocket, .32 ACP, Clip Fed, *Modern*	25	50	75

AUTOMATIC POLICE

See Forehand & Wadsworth.

AUTO-ORDNANCE CORP

Presently West Hurley, New York; formerly Bridgeport, Connecticut. See also Thompson and Numrich Arms Co. A native of Kentucky, John Taliaferro Thompson graduated from the U.S. Military Academy, West Point, in 1882. Beginning in 1890 he served in the Ordnance Department of the U.S. Army. After the Spanish-American War Thompson's services became paramount in the modernization of U.S. service small arms and ammunition. He developed a position of distinction as a designer and military arms expert, and was a key figure in the evolution of the Model 1911 Colt Automatic Pistol and the .45 ACP cartridge, and in their adoption by U.S. forces. Following retirement from the Army, Thompson joined the Remington Arms Co. (1914) as chief consulting engineer. Thompson formed the Auto-Ordnance Corporation in 1916, with the financial backing of venture capital businessman and entrepreneur Thomas Fortune Ryan. Ryan was later described by an associate as "the most adroit, suave, and noiseless man American finance has ever known." In the process of designing a practical automatic rifle, Thompson's tests and research concluded that a hand-held gun in the .45 ACP cartridge would be superior to all competition. His new gun became the Thompson Submachine Gun, in .45 ACP caliber—one of the world's first. Initially termed by its inventor as a "trench broom" the Thompson, or Tommy Gun, quickly became popular. But in 1917 plans by Thompson for the new firearm were interrupted by his return to active miltary service during the U.S. involvement in World War I. Wartime experience convinced the inventor, more than he ever realized, that his design had a bright future. In December 1918, returning to a civilian career, Thompson retired with the rank of Brigadier General. Friendly with Colt's president W.C. Skinner, Thompson soon saw his submachine gun entered into production by Colt's Pt. F.A. Mfg. Co. The Auto-Ordnance advertisement of 1921 noted: "The ideal weapon for the protection of large estates, ranches, plantations, etc." Purchases were made by police departments and other law enforcement agencies (Texas Rangers included), mining companies and steel makers, a number of foreign governments, and the U.S. government and selected armed services. Automaker Henry Ford acquired a few examples, a reflection of his fascination with firearms; also he wanted to be ready to deal with the potential problem of strikes at Ford Motor Company. Regrettably, particularly to the inventor and manufacturer, the Tommy Gun got its reputation in the hands of Prohibition-era gangsters. Bonnie and Clyde, John Dillinger, Machine Gun Kelly, Baby Face Nelson, Ma Barker and her sons, and Pretty Boy Floyd contributed to the renown of the "chopper," "Chicago piano," "typewriter" or "Tommygun." The most infamous of all incidents, in which two Thompsons played key roles, was the Valentine's Day Massacre of February 14, 1929. Thompson sales shot back up during World War II, with the new majority owner of Auto-Ordnance, Wall Street businessman Russell Maguire. Great Britain, France, and the U.S. Army ordered a large number of guns: over 1,750,000 were built, plus the equivalent of another quarter million in the form of spare parts. These were made in Utica, New York (on contract by Savage Arms) and Bridgeport, Connecticut (by Auto-Ordnance). Among the employees of the firm in Bridgeport was the young inventor and designer William B. Ruger, then a fledgling, but brilliant, gun designer. With its popularity in film and TV programs, the Thompson became one of the world's best-known firearms. The gun became as much a symbol of the Roaring '20s era as did jazz, flappers, speakeasies, and bathtub gin. The Tommy Gun's role in America has earned it a monumental status on all fronts: as a cultural icon and historically, socially, criminally, militarily, and cinematically.

	Fair	*V. Good*	*Excellent*
AUTOMATIC WEAPON, SUBMACHINE GUN			
M1 (not Colt made)	$1000	$2000	$3000
M1A (not Colt made)	750	1250	2500
Model 1921, Submachine Gun (Colt-made)	3000	7500	10000
Model 1927, Submachine Gun (Colt-made)	5000	10000	15000
Model 1928, Submachine Gun (Colt-made)	2000	5000	7500
HANDGUN, SEMI-AUTOMATIC			
1991 A1 Various Calibers, Based on the Colt Pistol, *Modern*	250	300	350
ZG-51 "Pit Bull,", Compact Model of the 1911 A1, 3.5" Barrel, *Modern*	275	325	375
CARBINE SEMI-AUTOMATIC (THOMPSON REPLICAS)			
1927 A1 "Submachine Gun," .45 ACP, 16" Barrel, *Modern*	$400	$450	$500
1927 A1 Deluxe "Submachine Gun," .45 ACP, Finned Barrel, Adjustable Sights, Pistol-Grip Forearm, *Modern*	500	600	700
1927 A1C "Submachine Gun," .45 ACP, Aluminum Alloy Receiver, *Modern*	450	525	600
1927 A3 "Submachine Gun," .22 LR, 16" Barrel, Aluminum Alloy Receiver, *Modern*	400	475	550
1927 A5 "Submachine Gun/Pistol," .45 ACP, Compact Variation, 13" Finned Barrel, Aluminum Alloy Receiver, No Shoulder Stock, *Modern*	450	525	600

AUTO-POINTER

Made by Yamamoto Mfg. Co., Imported by Sloans.

	Fair	*V. Good*	*Excellent*
SHOTGUN, SEMI-AUTOMATIC			
12 and 20 Gauges, Tube Feed, Checkered Stock, *Modern*	100	200	300

AUTOSTAND

Made for ManuFrance by Mre. d'Armes des Pyrenees.

	Fair	*V. Good*	*Excellent*
HANDGUN, SINGLESHOT			
E-1 (Unique), .22 L.R.R.F., Target Pistol, Adjustable Sights, *Curio*	25	50	75

AVENGER

	Fair	*V. Good*	*Excellent*
HANDGUN, REVOLVER			
.32 Long R.F., 5 Shot, Single Action, Spur Triggers, *Antique*	35	75	125

AVION

Azpiri y Cia., Eibar, Spain, c. 1915.

	Fair	*V. Good*	*Excellent*
HANDGUN, SEMI-AUTOMATIC			
Vest Pocket, .25 ACP, Clip Fed, *Curio*	35	75	125

A Y A

Aguirre y Aranzabal, Spain. Now Imported by Ventura.

	Fair	*V. Good*	*Excellent*
SHOTGUN, DOUBLE BARREL, OVER-UNDER			
Model 37 Super, Various Gauges, Single Selective Trigger, Automatic Ejectors, Fancy Engraving, Sidelock, *Modern*	1000	1750	2500
SHOTGUN, DOUBLE BARREL, SIDE-BY-SIDE			
Bolero, Various Gauges, Single Trigger, Checkered Stock, *Modern*	300	325	350

	Fair	V. Good	Excellent
Matador, Various Gauges, Single Selective Trigger, Checkered Stock, Selective Ejector, *Modern*	$275	$325	$375
Matador II, Various Gauges, Single Selective Trigger, Checkered Stock, Selective Ejector, Vent Rib, *Modern*	275	350	425
Model 1, Various Gauges, Automatic Ejectors, Sidelock, Fancy Checkering, Engraved, Lightweight, *Modern*	1750	2250	2750
Model 117, 12 Gauge, Sidelock, Single Selective Trigger, Engraved, Checkered Stock, *Modern*	575	650	725
Model 2, Various Gauges, Automatic Ejector, Sidelock, Engraved, Checkered Stock, Double Trigger, *Modern*	650	950	1250
Model 53E, 12 and 20 Gauges, Sidelock, Single Selective Trigger, Fancy Checkering, Fancy Engraving, *Modern*	1050	1500	1950
Model 56, 12 and 20 Gauges, Sidelock, Raised Matted Rib, Fancy Checkering, Fancy Engraving, *Modern*	2000	2500	3000
Model 76, 12 and 20 Gauges, Automatic Ejectors, Single Selective Trigger, Engraved, Checkered Stock, *Modern*	185	375	650
Model 76, .410 Gauge, Double Triggers, Engraved, Checkered Stock, *Modern*	200	375	550
Model 400, Various Gauges, Single Trigger, Checkered Stock, *Modern*	$165	$325	$575
Model 400E, Various Gauges, Single Selective Trigger, Checkered Stock, Selective Ejector, *Modern*	300	375	450
Model XXV/SL, 12 Ga., Sidelock, Automatic Ejector, Engraved Checkered Stock, *Modern*	900	1250	1600

AZANZA Y ARRIZABALAGA

Eibar, Spain, c. 1916.

HANDGUN, SEMI-AUTOMATIC

	Fair	V. Good	Excellent
M1916, .32 ACP, Clip Fed, Long Grip, *Curio*	50	100	150

AZUL

Eulegio Aristegui, Eibar, Spain, c. 1930.

HANDGUN, SEMI-AUTOMATIC

	Fair	V. Good	Excellent
Azul, .25 ACP, Clip Fed, Hammerless, *Curio*	35	75	125
Azul, .32 ACP, Clip Fed, Hammer, *Curio*	50	100	150
Azul, .32 ACP, Clip Fed, Hammerless, *Curio*	35	75	125
Azul, 7.63mm Mauser, Copy of Broomhandle Mauser, *Curio*	275	550	950

B

BABCOCK
c. 1880.

HANDGUN, REVOLVER

	Fair	V. Good	Excellent
.32 Short R.F., 5 Shot, Spur Trigger, Solid Frame, Single Action, *Antique*	$35	$75	$150

BABY BULLDOG

HANDGUN, REVOLVER

	Fair	V. Good	Excellent
.22 L.R.R.F., Double Action, Hammerless, Folding Trigger, *Modern*	35	75	150
.32 Short R.F., Double Action, Hammerless, Folding Trigger, *Modern*	35	75	125

BABY RUSSIAN
Made by American Arms Co., c. 1890.

HANDGUN, REVOLVER

	Fair	V. Good	Excellent
.38 S & W, 5 Shot, Single Action, Spur Trigger, Top Break, *Curio*	65	125	225

BACKHOUSE, RICHARD
Easton, Pa. 1774-1781. See Kentucky Rifles.

BACKUP
See TDE and AMT.

BACON ARMS CO.
Norwich, Conn. 1858–1891. Also known as Bacon & Co. and Bacon Mfg. Co. The role of James Bacon in the development of Manhattan Fire Arms Co. is part of the reason that his firearms are increasingly in demand. Civil War identification and association with the Old West will increasingly impact Bacon values. It is possible to purchase these arms at a reasonable cost now, but as Colts continue to head out-of-sight, the Bacon, in its revolver configuration, is a Colt look-alike that has its own genuine and worthwhile appeal. Also made handguns marked with trade names as follows, q.v.: Big Bonanza, Bonanza, Conqueror, Daisy, Express, Fitch & Waldo, Gem, Governor, C.W. Hopkins, Little Giant.

HANDGUN, PERCUSSION

	Fair	V. Good	Excellent
.34, Boot Gun, Underhammer, Half-Octagon Barrel, *Antique*	$100	$200	$350
6 Shot, Fluted Barrel, Pepperbox, Underhammer, Pocket Pistol, *Antique*	400	625	850

HANDGUN, REVOLVER

	Fair	V. Good	Excellent
.22 Short R.F., 7 Shot, Spur Trigger, Solid Frame, Single Action, *Antique*	75	150	250
.32 Short R.F, 6 Shot, Solid Frame, Single Action with Trigger Guard, *Antique*	75	150	300
.32 Short R.F., 5 Shot, Spur Trigger, Solid Frame, Single Action, *Antique*	75	150	250
.32 Short R.F., 6 Shot, Solid Frame, Spur Trigger, Single Action, *Antique*	85	175	300
"Navy," .38 Long R.F., 6 Shot, $7^1/_2$" Barrel, Solid Frame, Spur Trigger, Single Action, *Antique*	100	200	425

HANDGUN, SINGLESHOT

	Fair	V. Good	Excellent
Derringer, .32 R.F., Spur Trigger, Side-Swing Barrel, *Antique*	85	175	350
SS Percussion, .31 Cal., Ring Trigger, *Antique*	85	175	275

BAIKAL
Made in U.S.S.R., imported by Commercial Trading Imports.

SHOTGUN, DOUBLE BARREL, OVER-UNDER

	Fair	V. Good	Excellent
IJ-27E1C, 12 or 20 Gauge, Boxlock, Engraved, Checkered Stock, Single Selective Trigger, Selective Ejectors, Vent Rib, *Modern*	115	225	375
IJ-27E1C Silver, 12 or 20 Gauge, Boxlock, Engraved, Checkered Stock, Single Selective Trigger, Selective Ejectors, Vent Rib, *Modern*	100	200	300
IJ-27E1C Super, 12 or 20 Gauge, Boxlock, Engraved, Checkered Stock, Single Selective Trigger, Selective Ejectors, Vent Rib, *Modern*	175	350	550
MC-109, 12 Gauge, Sidelock, Engraved, Checkered Stock, Single Selective Trigger, Selective Ejectors, Vent Rib, *Modern*	2000	2500	3000

	Fair	V. Good	Excellent
MC-5-105, 20 Gauge, Boxlock, Engraved, Checkered Stock, Double Triggers, Solid Rib, Cased, *Modern*	$800	$875	$950
MC-6-105, 12 Gauge, Boxlock, Engraved, Checkered Stock, Double Triggers, Solid Rib, Cased, *Modern*	475	950	1500
MC-7-105, 12 or 20 Gauge, Boxlock, Engraved, Checkered Stock, Single Triggers, Selective Ejectors, Solid Rib, Cased, *Modern*	1100	1700	2300
MC-8-105, 12 Gauge, Trap or Skeet, Boxlock, Engraved, Checkered Stock, Single Trigger, Solid Rib, Cased, *Modern*	900	1400	1900
TOZ-34E, 12 or 28 Gauge, Boxlock, Engraved, Checkered Stock, Double Triggers, Vent Rib, *Modern*	200	325	450

SHOTGUN, DOUBLE BARREL, SIDE-BY-SIDE

	Fair	V. Good	Excellent
IJ-58MAE, 12 or 20 Gauge, Boxlock, Engraved, Checkered Stock, Double Triggers, *Modern*	50	100	200
MC-110, 12 or 20 Gauge, Boxlock, Engraved, Checkered Stock, Double Triggers, Solid Rib, Cased, *Modern*	1000	1500	2000
MC-111, 12 Gauge, Sidelock, Engraved, Checkered Stock, Single Selective Trigger, Selective Ejectors, Cased, *Modern*	2000	2500	3000

SHOTGUN, SINGLESHOT

	Fair	V. Good	Excellent
IJ-18E, 12 or 20 Gauge, Checkered Stock, *Modern*	25	50	75

BAKER GUN & FORGING CO.

Batavia, N.Y. 1886–1919.

RIFLE, SEMI-AUTOMATIC

	Fair	V. Good	Excellent
Batavia, .22 Short, Clip Fed, *Curio*	135	275	450

SHOTGUN, DOUBLE BARREL, SIDE-BY-SIDE

Single Trigger, Add $90.00-165.00
Deduct 50% for Damascus Barrels
Automatic Ejectors, Add $110.00-225.00

	Fair	V. Good	Excellent
Batavia Leader, Various Gauges, Sidelock, Double Trigger, Checkered Stock, *Curio*	350	425	500
Batavia Special, Various Gauges, Sidelock, Double Trigger, Checkered Stock, Automatic Ejectors, *Curio*	200	300	400
Black Beauty, Various Gauges, Sidelock, Double Trigger, Checkered Stock, *Curio*	225	450	675
Black Beauty Special, Various Gauges, Sidelock, Double Trigger, Checkered Stock, Automatic Ejectors, *Curio*	650	750	850
Deluxe ($1,000 Grade), Various Gauges, Sidelock, Fancy Wood, Fancy Engraving, Fancy Checkering, Automatic Ejector, *Curio*	$2000	$3500	$5000
Deluxe ($300 Grade), Various Gauges, Sidelock, Fancy Wood, Fancy Engraving, Fancy Checkering, Automatic Ejectors, *Curio*	2650	2950	3250
Expert, Various Gauges, Sidelock, Fancy Wood, Fancy Engraving, Fancy Checkering, Automatic Ejectors, *Curio*	1600	1850	2100
Grade A, Various Gauges, Sidelock, Hammerless, Engraved, Damascus Barrel, *Curio*	100	200	350
Grade B, Various Gauges, Sidelock, Hammerless, Engraved, Damascus Barrels, *Curio*	85	175	310
Grade C Batavia, Various Gauges, Boxlock, Hammerless, Engraved, Damascus Barrels, *Curio*	100	175	250
Grade H Deluxe, Various Gauges, Sidelock, Fancy Engraving, *Curio*	2050	2850	3650
Grade L Pigeon, Various Gauges, Sidelock, Fancy Engraving, *Curio*	950	1550	2150
Grade N Krupp Trap, 12 Ga., Sidelock, Engraved, *Curio*	500	950	1400
Grade R, Various Gauges, Sidelock, Light Engraving, *Curio*	500	1000	1500
Grade S, Various Gauges, Sidelock, Light Engraving, *Curio*	700	850	1000
Model 1896, 10 and 12 Gauges, Hammers, *Curio*	115	225	400
Model 1897, Various Gauges, Hammers, *Curio*	115	225	400
New Baker Model, 10 and 12 Gauges, Hammers, *Curio*	130	260	400
Paragon, Various Gauges, Sidelock, Double Trigger, Engraved, Fancy Checkering, *Curio*	1250	1350	1450
Paragon, Various Gauges, Sidelock, Double Trigger, Engraved, Fancy Checkering, Automatic Ejectors, *Curio*	1375	1475	1575
Paragon Special, *Curio*	625	1250	1950

SHOTGUN, SINGLESHOT

	Fair	V. Good	Excellent
Elite, 12 Ga., Vent Rib, Fancy Engraving, *Curio*	385	775	1250
Sterling, 12 Ga., Vent Rib, Light Engraving, *Curio*	325	550	775
Superba 12 Ga., Trap Grade, Fancy Wood, Fancy Engraving, Fancy Checkering, Automatic Ejectors, *Antique*	1125	1950	2775

BAKER GUN CO.

Made in Belgium for H & D Folsom Arms Co.

SHOTGUN, DOUBLE BARREL, SIDE-BY-SIDE

	Fair	V. Good	Excellent
Various Gauges, Hammerless, Damascus Barrel, *Antique*	$50	$100	$175
Various Gauges, Hammerless, Steel Barrel, *Antique*	65	125	200
Various Gauges, Outside Hammers, Damascus Barrel, *Antique*	35	75	175
Various Gauges, Outside Hammers, Steel Barrel, *Antique*	50	100	200

SHOTGUN, SINGLESHOT

	Fair	V. Good	Excellent
Various Gauges, Hammer, Steel Barrel, *Antique*	25	50	75

BAKER, EZEKIEL

London, England 1784–1825.

HANDGUN, PERCUSSION

	Fair	V. Good	Excellent
.58, Holster Pistol, Round Barrel, Light Ornamentation, *Antique*	350	550	750

BAKER, JOHN

Providence, Pa. 1768–1775. See Kentucky Rifles.

BAKER, W. H. & CO.

Marathon, N.Y. 1870, Syracuse, N.Y. 1878–1886.

COMBINATION WEAPON, DRILLING

	Fair	V. Good	Excellent
Hammer Drilling, Various Gauges, Damascus Barrels. Front Trigger Break, *Antique*	225	450	725

RIFLE, PERCUSSION

	Fair	V. Good	Excellent
.60, Brass Furniture, Scope Mounted, Target, Octagon Barrel, *Antique*	1250	2000	2750

SHOTGUN, DOUBLE BARREL, SIDE-BY-SIDE

	Fair	V. Good	Excellent
Hammer Double, 10 and 12 Gauges, Damascus Barrels, Front Trigger Break, *Antique*	175	275	375

BALL & WILLIAMS

Worcester, Mass. 1861–1866.

RIFLE, SINGLESHOT

	Fair	V. Good	Excellent
Ballard, .44 Long R.F., Milliary, Carbine, Falling Block, *Antique*	300	600	1200
Ballard, .46 Long R.F., Kentucky Rifle, Falling Block, *Antique*	625	750	875
Ballard, Various Rimfires, Falling Block, Sporting Rifle, *Antique*	325	425	525
Ballard, Various Rimfires, Military, Falling Block, *Antique*	335	675	1200
Merwin & Bray, .54 Ballard R.F., Military, Carbine, Falling Block, *Antique*	315	625	1200
Merwin & Bray, Various Rimfires, Falling Block, Sporting Rifle, *Antique*	$400	$525	$650

BALLARD & CO.

Worcester, Mass 1861–1971. Also see U.S. Military.

RIFLE, SINGLESHOT

	Fair	V. Good	Excellent
#2 (Marlin), Various Calibers, Falling Block, Sporting Rifle, *Antique*	800	1000	1200
#3 Gallery (Marlin), Various Calibers, Falling Block, Target Rifle, *Antique*	50	100	1200
#3 Gallery (Marlin), Various Rimfires, Falling Block, Target Rifle, *Antique*	800	1000	1200
#3-F Gallery (Marlin), .22 Long R.F., Falling Block, Target Rifle, Fancy Wood, *Antique*	800	1000	1200
#4 Perfection (Marlin), Various Calibers, Falling Block, Target Rifle, Target Sights, Set Triggers, Octagon Barrel, *Antique*	1000	1500	2000

BALLARD RIFLE

Made by Ball & Williams 1861–1866, Merrimack Arms & Mfg. Co. 1866–1869, Brown Mfg. Co. 1869–1873, J. M. Marlin from 1875. Although definitely an "also-ran" in the pantheon of 19th-century American long-gun makers, the Ballard stands as one of the most important and successful of U.S. singleshots, and was a well-made and designed competitior in that market. Civil War, Wild West, and target match identifications will contribute to the steady rise in and demand by collectors in these arms. James J. Grant's series on singleshot rifles are vital to the collector who wishes to pursue the Ballards, which fit into this highly popular area of the fine and historic in firearms.

RIFLE, SINGLESHOT

	Fair	V. Good	Excellent
#1½ Hunter (Marlin), .40-65 Ballard Everlasting, Falling Block, Sporting Rifle, Open Rear Sight, *Antique*	300	600	1500
#1 Hunter (Marlin), .44 Long R F/C F, Falling Block, Sporting Rifle, Recoil Pad, *Antique*	800	1000	1200
#2 (Marlin), .44-40 WCF, Falling Block, Sporting Rifle, Open Rear Sight, *Antique*	800	1000	1200
#2 (Marlin), Various Calibers, Falling Block, Sporting Rifle, Recoil Pad, Early Model, *Antique*	800	1000	1200
#3½ (Marlin), .40-65 Ballard Everlasting, Falling Block, Target Rifle, Target Sights, Octagon Barrel, *Antique*	500	1000	2000
#3 Gallery (Marlin), .22 Short R.F., Falling Block, Target Rifle, Early Model, *Antique*	800	1000	1200
#4½ (Marlin), .40-65 Ballard Everlasting, Falling Block, Mid-Range Target Rifle, Checkered Stock, *Antique*	1000	1500	2000

	Fair	V. Good	Excellent
#4 1/2 (Marlin), .45-70 Government, Falling Block, Sporting Rifle, *Antique*	$1000	$1500	$2000
#4 1/2 (Marlin), Various Calibers, Falling Block, Mid-Range Target Rifle, Target Sights, Fancy Wood, *Antique*	1250	2500	4000
#4 1/2 (Marlin), Various Calibers, Falling Block, Sporting Rifle, *Antique*	800	1000	1200
#4 Perfection (Marlin), Various Calibers, Falling Block, Target Rifle, Target Sights, Set Trigger, Early Model, *Antique*	800	1000	1200
#5 Pacific (Marlin), .45-70 Government, Falling Block, Target Rifle, Open Rear Sight, Set Trigger, Octagon Barrel, *Antique*	1500	2000	2500
#5 Pacific (Marlin), Various Calibers, Falling Block, Target Rifle, Open Rear Sight, Set Trigger, Octagon Barrel, *Antique*	1250	1750	2250
#6 1/2 (Marlin), .40-65 Ballard Everlasting, Falling Block, Off-Hand Target Rifle, Target Sights, Set Trigger, *Antique*	1000	2700	3500
#6 1/2 (Marlin), Various Calibers, Falling Block, Mid-Range Target Rifle, *Antique*	1000	2700	3500
#6 Pacific (Marlin), Various Calibers, Falling Block, Schutzen Rifle, Target Sights, Fancy Wood, Set Triggers, *Antique*	2000	3500	5000
#7 A (Marlin), .44-100 Ballard Everlasting, Falling Block, Long Range Target Rifle, Target Sights, Set Trigger, *Antique*	1100	2200	4500
#7 A-1 (Marlin), .44-100 Ballard Everlasting, Falling Block, Long Range Target Rifle, Target Sights, Set Trigger, Fancy Wood, *Antique*	1000	2000	5000
#7 A-1 (Marlin), .44-75 Ballard Everlasting, Falling Block, Creedmore Long Range, Target Sights, Fancy Wood, Set Trigger, *Antique*	1250	2500	5000
#7 A-1 Extra Deluxe, .44-100 Ballard Everlasting, Falling Block, Long Range Target Rifle, Target Sights, Set Trigger, Fancy Wood, *Antique*	1250	2500	6000
#8 (Marlin), .44-75 Ballard Everlasting, Falling Block, Creedmore Long Range, Target Sights, Pistol-Grip Stock, Set Trigger, *Antique*	1000	2000	2500
#9 (Marlin), .44-75 Ballard Everlasting, Falling Block, Creedmore Long Range, Target Sights, Set Trigger, *Antique*	1000	2000	2500
(Ball & Williams), .54 Ballard R.F., Military, Carbine, Falling Block, *Antique*	335	675	1200
(Ball & Williams), .44 Long R.F., Military, Carbine, Falling Block, *Antique*	335	675	1200

Three variations of Ballard single-shot sporting rifles. Note barrel bands of center rifle, indicating military styling. Top, *rifle with Ball & Williams markings.* Center, *an early military model with Brown Mfg. Co. markings.* Bottom, *a Hunters rifle.*

	Fair	V. Good	Excellent
(Ball & Williams), .46 Long R.F., Kentucky Rifle, Falling Block, *Antique*	$675	$850	$1025
(Ball & Williams), Various Rimfires, Falling Block, Sporting Rifle, *Antique*	275	475	675
(Ball & Williams), Various Rimfires, Military, Falling Block, *Antique*	375	750	1200
1 1/2 Hunter (Marlin), .45-70 Government, Falling Block, Sporting Rifle, Open Rear Sight, Set Trigger, *Antique*	350	700	1750
1 3/4 Far West (Marlin), .40-65 Ballard Everlasting, Falling Block, Sporting Rifle, Open Rear Sight, Set Trigger, *Antique*	315	625	1750
1 3/4 Far West (Marlin), .45-70 Government, Falling Block, Sporting Rifle, Open Rear Sight, Set Trigger, *Antique*	335	675	1750
5 1/2 Montana (Marlin), .45-100 Sharps, Falling Block, Sporting Rifle, Octagon Barrel, *Antique*	750	1500	4500
Brown Mfg. Co., .44 Long R.F., Falling Block, Mid-Range Target Rifle, *Antique*	550	875	1200
Hunter, .44 Long R F/C F, Falling Block, Sporting Rifle, Recoil Pad, *Antique*	350	675	1000
Merrimack Arms, .44 Long R.F., Falling Block, Carbine, *Antique*	335	675	1200
Merrimack Arms, .46 Long R.F., Falling Block, Military, *Antique*	385	775	1200
Merrimack Arms, .56-52 Spencer R.F., Falling Block, Military, *Antique*	350	675	1000
Merrimack Arms, Various Rimfires, Falling Block, Sporting Rifle, *Antique*	350	675	1000

	Fair	V. Good	Excellent
Merwin & Bray, Various Rimfires, Falling Block, Sporting Rifle, *Antique*	$285	$575	$1000

BANG-UP
Made by Hopkins & Allen, c. 1880.

HANDGUN, REVOLVER

	Fair	V. Good	Excellent
.22 Short R.F., 7 Shot, Spur Trigger, Solid Frame, Single Action, *Antique*	50	100	150

BARKER, F.A.
Fayetteville, N.C. 1860–1864. See Confederate Military.

BARKER, T.
Made by Crescent; also made in Belgium. See Crescent Fire Arms Co., Shotgun, Double Barrel, Side-By-Side; Shotgun, Singleshot.

BARLOW, J.
Moscow, Ind. 1836–1840. See Kentucky Rifles.

BARNETT & SON
London, England 1750–1832.

RIFLE, FLINTLOCK

	Fair	V. Good	Excellent
.75, 3rd. Model Brown Bess, Musket, Military, *Antique*	650	1250	1850

BARNETT, J. & SONS
London, England 1835–1875.

RIFLE, PERCUSSION

	Fair	V. Good	Excellent
.577, C.W. Enfield, Rifled, Musket, Military, *Antique*	250	500	750

BARRETT, J.
Wythesville, Va. 1857–1865. See Confederate Military.

BAUER FIREARMS (FRASER ARMS CO.)
Fraser, Mich.

HANDGUN, SEMI-AUTOMATIC

	Fair	V. Good	Excellent
25-Bicentennial, .25 ACP, Clip Fed, Pocket Pistol, Stainless Steel, Hammerless, Engraved, *Modern*	75	150	225
25-SS, .25 ACP, Clip Fed, Pocket Pistol, Stainless Steel, Hammerless, *Modern*	65	125	200

COMBINATION WEAPON, OVER-UNDER

	Fair	V. Good	Excellent
Rabbit, .22/.410, Metal Frame, Survival Gun, *Modern*	75	100	125

BAUER, GEORGE
Lancaster, Pa. 1770–1781. See Kentucky Rifles.

BAY STATE ARMS CO.
Uxbridge & Worcester, Mass. 1873–1874.

RIFLE, SINGLESHOT

	Fair	V. Good	Excellent
.32 Long R.F., Dropping Block, *Antique*	$75	$125	$175
Various Calibers, Target Rifle, *Antique*	325	600	875

SHOTGUN, SINGLESHOT

	Fair	V. Good	Excellent
Davenport Patent, 12 Ga., *Antique*	125	200	275

BAYARD
Belgium. Made by Anciens Etablissments Pieper, c. 1900. Also see Bergmann and Danish Military.

HANDGUN, REVOLVER

	Fair	V. Good	Excellent
S & W Style, .32 S&W Long, Double Action, *Curio*	25	50	100
S & W Style, .38 S&W, Double Action, *Curio*	25	50	100

HANDGUN, SEMI-AUTOMATIC

	Fair	V. Good	Excellent
Bergmann/Bayard 1910, 9mm Bayard, Clip Fed, Blue, Commercial, *Curio*	500	1000	1500
Bergmann/Bayard 1910, 9mm Bayard, Clip Fed, Blue, Commercial, with Holster/Stock, *Curio*	1250	1500	1750
Model 1908 (1910) Pocket, .32 ACP, Blue, Clip Fed, *Curio*	200	275	350
Model 1908 (1910) Pocket, .32 ACP, Blue, Clip Fed, German Military, *Curio*	225	300	375

Bayard Model 1908 (1910) .32 ACP

	Fair	V. Good	Excellent
Model 1908 (1910) Pocket, .32 ACP, Nickel, Clip Fed, *Curio*	225	300	375
Model 1908 (1911) Pocket, .380 ACP, Blue, Clip Fed, *Curio*	225	300	375
Model 1908 (1911) Pocket, .380 ACP, Nickel, Clip Fed, *Curio*	250	325	400

	Fair	V. Good	Excellent
Model 1908 (1912) Pocket, .25 ACP, Blue, Clip Fed, *Curio*	$250	$300	$350
Model 1908 (1912) Pocket, .25 ACP, Nickel, Clip Fed, *Curio*	250	325	400
Model 1923 Pocket, Early, .25 ACP, Blue, Clip Fed, With Magazine Safety, *Curio*	125	200	275
Model 1923 Pocket, Early, .32 ACP, Blue, Clip Fed, With Magazine Safety, *Curio*	175	225	275
Model 1923 Pocket, Early, .380 ACP, Blue, Clip Fed, With Magazine Safety, *Curio*	300	375	450
Model 1923 Pocket, Standard, .25 ACP, Blue, Clip Fed, No Magazine Safety, *Curio*	150	200	250
Model 1923 Pocket, Standard, .32 ACP, Blue, Clip Fed, No Magazine Safety, *Curio*	200	250	300
Model 1923 Pocket, Standard, .380 ACP, Blue, Clip Fed, No Magazine Safety, *Curio*	200	275	350
Model 1930 Pocket, .25 ACP, Blue, Clip Fed, *Curio*	125	200	275

Bayard Model 1930

	Fair	V. Good	Excellent
Model 1930 Pocket, .32 ACP, Blue, Clip Fed, *Curio*	125	200	275
Model 1930 Pocket, .380 ACP, Blue, Clip Fed, *Curio*	225	300	375

RIFLE, SINGLESHOT

	Fair	V. Good	Excellent
Boy's Rifle, .22 L.R.R.F., Plain, Takedown, *Curio*	25	50	75
Half-Auto Carbine, .22 Short, Checkered Stock, *Curio*	25	50	75
Half-Auto Carbine, .22 Short, Plain, *Curio*	25	50	75

SHOTGUN, DOUBLE BARREL, SIDE-BY-SIDE

	Fair	V. Good	Excellent
Hammer, 12 Gauge, Double Triggers, Fancy Engraving, Boxlock, Steel Barrels, *Curio*	65	125	225
Hammer, 12 Gauge, Double Triggers, Light Engraving, Boxlock, Damascus Barrels, *Curio*	35	75	150
Hammer, 12 Gauge, Double Triggers, Light Engraving, Boxlock, Steel Barrels, *Curio*	$35	$75	$150
Hammerless, 12 Gauge, Double Triggers, Light Engraving, Boxlock, Steel Barrels, *Curio*	65	125	200

BECK, GIDEON

Lancaster, Pa. 1780–1788. See Kentucky Rifles and Pistols.

BECK, ISAAC

Miffinberg, Pa. 1830–1840.

RIFLE, PERCUSSION

	Fair	V. Good	Excellent
.47, Octagon Barrel, Brass Furniture, *Antique*	900	1200	1500

BECK, JOHN

Lancaster, Pa. 1772–1777. See Kentucky Rifles and Pistols.

BEEMAN PRECISION FIREARMS

San Raphael, Calif., Importers.

HANDGUN, PERCUSSION

	Fair	V. Good	Excellent
Hege-Siber, English, .33, Checkered Stock, Light Engraving, Cased, Reproduction, *Antique*	250	500	750
Hege-Siber, French, .33, Checkered Stock, Engraved, Gold Inlays, Cased, Reproduction, *Antique*	375	750	1250
PB Aristocrat, .36 or .44, Single Set Trigger, Fluted Stock, Reproduction, *Antique*	100	175	250

HANDGUN, SEMI-AUTOMATIC

	Fair	V. Good	Excellent
Agner M80, .22 L.R.R.F., Clip Fed, Stainless Steel, Adjustable Target Grips, Adjustable Trigger, *Modern*	850	925	1000

Beeman Agner M80

	Fair	V. Good	Excellent
FAS Model 601, .22 Short R.F., Clip Fed, Target Grip, Rapid Fire, Target Pistol, *Modern*	$325	$650	$1000

Beeman FAS Model 601

	Fair	V. Good	Excellent
FAS Model 602, .22 L.R.R.F., Clip Fed, Target Grip, Match Pistol, *Modern*	500	750	1000
FAS Model 603, .32 S&W Wadcutter, Clip Fed, Target Grips, Match Pistol, *Modern*	550	775	1000
Unique Model 69, .22 L.R.R.F., Clip Fed, Adjustable Target Grips, Match Pistol, *Modern*	400	700	1000
Unique Model 823-U, .22 Short R.F., Clip Fed, Adjustable Target Grips, Rapid Fire Match Pistol, *Modern*	400	700	1000

RIFLE, BOLT ACTION

	Fair	V. Good	Excellent
Feinwerkbau 2000 Match, .22 L.R.R.F., Singleshot, Adjustable Trigger, Adjustable Target Stock, *Modern*	650	750	850

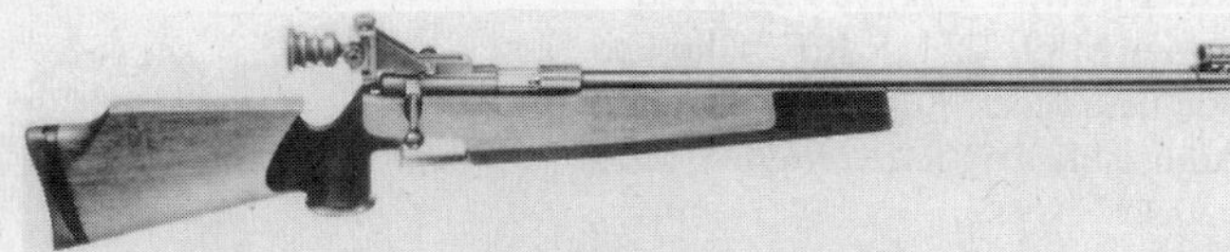

Beeman Feinwerkbau 2000 Match

	Fair	V. Good	Excellent
Feinwerkbau 2000 Mini, .22 L.R.R.F., Singleshot, Adjustable Trigger, Adjustable Target Stock, *Modern*	600	700	800
Feinwerkbau 2000 Running Target, .22 L.R.R.F., Singleshot, Adjustable Trigger, Adjustable Target Stock, *Modern*	650	750	850
Feinwerkbau 2000 Universal, .22 L.R.R.F., Singleshot, Adjustable Trigger, Adjustable Target Stock, *Modern*	650	750	850
Feinwerkbau Free Rifle, .22 L.R.R.F., Singleshot, Adjustable Electric Trigger, Adjustable Target Stock, Counterweights, Hook Buttplate, *Modern*	$750	$1000	$1250
Krico Model 302, .22 L.R.R.F., Clip Fed, Checkered Stock, Open Sights, *Modern*	350	400	450
Krico Model 304, .22 L.R.R.F., Clip Fed, Checkered Stock, Mannlicher Stock, Set Triggers, Open Sights, *Modern*	400	450	500
Krico Model 340, .22 L.R.R.F., Metallic Silhouette Match Rifle, Clip Fed, Checkered Stock, Target Stock, *Modern*	550	625	700
Krico Model 340, .22 L.R.R.F., Mini-Sniper Match Rifle, Clip Fed, Checkered Stock, Target Stock, *Modern*	575	650	725
Krico Model 400, .22 Hornet, Clip Fed, Checkered Stock, Open Sights, *Modern*	625	650	675
Krico Model 420, .22 Hornet, Clip Fed, Checkered Stock, Set Triggers, Mannlicher Stock, Open Sights, Sling Swivels, *Modern*	575	650	725
Krico Model 600, Various Calibers, Clip Fed, Checkered Stock, Open Sights, Sling Swivels, Recoil Pads, *Modern*	700	800	900
Krico Model 620, Various Calibers, Clip Fed, Checkered Stock, Set Triggers, Mannlicher Stock, Open Sights, Sling Swivels, *Modern*	675	775	875
Krico Model 640, Various Calibers, Deluxe Varmint Rifle, Clip Fed, Checkered Stock, Target Stock, *Modern*	$550	$625	$700
Krico Model 650, Various Calibers, Sniper/Match Rifle, Clip Fed, Checkered Stock, Target Stock, *Modern*	700	850	1000

Beeman Krico Model 650

	Fair	V. Good	Excellent
Krico Model 700, Various Calibers, Clip Fed, Checkered Stock, Open Sights, Sling Swivels, Recoil Pad, *Modern*	700	850	1000
Krico Model 720, Various Calibers, Clip Fed, Checkered Stock, Set Triggers, Mannlicher Stock, Open Sights, Sling Swivels, *Modern*	700	800	900

	Fair	V. Good	Excellent
Weihrauch HW60, .22 L.R.R.F., Singleshot Target Rifle, Target Sights, Target Stock, Heavy Barrel, *Modern*	$500	$525	$550

SHOTGUN, DOUBLE BARREL, OVER-UNDER

	Fair	V. Good	Excellent
Fabarm Gamma, 12 Gauge, Field Model, Single Selective Trigger, Checkered Stock, Vent Rib, *Modern*	625	700	775

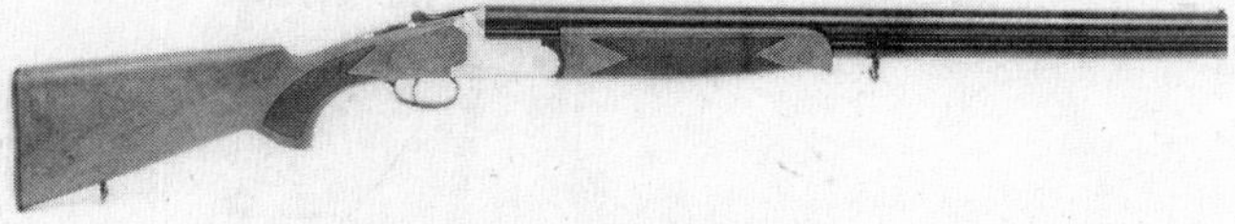

Beeman Fabarm Gamma

	Fair	V. Good	Excellent
Fabarm Gamma, 12 Gauge, Skeet Model, Single Selective Trigger, Checkered Stock, Vent Rib, *Modern*	750	775	800
Fabarm Gamma, 12 Gauge, Trap/Skeet Combo, 2 Barrels, Single Selective Trigger, Checkered Stock, Vent Rib, *Modern*	725	800	875

BEERSTECHER, FREDERICK

Lewisburg, Pa. 1849–1860.

HANDGUN, PERCUSSION

	Fair	V. Good	Excellent
.40, Double Shot, Superimposed Loading, Derringer Style, *Antique*	3250	4000	4750

BEHOLLA

Made by Becker & Hollander, Suhl, Germany c. 1910. Also made under this patent were the Stenda, Leonhardt, and Menta.

HANDGUN, SEMI-AUTOMATIC

	Fair	V. Good	Excellent
.32 ACP, Clip Fed, Commercial, Blue, Hard Rubber Grips, *Curio*	200	250	300
.32 ACP, Clip Fed, Commercial, Blue, Wood Grips, *Curio*	150	200	250
.32 ACP, Clip Fed, Military, Blue, Hard Rubber Grips, *Curio*	150	200	250
.32 ACP, Clip Fed, Military, Blue, Wood Grips, *Curio*	150	200	250

BELGIAN MILITARY

Also see Browning, Fabrique Nationale.

RIFLE, BOLT ACTION

	Fair	V. Good	Excellent
M 1889 Mauser, Carbine, Military, *Curio*	300	325	350
M 1889 Mauser, Military, *Curio*	275	300	325
M 1924, Various Calibers, Military, *Curio*	200	225	250
M 1930, Various Calibers, Military, *Curio*	$200	$225	$250
M 1934/30, Various Calibers, Military, *Curio*	175	200	225
M 1935 Mauser, Military, *Curio*	250	275	300
M 1936 Mauser, Military, *Curio*	125	150	175
M 1950, .30-06 Springfield, Military, *Curio*	225	250	275

RIFLE, SEMI-AUTOMATIC

	Fair	V. Good	Excellent
M 1949, .30-06 Springfield, Military, *Curio*	150	300	450
M 1949, Various Calibers, Military, *Curio*	125	250	375

BELL, JOHN

Carlisle, Pa., c. 1800. See Kentucky Rifles and Pistols.

BELLMORE GUN CO.

Made by Crescent, c. 1900. See Crescent Fire Arms Co., Shotgun, Double Barrel, Side-By-Side; Shotgun, Singleshot.

BENELLI

Made in Italy, imported by H & K Inc. and Sile.

HANDGUN, SEMI-AUTOMATIC

	Fair	V. Good	Excellent
B 76, 9mm Luger, Clip Fed, Blue, *Modern*	$300	$375	$450

RIFLE, SEMI-AUTOMATIC

	Fair	V. Good	Excellent
Model 940, .30-06 Springfield, Clip Fed, Open Sights, Recoil Pad, Sling Swivels, *Modern*	325	400	475

SHOTGUN, SEMI-AUTOMATIC

	Fair	V. Good	Excellent
Model 123V Deluxe, 12 Gauge, Engraved Model, Checkered Stock, Vent Rib, *Modern*	275	350	425
Model 123V, 12 Gauge, Standard Model, Checkered Stock, Vent Rib, *Modern*	250	325	400
Model SL 121MI, 12 Gauge, Police, Open Sights, Checkered Stock, Recoil Pad, *Modern*	225	300	375
Model SL 121V, 12 Gauge, Slug Gun, Open Sights, Checkered Stock, Recoil Pad, *Modern*	225	300	375
Model SL 201, 20 Gauge, Checkered Stock, Plain Barrel, *Modern*	200	275	350
Special Skeet, 12 Gauge, White Receiver, Checkered Stock, Vent Rib, *Modern*	325	400	475
Special Trap, 12 Gauge, White Receiver, Checkered Stock, Vent Rib, *Modern*	300	375	450

BENFER, AMOS

Beaverstown, Pa. c. 1810. See Kentucky Rifles and Pistols.

BERETTA

Pietro Beretta; Gardone V.T., Italy. Company history extends back to 1526. Beretta U.S.A. Corp. formed in 1977. Truly the Gucci, Armani or Ferrari of firearms, the company has remained in the hands of the same family for 13 generations, and is currently under the leadership of Ugo Gussalli Beretta and his sons Piero and Franco. Beretta is known to have been an active and successful business as early as 1526, as documented by a transaction between the firm and the City of Venice for the production of gun barrels. Later the Berettas developed state-of-the-art production and marketing skills, particularly in the 19th and 20th centuries, and today it boasts landmark stores in New York City and Dallas, Texas, and a factory in the U.S., in addition to its truly impressive world headquarters in Gardone, Val Trompia, Italy. The company's museum, available for visits by appointment, is considered by many to be the finest of its type of any contemporary gunmaker. Despite the size of the company, Beretta's master gunmakers are also capable of producing some of the world's most beautiful, accurate, and mechanically brilliant firearms. The fact that it is a Beretta handgun, the XM9, which is the standard sidearm of the U.S. government armed forces speaks volumes for the firm's designing, manufacturing, and marketing abilities.

HANDGUN, SEMI-AUTOMATIC

	Fair	*V. Good*	*Excellent*
1910, .25 ACP, Clip Fed, *Curio*	$200	$250	$300
1915, .32 ACP, Clip Fed, Military, *Curio*	250	300	350
1915, 9mm Glisenti, Clip Fed, Military, *Curio*	325	375	425
1915/1919, .32 ACP, Clip Fed, Military, *Curio*	200	250	300
1919 V P, .25 ACP, Clip Fed, *Curio*	200	250	300
Cougar, .380 ACP, Clip Fed, *Modern*	125	175	225
Jaguar, .22 L.R.R.F., Clip Fed, *Modern*	100	150	200
Jetfire, .25 ACP, Clip Fed, Blue, *Modern*	50	100	150
Jetfire, .25 ACP, Clip Fed, Nickel, *Modern*	50	100	150
Minx, .22 Short, Clip Fed, Blue, *Modern*	50	100	150
Minx, .22 Short, Clip Fed, Nickel, *Modern*	50	100	150
Model 100, .32 ACP, Clip Fed, *Modern*	150	175	200
Model 101, .22 L.R.R.F., Clip Fed, Adjustable Sights, *Modern*	150	175	200
Model 1923, 9mm Luger, Clip Fed, Military, *Curio*	325	375	425
Model 1923, 9mm Luger, Clip Fed, Military, with Detachable Shoulder Stock, *Curio*	500	575	650
Model 1931 Navy, .32 ACP, Clip Fed, Military, *Curio*	250	300	350

	Fair	*V. Good*	*Excellent*
Model 1934, .380 ACP, Clip Fed, Commercial, *Curio*	$275	$325	$375
Model 1934, .380 ACP, Clip Fed, Military, *Curio*	200	250	300
Model 1935, .32 ACP, Clip Fed, Commercial, *Curio*	225	275	325

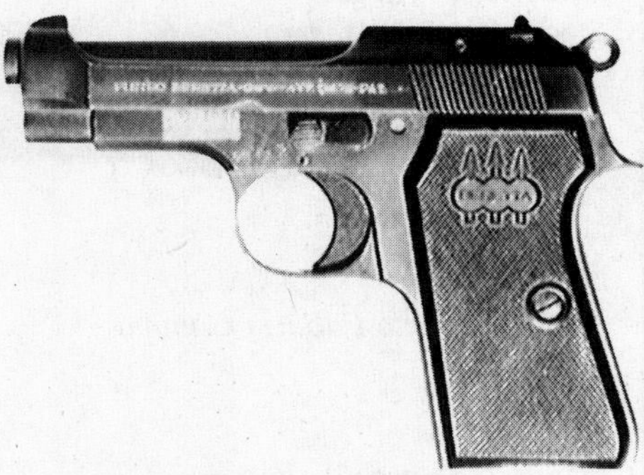

Beretta Model 1935.32 ACP

	Fair	*V. Good*	*Excellent*
Model 1935, .32 ACP, Clip Fed, Military, *Curio*	175	225	275
Model 318, .25 ACP, Clip Fed, *Modern*	225	250	275
Model 418, .25 ACP, Clip Fed, *Modern*	175	200	225
Model 420, .25 ACP, Clip Fed, Chrome, Light Engraving, *Modern*	200	250	300
Model 421, .25 ACP, Clip Fed, Gold Plated, Fancy Engraving, *Modern*	400	450	500
Model 70S, .380 ACP, Clip Fed, *Modern*	200	225	250
Model 70T, .32 ACP, Clip Fed, Adjustable Sights, *Modern*	175	200	225
Model 76, .22 L.R.R.F., Clip Fed, Adjustable Sights, *Modern*	200	250	300
Model 81, .32 ACP, Clip Fed, Double Action, *Modern*	250	300	350
Model 82, .32 ACP, Clip Fed, Double Action, *Modern*	225	275	325
Model 84, .380 ACP, Clip Fed, Double Action, *Modern*	325	375	425
Model 84 Tercentennial, .380 ACP, Clip Fed, Double Action, Engraved, Cased, *Modern*	500	750	1000
Model 85, .380 ACP, Clip Fed, Double Action, *Modern*	300	350	400
Model 90, .32 ACP, Clip Fed, Double Trigger, *Modern*	175	200	225
Model 92, 9mm Luger, 14 Shot Clip Fed, Double Action, *Modern*	325	375	425
Model 92, 9mm Luger, 16 Shot Clip Fed, Double Action, *Modern*	400	450	500
Model 948, .22 L.R.R.F., Clip Fed, Lightweight, *Modern*	125	150	175
Model 949 Olympic, .22 L.R.R.F., Clip Fed, Target Pistol, *Modern*	450	550	650

	Fair	V. Good	Excellent
Model 949 Olympic, .22 Short R.F., Clip Fed, Target Pistol, *Modern*	$450	$550	$650
Model 950 Minx, .22 Short R.F., Clip Fed, 2" Barrel, *Modern*	50	100	150
Model 950B Minx, .22 Short R.F., Clip Fed, 4" Barrel, *Modern*	50	100	150
Model 951 Brigadier, 9mm Luger, Clip Fed, Commercial, *Modern*	225	275	325
Model 951 Egyptian, 9mm Luger, Clip Fed, Military, *Curio*	125	250	375
Model 951 Israeli, 9mm Luger, Clip Fed, Military, *Curio*	125	250	375
Puma, .32 ACP, Clip Fed, *Modern*	150	175	200

RIFLE, SEMI-AUTOMATIC

	Fair	V. Good	Excellent
Olympia, .22 L.R.R.F., Clip Fed, Tangent Sights, Checkered Stock, *Modern*	100	150	200
Silver Gyrfalcon, .22 L.R.R.F., Checkered Stock, *Modern*	75	150	225
Super Sport, .22 L.R.R.F., Fancy Checkering, Clip Fed, *Modern*	75	150	225

SHOTGUN, DOUBLE BARREL, OVER-UNDER

	Fair	V. Good	Excellent
Golden Snipe Deluxe, 12 and 20 Gauges, Single Selective Trigger, Automatic Ejector, Fancy Engraving, Fancy Checkering, *Modern*	500	625	750
Golden Snipe, 12 and 20 Gauges, Single Selective Trigger, Automatic Ejector, Engraved, Fancy Checkering, *Modern*	525	600	675
Golden Snipe, 12 and 20 Gauges, Single Trigger, Automatic Ejector, Engraved, Fancy Checkering, *Modern*	500	550	600
Model 680, 12 Gauge, Mono Trap Grade, Automatic Ejector, Single Trigger, Checkered Stock, Light Engraving, *Modern*	800	950	1100
Model 680, 12 Gauge, Skeet Grade, Automatic Ejector, Single Selective Trigger, Engraved, Checkered Stock, Light Engraving, *Modern*	800	875	950
Model 680, 12 Gauge, Trap Grade, Automatic Ejector, Single Selective Trigger, Checkered Stock, Light Engraving, *Modern*	700	850	1000
Model 686, 12 Gauge, Field Grade, Automatic Ejector, Single Selective Trigger, Checkered Stock, Light Engraving, *Modern*	700	800	900
Model 687EL, 12 Gauge, Skeet Grade, Automatic Ejector, Single Selective Trigger, Checkered Stock, Fancy Engraving, *Modern*	1500	1750	2000
Model ASEL, 12 Gauge, Single Trigger, Checkered Stock, *Modern*	750	1000	1250
Model BL 1, *Modern*	200	275	350
Model BL 2, 12 Ga., Field Grade, Single Selective Trigger, Checkered Stock, *Modern*	$275	$325	$375
Model BL 3, 12 Ga., Trap Grade, Single Selective Trigger, Checkered Stock, Light Engraving, Vent Rib, *Modern*	400	475	550
Model BL 3, Various Gauges, Field Grade, Single Selective Trigger, Checkered Stock, Light Engraving, Vent Rib, *Modern*	450	500	550
Model BL 3, Various Gauges, Skeet Grade, Single Selective Trigger, Checkered Stock, Light Engraving, Vent Rib, *Modern*	500	550	600
Model BL 4, 12 Ga., Trap Grade, Single Selective Trigger, Selective Ejector, Engraved, Vent Rib, *Modern*	450	600	750
Model BL 4, Various Gauges, Field Grade, Single Selective Trigger, Selective Ejector, Engraved, Vent Rib, *Modern*	450	600	750
Model BL 4, Various Gauges, Skeet Grade, Single Selective Trigger, Selective Ejector, Engraved, Vent Rib, *Modern*	450	625	800
Model BL 5, 12 Ga., Trap Grade, Single Selective Trigger, Selective Ejector, Fancy Engraving, Vent Rib, *Modern*	400	700	1000
Model BL 5, Various Gauges, Field Grade, Single Selective Trigger, Selective Ejector, Fancy Engraving, Vent Rib, *Modern*	500	750	1000
Model BL 5, Various Gauges, Skeet Grade, Single Selective Trigger, Selective Ejector, Fancy Engraving, Vent Rib, *Modern*	575	725	875
Model BL 6, 12 Ga., Trap Grade, Single Selective Trigger, Selective Ejector, Fancy Engraving, Vent Rib, *Modern*	850	925	1000
Model BL 6, Various Gauges, Field Grade, Single Selective Trigger, Selective Ejector, Fancy Engraving, Vent Rib, *Modern*	900	1000	1100
Model BL 6, Various Gauges, Skeet Grade, Single Selective Trigger, Selective Ejector, Fancy Engraving, Vent Rib, *Modern*	975	1050	1125
Model S55B, 12 and 20 Gauges, Single Selective Trigger, Automatic Ejector, Vent Rib, Checkered Stock, *Modern*	375	425	475
Model S56E, 12 and 20 Gauges, Single Selective Trigger, Automatic Ejector, Engraved, Checkered Stock, *Modern*	425	475	525

	Fair	V. Good	Excellent
Model S58, 12 and 20 Gauges, Skeet Grade, Automatic Ejector, Single Selective Trigger, Engraved, Checkered Stock, Light Engraving, *Modern*	$550	$600	$650
Model S58, 12 Ga., Trap Grade, Automatic Ejector, Single Selective Trigger, Engraved, Checkered Stock, *Modern*	500	550	600
Model SO2, 12 Ga., Sidelock, Selective Ejector, Single Trigger, Checkered Stock, Engraved, *Modern*	2500	3000	3500
Model SO3 EELL, 12 Ga., Sidelock, Automatic Ejector, Single Selective Trigger, Fancy Engraving, Fancy Wood, *Modern*	5500	6500	7500
Model SO3 EL, 12 Ga., Sidelock, Automatic Ejector, Single Selective Trigger, Fancy Engraving, Fancy Wood, *Modern*	4500	5500	6500
Model SO3, 12 Ga., Sidelock, Automatic Ejector, Single Selective Trigger, Fancy Engraving, Fancy Wood, *Modern*	4000	5000	6000
Model SO4, 12 Ga., Sidelock, Automatic Ejector, Single Trigger, Fancy Engraving, Fancy Wood, *Modern*	4000	5000	6000
Model SO5, 12 Ga., Sidelock, Selective Ejector, Single Trigger, Fancy Engraving, Fancy Checkering, *Modern*	5000	6500	8000
Silver Snipe, 12 and 20 Gauges, Single Selective Trigger, Checkered Stock, Light Engraving, *Modern*	350	400	450
Silver Snipe, 12 and 20 Gauges, Single Selective Trigger, Light Engraving, Vent Rib, *Modern*	400	450	500
Silver Snipe, 12 and 20 Gauges, Single Trigger, Checkered Stock, Light Engraving, *Modern*	350	375	400
Silver Snipe, 12 and 20 Gauges, Single Trigger, Checkered Stock, Light Engraving, Vent Rib, *Modern*	350	400	450

SHOTGUN, DOUBLE BARREL, SIDE-BY-SIDE

	Fair	V. Good	Excellent
Model 409PB, Various Gauges, Double Trigger, Light Engraving, Checkered Stock, *Modern*	525	600	675
Model 410 E, 10 Ga. 3½", Double Trigger, Engraved, Checkered Stock, *Modern*	600	675	750
Model 410, 10 Ga. 3½", *Modern*	775	875	975
Model 411E, Various Gauges, Double Trigger, Engraved, Fancy Checkering, Automatic Ejector, *Modern*	975	1050	1125
Model 424, 12 and 20 Gauges, Double Trigger, Light Engraving, Checkered Stock, *Modern*	550	625	700
Model 426E, 12 and 20 Gauges, Single Selective Trigger, Automatic Ejector, Engraved, Checkered Stock, *Modern*	$675	$775	$875
Model GR 2, 12 and 20 Gauges, Double Trigger, Checkered Stock, Light Engraving, *Modern*	350	475	600
Model GR 3, 12 and 20 Gauges, Single Selective Trigger, Checkered Stock, Light Engraving, *Modern*	475	575	675
Model GR 4, 12 Ga., Single Selective Trigger, Selective Ejector, Checkered Stock, Engraved, *Modern*	575	650	725
Silver Hawk, 10 Ga. 3½", Double Trigger, Magnum, *Modern*	375	425	475
Silver Hawk, 12 Ga. Mag. 3", Magnum, *Modern*	300	350	400
Silver Hawk, 12 Ga., Mag. 3", Double Trigger, Magnum, *Modern*	275	325	375
Silver Hawk, Various Gauges, Double Trigger, Lightweight, *Modern*	300	375	450
Silver Hawk, Various Gauges, Single Trigger, Lightweight, *Modern*	400	450	500

SHOTGUN, SEMI-AUTOMATIC

	Fair	V. Good	Excellent
Gold Lark, 12 Ga., Vent Rib, Light Engraving, Checkered Stock, *Modern*	275	350	425
Model A301, 12 and 20 Gauges, Field Grade, Vent Rib, *Modern*	250	300	350
Model A301, 12 and 20 Gauges, Skeet Grade, Vent Rib, *Modern*	250	300	350
Model A301, 12 Ga., Mag. 3", Field Grade, Vent Rib, *Modern*	275	325	375
Model A301, 12 Ga., Slug, Open Rear Sight, *Modern*	250	300	350
Model A301, 12 Ga., Trap Grade, Vent Rib, *Modern*	225	275	325
Model A302, 12 and 20 Gauges, Field Grade, Vent Rib, *Modern*	250	300	350
Model A302, 12 and 20 Gauges, Skeet Grade, Vent Rib, *Modern*	250	300	350
Model A302, 12 Ga., Mag. 3", Field Grade, Vent Rib, *Modern*	275	325	375
Model A302, 12 Ga., Slug, Open Rear Sight, *Modern*	275	325	375
Model A302, 12 Ga., Trap Grade, Vent Rib, *Modern*	250	300	350
Model AL 1, 12 and 20 Gauges, Checkered Stock, *Modern*	250	300	350
Model AL 2, 12 and 20 Gauges, Vent Rib, Checkered Stock, *Modern*	250	275	300
Model AL 2, 12 and 20 Gauges, Vent Rib, Skeet Grade, Checkered Stock, *Modern*	300	325	350
Model AL 2, 12 Ga., Vent Rib, Trap Grade, Checkered Stock, *Modern*	225	275	325
Model AL 3, 12 and 20 Gauges, Vent Rib, Checkered Stock, Light Engraving, *Modern*	250	300	350

	Fair	V. Good	Excellent
Model AL 3, 12 and 20 Gauges, Vent Rib, Checkered Stock, Light Engraving, Skeet Grade, *Modern*	$250	$300	$350
Model AL 3, 12 Ga. Mag. 3", Vent Rib, Checkered Stock, Light Engraving, *Modern*	275	325	375
Model AL 3, 12 Ga., Vent Rib, Checkered Stock, Light Engraving, Trap Grade, *Modern*	225	275	325
Ruby Lark, *Modern*	375	450	525
Silver Lark, 12 Ga., Checkered Stock, *Modern*	150	200	250

SHOTGUN, SINGLESHOT

	Fair	V. Good	Excellent
Companion FS 1, Various Gauges, Folding Gun, *Modern*	100	125	150
Model Mark II, 12 Ga., Trap Grade, Vent Rib, Light Engraving, Checkered Stock, Monte Carlo Stock, *Modern*	300	375	450
Model TR 1, 12 Ga., Trap Grade, Vent Rib, Light Engraving, Checkered Stock, Monte Carlo Stock, *Modern*	150	200	250

SHOTGUN, SLIDE ACTION

	Fair	V. Good	Excellent
Gold Pigeon, 12 Ga., Vent Rib, Checkered Stock, Engraved, *Modern*	250	300	350
Gold Pigeon, 12 Ga., Vent Rib, Fancy Engraving, Fancy Checkering, *Modern*	325	375	425
Model SL 2, 12 Ga., Vent Rib, Checkered Stock, *Modern*	225	250	275
Ruby Pigeon, 12 Ga., Vent Rib, Fancy Engraving, Fancy Checkering, *Modern*	375	425	475
Silver Pigeon, 12 Ga., Light Engraving, Checkered Stock, *Modern*	100	150	200

BERETTA, GIOVANNI

Brescia, Italy, c. 1700.

HANDGUN, SNAPHAUNCE

	Fair	V. Good	Excellent
Belt Pistol, Engraved, Carved, Light Ornamentation, *Antique*	1750	3000	4250

BERGMANN

Gaggenau, Germany 1892–1944: Company renamed Bergmann Erben 1931. Also see Bayard.

HANDGUN, SEMI-AUTOMATIC

	Fair	V. Good	Excellent
Bergmann Mars, 9mmB, Clip Fed, *Curio*	3000	3250	3500
Bergmann/Bayard, Model 1908, 9mmB, Clip Fed, *Curio*	1250	1500	1750
Bergmann/Bayard, Model 1910, 9mmB, Clip Fed, *Curio*	500	1000	1500
Bergmann/Bayard, Model 1910/21, 9mmB, Clip Fed, *Curio*	1350	1600	1850
Erben Model I, .25 ACP, Clip Fed, *Modern*	$225	$275	$325
Erben Model II, .25 ACP, Clip Fed, *Modern*	250	300	350
Erben Special, .32 ACP, Clip Fed, *Modern*	275	325	375
Model 1894, 5mm, Blow Back, Clip Fed, *Antique*	3500	5000	6500
Model 1894, 8mm, Blow Back, Clip Fed, *Antique*	3000	3500	4000
Model 1896 #2, 5mm, Small Frame, Clip Fed, *Curio*	1700	2200	2700
Model 1896 #3, 6.5mm, Clip Fed, *Curio*	1500	2000	2500
Model 1896 #4, 8mm, Military, Clip Fed, *Curio*	1600	2100	2600
Model 1897 #5, 7.8mm, Clip Fed, *Curio*	1700	2200	2700
Model 1899 #6, 8mm, Clip Fed, *Curio*	1500	1750	2000
Model 2, .25 ACP, Clip Fed, *Modern*	150	250	350
Model 2A, .25 ACP, Einhand, Clip Fed, *Modern*	200	300	400
Model 3, .25 ACP, Long Grip, Clip Fed, *Modern*	200	250	300
Model 3A, .25 ACP, Einhand, Long Grip, Clip Fed, *Modern*	150	250	350

RIFLE, SEMI-AUTOMATIC

	Fair	V. Good	Excellent
Model 1897, Karabiner, 7.8mm, Long Barrel, Detachable Stock, *Modern*	3550	4400	5250

BERLIN, ABRAHAM

Caston, Pa. 1773–1786. See Kentucky Rifles and Pistols.

BERNARDELLI

Vincenzo Bernardelli, Gardone, V.T., Italy.

HANDGUN, REVOLVER

	Fair	V. Good	Excellent
Standard, .22 L.R.R.F., or .32 S & W Long, Double Action, Blue, *Modern*	125	200	275
Target, .22 L.R.R.F., Double Action, Blue, Target Sights, *Modern*	125	200	275
Target, .22 L.R.R.F., Double Action, Engraved, Chrome Plated, Target Sights, *Modern*	275	350	425

HANDGUN, SEMI-AUTOMATIC

	Fair	V. Good	Excellent
M1956, 9mm Luger, Clip Fed, *Curio*	700	975	1250
Model 100, .22 L.R.R.F., Clip Fed, Blue, Target Pistol, *Modern*	200	250	300
Model 60, .22 L.R.R.F., Clip Fed, Blue, *Modern*	75	125	175
Model 60, .22 L.R.R.F., Clip Fed, Blue, 8" Barrel, Detachable Front Sight, Adjustable Sights, *Modern*	200	275	350
Model 60, .32 ACP, Clip Fed, Blue, *Modern*	100	150	200

	Fair	V. Good	Excellent
Model 60, .380 ACP, Clip Fed, Blue, *Modern*	$100	$150	$200
Model 80, .22 L.R.R.F., Clip Fed, Blue, *Modern*	75	125	175
Model 80, .22 L.R.R.F., Clip Fed, Blue, 6" Barrel, *Modern*	62	125	200
Model 80, .32 ACP, Clip Fed, Blue, *Modern*	75	125	175
Model 80, .380 ACP, Clip Fed, Blue, *Modern*	62	125	200
Model V P, .22 L.R.R.F., Clip Fed, Blue, *Modern*	100	150	200
Model V P, .25 ACP, Clip Fed, Blue, *Modern*	50	100	175
Standard, .22 L.R.R.F., Clip Fed, Blue, *Modern*	50	100	175
Standard, .22 L.R.R.F., Clip Fed, Blue, 6" Barrel, Detachable Front Sight, *Modern*	75	150	225
Standard, .22 L.R.R.F., Clip Fed, Blue, 10" Barrel, Detachable Front Sight, *Modern*	112	225	350
Standard, .22 L.R.R.F., Clip Fed, Blue, 8" Barrel, Detachable Front Sight, *Modern*	75	150	275
Standard, .32 ACP, Clip Fed, Blue, *Modern*	100	150	200
Standard, .32 ACP, Clip Fed, Blue, 10" Barrel, Detachable Front Sight, *Modern*	275	350	425
Standard, .32 ACP, Clip Fed, Blue, 6" Barrel, Detachable Front Sight, *Modern*	150	225	300

Bernardelli Standard .32, 8" Barrel

	Fair	V. Good	Excellent
Standard, .32 ACP, Clip Fed, Blue, 8" Barrel, Detachable Front Sight, *Modern*	250	325	400
Standard, .380 ACP, Clip Fed, Blue, *Modern*	75	150	250
Standard, 9mm Luger, Clip Fed, Blue, *Modern*	200	325	450

RIFLE, DOUBLE BARREL, OVER-UNDER

	Fair	V. Good	Excellent
Various Calibers, Checkered Stock, Engraved, *Modern*	800	975	1150

SHOTGUN, DOUBLE BARREL, SIDE-BY-SIDE

	Fair	V. Good	Excellent
Brescia, 12 and 20 Gauges, Checkered Stock, Hammer, *Modern*	$750	$1200	$1650
Elio, 12 Ga., Checkered Stock, Light Engraving, Lightweight Selective Ejector, *Modern*	600	775	950
Game Cock Premier, 12 and 20 Gauges, Checkered Stock, Single Trigger, Selective Ejector, *Modern*	550	700	850
Game Cock, *Modern*	475	575	675
Holland Deluxe, Various Gauges, Sidelock, Fancy Engraving, Fancy Checkering, Automatic Ejector, *Modern*	3450	3850	4250
Holland Presentation, Various Gauges, Sidelock, Fancy Engraving, Fancy Checkering, Automatic Ejector, *Modern*	4350	5250	6150
Holland, Various Gauges, Sidelock, Engraved, Checkered Stock, Automatic Ejector, *Modern*	2750	3350	3950
Italia, 12 and 20 Gauges, Checkered Stock, Hammer, Light Engraving, *Modern*	$575	$725	$875
Roma #3, Various Gauges, Engraved, Checkered Stock, Automatic Ejector, *Modern*	675	750	825
Roma #4, Various Gauges, Fancy Engraving, Fancy Checkering, Automatic Ejector, *Modern*	425	650	875
Roma #6, Various Gauges, Fancy Engraving, Fancy Checkering, Automatic Ejector, *Modern*	700	825	950
St. Uberto F.S., 12 and 16 Gauges, Checkered Stock, Double Trigger, Automatic Ejector, *Modern*	625	750	875
Wesley Richards, Various Gauges, Checkered Stock, Light Engraving, Double Trigger, *Modern*	1150	1650	2150
Wesley Richards, Various Gauges, Fancy Checkering, Fancy Engraving, Single Trigger, Selective Ejector, Vent Rib, *Modern*	2100	2875	3650

BERNARDON-MARTIN

St. Etienne, France 1906–1912.

HANDGUN, SEMI-AUTOMATIC

	Fair	V. Good	Excellent
Automatique Francais, .32 ACP, Clip Fed, *Curio*	175	225	275

BERSA

Baraldo S.A.C.I. Argentina.

HANDGUN, SEMI-AUTOMATIC

	Fair	V. Good	Excellent
Model 62, .22 L.R.R.F., Clip Fed, Blue, *Modern*	75	100	125
Model 622, .22 L.R.R.F., Clip Fed, Blue, *Modern*	50	100	150

	Fair	V. Good	Excellent
Model 644, .22 L.R.R.F., Clip Fed, Blue, *Modern*	$50	$100	$150
Model 97, .380 ACP, Clip Fed, Blue, *Modern*	75	125	175

BERTUZZI
Gardone, V.T., Italy; Imported by Ventura.

SHOTGUN, DOUBLE BARREL, OVER-UNDER

Zeus, 12 Ga., Sidelock, Automatic Ejector, Single Selective Trigger, Fancy Checkering, Fancy Engraving, *Modern*	5500	6500	7500
Zeus Extra Lusso, 12 Ga., Sidelock, Automatic Ejector, Single Selective Trigger, Fancy Checkering, Fancy Engraving, *Modern*	6500	8500	10500

BICYCLE
Bicycle by Harrington & Richardson, c. 1895.

HANDGUN, REVOLVER

.22 L.R.R.F., Top Break, Double Action, *Curio*	50	100	150
.32 S & W, 5 Shot, Double Action, Top Break, *Curio*	35	75	125

BICYCLE
French.

HANDGUN, SINGLESHOT

.22 L.R.R.F., Auto Styling, *Modern*	200	275	350

BIG BONANZA
Made by Bacon Arms Co., c. 1880.

HANDGUN, REVOLVER

.22 Short R.F., 7 Shot, Spur Trigger, Solid Frame, Single Action, *Antique*	75	125	175

BIG HORN ARMS CO.
Watertown, S.D.

HANDGUN, SINGLESHOT

Target Pistol, .22 Short, Plastic Stock, Vent Rib, *Modern*	50	100	150

SHOTGUN, SINGLESHOT

12 Ga. Short, Plastic Stock, *Modern*	50	75	100

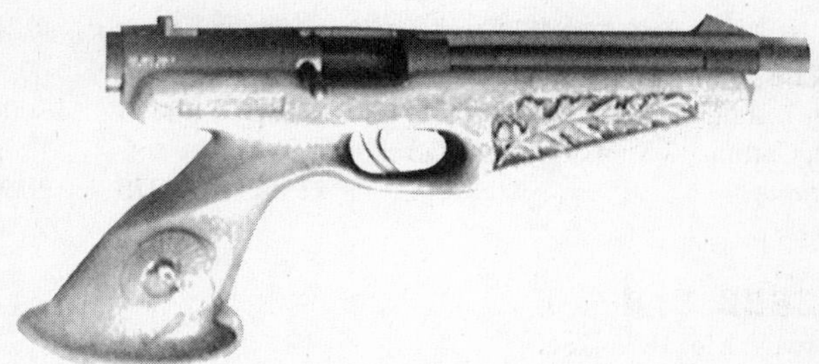

Big Horn .22 Pistol

BILLINGHURST, WILLIAM
Rochester, N.Y. 1843–80. A relatively small group of devotees specializes in American revolving rifles. The tremendous variety in these arms, coupled with their intriguing mechanisms, are a challenge to even the most advanced of arms collectors. Overshadowed largely by Colt revolving longarms, the competitor arms have not yet got in stride in terms of collector value. Billinghurst was one of the best makers, even having assistants who left to make their own revolving longarms. Some Billinghurst revolving rifles have a California connection, and they are deserving of a premium of at least 20 percent. The type also includes the relatively scarce transition ignition system variation, dating between the flintlock and the percussion known as the pill lock.

HANDGUN, PERCUSSION

	Fair	V. Good	Excellent
Buggy Pistol, Various Calibers, Detachable Stock, Heavy Barrel, *Antique*	$500	$1000	$2500

RIFLE, PERCUSSION

.36, Revolver, 7 Shot, Octagon Barrel, *Antique*	1075	2150	3500
.40, Revolver, 7 Shot, Octagon Barrel, *Antique*	935	1875	3500

Two Revolving Rifles of Billinghurst style, the top, *a pill-lock by T. P. Cherington, 7-shot cylinder, manual operation; .40 caliber rifled, c. 1830s;* the bottom, *a percussion by H. Volpius, in .36 caliber, also 7-shot, manual operation, c.* 1850.

	Fair	V. Good	Excellent
RIFLE, PILL LOCK			
.40, 7 Shot, Octagon Barrel, *Antique*	$1850	$2425	$3000
.40, Carbine, 7 Shot, Octagon Barrel, *Antique*	1550	2275	3000

BISBEE, D. H.

Norway, Me. 1835–1860.

	Fair	V. Good	Excellent
RIFLE, PERCUSSION			
.44, Octagon Barrel, Silver Inlay, *Antique*	1325	1750	2175

BISON

Imported from Germany by Jana International, c. 1971.

	Fair	V. Good	Excellent
HANDGUN, REVOLVER			
.22 L.R.R.F., Adjustable Sights, Western Style, Single Action, *Modern*	25	50	75
.22 LR/.22 WMR Combo, Adjustable Sights, Western Style, Single Action, *Modern*	25	50	75

BITTERLICH, FRANK J.

Nashville, Tenn. from about 1855 until about 1867.

	Fair	V. Good	Excellent
HANDGUN, PERCUSSION			
Derringer, .40, Plain, *Antique*	1050	1200	1350

BITTNER, GUSTAV

Vejprty, Bohemia, Austria-Hungary, c. 1893.

	Fair	V. Good	Excellent
HANDGUN, MANUAL REPEATER			
Model 1893, 7.7mm Bittner, Box Magazine, Checkered Stocks, *Antique*	2200	2500	2800

BLAKE, ANN

London, England, c. 1812.

	Fair	V. Good	Excellent
HANDGUN, FLINTLOCK			
Holster Pistol, .62, Walnut Stock, *Antique*	425	575	725

BLANCH, JOHN A.

London, England 1809–1835.

	Fair	V. Good	Excellent
HANDGUN, PERCUSSION			
.68 Pair, Double Barrel, Side by Side, Officer's Belt Pistol, Engraved, Silver Inlay, Steel Furniture, Cased with Accessories, *Antique*	2750	3500	4250
Pair, Pocket Pistol, Converted from Flintlock, High Quality, Cased with Accessories, *Antique*	$2000	$2500	$3000

BLAND, T & SONS

London & Birmingham, England, from 1876.

	Fair	V. Good	Excellent
SHOTGUN, DOUBLE BARREL, SIDE-BY-SIDE			
12 Ga., Boxlock, Adjustable Choke, Color Case Hardened Frame, Engraved, *Antique*	1500	1875	2250

BLANGLE, JOSEPH

Gratz, Styria, Austria, c. 1670.

	Fair	V. Good	Excellent
RIFLE, WHEELLOCK			
Brass Furniture, Engraved, Silver Inlay, Light Ornamentation, Full-Stocked, *Antique*	5100	5800	6500

BLEIBERG

London, England, c. 1690.

	Fair	V. Good	Excellent
HANDGUN, FLINTLOCK			
Holster Pistol, Engraved, Silver Inlay, High Quality, *Antique*	6300	7900	9500

BLICKENSDOERFER & SCHILLING

St. Louis, Mo. 1871–1875.

	Fair	V. Good	Excellent
RIFLE, PERCUSSION			
.48, Octagon Barrel, Fancy Wood, Brass Furniture, *Antique*	575	950	1325

BLISS & GOODYEAR

Connecticut, also made guns under trade names America, American Boy, and Challenge.

BLOODHOUND

Made by Hopkins & Allen, c. 1880.

	Fair	V. Good	Excellent
HANDGUN, REVOLVER			
.22 Short R.F., 7 Shot, Spur Trigger, Solid Frame, Single Action, *Antique*	50	100	200

BLUE JACKET

Made by Hopkins & Allen, c. 1880.

	Fair	V. Good	Excellent
HANDGUN, REVOLVER			
Model 1, .22 Short R.F., 7 Shot, Spur Trigger, Solid Frame, Single Action, *Antique*	50	100	200

	Fair	V. Good	Excellent
Model 2, .32 Short R.F., 5 Shot, Spur Trigger, Solid Frame, Single Action, *Antique*	$50	$100	$200

BLUE WHISTLER

Made by Hopkins & Allen, c. 1880.

HANDGUN, REVOLVER

	Fair	V. Good	Excellent
.32 Short R.F., *Antique*	50	100	200

BLUMENFELD

Memphis, Tenn., c. 1970.

SHOTGUN, DOUBLE BARREL, SIDE-BY-SIDE

	Fair	V. Good	Excellent
Arizaga, 20 Gauge, Double Triggers, Checkered Stock, *Modern*	65	125	200

SHOTGUN, SEMI-AUTOMATIC

	Fair	V. Good	Excellent
Volunteer Pointer, 12 Gauge, Checkered Stock, *Modern*	65	125	225

BLUNT, ORISON, & SYMS

N.Y.C. 1837–1865. An important gunmaker and dealer of its time, the firm of Blunt & Syms was significant for several reasons, not the least of which was its capability to manufacture prototype firearms for budding inventors–among them Samuel Colt. The prototype Walker model revolver, preserved in the Colt Collection of Firearms, Raymond Baldwin Museum of Connecticut History, was built for Colt by Blunt & Syms, and is so documented in the transcript of the Colt vs. Massachussetts Arms Co. trial of 1851. Blunt & Syms also made a working example of the Artemus Wheeler patent flintlock revolving longarm, which has survived in excellent condition, and is considered likely to have been built as an exhibit in that same trial.

HANDGUN, PERCUSSION

	Fair	V. Good	Excellent
Belt Pepperbox, Various Calibers, Ring Trigger, *Antique*	325	375	425
Boot Pistol, Various Calibers, Bar Hammer, *Antique*	275	325	375
Boot Pistol, Various Calibers, Ring Trigger, *Antique*	325	375	425
Boot Pistol, Various Calibers, Side Hammer, *Antique*	300	350	400
Boot Pistol, Various Calibers, Side Hammer, Ramrod, *Antique*	300	350	400
Boot Pistol, Various Calibers, Underhammer, *Antique*	275	325	375
Dragoon Pepperbox, Various Calibers, Ring Trigger, *Antique*	350	600	850
Pocket Pepperbox, Various Calibers, Ring Trigger, *Antique*	350	400	450

RIFLE, PERCUSSION

	Fair	V. Good	Excellent
.37, Octagon Barrel, Brass Furniture, *Antique*	425	525	625

BOITO

Brazil.

HANDGUN, SINGLESHOT

	Fair	V. Good	Excellent
.44 C.F., Break-Open, Hammer, Blue, *Modern*	$50	$75	$100

SHOTGUN, DOUBLE BARREL, OVER-UNDER

	Fair	V. Good	Excellent
O/U, 12 or 20 Gauge, Checkered Stock, *Modern*	50	100	175

SHOTGUN, DOUBLE BARREL, SIDE-BY-SIDE

	Fair	V. Good	Excellent
S/S, 12 or 20 Gauge, Checkered Stock, *Modern*	35	75	150

SHOTGUN, SINGLESHOT

	Fair	V. Good	Excellent
SS, 12 or 20 Gauge, Checkered Stock, *Modern*	12	25	50

BONANZA

Made by Bacon Arms Co.

HANDGUN, REVOLVER

	Fair	V. Good	Excellent
Model 1½, .22 Short R.F., 7 Shot, Spur Trigger, Solid Frame, Single Action, *Antique*	50	100	200

BOND, EDWARD

London, England 1800–1830.

HANDGUN, FLINTLOCK

	Fair	V. Good	Excellent
.68, Pair Officers' Type, Holster Pistol, Brass Furniture, Plain, *Antique*	1400	2450	3500

BOND, WM.

London, England 1798–1812.

HANDGUN, FLINTLOCK

	Fair	V. Good	Excellent
Pair, Folding Bayonet, Belt Pistol, Box Lock, Cannon Barrel, Brass Frame and Barrel, Cased with Accessories, *Antique*	4600	5225	5850

BONEHILL, C.G.

Birmingham, England, c. 1880.

SHOTGUN, DOUBLE BARREL, OVER-UNDER

	Fair	V. Good	Excellent
.450 N.E. 3¼", Under-Lever, Recoil Pad, Plain, *Modern*	625	1250	2500

BONIWITZ, JAMES

Lebanon, Pa., c. 1775. See Kentucky Rifles.

BOOWLES, R.

London, England, c. 1690.

HANDGUN, FLINTLOCK

	Fair	V. Good	Excellent
Holster Pistol, Engraved, Iron Mounts, Medium Quality, *Antique*	$525	$975	$1425

BORCHARDT

Made by Ludwig Lowe, Berlin, Germany 1893–1897. In 1897 acquired by D.W.M., superseded by the Luger in 1900. Lowe was an American gun designer who spent quite a few years in Europe, and the Borchardt self-loading pistol is truly a brilliant piece of engineering, as well as an example of gunmaking ingenuity of the application of machine tools. A student of modern art would find the Borchardt very sculptural, and a quite beautiful engraved and gold inlaid example by Raymond Wielgus is part of the Art Institute of Chicago's firearms collection.

HANDGUN, SEMI-AUTOMATIC

	Fair	V. Good	Excellent
DWM, 7.65mm, Borchardt, 8 Shot Magazine, Blue, with 6½" Barrel and Walnut Grips, Cased with Accessories, *Curio*	12500	15000	17500
Lowe, 7.65mm, Borchardt, 8 Shot Magazine, Blue, with 6½" Barrel and Walnut Grips, Cased with Accessories, Deduct 40% without Case and Accessories	15000	17500	20000

BOSS & CO. LTD.

London, England 1832 to Date.

SHOTGUN, DOUBLE BARREL, OVER-UNDER

	Fair	V. Good	Excellent
12 Ga., Single Selective Trigger, Straight Grip, Vent Rib, Trap Grade, Cased, *Curio*	13275	18750	24225
16 Ga., Double Trigger, Plain, *Curio*	8000	10000	12000
20 Ga., Single Selective Trigger, Vent Rib, High Quality, *Curio*	15000	25000	27,500

SHOTGUN, DOUBLE BARREL, SIDE-BY-SIDE

	Fair	V. Good	Excellent
12 Ga., Vent Rib, Fancy Wood, Fancy Checkering, Fancy Engraving, *Curio*	8000	10000	12000
Pair, 12 Ga., Straight Grip, Plain, Cased, *Curio*	15000	25000	-30536

BOSTON BULLDOG

Made by Iver Johnson, sold by J. P. Lovell & Sons, Boston, Mass.

HANDGUN, REVOLVER

	Fair	V. Good	Excellent
.22 Short R.F., 7 Shot, Double Action, Solid Frme *Curio*	35	75	150
.32 S & W, 5 Shot, Double Action, Solid Frame, *Curio*	35	75	150
.32 Short R.F., 5 Shot, Double Action, Solid Frame, *Curio*	$35	$75	$150
.38 S & W, 5 Shot, Double Action, Solid Frame, *Curio*	35	75	150
.38 Short R.F., 5 Shot, Double Action, Solid Frame, *Curio*	25	50	150

BOSWORTH

Lancaster Pa. 1760–1775. See Kentucky Rifles.

BOUTET, NICHOLAS NOEL

Workshops at Versailles, under appointment from the Emperor Napoleon. As gunmaker to the Emperor, Boutet was one of the greatest of all artist in arms, and actually bore the title Director Artiste. His artistry spanned the years from the pre–French Revolution (1785) through the Revolution, Directory, Consulate, Empire, Restoration and Paris periods. The total aesthetic philosophy of Boutet's attention to exquisite form and detail utilizing the finest materials available while reflecting the influences of rococo and neoclassicism figure in an appreciation of these magnificent firearms. Several of Boutet's design drawings have survived, adding to the fascination with this great gunmaker and artist. Boutet arms represent the decorative arts at their finest level of development in a functional artifact, and other than in specialized studies, the field is largely unknown and studied outside of curators and collectors. Many of the renowned Boutet pieces are in institutions such as the Army Museum (Paris), the Royal Armouries Museum, The Hermitage Museum, the Wallace Collection, The Victoria and Albert Museum and The Metropolitan Museum of Art that contain extraordinary examples of the finest of Boutet's work. A few private collections also contain exceptional specimens. In addition to the grand presentation and ultra-fine pieces, firearms of the Imperial Guard of Napoleon figure prominently in the pantheon of Boutet firearms. There are four grades of quality which have been established for Boutet arms. These are as follows: Plain, with no ornamentation on stocks or checkering; blued or browned barrels; minimal engraving. Medium, with stocks checkered; engraving more elaborate; blued barrels. High, with choice select woods; checkering more refined with bordering; carving on stocks; elaborate engraving in combination with silver wire inlays or minimal engraved silver plaques; tooled barrels; blued or browned; edges engraved; mounts deluxe, engraved or sculptured steel. Deluxe, with inlaid gold or silver engraved plaques; mounts cast silver or gold. High presentation provenance with fish-scale checkering on stocks; combination of choice woods. The author is grateful to Professor Dean Taylor for his assistance in preparing the Boutet section and values.

MUSKET

	Fair	V. Good	Excellent
Civilian Blunderbuss, Full-stocked; high quality; bayonet sometimes present; engraved mounts; "Entse Boutet/manufre A Versailles."	15000	20000	30000
Flint Musket (Velites De La Guarde An XII. 1803), Three brass barrel bands; "Manufre A Versailles"	4000	6000	8000

	Fair	V. Good	Excellent
Flint Musket Fusil D'Infanterie De La Guarde, Three brass bands; "Manufre A Versailles" (Consular) Note: Marked: "Mre Imple De Versailles" for Imperial Guard.	$4000	$6000	$7000
Flint Musketoon, (Chasseur A Cheval/Consular and Imperial Guard); Two brass bands; half-stocked; "Manufre A Versailles."	4000	6000	10000
Flint Musketoon, (Consular and Imperial Guard Grenadier A Cheval); Three brass bands; full-stocked; "Manufre A Versailles."	5000	7000	12000
Flintlock Mousqueton Imperial Guard (Arm of Honour), Two silver barrel bands; round barrel rifled; all mounts silver with presentation plaque in stock; inscribed "Mre. Imple De Versailles"	10000	20000	40,000
Flintlock Mousqueton Imperial Guard (Chasseurs), Two brass barrel bands; round barrel rifled; "Manufre Imple De Versailles."	5000	9000	16000
Flintlock Musket (De Gardes Du Corp); Guards of the King, 2nd type; special pan (Bassinet Laiton A Tambour)	8000	10000	12250
Flintlock Musket (Des Ecoles Militaires), Military School Cadets; Special pan, of rotary pattern.	2500	3000	5000
Flintlock Musket (Fusil), Model 1777 (Infantry)	1800	2000	3500
Flintlock Musket Model ANIX (Dragoon)	2000	2500	3500
Flintlock Musket of Reward (De Recompense), Honor Presentation. Silver mounts and commemorative plaque in butt.	8000	10000	15000
Flintlock Musketoon of Reward, (as above)	8000	15000	25000
High Grade Flintlock Blunderbuss Pistol, Blued Barrel; engraved iron mounts.	8000	12000	20000
High Grade Officer's Musket, Iron Mounts; spurred hammer; three barrel mounts; "Manufre A Versailles."	5000	7000	10000
Military Blunderbuss (Mamelukes), Half-stocked; brass mounts; swan hammer; octagonal; round barrel; "Entse Boutet. Mre Imple De Versailles." (overlapped into Empire).	10000	15000	20000
Musket of the Consular Dragoons, Open pan; three brass bands; middle one large.	2500	3000	3500
Musket of the Infantry (Consular Guard), Open pan; three brass barrel bands.	2000	2500	3000

	Fair	V. Good	Excellent
Musket of the Infantry (Guard Imperial), Open pan; three brass barrel bands.	$4000	$8000	$12000
Officer's Blunderbuss Flintlock, High to deluxe quality; full-stocked; iron engraved mounts; swan hammer.	10000	15000	20000
Officer's Blunderbuss Flintlock, Half-stocked; brass mounts; iron barrel; "Manfre De Versailles."	6000	8000	10000
Pill Lock High Grade Pistol, "Boutet A Versailles"; sculptured iron mounts; half-stocked; c. 1825.	8000	10000	15000

HANDGUN, PERCUSSION

	Fair	V. Good	Excellent
Half-Stocked High Grade Percussion Pistol, Gold carving on hammer; fish scale checkering; barrel "Boutet A Versailles"; circa 1818, *Antique*	10000	12000	20000
Percussion Back Action Lock Officer's Pistol, Medium to high quality; "Boutet A Paris"; silver mounts; ebony stock; c. 1828, *Antique*	6000	7000	8000

HANDGUN, POCKET PISTOL

	Fair	V. Good	Excellent
Flintlock Double Barrel Pocket Pistol, High grade checkering and carving; frizzen spring integral with barrel; "Boutet Directeur Artiste"; "Manufre De Versaille, *Antique*	15000	20000	25000
Flintlock Over-and-Under Deluxe Grade Presentation Pistol, c. 1814; gold engraved plaques; gold work breech and barrels. Note: cased with all accessories: $250,000 Excellent, *Antique*	30000	60000	80000
Flintlock Pocket Pistol, Converted 1820s; high butt spurs; carving at barrel tang. "Boutet/Arqre Ordre Du Roi, Versailles"; c. 1788, *Antique*	7000	10000	15000
Pocket/Muff Flintlock Pistol, Medium to high quality; checkering and minimal carving; short smooth bores; no spring on frizzen (built-in barrel), *Antique*	6000	8000	15000
Pocket/Muff Flintlock Pistol, Plain to medium quality; short smooth bores; spring on frizzen; no checkering, *Antique*	$4000	$7000	$10000

HANDGUN, MULTI-BARREL

	Fair	V. Good	Excellent
Flintlock Four Barrel Pistol with Tap Action Lock, Plain quality; "Boutet A Versailles."	5000	7000	9000

TARGET PISTOLS

	Fair	V. Good	Excellent
Officer's Flintlock Target Pistol, Full stocked; medium quality; set triggers as in Austrian Yaeger rifles; high quality lock "Manuf. A Versailles"; multi-groove rifling; barrel marked "Manufacture D'Armes De Versailles," *Antique*	$6000	$8000	$10000

RIFLE, FLINTLOCK

	Fair	V. Good	Excellent
Carbine (Cavalry Model); Model 1793 (short), Model 1793 (short), swan hammer, one brass barrel band; octagonal rifled barrel; full-stocked, *Antique*	8000	12000	15000
Carbine (Civilian) High Grade, Plain wood; iron mounts; "Manufre Versailles"; octagonal rifled barrel.	8000	10000	20000
Carbine (Infantry Model), Model 1793 (long); swan hammer; two brass barrel bands; octagonal rifled barrel; full-stocked.	4500	6500	10000
Carbine (Infantry); Model AN XII (1803–1804), Reinforced hammer; two barrel bands; octagonal rifled barrel; full-stocked.	8000	12000	15000
Deluxe Grade Flintlock Rifle, Full-stocked; engraved silver inlaid plaques; silver-mounted ebony sculpture behind triggerguard; octagonal gold ornamented barrel, *Antique*	20000	40000	80000
Flintlock Carbines, Plain to medium quality; octagonal rifled barrels; full stocked, *Antique*	10000	15000	20000
Flintlock Deluxe Carbines, Octagonal rifled barrels; medium to high quality, *Antique*	15000	25000	60000
Flintlock Rifle, "Manufacture Royale A Versailles" Silver mounts (c. 1815); plain stock, well carved behind triggerguard; engraved animals on lockplate; spurred hammer, *Antique*	12000	25000	50000
Takedown Carriage Carbine, Engraved "Equipage De, S.A.R. Monseigneur Le Duc de Berri" and "Manufre Royale A Versailles"; spurred hammer; c. 1815.	10000	12000	15000

RIFLE, DOUBLE BARREL, OVER-UNDER

	Fair	V. Good	Excellent
Cased Double Barrel, Over-and-Under Rifle, High deluxe grade with horn flasks and full accessories; "Manufacture Imperiale D'Armes De Versailles."	60000	150000	250000

PISTOLS, FLINTLOCK

	Fair	V. Good	Excellent
Cavalry Flintlock Pistol; Model AN XIII, Half-stocked; brass mounts; "Manufre Imp. Versailles."	4000	6000	7500
Cavalry Trooper's Model AN IX (1800–1801), Full-stocked; brass mounts; "Mre Nle. A. Versailles."	$4000	$6000	$7500
Civilian Flintlock Belt Pistol, With Spring Bayonet; Queen Anne style lock; "Boutet A Versailles	5000	7000	12000
Consular Guard Flintlock Dragoon Pistol, Full-stocked; plain brass butt; smoothbore., *Antique*	6500	8000	10000
Deluxe Grade Muff Flintlock Pistols, (1804–14)	15000	20000	30000
Flintlock Holster Pistol, Bright chiseled iron mounts; "Boutet A Versailles"; High butt spurs; wood carved at barrel tang; c. 1789.	6000	8000	10000
Flintlock Long Horse Pistol in Oriental, Far Eastern manner, Deluxe grade; silver and gold plaques; silver wire inlays; round smooth bore; barrel profuse gold ornamentation, *Antique*	15000	20000	30000
Flintlock Muff Pistol, Cannon barrel, plain grade; c. 1819, *Antique*	4000	6000	7000
Flintlock Naval Presentation Pistol (AN X), 1801, Deluxe quality; silver butt naval themes; extensive silver plaques and wire inlay work; "Boutet Directeur Artiste" and "Boutet A Versailles." Note: cased with full accesories and provenance: $200,000.	15000	30000	60000
Flintlock Pistol (Military-Gardes Du Corps Du Roi), 2nd Model (1816); Blued plain barrel; three fleurs-de-lis on, *Antique*	6000	7500	10000
Flintlock Pistol (Military: "National Guard"), c. 1816. Plain brass butt; "Mre Royale De Versailles," *Antique*	8000	12000	15000
Flintlock Pistol (Model 1763–1766), Brass mounts; round barrel smoothbore; full stocked; "Manufre Royale De Versailles," *Antique*	6500	10000	12000
Grade Deluxe Flint Dueling Pistols, Chased silver mounts; gold-engraved inlaid plaques, roller on frizzen. Gold work on octagonal barrel. Note: cased with full accessories; Excellent: $300,000.	15000	20000	30000
Half-Stocked High Grade Flintlock Pistol, Gold carving on hammer; fish scale checkering; barrel "Boutet A Versailles"; circa 1818, *Antique*	15000	20000	30000
High Grade Flintlock Blunderbuss Pistol, Blued barrel; engraved iron mounts.	8000	12000	20000

	Fair	V. Good	Excellent
High-grade flint dueling pistols, Double cased with flint seconds pistols. Full accessories; half-stocked; "Manufre A Versailles/Boutet Directeur Artiste."	$60000	$185000	$250000
Holster Pistol, Bright chiseled iron mounts; "Boutet A Versailles"; high butt spurs; wood carved at barrel tang; c. 1789, *Antique*	6000	8000	10000
Mameluke Guard Flintlock (Flagbearer), Full-stocked; round barrel; smoothbore; brass mounts.	10000	15000	20000
Mameluke Guard Flintlock Belt Pistol, Half-stocked; brass mounts; "Ent. se Boutet," "Manuf. De Versailles," *Antique*	6000	15000	17500
Mameluke Guard Flintlock Horse Pistol, Full-stocked; brass mounts; rifled bore, *Antique*	9000	16000	18000
Mameluke Guard Flintlock Officer's Pistol, Half-stocked; iron mounts; rifled bore, *Antique*	10000	18000	20000
Medium to High Grade Half-Stocked Flintlock Pistol, "Boutet Directeur Artiste, Manufacture A Versailles"; checkered stock; ebony butt inlay.	8000	15000	20000
Medium to High Grade Muff Flintlock Pistols, (1804–14), *Antique*	8000	12000	15000
Officer's Flintlock Belt Pistol, Iron mounted; plain quality; "Mre De Versailles," *Antique*	4000	5000	6000
Officer's Flintlock Pistol, Iron mounted; plain quality; triggerguard extension (a battle axe); "Manufre De Versailles."	6000	7000	8000
Officer's Flintlock Pistol, Octagonal barrel, marked "Manufre Royale"; lockplate "Manufre A Versailles"; engraved iron mounts; multi-groove rifling, *Antique*	4000	6000	8000
Officer's Flintlock Pistol, Plain quality, "Boutet A Versailles"; c. 1785, *Antique*	4000	6000	8000
Officer's Flintlock Pistol (Admiral's), Butt cap in silver (head of Neptune and Anchor); full silver	15000	20000	30000
Officer's Flintlock Pistol (Cheveau Leger), Light Horse Cavalry of the King; "Mfre Royale De Versailles" reinforced hammer; Fleur De Lis front of triggerguard, brass mounts, *Antique*	8000	12000	15000
Officer's Flintlock Pistol (Eagle Bearer Model 1809), Butt cap in silver (crown, "N", crossed oak, laurel branches); half-stocked; round barrel; rifled, iron mounts.	12000	20000	30000

	Fair	V. Good	Excellent
Officer's Flintlock Pistol (Empress Dragoons), Butt cap in silver (crown, "N" and crossed oak; laurel branches); round blued barrel; smoothbore; iron mounts.	$8000	$10000	$15000
Officer's Flintlock Pistol (Fortress Staff Officers Model), Iron mounts and plain iron butt cap; overall proportions as in Medusa pistol.	5000	7000	10000
Officer's Flintlock Pistol (Gendarmerie De La Maison Du Roi), King's Special Police; full-stocked; octagonal barrel; "Gendarmerie Du Roi" and "Manufre Royale De Versailles," *Antique*	8000	12000	15000
Officer's Flintlock Pistol (General Staff Officers Model), Plain silver butt cap; iron mounts.	6000	8000	15000
Officer's Flintlock Pistol (General's), Butt cap in silver (head of Medusa); octagon rifled bore; plain iron mounts; regulation issue. With deluxe silver mounts and cased: Excellent: $60,000	8000	10000	20000
Officer's Flintlock Pistol (Hussards), Butt cap in silver (head of Jupiter with lightning bolts); plain iron mounts; octagonal round barrel; half-stocked	12000	20000	30000
Officer's Flintlock Pistol (Infantry Officer), Butt cap in silver, crown, "N," crossed oak, laurel branches; longer barrel than eagle bearer. Marked "Boutet A Versailles"; iron mounts; round rifled barrel; half-stocked.	12000	20000	30000
Officer's Flintlock Pistol (Infantry Officer), Iron plain buttcap; half stocked; marked "Boutet A Versailles" or "Manuf. Imple De Versailles."; mounts or iron; round barrel; rifled.	6000	10000	15000
Officer's Flintlock Pistol (Line Officer), Same as Infantry Officer only with hammer and iron buttcap.	6000	10000	25000
Officer's Flintlock Pistol (Marshal's), Butt cap in silver (head of Jupiter or Zeus with lightning bolts); plain iron mounts; octagon blued rifles bore; regulation issue.	10000	15000	25000
Officer's Flintlock Pistol (Model IX); 1800–1801, Custom High Grade; silver-fluted butt; silver mounts; slender proportions; checkered; "Mre Nle Versailles."	8000	12000	15000

	Fair	V. Good	Excellent
Officer's Pistol ("General" Level), Full-stocked; round barrel, rifled; silver butt cap (axe and sword motif).	$15000	$20000	$25000
Officer's Pistol of Reward, Full stocked; medium to high quality; multi-groove rifling; "Entreprise Boutet" and "Boutet Directeur Artiste," *Antique*	5000	7000	12000
Officer's Pistol of Reward (Pistolet de Recompence), Full-stocked; multi-groove rifling; iron mounts; medium to high quality; "Boutet et Fils A Versailles."	10000	15000	20000
Officer's Pistol of Reward, Flintlock Model, Full stocked; medium to high quality; multi-groove rifling; "Enterprise Boutet" and "Boutet Directeur Artiste," *Antique*	5000	7000	12000
Officer's Presentation Deluxe Cased Flintlock Sets, With accessories, full-stocked, much wood carving; sculptured hammers; "Boutet A Versailles," *Antique*	60000	90000	180000
Pistols of Reward, Single piece; flintlock; full-stocked and "high" quality (double price for a cased pair), *Antique*	10000	20000	30000

PISTOL, PERCUSSION (ORIGINAL)

	Fair	V. Good	Excellent
Half-stocked High Grade Percussion Pistol, Gold carving on hammer; fish scale checkering; barrel "Boutet A Versailles"; c. 1818.	10000	12000	20000

SHOTGUN, FLINTLOCK

	Fair	V. Good	Excellent
Civilian Double Barrel Flintlock Fowler, Sculptured silver mounts; "Boutet Arq. Du Monsieur A. Versailles"; gold ornamentation on barrels; c. 1785.	8000	15000	30000
Flintlock Fowlers, Medium to high quality grades; "Manufre Royale A Versailles"	10000	15000	30000

BOY'S CHOICE

Made by Hood Firearms Co., c. 1875.

HANDGUN, REVOLVER

	Fair	V. Good	Excellent
.22 Short R.F., 7 Shot, Spur Trigger, Solid Frame, Single Action, *Antique*	50	100	175

BOYINGTON, JOHN

S. Coventry, Conn. 1841–1847.

RIFLE, PERCUSSION

	Fair	V. Good	Excellent
.50, Octagon Barrel, Brass Furniture, *Antique*	625	775	925

BREDA

Brescia, Italy, Diana Import Co., Current.

SHOTGUN, DOUBLE BARREL, OVER-UNDER

	Fair	V. Good	Excellent
.410 Ga., Light Engraving, Checkered Stock, *Modern*	$375	$425	$475

SHOTGUN, SEMI-AUTOMATIC

	Fair	V. Good	Excellent
"Magnum," 12 Ga., Mag. 3", Checkered Stock, Vent Rib, Lightweight, *Modern*	325	400	475
Grade 1, 12 Ga., Checkered Stock, Vent Rib, Lightweight, Engraved, *Modern*	350	425	500
Grade 2, 12 Ga., Fancy Checkering, Vent Rib, Lightweight, Fancy Engraving, *Modern*	500	575	650
Grade 3, 12 Ga., Fancy Checkering, Vent Rib, Lightweight, Fancy Engraving, *Modern*	675	750	825
Standard, 12 Ga., Checkered Stock, Plain Barrel, Lightweight, *Modern*	225	300	375
Standard, 12 Ga., Checkered Stock, Vent Rib, Lightweight, *Modern*	175	250	325

BRETTON

St. Etienne, France.

SHOTGUN, DOUBLE BARREL, OVER-UNDER

	Fair	V. Good	Excellent
Deluxe, 12 Gauge, Engraved, Dural Frame, Double Triggers, Barrels Can Be Unscrewed, *Modern*	450	600	750
Standard, 12 gauge, Dural Frame, Double Triggers, Barrels Can Be Unscrewed, *Modern*	375	500	625

B.R.F.

Successor to Pretoria Arms Factory, South Africa, 1950s.

SHOTGUN, SEMI-AUTOMATIC

	Fair	V. Good	Excellent
"Junior," .25 ACP, Clip Fed, Blue, *Modern*	150	225	300
"Junior," .25 ACP, Clip Fed, Blue, Low Slide, *Modern*	125	175	225
"Junior," .25 ACP, Clip Fed, Blue, PAF Logo on Slide, *Modern*	100	200	300
"Junior," .25 ACP, Clip Fed, Blue, Raised Sight Rib, *Modern*	$175	$225	$275
"Junior," .25 ACP, Clip Fed, Blue, Rough Ground Slide, *Modern*	150	175	200
"Junior," .25 ACP, Clip Fed, Factory Chrome Plated, *Modern*	250	325	400
"Junior", for Cocking Indicator, Add $75-$125			

BRIGGS, WILLIAM

Norristown, Pa. 1848–1875.

	Fair	V. Good	Excellent
SHOTGUN, PERCUSSION			
12 Ga., Underhammer, *Antique*	$200	$275	$350

BRITARMS
Aylesbury, England.

	Fair	V. Good	Excellent
HANDGUN, SEMI-AUTOMATIC			
M2000 Mk.II, .22 L.R.R.F., Clip Fed, Target Pistol, *Modern*	525	650	775

BRITISH BULLDOG
Made by Forehand & Wadsworth.

	Fair	V. Good	Excellent
HANDGUN, REVOLVER			
.32 S & W, 5 Shot, Double Action, Solid Frame, *Modern*	35	75	150
.38 S & W, 5 Shot, Double Action, Solid Frame, *Modern*	35	75	150
.44 S & W, 5 Shot, Double Action, Solid Frame, *Modern*	50	100	200

BRITISH MILITARY
British Military.

	Fair	V. Good	Excellent
HANDGUN, FLINTLOCK			
.58, New Land M1796 Tower, Long Tapered Round Barrel, Belt Hook, Brass Furniture, *Antique*	1000	1750	2500
.67, George III Tower, Cavalry Pistol, Military, Tapered Round Barrel, Brass Furniture, *Antique*	625	1250	2000
.80, Modified M1796 Spooner, Holster Pistol, Plain Brass Furniture, *Antique*	725	1450	2500
HANDGUN, REVOLVER			
#2 Mk I R.A.F., .38 S & W, Military, Top Break, *Curio*	200	250	300
#2 Mk I, .38 S & W, Military, Top Break, *Curio*	200	250	300
S & W M38/200, .38 S & W, Solid Frame, Swing-Out Cylinder, Double Action, Military, *Curio*	75	150	250
Webley Mk I, .455 Revolver Mk I, Top Break, Round Butt, Military, *Antique*	115	225	450
Webley Mk I*, .455 Revolver Mk I, Top Break, Round Butt, Military, *Antique*	115	225	450
Webley Mk I,** .455 Revolver Mk I, Top Break, Round Butt, Military, *Curio*	150	225	300
Webley Mk II, .455 Revolver Mk I, Top Break, Round Butt, Military, *Curio*	135	275	550
Webley Mk II*, .455 Revolver Mk I, Top Break, Round Butt, Military, *Curio*	200	250	300
Webley Mk II,** .455 Revolver Mk I, Top Break, Round Butt, Military, *Curio*	100	200	300

British Military Webley MK 1 No. 2.455

	Fair	V. Good	Excellent
Webley Mk III, .455 Revolver Mk I, Top Break, Round Butt, Military, *Curio*	$200	$250	$300
Webley Mk IV, .455 Revolver Mk I, Top Break, Round Butt, Military, *Curio*	150	225	300
Webley Mk V, .455 Revolver Mk I, Top Break, Round Butt, Military, *Curio*	200	250	300
Webley Mk VI, .455 Revolver Mk I, Top Break, Square Butt, Military, *Curio*	300	350	400
HANDGUN, SEMI-AUTOMATIC			
M1911A1 Colt, .455 Webley Auto, Clip Fed, Military, *Curio*	1000	1250	1500
Webley Mk.I, .455 Webley Auto, Clip Fed, *Curio*	700	850	1000
Webley Mk.I No. 2 R.A.F., .455 Webley Auto, Clip Fed, Cut for Shoulder Stock, *Curio*	3500	4000	4500
RIFLE, BOLT ACTION			
Lee Metford Mk I, .303 British, Clip Fed, *Curio*	150	175	200
Lee Metford Mk I, .303 British, Clip Fed, Carbine, *Curio*	175	200	225
Lee Metford Mk I*, .303 British, Clip Fed, Carbine, *Curio*	75	125	175
Lee Metford Mk II, .303 British, Clip Fed, *Curio*	125	150	175
Lee Metford Mk II*, .303 British, Clip Fed, *Curio*	150	175	200
M1896 Lee Metford, .303 British, Clip Fed, Military, Carbine, *Curio*	150	175	200
Pattern 14 (U.S.), .303 British, *Curio*	200	250	300
Santa Fe Jungle Carbine Mk.I MD12011, .303 British, Peep Sights, No Flash Hider, Commercial, *Modern*	75	125	175
SMLE #1 MK I, .303 British, Military, *Curio*	200	225	250
SMLE #1 MK III, .303 British, Military, *Curio*	175	200	225
SMLE #1 MK III*, .303 British, Military, *Curio*	200	225	250

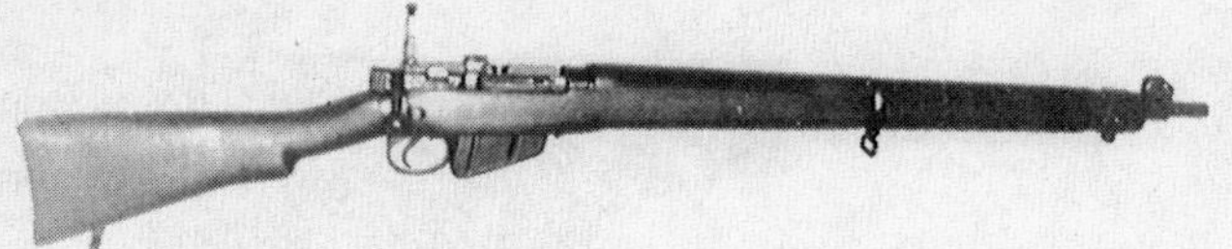

British Military #1 MK III

	Fair	V. Good	Excellent
SMLE #1 MK III*, .303 British, Tangent Sights, Military, Ishapore, *Curio*	$150	$175	$200
SMLE #2 MK IV, .22 L.R.R.F., Singleshot, Training Rifle, *Curio*	150	175	200
SMLE #3 MK I* (1914 Enfield), .303 British, Military, *Curio*	150	175	200
SMLE #4 MK I*, .303 British, Military, *Curio*	150	175	200
SMLE #4 MK I*, .303 British, Military, Canadian, Lightweight, *Curio*	100	125	150
SMLE #4 MK I*, .303 British, Military, Lightweight, *Curio*	150	175	200
SMLE #4 MK I*, .303 British, Military, New Zealand, Lightweight, *Curio*	150	175	200
SMLE #4 Sniper, .303 British, Military, Scope Mounted, *Curio*	400	475	550
SMLE #7, .22 L.R.R.F., Singleshot, Training Rifle, *Curio*	35	75	150
SMLE #8, .22 L.R.R.F., Singleshot, Training Rifle, *Curio*	50	100	150
SMLE #9, .22 L.R.R.F., Singleshot, Training Rifle, *Curio*	50	100	150
SMLE #MK V Jungle Carbine, .303 British, Peep Sights, Military, *Curio*	200	250	300

RIFLE, FLINTLOCK

	Fair	V. Good	Excellent
.75, 1st Model Brown Bess, Musket, Brass Furniture, *Antique*	2100	4200	6500
.75, 2nd Model Brown Bess, Musket, Military, *Antique*	1400	2800	4500
.75, 3rd Model Brown Bess, Musket, Military, *Antique*	800	1500	2500

RIFLE, PERCUSSION

	Fair	V. Good	Excellent
.58 Snider-Enfield, Military, Musket, *Antique*	265	525	800
.60 M1856 Tower, Military, Musket, *Antique*	175	350	800
.60 M1869 Enfield, Military, Musket, *Antique*	175	350	800

RIFLE, SINGLESHOT

	Fair	V. Good	Excellent
Martini-Henry, .303 British, *Antique*	225	275	325
Martini-Henry, .303 British, Carbine, *Antique*	85	175	275
Martini-Henry, .577/.450 Martini-Henry, *Antique*	175	225	275
Martini-Henry, .577/.450 Martini-Henry, Carbine, *Antique*	$100	$175	$250
Martini-Henry, .577/.450 Martini-Henry, Long Lever, *Antique*	150	200	250

SHOTGUN, SINGLESHOT

	Fair	V. Good	Excellent
Martini-Henry, .12 Gauge Special, Long Lever, *Antique*	75	125	175

BRNO

Ceska Zbrojovka, Brno, Czechoslovakia since 1922. Widely recognized and respected within the universe of arms manufacturing, BRNO has developed, over the years, some highly reliable and straight-shooting designs, deserving of distinction worldwide. The professional hunter Ian Manning of Zambia, South Africa and Botswana, swore by this piece, and said it rivaled any bolt action sporting rifle he had ever used.

RIFLE, BOLT ACTION

	Fair	V. Good	Excellent
21 H, Various Calibers, Sporting Rifle, Express Sights, Cheekpiece Checkered Stock, Set Trigger, *Modern*	600	675	750
22 F, Various Calibers, Sporting Rifle, Express Sights, Mannlicher Checkered Stock, Set Trigger, *Modern*	475	650	825
Model I, .22 L.R.R.F., Sporting Rifle, Express Sights, 5 Shot Clip, Checkered Stock, Set Trigger, *Modern*	300	350	400
Model II, .22 L.R.R.F., Sporting Rifle, Express Sights, 5 Shot Clip, Fancy Wood, Set Trigger, *Modern*	175	275	375
Z-B Mauser, .22 Hornet, Sporting Rifle, Express Sights, 5 Shot Clip, Checkered Stock, Set Trigger, *Modern*	350	575	800
ZKB 680 Fox, .22 Rem., Clip Fed, Checkered Stock, Sling Swivels, *Modern*	225	350	475
ZKM 452, .22 L.R.R.F., Clip Fed, Checkered Stock, Tangent Sights, *Modern*	50	100	150

RIFLE, SEMI-AUTOMATIC

	Fair	V. Good	Excellent
ZKM 581, .22 L.R.R.F., Clip Fed, Checkered Stock, Tangent Sights, *Modern*	225	300	375

RIFLE, DOUBLE BARREL, OVER-UNDER

	Fair	V. Good	Excellent
Super Express, Various Calibers, Fancy Checkering, Sidelock, Engraved, Double Triggers, *Modern*	950	1600	2250
Super Express Grade III, Various Calibers, Fancy Checkering, Sidelock, Fancy Engraving, Double Triggers, *Modern*	2750	3250	3750

	Fair	V. Good	Excellent
Super Express Grade IV, Various Calibers, Fancy Checkering, Sidelock, Fancy Engraving, Double Triggers, *Modern*	$2050	$2650	$3250

SHOTGUN, DOUBLE BARREL, OVER-UNDER

	Fair	V. Good	Excellent
Super, 12 Gauge, Fancy Checkering Sidelock, Plain, Ejectors, Double Triggers, *Modern*	235	475	725
Super Grade I, 12 Gauge, Fancy Checkering, Sidelock, Fancy Engraving, Ejectors, Double Triggers, *Modern*	700	1275	1850
Super Grade IV, 12 Gauge, Fancy Checkering, Sidelock, Engraved, Ejectors, Double Triggers, *Modern*	375	625	875
ZH 303 Field, 12 Gauge, Boxlock, Checkered Stock, *Modern*	300	400	500

SHOTGUN, DOUBLE BARREL, SIDE-BY-SIDE

	Fair	V. Good	Excellent
ZP 47, 12 Gauge, Sidelock, Double Triggers, Extractors, Checkered Stock, *Modern*	200	275	350
ZP 49, 12 Gauge, Sidelock, Double Triggers, Ejectors, Checkered Stock, *Modern*	375	450	525

BROCKWAY, NORMAN S.

West Brookfield, Mass. 1861–1867, Bellows Falls, Vt. 1867-1900.

RIFLE, PERCUSSION

	Fair	V. Good	Excellent
Various Calibers, Target Rifles, *Antique*	875	1750	3000

BRONCO

Echave y Arizmendi, Eibar, Spain 1911–1974.

HANDGUN, SEMI-AUTOMATIC

	Fair	V. Good	Excellent
1918 Vest Pocket, .32 ACP, Clip Fed, *Curio*	50	100	150
Vest Pocket, .25 ACP, Clip Fed, *Modern*	50	100	150
Vest Pocket, .25 ACP, Clip Fed, Light Engraving, *Modern*	65	125	200

BRONCO

Imported by Garcia, c. 1970.

COMBINATION WEAPON, OVER-UNDER

	Fair	V. Good	Excellent
.22/.410, Skeleton Stock, *Modern*	50	75	100

RIFLE, SINGLESHOT

	Fair	V. Good	Excellent
Skeleton Stock, *Modern*	25	50	75

SHOTGUN, SINGLESHOT

	Fair	V. Good	Excellent
.410 Ga., Skeleton Stock, *Modern*	25	50	75

BROOKLYN ARMS

Brooklyn, N.Y. 1863–1867. Not generally known in the firearms collecting field, or often thought of, the City of Brooklyn played a vital role in the history of American gunmaking. Revolvers like the Slocum are extremely well made, and were among several makes of revolving arms developed to try to take advantage of the expiration of Colonel Colt's master revolver patent, and the demand for arms developing during the Civil War. Brooklyn-made arms are a worthy subject for collecting.

HANDGUN, REVOLVER

	Fair	V. Good	Excellent
Slocum Patent, .32 R.F., 5 Shot Cylinder with Sliding Chambers, Spur Trigger, Single Action, Engraved, *Antique*	$155	$275	$395

BROWN MFG. CO.

Newburyport, Mass. 1869–73. Also see Ballard Rifle.

HANDGUN, SINGLESHOT

	Fair	V. Good	Excellent
Southerner Derringer, .41 R.F., Side-Swing Barrel, Spur Trigger, Brass Frame, *Antique*	150	250	350

RIFLE, BOLT ACTION

	Fair	V. Good	Excellent
1853 Long Enfield, .58 U.S. Musket, Converted from Percussion, Brass Furniture, *Antique*	165	325	750
U.S. M1861 Musket, .58 U.S. Musket, Converted from Percussion, Brass Furniture, *Antique*	175	350	750

BROWN PRECISION CO.

San Jose, Calif. since 1975.

RIFLE, BOLT ACTION

	Fair	V. Good	Excellent
Sporter, Various Calibers, Fiberglass Stock, Rem. 700 Action, Sling Swivels, *Modern*	650	750	850

BROWN, JOHN & SONS

Fremont, N.J. 1840–1871.

RIFLE, PERCUSSION

	Fair	V. Good	Excellent
.50, Target Rifle, Scope Mounted, Set Trigger, *Antique*	825	1650	4500
Various Calibers, Sporting Rifle, *Antique*	425	850	3500

BROWNING

Established 1870 in St. Louis, Mo., 1880 to Date, Ogden/Morgan, Utah. (See Fabrique Nationale.) Primary Manufacturer Fabrique National in Herstal and Liege, Belgium. Also see Commemoratives. The unique role of John M. Browning in the history of firearms presents an extraordinary chapter that has never fully been documented. The author has visited the Browning/FN complex in Herstal, Belgium, as well as the Browning Museum in Ogden, Utah. Both are a must for any dedicated arms collector, whether or not one is keen on Brownings per se. This company has not lost its touch in the manufacture of high-quality firearms. Browning firearms are among the finest mass-produced products ever made, and continue to attract hundreds of thousands of clients on a worldwide basis. As more books appear, and more collectors realize there is a small but determined army of Browning collectors and devotees, prices will exceed their present steady rise. Playing a further role in promoting Browning arms as collectibles is the Browning Collectors Association.

HANDGUN, SEMI-AUTOMATIC

	Fair	V. Good	Excellent
Baby Standard, .25 ACP, Clip Fed, *Modern*	$175	$225	$275
Baby, .25 ACP, Clip Fed, Lightweight, Nickel Plated, *Modern*	250	300	350
Baby, .25 ACP, Clip Fed, Renaissance, Nickel Plated, Engraved, *Modern*	400	600	800
BDA 38 Super, .38 Super, Clip Fed, Double Action, Fixed Sights, *Modern*	400	475	550
BDA 380, .380 ACP, Clip Fed, Double Action, Fixed Sights, *Modern*	250	300	350
BDA 380, .380 ACP, Clip Fed, Double Action, Fixed Sights, Nickel, *Modern*	225	300	375
BDA 45, .45 ACP, Clip Fed, Double Action, 7 Shot, *Modern*	250	325	400
BDA 9, 9mm Luger, Clip Fed, Double Action, 9 Shot, *Modern*	250	300	350
Challenger II, .22 L.R.R.F., Clip Fed, Adjustable Sights, *Modern*	125	175	225
Challenger III, .22 L.R.R.F., Clip Fed, Adjustable Sights, *Modern*	100	150	200

Browning Challenger III

	Fair	V. Good	Excellent
Challenger, .22 L.R.R.F., Clip Fed, Checkered Wood Grips, Adjustable Sights, *Modern*	200	250	300
Challenger, .22 L.R.R.F., Clip Fed, Gold Line, Checkered Wood Grips, Gold Inlays, Engraved, *Modern*	425	850	1500
Challenger, .22 L.R.R.F., Clip Fed, Renaissance, Checkered Wood Grips, Fancy Engraving, Nickel Plated, *Modern*	325	650	1200

	Fair	V. Good	Excellent
Classic Hi Power Pistol, 9mm, Engraved with Lynx and Bald Eagle, *Modern*	$375	$750	$1500
Gold Classic Hi Power Pistol, 9mm, Engraved with Lynx and Bald Eagle, *Modern*	750	1250	1750

Browning—Gold Classic Hi Power Pistol

	Fair	V. Good	Excellent
Hi Power "FM" Argentine, 9mm, Clip Fed, Made under License, Military, *Modern*	375	425	475
Hi Power Estonian, 9mm, Clip Fed, Military, *Curio*	385	775	1250
Hi Power Inglis #1 Mk I*, 9mm, Tangent Stocks, Slotted for Shoulder Stock, Military, *Curio*	350	550	750
Hi Power Inglis #1 Mk I*, 9mm, Tangent Stocks, with Shoulder Stock, Military, *Curio*	600	825	1050
Hi Power Inglis #1 Mk I, 9mm, Tangent Stocks, Slotted for Shoulder Stock, Military, *Curio*	400	675	950
Hi Power Inglis #2 Mk I*, 9mm, Fixed Sights, Slotted for Shoulder Stock, Military, *Curio*	600	750	900
Hi Power Inglis #2 Mk I, 9mm, Fixed Sights, Military, *Curio*	450	550	650
Hi Power Louis XVI, Fancy Engraving, Nickel Plated, Adjustable Sights, Cased, *Modern*	700	875	1050
Hi Power Louis XVI, Fancy Engraving, Nickel Plated, Fixed Sights, Cased, *Modern*	700	850	1000
Hi Power Renaissance, 9mm, Clip Fed, Nickel Plated, Engraved, *Modern*	365	725	1100
Hi Power Renaissance, 9mm, Clip Fed, Nickel Plated, Engraved, Adjustable Sights, *Modern*	500	850	1200
Hi Power Renaissance, 9mm, Clip Fed, with Ring Hammer, Nickel Plated, Engraved, *Modern*	500	875	1250
Hi Power Standard, 9mm, Clip Fed, with Ring Hammer, *Modern*	350	400	450
Hi Power Standard, 9mm, Clip Fed, with Spur Hammer, *Modern*	350	375	400

	Fair	V. Good	Excellent
Hi Power Standard, 9mm, Clip Fed, with Spur Hammer, Adjustable Sights, *Modern*	$300	$375	$450
Hi Power Standard, 9mm, Clip Fed, with Spur Hammer, with Tangent Sights, *Modern*	500	575	650
Hi Power Standard, 9mm, Clip Fed, with Spur Tangent Sights, Slotted for Shoulder Stock, *Modern*	750	850	950
Hi Power Standard, 9mm, Nickel Plating, Add 5%			
Hi Power, 9mm, Clip Fed, Military, *Curio*	300	375	450
Hi Power, 9mm, Clip Fed, Military, Tangent Sights, *Curio*	550	650	750

Browning Hi Power 9mm Military

	Fair	V. Good	Excellent
Hi Power, 9mm, Clip Fed, Military, Tangent Sights, with Detachable Shoulder Stock, *Curio*	400	575	750
Hi Power, 9mm, Clip Fed, Nazi-Marked Military, *Curio*	450	500	550
Hi Power, 9mm, Clip Fed, Nazi-Marked Military, Tangent Sights, *Curio*	700	850	1000
Hi Power, 9mm, Clip Fed, Nazi-Marked Military, Tangent Sights, *Curio*	700	850	1000
Hi Power, 9mm, Clip Fed, Nazi-Marked Military, Tangent Sights, with Detachable Shoulder Stock, *Curio*	2000	2250	2500
Hi Power, 9mm, Clip Fed, Pre-War Military, Tangent Sights, *Curio*	500	750	1000
Hi Power, 9mm, Clip Fed, Pre-War Military, Tangent Sights, with Detachable Shoulder Stock, *Curio*	1000	1250	1500
Medalist Goldline, .22 L.R.R.F., Clip Fed, Checkered Wood Target Grips, Wood Forestock, Gold Inlays, Engraved, *Modern*	375	750	2000

	Fair	V. Good	Excellent
Medalist International Early Model, .22 L.R.R.F., Clip Fed, Checkered Wood Target Grips, Target Sights, *Modern*	$450	$600	$750
Medalist International Second Model, .22 L.R.R.F., Clip Fed, Checkered Wood Target Grips, Gold Inlays, Engraved, Target Sights, *Modern*	500	550	600
Medalist Renaissance, .22 L.R.R.F., Clip Fed, Checkered Wood Target Grips, Fancy Engraving, Target Sights, *Modern*	500	1000	1750
Medalist, .22 L.R.R.F., Clip Fed, Checkered Wood Target Grips, Wood Forestock, Target Sights, *Modern*	400	575	750
Model 1900, .32 ACP, Clip Fed, *Curio*	125	200	275
Model 1900, .32 ACP, Clip Fed, Military, *Curio*	225	275	325
Model 1900, .32 ACP, Clip Fed, Early Type, No Lanyard Ring, *Curio*	225	325	425
Model 1903, 9mm Browning Long, Clip Fed, *Curio*	250	350	450

Browning M1903 9mm

	Fair	V. Good	Excellent
Model 1903, 9mm Browning Long, Clip Fed, Cut for Shoulder Stock, Military, *Curio*	650	750	850
Model 1903, 9mm Browning Long, Clip Fed, Cut for Shoulder Stock, with Holster Stock, Military, *Curio*			
Model 1903, 9mm Browning Long, Clip Fed, Light Engraving, *Curio*	250	450	650
Model 1903, 9mm Browning Long, Clip Fed, Military, *Curio*	400	450	500
Model 1903, 9mm Browning Long, Swedish Contract, Clip Fed, *Curio*	225	250	275
Model 1905, First Variation, .25 ACP, Clip Fed, Grip Safety, Nickel, *Modern*	175	250	325
Model 1905, First Variation, .25 ACP, Clip Fed, Grip Safety, *Modern*	175	225	275
Model 1905, Second Variation, .25 ACP, Clip Fed, Grip Safety, Nickel, *Modern*	150	200	250
Model 1910, .32 ACP, Clip Fed, *Curio*	150	225	300

	Fair	V. Good	Excellent
Model 1910, .32 ACP, Clip Fed, Military, *Curio*	$250	$325	$400
Model 1910, .32 ACP, Clip Fed, German Police, *Modern*	225	275	325
Model 1910, .32 ACP, Clip Fed, Japanese Military, *Curio*	125	225	325
Model 1910, .32 ACP, Clip Fed, Peruvian Military, *Curio*	225	275	325
Model 1910, .32 ACP, Clip Fed, Syrian Police, *Curio*	250	300	350
Model 1910, .380 ACP, Clip Fed, *Curio*	250	300	350
Model 1922, .32 ACP, Clip Fed, *Curio*	150	200	250
Model 1922, .32 ACP, Clip Fed, Nazi-Marked Military, *Curio*	200	250	300
Model 1922, .32 and .380 ACP, Clip Fed, *Curio*	125	175	225
Model 1922, .32 and .380 ACP, Clip Fed, Renaissance, Nickel Plated, Engraved, *Curio*	550	750	950
Model 1922, .380 ACP, Clip Fed, *Curio*	175	225	275
Model 1922, .380 ACP, Clip Fed, Dutch Military, *Curio*	200	250	300

Browning BBR

	Fair	V. Good	Excellent
Model 1922, .380 ACP, Clip Fed, Nazi-Marked, Military, *Curio*	250	300	350
Model 1922, .380 ACP, Clip Fed, Turkish Military, *Curio*	150	225	300
Model 1922, .380 ACP, Clip Fed, Waffenampt Proofed, *Curio*	200	250	300
Model 1922, .380 ACP, Clip Fed, Yugoslavian Military, *Curio*	150	225	300
Nomad, .22 L.R.R.F., Clip Fed, Plastic Grips, Adjustable Sights, *Modern*	200	250	300
Renaissance Set, Baby .389 Hi Power, Nickel Plated, Engraved, *Modern*	1500	2500	3500

RIFLE, BOLT ACTION

	Fair	V. Good	Excellent
Model BBR, Various Calibers, Checkered Stock, *Modern*	300	350	400
Exhibition Olympian Grade, Various Calibers, Gold Inlays, Fancy Wood, Fancy Checkering, Engraved, *Modern*	7500	8500	9500
Medallion Grade, .458 Win. Mag., Long Action, Fancy Wood, Fancy Checkering, Engraved, Open Rear Sight, *Modern*	1000	1250	1500
Medallion Grade, Various Calibers, Long Action, Magnum, Fancy Wood, Fancy Checkering, Engraved, *Modern*	900	1250	1600
Medallion Grade, Various Calibers, Short Action, Fancy Wood, Fancy Checkering, Engraved, *Modern*	$900	$1150	$1400
Olympian Grade, .458 Win. Mag., Long Action, Fancy Wood, Fancy Checkering, Engraved, *Modern*	2000	2750	3500
Olympian Grade, Various Calibers, Long Action, Fancy Wood, Fancy Checkering, Fancy Engraving, *Modern*	2000	2500	3000
Olympian Grade, Various Calibers, Long Action, Magnum, Fancy Wood, Fancy Checkering, Fancy Engraving, *Modern*	2250	2750	3250
Olympian Grade, Various Calibers, Medium Action, Fancy Wood, Fancy Checkering, Fancy Engraving, *Modern*	2000	2500	3000
Olympian Grade, Various Calibers, Short Action, Fancy Wood, Fancy Checkering, Engraved, *Modern*	1750	2250	2750
Safari Grade, Various Calibers, Long Action, Checkered Stock, *Modern*	600	725	850
Safari Grade, Various Calibers, Long Action, Magnum, Checkered Stock, *Modern*	400	800	1200
Safari Grade, Various Calibers, Medium Action, Checkered Stock, *Modern*	575	700	825
Safari Grade, Various Calibers, Short Action, Checkered Stock, *Modern*	550	675	800
T-Bolt T-1, .22 L.R.R.F., 5 Shot Clip, Plain, Open Rear Sight, *Modern*	200	250	300
T-Bolt T-1, .22 L.R.R.F., 5 Shot Clip, Plain, Open Rear Sight, Left-Hand, *Modern*	225	275	325
T-Bolt T-2, .22 L.R.R.F., 5 Shot Clip, Checkered Stock, Fancy Wood, Open Rear Sight, *Modern*	250	325	400

RIFLE, LEVER ACTION

	Fair	V. Good	Excellent
BL-22 Grade 1, .22 L.R.R.F., Tube Feed, Checkered Stock, *Modern*	150	200	250
BL-22 Grade 2, .22 L.R.R.F., Tube Feed, Checkered Stock, Light Engraving, *Modern*	175	225	275
BL-22, Belgian Manufacture, Add 15%-25%			
Model 81 BLR, Various Calibers, Center-Fire, Plain, Clip Fed, Checkered Stock, *Modern*	250	300	350
Model 92 Centennial, Tube Feed, Open Sights, *Modern*	275	325	375
Model 92, .357 Mag., Tube Feed, Open Sights, *Modern*	225	275	325
Model 92, .44 Mag., Tube Feed, Open Sights, *Modern*	250	300	350

Browning B-92

RIFLE, PERCUSSION

	Fair	V. Good	Excellent
J. Browning Mountain Rifle, Various Calibers, Singleshot, Octagon Barrel, Open Rear Sight, Single Set Trigger, Brass Finish, Reproduction, *Antique*	$175	$350	$600
Mountain Rifle, Various Calibers, Singleshot, Octagon Barrel, Open Rear Sight, Single Set Trigger, Browned Finish, Reproduction, *Antique*	125	250	400

RIFLE, SEMI-AUTOMATIC

	Fair	V. Good	Excellent
Auto-Rifle Grade I, .22 L.R.R.F., Tube Feed, Takedown, Open Rear Sight, Checkered Stock, *Modern*	225	300	375
Auto-Rifle Grade I, .22 Short, Tube Feed, Takedown, Open Rear Sight, Checkered Stock, *Modern*	250	350	450

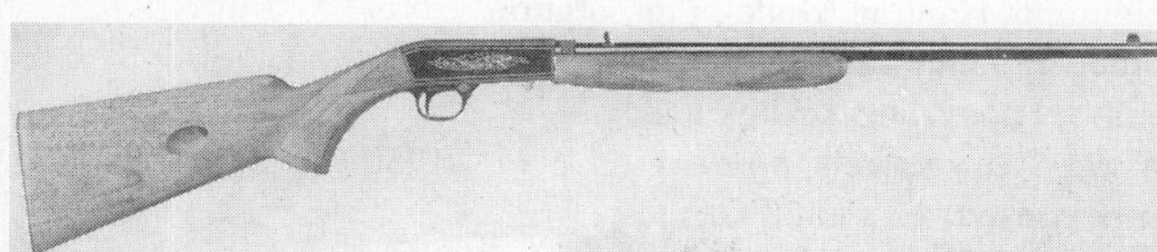

Browning Auto-Rifle Grade I

	Fair	V. Good	Excellent
Auto-Rifle Grade II, .22 L.R.R.F., Tube Feed, Takedown, Open Rear Sight, Satin Chrome Receiver, Engraved, *Modern*	275	550	1250
Auto-Rifle Grade III, .22 L.R.R.F., Takedown, Satin Chrome Receiver, Fancy Wood, Fancy Checkering, Fancy Engraving, Cased, *Modern*	500	1000	2250
Auto-Rifle, Belgian Mfg., Add 20%-30%			
BAR Grade 1, Various Calibers, Center-Fire, Checkered Stock, Plain, *Modern*	350	400	450

Browning BAR 22

	Fair	V. Good	Excellent
BAR Grade 2, Various Calibers, Center-Fire, Checkered Stock, Light Engraving, *Modern*	425	500	575
BAR Grade 3, Various Calibers, Center-Fire, Fancy Wood, Fancy Checkering, Engraved, *Modern*	$500	$650	$800
BAR Grade 4, Various Calibers, Center-Fire, Fancy Wood, Fancy Checkering, Fancy Engraving, *Modern*	565	1125	2000
BAR Grade 5, Various Calibers, Center-Fire, Fancy Wood, Fancy Checkering, Fancy Engraving, Gold Inlays, *Modern*	1125	2250	3500

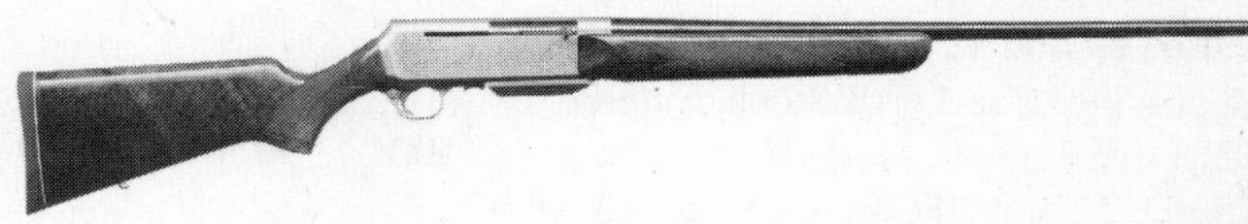

Browning BAR

	Fair	V. Good	Excellent
BAR, Various Calibers, Center-Fire, Belgian Mfg., Add 15%-25%			
BAR, Various Calibers, Center-Fire, Magnum Calibers, Add 10%			
BAR-22 Grade I, .22 L.R.R.F., Checkered Stock, *Modern*	175	200	225
BAR-22 Grade II, .22 L.R.R.F., Checkered Stock, *Modern*	225	275	325
Classic Light, 12 Gauge, Engraved with Mallard Ducks, Labrador Retriever, and Portrait of John M. Browning, *Modern*	1000	1250	1500
Gold Classic Light, 12 Gauge, Engraved with Mallard Ducks, Labrador Retriever, and Portrait of John M. Browning, *Modern*	3000	3750	4500

RIFLE, SINGLESHOT

	Fair	V. Good	Excellent
Model 78, .30-06, 1 of 50 Bicentennial Rifle, .30-06 Caliber, Commemorative, *Curio*	1500	3500	5000
Model 78, Various Calibers, Various Barrel Styles, Checkered Stock, *Modern*	7000	12500	17500

RIFLE, DOUBLE BARREL, OVER-UNDER

	Fair	V. Good	Excellent
Express Rifle, .30/06 or .270 Win., Engraved, Fancy Wood, Fancy Checkering, Cased, *Modern*	1200	1850	2500

RIFLE, SLIDE ACTION

	Fair	V. Good	Excellent
BPR, .22 L.R.R.F., Grade I, Checkered Stock, *Modern*	100	150	200
BPR, .22 Mag., Grade I, Checkered Stock, *Modern*	125	175	225
BPR, .22 Mag., Grade II, Checkered Stock, Engraved, *Modern*	325	350	375

	Fair	V. Good	Excellent
SHOTGUN, DOUBLE BARREL, OVER-UNDER			
Citori Grade I, 12 Ga., Skeet Grade, Vent Rib, Checkered Stock, *Modern*	$650	$750	$850
Citori Grade I, 12 Ga., Trap Grade, Vent Rib, Checkered Stock, *Modern*	700	850	1000
Citori Grade II, Trap and Skeet Models, Add 10%			
Citori Grade II, Various Gauges, Hunting Model, Engraved, Checkered Stock, Single Selective Trigger, *Modern*	650	800	950
Citori Grade V, Trap and Skeet Models, Add 10%			
Citori Grade V, Various Gauges, Fancy Engraving, Checkered Stock, Single Selective Trigger, *Modern*	1100	1250	1400
Citori, 12 and 20 Gauges, Standard Grade, Vent Rib, Checkered Stock, *Modern*	600	725	850

Browning Citori Superlight

	Fair	V. Good	Excellent
Citori, 12 Ga., Early Model, Vent Rib, Checkered Stock, *Modern*	650	700	750
Citori, 12 Gauge, Magnum, Vent Rib, Checkered Stock, *Modern*	700	850	1000
Classic, 20 Gauge, 26" Barrel, Engraved with Bird Dogs, Pheasant, and Quail, *Modern*	1250	1500	1750
Gold Classic, 20 Gauge, 26" Barrel, Engraved with Bird Dogs, Pheasant, and Quail, *Modern*	4000	4500	5000

Browning Gold Classic Light

	Fair	V. Good	Excellent
Grand Liege, 12 Ga., Engraved, Single Trigger, Checkered Stock, *Modern*	600	700	800
Liege, 12 Ga., Engraved, Single Trigger, Checkered Stock, *Modern*	$450	$525	$600
ST-100, 12 Ga., Trap Special, Engraved, Checkered Stock, *Modern*	1500	1750	2000
Superposed Bicentennial, Fancy Engraving, Gold Inlays, Fancy Wood, Fancy Checkering, Cased, Commemorative, *Modern*	6500	7500	8500
Superposed, 12 and 20 Gauges, Lightning Hunting Model, Presentation Grade 4, Fancy Engraving, with Sideplates, Gold Inlays, Fancy Checkering, Fancy Wood, Extra Barrels, *Modern*	4750	5750	6750
Superposed, 12 and 20 Gauges, Lightning Hunting Model, Presentation Grade 4, Fancy Engraving, with Sideplates, Fancy Checkering, Fancy Wood, Extra Barrels, *Modern*	4500	5250	6000
Superposed, 12 and 20 Gauges, Lightning Hunting Model, Presentation Grade 2, Fancy Engraving, Fancy Checkering, Fancy Wood, Extra Barrels, *Modern*	3250	3500	3750
Superposed, 12 and 20 Gauges, Lightning Hunting Model, Presentation Grade 2, Fancy Engraving, Gold Inlays, Fancy Checkering, Fancy Wood, Extra Barrels, *Modern*	1750	2750	3750
Superposed, 12 and 20 Gauges, Lightning Hunting Model, Presentation Grade 1, Engraved, Gold Inlays, Fancy Checkering, Fancy Wood, *Modern*	2000	2250	2500
Superposed, 12 and 20 Gauges, Lightning Hunting Model, Presentation Grade 1, Engraved, Fancy Checkering, Fancy Wood, *Modern*	1750	2000	2250
Superposed, 12 and 20 Gauges, Lightning Skeet Model, Presentation Grade 4, Fancy Engraving, with Sideplates, Gold Inlays, Fancy Checkering, Fancy Wood, *Modern*	4500	5500	6500
Superposed, 12 and 20 Gauges, Lightning Skeet Model, Presentation Grade 4, Fancy Engraving, with Sideplates, Fancy Checkering, Fancy Wood, Extra Barrels, *Modern*	4500	5500	6500
Superposed, 12 and 20 Gauges, Lightning Skeet Model, Presentation Grade 3, Fancy Engraving, Gold Inlays, Fancy Checkering, Fancy Wood, *Modern*	4000	4750	5500
Superposed, 12 and 20 Gauges, Lightning Skeet Model, Presentation Grade 2, Fancy Engraving, Gold Inlays, Fancy Checkering, Fancy Wood, *Modern*	2500	3000	3500

	Fair	V. Good	Excellent
Superposed, 12 and 20 Gauges, Lightning Skeet Model, Presentation Grade 1, Engraved, Gold Inlays ...	$1000	$2000	$2750
Superposed, 12 and 20 Gauges, Lightning Skeet Model, Presentation Grade 1, Engraved, Fancy Checkering, Fancy Wood, *Modern*	900	1900	2500
Superposed, 12 and 20 Gauges, Super-Light Hunting Model, Presentation Grade 4, Extra Barrels, Fancy Engraving, with Sideplates, Gold Inlays, Fancy Checkering, Fancy Wood, *Modern*	3000	5750	6750
Superposed, 12 and 20 Gauges, Super-Light Hunting Model, Presentation Grade 4, Fancy Engraving, with Sideplates, Fancy Checkering, Fancy Wood, Extra Barrels, *Modern*	3000	5000	6250
Superposed, 12 and 20 Gauges, Super-Light Hunting Model, Presentation Grade 2, Fancy Engraving, Fancy Checkering, Fancy Wood, Extra Barrels, *Modern*	1500	3000	4000
Superposed, 12 and 20 Gauges, Super-Light Hunting Model, Presentation Grade 2, Fancy Engraving, Gold Inlays, Fancy Checkering, Fancy Wood, Extra Barrels, *Modern*	1250	2500	3750
Superposed, 12 and 20 Gauges, Super-Light Hunting Model, Presentation Grade 1, Engraved, Gold Inlays, Fancy Checkering, Fancy Wood, *Modern*	1000	2000	2750
Superposed, 12 and 20 Gauges, Super-Light Hunting Model, Presentation Grade 1, Engraved, Fancy Checkering, Fancy Wood, *Modern*	900	1900	2500
Superposed, 12 Ga., Broadway Trap Model, Presentation Grade 4, Fancy Engraving, with Sideplates, Gold Inlays, Fancy Checkering, Fancy Wood, *Modern*	3000	5000	6500
Superposed, 12 Ga., Broadway Trap Model, Presentation Grade 4, Fancy Engraving, with Sideplates, Fancy Checkering, Fancy Wood, *Modern*	2700	4500	6000
Superposed, 12 Ga., Broadway Trap Model, Presentation Grade 3, Fancy Engraving, Gold Inlays, Fancy Checkering, Fancy Wood, *Modern*	2500	3500	5000
Superposed, 12 Ga., Broadway Trap Model, Presentation Grade 2, Fancy Engraving, Fancy Checkering, Fancy Wood, *Modern*	1500	3000	4000
Superposed, 12 Ga., Broadway Trap Model, Presentation Grade 2, Fancy Engraving, Gold Inlays, Fancy Checkering, Fancy Wood, *Modern*	1200	2500	3500
Superposed, 12 Ga., Broadway Trap Model, Presentation Grade 1, Engraved, Gold Inlays, Fancy Checkering, Fancy Wood, *Modern*	$900	$2000	$3000
Superposed, 12 Ga., Broadway Trap Model, Presentation Grade 1, Engraved, Fancy Checkering, Fancy Wood, *Modern*	800	1800	2750
Superposed, 12 Ga., Lightning Trap Model, Presentation Grade 4, Fancy Engraving, with Sideplates, Gold Inlays, Fancy Checkering, Fancy Wood, *Modern*	2700	4500	6000
Superposed, 12 Ga., Lightning Trap Model, Presentation Grade 4, Fancy Engraving, with Sideplates, Fancy Checkering, Fancy Wood, *Modern*	2700	4000	5500
Superposed, 12 Ga., Lightning Trap Model, Presentation Grade 3, Fancy Engraving, Gold Inlays, Fancy Checkering, Fancy Wood, *Modern*	2000	3000	4500
Superposed, 12 Ga., Lightning Trap Model, Presentation Grade 2, Fancy Engraving, Fancy Checkering, Fancy Wood, *Modern*	1200	2500	3750
Superposed, 12 Ga., Lightning Trap Model, Presentation Grade 2, Fancy Engraving, Gold Inlays, Fancy Checkering, Fancy Wood, *Modern*	1000	2200	3250
Superposed, 12 Ga., Lightning Trap Model, Presentation Grade 1, Engraved, Gold Inlays, Fancy Checkering, Fancy Wood, *Modern*	800	2000	2750
Superposed, 12 Ga., Lightning Trap Model, Presentation Grade 1, Engraved, Fancy Checkering, Fancy Wood, *Modern*	700	1800	2500
Superposed, 28 Ga. or .410 Ga., Lightning Hunting Model, Presentation Grade 4, Fancy Engraving, with Sideplates, Gold Inlays, Fancy Checkering, Fancy Wood, *Modern*	2700	4000	5500
Superposed, 28 Ga. or .410 Ga., Lightning Hunting Model, Presentation Grade 4, Fancy Engraving, with Sideplates, Gold Inlays, Fancy Checkering, Fancy Wood, *Modern*	2500	4000	5250
Superposed, 28 Ga. or .410 Ga., Lightning Hunting Model, Presentation Grade 4, Fancy Engraving, with Sideplates, Fancy Checkering, Fancy Wood, *Modern*	2000	3700	5000
Superposed, 28 Ga. or .410 Ga., Lightning Hunting Model, Presentation Grade 3, Fancy Engraving, Gold Inlays, Fancy Checkering, Fancy Wood, *Modern*	2000	3000	4500

	Fair	V. Good	Excellent
Superposed, 28 Ga. or .410 Ga., Lightning Hunting Model, Presentation Grade 2, Fancy Engraving, Fancy Checkering, Fancy Wood, *Modern*	$1500	$2500	$3500
Superposed, 28 Ga. or .410 Ga., Lightning Hunting Model, Presentation Grade 2, Fancy Engraving, Gold Inlays, Fancy Checkering, Fancy Wood, *Modern*	1500	2500	4000
Superposed, 28 Ga. or .410 Ga., Lightning Hunting Model, Presentation Grade 1, Engraved, Gold Inlays, Fancy Checkering, Fancy Wood, *Modern*	1000	2000	3000
Superposed, 28 Ga. or .410 Ga., Lightning Hunting Model, Presentation Grade 1, Engraved, Fancy Checkering, Fancy Wood, *Modern*	900	1800	2500
Superposed, 28 Ga. or .410 Ga., Lightning Skeet Model, Presentation Grade 4, Fancy Engraving, with Sideplates, Gold Inlays, Fancy Checkering, Fancy Wood, *Modern*	2700	4000	5500
Superposed, 28 Ga. or .410 Ga., Lightning Skeet Model, Presentation Grade 4, Fancy Engraving, with Sideplates, Gold Inlays, Fancy Checkering, Fancy Wood, *Modern*	2500	4000	5250
Superposed, 28 Ga. or .410 Ga., Lightning Skeet Model, Presentation Grade 4, Fancy Engraving, with Sideplates, Fancy Checkering, Fancy Wood, *Modern*	2000	3700	5000
Superposed, 28 Ga. or .410 Ga., Lightning Skeet Model, Presentation Grade 3, Fancy Engraving, Gold Inlays, Fancy Checkering, Fancy Wood, *Modern*	1700	3500	4500
Superposed, 28 Ga. or .410 Ga., Lightning Skeet Model, Presentation Grade 2, Fancy Engraving, Fancy Checkering, Fancy Wood, *Modern*	1000	2500	3500
Superposed, 28 Ga. or .410 Ga., Lightning Skeet Model, Presentation Grade 2, Fancy Engraving, Gold Inlays, Fancy Checkering, Fancy Wood, *Modern*	1200	2700	4000
Superposed, 28 Ga. or .410 Ga., Lightning Skeet Model, Presentation Grade 1, Engraved, Gold Inlays, Fancy Checkering, Fancy Wood, *Modern*	1000	2000	3250
Superposed, 28 Ga. or .410 Ga., Lightning Skeet Model, Presentation Grade 1, Engraved, Fancy Checkering, Fancy Wood, *Modern*	900	1800	2750
Superposed, For .410 or 28 Gauge, Add 15%-25%			
Superposed, For 20 Gauge, Add 10%-15%			
Superposed, Pre-1977, Lightning Skeet, Add 5%-10%			
Superposed, Pre-1977, 4-Barrel, Skeet Set, Add 275%-300%			
Superposed, Pre-1977, Broadway Trap Model, Add 8%-13%			
Superposed, Pre-1977, Extra Barrel, Add 35%-40%			
Superposed, Pre-1977, Lightning Trap Model, Add 5%-10%			
Superposed, Pre-1977, Super-Light Lightning, Add 15%-20%			
Superposed, Pre-1977, Vent Rib, Pre-War, Add 10%-15%			
Superposed, Pre-War, Raised Solid Rib, Add $60.00-$90.00			
Superposed, Various Gauges, Pre-1977, Diana Grade Hunting Model, Satin Nickel-Plated Frame, Fancy Engraving, Fancy Checkering, Fancy Wood, *Modern*	$1500	$3000	$4500
Superposed, Various Gauges, Pre-1977, Exhibition Grade, Fancy Engraving, Fancy Checkering, Fancy Wood, Gold Inlays, *Modern*	5000	8000	10000
Superposed, Various Gauges, Pre-1977, Grade 1, Engraved, Checkered Stock, Vent Rib, Single Selective Trigger, *Modern*	700	1200	2000
Superposed, Various Gauges, Pre-1977, Midas Grade Hunting Model, Fancy Engraving, Fancy Checkering, Fancy Wood, Gold Inlays, *Modern*	3000	5000	6500
Superposed, Various Gauges, Pre-1977, Pigeon Grade Hunting Model, Satin Nickel-Plated Frame, Fancy Engraving, Fancy Checkering, Fancy Wood, *Modern*	1000	2000	3000
Superposed, Various Gauges, Pre-1977, Pointer Grade, Fancy Engraving, Fancy Checkering, Single Selective Trigger, *Modern*	1000	2000	3500
Superposed, Various Gauges, Pre-1977, Super Exhibition Grade, Fancy Wood, Fancy Checkering, Fancy Engraving, Gold Inlays, *Modern*	10000	20000	25000
Superposed, Various Gauges, Presentation Grade 1, Extra Sets of Barrels, Add for each: $725.00-$1100.00			
Superposed, Various Gauges, Presentation Grade 2, Extra Sets of Barrels, Add for each: $825.00-$1250.00			
Superposed, Various Gauges, Presentation Grade 3, Extra Sets of Barrels, Add for each: $900.00-$1500.00			
Superposed, Various Gauges, Presentation Grade 4, Extra Sets of Barrels, Add for each: $1200.00-$1700.00			

SHOTGUN, DOUBLE BARREL, SIDE-BY-SIDE

	Fair	V. Good	Excellent
B-SS, 12 and 20 Gauges, Checkered Stock, Field Grade, *Modern*	$250	$400	$500
B-SS, 12 and 20 Gauges, Checkered Stock, Grade II, Engraved, *Modern*	575	775	975
B-SS, 12 and 20 Gauges, Checkered Stock, Sporter Grade, *Modern*	300	500	600

SHOTGUN, SEMI-AUTOMATIC

	Fair	V. Good	Excellent
Auto-5, Various Gauges, Vent Rib, Add $50.00-$75.00			
Auto-5, 12 and 20 Gauges, Magnum, Checkered Stock, Light Engraving, Plain Barrel, *Modern*	250	350	450
Auto-5, 12 and 20 Gauges, Skeet Grade, Checkered Stock, Light Engraving, Vent Rib, *Modern*	250	350	550
Auto-5, 12 Ga., Trap Grade, Vent Rib, Checkered Stock, *Modern*	200	350	475
Auto-5, 16 Ga., 29/16", Pre-WW2, Checkered Stock, Light Engraving, Plain Barrel, *Modern*	150	200	275
Auto-5, 16 Gauge, Sweet Sixteen, Lightweight, Checkered Stock, Light Engraving, Plain Barrel, *Modern*	150	300	400
Auto-5, For Belgian Make Add 15%-25%			
Auto-5, Various Gauges, Buck Special, Checkered Stock, Light Engraving, Plain Barrel, *Modern*	250	400	525
Auto-5, Various Gauges, Grade 2, Pre-WW2, Plain Barrel, Fancy Engraving, *Modern*	425	850	1500
Auto-5, Various Gauges, Grade 2, Pre-WW2, Plain Barrel Fancy Engraving, Gold Inlays, *Modern*	900	2000	2750
Auto-5, Various Gauges, Grade IV, Plain Barrel, Fancy Engraving, *Modern*	1500	3000	3750
Auto-5, Various Gauges, Lightweight, Checkered Stock, Light Engraving, Plain Barrel, *Modern*	300	450	525
Auto-5, Various Gauges, Raised Solid Rib, Add $50.00-$75.00			
B-80, 12 Gauge, Lightweight, Checkered Stock, Vent Rib, *Modern*	150	300	$375

Browning B-80

	Fair	V. Good	Excellent
Double-Auto, 12 and 20 Gauges, Checkered Stock, Engraved, Plain Barrel, *Modern*	150	300	375
Double-Auto, 12 Ga., Trap Model, Add 10%-15%			
Double-Auto, 12 Gauge, Checkered Stock, Engraved, Vent Rib, Barrel, *Modern*	$200	$400	$475
Double-Auto, Skeet Model, Add 10%-15%			
Double-Auto, Vent Rib, Add $50.00-$75.00			
Model 2000 Montreal Olympic, 12 Ga., Trap Grade, Vent Rib, Engraved, Gold Inlays, Commemorative, Tube Feed, Checkered Stock, *Modern*	400	700	1000
Model 2000, 12 and 20 Gauges, Buck Special, Open Rear Sight, Tube Feed, Checkered Stock, *Modern*	175	250	325
Model 2000, 12 and 20 Gauges, Skeet Grade, Vent Rib, Tube Feed, Checkered Stock, *Modern*	200	275	350
Model 2000, 12 and 20 Gauges, Vent Rib, Tube Feed, Checkered Stock, *Modern*	175	250	325
Model 2000, 12 Ga., Trap Grade, Vent Rib, Tube Feed, Checkered Stock, *Modern*	200	275	325

SHOTGUN, SINGLESHOT

	Fair	V. Good	Excellent
BT-99, 12 Ga., Pigeon Grade, Checkered Stock, Engraved, Vent Rib, *Modern*	700	850	1000
BT-99, 12 Ga., Trap Grade, Vent Rib, Checkered Stock, Engraved, *Modern*	400	650	750
BT-99, 12 Ga., Trap Grade, Vent Rib, with extra Single Trap Barrel, Checkered Stock, Engraved, *Modern*	400	675	850

SHOTGUN, SLIDE ACTION

	Fair	V. Good	Excellent
BPS, 12 Ga., Buck Special, Rifle Sights, *Modern*	200	300	375
BPS, 12 Ga., Checkered Stock, Vent Rib, *Modern*	200	300	375
BPS, 12 Ga., Invector Trap, Checkered Stock, Vent Rib, *Modern*	175	275	300

BRUTUS

Made by Hood Firearms Co., c. 1875-76.

HANDGUN, REVOLVER

	Fair	V. Good	Excellent
.22 Short R.F., 7 Shot, Spur Trigger, Solid Frame, Single Action, *Antique*	50	100	175

BSA

Birmingham Small Arms, Ltd., Birmingham, England, from 1885.

RIFLE, BOLT ACTION

	Fair	V. Good	Excellent
Imperial, Various Calibers, Sporting Rifle, Muzzle Brake, Checkered Stock, Open Rear Sight, *Modern*	85	175	275

	Fair	V. Good	Excellent
Imperial, Various Calibers, Sporting Rifle, Muzzle Brake, Checkered Stock, Open Rear Sight, Lightweight, *Modern*	$150	$200	$275
Majestic Deluxe, .458 Win. Mag., Sporting Rifle, Muzzle Brake, Lightweight, Checkered Stock, Open Rear Sight, *Modern*	125	225	325
Majestic Deluxe, Various Calibers, Sporting Rifle, Checkered, Stock, Open Rear Sight, *Modern*	85	175	275
Majestic Deluxe, Various Calibers, Sporting Rifle, Muzzle Brake, Lightweight, Checkered Stock, Open Rear Sight, *Modern*	85	175	275
Model CF-2, Various Calibers, Sporting Rifle, Checkered Stock, Open Rear Sights, *Modern*	115	225	375
Model CF-2, Various Calibers, Sporting Rifle, Checkered Stock, Double Set Triggers, Open Rear Sights, *Modern*	150	275	400
Monarch Deluxe, Various Calibers, Sporting Rifle, Checkered Stock Open Rear Sight, *Modern*	100	200	300
Monarch Deluxe, Various Claibers, Varmint, Heavy Barrel, Checkered Stock, Open Rear Sight, *Modern*	150	225	300

RIFLE, SINGLESHOT

	Fair	V. Good	Excellent
#12 Martini, *Modern*	100	200	300
#12/15 Martini, .22 L.R.R.F., Target, Target Sights, Target Stock, *Modern*	150	250	350
#12/15 Martini, .22 L.R.R.F., Target, Target Sights, Target Stock, Heavy Barrel, *Modern*	125	250	375
#13 Martini, .22 Hornet, Sporting Rifle, Checkered Stock, *Modern*	175	275	375
#13 Martini, .22 L.R.R.F., Target, Target Sights, Checkered Stock, *Modern*	125	200	275
#15 Martini, .22 L.R.R.F., Target, Target Sights, Target Stock, *Modern*	250	350	450
Centurian Martini, .22 L.R.R.F., Target, Target Sights, Target Stock, Target Barrel, *Modern*	125	250	375
International Martini, .22 L.R.R.F., Target, Target Sights, Heavy Barrel, Target Stock, *Modern*	125	250	400
International MK 2 Martini, .22 L.R.R.F., Target, Target Sights, Target Stock, *Modern*	150	275	400
International MK 2 Martini, .22 L.R.R.F., Target, Target Sights, Target Stock, Heavy Barrel, *Modern*	125	250	375
International MK 3 Martini, .22 L.R.R.F., Target, Target Sights, Target Stock, Heavy Barrel, *Modern*	$250	$325	$400
Mark V, .22 L.R.R.F., Heavy Barrel, Target Rifle, Target Sights, Target Stock, *Modern*	225	350	475
Martini I S U, .22 L.R.R.F., Target Rifle, Target Sights, Target Stock, *Modern*	125	250	475

RIFLE, SLIDE ACTION

	Fair	V. Good	Excellent
.22 L.R.R.F., Clip Fed, Takedown, *Modern*	35	75	150
.22 L.R.R.F., Tube Feed, Takedown, *Modern*	50	100	150

BUCHEL, ERNST FRIEDRICH

Zella Mehlis, Germany, 1919–1926.

HANDGUN, SINGLESHOT

	Fair	V. Good	Excellent
Luna, .22 L.R.R.F., Rotary Breech, Free Pistol, Set Triggers, Light Engraving, *Curio*	400	650	750
Model W.B., .22 L.R.R.F., Roux Action, Target Pistol, Hammerless, Tip-Down Barrel, *Curio*	225	350	475
Practice, .22 Short R.F., Warnant Action, Hammer, Target Pistol, *Curio*	150	225	300
Tell I, .22 L.R.R.F., Rotary Breech, Free Pistol, Set Triggers, Light Engraving, *Curio*	400	700	850
Tell II, .22 L.R.R.F., Rotary Breech, Free Pistol, Set Triggers, Light Engraving, *Curio*	400	700	850

BUDDY ARMS

Fort Worth, Tex., during the early 1960s.

HANDGUN, DOUBLE BARREL, OVER-UNDER

	Fair	V. Good	Excellent
Double Deuce, .22 L.R.R.F., Remington Derringer Copy, *Modern*	25	50	75

BUDISCHOWSKY

Made by Norton Armament (Norarmco), Mt. Clemens, Mich. 1973-1977.

HANDGUN, SEMI-AUTOMATIC

	Fair	V. Good	Excellent
TP-70, .22 L.R.R.F., Clip Fed, Double Action, Pocket Pistol, Stainless Steel, Steel Hammer, *Modern*	200	350	425
TP-70, .25 ACP, Clip Fed, Double Action, Pocket Pistol, Stainless Steel, Hammer, Presentation, Custom Serial Number, *Curio*	550	750	950

	Fair	V. Good	Excellent
TP-70, .25 ACP, Clip Fed, Double Action, Pocket Pistol, Stainless Steel, Hammer, *Modern*	$175	$250	$325

Budischowsky TP-70

BUFALO

Gabilondo y Cia., Elgobar, Spain.

HANDGUN, SEMI-AUTOMATIC

	Fair	V. Good	Excellent
Model 1920, .25 ACP, Clip Fed, *Modern*	50	100	150
Pocket, .32 ACP, Clip Fed, *Modern*	50	100	150

BUFFALO ARMS

Tonawanda, N.Y.

HANDGUN, DOUBLE BARREL, OVER-UNDER

	Fair	V. Good	Excellent
Model 1, .357 Mag., Hammer, Blue or Nickel, *Modern*	50	75	100

BUFFALO BILL

Sold by Homer Fisher Co.

HANDGUN, REVOLVER

	Fair	V. Good	Excellent
.22 Short R.F., 7 Shot, Spur Trigger, Solid Frame, Single Action, *Antique*	50	100	150

BUFFALO STAND

Tradename used by ManuFrance.

HANDGUN, SINGLESHOT

	Fair	V. Good	Excellent
Bolt Action, .22 L.R.R.F., Target Pistol, *Modern*	25	50	100

BUHAG

Buchsenmacher-Handwerkgenossenschaft M.B.H. of Suhl, East Germany.

HANDGUN, SEMI-AUTOMATIC

	Fair	V. Good	Excellent
Olympia, .22 Short R.F., Clip Fed, Target Pistol, *Modern*	$200	$375	$550

BULL DOZER

Made by Norwich Pistol Co., Sold by J. McBride & Co., c. 1875–1883.

HANDGUN, REVOLVER

	Fair	V. Good	Excellent
.22 Short R.F., 7 Shot, Spur Trigger, Solid Frame, Single Action, *Antique*	50	100	175
.38 Short R.F, 5 Shot, Spur Trigger, Solid Frame, Single Action, *Antique*	50	100	200
.41 Short R.F., 5 Shot, Spur Trigger, Solid Frame, Single Action, *Antique*	65	125	200
.44 Short R.F., 5 Shot, Spur Trigger, Solid Frame, Single Action, *Antique*	85	175	275

BULLARD REPEATING ARMS CO.

Springfield, Mass., 1987–1989 Designed and built by an S & W alumnus, the Bullard rifle was perceived as a viable competitor to the lever-action Winchester. The rifle was even popular with such dignitaries as Theodore Roosevelt, who posed with one and some thieves he had captured while out West in the Dakotas. That rifle, with a distinctive engraved plaque on the right side of the butt-stock, has yet to be discovered. One of Gustave Young's master-works as an arms engraver was a Bullard rifle, exquisitely engraved and evidently used as a promotional and display piece. Of further importance, Bullard rifles represent some of the finest American gunmaking of the second half of the 19th century, although they simply do not have the aesthetic appeal of a Winchester or a Marlin lever-action.

RIFLE, LEVER ACTION

Various Calibers, Light Engraving, Add $55.00-$160.00
Various Calibers, Medium Engraving, Add $220.00-$435.00
Various Calibers, Octagon Barrel, Add $75.00-$110.00
Various Calibers, Ornate Engraving, Add $775.00-$1150.00
Various Calibers, Target Sights, Add $125.00-$185.00
Various Calibers, Fancy Checkering, Add $75.00-$110.00
Various Calibers, for Express Sights, Add $110.00-$160.00
Various Calibers, for Fancy Wood, Add $30.00-$50.00
Various Calibers, for Lyman Sights, Add $45.00-$75.00
Various Calibers, for Standard Checkering, Add $35.00-$50.00
Various Calibers, Full Nickel Plating, Add $55.00-$80.00
Various Calibers, Half-Octagon Barrel, Add $35.00-$65.00

	Fair	V. Good	Excellent
Carbine, Various Calibers, Open Rear Sight, Carbine, *Antique*	$2500	$3750	$5000
Military, Musket, with Bayonet, Open Rear Sight, *Antique*	2500	3250	4000
Various Calibers, Large Frame, Tube Feed, Round Barrel, Plain, Open Rear Sight, Sporting Rifle, *Antique*	1000	2000	3000
Various Calibers, Small Frame, Tube Feed, Round Barrel, Plain, Open Rear Sights, Sporting Rifle, *Antique*	1000	1750	2500

RIFLE, SINGLESHOT

	Fair	V. Good	Excellent
Military, Full-Stocked, with Bayonet, Open Rear Sight, *Antique*	4000	6500	7500
Military, Full-Stocked, with Bayonet, Open Rear Sight, Carbine, *Antique*	5000	8000	10000
Various Calibers, Schuetzen Target Rifle, Octagon Barrel, Target Sights, Swiss Buttplate, Checkered Stock, *Antique*	1200	2500	3500
Various Calibers, Target Gallery/Hunting, Lightweight, Open Rear Sights, *Antique*	900	1800	2500
Various Rimfires, Target Gallery/Hunting, .22 Caliber, Open Rear Sights, *Antique*	600	1200	1750
Various Rimfires, Target Rifle, Octagon Barrel, Target Sights, Swiss Buttplate, Checkered Stock, *Antique*	1200	2500	3500

BULLDOG

Made by Forehand & Wadsworth.

HANDGUN, REVOLVER

	Fair	V. Good	Excellent
.32 S & W, 7 Shot, Double Action, Solid Frame, *Curio*	50	75	100
.38 S & W, 6 Shot, Double Action, Solid Frame, *Curio*	50	75	100
.44 S & W, 5 Shot, Double Action, Solid Frame, *Curio*	35	75	125

BULLS EYE

c. 1875.

HANDGUN, REVOLVER

	Fair	V. Good	Excellent
.22 Short R.F., 7 Shot, Spur Trigger, Solid Frame, Single Action, *Antique*	50	100	150

BULWARK

Beistegui Hermanos, Eibar, Spain.

HANDGUN, SEMI-AUTOMATIC

	Fair	V. Good	Excellent
.25 ACP, External Hammer, Clip Fed, Blue, *Curio*	125	225	325
.25 ACP, Hammerless, Clip Fed, Blue, *Curio*	$50	$100	$150
.32 ACP, External Hammer, Clip Fed, Blue, *Curio*	85	175	300
.32 ACP, Hammerless, Clip Fed, Blue, *Curio*	50	100	150

BUMFORD

London, England 1730–1760.

HANDGUN, FLINTLOCK

	Fair	V. Good	Excellent
.38, Pocket Pistol, Boxlock, Queen Anne Style, Screw Barrel, Silver Inlay, *Antique*	325	550	775

BURGESS, ANDREW

Oswego, N.Y. 1874–1887. A prolific inventor of great ingenuity and talent, Burgess was also an adept marketer. Once, with a new collapsible and quick takedown shotgun, Burgess gave a demonstration before Theodore Roosevelt in his own office (TR was then commissioner, New York Police Department). That masterfully orchestrated and dramatic showing, which proved to Roosevelt the cleverness of Burgess's design, is a classic story of firearms audacity and entrepreneurship! An entire book has been written, by researcher and collector Sam Maxwell, on the Burgess patents and the inventor's widespread influence in the firearms field.

RIFLE, LEVER ACTION

	Fair	V. Good	Excellent
Model 1876, .45-70 Government, Tube Feed, Octagon Barrel, *Antique*	475	950	2500

RIFLE, SLIDE ACTION

	Fair	V. Good	Excellent
Various Calibers, Folding Gun, with Case, *Antique*	425	850	1475

SHOTGUN, SLIDE ACTION

	Fair	V. Good	Excellent
12 Ga., Folding Gun, with Case, *Antique*	300	700	1000
12 Ga., Takedown, Solid Rib, Light Engraving, *Antique*	200	500	750

BUSHMASTER

Gwinn Arms Co., Winston-Salem, N.C.

HANDGUN, SEMI-AUTOMATIC

	Fair	V. Good	Excellent
Bushmaster, .223 Rem., Clip Fed, *Modern*	175	250	325

RIFLE, SEMI-AUTOMATIC

	Fair	V. Good	Excellent
.223 Rem., Clip Fed, Folding Stock, *Modern*	200	275	350
.223 Rem., Clip Fed, Wood Stock, *Modern*	200	250	300

C

C.A.C.

Made by A.I.G. Corp., North Haven, Conn. Distributed by Mossberg.

	Fair	V. Good	Excellent
HANDGUN, SEMI-AUTOMATIC			
Combat, .45 ACP, Clip Fed, Stainless Steel, *Modern*	$200	$375	$450

CADET

Sold by Maltby-Curtis Co.

	Fair	V. Good	Excellent
HANDGUN, REVOLVER			
.22 Long R.F., 7 Shot, Single Action, Solid Frame, Spur Trigger, *Antique*	50	100	150

CALDERWOOD, WILLIAM

Phila., Pa. 1808–1816. See Kentucky Rifles and Pistols and U.S. Military.

CANADIAN MILITARY

Canadian Military.

	Fair	V. Good	Excellent
HANDGUN, SEMI-AUTOMATIC			
Hi Power Inglis #1 Mk I, 9mm, Tangent Sights, Slotted for Shoulder Stock, Military, *Curio*	600	850	1000
Hi Power Inglis #1 Mk I*, 9mm, Tangent Sights, Slotted for Shoulder Stock, Military, *Curio*	350	550	750
Hi Power Inglis #2 Mk I, 9mm, Fixed Sights, Military, *Curio*	300	400	550
Hi Power Inglis #2 Mk I*, 9mm, Tangent Sights, Slotted for Shoulder Stock, Military, *Curio*	200	350	450
RIFLE, BOLT ACTION			
1907 MK 2 Ross, .303 British, Full-Stocked, Military, *Curio*	150	250	300
1910 MK 3 Ross, .303 British, Full-Stocked, Military, *Curio*	150	275	325
SMLE #4 Mk.1*, .303 British, Clip Fed, *Curio*	75	150	175

CAPT. JACK

Made by Hopkins & Allen 1871–1875.

	Fair	V. Good	Excellent
HANDGUN, REVOLVER			
.22 Short R.F., 7 Shot, Spur Trigger, Solid Frame, Single Action, *Antique*	$35	$75	$150

CAROLINE ARMS

Made by Crescent Firearms Co. 1892–1900. See Crescent Fire Arms Co., Shotgun, Double Barrel, Side-By-Side; Shotgun, Single Shot.

	Fair	V. Good	Excellent
SHOTGUN, SINGLESHOT			
Various Gauges, Hammer, Steel Barrel, *Modern*	25	50	75

CARPENTER, JOHN

Lancaster, Pa. 1771–1790. See Kentucky Rifles.

CARROLL, LAWRENCE

Philadelphia, Pa. 1786–1790. See Kentucky Rifles.

CARTRIDGE FIREARMS

Cartridge Firearms.

	Fair	V. Good	Excellent
COMBINATION WEAPON, DRILLING			
German, Various Calibers, Light Engraving, *Modern*	250	500	850
HANDGUN, REVOLVER			
.22 Short, Small Pocket Pistol, Double Action, *Modern*	25	50	75
.22 Short, Small Pocket Pistol, Folding Trigger, *Modern*	25	50	125
.25 ACP, Small Pocket Pistol, Double Action, *Modern*	12	25	75
.25 ACP, Small Pocket Pistol, Folding Trigger, *Modern*	25	50	100
11mm Pinfire, Lefaucheux Military Style, *Antique*	75	150	225
11mm Pinfire, Lefaucheux Military Style, Engraved, *Antique*	112	225	375
7.62mm Nagent, Nagent Style Gas Seal, Solid Frame, Double Action, *Modern*	35	75	150
7mm Pinfire, Pocket Pistol, Folding Trigger, Engraved, *Antique*	35	75	125

	Fair	V. Good	Excellent
Belgian Proofs, Various Calibers, Top Break, Double Action, Medium Quality, *Modern*	$25	$50	$75
Belgian Proofs, Various Calibers, Top Break, Double Action, Engraved, Medium Quality, *Modern*	35	75	125
Belgian Proofs, Various Calibers, Top Break, Double Action, Folding Trigger, Medium Quality, *Modern*	50	75	100
Chinese Copy of Colt Police Positive, .38 Special, Double Action, Solid Frame, Swing-Out Cylinder, Low Quality, *Modern*	25	50	75
Chinese Copy of Police Positive, 9mm Luger, Double Action, Solid Frame, Swing-Out Cylinder, Low Quality, *Modern*	25	50	75
Chinese Copy of S&W M-10, .38 Special, Double Action, Solid Frame, Swing-Out Cylinder, Low Quality, *Modern*	25	50	75
Copy of Colt SAA, Various Calibers, Western Style, Single Action, Low Quality, *Modern*	25	50	100
Copy of Colt SAA, Various Calibers, Western Style, Single Action, Medium Quality, *Modern*	35	75	125
Copy of S&W Russian Model, Various Calibers, Break, Single Action, Low Quality, *Antique*	35	75	150
Copy of S&W Russian Model, Various Calibers, Top Break, Single Action, Medium Quality, *Antique*	75	150	250
Copy of S&W Russian Model, Various Calibers, Top Break, Single Action, High Quality, *Antique*	200	350	500
Spanish Copy of S&W M-10, .38 Special, Double Action, Solid Frame, Swing-Out Cylinder, Low Quality, *Modern*	25	50	75
Spanish Copy of S&W M-10, .32-20 WCF, Double Action, Solid Frame, Swing-Out Cylinder, Low Quality, *Modern*	25	50	75
Spanish Copy of S&W M-10, .38 Special, Double Action, Solid Frame, Swing-Out Cylinder, Low Quality, *Modern*	25	50	75
Various Centerfire Calibers, Bulldog Style, Double Action, Solid Frame, *Modern*	25	50	75
Various Centerfire Calibers, European Military Style, Double Action, Solid Frame, *Modern*	35	75	150
Various Centerfire Calibers, Folding Trigger, Open Top Frame, *Modern*	50	75	100
Various Centerfire Calibers, Gasser Style, Solid Frame, Double Action, *Modern*	35	75	150
Various Centerfire Calibers, Small Pocket Pistol, Hammerless, Folding Trigger, with Safety, *Modern*	$50	$75	$100
Various Centerfire Calibers, Warnant Style, Top Break, Double Action, *Modern*	35	75	150

HANDGUN, SEMI-AUTOMATIC

	Fair	V. Good	Excellent
Chinese Broomhandle, 7.63 Mauser, Low Quality, *Modern*	50	100	700
Chinese Copy of FN 1900, Various Calibers, Clip Fed, Low Quality, *Modern*	50	75	100
Chinese Pocket Pistols, Various Calibers, Clip Fed, Low Quality, *Modern*	50	75	100
Copy of Colt M1911, .45 ACP, Clip Fed, Military, High Quality, *Modern*	100	175	250
Spanish Pocket Pistols, .25 ACP, Clip Fed, Low Quality, *Modern*	50	75	100
Spanish Pocket Pistols, .32 ACP, Clip Fed, Low Quality, *Modern*	35	75	125
Spanish Pocket Pistols, .32 ACP, Clip Fed, Low Quality, Ruby Style, *Modern*	35	75	125

HANDGUN, SINGLESHOT

	Fair	V. Good	Excellent
Flobert Style, Various Configurations, *Modern*	25	50	100
.22 R.F, Fancy Target Pistol, Hammerless, Set Triggers, *Modern*	137	275	425
.22 Short, Fancy German Target Pistol, Tip-Up Barrel, Engraved, Set Triggers, *Modern*	250	350	450
.22 Short, Target Pistol, Tip-Up Barrel, Plain, *Modern*	35	75	125

RIFLE, BOLT ACTION

	Fair	V. Good	Excellent
Various Centerfire Calibers, Commercial Sporting Rifle, Low Quality, *Modern*	35	75	125
Various Rimfire Calibers, Singleshot, Checkered Stock, European, *Modern*	12	25	50
Arabian Copies, Various Calibers, Military, Reproduction, Low Quality, *Modern*	25	50	75

RIFLE, SINGLESHOT

	Fair	V. Good	Excellent
Various Calibers, Flobert Style, Checkered Stock, *Modern*	50	75	100
Various Calibers, Warnant Style, Checkered Stock, *Modern*	35	75	125
Belgian Proofs, .22 Long R.F., Tip-Up, Octagon Barrel, Medium Quality, *Antique*	50	75	100

SHOTGUN, DOUBLE BARREL, SIDE-BY-SIDE

	Fair	V. Good	Excellent
Belgian Proofs, Various Gauges, Damascus Barrel, Low Quality, Outside Hammers, *Modern*	50	75	100

	Fair	V. Good	Excellent
English Proofs, Various Gauges, Damascus Barrel, Low Quality, Outside Hammers, *Modern*	$35	$75	$125
No Proofs, Various Gauges, Damascus Barrel, Low Quality, Outside Hammers, *Modern*	25	50	100
Various Gauges, American, Hammerless, Damascus Barrel, *Modern*	35	75	150
Various Gauges, American, Hammerless, Steel Barrel, *Modern*	50	100	175
Various Gauges, American, Outside Hammers, Damascus Barrel, *Modern*	35	75	150
Various Gauges, American, Outside Hammers, Steel Barrel, *Modern*	35	75	175

SHOTGUN, SINGLESHOT

"Zulu,", 12 Ga., Converted from Perc. Musket, Trap Door Action, *Antique*	35	75	125
Various Gauges, American, Hammer, Steel Barrel, *Modern*	25	50	75
Various Gauges, Warnant Style, Checkered Stock, *Modern*	25	50	75

CEBRA

Arizmendi, Zulaika y Cia., Eibar, Spain.

HANDGUN, SEMI-AUTOMATIC

Pocket, .25 ACP, Clip Fed, *Curio*	35	75	125

CELTA

Tomas de Urizar y Cia., Eibar, Spain, c. 1935.

HANDGUN, SEMI-AUTOMATIC

Pocket, .25 ACP, Clip Fed, *Curio*	35	75	125

CENTENNIAL

Made by Deringer Rifle & Pistol Works 1876.

HANDGUN, REVOLVER

.22 Short R.F., 7 Shot, Spur Trigger, Tip-Up, *Antique*	150	250	350
.32 Short R.F., 5 Shot, Spur Trigger, Solid Frame, Single Action, *Antique*	50	100	175
.38 Short R.F., 5 Shot, Spur Trigger, Solid Frame, Single Action, *Antique*	50	100	175
Centennial '76, .38 Long R.F., 5 Shot, Single Action, Spur Trigger, Tip-Up, *Antique*	100	250	350
Model 2, .32 R.F., 5 Shot, Single Action, Spur Trigger, Tip-Up, *Antique*	150	250	350

CENTRAL

Made by Stevens Arms.

SHOTGUN, DOUBLE BARREL, SIDE-BY-SIDE

	Fair	V. Good	Excellent
Model 215, 12 and 16 Gauges, Outside Hammers, Steel Barrel, *Modern*	$50	$100	$175
Model 311, Various Gauges, Hammerless, Steel Barrel, *Modern*	50	100	175
Model 315, Various Gauges, Hammerless, Steel Barrel, *Modern*	50	100	175

SHOTGUN, SINGLESHOT

Model 94, Various Gauges, Takedown, Automatic Ejector, Plain Hammer, *Modern*	25	50	75

CENTRAL ARMS CO.

Made by Crescent for Shapleigh Hardware Co., c. 1900. See Crescent Fire Arms Co., Shotgun, Double Barrel, Side-by-Side; Shotgun, Single Shot.

CHALLENGE

Made by Bliss & Goodyear, c. 1878.

HANDGUN, REVOLVER

.32 Short R.F., 5 Shot, Spur Trigger, Solid Frame, Single Action, *Antique*	50	100	150

CHAMPION

c. 1870.

HANDGUN, REVOLVER

.22 Short R.F., *Antique*	50	100	150

CHAMPLIN FIREARMS

Enid, Oklahoma. The author was privileged to have visited this fine and important firm of riflemakers and dealers. The expertise present is impressive, under the direction of George Caswell, veteran of many hunts in Africa and shooter of virtually every double rifle type and cartridge known to humanity. Probably America's leading expert on double rifles, this company deals in more of those guns than perhaps any other firm in the world. You can also fly in with your double rifles and have the experts help select the proper loads for truly accurate shooting and best performance. Not a few of these arms over the years have lost the accompanying data on the proper bullets and powders; and quite a few have lost the original ammunition sold with the rifles. Further, after about 25 to 30 years a centerfire rifle cartridge may well no longer work properly. Answers to questions on subjects of that nature are a specialty of Champlin Firearms. The firm's custom-made sporting rifles and shotguns are also of a high quality; those too can be tested with Champlin's expertise available, to guarantee a faultless hunt. The company publishes a catalogue and also handles selected reference books and videos.

RIFLE, BOLT ACTION

Basic Rifle, with Quarter Rib, Express Sights, Add $185.00-$270.00

	Fair	V. Good	Excellent
Basic Rifle, Fancy Checkering, Add $30.00-$45.00			
Basic Rifle, Fancy Wood, Add $55.00-$90.00			
Basic Rifle, Various Calibers, Adjustable Trigger, Round or Octagon Tapered Barrel, Checkered Stock, *Modern*	$1500	$2750	$3500

SHOTGUN, DOUBLE BARREL, OVER-UNDER

	Fair	V. Good	Excellent
12 Ga., Extra Barrels, Add $175.00-$250.00			
Model 100, 12 Ga., Field Grade, Checkered Stock, Vent Rib, Single Selective Trigger, Engraved, *Modern*	265	525	850
Model 100, 12 Ga., Skeet Grade, Checkered Stock, Vent Rib, Single Selective Trigger, Engraved, *Modern*	285	575	925
Model 100, 12 Ga., Trap Grade, Checkered Stock, Vent Rib, Single Selective Trigger, Engraved, *Modern*	285	575	925
Model 500, 12 Ga., Field Grade, Checkered Stock, Vent Rib, Single Selective Trigger, Engraved, *Modern*	425	850	1375
Model 500, 12 Ga., Skeet Grade, Checkered Stock, Vent Rib, Single Selective Trigger, Engraved, *Modern*	450	900	1500
Model 500, 12 Ga., Trap Grade, Checkered Stock, Vent Rib, Single Selective Trigger, Engraved, *Modern*	485	975	1600

SHOTGUN, SINGLESHOT

	Fair	V. Good	Excellent
Model SB 100, 12 Ga., Trap Grade, Checkered Stock, Vent Rib, Single Selective Trigger, Engraved, *Modern*	285	575	875
Model SB 500, 12 Ga., Trap Grade, Checkered Stock, Vent Rib, Single Selective Trigger, Engraved, *Modern*	435	875	1350

CHAPUIS

St. Bonnet-le-Chateau, France.

SHOTGUN, DOUBLE BARREL, SIDE-BY-SIDE

	Fair	V. Good	Excellent
Progress RBV, R20, 12 or 20 Gauge, Automatic Ejectors, Sideplates, Double Triggers, Checkered Stock, *Modern*	800	1275	1450
Progress RG, 12 or 20 Gauge, Automatic Ejectors, Double Triggers, Checkered Stock, *Modern*	1000	1800	2000
Progress Slug, 12 or 20 Gauge, Automatic Ejectors, Slug Barrel, Double Triggers, Checkered Stock, *Modern*	1000	1800	2200

CHARLES DALY

Trade name on guns made in Suhl, Germany, prior to WWII, and by Miroku and Breda after WWII. The quality of Daly guns kept their firm's name brand recognition, and value, at a high level. These arms continue in demand primarily as shooters, rather than as collectors' items. The products of this firm reflect an enlightened management, and Daly was one of the first to capitalize on the talented gunmaking industry evolved in Japan after World War II. Among firms of distinction who sold Daly guns were Abercrombie & Fitch, whose reputation as a knowledgeable source of high-grade arms continued into the 1980s.

COMBINATION WEAPON, DRILLING

	Fair	V. Good	Excellent
Diamond, Various Calibers, Fancy Engraving, Fancy Checkering, *Modern*	$4000	$5500	$6700
Regent Diamond, Various Calibers, Fancy Engraving, Fancy Checkering, Fancy Wood, *Modern*	2000	4000	4800
Superior, Various Calibers, Engraved, *Modern*	1000	2000	2600

RIFLE, BOLT ACTION

	Fair	V. Good	Excellent
.22 Hornet, 5 Shot Clip, Checkered Stock, *Modern*	475	550	625

SHOTGUN, DOUBLE BARREL, OVER-UNDER

	Fair	V. Good	Excellent
For 28 Ga., Add 10%-15%			
12 Ga., For Wide Vent Rib, Add $25.00-$45.00			
Various Gauges, Field Grade, Light Engraving, Single Selective Trigger, Automatic Ejector, Post-War, *Modern*	175	300	425
Commander 100, Various Gauges, Automatic Ejector, Checkered Stock, Single Trigger, *Modern*	250	375	500
Commander 100, Various Gauges, Automatic Ejector, Checkered Stock, Double Trigger, *Modern*	200	325	450
Commander 200, Various Gauges, Automatic Ejector, Checkered Stock, Engraved, Single Trigger, *Modern*	375	550	725
Commander 200, Various Gauges, Double Trigger, *Modern*	300	475	650
Diamond, 12 Ga., Trap Grade, Selective Ejector, Single Selective Trigger, Post-War, *Modern*	300	500	700
Diamond, 12 or 20 Gauges, Field Grade, Trap Grade, Selective Ejector, Single Selective Trigger, Post-War, *Modern*	250	500	750
Diamond, 12 or 20 Gauges, Skeet Grade, Trap Grade, Selective Ejector, Single Selective Trigger, Post-War, *Modern*	250	500	750
Diamond, Various Gauges, Double Trigger, Automatic Ejector, Fancy Engraving, Fancy Checkering, *Modern*	1250	2500	4575

	Fair	V. Good	Excellent
Empire, Various Gauges, Double Trigger, Automatic Ejector, Checkered Stock, Engraved, *Modern*	$935	$2200	$3650
Superior, 12 Ga., Trap Grade, Automatic Ejector, Single Selective Trigger, Post-War, *Modern*	200	350	475
Superior, Various Gauges, Field Grade, Trap Grade, Automatic Ejector, Single Selective Trigger, Post-War, *Modern*	200	350	475
Superior, Various Gauges, Skeet Grade, Trap Grade, Automatic Ejector, Single Selective Trigger, Post-War, *Modern*	200	350	475
Venture, 12 Ga., Trap Grade, Single rigger, Monte Carlo Stock, Post-War, *Modern*	125	250	375
Venture, 12 or 20 Gauges, Field Grade, Single Trigger, Trap Grade, Post-War, *Modern*	125	250	375
Venture, 12 or 20 Gauges, Skeet Grade, Single Trigger, Trap Grade, Post-War, *Modern*	175	275	375

SHOTGUN, DOUBLE BARREL, SIDE-BY-SIDE

	Fair	V. Good	Excellent
Diamond, Various Gauges, Double Trigger, Fancy Engraving, Fancy Checkering, Fancy Wood, Automatic Ejector, *Modern*	2600	3275	3950
Empire, Various Gauges, Double Trigger, Engraved, Checkered Stock, Automatic Ejector, *Modern*	900	1825	2525
Empire, Various Gauges, Vent Rib, Single Trigger, Checkered Stock, Engraved, Post-War, *Modern*	150	250	350
Regent Diamond, Various Gauges, Double Trigger, Fancy Engraving, Fancy Checkering, Fancy Wood, Automatic Ejector, *Modern*	1435	2875	5250
Superior, Various Gauges, Double Trigger, Light Engraving, Checkered Stock, *Modern*	425	850	1275

SHOTGUN, SEMI-AUTOMATIC

	Fair	V. Good	Excellent
Novamatic, 12 Ga., Mag. 3", Takedown, Vent Rib, Checkered Stock, Magnum, *Modern*	250	275	300
Novamatic, 12 Ga., Takedown, Trap Grade, Vent Rib, Checkered Stock, Monte Carlo Stock, *Modern*	225	275	325
Novamatic, 12 or 20 Gauges, Takedown, Plain Barrel, Checkered Stock, Lightweight, *Modern*	175	225	275
Novamatic, 12 or 20 Gauges, Takedown, Plain Barrel, Checkered Stock, Lightweight, Interchangeable Choke Tubes, *Modern*	225	250	275
Novamatic, 12 or 20 Gauges, Takedown, Vent Rib, Checkered Stock, Lightweight, *Modern*	150	200	250
Novamatic, 12 or 20 Gauges, Takedown, Vent Rib, Checkered Stock, Lightweight, Interchangable Choke Tubes, *Modern*	$125	$225	$275
Novamatic, 20 Ga., Takedown, Checkered Stock, Magnum, Lightweight, *Modern*	200	250	300
Novamatic Super Light, 12 and 20 Gauges, Takedown, Plain Barrel, Checkered Stock, *Modern*	125	200	275
Novamatic Super Light, 12 and 20 Gauges, Takedown, Plain Barrel, Checkered Stock, Interchangeable Choke Tubes, *Modern*	100	175	250
Novamatic Super Light, 12 and 20 Gauges, Takedown, Vent Rib, Checkered Stock, *Modern*	75	150	325

SHOTGUN, SINGLESHOT

	Fair	V. Good	Excellent
Empire, 12 Ga., Trap Grade, Fancy Engraving, Fancy Wood, Automatic Ejector, *Modern*	2150	3450	4750
Sextuple Empire, 12 Ga., Trap Grade, Fancy Checkering, Fancy Engraving, Fancy Wood, Automatic Ejector, *Modern*	2000	3675	4975
Sextuple Regent Diamond, 12 Ga., Trap Grade, Fancy Checkering, Fancy Engraving, Fancy Wood, Automatic Ejector, *Modern*	2575	4625	6675
Superior, 12 Ga., Trap Grade, Monte Carlo Stock, Selective Ejector, Engraved, Post-War, *Modern*	175	275	375

CHAROLA Y ANITUA

Garate, Anitua y Cia., Eibar, Spain, c. 1898.

HANDGUN, SEMI-AUTOMATIC

	Fair	V. Good	Excellent
Charola, 5mm Clement, Locked Breech, Box Magazine, Belgian Made, *Curio*	225	450	1000
Charola, 5mm Clement, Locked Breech, Box Magazine, Spanish Made, *Curio*	285	575	1000

Charola y Anitua, Spanish

CHARTER ARMS

Stratford, Conn. since 1965. The brainchild of engineer and gun designer Doug McLanahan, aided in time by business head Dave Ecker, Charter Arms developed a solid line of handguns, beginning with the Undercover. When misguided thinking at the Colt company led to their reducing production and marketing of snub-nosed, self-defense revolvers (like the Cobra and Detective Special), Doug McLanahan, an employee of Sturm, Ruger & Co—recognizing Ruger's own hesitation to produce snub-nose revolvers—stepped into a ready market. McLanahan used to vacation on Mississippi paddle-wheelers as a means of relaxing and increasing his output of designs and innovative products. In the late 1960s the author was involved in helping Charter Arms to develop an engraving line, even to the point of the company's advertising deluxe examples, in different grades. One deluxe example, engraved and with gold inlay and executed for Dave Ecker, was featured on the cover of *Shooting Times* magazine. Brochures were also printed up in promoting the new concept. Production was extremely limited, however, and these arms will bring a premium of five to seven times the value of the standard unembellished models.

HANDGUN, REVOLVER

	Fair	V. Good	Excellent
Milestone Limited Edition, .44 Special, Bulldog, Engraved, Silver Plated, Cased with Accessories, *Modern*	$555	$775	$995
Bulldog Tracker, .357 Magnum, Double Action, Blue, Adjustable Sights, *Modern*	125	200	225

Charter Arms Bulldog Tracker.357 Magnum, 6" Barrel

	Fair	V. Good	Excellent
Bulldog, .44 Special, Double Action, Blue, *Modern*	125	175	200
Bulldog, .44 Special, Double Action, Nickel Plated, *Modern*	125	200	225
Bulldog, .44 Special, Double Action, Stainless, *Modern*	125	225	250
Off-Duty, .38 SPL, 5 Shot, 2" Barrel, Stainless, *Modern*	125	225	275
Off-Duty, .38 SPL, 5 Shot, 2" Barrel, Steel Frame, *Modern*	100	150	175
Pathfinder, .22 L.R.R.F., Adjustable Sights, Bulldog Grips, Double Action, *Modern*	100	175	200
Pathfinder, .22 L.R.R.F., Adjustable Sights, Bulldog Grips, Double Action, Stainless Steel, *Modern*	$125	$225	$275
Pathfinder, .22 L.R.R.F., Adjustable Sights, Square-Butt, Double Action, *Modern*	75	125	175
Pathfinder, .22 WMR, Adjustable Sights, Double Action, Bulldog Grips, *Modern*	75	125	175
Pathfinder, .22 WMR, Adjustable Sights, Double Action, Square-Butt, *Modern*	75	125	175
Police Bulldog, .32 H&R Magnum, 4" Bull Barrel, Checkered Grips, Blue, *Modern*	125	175	225
Police Bulldog, .38 Special, 1" Bull Barrel, Stainless, *Modern*	150	250	275
Police Bulldog, .38 Special, 4" Tapered Barrel, Square Grips, Stainless, *Modern*	100	175	250
Police Bulldog, .38 Special, Double Action, Blue, Adjustable Sights, *Modern*	65	125	200

Charter Arms Police Bulldog

	Fair	V. Good	Excellent
Police Bulldog Tracker, .357 Magnum, 2½" Barrel, Blue, *Modern*	100	200	250
Police Bulldog Tracker, .357 Magnum, 4" Barrel, Bulldog Grips, Blue, *Modern*	100	200	250
Police Undercover, .32 H&R Magnum, 2" Barrel, Checkered Panel Grips, Blue, *Modern*	100	175	200
Police Undercover, .38 Special, 2" Barrel, Blue, Pocket Hammer, *Modern*	100	175	200
Police Undercover, Law Enforcement Version, .38 Special, Five Shot, Neoprene Grips, *Modern*	125	250	275
Target Bulldog, .357 Magnum, Double Action, Blue, Adjustable Sights, *Modern*	75	150	175

	Fair	V. Good	Excellent
Target Bulldog, .44 Special, Double Action, Blue, Adjustable Sights, *Modern*	$75	$150	$200
Undercover, .38 Special, Double Action, Blue, Bulldog Grips, *Modern*	75	125	175
Undercover, .38 Special, Double Action, Blue, *Modern*	75	125	175
Undercover, .38 Special, Double Action, Nickel Plated, *Modern*	75	125	175
Undercover, .38 Special, Double Action, Stainless Steel, *Modern*	100	175	225
Undercoverette, .32 S & W Long, Double Action, Blue, Bulldog Grips, *Modern*	50	100	150

HANDGUN, SEMI-AUTOMATIC

	Fair	V. Good	Excellent
Explorer II, .22 L.R.R.F., Clip Fed, Takedown, *Modern*	50	75	100
Explorer SII, .22 L.R.R.F., Clip Fed, Takedown, 6" and 10" Optional Barrels, *Modern*	75	100	125
Model 40, .22 L.R., 8 Shot Mag, Checkered Walnut Gripstock, Stainless, *Modern*	$125	$200	$225
Model 79K, .380 Autoloader, 7 Shot Mag, Checkered Gripstock, Stainless, *Modern*	150	250	300
Model 79K32, .32 Caliber Autoloader, 7 Shot Mag, Stainless, *Modern*	200	350	400

Charter Arms M40 Double Action Pistol

Charter Arms M79K, .380 Caliber

RIFLE, SEMI-AUTOMATIC

	Fair	V. Good	Excellent
AR-7 Explorer, .22 L.R.R.F., Clip Fed, Takedown, *Modern*	75	100	125

CHASE, WILLIAM

Pandora, Ohio 1854–1860.

COMBINATION WEAPON, PERCUSSION

	Fair	V. Good	Excellent
Various Calibers, Double Barrel, *Antique*	450	850	1250

CHEROKEE ARMS CO.

Made by Crescent, C. M. McClung & Co., Tennessee, c. 1900. See Crescent Fire Arms Co., Shotgun, Double Barrel, Side-By-Side; Shotgun, Singleshot.

CHERRINGTON, THOMAS P.

Cattawissa, Pa. 1847–1858.

RIFLE, PILL LOCK

	Fair	V. Good	Excellent
.40, Revolver, Octagon Barrel, *Antique*	1000	2000	2500

CHESAPEAKE GUN CO.

Made by Crescent, c. 1900.

SHOTGUN, DOUBLE BARREL, SIDE-BY-SIDE

	Fair	V. Good	Excellent
Various Gauges, Hammerless, Damascus Barrel, *Modern*	35	75	150
Various Gauges, Hammerless, Steel Barrel, *Modern*	50	100	175
Various Gauges, Outside Hammers, Damascus Barrel, *Modern*	35	75	150
Various Gauges, Outside Hammers, Steel Barrel, *Modern*	50	100	175

SHOTGUN, SINGLESHOT

	Fair	V. Good	Excellent
Various Gauges, Hammer, Steel Barrel, *Modern*	25	50	75

CHICAGO ARMS CO.

Sold by Fred Bifflar Co. Made by Meriden Firearms Co. 1870–1890.

	Fair	V. Good	Excellent
HANDGUN, REVOLVER			
.32 S & W, 5 Shot, Double Action, Top Break, *Antique*	$25	$50	$100
.38 S & W, 5 Shot, Double Action, Top Break, *Antique*	25	50	100
.38 S & W, Top Break, Hammerless, Double Action, Grip Safety, *Antique*	35	75	125

CHICAGO FIRE ARMS CO.

Chicago, Ill. 1883–1894. One of the most intriguing of oddities in the history of American firearms, these bizarre little handguns were sometimes built with deluxe grip panels, like mother-of-pearl, and were supremely well made. Loading was achieved by unscrewing one of the side panels and then inserting the cartridges from the center of a radiating chamber. It is not uncommon to find these arms in excellent condition, since it appears that not too many were ever fired. The mechanisms were quite simple, but the type had fierce competition, and sales proved disappointing. Examples found in the original pasteboard box will bring a premium of at least an additional 25 percent.

	Fair	V. Good	Excellent
HANDGUN, PALM PISTOL			
.32 Extra Short R.F., Blued, *Antique*	500	1000	1500

Chicago Fire Arms Palm Pistol

	Fair	V. Good	Excellent
.32 Extra Short R.F., Nickel, *Antique*	325	650	1200

CHICNESTER

Made by Hopkins & Allen, c. 1880.

	Fair	V. Good	Excellent
HANDGUN, REVOLVER			
.38 Short R.F., 5 Shot, Spur Trigger, Solid Frame, Single Action, *Antique*	$50	$100	$175

CHIEFTAIN

Made by Norwich Pistol Co., c. 1880.

	Fair	V. Good	Excellent
HANDGUN, REVOLVER			
.32 Short R.F., 5 Shot, Spur Trigger, Solid Frame, Single Action, *Antique*	50	100	150

CHILEAN MILITARY

	Fair	V. Good	Excellent
RIFLE, BOLT ACTION			
M1895 Carbine, 7mm Mauser, Military, *Curio*	$150	$275	$300
M1895 Rifle, 7mm Mauser, Military, *Curio*	150	225	250
M1895 Short Rifle, 7mm Mauser, Military, *Curio*	150	250	275

CHINESE MILITARY

	Fair	V. Good	Excellent
HANDGUN, SEMI-AUTOMATIC			
Makarov, 9mm Mak., Clip Fed, *Modern*	300	650	750
Tokarev, 7.62mm Tokarev, Clip Fed, *Modern*	200	300	350

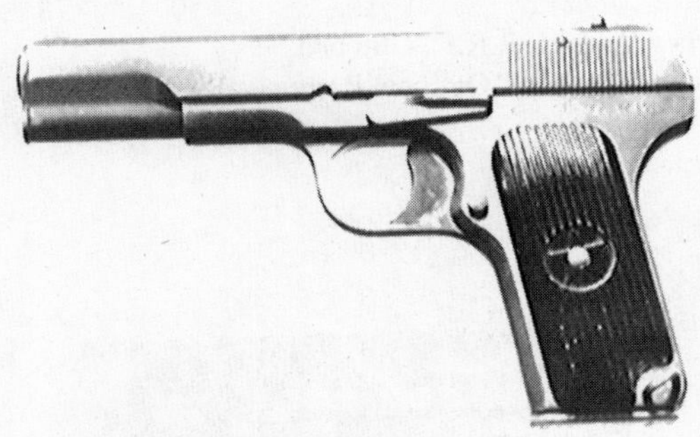

Chinese Military Tokarev

	Fair	V. Good	Excellent
Walther PPK Type, .32 A.C.P., Double Action, Blue, Clip Fed, Military, *Modern*	300	650	750
RIFLE, BOLT ACTION			
Type 53 (Nagent), 7.62 × 54R Russian, *Modern*	35	75	175
RIFLE, SEMI-AUTOMATIC			
SKS, 7.62 × 39 Russian, Folding Bayonet, Military, *Modern*	125	250	375

CHINESE NATIONALIST MILITARY

	Fair	V. Good	Excellent
HANDGUN, SEMI-AUTOMATIC			
Hi Power, 9mm Luger, Clip Fed, Military, Tangent Sights, *Curio*	300	650	750
Hi Power, 9mm Luger, Clip Fed, Military, Tangent Sights, with Detachable Shoulder Stock, *Curio*	500	1000	1250
RIFLE, BOLT ACTION			
Kar 98k Type 79, 8mm Mauser, *Modern*	150	275	300

	Fair	V. Good	Excellent
M1871 Mauser, .43 Mauser, Carbine, *Antique*	$175	$325	$350
M1888, Hanyang, 8mm Mauser, 5 Shot, *Curio*	150	250	275
M98 Mukden, 8mm Mauser, *Modern*	200	350	375

CHIPMUNK

Medford, Ore., since 1982.

RIFLE, BOLT ACTION

.22 L.R.R.F., Singleshot, Manual Cocking, *Modern*	50	75	100

CHURCHILL, E. J. LTD.

London, England, 1892 to date. This capable London gunmaker enjoys a justly deserved reputation as a respected member of the trade specializing in best quality firearms. For several years Churchill belonged to Sam Cummings, the first American member of the London Gunmaker's Guild. Cummings is more generally known as the founder and chairman of Interarms, an international small arms and armaments company headquartered in Monaco.

RIFLE, BOLT ACTION

One of 1,000, Various Calibers, Checkered Stock, Recoil Pad, Express Sights, Cartridge Trap, *Modern*	200	600	1250
One of 1,000, Various Calibers, Fancy Checkering, Engraved Expressed Sights, Cartridge Trap, Cased with Accessories, *Modern*	900	1850	2575

SHOTGUN, DOUBLE BARREL, OVER-UNDER

Premier Quality, for Raised Vent Rib, Add $350.00-$520.00

Premier Quality, for Single Selective Trigger, Add $400.00-$535.00

Premier Quality, Various Gauges, Hammerless Sidelock, Fancy Checkering, Automatic Ejectors, Engraved, *Modern*	7000	12000	15000

SHOTGUN, DOUBLE BARREL, SIDE-BY-SIDE

	Fair	V. Good	Excellent
Field Model, Various Gauges, Hammerless Sidelock, Fancy Checkering, Automatic Ejectors, Engraved, *Modern*	3500	6000	7000
Hercules Model XXV, Various Gauges, Hammerless Sidelock, Engraved, Fancy Checkering, Fancy Wood, Cased, *Modern*	3500	6000	7000
Imperial Model XXV, Various Gauges, Hammerless Sidelock, Fancy Checkering, Automatic Ejectors, Engraved, *Modern*	4000	7500	9500
Premier Quality, Various Gauges, Hammerless Sidelock, Fancy Checkering, Automatic Ejectors, Engraved, *Modern*	$6000	$10000	$12000
Regal Model XXV, Various Gauges, Hammerless Sidelock, Fancy Checkering, Automatic Ejectors, Engraved, *Modern*	2000	3750	4300
Utility Model, Various Gauges, Boxlock, Double Triggers, Color Case with Hardened Frame, Engraved, *Modern*	2000	3500	4500

For Single Selective Trigger, Add $375.00-$535.00

CHYLEWSKI, WITOLD

Austria, 1910–1918. Pistols made by S.I.G.

HANDGUN, SEMI-AUTOMATIC

Einhand, .25 A.C.P., Clip Fed, Blue, No Locking Screw, *Curio*	400	650	875
Einhand, .25 A.C.P., Clip Fed, Blue, with Locking Screw, *Curio*	500	675	750

Chylewski .25 with Locking Screw

CLARK, F. H.

Memphis, Tenn., c. 1860.

HANDGUN, PERCUSSION

Derringer, .41, German Silver Mountings, *Antique*	400	750	1100

CLARKSON, J.

London, England 1680–1740.

HANDGUN, FLINTLOCK

.32, Pocket Pistol, Queen Anne Style, Box Lock, Screw Barrel, Silver Furniture, *Antique*	250	475	700

CLASSIC ARMS

Palmer, Mass.

HANDGUN, PERCUSSION

.36 Duckfoot, 3 Shot, Brass Frame, Reproduction, *Antique*	15	25	50

	Fair	V. Good	Excellent
.36 Ethan Allen, Pepperbox, 4 Shot, Brass Frame, Reproduction, *Antique*	$15	$25	$50
.36 Snake-Eyes, Double Barrel, Side by Side, Brass Frame, Reproduction, *Antique*	15	25	50
.36 Twister, 2 Shot, Brass Frame, Reproduction, *Antique*	15	25	50
.44 Ace, Rifled, Brass Frame, Reproduction, *Antique*	15	25	50

CLEMENT, CHARLES

Liege, Belgium 1886–1914.

HANDGUN, SEMI-AUTOMATIC

	Fair	V. Good	Excellent
M1903, 5.5mm Clement, Clip Fed, Blue, *Curio*	200	375	500

Clement M1903 5mm

	Fair	V. Good	Excellent
M1907, .25 ACP, Clip Fed, Blue, *Curio*	125	250	325
M1907, .32 ACP, Clip Fed, Blue, *Curio*	125	275	375
M1908, .25 ACP, Clip Fed, Blue, *Curio*	200	325	400
M1910, .25 ACP, Clip Fed, Blue, *Curio*	125	225	325
M1910, .32 ACP, Clip Fed, Blue, *Curio*	125	275	375
M1912 Fulgor, .32 ACP, Clip Fed, Blue, *Curio*	200	450	650

RIFLE, SEMI-AUTOMATIC

	Fair	V. Good	Excellent
Clement-Neumann, .401 Win., Clip Fed, Checkered Stock, Matted Rib, *Curio*	250	450	650

SHOTGUN, DOUBLE BARREL, SIDE-BY-SIDE

	Fair	V. Good	Excellent
Various Gauges, Hammerless, Damascus Barrel, *Curio*	65	125	200
Various Gauges, Hammerless, Steel Barrel, *Curio*	75	150	225
Various Gauges, Outside Hammers, Damascus Barrel, *Curio*	65	125	200

CLEMENT, J. B.

Belgium.

SHOTGUN, DOUBLE BARREL, SIDE-BY-SIDE

	Fair	V. Good	Excellent
Various Gauges, Hammerless, Steel Barrel, *Modern*	$75	$150	$225
Various Gauges, Outside Hammers, Steel Barrel, *Modern*	100	150	200

CLERKE

Santa Monica, Calif.

HANDGUN, REVOLVER

	Fair	V. Good	Excellent
32-200, .32 S & W, Nickel Plated, *Modern*	15	25	50
CF200, .22 L.R.R.F., Nickel Plated, *Modern*	15	25	50

RIFLE, SINGLESHOT

	Fair	V. Good	Excellent
Hi-Wall, Various Calibers, Fancy Wood, *Modern*	150	200	250
Hi-Wall Deluxe, Various Calibers, Octagon Barrel, Fancy Wood, *Modern*	150	250	300
Hi-Wall Deluxe, Various Calibers, Octagon Barrel, Set Trigger, Fancy Wood, *Modern*	150	275	325

CLIMAS

Made by Stevens Arms.

SHOTGUN, SINGLESHOT

	Fair	V. Good	Excellent
Model 90, Various Gauges, Takedown, Automatic Ejector, Plain Hammer, *Modern*	25	50	75

CLIPPER

Maker unknown, c. 1880.

HANDGUN, REVOLVER

	Fair	V. Good	Excellent
.22 Short R.F., 7 Shot, Spur Trigger, Solid Frame, Single Action, *Antique*	50	100	150

CODY MANUFACTURING CO.

Chicopee, Mass. 1957–1959.

HANDGUN, REVOLVER

	Fair	V. Good	Excellent
Thunderbird, .22 R.F., 6 Shot, Double Action, Aluminum with Steel Liners, *Modern*	75	125	175

COGSWELL & HARRISON

London, England 1770 to date; Branch in Paris 1924–1938. Cogswell & Harrison was another respected member of the London gun trade. Due to increased competition and operating costs, and gradually worsening U.K gun laws, Cogswell finally closed its doors in the early 1990s.

HANDGUN, REVOLVER

	Fair	V. Good	Excellent
S & W Victory, .38 Special, Double Action, Swing-Out Cylinder, Refinished and Customized, Rebored from .38 S & W and may be unsafe with .38 Spec., *Modern*	$75	$150	$250

RIFLE, BOLT ACTION

	Fair	V. Good	Excellent
BSA-Lee Speed, .303 British, Sporting Rifle, Express Sights, Engraved, Checkered Stock, Commercial, *Modern*	275	550	825

Cogswell & Harrison Lee Speed

SHOTGUN, DOUBLE BARREL, SIDE-BY-SIDE

	Fair	V. Good	Excellent
Avant Tout (Konor), Various Gauges, Box Lock, Automatic Ejector, Fancy Checkering, Fancy Engraving, Double Trigger, *Modern*	1675	2025	2375
Avant Tout (Konor), Various Gauges, Box Lock, Automatic Ejector, Fancy Checkering, Fancy Engraving, Single Trigger, *Modern*	1500	2350	2750
Avant Tout (Konor), Various Gauges, Box Lock, Automatic Ejector, Fancy Checkering, Fancy Engraving, Single Selective Trigger, *Modern*	1500	2500	2925
Avant Tout (Rex), Various Gauges, Box Lock, Automatic Ejector, Checkered Stock, Light Engraving, Double Trigger, *Modern*	1150	1450	1750
Avant Tout (Rex), Various Gauges, Box Lock, Automatic Ejector, Checkered Stock, Light Engraving, Single Trigger, *Modern*	800	1275	1750
Avant Tout (Rex), *Modern*	1200	1700	1925
Avant Tout (Sandhurst), Various Gauges, Box Lock, Automatic Ejector, Fancy Checkering, Engraved, Double Trigger, *Modern*	1300	1875	2450
Avant Tout (Sandhurst), Various Gauges, Box Lock, Automatic Ejector, Fancy Checkering, Engraved, Single Trigger, *Modern*	1025	1850	2675
Avant Tout (Sandhurst), Various Gauges, Box Lock, Automatic Ejector, Fancy Checkering, Engraved, Single Selective Trigger, *Modern*	1500	2275	2850
Huntic, Various Gauges, Sidelock, Automatic Ejector, Checkered Stock, Double Trigger, *Modern*	$1200	$2000	$3200
Huntic, Various Gauges, Sidelock, Automatic Ejector, Checkered Stock, Single Trigger, *Modern*	1500	2675	3350
Huntic, Various Gauges, Sidelock, Automatic Ejector, Checkered Stock, Single Selective Trigger, *Modern*	1500	2500	3325
Markor, Various Gauges, Box Lock, Automatic Ejector, Checkered Stock, Double Trigger, *Modern*	800	1000	1500
Markor, Various Gauges, Box Lock, Checkered Stock, Double Trigger, *Modern*	500	800	1350
Primic, Various Gauges, Sidelock, Automatic Ejector, Fancy Engraving, Fancy Checkering, Double Trigger, *Modern*	1500	2750	3850
Primic, Various Gauges, Sidelock, Automatic Ejector, Fancy Engraving, Fancy Checkering, Single Trigger, *Modern*	1700	3000	4150
Primic, Various Gauges, Sidelock, Automatic Ejector, Fancy Engraving, Fancy Checkering, Single Selective Trigger, *Modern*	1700	3000	4275
Victor, Various Gauges, Sidelock, Automatic Ejector, Engraved, Checkered Stock, Double Trigger, *Modern*	2000	4000	5125
Victor, Various Gauges, Sidelock, Automatic Ejector, Engraved, Checkered Stock, Single Trigger, *Modern*	3000	4500	5875
Victor, Various Gauges, Sidelock, Automatic Ejector, Engraved, Checkered Stock, Single Selective Trigger, *Modern*	3200	4675	6150

COLON

Antonio Azpiri y Cia. Eibar, Spain 1914–1918.

HANDGUN, SEMI-AUTOMATIC

	Fair	V. Good	Excellent
Pocket, .25 ACP, Clip Fed, *Curio*	75	100	125

COLON

Made by Orbea Hermanos Eibar, Spain, c. 1925.

HANDGUN, REVOLVER

	Fair	V. Good	Excellent
Colt Police Positive Copy, .32/20 Double Action, Blue, *Curio*	75	100	125

COLONIAL

Fabrique d'Armes de Guerre de Grand Precision, Eibar, Spain.

	Fair	V. Good	Excellent
HANDGUN, SEMI-AUTOMATIC			
.25 ACP, Clip Fed, Blue, *Modern* .	$35	$75	$125
.32 ACP, Clip Fed, Blue, *Modern* .	50	100	150

COLT

Paterson, N.J. 1836–1841. Whitneyville, Conn. 1847–1848. Hartford, Conn. 1848 to Date; London, England 1853–1857. Also see U.S. Military. Also see Commemorative Section. Founded by Samuel Colt in 1836, the company that bears his name is the original manufacturer of the world's first successful revolving firearms. One of America's oldest gunmakers, and possessor of one of history's most respected brand names, Colt is to firearms as Kodak is to the camera, Ford to the automobile, and Rolex to the wristwatch. Most famous—and most attractive—of all Colt revolvers is the Single Action Army—known popularly as the Peacemaker, Thumb-Buster, Hogleg, Equalizer and Plowhandle. Popular Colt factory designations are the Bisley (a distinct variation) and the Frontier Six-Shooter (both noted in barrel markings on specific examples). Collectors have added their own array of appellations: U.S. Martial, Buntline, Long-Flute, Rimfire, and Sheriff's or Storekeeper's model. U.S. Ordnance tests of the predecessor arm, the Model 1872 Open Top .44, had not proved successful. But within a matter of months Colt followed up with the Single Action Army. The new design featured solid-frame construction, .45 caliber, 7$^1/_2$" barrel, with blued and case-hardened finish, and grips of oil-stained one-piece walnut. The new revolver combined the most practical attributes of the Open Top .44, sharing a similar interior mechanism and frame size as the 1851 Navy and 1860 Army cap and ball predecessor models. Samuel Colt's design expertise was therefore carried over into the Single Action, a model introduced 10 years after the Colonel's death. Unlike the majority of cap and ball Colt revolvers, the barrel was a screw-in type. The ejector mechanism, for the breech-loading metallic cartridges, was mounted alongside the barrel. In 1873 the U.S. Ordnance adopted the new revolver for service. The Ordnance Department's favorable reception was followed up by contracts from the government totaling 37,063, from 1873 to 1891. The revolvers accepted by Ordnance are clearly marked with the U.S. stamped on the left side of the frame, inspector initials on the grips (often with date markings denoting year of acceptance), and minute inspector initial stampings on various other parts. Collectors pursue variations based on calibers, barrel lengths, markings, technical features (like machine cuts), low and otherwise special serial numbers, engraving, finishes, grips, and such an exotic rarity as the long-barreled Buntline Special. Manufacture was from 1873 to 1940, and from 1956 to date. Researching shipping ledgers of the Colt plant (a service of Colt's Historical Department) allows for tracing most of the prewar and all of the postwar production. Unfortunately, factory records are missing on the majority of the first 30,000 revolvers shipped, which were primarily government purchases. With its enormous appeal and striking beauty, more enthusiasts and collectors specialize in the Single Action Army than any other Colt revolver. Historically and artistically this is the ne plus ultra of all Colt firearms. The model's popularity is reflected in the total production from its introduction until modern times, including prewar, postwar, commemorative, Bisleys, Flattop Targets, the Buntlines, and special order guns from the Colt Custom Shop in excess of 650,000. Initially advertised as "The Most Powerful Automatic Pistol Made," the Model 1911 is the most famous of all handgun designs by John Browning, and is a bona fide firearms masterpiece. This classic pistol stands to this day as one of Colt's and Browning's major contributions to the long and complex history of firearms development. The first .45ACP pistol, however, was not the Model 1911. Its predecessor model was the 1905, of which only 6100 were manufactured. The U.S. government ordered 200 of these, followed by another 201, in a variant known as the Model 1907. The latter were for tests by the Springfield Armory. As exemplified in a fascinating series of development types, including the rare 1909 and 1910, Colt engineers and John Browning created the Model 1911. The resultant pistol is a classic in simplicity, design, performance, and manufacturability. From the basic Model 1911 eventually evolved a veritable industry of clones, in a variety of calibers, intended for sport hunting, target shooting, combat pistol shooting, self-defense, law enforcement and special issue "commemorative" collecting. The Colt-made Model 1911 and its successors are the record holder as the largest quantity ever made of any Colt handgun: over four million, and still going strong. The technical features which differentiate the Model 1911 from the Model 1911A1 successor variation are the arched mainspring housing, the decreased trigger width, and the grip safety increased in its rearward projection. Because of the demand for service in the First World War, government orders totaling 2,550,000 Model 1911s were placed. Only a relatively small number of pistols were delivered. American service involvement in the war was limited to the years 1917–18. Tooling up time by contracted companies proved lengthy, and among those who had been awarded contracts were the Winchester Repeating Arms Co., Lanston Monotype Machine Co., National Cash Register Co., Burroughs Adding Machine Co., Savage Arms Co., A.J. Savage Munitions Co., Caron Brothers Mfg. Co., and Dominion Rifle Plant—North American Arms Co., Ltd. The Springfield Armory, also under contract for licensed manufacture, performed best by far; the historic institution produced a total of 25,767, from 1914–18. Manufacture was from 1911 to late 1923; then succeeded by the M1911A1; approximately 130,000 civilian and 700,000 military Model 1911s were produced. The civilian range is relatively simple; the military rather complex, with individual ranges of the Colt factory, from 1911 (1 on up to approximately 700,000 range in 1924); the Remington-UMC, 1918–19 (1-21676), and specific range by Springfield Armory (began 1914, with 72751; and completed, with gaps, in 1918 with the high serial 133186). Since adoption of the Model 1911A1, production soared, with an estimated number of that variation and its successors in excess of 3,000,000. Note: the assistance of Martin J. Lane (Martin Lane Historical Americana Gallery) in review of the Colt section is gratefully appreciated. Note: For more detailed information concerning rarity, see *The Book of Colt Firearms.*

	Fair	V. Good	Excellent
PATERSON HANDGUNS			
.28 caliber Baby Paterson revolver, approximately 500 manufactured; serial number from 1 on up; various barrel lengths; octagonal barrel; no loading lever. *Antique*	$7000	$17500	$30000

	Fair	V. Good	Excellent
.31 caliber Belt Model No. 2 Paterson, straight grip, without loading lever; approximately 850 manufactured (including No. 3 with flared grip), serial number from 1 on up; various barrel lengths; octagonal barrel. *Antique*	$9500	$22500	$37500
.31 caliber Belt Model No. 3 Paterson, flared grip, without loading lever; approximately 850 manufactured (including No. 2 Model with straight grip); serial number from 1 on up; various barrel lengths; octagonal barrel. Added premium if cased set with extra cylinder and accessories. *Antique*	10000	27500	42500
.31 caliber Belt Model No. 3 Paterson, flared grip and loading lever; relatively limited number from approximately 850 manufactured (including No. 2 Model with straight grip); various barrel lengths; octagonal barrel. Added premium if cased set with extra cylinder and accessories. *Antique*	12500	35000	50000
.36 caliber Holster Model or Texas Paterson, flared grip, without loading lever; approximately 1,000 manufactured; serial number from 1 on up; various barrel lengths, but 7 1/2" and 9" standard; octagonal barrel. Added premium if cased set with extra cylinder and accessories. *Antique*	17500	45000	67500
.36 caliber Holster Model or Texas Paterson, flared grip and loading lever; relatively limited production from approximately 1,000 manufactured; various barrel lengths, but 7 1/2" and 9" standard; octagonal barrel. Added premium if cased set with extra cylinder and accessories; different contents when loading lever present. *Antique*	20000	50000	75000
.28 caliber Ehlers Model, round back cylinder and loading lever. Barrel address does not include "Mfg. Co." in marking. Added premium if cased set with accessories. Limited production of 500 (including .31 caliber Ehlers Model); serial number from 1 on up; octagonal barrel. *Antique*	10500	25000	45000

	Fair	V. Good	Excellent
.31 caliber Ehlers Model, round back cylinder and loading lever. Barrel address does not include "Mfg. Co." in marking. Added premium if cased set with accessories. Limited production of 500 (including .28 caliber Ehlers Model); serial number from 1 on up; octagonal barrel. *Antique*	$10500	$27500	$47500

PATERSON LONGARMS

	Fair	V. Good	Excellent
No. 1 Ring Lever Revolving Rifle, topstrap over cylinder; 200 only manufactured, in .34, .36, .38, .40 and .44 caliber (8 or 10 shots); serial number from 1 on up; octagonal barrel. *Antique*	6500	15000	40000

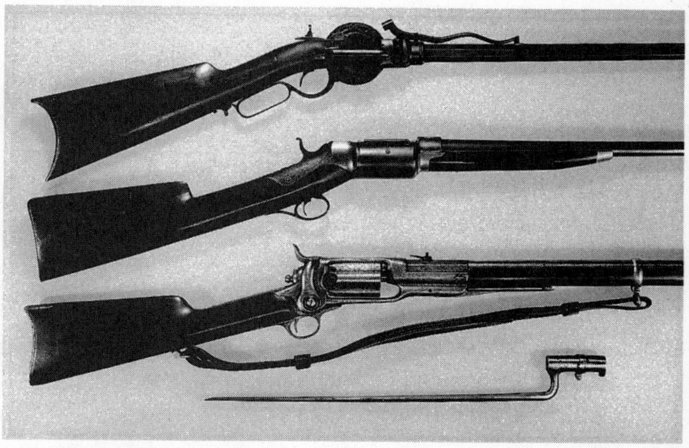

Three American Revolving rifles of the second half of the 19th century: from the top, *a P. W. Porter 9-shot pill-lock in .50 caliber (dated 1851); a 4-shot Roper in 12-gauge; and a Model 1855 Colt Sidehammer Rifled Musket with angular bayonet accessory, 5-shot, .56 caliber.*

	Fair	V. Good	Excellent
No. 2 Ring Lever Revolving Rifle, without topstrap over cylinder; 500 manufactured, in .44 caliber (8 or 10 shots); serial number from 1 on up; octagonal barrel. *Antique*	5500	12500	35000
Model 1839 Revolving Carbine, .525 smoothbore caliber; approximately 950 produced; serial number from 1 on up; 6 shots; round barrel with faceted breech. *Antique*	5500	17500	37500

	Fair	V. Good	Excellent
Variation with smooth cylinders (no roll engraved scene), formerly known as Albert Foster Jr. Carbines; sold by Colt in early Hartford period; often found in excellent condition. *Antique*	$5000	$12500	$30000
Model 1839 Revolving Shotgun, .62 caliber; approximately 225 produced; serial number from 1 on up; 6 shots; round barrel, faceted breech. *Antique*	4000	10000	25000

THE WALKER COLT, MADE IN WHITNEYVILLE, CONNECTICUT, IN THE WHITNEY ARMORY.

	Fair	V. Good	Excellent
Walker Colt Revolver, .44 caliber, 6 shots, 9″ part round/part octagonal barrel; with military markings of Cos. A, B, C, D from 1 to approximately 220, and E Co. from 1 to 120. *Antique*	20000	55000	95000
Walker Colt revolver, .44 caliber, 6 shots, 9″ part round/part octagonal barrel; with civilian serial range of 1001 up to 1100. *Antique*	20000	55000	95000

HANDGUNS AND LONGARMS OF HARTFORD MANUFACTURE

	Fair	V. Good	Excellent
Whitneyville-Hartford Transition Dragoon revolver, .44 caliber, 6 shots, 7½″ half round/half octagonal barrel; serial range approximately 1101 through 1340. One of the most rare of all Colt revolvers. Variations primarily of Walker style grip profiling into frame at rear or of straight-backed frame at juncture with front of grip. *Antique*	15000	40000	75000
First Model Dragoon Revolver, .44 caliber, 6 shots, 7½″ half round/half octagonal barrel; round cylinder stop grooves on cylinder; squareback triggerguard; serial range approximately 1341 through 8000; total production approximately 7,000. *Antique*	4000	19000	45000
Fluck pre-First Model Dragoon Revolver, .44 caliber, 6 shots, 7½″ half round/half octagonal barrel; serial range approximately 2216 through 2215; round stop grooves on cylinder; believed made to replace Walker Models which failed in service. Small serial numbers, some reworked Walker parts; with Ordnance stamps. *Antique*	4500	20000	50000

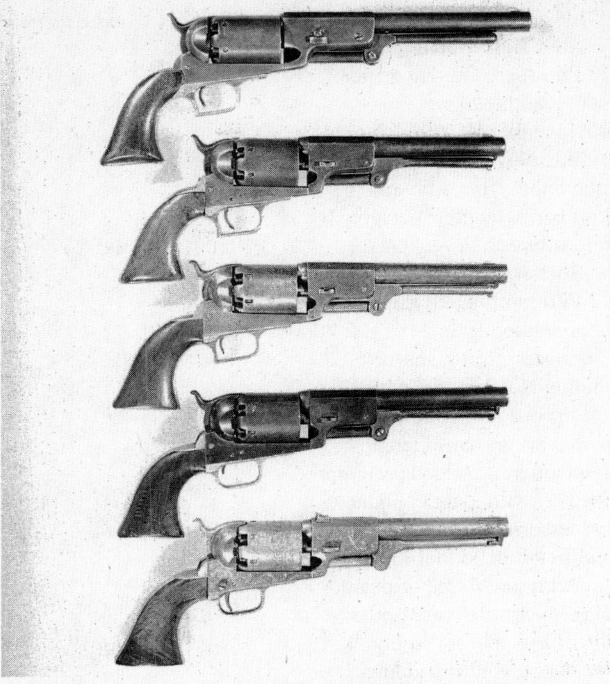

Colt .44 caliber percussion revolvers, from top, *the Walker Model, First Model Dragoon, Second Model, Third Model with vertical loading lever latch, and Third Model cut for attachable shoulder stock and with horizontal lever latch (and deluxe engraved by Nimschke).*

	Fair	V. Good	Excellent
Second Model Dragoon revolver, .44 caliber, 6 shots, 7½″ half round/half octagonal barrel, squared cylinder stop slots, squareback triggerguard; serial range approximately 8000 through 10700; approximately 2,700 made. Premium for Massachusetts or C.L. Dragoon specimens. *Antique*	$3750	$16000	$35000
Third Model Dragoon Revolver, .44 caliber, 6 shots, 7½″ half round/half octagonal barrel, squared cylinder stop slots, roundback triggerguard; serial range approximately 10500 through 19500. Premium paid for variation with attachable shoulder stock, revolvers with steel gripstraps, and 8″ barrel specimens. *Antique*	2750	12500	27500
Shoulder Stock, First Model, two projections engaging two slots on backstrap. *Antique*	2500	4500	8000
Shoulder Stock, Second Model, one projection into backstrap; clamp on butt. *Antique*	1700	3500	7500
Shoulder Stock, Third Model, hooks into cutouts on recoil shield, and clamp on butt. *Antique*	1250	2700	6000

	Fair	V. Good	Excellent
Hartford-English Dragoon Revolver, .44 caliber, 6 shots, 7 1/2″ half round/half octagonal barrel, squared cylinder stop slots, roundback triggerguard, serial range from 1 to 700, most have New York barrel address markings. Premium paid for early examples, some of which have hand-engraved frame and barrel address markings, and some of which have squareback triggerguards. *Antique*	$2500	$10000	$22500
Model 1848 Baby Dragoon Pocket Model Revolver, .31 caliber, 5 shots; 3″, 4″, 5″ and 6″ octagonal barrel lengths; squareback triggerguards; early production without loading levers. Some of later production built with levers; some levers added later by private gunsmiths. Serial range 1 through approximately 14000 (overlap with Model 1849 Pocket Model); made c. 1848 to 1850. *Antique*	1500	4500	12500
Model 1849 Pocket Model Revolver, .31 caliber, 5 or 6 shots, 3″, 4″, 5″ and 6″ octagonal barrel lengths; with loading levers. Serial range approximately 12000 (overlap with Baby Dragoon) to approximately 340000; made c. 1850 to 1873. Numerous variations; premium paid for some of these, such as revolver with steel gripstraps, full nickel-plating, and 3″ barrel version with loading lever. *Antique*	700	800	2250
Model 1849 Pocket Model Revolver, Wells Fargo variation, generally 3″ or 4″ barrels, without loading levers; .31 caliber. 5 or 6 shots. *Antique*	900	2750	7500
Model 1849 Pocket Revolver, London manufacture, 4″, 5″ and 6″ barrel lengths; 5 shots; generally with Col. Colt London barrel address markings. Approximately 11,000 produced, in own serial range from 1 on up. *Antique*	450	750	2250
Model 1851 Navy or Belt Revolver, .36 caliber, 7 1/2″ barrel, 6 shots; total made approximately 215,000, in own serial range from 1 on up. Numerous variations bring premiums, including specimens with barrels exceeding 7 1/2″ or shorter than 7 1/2″, cutaways, specially marked examples, full nickel-plating.			
Model 1851 early production, First Model, squareback triggerguard, wedge over screw in barrel; serial range approximately 1 to 1250. *Antique*	$3500	$12500	$20000
Model 1851 early production, Second Model, squareback triggerguard, screw over wedge in barrel; serial range approximately 1250 to 4,200. *Antique*	1700	3750	15000
Model 1851 standard production, so-called Third Model, small round triggerguard; serial range approximately 4200 to 85000. *Antique*	800	2500	7500
As above, with U.S. markings and Ordnance inspector stampings; steel gripstraps. *Antique*	950	3000	9500
Model 1851 standard production, Fourth Model, large round triggerguard; serial range approximately 85000 to 215000. *Antique*	750	2500	7500
As above, with U.S. markings and Ordnance inspector stampings; steel gripstraps. *Antique*	2250	4500	12000
Third and Fourth Model Navy Specimen, cut for attachable shoulder stocks. *Antique*	1500	3000	11500
Shoulder stock, First Model, two projections engaging two slots on backstrap. *Antique*	1500	3500	6500
Shoulder stock, Second Model, one projection into backstrap; clamp on butt. *Antique*	1200	3000	5500
Shoulder Stock, Third Model, hooks into cutouts on recoil shield, and clamp on butt. *Antique*	950	2250	4000
London Model 1851 Revolver, .36 caliber, 7 1/2″ octagonal barrel, with blued or silver-plated steel gripstraps. Manufactured in London, c. 1853–57; total of approximately 42,000. Not to be confused with examples made in Hartford with London barrel addresses and proof stampings. Premium paid for variations, such as early examples with special barrel markings, squareback triggerguards. *Antique*	800	2200	6000
Model 1855 Sidehammer Revolver, .28 caliber (Model 3A in .31 caliber), 5 shots; 3 1/2″ octagonal barrels (3 7/16″ for Model 1A), blued. Manufactured c. 1855–1861; total of 28,000. Variations 1 and 1A, 2, and 3A. Premium for 1, 1A and 3A due to rarity. *Antique*	400	1200	3000

	Fair	V. Good	Excellent
Model 1855 Sidehammer Revolver, .31 caliber (Models 4, 5 and 5A, 6 and 6A, and 7 and 7A); 5 shots; 3½″ and 4½″ barrels (3½″ for Model 4; octagonal for Model 4; balance of variations round), blued. Manufactured c. 1860–1870; total of 14,000. Premium for Model 4, Model 6 and 6A, and Model 7 and 7A (screw in cylinder variation). *Antique*	$350	$950	$3750
Model 1855 Sidehammer Revolving Longarms, various calibers and barrel lengths. Two basic frame types, one having 5 shots generally and the other 6 shots. Several variations:			
Sporting Rifles, total of approximately 3,500, in .36, .40, .44, .50, and .56 calibers. Premium paid for rare calibers and unusual barrel lengths. *Antique*	950	3000	8500
Military Rifles, sling swivels and barrel bands; total of approximately 9,310 made, in calibers .44 and .56 (with 25 or less only in .64 caliber). Premium for rare caliber and unusual barrel lengths; and when bayonet present. *Antique*	2260	4250	16000
Carbines, total of approximately 4,435 made, in calibers .36, .40, .44, .50, and .56 (.36, .40 and .50 rare). Premium for rare caliber and unusual barrel lengths. *Antique*	1000	3750	11500
Shotguns, in 10 gauge (.75 caliber) and 20 gauge (.60 caliber); approximately 1,100 made, in own serial number range. Premium for unusual barrel lengths. *Antique*	900	2500	6000
Model 1861 Single Shot Rifled Musket; .58 caliber; standard with 40″ barrel; finished bright. Colt markings on lockplate and date 1861, 1862, 1863 or 1864. Not serial numbered. *Antique*	400	1200	2750
Single Shot Target Rifle, only a handful produced. .52 caliber (approx.); 28½″ barrel (will vary); not serial numbered. Premium if false muzzle present. *Antique*	1200	3250	8750

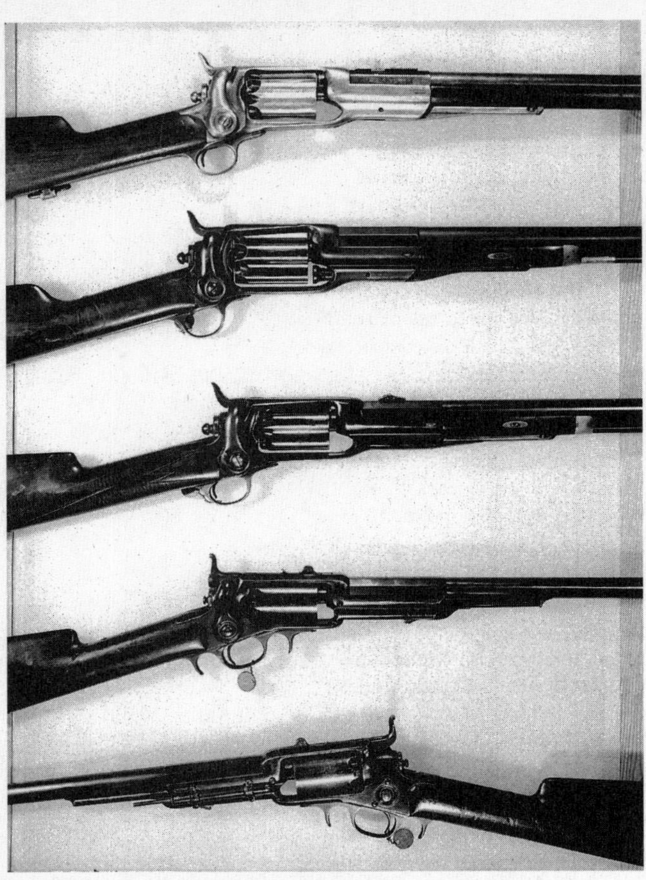

Colt Model 1855 longarms, from the top, *Rifled Musket, Shotgun, Sporting Rifle, and the First Model Sporting Rifle (lacking fore end, and fitted with automatic oiler for charges in cylinder).*

	Fair	V. Good	Excellent
Model 1860 Army Revolver, .44 caliber, 6 shot rebated cylinder; total production 200,500. Standard model with 8″ round barrel with creeping style ramrod, cylinder engraved with naval engagement roll scene; Army-size grips of walnut. *Antique*	$850	$3000	$8500
Military variation of the above, 4-screw frame, cut for shoulder stock; premium if inspector markings on grips and various metal parts. *Antique*	850	4000	10000
7½″ barrel, fluted cylinder, rare early production with Army size grips; Navy size grips bring premium. *Antique*	900	4500	12500
8″ barrel, fluted cylinder, scarce early production. *Antique*	850	4000	11000
Model 1860 Army Revolver, London barrel address. *Antique*	850	4000	11000

	Fair	V. Good	Excellent
Model 1860 attachable shoulder stock, First Model, two projections engaging two slots on backstrap. *Antique*	$1000	$2500	$6000
Model 1860 attachable shoulder stock, Second Model, one projection into backstrap; clamp on butt. *Antique*	900	2000	5000
Model 1860 attachable shoulder stock, Third Model, hooks into cutouts on recoil shield, and clamp on butt. *Antique*	850	1700	4500
Model 1861 Navy Revolver, .36 caliber, 6 shots, 7 1/2" barrel. 38,843 made (some converted to metallic cartridge). *Antique*	700	2000	6000
Model 1861 Navy Revolver, rare early variation with half-fluted cylinder. *Antique*	2500	15000	25000
Model 1861 Navy Revolver, U.S. martial markings. *Antique*	900	3000	14000
Model 1861 Navy Revolver, London barrel address markings. *Antique*	1100	2500	9000
Model 1862 Police Revolver, .36 caliber, 5 shot half fluted, rebated cylinders, 4 1/2", 5 1/2" and 6 1/2" round barrels. Approximately 47,000 made (40 percent were the 1862 Pocket Navy; some built as metallic cartridge conversions). Early specimens bring premium and have Hartford barrel address and low serial numbers. Premium for steel-grip revolvers and London barrel address markings. *Antique*	425	1200	3000
Trapper's Model, 3 1/2" barrel variation, without attachable loading lever; about 50 produced. *Antique*	1000	3500	10000
Model 1862 Pocket Pistol of Navy Caliber Revolver; .36 caliber, 5 shots, 4 1/2", 5 1/2" and 6 1/2" octagonal barrels; stagecoach holdup roll scene on rebated cylinder. Premium paid for London barrel address variation. *Antique*	400	1200	3700

CONVERSIONS AND EARLY SINGLE ACTION REVOLVERS

(Conversions of revolvers from percussion models. Total by factory estimated at approximately 46,000, built primarily c. 1869–c. 1878.)

	Fair	V. Good	Excellent
Thuer conversions: all handguns with 6 shot cylinders; any conversions of this type done on any models other than those listed below are rare and will bring premium; estimated total of all types 5,000			
Model 1849 Pocket Revolver, *Antique*	$1700	$3800	$9000
Model 1851 Navy Revolver, *Antique*	1500	4000	10000
Model 1860 Army Revolver, *Antique*	1800	4500	10000
Model 1861 Navy Revolver. *Antique*	3000	4500	10000
Model 1862 Police Revolver. *Antique*	1500	4000	10000
Model 1860 Army Revolver, Richards Conversion, .44 Colt c.f.; 6 shots; 8" barrels; approximately 9,000 made, most in range from 1 on up. *Antique*	500	2000	5000
Model 1860 Army Revolver, Richards-Mason Conversion, .44 Colt c.f.; 6 shots; 7 1/2" and 8" barrels; approximately 2,100 made, within high range of Richards Conversions. *Antique*	600	2400	8000
Model 1851 Navy Conversions, .38 r.f. and .38 c.f. calibers; 6 shots; 7 1/2" barrels; approximately 3,800 made. Premium for U.S. Navy markings. *Antique*	600	1700	4500
Model 1861 Navy Conversions, .38 r.f. and .38 c.f. calibers; 6 shots; 7 1/2" barrels; approximately 2,200 made). Premium for .38 r.f. and for U.S. Navy marked revolvers. *Antique*	650	2000	4750
Model 1862 Police and Pocket Navy conversions, .38 r.f. and .38 c.f. calibers; 5 shots; 3 1/2", 4 1/2", 5 1/2" and 6 1/2" barrel lengths. Total of approximately 24,000 in various configurations.			
4 1/2" Octagonal Barrel Model, .38 rimfire (built from Pocket Navy). *Antique*	400	1150	2500
Round Barrel Pocket Navy with Ejector, .38 r.f. and c.f. *Antique*	375	1000	2500
Model 1862 Police/Pocket Navy with Ejector, .38 r.f. and c.f. *Antique*	375	1000	2500
Round (Cartridge) Barrel Model with Ejector, .38 r.f. and c.f. *Antique*	350	950	2500
3 1/2" Round (Cartridge) Barrel Model, .38 r.f. and c.f. *Antique*	275	800	1800

	Fair	V. Good	Excellent
Model 1871–72 Open Top Frontier .44 Single Action Revolver, .44 rimfire; 6 shot cylinder with naval engagement roll scene; 7$^1/_2$" round barrels (8" barrels bring premium); total of approximately 7,000 in own serial range from 1 on up. *Antique*	$1000	$4000	$10000
Single Action Army Revolver, first generation, built from 1873 until c. 1940; in a total of approximately 30 calibers (.32-20, .38-40, .44-40 and .45 Colt the most common); and several barrel lengths from 2" up to 16" (4$^3/_4$", 5$^1/_2$" and 7$^1/_2$" most common); serial numbered from 1 on up to 357859 (310386 with standard frame; 917 flattop target models; 44,350 Bisley models, and 976 Bisley flattop target models)			
Standard production model, 4$^3/_4$", 5$^1/_2$" and 7$^1/_2$" barrel lengths, in common calibers, with walnut or hard rubber grips. Early production bring premium. *Antique*	700	2500	7500
Early production revolvers, with so-called "pinched frame" feature; serial range 1 to approximately 165. *Antique*	7000	22500	60000
U.S. Martial, with U.S. frame stamping and inspector markings; .45 caliber, 7$^1/_2$" barrel. *Antique*	1200	3700	14500
U.S. Martial variation, "Artillery Model," 5$^1/_2$", rebuilt revolvers sent back to Colt factory; are refinished and with mixed serial numbers. *Antique*	800	1500	4500
Rimfire, own serial range from 1 to approximately 1800; premium for .22 caliber; most were made in .44 caliber and with 7$^1/_2$" barrels. *Antique*	1000	5000	22000
Colt Frontier Six-Shooter, with etched barrel marking of that legend on left side; .44-40 caliber; serial range 21000 to 65000. *Antique*	900	2800	10000
Sheriff's Model, Storekeeper variation, without ejector rod or rod housing; customary barrel length 3" or 4". *Antique*	1500	5000	17500
Long-Flute Cylinder variation, found in serial range 330001 to 331480; cylinders from double action revolver production. *Antique*	1250	4000	12000

	Fair	V. Good	Excellent
Single Action Army Flattop Target Model Revolver, various calibers from .22 rimfire up to .476 Eley; various barrel lengths. Premiums for unusual barrel lengths and calibers. *Antique*	$1200	$4500	$8500
Bisley Model Single Action Army Revolver, various calibers from .32 Colt up to .455 Eley; various barrel lengths. Premiums for unusual barrel lengths and calibers, and for Sheriff's Model. *Antique*	700	1500	3000
Bisley Flattop Target Model Revolver, various calibers from .32 Colt rimfire up to .455 Eley; various barrel lengths. Premiums for unusual barrel lengths and calibers. *Antique*	1000	2700	7500
Post–World War II Single Action Army Revolver, from 1956 to date; serial range began at 0001SA, when reached total of approximately 100000 the company placed SA in front of the serial number, e.g., SA00001. Calibers .38 Special, .357 Magnum, .44 Special, and .45 Colt; 4$^3/_4$", 5$^1/_2$", and 7$^1/_2$" barrels. Premium for Sheriff's Models, unusual barrel lengths, and special calibers. *Modern*	300	600	1000
New Frontier Single Action Army Revolver, 1961 into 1970s. .357 Magnum, .44 Special and .45 Colt calibers, 4$^3/_4$", 5$^1/_2$" and 7$^1/_2$" barrels. *Modern*	400	750	1250
Frontier Scout Revolvers, .22 rimfire and .22 magnum rimfire; 6 shots, 4$^3/_4$" and 9$^1/_2$" barrels standard. Serial numbers began with 1000Q; suffix changed to F, 1958. *Modern*	200	400	850

Colt New Frontier

	Fair	V. Good	Excellent
K Series Frontier Scout Revolver, as above; production began with P suffix, beginning with 999P, 1962; then changed to K, beginning with 1K, 1960. *Modern*	$200	$400	$850

DERRINGERS AND POCKET REVOLVERS

	Fair	V. Good	Excellent
First Model Derringer pistol, .41 short rimfire; 2½]″ barrel; all metal construction; total made 6,500, from 1 on up; 1870–90. *Antique*	350	1250	3000
Second Model Derringer pistol, .41 short rimfire (approx. 200 in c.f.); 2½″ barrel; with checkered walnut grips; total made 9,000, from 1 on up; 1870–90. *Antique*	300	1200	2500
Third Model (Thuer) Derringer pistol, .41 short rimfire (limited number in .41 c.f.); 2½″ barrel; total production approximately 45,000, from 1 on up; c. 1875 through early 20th century. *Antique*	250	475	975
Fourth Model Derringer, .22 rimfire; 2½″ barrel; D and N suffix to serial numbers; total made of approximately 112,000, from 1959–63. *Modern*	100	350	600
Lord and Lady Derringer, .22 short rimfire; 2½″ barrel; from 1001 on up, with DER suffix; approximately 12,000 cased pairs of Lord and 3,000 cased pairs of Lady Model made in 1970, with some production thereafter; valued as cased pairs. *Modern*	200	700	1000
Cloverleaf House Model Revolver, .41 short and long rimfire; 4 shots (Cloverleaf), 5 shots (House Pistol); 1½″ and 3″ barrels; House Pistol with 2⅝″ barrel only; approximately 10,000 made, from 1 on up. Premium for 1½″ barrel.			
Cloverleaf House Model, 4-shot cylinder. *Antique*	300	575	1400
House Model, 5-shot cylinder. *Antique*	275	500	1250
Open Top Pocket Model Revolver, .22 short and long rimfire, 7 shots; 2¾″ and 2⅞″ barrels; approximately 114,200 made, from 1 on up. Premium for early model with integral ejector. *Antique*	125	275	650
New Line .22 Revolver, .22 short and long rimfire; 7 shots; 2¼″ barrel; approximately 55,343 made, from 1 on up. Premium for first model (1 through 16000 serial range); c. 1873–77. *Antique*	100	250	575
New Line .30 Caliber Revolver, .30 short and long rimfire; 5 shots; 1¾″ and 2¼″ barrels; approximately 11,000 made, from 1 on up; c. 1874–76. *Antique*	$150	$350	$1000
New Line .32 Caliber Revolver, .32 short and long rimfire, 32 short and long centerfire; 5 shots; 2¼″ and 4″ barrels; approximately 22,000 made, from 1 on up; c. 1873–84. *Antique*	125	325	875
New Line .38 Caliber Revolver, .38 short and long rimfire, .38 short and long centerfire; 2¼″ and 4″ barrels; approximately 5,500 made, serial numbered with .41 New Lines, from 1 on up; c. 1874–80. *Antique*	125	325	950
New Line .41 Caliber Revolver, .41 short and long rimfire, .41 short and long centerfire; 2¼″ and 4″ barrels; approximately 7,000 made, serial numbered with .38 New Line, from 1 on up; c. 1874–79. *Antique*	150	400	1200
New House Model Revolver, .38 and .41 short and long centerfire (premium for .32 short and long centerfire); 5 shots; 2¼″ barrel; approximately 4,000 made, numbered with New Line .32, .38 and .41 pistols and Police Model pistols; c. 1880–86. *Antique*	125	450	1500
New Police Model Revolver, .32, .38 and .41 short and long centerfire; 5 shots; 2¼″ (without ejector) and 4½″, 5″ and 6″ barrels (with ejector); approximately 3,500 to 4,000 made (.32 and .41 rare), numbered with .32 New Line and .38 and .41 House pistols; c. 1882–86. Known as Cop & Thug Model, due to depiction on composition hard rubber grips of policeman and thug. *Antique*	200	900	3500

DOUBLE ACTION REVOLVERS

	Fair	V. Good	Excellent
Model 1877 Lightning Revolver, .38 Colt, .41 Colt (rare in .32 Colt, about 200 made, brings premium); 6 shots; 2½″, 3½″ (without ejector), 4½″, 6″ barrels standard, various lengths from 1½″ to 10″; 166,849 made; c. 1877–09.			
Standard model, without ejector; premium for checkered rosewood grips, early serial numbers. *Antique*	200	350	850

	Fair	V. Good	Excellent
Standard model, ejector; premium for checkered rosewood grips, early serial numbers. *Antique*	$200	$350	$850
Specimens with London barrel address markings and British proof stampings. *Antique*	250	450	1000
Model 1878 Frontier Revolver, .22 rimfire, .32-20, .38-40, .38 Colt, .44 Russian, .44 German Government, .44 S & W, .44-40, .45 Colt, and .450, .455 and .476 Eley; 6 shots; 2½″ to 12″ barrels (standard 3″ and 4″ without ejector and 4¾″, 5½″ and 7½″ with ejector); 51,210 made; c. 1878–1905.			
Standard model, without ejector. *Antique*	300	550	1000
Standard model, ejector. *Antique*	350	600	1200
Specimens with London barrel address markings and British proof stampings. *Antique*	350	600	1200
Alaskan or Philippine variation, with oversize triggerguard; U.S. inspector markings; .45 caliber; lanyward swivel on butt; 4,600 made (range 43401–48097). *Antique*	400	650	1650

DOUBLE ACTION SWINGOUT CYLINDER MODELS

	Fair	V. Good	Excellent
Model 1889 Navy Revolver, .38 Colt, .38 S & W (scarce), and .41 Colt calibers; 6 shots; 3″, 4½″ and 6″ barrels; 31,000 made, from 1 on up; c. 1889–94. *Antique*	225	750	1750
Model 1889 Navy Revolver, U.S. Navy contract. *Antique*	350	950	2000
Models 1892, 1894, 1895, 1896, 1901 and 1903 New Army and Navy Revolvers, .38 Colt, .38 S & W, .41 Colt and .32-20; 6 shots; barrel lengths from 2″ to 6″; 291,000 made, from 1 on up; c. 1892–1907 (succeeded by Army Special). *Antique and modern*	125	250	650
As above, U.S. Navy purchases. *Antique*	225	450	1000
As above, U.S. Army purchases. *Antique and modern*	200	350	900
Army Special Revolver, .32-20, .38 Colt, .38 S & W Special, .41 Colt; 6 shots; barrel lengths from 4″ to 6″; 240,000 made, from 291000 to 540000 (overlaps with Official Police Model); c. 1908–28. *Modern*	175	300	850
Model 1905 Marine Corps Revolver, .38 Colt, .38 S & W Special; 6 shots; 6″ barrel; 926 made; from 10001 on up; c. 1905–09. *Modern*	650	1250	2500
Official Police Revolver, .32-20, .38 Colt, .38 Colt Special, .38-44 S & W; 6 shots; 4″, 5″ and 6″ barrels; more than 400,000 made, range continued from Army Special (with overlap) at 513216 to approximately 9828163 (some numbers not used); plus a series of .22 revolvers numbered in own range (30,000 made; 1930 to 1967); c. 1927 to early 1970s. Succeeded by J series revolvers, which began 1969. Premium for military and police marked specimens. *Modern*	$150	$250	$450
Commando Revolver, .38 Special; 6 shots; 2″, 4″ and 6″ barrels (4″ standard); 50,617 made; from 1 on up; c. 1942–45; parkerized finish. *Modern*	100	200	400
Marshal Revolver, .38 Special; 6 shots; 2″ and 4″ barrels; 2,500 made, in range from 833352-M, from Official Police range; c. 1954–56. *Modern*	150	250	500
Officers Model Revolver, Officers Model Target, Officers Model Special and **Officers Model Match**, various calibers, from .32 Colt Police Positive to .38 Special, with several chamberings; 4″ and 6″ barrels most common, but range of from 4″ to 7½″ lengths; 15,000 made, beginning at 229881 in Army Special and continuing in Official Police ranges); c. 1904–49; and resumed with serial changes in 1950, 1953 and 1970; complex sequence of models and serial sequences. Premium for earlier revolvers, pre–World War II, with better quality finish. *Modern*	175	300	600
New Service and Shooting Master Revolvers, New Service in production from 1898 through 1944; total 356,000 made, from 1 on up; calibers .38 Colt on up to .476 Eley; 6 shots; 2″ up to 7½″ barrels. Earlier production brings premium.			
Standard Model. *Modern*	200	350	850
Shooting Master (flattop target) Model. *Modern*	250	400	950
Model 1909 U.S. Army and U.S. Navy variation, .45 caliber, 5½″, serial range 30000 to 50000. *Modern*	300	500	1000
Model 1909 U.S. Marine Corps, USMC marked; varnished and checkered walnut grips. *Modern*	300	500	1000

	Fair	V. Good	Excellent
Model 1917 U.S. Army, serial range 150000 to 310000; .45 and .45 ACP; 5 1/2". *Modern*	$200	$400	$850
Camp Perry Single Shot Pistol, .22 long rifle; 8" and 10" barrels; 2,488 made; from 1 on up; c. 1920–41. *Modern*	500	750	1250
New Pocket Model Revolver, .32 Colt, .32 S & W; 6 shot; 2 1/2" to 6" barrels; 30,000 made, from 1 on up; c. 1893–1905; Pocket Positive continued serial number from 30000. *Modern*	150	250	500
Pocket Positive Model Revolver, several variants of .32 centerfire cartridge; 2" to 6" barrels; 6 shot; 130,000 made, from 30000 up to 159000; c. 1905–43. *Modern*	150	300	550
New Police .32 and New Police Target Model Revolvers, .32 Colt, .32 S & W, .32 Colt New Police; 6 shot; 2 1/2", 4", and 6" barrels; 49,500 made, from 1 on up; c. 1896–1907. Majority of production New Police; premium for Police Target (was in 6" barrel only). *Modern*	175	325	600

Colt Police Positive, Late

	Fair	V. Good	Excellent
Police Positive .32 and Police Positive Target Model Revolvers, various .32 caliber cartridges; 6 shot; 2 1/2", 4", 5" and 6" barrels; 199,000 made, from 49500 on up to 238623; c. 1907–43. Majority of production Police Positive; premium for Police Positive Target (was in 6" barrel only and totalled only 3351 made). *Modern*	175	325	600
Pequano Model Police Positive Revolver, .32 Police Positive; 2", 2 1/2", 4", 5" and 6" barrels; few thousand only made; c. 1933–1941, in serial range 226000 to 237000. *Modern*	$200	$350	$700
Police Positive .22 Target Revolver, Models G and C, .22 rimfire and various .32 c.f. calibers; 6" barrel; four series of serial numbers used; most of production in range from 1 on up to approximately 45741; c. 1910–41. *Modern*	200	350	700
Police Positive .38 Model Revolver, .38 Colt Police Positive (New Police) and .38 S & W calibers; 6 shot; 2", 4", 5" and 6" barrels; 200,000 made, from 1 to 177000, then 329000 on (latter shared with Bankers Special and .32 Police Positive on .38 frame); c. 1905–43. *Modern*	200	350	750
Bankers' Special Revolver, .22 long rifle, .38 Colt Police Positive (New Police) and .38 S & W; 6 shot; 2" barrel; more than 35,000 made, in Police Positive .38 range from 177000 through 185000 and 329000 through 406725; c. 1928–43. *Modern*	200	400	800
Police Positive Special Revolver, .32-20, .32 New Police, .38 Colt, .38 Special, .38 New Police, .38 S & W Special, .38-44 S & W Special and .38 smoothbore (rare); 6 shot; 2", 4", 4 1/2", 5" and 6" barrels; over 650,000 made, from 1 on up; c. 1908 into the 1970s; note variations in serial numbers, including with letter prefixes beginning 1969 (A10000 to A59999). Premium for pre–World War II revolvers, which show better quality of manufacture. Late model has special barrel design, with shrouded ejector rod. *Modern*	200	400	800
Detective Special Revolver, various .32 and .38 calibers; 6 shot; 2" and 3" (latter for .38 only) barrels; over 350,000 made; serial numbered with Police Positive Special from 331000; A prefix numbers began 1969; c. 1927 into the 1970s. *Modern*	200	400	850
Border Patrol Revolver, .38 Special; 6 shot; 4" heavy bull barrel; 400 made, in range of 610000 through 620000; c. 1952. *Modern*	350	500	1000

Colt Detective Special

	Fair	V. Good	Excellent
Diamondback Revolver, .22 long rifle, .38 Special; 6 shot; 2½″ and 4″ barrel; Python styling with distinctive weighted and ventilated rib barrel; more than 50,000 made, c. 1966 into the 1970s; from D1001 on up. *Modern*	$200	$350	$750
Cobra Revolver, .22 long rifle, .32 Colt New Police; .38 Colt New Police, .38 Special; 6 shot; 2″, 3″ 4″ and 5″ barrels; aluminum alloy frame; over 240,000 made, from 1LW on up (numbered with Agent, Courier, and Aircrewman models); from 1950 into the 1970s; A prefix serial numbers begun in 1969. *Modern*	200	350	750
Aircrewman Revolver, .38 Special; 6 shot; 2″ barrel; aluminum alloy barrel and cylinder; 1,189 made; majority destroyed due to safety problem with ammunition; numbered in Cobra and Courier serial range with LW suffix; most in 2901LW to 7775LW serial group; Air Force buttstrap numbers, from 1 to 1189; made 1951. *Modern*	650	1,000	2500
Courier Revolver, .22 long rifle, .32 S & W long and short and .32 New Police; 6 shot; 3″ barrel; aluminum alloy frame; approximately 3,000 made; in serial range of Cobra and Agent revolvers; c. 1953–56. *Modern*	200	400	700
Agent Revolver, .38 Special; 6 shot; 2″ barrel; aluminum alloy frame with diminuitive grip; over 50,000 made; c. 1962 into 1970s; in serial range of Cobra Model. *Modern*	200	350	650

	Fair	V. Good	Excellent
Trooper Revolver, .22 long rifle, .38 Special, .357 Magnum; 4″ and 6″ barrels; production began 1954, from 1 on up; serial range with .357 Model through 1961; shared with Officer's Model Match from 1953 into 1970s; J series began 1969 with J1001. *Modern*	$150	$250	$450
.357 Magnum Revolver, .38 Special and .357 Magnum; 6 shot; 4″ and 6″ barrels; from 1953 to 1961, from 1 on up; rare early production of 259 in 1953; number shared with Trooper Model; discontinued in 28000 range, 1961. *Modern*	150	250	450
Python Revolver, .357 Magnum; 6 shots; 2½″, 4″ and 6″ barrels; from 1955 to date, from 1 on up; prefix E begun in 1969 with five digit number. Over 200,000 made to date. Python Hunter variation will bring premium, as will earlier specimens. *Modern*	250	350	500

Colt Python .357 Magnum

MK III Series, Trooper, Metropolitan, Lawman, Official Police and Officers Model Match, production began with J-serial prefix in 1969; revolvers often called the J-series; .38 Special and .357 Magnum calibers, with some models in .22 Long Rifle. Premium for nickel plating.

	Fair	V. Good	Excellent
Lawman MK III, .357 Magnum, various barrel lengths, 6 shots. *Modern*	100	250	500
Lawman MK V, .357 Magnum, various barrel lengths, 6 shots. *Modern*	100	250	500

Colt Lawman MK V

	Fair	V. Good	Excellent
Metropolitan MK III, .38 Special, 4″ barrel, 6 shots. *Modern*	$150	$250	$500
Official Police MK III, .38 Special, 6 shot. *Modern*	150	250	500

SEMI-AUTOMATIC PISTOLS

	Fair	V. Good	Excellent
Model 1900 Automatic, .38 rimless, smokeless; 7-shot magazine; 6″ barrel; 3,500 made, from 1 on up; c. 1900–03; serial range continued by Sporting Model 1902 pistols. Premium for rear sight functioning as hammer safety. *Modern*	1000	2000	5000
Navy contract of above pistols, USN numbers as well as commercial serial numbers; rare. *Modern*	1500	3500	7500
Army contract of above pistols, first series, 75 only; J.T.T. inspector marking; scarce. *Modern*	3000	7500	17500
Army contract of above pistols, second series; 200 only; R.A.C. inspector marking; scarce. *Modern*	3500	4500	15000
Model 1902 Sporting Automatic, .38 rimless, smokeless; 7-shot magazine; 6″ barrel; 7,500 made, from approximately 3500 up to 10999 and from 30000 to 30190; c. 1903–08; premium for location of serrations on front of slide. *Modern*	500	750	2000
Model 1902 Military Automatic, .38 rimless, smokeless; 8-shot magazine; 6″ barrel; 18,000 made, from 15001 back to 11000; then from 30200 to 47266 (numbered with Model 1903 Pocket Automatic c. 1918–29); c. 1902–29; premium for location of serrations on front of slide. *Modern*	500	750	2000
Model 1902 Military Automatic with U.S. Army markings (R.A.C. and J.T.T. inspectors); serial range 15001 to 15200. *Modern*	1000	4000	10000

	Fair	V. Good	Excellent
Model 1903 Pocket (Hammer) Automatic, .38 rimless, smokeless; 7-shot magazine; $4^1/_2$″ barrel; 26,000 made, from 16001 to 47226 (shared numbers from 30200 on up with Model 1902 Military Pistol); c. 1903–29. *Modern*	$200	$650	$1250
Model 1903 Hammerless .32 Pocket Automatic, .32 ACP; 8-shot magazine; 4″ and $3^3/_4$″ barrel; 572,215 made; from 1 on up; c. 1903–45.			
1st Model, serial range 1 to 71999. *Modern*	200	300	700
2nd Model, range 72000 to 105050. *Modern*	150	250	650
3rd Model, range 105051 to 468096. *Modern*	125	200	500
4th Model (commercial), range 468097 to 554000. *Modern*	150	250	550
4th Model (military), U.S. PROPERTY marking on frame; range 554001 to 572214. *Modern*	250	600	1250
Model 1908 .38 Hammerless Pocket Automatic, .380 ACP; 7-shot magazine; $3^3/_4$″ barrel; 138,009 made; from 1 on up; c. 1908–45.			
1st Model, range 1 to 6251. *Modern*	200	350	650
2nd Model, range 6252 to 92893. *Modern*	150	275	500
3rd Model (Commercial), range 92894 to 133649. *Modern*	125	200	450
3rd Model (Military), range 133650 to 138009; marked U.S. PROPERTY on frame. *Modern*	500	950	2000
Model 1908 .25 Hammerless Automatic, .25ACP; 6-shot magazine; 2″ barrel; 409,061 made, from 1 on up; c. 1908–41.			
Early model, up through approximately serial 20000. *Modern*	150	250	500
Standard model, post 20000 serial range, with 1910 or 1910 and 1917 patent dates on slide. *Modern*	125	200	450
Military variation, U.S. PROPERTY marking on frame; limited production of less than 1,000. *Modern*	500	1750	3250
Junior Colt .25/22 Automatic and **Colt Automatic Caliber .25**, .22 short and .25ACP; 6-shot magazines; $2^1/_4$″ barrel; over 75,000 made; serial range began with 1CC, shared between both models. *Modern*	150	250	350

	Fair	V. Good	Excellent
Model 1905 .45 Automatic, .45 rimless, smokeless; 7-shot magazine; 5″ barrel; 6,100 made, from 1 on up. Premium for early production with 1897 and 1902 patent markings on slide.			
Standard model. *Modern*	$500	$1000	$2750
U.S. Government Contract, 1907, numbered 1 to 200; K.M. inspector marking. *Modern*	4000	7500	12500
Shoulder stock variation, with stock designed to also act as holster. *Modern*	4000	7500	12500
Model 1909 Prototype/ Experimental Automatic, .45ACP; 7-shot magazine; 5″ barrel; approximately 23 made, from 1 on up; c. 1909. *Curio*	7500	12500	20000
Model 1911 Automatic, Commercial serial series (with C prefix from C1 through C240227 and C suffix from 240228C through 1970 at 336169C); 7-shot magazine; 5″ barrel.			
Early specimens, with 1897, 1902, 1905, 1911 patent dates on slide; C1 to approximately C4500. *Modern*	500	750	1500
Standard production, range C4500 to C130000; straight mainspring housing. *Modern*	400	600	1250
.455 British Contract, own serial range W10001 to W21000; c. 1915–16. *Modern*	400	600	1250
Russian Contract, marked ANGLO ZAKAZIVAT in cyrilic; about 14,500 made, within serial range C50000 to C85000. *Modern*	750	2250	4500
Military Serial Series, complex numbering. Early production, range from 1 to 629500; straight mainspring housing; premium for low numbers. *Modern*	350	750	1250
As above, but with U.S.N. markings. *Modern*	650	1750	2750
Model 1911A1, serial range 700001 to 2380013; RS inspector stamp; arched mainspring housing. Premium for blued over Parkerized finish. *Modern*	250	650	1000
Ithaca Gun Co. variation, ITHACA GUN CO. on slide. *Modern*	250	500	1000
North American Arms Co. variation, approximately 100 only made. *Modern*	4000	7500	12500
Remington Rand, Inc. variation, several ranges of numbers; approximately 900,000 made. *Modern*	250	650	1000
Remington-UMC variation, serial range 1 to 21676, with Colt and Remington-UMC slide marks. *Modern*,	$300	$750	$1500
Singer Mfg. Co. variation, range S800001 to S800500; 500 only made. *Modern*	3500	6500	10000
Springfield Armory variation, range 72751 to 133186; 25,767 made. *Modern*	650	1250	2000
Union Switch & Signal Co. variation, range 1041405 to 1096404; approximately 40,000 made. *Modern*	350	550	1000
First Model National Match .45 Automatic, .45ACP, 7-shot magazine; 5″ barrel; approximately 10,000 made; serial within commercial series pistols, with C prefix; c. 1933–41. *Modern*	850	1750	2750
Ace .22 Automatic, .22 long rifle; 10-shot magazine; $4^{3}/_{4}$″ barrel; approximately 11,000 made; from 1 on up; c. 1931–41. *Modern*	500	1500	2500
Service Model Ace Automatic Pistol, .22 long rifle; 10-shot magazine; 5″ barrel; approximately 13,500 made, with SM prefix to serial numbers; c. 1937–45. *Modern*	500	1500	2500
.22-.45 Conversion Unit, .22 long rifle; 10-shot magazine; 5″ barrel; more than 5,000 made; c. 1938–1970s. *Modern*	250	400	750
.45-.22 Conversion Unit, .45 ACP; 7-shot magazine; serial range U1 to U112; made 1938–1940. *Modern*	350	1000	1750
.38 AMU Automatic (Kit), .38 AMU caliber; 9-shot magazine; 5″ barrel; from Model 1911 and 1911A1 serial ranges; some from Super .38 serial range; limited production, from c. 1958. *Modern*	500	1750	2500
.38 Special Kit, made for dealer Gil Hebard; c. 1964 to early 1970s; .38 Special and .45ACP; variation from .38 AMU; approximately 500 .38 Special Kits (suffix H) and over 1,200 .45ACP (suffix O). *Modern*	500	1750	2500
Super .38 Automatic, .38 rimless, smokeless (.38ACP) and .38 Super; 9-shot magazine; 5″ barrel; in excess of 200,000 made, from 1 on up; production into 1970s; CS prefix begun 1969. *Modern*	1000	2000	3000

	Fair	V. Good	Excellent
Super Match .38 Automatic, scarce variation of the Super 38; from c. 1935 to 1941, serial numbered in Super 38 sequence; production estimated at 3,000 to 5,000. *Modern*	$1250	$2500	4000
Gold Cup National Match Automatic, .45 mid range, .45ACP, .38 Special mid range or wad-cutter; 5-shot magazines; 5″ barrels; more than 40,000 made in .45, more than 10,000 in .38; .45 range 10NM on up, in 1970 new series began with 70N prefix; .38 range 100NMR to 7000NMR; .38 National Match with MS suffix, in 1961, 101 through 855MS only (premium for this scarce variation). *Modern*	400	700	1000
Gold Cup MK III, 9mm Luger, .38 Special, .45ACP. *Modern*	400	700	1000
Mark IV/80 Gold Cup National Match, .45ACP. *Modern*	400	700	1000
Springfield Armory National Match, from 1955 through 1965; total of approximately 16,000 made; made from service pistols. *Modern*	350	700	1000
Government Model Mark IV, .38 Super, .45ACP. *Modern*	400	750	1100
Government Model Mark IV/ Series 80, various calibers including 9mm Luger and .45ACP. *Modern*	400	700	1000
Officer's Model ACP MK IV/80, .45ACP; 6-shot magazine. *Modern*	400	700	1000
Commander Model Automatic, 9mm Luger, .38 Super, .45ACP; 9-shot (38 and 9mm) and 7-shot magazines; 4¼″ barrels; in excess of 100,000; serial markings with 00 prefix through 65; LW suffix through 1968; CLW prefix from 1969; aluminum alloy frame. *Modern*	300	500	750
Combat Commander variation, with steel frame. *Modern*	350	550	850
Mark IV/80 Combat Commander, 9mm Luger, .45ACP. *Modern*	350	550	850
Government Model Mark IV/80, .380; 7-shot magazine. *Modern*	200	400	700
Government Model Mark IV/ 80 Combat, .380; 7-shot magazine; light weight. *Modern*	200	400	700

	Fair	V. Good	Excellent
Woodsman Automatic Target Pistol, .22 long rifle; 10-shot magazine; 4½″ and 6½″ barrels; total made through 1932, approximately 84,000; from 1 on up; from 1915. Sport and Target Models made from 1943. Original Woodsman series obsolete after serial range 157000 (1943). *Modern*	$250	$400	$750
Woodsman Target and Sport Model, .22 long rifle; 10-shot magazine; 4½″ and 6½;" (later 6″; Target Model) barrels; 35,000 Sport and 38,000 Target pistols from 1932 through 1943, serial numbers from 1-S on up, to 241811-S; approximately 90,000 Sport and 90,000 Target pistols from 1947 through 1970. Postwar pistols identified by S suffix; new series begun 1969, 001001-S on up. *Modern*	200	350	750
First Model Match Target Woodsman, .22 long rifle; 10-shot magazine; 6½″ heavy target barrel; from 1938 to 1942, 15,100 made; serials with MT prefix, from MT-1 on up. *Modern*	500	1000	1750
Second and Third Model Match Target Woodsman, .22 long rifle; 10-shot magazine; 4½″ and 6½″ barrels; from 1948 into 1970s more than 100,000 made; S-suffix in range begun 1947, shared with postwar Sport and Target Model pistols. *Modern*	200	350	750
Challenger and Huntsman Models, .22 long rifle; 10-shot magazine; 4½″ and 6″ barrels; total of Challenger (1950–55) at 77,143, numbering began with 1-C; total of Huntsman (c. 1955 into 1970s) more than 70,000, numbering continued C suffix series, with 90001-C. *Modern*	200	350	750
Woodsman Targetsman Model, .22 long rifle; 10-shot magazine; 6″ barrel; made from 1959, with serial range 129300-C; total made into early 1970s in excess of 40,000. *Modern*	200	350	750

CARTRIDGE LONGARMS

	Fair	V. Good	Excellent
Berdan Military Rifle and Carbine, .42 caliber bottle necked c.f.; single shot; $32^{1}/_{2}$″ (rifle) and $14^{1}/_{4}$″ (carbine) barrel lengths; approximately 30,000 made, from 1 on up; c. 1866–70.			
Russian marked military rifles, approximately 30,000 made. *Antique*	$225	$600	$1200
Russian marked carbines, approximately not more than 25 made. *Antique*	1000	3000	6500
Carbines marked with Colt and Hartford, Connecticut address, not more than 25 made. *Antique*	1250	4000	7500
Military rifles marked with Colt, Hartford, not more than 100. *Antique*	1000	2500	4500
Custom-made Target Rifles on the Berdan action, not more than 30 (three models, 1st, 2nd and 3rd type), *Antique*	1500	4000	8500
Colt-Laidley Military Rifle, single shot rolling block breechloading rifle; .45 c.f. and .50 c.f., 25 of each caliber; c. 1867. *Antique*	1000	2000	5000
Colt-Franklin Military Rifle, .45-70 caliber; 9-shot gravity feed magazine; $32^{1}/_{2}$″ barrel; bolt action; approximately 50 made; c. 1887–88. *Antique*	1750	4500	7500
Model 1878 Double Barrel Hammer Shotgun, 10 and 12 gauge; 28″, 30″ and 32″ standard barrel lengths (known lengths from 18″ to 34″); 22,683 made, from 1 on up; c. 1878–89.			
Standard model, with moderate embellishments and checkered stocks. *Antique*	450	850	1750
Better-grade guns, panel scene engraving; higher grade stockwork and checkering. *Antique*	650	1500	3250
Model 1878 Double Barrel Sporting Rifle, .45-70, .45-85 Express, .45-90 and .45-100 calibers; approximately 40 made, serial numbers from 1 on up, and nos. 293 and 397 from Model 1878 shotgun range; c. 1879–85 (appear to be special order only). *Antique*	3500	12500	20000
Model 1883 Double Barrel Shotgun, 8, 10 and 12 gauge; standard barrel lengths 28″, 30″ and 32″ (known lengths from 18″ to 36″); approximately 7366 made, from 1 on up, with gap from 3056-4057; c. 1883–95.			
Standard model, moderate embellishments and checkered stocks. *Antique*	$450	$850	$1750
Better-grade guns, panel scene engraving; higher grade stockwork and checkering. *Antique*	650	1500	3250
Colt-Burgess Lever Action Rifle, .44-40 caliber; $25^{1}/_{2}$″ (rifle) and 20″ (carbine) barrels; 6403 made, from 1 on up; c. 1883–85. *Antique*	500	1250	3500

LIGHTNING SLIDE ACTION MAGAZINE RIFLES

	Fair	V. Good	Excellent
Medium Frame Model, .32-20, .38-40, and .44-40 calibers; 20″ (carbine) and 26″ (rifle) barrels, with some variations; shortest from 8″ to longest of 34″; 89,777 made, from 1884–1902.			
Standard rifle, 1883 patent dates on barrel; lacks cover on top of breech. *Antique*	350	650	1500
Standard rifle, with 1883, ’85, ’86 and ’87 patent date markings; and sliding cover on top of breech. *Antique*	300	600	1350
Carbine, .44-40. *Antique*	400	1250	2500
Baby Carbine, $5^{1}/_{4}$ lbs. weight, with special lightweight barrel. *Antique*	500	1750	3000
Military Rifle or Carbine, .44-40; with bayonet lug and sling swivel. *Antique*	600	2000	3750
San Francisco Police Department Rifles, .44-40; markings of SFP 1 to SFP 401, on lower tang; blued finish. *Antique*	400	1250	2250
Small Frame Model, .22 short and long rifle; 24″ barrel length standard lengths known from $9^{1}/_{2}$″ to 26″; total 89,912 made, serials from 1 on up; c. 1887/1904. *Antique*	275	500	1000
Large Frame or Express Model, .38-56, .40-60, .45-60, .45-65, .45-85 and .50-95 Express; 22″ (carbine) and 28″ (rifle) barrels; variations from 22″ to 36″ standard length for .50-95 Express; total 6,496 made, from 1 on up; c. 1887–94.			
Standard Rifle, round or octagonal barrel. *Antique*	400	1250	2500

Medium and small frame Colt Lightning slide action rifles; from the top, *deluxe medium frame with semi-pistol grip stock; standard model with plain stocks; two .22 rimfire rifles (small frame) in deluxe and standard stock versions; and a medium frame Saddle Ring carbine.*

	Fair	V. Good	Excellent
Carbine, weight 9 lbs. *Antique*	$750	$2750	$6500
Baby Carbine, lightweight barrel; weight 8 lbs. *Antique*	850	3000	7500
Colt '57" Bolt Action Sporting Rifle, .30-06 and .243 calibers, with FN Mauser actions; serial nos. from 1 on up; approximately 5,000 made, in 1957. *Modern*	300	550	850
Coltsman Bolt Action Rifle, Standard, Deluxe and Custom grades, .30-06, .300 Magnum, .243, and .308 calibers, with Sako and FN actions; approximately 10,000 made (including the Standard and Custom rifles of 1963–65); 1958–62. *Modern*	350	600	950

	Fair	V. Good	Excellent
Coltsman Bolt Action Rifle, Standard and Custom grades, .223, .243, .308, .264, and .30-06 calibers; with Sako actions; approximately 10,000 made (including Standard, Deluxe and Custom grades made 1958–62); 1963–65; premum for Custom grade. *Modern*	$350	$600	$950
Colt Sauer Bolt Action Sporting Rifle, Grand African, .458 Magnum; box magazine. *Modern*	650	1000	1500
Colt Sauer Bolt Action Sporting Rifle, Grand Alaskan, .375 H & H Magnum; box magazine. *Modern*	550	900	1350
Colteer 1-22 Bolt Action Rifle, .22 short, long, long rifle and .22 magnum; single shot; 20" and 22" barrels; made without serial numbers; approximately 25,000 made, c. 1957–66. *Modern*	100	200	400
Colteer, Stagecoach and Courier .22 Autoloader Rifles, .22 long rifle; over 85,000 made in total of the three models; c. 1964–early 1970s. Colteer; 15 shots, with 19$^3/_8$" barrel; over 50,000 made. *Modern*	150	250	350
Stagecoach, 13 shots; with 16$^1/_2$" barrel; over 25,000 made, from 1965. *Modern*	250	325	550
Courier, made from 1970. *Modern*	150	250	350
AR-15 Semi-Automatic Sporter Rifle, .223 (5.56mm) caliber; 21" barrel with flash supressor; serial numbers from SP0001 on up; c. 1964 to present; over 100,000 made.			

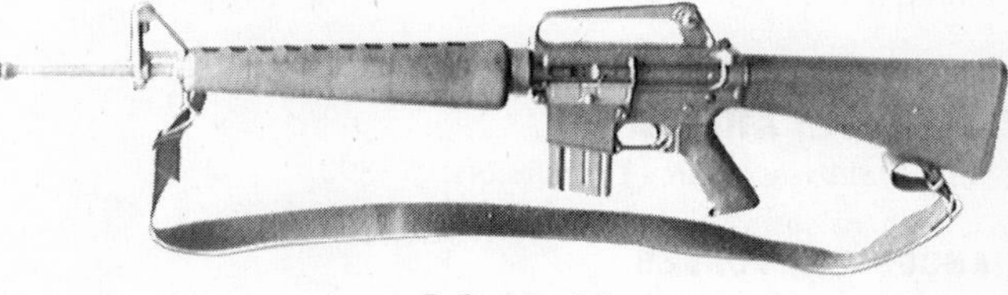

Colt AR- 15

	Fair	V. Good	Excellent
Standard Semi-automatic Rifle configuration, early model with smooth composition stocks. *Modern*	750	1000	2500
Later version, with ribbed forend; standard barrel length. *Modern*	750	1000	2000
Carbine Variation, with ribbed forend. *Modern*	750	1250	2250

	Fair	V. Good	Excellent
Pump Shotgun, 12, 16 and 20 gauges; 3-shot tubular magazine; 26″ and 28″ barrels; various chokes; total of approximately 2,000; serial numbers from supplier's range, vary from as low as 15000 to as high as 105000 (most within range 60000 to 62600, or higher; c. 1961–65. *Modern*	$100	$250	$450
Semi-Automatic Shotgun, 12 and 20 gauges; 4-shot tubular magazine; 26″, 28″, 30″ and 32″ barrels; 5,293 made, numbered in unusual ranges, with C0 prefix; c. 1962–66. *Modern*	150	250	450
Double Barrel Shotgun, 12, 12 magnum and 16 gauges; 26″, 28″ and 30″ barrels; 25 to 50 made, in range 47000 to 469000; c. 1961–62. *Modern*	250	450	850
Colt-Sharps Single Shot Falling Block Sporting Rifle, .17, .22-250 Remington, .243 Winchester, .25.06 Remington, 7mm Remington Magnum, .30-06 Springfield, .375 H & H Magnum; 25″, 26″ and 28″ barrels; approximately 500 made, from 1 on up (CS prefix to numbers); c. 1970 into early 1970s. *Modern*	750	1250	1950
Gatling Gun, crank-operated mechanical repeating firearm, with box and Accles feed magazines; made in a variety of calibers from .30 to 1″. See Gatling Gun Co. for historical information. Values vary somewhat, based on popularity of calibers, markings, presence of original carriage, mounts, and accessories, and condition. Approximate value range. *Antique*	15000	35000	65000

COLUMBIA ARMORY

Tenn., Maltby & Henley Distributors, c. 1890.

HANDGUN, REVOLVER

New Safety, .22 L.R.R.F., 7 Shot, Double Action, Solid Frame, Grip Safety, *Modern*	75	100	125
New Safety, .32 S & W, 5 Shot, Double Action, Solid Frame, Grip Safety, *Modern*	75	100	125
New Safety, .38 S & W, 5 Shot, Double Action, Solid Frame, Grip Safety, *Modern*	100	125	150

COLUMBIAN

Made by Foehl & Weeks, Philadelphia, Pa., c. 1890.

HANDGUN, REVOLVER

	Fair	V. Good	Excellent
.32 S & W, 5 Shot, Double Action, Solid Frame, *Curio*	$50	$75	$100
.38 S & W, 5 Shot, Double Action, Solid Frame, *Curio*	50	75	100

COMBINATION WEAPONS DRILLING

German, Various Calibers, Light Engraving, Modern. For whatever reason, Drillings have never proven a popular collectors' item in the U.S. The author has seen many of these over the years, most wanting in condition, and most of odd calibers by American standards. Although Theodore Roosevelt himself, one of the world's most experienced hunters, had at least one Drilling in his sporting arsenal, the type never caught on in the U.S. Hardly any were manufactured by American gunmakers. The combination of a rifle with a double-barrel shotgun made the weapon generally too heavy. Further, when Americans go hunting, they are either going after something that would require a rifle or shotgun—but not both. Therefore one would buy rifles of various calibers for certain types of game, and shotguns of different gauges and chokes for bird shooting—and not buy a gun that could take birdshot in two barrels and rifle bullets in the third. The author has shot in Europe, where many of the hunters used Drillings. Even then he preferred to have a rifle and a shotgun handy, and rarely did he miss the chance to fire at something because he had the wrong gun in hand. The Drilling is, therefore, mainly of interest to Europeans, and has yet to capture the collecting imagination of Americans.

COMET

HANDGUN, REVOLVER

.32 Long R.F., 7 Shot, Single Action, Spur Trigger, Solid Frame, *Antique*	35	75	150

COMINAZZO OR COMINAZZI

Family of Armorers in Brescia, Italy from c. 1593 to c. 1875. Barrels by this distinguished dynasty of Brescian gunmakers were instrumental in earning a deserved worldwide reputation for quality, continued today by such august gunmakers as Beretta, Rizzini and Fabbri. The author visited the palazzo of Brescian industrialist Luigi Marzolli in 1960, and was proudly shown glass display cases filled with Brescian steel-mounted wheel lock, miquelet and flintlock pistols, many of them with barrels marked Cominazzo or Cominazzi. Marzolli was so proud of his collection that on his death a number of the pieces, including miscellaneous arms and armor (primarily Italian) became a special display of the city of Brescia, where they were installed in the Castle overlooking the city. These barrels were respected for accuracy, sturdiness, reliability and beauty. Some of the most exquisite Brescian, steel-mounted firearms are featured in the Arms and Armor galleries of the Metropolitan Museum of Art, as well as certain of the European and British museums featuring arms and armor.

	Fair	V. Good	Excellent
HANDGUN, FLINTLOCK			
.54, Mid-1600s, Belt Pistol, Brass Furniture, Ornate, *Antique*	$2550	$4150	$5750
HANDGUN, WHEEL LOCK			
Ebony Full Stock, Ivory Pom, Holster Pistol, German Style, Military, Engraved, *Antique*	2550	4250	5950

COMMANDER

	Fair	V. Good	Excellent
HANDGUN, REVOLVER			
.32 Long R.F., 7 Shot, Single Action, Spur Trigger, Solid Frame, *Antique*	50	100	150

COMMANDO ARMS

Made by Volunteer Enterprises in Knoxville, Tenn., since 1969. Company name changed to Commando Arms in 1978.

	Fair	V. Good	Excellent
RIFLE, SEMI-AUTOMATIC			
Commando MK III, .45 ACP, Clip Fed, Horizontal Fore end, with Compensator, Carbine, *Modern* ...	175	225	275
Commando MK III, .45 ACP, Clip Fed, Vertical Fore end, with Compensator, Carbine, *Modern* ...	200	250	300
Commando MK 9, 9mm Luger, Clip Fed, Horizontal Fore end, with Compensator, Carbine, *Modern* ...	175	225	275
Commando MK 9, 9mm Luger, Clip Fed, Vertical Fore end, with Compensator, Carbine, *Modern* ...	200	250	300
Commando MK 45, .45 ACP, Clip Fed, Horizontal Fore end, with Compensator, Carbine, *Modern* ...	175	225	275
Commando MK 45, .45 ACP, Clip Fed, Vertical Fore end, with Compensator, Carbine, *Modern* ...	200	250	300

COMMERCIAL

See Smith, Otis A.

COMPEER

Made by Crescent for Van Camp Hardware, c. 1900. See Crescent Fire Arms Co., Shotgun, Double Barrel, Side-By-Side; Shotgun, Singleshot.

CONE, D.D.

Washington, D.C., c. 1865.

	Fair	V. Good	Excellent
HANDGUN, REVOLVER			
.22 Long R.F., 7 Shot, Single Action, Spur Trigger, Solid Frame, *Antique*	65	125	200

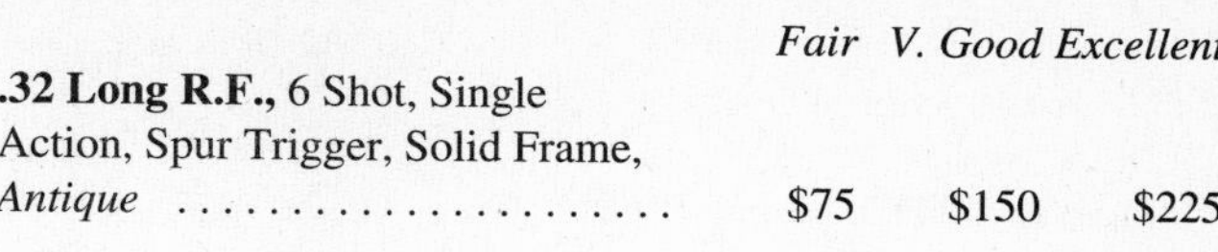

	Fair	V. Good	Excellent
.32 Long R.F., 6 Shot, Single Action, Spur Trigger, Solid Frame, *Antique*	$75	$150	$225

From top, a Lindsay two-shot single-barrel Musket in .58 caliber; a Confederate rifled Musket of the Model 1861 style, .58 caliber, with brass trim, the lock marked Fayetteville, *with an eagle and C.S.A., 1862; and a .58 caliber U.S. rifled Musket by Providence Tool Co., dated 1864.*

CONFEDERATE MILITARY

	Fair	V. Good	Excellent
HANDGUN, PERCUSSION			
.36 Columbus, Revolver, Brass Trigger Guard, 6 Shot, *Antique* ...			Rare
.36 Dance Box, Revolver, Iron Frame, 6 Shot, *Antique*			Rare
.36 Griswold & Gunnison, Revolver, Brass Frame, 6 Shot, Serial No. is the Only Marking, *Antique*			Rare
.36 Leech & Co., Revolver, Brass Grip Frame, 6 Shot, *Antique*			Rare
.36 Leech & Rigdon, Revolver, Brass Grip Frame, 6 Shot, *Antique* .			Rare
.36 Rigdon & Ansley, Revolver, Brass Grip Frame, 6 Shot, *Antique* .			Rare
.36 Shawk & McLanahan, Revolver, Brass Frame, 6 Shot, *Antique*			Rare
.36 Spiller & Burr, Revolver, Brass Frame, 6 Shot, *Antique*			Rare
.36 T.W. Cofer, Revolver, Brass Frame, 6 Shot, *Antique*			Rare
.44 Dance Bros., Revolver, Brass Grip Frame, 6 Shot, *Antique*			Rare
.44 Tucker & Sherrod, Revolver, Copy of Colt Dragoon, serial number is the only marking, *Antique*			Rare
.54 J. and F. Garrett, Singleshot, Brass Barrel, Converted from Flintlock, *Antique*	725	1450	2500

	Fair	V. Good	Excellent
.54 Palmetto, Singleshot, Brass Furniture, *Antique*			Rare
.58 Fayetteville, Singleshot, Rifled, *Antique*			Rare
.58 Fayetteville, Singleshot, Rifled, with Shoulder Stock, *Antique*			Rare

RIFLE, PERCUSSION

	Fair	V. Good	Excellent
.52, "P," Tallahassee, Breech Loader, Carbine, *Antique*			Rare
.52, Tarpley, Breech Loader, Carbine, Brass Breech, *Antique*			Rare

From the top, *Confederate percussion carbine marked* Richmond Va. 1864, *.58 caliber; with a Model 1854–type Confederate carbine marked* C.S.A. *and* P; *and a Confederate carbine, looking very much like a Maynard, but with brass frame; .52 caliber.*

	Fair	V. Good	Excellent
.54, L.G. Sturdivant, Brass Furniture, Rifled, Serial No. is the Only Marking, *Antique*			Rare
.54, Wytheville-Hall, Muzzle Loader, Rifled, Brass Frame, *Antique*			Rare
.57, Tyler, Texas Enfield, Brass Furniture, *Antique*			Rare
.58, Cook & Brother, Artillery Carbine, Brass Furniture, Military, *Antique*			Rare
.58, Cook & Brother, Infantry Type, Brass Furniture, Military, *Antique*			Rare
.58, Cook & Brother, Musketoon, Brass Furniture, Military, *Antique*			Rare
.58, D.C., Hodgkins & Co., Iron Mounts, Rifled, Carbine, *Antique*			Rare
.58, Dickson, Nelson & Co., Military, Carbine, *Antique*			Rare
.58, Dickson, Nelson & Co., Military, Rifle, *Antique*			Rare
.58, Fayetteville, Brass Furniture, 2 Bands, Rifled, *Antique*			Rare
.58, Georgia, Brass Furniture, Rifled, *Antique*			Rare
.58, H.C. Lamb & Co., Brass Furniture, 2 Bands, Rifled, *Antique*			Rare
.58, Palmetto, "Mississippi" Rifle, *Antique*			Rare
.58, Richmond, Carbine, *Antique*			Rare
.58, Richmond, Musket, Rifled, *Antique*			Rare
.58, Tallahassee, Carbine, Brass Furniture, 2 Bands, *Antique*			Rare
.58, Whitney, U.S. Contract 1861, Rifle, Musket, *Antique*			Rare
.62, Richmond Navy, Musketoon, Smoothbore, *Antique*			Rare
.69, Prussian Musket, Brass Furniture, Military, *Antique*			Rare
.69, Whitney, Model 1861, Rifled, Brass Furniture, *Antique*			Rare

RIFLE, SINGLESHOT

	Fair	V. Good	Excellent
.50, Morse, Musket, Breech Loader, *Antique*			Rare
.58, S.C. Robinson, Model 1861, Brass Furniture, Breech Loader, Carbine, Imitation Sharps, *Antique*			Rare
.71, Morse, Carbine, Breech Loader, *Antique*			Rare

CONN. ARMS & MFG. CO.

Naubuc, Conn. 1863–1869. The Hammond Bulldog was a well-built, relatively hard-hitting handgun, with but one drawback: it was a singleshot only, and therefore was no competition in terms of firepower with arms like the Colt 1860 Army or the mammoth Colt Dragoons. A legitimate Civil War handgun, though none was issued to troops; a foot soldier might well have one as a backup piece. The mechanism was simple, and the design is reflected by the Bulldog name. This arm is one that will often turn up in excellent condition, suggesting that relatively few were ever put to service use. If found in the original pasteboard box, add a premium of 25 percent.

HANDGUN, SINGLESHOT

	Fair	V. Good	Excellent
Hammond Patent Bull-Dozer, .44 R.F., Pivoting Breechblock, Hammer, Spur Trigger, *Antique*	125	225	325
Hammond Patent Bulldog, .44 R.F., Pivoting Breechblock, Hammer, Spur Trigger, *Antique*	100	200	325
Hammond Patent Bulldog, .44 R.F., Pivoting Breechblock, Hammer, Spur Trigger, Very Long Barrel, *Antique*	150	300	450

CONN. ARMS CO.

Norfolk, Conn. 1862–1869.

HANDGUN, REVOLVER

	Fair	V. Good	Excellent
Wood's Patent, .28 T.F., Tip-Up Barrel, 6 Shot, Spur Trigger, *Antique*	85	175	325

	Fair	V. Good	Excellent

CONNECTICUT SHOTGUN MFG. CO.,

New Britain, Connecticut. See also A.H. Fox Gun Co. Founded by Tony Galazan, accomplished dealer and expert in best-quality sporting arms, Connecticut Shotgun Mfg. Co. specializes in producing the highest grade of over-and-under and side-by-side shotguns, with the top of their line a Fabbri look-alike, also influenced by Boss & Co. styling. Priced competitively, the design and workmanship is on a par with any sporting gun in the world today, and a visit to the workshop reminds one of Old World European standards of excellence. Without taking a nickel of aid or a moment of time from the State of Connecticut, Galazan has created a Mecca for the connoisseur of fine guns, in a state that was known for years as a trasher of industrial companies, through high taxes and truly idiotic politics. See also A.H. Fox Gun Co.

CONQUERER

Made by Bacon Arms Co., c. 1880.

HANDGUN, REVOLVER

	Fair	V. Good	Excellent
.22 Short R.F., 7 Shot, Spur Trigger, Solid Frame, Single Action, *Antique*	$50	$100	$175
.32 Short R.F., 5 Shot, Spur Trigger, Solid Frame, Single Action, *Antique*	50	100	175

CONSTABLE, RICHARD

Philadelphia, Pa. 1817–1851.

HANDGUN, PERCUSSION

	Fair	V. Good	Excellent
Dueling Pistols, Cased Pair, with Accessories, *Antique*	900	2500	3500

RIFLE, PERCUSSION

	Fair	V. Good	Excellent
.44, Octagon Barrel, Brass Furniture, *Antique*	700	1500	1800

CONTENTO

See Ventura Imports.

CONTINENTAL

Made by Hood Firearms Co., successors to Continental Arms Co.; Sold by Marshall Wells Co., Duluth, Minn., c. 1870.

HANDGUN, REVOLVER

	Fair	V. Good	Excellent
.22 Short R.F., 7 Shot, Spur Trigger, Solid Frame, Single Action, *Antique*	50	100	175
.32 Short R.F., 5 Shot, Spur Trigger, Solid Frame, Single Action, *Antique*	50	100	175

CONTINENTAL

Made by Jules Bertrand, Liege, Belgium, c. 1910.

HANDGUN, SEMI-AUTOMATIC

	Fair	V. Good	Excellent
Pocket, .25 ACP, Clip Fed, *Curio*	100	175	250

CONTINENTAL

Made by Stevens Arms.

RIFLE, BOLT ACTION

	Fair	V. Good	Excellent
Model 52, .22 L.R.R.F., Singleshot, Takedown, *Modern*	$25	$50	$75

SHOTGUN, DOUBLE BARREL, SIDE-BY-SIDE

	Fair	V. Good	Excellent
Model 215, 12 and 16 Gauges, Outside Hammers, Steel Barrel, *Modern*	50	100	175
Model 311, Various Gauges, Hammerless, Steel Barrel, *Modern*	65	125	200
Model 315, Various Gauges, Hammerless, Steel Barrel, *Modern*	75	125	175

SHOTGUN, SINGLESHOT

	Fair	V. Good	Excellent
Model 90, Various Gauges, Takedown, Automatic Ejector, Plain Hammer, *Modern*	25	50	75

CONTINENTAL

Rheinische Waffen u. Munitionsfabrik. Cologne, Germany.

HANDGUN, SEMI-AUTOMATIC

	Fair	V. Good	Excellent
.25 ACP, Clip Fed, Blue, *Curio*	75	150	225
.32 ACP, Clip Fed, Webley Copy, Blue, *Curio*	125	200	275

CONTINENTAL ARMS CO.

Norwich, Conn. 1866–1867.

HANDGUN, PEPPERBOX

	Fair	V. Good	Excellent
Continental 1, .22 R.F., 7 Shot, Spur Trigger, Solid Frame, *Antique*	325	450	575
Continental 2, .32 R.F., 5 Shot, Spur Trigger, Solid Frame, *Antique*	450	525	600

CONTINENTAL ARMS CO.,

New York City. Founded by the brothers Joe and Ted Tonkin, and located at a site on exclusive Fifth Avenue, Continental Arms ordered double rifles and fine side-by-side and over-and-under shotguns for a discriminating clientele—among them Prince Abdul Reza of Iran, President Dwight D. Eisenhower, and the first violinist of the Berlin Philharmonic Orchestra. The author met both Joe and Ted, and made a habit of visiting their walnut-paneled showroom while on trips to New York City. Ted died trying to fight back a robber in a theft in their fourth-floor emporium, while Joe's gun failed to fire. Joe carried on for years, finally retiring early in the 1990s when he was into his 80s. Both Ted and Joe were charming gentlemen of the old school, with Ted the arms expert and buyer and Joe the businessman. You never knew who you would encounter in the store, and the author was interviewed there for the BBC-TV by English broadcaster, critic, and columnist Bernard Levin. The piece was for a television program based on Levin's book *A Walk Down Fifth Avenue*. Considering the anti-gun bias of the British press, the segment in the book was quite flattering, to some extent the result of the author having brought along a rather stunning Colt Third Model Dragoon revolver decorated by Tiffany & Co., described by Levin as "absolutely beautiful."

COONAN ARMS, INC.

St. Paul, Minn. since 1982.

HANDGUN, SEMI-AUTOMATIC

	Fair	V. Good	Excellent
Comp. 1, .357 Magnum, Standard Production Model, Stainless Steel, Clip Fed, Adjustable Sights, *Modern*	$750	$900	$1050
Model A, .357 Magnum, Single Action, Stainless, *Modern*	450	550	650
Model B, .357 Magnum, Pre-Production Model, Serial Numbers under 1000, Stainless Steel, Clip Fed, Adjustable Sights, *Modern*	175	350	675

COOPER FIREARMS MFG. CO.

Philadelphia, Pa. 1851–1869. This cleverly produced Colt look-alike was basically a double-action copy of the Colt Model 1849 Pocket. Philadelphia was a gunmaking center of no little skill and ingenuity. Among prominent gunmakers, the city also boasted, for a while at least, the Sharps company, and had prominent dealers the likes of J.C. Grubb & Co., E.K. Tryon, and Krider. Cooper not only made a fair quantity of Navy and Pocket handguns, the company manufactured a handful of exquisitely embellished and cased pairs. Two such sets were richly engraved, plated in silver, with ivory grips; fitted in velvet-lined, contour-fitted cases of carefully crafted woods.

HANDGUN, PERCUSSION

	Fair	V. Good	Excellent
Navy, .31, 5 Shots, Double Action, *Antique*	300	475	650
Pocket, .31, 5 or 6 Shots, Double Action, *Antique*	250	425	600

C.O.P.

M & N Distributers, Torrance, Calif.

HANDGUN, REPEATER

	Fair	V. Good	Excellent
Model Mini, .22 L.R.R.F., Four Barrels, Aluminum Frame, Hammerless, Double Action, *Modern*			
Model Mini, .22 W.M.R., Four Barrels, Stainless Steel, Hammerless, Double Action, *Modern*			Rare
Model SS-1, .357 Mag., Four Barrels, Stainless Steel, Hammerless, Double Action, *Modern*	200	250	300

HANDGUN, SEMI-AUTOMATIC

	Fair	V. Good	Excellent
TP-70 AAI, .22 L.R.R.F., Double Action, Clip Fed, Stainless Steel, Hammer, *Modern*	75	125	175
TP-70 AAI, .25 A.C.P., Double Action, Clip Fed, Stainless Steel, Hammer, *Modern*	$75	$125	$175

COPELAND, F.

Made by Frank Copeland, Worcester, Mass. 1868-1874.

HANDGUN, REVOLVER

	Fair	V. Good	Excellent
.22 Short R.F., 7 Shot, Spur Trigger, Solid Frame, Single Action, *Antique*	150	200	250
.32 Short R.F., 5 Shot, Spur Trigger, Solid Frame, Single Action, *Antique*	125	175	225

COQ

Spain, c. 1900.

HANDGUN, SEMI-AUTOMATIC

	Fair	V. Good	Excellent
K-25, .25 ACP, Clip Fed, *Modern*	35	75	125

CORNFORTH

London, England 1725–1760.

HANDGUN, FLINTLOCK

	Fair	V. Good	Excellent
Pair, Belt Pistol, Brass Barrel, Brass Furniture, Plain, *Antique*	1400	2700	4000

COSENS, JAMES

Gunmaker in Ordinary to Charles II, England, Late 1600s.

HANDGUN, FLINTLOCK

	Fair	V. Good	Excellent
Pair, Holster Pistol, Silver Furniture, Engraved Silver Inlay, High Quality, *Antique*	4675	9350	16000

COSMI

Made for Abercrombie & Fitch, c. 1960.

SHOTGUN, SEMI-AUTOMATIC

	Fair	V. Good	Excellent
12 or 20 Gauge, Top Break, Engraved, Checkered Stock, Vent Rib, *Modern*	2500	3000	3500

COSMOPOLITAN ARMS CO.

Hamilton, Ohio 1860-1865. Also see U.S. Military.

RIFLE, PERCUSSION

	Fair	V. Good	Excellent
.45, Sporting Rifle, *Antique*	900	1200	1500
.50, Carbine, *Antique*	500	850	1200

COWELS & SMITH

Chicopee Falls, Mass. 1863–1876. Became Cowels & Son in 1871.

	Fair	V. Good	Excellent
HANDGUN, SINGLESHOT			
.22 R.F., Side-Swing Barrel, Hammer, Spur Trigger, *Antique*	$75	$150	$225
.30 R.F., Side-Swing Barrel, Hammer, Spur Trigger, *Antique*	75	150	250

COWLES & SON

Cowles & Smith, 1866–1871, Cowles & Son 1871–1876 in Chicopee Falls, Mass.

	Fair	V. Good	Excellent
HANDGUN, SINGLESHOT			
.22 Short R.F., Brass Frame, Side Swing Barrel, *Antique*	100	175	250

CRAFT PRODUCTS

	Fair	V. Good	Excellent
HANDGUN, SEMI-AUTOMATIC			
.25 ACP, Clip Fed, *Modern*	35	75	125

CREEDMORE

Made by Hopkins & Allen, c. 1870.

	Fair	V. Good	Excellent
HANDGUN, REVOLVER			
#1, .22 Short R.F., 7 Shot, Spur Trigger, Solid Frame, Single Action, *Antique*	50	100	175

CRESCENT

Made by Norwich Falls Pistol Co., c. 1880.

	Fair	V. Good	Excellent
HANDGUN, REVOLVER			
.32 Short R.F, 5 Shot, Spur Trigger, Solid Frame, Single Action, *Antique*	50	100	175

CRESCENT FIRE ARMS CO.

Norwich, Conn., 1892; purchased by H & D Folsom in 1893, and absorbed by Stevens Arms & Tool 1926. Also manufactured single and double barrel shotguns marked with the following tradenames: American Barlock Wonder, American Gun Co., T. Barker, Bellmore Gun Co., Carolina Arms Co., Elgin Arms Co., Empire Arms Co., Enders Oakleaf, Essex, Faultless Goose Gun, F. F. Forbes, Harrison Arms Co., Hartford Arms Co., Hermitage Arms Co., Howard Arms, Interstate Arms Co., Lee Special, Metropolitan, Mississippi Valley Arms Co., Mohawk, National Arms Co., New Rival, New York Arms Co., Not-Nac Mfg. Co., Oxford Arms Co., Peerless, Perfection, Piedmont, Pioneer, Quail, Queen City, Rev-O-Noc, Charles Richter, Rickard Arms, Rummel, Southern, Sportsman, Springfield Arms, Square Deal, State Arms Co., Sterling Arms Co., Sullivan Arms Co., Tiger, U.S. Arms Co., Victor, Victor Special, Virginia Arms Co., Winfield Arms Co., Winoca Arms Co., Wolverine Arms Co., Worthington Arms Co.

	Fair	V. Good	Excellent
SHOTGUN, DOUBLE BARREL, SIDE-BY-SIDE			
Various Gauges, Hammerless, Damascus Barrel, *Modern*	125	175	225
Various Gauges, Hammerless, Steel Barrel, *Modern*	$150	$225	$300
Various Gauges, Outside Hammers, Damascus Barrel, *Modern*	125	175	225
Various Gauges, Outside Hammers, Steel Barrel, *Modern*	125	200	275
SHOTGUN, SINGLESHOT			
Various Gauges, Hammer, Steel Barrel, *Modern*	50	75	100

CRIOLLA

Hispano Argentine Automoviles, Buenos Aires, Argentina, c. 1935.

	Fair	V. Good	Excellent
HANDGUN, SEMI-AUTOMATIC			
La Criolla, .22 L.R.R.F., Colt M1911, Ace Copy, Clip Fed, Blue, *Modern*	175	250	325

CROWN JEWEL

Made by Norwich Falls Pistol Co., c. 1880.

	Fair	V. Good	Excellent
HANDGUN, REVOLVER			
.32 Short R.F., 5 Shot, Spur Trigger, Solid Frame, Single Action, *Antique*	50	100	175

CRUCELEGUI

Spain, Imported by Mandall Shooting Supplies, Scottsdale, Ariz.

	Fair	V. Good	Excellent
SHOTGUN, DOUBLE BARREL, SIDE-BY-SIDE			
Model 150, 12 or 20 Gauges, Outside Hammers, Double Trigger, *Modern*	100	150	200

CRUSO

Made by Stevens Arms.

	Fair	V. Good	Excellent
RIFLE, BOLT ACTION			
Model 53, .22 L.R.R.F., Singleshot, Takedown, *Modern*	25	50	75
SHOTGUN, SINGLESHOT			
Model 90, Various Gauges, Takedown, Automatic Ejector, Plain Hammer, *Modern*	25	50	75

CUMBERLAND ARMS CO.

Made by Crescent for Hibbard- Spencer Bartlett Co., c. 1900. See Crescent Fire Arms Co., Shotgun, Double Barrel, Side-By-Side; Shotgun, Single Shot.

C.V.A.

(Connecticut Valley Arms), Norcross, Ga.

	Fair	V. Good	Excellent
HANDGUN, FLINTLOCK			
.45 Kentucky, Brass Furniture, Reproduction	$25	$50	$75

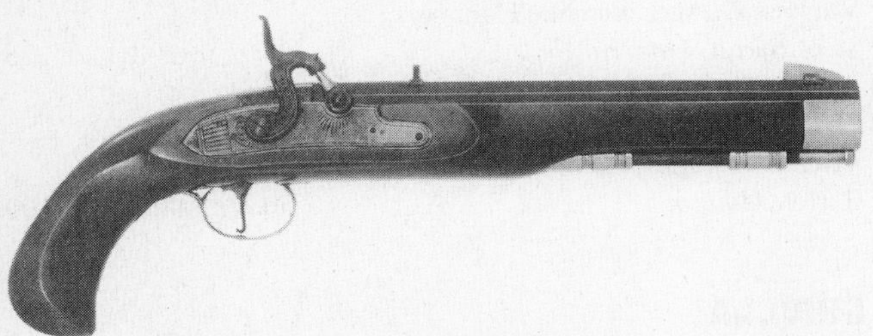

CVA Kentucky Pistol

	Fair	V. Good	Excellent
.50 Hawken, Brass Furniture, Reproduction	35	75	125
HANDGUN, PERCUSSION			
.45 Kentucky, Brass Furniture, Reproduction	25	50	75
.45 or .50 Mountain Pistol, Brass Furniture, Reproduction	25	50	100

CVA Mountain Pistol

	Fair	V. Good	Excellent
.45 Philadelphia Derringer, Reproduction	12	25	75
.45 Tower Pistol, Brass Furniture, Reproduction	12	25	75
.50 Hawken, Brass Furniture, Set Triggers, Reproduction	25	50	100
.45 Colonial Pistol, Brass Furniture, Reproduction	12	25	50
PP258, Pioneer, .32 Caliber, Octagonal Barrel, Reproduction	50	75	100
PP640, Prospector, .44 Caliber, Single-shot, Reproduction	50	75	100
HANDGUN, REVOLVER			
RV 630, 1858 Remington Army, .44 Caliber, One Piece Frame, Reproduction	100	150	200

CVA Prospector Pistol

	Fair	V. Good	Excellent
RV 632, 1858 Remington Army, .44 Caliber, Brass Frame, Reproduction	$100	$125	$150
RV600, 1851 Colt Navy, .36 Caliber, Six Shot, Brass Frame, Reproduction	35	75	125
RV610, 1860 Colt Army, .44 Caliber, Six Shot, Reproduction	100	150	200
RV650, New Model Pocket Remington, .31 Caliber, Spur Trigger, Reproduction	50	75	100

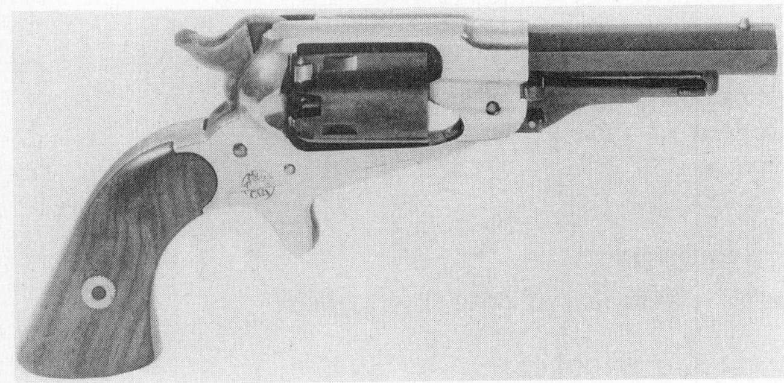

CVA New Pocket Remington

	Fair	V. Good	Excellent
RVF620, 1861 Colt Navy, .44 Caliber, Steel Frame, Reproduction	75	125	175
RVF622, 1861 Colt Navy, .44 Caliber, Steel Frame, Reproduction	35	75	125
RIFLE, FLINTLOCK			
.45 Kentucky Rifle, Brass Furniture, Reproduction	50	100	150
.45 or .50 Mountain Rifle, German Silver Furniture, Reproduction	65	125	200
.50 Frontier Rifle, Brass Furniture, Reproduction	50	100	150
.50 or .54 Hawken Rifle, Brass Furniture, Reproduction	75	125	175
FR503, Squirrel Rifle, .32 Caliber, Double Set Triggers, Reproduction	150	200	250
FR504, Pennsylvania Long Rifle, .50 Caliber, Brass Butt Plate, Reproduction	225	300	375

	Fair	V. Good	Excellent
RIFLE, PERCUSSION			
.45 Kentucky Rifle, Brass Furniture, Reproduction	$35	$75	$125
.45 or .50 Frontier Rifle, Brass Furniture, Reproduction	50	100	150
.45, .50, .54, or.58 Mountain Rifle, German Silver Furniture, Reproduction	75	125	175
.50 .54 Hawken Rifle, Brass Furniture, Reproduction	75	125	175
.58 Zouave, Brass Furniture, Reproduction	50	100	150
PR403, Squirrel Rifle, .32 Caliber, Right Handed Model, Reproduction	125	175	225
PR404, Pennsylvania Long Rifle, .50 Caliber, Brass Butt Plate, Reproduction	225	300	375

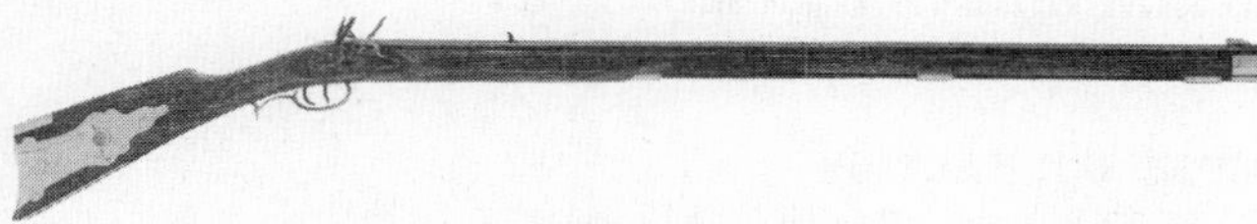

CVA Pennsylvania Long Rifle

PR407, Big Bore Mountain Rifle, .54 Caliber, Undecorated Stock, Beavertail Cheekpiece, Reproduction	250	300	350
PR456, Squirrel Rifle, .32 Caliber, Left Handed Model, Reproduction	125	175	225
SHOTGUN, DOUBLE BARREL, SIDE-BY-SIDE			
PS409, .12 Gauge, Percussion, Muzzleloading, Reproduction	175	225	275
SHOTGUN, SINGLE BARREL			
FB557, Blunderbuss, .69 Caliber, Flintlock, Brass Trigger, Reproduction	175	225	275

CZ

Czechoslovakia from 1918 to date. This listing includes both Ceska Zbrojovka Brno and Cesksloveska Zbrojovka. Also see Brno.

HANDGUN, REVOLVER			
Grand, .357 Mag., Double Action, Swing-Out Cylinder, *Modern*	75	125	175
Grand, .38 Spec., Double Action, Swing-Out Cylinder, *Modern*	75	125	175
ZKR 551, .38 Spec., Single Action, Swing-Out Cylinder, Target Pistol, *Modern*	100	175	250
HANDGUN, SEMI-AUTOMATIC			
"Vest Pocket" CZ 1945, .25 ACP, Clip Fed, *Modern*	125	150	175
CZ 1924 Navy, .380 ACP, Clip Fed, Nazi-Proofed, *Curio*	700	950	1200

CZ VZ 38

	Fair	V. Good	Excellent
CZ 1938, .380 ACP, Clip Fed, Double Action, *Curio*	$200	$250	$300
CZ 1938, .380 ACP, Clip Fed, Double Action, Nazi-Proofed, *Curio*	1250	1300	1350
CZ 1938, .380 ACP, Clip Fed, Double Action, with Safety, *Curio*	550	750	950
CZ 70, .32 ACP, Clip Fed, Blue, Double Action, *Modern*	125	150	175
CZ 75, 9mm P. Clip Fed, Double Action, Blue, *Modern*	250	300	350
CZ NB 50 Police, .32 ACP, Clip Fed, Double Action, *Curio*	200	275	350
CZ1922, .380 ACP, Clip Fed, *Curio*	225	300	375
CZ1922, .380 ACP, Clip Fed, *Curio*	175	250	325
CZ1924, .380 ACP, 10 Shot, Long Grip, Clip Fed, *Curio*	450	550	650
CZ1924, .380 ACP, Clip Fed, *Curio*	250	300	350
CZ1924, .380 ACP, Clip Fed, *Curio*	175	250	325
CZ1936, .25 ACP, Clip Fed, *Curio*	200	225	250

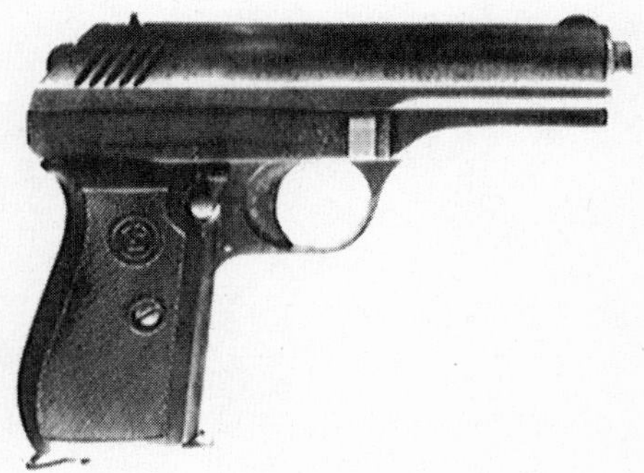

CZ VZ 27

CZ27 Communist, .32 ACP, Clip Fed, *Curio*	125	150	175
CZ27 Early Luftwaffe, .32 ACP, Clip Fed, Nazi-Proofed, *Curio*	275	350	425
CZ27 Late Luftwaffe, .32 ACP, Clip Fed, Nazi-Proofed, *Curio*	225	300	375
CZ27 Navy, .32 ACP, Clip Fed, Nazi-Proofed, *Curio*	300	400	500
CZ27 Police, .32 ACP, Clip Fed, Nazi-Proofed, *Curio*	250	350	450

	Fair	V. Good	Excellent
CZ27 Postwar, .32 ACP, Clip Fed, Commercial, *Curio*	$150	$175	$200
CZ27 Pre-War, .32 ACP, Clip Fed, Commercial, *Curio*	200	300	400
CZ50, .32 ACP, Clip Fed, Double Action, Military, *Modern*	100	125	150
CZ52, 7.62mm Tokarev, Clip Fed, Single Action, *Curio*	65	100	135
Duo, .25 ACP, Clip Fed, *Modern*	75	125	175
Fox, .25 ACP, Clip Fed, *Curio*	225	275	325
Niva, .25 ACP, Clip Fed, *Curio*	225	275	325
PAV, .22 ACP, Clip Fed, *Modern*	65	75	85

HANDGUN, SINGLESHOT

	Fair	V. Good	Excellent
Drulov 75, .22 L.R.R.F., Top Break, Target Pistol, Target Sights, *Modern*	150	200	250
Model P, .22 L.R.R.F., Top Break, Target Pistol, *Modern*	100	175	250
Model P, 6mm Flobert, Top Break, Target Pistol, *Modern*	75	150	225

RIFLE, BOLT ACTION

	Fair	V. Good	Excellent
ZKK 600, Various Calibers, Checkered Stock, Express Sights, *Modern*	300	400	500
ZKK 602, Various Magnum Calibers, Checkered Stock, Express Sights, *Modern*	400	500	600

SHOTGUN, DOUBLE BARREL, OVER-UNDER

	Fair	V. Good	Excellent
Model 581, 12 Gauge, Checkered Stock with Cheekpiece, *Modern*	350	450	550

CZAR

Made by Hood Firearms Co., c. 1876.

HANDGUN, REVOLVER

	Fair	V. Good	Excellent
.22 Short R.F., 7 Shot, Spur Trigger, Solid Frame, Single Action, *Antique*	$50	$100	$175

CZAR

Made by Hopkins & Allen, c. 1880.

HANDGUN, REVOLVER

	Fair	V. Good	Excellent
.22 Short R.F., 7 Shot, Spur Trigger, Solid Frame, Single Action, *Antique*	50	100	150
.32 Short R.F., 5 Shot, Spur Trigger, Solid Frame, Single Action, *Antique*	75	125	175

CZECHOSLOVAKIAN MILITARY

Also see German Military, CZ.

RIFLE, BOLT ACTION

	Fair	V. Good	Excellent
GEW 33 /40, 8mm Mauser, Military, Nazi-Proofed, Carbine, *Curio*	150	225	300
Gewehr 24 T, 8mm Mauser, Military, Nazi-Proofed, *Curio*	75	150	250
VZ 24, 8mm Mauser, Military, *Curio*	65	125	200
VZ 33, 8mm Mauser, Military, Carbine, *Curio*	75	125	175

D

DAISY

Made by Bacon Arms Co., c. 1880.

HANDGUN, REVOLVER

	Fair	V. Good	Excellent
.22 Short R.F., 7 Shot, Spur Trigger, Solid Frame, Single Action, *Antique*	$35	$75	$250

DAKIN GUN CO.

San Francisco, Ca., c. 1960.

SHOTGUN, DOUBLE BARREL, OVER-UNDER

	Fair	V. Good	Excellent
Model 170, Various Gauges, Light Engraving, Checkered Stock, Double Triggers, Vent Rib, *Modern*	350	450	550

SHOTGUN, DOUBLE BARREL, SIDE-BY-SIDE

	Fair	V. Good	Excellent
Model 100, 12 or 20 Gauges, Boxlock, Light Engraving, Double Triggers, *Modern*	250	300	350
Model 147, Various Magnum Gauges, Boxlock, Light Engraving, Double Triggers, Vent Rib, *Modern*	300	350	400
Model 215, 12 or 20 Gauges, Sidelock, Fancy Engraving, Fancy Wood, Ejectors, Single Selective Trigger, Vent Rib, *Modern*	625	800	975

DALBY, DAVID

Lincolnshire, England, c. 1835.

HANDGUN, FLINTLOCK

	Fair	V. Good	Excellent
.50, Pocket Pistol, Box Lock, Screw Barrel, Folding Trigger, Silver Inlay, *Antique*	300	350	400

DALY ARMS CO.

New York City, c. 1890.

HANDGUN, REVOLVER

	Fair	V. Good	Excellent
.22 Long R.F., 6 Shot, Double Action, Ring Trigger, Solid Frame, *Antique*	100	175	250
Peacemaker, .32 Short R.F., 5 Shot, Spur Trigger, Solid Frame, Single Action, *Antique*	50	100	175

DAN WESSON ARMS

Monson, Mass. since 1970.

HANDGUN, REVOLVER

10", 15-2 $20.00-$40.00; 15-2H $35.00-$55.00; 15-2V $35.00-$55.00; 15-2VH $40.00-$70.00; 44-V $55.00-$85.00; 44-VH; 715 $35.00-$55.00; 715V $45.00-$65.00; 715VH $50.00-$80.00; 744V $60.00-$100.00; 44-VH $70.00- $110.00

12", 15-2 $50.00-$80.00; 15-2VH $75.00-$110.00; 715 $75.00-$110.00; 715V $80.00-$120.00; 715VH $95.00-$140.00

15", 15-2 $75.00-$110.00; 15-2H $95.00-$135.00; 15-2V $95.00-$135.00; 15-2VH $120.00-$160.00; 715 $80.00-$120.00; 715V $95.00-$140.00; 715VH $100.00-$155.00

Extra Barrel Assemblies, Add:

	Fair	V. Good	Excellent
Model 11, .357 Magnum, Double Action, 3-Barrel Set, Nickel Plated, *Modern*	$150	$200	$250
Model 11, .357 Magnum, Double Action, 3-Barrel Set, Satin Blue, *Modern*	40	45	50
Model 11, .357 Magnum, Various Barrel Lengths, Nickel Plated, Double Action, *Modern*	75	150	225
Model 11, .357 Magnum, Various Barrel Lengths, Satin Blue, Double Action, *Modern*	100	150	200
Model 11, .38 Special, Various Barrel Lengths, Nickel Plated, Double Action, *Modern*	65	125	200
Model 11, .38 Special, Various Barrel Lengths, Satin Blue, Double Action, *Modern*	125	150	175
Model 12, .357 Magnum, 3-Barrel Set, Satin Blue, Adjustable Sights, *Modern*	150	225	300
Model 12, .357 Magnum, Various Barrel Lengths, Double Action, Blue, Adjustable Sights, *Modern*	150	200	250
Model 12, .357 Magnum, Various Barrel Lengths, Double Action, Nickel Plated, Adjustable Sights, *Modern*	85	175	300
Model 12, .38 Special, Various Barrel Lengths, Double Action, Blue, Adjustable Sights, *Modern*	50	100	150
Model 12, .38 Special, Various Barrel Lengths, Double Action, Nickel Plated, Adjustable Sights, *Modern*	50	100	175
Model 14, .357 Magnum, Double Action, 3-Barrel Set, Nickel Plated, *Modern*	150	225	300

	Fair	V. Good	Excellent
Model 14, .357 Magnum, Double Action, 3-Barrel Set, Satin Blue, *Modern*	$175	$225	$275
Model 14, .357 Magnum, Various Barrel Lengths, Double Action, Satin Blue, *Modern*	125	175	225
Model 14, .357 Magnum, Various Barrel Lengths, Double Action, Nickel Plated, *Modern*	75	125	175
Model 14, .38 Special, Various Barrel Lengths, Double Action, Satin Blue, *Modern*	50	100	150
Model 14, .38 Special, Various Barrel Lengths, Double Action, Nickel Plated, *Modern*	50	100	150
Model 14-2, .357 Magnum, Double Action, 4-Barrel Set, Blue, *Modern*	175	250	325
Model 14-2, .357 Magnum, Various Barrel Lengths, Double Action, Satin Blue, *Modern*	100	125	150
Model 14-2B, .357 Magnum, Double Action, 4-Barrel Set, Brite Blue, *Modern*	200	275	350
Model 14-2B, .357 Magnum, Various Barrel Lengths, Double Action, Brite Blue, *Modern*	50	100	150
Model 15, .357 Magnum, Double Action, 3-Barrel Set, Satin Blue, Adjustable Sights, *Modern*	175	250	325
Model 15, .357 Magnum, Double Action, 3-Barrel Set, Blue, Adjustable Sights, *Modern*	150	250	350
Model 15, .357 Magnum, Various Barrel Lengths, Double Action, Nickel Plated, Adjustable Sights, *Modern*	85	175	275
Model 15, .357 Magnum, Various Barrel Lengths, Double Action, Satin Blue, Adjustable Sights, *Modern*	125	175	225
Model 15, .357 Magnum, Various Barrel Lengths, Double Action, Blue, Adjustable Sights, *Modern*	150	200	250
Model 15, .38 Special, Various Barrel Lengths, Double Action, Nickel Plated, Adjustable Sights, *Modern*	100	175	250
Model 15, .38 Special, Various Barrel Lengths, Double Action, Satin Blue, Adjustable Sights, *Modern*	100	150	200
Model 15, .38 Special, Various Barrel Lengths, Double Action, Blue, Adjustable Sights, *Modern*	125	175	225
Model 15-2, .357 Magnum or .22 L.R.R.F., Double Action, 4-Barrel Set, Blue, Adjustable Sights, *Modern*	200	275	350
Model 15-2, .357 Magnum or .22 L.R.R.F., Various Barrel Lengths, Double Action, Blue, Adjustable Sights, *Modern*	100	150	200

	Fair	V. Good	Excellent
Model 15-2H, .357 Magnum or .22 L.R.R.F., Double Action, 4-Barrel Set, Blue, Adjustable Sights, Heavy Barrel, *Modern*	$200	$275	$350
Model 15-2H, .357 Magnum or .22 L.R.R.F., Various Barrel Lengths, Double Action, Blue, Adjustable Sights, Heavy Barrel, *Modern*	75	150	225
Model 15-2V, .357 Magnum or .22 L.R.R.F., Double Action, 4-Barrel Set, Blue, Adjustable Sights, Vent Rib, *Modern*	250	325	400
Model 15-2V, *Modern*	75	150	225
Model 15-2VH, .357 Magnum or .22 L.R.R.F., Double Action, 4-Barrel, Vent Rib, *Modern*	225	300	375
Model 15-2VH, .357 Magnum or .22 L.R.R.F., Various Barrel Lengths, Double Action, Adjustable Sights, Heavy Barrel, Vent Rib, *Modern*	125	200	275
Model 44-V, .44 Magnum, Double Action, 4-Barrel Set, Blue, Adjustable Sights, Vent Rib, *Modern*	175	350	750
Model 44-V, .44 Magnum, Various Barrel Lengths, Double Action, Blue, Adjustable Sights, Vent Rib, *Modern*	350	500	650
Model 44-VH, .44 Magnum, Double Action, 4-Barrel Set, Blue, Adjustable Sights, Heavy Barrel, Vent Rib, *Modern*	475	700	925
Model 44-VH, .44 Magnum, Various Barrel Lengths, Double Action, Adjustable Sights, Heavy Barrel, Vent Rib, *Modern*	225	450	675
Model 714, .357 Magnum, Double Action, 4-Barrel Set, Stainless Steel, Fixed Sights, *Modern*	200	300	400
Model 714, .357 Magnum, Various Barrel Lengths, Double Action, Stainless Steel, Fixed Sights, *Modern*	200	250	300
Model 715-2, .357 Magnum, Double Action, 4-Barrel Set, Stainless Steel, Adjustable Sights, *Modern*	250	325	400
Model 715-2, .357 Magnum, Various Barrel Lengths, Double Action, Stainless Steel, Adjustable Sights, *Modern*	175	225	275
Model 715-2V, .357 Magnum, Double Action, 4-Barrel Set, Stainless Steel, Adjustable Sights, Vent Rib, *Modern* .325	400	475	
Model 715-2V, .357 Magnum, Various Barrel Lengths, Double Action, Stainless Steel, Adjustable Sights, Vent Rib, *Modern*	200	275	350

	Fair	V. Good	Excellent
Model 715-2VH, .357 Magnum, Double Action, 4-Barrel Set, Stainless Steel, Adjustable Sights, Vent Rib, Heavy Barrel, *Modern*	$300	$400	$500
Model 744-V, .44 Magnum, Double Action, 4-Barrel Set, Stainless, Adjustable Sights, Vent Rib, *Modern*	500	700	900
Model 744-V, .44 Magnum, Various Barrel Lengths, Double Action, Stainless, Adjustable Sights, Vent Rib, *Modern*	475	600	725
Model 744-VH, .44 Magnum, Various Barrel Lengths, Double Action, Adjustable Sights, Stainless, Heavy Barrel, Vent Rib, *Modern*	500	650	800
Model 744-VH, .44 Magnum, Various Barrel Lengths, Double Action, Adjustable Sights, Stainless, Heavy Barrel, Vent Rib, *Modern*	525	725	925

Others:, 15-2 $20.00-$40.00; 15-2H $35.00-$55.00; 15-2V $35.00-$55.00; 15-2VH $40.00-$70.00; 44-V $55.00-$85.00; 44-VH; 715 $35.00-$55.00; 715V $45.00-$65.00; 715VH $50.00-$80.00; 744-V $60.00-$100.00; 44-VH $70.00-$110.00

DANIELS, HENRY & CHARLES

Chester, Conn., 1835–1850.

RIFLE, PERCUSSION

	Fair	V. Good	Excellent
Turret Rifle, .40, Underhammer, 8 Shot, Manual Repeater, Octagon Barrel, *Antique*	5500	6500	7500

DANISH MILITARY

HANDGUN, REVOLVER

	Fair	V. Good	Excellent
9.1mm Ronge 1891, Military, Top Break, Hammer-Like Latch, *Antique*	350	400	450

HANDGUN, SEMI-AUTOMATIC

	Fair	V. Good	Excellent
M1910, 9mm B, Made by Pieper, Clip Fed, *Curio*	300	475	650
M1910/21, 9mm B, Converted from M1910, Clip Fed, *Curio*	350	400	450
M1910/21, 9mm B, Made by Danish Army Arsenal, Clip Fed, *Curio*	450	500	550
S.L.G. SG/8 9mm Luger, Clip Fed, Military, *Curio*	750	1000	1250

RIFLE, BOLT ACTION

	Fair	V. Good	Excellent
M1889 Krag, 8 × 54 Krag-Jorgensen, Carbine, *Antique*	550	650	750
M98 Mauser, 6.5 × 57, Haerens Vabenarsenal, *Curio*	150	250	350

RIFLE, SINGLESHOT

	Fair	V. Good	Excellent
M1867, Remington Rolling Block, Full Stock, *Antique*	400	850	950

DANTON

Made by Gabilondo y Cia., Elgoibar, Spain, 1925–1933.

HANDGUN, SEMI-AUTOMATIC

	Fair	V. Good	Excellent
Pocket, .25 ACP, Clip Fed, *Curio*	$50	$100	$150
Pocket, .25 ACP, Grip Safety, Clip Fed, *Curio*	75	125	175
Pocket, .32 ACP, Clip Fed, *Curio*	50	100	175

Danton.25

	Fair	V. Good	Excellent
Pocket, .32 ACP, Grip Safety, Clip Fed, *Curio*	75	125	175

DARDICK

Hamden, Conn., 1954–1962.

HANDGUN, REVOLVER

	Fair	V. Good	Excellent
Series 1100, .38 Dardick Tround, Double Action, Clip Fed, 3" Barrel, 11 Shot, *Modern*	350	550	750
Series 1500, .22, Double Action, Clip Fed, 2" and 11" Barrels, *Modern*	550	750	950
Series 1500, .30, Double Action, Clip Fed, 4 3/4" Barrel, *Modern*	550	750	950
Series 1500, .38 Dardick Tround, Double Action, Clip Fed, 6" Barrel, 15 Shot, *Modern*	250	450	650

For Carbine Conversion Unit .22, Add $25.00-$395.00

For Carbine Conversion Unit .38, Add $215.00-$325.00

DARNE

St. Etienne, France.

SHOTGUN, DOUBLE BARREL, SIDE-BY-SIDE

	Fair	V. Good	Excellent
Bird Hunter, Various Gauges, Sliding Breech, Ejectors, Double Triggers, Checkered Stock, *Modern*	600	800	1000
Hors Serie #1, Various Gauges, Sliding Breech, Ejectors, Fancy Engraving, Checkered Stock, *Modern*	1900	3200	4500

	Fair	V. Good	Excellent
Magnum, 12 or 20 Gauges 3", Sliding Breech, Ejectors, Double Triggers, Checkered Stock, *Modern*	$1250	$2250	$3250
Pheasant Hunter, Various Gauges, Sliding Breech, Ejectors, Light Engraving, Checkered Stock, *Modern*	1500	2000	2500
Quail Hunter, Various Gauges, Sliding Breech, Ejectors, Engraved, Checkered Stock, *Modern*	1750	2750	3750

DAVENPORT, W. H.

Providence, R.I. 1880–1883, Norwich, Conn. 1890–1900.

SHOTGUN, DOUBLE BARREL, SIDE-BY-SIDE

	Fair	V. Good	Excellent
8 Ga., *Modern*	200	250	300

SHOTGUN, SINGLESHOT

	Fair	V. Good	Excellent
Various Gauges, Hammer, Steel Barrel, *Modern*	75	150	300

DAVIDSON

Spain Mfg. by Fabrica de Armas, imported by Davidson Firearms Co., Greensboro, N.C.

SHOTGUN, DOUBLE BARREL, SIDE-BY-SIDE

	Fair	V. Good	Excellent
73 Stagecoach, 12 or 20 Gauges, Magnum, Checkered Stock, *Modern*	175	225	275
Model 63B, 12 and 20 Gauges, Magnum, Engraved, Nickel Plated, Checkered Stock, *Modern*	100	175	250
Model 63B, Various Gauges, Engraved, Nickel Plated, Checkered Stock, *Modern*	65	125	200
Model 673B, 10 Ga. $3\frac{1}{2}$", Magnum, Engraved, Nickel Plated, Checkered Stock, *Modern*	125	200	275
Model 69 SL, 12 and 20 Gauges, Sidelock, Light Engraving, Checkered Stock, *Modern*	250	325	400

DAVIS INDUSTRIES

Current manufacturer in Chino, Calif.

HANDGUN, DOUBLE BARREL, OVER-UNDER

	Fair	V. Good	Excellent
Model D-22, *Modern*	25	50	75
Model D-22, .22 L.R.R.F., Remington Derringer Style, Black, Teflon, *Modern*	25	50	75
Model D-22, .25 ACP, Remington Derringer Style, Black Teflon, *Modern*	25	50	75
Model D-22, .25 ACP, Remington Derringer Style, Chrome, *Modern* .	25	50	75

DAVIS, N. R. & CO.

Freetown Mass., 1853–1917. Merged with Warner Co. of Norwich, Conn., and became Davis-Warner Arms Co. It was not active between 1920 and 1922, but in 1930 started again as Crescent-Davis Arms Co., Norwich. This included Crescent Fire Arms Co. They relocated in Springfield, Mass., 1931–1932, and were taken over in 1932 by Stevens Arms.

RIFLE, PERCUSSION

	Fair	V. Good	Excellent
.45, Octagon Barrel, *Antique*	$200	$400	$675

SHOTGUN, PERCUSSION

	Fair	V. Good	Excellent
#1 Various Gauges, Double Barrel, Side by Side, Damascus Barrel, Outside Hammers, *Antique*	175	325	475
#3 Various Gauges, Double Barrel, Side by Side, Damascus Barrel, Outside Hammers, *Antique*	150	275	400

SHOTGUN, DOUBLE BARREL, SIDE-BY-SIDE

	Fair	V. Good	Excellent
Various Gauges, Hammerless, Damascus Barrel, *Modern*	50	100	175
Various Gauges, Hammerless, Steel Barrel, *Modern*	62	125	200
Various Gauges, Outside Hammers, Damascus Barrel, *Modern*	50	100	175
Various Gauges, Outside Hammers, Steel Barrel, *Modern*	50	100	200

SHOTGUN, SINGLE BARREL

	Fair	V. Good	Excellent
Various Gauges, Hammer, Steel Barrel, *Modern*	25	50	100

DAY ARMS CO.

San Antonio, Tex.

HANDGUN, SEMI-AUTOMATIC

	Fair	V. Good	Excellent
Conversion Unit Only, .22 L.R.R.F., For Colt M1911, Clip Fed	100	125	150

DEAD SHOT

L. W. Pond Co.

HANDGUN, REVOLVER

	Fair	V. Good	Excellent
.22 Long R.F., 6 Shot, Single Action, Solid Frame, Spur Trigger, *Antique*	175	225	275

DEANE, ADAMS & DEANE

See Adams.

DEBATIR

HANDGUN, SEMI-AUTOMATIC

	Fair	V. Good	Excellent
.25 ACP, Clip Fed, *Curio*	75	150	225
.32 ACP, Clip Fed, *Curio*	100	175	250

DEBERIERE, HENRY

Phila., Pa. 1769–1774. See Kentucky Rifles and Pistols.

Debatir .25

DECKER, WILHELM

Zella St. Blasii, Germany, c. 1913.

HANDGUN, REVOLVER

	Fair	V. Good	Excellent
Decker, .25 ACP, Hammerless, 6 Shot, *Curio*	$425	$650	$875
Mueller Special, .25 ACP, Hammerless, 6 Shot, *Curio*	375	675	975

DEFENDER

Made by Iver-Johnson, sold by J.P. Lovell Arms 1875–1895.

HANDGUN, REVOLVER

	Fair	V. Good	Excellent
#89, .22 Short R.F., 7 Shot, Spur Trigger, Solid Frame, Single Action, *Antique*	50	100	150
#89, .32 Short R.F., 5 Shot, Spur Trigger, Solid Frame, Single Action, *Antique*	75	125	175
.22 Short R.F., 7 Shot, Spur Trigger, Solid Frame, Single Action, *Antique*	50	100	175
.32 Short R.F., 5 Shot, Spur Trigger, Solid Frame, Single Action, *Antique*	75	125	175

DEFENDER

N. Shore & Co., Chicago, Ill., c. 1922.

HANDGUN, KNIFE PISTOL

	Fair	V. Good	Excellent
#215, .22 R.F., 3" Overall Length, 1 Blade	50	100	175

DEFIANCE

Made by Norwich Falls Pistol Co., c. 1880.

HANDGUN, REVOLVER

	Fair	V. Good	Excellent
.22 Short R.F., 7 Shot, Spur Trigger, Solid Frame, Single Action, *Antique*	50	100	175

DEHUFF, ABRAHAM

Lancaster, Pa., c. 1779. See Kentucky Rifles and Pistols.

DEK-DU

Tomas de Urizar y Cia., Eibar, Spain, c. 1910.

HANDGUN, REVOLVER

	Fair	V. Good	Excellent
Velo Dog, .25 ACP, 12 Shots, Folding Trigger, *Curio*	$75	$125	$175
Velo Dog, 5.5mm Velo Dog, 12 Shots, Folding Trigger, *Curio*	50	100	150

DELPHIAN

Made by Stevens Arms.

SHOTGUN, SINGLESHOT

	Fair	V. Good	Excellent
Model 90, Various Gauges, Takedown, Automatic Ejector, Plain Hammer, *Modern*	25	50	75

DELU

Fab. d'Armes Delu & Co.

HANDGUN, SEMI-AUTOMATIC

	Fair	V. Good	Excellent
.25 ACP, Clip Fed, *Curio*	125	150	175

DEMRO

Manchester, Conn.

HANDGUN, SEMI-AUTOMATIC

	Fair	V. Good	Excellent
T.A.C. XF-7 Wasp, .45 ACP or 9mm Luger, Clip Fed, *Modern*	250	300	350

RIFLE, SEMI-AUTOMATIC

	Fair	V. Good	Excellent
T.A.C. Model 1 Carbine, .45 ACP or 9mm Luger, Clip Fed, Fixed Stock, *Modern*	112	225	350
T.A.C. XF-7 Wasp Carbine, .45 ACP or 9mm Luger, Clip Fed, Folding Stock, *Modern*	300	350	400

DERINGER RIFLE AND PISTOL WORKS

Philadelphia, Pa. 1870–1880.

HANDGUN, REVOLVER

	Fair	V. Good	Excellent
Centennial '76, .38 Long R.F., 5 Shot, Single Action, Spur Trigger, Tip-up, *Antique*	300	350	400
Model 1, .22 Short R.F., 7 Shot, Spur Trigger, Tip-up, *Antique*	225	300	375
Model 2, .22 Short R.F., 7 Shot, Spur Trigger, Tip-up, *Antique*	125	200	275
Model 2, .32 Long R.F., 5 Shot, Single Action, Spur Trigger, Tip-up, *Antique*	125	200	275

DERINGER, HENRY, JR.

Philadelphia, Pa. 1806–1868. Also see U.S. Military. The inventor, designer, and gunmaker Henry Deringer, Jr., testified on his own behalf in the celebrated trademark trial of *Henry Deringer* v. *Adolphus J. Plate,* a suit brought against dealer A. J. Plate, for his role in the manufacture of spurious pistols (by Slotter & Co.) that were marked with the Deringer trademark. The stamp, marked on the breech of the barrel and the lockplate, precisely duplicated the original. In fact, this was likely a stamp made for Deringer himself: DERINGER PHILA—The percussion ignition system was only coming into use in the 1830s, and Deringer was among the first to employ it. The use of the percussion system was instrumental in making practical, concealable firearms, like the Deringer pistol, as they were also in the evolution of practical revolvers, like the Colt. Deringer's role in manfacturing military and naval arms under government contract was crucial in his awareness and knowledge of developments in firearms technology. Among the most famous names in firearms history, Henry Deringer developed his pocket pistols beginning around 1826, proceeding through an evolution to a design which had been firmly established by the mid-19th century. By the time of his death, in 1868, over 15,000 pairs had been manufactured. The type became so recognizable that "Deringer's pistols" achieved worldwide renown to become "the derringer pistol"—a specific type and style of pocket protector recognized wherever men knew about guns. Competitors quickly seized upon the popularity of the derringer. Within a short time, a flood of counterfeit arms hit the market, a problem which plagued the inventor until his death, at the age of 82. It is due to this dilemma that much more is known about Deringer and his rivals than about many other American gunmakers: Deringer sued the most blatant counterfeiter, and won. The civil suit he initiated was successfully prosecuted by his estate, and remains today as a landmark in trademark infringement law. This was the first case to award the amount of profit by the defendant as the damages to the plaintiff—in Deringer's case this was $1,700. Deringer also made military arms, as well as a variety of civilian types: holster and belt pistols, a box-lock martial model (for the U.S. Navy), and even long arms—especially military rifles of the 1814 and 1817 patterns. His Kentucky rifles were often exquisite, with rich tiger-stripe maple stocks and handsome inlays. An elegant Deringer Kentucky rifle was used in an infamous duel between Congressman Cilley of Maine, and a Mr. Graves (1838); they fought at a range of 80 yards; Cilley was killed on the third round of the engagement. The last of the Deringer production were .22 and .32 rimfire, single action pocket revolvers of which approximately 6,900 were made in .22 caliber (1873–79), and 4,000 in .32 (1874–79). But the percussion pocket pistol remains Henry Deringer's greatest legacy. These were carried by ladies and gentlemen, soldiers, gold miners, riverboat gamblers, and a broad array of other humanity, occasionally as a final arbiter in a dispute. Among the first pairs was that made for U.S. Army officer and Ordnance official Colonel George Talcott, dating from the 1830s. Among other well-known owners were pioneer Minnesota governor Alexander Ramsey (a gift from one of Deringer's sons, Calhoun) and the soon-to-be internationally celebrated William F. Cody. The most infamous of all Deringers is the pistol used by John Wilkes Booth in the assassination of President Abraham Lincoln, April 14, 1865. Ironically, Lincoln's opponent in the Presidential campaign of 1860, Senator Stephen A. Douglas, carried a pair of Deringers, and it has been speculated that Lincoln himself may well have owned a pair. Manufacture of the percussion Deringer was from the 1830s to 1868. Production of the metallic cartridge Deringer revolvers was under supervision of I. Jones Clark, from c. 1870 to 1880.

HANDGUN, PERCUSSION

	Fair	V. Good	Excellent
Dueller, .41, Back Lock, German Silver Mounts, *Antique*	$1500	$2000	$2500
Medium Pocket, .41, Back Lock, German Silver Mounts, *Antique*	500	1000	1500
Pocket, .41, Back Lock, German Silver Mounts, *Antique*	375	750	1250

DERINGER, HENRY, SR.

Richmond, Va. & Philadelphia, Pa. 1768–1814. See Kentucky Rifles and Pistols; U.S. Military.

DERR, JOHN

Lancaster, Pa. 1810–1844. See Kentucky Rifles and Pistols.

DESPATCH

Made by Hopkins & Allen, c. 1875.

HANDGUN, REVOLVER

	Fair	V. Good	Excellent
.22 Short R.F., 7 Shot, Spur Trigger, Solid Frame, Single Action, *Antique*	75	125	175

DESTROYER

Made in Spain by Isidro Gaztanaga 1914–1933, reorganized as Gaztanaga, Trocoala y Ibarzabal 1933–1936.

HANDGUN, SEMI-AUTOMATIC

	Fair	V. Good	Excellent
Destroyer, .25 ACP, Clip Fed, *Curio*	75	125	175

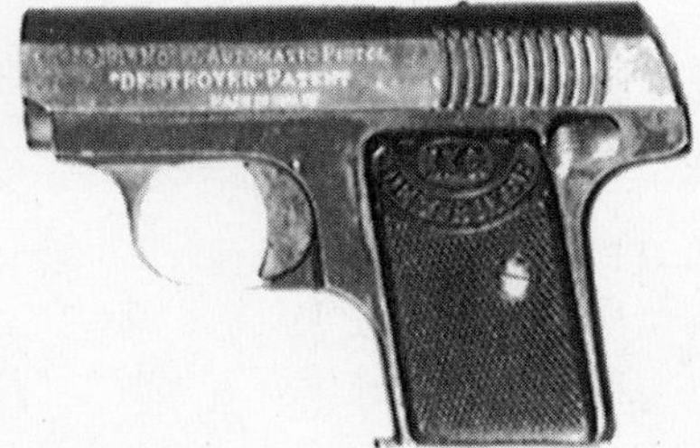

Destroyer .25

	Fair	V. Good	Excellent
Destroyer, .32 ACP, Clip Fed, Long Grip, *Curio*	100	150	200
Model 1913, .25 ACP, Clip Fed, *Modern*	75	125	175
Model 1919, .32 ACP, Clip Fed, *Modern*	75	125	175
Super Destroyer, .32 ACP, Clip Fed, *Modern*	125	175	225

DESTRUCTOR

Iraola Salaverria, Eibar, Spain.

HANDGUN, SEMI-AUTOMATIC

	Fair	V. Good	Excellent
.25 ACP, Clip Fed, *Modern*	$50	$100	$150
.32 ACP, Clip Fed, *Modern*	75	125	175

DETONICS

Seattle, Washington. This cleverly designed series of pistols features the scaled down Government Model .45, designed for concealment. Although recoil is substantial, the .45 ACP cartridge is so powerful that the mini-arm proved instantly popular, and received an enormous amount of publicity. Eventually the Colt company introduced its own scaled-down pistol, the Officer's Model ACP; that too became extremely popular. The Detonics is only one of several knock-offs of the orginal Colt/Browning Government Model .45.

HANDGUN, SEMI-AUTOMATIC

	Fair	V. Good	Excellent
Mark I, .45 ACP, Combat Modifications, Clip Fed, Pocket Pistol, Matt Blue, *Modern*	325	450	575
Mark II, 9mm P., Combat Modifications, Clip Fed, Pocket Pistol, Matt Blue, *Modern*	300	375	450
Mark III, .38 Super, Combat Modifications, Clip Fed, Pocket Pistol, Matt Blue, *Modern*	300	400	500
Combat Master, .45 ACP, Combat Modifications, Clip Fed, Pocket Pistol, Matt Blue, *Modern*	600	675	750
Combat Master, .45 ACP, Combat Modifications, Clip Fed, Pocket Pistol, Matt Blue, Adjustable Sights, *Modern*	650	725	800
Combat Master Mk. V, .38 Super, Combat Modifications, Clip Fed, Pocket Pistol, Matt Stainless, *Modern*	625	700	775
Combat Master Mk. V, .45 ACP, Combat Modifications, Clip Fed, Pocket Pistol, Matt Stainless, *Modern*	450	600	750
Combat Master Mk. V, 9mm P., Combat Modifications, Clip Fed, Pocket Pistol, Matt Stainless, *Modern*	625	700	775
Combat Master Mk. VI, .45 ACP, Combat Modifications, Clip Fed, Pocket Pistol, Polished Stainless, Adjustable Sights, *Modern*	650	725	800
Combat Master Mk. VI, .451 Mag., Combat Modifications, Clip Fed, Pocket Pistol, Polished Stainless, Adjustable Sights, *Modern*	625	800	975
Combat Master Mk. VI, 9mm P., Combat Modifications, Clip Fed, Pocket Pistol, Polished Stainless, Adjustable Sights, *Modern*	675	750	825

Detonics Mark VI

	Fair	V. Good	Excellent
Combat Master Mk. VII, .38 Super, Combat Modifications, Clip Fed, Pocket Pistol, Matt Stainless, No Sights, Lightweight, *Modern*	$775	$850	$925
Combat Master Mk. VII, .45 ACP, Combat Modifications, Clip Fed, Pocket Pistol, Matt Stainless, No Sights, Lightweight, *Modern*	750	825	900
Combat Master Mk. VII, .451 Mag., Combat Modifications, Clip Fed, Pocket Pistol, Matt Stainless, No Sights, Lightweight, *Modern*	600	900	1200
Combat Master Mk. VII, 9mm P., Combat Modifications, Clip Fed, Pocket Pistol, Matt Stainless, No Sights, Lightweight, *Modern*	775	850	925
MC2 Military Combat, .38 Super, Clip Fed, Pocket Pistol, Matt Stainless, *Modern*	550	600	650
MC2 Military Combat, .45 ACP, Clip Fed, Pocket Pistol, Matt Stainless, *Modern*	525	575	625
MC2 Military Combat, 9mm P., Clip Fed, Pocket Pistol, Matt Stainless, *Modern*	550	600	650
Scoremaster, .45 ACP, I.P.S.C. Target Pistol, Target Sights, Stainless Steel, *Modern*	550	750	950
Scoremaster, .451 Mag., I.P.S.C. Target Pistol, Target Sights, Stainless Steel, *Modern*	750	1000	1250

DIAMOND

Made by Stevens Arms.

SHOTGUN, SINGLESHOT

	Fair	V. Good	Excellent
Model 89 Dreadnaught, Various Gauges, Hammer, *Modern*	50	75	100
Model 90, Various Gauges, Takedown, Automatic Ejector, Plain Hammer, *Modern*	25	50	75
Model 95, 12 and 16 Gauge, Takedown, *Modern*	25	50	75

	Fair	V. Good	Excellent

DIANE

Erquiaga, Muguruzu, y Cia., Eibar, Spain, c. 1923.

HANDGUN, SEMI-AUTOMATIC

	Fair	V. Good	Excellent
.25 ACP, Clip Fed, Blue, *Curio*	$175	$225	$275

DIANE

Made by Wilkinson Arms, Covina, Calif.

HANDGUN, SEMI-AUTOMATIC

	Fair	V. Good	Excellent
Standard Model, .25 ACP, Clip Fed, *Modern*	75	100	125

DICKINSON, J. & L.

Also E. L. & J. Dickinson, Springfield, Mass. 1863–1880.

HANDGUN, SINGLESHOT

	Fair	V. Good	Excellent
.22 R.F., Brass Frame, Pivoting Barrel, Rack Ejector, *Antique*	300	350	400
.32 R.F., Brass Frame, Pivoting Barrel, Rack Ejector, *Antique*	200	250	300

DICKSON

Made in Italy for American Import Co. until 1968.

HANDGUN, SINGLESHOT

	Fair	V. Good	Excellent
Detective, .25 ACP, Clip Fed, *Modern*	75	100	125

DICTATOR

Made by Hopkins & Allen, c. 1880.

HANDGUN, REVOLVER

	Fair	V. Good	Excellent
.22 Short R.F., 7 Shot, Spur Trigger, Solid Frame, Single Action, *Antique*	75	125	175
.32 Short R.F., 5 Shot, Spur Trigger, Solid Frame, Single Action, *Antique*	75	125	175
#2, .32 Short R.F., 5 Shot, Spur Trigger, Solid Frame, Single Action, *Antique*	100	150	200

DIXIE GUN WORKS

Union City, Tenn. The author remembers a trip to Tennessee as a boy to visit relatives living in Memphis, when the unending pleas of brother Jack and self led to a detour in order to visit the operations of Turner Kirkland's Dixie Gun Works at Union City. The trip was in 1953 and Kirkland had already developed his own empire. We were amazed at the vast quantities of replacement parts, replica guns, antique arms, and even collectors' cars. Years later, when *Sports Afield* magazine compiled a list of the most important firearms personalities in that publication's 100 years of existence, Turner's name was among them. Today the Dixie Gun Works annual catalogue is massive. The firm exhibits at the NRA Show and at IWA, as well as the SHOT Show, and has developed a book line, continues to deal in antique arms, and remains at the forefront of replica and muzzle-loading firearms interests.

HANDGUN, FLINTLOCK

	Fair	V. Good	Excellent
Tower, .67, Brass Furniture, Reproduction	$12	$25	$50

HANDGUN, PERCUSSION

	Fair	V. Good	Excellent
Army, .44 Revolver, Buntline, Reproduction	100	125	150
Navy, .36 Revolver, Buntline, Brass Frame, Engraved, Reproduction	125	175	225
Navy, .36 Revolver, Buntline, Brass Frame, Reproduction	100	150	200
Spiller & Burr, .36 Revolver, Buntline, Brass Frame, Reproduction	50	75	100
Wyatt Earp, .44 Revolver, Buntline, Brass Frame, Reproduction	50	75	100
Wyatt Earp, .44 Revolver, Buntline, Brass Frame, with Shoulder Stock, Reproduction	125	150	175

RIFLE, LEVER ACTION

	Fair	V. Good	Excellent
Win. 73 (Italian), .44-40 WCF, Tube Feed, Octagon Barrel, Carbine, *Modern*	350	475	600
Win. 73 (Italian), .44-40 WCF, Tube Feed, Octagon Barrel, Color Cased Hardened Frame, Engraved, *Modern*	350	475	600

RIFLE, FLINTLOCK

	Fair	V. Good	Excellent
1st. Model Brown Bess, .75, Military, Reproduction	250	325	400
2nd. Model Brown Bess, .74, Military, Reproduction	350	425	500
Coach Guard, .95, Blunderbuss, Brass Furniture, Reproduction	50	100	150
Day Rifle, .45, Double Barrel, Over-Under, Swivel Breech, Brass Furniture, Reproduction	225	300	375
Deluxe Pennsylvania, .45, Kentucky Rifle, Full-Stocked, Brass Furniture, Light Engraving, Reproduction	200	275	350
Deluxe Pennsylvania, .45, Kentucky Rifle, Full-Stocked, Brass Furniture, Reproduction	175	250	325
Kentuckian, .45, Kentucky Rifle, Full-Stocked, Brass Furniture, Reproduction	50	100	150
Kentuckian, .45, Kentucky Rifle, Full-Stocked, Brass Furniture, Reproduction, Carbine	75	150	225
Musket, .67, Smoothbore, Reproduction, Carbine	35	75	125

	Fair	V. Good	Excellent
Squirrel Rifle, .45, Kentucky Rifle, Full-Stocked, Brass Furniture, Reproduction	$175	$275	$375
York County, .45, Kentucky Rifle, Full-Stocked, Brass Furniture, Reproduction	125	150	175

RIFLE, PERCUSSION

	Fair	V. Good	Excellent
Day Rifle, .45, Double Barrel, Over-Under, Swivel Breech, Brass Furniture, Reproduction	175	225	275
Deluxe Pennsylvania, .45, Kentucky Rifle, Full-Stocked, Brass Furniture, Reproduction	225	275	325
Deluxe Pennsylvania, .45, Kentucky Rifle, Full-Stocked, Brass Furniture, Light Engraving, Reproduction	200	275	350
Dixie Hawkin, .45, Half-Stocked, Octagon Barrel, Set Trigger, Brass Furniture, Reproduction	100	150	200
Dixie Hawkin, .50, Half-Stocked, Octagon Barrel, Set Trigger, Brass Furniture, Reproduction	100	150	200
Enfield Two-Band, .577, Musketoon, Military, Reproduction	65	125	200
Kentuckian, .45, Kentucky Rifle, Full-Stocked, Brass Furniture, Reproduction	75	125	175
Kentuckian, .45, Kentucky Rifle, Full-Stocked, Brass Furniture, Reproduction, Carbine	150	200	250
Musket, .66, Smoothbore, Reproduction	75	125	175
Plainsman, .45, Half-Stocked, Octagon Barrel, Reproduction	150	200	250
Plainsman, .50, Half-Stocked, Octagon Barrel, Reproduction	75	150	275
Squirrel Rifle, .45, Kentucky Rifle, Full-Stocked, Brass Furniture, Reproduction	225	300	375
Target, .45, Half-Stocked, Octagon Barrel, Reproduction	35	75	125
York County, .45, Kentucky Rifle, Full-Stocked, Brass Furniture, Reproduction	75	125	175
Zouave M 1863, .58, Military, Reproduction	100	175	250

SHOTGUN, PERCUSSION

	Fair	V. Good	Excellent
12 Gauge, Double Barrel, Side by Side, Double Trigger, Reproduction	50	75	100
28 Gauge, Single Barrel, Reproduction	50	75	100

SHOTGUN, FLINTLOCK

	Fair	V. Good	Excellent
Fowling Piece, 14 Gauge, Single Barrel, Reproduction	95	100	105

DOBSON T.

London, England, c. 1780.

HANDGUN, FLINTLOCK

	Fair	V. Good	Excellent
.64, Presentation, Holster Pistol, Gold Inlays, Engraved, Half- Octagon Barrel, High Quality, *Antique*	$1250	$2500	$4000

DOMINO

Made in Italy, imported by Mandell Shooting Sports. Also see Beeman.

Precision Firearms

HANDGUN, SEMI-AUTOMATIC

	Fair	V. Good	Excellent
Model O.P. 601, .22 Short, Target Pistol, Adjustable Sights, Target Grips, *Modern*	700	900	1100
Model O.P. 602, .22 L.R., Target Pistol, Adjustable Sights, Target Grips, *Modern*	800	1000	1200

DREADNOUGHT

Made by Hopkins & Allen, c. 1880.

HANDGUN, REVOLVER

	Fair	V. Good	Excellent
.22 Short R.F., 7 Shot, Spur Trigger, Solid Frame, Single Action, *Antique*	50	100	150
.32 Short R.F., 5 Shot, Spur Trigger, Solid Frame, Single Action, *Antique*	75	125	175

DREYSE

Dreyse Rheinische Metallwaren Machinenfabrik, Sommerda, Germany, since 1889. In 1936 merged and became Rheinmetall-Borsig, Dusseldorf, Germany.

HANDGUN, SEMI-AUTOMATIC

	Fair	V. Good	Excellent
M1907, .32 ACP, Clip Fed, *Curio*	75	125	175

Dreyse Model 1907 Late

	Fair	V. Good	Excellent
M1907, .32 ACP, Clip Fed, Early Model, *Curio*	100	150	200
M1910, 9mm Luger, Clip Fed, *Curio*	2000	2500	3000

	Fair	V. Good	Excellent
Rheinmetall, .32 ACP, Clip Fed, *Curio*	$175	$225	$275
Vest Pocket, .25 ACP, Clip Fed, *Curio*	100	150	200
Vest Pocket, .25 ACP, Clip Fed, Early, *Curio*	125	175	225

RIFLE, SEMI-AUTOMATIC

Carbine, .32 ACP, Clip Fed, Checkered Stock, *Curio*	300	375	450

DRIPPARD, F.

Lancaster, Pa., 1767–1773. See Kentucky Rifles and Pistols.

DRISCOLL, J. B.

Springfield, Mass., c. 1870.

HANDGUN, SINGLESHOT

.22 R.F., Brass Frame, Spur Trigger, *Antique*	250	300	350

DUBIEL ARMS CO.

Sherman, Tex., since 1975.

RIFLE, BOLT ACTION

Custom Rifle, Various Calibers, Various Styles, Fancy Wood, *Modern*	1500	2000	2500

DUMARESD, B.

Marseille, France, probably c. 1730.

HANDGUN, FLINTLOCK

Holster Pistol, Engraved, Horn Inlays, Ornate, Silver Furniture, *Antique*	1000	1500	2000

DUMOULIN & DELEYE

Liege, Belgium. Makers of best quality double rifles and bolt action sporting rifles, this firm manufactured a magnificent double barrel rifle for the author in 1972. The rifle was similar to the style of Holland & Holland and was made up partly for hunting use, and partly as a sample of engraving for the author's A.A. White Engravers, Inc. This exquisite rifle has taken Cape Buffalo, leopard, lion and elephant, and remains one of the author's most prized possessions. Engraving was by K.C. Hunt, A.A. White, Rene Delcour, Philippe Grifnee, Denise Thirion, and Hans Obiltschnig. Although gunmaker Dumoulin (son of the gunmaker running Dumoulin Freres et. Cie.) referred to the rifle as a "jungle" (due to the combination of six engravers on one piece), it nevertheless must rank among the finest rifles ever built by that firm.

DUMOULIN FRERES ET CIE

Milmort, Belgium since 1849.

	Fair	V. Good	Excellent
RIFLE, BOLT ACTION			
African Pro, Various Calibers, Fancy Checkering, Fancy Engraving, Fancy Wood, *Modern*	$2500	$4000	$4500
Safari Sportsman, Various Calibers, Fancy Checkering, Engraved, Fancy Wood, *Modern*	2000	3000	3500
Safari, Various Calibers, Fancy Checkering, Engraved, *Modern*	1200	2000	2500

RIFLE, DOUBLE BARREL, SIDE-BY-SIDE

Europa, Various Calibers, Fancy Checkering, Engraved, Fancy Wood, *Modern*	2000	3500	4500

DUO FRANTISEK DUSEK

Opocno, Czechoslovakia, 1926–1948. Ceska Zbrojovka from 1948 to date.

HANDGUN, SEMI-AUTOMATIC

Duo, .25 ACP, Clip Fed, *Modern*	150	200	250

DUTCH MILITARY

HANDGUN, REVOLVER

Model 1871 Hemberg, 9.4mm, Military, *Antique*	250	300	350

RIFLE, BOLT ACTION

Beaumont-Vitale M1871/88, Military, *Antique*	100	150	200
Model 95, 6.5mm Mannlicher, Carbine, Full Stock, *Curio*	75	100	125
Model 95, 6.5mm Mannlicher, Full Stock, *Curio*	100	125	150

RIFLE, FLINTLOCK

.70, Officer's Type, Musket, Brass Furniture, *Antique*	1000	1250	1500

DUTTON, JOHN S.

Jaffrey, N.H. 1855–1870.

RIFLE, PERCUSSION

.36, Target Rifle, Swiss Buttplate, Octagon Barrel, Target Sights, *Antique*	450	900	1600

DWM

Deutsche Waffen und Munitionsfabrik, Berlin, Germany, 1896–1945. Also see Luger and Borchardt.

HANDGUN, SEMI-AUTOMATIC

Pocket, .32 ACP, Clip Fed, *Curio*	150	250	350

E

	Fair	V. Good	Excellent

E.A.

Echave y Arizmendi, Eibar, Spain 1911-1975. Also see Echasa and MAB.

HANDGUN, SEMI-AUTOMATIC

	Fair	V. Good	Excellent
1916 Model, .25 ACP, Clip Fed, *Curio*	$35	$75	$125

E.A.

Eulogio Arostegui, Eibar, Spain, c. 1930.

HANDGUN, SEMI-AUTOMATIC

	Fair	V. Good	Excellent
.25 ACP, Clip Fed, Blue, Dog Logo on Grips, *Modern*	37	75	125

EAGLE

Made by Iver Johnson, c. 1879–1886.

HANDGUN, REVOLVER

	Fair	V. Good	Excellent
.22 Short F.F., 7 Shot, Spur Trigger, Solid Frame, Single Action, *Antique*	50	100	150
.32 Short R.F., 5 Shot, Spur Trigger, Solid Frame, Single Action, *Antique*	50	100	150
.38 Short R.F., 5 Shot, Spur Trigger, Solid Frame, Single Action, *Antique*	75	125	175
.44 Short R.F., 5 Shot, Spur Trigger, Solid Frame, Single Action, *Antique*	125	200	275

EAGLE ARMS CO.

New York City, c. 1865. Marketed by Plant's Manufacturing Company, New Haven, Conn.

HANDGUN, REVOLVER

	Fair	V. Good	Excellent
.30 Cup Primed Cartridge, 6 Shot, Single Action, Spur Trigger, Solid Frame, *Antique*	300	400	500
.30 Cup Primed Cartridge, 6 Shot, Single Action, Spur Trigger, Tip-up, *Antique*	400	525	650
.42 Cup Primed Cartridge, 6 Shot, Single Action, Spur Trigger, Iron Frame, *Antique*	750	850	950
.42 Cup Primed Cartridge, 6 Shot, Single Action, Spur Trigger, Tip-up, *Antique*	750	950	1150

EARLHOOD

Made by E.L. Dickinson Co., Springfield, Mass. 1870–1880.

HANDGUN, REVOLVER

	Fair	V. Good	Excellent
.32 Short R.F., 5 Shot, Spur Trigger, Solid Frame, Single Action, *Antique*	$50	$125	$175

EARLY, AMOS

Dauphin Co. Pa. See Kentucky Rifles.

EARLY, JACOB

Dauphin Co. Pa. See Kentucky Rifles.

EARTHQUAKE

See Earlhood.

EASTERN

Made by Stevens Arms.

SHOTGUN, DOUBLE BARREL, SIDE-BY-SIDE

	Fair	V. Good	Excellent
Model 311, Various Gauges, Hammerless, Steel Barrel, *Modern*	125	150	175

SHOTGUN, SINGLESHOT

	Fair	V. Good	Excellent
Model 94, Various Gauges, Takedown, Automatic Ejector, Plain Hammer, *Modern*	25	50	75

EASTERN ARMS CO.

Made by Meriden Firearms and sold by Sears, Roebuck.

HANDGUN, REVOLVER

	Fair	V. Good	Excellent
.32 S & W, 5 Shot, Double Action, Top Break, *Modern*	50	75	100
.38 S & W, 5 Shot, Double Action, Top Break, *Modern*	75	100	125

EASTFIELD

See Smith & Wesson.

ECHABERRIA, ARTURA

Spain, c. 1790.

	Fair	V. Good	Excellent
HANDGUN, MIQUELET-LOCK			
Pair, Holster Pistol, Plain, Brass Furniture, *Antique*	$2500	$3500	$4500

ECHASA

Tradename used in the 1950s by Echave, Arizmendi y Cia., Eibar, Spain.

	Fair	V. Good	Excellent
HANDGUN, SEMI-AUTOMATIC			
Model GZ MAB, .22 L.R.R.F., Clip Fed, Hammer, *Modern*	50	100	150

Echasa GZ-MAB

	Fair	V. Good	Excellent
Model GZ MAB, .25 ACP, Clip Fed, Hammer, *Modern*	100	125	150
Model GZ MAB, .32 ACP, Clip Fed, Hammer, *Modern*	75	125	175

ECLIPSE

Made by Johnson, Bye & Co., c. 1875.

	Fair	V. Good	Excellent
HANDGUN, SINGLESHOT			
.25 Short R.F., Derringer, Spur Trigger, *Antique*	35	75	125

EDGESON

Lincolnshire, England, 1810–1830.

	Fair	V. Good	Excellent
HANDGUN, FLINTLOCK			
.45, Pair, Box Lock, Screw Barrel, Pocket Pistol, Folding Trigger, Plain, *Antique*	500	1000	1800

EDMONDS, J.

See Kentucky Rifles.

EGG, CHARLES

London, England, c. 1850.

	Fair	V. Good	Excellent
HANDGUN, PERCUSSION			
Pepperbox, .36, 6 Shot, $3^1/_2$" Barrels, *Antique*	$165	$325	$600

EGG, DURS

London, England 1770–1840. Also see British Military.

	Fair	V. Good	Excellent
HANDGUN, FLINTLOCK			
.50, Dueling Type, Holster Pistol, Octagon Barrel, Steel Furniture, Light Ornamentation, *Antique*	750	1500	2500
HANDGUN, PERCUSSION			
6 Shot, Pepperbox, Fluted Barrel, Pocket Pistol, Engraved, *Antique*	1000	1500	2000

EGYPTIAN MILITARY

	Fair	V. Good	Excellent
HANDGUN, SEMI-AUTOMATIC			
Tokagypt M-58, 9mm Luger, Clip Fed, *Curio*	250	300	350
RIFLE, SEMI-AUTOMATIC			
Hakim, .22 L.R.R.F., Training Rifle, Military, *Modern*	225	250	275
Hakim, 8mm Mauser, Military, *Modern*	250	300	350

84 GUN CO.

Eighty Four, Pa., c. 1973.

	Fair	V. Good	Excellent
RIFLE, BOLT ACTION			
Classic Rifle, Various Calibers, Checkered Stock, Grade 1, *Modern*	200	250	300
Classic Rifle, Various Calibers, Checkered Stock, Grade 2, *Modern*	200	500	600
Classic Rifle, Various Calibers, Checkered Stock, Grade 3, *Modern*	350	550	650
Classic Rifle, Various Calibers, Checkered Stock, Grade 4, *Modern*	600	1000	1200
Lobo Rifle, Various Calibers, Checkered Stock, Grade 1, *Modern*	300	375	400
Lobo Rifle, Various Calibers, Checkered Stock, Grade 2, *Modern*	350	500	575
Lobo Rifle, Various Calibers, Checkered Stock, Grade 3, *Modern*	600	1000	1200
Lobo Rifle, Various Calibers, Checkered Stock, Grade 4, *Modern*	700	1500	1800
Pennsy Rifle, Various Calibers, Checkered Stock, Grade 1, *Modern*	250	350	400
Pennsy Rifle, Various Calibers, Checkered Stock, Grade 2, *Modern*	300	450	600
Pennsy Rifle, Various Calibers, Checkered Stock, Grade 3, *Modern*	650	950	1250
Pennsy Rifle, Various Calibers, Checkered Stock, Grade 4, *Modern*	750	1250	1750

	Fair	V. Good	Excellent
Pennsy Rifle, Various Calibers, Checkered Stock, Standard Grade, *Modern*	$175	$250	$325

EL FAISAN

SHOTGUN, DOUBLE BARREL, SIDE-BY-SIDE

	Fair	V. Good	Excellent
El Faisan, .410 Gauge, Folding Gun, Double Trigger, Outside Hammers, *Modern*	50	75	100

EL TIGRE

RIFLE, LEVER ACTION

	Fair	V. Good	Excellent
Copy of Winchester M1892, 44-40 WCF, Tube Feed, *Modern*	100	200	450

ELECTOR

Made by Hopkins & Allen, c. 1880.

HANDGUN, REVOLVER

	Fair	V. Good	Excellent
.22 Short R.F., 7 Shot, Spur Trigger, Solid Frame, Single Action, *Antique*	50	100	150
.32 Short R.F., 5 Shot, Spur Trigger, Solid Frame, Single Action, *Antique*	75	125	175

ELECTRIC

Made by Forehand & Wadsworth 1871–1880.

HANDGUN, REVOLVER

	Fair	V. Good	Excellent
.32 Short R.F., 5 Shot, Spur Trigger, Solid Frame, Single Action, *Antique*	75	125	175

ELGIN ARMS CO.

Made by Crescent for Fred Bifflar & Co., Chicago, Ill. See Crescent Fire Arms Co., Shotgun, Double Barrel, Side-by-Side; Shotgun, Single Shot.

ELGIN CUTLASS PISTOLS

Springfield, Mass. Made by C.B. Allen, and Merrill, Mossman & Blair. Blades made by Ames Sword Co. c. 1835. One of the more unusual oddities and among the most sought-after of rarities in arms collecting, the most desirable of Elgin Cutlass pistols were those made for U.S. Navy service on the Wilkes South Seas Expedition of 1838–42; some of these arms also made their way to the American West. Touted as the "Elgin patent Bowie knives with pistol attached will shoot and cut at the same time," the unusual pistol was protected by a patent of 1837. The naval design was made in a total of about 150, by C.B. Allen, Springfield, Massachusetts; and examples are known to have been sold in St. Louis in December 1838. The stylings by Merrill, Mossman & Blair and by Mossman & Blair, made in nearby Amherst, Massachusetts, had barrels of approximately 3 to 6 inches, and were chambered for .34 to .54 calibers.

HANDGUN, PERCUSSION

	Fair	V. Good	Excellent
Allen Small Frame, 35-41 Cal., 4"- 5" Octagonal Barrel and 7½" - 10" Blade, *Antique*	$4000	$5000	$6000
M.M.&B. Medium Frame, .31-36 Cal., 4" Round Barrel and 8¾" - 9½" Blade, *Antique*	3500	4500	5500
U.S. Navy Model (Allen), 54 Cal., 5" Octagonal Barrel and 11" Blade, *Antique*	8000	12500	15000

Elgin Cutlass Pistol, .54 Caliber

ELLIS, REUBEN

Albany, N.Y. 1808–1829.

RIFLE, FLINTLOCK

	Fair	V. Good	Excellent
Ellis-Jennings, .69, Sliding Lock for Multiple Loadings, 4 shot, *Antique*	10000	15000	20000
Ellis-Jennings, .69, Sliding Lock for Multiple Loadings, 10 shot, *Antique*	20000	25000	30000

E.M.F.

(Early and Modern Firearms Co., Inc.) Studio City, Calif.

HANDGUN, REVOLVER

	Fair	V. Good	Excellent
California Dragoon, .44 Magnum, Single Action, Western Style, Engraved, *Modern*	175	225	275
Dakota, Various Calibers, Single Action, Western Style, *Modern*	125	175	225
Dakota, Various Calibers, Single Action, Western Style, Engraved, *Modern*	175	250	325
Dakota, Various Calibers, Single Action, Western Style, Nickel Plated, *Modern*	125	200	275
Dakota, Various Calibers, Single Action, Western Style, Nickel Plated, Engraved, *Modern*	200	275	350
Dakota Buntline, Various Calibers, 12" Barrel, Single Action, Western Style, *Modern*	150	200	250
Dakota Buckhorn, Various Calibers, 16¼" Barrel, Single Action, Western Style, *Modern*	125	200	275
Dakota Buckhorn, Various Calibers, 16¼" Barrel, Single Action, Western Style, with Shoulder Stock, *Modern*	100	200	300
Dakota Sheriff, Various Calibers, Single Action, Western Style, *Modern*	175	225	275

	Fair	V. Good	Excellent
Super Dakota, Various Calibers, Single Action, Western Style, Magnum, *Modern*	$150	$225	$300
Outlaw 1875, Various Calibers, Single Action, Remington Style, Engraved, *Modern*	100	175	250
Outlaw 1875, Various Calibers, Single Action, Remington Style, Engraved, *Modern*	125	225	325
Thermodynamics, .357 Magnum, Solid Frame, Swing-out Cylinder, Vent Rib, Stainless Steel, *Modern*	75	150	225

HANDGUN, SINGLESHOT

	Fair	V. Good	Excellent
Baron, .22 Short R.F., Derringer, Gold Frame, Blue Barrel, Wood Grips, *Modern*	25	50	75
Baron, Count, Etc., Derringer, if Cased Add $10.00-$15.00			
Baroness, .22 Short R.F., Derringer, Gold Plated, Pearl Grips, *Modern*	25	50	75
Count, .22 Short R.F., Derringer, Blue, Wood Grips, *Modern*	12	25	50
Rolling Block, .357 Magnum, Remington Copy, *Modern*	50	100	150

RIFLE, LEVER ACTION

	Fair	V. Good	Excellent
1866 Yellowboy Carbine, Various Calibers, Brass Frame, Winchester Copy, *Modern*	300	375	450
1866 Yellowboy Carbine, Various Calibers, Brass Frame, Winchester Copy, Engraved, *Modern*	300	450	600
1873 Carbine, Various Calibers, Winchester Copy, *Modern*	300	375	450
1873 Rifle, Various Calibers, Winchester Copy, *Modern*	400	500	600
1873 Rifle, Various Calibers, Winchester Copy, Engraved, *Modern*	250	450	650

EM-GE

Gerstenberger & Eberwein, Gussenstadt, Germany.

HANDGUN, REVOLVER

	Fair	V. Good	Excellent
Model 220 KS, .22 L.R.R.F., Double Action, *Modern*	25	50	75
Model 223, .22 W.M.R., Double Action, *Modern*	25	50	75
Target Model 200, .22 L.R.R.F., Double Action, Target Sights, Vent Rib, *Modern*	50	75	100

EMPIRE

Made by Jacob Rupertus 1858-1888.

HANDGUN, REVOLVER

	Fair	V. Good	Excellent
.22 Short R.F., 7 Shot, Spur Trigger, Solid Frame, Single Action, *Antique*	50	100	175
.38 Short R.F., 5 Shot, Spur Trigger, Solid Frame, Single Action, *Antique*	$100	$150	$200
.41 Short R.F., 5 Shot, Spur Trigger, Solid Frame, Single Action, *Antique*	125	175	225

EMPIRE ARMS

Made by Meriden and distributed by H. & D. Folsom.

HANDGUN, REVOLVER

	Fair	V. Good	Excellent
.32 S & W, 5 Shot, Double Action, Top Break, *Modern*	35	75	125
.38 S & W, 5 Shot, Double Action, Top Break, *Modern*	35	75	125

EMPIRE ARMS CO.

Made by Crescent for Sears, Roebuck & Co., c. 1900. See Crescent Fire Arms Co., Shotgun, Double Barrel, Side-By-Side; Shotgun, Singleshot.

EMPIRE STATE

Made by Meriden Firearms, and distributed by H & D Folsom.

HANDGUN, REVOLVER

	Fair	V. Good	Excellent
.32 S & W, 5 Shot, Double Action, Top Break, *Modern*	50	75	100
.38 S & W, 5 Shot, Double Action, Top Break, *Modern*	50	75	100

EMPRESS

Made by Jacob Rupertus 1858–1888.

HANDGUN, REVOLVER

	Fair	V. Good	Excellent
.32 Short R.F., 5 Shot, Spur Trigger, Solid Frame, Single Action, *Antique*	100	125	150

ENCORE

Made by Johnson-Bye, also by Hopkins & Allen 1847–1887.

HANDGUN, REVOLVER

	Fair	V. Good	Excellent
.22 Short R.F., 7 Shot, Spur Trigger, Solid Frame, Single Action, *Antique*	50	100	150
.32 Short R.F., 5 Shot, Spur Trigger, Solid Frame, Single Action, *Antique*	75	125	175
.38 R.F., 5 Shot, Spur Trigger, Solid Frame, Single Action, *Antique*	100	150	200

ENDERS OAKLEAF

Made by Crescent for Shapleigh Hardware Co., St. Louis, Mo. See Crescent Fire Arms Co., Shotgun, Double Barrel, Side-By-Side; Shotgun, Singleshot.

ENTERPRISE

Made by Enterprise Gun Works, Pittsburgh, Pa., c. 1875.

HANDGUN, REVOLVER

	Fair	V. Good	Excellent
#1, .22 Short R.F., 7 Shot, Spur Trigger, Solid Frame, Single Action, *Antique*	$75	$125	$175
#2, .32 Short R.F., 5 Shot, Spur Trigger, Solid Frame, Single Action, *Antique*	100	150	200
#3, .38 Short R.F., 5 Shot, Spur Trigger, Solid Frame, Single Action, *Antique*	125	175	225
#4, .41 Short R.F., 5 Shot, Spur Trigger, Solid Frame, Single Action, *Antique*	150	200	250

ERBI

SHOTGUN, DOUBLE BARREL, SIDE-BY-SIDE

	Fair	V. Good	Excellent
Deluxe Ejector Grade, 12 and 20 Gauge, Raised Matted Rib, Double Trigger, Checkered Stock, Beavertail Fore End, Automatic Ejector, *Modern*	100	175	250
Field Grade, 12 and 20 Gauge, Raised Matted Rib, Double Trigger, Checkered Stock, *Modern*	100	150	200

ERIKA

Francios Pfannl, Krems, Austria 1913–1926.

HANDGUN, SEMI-AUTOMATIC

	Fair	V. Good	Excellent
4.25mm, Clip Fed, Blue, *Curio*	250	450	650

ERMA

Erfurter Maschinen u. Werkzeugfabrik, Erfurt, Germany, prior to WWII, and after the war became Erma-Werke, Munich-Dachau, West Germany. Imported by Excam, Miami, Fla.

HANDGUN, REVOLVER

	Fair	V. Good	Excellent
Model 440, .38 Spec., Double Action, Swing-Out Cylinder, Stainless, *Modern*	100	175	225
Model 442, .22 L.R.R.F., Double Action, Swing-Out Cylinder, Blue, *Modern*	75	125	175
Model 443, .22 W.M.R., Double Action, Swing-Out Cylinder, Blue, *Modern*	75	125	175

HANDGUN, SEMI-AUTOMATIC

	Fair	V. Good	Excellent
EP-22, .22 L.R.R.F., Clip Fed, *Modern*	75	150	275
EP-25, .25 ACP, Clip Fed, *Modern*	100	175	250
ET-22 Luger, .22 L.R.R.F., Clip Fed, *Modern*	200	275	350
ET-22 Luger, .22 L.R.R.F., Clip Fed, with Conversion Kit, Cased with Accessories, *Modern*	$275	$350	$425
FB-1, .25 ACP, Clip Fed, *Modern*	35	75	125
KGP-68 (Baby), .32 ACP, Clip Fed, *Modern*	175	250	325
KGP-68 (Baby), .380 ACP, Clip Fed, *Modern*	200	275	350
KGP-69, .22 L.R.R.F., Clip Fed, *Modern*	200	275	350
LA-22 PO 8, .22 L.R.R.F., Clip Fed, *Modern*	125	200	275
New Model Target, .22 L.R.R.F., Clip Fed, *Modern*	225	250	275
Old Model Target, .22 L.R.R.F., Clip Fed, *Modern*	200	225	250
RX-22, .22 L.R.R.F., Double Action, Clip Fed, *Modern*	150	175	200

RIFLE, BOLT ACTION

	Fair	V. Good	Excellent
EG-61, .22 L.R.R.F., Singleshot, Open Sights, *Modern*	50	75	100
M1957 KK, .22 L.R.R.F., Military Style Training Rifle, *Modern*	50	75	100
M98 Conversation Unit, .22 L.R.R.F., Clip Fed, Cased, *Modern*	175	250	325
Master Target, .22 L.R.R.F., Checkered Stock, Peep Sights, *Modern*	75	125	175

RIFLE, LEVER ACTION

	Fair	V. Good	Excellent
EG-71, .22 L.R.R.F., Tube Feed, *Modern*	50	100	150
EG-712, .22 L.R.R.F., Tube Feed, *Modern*	75	125	175
EG-712 L, .22 L.R.R.F., Tube Feed, Octagon Barrel, Nickel Silver Receiver, *Modern*	125	200	275
EG-73, .22 W.M.R., Tube Feed, *Modern*	100	150	200

RIFLE, SEMI-AUTOMATIC

	Fair	V. Good	Excellent
EGM-1, .22 L.R.R.F., Clip Fed, *Modern*	100	125	150
EM-1, .22 L.R.R.F., Clip Fed, *Modern*	100	125	150
ESG22, .22 L.R.R.F., Clip Fed, *Modern*	100	125	150
ESG22, .22 W.M.R., Clip Fed, *Modern*	100	175	250

ESSEX

Made by Crescent for Belknap Hardware Co. Louisville, Ky. See Crescent Fire Arms Co., Shotgun, Double Barrel, Side-by-Side; Shotgun, Single Shot.

ESSEX

Made by Stevens Arms.

	Fair	V. Good	Excellent
RIFLE, BOLT ACTION			
Model 50, .22 L.R.R.F., Singleshot, Takedown, *Modern*	$12	$25	$50
Model 53, .22 L.R.R.F., Singleshot, Takedown, *Modern*	12	25	50
Model 56 Buckhorn, .22 L.R.R.F., 5 Shot Clip, Open Rear Sights, *Modern*	12	25	50
SHOTGUN, DOUBLE BARREL, SIDE-BY-SIDE			
Model 515, Various Gauges, Hammerless, *Modern*	50	100	150

ESSEX

Makers of pistol frames in Island Pond, Vt.

	Fair	V. Good	Excellent
HANDGUN, SEMI-AUTOMATIC			
Colt M1911 Copy, .45 ACP, Parts Gun, *Modern*	125	200	275

ESTEVA, PEDRO

Spain, c. 1740.

	Fair	V. Good	Excellent
HANDGUN, FLINTLOCK			
Pair, Belt Pistol, Silver Inlay, Silver Furniture, Engraved, Half-Octagon Barrel, *Antique*	4000	7500	9000

EVANS RIFLE MFG. CO.

Mechanics Falls, Maine, 1868–1880. Not known particularly for its grace and beauty, nevertheless the Evans lever-action repeating magazine rifle was one of the most intriguing of designs from the second half of the 19th century. With a spiral magazine design, a total of 28 or 34 cartridges could be inserted in the rifle loading port (located in the butt), allowing the shooter a substantial supply of ammunition—far more than conventional Winchesters. Despite the mechanical innovations, the Evans production had the distinct disadvantage of exceptional weight, and poor, butt-heavy balance. Among celebrity owners of Evans rifles were W. F. "Buffalo Bill" Cody and Mexican President and keen arms collector Porfirio Diaz. At present Cody's Evans, a gift from the factory, is on display at the Cody Firearms Museum, and perhaps the most exquisitely engraved specimen known is at the Royal Military College Museum, Kingston, Ontario. The L.D. Nimschke engraving record illustrates some handsome designs developed by L.D.N. and engraved on a few specimens.

	Fair	V. Good	Excellent
RIFLE, LEVER ACTION			
New Model, .44 C.F., Tube Feed, Dust Cover, Carbine, *Antique*	375	750	1200
New Model, .44 C.F., Tube Feed, Dust Cover, Military Musket, *Antique*	500	1000	1500
New Model, .44 C.F., Tube Feed, Dust Cover, Sporting Rifle, *Antique*	325	650	1000
Old Model, .44 C.F., Upper Buttstock Only, Tube Feed, Sporting Rifle, *Antique*	500	1000	1500

Two Spencer lever-action breechloading carbines, the top *an early .52 rimfire example, and the* center *an example in .50 caliber, the Model 1865, by Burnside Rifle Co., sometimes known as "The Indian Model."* At bottom, *an Evans lever-action carbine in .44 caliber, made at Mechanics Falls, Maine; capacity of 26 cartridges.*

EVANS, STEPHEN

Valley Forge, Pa. 1742–1797. See Kentucky Rifles and U.S. Military.

EVANS, WILLIAMS

London, England 1883–1900.

	Fair	V. Good	Excellent
SHOTGUN, DOUBLE BARREL, SIDE-BY-SIDE			
Pair, 12 Gauge, Double Trigger, Plain, Cased, *Modern*	$2500	$5000	$7500
Pair, 12 Gauge, Double Trigger, Straight Grip, Cased, *Modern*	4000	6000	8000

EXCAM

Importers, Hialeah, Fla. Also see Erma and Tanarmi.

	Fair	V. Good	Excellent
HANDGUN, DOUBLE BARREL, OVER-UNDER			
TA-38, .38 Special, 2 Shot, Derringer, *Modern*	65	75	85
HANDGUN, REVOLVER			
Buffalo Scout TA-22, .22 L.R.R.F., Western Style, Single Action, Brass Backstrap, *Modern*	55	65	75
Buffalo Scout TA-22, .22 LR/.22 WMR Combo, Western Style, Single Action, Brass Backstrap, *Modern*	70	85	100
Buffalo Scout TA-22, .22 LR/.22 WMR Combo, Western Style, Single Action, Brass Backstrap, Target Sights, *Modern*	60	80	100
Buffalo Scout TA-76, .22 L.R.R.F., Western Style, Single Action, *Modern*	55	70	85

	Fair	V. Good	Excellent
Buffalo Scout TA-76, .22 LR/.22 WMR Combo, Western Style, Single Action, *Modern*	$55	$70	$85
Warrior, .22 L.R.R.F., Double Action, Blue, Vent Rib, *Modern*	25	50	75
Warrior, .22 LR/.22 WMR Combo, Double Action, Blue, Vent Rib, *Modern*	75	100	125
Warrior, .357 Magnum, Double Action, Blue, Vent Rib, Target Sights, *Modern*	50	100	150
Warrior, .38 Spec., Double Action, Blue, Vent Rib, Target Sights, *Modern*	50	75	100

HANDGUN, SEMI-AUTOMATIC

	Fair	V. Good	Excellent
GT-22, .22 L.R.R.F., Clip Fed, *Modern*	35	75	150
GT-26, .25 ACP, Clip Fed, Steel Frame, *Modern*	12	25	50
GT-27, .25 ACP, Clip Fed, *Modern*	12	25	50
GT-27, .25 ACP, Clip Fed, Steel Frame, *Modern*	25	50	75
GT-32, .32 ACP, Clip Fed, *Modern*	100	125	150
GT-32, .32 ACP, Clip Fed, 12 Shot, *Modern*	100	125	150
GT-380, .25 ACP, Clip Fed, Engraved, *Modern*	100	125	150
GT-380, .380 ACP, Clip Fed, *Modern*	75	100	125
GT-380, .380 ACP, Clip Fed, 11 Short, *Modern*	$100	$125	$150
RX-22, .22 L.R.R.F., Clip Fed, *Modern*	75	100	125

EXCELSIOR

Made by Norwich Pistol Co., c. 1880.

HANDGUN, REVOLVER

	Fair	V. Good	Excellent
.32 Short R.F., 5 Shot, Spur Trigger, Solid Frame, Single Action, *Antique*	75	125	175

EXCELSIOR

Made in Italy.

SHOTGUN, DOUBLE BARREL, SIDE-BY-SIDE

	Fair	V. Good	Excellent
Super 88, 12 Ga. Mag 3", Boxlock, Checkered Stock, *Modern*	200	275	350

EXPRESS

Made by Bacon Arms Co., c. 1880.

HANDGUN, REVOLVER

	Fair	V. Good	Excellent
.22 Short R.F., 7 Shot, Spur Trigger, Solid Frame, Single Action, *Antique*	75	125	175

F

F.I.E.

Firearms Import & Export Corp., Miami, Fla.

HANDGUN, DOUBLE BARREL, OVER-UNDER

	Fair	V. Good	Excellent
D 38, .38 Special, Derringer, *Modern*	$35	$50	$65
D 86, .38 Special, Derringer, *Modern*	55	70	85

HANDGUN, FLINTLOCK

	Fair	V. Good	Excellent
Kentucky, .44, Belt Pistol, Engraved, Reproduction	12	25	50
Kentucky, .44, Belt Pistol, Reproduction	12	25	50
Tower, .69	25	25	25

HANDGUN, PERCUSSION

	Fair	V. Good	Excellent
Baby Dragoon, .31, Revolver, Engraved, Reproduction	12	25	50
Baby Dragoon, .31, Revolver, Reproduction	12	25	50
Kentucky, .44, Belt Pistol, Engraved, Reproduction	12	25	50
Kentucky, .44, Belt Pistol, Reproduction	12	25	50
Navy, .36, Revolver, Engraved, Reproduction	12	25	50
Navy, .36, Revolver, Reproduction.	25	25	25
Navy, .44, Revolver, Engraved, Reproduction	12	25	50
Navy, .44, Revolver, Reproduction	12	25	50
Remington, .36, Revolver, Engraved, Reproduction	12	25	50
Remington, .36, Revolver, Reproduction	12	25	50
Remington, .44, Revolver, Engraved, Reproduction	12	25	50
Remington, .44, Revolver, Reproduction	12	25	50

HANDGUN, REVOLVER

	Fair	V. Good	Excellent
Arminius, .22 L.R.R.F., Double Action, Swing-out Cylinder, Fixed Sights, Chrome, *Modern*	50	75	100
Arminius, .22 L.R.R.F., Double Action, Swing-out Cylinder, Adjustable Sights, Blue, *Modern*	25	50	75
Arminius, .22 L.R.R.F., Double Action, Swing-out Cylinder, Adjustable Sights, Chrome, *Modern*	50	75	100
Arminius, .22 L.R.R.F., Double Action, Swing-out Cylinder, Adjustable Sights, Blue, Target, *Modern*	$50	$75	$100
Arminius, .22 L.R.R.F., Double Action, Swing-out Cylinder, Adjustable Sights, Chrome, Target, *Modern*	50	75	100
Arminius, .22 LR/.22 WMR Combo, Double Action, Swing-out Cylinder, Fixed Sights, Chrome, *Modern*	50	75	100
Arminius, .22 LR/.22 WMR Combo, Double Action, Swing-out Cylinder, Adjustable Sights, Chrome, *Modern*	50	75	100
Arminius, .22 LR/.22 WMR Combo, Double Action, Swing-out Cylinder, Adjustable Sights, Blue, *Modern*	50	75	100
Arminius, .22 LR/.22 WMR Combo, Double Action, Swing-out Cylinder, Adjustable Sights, Blue, Target, *Modern*	25	50	75
Arminius, .32 S & W, Double Action, Swing-out Cylinder, Adjustable Sights, Blue, Target, *Modern*	50	75	100
Arminius, .32 S & W, Double Action, Swing-out Cylinder, Adjustable Sights, Chrome, Target, *Modern*	50	75	100
Arminius, .357 Magnum, Double Action, Swing-out Cylinder, Adjustable Sights, Chrome, Target, *Modern*	75	100	125
Arminius, .357 Magnum, Double Action, Swing-out Cylinder, Adjustable Sights, Blue, Target, *Modern*	75	100	125
Arminius, .38 Special, Double Action, Swing-out Cylinder, Adjustable Sights, Blue, Target, *Modern*	50	75	100
Arminius, .38 Special, Double Action, Swing-out Cylinder, Adjustable Sights, Chrome, Target, *Modern*	50	75	100
Arminius, .38 Special, Double Action, Swing-out Cylinder, Blue, *Modern*	25	50	75
Arminius, .38 Special, Double Action, Swing-out Cylinder, Chrome, *Modern*	25	50	75
Buffalo Scout, .22LR/.22 WMR Combo, Single Action, Western Style, *Modern*	55	65	75
Buffalo, .22 L.R.R.F., Single Action, Western Style, ., *Modern*	12	25	50
Guardian, .22 L.R.R.F., Double Action, Swing-out Cylinder, *Modern*	12	25	50
Guardian, .22 L.R.R.F., Double Action, Swing-out Cylinder, Chrome, *Modern*	12	25	50

	Fair	V. Good	Excellent
Guardian, .32 S & W, Double Action, Swing-out Cylinder, *Modern*	$12	$25	$50
Guardian, .32 S & W, Double Action, Swing-out Cylinder, Chrome, *Modern*	12	25	50
Hombre, .357 Magnum, Single Action, Western Style, Steel Frame, *Modern*	100	150	200
Hombre, .44 Mag, Single Action, Western Style, Steel Frame, *Modern*	100	150	200
Hombre, .45 L.C., Single Action, Western Style, Steel Frame, *Modern*	100	150	200
Legend, .22 L.R.R.F., Single Action, Western Style, Steel Frame, *Modern*	70	85	100
Legend, .22LR/.22 WMR Combo, Single Action, Western Style, Steel Frame, *Modern*	70	85	100
Texas Ranger, .22LR/.22 WMR Combo, Single Action, Western Style, Steel Frame, *Modern*	55	65	75

HANDGUN, SEMI-AUTOMATIC

	Fair	V. Good	Excellent
Best, .25 ACP, Hammer, Steel Frame, Blue, *Modern*	50	75	100
Guardian, .25 ACP, Hammer, Blue, *Modern*	12	25	50
Guardian, .25 ACP, Hammer, Chrome, *Modern*	12	25	50
Guardian, .25 ACP, Hammer, Gold Plated, *Modern*	12	25	50
Interdynamics KG-9, 9mm Luger, Clip Fed, *Modern*	300	325	350
Interdynamics Mini-99, 9mm Luger, Clip Fed, *Modern*	175	200	225
Super Titan II, .32 ACP, Hammer, Steel Frame, Blue, 13 Shot, *Modern*	75	100	125
Super Titan II, .380 ACP, Hammer, Steel Frame, Blue, 12 Shot, *Modern*	100	125	150
Titan, .25 ACP, Hammer, Blue, *Modern*	12	25	50
Titan, .25 ACP, Hammer, Chrome, *Modern*	12	25	50
Titan, .32 ACP, Hammer, Steel Frame, Blue, *Modern*	50	75	100
Titan, .32 ACP, Hammer, Steel Frame, Chrome, *Modern*	50	75	100
Titan, .32 ACP, Hammer, Steel Frame, Engraved, Blue, *Modern*	50	75	100
Titan, .32 ACP, Hammer, Steel Frame, Engraved, Chrome, *Modern*	50	75	100
Titan, .380 ACP, Hammer, Steel Frame, Blue, *Modern*	50	75	100
Titan, .380 ACP, Hammer, Steel Frame, Chrome, *Modern*	75	100	125
Titan, .380 ACP, Hammer, Steel Frame, Engraved, Blue, *Modern*	100	125	150
Titan, .380 ACP, Hammer, Steel Frame, Engraved, Chrome, *Modern*	100	125	150
TZ-75, 9mm. Luger, Clip Fed, Double Action, Hammer, Adjustable Sights, Wood Grips, *Modern*	$200	$225	$250

RIFLE, FLINTLOCK

	Fair	V. Good	Excellent
Kentucky, .45, Engraved, Reproduction	25	50	75
Kentucky, .45, Reproduction	25	50	75

RIFLE, PERCUSSION

	Fair	V. Good	Excellent
Berdan, .45, Reproduction	25	50	75
Kentucky, .45, Engraved, Reproduction, *Antique*	25	50	75
Kentucky, .45, Reproduction, *Antique*	25	50	75
Zoave, .58, Reproduction, *Antique*	50	75	100

COMBINATION WEAPON, OVER-UNDER

	Fair	V. Good	Excellent
Combo, 30/30-20 Ga., *Modern*	50	75	100

SHOTGUN, DOUBLE BARREL, OVER-UNDER

	Fair	V. Good	Excellent
OU, 12 and 20 Ga., Field Grade, Vent Rib, *Modern*	125	150	175
OU 12 T, 12 Ga., Trap Grade, Vent Rib, *Modern*	125	150	175
OU-S, 12 and 20 Ga., Skeet Grade, Vent Rib, *Modern*	125	150	175

SHOTGUN, DOUBLE BARREL, SIDE-BY-SIDE

	Fair	V. Good	Excellent
Brute, Various Gauges, Short Barrels, Short Stock, *Modern*	50	100	175
DB, Various Gauges, Hammerless, *Modern*	35	75	125
DB Riot, Various Gauges, Hammerless, *Modern*	35	75	150

SHOTGUN, SINGLESHOT

	Fair	V. Good	Excellent
S.O.B., 12 and 20 Gauges, Short Barrel, Short Stock, *Modern*	12	25	50
SB 12 16 20.410, Various Gauges, Hammer, *Modern*	12	25	50
SB 40, 12 Ga., Hammer, Button Break, *Modern*	12	25	50
SB 41, 20 Ga., Hammer, Button Break, *Modern*	12	25	50
SB 42, .410 Ga., Hammer, Button Break, *Modern*	12	25	50
SB Youth, Various Gauges, Hammer, *Modern*	12	25	50

FABRIQUE D'ARMES DE GUERRE

Spain, c. 1900.

HANDGUN, SEMI-AUTOMATIC

	Fair	V. Good	Excellent
Paramount, .25 ACP, Clip Fed, *Modern*	100	125	150

FABRIQUE D'ARMES DE GUERRE DE GRAND

HANDGUN, SEMI-AUTOMATIC

	Fair	V. Good	Excellent
Bulwak, .25 ACP, Clip Fed, *Modern*	$100	$125	$150
Colonial, .25 ACP, Clip Fed, *Modern*	125	150	175
Colonial, .32 ACP, Clip Fed, *Modern*	150	175	200
Helvece, .25 ACP, Clip Fed, *Modern*	100	125	150
Jupiter, .32 ACP, Clip Fed, *Modern*	100	125	150
Libia, .32 ACP, Clip Fed, *Modern*	125	150	175
Looking Glass, .32 ACP, Clip Fed, *Modern*	125	150	175
Looking Glass, .32 ACP, Clip Fed, Grip Safety, *Modern*	150	175	200
Trust, .25 ACP, Clip Fed, *Modern*	100	125	150

FABRIQUE NATIONALE

Herstal, Belgium from 1889. Also see Browning and Belgian Military. One of Europe's most historic gunmakers, FN was given a boost in its product line by the willingness of John M. Browning to license the firm to manufacture shotguns, handguns and other arms of his invention. In 1967 the author was on a firearms tour of Europe, and through his friend, arms engraver Rene Delcour, was given a tour of the FN workshops. The enormity of the firm was truly impressive and the engraving studio alone then employed over 125 artisans in the FN section, and about 50 in the Browning Arms Co. studio. There was some consternation at the time, since management had entered into arrangements of having production of some products done in Japan. Employees in Herstal saw the demise of their national operations, due to the less expensive, but high quality Japanese work. Some workmen from Belgium were actually chastised for going to Japan to teach the new machinists. Alas, the concerns of the Belgian workers were well founded. Today FN is much smaller than in those days—the bulk of the engraving is now executed by a consortium of craftsmen; that substantial studio no longer exists. John Browning became a national hero in Belgium, and was responsible for the employment of literally thousands of workmen over the years. It was, in fact, in Belgium, in 1926, while working at the FN factory on a new project, where the brilliant inventor and designer died.

RIFLE, BOLT ACTION

	Fair	V. Good	Excellent
Mauser 98 Military Style, 30/06, Military Finish, Military Stock, Commercial, *Modern*	150	200	250
Mauser 98 Military Style, Various Military Calibers, Military Finish, Military Stock, Commercial, *Modern*	100	125	150
Mauser Deluxe Presentation, Various Calibers, Sporting Rifle, Fancy Wood, Engraved, *Modern*	500	850	1000
Mauser Deluxe, Various Calibers, Sporting Rifle, Checkered Stock, Engraved, *Modern*	300	525	600
Mauser Supreme, Various Calibers, Sporting Rifle, Checkered Stock, *Modern*	$300	$500	$575
Mauser Supreme, Various Calibers, Sporting Rifle, Checkered Stock, Magnum, *Modern*	300	575	650
Model 1925 Deluxe, .22 L.R.R.F., Singleshot, Checkered Stock, *Modern*	50	75	100
Model 1925, .22 L.R.R.F., Singleshot, *Modern*	25	50	75

RIFLE, SEMI-AUTOMATIC

	Fair	V. Good	Excellent
FN FAL, .308 Win., Clip Fed, Commercial, *Modern*	400	750	950
FN LAR Competition, .308 Win., Clip Fed, Commercial, Flash Hider, *Modern*	700	1400	1650
FN LAR Heavy Barrel, .308 Win., Clip Fed, Commercial, Synthetic Stock, Bipod, *Modern*	800	1650	1850
FN LAR Heavy Barrel, .308 Win., Clip Fed, Commercial, Wood Stock, Bipod, *Modern*	800	1750	2000
FN LAR Paratrooper, .308 Win., Clip Fed, Commercial, Folding Stock, *Modern*	500	800	950
FNC Competition, .223 Rem., Clip Fed, Commercial, Flash Hider, *Modern*	500	850	1000
FNC Paratrooper, .223 Rem., Clip Fed, Commercial, Folding Stock, *Modern*	600	1000	1150
M-49 Egyptian, 8mm Mauser, Clip Fed, Military, *Modern*	200	275	325
Model 1949, 30/06, Clip Fed, Military, *Modern*	250	350	400
Model 1949, 7mm or 9mm Mauser, Clip Fed, Military, *Modern*	200	275	325

SHOTGUN, BOLT ACTION

	Fair	V. Good	Excellent
9mm Shotshell, *Modern*	100	125	150

FALCON FIREARMS

Northridge, Calif.

HANDGUN, SEMI-AUTOMATIC

	Fair	V. Good	Excellent
Portsider, .45 ACP, Clip Fed, Stainless Steel, *Modern*	250	400	475

FAMARS

Gardone, Val Trompia, Italy. The joint creation of Mario Abbiatico and Remo Salvinelli, Famars rapidly built an international reputation as one of Europe's finest gunmakers. When the author first visited the firm's factory, in the early 1970s, it was a relatively small operation, along a quiet street in Gardone, Val Trompia. In the 1980s the company built an impressive, modern structure along the main highway through Gardone. This new building has more than ample space, with the most modern equipment in a comfortable production complex, with a handsome showroom and offices.

	Fair	V. Good	Excellent

Abbiatico's books on fine guns were instantly popular, and alerted the world to the extraordinary work carried on in Val Trompia, not only by Famars, but by such companies as Fabbri, Rizzini, Piotti, and of course Beretta. Many would argue that considering price and quality, performance and reliability, the Italian best quality shotgun is as good as, if not better than, any made anywhere in the world today.

SHOTGUN, DOUBLE BARREL, SIDE-BY-SIDE

	Fair	V. Good	Excellent
Hammer Gun, Various Gauges, Automatic Ejector, Fancy Wood, Fancy Engraving, Double Trigger, *Modern*	$4500	$7000	$7750
Sidelock Gun, Various Gauges, Automatic Ejector, Double Trigger, Fancy Engraving, Fancy Wood, *Modern*	5000	9000	10500

FARNOT, FRANK

Lancaster, Pa. 1779–1783. See Kentucky Rifles and Pistols.

FARNOT, FREDERICK

Lancaster, Pa. 1779–1782. See Kentucky Rifles and Pistols.

FARROW ARMS CO.

Holyoke, Mass. Established by William Farrow 1878–1885. Became Farrow Arms Co. about 1885 and moved to Mason, Tenn. in 1904, then to Washington, D.C., in 1904 and remained in business until 1917.

RIFLE, SINGLESHOT

	Fair	V. Good	Excellent
#1, .30 Long R.F., Target Rifle, Octagon Barrel, Target Sights, Fancy Wood, *Antique*	3000	4000	4500
#2, .30 Long R.F., Target Rifle, Octagon Barrel, Target Sights, *Antique*	2000	3000	3500

FAST

Echave, Arizmendi y Cia, Eibar, Spain.

HANDGUN, SEMI-AUTOMATIC

	Fair	V. Good	Excellent
Model 221, .22 L.R.R.F., Clip Fed, Blue, *Modern*	45	95	150
Model 221, .22 L.R.R.F., Clip Fed, Chrome, *Modern*	125	150	175
Model 631, .25 ACP, Clip Fed, Blue, *Modern*	100	125	150
Model 631, .25 ACP, Clip Fed, Chrome, *Modern*	100	125	150
Model 761, .32 ACP, Clip Fed, Blue, *Modern*	125	150	175
Model 761, .32 ACP, Clip Fed, Chrome, *Modern*	125	150	175
Model 901, .380 ACP, Clip Fed, Blue, *Modern*	125	150	175
Model 901, .380 ACP, Clip Fed, Chrome, *Modern*	$125	$150	$175

FAULTLESS GOOSE GUN

Made by Crescent for John M. Smythe Hdw. Co., Chicago, Ill. See Crescent Fire Arms Co., Shotgun, Double Barrel, Side-by-Side; Shotgun, Singleshot.

FAVORITE

Made by Johnson-Bye Co., c. 1874–1884.

HANDGUN, REVOLVER

	Fair	V. Good	Excellent
#1, .22 Short R.F., 7 Shot, Spur Trigger, Solid Frame, Single Action, *Antique*	75	125	175
#2, .32 Short R.F., 5 Shot, Spur Trigger, Solid Frame, Single Action, *Antique*	75	125	175
#3, .38 Short R.F., 5 Shot, Spur Trigger, Solid Frame, Single Action, *Antique*	100	150	200
#4, .41 Short R.F., 5 Shot, Spur Trigger, Solid Frame, Single Action, *Antique*	125	175	225

FAVORITE NAVY

Made by Johnson-Bye Co., c. 1874–1884.

HANDGUN, REVOLVER

	Fair	V. Good	Excellent
.44 Short R.F., 5 Shot, Spur Trigger, Solid Frame, Single Action, *Antique*	200	250	300

FAY, HENRY C.

Lancaster, Mass., c. 1837.

RIFLE, PERCUSSION

	Fair	V. Good	Excellent
.58, Military, *Antique*	2000	2750	3500

FECHT, G. VAN DER

Berlin, Germany, c. 1733.

RIFLE, FLINTLOCK

	Fair	V. Good	Excellent
Yaeger, Half-Octagon Barrel, Brass Furniture, Engraved, Carved, *Antique*	4000	4500	5000

FEDERAL ARMS

Made by Meriden Firearms, sold by Sears-Roebuck.

HANDGUN, REVOLVER

	Fair	V. Good	Excellent
.32 S & W, 5 Shot, Double Action, Top Break, *Modern*	50	75	100
.38 S & W, 5 Shot, Double Action, Top Break, *Modern*	50	75	100

FEMARU

Made by Femaru Fegyver es Gepgyar (Fegyvergyar) Pre-War; Post-War Made by Femaru es Szerszamgepgyar, N.V., Budapest, Hungary. Also see Frommer, Hungarian Military.

HANDGUN, SEMI-AUTOMATIC

	Fair	V. Good	Excellent
M 29, .380 ACP, Clip Fed, Military, *Curio*	$125	$175	$225
M 37, .32 ACP, Clip Fed, Nazi-Proofed, *Modern*	150	200	250
M 37, .380 ACP, Clip Fed, Military, *Modern*	150	200	250
M 37, .380 ACP, Clip Fed, Nazi-Proofed, *Modern*	175	225	275

FENNO

Lancaster Pa. 1790–1800. See Kentucky Rifles and Pistols.

FERLACH

Genossenschaft der Buchsenmachermeister, Ferlach, Austria. One of the world's great gun centers, like Val Trompia in Italy, Ferlach is in a remote part of Austria, and is only reachable by car. The author visited this small city in 1972, and was quite overwhelmed by the quality of workmanship, and the number of dedicated craftsmen and gunmakers. A visit to the gunmaking school demonstrated that the future of fine gunmaking in Ferlach was assured. In the intervening years, a magnificent book was published on German and Austrian gun engravers, and the style of Ferlach guns has undergone a significant transformation. Fine makers like Peter Hofer, Wilfried Glanzning, Ludwig Borovnik and Schiering have built some of the most exquisite arms of all time. The style and ingenuity of the work of some makers reveals not only mechanical wizardry, but the artistic influence of British and Italian gunmakers. As a result, not all Ferlach arms have that old strongly Germanic look. One of the most appealing aspects of contemporary gunmaking is that the creations of the best of these craftsmen rival the work of the finest gunmakers in history. In the exalted realm of the world's greatest gunmakers, the Ferlach masters play a significant role.

RIFLE, DOUBLE BARREL, SIDE-BY-SIDE

	Fair	V. Good	Excellent
Standard Grade, Various Calibers, Boxlock, Engraved, Checkered Stock, Fancy Wood, *Modern*	2000	3000	3500
Standard Grade, Various Calibers, Sidelock, Engraved, Checkered Stock, Fancy Wood, *Modern*	3000	4500	5000

FERREE, JACOB

Lancaster, Pa. 1774–1784. See Kentucky Rifles and U.S. Military.

FESIG, CONRAD

Reading, Pa. 1779–1790. See Kentucky Rifles and Pistols.

FIALA

Made for Fiala Arms & Equipment Co. by Blakslee Forging Co., New Haven, Conn.

HANDGUN, MANUAL REPEATER

	Fair	V. Good	Excellent
.22 L.R.R.F., Clip Fed, Target Pistol, *Curio*	$350	$400	$450
.22 L.R.R.F., Clip Fed, Target Pistol, with Shoulder Stock, 20" Barrel, 3" Barrel, Cased, *Curio*	600	1000	1150

FIEHL & WEEKS FIRE ARMS MFG. CO.

Philadelphia, Pa., c. 1895.

HANDGUN, REVOLVER

	Fair	V. Good	Excellent
.32 S & W, 5 Shot, Top Break, Hammerless, Double Action, *Modern*	50	75	100

FIEL

Erquiaga, Muguruzu y Cia., Eibar, Spain, c., 1920.

HANDGUN, SEMI-AUTOMATIC

	Fair	V. Good	Excellent
Fiel #1, .25 ACP, Clip Fed, Eibar Style, *Curio*	100	125	150
Fiel #1, .32 ACP, Clip Fed, Eibar Style, *Curio*	100	125	150
Fiel #2, .25 ACP, Clip Fed, Breech Bolt, *Curio*	125	175	225

FIGTHORN, ANDREW

Reading, Pa. 1779–1790. See Kentucky Rifles.

FINNISH LION

Made by Valmet, Jyvaskyla, Finland.

RIFLE, BOLT ACTION

	Fair	V. Good	Excellent
Champion, .22 L.R.R.F., Singleshot, Free Rifle, Thumbhole Stock, Target Sights, Heavy Barrel, *Modern*	400	450	500
Match, .22 L.R.R.F., Singleshot, Target Rifle, Thumbhole Stock, Target Sights, *Modern*	250	350	400
Standard, .22 L.R.R.F., Singleshot, Target Rifle, Target Stock, Target Sights, U.I.T. Rifle, *Modern*	175	225	275

FIREARMS CO. LTD.

Made in England for Mandall Shooting Supplies.

RIFLE, BOLT ACTION

	Fair	V. Good	Excellent
Alpine Custom, Various Calibers, Checkered Stock, Recoil Pad, Open Rear Sight, *Modern*	200	275	325

	Fair	V. Good	Excellent
Alpine Standard, Various Calibers, Checkered Stock, Recoil Pad, Open Rear Sight, *Modern*	$200	$250	$300

FIREARMS INTERNATIONAL

Washington, D.C.

HANDGUN, REVOLVER

	Fair	V. Good	Excellent
Regent, .22 L.R.R.F., 7 Shot, Various Barrel Lengths, Blue, *Modern*	50	75	100
Regent, .22 L.R.R.F., 8 Shot, Various Barrel Lengths, Blue, *Modern*	50	75	100

HANDGUN, SEMI-AUTOMATIC

	Fair	V. Good	Excellent
Combo, .22 L.R.R.F., Unique Model L Pistol with Conversion Kit for Stocked Rifle, *Modern*	75	125	150
Model D, .380 ACP., Clip Fed, Adjustable Sights, Blue, *Modern*	75	125	175
Model D, .380 ACP., Clip Fed, Adjustable Sights, Chrome, *Modern*	125	150	175
Model D, .380 ACP., Clip Fed, Adjustable Sights, Matt Blue, *Modern*	75	125	175

SHOTGUN, DOUBLE BARREL, SIDE-BY-SIDE

	Fair	V. Good	Excellent
Model 400, Various Gauges, Single Trigger, Checkered Stock, *Modern*	125	175	225
Model 400E, Various Gauges, Single Selective Trigger, Checkered Stock, Selective Ejector, Vent Rib, *Modern*	175	225	275
Model 400E, Various Gauges, Single Selective Trigger, Selective Ejector, *Modern*	150	200	250

FIREARMS SPECIALTIES

Owosso, Mich., c. 1972.

HANDGUN, REVOLVER

	Fair	V. Good	Excellent
.45/70 Custom Revolver, Brass Frame, Single Action, Western Style, *Modern*	300	500	550

FIREARMS, CUSTOM-MADE

This category covers some of the myriad special firearms that are built to an individual's specifications by a competent gunsmith, and not by the original factory. Most firearms in this class will appeal only to a person who happens to want the same special features, and because of this many of these guns will sell for less than the cost of the conversion. The collector or investor in this area of firearms should bear in mind that something built to his own specifications may or may not appreciate significantly in value. Most crucial in determining long-term value are such factors as the reputation and quality of the gunmaker, the make and the action, the caliber, barrel length, type wood, quality of the wood grain and finish, and amount of personalization evident in the decoration or inscriptions. Unless the client is famous or renowned for one reason or another, the monogram or name on a piece might be detrimental to future salability, although in some instances the monogram or name could be removed and replaced by that of the new owner or by some other decoration or inscription.

HANDGUN, PERCUSSION

	Fair	V. Good	Excellent
Target Revolver, Various Calibers, Tuned, Target Sights, Reproduction			Rare

HANDGUN, REVOLVER

	Fair	V. Good	Excellent
"F.B.L." Conversion, .38 Special, Cut Trigger Guard, Spurless Hammer, Short Barrel, *Modern*			Rare
P.P.C. Conversion, .38 Special, Heavy Barrel, Rib with Target Sights, Target Trigger, Target Grips, *Modern*			Rare
Recoil Compensation Devices or Ports, Add $25.00-$45.00			

HANDGUN, SEMI-AUTOMATIC

	Fair	V. Good	Excellent
M1911A1, Combat Conversion, Extended Trigger Guard, Ambidextrous Safety, Special Slide Release, Ported, Combat Sights, *Modern*			Rare
M1911A1, Double Action Conversion, Add $95.00-$175.00			
M1911A1, I.P.S.C. Conversion, Extended Trigger Guard, Ambidextrous Safety, Special Slide Release, Ported, Target Sights, Extended Grip Safety, *Modern*			Rare

HANDGUN, SINGLESHOT

	Fair	V. Good	Excellent
Silhouette Pistol, Various Calibers, Bolt Action, Thumbhole Stock, Target Sights, Target Trigger, *Modern*			Rare

RIFLE, BOLT ACTION

	Fair	V. Good	Excellent
Sporting Rifle, Various Calibers, Checkered Stock, Recoil Pad, Simple Military Conversion, *Modern*			Rare
Sporting Rifle, Various Calibers, Fancy Stock, High Quality Commercial Parts, Fancy Checkering, Stock Inlays, *Modern*			Rare
Sporting Rifle, Various Calibers, Fancy Stock, High Quality Commercial Parts, Fancy Checkering, Stock Inlays, Engraved, *Modern*			Rare
Sporting Rifle, Various Calibers, Fancy Stock, High Quality Commercial Parts, Fancy Checkering, Stock Inlays, Engraved, Gold Inlays, *Modern*			Rare
Sporting Rifle, Various Calibers, Fancy Wood, Recoil Pad, Fancy Military Conversion, *Modern*			Rare

	Fair	V. Good	Excellent
Sporting Rifle, Various Calibers, Mauser 1871 Action, Checkered Stock, *Antique*			Rare
Sporting Rifle, Various Calibers, Plain Stock, Commercial Parts, *Modern*			Rare

RIFLE, SINGLESHOT

Target Rifle, Centerfire Calibers, Fancy, Target Sights, Built on Various Moving Block Actions, *Modern*			Rare
Target Rifle, Centerfire Calibers, Plain, Target Sights, Built on Various Bolt Actions, *Modern*			Rare
Target Rifle, Centerfire Calibers, Plain, Target Sights, Built on Various Moving Block Actions, *Modern*			Rare
Target Rifle, Rimfire Calibers, Plain, Target Sights, Built on Various Moving Block Actions, *Modern*			Rare

SHOTGUN, DOUBLE BARREL, OVER-UNDER

Trap Conversion, 12 Ga., Recoil Reducer in Stock, Release Triggers, Throated Chambers, Trap Pad, Add $275.00-$400.00

SHOTGUN, SLIDE ACTION

Combat Conversion, 12 Ga., Short Barrel, Extended Magazine Tube, Folding Stock, Rifle Sights, *Modern*			Rare
Competition Conversion, Various Gauges, High Rib, Recoil Reducer in Stock, Fancy Wood, *Modern*			Rare

FIREBIRD

Made by Femaru for German exporter for U.S. Sales.

HANDGUN, SEMI-AUTOMATIC

Tokagypt Type, 9mm Luger, Clip Fed, Blue, *Modern*	$200	$400	$600

FITCH & WALDO

New York City, c. 1862–67. Made by Bacon Mfg. Co., Norwich, Conn.

HANDGUN, REVOLVER

Pocket Model, .31, 5 Shot, *Antique*	200	400	600

FLINTLOCK

Establishing values in this area is worthy of a book unto itself. Variables in the reputation of makers, national and regional styles, quality of workmanship, calibers, dates of manufacture, technical features of mechanisms and mounts, and many other features present a challenge to the appraiser. The figures presented herewith are approximate only. As an example, the author was privileged to have found a flintlock pistol by the renowned French maker Piraube at a bar near New Haven, Connecticut. Piraube was one of the most respected gunmakers of his day and was honored with apartments in the Louvre, where his shop could manufacture arms under appointment to the king. The barrel of this truly exceptional pistol was gold damascened with an inscription indicating Piraube's address at the Louvre, and testifying to his status as gunmaker to Louis XIV. Furthermore, the pistol bore the coat of arms of the Swedish King, to whom a garniture of guns by Piraube had been presented by Louis XIV. For some time the owner of the bar was reluctant to sell this pistol. He knew the gun was valuable, but had been frustrated in his attempts to determine its true worth. Finally, he had exhausted the patience of several collector/dealers and dealers, all of whom had been knocking on the bar owner's door. Norm Flayderman bought the pistol, and it was soon sold to the author, acting on behalf of client and friend, John B. Solley III. Despite the fact that the Piraube had been restocked in the 18th century, the workmanship was so magnificent that the pistol is a featured piece in the magnificent collections of the Metropolitan Museum of Art. The Piraube is a classic example of the difficulty of determining value for some arms, even though this pistol is an extreme case, in value far more exalted than most flintlocks that the reader is likely to encounter.

Fitch & Waldo Pocker Revolver, .31 Caliber

HANDGUN, FLINTLOCK

	Fair	V. Good	Excellent
.28, English, Pocket Pistol, Queen Anne Style, Box Lock, Screw Barrel, Plain, *Antique*	$375	$475	$575
.40, Herdsman Pistol, Long Tapered Round Barrel, Silver Furniture, *Antique*	150	200	250
.45, French, Mid-1700s, Screw Barrel, Long Cannon Barrel, Silver Furniture	700	1500	1750
.60, Continental, Early 1700s, Holster Pistol, Half-Octagon Bar Engraved, High Quality	1500	2500	2750
.60, Oval Bore, Box Lock, Pocket Pistol, Steel Furniture	500	750	1000
.62, Crantham English, Holster Pistol, Brass Furniture, Plain	400	650	750
.63, Spanish, Mid-1600s, Holster Pistol, Silver Inlay, Engraved	2000	4000	4250
.65, Arabian, Holster Pistol, Flared, Round Barrel, Low Quality	150	200	250
.68, Tower, Continental, Plain	300	350	400
English Lock, mid-1600s, Military, Holster Pistol, Iron Mounts, Plain	1700	3000	3500

	Fair	V. Good	Excellent
English, Early 1700s, Pocket Pistol, Box Lock, Double Barrel, Screw Barrel, Low Quality	$400	$600	$650
English, Early 1700s, Pocket Pistol, Queen Anne Style, Box Lock, Screw Barrel, All Metal	500	800	850
English, Mid-1600s, Button Trigger, Brass Barrel, Octagon Fish-tail Butt	1500	2500	3000
French Officer's Type, c. 1650, Steel Furniture, Rifled	1500	2700	3000
French Sedan Mid-1600s, Long Screw Barrel, Rifled, Plain	1500	2500	3000

RIFLE, FLINTLOCK

	Fair	V. Good	Excellent
.64, Continental, Carbine, Musket, Brass Furniture	400	600	675
.72, Continental, 1650, Musket, Brass Furniture, Plain	700	1000	1250

SHOTGUN, FLINTLOCK

	Fair	V. Good	Excellent
.65, American Hudson Valley	800	1250	1650

FOLGER, WILLIAM H.

Barnsville, Ohio 1830–1854. Also see Kentucky Rifles.

FOLK'S GUN WORKS

Bryan, Ohio 1860–1891.

RIFLE, SINGLESHOT

	Fair	V. Good	Excellent
.32 L.R.R.F., Side Lever, Octagon Barrel, *Antique*	200	325	375

FONDERSMITH, JOHN

Strasburg, Pa. 1749–1801. See Kentucky Rifles, U.S. Military.

FORBES, F. F.

Made by Crescent, c. 1900. See Crescent Fire Arms Co., Shotgun, Double Barrel, Side-by-side; Shotgun, Singleshot.

FOREHAND & WADSWORTH

Worchester, Mass. Successors and sons-in-law to Ethan Allen 1871–1902. In 1872 the name was changed to Forehand & Wadsworth, in 1890 to Forehand Arms. Co.

HANDGUN, REVOLVER

	Fair	V. Good	Excellent
.22 Short R.F. Side Hammer, 7 Shot, Single Action, Solid Frame, *Antique*	150	175	200
.41 Short R.F. Center Hammer, Single Action, Spur Trigger, Solid Frame, *Antique*	50	100	200
American Bulldog, .32 S & W, 6 Shot, Double Action, Solid Frame, *Antique*	75	100	125
British Bulldog, .38 S & W, 6 Shot, Double Action, Solid Frame, *Antique*	$200	$225	$250
British Bulldog, .44 S & W, 6 Shot, Double Action, Solid Frame, *Antique*	225	250	275
New Army, .44 Russian, 6 Shot, Single Action, Solid Frame, *Antique*	650	1200	1750
Old Army, .44 Russian, 6 Shot, Single Action, Solid Frame, 7½" Barrel, *Antique*	500	1000	1750
Swamp Angel, .41 Short R.F., 5 Shot, Single Action, Solid Frame, Spur Trigger, *Antique*	65	125	250
Terror, .32 Short R.F., 5 Shot, Single Action, Solid Frame, Spur Trigger, *Antique*	62	125	200

HANDGUN, SINGLESHOT DERRINGER

	Fair	V. Good	Excellent
.22 Short R.F., Spur Trigger, Side-swing Barrel, *Antique*	250	300	350
.41 Short R.F., Spur Trigger, Side-swing Barrel, *Antique*	450	550	650

FOREHAND ARMS CO.

HANDGUN, REVOLVER

	Fair	V. Good	Excellent
.32 S & W, 5 Shot, Double Action, Solid Frame, 2" Barrel, *Antique*	50	75	100

Forehand Arms Co., .32 S&W

	Fair	V. Good	Excellent
.38 S & W, 5 Shot, Double Action, Solid Frame, 2" Barrel, *Antique*	50	75	100
Perfection Automatic, .32 S & W, 5 Shot, Double Action, Top Break, Hammerless, *Antique*	100	125	150
Perfection Automatic, .32 S & W, 5 Shot, Double Action, Top Break, *Antique*	75	100	125

FOREVER YOURS

Flaig's Lodge, Millvale, Pa.

	Fair	V. Good	Excellent
SHOTGUN, DOUBLE BARREL, OVER-UNDER			
Various Gauges, Automatic Ejector, Checkered Stock, Vent Rib, Double Trigger, *Modern*	$450	$550	$650
Various Gauges, Automatic Ejector, Checkered Stock, Vent Rib, Single Trigger, *Modern*	400	550	700

FOULKES, ADAM

Easton & Allentown, Pa. 1773–1794. See Kentucky Rifles and U.S. Military.

FOUR ACE CO.

Brownsville, Texas.

	Fair	V. Good	Excellent
HANDGUN, SINGLESHOT			
Four Ace, Derringer, Presentation Case Add $10.00-$15.00			
Four Ace Model 200, .22 Short R.F., Derringer, 4 Shot, Spur Trigger, *Modern*	12	25	50
Four Ace Model 200, .22 Short R.F., Derringer, 4 Shot, Spur Trigger, Nickel Plated, Gold Plated, *Modern*	12	25	50
Four Ace Model 202, .22 L.R.R.F., Derringer, 4 Shot, Spur Trigger, Nickel Plated, Gold Plated, *Modern*	25	50	75
Four Ace Model 202, .22 L.R.R.F., Derringer, 4 Shot, Spur Trigger, *Modern*	12	25	50
Four Ace Model 204, .22 L.R.R.F., Derringer, 4 Shot, Spur Trigger, Stainless Steel, *Modern*	25	50	75
Little Ace Model 300, .22 Short R.F., Derringer, Side-swing Barrel, Spur Trigger, *Modern*	12	25	50

FOX

Foxco Products, Inc. Manchester, Conn. Also see Demro, T.A.C.

	Fair	V. Good	Excellent
RIFLE, SEMI-AUTOMATIC			
Model #1, 9mm Luger or .45 ACP, Carbine, Clip Fed, *Modern*	85	175	275

FOX, A.H. GUN CO.

Philadelphia, Pa. Formerly Philadelphia Arms Co., from 1903. A subsidiary of Savage Arms Co., 1930–1942. Also see Savage Arms Co., and Connecticut Shotgun Mfg. Co. Though famous today for his fine shotguns, Ansley H. Fox (1875–1948) was also a prolific designer and inventor and an entrepreneurial businessman, who excelled in automobiles, munitions, machine guns, real estate, and fishing reels. Fox lived in times which saw extraordinary advancements in science and technology, two devastating world wars, and rapid changes in virtually every sphere of human interest. Of all his achievements, the most distinguished were in the field of firearms, and the Fox was promoted as "The Finest Gun in the World." At the age of eighteen, Fox applied to the U.S. Patent Office for protection on a break-open open side-by-side shotgun, with concealed hammers, which were cocked by the opening action of the barrels. The innovative design revealed a simplicity and functionalism reflecting true mechanical brilliance—there were no less than 19 patentable features, as issued July 3, 1894 (No. 522,464). Soon thereafter, the youthful inventor submitted still another design, an improvement on the original, with twelve more specific features! Fox was on his way. Beginning his arms-making enterprise under the name of the National Arms Company, in Baltimore, in 1897, the firm went through several evolutionary steps, and what eventually emerged, in 1904, was the A.H. Fox Gun Co. of Philadelphia. Importantly, the firearms industry was experiencing the dramatic change from black to smokeless powders, an improvement which also meant added stress to materials, and the resultant likelihood of breakdowns—particularly so with shotguns fired repeatedly, as in competitive shotgun shooting. The inventor himself was destined to become one of America's leading live pigeon shooters, but his gunmaking and designing interests were a distraction. Accordingly, he was described in an 1896 *American Field* article as "something of a shot, but, having devoted more of his time to developing his mechanical ideas than to shooting, does not rank as an expert. No doubt in time this will be rectified." From 1900 through 1902 Fox was a sales representative and professional shotgun shooter, an employee of the Winchester Repeating Arms Co. With innovations in gun designs, augmented by a national reputation as an experienced and highly competitive shotgunner, Fox (termed by some the "boy inventor") quickly made a name for himself and his guns. In fact, it appears that Fox's tournament shooting was done with guns of his own designs. In 1909 the company was the first gunmaker to exhibit at the Grand American Handicap Tournament, the World Series of trapshooting. The same year, a special 12-gauge side-by-side gun was built for President Theodore Roosevelt to take on his celebrated safari to Africa. TR wrote Fox that it was "the most beautiful gun I have ever seen. I am extremely proud that I am to have such a beautiful bit of American workmanship with me." Still another satisfied Fox gun owner was the legendary Ty Cobb, one of the greatest stars in the annals of baseball. Fox guns were awarded the Gold Medal at the Panama-Pacific International Exposition, in San Francisco (1915), for the best double shotguns and single trigger mechanism. The company capitalized on awards and quotations from satisfied shooters. Contemporary Fox guns, made by the Connecticut Shotgun Manufacturing Co., rival and sometimes surpass the artistry of the original A.H. Fox firm. The author has toured the new firm's factory in New Britain, Connecticut, and was amazed at the quality of workmanship, and at the collection of talent, many of them artisans from European gunmaking centers. Tony Galazan, founder of the company, has made Connecticut again a center of manufacture of some of the world's finest and most innovative shotguns.

SHOTGUN, DOUBLE BARREL, SIDE-BY-SIDE

Various Gauges, Beavertail Forend Add 10%-15%

Various Gauges, For Single Trigger Add $200.00-$300.00

Various Gauges, For Vent Rib Add $295.00-$495.00

	Fair	V. Good	Excellent
Various Gauges, Single Selective Trigger Add $295.00-$495.00			
Various Grades, for 20 Ga. Add 50%-75%			
A Grade, Various Gauges, Box Lock, Light Engraving, Checkered Stock, *Modern*	$600	$1150	$1400
AE Grade, Various Gauges, Box Lock, Light Engraving, Checkered Stock, Automatic Ejector, *Modern*	800	1500	1700
BE Grade, Various Gauges, Box Lock, Engraved, Checkered Stock, Automatic Ejector, *Modern*	1500	2000	2100
CE Grade, Various Gauges, Box Lock, Engraved, Fancy Checkering, Automatic Ejector, *Modern*	3000	4500	6000
DE Grade, Various Gauges, Box Lock, Fancy Engraving, Fancy Checkering, Fancy Wood, Automatic Ejector, *Modern*	5000	7000	9000
FE Grade, Various Gauges, Box Lock, Fancy Engraving, Fancy Checkering, Fancy Wood, Automatic Ejector, *Modern*	7500	10000	12500
HE Grade, 12 and 20 Gauge, Box Lock, Light Engraving, Checkered Stock, Automatic Ejector, *Modern*	1200	2200	2500
SP Grade, Various Gauges, Box Lock, Checkered Stock, *Modern*	600	800	1000
SP Grade, Various Gauges, Box Lock, Checkered Stock, Automatic Ejector, *Modern*	600	900	1200
SP Grade, Various Gauges, Box Lock, Skeet Grade, Automatic Ejector, Checkered Stock, *Modern*	650	950	1250
SP Grade, Various Gauges, Box Lock, Skeet Grade, Checkered Stock, *Modern*	550	750	950
Sterlingworth, Various Gauges, Box Lock, Checkered Stock, Hammerless, *Modern*	600	800	1000
Sterlingworth, Various Gauges, Box Lock, Checkered Stock, Hammerless, Automatic Ejector, *Modern*	750	1000	1250
Sterlingworth, Various Gauges, Box Lock, Skeet Grade, Checkered Stock, *Modern*			Rare
Sterlingworth, Various Gauges, Box Lock, Skeet Grade, Checkered Stock, Automatic Ejector, *Modern*			Rare
Sterlingworth Deluxe, Various Gauges, Box Lock, Checkered Stock, Hammerless, Recoil Pad, *Modern*	750	1000	1250
Sterlingworth Deluxe, Various Gauges, Box Lock, Checkered Stock, Hammerless, Recoil Pad, Automatic Ejector, *Modern*	1000	1250	1500
XE Grade, Various Gauges, Box Lock, Fancy Engraving, Fancy Checkering, Fancy Wood, Automatic Ejector, *Modern*	2750	5500	8500

SHOTGUN, SINGLESHOT

	Fair	V. Good	Excellent
JE Grade, 12 Gauge, Trap Grade, Vent Rib, Automatic Ejector, Engraved, Fancy Checkering, *Modern*	$1175	$1475	$1775
KE Grade, 12 Gauge, Trap Grade, Vent Rib, Automatic Ejector, Engraved, Fancy Checkering, *Modern*	1950	2250	2550
LE Grade, 12 Gauge, Trap Grade, Vent Rib, Automatic Ejector, Fancy Engraving, Fancy Checkering, *Modern*	2500	3000	3500
ME Grade, 12 Gauge, Trap Grade, Vent Rib, Automatic Ejector, Fancy Engraving, Fancy Checkering, *Modern*	5500	6500	7500

FRANCAIS

France. Made by Manufacture d'Armes Automatiques Francaise.

HANDGUN, SEMI-AUTOMATIC

	Fair	V. Good	Excellent
Prima, .25 ACP, Clip Fed, *Modern*	75	100	125

FRANCHI

Brescia, Italy. In addition to its own production, Franchi built guns to the specifications of other companies, among these Colt's of Hartford. In the 1990s, Franchi became a subsidary of P. Beretta & Co.

RIFLE, SEMI-AUTOMATIC

	Fair	V. Good	Excellent
Centennial, .22 L.R.R.F., Checkered Stock, Tube Feed, Takedown, *Modern*	150	275	325
Centennial Deluxe, .22 L.R.R.F., Checkered Stock, Tube Feed, Takedown, Light Engraving, *Modern*	200	325	400
Centennial Gallery, .22 Short R.F., Checkered Stock, Tube Feed, Takedown, *Modern*	125	200	250

SHOTGUN, DOUBLE BARREL, OVER-UNDER

	Fair	V. Good	Excellent
Alcione, 12 Ga., Field Grade, Automatic Ejectors, Single Selective Trigger, Vent Rib, *Modern*	200	400	500
Alcione, 12, Vent Rib, Single Selective Trigger, Automatic Ejector, Engraved, *Modern*	200	450	550
Alcione, 12, Vent Rib, Single Selective Trigger, Automatic Ejector, Engraved, *Modern*	500	875	975
Aristocrat, 12 Ga., Imperial Grade, Automatic Ejectors, Single Selection Trigger, Vent Rib, *Modern*	1500	1800	2100
Aristocrat, 12 Ga., Monte Carlo Grade, Automatic Ejectors, Single Selective Trigger, Vent Rib, *Modern*	1500	2500	3000

	Fair	V. Good	Excellent
Barrage Skeet, 12 Ga., Vent Rib, Single Selective Trigger, Automatic Ejector, Recoil Pad, *Modern*	$500	$900	$1100
Barrage Trap, 12 Ga., Vent Rib, Single Selective Trigger, Automatic Ejector, Recoil Pad, *Modern*	500	900	1100
Dragon Skeet, 12 Ga., Vent Rib, Single Selective Trigger, Automatic Ejector, Recoil Pad, *Modern*	400	800	950
Dragon Trap, 12 Ga., Vent Rib, Single Selective Trigger, Automatic Ejector, Recoil Pad, *Modern*	400	800	950
Falconet Buckskin, 12 and 20 Ga., Vent Rib, Single Selective Trigger, Automatic Ejector, *Modern*	300	475	550
Falconet Ebony, 12 and 20 Ga., Vent Rib, Single Selective Trigger, Automatic Ejector, *Modern*	250	425	500
Falconet Peregrine 400, 12 and 20 Ga., Vent Rib, Single Selective Trigger, Automatic Ejector, *Modern*	300	575	650
Falconet Peregrine 451, 12 and 20 Ga., Vent Rib, Single Selective Trigger, Automatic Ejector, *Modern*	250	500	600
Falconet Pigeon, 12 Ga., Vent Rib, Single Selective Trigger, Automatic Ejector, Fancy Engraving, Fancy Checkering, *Modern*	600	1000	1200
Falconet Silver, 12 Ga., Vent Rib, Single Selective Trigger, Automatic Ejector, *Modern*	300	550	625
Falconet Super, 12 Ga., Vent Rib, Single Selective Trigger, Automatic Ejector, *Modern*	350	650	725
Falconet Super Deluxe, 12 Ga., Vent Rib, Single Selective Trigger, Automatic Ejector, *Modern*	400	750	950
Model 2003, 12 Ga., Trap Grade, Vent Rib, Single Selective Trigger, Automatic Ejector, *Modern*	500	1075	1250
Model 2005/2, 12 Ga., Trap Grade, Vent Rib, Single Selective Trigger, Automatic Ejector, Extra Shotgun Barrel, *Modern*	1000	2000	2250
Model 2005/3, 12 Ga., Trap Grade, Vent Rib, Single Selective Trigger, Automatic Ejector, Extra Shotgun Barrel, Custom Choke, *Modern*	1000	2250	2500
Model 255, 12 Ga., Vent Rib, Single Selective Trigger, Automatic Ejector, *Modern*	250	500	525

SHOTGUN, DOUBLE BARREL, SIDE-BY-SIDE

	Fair	V. Good	Excellent
Airone, 12 Ga., Box Lock, Hammerless, Checkered Stock, Automatic Ejector, *Modern*	450	800	1000
Astore, 12 Ga., Box Lock, Hammerless, Checkered Stock, *Modern*	350	700	800
Astore 5, 12 Ga., Box Lock, Hammerless, Checkered Stock, Light Engraving, *Modern*	$700	$1500	$1700
Condor, Various Gauges, Sidelock, Engraved, Checkered Stock, Automatic Ejector, *Modern*	2500	5000	6000
Imperial, Various Gauges, Sidelock, Engraved, Checkered Stock, Automatic Ejector, *Modern*	4500	8500	9500
Imperial Monte Carlo #11, Various Gauges, Sidelock, Fancy Engraving, Fancy Checkering, Automatic Ejector, *Modern*	7000	12000	14000
Imperial Monte Carlo #5, Various Gauges, Sidelock, Fancy Engraving, Fancy Checkering, Automatic Ejector, *Modern*	6500	10000	12500
Imperial Monte Carlo Extra, Various Gauges, Sidelock, Fancy Engraving, Fancy Checkering, Automatic Ejector, *Modern*	8000	15000	18000
Imperiales, Various Gauges, Sidelock, Engraved, Checkered Stock, Automatic Ejector, *Modern*	4500	8500	9500

SHOTGUN, SEMI-AUTOMATIC

	Fair	V. Good	Excellent
Dynamic (Heavy), 12 Ga., Checkered Stock, Slug, Open Rear Sight, *Modern*	175	275	375
Dynamic (Heavy), 12 Ga., Plain Barrel, *Modern*	175	250	325
Dynamic (Heavy), 12 Ga., Skeet Grade, Vent Rib, Checkered Stock, *Modern*	175	275	375
Dynamic (Heavy), 12 Ga., Vent Rib, *Modern*	150	300	350
Eldorado, 12 and 20 Ga., Vent Rib, Engraved, Fancy Checkering, Lightweight, *Modern*	150	350	450
Hunter, 12 and 20 Ga., Vent Rib, Engraved, Checkered Stock, Lightweight, *Modern*	200	400	500
Model 500, 12 Ga., Vent Rib, Checkered Stock, *Modern*	150	250	350
Model 500, 12 Ga., Vent Rib, Checkered Stock, Engraved, *Modern*	200	350	450
Slug Gun, 12 and 20 Ga., Open Rear Sights, Sling Swivels, *Modern*	200	350	450
SPAS 12, 12 gauge, Combat Shotgun, Folding Stock, Rifle Sights, Lightweight, *Modern*	250	400	500
Standard, 12 and 20 Ga., Plain Barrel, Lightweight, Checkered Stock, *Modern*	200	325	425
Standard, 12 and 20 Ga., Solid Rib, Lightweight, Checkered Stock, *Modern*	200	350	450
Standard, 12 and 20 Ga., Vent Rib, Lightweight, Checkered Stock, *Modern*	200	375	475

	Fair	V. Good	Excellent
Standard Magnum, 12 and 20 Gauges, Vent Rib, Lightweight, Checkered Stock, *Modern*	$150	$250	$350
Superange (Heavy), 12 and 20 Gauges, Magnum, Plain Barrel, Checkered Stock, *Modern*	150	250	350
Superange (Heavy), 12 and 20 Gauges, Magnum, Vent Rib, Checkered Stock, *Modern*	200	375	425
Wildfowler (Heavy), 12 and 20 Gauges, Magnum, Vent Rib, Checkered Stock, Engraved, *Modern*	200	375	450

SHOTGUN, SINGLESHOT

	Fair	V. Good	Excellent
Model 2004, 12 Ga., Trap Grade, Vent Rib, Automatic Ejector, *Modern*	500	900	1050
Model 3000/2, 12 Ga., Trap Grade, Vent Rib, Automatic Ejector, with Choke Tubes, *Modern*	1000	2000	2600

FRANCI, PIERO INZI

Brescia, Italy, c. 1640.

HANDGUN, WHEEL LOCK

	Fair	V. Good	Excellent
Octagon-Barrel, Dagger, Handle Butt, *Antique*	2000	4000	5000

FRANCOTTE, AUGUST

Liege, Belgium, 1844 to date, also London, England, 1877–1893. One of the most memorable moments in the author's career in the arms field was visiting Francotte while the last of the family was still at the helm. Monsieur Francotte, a direct descendant of the founder, gave the writer a tour of the old facility, and signed some original photographs taken of specially built display guns exhibited by the firm at world's fairs and expositions. This gracious old gentleman, then in his 70s, took justifiable pride in the creations of his family, but his sadness at having no heirs who could carry on the business was clearly evident. Francotte was then much like the J. Purdey & Sons of continental Europe, still making superior sporting arms for a discriminating clientele—many of these clients decendants of clients of Francotte from earlier generations. The new owners have done an admirable job of maintaining the quality and reputation of the firm although the factory site is now primarily a showroom, with much of the work sub-contracted to highly competent artisans from Liege and surrounding locales.

HANDGUN, REVOLVER

	Fair	V. Good	Excellent
Bulldog, Various Calibers, Double Action, Solid Frame, *Curio*	50	100	200
Military Style, Various Calibers, Double Action, *Antique*	50	100	200

HANDGUN, SEMI-AUTOMATIC

	Fair	V. Good	Excellent
Vest Pocket, .25 ACP, Clip Fed, *Curio*	100	200	250

Francotte Bulldog Revolver

HANDGUN, SINGLESHOT

	Fair	V. Good	Excellent
Target Pistol, .22 L.R.R.F., Toggle Breech, *Modern*	$200	$300	$375

RIFLE, DOUBLE BARREL, SIDE-BY-SIDE

	Fair	V. Good	Excellent
Luxury Double, .458 Win., Sidelock, Hammerless, Double Triggers, Fancy Engraving, *Curio*	9000	17500	20000

SHOTGUN, DOUBLE BARREL, SIDE-BY-SIDE

	Fair	V. Good	Excellent
A & F #14, Various Gauges, Box Lock, Automatic Ejector, Checkered Stock, Engraved, Hammerless, *Curio*	900	1750	2000
A & F #20, Various Gauges, Box Lock, Automatic Ejector, Checkered Stock, Engraved, Hammerless, *Curio*	1100	2750	3250
A & F #25, Various Gauges, Box Lock, Automatic Ejector, Checkered Stock, Engraved, Hammerless, *Curio*	1500	3200	3500
A & F #30, Various Gauges, Box Lock, Automatic Ejector, Checkered Stock, Engraved, Hammerless, *Curio*	2000	3800	4500
A & F #45, Various Gauges, Box Lock, Automatic Ejector, Checkered Stock, Engraved, Hammerless, *Curio*	1600	3500	4000
A & F Jubilee, Various Gauges, Box Lock, Automatic Ejector, Checkered Stock, Light Engraving, Hammerless, *Curio*	600	1250	1500
A & F Knockabout, Various Gauges, Box Lock, Automatic Ejector, Checkered Stock, Hammerless, *Curio*	500	1000	1250
Francotte Original, Various Gauges, Box Lock, Automatic Ejector, Checkered Stock, Hammerless, Engraved, *Curio*	900	2000	3000
Francotte Special, Various Gauges, Box Lock, Automatic Ejector, Checkered Stock, Hammerless, Light Engraving, *Curio*	750	1500	2500

	Fair	V. Good	Excellent
Model 10/18E/628, Various Gauges, Box Lock, Automatic Ejector, Checkered Stock, Hammerless, Light Engraving, *Curio*	$1500	$3000	$4000
Model 10594, Various Gauges, Box Lock, Automatic Ejector, Checkered Stock, Hammerless, Engraved, *Curio*	1500	2500	3000
Model 11/18E, Various Gauges, Box Lock, Automatic Ejector, Checkered Stock, Hammerless, Engraved, *Curio*	1500	2500	3000
Model 120.HE/328, Various Gauges, Sidelock, Automatic Ejector, Checkered Stock, Hammerless, Fancy Engraving, *Curio*	3500	7000	8500
Model 4996, Various Gauges, Box Lock, Automatic Ejector, Checkered Stock, Hammerless, Light Engraving, *Curio*	750	1500	2500
Model 6886, Various Gauges, Box Lock, Automatic Ejector, Checkered Stock, Hammerless, *Curio*	750	1500	2500
Model 6930, Various Gauges, Box Lock, Automatic Ejector, Checkered Stock, Hammerless, Light Engraving, *Curio*	750	1500	2500
Model 6982, Various Gauges, Box Lock, Automatic Ejector, Checkered Stock, Hammerless, Engraved, *Curio*	1200	2500	3500
Model 8455, Various Gauges, Box Lock, Automatic Ejector, Checkered Stock, Hammerless, *Curio*	1000	2500	3500
Model 8457, Various Gauges, Box Lock, Automatic Ejector, Checkered Stock, Hammerless, Engraved, *Curio*	1000	2500	3000
Model 9/40.SE, Various Gauges, Box Lock, Automatic Ejector, Checkered Stock, Hammerless, Fancy Engraving, *Curio*	3500	7000	9500
Model 9/40E/38321, Various Gauges, Box Lock, Automatic Ejector, Checkered Stock, Hammerless, Engraved, *Curio*	1500	3000	4000
Model SOB.E/11082, Various Gauges, Box Lock, Automatic Ejector, Checkered Stock, Hammerless, Engraved, *Curio*	2500	5000	6000

FRANKLIN, C. W.

Belgium, c. 1900.

SHOTGUN, DOUBLE BARREL, SIDE-BY-SIDE

	Fair	V. Good	Excellent
Various Gauges, Hammerless, Damascus Barrel, *Modern*	75	125	175
Various Gauges, Hammerless, Steel Barrel, *Modern*	$100	$150	$200
Various Gauges, Outside Hammers, Damascus Barrel, *Modern*	75	125	175
Various Gauges, Outside Hammers, Steel Barrel, *Modern*	75	125	175

SHOTGUN, SINGLESHOT

	Fair	V. Good	Excellent
Various Gauges, Hammer, Steel Barrel, *Modern*	50	75	100

FRANKONIA

Franconia Jagd, arms dealers and manufacturers in West Germany. Publishers of one of the most beautiful and comprehensive arms-related catalogues in the world, Frankonia remains in the family of the founders. The author has had the pleasure of meeting the patriarch of the family, and one of his sons, at the IWA show in Nuremberg. Among manufacturers represented by Frankonia are a wide array of European and American gunmakers, not the least of which, Sturm, Ruger & Co., has been a featured Frankonia brand for many years. The company's significance in today's sporting Germany is broad-based, having several stores located throughout the country, catering to a dedicated and enthusiastic clientele.

RIFLE, BOLT ACTION

	Fair	V. Good	Excellent
Favorit, Various Calibers, Set Triggers, Checkered Stock, *Modern*	100	275	325
Favorit Deluxe, Various Calibers, Set Triggers, Checkered Stock, *Modern*	200	350	425
Favorit Leichtmodell, Various Calibers, Lightweight, Set Triggers, Checkered Stock, *Modern*	200	400	450
Safari, Various Calibers, Target Trigger, Checkered Stock, *Modern*	250	425	475
Stutzen, Various Calibers, Carbine, Set Triggers, Full Stock, *Modern*	250	400	450

RIFLE, SINGLESHOT

	Fair	V. Good	Excellent
Heeren Rifle, Various Calibers, Fancy Engraving, Fancy Wood, Octagon Barrel, *Modern*	1200	2500	3250
Heeren Rifle, Various Calibers, Fancy Engraving, Fancy Wood, Round Barrel, *Modern*	1000	2000	2500

FRASER

Formerly Bauer Firearms, Fraser, Mich.

HANDGUN, SEMI-AUTOMATIC

	Fair	V. Good	Excellent
.25 ACP, Stainless Steel, Clip Fed, Hammerless, Browning Baby Style, *Modern*	75	100	125

	Fair	V. Good	Excellent

FRASER, D. & J.

Edinburgh, Scotland 1870–1900.

RIFLE, DOUBLE BARREL, SIDE-BY-SIDE

	Fair	V. Good	Excellent
.360 N.E. #2, Automatic Ejector, Express Sights, Engraved, Extra Set of Barrels, Cased with Accessories, *Modern*	$4500	$8500	$10000

FRAZIER, CLARK K.

Rawson, Ohio.

RIFLE, PERCUSSION

	Fair	V. Good	Excellent
Matchmate Offhand, Various Calibers, Under-Hammer, Thumbhole Stock, Heavy Barrel, Reproduction, *Antique*	250	450	650

FRAZIER, JAY

Tyler, Wash., c. 1974.

RIFLE, SINGLESHOT

	Fair	V. Good	Excellent
Creedmore Rifle, Various Calibers, Single Set Trigger, Vernier Sights, Skeleton Buttplate, Pistol Grip Stock, *Modern*	300	600	800
Schuetzen Rifle, Various Calibers, Single Set Trigger, Vernier Sights, Helm Buttplate, Palm Rest, False Muzzle, *Modern*	300	600	800

FREEDOM ARMS

Freedom, Wyo.

HANDGUN, REVOLVER

	Fair	V. Good	Excellent
FA-BG, "Minute Man,".22 L.R.R.F., Spur Trigger, 3" Barrel, Single Action, *Modern*	125	175	225
FA-S, "Bostonian,".22 L.R.R.F., Spur Trigger, 3" Barrel, Single Action, *Modern*	100	175	250
FA-S, "Ironsides,".22 W.M.R., Matte Finish, Spur Trigger, 1" Barrel, Single Action, *Modern*	125	175	225
FA-S, "Patriot,".22 L.R.R.F., Matte Finish, Spur Trigger, 1" Barrel, Single Action, *Modern*	75	125	175
FA-S, .22 L.R.R.F., Stainless Steel, Matte Finish, Spur Trigger, 1¾" Barrel, Single Action, Buckel/Rev. Combo, *Modern*	150	200	250

For High Gloss Finish, Add $5.00-$10.00

FRENCH MILITARY

HANDGUN, FLINTLOCK

	Fair	V. Good	Excellent
.69 AN XIII, Officer's Pistol, Made in France, *Antique*	$375	$750	$1200

French Military AN XIII

	Fair	V. Good	Excellent
.69 AN XIII, Officer's Pistol, Made in Occupied Country, *Antique*	375	750	1200

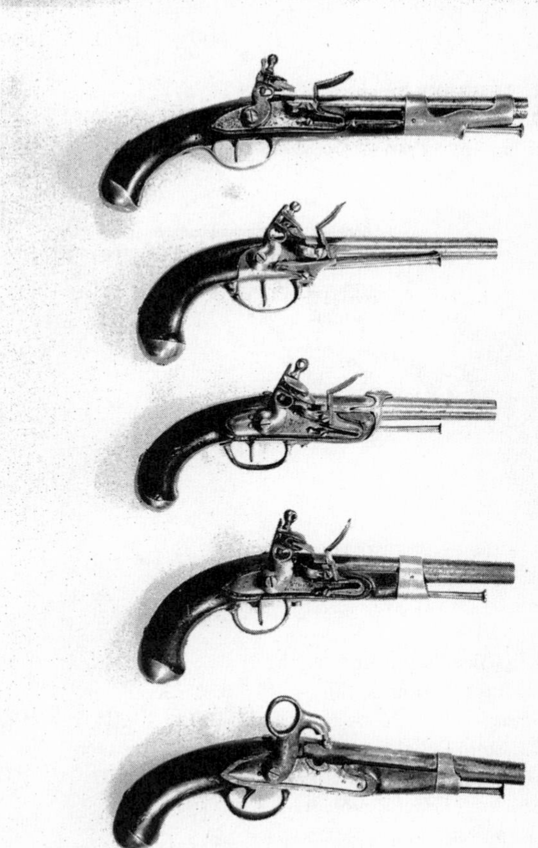

French military flintlock pistols; from top, *Model 1763, dated 1793; Model 1777, St. Etienne markings, this the type on which North & Cheney U.S. martial pistol based; Model 1799 known as "Depareille" model; Model AN 13 (1804), with lock marking* Mre Imple de Versailles*; converted flintlock Model 1815, with odd ring-type hammer.*

	Fair	V. Good	Excellent
.69 Charleville 1777, Cavalry Pistol, Brass Furniture, Belt Hook, *Antique*	$450	$1050	$1500

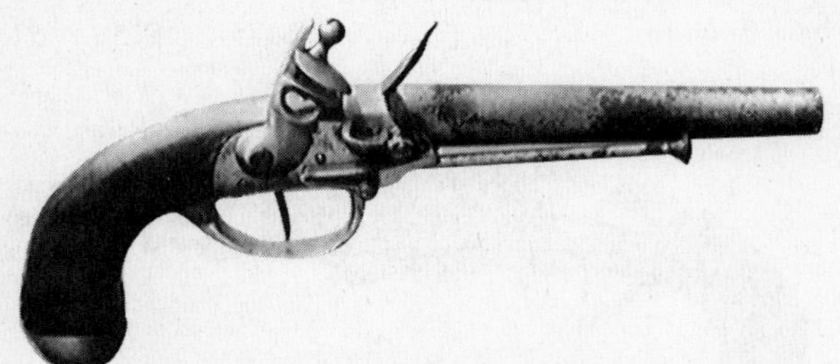

French Military M1777 Charleville

	Fair	V. Good	Excellent
.69 Charleville 1810, Cavalry Pistol, Brass Furniture, Plain, *Antique*	400	800	1200
.69 Charleville 1810, Cavalry Pistol, Brass Furniture, Converted from Flintlock, Plain, *Antique*	200	400	650
.69 Model 1763, Belt Pistol, Military, *Antique*	500	1000	1500

HANDGUN, REVOLVER

	Fair	V. Good	Excellent
Model 1873, 11mm French Ordnance, Double Action, Solid Frame, *Antique*	100	200	350

French Military M1873 Revolver

	Fair	V. Good	Excellent
Model 1873 Officer's, 11mm French Ordnance, Double Action, Solid Frame, *Antique*	100	225	350
Model 1892, 8mm Lebel Revolver, Double Action, Solid Frame, *Curio*	75	150	250
Model 1915, 8mm Lebel Revolver, Double Action, Solid Frame, Spanish Contract, *Curio*	100	200	250

HANDGUN, SEMI-AUTOMATIC

	Fair	V. Good	Excellent
M.A.B. Model C, 7.65mm, Clip Fed, *Curio*	100	225	250
M.A.B. Model C, 7.65mm, Clip Fed, Nazi Proofed, *Curio*	150	325	350
M.A.B. Model D, 7.65mm, Clip Fed, *Curio*	$100	$200	$225
M.A.B. Model D, 7.65mm, Clip Fed, Nazi Proofed, *Curio*	125	250	300
Model 1935-A, 7.65 MAS, Clip Fed, Black Paint, *Curio*	75	125	150

French Military M1935A

	Fair	V. Good	Excellent
Model 1935-A, 7.65 MAS, Clip Fed, Blued, *Curio*	75	150	175
Model 1935-A, 7.65 MAS, Clip Fed, Nazi Proofed, *Curio*	125	225	250
Model 1935-A, 7.65 MAS, M.A.C., Clip Fed, *Curio*	125	250	300
Model 1935-S, 7.65 MAS, M.A.C. M-1, Clip Fed, *Curio*	150	325	350
Model 1935-S, 7.65 MAS, M.A.C., Clip Fed, Nazi Proofed, *Curio*	150	400	450
Model 1935-S, 7.65 MAS, SACM, Clip Fed, *Curio*	125	200	225
Model 1935-S, 7.65 MAS, SAGEM M-1, Clip Fed, Nazi Proofed, *Curio*	125	250	300
Model 1950, 9mm Luger, M.A.S., Clip Fed, *Modern*	150	350	475

French Military M1950

RIFLE, BOLT ACTION

	Fair	V. Good	Excellent
6.5 X 53.5 Daudetau, Carbine, *Curio*	40	80	100
Model 1874, 11 × 59R Gras, *Antique*	65	125	250

French Military Daudetau Rifle

	Fair	V. Good	Excellent
Model 1874, 11 × 59R Gras, Carbine, *Antique*	$75	$150	$300
Model 1886/93 Lebel, 8 × 50R Lebel, *Curio*	50	75	100
Model 1907/15 Remington, 8 × 50R Lebel, *Curio*	75	125	150
Model 1916 St. Etienne, 8 × 50R Lebel, Carbine, *Curio*	50	125	175
Model 1936 MAS, 7.5 × 54 MAS, with Bayonet, *Curio*	50	75	125

RIFLE, FLINTLOCK

.69, Model 1763 Charleville 1st. Type, Musket, Model 1763/66 Charleville, Musket, *Antique*	425	1700	2000

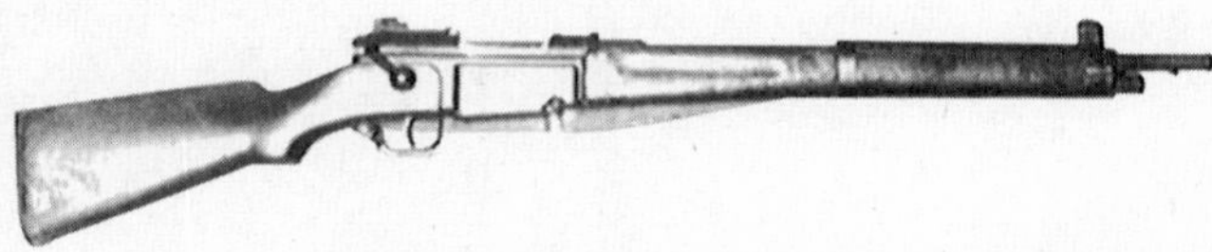

French Military Model 1935 MAS Rifle

RIFLE, PERCUSSION

Model 1840, Short Rifle, *Antique*	400	800	1000

FROMMER

Made by Femaru-Fegyver-Es Gepgyar R.T. (Fegyvergyar), Budapest, Hungary. Also see Femaru.

HANDGUN, SEMI-AUTOMATIC

	Fair	V. Good	Excellent
Baby Pocket, .32 ACP, Clip Fed, *Curio*	100	150	200
Baby Pocket, .380 ACP, Clip Fed, *Curio*	125	175	225
Liliput, .22 L.R.R.F., Clip Fed, *Curio*			Rare
Liliput, .25 ACP, Clip Fed, *Curio*	150	200	250

Frommer Liliput

	Fair	V. Good	Excellent
Roth-Frommer Model 1901, 8mm Roth Sauer, Fixed Magazine, Commercial, *Curio*	$700	$1500	$1750
Roth-Frommer Model 1901, 8mm Roth Sauer, Fixed Magazine, Military Test, *Curio*			Rare
Roth-Frommer Model 1906, 7.65mm Roth Sauer, Clip Fed, Commercial, *Curio*	700	1250	1500
Roth-Frommer Model 1906, 7.65mm Roth Sauer, Fixed Magazine, Commercial, *Curio*	500	1100	1300
Roth-Frommer Model 1910, .32 ACP, Fixed Magazine, Commercial, *Curio*	500	1250	1500

Frommer Roth-Frommer 1910

Roth-Frommer Model 1910, .32 ACP, Fixed Magazine, Police, *Curio*	600	1500	1750
Stop Pocket, .32 ACP, Commercial, Clip Fed, *Curio*	100	200	250
Stop Pocket, .32 ACP, M-19 Military, Clip Fed, *Curio*	100	175	225
Stop Pocket, .32 ACP, Police, Clip Fed, *Curio*	125	225	275
Stop Pocket, .32 ACP, WW-1 Military, Clip Fed, *Curio*	100	175	225
Stop Pocket, .380 ACP, Military, Clip Fed, *Curio*	150	275	325

FRONTIER

Made by Norwich Falls Pistol Co., c. 1880.

HANDGUN, REVOLVER

.32 Short R.F., 5 Shot, Spur Trigger, Solid Frame, Single Action, *Antique*	50	100	175

FRYBERG, ANDREW

Hopkintown, Mass., c. 1905.

	Fair	V. Good	Excellent
HANDGUN, REVOLVER			
.32 S & W, 5 Shot, Top Break, Double Action, *Modern*	$75	$100	$125
.32 S & W, 5 Shot, Top Break, Hammerless, Double Action, *Modern*	75	100	125
.38 S & W, 5 Shot, Top Break, Double Action, *Modern*	75	100	125
.38 S & W, 5 Shot, Top Break, Hammerless, Double Action, *Modern*	75	100	125

FTL

Covina, Calif.

	Fair	V. Good	Excellent
HANDGUN, SEMI-AUTOMATIC			
.22 L.R.R.F., Clip Fed, Chrome Plated, *Modern*	$50	$100	$150

G

GALAND, CHARLES FRANCOIS

From 1865 until about 1910 with plants in London, England, Paris, France, and Liege, Belgium.

HANDGUN, REVOLVER

	Fair	V. Good	Excellent
Galand, Various Calibers, Double Action, Underlever Extraction, *Curio*	$125	$275	$450
Galand-Perrin, Various Calibers, Double Action, Underlever Extraction, *Curio*	125	250	450
Galand-Sommerville, 7-12mm, Double Action, Underlevel Extraction, *Curio*	125	275	450
Galand-Sommerville, 7-12mm, Double Action, Underlever Extraction, *Curio*	150	300	450
Le Novo, .25 ACP, Double Action, Folding Trigger, *Curio*	100	150	200

SHOTGUN, PERCUSSION

	Fair	V. Good	Excellent
Various Gauges, Checkered Stock, Double Barrel, Plain, *Antique*	100	200	250

SHOTGUN, DOUBLE BARREL, SIDE-BY-SIDE

	Fair	V. Good	Excellent
Various Gauges, Checkered Stock, Plain, Hammers, *Curio*	75	125	175

GALEF

Importers in New York City.

HANDGUN, REVOLVER

	Fair	V. Good	Excellent
Stallion, 22LR/.22 WMR Combo, Western Style, Single Action, *Modern*	50	75	100

HANDGUN, SEMI-AUTOMATIC

	Fair	V. Good	Excellent
Brigadier, 9mm Luger, Beretta, Clip Fed, *Modern*	100	200	300
Cougar, .380 ACP, Beretta, Clip Fed, *Modern*	100	175	225
Jaguar, .22 L.R.R.F., Beretta, Clip Fed, *Modern*	100	150	200
Puma, .32 ACP, Beretta, Clip Fed, *Modern*	100	150	200
Sable, .22 L.R.R.F., Beretta, Clip Fed, Adjustable Sights, *Modern*	75	150	225

RIFLE, BOLT ACTION

	Fair	V. Good	Excellent
BSA Monarch, Various Calibers, Checkered Stock Magnum Action, *Modern*	$125	$225	$275
BSA Monarch, Various Calibers, Checkered Stock, *Modern*	100	200	250
BSA Monarch Varmint, Various Calibers, Checkered Stock, Heavy Barrel, *Modern*	125	250	300

SHOTGUN, DOUBLE BARREL, OVER-UNDER

	Fair	V. Good	Excellent
Golden Snipe, 12 and 20 Gauges, Beretta, Single Selective Trigger, Automatic Ejector, Engraved, Fancy Checkering, *Modern*	200	425	475
Golden Snipe, 12 and 20 Gauges, Beretta, Single Trigger, Automatic Ejector, Engraved, Fancy Checkering, *Modern*	150	350	400
Golden Snipe, 12 and 20 Gauges, Skeet Grade, Single Trigger, Automatic Ejector, Engraved, Checkered Stock, *Modern*	200	450	500
Golden Snipe, 12 Ga., Trap Grade, Single Trigger, Automatic Ejector, Engraved, Checkered Stock, *Modern*	200	450	500
Golden Snipe Deluxe, 12 and 20 Gauges, Beretta, Single Selective Trigger, Automatic Ejector, Fancy Engraving, Fancy Checkering, *Modern*	200	475	525
Silver Snipe, 12 and 20 Gauges, Beretta, Single Selective Trigger, Checkered Stock, Light Engraving, *Modern*	150	325	375
Silver Snipe, 12 and 20 Gauges, Beretta, Single Trigger, Checkered Stock, *Modern*	150	300	350
Silver Snipe, 12 and 20 Gauges, Skeet Grade, Single Trigger, Vent Rib, Engraved, Checkered Stock, *Modern*	200	375	425
Silver Snipe, 12 Ga., Trap Grade, Single Trigger, Vent Rib, Engraved, Checkered Stock, *Modern*	175	375	425
Zoli Golden Snipe, 12 and 20 Gauges, Vent Rib, Single Trigger, Adjustable Choke, Engraved, Checkered Stock, *Modern*	175	400	450

	Fair	V. Good	Excellent
Zoli Silver Snipe, 12 and 20 Gauges, Vent Rib, Single Trigger, Engraved, Checkered Stock, *Modern*	$150	$350	$400

SHOTGUN, DOUBLE BARREL, SIDE-BY-SIDE

	Fair	V. Good	Excellent
M213CH, 10 Ga. 3½", Double Trigger, Checkered Stock, Light Engraving, Recoil Pad, *Modern*	100	200	250
M213CH, Various Gauges, Double Trigger, Checkered Stock, Light Engraving, Recoil Pad, *Modern*	75	125	175
Silver Hawk, 10 Ga. 3½", Beretta, Double Trigger, Magnum, *Modern*	200	450	500
Silver Hawk, 12 and 20 Gauges, Double Trigger, Engraved, Checkered Stock, *Modern*	200	325	375
Silver Hawk, 12 Ga. Mag. 3", Beretta, Double Trigger, Magnum, *Modern*	150	325	375
Silver Hawk, 12 Ga. Mag. 3", Beretta, Single Trigger, Magnum, *Modern*	175	375	425
Silver Hawk, Various Gauges, Beretta, Double Trigger, Lightweight, *Modern*	150	275	325
Silver Hawk, Various Gauges, Beretta, Double Trigger, Lightweight, *Modern*	150	350	400
Zabala 213, 10 Ga. 3½", Double Trigger, *Modern*	75	150	200
Zabala 213, 12 and 20 Gauges, Double Trigger, *Modern*	75	125	175
Zabala 213, 12 and 20 Gauges, Double Trigger, Vent Rib, *Modern*	75	125	175
Zabala Police, 12 and 20 Gauges, Double Trigger, *Modern*	75	125	175

SHOTGUN, SEMI-AUTOMATIC

	Fair	V. Good	Excellent
Gold Lark, 12 Ga., Beretta, Vent Rib, Light Engraving, Checkered Stock, *Modern*	100	200	250
Ruby Lark, 12 Ga., Beretta, Vent Rib, Fancy Engraving, Fancy Checkering, *Modern*	150	300	350
Silver Gyrfalcon, 12 Ga., Beretta, Checkered Stock, *Modern*	50	100	125
Silver Lark, 12 Ga., Beretta, Checkered Stock, *Modern*	75	125	150

SHOTGUN, SINGLESHOT

	Fair	V. Good	Excellent
Companion, Various Gauges, Folding Gun, Checkered Stock, *Modern*	25	50	75
Companion, Various Gauges, Folding Gun, Checkered Stock, Vent Rib, *Modern*	25	50	75
Monte Carlo, 12 Ga., Trap Grade, Vent Rib, Engraved, Checkered Stock, *Modern*	100	175	225

SHOTGUN, SLIDE ACTION

	Fair	V. Good	Excellent
Gold Pigeon, 12 Ga., Beretta, Vent Rib, Fancy Engraving, Fancy Checkering, *Modern*	150	300	350
Ruby Pigeon, 12 Ga., Beretta, Vent Rib, Fancy Engraving, Fancy Checkering, *Modern*	$200	$400	$450
Silver Pigeon, 12 Ga., Beretta, Light Engraving, Checkered Stock, *Modern*	75	125	150

GALESI

Industria Armi Galesi, Brescia, Italy, since 1910.

HANDGUN, SEMI-AUTOMATIC

	Fair	V. Good	Excellent
Galesi, 6.35mm, Clip Fed, *Curio*	100	200	250
Model 30, 6.35mm, Clip Fed, *Curio*	100	200	250
Model 30, 7.65mm, Clip Fed, *Curio*	100	200	250
Model 9, .22 L.R.R.F., Clip Fed, *Curio*	75	150	175

Galesi Model 9 Pistol

	Fair	V. Good	Excellent
Model 9, .32 ACP, Clip Fed, *Curio*	75	125	150
Model 9, .380 ACP, Clip Fed, *Curio*	75	150	175

GALLATIN, ALBERT

See Kentucky Rifles and Pistols.

GALLUS

Retoloza Hermanos, Eibar, Spain, c. 1920.

HANDGUN, SEMI-AUTOMATIC

	Fair	V. Good	Excellent
.25 ACP, Clip Fed, Blue, *Curio*	75	100	125

GAMBA

Renato Gamba, Brescia, Italy.

RIFLE, SINGLESHOT

	Fair	V. Good	Excellent
Mustang, Various Calibers, Holland Type Sidelock Action, Set Triggers, Checkered Stock, Engraved, Zeiss Scope, *Modern*	3500	7000	10000

	Fair	V. Good	Excellent
RIFLE, DOUBLE BARREL, OVER-UNDER			
Safari, Various Calibers, Boxlock, Checkered Stock, Engraved, Double Triggers, *Modern*	$1500	$3000	$4000
SHOTGUN, DOUBLE BARREL, SIDE-BY-SIDE			
London, 12 or 20 Ga., Sidelock, Checkered Stock, Engraved, *Modern*	3000	6500	8000
Oxford, 12 or 20 Ga., Boxlock, Checkered Stock, Engraved, *Modern*	1100	2500	3000

GANDER, PETER

Lancaster, Pa. 1779–1782. See Kentucky Rifles.

GARATE, ANITUA

Eibar, Spain, c. 1915.

	Fair	V. Good	Excellent
HANDGUN, REVOLVER			
Pistol O.P. #Mk.I, .455 Webley, British Military, *Curio*	150	250	275
HANDGUN, SEMI-AUTOMATIC			
.32 ACP, Clip Fed, Long Grip, *Curio*	75	125	150

GARBI

Amas Garbi, Eibar, Spain.

	Fair	V. Good	Excellent
SHOTGUN, DOUBLE BARREL, SIDE-BY-SIDE			
Model 51-A, Various Gauges, Boxlock, Checkered Stock, Engraved, *Modern*	200	400	450
Model 60-A, Various Gauges, Sidelock, Checkered Stock, Engraved, *Modern*	225	550	650
Model 60-B, Various Gauges, Sidelock, Checkered Stock, Engraved, Automatic Ejectors, *Modern*	600	1250	1500

GARRISON

Made by Hopkins & Allen, c. 1880–1890.

	Fair	V. Good	Excellent
HANDGUN, REVOLVER			
.22 Short R.F., 7 Shot, Spur Trigger, Solid Frame, Single Action, *Antique*	75	125	175

GARRUCHA

Made by Amadeo Rossi, São Leopoldo, Brazil.

	Fair	V. Good	Excellent
HANDGUN, DOUBLE BARREL, SIDE-BY-SIDE			
.22 L.R.R.F., Double Triggers, Outside Hammers, *Modern*	25	50	75

GASSER

Leopold Gasser, Vienna, Austria.

	Fair	V. Good	Excellent
HANDGUN, REVOLVER			
Montenegrin Gasser, 10.7mm Montenegrin, Double Action, Break Top, Ring Extractor, *Antique*	$175	$375	$425
Rast & Gasser, 8mm R&G, Double Action, Solid Frame, *Curio*	100	200	250

GASTINNE RENETTE

Paris, France since 1812. Like his Uncle Napoleon Bonaparte, Napoleon III was a keen arms devotee and collector, and was also renowned for his skills as a bird shooter. Napoleon III was a patron of such distinguished gunmakers as Gastinne Renette and Galvain, and was presented some fine American-made guns by various makers. The author has had the pleasure of owning, if only briefly, an extraordinary cased fowling piece and a cased pair of exquisite percussion pistols made for Napoleon III by Gastinne Renette. While visiting Paris in the late 1980s, the author was invited to fire a Colt Python at the Gastinne Renette private shooting gallery, a vestige from the original company used in the 19th century to practice target shooting and dueling! The gallery is located below street level of the store, and has much of the original decorative interior intact. Gastinne Renette today is one of the most elegant showrooms of any arms dealer in the world, and remains at a Paris address used by the firm since the 19th century. The sport of game shooting is alive and well in France, ably assisted and encouraged by the remarkable and historic firm of Gastinne Renette.

	Fair	V. Good	Excellent
RIFLE, DOUBLE BARREL, SIDE-BY-SIDE			
Chapuis Standard, Various Calibers, Boxlock Action, Engraved, Checkered Stock, Double Trigger, Open Sights, *Modern*	1000	2000	2200
Chapuis de Luxe, Various Calibers, Boxlock Action with Sideplates, Fancy Engraving, Checkered Stock, Double Trigger Open Sights, *Modern*	1000	2250	2600
Chapuis President, Various Calibers, Boxlock Action with Sideplates, Engraved, Gold Inlays, Checkered Stock, Double Trigger, Open Sights, *Modern*	1200	2500	3200
Chapuis, For Claw Mounts Add $150.00-$250.00			
Chapuis, With 20 Gauge Barrels Add $550.00-$850.00			
SHOTGUN, DOUBLE BARREL, OVER-UNDER			
Bretton Baby Luxe, Lightweight, Double Trigger, Checkered Stock, Engraved, Chrome Frame, *Modern*	200	400	450
Bretton Baby Standard, Lightweight, Double Trigger, Checkered Stock, *Modern*	150	350	400
Bretton Baby-Elite, Lightweight, Double Trigger, Checkered Stock, *Modern*	150	375	425

	Fair	V. Good	Excellent
SHOTGUN, DOUBLE BARREL, SIDE-BY-SIDE			
Model 105, 12 or 20 Gauge, Boxlock Action, Engraved, Fancy Wood, Checkered Stock, Double Trigger, *Modern*	$600	$1250	$1500
Model 202, 12 or 20 Gauge, Boxlock Action with Sideplates, Fancy Engraving, Fancy Wood, Checkered Stock, Double Trigger, *Modern*	1700	3500	4000
Model 353, 12 or 20 Gauge, Sidelock Action, Fancy Engraving, Fancy Wood, Checkered Stock, Double Trigger, *Modern*	5000	10000	14000
Model 98, 12 or 20 Gauge, Boxlock Action, Engraved, Fancy Wood, Checkered Stock, Double Trigger, *Modern*	1100	2000	2250

GATLING ARMS & AMMUNITION CO

Birmingham, England, c. 1890.

	Fair	V. Good	Excellent
HANDGUN, REVOLVER			
Dimancea, .38 &.45 Caliber, Hammerless, Twist Opening, Double Action, *Antique*	400	800	900

GATLING GUN COMPANY

Hartford, Connecticut; production est. 1866, in conjunction with the Colt's Patent Fire Arms Mfg. Co., Inc. Inventor of the first successful crank-operated repeating gun, Dr. Richard Gatling (1818–1903) created the machine while he was residing in Indianapolis, Indiana, a successful doctor of medicine. A prolific inventor who also patented a bicycle, a flush toilet, torpedo boats, a cultivator, a cleaning system, a casting system, and a cast steel gun, the Gatling Gun was designed for defense of buildings, bridges, and causeways. Gatling demonstrated his first working model in 1862, with six revolving barrels, each with its own bolt. Cocking and firing were by a cam action, via a gear-drive mechanism. The original design fired paper cartridges, ignited by percussion caps. Rimfire ammunition soon succeeded the percussion and the Gatling was adopted by the U.S. Army in 1866, with the first example chambered for the newly adopted .50 caliber government cartridge. With adequate protection for his designs from the U.S. Patent Office, Gatling approached the Colt's Patent Fire Arms Mfg. Co., known to be receptive to creative inventors, to contract their production of his revolutionary design. Accordingly, all the Gatling Guns made in America, from the Model 1866 onward, were built by Colt's. The company marking appears on the breeches either in hand-engraved inscriptions, or embossed on cast bronze plaques. Until Gatling Guns became obsolete and the company was dissolved in 1912, most of the officers of the Colt company were one and the same as those of the Gatling Gun Co. The inventor himself served as Gatling Gun Co. president until 1897, when he was succeeded by Colt's president, John H. Hall. In the same year, the Gatling Gun Co. was absorbed by Colt's. Evolutionary design changes led from the first guns, the Models of 1862, to the Models 1865, 1866, 1871–73, '74, '75, '76, '77, '79, '81, '83, '85, '86, '87, '89, '91, '92, '93, '93 Electric, the Police Gatling (Model 1893 Bulldog), '95, 1900, '03, and the Models 1903–06. Gatlings earned worldwide popularity, primarily in the armed services of many European countries, as well as in South America, and even in Africa and China. Gatlings were chambered for nearly every major military cartridge in use during their period of manufacture: from the smallest of these, the .30, on up to the largest, the 1". The name "gat" was derived from an abbreviation of the Gatling Gun, as a generic term for firearms. By the end of the gun's production, examples had even been adapted for operating under electric power, with a cyclic rate of 3,000 rounds per minute. Colt's had entered into agreements with the inventor John M. Browning for manufacture of a gas-operated, belt-feed machine gun, in 1895. Those arrangements assured the company's dominance in machine guns until well into the Twentieth Century. See Colt for value listings.

GAULOIS

Tradename used by Mrs. Francaise de Armes et Cycles de St. Etienne, France 1897–1910.

	Fair	V. Good	Excellent
HANDGUN, MANUAL REPEATER			
Palm Pistol, 8mm, Engraved, *Curio*	$250	$500	$850

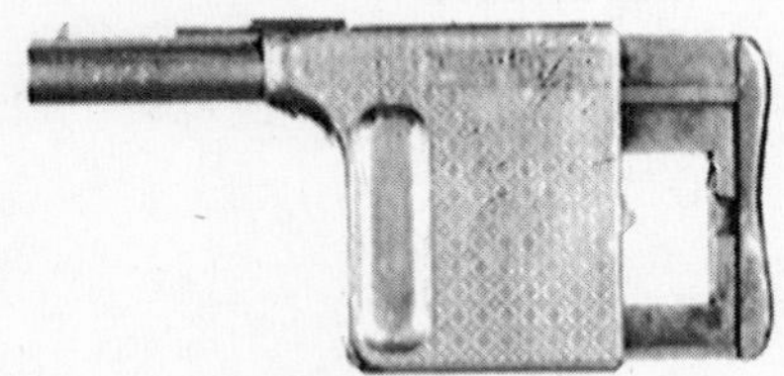

Gaulois Palm Pistol

GAUTEC, PETER

Lancaster, Pa., c. 1780 Kentucky Rifles and Pistols.

GAVAGE

Fab. d'Armes de Guerre de Haute Precision Armand Gavage, Liege, Belgium, c. 1940.

	Fair	V. Good	Excellent
HANDGUN, SEMI-AUTOMATIC			
7.65mm, Clip Fed, Blue, *Curio*	150	300	350

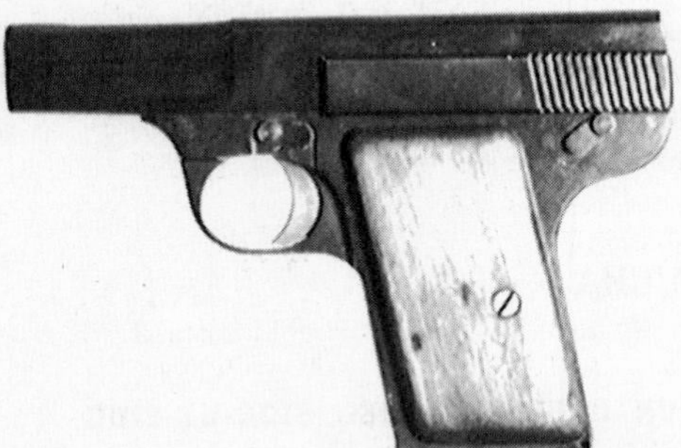

Gavage .32 Pistol

	Fair	V. Good	Excellent
7.65mm, Clip Fed, Blue, Nazi-Proofed, *Curio*	$200	$400	$450

GECADO

Suhl, Germany, by G. C. Dornheim.

HANDGUN, SEMI-AUTOMATIC

	Fair	V. Good	Excellent
Model 11, .25 ACP, Clip Fed, *Modern*	75	100	125

GECO

Tradename used by Gustav Genschow, Hamburg, Germany.

HANDGUN, REVOLVER

	Fair	V. Good	Excellent
Bulldog, .32 ACP, Double Action, *Modern*	75	100	125
Velo Dog, .25 ACP, Double Action, *Modern*	75	100	125

SHOTGUN, DOUBLE BARREL, SIDE-BY-SIDE

	Fair	V. Good	Excellent
12 Gauge, Checkered Stock, Double Triggers, Plain, *Modern*	75	125	175

GEM

Made by Bacon Arms Co., c. 1880.

HANDGUN, REVOLVER

	Fair	V. Good	Excellent
.22 Short R.F., 7 Shot, Spur Trigger, Solid Frame, Single Action, *Antique*	100	175	225

GEM

Made by J. Stevens Arms & Tool, Chicopee Falls, Mass.

HANDGUN, SINGLESHOT

	Fair	V. Good	Excellent
.22 or .30 R.F., Side-Swing Barrel, Spur Trigger, *Antique*	75	125	175

GERMAN MILITARY

Also see: Walther, Mauser, Luger. For centuries Germany was a militaristic country. German military firearms have a distinctive businesslike style, but also exhibit the Germanic qualities of practicality and serviceability. Although there is a tremendous interest in World War II Nazi arms and memorabilia, some gun shows are reluctant to permit the display and sale of these artifacts. Ironically, not a few of the collectors interested in such material are Jewish, despite the horrendous treatment of Jews by Hitler and his minions. Interest in Nazi material should by no means be considered a reflection of political bent in favor of Nazi philosophies. The relics of that period often reveal solid craftsmanship, interesting designs, and engineering orginality. One of the specialists in Nazi and Imperial German collectibles, for many years, has been the Mohawk Arms firm in Utica, New York. Catalogues the company has produced have been substantial and are at times like a textbook of that field of interest.

HANDGUN, FLINTLOCK

	Fair	V. Good	Excellent
Model 1830, .63, Military, *Antique*	$450	$800	$950

HANDGUN, PERCUSSION

	Fair	V. Good	Excellent
Model 1860, .63, Military, *Antique*	250	550	600

HANDGUN, REVOLVER

	Fair	V. Good	Excellent
Model 1879 Troopers Model, 11mm German Service, Solid Frame, Single Action, Safety, 7" Barrel, 6 Shot, *Antique*	175	375	650

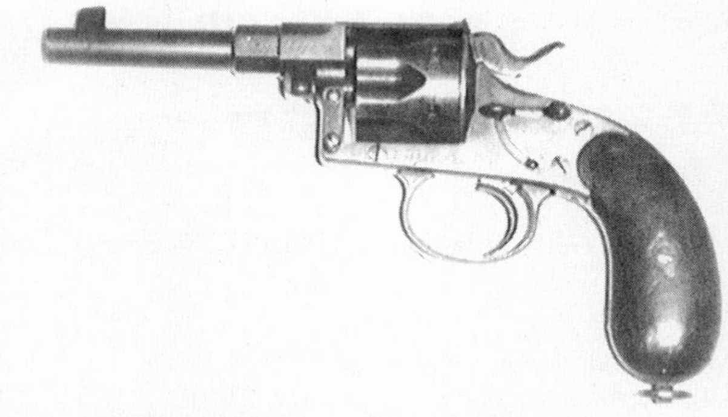

German Military Model 1879 Revolver

	Fair	V. Good	Excellent
Model 1883 Officer's Model, 11mm German Service, Solid Frame, Single Action, Safety, 5" Barrel, 6 Shot, *Antique*	150	300	550

RIFLE, BOLT ACTION

	Fair	V. Good	Excellent
GEW 88 Commission, 8 × 57 JRS, Clip Fed, *Antique*	35	75	125
GEW 98 (Average), 8mm Mauser Military, *Curio*	100	175	250
GEW 98 Sniper, 8mm Mauser, Scope Mounted, Military, *Curio*	200	650	750
K98K Sniper, 8mm Mauser, Scope Mounted, Military, *Curio*	225	475	550
KAR 98 (Average), 8mm Mauser Military, Carbine, *Curio*	100	150	175
KAR 98A (Average), 8mm Mauser Military, Carbine, *Curio*	100	150	175
M-95, 8mm Mauser, Steyr-Mannlicher, German Military, Nazi- Proofed, *Curio*	75	125	150
M-95, 8mm Mauser, Steyr-Mannlicher, German Military, Carbine Nazi-Proofed, *Curio*	50	100	125
Model 1871 Mauser, .43 Mauser, Carbine, Singleshot, Military, *Antique*	250	400	550

German Military Model 1871 Rifle

	Fair	V. Good	Excellent
Model 1871 Mauser, .43 Mauser, Singleshot, Military, *Antique*	$150	$300	$450
Model 1936 Falke KK, .22 L.R.R.F., Training Rifle, Military, *Curio*	35	75	225
Model 29/40, 8mm Mauser, Nazi-Proofed, Military, *Curio*	50	100	225
Model 3 3/40, 8mm Mauser, Nazi-Proofed, Military, *Curio*	65	125	225
Model 45 Mauser, .22 L.R.R.F., Training Rifle, Military, *Curio*	75	150	225
Model 71/84 Mauser, .43 Mauser, Tube Feed, Military, *Antique*	175	325	550

German Military Model 1871/84 Rifle

	Fair	V. Good	Excellent
Needle Gun, 11mm, Singleshot, Military, *Antique*	250	525	900
VK-98, 8mm Mauser, Nazi-Proofed, Military, *Curio*	75	175	300
VZ-24 BRNO, 8mm Mauser, Nazi-Proofed, Military, *Curio*	65	125	250

RIFLE, PERCUSSION

	Fair	V. Good	Excellent
M1839, .69, Musket, Brass Furniture, Military, *Antique*	200	400	600
M1842, .75, Musket, Brass Furniture, Military, *Antique*	150	325	600

RIFLE, SEMI-AUTOMATIC

	Fair	V. Good	Excellent
G43, 8mm Mauser, Clip Fed, 10 Shot, Military, *Curio*	125	275	450
GEW 41, 8mm Mauser, 10 Shot, Military, *Curio*	250	425	600
GEW 41(W), 8mm Mauser, 10 Shot, Military, *Curio*	175	375	600
KAR 43 Sniper, 8mm Mauser, Scope Mounted, Clip Fed, 10 Shot, Military, *Curio*	325	675	1200
VG 2, 8mm Mauser, Clip Fed, 10 Shot, Military, *Curio*	150	300	600

RIFLE, SINGLESHOT

	Fair	V. Good	Excellent
Model 1869 Werder, 11.5mm, Bavarian, *Antique*	350	700	850

GESSCER, GEORG

Saxony, 1591–1611.

HANDGUN, WHEEL LOCK

	Fair	V. Good	Excellent
Pair, Military, Inlays, Pear Pommel, Medium Ornamentation, *Antique*	8000	15000	20000

GEVARM

Gevelot, St. Etienne, France.

RIFLE, SEMI-AUTOMATIC

	Fair	V. Good	Excellent
Model A3, .22 L.R.R.F., Target Sights, Clip Fed, *Modern*	$50	$100	$150
Model A6, .22 L.R.R.F., Open Sights, Clip Fed, *Modern*	75	100	125
Model A7, .22 L.R.R.F., Target Sights, Clip Fed, *Modern*	50	100	150

GIBRALTER

Made by Stevens Arms.

SHOTGUN, SINGLESHOT

	Fair	V. Good	Excellent
Model 116, Various Gauges, Hammer, Automatic Ejector, Raised Matted Rib, *Modern*	25	50	75

GILL, THOMAS

London, England 1770–1812.

HANDGUN, FLINTLOCK

	Fair	V. Good	Excellent
.68, Pocket Pistol, Octagon Barrel, Plain, High Quality, *Antique*	400	800	1000

GLASER WAFFEN

Zurich, Switzerland.

HANDGUN, SINGLESHOT

	Fair	V. Good	Excellent
Target Pistol, .22 L.R.R.F., Toggle Breech, Francotte, *Modern*	150	350	400

RIFLE, BOLT ACTION

	Fair	V. Good	Excellent
Custom Rifle, Various Calibers, Fancy Wood, *Modern*	500	1000	1200

RIFLE, SINGLESHOT

	Fair	V. Good	Excellent
Heeren Rifle, Various Calibers, Engraved, Fancy Wood, *Modern*	900	2000	2500

GLASSBRENNER, DAVID

Lancaster, Pa., c. 1800. See Kentucky Rifles.

GLAZIER, JOHN

Belleville, Ind., c. 1820. See Kentucky Rifles.

GLENFIELD

See Marlin.

GLENN, ROBERT

Edinburgh, Scotland, c. 1860. Made fine copies of Highland Pistols.

HANDGUN, SNAPHAUNCE

	Fair	V. Good	Excellent
Replica Highland, All Brass, Engraved, Ovoid Pommel, *Antique*	$1100	$2500	$3000

GLISENTI

Soc. Siderugica Glisenti, Turin, Italy, c. 1889–1930.

HANDGUN, REVOLVER

	Fair	V. Good	Excellent
M1889, 10.4mm Glisenti, Double Action, Folding Trigger, Military, *Curio*	75	125	150
M1889, 10.4mm Glisenti, Double Action, Trigger Guard, Military, *Curio*	75	125	150

HANDGUN, SEMI-AUTOMATIC

	Fair	V. Good	Excellent
Brixia, 9mm Glisenti, Clip Fed, Hard Rubber Grips, *Curio*	200	375	425
M1906, 7.63 Mauser, Clip Fed, Military, *Curio*	200	475	550
M1910 Army, 9mm Glisenti, Clip Fed, Wood Grips, *Curio*	200	500	550
M1910 Navy, 9mm Glisenti, Clip Fed, Hard Rubber Grips, *Curio*	250	575	650

GOFF, DANIEL

London, England 1779-1810.

HANDGUN, FLINTLOCK

	Fair	V. Good	Excellent
Dueling Pistols, .50, Cased pair, with Accessories, *Antique*	900	2000	4000

GOLCHER, JAMES

Philadelphia, Pa. 1820–1833. Locks with Golcher markings are often seen on arms made by other gunmakers, which sometimes is the source of confusion in trying to identify the maker of a particular firearm. The name on the barrel generally is indicative, in this period, of the gunmaker's identity; the name on the lock often merely identifies the maker of the lock only.

GOLCHER, JOHN

Easton, Pa., c. 1775.

GOLCHER, JOSEPH

Philadelphia, Pa., c. 1800.

GOLDEN EAGLE

Nikko Arms Co. Ltd., Tochigi, Japan.

RIFLE, BOLT ACTION

	Fair	V. Good	Excellent
Model 7000, Various African Calibers, Grade 1, Checkered Stock, *Modern*	$225	$475	$550
Model 7000, Various African Calibers, Grade 2, Checkered Stock, *Modern*	300	625	700
Model 7000, Various Calibers, Grade 1, Checkered Stock, *Modern*	200	425	500
Model 7000, Various Calibers, Grade 2, Checkered Stock, *Modern*	250	575	650

SHOTGUN, DOUBLE BARREL, OVER-UNDER

	Fair	V. Good	Excellent
Model 5000 Grandee, 12 and 20 Gauges, Field Grade 3, Vent Rib, Checkered Stock, Fancy Engraving, Gold Overlay, *Modern*	900	2250	2750
Model 5000 Grandee, 12 and 20 Gauges, Skeet Grade 3, Vent Rib, Checkered Stock, Fancy Engraving, Gold Overlay, *Modern*	900	2000	2250
Model 5000 Grandee, 12 and 20 Gauges, Trap Grade 3, Vent Rib, Checkered Stock, Fancy Engraving, Gold Overlay, *Modern*	900	2000	2250
Model 5000, 12 and 20 Gauges, Field Grade 2, Vent Rib, Checkered Stock, Light Engraving, Gold Overlay, *Modern*	500	1000	1250
Model 5000, 12 and 20 Gauges, Field Grade, Vent Rib, Checkered Stock, Light Engraving, Gold Overlay, *Modern*	350	725	850
Model 5000, 12 and 20 Gauges, Skeet Grade 2, Vent Rib, Checkered Stock, Light Engraving, Gold Overlay, *Modern*	425	950	1100
Model 5000, 12 and 20 Gauges, Skeet Grade, Vent Rib, Checkered Stock, Light Engraving, Gold Overlay, *Modern*	350	800	900
Model 5000, 12 and 20 Gauges, Trap Grade 2, Vent Rib, Checkered Stock, Light Engraving, Gold Overlay, *Modern*	400	950	1050
Model 5000, 12 and 20 Gauges, Trap Grade, Vent Rib, Checkered Stock, Light Engraving, Gold Overlay, *Modern*	400	875	950

GONTER, PETER

Lancaster, Pa. 1770–1778. See Kentucky Rifles.

GOOSE GUN

Made by Stevens Arms.

	Fair	V. Good	Excellent
SHOTGUN, SINGLESHOT			
Model 89 Dreadnaught, Various Gauges, Hammer, *Modern*	$25	$50	$75

GOVERNOR

Made by Bacon Arms Co.

HANDGUN, REVOLVER			
.22 Short R.F., 7 Shot, Spur Trigger, Solid Frame, Single Action, *Antique*	75	125	175

GOVERNOR

Various makers, c. 1880.

HANDGUN, REVOLVER			
.32 S & W, 5 Shot, Double Action, Top Break, *Modern*	50	75	100
.38 S & W, 5 Shot, Double Action, Top Break, *Modern*	35	75	125

GRAEFF, WM.

Reading, Pa. 1751–1784. See Kentucky Rifles.

GRANT HAMMOND

New Haven, Conn. 1915–1917.

HANDGUN, SEMI-AUTOMATIC			
U.S. Test, .45 ACP, Clip Fed, Hammer, *Curio*	3000	7000	10000

GRANT, W. L.

Manufactured by Wm. Uhlinger, Phil., Penn.

HANDGUN, REVOLVER			
.22 Long R.F., 6 Shot, Single Action, Solid Frame, Spur Trigger, *Antique*	100	200	350
.22 Short R.F., 6 Shot, Single Action, Solid Frame, Spur Trigger, *Antique*	100	200	375

GRAVE, JOHN

Lancaster, Pa. 1769–1773. See Kentucky Rifles.

GREAT WESTERN ARMS CO.

Venice, Calif. Moved to North Hollywood, Calif. in 1959. Last address Los Angeles, Calif. 1953–1961. See also Hy Hunter. The Great Western firm was the operation of Hy Hunter, a flamboyant arms dealer and entrepreneur with a great many Hollywood connections. As a boy the author remembers seeing advertisements of Hy Hunter, and articles and pictures of him with such show business types as Mel Tormé, Audie Murphy, and several of the TV and movie Western stars. Although relatively short-lived, Hunter and his company had a strong impact on the popularity of single action style firearms, on guns as collectibles, and on the use of the single action for sport and target shooting and in the rapidly growing hobby of quick-draw.

	Fair	V. Good	Excellent
HANDGUN, DOUBLE BARREL, OVER-UNDER			
Double Derringer, .38 Spec., Remington Copy, *Modern*	$150	$300	$350
HANDGUN, REVOLVER			
Buntline, Various Calibers, Single Action, Western Style, *Modern*	300	650	750
Deputy, .22 L.R.R.F., Single Action, Western Style, *Modern*	600	1200	1500
Frontier, .22 L.R.R.F., Target Model, Single Action, Western Style, *Modern*	500	1000	1250
Frontier, Various Calibers, Single Action, Western Style, *Modern*	300	500	600

GREAT WESTERN GUN WORKS

Pittsburgh, Pa., 1860 to about 1923. Catalogs by the Great Western Gun Works have proven a valuable source in researching various arms built and sold in the period of this firm's years of operation. Well illustrated, and covering a breadth of guns, these catalogs are among the most comprehensive and informative of arms-related publications from the 19th and early 20th century.

HANDGUN, REVOLVER			
.22 Short R.F., 7 Shot, Spur Trigger, Solid Frame, Single Action, *Antique*	75	125	175
RIFLE, PERCUSSION			
No. 5, Various Calibers, Various Barrel Lengths, Plains Rifle, Octagon Barrel, Brass Fittings, *Antique*	250	575	650

GREEK MILITARY

RIFLE, BOLT ACTION			
M 1903 Mannlicher Schoenauer, 6.5mm M.S., Military, *Curio*	100	225	275
M 1903 Mannlicher Schoenauer, 8mm Mauser, Military, *Curio*	125	225	275
M 1930 F N Short Rifle, 8mm Mauser, Military, *Curio*	125	250	300

GREENER, W. W.

Established in 1829 in Northumberland, England, as W. Greener, moved to Birmingham, England, in 1844; name changed to W. W. Greener in 1860, and to W. W. Greener & Son in 1879. William Greener was author of one of the most widely read arms books of all time: *The Gun, or a Treatise on the Various Descriptions of Small Fire-Arms,* published in London, 1835, and in numerous editions thereafter. This book is a must for any enthusiast of collectors firearms. The text includes a history of firearms, with illustrations based on Greener's own experience, as well as expositions on a variety of matters involving gun design, performance and ammunition. Later editions are of particular interest due to developments in firearms technology, a science in which Greener was well informed. When the Greener firm closed its doors, Val Forgett was the successful purchaser of the remaining stock and numerous records and files.

SHOTGUN, DOUBLE BARREL, SIDE-BY-SIDE

	Fair	V. Good	Excellent
Various Gauges, Single Non-Selective Trigger Add $280.00-$400.00			
Various Gauges, Single Selective Trigger Add $385.00-$475.00			
Crown DH-55, Various Gauges, Box Lock, Automatic Ejector, Checkered Stock, Fancy Engraving, *Modern*	$1600	$3000	$3250
Empire, 12 Ga., Mag. 3", Box Lock, Hammerless, Light Engraving, Checkered Stock, *Modern*	600	1250	1500
Empire, 12 Ga., Mag. 3", Box Lock, Hammerless, Light Engraving, Checkered Stock, Automatic Ejector, *Modern*	700	1500	1700
Empire Deluxe, 12 Ga., Mag. 3", Box Lock, Hammerless, Engraved, Checkered Stock, *Modern*	600	1400	1600
Empire Deluxe, 12 Ga., Mag. 3", Box Lock, Hammerless, Engraved, Checkered Stock, Automatic Ejector, *Modern*	700	1550	1800
Farkiller F35, 10 Ga. 3½", Box Lock, Hammerless, Engraved, Checkered Stock, *Modern*	1100	2500	3000
Farkiller F35, 10 Ga. 3½", Box Lock, Hammerless, Engraved, Checkered Stock, Automatic Ejector, *Modern*	1500	3250	4000
Farkiller F35, 12 Ga., Mag. 3", Box Lock, Hammerless, Engraved, Checkered Stock, *Modern*	1100	2250	3000
Farkiller F35, 12 Ga., Mag. 3", Box Lock, Hammerless, Engraved, Checkered Stock, Automatic Ejector, *Modern*	1600	3000	3750
Farkiller F35, 8 Ga., Box Lock, Hammerless, Engraved, Checkered Stock, *Modern*	1100	2500	3000
Farkiller F35, 8 Ga., Box Lock, Hammerless, Engraved, Checkered Stock, Automatic Ejector, *Modern*	1600	3250	4000
Jubilee DH-35, Various Gauges, Box Lock, Automatic Ejector, Checkered Stock, Engraved, *Modern*	900	2000	2500
Royal DH-75, Various Gauges, Box Lock, Automatic Ejector, Checkered Stock, Fancy Engraving, *Modern*	1700	3700	4500
Sovereign DH-40, Various Gauges, Box Lock, Automatic Ejector, Checkered Stock, Engraved, *Modern*	900	2150	2600

SHOTGUN, SINGLESHOT

	Fair	V. Good	Excellent
G.P. Martini, 12 Ga., Checkered Stock, Takedown, *Modern*	175	300	350

GREGORY

Mt. Vernon, Ohio 1837–1842. See Kentucky Rifles.

GREIFELT & CO

Suhl, Germany, from 1885.

COMBINATION WEAPON, DRILLING

	Fair	V. Good	Excellent
Various Calibers, Engraved, Checkered Stock, *Curio*	$1200	$3000	$3500
Various Calibers, Fancy Wood, Fancy Checkering, Engraved, *Curio*	1700	4000	4500

RIFLE, BOLT ACTION

	Fair	V. Good	Excellent
Sport, .22 Hornet, Checkered Stock, Express Sights, *Curio*	450	850	1250

COMBINATION WEAPON, OVER-UNDER

	Fair	V. Good	Excellent
Various Calibers, Solid Rib, Engraved, Checkered Stock, *Curio*	2700	5000	6000
Various Calibers, Solid Rib, Engraved, Checkered Stock, Automatic Ejector, *Curio*	3000	5800	6500

SHOTGUN, DOUBLE BARREL, OVER-UNDER

	Fair	V. Good	Excellent
Various Gauges, For Vent Rib Add $300.00-$400.00			
Various Gauges, Single Trigger, Add $350.00-$450.00			
#1, .410 & 28 Ga., Automatic Ejector, Fancy Engraving, Checkered Stock, Fancy Wood, Solid Rib, *Modern*	1300	3000	4000
#1, Various Gauges, Automatic Ejector, Fancy Engraving, Checkered Stock, Fancy Wood, Solid Rib, *Modern*	1300	2750	3250
#3, .410 & 28 Ga., Automatic Ejector, Engraved, Checkered Solid Rib, *Modern*	1000	2500	3000
#3, Various Gauges, Automatic Ejector, Engraved, Checkered Stock, Solid Rib, *Modern*	800	1750	2250
Model 143E, Various Gauges, Automatic Ejector, Engraved, Checkered Stock, Solid Rib, Double Trigger, *Modern*	900	2000	2500
Model 143E, Various Gauges, Automatic Ejector, Engraved, Checkered Stock, Vent Rib, Single Selective Trigger, *Modern*	900	2250	2750

SHOTGUN, DOUBLE BARREL, SIDE-BY-SIDE

	Fair	V. Good	Excellent
Model 103, 12 and 16 Gauge, Box Lock, Double Trigger, Checkered Stock, Light Engraving, *Modern*	700	1500	1750

	Fair	V. Good	Excellent
Model 103E, 12 and 16 Gauge, Box Lock, Double Trigger, Checkered Stock, Light Engraving, Automatic Ejector, *Modern*	$700	$1600	$1850
Model 22, 12 and 16 Gauge, Box Lock, Double Trigger, Checkered Stock, Engraved, *Modern*	700	1500	1750
Model 22E, 12 and 16 Gauge, Box Lock, Double Trigger, Checkered Stock, Engraved, Automatic Ejector, *Modern*	700	1750	2000

GREYHAWK ARMS CORP.

South El Monte, Calif., c. 1975.

RIFLE, SINGLESHOT

Model 74, Various Calibers, Rolling Block, Octagon Barrel, Open Rear Sight, Reproduction, *Modern*	75	100	125

GRIFFIN & HOWE

N.Y.C., 1923–1976, subsidiary of Abercrombie & Fitch 1930–1976, privately held company after 1976. Maker of custom rifles. Showrooms and shop opened in Bernardsville, N.J., 1987. Rifles by Griffin & Howe rank among the finest custom-made arms in the history of American gunmaking—and among the finest bolt action rifles made anywhere. Built on a variety of actions—though Mausers have been the primary type—G & H rifles have their own designated serial range, and a classic quality and style. The present showroom is at 36 West 44th Street, New York City, and a New Jersey showroom and workshops are in Bernardsville. Griffin himself was a cabinet maker, who had a keen appreciation of fine guns. His preference in stock styling was the traditional English, and that's what he set out to make. Other gunsmithing firms then rebuilding Springfield bolt action rifles, in the World War I period, included Fred Adolph of New York state, Louis Wundhammer of Los Angeles, and R.F. Sedgely of Philadelphia. Riflemen Townsend Whelen and E.C. Crossman wrote about the new sporter Springfields, which had a positive affect on the demand. Colonel Whelen was instrumental in putting Griffin together with master metal worker James V. Howe, then foreman of Frankford Arsenal's machine shop. At a May 1923 meeting which included Griffin, Howe, Whelen, James M. Holsworth and James L. Gerry, Griffin & Howe was established, with a shop and showroom set up at 234 East 39th Street, New York City. Howe, in a matter of months, left to join a competitor, Hoffman Arms Co., of Cleveland, Ohio, and would later write a classic work on gun and stock making, metalwork and engraving: *The Modern Gunsmith.* Griffin, then the only active employee, continued toiling for another five years, uncertain if the business would prove a success. Despite the stock market crash of 1929, Griffin & Howe remained active, aided by a significant order from the Springfield Armory, to build stocks for international match rifles. By c. 1930 approximately 840 G & H rifles had been made. From March to October 1930 the company was known as Griffin & Hobbs, Inc., at which time G & H serial numbers started with 1000. The company name reverted back to Griffin & Howe soon after the firm became a subsidiary of Abercrombie & Fitch, in September of 1930. Springfield Conversions to sporting rifles continued to be the main output, but Mauser actions became increasingly popular. During World War II the company devoted its time and talents to defense work, including triggers for anti-aircraft guns, as well as parts for airplane factories, sidemounts for Garand M1 rifles (23,000 of them by war's end), and special mounts for telescopic sights for the British Enfield bolt action rifle (only 50 prototypes were delivered due to the abrupt end of war). After World War II Griffin & Howe returned to the manufacture of big game sporting rifles. However, by 1975 Abercrombie & Fitch was in liquidation, and employee Bill Ward was able to buy G & H. From 1960 through 1987 the workshop and later showrooms were located in downtown New York.

GROOM, RICHARD

London, England, c. 1855.

HANDGUN, FLINTLOCK

	Fair	V. Good	Excellent
.68, East India Company, Calvary Pistol, Military, Tapered Round Barrel, Brass Furniture, *Antique*	$800	$1800	$2000

GROSS ARMS CO.

Tiffin, Ohio 1862–1865.

HANDGUN, POCKET REVOLVER

.25 Short R.F., 7 Shot, Spur Trigger, Tip-Up, *Antique*	400	750	900
.30 Short R.F., 7 Shot, Spur Trigger, Tip-Up, *Antique*	400	800	1000

GRUENEL

Gruenig & Elmiger, Malters, Switzerland.

RIFLE, BOLT ACTION

Match 300m, Various Calibers, Offhand Target Rifle, Target Sights, Ventilated Forestock, Palm Rest, Hook Buttplate, *Modern*	600	1000	1200
Model K 31, .308 Win., U.I.T. Target Rifle, Target Sights, Ventilated Forestock, *Modern*	350	750	900
U.L.T. Standard, .308 Win., Target Rifle, Target Sights, Ventilated Forestock, *Modern*	350	700	800

GUARDIAN

Made by Bacon Arms Co., c. 1880.

HANDGUN, REVOLVER

.22 Short R.F., 7 Shot, Spur Trigger, Solid Frame, Single Action, *Antique*	75	125	175
.32 Short R.F., 5 Shot, Spur Trigger, Solid Frame, Single Action, *Antique*	75	150	200

GUMPH, CHRISTOPHER

Lancaster, Pa. 1779–1803. See Kentucky Rifles and Pistols.

GUSTAF, CARL

See Husqvarna Vapenfabrik Akitiebolag.

GUSTLOFF WERKE

Suhl, Germany.

HANDGUN, SEMI-AUTOMATIC

	Fair	V. Good	Excellent
.32 ACP, Clip Fed, Hammer, Single Action, *Modern*	$600	$1200	$1500
.380 ACP, Clip Fed, Hammer, Single Action, *Modern*	1200	2500	3000

RIFLE, BOLT ACTION

	Fair	V. Good	Excellent
Mauser M98, 8mm Mauser, Military, *Curio*	$50	$75	$100
Model KKW, .22 L.R.R.F., Pre-WW2, Singleshot, Tangent Sights, Military Style Stock, *Modern*	150	350	400

SHOTGUN, DOUBLE BARREL, SIDE-BY-SIDE

	Fair	V. Good	Excellent
16 Ga., Engraved, Color Case Hardened Floor, *Modern*	150	400	500

GYROJET

See M.B. Associates.

H

	Fair	V. Good	Excellent

H & D
Henrion & Dassy, Liege, Belgium, c. 1900.

HANDGUN, SEMI-AUTOMATIC

H & D Patent, .25 ACP, Clip Fed, *Curio*	$150	$400	$500

HACKET, EDWIN AND GEORGE
London, England, c. 1870.

SHOTGUN, DOUBLE BARREL, SIDE-BY-SIDE

10 Ga. 2⅞", Damascus Barrel, Plain, *Antique*	75	150	200

HADDEN, JAMES
Philadelphia, Pa. c. 1769. See Kentucky Rifles and Pistols.

HAEFFER, JOHN
Lancaster, Pa., c. 1800. See Kentucky Rifles and Pistols.

HAENEL, C. G.
C. G. Haenel Waffen und Fahrradfabrik, Suhl, Germany 1840–1945.

HANDGUN, SEMI-AUTOMATIC

Schmiesser Model 1, .25 ACP, Clip Fed, *Curio*	125	225	275

Haenel Schmeisser Model I

Schmeisser Model 2, .25 ACP, Clip Fed, *Curio*	125	250	300

	Fair	V. Good	Excellent

RIFLE, BOLT ACTION

Model 88, Various Calibers, Sporting Rifle, Half-Octagon Barrel, Open Rear Sights, *Curio*	$150	$300	$350
Model 88 Sporter, Various Calibers, 5 Shot Clip, Half-Octagon Barrel, Open Rear Sights, *Curio*	150	350	400

HAFDASA
Hispano Argentina Fab. de Automoviles, Buenos Aires, Argentina, c. 1935.

HANDGUN, SEMI-AUTOMATIC

.22 L.R.R.F., Blowback, *Curio*	150	375	400

Hafdasa

HALF-BREED
Made by Hopkins & Allen, c. 1880.

HANDGUN, REVOLVER

.32 Short R.F., 5 Shot, Spur Trigger, Solid Frame, Single Action, *Antique*	75	125	175

HAMMERLI
Lenzburg, Switzerland. One of the world leaders in highly accurate target guns, the Hammerli name is synonymous with Olympic level target shooting.

HANDGUN, REVOLVER

Dakota, Various Calibers, Single Action, Western Style, *Modern*	100	250	275
Virginian, Various Calibers, Single Action, Western Style, *Modern*	100	225	250

	Fair	V. Good	Excellent
HANDGUN, SEMI-AUTOMATIC			
Model 200 Walther Olympia, .22 L.R.R.F., Target Pistol, *Modern*	$325	$600	$625
Model 200 Walther Olympia, .22 L.R.R.F., Target Pistol, Muzzle Brake, *Modern*	325	650	675
Model 201 Walther Olympia, .22 L.R.R.F., Target Pistol, Adjustable Grips, *Modern*	300	600	625
Model 202 Walther Olympia, .22 L.R.R.F., Target Pistol, Adjustable Grips, *Modern*	350	700	750
Model 203 Walther Olympia, .22 L.R.R.F., Target Pistol, Adjustable Grips, *Modern*	350	650	700
Model 203 Walther Olympia, .22 L.R.R.F., Target Pistol, Adjustable Grips, Muzzle Brake, *Modern*	350	725	775
Model 204 Walther Olympia, .22 L.R.R.F., Target Pistol, *Modern*	325	700	750
Model 205 Walther Olympia, .22 L.R.R.F., Target Pistol, Fancy Wood, *Modern*	350	775	850
Model 205 Walther Olympia, .22 L.R.R.F., Target Pistol, Fancy Wood, Muzzle Brake, *Modern*	400	900	950
Model 206, .22 L.R.R.F., Target Pistol, *Modern*	300	650	700
Model 207, .22 L.R.R.F., Target Pistol, Adjustable Grips, *Modern*	300	650	725
Model 208 Deluxe, .22 L.R.R.F., Target Pistol, Clip Fed, Adjustable Grips, *Modern*	1600	3000	3250
Model 208, .22 L.R.R.F., Target Pistol, Clip Fed, Adjustable Grips, *Modern*	700	1500	1850
Model 209, .22 Short R.F., Target Pistol, 5 Shot Clip, Muzzle Brake, *Modern*	325	700	775
Model 210, .22 L.R.R.F., Target Pistol, Adjustable Grips, *Modern*	400	800	875
Model 211, .22 L.R.R.F., Target Pistol, Clip Fed, *Modern*	700	1500	1800
Model 212, .22 L.R.R.F., Target Pistol, Clip Fed, *Modern*	700	1500	1600
Model 215, .22 L.R.R.F., Target Pistol, Clip Fed, *Modern*	400	850	900
Model 230, .22 Short R.F., Target Pistol, 5 Shot Clip, *Modern*	300	575	650
Model 232, .22 Short R.F., Target Pistol, 5 Shot Clip, Adjustable Grips, *Modern*	300	625	675
Model 232, .22 Short R.F., Target Pistol, 5 Shot Clip, Adjustable Grips, Left-Hand, *Modern*	275	600	675
280, .22 L.R.R.F., Target Pistol, Clip Fed, Conversion Unit Only, *Modern*	250	525	600
280, .22 Short, Clip Fed, Target Pistol, Cased with Accessories, *Modern*	800	1500	1750
280, .32 Wadcutter, Clip Fed, Target Pistol, Cased with Accessories, *Modern*	$800	$1750	$2000
HANDGUN, SINGLESHOT			
Match Pistol, .22 L.R.R.F., Target Pistol, Round Barrel, *Modern*	300	500	600
Model 100, .22 L.R.R.F., Target Pistol, *Modern*	350	750	800
Model 100 Deluxe, .22 L.R.R.F., Target Pistol, *Modern*	425	800	850
Model 101, .22 L.R.R.F., Target Pistol, *Modern*	350	775	825
Model 102, .22 L.R.R.F., Target Pistol, *Modern*	400	800	850
Model 102 Deluxe, .22 L.R.R.F., Target Pistol, *Modern*	400	825	875
Model 103, .22 L.R.R.F., Target Pistol, Carved, *Modern*	400	850	925
Model 103, .22 L.R.R.F., Target Pistol, Carved, Inlays, *Modern*	425	1000	1250
Model 104, .22 L.R.R.F., Target Pistol, Round Barrel, *Modern*	300	750	850
Model 105, .22 L.R.R.F., Target Pistol, Octagon Barrel, *Modern*	400	875	950
Model 107, .22 L.R.R.F., Target Pistol, Octagon Barrel, *Modern*	400	850	950
Model 107 Deluxe, .22 L.R.R.F., Target Pistol, Octagon Barrel, Engraved, *Modern*	525	1150	1250
Model 120 H.B., .22 L.R.R.F., Target Pistol, Heavy Barrel, Left-Hand, Adjustable Grips, *Modern*	225	550	600
Model 120-1, .22 L.R.R.F., Target Pistol, Heavy Barrel, *Modern*	200	400	450
Model 120-1, .22 L.R.R.F., Target Pistol, Heavy Barrel, Adjustable Grips, *Modern*	200	400	475
Model 150, .22 L.R.R.F., Target Pistol, *Modern*	700	1500	1750
Model 152 Electronic, .22 L.R.R.F., Target Pistol, *Modern*	800	1750	2000
RIFLE, BOLT ACTION			
Model 45, .22 L.R.R.F., Singleshot, Thumbhole Stock, Target Sights, with Accessories, *Modern*	250	500	550
Model 54, .22 L.R.R.F., Singleshot, Thumbhole Stock, Target Sights, with Accessories, *Modern*	250	525	575
Model 503, .22 L.R.R.F., Singleshot, Thumbhole Stock, Target Sights, with Accessories, *Modern*	250	500	550
Model 506, .22 L.R.R.F., Singleshot, Thumbhole Stock, Target Sights, with Accessories, *Modern*	250	550	600
Olympia 300 Meter, Various Calibers, Singleshot, Thumbhole Stock, Target Sights, with Accessories, *Modern*	300	675	750
Sporting Rifle, Various Calibers, Set Triggers, Fancy Wood, Checkered Stock, Open Sights, *Modern*	250	525	600

	Fair	V. Good	Excellent
Tanner, Various Calibers, Singleshot, Thumbhole Stock, Target Sights, with Accessories, *Modern*	$300	$750	$825

HAMPTON, JOHN

Dauphin County, Pa. See Kentucky Rifles and Pistols.

HARD PAN

Made by Hood Firearms Co., c. 1875.

HANDGUN, REVOLVER

	Fair	V. Good	Excellent
.22 Short R.F., 7 Shot, Spur Trigger, Solid Frame, Single Action, *Antique*	50	100	150
.32 Short R.F., 5 Shot, Spur Trigger, Solid Frame, Single Action, *Antique*	75	125	175

HARPERS FERRY ARMS CO.

RIFLE, FLINTLOCK

	Fair	V. Good	Excellent
.72 Lafayette, Musket, Reproduction	150	250	300

RIFLE, PERCUSSION

	Fair	V. Good	Excellent
.51 Maynard, Carbine, Breech Loader, Reproduction	100	150	200
.58, 1861 Springfield, Rifled, Musket, Reproduction	100	150	200

HARRINGTON & RICHARDSON ARMS CO.

HANDGUN, REVOLVER

	Fair	V. Good	Excellent
Abilene Anniversary, .22 L.R.R.F., Commemorative, *Curio*	50	75	100
American, Various Calibers, Double Action, Solid Frame, *Modern*	25	50	75
Auto Ejecting, Various Calibers, Top Break, Hammer, Double Action, *Modern*	75	100	125
Bobby, Various Calibers, 6 Shot, Top Break, Double Action, *Modern*	35	75	100
Bulldog, Various Calibers, Double Action, Solid Frame, *Modern*	$50	$75	$100
Defender, .38 S & W, Top Break, 6 Shot, Double Action, Adjustable Sights, *Modern*	75	100	125
Expert, .22 L.R.R.F., Top Break, 9 Shot, Double Action, Wood Grips, *Modern*	75	125	150
Expert, .22 W.R.F., Top Break, 9 Shot, Double Action, Wood Grips, *Modern*	75	125	150
Hammerless, Various Calibers, Double Action, Solid Frame, *Modern*	50	75	100
Hunter (Early), .22 L.R.R.F., 7 Shot, Solid Frame, Wood Grips, Double Action, *Modern*	50	75	100
Hunter (Late), .22 L.R.R.F., 9 Shot, Solid Frame, Wood Grips, Double Action, *Modern*	50	75	100
Model 4, Various Calibers, Double Action, Solid Frame, *Modern*	50	75	100
Model 40, Various Calibers, Top Break, Hammerless, Double Action, *Modern*	75	100	125
Model 5, .32 S & W Double Action, 5 Shot, Solid Frame, *Modern*	50	75	100
Model 6, .22 L.R.R.F., Double Action, 7 Shot, Solid Frame, *Modern*	50	75	100
Model 603, .22 W.M.R., 9 Shot, Solid Frame, Double Action, Swing-Out Cylinder, Adjustable Sights, *Modern*	50	100	125
Model 604, .22 W.M.R., 9 Shot, Solid Frame, Double Action, Swing-Out Cylinder, Adjustable Sights, *Modern*	75	125	150
Model 622, .22 L.R.R.F., Solid Frame, 6 Shot, Double Action, *Modern*	25	50	75
Model 632, .32 S & W Long, Solid Frame, 6 Shot, Double Action, *Modern*	50	75	100
Model 633, .32 S & W Long, Solid Frame, 6 Shot, Chrome, Double Action, *Modern*	25	50	75
Model 649, .22LR/.22 W.M.R. Combo, Western Style, 9 Shot, Double Action, Adjustable Sights, *Modern*	75	100	125

Harrington & Richardson Auto Ejecting

Harrington & Richardson M649, .22 Caliber

	Fair	V. Good	Excellent
Model 650, .22LR/.22 W.M.R. Combo, Western Style, 9 Shot, Double Action, Adjustable Sights, *Modern*	$75	$125	$150
Model 666, .22LR/.22 W.M.R. Combo, Solid Frame, 9 Shot, Double Action, *Modern*	25	50	75
Model 676, .22LR/.22 W.M.R. Combo, Western Style, 9 Shot, Double Action, Adjustable Sights, *Modern*	50	75	100
Model 676-12", .22LR/.22 W.M.R. Combo, Western Style, 9 Shot, Double Action, Adjustable Sights, *Modern*	75	100	125
Model 686, .22LR/.22 W.M.R. Combo, Western Style, 9 Shot, Double Action, Adjustable Sights, *Modern*	75	125	175
Model 732, .32 S & W Long, Solid Frame, 6 Shot, Double Action, Swing-Out Cylinder, *Modern*	50	75	100
Model 733, .32 S & W Long, Solid Frame, 6 Shot, Double Action, Swing-Out Cylinder, *Modern*	75	100	125
Model 766, .22 L.R.R.F., Top Break, 7 Shot, Double Action, Wood Grips, *Modern*	75	100	125
Model 766, .22 W.M.F., Top Break, 7 Shot, Double Action, Wood Grips, *Modern*	75	100	125
Model 826, .22 W.M.R., 6 Shot, Double Action, Adjustable Sights, Swing-Out Cylinder, *Modern*	50	75	100
Model 829, .22 L.R.R.F., 9 Shot, Double Action, Adjustable Sights, Swing-Out Cylinder, *Modern*	50	75	100
Model 832, .32 S & W, 6 Shot, Double Action, Adjustable Sights, Swing-Out Cylinder, *Modern*	50	75	100
Model 900, .22 L.R.R.F., Solid Frame, 9 Shot, Double Action, *Modern*	75	75	75
Model 901, .22 L.R.R.F., Solid Frame, 9 Shot, Double Action, *Modern*	50	75	100
Model 922 (Early), .22 L.R.R.F., 9 Shot, Solid Frame, Wood Grips, Octagon Barrel, Double Action, *Modern*	50	75	100
Model 922 (Early), .22 L.R.R.F., 9 Shot, Solid Frame, Double Action, *Modern*	25	50	75
Model 922 (Late), .22 L.R.R.F., 9 Shot, Solid Frame, Swing-Out Cylinder, Double Action, *Modern*	25	50	75
Model 925, .22 L.R.R.F., 9 Shot, Solid Frame, Double Action, Swing-Out Cylinder, *Modern*	50	75	100
Model 925, .38 S & W, Solid Frame, 5 Shot, Adjustable Sights, *Modern*	50	75	100
Model 926, .22 L.R.R.F., 5 Shot, Solid Frame, Adjustable Sights, *Modern*	75	100	125
Model 926, .38 S & W, Solid Frame, 5 Shot, Adjustable Sights, *Modern*	50	75	100
Model 929, .22 L.R.R.F., 9 Shot, Solid Frame, Double Action, Swing-Out Cylinder, *Modern*	$25	$50	$75

Harrington & Richardson M929, .22 Caliber

	Fair	V. Good	Excellent
Model 930, .22 L.R.R.F., 9 Shot, Solid Frame, Double Action, Swing-Out Cylinder, Adjustable Sights, *Modern*	50	75	100
Model 939, .22 L.R.R.F., 9 Shot, Solid Frame, Double Action, Swing-Out Cylinder, Adjustable Sights, *Modern*	50	75	100
Model 940, .22 L.R.R.F., 9 Shot, Solid Frame, Double Action, Swing-Out Cylinder, *Modern*	25	50	75
Model 949, .22 L.R.R.F., 9 Shot, Western Style, Double Action, Adjustable Sights, *Modern*	50	75	100
Model 950, .22 L.R.R.F., 9 Shot, Western Style, Double Action, Adjustable Sights, *Modern*	50	75	100
Model 976, .22 Checkered Grip, Case Hardened Frame, *Modern*	25	50	75
Model 999 (Early), .22 L.R.R.F., 9 Shot, Top Break, Double Action, Adjustable Sights, *Modern*	75	125	150
Model 999 (Early), .22 W.R.F., Top Break, 9 Shot, Double Action, Adjustable Sights, *Modern*	75	125	150
Model 999 (Engraved), .22 L.R.R.F., Top Break, 9 Shot, Double Action, Adjustable Sights, *Modern*	100	250	350
New Defender, .22 L.R.R.F., Top Break, 9 Shot, Double Action, Wood Grips, Adjustable Sights, *Modern*	75	150	175
Special, .22 L.R.R.F., Top Break, 9 Shot, Double Action, Wood Grips, *Modern*	50	100	125
Special, .22 W.R.F., Top Break, 9 Shot, Double Action, Wood Grips, *Modern*	75	125	150
Sportsman No. 199, .22 L.R.R.F., Single Action, 9 Shot, Top Break Adjustable Sights, *Modern*	50	75	100

	Fair	V. Good	Excellent
Target (Early), .22 L.R.R.F., Top Break, 9 Shot, Double Action, Wood Grips, *Modern*	$75	$100	$125
Target (Early), .22 W.R.F., Top Break, 9 Shot, Double Action, Wood Grips, *Modern*	75	100	125
Target (Hi Speed), .22 L.R.R.F., Top Break, 9 Shot, Double Action, Wood Grips, *Modern*	75	125	150
Target (Hi Speed), .22 W.R.F., Top Break, 9 Shot, Double Action, Wood Grips, *Modern*	75	125	150
Trapper, .22 L.R.R.F., 7 Shot, Solid Frame, Wood Grips, Double Action, *Modern*	50	100	125
Vest Pocket, Various Calibers, Double Action, Solid Frame, Spurless Hammer, *Modern*	25	50	75
Young America, Various Calibers, Double Action, Solid Frame, *Modern*	25	50	75

HANDGUN, SEMI-AUTOMATIC

	Fair	V. Good	Excellent
Self-Loading, .25 ACP, Clip Fed, *Modern*	150	275	325
Self-Loading, .32 ACP, Clip Fed, *Modern*	150	225	275

Harrington & Richardson .32 Pistol

HANDGUN, SINGLESHOT

	Fair	V. Good	Excellent
U.S.R.A. Target, .22 L.R.R.F., Top Break, Adjustable Sights, Wood Grips, *Modern*	175	325	375

RIFLE, BOLT ACTION

	Fair	V. Good	Excellent
Model 250 Sportster, .22 L.R.R.F., 5 Shot Clip, Open Rear Sight, *Modern*	25	50	75
Model 251 Sportster, .22 L.R.R.F., 5 Shot Clip, Open Rear Sight, *Modern*	25	50	75
Model 265 Reg'lar, .22 L.R.R.F., Clip Fed, Peep Sights, *Modern*	25	50	75
Model 300, Various Calibers, Cheekpiece, Monte Carlo Stock, Checkered Stock, *Modern*	150	300	350
Model 301, Various Calibers, Checkered Stock, Mannlicher, *Modern*	$150	$350	$400
Model 317, Various Calibers, Checkered Stock, Monte Carlo Stock, *Modern*	150	275	325
Model 317P, .223 Rem., Fancy Checkering, Monte Carlo Stock, Fancy Wood, *Modern*	200	450	500
Model 330, Various Calibers, Checkered Stock, Monte Carlo Stock, *Modern*	150	225	275
Model 333, Various Calibers, Monte Carlo Stock, *Modern*	150	225	275
Model 340, Various Calibers, Monte Carlo Stock, Recoil Pad, *Modern*	150	250	300
Model 365 ACE, .22 L.R.R.F., Singleshot, Peep Sights, *Modern*	25	50	75
Model 370, Various Calibers, Target Stock, Heavy Barrel, *Modern*	150	300	350
Model 450 Medalist, .22 L.R.R.F., 5 Shot Clip, No Sights, Target Stock, *Modern*	75	125	150
Model 451 Medalist, .22 L.R.R.F., 5 Shot Clip, Lyman Sights, Target Stock, *Modern*	75	125	175
Model 465 Targeteer, .22 L.R.R.F., Clip Fed, Peep Sights, *Modern*	50	75	100
Model 465 Targeteer Jr., .22 L.R.R.F., Clip Fed, Peep Sights, *Modern*	50	75	100
Model 5200 Match, .22 L.R.R.F., Target Rifle, Single Shot, Heavy Barrel, No Sights, *Modern*	125	225	275
Model 5200 Sporter, .22 L.R.R.F., Targert Rifle, Clip Fed, Target Sights, Checkered Stock, *Modern*	125	225	275
Model 750 Pioneer, .22 L.R.R.F., Singleshot, Open Rear Sight, *Modern*	25	50	75
Model 751 Pioneer, .22 L.R.R.F., Singleshot, Open Rear Sight, Mannlicher, *Modern*	25	50	75
Model 765 Pioneer, .22 L.R.R.F., Singleshot, Open Rear Sight, *Modern*	25	50	75
Model 852 Fieldsman, .22 L.R.R.F., Tube Feed, Open Rear Sight, *Modern*	25	50	75
Model 865 Plainsman, .22 L.R.R.F., 5 Shot Clip, Open Rear Sights, *Modern*	25	50	75
Model 866 Plainsman, .22 L.R.R.F., 5 Shot Clip, Open Rear Sight, Mannlicher, *Modern*	25	50	75

RIFLE, PERCUSSION

	Fair	V. Good	Excellent
Huntsman .45, Top Break, Side Lever, Rifled, Reproduction, *Antique*	50	75	100

	Fair	V. Good	Excellent
Huntsman .50, Top Break, Side Lever, Rifled, Reproduction, *Antique*	$50	$75	$100
Model 175, .45 or .58 Caliber, Springfield Style, Open Sights, Reproduction, *Antique*	75	125	175
Model 175 Deluxe, .45 or .58 Caliber, Springfield Style, Open Sights, Checkered Stock, Reproduction, *Antique*	125	225	275

RIFLE, SEMI-AUTOMATIC

	Fair	V. Good	Excellent
Model 150 Leatherneck, .22 L.R.R.F., 5 Shot Clip, Open Rear Sight, *Modern*	50	75	100
Model 151 Leatherneck, .22 L.R.R.F., 5 Shot Clip, Peep Sights, *Modern*	50	75	100
Model 165 Leatherneck, .22 L.R.R.F., Clip Fed, Heavy Barrel, Peep Sights, *Modern*	75	100	125
Model 308, Various Calibers, Checkered Stock, Monte Carlo Stock, *Modern*	150	275	325
Model 360, Various Calibers, Checkered Stock, Monte Carlo Stock, *Modern*	125	250	300
Model 361, Various Calibers, Checkered Stock, Monte Carlo Stock, *Modern*	150	275	325
Model 60 Reising, .45 ACP, Clip Fed, Carbine, Open Rear Sight, *Modern*	150	350	400
Model 65 General, .22 L.R.R.F., Clip Fed, Heavy Barrel, Peep Sights, *Modern*	100	200	250
Model 700, .22 W.M.R., Monte Carlo Stock, 5 Shot Clip, *Modern*	75	125	150
Model 700 Deluxe, .22 W.M.R., Monte Carlo Stock, 5 Shot Clip, *Modern*	125	200	225
Model 800 Lynx, .22 L.R.R.F., Clip Fed, Open Rear Sight, *Modern*	50	75	100

RIFLE, SINGLESHOT

	Fair	V. Good	Excellent
1871 Springfield Deluxe, .45-70 Government, Trap Door Action, Carbine, Light Engraving, *Modern*	75	300	350
1871 Springfield Officers', .45-70 Government, Commemorative, Trap Door Action, *Curio*	150	275	300
1871 Springfield Standard, .45-70 Government, Trap Door Action, Carbine, *Modern*	100	250	300
1873 Springfield Officers', .45-70 Government, Trap Door Action, Light Engraving, Peep Sights, *Modern*	100	250	300
1873 Springfield Standard, .45-70 Government, Trap Door Action, Commemorative, *Modern*	$100	$200	$300
Custer Memorial Enlisted Model, .45-70 Government, Commemorative, Trap Door Action, Carbine, Fancy Engraving, Fancy Wood, *Curio*	500	1000	1200
Custer Memorial Officers' Model, .45-70 Government, Commemorative, Trap Door Action, Carbine, Fancy Engraving, Fancy Wood, *Curio*	$1100	$2200	$2500
Little Big Horn Springfield Standard, .45-70 Government, Commemorative, Trap Door Action, Carbine, *Curio*	150	300	350
Model 157, Various Calibers, Top Break, Side Lever, Automatic Ejector, Open Rear Sights, Mannlicher, *Modern*	25	50	75
Model 158 Topper, Various Calibers, Top Break, Side Lever, Automatic Ejector, Open Rear Sight, *Modern*	25	50	75
Model 158 Topper, Various Calibers, Top Break, Side Lever, Automatic Ejector, Open Rear Sight, Extra Set of Rifle Barrels, *Modern*	50	75	100
Model 158 Topper, Various Calibers, Top Break, Side Lever, Automatic Ejector, Open Rear Sight, Extra Shotgun Barrel, *Modern*	50	75	100
Model 163, Various Calibers, Top Break, Side Lever, Automatic Ejector, Open Rear Sight, *Modern*	25	50	75
Model 172 Springfield, .45-70 Government, Trap Door Action, Carbine, Engraved, Silver Plated, Tang Sights, Checkered Sights, *Modern*	150	350	400
Model 755 Sahara, .22 L.R.R.F., Singleshot, Open Rear Sight, Mannlicher, *Modern*	25	50	75
Model 760 Sahara, .22 L.R.R.F., Singleshot, Open Rear Sight, *Modern*	25	50	75
Shikari, .44 Magnum, Top Break, Side Lever, Automatic Ejector, *Modern*	25	50	75
Shikari, .45-70 Government, Top Break, Side Lever, Automatic Ejector, *Modern*	50	75	100

RIFLE, SLIDE ACTION

	Fair	V. Good	Excellent
Model 422, .22 L.R.R.F., Tube Feed, Open Rear Sight, *Modern*	75	100	125

SHOTGUN, BOLT ACTION

	Fair	V. Good	Excellent
Model 348 Gamemaster, 12 and 16 Gauges, Tube Feed, Takedown, *Modern*	25	50	75
Model 349 Deluxe, 12 and 16 Gauges, Tube Feed, Takedown, Adjustable Choke, *Modern*	25	50	75
Model 351 Huntsman, 12 and 16 Gauges, Tube Feed, Takedown, Monte Carlo Stock, Adjustable Choke, *Modern*	25	50	75

	Fair	V. Good	Excellent
SHOTGUN, PERCUSSION			
Huntsman 12 Ga., Top Break, Side Lever, Reproduction, *Antique*	$50	$75	$100
SHOTGUN, DOUBLE BARREL, OVER-UNDER			
Model 1212, 12 Ga., Field Grade, Vent Rib, Single Selective Trigger, *Modern*	150	325	375
Model 1212 Waterfowl, Ga. Mag. 3", Field Grade, Vent Rib, Single Selective Trigger, *Modern*	150	350	400
SHOTGUN, DOUBLE BARREL, SIDE-BY-SIDE			
Model 404, Various Gauges, Hammerless, *Modern*	75	150	175
Model 404C, Various Gauges, Hammerless, Checkered Stock, *Modern*	75	125	175
SHOTGUN, SEMI-AUTOMATIC			
Model 403, .410 Ga., Takedown, *Modern*	75	150	200
SHOTGUN, SINGLESHOT			
Folding Gun, Various Gauges, Top Break, Hammer, Automatic Ejector, *Modern*	25	50	75
Model #1 Harrich, 12 Ga., Vent Rib, Engraved, Fancy Checkering, *Modern*	600	1250	1550
Model 148, Various Gauges, Top Break, Side Lever, Automatic Ejector, *Modern*	25	50	75
Model 158, Various Gauges, Top Break, Side Lever, Automatic Ejector, *Modern*	25	50	75
Model 159, Various Gauges, Top Break, Side Lever, Automatic Ejector, *Modern*	25	50	75
Model 162 Buck, 12 Ga., Top Break, Side Lever, Automatic Ejector, Peep Sights, *Modern*	25	50	75
Model 176, 10 Ga. 3½", Top Break, Side Lever, Automatic Ejector, *Modern*	25	50	75
Model 188 Deluxe, Various Gauges, Top Break, Side Lever, Automatic Ejector, *Modern*	15	25	50
Model 198 Deluxe, Various Gauges, Top Break, Side Lever, Automatic Ejector, *Modern*	15	25	50
Model 3, Various Gauges, Top Break, Hammerless, Automatic Ejector, *Modern*	25	50	75
Model 459 Youth, Various Gauges, Top Break, Side Lever, Automatic Ejector, *Modern*	25	50	75
Model 48, Various Gauges, Top Break, Hammer, Automatic Ejector, *Modern*	25	50	75
Model 480 Youth, Various Gauges, Top Break, Side Lever, Automatic Ejector, *Modern*	$25	$50	$75
Model 488 Deluxe, Various Gauges, Top Break, Hammer, Automatic Ejector, *Modern*	25	50	75
Model 490 Youth, Various Gauges, Top Break, Side Lever, Automatic Ejector, *Modern*	25	50	75
Model 5, Various Gauges, Top Break, Lightweight, Automatic Ejector, *Modern*	50	75	100
Model 6, Various Gauges, Top Break, Heavyweight, Automatic Ejector, *Modern*	50	75	100
Model 7, Various Gauges, Top Break, Automatic Ejector, *Modern*	25	50	75
Model 8 Standard, Various Gauges, Top Break, Automatic Ejector, *Modern*	25	50	75
Model 9, Various Gauges, Top Break, Automatic Ejector, *Modern*	25	50	75
Model 98, Various Gauges, Top Break, Side Lever, Automatic Ejector, *Modern*	25	50	75
SHOTGUN, SLIDE ACTION			
Model 400, Various Gauges, Solid Frame, *Modern*	75	150	175
Model 400, Various Gauges, Solid Frame, Vent Rib, *Modern*	75	150	175
Model 401, Various Gauges, Solid Frame, Adjustable Choke, *Modern*	75	150	175
Model 402, .410 Ga., Solid Frame, *Modern*	75	150	175
Model 440, Various Gauges, Solid Frame, *Modern*	75	150	175

HARRIS, HENRY

Payton, Pa. 1779–1783. See Kentucky Rifles.

HARRISON ARMS CO.

Made in Belgium for Sickles & Preston, Davenport, Iowa. See Crescent Fire Arms Co., Shotgun, Double Barrel, Side-by-Side; Shotgun, Singleshot.

HARTFORD ARMS & EQUIPMENT CO.

Hartford, Conn. 1929–1932. Acquired by High Standard Arms Co. in 1932.

	Fair	V. Good	Excellent
HANDGUN, MANUAL REPEATER			
.22 L.R.R.F., Singleshot Target, Clip Fed, Target Pistol, *Curio*	300	700	800
HANDGUN, SEMI-AUTOMATIC			
1st Model, .22 L.R.R.F., Clip Fed, Target Pistol, *Curio*	300	650	750
2nd Model, .22 L.R.R.F., Target Pistol, *Curio*	300	600	700

HARTFORD ARMS CO.

Made by Crescent for Simmons Hardware Co., St. Louis, Mo. See Crescent Fire Arms Co., Shotgun, Double Barrel, Side-by-Side; Shotgun, Singleshot.

HARTFORD ARMS CO.

Made by Norwich Falls Pistol Co., c. 1880.

HANDGUN, REVOLVER

	Fair	V. Good	Excellent
.32 Short R.F., 5 Shot, Spur Trigger, Solid Frame, Single Action, *Antique*	$75	$125	$175

HARVARD

Made by Crescent, c. 1900. See Crescent Fire Arms Co., Shotgun, Double Barrel, Side-By-Side; Shotgun, Singleshot.

HAUCK, WILBUR

West Arlington, Vt., c. 1950.

RIFLE, SINGLESHOT

	Fair	V. Good	Excellent
Target Rifle, Various Calibers, Target Sights, Target Stock, Adjustable Trigger, *Modern*	200	450	550

HAWES FIREARMS

Van Nuys, Calif. Manufactured by J. P. Sauer und Sohn, Eckernforde, Germany.

HANDGUN, REVOLVER

	Fair	V. Good	Excellent
Chief City Marshall, .25 Colt, Western Style, Single Action, Brass Grip Frame, Adjustable Sights, *Modern*	65	125	200
Chief Marshall, .357 Magnum, Western Style, Single Action, Brass Grip Frame, Adjustable Sights, *Modern*	65	125	200
Chief Marshall, .44 Magnum, Western Style, Single Action, Brass Grip Frame, Adjustable Sights, *Modern*	65	125	200
Denver Marshall, .22 L.R.R.F., Western Style, Single Action, Brass Grip Frame, Adjustable Sights, *Modern*	50	75	100
Denver Marshall, .22 L.R.R.F./ .22 W.M.R. Combo, Western Style, Single Action, Adjustable Sights, *Modern*	100	125	150
Montana Marshall, .22 L.R.R.F., Western Style, Single Action, Brass Grip Frame, *Modern*	50	75	100
Montana Marshall, .22 L.R.R.F./ .22 W.M.R. Combo, Western Style, Single Action, Brass Grip Frame, *Modern*	75	100	125
Montana Marshall, .357 Magnum/ 9mm Combo, Western Style, Single Action, Brass Grip Frame, *Modern*	$100	$175	$225
Montana Marshall, .44 Magnum, Western Style, Single Action, Brass Grip Frame, *Modern*	75	150	200
Montana Marshall, .44 Magnum/ .44-40 Combo, Western Style, Single Action, Brass Grip Frame, *Modern*	100	175	225
Montana Marshall, .45 Colt, Western Style, Single Action, Brass Grip Frame, *Modern*	75	150	200
Montana Marshall, .45 Colt/.45 ACP Combo, Western Style, Single Action, Brass Grip Frame, *Modern*	75	175	250
Silver City Marshall, .22 L.R.R.F., Western Style, Single Action, Brass Grip Frame, *Modern*	50	75	100
Silver City Marshall, .22 L.R.R.F./ .22 W.M.R., Western Style, Single Action, Brass Grip Frame, *Modern*	50	100	150
Silver City Marshall, .357 Magnum/ 9mm Combo, Western Style, Single Action, Brass Grip Frame, *Modern*	75	150	225
Silver City Marshall, .44 Magnum, Western Style, Single Action, Brass Grip Frame, *Modern*	75	150	225
Silver City Marshall, .44 Magnum/ .44-40 Combo, Western Style, Single Action, Brass Grip Frame, *Modern*	75	150	225
Silver City Marshall, .45 Colt, Western Style, Single Action, Brass Grip Frame, *Modern*	65	150	200
Silver City Marshall, .45 Colt/.45 ACP Combo, Western Style, Single Action, Brass Grip Frame, *Modern*	75	200	250
Texas Marshall, .22 L.R.R.F., Western Style, Single Action, Nickel Plated, *Modern*	50	75	100
Texas Marshall, .22 L.R.R.F./ 22 W.M.R., Combo, Western Style, Single Action, Nickel Plated, *Modern*	75	125	150
Texas Marshall, .357 Magnum, Western Style, Single Action, Nickel Plated, *Modern*	65	125	200
Texas Marshall, .357 Magnum/ 9mm Combo, Western Style, Single Action, Nickel Plated, *Modern*	75	150	225
Texas Marshall, .44 Magnum, Western Style, Single Action, Nickel Plated, *Modern*	65	125	200
Texas Marshall, .44 Magnum/ .44-40 Combo, Western Style, Single Action, Nickel Plated, *Modern*	100	175	250
Texas Marshall, .45 Colt, Western Style, Single Action, Nickel Plated, *Modern*	65	125	200

	Fair	V. Good	Excellent
Texas Marshall, .45 Colt/.45 ACP Combo, Western Style, Single Action, Nickel Plated, *Modern*	$100	$175	$250

HANDGUN, SEMI-AUTOMATIC

.25 ACP, Clip Fed, *Modern*	75	100	125

HANDGUN, SINGLESHOT

Stevens Favorite Copy, .22 L.R.R.F., Tip-Up, Plastic Grips, *Modern*	75	100	125
Stevens Favorite Copy, .22 L.R.R.F., Tip-Up, Plastic Grips, Target Sights, *Modern*	75	100	125
Stevens Favorite Copy, .22 L.R.R.F., Tip-Up, Rosewood Grips, *Modern*	75	100	125

HAWKEN, J. & S.

Jacob and Samuel Hawken, St. Louis, Mo. 1822–1862. John Gemmer purchased the business and continued it until 1890. Jacob Hawken came to St. Louis, Missouri from Maryland, having once been employed by the Harpers Ferry Armory. Hawken and James Lakenen, of Virginia, were in St. Louis as early as 1819, evidently in business as partners. Gunmakers in St. Louis had distinct advantages over those back East, since having the opportunity to speak directly with clients off the frontier allowed for convenient access to the market, and the benefit of their expertise on design and performance. Samuel Hawken joined his older brother in St. Louis, in 1822, setting up a business a few blocks distant. On the death of Lakenen, the brothers established the J & S Hawken shop. Guns so marked are within the years c. 1825 to 1850. Of rugged proportions and substantial calibers, Hawken rifles could stand up to the demands of tough frontier service. Furthermore, these handsomely styled arms were renowned for their accuracy. The Hawken soon became the standard by which all so-called "Rocky Mountain" rifles were judged. Customary mounts on the Hawkens were of iron, proving stronger than brass. The supreme Hawken rifle, made from the late 1830s into the 1840s, customarily had a barrel of about 38" length, heavy in weight, and of about .50 to .53 caliber. The stock was of maple, of half length in the forend, with an oval contoured cheekpiece. Average weight was a substantial 11 pounds. Hawkens were considered accurate up to and somewhat beyond 200 yards. Considering the tremendous interest in the great American West, Hawken rifles, made in limited numbers, and suffering from a high attrition rate, are among the most prized of frontier weaponry—a sure thing to increase in value and demand over the years. And with these arms, condition is not particularly important, since each dent, scratch, mar and scar likely represents some unknown adventure in the hands of some of the most fearsome men who courageously trod the frontier.

RIFLE, PERCUSSION

Gemmer Plains Rifle, Various Calibers, Hawken Style, *Antique* ..			Rare
Hawken Plains Rifle, Various Calibers, Hawken Style, *Antique* ..			Rare

From top, an S. Hawken percussion Plains rifle, made in .54 caliber, with iron mounts and without patchbox; a Leman, Lancaster, Plains rifle in .42 caliber and with artifically striped maple halfstock; and an A. Wurfflein, Philadelphia Plains rifle with back-action lock and in .50 caliber.

HAWKINS, HENRY

Schenectady, N.Y. 1769–1775. See Kentucky Rifles.

H.D.H.

Mre. d'Armes HDH, Liege, Belgium, c. 1910.

HANDGUN, REVOLVER

	Fair	V. Good	Excellent
10 Shot, Various Calibers, Double Action, *Curio*	$200	$400	$500
20 Shot, Various Calibers, Over-Under Barrels, Two Row Cylinder, Double Action, *Curio*	250	600	700
Constabulary Type, Various Calibers, Double Action, *Curio*	100	125	150
Ordnance Type, Various Calibers, Double Action, *Curio*	100	150	175
"Velo-Dog," Various Calibers, Folding Trigger, Double Action, Hammerless, *Curio*	50	100	200

HECKERT, PHILIP

York, Pa. 1769–1779. See Kentucky Rifles and Pistols.

HECKLER & KOCH

Oberndorf/Neckar, Germany. Recognized and respected for their quality, design, and engineering, H & K arms are rated amongst the finest performing sporting, target, self-defense and military arms made today.

HANDGUN, SEMI-AUTOMATIC

HK, Various Calibers, Clip Fed, Conversion Kit Only, *Each*	15	25	50

	Fair	V. Good	Excellent
HK, Various Calibers, Clip Fed, Double Action, with Conversion Kits All 4 Calibers, *Modern*	$250	$500	$600
HK P-7(PSP), 9mm Luger, Squeeze Cocking, *Modern*	250	575	675
HK P-9S, .45 ACP, Clip Fed, Double Action, *Modern*	175	325	400

Heckler & Koch P-9S Sport Competition

	Fair	V. Good	Excellent
HK P-9S, .45 ACP, Target Model, Clip Fed, Double Action, *Modern*	150	350	450
HK P-9S, .45 ACP, with Extra 8" Barrel, Clip Fed, Double Action, *Modern*	200	400	500
HK-4, .22 L.R.R.F., Clip Fed, Double Action, *Modern*	200	400	475
HK-4, .25 ACP, Clip Fed, Double Action, *Modern*	150	275	350
HK-4, .32 ACP, Clip Fed, Double Action, *Modern*	150	225	300
HK-4, .32 ACP, Clip Fed, Double Action, French Made, *Modern*	125	250	300
HK-4, .32 ACP, Clip Fed, Double Action, German Police, *Modern*	150	300	400
HK-4, .380 ACP, Clip Fed, Double Action, *Modern*	150	375	450
P-9S, 9mm Luger, Clip Fed, Double Action 5½" Barrel, Target Sights, *Modern*	150	350	450
P-9S Combat, 9mm Luger, Clip Fed, Double Action 4" Barrel, *Modern*	200	425	500
P-9S Combat, 9mm Luger, Clip Fed, Double Action 4" Barrel with .30 Luger Conversion Kit, *Modern*	300	625	700
P-9S Competition Kit, 9mm Luger, Clip Fed, Double Action, Extra Barrel, Target Sights, Target Grips, *Modern*	300	650	750
VP-70Z, 9mm Luger, Clip Fed, Double Action, 18 Shot Clip, *Modern*	150	300	350

RIFLE, SEMI-AUTOMATIC

	Fair	V. Good	Excellent
HK 770, .308 Win., Sporting Rifle, Checkered Stock, Monte Carlo Stock, *Modern*	250	550	650
HK 91 A-2 Package, .308 Win., Clip Fed, Sporting Version of Military Rifle, with Compensator, Polygonal Rifling, *Modern*	$700	$1500	$1750
HK 91 A-2, .308 Win., Clip Fed, Sporting Version of Military Rifle, with Compensator, *Modern*	600	1000	1250
HK 91 A-2, .308 Win., Clip Fed, Sporting Version of Military Rifle, Folding Stock with Compensator, Polygonal Rifling, *Modern*	600	1250	1500
HK 91 A-3, .308 Win., Clip Fed, Sporting Version of Military Rifle, Folding Stock with Compensator, *Modern*	600	1250	1500
HK 91, .22 L.R.R.F., Clip Fed, Conversion Kit Only	300	600	750
HK 91/93, For Scope Mount Add $75.00-$120.00			
HK 91/93, Light Bipod, Add $40.00-$60.00			
HK 93 A-2, .223 Rem., Clip Fed, Sporting Version of Military Rifle, with Compensator, *Modern*	500	1000	1250
HK 93 A-3, .223 Rem., Clip Fed, Sporting Version of Military Rifle, Folding Stock with Compensator, *Modern*	550	1250	1500

Heckler & Koch HK 93 A-3

	Fair	V. Good	Excellent
HK 94 A-2, 9mm Luger, Clip Fed, Carbine, Standard Stock, *Modern*	750	1750	2000

Heckler & Koch HK 94 A-2

	Fair	V. Good	Excellent
HK 94 A-3, 9mm Luger, Clip Fed, Carbine, Folding Stock, *Modern*	800	1850	2150
Model 270, .22 L.R.R.F., Clip Fed, Checkered Stock, Open Rear Sight, *Modern*	150	300	325
Model 300, .22 WMR, Clip Fed, Checkered Stock, Open Rear Sight, *Modern*	200	425	500

	Fair	V. Good	Excellent
Model 630, .223 Rem., Clip Fed, Checkered Stock, Open Rear Sight, *Modern*	$250	$500	$600
Model 940, .30/06, Clip Fed, Checkered Stock, Open Rear Sight, *Modern*	250	550	650
Model SL 6, .223 Rem., Clip Fed, Military Style Carbine, Open Rear Sight, *Modern*	200	450	575
Model SL 7, .308 Win., Clip Fed, Military Style Carbine, Open Rear Sight, *Modern*	175	425	550

Heckler & Koch SL 7

HEGE

Tradename of Hebsacker Gesellschaft and Hege GmbH, established in 1959 in Schwabisch Halle, West Germany. Now in Uberlingen/Bodensee, West Germany. Also see Beeman Precision Firearms. Founder and president Frederick Hebsacker, a talented master gunsmith, is also a master marketer and consummate entrepreneur in the domain of muzzle loading and replica firearms. His highly detailed catalog and stock of arms and accessories rank among the finest in the world. Among the exquisite products in the Hege catalog are finely made muzzle loaders, built to Hebsacker's own specifications, and based on such original arms as Manton flintlock dueling pistols and a complete line of muzzle loading revolvers. Some of the more refined of these arms are partially built by such best-quality gunmakers Uberti, and then perfected still further in the Hege workshops.

HANDGUN, PERCUSSION

	Fair	V. Good	Excellent
Silber Pistol, .33 Caliber, British Style, Engraved, Cased, Reproduction, *Antique*	150	375	425
Silber Pistol, .33 Caliber, French Style, Engraved, Gold Inlays, Cased, Reproduction, *Antique*	300	600	650

HANDGUN, SEMI-AUTOMATIC

	Fair	V. Good	Excellent
AP-63, .32 ACP, Clip Fed, Double Action, *Modern*	150	275	325
AP-66, .32 ACP, Clip Fed, Double Action, *Modern*	150	225	275
AP-66, .380 ACP, Clip Fed, Double Action, *Modern*	100	250	300

COMBINATION WEAPON, OVER-UNDER

	Fair	V. Good	Excellent
President, Various Calibers, Box Lock, Solid Rib, Double Trigger, Checkered Stock, *Modern*	300	675	725

Hege AP-66.32

RIFLE, MATCHLOCK

	Fair	V. Good	Excellent
Zeughaus Musket, .63 Caliber, Heavy Swiss Style, Plain, Reproduction, *Antique*	$100	$250	$300

HEINZELMANN, C.E.

Plochigen, Germany 1921-1928.

HANDGUN, SEMI-AUTOMATIC

	Fair	V. Good	Excellent
Heim, .25 ACP, Clip Fed, Blue, *Curio*	100	200	250

HELFRICHT

Alfred Krauser Waffenfabrik, Zella Mehlis, Germany 1921–1929.

HANDGUN, SEMI-AUTOMATIC

	Fair	V. Good	Excellent
Model 1, .25 ACP, Clip Fed, *Curio*	200	425	475
Model 2, .25 ACP, Clip Fed, *Curio*	200	400	450
Model 3, .25 ACP, Clip Fed, *Curio*	200	400	450
Model 4, .25 ACP, Clip Fed, *Curio*	150	350	400

HELVICE

Fab. d'Armes de Guerre de Grand Precision, Eibar, Spain.

HANDGUN, SEMI-AUTOMATIC

	Fair	V. Good	Excellent
.25 ACP, Clip Fed, *Modern*	50	125	150

HENNCH, PETER

Lancaster, Pa. 1770–1774. See Kentucky Rifles.

HENRY GUN CO.

Belgium, c. 1900.

SHOTGUN, DOUBLE BARREL, SIDE-BY-SIDE

	Fair	V. Good	Excellent
Various Gauges, Hammerless, Damascus Barrel, *Modern*	100	150	200
Various Gauges, Hammerless, Steel Barrel, *Modern*	125	175	225
Various Gauges, Outside Hammers, Damascus Barrel, *Modern*	100	150	200

Greg Martin, acknowledged leading dealer (and one of the top collectors) in the contemporary antique firearms scene. Treasures are from Butterfield & Butterfield auctions, the success of which is directly due to his leadership role.

Deluxe engraved presentation set of Colt Third Model Dragoon revolvers, by Gustave Young, and with U.S. cavalry history and backstrap inscriptions documenting shooting prize; realized $299,500 at the Repaire sale, April 1997.

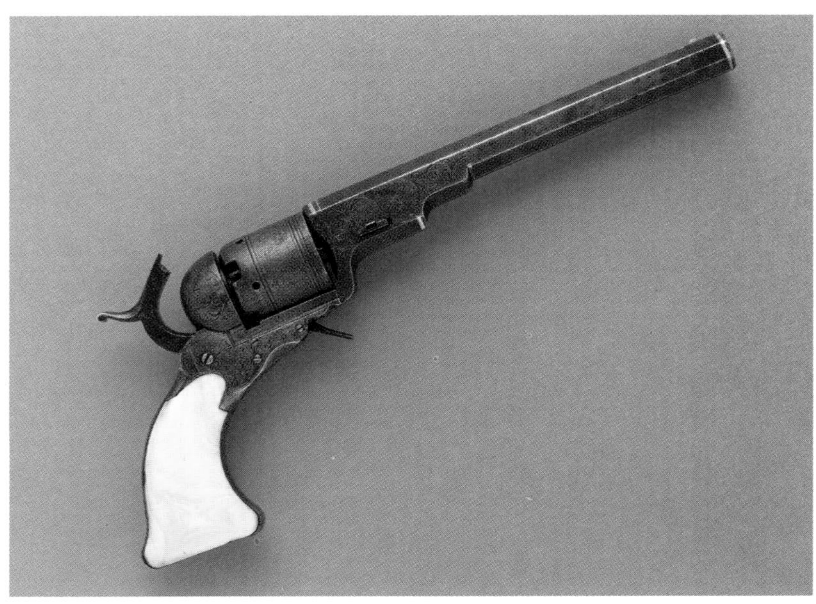

Engraved and silver-banded Colt Texas Paterson revolver, with ivory grips; also from the Repaire collection, sold for $200,500.

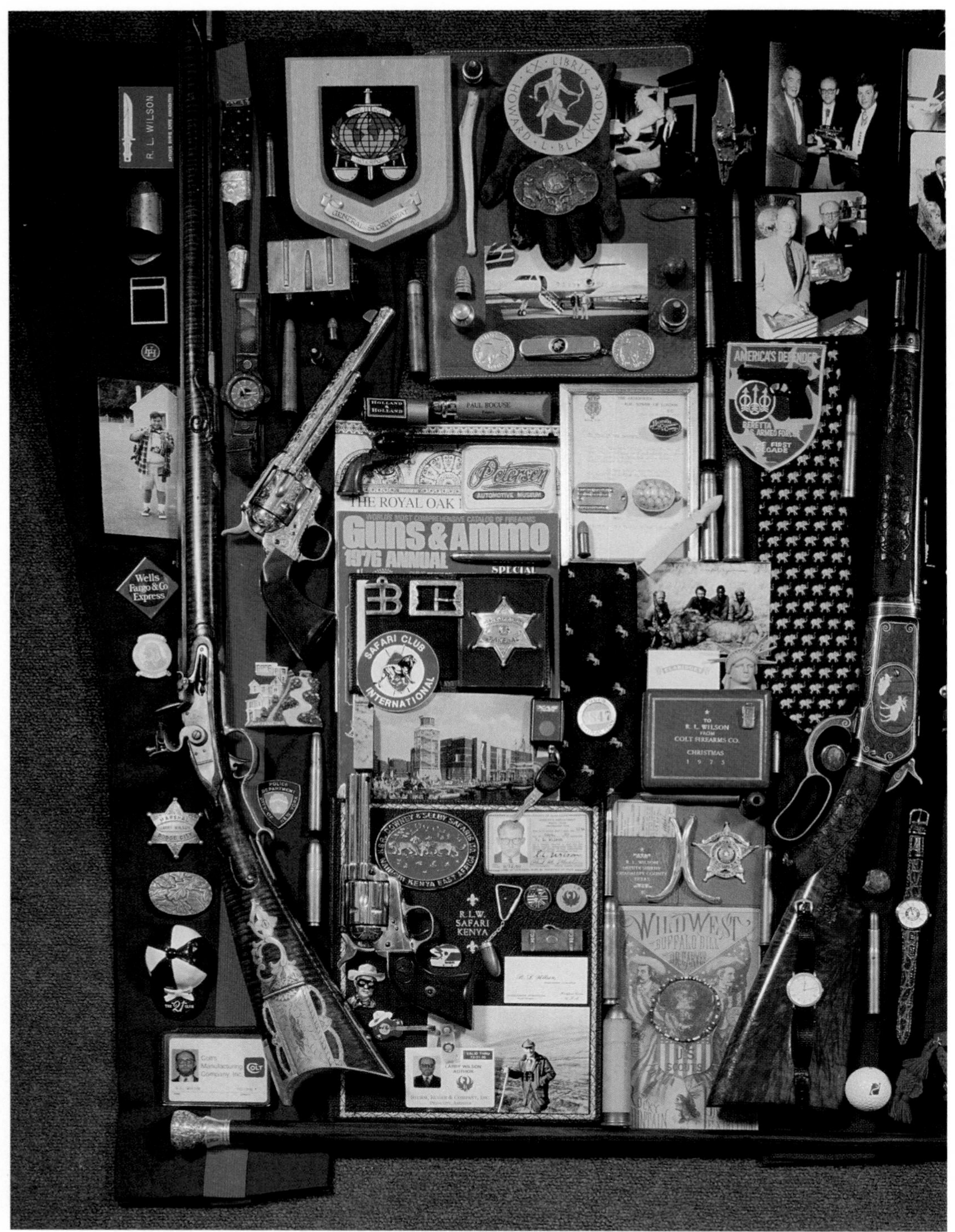

Memorabilia and images from a lifetime in gun collecting: longarms from left, *flintlock Kentucky rifle by Alvin White, Winchester Model 1886 engraved, gold and platinum inlaid and signed by John Ulrich (serial no. 129066), .35 Whelen Alaskan Guide rifle by Steve Berg, .375 H & H double rifle by Dumoulin & DeLeye; 7½" Single Action at* left *based on* Peacemaker *book cover gun, S.A.A. at* bottom *cutaway on other side, made for author when employed at Colt factory (1964–65); revolvers at* far right, *a magnificent Diamondback made for the author by Tiffany & Co. and gold inlaid by gifted engraver Andrew Bourbon, one of a pair of Belgian Navy Brevete revolvers (made for the emperor of Haiti), and a Texas Longhorn Arms prototype to the Alvin White deluxe series.*

The three sets of trousers from the author's service in the 1st Company, Governors Foot Guard, of Hartford, Connecticut, oldest continuous service military organization in the Western Hemisphere.

Richly decorated Bowie knife (with gold-tooled blue and silver-mounted scabbard) by Alvin White, as is ivory turtle netsuke, miniature sterling silver Wells Fargo & Co. treasure chest, and Scottish kilt dagger. Cane at bottom *gift to author*

from Andrew Bourbon. Ties by Hermes, J. Press and Hunting World, Inc. Honorary Deputy U.S. Marshal badge at left center.

Among celebrities pictured are Charles Addams and U.S. Historical Society chairman Robert Kline, James Stewart, Roger Mitchell (vice chairman, Holland & Holland, Ltd.), Hunting World founder/president Robert M. Lee, Tiffany & Co. chairman William R. Chaney and wife Carolyn, author/publisher Steven Fjestad, writer/wild West performer Phil Spangenberger, Mel Torme with former Colt's vice president Bob Morrison, Colt Historian Emeritus Martin S. Huber, Hartford real estate tycoon Thomas Standish (with rampant colt from factory dome), former Royal Army Museum director William Reid and wife Nina, and author's editor Robert Loomis. Author's oil-painting portrait by the talented C. Bourbeau.

Charging elephant photo at lower center *from author's first African safari, in Zambia, 1970.*

PHOTOGRAPH BY G. ALLAN BROWN.

From a lifetime in gun collecting: longarms from left, *Stephen Alexander mid-19th-century style English percussion sporting rifle, deluxe Henry rifle by A. Uberti & Co., Winchester Model 70 deluxe by David Miller (.375 H & H Magnum, engraved, gold inlaid by Leonard Francolini), and Rizzini side by side in .410 gauge, engraved by Bottega dell Artigiano. Flintlock pistol at* left, *a Kentucky style by A. A. White; Paterson at right by Uberti for U.S. Historical Society (above photograph showing William B. Ruger, editor Paul McCarthy and author at Holland & Holland, Ltd., New York, on occasion of book party for* Ruger & His Guns; *photo to* left *shows author at Hunting World book party for* Steel Canvas, *with Nathaniel de Rothschild, Wayne Sheets, and Colt chairman Donald Zilkha).*

Tower of London miniature at right center, *representing early museum training of author. Bronze of Texas Longhorn, a copyrighted polychrome work by the brilliant Harry Jackson. Engraved powder horn by Alvin White, as are sterling silver tankard, ivory and abalone hilted and silver-mounted California style knife, blued steel gold and silver eagle paperweight, and monogrammed gold belt buckle. Tooled leather western-style cuff by James Nottage, chief curator, Autry Museum of*

Western Heritage. Matchbooks reminiscent of restaurants and hotels patronized over the years. Photo of author with late father-in-law Arno Werner, and sons Peter, Christopher, and Stephen, by renowned photographer Steven Begleiter.

Among arms enthusiasts illustrated: radio talk-show host Barry Gray, comedian/entertainer Jerry Lewis (on occasion of visit to Colt factory), Chuck Yaeger, chef/restaurateur Paul Bocuse, shooting editor Jim Carmichel, photographer Peter Beard, Hunting World founder/president Robert M. Lee, Colt Historian Emeritus Ron Wagner, William B. Ruger grandchildren Amy, Adrienne, and Charlie Ruger, music industry executive Arma Andon and son, editor Angus Cameron and friend Joe Conte, Mel Torme, Gene Autry, author Harold L. Peterson, professional hunter Harry Mueller, Indy 500 winner Gordon Johncock, splendid gun photographer G. Allan Brown, friends Peter Buxtun and Angie Lussing (in Belgium, at the Royal Army Museum, Brussels), author's secretary, Barbara Cromeenes, and author's parents, Dr. and Mrs. John M. Wilson.

PHOTOGRAPH BY G. ALLAN BROWN.

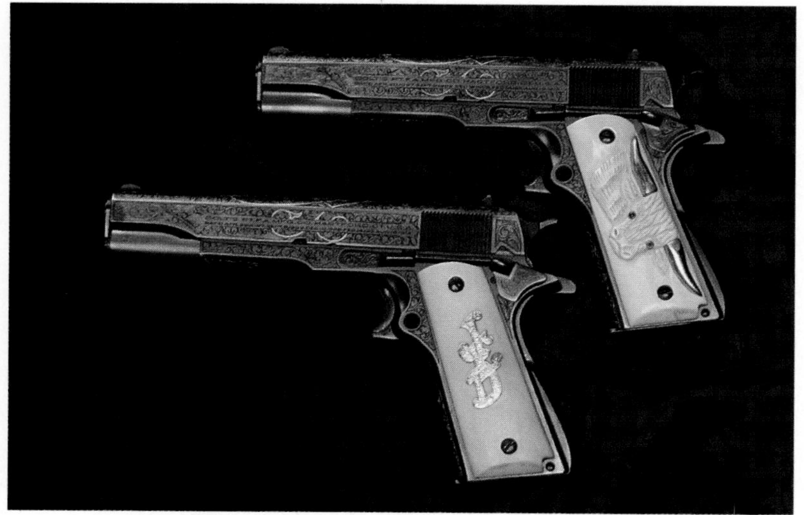

Factory engraved and gold inlaid pair of Colt National Match .45 semi-automatic pistols, decorated by Wilbur Glahn. Note relief-carved ivory grips, with JED monograms. Numerous special-order features. Custom made for J. E. Decker, Sheriff of Dallas County, Texas, with full factory documentation. Decker held Texas sheriff's badge #1 for life, and was one of Texas' most renowned lawmen, even having been involved in the pursuit of Bonnie and Clyde, along with Texas Ranger Frank Hamer. Serial numbers C201178 and C201184. Sold by Little John's for $187,000.

Exceptional Smith & Wesson 2nd Model American revolver, in .44 Henry rimfire caliber, Nimschke engraved, and plated in silver and gold; note Mexican eagle and snake ivory grips. Historic revolver, with knives, from Mariono Escobedo, the general in charge of the execution of Maximilian, Emperor of Mexico. Serial number 18054. Sold by Little John's, February 16th, 1997, at $44,000.

Rare Colt Model 1910/13 Patent Prototype semi-automatic pistol serial number 3, shown to Colt's board of directors by John M. Browning, to explain his 1913 patent modifications. Includes copy of August 19th, 1913, patent application. Realized $214,500 at Little John's sale of February 16th.

The sensational cover illustration for Christie's sale of November 8th, 1995, of selections from the W. Keith Neal Collection. The auction realized a total of approximately $1,700,000.

Below: Rare .38 bore French flintlock turnover sporting carbine, by Nicholas-Noel Boutet, Versailles, c. 1805. Realized approximately $32,000 at Christie's sale of the A. N. Kennard Collection, March 7th, 1996. Kennard was late deputy master of the Armouries, H.M. Tower of London.

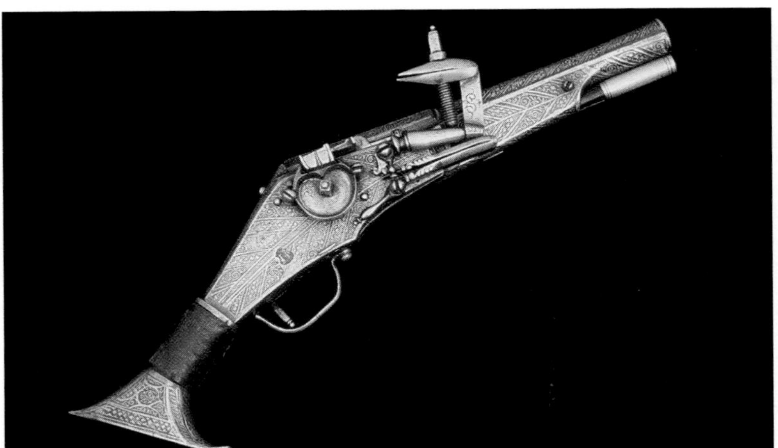

Rare 40-bore Nuremberg all-steel wheel lock belt pistol, of the late 16th century. Etched and gilt two-stage barrel with mauresques and chevron designs; the breech stamped with initials PD (for Peter Danner), and an N. Believed from a group of all-steel pistols in the Arsenal of the Council of Ten, Palazzo Ducale, Venice. Sold at Christie's November 20th, 1996, sale, for approximately $18,000.

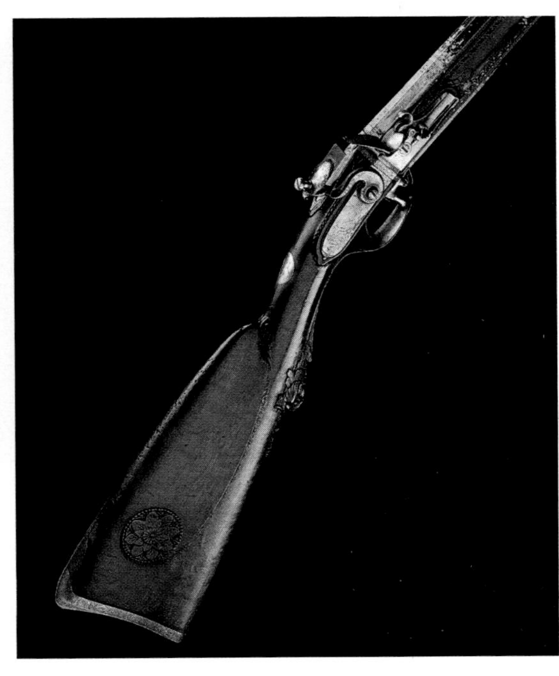

FROM CHRISTIE'S, LONDON

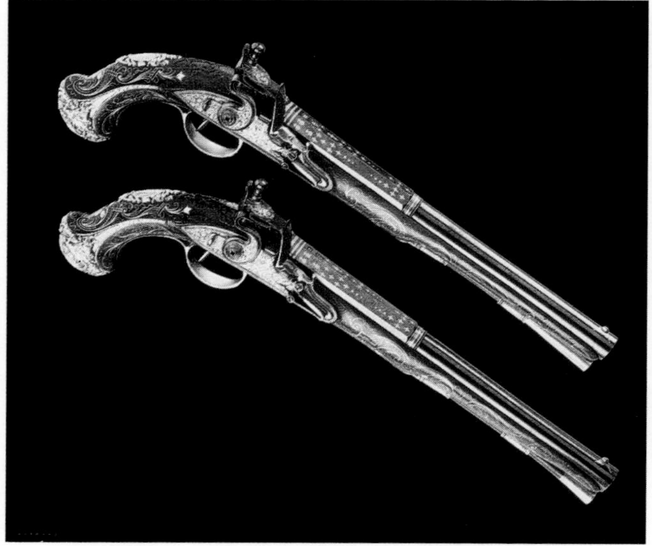

Magnificent pair of 20-bore silver-mounted flintlock pistols, by Henry Hadley, London, c. 1765. Spanish-style barrels. Escutcheons engraved with the arms of Clerk of Penicuik (Scotland); pistols were likely made for George, second son of Sir John Clerk, who became 4th Baronet; he died in 1784. Reached a record auction price for European guns or pistols, in excess of $260,000, at Christie's auction of March 27th, 1996.

Cased gold-mounted Royal presentation .54 caliber Tranter patent five-shot double-action percussion revolver, supplied by crown jewelers Garrards to the Prince of Wales, later King Edward VII, in 1869. Serial number 14031T. Barrel with signature "R.S. Garrard. & Co. London." Believed presented by Albert Edward, Prince of Wales, to Prince Abdulhamid (later Sultan Abdulhamid II (reign from 1876 to 1909), April 1869, on a state visit to Constantinople. To be sold July 16th, 1997, by Christie's, London, with estimate of approximately $18,000 to $28,000.

Book signing party by Hunting World's New York flagship store, November 1995, on publication of Steel Canvas. *From the* left, *Wayne Sheets, executive director, NRA Foundation, William R. Chaney, Chairman of the Board, Tiffany & Co., author, celebrated photographer (later stomped on by enraged female elephant), Peter Beard, and host Robert M. Lee, founder, president of Hunting World, Inc. Everyone in the picture is a keen shooter and firearms enthusiast.*

FROM A PRIVATE SALE

One of the most extraordinary and sought-after of all firearms rarities: Texas or Holster Model Paterson revolver, serial number 525, with rare extra 12-inch barrel; the cased set with 4$^{11}/_{16}$" barrel, extra cylinder, and various accessories. Discovered in 1996 in France, and now in a private American collection. A private sale by Greg Martin, and brought to America by Martin Lane.

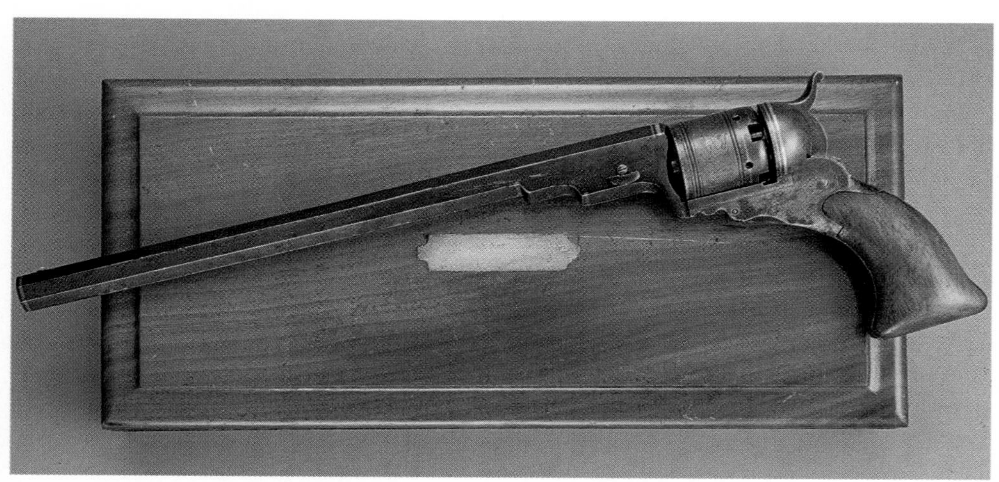

	Fair	V. Good	Excellent
Various Gauges, Outside Hammers, Steel Barrel, *Modern*	$100	$150	$200

SHOTGUN, SINGLESHOT

	Fair	V. Good	Excellent
Various Gauges, Hammer, Steel Barrel, *Modern*	50	75	100

HENRY, ALEXANDER

Edinburgh, Scotland 1869–1895. One of the most respected of British gunmakers, Alexander Henry's influence continues to this day, as reflected in such contemporary arms as the Ruger No. 1 Sporting rifle, which features a "Henry-style forend." A number of Henry sporting rifles are in the private arms collection of William B. Ruger, some of which appear in the author's *Ruger & His Guns.* The design and quality of Alexander Henry rifles reflects the masterful skills of British Empire gunmakers. Collecting in this area of interest tends to be expensive, although specimens are available showing a fair amount of use, and thus at more reasonable prices.

RIFLE, DOUBLE BARREL, SIDE-BY-SIDE

	Fair	V. Good	Excellent
.500/450 Mag. BPE, Damascus Barrel, Engraved, Fancy Checkering, Ornate, Cased with Accessories, Hammerless, *Antique*	2500	4750	5250

HERCULES

Made by Stevens Arms.

SHOTGUN, DOUBLE BARREL, SIDE-BY-SIDE

	Fair	V. Good	Excellent
M 315, Various Gauges, Hammerless, Steel Barrel, *Modern*	75	150	175
Model 215, 12 and 16 Gauges, Outside Hammers, Steel Barrel, *Modern*	75	150	175
Model 311, Various Gauges, Hammerless, Steel Barrel, *Modern*	75	175	200
Model 3151, Various Gauges, Hammerless, Recoil Pad, Front & Rear Bead Sights, *Modern*	75	175	200
Model 5151, Various Gauges, Hammerless, Steel Barrel, *Modern*	75	175	200

SHOTGUN, SINGLESHOT

	Fair	V. Good	Excellent
Model 94, Various Gauges, Takedown, Automatic Ejector, Plain Hammer, *Modern*	25	50	75

HERMETIC

Tradename used by Bernadon-Martin, St. Etienne, France, c. 1912.

HANDGUN, SEMI-AUTOMATIC

	Fair	V. Good	Excellent
B.M., .32 ACP, Clip Fed, *Curio*	150	275	325

HERMITAGE

Made by Stevens Arms.

SHOTGUN, SINGLESHOT

	Fair	V. Good	Excellent
Model 90, Various Gauges, Takedown, Automatic Ejector, Plain Hammer, *Modern*	$25	$50	$75

HERMITAGE ARMS CO.

Made by Crescent for Grey & Dudley Hdw. Co., Nashville, Tenn. See Crescent Fire Arms Co., Shotgun, Double Barrel, Side-By-Side; Shotgun, Singleshot.

HERO

Made by Manhattan/American Standard.

HANDGUN, SINGLESHOT PISTOL

	Fair	V. Good	Excellent
.34 Caliber, American Standard, Spur Trigger, Solid Frame, Single Action, *Antique*	100	200	275
.34 Caliber, Manhattan, Spur Trigger, Solid Frame, Single Action, *Antique*	100	225	300

HEROLD

Tradename of Franz Jager & Co., Suhl, Germany 1923–1939.

RIFLE, BOLT ACTION

	Fair	V. Good	Excellent
Herold Repetierbuchse, .22 Hornet, Set Triggers, Checkered Stock, *Modern*	400	750	800

HERTERS

Distributor & Importer in Waseca, Minn.

HANDGUN, REVOLVER

	Fair	V. Good	Excellent
Guide, .22 L.R.R.F., Swing-Out Cylinder, Double Action, *Modern*	50	75	100
Power-Mag, .357 Magnum, Western Style, Single Action, *Modern*	75	100	125
Power-Mag, .401 Herter Mag., Western Style, Single Action, *Modern*	75	100	125
Power-Mag, .44 Magnum, Western Style, Single Action, *Modern*	75	125	150
Western, .22 L.R.R.F., Single Action, Western Style, *Modern*	25	50	75

RIFLE, BOLT ACTION

	Fair	V. Good	Excellent
Model J-9 Hunter, Various Calibers, Plain, Monte Carlo Stock, *Modern*	75	150	200
Model J-9 Presentation, Various Calibers, Checkered Stock, Monte Carlo Stock, Sling Swivels, *Modern*	75	175	225
Model J-9 Supreme, Various Calibers, Checkered Stock, Monte Carlo Stock, Sling Swivels, *Modern*	100	200	250
Model U-9 Hunter, Various Calibers, Plain, Monte Carlo Stock, *Modern*	75	125	175

	Fair	V. Good	Excellent
Model U-9 Presentation, Various Calibers, Checkered Stock, Monte Carlo Stock, Sling Swivels, *Modern*	$75	$150	$200
Model U-9 Supreme, Various Calibers, Checkered Stock, Sling Swivels, Monte Carlo Stock, *Modern*	75	175	225

SHOTGUN, SEMI-AUTOMATIC

Model SL-18, 12 Ga. 3", Checkered Stock, *Modern*	125	225	275

SHOTGUN, SINGLESHOT

Model 151, Various Gauges, Hammer, *Modern*	50	75	100

HESS, JACOB

Stark Co., Ohio 1842–1860. See Kentucky Rifles.

HESS, SAMUEL

Lancaster, Pa., c. 1771. See Kentucky Rifles.

HEYM

Franz W. Heym, 1934–1945 in Suhl, Germany, now in Munnerstadt, Germany.

COMBINATION WEAPON, DRILLING

Model 33, Various Calibers, Hammerless, Double Triggers, Engraved, Checkered Stock, Express Sights, *Curio*	2000	4500	5000
Model 37, Various Calibers, Hammerless, Sidelock, Double Rifle Barrels, Engraved, Checkered Stock, *Curio*	3500	8000	9000
Model 37, Various Calibers, Hammerless, Sidelock, Engraved, Checkered Stock, *Curio*	3500	7500	8500
Model 37 Deluxe, Various Calibers, Hammerless, Sidelock, Double Rifle Barrels, Engraved, Checkered Stock, *Curio*	4000	8500	9500

RIFLE, BOLT ACTION

Model SR-20, Various Calibers, Fancy Wood, Double Set Triggers, *Curio*	600	1000	1250
Model SR-20 Hunter, Various Calibers, Fancy Wood, Double Set Triggers, *Curio*	450	950	1100

COMBINATION WEAPON, OVER-UNDER

Model 22S, Various Calibers, Single Set Trigger, Checkered Stock, Light Engraving, *Curio*	900	2000	2500
Model 55BF (77BF), Various Calibers, Boxlock, Double Triggers, Checkered Stock, Engraved, *Curio*	1800	4000	4500

	Fair	V. Good	Excellent
Model 55BFSS (77BFSS), Various Calibers, Sidelock, Double Triggers, Checkered Stock, *Curio*	$1500	$3500	$4000

RIFLE, SINGLESHOT

Model HR-30, Various Calibers, Fancy Wood, Engraved, Single Set Trigger, Ruger Action, Round Barrel, *Curio*	1200	2000	2500
Model HR-38, Various Calibers, Fancy Wood, Engraved, Single Set Trigger, Ruger Action, Octagon Barrel, *Curio*	1300	2500	3000

RIFLE, DOUBLE BARREL, OVER-UNDER

Model 88-B, Various Calibers, Boxlock, Engraved, Checkered Stock, *Curio*	3000	7500	9000
Model 88-B Safari, Various Calibers, Sidelock, Engraved, Checkered Stock, *Curio*	3500	8500	11000

SHOTGUN, DOUBLE BARREL, OVER-UNDER

Model 55F (77F), Various Gauges, Boxlock, Engraved, Checkered Stock, Double Triggers, *Curio*	2000	3750	4250
Model 55FSS (77FSS), Various Gauges, Sidelock, Engraved, Checkered Stock, Double Triggers, *Curio*	1700	4000	4500

HIGGINS, J.C.

Tradename used by Sears-Roebuck, 1946–1962.

HANDGUN, REVOLVER

Model 88, .22 L.R.R.F., *Modern*	25	50	75
Model 88 Fisherman, .22 L.R.R.F., *Modern*	25	50	75
Ranger, .22 L.R.R.F., *Modern*	25	50	75

HANDGUN, SEMI-AUTOMATIC

Model 80, .22 L.R.R.F., Clip Fed, Hammerless, *Modern*	50	75	100
Model 85, .22 L.R.R.F., Clip Fed, Hammer, *Modern*	75	100	125

RIFLE, BOLT ACTION

Model 228, .22 L.R.R.F., Clip Fed, *Modern*	15	25	50
Model 229, .22 L.R.R.F., Tube Feed, *Modern*	15	25	50
Model 245, .22 L.R.R.F., Singleshot, *Modern*	15	25	50
Model 51, Various Calibers, Checkered Stock, *Modern*	100	175	225
Model 51 Special, Various Calibers, Checkered Stock, Light Engraving, *Modern*	125	225	275

	Fair	V. Good	Excellent
RIFLE, LEVER ACTION			
.22 WMR, *Modern*	$25	$50	$75
Model 45, Various Calibers, Tube Feed, Carbine, *Modern*	25	50	75
RIFLE, SEMI-AUTOMATIC			
Model 25, .22 L.R.R.F., Clip Fed, *Modern*	15	25	50
Model 31, .22 L.R.R.F., Tube Feed, *Modern*	25	50	75
RIFLE, SLIDE ACTION			
Model 33, .22 L.R.R.F., Tube Feed, *Modern*	25	50	75
SHOTGUN, BOLT ACTION			
Model 10, Various Gauges, Tube Feed, 5 Shot, *Modern*	25	50	75
Model 11, Various Gauges, Tube Feed, 3 Shot, *Modern*	50	50	50
SHOTGUN, DOUBLE BARREL, SIDE-BY-SIDE			
Various Calibers, Plain, Takedown, Hammerless, *Modern*	75	150	175
SHOTGUN, SEMI-AUTOMATIC			
Model 66, 12 Ga., Plain Barrel, *Modern*	75	125	175
Model 66, 12 Ga., Plain Barrel, Adjustable Choke, *Modern*	75	150	175
Model 66, 12 Ga., Vent Rib, Adjustable Choke, *Modern*	75	150	175
Model 66 Deluxe, 12 Ga., *Modern*	75	150	175
SHOTGUN, SINGLESHOT			
Various Calibers, Takedown, Adjustable Choke, Plain, Hammer, *Modern*	25	50	75
SHOTGUN, SLIDE ACTION			
Model 20 Deluxe, 12 Ga., *Modern*	75	125	150
Model 20 Deluxe, 12 Ga., Vent Rib, Adjustable Choke, *Modern*	75	125	150
Model 20 Special, 12 Ga., Vent Rib, Adjustable Choke, *Modern*	75	150	200
Model 20 Standard, 12 Ga., *Modern*	50	100	150

HIGH STANDARD

High Standard Mfg. Co. 1926 to the present, first in New Haven, Conn., then as High Standard Sporting Firearms in Hamden, Conn., now as High Standard, Inc. in East Hartford, Conn.; reorganized and factory now in Dallas, Texas, with office in Hartford. The product lines of the High Standard company commenced with .22 rimfire self-loading pistols, and developed into one of the finest lines in the history of target and sport handguns of that caliber. In the post–World War II years, attempts were made to fill out the product line, eventually contributing to the company's temporary demise. One of the most capable engineers and designers to work for High Standard was Harry Sefried II, whose years of creative engineering at Winchester (assisting "Carbine" Williams) and at Sturm, Ruger, & Co. (under William B. Ruger) established him as one of the 20th century's most talented arms innovators. The High Standard Sentinel series of revolvers was one of Sefried's creations, achieving over the million mark in sales. After difficulties with the East Hartford operation, the company was reorganized, and presently has a production facility in Dallas, Texas, and office in Hartford, Connecticut.

	Fair	V. Good	Excellent
HANDGUN, DOUBLE BARREL, OVER-UNDER			
Derringer, .22 L.R.R.F., Double Action, Top Break, Electroless, Nickel Plated, Hammerless, Walnut Grips, Cased, *Modern*	$75	$150	$175
Derringer, .22 L.R.R.F., Double Action, Top Break, Nickel Plated, Hammerless, Cased, *Modern*	75	150	175
Derringer, .22 WMR, Double Action, 2 Shot, *Modern*	75	150	175
Derringer, .22 WMR, Double Action, Top Break, Electroless, Nickel Plated, Hammerless, Walnut Grips, Cased, *Modern*	75	175	200
Derringer, .22 WMR, Double Action, Top Break, Nickel Plated, Hammerless, Cased, *Modern*	75	175	200
Derringer, 22 L.R.R.F., Double Action, 2 Shot, *Modern*	75	125	150
Gold Derringer, .22 WMR, Double Action, 2 Shot, *Modern*	125	300	400
Silver Derringer, .22 WMR, Double Action, Top Break, Hammerless, Cased, *Modern*	100	250	350
HANDGUN, PERCUSSION			
.36, Griswald & Gunnison, Revolver, Commemorative, Cased, Reproduction, *Antique*	100	200	225
.36 Leech & Rigdon, Revolver, Commemorative, Cased, Reproduction, *Antique*	100	200	225
.36 Schneider & Glassick, Revolver, Commemorative, Cased, Reproduction, *Antique*	100	250	275
HANDGUN, REVOLVER			
For Nickel Plating, Add $7.50-$12.50			
Crusader, Deluxe Pair, .44 Mag. & .45 Colt, Commemorative, Double Action, Swing-Out Cylinder, Gold Inlays, Engraved, *Modern*	900	2000	2500
Double-Nine, .22 L.R.R.F., Double Action, Western Style, *Modern*	75	125	150
Double-Nine, .22 LR/.22 WMR Combo, Double Action, Western Style, Alloy Frame, *Modern*	75	150	175
Double-Nine, .22 LR/.22 WMR Combo, Double Action, Western Style, *Modern*	75	150	200

	Fair	V. Good	Excellent
Double-Nine Deluxe, .22 LR/.22 WMR Combo, Double Action, Western Style, Adjustable Sights, *Modern*	$100	$200	$225
Durango, .22 L.R.R.F., Double Action, Western Style, *Modern*	50	100	125
High Sierra, .22 LR/.22 WMR Combo, Double Action, Western Style, Octagon Barrel, *Modern*	75	125	150
High Sierra Deluxe, .22 LR/.22 WMR Combo, Double Action, Western Style, Octagon Barrel, Adjustable Sights, *Modern*	75	150	175
Kit Gun, .22 L.R.R.F., Double Action, 9 Shot, Swing-Out Cylinder, Adjustable Sights, *Modern*	75	125	175
Longhorn, .22 LR/.22 WMR Combo, Double Action, Adjustable Sights, Western Style, *Modern*	100	150	175
Longhorn, .22 LR/.22 WMR Combo, Double Action, Western Style, Alloy Frame, *Modern*	75	100	125
Longhorn, .22 LR/.22 WMR Combo, Double Action, Western Style, *Modern*	75	125	150

High Standard Longhorn

	Fair	V. Good	Excellent
Natchez, .22 LR/.22 WMR Combo, Double Action, Western Style, Birdshead Grip, Allow Frame, *Modern*	$50	$75	$100
Posse, .22 LR/.22 WMR Combo, Double Action, Western Style, Brass Gripframe, *Modern*	50	75	100
Sentinel, .22 L.R.R.F., Double Action, Swing-Out Cylinder, *Modern*	75	125	150
Sentinel Deluxe, .22 L.R.R.F., Double Action, Swing-Out Cylinder, *Modern*	75	150	175
Sentinel Imperial, .22 L.R.R.F., Double Action, Swing-Out Cylinder, *Modern*	75	150	175
Sentinel Mk I, .22 L.R.R.F., Double Action, Swing-Out Cylinder, *Modern*	75	125	175

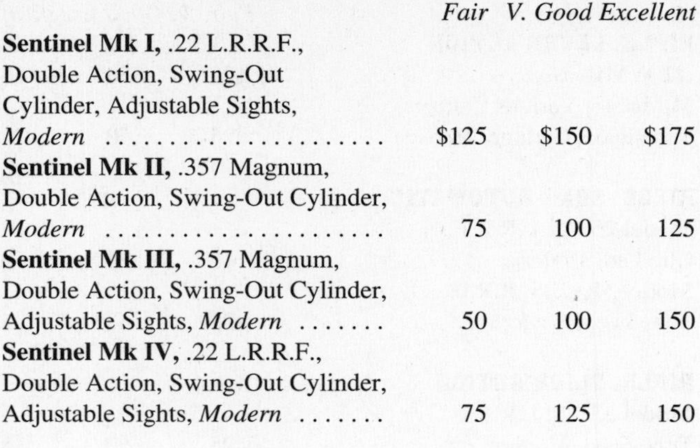

	Fair	V. Good	Excellent
Sentinel Mk I, .22 L.R.R.F., Double Action, Swing-Out Cylinder, Adjustable Sights, *Modern*	$125	$150	$175
Sentinel Mk II, .357 Magnum, Double Action, Swing-Out Cylinder, *Modern*	75	100	125
Sentinel Mk III, .357 Magnum, Double Action, Swing-Out Cylinder, Adjustable Sights, *Modern*	50	100	150
Sentinel Mk IV, .22 L.R.R.F., Double Action, Swing-Out Cylinder, Adjustable Sights, *Modern*	75	125	150

High Standard Sentinel

	Fair	V. Good	Excellent
Sentinel Mk IV, .22 WMR, Double Action, Swing-Out Cylinder, Adjustable Sights, *Modern*	50	100	150
Sentinel Mk IV, .22 WMR, Double Action, Swing-Out Cylinder, *Modern*	75	100	125
Sentinel Snub, .22 L.R.R.F., Double Action, Swing-Out Cylinder, *Modern*	50	75	100

HANDGUN, SEMI-AUTOMATIC

	Fair	V. Good	Excellent
"Benner Olympic," .22 L.R.R.F., Supermatic, Military, Engraved, *Curio*	300	650	750
10-X Custom, .22 L.R.R.F., Heavy Barrel, Military Grip, Target Sights, *Modern*	700	1500	1750
Citation (Early), .22 L.R.R.F., Supermatic, Clip Fed, Hammerless, Tapered Barrel, *Modern*	150	350	450
Citation (Early), .22 L.R.R.F., Supermatic, Clip Fed, Hammerless, Heavy Barrel, *Modern*	150	375	475
Citation (Late), .22 L.R.R.F., Supermatic, Clip Fed, Hammerless, Frame-Mounted Rear Sight, Heavy Barrel, *Modern*	175	375	425
Citation (Late), .22 L.R.R.F., Supermatic, Military, Hammerless, Frame-Mounted Rear Sight, Fluted Barrel, *Modern*	175	350	425

	Fair	V. Good	Excellent
Citation (Late), .22 L.R.R.F., Supermatic, Military, Hammerless, Frame-Mounted Rear Sight, Heavy Barrel, *Modern*	$175	$375	$450
Duramatic, .22 L.R.R.F., Clip Fed, Hammerless, *Modern*	125	275	350
Field King, .22 L.R.R.F., Clip Fed, Hammerless, Heavy Barrel, *Modern*	150	300	350
Flight King, .22 Short R.F., Clip Fed, Hammerless, *Modern*	125	275	325
Flight King, .22 Short R.F., Clip Fed, Hammerless, Extra Barrel, *Modern*	150	300	350
Flight King, .22 Short R.F., Clip Fed, Hammerless, Lightweight, *Modern*	125	275	350
Flight King, .22 Short R.F., Clip Fed, Hammerless, Lightweight, Extra Barrel, *Modern*	150	300	375
For Nickel Plating, Add $20.00-$35.00			
Model A, .22 L.R.R.F., Clip Fed, Hammerless, *Curio*	175	400	450
Model B, .22 L.R.R.F., Clip Fed, Hammerless, *Curio*	175	350	400
Model B, .22 L.R.R.F., Navy, Clip Fed, Hammerless, *Curio*	200	475	550
Model C, .22 Short R.F., Clip Fed, Hammerless, *Curio*	200	450	525
Model D, .22 L.R.R.F., Clip Fed, Hammerless, Heavy Barrel, *Curio*	225	450	525
Model E, .22 L.R.R.F., Clip Fed, Hammerless, Heavy Barrel, Target Grips, *Curio*	300	650	750
Model G-380, .380 ACP, Clip Fed, Hammer, Takedown, *Curio*	200	425	500
Model G-B, .22 L.R.R.F., Clip Fed, Hammerless, Takedown, *Curio*	200	400	450
Model G-B, .22 L.R.R.F., Clip Fed, Hammerless, Takedown, Extra Barrel, *Curio*	200	450	525
Model G-D, .22 L.R.R.F., Clip Fed, Hammerless, Takedown, *Curio*	225	500	600
Model G-D, .22 L.R.R.F., Clip Fed, Hammerless, Takedown, Extra Barrel, *Curio*	250	550	650
Model G-E, .22 L.R.R.F., Clip Fed, Hammerless, Takedown, Extra Barrel, *Curio*	400	800	950
Model G-E, .22 L.R.R.F., Clip Fed, Hammerless, Takedown, *Curio*	350	750	900
Model G-O, .22 Short, Clip Fed, Hammerless, Takedown, Extra Barrel, *Curio*	450	900	1050
Model G-O, .22 Short, Clip Fed, Hammerless, Takedown, *Curio*	400	850	1000
Model H-A, .22 L.R.R.F., Clip Fed, Hammer, *Curio*	250	550	650
Model H-B, .22 L.R.R.F., Clip Fed, Hammer, *Curio*	175	375	450

	Fair	V. Good	Excellent
Model H-D Military, .22 L.R.R.F., Clip Fed, Hammer, Heavy Barrel, Thumb Safety, *Curio*	$175	$375	$425
Model H-D, .22 L.R.R.F., Clip Fed, Hammer, Heavy Barrel, *Curio*	400	850	1000
Model H-E, .22 L.R.R.F., Clip Fed, Hammer, Heavy Barrel, Target Grips, *Curio*	600	1250	1500
Model SB, .22 L.R.R.F., Clip Fed, Hammerless, Smoothbore, Class 3	200	400	475
Olympic I.S.U., .22 Short R.F., Clip Fed, Hammerless, Military, Frame-Mounted Rear Sights, *Modern*	225	500	600
Olympic I.S.U., .22 Short R.F., Clip Fed, Hammerless, Frame- Mounted Rear Sights, *Modern*	250	525	600
Olympic I.S.U., .22 Short R.F., Supermatic, Clip Fed, Hammerless, Military, *Modern*	250	550	650
Olympic I.S.U., .22 Short R.F., Supermatic, Clip Fed, Hammerless, *Modern*	250	525	600
Olympic, .22 Short R.F., Clip Fed, Hammerless, *Modern*	250	475	550
Olympic, .22 Short R.F., Clip Fed, Hammerless, Extra Barrel, *Modern*	250	575	650
Plinker, .22 L.R.R.F., Clip Fed, Hammer, *Modern*	125	200	250
Sharpshooter (Late), .22 L.R.R.F., Military Grip, Clip Fed, Hammerless, *Modern*	150	375	425
Sharpshooter, .22 L.R.R.F., Clip Fed, Hammerless, *Modern*	150	350	400

High Standard Sharpshooter

	Fair	V. Good	Excellent
Sport King (Late), .22 L.R.R.F., Military Grip, Clip Fed, Hammerless, *Modern*	125	225	275
Sport King, .22 L.R.R.F., Clip Fed, Hammerless, *Modern*	100	250	300
Sport King, .22 L.R.R.F., Clip Fed, Hammerless, Extra Barrel, *Modern*	125	250	325
Sport King, .22 L.R.R.F., Clip Fed, Hammerless, Lightweight, *Modern*	125	250	300

	Fair	V. Good	Excellent
Sport King, .22 L.R.R.F., Clip Fed, Hammerless, Lightweight, Extra Barrel, *Modern*	$125	$250	$325
Supermatic, .22 L.R.R.F., Clip Fed, Hammerless, *Modern*	200	450	525
Supermatic, .22 L.R.R.F., Clip Fed, Hammerless, Extra Barrel, *Modern*	200	450	550
Survival Pack, .22 L.R.R.F., Sharpshooter (Late), Electroless Nickel Plated, Cased with Accessories, *Modern*	175	375	450
Tournament, .22 L.R.R.F., Supermatic, Clip Fed, Hammerless, *Modern*	175	375	425
Tournament, .22 L.R.R.F., Supermatic, Clip Fed, Hammerless, Military, *Modern*	175	350	400
Trophy (Early), .22 L.R.R.F., Supermatic, Clip Fed, Hammerless, *Modern*	200	475	525
Trophy (Late), .22 L.R.R.F., Supermatic, Military, Hammerless, Frame-Mounted Rear Sight, Fluted Barrel, *Modern*	200	400	500
Trophy (Late), .22 L.R.R.F., Supermatic, Military, Hammerless, Frame-Mounted Rear Sight, Heavy Barrel, *Modern*	225	500	575
Victor, .22 L.R.R.F., Heavy Barrel, Military Grip, Solid Rib, Target Sights, *Modern*	225	450	550
Victor, .22 L.R.R.F., Heavy Barrel, Military Grip, Vent Rib, Target Sights, *Modern*	250	500	575

RIFLE, BOLT ACTION

	Fair	V. Good	Excellent
Hi Power Deluxe, Various Calibers, Monte Carlo Stock, Checkered Stock, *Modern*	100	200	250
High Power, Various Calibers, Field Grade, *Modern*	75	175	225

RIFLE, SEMI-AUTOMATIC

	Fair	V. Good	Excellent
Sport King, .22 L.R.R.F., Field Grade, Carbine, Tube Feed, *Modern*	50	75	100
Sport King, .22 L.R.R.F., Field Grade, Tube Feed, *Modern*	25	50	75
Sport King Deluxe, .22 L.R.R.F., Tube Feed, Monte Carlo Stock, Checkered Stock, *Modern*	50	100	150
Sport King Special, .22 L.R.R.F., Tube Feed, Monte Carlo Stock, *Modern*	50	75	100

RIFLE, SLIDE ACTION

	Fair	V. Good	Excellent
.22 L.R.R.F., Flight-King, Tube Feed, Monte Carlo Stock, *Modern*	50	75	100

SHOTGUN, DOUBLE BARREL, OVER-UNDER

	Fair	V. Good	Excellent
Shadow Indy, 12 Ga., Single Selective Trigger, Selective Ejectors, Checkered Stock, Engraved, *Modern*	$300	$650	$750
Shadow Seven, 12 Ga., Single Selective Trigger, Selective Ejectors, Checkered Stock, Light Engraving, *Modern*	250	550	650

SHOTGUN, SEMI-AUTOMATIC

	Fair	V. Good	Excellent
12 Ga., Supermatic, Field Grade, *Modern*	75	150	175
20 Ga. Mag., Supermatic, Field Grade, *Modern*	75	150	175
20 Ga. Mag., Supermatic, Skeet Grade, Vent Rib, *Modern*	75	145	225
Deer Gun, 12 Ga., Supermatic, Open Rear Sight, Recoil Pad, *Modern*	100	175	200
Deluxe, 20 Ga. Mag., Supermatic, Recoil Pad, *Modern*	100	175	225
Deluxe, 20 Ga. Mag., Supermatic, Recoil Pad, Vent Rib, *Modern*	100	175	225
Deluxe, Recoil Pad, *Modern*	75	150	175
Deluxe, Recoil Pad, Vent Rib, *Modern*	100	175	200
Duck Gun, 12 Ga. Mag., 3", Supermatic, Recoil Pad, Field Grade, *Modern*	100	175	200
Duck Gun, 12 Ga. Mag., 3", Supermatic, Vent Rib, Recoil Pad, *Modern*	100	175	225
Model 10B, 12 Ga., Riot Gun, *Modern*	225	475	550
Skeet Grade, Vent Rib, Recoil Pad, *Modern*	125	225	250
Special, 12 Ga., Field Grade, Adjustable Choke, *Modern*	100	175	200
Special, 20 Ga. Mag., Supermatic, Field Grade, Adjustable Choke, *Modern*	100	175	200
Trap Grade, Vent Rib, Recoil Pad, *Modern*	100	200	225
Trophy, 20 Ga. Mag., Supermatic, Recoil Pad, Vent Rib, Adjustable Choke, *Modern*	100	200	225
Trophy, Recoil Pad, Vent Rib, Adjustable Choke, *Modern*	100	175	200

SHOTGUN, SLIDE ACTION

	Fair	V. Good	Excellent
.410 Ga. 3", Flight-King, Field Grade, *Modern*	75	125	150
.410 Ga. 3", Flight-King, Skeet Grade, *Modern*	75	150	175
12 and 20 Gauges, Flight-King, Field Grade, *Modern*	75	125	150
12 Ga., Flight-King, Trap Grade, Vent Rib, Recoil Pad, *Modern*	75	150	175

	Fair	V. Good	Excellent
12 Ga., Flight-King, Skeet Grade, Vent Rib, Recoil Pad, *Modern*	$75	$150	$175
28 Ga., Flight-King, Field Grade, *Modern*	75	150	175
28 Ga., Flight-King, Skeet Grade, Vent Rib, *Modern*	75	150	175
Brush Gun, 12 Ga., Flight-King, Open Rear Sight, *Modern*	75	125	150
Deluxe, .28 Ga., Flight-King, Vent Rib, *Modern*	75	150	175
Deluxe, .410 Ga. 3", Flight-King, Vent Rib, *Modern*	75	150	175
Deluxe, 12 and 20 Gauges, Flight-King, Recoil Pad, Vent Rib, *Modern*	75	150	175
Deluxe, 12 and 20 Gauges, Flight-King, Recoil Pad, *Modern*	65	125	150
Deluxe Brush Gun, 12 Ga., Flight-King, Peep Sights, Sling Swivels, *Modern*	100	175	200
Riot, 12 Ga., Flight-King, Open Rear Sight, *Modern*	100	150	175
Riot, 12 Ga., Flight-King, Plain Barrel, *Modern*	100	150	175
Special, 12 and 20 Gauges, Flight-King, Field Grade, Adjustable Choke, *Modern*	100	150	175
Trophy, 12 and 20 Gauges, Flight-King, Recoil Pad, Vent Rib, Adjustable Choke, *Modern*	100	150	175

HIJO

Tradename used by Sloan's of N.Y.C.

HANDGUN, SEMI-AUTOMATIC

	Fair	V. Good	Excellent
Hijo, .25 ACP, Clip Fed, *Modern*	50	75	100
Hijo Military, .22 L.R.R.F., Clip Fed, *Modern*	75	100	125

HILL, S.W.

See Kentucky Rifles and Pistols.

HILLEGAS, J.

Pottsville, Pa. 1810–1830. See Kentucky Rifles.

HILLIARD, D.H. & GEORGE C.

D. H. Hilliard, Cornish, New Hampshire, 1842-1877, taken over by George C. Hilliard and operated 1877-1880.

HANDGUN, PERCUSSION

	Fair	V. Good	Excellent
.34, Underhammer Target Pistol, *Antique*	300	700	850

HINO-KOMORO

Kumaso Hino and Tomisiro Komoro, Tokyo, Japan, c. 1910.

HANDGUN, SEMI-AUTOMATIC

	Fair	V. Good	Excellent
Blow-Forward, 7.65mm, Clip Fed, *Curio*	$1600	$3000	$3250

HOCKLEY, JAMES

Chester County, Pa. 1769–1771. See Kentucky Rifles.

HOLDEN, CYRUS B.

Worchester, Mass., c. 1861–1880.

RIFLE, SINGLESHOT

	Fair	V. Good	Excellent
Model 1862, .44 Henry, Octagon Barrel, *Antique*	325	650	775
Tip-Up, .22 R.F., Nickel Plated Frame, Blued Barrel, *Antique*	225	500	600

HOLLAND & HOLLAND

London, England since 1835; showrooms later opened in New York and Paris. One of the world's most respected gunmakers, Holland & Holland remained in the hands of the family until well into the 20th century. In the early 1990s, after a period of years as a stock-ownership company, the firm was bought 100 percent by Chanel. President of Chanel Alain Wertheimer is a devoted firearms enthusiast, a keen shot, and a highly talented entrepreneur. Under his patronage Holland & Holland has entirely modernized its London factory, created some of the finest showrooms for any product in London, Paris, and New York City, and is spearheading a revival in the British arms trade.

RIFLE, BOLT ACTION

	Fair	V. Good	Excellent
Best Quality, Various Calibers, Express Sights, Checkered Stock, *Modern*			Rare
Best Quality, Various Calibers, Express Sights, Fancy Checkering, Engraved, *Modern*			Rare

RIFLE, DOUBLE BARREL, SIDE-BY-SIDE

	Fair	V. Good	Excellent
#2, Various Calibers, Sidelock, Checkered Stock, Engraved, Hammerless, *Modern*			Rare
Deluxe, Various Calibers, Sidelock, Automatic Ejector, Fancy Engraving, Fancy Checkering, Double Trigger, *Modern*			Rare
Royal, Various Calibers, Sidelock, Automatic Ejector, Fancy Engraving, Fancy Checkering, Double Trigger, *Modern*			Rare

SHOTGUN, DOUBLE BARREL, OVER-UNDER

	Fair	V. Good	Excellent
Deluxe Royal, 12 Ga., Sidelock, Automatic Ejector, Fancy Engraving, Fancy Checkering, Double Triggers, *Modern*	12000	27000	30000

	Fair	V. Good	Excellent
Deluxe Royal, 12 Ga., Sidelock, Automatic Ejector, Fancy Engraving, Fancy Checkering, Single Trigger, *Modern*	$15000	$30000	$35000
Royal Model (Late), 12 Ga., Sidelock, Automatic Ejector, Fancy Engraving, Fancy Checkering, Double Triggers, *Modern*	12000	22500	25000
Royal Model (Late), 12 Ga., Sidelock, Automatic Ejector, Fancy Engraving, Fancy Checkering, Single Trigger, *Modern*	12500	25000	27500
Royal Model (Old), 12 Ga., Sidelock, Automatic Ejector, Fancy Engraving, Fancy Checkering, Double Triggers, *Modern*	8000	17500	20000
Royal Model (Old), 12 Ga., Sidelock, Automatic Ejector, Fancy Engraving, Fancy Checkering, Single Trigger, *Modern*	9000	20000	22000

SHOTGUN, DOUBLE BARREL, SIDE-BY-SIDE

	Fair	V. Good	Excellent
Badminton, Various Gauges, Sidelock, Automatic Ejector, Fancy Engraving, Fancy Checkering, Double Triggers, *Modern*	3500	7500	8500
Badminton, Various Gauges, Sidelock, Automatic Ejector, Fancy Engraving, Fancy Checkering, Single Trigger, *Modern*	4000	8000	9250
Centenary Royal, 12 Ga. 2", Sidelock, Automatic Ejector, Fancy Engraving, Fancy Checkering, Double Triggers, *Modern*	5750	12500	15000
Deluxe, Various Gauges, Sidelock, Automatic Ejector, Fancy Engraving, Fancy Checkering, Double Triggers, *Modern*	5750	12500	15000
Deluxe, Various Gauges, Sidelock, Automatic Ejector, Fancy Engraving, Fancy Checkering, Single Trigger, *Modern*	6500	15000	17500
Dominion, 12 Ga. 2", Sidelock, Automatic Ejector, Engraved, Checkered Stock, Double Triggers, *Modern*	2750	5000	5500
Dominion, Various Gauges, Sidelock, Automatic Ejector, Engraved, Checkered Stock, Double Triggers, *Modern*	1900	4000	4500
Northwood, Various Gauges, Boxlock, Automatic Ejector, Checkered Stock, Engraved, *Modern*	2000	4500	5000
Riviera, Various Gauges, Extra Shotgun Barrel, Automatic Ejector, Fancy Engraving, Fancy Checkering, Double Triggers, *Modern*	4000	8000	10000
Royal, Various Gauges, Sidelock, Automatic Ejector, Fancy Engraving, Fancy Checkering, Double Triggers, *Modern*	$3750	$10000	$12500
Royal, Various Gauges, Sidelock, Automatic Ejector, Fancy Engraving, Fancy Checkering, Single Trigger, *Modern*	5500	12000	15000
Royal Ejector Grade, 12 Ga. Mag. 3", Single Selective Trigger, Vent Rib, Pistol-Grip Stock, Cased with Accessories, *Modern*	5000	10000	12500

SHOTGUN, SINGLESHOT

	Fair	V. Good	Excellent
Standard Super Trap, 12 Ga., Boxlock, Automatic Ejector, Vent Rib, Fancy Engraving, Checkered Stock, *Modern*	1800	3500	4000
Deluxe Super Trap, 12 Ga., Boxlock, Automatic Ejector, Vent Rib, Fancy Engraving, Checkered Stock, *Modern*	2000	5500	6500
Exhibition Super Trap, 12 Ga., Boxlock, Automatic Ejector, Vent Rib, Fancy Engraving, Checkered Stock, *Modern*	3500	7500	8000

HOLLIS, CHAS. & SONS

London, England.

SHOTGUN, DOUBLE BARREL, SIDE-BY-SIDE

	Fair	V. Good	Excellent
12 Ga., Hammerless, Engraved, Fancy Checkering, Fancy Wood, *Modern*	1200	2500	3000

HOLLIS, RICHARD

London, England 1800-1850.

HANDGUN, FLINTLOCK

	Fair	V. Good	Excellent
.68, Holster Pistol, Round Barrel, Brass Furniture, Plain, *Antique*	250	550	775

SHOTGUN, PERCUSSION

	Fair	V. Good	Excellent
12 Ga., Double Barrels, Double Triggers, Hook Breech, Light Engraving, Checkered Stock, *Antique*	225	450	550

HOLMES, BILL

Fayetteville, Ark.

SHOTGUN, SINGLESHOT

	Fair	V. Good	Excellent
Supertrap, 12 Ga., Various Action Types, Checkered Stock, *Modern*	800	1650	1800

HOOD FIREARMS CO.

Norwich, Conn., c. 1875. Also made handguns with selected trade name markings, as follows: Alaska, Alert, Alexis, Boy's Choice, Continental, Czar, Hard Pan, International, Liberty, Little John, Marquis of Lorne, Rob Roy, Robin Hood, Scout, Tramps Terror, Turner & Ross, Union Jack, Victoria, Wide Awake.

HANDGUN, REVOLVER

	Fair	*V. Good*	*Excellent*
.32 Short R.F., 5 Shot, Spur Trigger, Solid Frame, Single Action, *Antique*	$75	$125	$175

HOPKINS & ALLEN

Norwich, Conn. 1868–1914, taken over by Marlin-Rockwell in 1914. Also see Bacon Arms Co. and Merwin Hulbert & Co. The following trade names also made by Hopkins & Allen, q.v.: Acme Hammerless, Alexia, Allen, American Eagle, American Gun Co., Aristocrat, Automatic, Bang-Up, Bloodhound, Blue Jacket, Blue Whistler, Capt. Jack, Chicnester, Creedmore, Czar, Despatch, Dictator, Elector, Encore, Garrison, Half-Breed, Imperial Arms, Mountain Eagle, Paragon, Parole, Ranger, Tower's Police Safety, Universal, You Bet. Although considered by some collectors as second-grade guns, Hopkins & Allen's production spread throughout the U.S. and proved to see active service in the American West. One of their most historic production was a pocket revolver, finely engraved on one of the ivory grip panels; A. Lincoln.

HANDGUN, PERCUSSION REVOLVER

	Fair	*V. Good*	*Excellent*
Dictator, .36 Caliber, 5 Shot, Octagon Barrel, *Antique*	150	375	450

HANDGUN, REVOLVER

	Fair	*V. Good*	*Excellent*
Model 1876 Army, .44-40 WCF, Solid Frame, Single Action, 6 Shot, Finger-Rest Trigger Guard, *Antique*	250	550	650
Safety Police, .22 L.R.R.F., Top Break, Double Action, Various Barrel Lengths, *Curio*	100	150	200
Safety Police, .32 S & W, Top Break, Double Action, Various Barrel Lengths, *Curio*	75	125	150
Safety Police, .38 S & W, Top Break, Double Action, Various Barrel Lengths, *Curio*	75	125	175
XL .30 Long, .30 Long R.F., Solid Frame, Spur Trigger, Single Action, 5 Shot, *Antique*	100	150	175
XL 1 Double Action, .22 Short R.F., Solid Frame, Folding Hammer, *Curio*	75	100	125
XL 3 Double Action, .32 S & W, Solid Frame, Folding Hammer, *Curio*	50	75	100
XL Bulldog, .32 S & W, Solid Frame, Folding Hammer, *Curio*	75	100	125
XL Bulldog, .32 Short R.F., Solid Frame, Folding Hammer, *Curio*	50	75	100
XL Bulldog, .38 S & W, Solid Frame, Folding Hammer, *Curio*	50	75	100
XL CR .22 Short R.F., Solid Frame, Spur Trigger, Single Action, 7 Shot, *Antique*	$125	$150	$175
XL Double Action, .32 S & W, Solid Frame, Folding Hammer, *Curio*	50	75	100
XL Double Action, .38 S & W, Solid Frame, Folding Hammer, *Curio*	50	75	100
XL Navy, .38 Short R.F., Solid Frame, Single Action, 6 Shot, *Antique*	250	500	650
XL No. 1, .22 Short R.F., Solid Frame, Spur Trigger, Single Action, 7 Shot, *Antique*	100	150	175
XL No. 2, .30 Short R.F., Solid Frame, Spur Trigger, Single Action, 5 Shot, *Antique*	100	175	200
XL No. 3, .32 Short R.F., Solid Frame, Spur Trigger, Single Action, 5 Shot, Safety Cylinder, *Antique*	100	175	200
XL No. 4, .38 Short R.F., Solid Frame, Spur Trigger, Single Action, 5 Shot, *Antique*	100	175	200
XL No. 5, .38 S & W, Solid Frame, Spur Trigger, Single Action, 5 Shot, *Antique*	150	350	400
XL No. 5, .38 Short R.F., Solid Frame, Spur Trigger, Single Action, 5 Shot, Safety Cylinder, Engraved, *Antique*	150	300	350
XL No. 6, .41 Short R.F., Solid Frame, Spur Trigger, Single Action, 5 Shot, *Antique*	100	175	225
XL No. 7, .41 Short R.F., Solid Frame, Spur Trigger, Single Action, 5 Shot, Swing-Out Cylinder, *Antique*	100	225	275
XL No. 8 Army, .44 R.F., Solid Frame, Single Action, 6 Shot, *Antique*	300	600	750
XL Police, .38 Short R.F., Solid Frame, Single Action, 6 Shot, *Antique*	200	400	450

HANDGUN, SINGLESHOT

	Fair	*V. Good*	*Excellent*
New Model Target, .22 L.R.R.F., Top Break, 10" Barrel, Adjustable Sights, Target Grips	150	300	350
Single Shot Derringer, .22 Short R.F., $1\frac{3}{4}$" Barrel Pivots Downward for Loading, Folding Trigger, Single Action, *Antique*	400	900	1000
XL Derringer, .41 Short R.F., Spur Trigger, Single Action, *Antique*	225	475	550

RIFLE, BOLT ACTION

	Fair	*V. Good*	*Excellent*
American Military, .22 L.R.R.F., Singleshot, Takedown, Open Rear Sight, Round Barrel, *Curio*	100	200	250

RIFLE, FLINTLOCK

	Fair	*V. Good*	*Excellent*
"Kentucky," .31, Octagon Barrel, Full-Stocked, Brass Furniture, Reproduction (Numrich), *Antique*	100	175	200

	Fair	V. Good	Excellent
"Kentucky," .36, Octagon Barrel, Full-Stocked, Brass Furniture, Reproduction (Numrich), *Antique*	$100	$175	$200
"Kentucky," .45, Octagon Barrel, Full-Stocked, Brass Furniture, Reproduction (Numrich), *Antique*	100	175	200
"Minute Brush," .50, Octagon Barrel, Full-Stocked, Carbine Reproduction (Numrich), *Antique*	100	175	200
"Minuteman Brush," .45, Octagon Barrel, Full-Stocked, Carbine Reproduction (Numrich), *Antique*	100	175	200
"Minuteman," .31, Octagon Barrel, Full-Stocked, Brass Furniture, Reproduction (Numrich), *Antique*	100	175	200
"Minuteman," .36, Octagon Barrel, Full-Stocked, Brass Furniture, Reproduction (Numrich), *Antique*	75	150	175
"Minuteman," .45, Octagon Barrel, Full-Stocked, Brass Furniture, Reproduction (Numrich), *Antique*	100	175	200
"Minuteman," .50, Octagon Barrel, Full-Stocked, Brass Furniture, Reproduction (Numrich), *Antique*	100	175	200
"Pennsylvania," .31, Octagon Barrel, Half-Stocked, Brass Furniture, Reproduction (Numrich), *Antique*	100	150	175
"Pennsylvania," .36, Octagon Barrel, Half-Stocked, Brass Furniture, Reproduction (Numrich), *Antique*	75	150	175
"Pennsylvania," .45, Octagon Barrel, Half-Stocked, Brass Furniture, Reproduction (Numrich), *Antique*	100	175	200
"Pennsylvania," .50, Octagon Barrel, Half-Stocked, Brass Furniture, Reproduction (Numrich), *Antique*	75	150	175

RIFLE, PERCUSSION

	Fair	V. Good	Excellent
"Buggy Deluxe," .36, Under-Hammer, Octagon Barrel, Carbine, Reproduction (Numrich), *Antique*	50	75	100
"Buggy Deluxe," .45, Under-Hammer, Octagon Barrel, Carbine, Reproduction (Numrich), *Antique*	50	100	125
"Deer Stalker," .58, Under-Hammer, Octagon Barrel, Reproduction (Numrich), *Antique*	50	75	100
"Heritage," .36, Under-Hammer, Octagon Barrel, Brass Furniture, Reproduction (Numrich), *Antique*	50	100	125

Hopkins & Allen Heritage Rifle

	Fair	V. Good	Excellent
"Heritage," .45, Under-Hammer, Octagon Barrel, Brass Furniture, Reproduction (Numrich), *Antique*	$50	$100	$125
"Kentucky," .31, Full-Stocked, Octagon Barrel, Brass Furniture, Reproduction (Numrich), *Antique*	75	150	175
"Kentucky," .36, Full-Stocked, Octagon Barrel, Brass Furniture, Reproduction (Numrich), *Antique*	75	150	175
"Kentucky," .45, Full-Stocked, Octagon Barrel, Brass Furniture, Reproduction (Numrich), *Antique*	75	150	175
"Minuteman Brush," .45, Full-Stocked, Octagon Barrel, Carbine, Reproduction (Numrich), *Antique*	75	150	175
"Minuteman Brush," .50, Full-Stocked, Octagon Barrel, Carbine, Reproduction (Numrich), *Antique*	75	175	200
"Minuteman," .31, Full-Stocked, Octagon Barrel, Brass Furniture, Reproduction (Numrich), *Antique*	75	150	175
"Minuteman," .36, Full-Stocked, Octagon Barrel, Brass Furniture, Reproduction (Numrich), *Antique*	75	150	175
"Minuteman," .45, Full-Stocked, Octagon Barrel, Brass Furniture, Reproduction (Numrich), *Antique*	75	150	175
"Minuteman," .50, Full-Stocked, Octagon Barrel, Brass Furniture, Reproduction (Numrich), *Antique*	75	125	175
"Offhand Deluxe," .36 Under-Hammer, Octagon Barrel, Reproduction (Numrich), *Antique*	50	75	100
"Offhand Deluxe," .45 Under-Hammer, Octagon Barrel, Reproduction (Numrich), *Antique*	50	75	100
"Offhand Deluxe," .45 Under-Hammer, Octagon Barrel, Reproduction (Numrich), *Antique*	50	75	100
"Pennsylvania," .31, Half-Stocked, Octagon Barrel, Brass Furniture, Reproduction (Numrich), *Antique*	75	125	150
"Pennsylvania," .36, Half-Stocked, Octagon Barrel, Brass Furniture, Reproduction (Numrich), *Antique*	75	150	175
"Pennsylvania," .45, Half-Stocked, Octagon Barrel, Brass Furniture, Reproduction (Numrich), *Antique*	75	150	175
"Pennsylvania," .50, Half-Stocked, Octagon Barrel, Brass Furniture, Reproduction (Numrich), *Antique*	75	150	175
"Target," .45, Under-Hammer, Octagon Barrel, Reproduction (Numrich), *Antique*	50	75	100
.45, Double Barrel, Over-Under, Swivel Breech, Brass Furniture, Reproduction (Numrich), *Antique*	50	100	125

	Fair	V. Good	Excellent
RIFLE, SINGLESHOT			
Model 1881 (XL), Various Calibers, Falling Block, Takedown, Lever Action, Round Barrel, Open Rear Sight, *Antique*	$150	$375	$450
Model 1881 Junior, .22 L.R.R.F., Falling Block, Takedown, Lever Action, Round Barrel, Open Rear Sight, *Antique*	150	350	500
No. 1922 New Model Junior, .22 L.R.R.F., Falling Block, Takedown, Lever Action, Octagon Barrel, Open Rear Sight, *Curio*	100	200	225
No. 1925 New Model Junior, .25 Short R.F., Falling Block, Takedown, Lever Action, Octagon Barrel, Open Rear Sight, *Curio*	125	250	275
No. 1932 New Model Junior, .32 Long R.F., Falling Block, Takedown, Lever Action, Octagon Barrel, Open Rear Sight, *Curio*	125	225	250
No. 1938 New Model Junior, .38 S & W, Falling Block, Takedown, Lever Action, Octagon Barrel, Open Rear Sight, *Curio*	125	250	275
No. 2922 New Model Junior, .22 L.R.R.F., Falling Block, Takedown, Lever Action, Octagon Barrel, Checkered Stock, Open Rear Sight, *Curio*	100	225	250
No. 2925 New Model Junior, .25 Short R.F., Falling Block, Takedown, Lever Action, Octagon Barrel, Checkered Stock, Open Rear Sight, *Curio*	125	250	275
No. 2932 New Model Junior, .32 Long R.F., Falling Block, Takedown, Lever Action, Octagon Barrel, Checkered Stock, Open Rear Sight, *Curio*	125	250	275
No. 2938 New Model Junior, .38 S & W, Falling Block, Takedown, Lever Action, Octagon Barrel, Checkered Stock, Open Rear Sight, *Curio*	125	275	300
No. 3922 Schüetzen Target, .22 L.R.R.F., Falling Block, Takedown, Lever Action, Octagon Barrel, Checkered Stock, Swiss Buttplate, *Antique*	600	1250	1500
No. 3925 Schüetzen Target, .25-20 WCF, Falling Block, Takedown, Lever Action, Octagon Barrel, Checkered Stock, Swiss Buttplate, *Antique*	550	1000	1250
No. 722, .22 L.R.R.F., Rolling Block, Takedown, Round Barrel, Open Rear Sight, *Curio*	50	100	125
No. 822, .22 L.R.R.F., Rolling Block, Takedown, Lever Action, Round Barrel, Open Rear Sight, *Curio*	75	125	150
No. 832, .32 Short R.F., Rolling Block, Takedown, Lever Action, Round Barrel, Open Rear Sight, Curio	$75	$150	$175
No. 922 New Model Junior, 22 L.R.R.F., Falling Block, Takedown, Lever Action, Round Barrel, Open Rear Sight, *Curio*	75	150	175
No. 925 New Model Junior, .25 Short R.F., Falling Block, Takedown, Lever Action, Round Barrel, Open Rear Sight, *Curio*	75	150	175
No. 932 New Model Junior, .32 Long R.F., Falling Block, Takedown, Lever Action, Round Barrel, Open Rear Sight, *Curio*	75	125	175
No. 938 New Model Junior, .38 S & W, Falling Block, Takedown, Lever Action, Round Barrel, Open Rear Sight, *Curio*	100	225	250
SHOTGUN, DOUBLE BARREL, SIDE-BY-SIDE			
No. 100, 12 and 16 Ga., Double Trigger, Outside Hammers, Checkered Stock, Steel Barrel, *Curio*	75	125	150
No. 110, 12 and 16 Ga., Double Trigger, Hammerless, Checkered Stock, Steel Barrel, *Curio*	75	150	175
SHOTGUN, SINGLESHOT			
New Model, Various Gauges, Hammer, Top Break, Damascus Barrel, Checkered Stock, *Curio*	50	75	100
New Model, Various Gauges, Hammer, Top Break, Steel Barrel, *Curio*	50	75	100
New Model, Various Gauges, Hammer, Top Break, Steel Barrel, Automatic Ejector, Checkered Stock, *Curio*	50	75	100

HOPKINS, C. W.

Made by Bacon Mfg. Co., Norwich, Conn.

	Fair	V. Good	Excellent
HANDGUN, REVOLVER			
.32 Short R.F., Single Action, Solid Frame, Swing-Out Cylinder, *Antique*	125	350	450
.38 Caliber (Navy), Single Action, Solid Frame, Swing-Out Cylinder, *Antique*	250	575	625

HOROLT, LORENZ

Nuremberg, Germany, c. 1600.

	Fair	V. Good	Excellent
HANDGUN, WHEEL LOCK			
Long Barreled, Holster Pistol, Hexagonal Ball Pommel, Light Ornamentation, *Antique*	3500	7500	8500

HOUILLER, BLANCHAR

Paris, France, c. 1845.

	Fair	V. Good	Excellent
HANDGUN, PERCUSSION			
Pepperbox, .48, 6 Shot, *Antique*	$175	$375	$500

HOWARD ARMS

Made by Crescent for Fred Bifflar & Co. See Crescent Fire Arms Co., Shotgun, Double Barrel, Side-By-Side; Shotgun, Singleshot.

HOWARD ARMS

Made by Meriden Firearms Co.

	Fair	V. Good	Excellent
HANDGUN, REVOLVER			
.32 S & W, 5 Shot, Double Action, Top Break, *Modern*	50	75	100
.38 S & W, 5 Shot, Double Action, Top Break, *Modern*	50	75	100

HOWARD BROTHERS

Detroit, Mich., c. 1868.

	Fair	V. Good	Excellent
RIFLE, SINGLESHOT			
.44 Henry R.F., Round Barrel, *Antique*	150	375	500

HUMBERGER, PETER JR.

Ohio 1791–1852. See Kentucky Rifles.

HUMBERGER, PETER SR.

Pa. 1774–1791, then Ohio 1791–1811. See Kentucky Rifles.

HUMMER

Belgium, for Lee Hdw., Kansas.

	Fair	V. Good	Excellent
SHOTGUN, DOUBLE BARREL, SIDE-BY-SIDE			
Various Gauges, Hammerless, Steel Barrel, *Modern*	100	175	200
Various Gauges, Outside Hammers, Damascus Barrel, *Modern*	75	150	175
Various Gauges, Outside Hammers, Steel Barrel, *Modern*	75	150	175
SHOTGUN, SINGLESHOT			
Various Gauges, Hammer, Steel Barrel, *Modern*	25	50	75

HUNGARIAN MILITARY

	Fair	V. Good	Excellent
HANDGUN, SEMI-AUTOMATIC			
29M Femaru, 7.65mm, Clip Fed, Blue, Miltary, *Curio*	175	350	375
37M Femaru, 7.65mm, Clip Fed, Blue, Military, *Curio*	$125	$250	$275
Frommer, Stop Pocket, .380 ACP, Clip Fed, Blue, Military, *Curio*	100	225	250
RIFLE, BOLT ACTION			
1935M, 8mm, Mannlicher, Military, *Curio*	100	225	250
1943M, 8mm Mauser, Mannlicher, Military, *Curio*	150	325	350

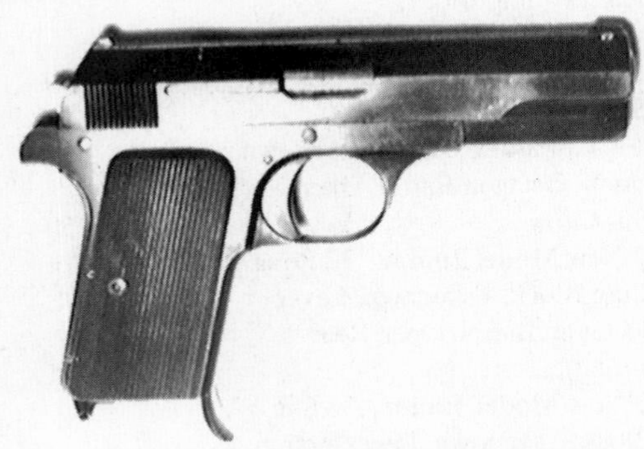

Hungarian Military 37M Femaru

HUNTER ARMS

See L. C. Smith.

HUNTING WORLD

New York City. A dedicated sportsman and gun enthusiast, Hunting World's founder and president Bob Lee began collecting custom-made rifles while still a youth, carrying on correspondence with prominent riflemen the likes of Jack O'Connor and Elmer Keith. Lee's knowledge of fine guns of all periods is prodigious, and his hunting experiences around the world have established him as one of the 20th century's premier sportsmen and firearms authorities. It was only natural, therefore, that he would venture into the world of gunmaking, with his own line of best-quality game guns. The relatively limited production was based on the Holland & Holland system, style and quality, even to the detail of having K. C. Hunt design and embellish the prototype gun. That sample piece served as the standard pattern for the remaining production, done in Spain by gunmakers at a high level of quality and performance. These game guns are no longer in production.

	Fair	V. Good	Excellent
SHOTGUN, DOUBLE BARREL, SIDE-BY-SIDE			
Royal Deluxe Game Gun, 12 or 20 Gauges, Sidelock, Fancy Wood, Engraved, *Modern*	1700	3500	4000

HUSQVARNA VAPENFABRIK AKITIEBOLAG

	Fair	V. Good	Excellent
HANDGUN, REVOLVER			
Model 1887 Swedish Nagent, 7.5mm, Double Action, Blue, Military, *Antique*	150	400	450

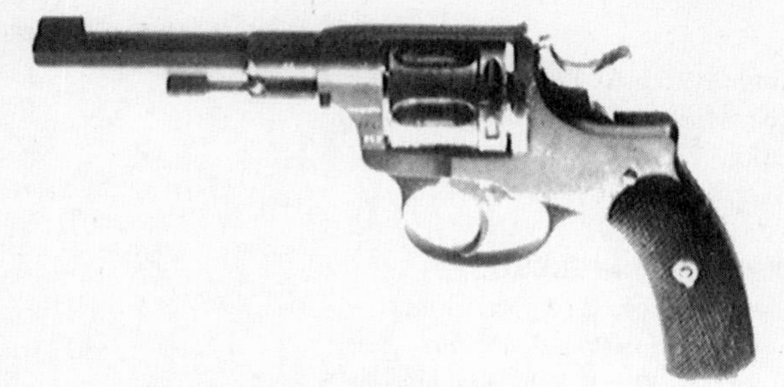

Husqvarna M1887 Revolver

	Fair	V. Good	Excellent
HANDGUN, SEMI-AUTOMATIC			
Model 40 "Lahti," 9mm Browning Long, Clip Fed, Swedish Military, *Curio*	$150	$300	$350
Model L-35 "Lahti," 9mm Browning Long, Clip Fed, Finnish Military, *Curio*	400	800	950
RIFLE, BOLT ACTION			
1000 Super Grade, Various Calibers, Sporting Rifle, Checkered Stock, Monte Carlo Stock, *Curio*	150	300	350
1100 Deluxe, Various Calibers, Sporting Rifle, Checkered Stock, *Curio*	150	300	350
1622, .22 L.R.R.F., Clip Fed, Sling Swivels, *Curio*	50	100	150
1951, Various Calibers, Sporting Rifle, Checkered Stock, *Curio*	150	300	375
3000 Crown Grade, Various Calibers, Sporting Rifle, Checkered Stock, Monte Carlo Stock, *Curio*	175	350	375
3100 Crown Grade, Various Calibers, Sporting Rifle, Checkered Stock, *Curio*	175	325	375
4000, Various Calibers, Sporting Rifle, Checkered Stock, Lightweight, Monte Carlo Stock, *Curio*	175	350	375
4100, Various Calibers, Sporting Rifle, Checkered Stock, Lightweight, *Curio*	175	325	375
456, Various Calibers, Sporting Rifle, Checkered Stock, Lightweight, Full-Stocked, *Curio*	175	375	400
6000 Imperial, Various Calibers, Sporting Rifle, Checkered Stock, Fancy Wood, Express Sights, *Curio*	200	425	475
8000 Imperial Grade, Various Calibers, Sporting Rifle, Checkered Stock, Engraved, Monte Carlo Stock, Fancy Wood, *Curio*	200	425	500
9000 Crown Grade, Various Calibers, Sporting Rifle, Checkered Stock, Monte Carlo Stock, *Curio*	150	325	375
Gustav CG-T, Various Calibers, Singleshot, Target Stock, Heavy Barrel, *Curio*	125	250	275
Gustav Grade II, Various Calibers, Sporting Rifle, Checkered Stock, *Curio*	$175	$375	$400
Gustav Grade II, Various Calibers, Sporting Rifle, Checkered Stock, Left-Hand, *Curio*	200	400	425
Gustav Grade II, Various Calibers, Sporting Rifle, Checkered Stock, Magnum Action, *Curio*	175	375	400
Gustav Grade III, Various Calibers, Sporting Rifle, Checkered Stock, Magnum Action, Left-Hand, *Curio*	200	400	425
Gustav Grade III, Various Calibers, Sporting Rifle, Checkered Stock, Magnum Action, Light Engraving, Left-Hand, *Curio*	200	400	475
Gustav Grade III, Various Calibers, Sporting Rifle, Checkered Stock, Magnum Action, Light Engraving, *Curio*	200	450	475
Gustav Grade III, Various Calibers, Sporting Rifle, Checkered Stock, Light Engraving, *Curio*	200	450	500
Gustav Grade III, Various Calibers, Sporting Rifle, Checkered Stock, Light Engraving, Left-Hand, *Curio*	200	425	475
Gustav Grade V, Various Calibers, Sporting Rifle, Checkered Stock, Engraved, *Curio*	300	600	650
Gustav Grade V, Various Calibers, Sporting Rifle, Checkered Stock, Engraved, Left-Hand, *Curio*	275	575	650
Gustav Grade V, Various Calibers, Sporting Rifle, Checkered Stock, Engraved, Magnum Action, *Curio*	300	600	675
Gustav Grade V, Various Calibers, Sporting Rifle, Checkered Stock, Engraved, Magnum Action, Left-Hand, *Curio*	300	625	675
Gustav Swede, Various Calibers, Sporting Rifle, Checkered Stock, *Curio*	150	300	325
Gustav Swede Deluxe, Various Calibers, Sporting Rifle, Checkered Stock, Light Engraving, *Curio*	150	300	350
Gustav V-T, Various Calibers, Varmint, Target Stock, Heavy Barrel, *Curio*	200	400	450
Hi Power, Various Calibers, Sporting Rifle, Checkered Stock, *Curio*	150	300	350
P 3000 Presentation, Various Calibers, Sporting Rifle, Checkered Stock, Engraved, Fancy Wood, *Curio*	300	625	650

HUTZ, BENJAMIN

Lancaster, Pa., c. 1802. See Kentucky Rifles.

HVA

See Husqvarna.

HY HUNTER

Burbank, Calif. See also Great Western Arms Co.

	Fair	V. Good	Excellent
HANDGUN, DOUBLE BARREL, OVER-UNDER			
Automatic Derringer, .22 L.R.R.F., Blue, *Modern*	$15	$25	$50
HANDGUN, REVOLVER			
Chicago Cub, .22 Short, 6 Shot, Folding Trigger, *Modern*	15	25	50
Detective, .22 L.R.R.F., Double Action, 6 Shot, *Modern*	25	50	75
Detective, .22 W.M.R., Double Action, 6 Shot, *Modern*	25	50	75
Frontier Six Shooter, .22 L.R.R.F., Single Action, Western Style, *Modern*	25	50	75
Frontier Six Shooter, .22 LR/.22 WRF Combo, Single Action, Western Style, *Modern*	25	50	75
Frontier Six Shooter, .357 Mag., Single Action, Western Style, *Modern*	50	125	150
Frontier Six Shooter, .44 Mag., Single Action, Western Style, *Modern*	75	150	175
Frontier Six Shooter, .45 Colt, Single Action, Western Style, *Modern*	50	125	150
HANDGUN, SEMI-AUTOMATIC			
Maxim, .25 ACP, Clip Fed, *Modern*	25	50	75
Militar, .22 L.R.R.F., Double Action, Hammer, Clip Fed, Blue, *Modern*	25	50	100
Militar, .32 ACP, Double Action, Hammer, Clip Fed, Blue, *Modern*	50	75	100
Militar, .380 ACP, Double Action, Hammer, Clip Fed, Blue, *Modern*	50	100	125
Panzer, .22 L.R.R.F., Clip Fed, Blue, *Modern*	25	50	75
Stingray, .25 ACP, Clip Fed, Blue, *Modern*	$25	$50	$75
Stuka, .22 Long, Clip Fed, Blue, *Modern*	25	50	75
HANDGUN, SINGLESHOT			
Accurate Ace, .22 Short, Flobert Type, Chrome Plated, *Modern*	15	25	50
Favorite, .22 L.R.R.F., Stevens Copy, *Modern*	25	50	75
Favorite, .22 W.M.R., Stevens Copy, *Modern*	25	50	75
Gold Rush Derringer, .22 L.R.R.F., Spur Trigger, *Modern*	15	25	50
Target, .22 L.R.R.F., Bolt Action, *Modern*	15	25	50
Target, .22 W.M.R., Bolt Action, *Modern*	15	25	50

HY SCORE ARMS

Brooklyn, N.Y.

	Fair	V. Good	Excellent
HANDGUN, REVOLVER			
.22 L.R.R.F., Double Action, *Modern*	15	25	50

HYPER

Jenks, Okla. Discontinued 1984.

	Fair	V. Good	Excellent
RIFLE, SINGLESHOT			
Hyper-Single Rifle, Various Calibers, Fancy Wood, No Sights, Falling Block, Fancy Checkering, *Modern*	800	1750	2000
Hyper-Single Rifle, Various Calibers, Fancy Wood, No Sights, Falling Block, Fancy Checkering, Stainless Steel Barrel, *Modern*	900	2000	2250

I

I G

Grey, of Dundee, c. 1630.

HANDGUN, SNAPHAUNCE

	Fair	V. Good	Excellent
Belt Pistol, Engraved, Ovoid Pommel, All Metal, *Antique*	$9000	$20000	$25000

I P

German, 1580–1600.

RIFLE, WHEELOCK

	Fair	V. Good	Excellent
.60, German Style, Brass Furniture, Light Ornamentation, Horn Inlays, Set Trigger, *Antique*	1900	4000	4500

IAB SHOTGUNS

Brescia, Italy. Imported by Puccinelli Co., San Anselmo, Calif.

SHOTGUN, DOUBLE BARREL, OVER-UNDER

	Fair	V. Good	Excellent
C-300 Super Combo, 12 Ga., Vent Rib, Single Selective Trigger, Checkered Stock, with 2 Extra Single Barrels, *Modern*	1100	2250	2750
C-3000 Combo, 12 Ga., Vent Rib, Single Selective Trigger, Checkered Stock, with 2 Extra Single Barrels, *Modern*	900	1750	2000

SHOTGUN, SINGLESHOT

	Fair	V. Good	Excellent
S-300, 12 Ga., Vent Rib, Checkered Stock, Trap Grade, *Modern*	450	1000	1250

IMPERIAL ARMS

Made by Hopkins & Allen, c. 1880.

HANDGUN, REVOLVER

	Fair	V. Good	Excellent
.32 Short R.F., 5 Shot, Spur Trigger, Solid Frame, Single Action, *Antique*	50	125	150
.38 Short R.F., 5 Shot, Spur Trigger, Solid Frame, Single Action, *Antique*	75	150	175

IMPERIAL REVOLVER

c. 1880.

HANDGUN, REVOLVER

	Fair	V. Good	Excellent
.22 Short R.F., 7 Shot, Spur Trigger, Solid Frame, Single Action, *Antique*	$50	$125	$150
.32 Short R.F., 5 Shot, Spur Trigger, Solid Frame, Single Action, *Antique*	75	150	175

I.N.A.

Industria Nacional de Armas, Sao Paulo, Brazil.

HANDGUN, REVOLVER

	Fair	V. Good	Excellent
Tiger, .22 L.R.R.F., Single Action, Western Style, *Modern*	25	50	75
Tiger, .32 S&W Long, Single Action, Western Style, *Modern*	25	50	75

INDIA MILITARY

RIFLE, BOLT ACTION

	Fair	V. Good	Excellent
No. 1 Mk.III, S.M.L.E., .303 British, Clip Fed, Ishapore, *Curio*	75	150	175

INDIAN ARMS

Detroit, Mich., c. 1976. Discontinued.

HANDGUN, SEMI-AUTOMATIC

	Fair	V. Good	Excellent
.380 ACP, Clip Fed, Stainless Steel, Vent Rib, Double Action, *Modern*	125	300	375

INDIAN SALES

Cheyenne, Wyo.

HANDGUN, REVOLVER

	Fair	V. Good	Excellent
HS-21, .22 L.R.R.F., Double Action, Blue, *Modern*	15	25	50

HANDGUN, SEMI-AUTOMATIC

	Fair	V. Good	Excellent
Model 4, .25 ACP, Clip Fed, Blue, *Modern*	25	50	75

INGRAM

Invented by Gordon Ingram. Made by Police Ordnance Co., Los Angeles, Calif. and Military Armament Corp., Georgia. Discontinued 1982.

	Fair	V. Good	Excellent
SEMI-AUTOMATIC WEAPON			
MAC 10, .45, ACP or 9mm, Clip Fed, Folding Stock, Open-Bolt, *Modern*	$300	$650	$750
MAC 10A1, 9mm Luger or .45 ACP, Clip Fed, Folding Stock, Closed Bolt, *Modern*	125	250	275
MAC 11, .380 ACP, Clip Fed, Folding Stock, Smaller Version of MAC 10, *Modern*	250	500	575

INGRAM, CHARLES

Glasgow, Scotland, c. 1860.

	Fair	V. Good	Excellent
SHOTGUN, DOUBLE BARREL, SIDE-BY-SIDE			
Extra Set of Rifle Barrels, High Quality, Cased with Accessories, Engraved, Checkered Stock, *Antique*	3000	6500	7500

INHOFF, BENEDICT

Berks County, Pa. 1781–1783. See Kentucky Rifles.

INTERARMS

Alexandria, Virginia. Founded by Samuel Cummings, the company also maintains facilities in the U.K., Europe, and the Far East. On the 40th anniversary, Richard S. Winter, Executive Vice President based in Alexandria, Virginia, wrote the following history, at the same time a tribute to the company founder: "The history of Interarms is colorful. To some it engages a degree of mystique. Founded in 1953, it gained physical permanency in 1957 with the establishment of offices and warehouses along the Potomac River in historic Alexandria, Virginia. Its beginning was stimulated by the introduction of completely new marketing concepts which were reflective of market interest. Many continue to reflect on an unprecedented decade of unequaled firearm values. Incoming shipments of Mausers, Enfields, Springfields, Garands, M-1 Carbines, Colts, Lugers, Walthers, Webleys, Smith & Wessons, Lahtis and all of the variations thereof, plus hundreds of other military/civilian models were virtual treasure hunts destined to please the hunter, plinker, targeteer, collector, history buff, and, above all, those in search of sound firearms at affordable prices. This era carried with it a boom to gunsmiths, hobbyists, accessory manufacturers, plus untold numbers of others directly or indirectly associated with our traditional enjoyment of firearms. These were also prized by large, time-honored chains, such as Sears and Montgomery Ward—yes, the list also included giant cosmopolitan retailers, such as Gimbels and Macy's. An added dimension was generated in satisfying a refreshing new surge in firearm interest. During this period, a few domestic manufacturers sought to curb an imagined threat to their industry through a petition filed with the Office of Civil and Defense Mobilization. This was successfully resisted by Interarms with the stalwart support of a few high brigades of firearms dealers. Ultimately, domestic manufacturers were also beneficiaries as manifested by the upswing in firearm sales during the years thereafter. Many who had purchased those reliable military obsoletes decided to trade upward for commercial counterparts with a bit more sophistication and cosmetic allure. Millions of military surplus bargains introduced thousands of shooters into the world of firearms due to an irresistible introductory investment. Some of these fine relics can still be found on dealer shelves or at gun shows at prices which have multiplied. Starting with Walther and Mauser, we moved our attention to Star, Astra, Rossi, Zastava, Howa, Norinco and many others. This signaled a corporate reorganization, which emphasized a restructuring of our Marketing Division. It called for an upgraded commercial approach, including the organizing of professional salesmen to make our products known to essentially every major distributor. This was concurrent with keeping in close contact with as many dealers as possible and upon whom we are dependent. Our specialized national sales organization is today second to none. Sales of new commercial products soon caught and surpassed previous sales revenue. Thanks to dealer and consumer responsiveness, this upward curve has continued without interruption."

INTERCHANGEABLE

Belgium, Tradename Schoverlin-Daley & Gales, c. 1880.

	Fair	V. Good	Excellent
SHOTGUN, DOUBLE BARREL, SIDE-BY-SIDE			
Various Gauges, Outside Hammers, Damascus Barrel, *Curio*	$50	$100	$150

INTERDYNAMIC

Miami, Fla., c. 1979. Sold by F.I.E.

	Fair	V. Good	Excellent
HANDGUN, SEMI-AUTOMATIC			
KG-99, 9mm Luger, Clip Fed, SMG Styling, *Modern*	225	475	550

INTERNATIONAL

Made by Hood Firearms, c. 1875.

	Fair	V. Good	Excellent
HANDGUN, REVOLVER			
.22 Short R.F., 7 Shot, Spur Trigger, Solid Frame, Single Action, *Antique*	75	125	175
.32 Short R.F., 5 Shot, Spur Trigger, Solid Frame, Single Action, *Antique*	75	125	175

INTERNATIONAL DISTRIBUTORS

Miami, Fla.

	Fair	V. Good	Excellent
RIFLE, BOLT ACTION			
Mauser Type, Various Calibers, Checkered Stock, Sling Swivels, Recoil Pad, *Modern*	75	150	200

INTERSTATE ARMS CO.

Made by Crescent for Townley Metal & Hdw., Kansas City, Mo. See Crescent Fire Arms Co., Shotgun, Double Barrel, Side-By-Side; Shotgun, Singleshot.

ISRAELI MILITARY

This list includes both military arms and the commercial arms made by Israeli Military Industries (I.M.I.). Also see Magnum Research, Inc. (M.R.I.).

	Fair	V. Good	Excellent
HANDGUN, REVOLVER			
S & W Model 10 Copy, 9mm Luger, Solid Frame, Swing-Out Cylinder, Double Action, Military, *Modern*	$250	$500	$575
RIFLE, SEMI-AUTOMATIC			
Galil, .223 Rem., Clip Fed, Assault Rifle, Folding Stock, *Modern*	400	800	950
Galil, .308 Win., Clip Fed, Assault Rifle, Folding Stock, *Modern*	425	900	1050
UZI, 9mm Luger, Clip Fed, Folding Stock, Commercial, *Modern*	400	850	950

ITALGUNS INTERNATIONAL

Cusago, Italy.

	Fair	V. Good	Excellent
HANDGUN, REVOLVER			
Western Style, Various Calibers, Single Action, *Modern*	50	125	150
Western Style, Various Calibers, Single Action, Automatic Hammer Safety, *Modern*	50	125	150
COMBINATION WEAPON, OVER-UNDER			
Various Calibers, Checkered Stock, Double Triggers, *Modern*	100	275	325
SHOTGUN, DOUBLE BARREL, OVER-UNDER			
Model 125, 12 Gauge, Checkered Stock, Vent Rib, Double Triggers, *Modern*	100	200	225
Model 150, 12 or 20 Gauges, Checkered Stock, Vent Rib, Single Trigger, *Modern*	100	225	250

ITALIAN MILITARY

Also See Beretta. Anyone who has visited Val Trompia, about a 90-minute drive northeast of Milan, comes away with a realization that Italian gunmakers are capable of designs and manufacture in the firearms genre rivaling, or surpassing, the work of any gunmakers anywhere in the world. The Beretta Museum, in Gardone, best exemplifies these exemplary craftsmen and mechanics. The collection of military arms on display there is of particular interest because it not only demonstrates Italian proficiency, but exhibits substantial numbers of military arms made in other nations, including the United States. The adoption by U.S. armed forces of the Beretta XM9 self-loading 9mm pistols is proof in itself of the extraordinary capability of Italian gunmakers in the military small arms arena.

	Fair	V. Good	Excellent
HANDGUN, REVOLVER			
Service Revolver, 10.4mm, Double Action, 6 Shot, Folding Trigger, *Curio*	$50	$100	$250

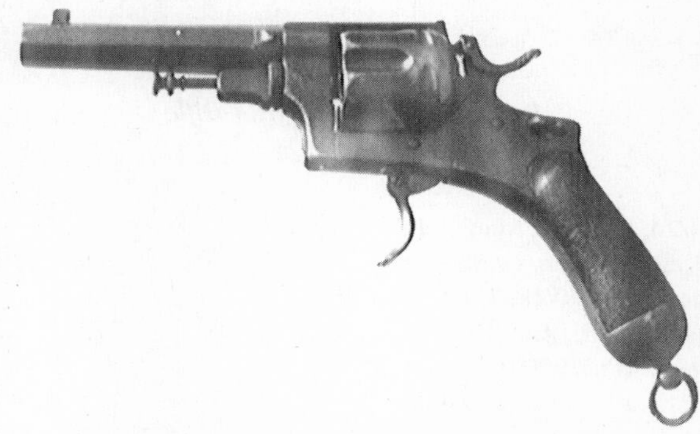

Italian Military Service Revolver Folding Trigger

	Fair	V. Good	Excellent
Service Revolver, 10.4mm, Double Action, 6 Shot, Trigger Guard, *Curio*	50	100	125
HANDGUN, SEMI-AUTOMATIC			
Brixia, 9mm Glisenti, Clip Fed, *Curio*	150	375	550
M1910 Glisenti Army, 9mm, Clip Fed, *Curio*	150	400	450

Italian Military M910

	Fair	V. Good	Excellent
M1934 Beretta, .380 ACP, Clip Fed, *Curio*	150	275	325
RIFLE, BOLT ACTION			
M1891, 6.5 × 52 Mannlicher-Carcano, *Curio*	50	75	100
M38, 7.35mm, Terni, Military, *Curio*	50	75	100
M91 T.S., 6.5 × 52 Mannlicher-Carcano, Carbine, Folding Bayonet, *Curio*	50	75	100
M91 T.S. (Late), 6.5 × 52 Mannlicher-Carcano, Carbine, Folding Bayonet, *Curio*	50	75	100

	Fair	V. Good	Excellent
M91/24, 6.5 × 52 Mannlicher-Carcano, *Curio*	$50	$75	$100

Italian Military M91/24 Rifle

	Fair	V. Good	Excellent
M91/24, 6.5 × 52 Mannlicher-Carcano, Carbine, *Curio*	50	75	100
Vetterli M1870/1887, 10.4 × 47R Italian Vetterli, *Antique*	100	175	225
Vetterli M1870/87/15, 6.5 × 52 Mannlicher-Carcano, *Antique*	50	125	150

ITHACA GUN CO.

Ithaca, N.Y. 1883–1986. Absorbed Lefever Arms Co., Syracuse Arms Co., Union Firearms Co., and Wilkes Barre Gun Co. Also see the commemorative section. The founders of Ithaca were William H. Baker, John VanNatta, Dwight McIntyre, and Leroy Smith, latter and associate George Livermore becoming sole owners and operators by 1894. Smith and Baker, a prolific gun designer, both took out patents for shotgun designs, and the growing concern, along a raceway from Fall Creek, had additions to the initial structure in 1890, 1904, and 1917. It is ironic that although Ithaca's Cornell University is a world-renowned educational institution, the city is often better known as the site of the Ithaca Gun Co. In 1986 Ithaca closed for a short period, reopening early in 1987, under the name Ithaca Acquisition Corporation. In Ithaca's long and distinguished past, gun companies the likes of Lefever, Syracuse, Union, and Wilkes-Barre were purchased or absorbed. Four generations of the Smith family and two generations of the Livermore family devoted time and energy to Ithaca Gun, which has, like many American gunmakers, a following of near cult proportions. The Wells Fargo & Co. Shotguns: The Flues Model was a variation of the Ithaca side-by-side double barrel hammer and hammerless gun which attracted the interest of the historic express agency, Wells Fargo & Co., beginning c. 1909. The company's directive No. 280, from the 1884 Book of Instructions, stated: "Guards and Messengers will be furnished with suitable firearms, if needed, by requisition on the Stationery and Supply Department, San Francisco." Directive No. 1056, from the 1902 Book of Instructions, further stated: "Messengers on all important routes are required to travel armed for defense, in case of attack." Ithaca's Flues Model joined the line in 1908, the year the first ten were built by employee Emil Flues. As detailed in company catalogues, the gun boasted a new three-piece lock, developed by Flues, "the noted inventor." Wells Fargo & Co. had its own arsenal, for issue to its agents and messengers, in dealing with the threat of hold-up men. Revolvers were usually by Colt or Smith & Wesson, rifles by Winchester, and shotguns by such makers as L. C. Smith, Remington, and Ithaca. From 1907 to 1917, approximately 749 shotguns were sold to Wells Fargo & Co. by the Ithaca Gun Co. From 1908 through 1925, approximately 223,000 shotguns of the Flues model were built (4,700 of them single barrel trap guns.) Among shooters of these guns, the two most famous were Annie Oakley and John Philip Sousa, whose "Stars and Stripes Forever" is a time-honored favorite of marching bands. Wells Fargo & Co. Markings: On lock plate and frame water table: W.F. & Co. EX., accompanied by property number. On barrel rib: Wells Fargo & Co. followed by property number. Ithaca records do not record all of the Wells Fargo & Co. numbers. Most of those numbers known are in the mid and late 400, late 500 and early 600 range. Variations: Grade X Hammer Models, frames heavily constructed, all barrels of A quality, guns in configuration of: 12 gauge, 26" fluid steel barrels; 10 gauge, 24" twisted steel barrels; 12 gauge, 24" fluid steel barrels. Dates of Orders: Between February of 1909 and 1917: steel barrels; 1911 through 1917, serial ranges 211000, 219000, 223000, 228000, 230000, 233000, 241000, 251000, 253000, 255000, 256000, 262000, 263000, 265000, 275000, 279000, 281000, 282000, 12 gauge, 24" fluid steel barrels. On cessation of express operations in 1918, the records of the Wells Fargo & Co. Express went to American Railway Express Co., later the Railway Express Agency. These records have been of virtually no assistance to collectors over the years. Because of imaginative faking not a few bogus markings of Wells Fargo & Co. stamps have been placed on guns never property of the firm. The exercise of caution is important to any enthusiast keen on possessing a genuine Wells Fargo shotgun. Thus, the records of the Ithaca Gun Co. are of immeasurable value in assessing express guns of their manufacture.

RIFLE, BOLT ACTION

	Fair	V. Good	Excellent
LSA 55, Various Calibers, Monte Carlo Stock, Cheekpiece, Heavy Barrel, *Modern*	$150	$350	$375
LSA 55, Various Calibers, Monte Carlo Stock, Open Rear Sight, *Modern*	150	325	350
LSA 55 Deluxe, Various Calibers, Monte Carlo Stock, Cheekpiece, No Sights, Scope Mounts, *Modern*	150	350	400
LSA 65 Deluxe, Various Calibers, Monte Carlo Stock, Cheekpiece, No Sights, Scope Mounts, *Modern*	150	325	375
LSA 65, Various Calibers, Monte Carlo Stock, Open Rear Sight, *Modern*	150	300	350

RIFLE, LEVER ACTION

	Fair	V. Good	Excellent
Model 49, .22 L.R.R.F., Singleshot, *Modern*	50	75	100
Model 49, .22 WMR, Singleshot, *Modern*	50	75	100
Model 49 Deluxe, .22 L.R.R.F., Singleshot, Fancy Wood, *Modern*	75	100	125
Model 49 Presentation, .22 L.R.R.F., Singleshot, Engraved, Fancy Checkering, *Modern*	75	125	150
Model 49 R, .22 L.R.R.F., Tube Feed, *Modern*	50	75	100
Model 49 St. Louis, .22 L.R.R.F., Bicentennial, Fancy Wood, Singleshot, *Curio*	35	75	150
Model 49 Youth, .22 L.R.R.F., Singleshot, *Modern*	25	50	75

	Fair	V. Good	Excellent
Model 72, .22 L.R.R.F., Tube Feed, *Modern*	$50	$100	$125
Model 72, .22 WMR, Tube Feed, *Modern*	75	125	150
Model 72 Deluxe, .22 L.R.R.F., Tube Feed, Octagon Barrel, *Modern*	75	125	175

COMBINATION WEAPON, OVER-UNDER

	Fair	V. Good	Excellent
LSA 55 Turkey Gun, 12 Ga./.222, Open Rear Sight, Monte Carlo Stock, *Modern*	250	500	550

RIFLE, SEMI-AUTOMATIC

	Fair	V. Good	Excellent
X-15 Lightning, .22 L.R.R.F., Clip Fed, *Modern*	75	100	125
X5-C Light Lightning, .22 L.R.R.F., Clip Fed, *Modern*	50	75	100
X5-T Lightning, .22 L.R.R.F., Tube Feed, *Modern*	50	75	100

SHOTGUN, DOUBLE BARREL, OVER-UNDER

	Fair	V. Good	Excellent
Model 500, 12 and 20 Gauges, Field Grade, Selective Ejector, Vent Rib, *Modern*	150	350	400
Model 500, 12 Ga. Mag. 3", Field Grade, Selective Ejector, Vent Rib, *Modern*	150	375	425
Model 600 Combo Set, Various Gauges, Skeet Grade, Selective Ejector, Vent Rib, Cased, *Modern*	400	950	1350
Model 600, 12 and 20 Gauges, Field Grade, Selective Ejector, Vent Rib, *Modern*	200	400	475
Model 600, 12 and 20 Gauges, Skeet Grade, Selective Ejector, Vent Rib, *Modern*	200	475	525
Model 600, 12 Ga., Trap Grade, Selective Ejector, Vent Rib, *Modern*	200	450	525
Model 600, 12 Ga., Trap Grade, Selective Ejector, Vent Rib, Monte Carlo Stock, *Modern*	225	475	550
Model 600, 28 and.410 Gauges, Skeet Grade, Selective Ejector, Vent Rib, *Modern*	250	575	650
Model 680 English, 12 and 20 Gauges, Field Grade, Selective Ejector, Vent Rib, Modern	275	575	625
Model 700 Combo Set, Various Gauges, Skeet Grade, Selective Ejector, Vent Rib, Cased, *Modern*	700	1500	1750
Model 700, 12 and 20 Gauges, Skeet Grade, Selective Ejector, Vent Rib, *Modern*	300	675	750
Model 700, 12 Ga., Trap Grade, Selective Ejector, Vent Rib, *Modern*	300	675	750
Model 700, 12 Ga., Trap Grade, Selective Ejector, Vent Rib, Monte Carlo Stock, *Modern*	300	725	775

	Fair	V. Good	Excellent
Parazzi MT-6, 12 Ga., Skeet Grade, Automatic Ejector, Vent Rib, Cased, *Modern*	$1500	$3250	$3750
Parazzi MT-6, 12 Ga., Trap Grade, Automatic Ejector, Vent Rib, Cased, *Modern*	1500	3000	3500
Perazzi Competition 1, 12 Ga., Skeet Grade, Automatic Ejector, Vent Rib, Single Trigger, Cased, *Modern*	1500	3000	3500
Perazzi Competition 1, 12 Ga., Trap Grade, Automatic Ejector, Vent Rib, Single Trigger, Cased, *Modern*	800	1750	2000
Perazzi Light Game Model, 12 Ga., Automatic Ejector, Vent Rib, Single Trigger, *Modern*	1500	3000	3500
Perazzi Mirage Special 4-Barrel Set, Various Gauges, Skeet Grade, Automatic Ejector, Vent Rib, Cased, *Modern*	4000	8000	9000
Perazzi Mirage Special, 12 Ga., Trap Grade, Automatic Ejector, Vent Rib, Cased, *Modern*	2000	4500	5000
Perazzi MX-7 Combo, 12 Ga., Trap Grade, Automatic Ejector, Vent Rib, Cased, *Modern*	2000	4000	4500

Ithaca Perazzi Combination

SHOTGUN, DOUBLE BARREL, SIDE-BY-SIDE

	Fair	V. Good	Excellent
Early Model, Serial Numbers under 425,000, Deduct 50%			
Outside Hammers, Deduct Another 20%-30%			
#2 Grade, 10 Ga. Magnum, Hammerless, Beavertail Forend, Double Trigger, *Modern*	700	1500	2200
#2 Grade, 12 Ga., Hammerless, Beavertail Forend, Double Trigger, Checkered Stock, *Modern*	500	1050	1100
#2 Grade, *Modern*	500	1000	1150
#2 Grade, *Modern*	550	1200	1350
#3 Grade, 10 Ga. Magnum, Hammerless, Beavertail Forend, Double Trigger, *Modern*	900	2000	2500
#3 Grade, 12 Ga., Hammerless, Double Trigger, Engraved, Checkered Stock, *Modern*	600	1125	1325
#3 Grade, 16 Ga., Hammerless, Beavertail Forend, Engraved, Checkered Stock, Double Trigger, *Modern*	500	1050	1250

	Fair	V. Good	Excellent
#3 Grade, 20 Ga., Hammerless, Double Trigger, Engraved, Checkered Stock, *Modern*	$700	$1500	$1750
#4 E Grade, 12 Ga., Hammerless, Automatic Ejector, Vent Rib, Beavertail Forend, *Modern*	1200	2750	3000
#4 E Grade, 16 Ga., Hammerless, Automatic Ejector, Vent Rib, Fancy Checkering, Engraving, *Modern*	1500	3250	3500
#4 E Grade, 20 Ga., Hammerless, Automatic Ejector, Beavertail Forend, Fancy Checkering, Engraving, *Modern*	1600	3500	3750
#5 E Grade, 10 Ga. Mag., Hammerless, Automatic Ejector, Vent Rib, Beavertail Forend, *Modern*			Rare
#5 E Grade, 12 Ga., Hammerless, Automatic Ejector, Vent Rib, Fancy Checkering, Engraving, *Modern*	1400	3250	3500
#5 E Grade, 16 Ga., Hammerless, Automatic Ejector, Beavertail Forend, Fancy Checkering, Fancy Engraving, *Modern*	1500	3250	3500
#5 E Grade, 20 Ga., Hammerless, Automatic Ejector, Fancy Checkering, Fancy Engraving, Double Trigger, *Modern*	1500	3750	4500
#7 E Grade, Various Gauges, Hammerless, Automatic Ejector, Vent Rib, Beavertail Forend, *Modern*			Rare
$1000 Grade, 12 Ga., Hammerless, Automatic Ejector, Single Selective Trigger, Vent Rib, Beavertail Forend, *Curio*	4000	9000	10500
$1000 Grade, 16 and 20 Gauges, Hammerless, *Curio*			Rare
$2000 Grade, 12 Ga., Hammerless, Automatic Ejector, Single Selective Trigger, Ornate, *Modern*	3500	8500	9500
$2000 Grade, 16 Ga., Hammerless, Automatic Ejector, Single Selective Trigger, Vent Rib, Ornate, *Modern*			Rare
$2000 Grade, 20 Ga., Hammerless, Automatic Ejector, Single Selective Trigger, Beavertail Forend, Ornate, *Modern*			Rare
Field Grade, Various Gauges, Hammerless, 10 Ga. Magnum, Beavertail Forend, *Modern*	700	1750	2000
Field Grade, Various Gauges, Hammerless, 10 Ga. Magnum, Double Trigger, *Modern*	600	1500	1750
Field Grade, Various Gauges, Hammerless, Beavertail Forend, Double Trigger, *Modern*	300	700	775
Field Grade, Various Gauges, Hammerless, Double Trigger, Checkered Stock, *Modern*	250	550	600

SHOTGUN, LEVER ACTION

	Fair	V. Good	Excellent
Model 66, Various Gauges, Singleshot, *Modern*	$50	$75	$100
Model 66, Various Gauges, Singleshot, Ventilated Rib, *Modern*	75	100	125
Model 66 Youth, Various Gauges, Singleshot, *Modern*	25	50	75

SHOTGUN, PISTOL

	Fair	V. Good	Excellent
Auto Burglar, Various Gauges, Double Barrel, Side by Side, Short Shotgun, *Curio*	300	650	850

SHOTGUN, SEMI-AUTOMATIC

	Fair	V. Good	Excellent
5KB 300 Standard, 12 and 20 Gauges, *Modern*	100	200	250
5KB 300 Standard, 12 and 20 Gauges, Vent Rib, *Modern*	100	225	275
5KB 300 XL Standard, 12 and 20 Gauges, *Modern*	125	275	300
5KB 300 XL Standard, 12 and 20 Gauges, Vent Rib, *Modern*	150	300	325
5KB 900 XL Deluxe, 12 and 20 Gauges, Vent Rib, *Modern*	125	275	300
5KB 900 XL MR Deluxe, 12 and 20 Gauges, Vent Rib, *Modern*	125	250	275
5KB 900 XL Slug, 12 and 20 Gauges, Open Rear Sight, *Modern*	125	275	300
5KB 900 XL, 12 and 20 Gauges, Skeet Grade, *Modern*	150	325	350
5KB 900 XL, 12 Ga., Trap Grade, *Modern*	150	325	350
5KB 900 XL, 12 Ga., Trap Grade, Monte Carlo Stock, *Modern*	150	350	375
Mag 10 Deluxe, 10 Ga. 3½", Takedown, Vent Rib, Fancy Wood, Checkered Stock, *Modern*	350	800	950
Mag 10 Standard, 10 Ga. 3½", Takedown, Recoil Pad, Checkered Stock, Sling Swivels, *Modern*	225	475	525
Mag 10 Standard, 10 Ga. 3½", Takedown, Vent Rib, Recoil Pad, Checkered Stock, Sling Swivels, *Modern*	300	600	650
Mag 10 Supreme, 10 Ga. 3½", Takedown, Vent Rib, Fancy Wood, Engraved, Checkered Stock, *Modern*	300	600	750
Model 51 Presentation, 12 and 20 Gauges, Skeet Grade, Takedown, Checkered Stock, Fancy Wood, Recoil Pad, *Modern*	325	750	1250
Model 51 Standard, 12 and 20 Gauges, Takedown, Checkered Stock, *Modern*	125	225	275
Model 51 Standard, 12 and 20 Gauges, Takedown, Vent Rib, Checkered Stock, *Modern*	150	300	375

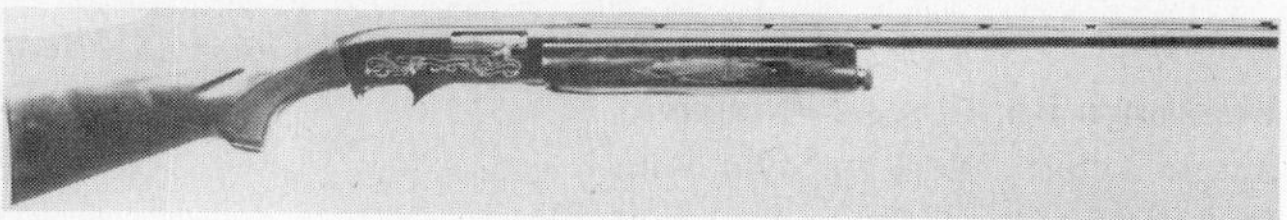

Ithaca Model 51

	Fair	V. Good	Excellent
Model 51 Turkey Gun, 12 Ga., Trap Grade, Takedown, Checkered Stock, Fancy Wood, Recoil Pad, *Modern*	$150	$375	$450
Model 51A Deerslayer, 12 Ga., Takedown, Open Rear Sight, Sling Swivels, *Modern*	125	275	325
Model 51A Waterfowler, 12 Ga., Trap Grade, Monte Carlo Stock, Fancy Wood, Recoil Pad, *Modern*	150	325	350
Model 51A, Magnum 12 Ga., Takedown, Vent Rib, Recoil Pad, *Modern*	150	325	375

SHOTGUN, SINGLESHOT

	Fair	V. Good	Excellent
$5000 Grade, 12 Ga., Trap Grade, Automatic Ejector, Ornate, *Modern*	3000	7500	9000
4 E Grade, 12 Ga., Trap Grade, Automatic Ejector, Engraved, Fancy Checkering, *Modern*	450	1000	1200
5 E Grade, 12 Ga., Trap Grade, Automatic Ejector, Fancy Engraving, Fancy Checkering, *Modern*	900	2000	2250
7 E Grade, 12 Ga., Trap Grade, Automatic Ejector, Fancy Engraving, Fancy Checkering, *Modern*	1700	4000	4500
Century 12 Ga., Trap Grade, Automatic Ejector, Engraved, Checkered Stock, *Modern*	200	425	475
Century II, 12 Ga., Trap Grade, Automatic Ejector, Engraved, Checkered Stock, *Modern*	225	475	525
Perazzi Competition, 12 Ga., Trap Grade, Automatic Ejector, Vent Rib, Cased, *Modern*	400	950	1250
Victory Grade, 12 Ga., Automatic Ejector, Checkered Stock, Vent Rib, Trap Grade, *Modern*	325	725	800

SHOTGUN, SLIDE ACTION

Model 37, Extra Vent Rib Barrel, Add $60.00-$85.00

Model 37, for Extra Barrel, Add $50.00-$75.00

	Fair	V. Good	Excellent
Model 37 Deerslayer, Various Gauges, Takedown, Checkered Stock, Recoil Pad, Open Rear Sight, *Modern*	125	275	350
Model 37 Deerslayer, Various Gauges, Takedown, Fancy Wood, Checkered Stock, Recoil Pad, Open Rear Sight, *Modern*	125	250	300
Model 37 DSPS, 12 Ga., Takedown, Checkered Stock, 5 Shot, Open Rear Sight, *Modern*	$100	$200	$225
Model 37 DSPS, 12 Ga., Takedown, Checkered Stock, 8 Shot, Open Rear Sight, *Modern*	100	225	250
Model 37 English Ultralite, 12 or 20 Gauge, Takedown, Checkered Stock, Recoil Pad, *Modern*	125	250	300
Model 37 Field Grade, Various Gauges, Takedown, Plain, *Modern*	75	150	200
Model 37 Presentation, Various Gauges, Takedown, Skeet Grade, Fancy Wood, Checkered Stock, *Modern*	450	1000	1250
Model 37 Riotgun, 12 Ga., Takedown, Parkerized, 5 Shot, *Modern*	700	1500	1750
Model 37 Standard, Various Gauges, Takedown, Checkered Stock, *Modern*	100	200	225
Model 37 Trenchgun, 12 Ga., Takedown, Parkerized, 5 Shot, *Modern*	1400	3000	3500
Model 37, 12 Ga., Takedown, Bicentennial, Engraved, Fancy Wood, Checkered Stock, *Modern*	150	325	350
Model 37-$1000 Grade, Various Gauges, Takedown, Fancy Wood, Fancy Checkering, Fancy Engraving, Gold Inlays, *Modern*	1700	4000	5000
Model 37-$5000 Grade, Various Gauges, Takedown, Fancy Wood, Fancy Checkering, Fancy Engraving, Gold Inlays, *Modern*	1500	3500	5500
Model 37-D, Various Gauges, Takedown, Checkered Stock, Beavertail Forend, *Modern*	100	225	250
Model 37-DV, Various Gauges, Takedown, Checkered Stock, Recoil Pad, *Modern*	100	225	275
Model 37-R Deluxe, Various Gauges, Takedown, Solid Rib, Fancy Wood, Checkered Stock, *Modern*	100	225	300
Model 37-R, Various Gauges, Takedown, Solid Rib, Checkered Stock, *Modern*	75	175	225
Model 37-R, Various Gauges, Takedown, Solid Rib, Plain, *Modern*	75	150	200
Model 37-S, Various Gauges, Takedown, Skeet Grade, Checkered Stock, Fancy Wood, *Modern*	150	325	400
Model 37-T, Various Gauges, Takedown, Trap Grade, Checkered Stock, Fancy Wood, *Modern*	150	325	400
Model 37-V Standard, Various Gauges, Takedown, Checkered Stock, Vent Rib, *Modern*	100	225	250
Model 37T Target, Various Gauges, Takedown, Trap Grade, Fancy Wood, Checkered Stock, *Modern*	150	350	400

IVER JOHNSON

Started as Johnson & Bye, 1871, in Worcester, Mass. In 1883 became Iver Johnson's Arms & Cycle Works. 1891–1982 at Fitchburg, Mass., relocated to Jacksonville, Ark. in 1982. Acquired by American Military Arms in 1987. All operations ceased in 1993. The following trade names also marked on selected handguns by this firm, q.v.: Automatic Hammerless, Boston Bulldog, Defender, Eagle. Although not one of the major gunmakers in terms of reputation, beauty or rarity, Iver Johnson produced a vast quantity of firearms, for a broad-based clientele, at reasonable prices. The latter years of Iver Johnson were under the ownership and direction of Louis Imperata, prominent New York arms dealer and gunmaker. Owners of John Jovino, Inc., Louis Imperata, later joined by his son Anthony, have been a major force in U.S. gunmaking. For years Jovino was the leading Colt jobber, and for much of the 1970s the Imperatas were involved, through Iver Johnson, in the production of Colt Blackpowder revolvers, the parts having been supplied from Gardone, Val Trompia, Italy, primarily by the Uberti Co. and Armi San Marco. Though no longer operating as Iver Johnson, the Imperatas are the licensed manufacturers of the Colt Blackpowder production of the 1990s.

HANDGUN, PERCUSSION

	Fair	V. Good	Excellent
.36 1861 Navy, Revolver, Reproduction, *Antique*	$25	$50	$75
.36 New Model Navy, Revolver, Reproduction, *Antique*	25	50	75
.36 Pocket Model, Revolver, Reproduction, *Antique*	25	50	75
.36 Remington Army, Revolver, Reproduction, *Antique*	25	50	75
.44 1860 Army, Revolver, Reproduction, *Antique*	25	50	75
.44 Confederate Army, Revolver, Reproduction, *Antique*	25	50	75
.44 Remington Army, Revolver, Reproduction, *Antique*	50	75	100
.44 Remington Target, Revolver, Reproduction, *Antique*	50	75	100
Prince, .30, Singleshot, Spur Trigger, Various Barrel Lengths, Screw Barrel, *Antique*	150	300	325
Uncle Sam 1871, .30, Singleshot, Spur Trigger, Various Barrel Lengths, *Antique*	125	250	300

HANDGUN, REVOLVER

	Fair	V. Good	Excellent
.22 Supershot, .22 L.R.R.F., 7 Shot, Blue, Wood Grips, Top Break, Double Action, *Modern*	50	75	100
Armsworth M855, .22 L.R.R.F., 8 Shot, Single Action, Top Break, Adjustable Sights, Wood Grips, *Modern*	50	100	125
Buckhorn Buntline, .357 Magnum, Single Action, Western Style, with Detachable Shoulder Stock, Adjustable Sights, 18" Barrel, *Modern*	125	275	300
Buckhorn Buntline, .44 Magnum, Single Action, Western Style, with Detachable Shoulder Stock, Adjustable Sights, 18" Barrel, *Modern*	$150	$300	$325
Buckhorn Buntline, .45 Colt, Single Action, Western Style, with Detachable Shoulder Stock, Adjustable Sights, 18" Barrel, *Modern*	150	275	300
Buckhorn, .357 Magnum, Single Action, Western Style, Color Case Hardened Frame, Adjustable Sights, 12" Barrel, *Modern*	100	175	200
Buckhorn, .357 Magnum, Single Action, Western Style, Color Case Hardened Frame, Adjustable Sights, Various Barrel Lengths, *Modern*	75	125	175
Buckhorn, .44 Magnum, Single Action, Western Style, Color Case Hardened Frame, Adjustable Sights, Various Barrel Lengths, *Modern*	100	175	200
Buckhorn, .45 Colt, Single Action, Western Style, Color Case Hardened Frame, Adjustable Sights, Various Barrel Lengths, *Modern*	75	150	175
Buckhorn, .45 Colt, Single Action, Western Style, Color Case Hardened Frame, Adjustable Sights, 12" Barrel, *Modern*	100	175	200
Cadet, .22 WMR, 8 Shot, Solid Frame, Double Action, Plastic Stock, Blue, *Modern*	25	50	75
Cadet, .32 S & W Long, 5 Shot, Solid Frame, Double Action, Plastic Stock, Nickel Plated, *Modern*	25	50	75
Cadet, .32 S & W, 5 Shot, Solid Frame, Double Action, Plastic Stock, Blue, *Modern*	25	50	75
Cadet, .38 Special, 5 Shot, Solid Frame, Double Action, Plastic Stock, Blue, *Modern*	25	50	75
Cadet, .38 Special, 5 Shot, Solid Frame, Double Action, Plastic Stock, Nickel Plated, *Modern*	25	50	75
Cattleman, .357 Magnum, Single Action, Western Style, Color Case Hardened Frame, Various Barrel Lengths, *Modern*	100	150	175
Cattleman, .447 Magnum, Single Action, Western Style, Color Case Hardened Frame, Various Barrel Lengths, *Modern*	100	175	200
Cattleman, .45 Colt, Single Action, Western Style, Color Case Hardened Frame, Various Barrel Lengths, *Modern*	75	125	150
Champion Target, .22 L.R.R.F., 8 Shot, Single Action, Top Break, Adjustable Sights, Wood Grips, *Modern*	50	100	125

	Fair	V. Good	Excellent
Model 1900 Target, .22 L.R.R.F., 7 Shot, Blue, Wood Grips, Solid Frame, Double Action, *Modern*	$65	$125	$150
Model 1900, .22 L.R.R.F., 7 Shot, Blue, Double Action, Solid Frame, *Modern*	50	75	100
Model 1900, .22 L.R.R.F., 7 Shot, Nickel Plated, Double Action, Solid Frame, *Modern*	50	75	100
Model 1900, .32 S & W Long, 6 Shot, Blue, Double Action, Solid Frame, *Modern*	50	75	100
Model 1900, .32 S & W Long, 6 Shot, Nickel Plated, Double Action, Solid Frame, *Modern*	50	75	100
Model 1900, .32 Short R.F., 6 Shot, Blue, Double Action, Solid Frame, *Modern*	50	75	100
Model 1900, .32 Short R.F., 6 Shot, Nickel Plated, Double Action, Solid Frame, *Modern*	50	100	125
Model 1900, .38 S & W, 5 Shot, Blue, Double Action, Solid Frame, *Modern*	50	100	125
Model 1900, .38 S & W, 5 Shot, Nickel Plated, Double Action, Solid Frame, *Modern*	50	100	125
Model 50A Sidewinder, .22 L.R.R.F., 8 Shot, Solid Frame, Double Action, Plastic Stock, Western Style, *Modern*	20	50	75
Model 50A Sidewinder, .22 L.R.R.F., 8 Shot, Solid Frame, Double Action, Wood Grips, Western Style, *Modern*	25	50	75
Model 55, .22 L.R.R.F., 8 Shot, Solid Frame, Double Action, Wood Grips, Blue, *Modern*	25	50	75
Model 55-S Cadet, .32 S & W, 5 Shot, Solid Frame, Double Action, Plastic Stock, Blue, *Modern*	25	50	75
Model 55-S Cadet, .38 S & W, 5 Shot, Solid Frame, Double Action, Plastic Stock, Blue, *Modern*	25	50	75
Model 55-SA Cadet, .22 L.R.R.F., 8 Shot, Solid Frame, Double Action, Plastic, Blue, *Modern*	25	50	75
Model 55-SA Cadet, .32 S & W, 5 Shot, Solid Frame, Double Action, Plastic Stock, Blue, *Modern*	25	50	75
Model 55-SA Cadet, .38 S & W, 5 Shot, Solid Frame, Double Action, Plastic Stock, Blue, *Modern*	25	50	75
Model 55A, .22 L.R.R.F., 8 Shot, Solid Frame, Double Action, Wood Grips, Blue, *Modern*	50	75	100
Model 55A, .22 L.R.R.F., 8 Shot, Solid Frame, Double Action, Wood Grips, Blue, *Modern*	50	75	100
Model 55A, .22 L.R.R.F., 8 Shot, Solid Frame, Double Action, Plastic Stock, Blue, *Modern*	$50	$75	$100
Model 55S, .22 L.R.R.F., 8 Shot, Solid Frame, Double Action, Plastic Stock, Blue, *Modern*	25	50	75
Model 57 Target, .22 L.R.R.F., 8 Shot, Solid Frame, Double Action, Plastic Stock, Adjustable Sights, *Modern*	50	75	100
Model 57 Target, .22 L.R.R.F., 8 Shot, Solid Frame, Double Action, Wood Grips, Adjustable Sights, *Modern*	50	75	100
Model 57-A Target, .22 L.R.R.F., 8 Shot, Solid Frame, Double Action, Plastic Stock, Adjustable Sights, *Modern*	50	75	100
Model 57-A Target, .22 L.R.R.F., 8 Shot, Solid Frame, Double Action, Wood Grips, Adjustable Sights, *Modern*	50	75	100
Model 66 Trailsman, .22 L.R.R.F., 8 Shot, Top Break, Double Action, Wood Grips, Adjustable Sights, *Modern*	50	75	100
Model 67 Viking, .22 L.R.R.F., 8 Shot, Top Break, Double Action, Plastic Stock, Adjustable Sights, *Modern*	50	75	100
Model 67S Viking, .32 S & W, 5 Shot, Top Break, Double Action, Plastic Stock, Adjustable Sights, *Modern*	50	75	100
Model 67S Viking, .38 S & W, 5 Shot, Top Break, Double Action, Plastic Stock, Adjustable Sights, *Modern*	25	50	75

Iver Johnson Trailsman

	Fair	V. Good	Excellent
Model 76S Viking, .22 L.R.R.F., 8 Shot, Top Break, Double Action, Plastic Stock, Adjustable Sights, *Modern*	50	75	100
Petite, .22 Short Nickel Plated, Folding Trigger, 5 Shot, "Baby" Style, *Antique*	100	200	250

	Fair	V. Good	Excellent
Safety, .22 L.R.R.F., 7 Shot, Top Break, Double Action, Hammer, Blue, *Modern*	$50	$100	$125
Safety, .22 L.R.R.F., 7 Shot, Top Break, Double Action, Hammer, Nickel Plated, *Modern*	50	125	150
Safety, .22 L.R.R.F., 7 Shot, Top Break, Double Action, Hammerless, Blue, *Modern*	50	125	150
Safety, .22 L.R.R.F., 7 Shot, Top Break, Double Action, Hammerless, Nickel Plated, *Modern*	50	125	150
Safety, .32 S & W Long, 6 Shot, Top Break, Double Action, Hammer, Blue, *Modern*	50	100	125
Safety, .32 S & W Long, 6 Shot, Top Break, Double Action, Hammer, Nickel Plated, *Modern*	50	100	125
Safety, .32 S & W Long, 6 Shot, Top Break, Double Action, Hammerless, Blue, *Modern*	50	100	125
Safety, .32 S & W, 5 Shot, Top Break, Double Action, Hammer, Nickel Plated, *Modern*	50	125	150
Safety, .32 S & W, 5 Shot, Top Break, Double Action, Hammer, Blue, *Modern*	50	100	125
Safety, .32 S & W, 5 Shot, Top Break, Double Action, Hammerless, Blue, *Modern*	50	125	150
Safety, .32 S & W, 5 Shot, Top Break, Double Action, Hammerless, Nickel Plated, *Modern*	50	125	150
Safety, .38 S & W, 5 Shot, Top Break, Double Action, Hammerless, Nickel Plated, *Modern*	50	125	150
Sealed 8 Protector, .22 L.R.R.F., 8 Shot, Blue, Wood Grips, Top Break, Double Action, *Modern*	50	125	150
Sealed 8 Supershot, .22 L.R.R.F., Adjustable Sights, Blue, Wood Grips, Top Break, Double Action, *Modern*	50	125	150
Sealed 8 Target, .22 L.R.R.F., 8 Shot, Blue, Wood Grips, Solid Frame, Double Action, *Modern*	50	100	125
Sidewinder, .22LR/.22 WMR Combo, Western Style, 4" Barrel, Adjustable Sights, *Modern*	25	75	100
Sidewinder, .22LR/.22 WMR Combo, Western Style, 6" Barrel, Adjustable Sights, *Modern*	25	75	100
Supershot 9, .22 L.R.R.F., 9 Shot, Adjustable Sights, Blue, Wood Grips, Top Break, *Modern*	50	100	125
Supershot M 844, .22 L.R.R.F., 8 Shot, Double Action, Top Break, Adjustable Sights, Wood Grips, *Modern*	25	75	100
Swing Out Model 1879, .38 S & W, 5 Shot, Swing Right, Forward Hinge, Solid Frame, *Antique*	100	275	300
Swing Out, .22 L.R.R.F., Swing-Out Cylinder, 4" Barrel, Double Action, Wood Grips, Blue, *Modern*	$25	$75	$100
Swing Out, .22 L.R.R.F., Swing-Out Cylinder, 4" Barrel, Double Action, Adjustable Sights, Blue, *Modern*	50	125	150
Swing Out, .22 L.R.R.F., Swing-Out Cylinder, 6" Barrel, Double Action, Adjustable Sights, Blue, *Modern*	50	100	125
Swing Out, .22 L.R.R.F., Swing-Out Cylinder, Various Barrel Lengths, Double Action, Wood Grips, Blue, *Modern*	25	75	100
Swing Out, .22 WMR, Swing-Out Cylinder, 4" Barrel, Double Action, Wood Grips, Blue, *Modern*	25	75	100
Swing Out, .22 WMR, Swing-Out Cylinder, 4" Barrel, Double Action, Adjustable Sights, Blue, *Modern*	50	125	150
Swing Out, .22 WMR, Swing-Out Cylinder, 6" Barrel, Double Action, Adjustable Sights, Blue, *Modern*	25	100	125
Swing Out, .22 WMR, Swing-Out Cylinder, Various Barrel, Lengths, Double Action, Wood Grips, Blue, *Modern*	50	75	100
Swing Out, .32 S & W Long, Swing-Out Cylinder, 4" Barrel, Double Action, Wood Grips, Blue, *Modern*	75	100	125
Swing Out, .32 S & W Long, Swing-Out Cylinder, 4" Barrel, Double Action, Adjustable Sights, Blue, *Modern*	75	125	150
Swing Out, .32 S & W Long, Swing-Out Cylinder, 6" Barrel, Double Action, Adjustable Sights, Blue, *Modern*	50	100	125
Swing Out, .32 S & W Long, Swing-Out Cylinder, Various Barrel Lengths, Double Action, Wood Grips, Blue, *Modern*	50	75	100
Swing Out, .32 S & W Long, Swing-Out Cylinder, Various Barrel Lengths, Double Action, Wood Grips, Nickel Plated, *Modern*	50	100	125
Swing Out, .38 Special, Swing-Out Cylinder, 4" Barrel, Double Action, Wood Grips, Blue, *Modern*	50	100	125
Swing Out, .38 Special, Swing-Out Cylinder, 4" Barrel, Double Action, Adjustable Sights, Blue, *Modern*	50	125	150
Swing Out, .38 Special, Swing-Out Cylinder, 6" Barrel, Double Action, Adjustable Sights, Blue, *Modern*	50	125	150
Swing Out, .38 Special, Swing-Out Cylinder, Various Barrel Lengths, Double Action, Wood Grips, Blue, *Modern*	50	100	125

	Fair	V. Good	Excellent
Swing Out, .38 Special, Swing-Out Cylinder, Various Barrel Lengths, Double Action, Wood Grips, Nickel Plated, *Modern*	$50	$100	$125
Target 9, .22 L.R.R.F., 9 Shot, Blue, Solid Frame, Wood Grips, Double Action, *Modern*	50	100	125
Trailblazer, .22LR/.22 WMR Combo, Single Action, Western Style, Color Case Hardened Frame, Adjustable Sights, *Modern*	50	125	150
Trigger-Cocking, .22 L.R.R.F., 8 Shot, Single Action, Top Break, Adjustable Sights, Wood Grips, *Modern*	50	125	150

HANDGUN, SEMI-AUTOMATIC

	Fair	V. Good	Excellent
Model TP-22, .22 L.R.R.F., Double Action, Hammer, Clip Fed, Blue, *Modern*	100	175	200
Model TP-25, .25 ACP, Double Action, Hammer, Clip Fed, Blue, *Modern*	100	150	175
Pony, .380 ACP, Hammer, Clip Fed, Blue, *Modern*	100	200	250
Pony, .380 ACP, Hammer, Clip Fed, Nickel Plated, *Modern*	100	175	225
Pony, .380 ACP, Hammer, Clip Fed, Stainless, *Modern*	100	225	275
PP30 Enforcer, .30 M1 Carbine, Clip Fed, Blue, *Modern*	100	200	225

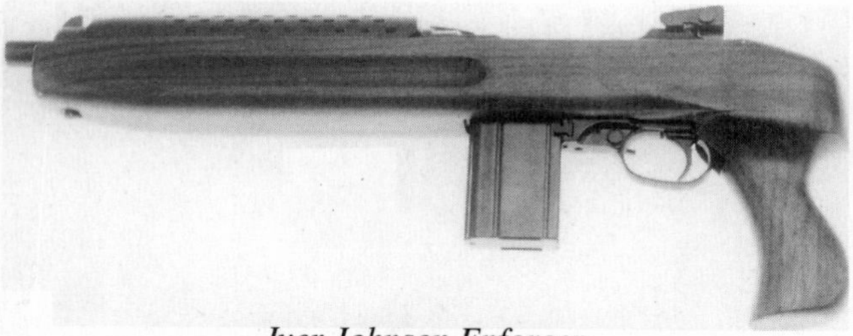

Iver Johnson Enforcer

	Fair	V. Good	Excellent
PP30S Enforcer, .30 M1 Carbine, Clip Fed, Stainless, *Modern*	100	225	250
Trailsman, .22 L.R.R.F., Clip Fed, Blue, *Modern*	75	125	150

HANDGUN, SINGLESHOT

	Fair	V. Good	Excellent
Eclipse 1872, .22 R.F., Spur Trigger, Side-Swing Barrel, Hammer, *Antique*	100	250	275

RIFLE, BOLT ACTION

	Fair	V. Good	Excellent
Model 2X, .22 L.R.R.F., Singleshot, Takedown, *Modern*	25	50	75
Model X, .22 L.R.R.F., Singleshot, Takedown, *Modern*	50	50	50

RIFLE, SEMI-AUTOMATIC

	Fair	V. Good	Excellent
PM30G, .30 Carbine, Clip Fed, Military Style, Carbine, *Modern*	$75	$150	$175

Iver Johnson PM30G

	Fair	V. Good	Excellent
PM30P, .30 Carbine, Clip Fed, Telescoping Stock, Carbine, *Modern*	75	175	200
PM30PS Paratrooper, .30 M1 Carbine, Clip Fed, Stainless, *Modern*	100	225	275
PM5.7 Spitfire, 5.7 Spitfire, Clip Fed, Military Style, *Modern*	75	150	175
SC30F, .30 Carbine, Clip Fed, Folding Stock, Carbine, *Modern*	100	175	200
SC30F, .30 Carbine, Clip Fed, Paratrooper, Carbine, Stainless, *Modern*	100	200	250
SC30S, .30 Carbine, Clip Fed, Plastic Stock, Carbine, Stainless, *Modern*	75	150	200

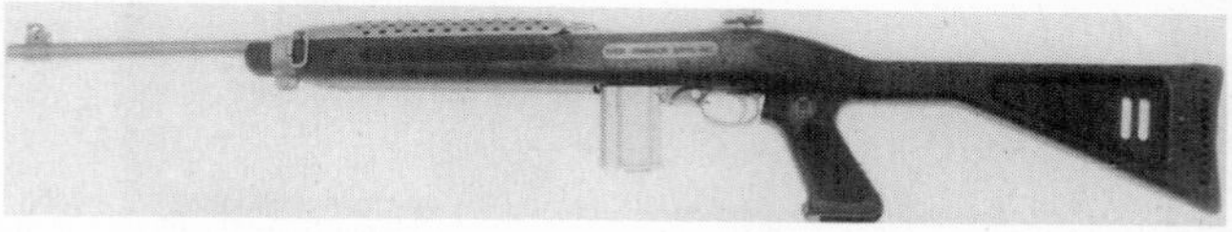

Iver Johnson SC30SS

	Fair	V. Good	Excellent
SC5.7S, 5.7 Spitfire, Clip Fed, Carbine, *Modern*	75	150	200
SC5.7S, 5.7 Spitfire, Clip Fed, Folding Stock, Carbine, *Modern*	75	150	175
SC5.7S, 5.7 Spitfire, Clip Fed, Plastic Stock, *Modern*	50	125	150
SC5.7S, 5.7 Spitfire, Clip Fed, Plastic Stock, Stainless, *Modern*	75	175	225

SHOTGUN, DOUBLE BARREL, OVER-UNDER

	Fair	V. Good	Excellent
Silver Shadow, 12 Gauge, Double Trigger, Checkered Stock, *Modern*	100	250	300
Silver Shadow, 12 Gauge, Double Trigger, Checkered Stock, Light Engraving, Vent Rib, *Modern*	125	300	350
Silver Shadow, 12 Gauge, Single Trigger, Checkered Stock, *Modern*	150	350	400
Silver Shadow, 12 Gauge, Single Trigger, Checkered Stock, Light Engraving, Vent Rib, *Modern*	150	375	425

SHOTGUN, DOUBLE BARREL, SIDE-BY-SIDE

	Fair	V. Good	Excellent
Hercules, Various Gauges, Double Trigger, Automatic Ejector, Hammerless, Checkered Stock, *Modern*	175	400	475

	Fair	V. Good	Excellent
Hercules, Various Gauges, Double Trigger, Checkered Stock, Hammerless, *Modern*	$175	$375	$375
Hercules, Various Gauges, Single Trigger, Automatic Ejector, Hammerless, Checkered Stock, *Modern*	175	450	575
Hercules, Various Gauges, Single Trigger, Hammerless, Checkered Stock, *Modern*	175	425	475
Knox-All, Various Gauges, Double Trigger, Hammer, Checkered Stock, *Modern*	150	300	350
Skeeter, Various Gauges, Double Trigger, Hammerless, *Modern*	300	700	800
Skeeter, Various Gauges, Skeet Grade, Single Selective Trigger, Hammerless, *Modern*	350	800	950
Skeeter, Various Gauges, Skeet Grade, Single Selective Trigger, Automatic Ejector, Hammerless, *Modern*	500	1000	1200
Skeeter, Various Gauges, Skeet Grade, Single Trigger, Hammerless, *Modern*	350	800	950
Super, *Modern*	300	700	750
Super, 12 Gauge, Trap Grade, Double Trigger, Hammerless, *Modern*	275	600	650
Super, 12 Gauge, Trap Grade, Single Trigger, Hammerless, Modern	$325	$700	$750

SHOTGUN, SINGLESHOT

	Fair	V. Good	Excellent
Champion, Various Gauges, Automatic Ejector, *Modern*	25	50	75
Mat Rib Grade, Various Gauges, Raised Matted Rib, Automatic Ejector, Checkered Stock, *Modern*	50	75	100
Side Snap, 12 Gauge, Damascus Barrel, Hammer, *Antique*	25	50	75
Side Snap, 12 Gauge, Steel Barrel, Hammer, *Antique*	50	75	100
Top Snap, 12 Gauge, Steel Barrel, Hammer, *Antique*	50	75	100
Trap Grade, 12 Gauge, Vent Rib, Checkered Stock, *Modern*	65	125	450

IZARRA

Made by Bonifacio Echeverra, Eibar, Spain, c. 1918.

HANDGUN, SEMI-AUTOMATIC

	Fair	V. Good	Excellent
.32 ACP, Clip Fed, Long Grip, *Curio*	100	150	175

J

J & R
Burbank, Calif.

RIFLE, SEMI-AUTOMATIC

	Fair	V. Good	Excellent
Model 68, 9mm Luger, Clip Fed, Flash Hider, Takedown, *Modern*	$100	$150	$175

JACKRABBIT
Continental Arms Corp., New York City, c. 1960.

RIFLE, SINGLESHOT

	Fair	V. Good	Excellent
Handy Gun, .44 Magnum, Detachable Shoulder Stock, *Modern*	50	75	100

SHOTGUN, SINGLESHOT

	Fair	V. Good	Excellent
Handy Gun, .410, Detachable Shoulder Stock, *Modern*	25	50	75

JACKSON ARMS CO.
Made by Crescent for C. M. McClung & Co., Knoxville, Tenn. See Crescent Fire Arms Co., Shotgun, Double Barrel, Side-by-Side; Shotgun, Single Shot.

JACKSON HOLE RIFLE CO.
Jackson Hole, Wyo., c. 1970.

RIFLE, BOLT ACTION

	Fair	V. Good	Excellent
Custom, Various Calibers, with 3 Interchangeable Barrels, Fancy Checkering, Fancy Wood, *Modern*	400	850	950
Presentation, Various Calibers, with 3 Interchangeable Barrels, Fancy Checkering, Fancy Wood, Engraved, *Modern*	450	1000	1250
Sportsman, Various Calibers, with 3 Interchangable Barrels, Checkered Stock, *Modern*	350	750	850

JAGA
Frantisek Dusek, Opocno, Czechoslovakia, c. 1930.

HANDGUN, SEMI-AUTOMATIC

	Fair	V. Good	Excellent
.25 ACP, Clip Fed, Blue, *Curio*	75	125	150

JAGER
Germany, 1960–1975.

HANDGUN, REVOLVER

	Fair	V. Good	Excellent
Jager, .22LR/.22 WMR Combo, Single Action, Western Style, Adjustable Sights, *Modern*	$50	$100	$125
Jager, .22LR/.22 WMR Combo, Single Action, Western Style, *Modern*	50	75	100
Jager Centerfire, Various Calibers, Single Action, Western Style, Adjustable Sights, *Modern*	75	125	150
Jager Centerfire, Various Calibers, Single Action, Western Style, *Modern*	50	100	125

JAGER
Suhl, Germany.

HANDGUN, SEMI-AUTOMATIC

	Fair	V. Good	Excellent
.32 ACP, Clip Fed, Commercial, *Curio*	150	350	375
.32 ACP, Clip Fed, Military, *Curio*	175	400	450

JAGER, F. & CO.
See Herold.

JANSSEN FRERES
Liege, Belgium, c. 1925.

SHOTGUN, DOUBLE BARREL, SIDE-BY-SIDE

	Fair	V. Good	Excellent
Various Gauges, Hammerless, Steel Barrel, *Curio*	100	175	200

JAPANESE MILITARY

HANDGUN, REVOLVER

	Fair	V. Good	Excellent
Model 26, 9mm, Military, *Curio*	125	250	275

HANDGUN, SEMI-AUTOMATIC

	Fair	V. Good	Excellent
Baby Nambu, 7mm Nambu, "TGE," Clip Fed, Military, *Curio*	1400	3000	3500
Baby Nambu, 7mm Nambu, Clip Fed, Military, *Curio*	1100	2250	2500
Type 14 Nambu, 8mm Nambu, Clip Fed, Large Trigger Guard, Military, *Curio*	150	350	375
Type 14 Nambu, 8mm Nambu, Clip Fed, Small Trigger Guard, Military, *Curio*	200	425	475

Japanese Military Type 26 Revolver

Japanese Military Type 14 Pistol

	Fair	V. Good	Excellent
Type 1902 "Grandpa," 8mm Nambu, Tokyo Arsenal, Clip Fed, Military, *Curio*	$1200	$3000	$3500
Type 1904 "Papa," 8mm Nambu, TGE Commercial, Clip Fed, *Curio*	700	1500	1750
Type 1904 "Papa," 8mm Nambu, TGE Navy, Clip Fed, Military, *Curio*	600	1250	1500
Type 1904 "Papa," 8mm Nambu, Thailand, Clip Fed, Military, *Curio*	450	1000	1250
Type 1904 "Papa," 8mm Nambu, Tokyo Arsenal, Clip Fed, Military, *Curio*	450	1000	1250
Type 94, 8mm Nambu, Clip Fed, Military, *Curio*	125	225	250

RIFLE, BOLT ACTION

	Fair	V. Good	Excellent
Japanese "Siamese Mauser," 8 × 52R Cal., Made by Japan for the Government of Siam in the Early 1920s. A Modified 98 Mauser, Bolt Action, 30-Inch Barrel, *Curio*	50	100	125
Model 38 (1905), 6.5 × 50 Arisaka, Military, *Curio*	50	125	150
Model 38 (1905), 6.5 × 50 Arisaka, Military, Carbine, *Curio*	75	150	250
Model 44 (1911), 6.5 × 50 Arisaka, Military, Carbine, *Curio*	100	225	350
Model 99 (1939), 7.7 × 58 Arisaka, Military, Open Rear Sight, *Curio*	75	125	150
Type 30 (1897), 6.5 Aisaka, Bolt Action, 31-Inch Barrel, Often Referred to as the "Hook Safety Rifle," *Curio*	$75	$150	$175
Type 38 Carbine, 6.5 Cal., Arisaka, 19-Inch Barrel, Modified for Paratroop Use by the addition of a Hinge to the Wrist of the Stock for Folding, Somewhat Rare, *Curio*	75	300	400
Type 38, 6.5 × 50 Arisaka, Late Model, Military, *Curio*	75	125	150
Type 44, 6.5 × 50 Arisaka, Folding Bayonet, Military, *Curio*	100	225	275
Type 97 Sniper Rifle, Arisaka, 31-Inch Barrel, Specially Selected for Extreme Accuracy and Then Fitted with Telescopic Sight, *Curio*	150	325	500
Type 99 Type 2 Take Down Rifle, 7.7 Cal., Arisaka, 25-Inch Barrel, A Standard Type 99 Rifle Modified to Break in Half for Compact Paratroop Use, Very Rare, *Curio*	125	275	450
Type 99, 7.7 Cal., Arisaka, 31-Inch Barrel, Five Shot Mauser Type Magazine, Bolt Action, Long Barrel Infantry Model, Becoming Scarce, *Curio*	75	125	150
Type 99, 7.7 × 58 Arisaka, Aircraft Sights Dust Cover, Military, *Curio*	100	225	250

Japanese Military Type 99 Rifle

JENNINGS FIREARMS, INC.

Carson City, Nev.

HANDGUN, SEMI-AUTOMATIC

	Fair	V. Good	Excellent
Model J-22, .22 L.R.R.F., Clip Fed, Black Teflon Plate, *Modern*	25	50	75
Model J-22, .22 L.R.R.F., Clip Fed, Satin Nickel Plate, *Modern*	25	50	75

JEWEL

Made by Hood Firearms Co., c. 1876.

HANDGUN, REVOLVER

	Fair	V. Good	Excellent
#1, .22 Short R.F., 7 Shot, Spur Trigger, Solid Frame, Single Action, *Antique*	75	150	175

J.G.L.

Jos. G. Landmann, Holstein, Germany, c. 1968.

	Fair	V. Good	Excellent
RIFLE, SEMI-AUTOMATIC			
JGL-68 Model 1, .22 L.R.R.F., Clip Fed, Carbine Style, *Modern*	$25	$50	$75
JGL-68 Model 2, .22 L.R.R.F., Clip Fed, Vertical Grip & Foregrip, *Modern*	25	50	75
JGL-68 Model 3, .22 L.R.R.F., Clip Fed, Vertical Grip, *Modern*	25	50	75

JIEFFCO

Mre. Liegoise d'Armes a Feu Robar et Cie, Liege, Belgium, c. 1912–1914.

	Fair	V. Good	Excellent
HANDGUN, SEMI-AUTOMATIC			
.25 ACP, Clip Fed, Blue, *Curio*	100	250	275
.32 ACP, Clip Fed, Blue, *Curio*	100	250	275

JIEFFCO

Tradename used by Davis-Warner on pistols made by Robar et Cie., c. 1920.

	Fair	V. Good	Excellent
HANDGUN, SEMI-AUTOMATIC			
New Model Melior, .25 ACP, Clip Fed, *Curio*	75	150	175

JO-JO-AR

Hijos de Arrizabalaga, Eibar, Spain, c. 1920.

	Fair	V. Good	Excellent
HANDGUN, SEMI-AUTOMATIC			
.380 ACP, Tip-up, Clip Fed, Hammer, Spur Trigger, Military, *Curio*	100	200	250
9mm Bergmann, Tip-up, Clip Fed, Hammer, Spur Trigger, Military, *Curio*	75	150	200

JOFFRE

Spain, c. 1900.

	Fair	V. Good	Excellent
HANDGUN, SEMI-AUTOMATIC			
M1916, .32 ACP, Clip Fed, *Modern*	50	100	125

JOHNSON & BYE CO.

Worcester, Mass. The following trade names also marked on selected guns made by this firm, q.v.: American Bulldog, Eclipse, Encore, Favorite, Favorite Navy, Lion, Tycoon.

JOHNSON AUTOMATICS

Providence, R.I. Also see U.S. Military.

	Fair	V. Good	Excellent
RIFLE, BOLT ACTION			
Diamond Cherry Featherweight, Various Calibers, Engraved, Carved Cherry Stock, Muzzle Brake, *Modern*	$450	$1000	$1250
Honey Featherweight, Various Calibers, Engraved, Carved Stock, Muzzle Brake, Gold and Silver Inlays, *Modern*	700	1500	1750
Laminar Sporter, Various Calibers, Laminated Stock, *Modern*	275	650	750
RIFLE, SEMI-AUTOMATIC			
Model 1941, .30-06 Springfield, Miliatry, *Curio*	500	1000	1700
Model 1941, 7mm Mauser, Military, *Curio*	400	850	950

JONES, CHARLES

Lancaster, Pa. 1780. See Kentucky Rifles.

JONES, J.N. & CO.

London, England, c. 1760.

	Fair	V. Good	Excellent
HANDGUN, FLINTLOCK			
.60, George III, Navy Pistol, Brass Barrel, Brass Furniture, Military, *Antique*	550	1250	1500
HANDGUN, PERCUSSION			
.58, Holster Pistol, Converted from Flintlock, Brass Furniture, Plain, *Antique*	500	1100	1400

JUPITER

Fabrique d'Armes de Guerre de Grand Precision, Eibar, Spain.

	Fair	V. Good	Excellent
HANDGUN, SEMI-AUTOMATIC			
.32 ACP, Clip Fed, Blue, *Curio*	50	125	150

K

KABA SPEZIAL

Made by August Menz, Suhl, Germany, for Karl Bauer & Co., Berlin, Germany, c. 1925.

HANDGUN, SEMI-AUTOMATIC

	Fair	V. Good	Excellent
Liliput, .25 ACP, Clip Fed, Blue, *Modern*	$100	$225	$250
Liliput, .32 ACP, Clip Fed, Blue, *Modern*	100	250	275

KABA SPEZIAL

Made by Francisco Arizmendi, Eibar, Spain.

HANDGUN, SEMI-AUTOMATIC

	Fair	V. Good	Excellent
.25 ACP, Clip Fed, Blue, *Modern*	75	150	175

KART

HANDGUN, SEMI-AUTOMATIC

	Fair	V. Good	Excellent
For Colt Government Target, .22 L.R.R.F., Conversion Unit Only	75	150	175
Target, .22 L.R.R.F., Clip Fed, M1911 Frame, 6" Barrel, *Modern*	250	575	650

KASSNAR IMPORTS

Harrisburg, Pa.

RIFLE, BOLT ACTION

	Fair	V. Good	Excellent
Model M-14S, .22 L.R.R.F., Clip Fed, Checkered Stock, *Modern*	25	50	75
Model M-15S, .22 WMR, Clip Fed, Checkered Stock, *Modern*	25	50	75
Model M-1400, .22 L.R.R.F., Clip Fed, Checkered Stock, *Modern*	25	50	75
Model M-1500, .22 WMR, Clip Fed, Checkered Stock, *Modern*	50	75	100
Parker Hale Midland, Various Calibers, Checkered Stock, Open Sights, *Modern*	100	200	225
Parker Hale Super, Various Calibers, Checkered Stock, Open Sights, Monte Carlo Stock, *Modern*	100	250	300
Parker Hale Varmint, Various Calibers, Checkered Stock, Open Sights, Varmint Stock, *Modern*	125	275	300

RIFLE, SEMI-AUTOMATIC

	Fair	V. Good	Excellent
Model M-16, .22 L.R.R.F., Clip Fed, Military Style, *Modern*	25	50	75
Model M-20S, .22 L.R.R.F., *Modern*	$25	$50	$75

SHOTGUN, DOUBLE BARREL, OVER-UNDER

	Fair	V. Good	Excellent
Fias SK-1, 12 and 20 Gauges, Double Trigger, Checkered Stock, *Modern*	150	350	375
Fias SK-3, 12 and 20 Gauges, Single Selective Trigger, Checkered Stock, *Modern*	150	350	400
Fias SK-4, 12 and 20 Gauges, Single Selective Trigger, Checkered Stock, Automatic Ejector, *Modern*	150	375	450
Fias SK-4D, 12 and 20 Gauges, Single Selective Trigger, Fancy Checkering, Fancy Wood, Engraved, Automatic Ejector, *Modern*	175	400	475
Fias SK-4T, 12 Ga., Trap Grade, Single Selective Trigger, Automatic Ejector, Checkered Stock, Wide Vent Rib, *Modern*	200	425	475

SHOTGUN, DOUBLE BARREL, SIDE-BY-SIDE

	Fair	V. Good	Excellent
Zabala, Various Gauges, Checkered Stock, Double Triggers, *Modern*	150	325	375

SHOTGUN, SINGLESHOT

	Fair	V. Good	Excellent
Taiyojuki, Various Gauges, Top Break, Plain, *Modern*	15	25	50

KEFFER, JACOB

Lancaster, Pa., c. 1802. See Kentucky Rifles and Pistols.

KEIM, JOHN

Reading, Pa. 1820–1839. See Kentucky Rifles and Pistols.

KENTUCKY RIFLES AND PISTOLS

The uniquely American "Kentucky" (or, as some prefer, "Pennsylvania") expressed in wood & metal, the attitude of strength and independence that fostered our young nation. For the most part Kentuckys are custom guns, and, aside from general similarities, virtually all are different, even those by the same maker. To add to the problem of price generalization, gunsmiths purchased parts from various makers and there may be three different names on a single gun or none at all. The main considerations in determining value are: 1. Type of ignition; 2. Quality of workmanship; 3. Decoration; 4. Originality; 5. Condition.

RIFLE, FLINTLOCK

	Fair	V. Good	Excellent
High Quality, Fancy Decoration, *Antique*	$5000	$12000	$15000
Moderate Quality, Medium Decoration, *Antique*	3000	8000	10000
Moderate Quality, Plain, *Antique*	1250	4000	5000
Over-Under, Swivel-Breech, High Quality, *Antique*	9000	20000	25000
Over-Under, Swivel-Breech, Medium Quality, *Antique*	8000	17500	20000
Over-Under, Swivel-Breech, Plain, *Antique*	4000	8500	10000
Deduct 30%-40%, if Converted from Percussion			

RIFLE, PERCUSSION

	Fair	V. Good	Excellent
Add 20%, if Converted from Flintlock Percussion			
High Quality, Fancy Decoration, *Antique*	4000	8500	10000

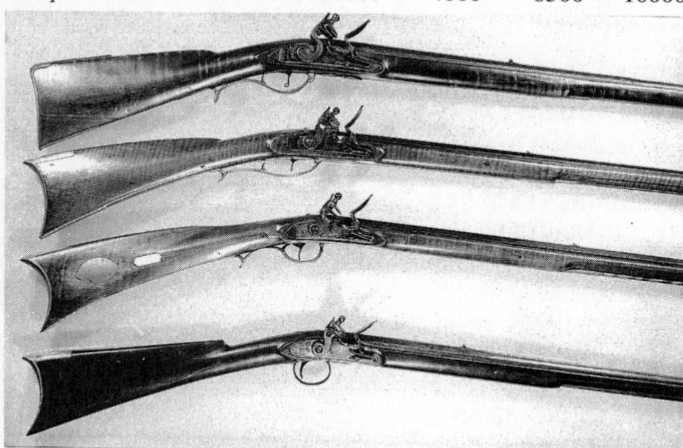

From the top, *flintlock Kentucky type rifles with Ketland lock but otherwise unmarked, next with barrel marked* S. Miller *and lock marked* Ross, *next marked* J. J. Henry-Boulton *on lock; and bottom with lock marked* A. W. Spies.

	Fair	V. Good	Excellent
Moderate Quality, Medium Decoration, *Antique*	2000	4000	5000
Moderate Quality, Plain, *Antique*	900	2000	2500
Over-Under, High Quality, Swivel Breech, *Antique*	6000	10000	12500
Over-Under, Medium Quality, Swivel Breech, *Antique*	3500	7500	8500
Over-Under, Medium Quality, Swivel Breech, Plain, *Antique*	2000	4000	5000

PISTOLS, FLINTLOCK

	Fair	V. Good	Excellent
High Quality, Fancy Decoration, *Antique*	4000	8000	10000
Moderate Quality, Medium Decoration, *Antique*	3000	6500	7500

PISTOL, PERCUSSION (ORIGINAL)

	Fair	V. Good	Excellent
High Quality, Fancy Decoration, *Antique*	$1600	$3000	$3500
Moderate Quality, Medium Decoration, *Antique*	800	1750	2000

PISTOLS, PERCUSSION (CONVERTED FLINTLOCK)

	Fair	V. Good	Excellent
High Quality, Fancy Decoration, *Antique*	2000	4000	4500
Moderate Quality, Medium Decoration, *Antique*	1500	3000	3500

KETLAND & CO

Birmingham & London, England 1760–1831. Also see Kentucky Rifles. The Ketland marking, a name not infrequently found marked on locks, is often mistakenly thought to be the manufacturer of a variety of arms. Generally speaking, Ketland supplied the lock only, while the identity of the maker needs to be determined either by identification through the barrel marking, or by interpreting the style.

HANDGUN, FLINTLOCK

	Fair	V. Good	Excellent
.58, Holster Pistol, Plain, Tapered Round Barrel, Brass Furniture, *Antique*	500	1200	1500
.62, Belt Pistol, Brass Barrel, Brass Furniture, Light Ornamentation, *Antique*	700	1700	2000

KETLAND, T.

Birmingham, England, 1750–1829.

HANDGUN, FLINTLOCK

	Fair	V. Good	Excellent
.69, Pair, Belt Pistol, Brass Furniture, Plain, *Antique*	1200	2700	3000

RIFLE, FLINTLOCK

	Fair	V. Good	Excellent
.65, Officers Model Brown Bess, Musket, Military, *Antique*	1500	3000	3500
.73, 2nd Model Brown Bess, Musket, Military, *Antique*	1000	2250	2500

KETLAND, WILLIAM & CO.

HANDGUN, FLINTLOCK

	Fair	V. Good	Excellent
.63, Holster Pistol, Round Barrel, Plain, *Antique*	600	1350	1500

KETTNER, ED

Suhl, Thuringia, Germany, 1922–1939.

COMBINATION WEAPON, DRILLING

	Fair	V. Good	Excellent
12 X 12 X 10.75 X 65R Collath, Engraved, Checkered Stock, Sling Swivels, *Curio*	900	2200	2500

KIMBALL, J. M. ARMS CO.
Detroit, Mich., c. 1955–1958.

HANDGUN, SEMI-AUTOMATIC

	Fair	V. Good	Excellent
Combat Model, .30 Carbine, 3" Barrel, Clip Fed, Blue, Short Barrel, *Modern*	$400	$800	$900
Target Model, .30 Carbine, 5" Barrel, Clip Fed, Blue, Adjustable Sights, *Modern*	400	800	900
Standard Model, .22 Hornet, Clip Fed, Blue, *Modern*			Rare

KIMBER
Clackamas, Ore. 1980–1991.

RIFLE, BOLT ACTION

	Fair	V. Good	Excellent
Model 82 Match, .22 L.R.R.F., Checkered Stock, Clip Fed, No Sights, *Modern*	600	1250	1500
Model 82 Varmint, .22 W.M.R., Checkered Stock, Clip Fed, No Sights, *Modern*	300	600	700
Model 82C Classic, .22 L.R.R.F., Checkered Stock, Clip Fed, No Sights, Monte Carlo Stock, *Modern*	400	800	900
Model 82C Super America, .22 L.R.R.F., Checkered Stock, Clip Fed, No Sights, Monte Carlo Stock, *Modern*	400	850	950

KIMEL INDUSTRIES
Mathews, N.C.

HANDGUN, DOUBLE BARREL, OVER-UNDER

	Fair	V. Good	Excellent
Twist, .22 Short R.F., Swivel Breech, Derringer, Spur Trigger, *Modern*	25	50	75

KING NITRO
Made by Stevens Arms.

RIFLE, BOLT ACTION

	Fair	V. Good	Excellent
Model 53, .22 L.R.R.F., Singleshot, Takedown, *Modern*	150	350	450

SHOTGUN, DOUBLE BARREL, SIDE-BY-SIDE

	Fair	V. Good	Excellent
M 315 Various Gauges, Hammerless, Steel Barrel, *Modern*	75	125	150

KINGLAND 10-STAR
Made by Crescent for Geller, Wards, & Hasner St. Louis, Mo. See Kingland Special.

KINGLAND SPECIAL
Made by Crescent for Geller, Wards & Hasner St. Louis, Mo. See Crescent Fire Arms Co., Shotgun, Double Barrel, Side-by-Side; Shotgun, Singleshot.

KIRIKKALE
Makina ve Kimya Endustrisi Kurumu Kirrikale, Ankara, Turkey.

HANDGUN, SEMI-AUTOMATIC

	Fair	V. Good	Excellent
MKE, 7.65mm & 9mmk, Clip Fed, Double Action, *Modern*	$150	$325	$375

KITTEMAUG
c. 1880.

HANDGUN, REVOLVER

	Fair	V. Good	Excellent
.32 Short R.F., 5 Shot, Spur Trigger, Solid Frame, Single Action, *Antique*	75	150	175

KLEINGUENTHER'S
Seguin, Texas.

HANDGUN, REVOLVER

	Fair	V. Good	Excellent
Reck R-18, .357 Magnum, Adjustable Sights, Western Style, Single Action, *Modern*	50	100	125

RIFLE, BOLT ACTION

	Fair	V. Good	Excellent
K-10, .22 L.R.R.F., Single Shot, Tangent Sights, *Modern*	25	50	75
K-12, .22 L.R.R.F., Clip Fed, Checkered Stock, *Modern*	25	50	75
K-13, .22 W.M.R., Clip Fed, Checkered Stock, *Modern*	50	100	125
K-14 Insta-fire, Various Calibers, Checkered Stock, No Sights, Recoil Pad, *Modern*	300	700	800
K-15, .22 L.R.R.F., Clip Fed, Checkered Stock, *Modern*	50	100	125
K-15 Insta-fire, Various Calibers, Checkered Stock, No Sights, Recoil Pad, *Modern*	400	800	1000
V2130, Various Calibers, Checkered Stock, Recoil Pad, *Modern*	100	200	225

RIFLE, DOUBLE BARREL, OVER-UNDER

	Fair	V. Good	Excellent
Model 222, .22 W.M.R., Plain, *Modern*	75	125	150

SHOTGUN, DOUBLE BARREL, OVER-UNDER

	Fair	V. Good	Excellent
Condor, 12 Gauge, Single Selective Trigger, Automatic Ejector, Vent Rib, *Modern*	150	375	425
Condor, 12 Gauge, Skeet Grade, Single Selective Trigger, Automatic Ejector, Wide Vent Rib, *Modern*	200	400	450

SHOTGUN, DOUBLE BARREL, SIDE-BY-SIDE

	Fair	V. Good	Excellent
Brescia, 12 Gauge, Hammerless, Light Engraving, Double Trigger, *Modern*	$100	$200	$250

SHOTGUN, SEMI-AUTOMATIC

	Fair	V. Good	Excellent
12 Ga., Checkered Stock, Vent Rib, Engraved, Left Hand, *Modern*	100	200	225
12 Ga., Checkered Stock, Vent Rib, Engraved, Right Hand, *Modern*	100	175	200

KLETT, SIMON

Leipzig, c. 1620.

RIFLE, WHEEL LOCK

	Fair	V. Good	Excellent
.54, Rifled, Octagon Barrel, Brass Furniture, Medium Ornamentation, Engraved, High Quality, *Antique*	4500	10000	12000

KNICKERBOCKER

Made by Crescent H & D Folsom, c. 1900. See Crescent Fire Arms Co., Shotgun, Double Barrel, Side-by-Side.

KNICKERBOCKER

Made by Stevens Arms.

SHOTGUN, DOUBLE BARREL, SIDE-BY-SIDE

	Fair	V. Good	Excellent
Model 311, Various Gauges, Hammerless, Steel Barrel, *Modern*	75	150	175

KNOCKABOUT

Made by Stevens Arms.

SHOTGUN, DOUBLE BARREL, SIDE-BY-SIDE

	Fair	V. Good	Excellent
Model 311, Various Gauges, Hammerless, Steel Barrel, *Modern*	75	150	175

KNOXALL

Made by Crescent, c. 1900.

SHOTGUN, DOUBLE BARREL, SIDE-BY-SIDE

	Fair	V. Good	Excellent
Various Gauges, Hammerless, Steel Barrel, *Modern*	100	175	200
Various Gauges, Outside Hammers, Steel Barrel, *Modern*	75	150	175

KODIAK MFG. CO.

North Haven, Conn., c. 1965. Despite the prodigious knowledge and experience with fine sporting arms of George Rowbottom, a principal in the company, the Mfg. Co. was relatively short-lived.

RIFLE, BOLT ACTION

	Fair	V. Good	Excellent
Model 98 Brush Carbine, Various Calibers, Checkered Stock, *Modern*	75	150	175
Model 99 Deluxe Brush Carbine, Various Calibers, Checkered Stock, *Modern*	$75	$150	$175
Model 100 Deluxe Rifle, Various Calibers, Checkered Stock, *Modern*	75	175	200
Model 100M Deluxe Rifle, Various Magnum Calibers, Checkered Stock, *Modern*	75	175	200
Model 101 Ultra, Various Calibers, Monte Carlo Stock, *Modern*	75	175	200
Model 101M Ultra, Various Magnum Calibers, Monte Carlo Stock, *Modern*	100	200	225
Model 102 Ultra Varmint, Various Calibers, Heavy Barrel, *Modern*	100	200	225

RIFLE, SEMI-AUTOMATIC

	Fair	V. Good	Excellent
Model 260 Autoloader, .22 L.R.R.F., Tube Feed, Open Sights, 22" Barrel, *Modern*	100	200	250
Model 260 Autoloader Carbine, .22 L.R.R.F., Tube Feed, Open Sights, 20" Barrel, *Modern*	100	225	275
Model 260 Magnum, .22 W.M.R., Tube Feed, Open Sights, 22" Barrel, *Modern*	125	250	300
Model 260 Magnum Carbine, .22 W.M.R., Tube Feed, Open Sights, 20" Barrel, *Modern*	100	225	275

KOHOUT & SPOL

Kdyne, Czechoslovakia, 1928–1945.

HANDGUN, SEMI-AUTOMATIC

	Fair	V. Good	Excellent
Mars, 6.35mm, Clip Fed, *Curio*	75	175	225
Mars, 7.65mm, Clip Fed, *Curio*	100	200	250

KOMMER, THEODOR

Zella Mehlis, Germany, c. 1920.

HANDGUN, SEMI-AUTOMATIC

	Fair	V. Good	Excellent
Model I, 6.35mm, Clip Fed, *Curio*	125	275	300

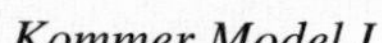

Kommer Model I

	Fair	V. Good	Excellent
Model II, 6.35mm, Clip Fed, *Curio*	125	250	275

	Fair	V. Good	Excellent
Model III, 6.35mm, Clip Fed, *Curio*	$100	$225	$250
Model IV, 7.65mm, Clip Fed, *Curio*	150	300	325

KORTH

Wilhelm Korth Waffenfabrik, Ratzburg, West Germany. One of the world's finest revolving handguns, the Korth has a well-deserved reputation for excellence in engineering, and for quality of manufacture. These arms also rank as one of the most expensive out-of-the-box revolvers produced today.

HANDGUN, REVOLVER

	Fair	V. Good	Excellent
Target, Various Calibers, 6 Shot, *Modern*	700	1750	2000

KRAFT, JACOB

Lancaster, Pa. 1771–1782. See Kentucky Rifles and Pistols.

KRICO

Stuttgart, West Germany. Also see Beeman's.

RIFLE, BOLT ACTION

	Fair	V. Good	Excellent
.22 Rem. Carbine, Checkered Stock, Double Set Triggers, *Modern*	250	575	625
.22 Rem. Rifle, Checkered Stock, Double Set Triggers, *Modern*	250	550	600
Model 302, .22 L.R.R.F., Clip Fed, Checkered Stock, Open Sights, *Modern*	300	625	675
Model 304, .22 L.R.R.F., Clip Fed, Checkered Stock, Mannlicher Stock, Set Triggers, Open Sights, *Modern*	300	625	675
Model 311, .22 L.R.R.F., Checkered Stock, Double Set Trigger, *Modern*	150	300	325
Model 340, .22 L.R.R.F., Metallic Silhouette Match Rifle, Clip Fed, Checkered Stock, Target Stock, *Modern*	300	600	650
Model 340, .22 L.R.R.F., Mini-Sniper Match Rifle, Clip Fed, Checkered Stock, Target Stock, *Modern*	300	650	700
Model 351, .22 WMR, Checkered Stock, Double Set Triggers, *Modern*	250	500	550
Model 354, .22 WMR, Checkered Stock, Double Set Triggers, *Modern*	300	600	650
Model 400, .22 Hornet, Clip Fed, Checkered Stock, Open Sights, *Modern*	300	625	700
Model 420, .22 Hornet, Clip Fed, Checkered Stock, Set Triggers, Mannlicher Stock, Open Sights, Sling Swivels, *Modern*	400	800	875
Model 600, Various Calibers, Clip Fed, Checkered Stock, Open Sights, Sling Swivels, Recoil Pad, *Modern*	$400	$800	$1000
Model 600 Export, Various Calibers, Checkered Stock, Double Set Triggers, *Modern*	200	400	450
Model 600 Luxus, Various Calibers, Checkered Stock, Double Set Triggers, *Modern*	225	475	525
Model 620, Various Calibers, Clip Fed, Checkered Stock, Set Triggers, Mannlicher Stock, Open Sights, Sling Swivels, *Modern*	425	900	1150
Model 620 Luxus, Various Calibers, Checkered Stock, Double Set Triggers, *Modern*	250	550	625
Model 640, Various Calibers, Deluxe Varmint Rifle, Clip Fed, Checkered Stock, Target Stock, *Modern*	500	1025	1175
Model 650, Various Calibers, Sniper/Match Rifle, Clip Fed, Checkered Stock, Target Stock, *Modern*	450	950	1200
Model 700, Various Calibers, Clip Fed, Checkered Stock, Open Sights, Sling Swivels, Recoil Pad, *Modern*	325	750	900
Model 700 Export, Various Calibers, Checkered Stock, Double Set Triggers, *Modern*	250	550	650
Model 700 Luxus, Various Calibers, Checkered Stock, Double Set Triggers, *Modern*	300	600	675
Model 720, Various Calibers, Clip Fed, Checkered Stock, Set Triggers, Mannlicher Stock, Open Sights, Sling Swivels, *Modern*	450	950	1100
Model 720 Luxus, Various Calibers, Checkered Stock, Double Set Triggers, *Modern*	350	775	850
Model DJV, .22 Various Calibers, Checkered Target Stock, Double Set Triggers, *Modern*	250	500	550
Special Varmint, .222 Rem., Checkered Stock, Heavy Barrel, Double Set Triggers, *Modern*	250	550	600

KRIEGHOFF GUN CO.

Suhl, Germany, 1886–1945, and from 1945 to date in Ulm, West Germany. Also see shotguns of Ulm. For many years these highly respected sporting guns have been imported by Hal Du Pont, of the Du Pont chemical family. With their Germanic styling, solid construction, and high-quality Krieghoffs are not inexpensive, but they have had a strong following for decades. The vast majority, however, are sold not to collectors, but to active shooters.

	Fair	V. Good	Excellent
COMBINATION WEAPON, DRILLING			
Neptun, Various Calibers, Hammerless, Engraved, Fancy Checkering, Sidelock, *Modern*	$3500	$8000	$10000
Neptun Dural, Various Calibers, Hammerless, Engraved, Fancy Checkering, Sidelock, *Modern*	3500	8000	10000
Neptun Primus, Various Calibers, Hammerless, Fancy Checkering, Fancy Engraving, Sidelock, *Modern*	6000	12000	15000

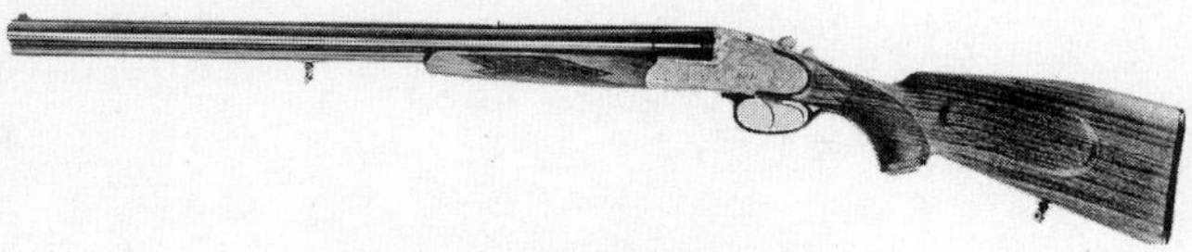

Krieghoff Neptun

	Fair	V. Good	Excellent
Neptun Primus Dural, Various Calibers, Hammerless, Fancy Checkering, Fancy Engraving, Sidelock, Lightweight, *Modern*	6000	12500	15500
Trumpf, Various Calibers, Hammerless, Engraved, Fancy Checkering, *Modern*	3000	6000	6500

Krieghoff Trumpf

	Fair	V. Good	Excellent
Trumpf Dural, Various Calibers, Hammerless, Engraved, Fancy Checkering, Lightweight, *Modern*	3000	6200	6700
RIFLE, DOUBLE BARREL, OVER-UNDER			
Teck, Various Calibers, Hammerless, Engraved, Fancy Checkering, *Modern*	2500	5500	6500
Teck Dural, Various Calibers, Hammerless, Engraved, Fancy Checkering, Lightweight, *Modern*	2500	6000	7000
Ulm, Various Calibers, Hammerless, Engraved, Fancy Checkering, Sidelock, *Modern*	3000	7500	8500
Ulm Dural, Various Calibers, Hammerless, Engraved, Fancy Checkering, Sidelock, *Modern*	3700	8000	9000
Ulm Primus, Various Calibers, Hammerless, Engraved, Fancy Checkering, Sidelock, *Modern*	3500	8000	10000

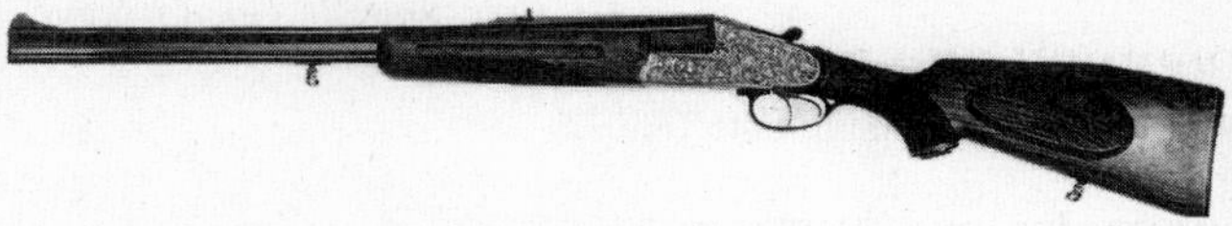

Krieghoff Ulm

	Fair	V. Good	Excellent
Ulm Primus Dural, Various Calibers, Hammerless, Engraved, Fancy Checkering, Sidelock, Lightweight, *Modern*	$3500	$8500	$10500
SHOTGUN, DOUBLE BARREL, OVER-UNDER			
Crown, 12 Gauge, Trap Grade, *Modern*	8000	16000	18000
Exhibition, 12 Gauge, Trap Grade, *Modern*	9000	25000	30000
Extra Barrel, Add $800.00–$1,000.00			
Monte Carlo, 12 Gauge, Trap Grade, *Modern*	5000	11000	13000
Munchen, Various Gauges, Skeet Grade, *Modern*	2500	5000	7000
San Remo, 12 Gauge, Trap Grade, *Modern*	2700	6000	8000
Standard, 12 Gauge, Field Grade, *Modern*	1400	3500	4000
Standard, 12 Gauge, Trap Grade, *Modern*	2000	4500	5000

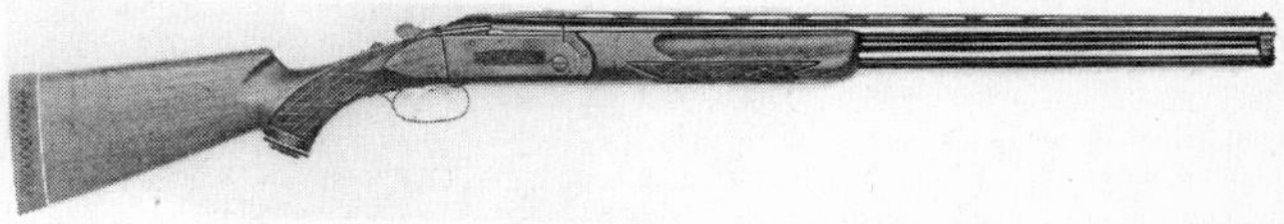

Krieghoff Standard

	Fair	V. Good	Excellent
Standard, Various Gauges, Skeet Grade, *Modern*	1600	3500	4000
Super Crown, 12 Gauge, Trap Grade, *Modern*	7000	15000	17000

KROYDEN

Tradename used by Savage Arms Corp.

	Fair	V. Good	Excellent
RIFLE, SEMI-AUTOMATIC			
.22 L.R.R.F., Tube Feed, Plain Stock, *Modern*	25	50	75

KRUSCHITZ

Vienna, Austria.

	Fair	V. Good	Excellent
RIFLE, BOLT ACTION			
Mauser 98, .30/06, Checkered Stock, Double Set Triggers, *Modern*	100	250	300

	Fair	V. Good	Excellent

KYNOCH GUN FACTORY
Birmingham, England. Late 1880s.

HANDGUN, REVOLVER

	Fair	V. Good	Excellent
Schlund, .32, .38 &.45 Calibers, Concealed Hammer, Top Break, Double Trigger, Cocking, *Antique* .	400	850	1000

Kynoch Schlund Revolver

L

LA SALLE

Tradename used by Manufrance.

	Fair	V. Good	Excellent
SHOTGUN, SEMI-AUTOMATIC			
Custom, 12 Ga., Checkered Stock, *Modern*	$100	$250	$300
SHOTGUN, SLIDE ACTION			
12 Gauge, Checkered Stock, Fancy Wood, *Modern*	100	250	275
12 Gauge, Field Grade, Plain, *Modern*	100	225	250
20 Gauge, Field Grade, Plain, *Modern*	75	150	200

LAHTI

Developed and made by Valtion Kivaarithedas, Jyvaskyla, Finland. Also made by Husqvarna in Sweden.

	Fair	V. Good	Excellent
HANDGUN, SEMI-AUTOMATIC			
L-35 Finnish, 9mm Luger, Clip Fed, Military, *Curio*	300	750	1000
M 40 Swedish, 9mm Luger, Clip Fed, Military, *Modern*	150	275	350

LAKESIDE

Made by Crescent for Montgomery Ward & Co., c. 1900. See Crescent Fire Arms Co., Shotgun, Double Barrel, Side-by-Side; Shotgun, Singleshot.

LAMES

Chiavari, Italy.

	Fair	V. Good	Excellent
SHOTGUN, DOUBLE BARREL, OVER-UNDER			
California, 12 Gauge, Trap Grade, Automatic Ejector, Single Selective Trigger, Vent Rib, Checkered Stock, *Modern*	300	675	725
Field Grade, 12 Gauge, Automatic Ejector, Single Selective Trigger, Vent Rib, Checkered Stock, *Modern*	150	350	400
Skeet Grade, 12 Gauge, Automatic Ejector, Single Selective Trigger, Vent Rib, Checkered Stock, *Modern*	200	500	575
Trap Grade, 12 Gauge, Automatic Ejector, Single Selective Trigger, Vent Rib, Monte Carlo Stock, *Modern*	$300	$625	$600

LANBER

Lanber Armas, S.A., Zaldibar, Spain.

	Fair	V. Good	Excellent
SHOTGUN, DOUBLE BARREL, OVER-UNDER			
Model 844 ST, 12 Gauge, Double Triggers, Checkered Stock, Light Engraving, *Modern*	150	275	325
Model 844 MST, 12 Gauge 3", Double Triggers, Checkered Stock, Light Engraving, *Modern*	150	300	350
Model 844 EST, 12 Gauge, Automatic Ejector, Double Triggers, Checkered Stock, Light Engraving, *Modern*	150	350	400
Model 844 EST CHR, 12 Gauge, Automatic Ejector, Double Triggers, Checkered Stock, Light Engraving, *Modern*	200	400	450
Model 2004 LCH, 12 Gauge, Trap Grade, Automatic Ejector, Single Trigger, Checkered Stock, Light Engraving, Lanber Choke, *Modern*	200	450	600
Model 2004 LCH, 12 Gauge, Skeet Grade, Automatic Ejector, Single Trigger, Checkered Stock, Light Engraving, Lanber Choke, *Modern*	200	450	600
Model 2004 LCH, 12 Gauge, Automatic Ejector, Single Trigger, Checkered Stock, Light Engraving, Lanber Choke, *Modern*	200	450	600

LANCASTER, CHARLES

London, England, 1889–1936.

	Fair	V. Good	Excellent
RIFLE, BOLT ACTION			
Various Calibers, Sporting Rifle, Checkered Stock, *Curio*	450	1000	1250

LANCELOT

	Fair	V. Good	Excellent
HANDGUN, SEMI-AUTOMATIC			
.25 ACP, Clip Fed, Blue, *Modern*	75	150	175

LANE & READ

Boston, Mass. 1826–1835.

SHOTGUN, PERCUSSION

	Fair	V. Good	Excellent
28 Gauge, Double Barrel, Side by Side, Light Engraving, Checkered Stock, *Antique*	$200	$400	$475

LANG, JOSEPH

London, England, established in 1821.

HANDGUN, PERCUSSION

	Fair	V. Good	Excellent
Pair, Double Barrel, Over-Under, Officer's Belt Pistol, Light Engraving, Cased with Accessories, *Antique*	1800	4000	4750

SHOTGUN, SINGLESHOT

	Fair	V. Good	Excellent
12 Gauge, Plain, Trap Grade, *Modern*	600	1200	1500

LANGENHAN

Friedrich Langenhan Gewehr u. Fahrradfabrik, Zella Mehlis, Germany.

HANDGUN, SEMI-AUTOMATIC

	Fair	V. Good	Excellent
Model I, 7.65mm, Clip Fed, Military, *Modern*	100	225	250

Langenhan Model I

	Fair	V. Good	Excellent
Model II, 6.35mm, Clip Fed, *Modern*	125	275	300
Model III, 6.35mm, Clip Fed, *Modern*	125	275	325

LAURONA

Spain.

SHOTGUN, DOUBLE BARREL, OVER-UNDER

	Fair	V. Good	Excellent
Model 67-G, 12 Gauge 3", Checkered Stock, Vent Rib, Double Triggers, *Modern*	75	150	225

LE BARON

RIFLE, FLINTLOCK

	Fair	V. Good	Excellent
.69 Presentation, Silver Furniture, Fancy Wood, Fancy Checkering, Fancy Engraving, *Antique*	$1900	$4000	$4500

LE BASQUE

HANDGUN, SEMI-AUTOMATIC

	Fair	V. Good	Excellent
7.65mm, Clip Fed, Blue, *Modern*	100	150	200

LE FRANCAISE

Mre. Francaise de Armes et Cycles de St. Etienne, St. Etienne, France.

HANDGUN, SEMI-AUTOMATIC

	Fair	V. Good	Excellent
Army Model, 9mm French Long, Clip Fed, *Curio*	400	800	950
Champion, 6.35mm, Clip Fed, Long Grip, *Curio*	125	250	275
Le Francais, 7.65mm, Clip Fed, *Curio*	150	350	400
Pocket Model, 6.35mm, Clip Fed, *Curio*	100	175	200
Policeman, 6.35mm, Clip Fed, *Curio*	300	650	750

Le Francaise Policeman

	Fair	V. Good	Excellent
Staff Officer's, 6.35mm, Clip Fed, *Curio*	150	300	350

LE MARTINY

HANDGUN, SEMI-AUTOMATIC

	Fair	V. Good	Excellent
6.35mm, Clip Fed, Blue, *Curio*	50	100	125

LE MONOBLOC

Jules Jacquemart, Liege, Belgium, c. 1910.

HANDGUN, SEMI-AUTOMATIC

	Fair	V. Good	Excellent
6.35mm, Clip Fed, *Curio*	100	200	250

	Fair	V. Good	Excellent

LE PAGE

Made by Manufacter d'Armes Le Page, Liege, Belgium.

HANDGUN, SEMI-AUTOMATIC

	Fair	V. Good	Excellent
7.65mm, Clip Fed, *Curio*	$150	$375	$400

Le Page

	Fair	V. Good	Excellent
9mm Browning Long, Clip Fed, Adjustable Sights, *Curio*	200	450	600
9mm Browning Long, Clip Fed, Adjustable Sights, Detachable Shoulder Stock, *Curio*	400	800	900
9mm Short, Clip Fed, Adjustable Sights, *Curio*	200	400	450

LE SANS PARIEL

Mre. d'Armes des Pyrenees.

HANDGUN, SEMI-AUTOMATIC

	Fair	V. Good	Excellent
6.35mm, Clip Fed, Blue, *Curio*	75	125	150

LE TOUTACIER

Mre. d'Armes des Pyrenees.

HANDGUN, SEMI-AUTOMATIC

	Fair	V. Good	Excellent
6.35mm, Clip Fed, Blue, *Curio*	50	125	150

LEADER

Possibly Hopkins & Allen, c. 1880.

HANDGUN, REVOLVER

	Fair	V. Good	Excellent
.22 Short R.F., 7 Shot, Spur Trigger, Solid Frame, Single Action, *Antique*	75	150	175
.32 Short R.F., 5 Shot, Spur Trigger, Solid Frame, Single Action, *Antique*	75	150	175

LEADER GUN CO.

Made by Crescent for Charles William Stores Inc., c. 1900. SEE Crescent Fire Arms Co., Shotgun, Double Barrel, Side-by-Side; Shotgun, Singleshot.

LEATHER, JACOB

York, Pa. 1779–1802. See U.S. Military, Kentucky Rifles.

LEBEAU-COURALLY

Lebeau-Courally Continental Firearms, Liege, Belgium since 1865.

RIFLE, DOUBLE BARREL, SIDE-BY-SIDE

	Fair	V. Good	Excellent
Ardennes, Various Calibers, Fancy Engraving, Double Triggers, Checkered Stock, Automatic Ejector, Boxlock, Fancy Wood, *Modern*	$6000	$12000	$14000
St. Hubert, Various Calibers, Fancy Engraving, Double Triggers, Checkered Stock, Automatic Ejector, Sidelocks, Fancy Wood, *Modern*	9000	20000	25000

SHOTGUN, DOUBLE BARREL, SIDE-BY-SIDE

	Fair	V. Good	Excellent
Grand Russe, 12 Gauge, Fancy Engraving, Double Triggers, Checkered Stock, Automatic Ejector, Boxlock, Fancy Wood, *Modern*	3250	8000	10000
Sologne, 12 Gauge, Medium Engraving, Double Triggers, Checkered Stock, Automatic Ejector, Boxlock with Sideplates, Fancy Wood, *Modern*	4000	9500	12000

LEBEAU-COURALLY

Liege, Belgium since 1865. One of the finest gunmakers of sporting arms in the world.

LEE ARMS CO.

Wilkes-Barre, Pa., c. 1870. Also see Red Jacket.

HANDGUN, REVOLVER

	Fair	V. Good	Excellent
.22 Short R.F., 7 Shot, Spur Trigger, Solid Frame, Single Action, *Antique*	75	150	175
.32 Short R.F., 5 Shot, Spur Trigger, Solid Frame, Single Action, *Antique*	75	150	175
.32 Short R.F., Spur Trigger, Nickel Plated, *Antique*	75	125	150

LEE SPECIAL

Made by Crescent for Lee Hardware, Salinas, Kans. c. 1900. See Crescent Fire Arms Co., Shotgun, Double Barrel, Side-by-Side; Shotgun, Singleshot.

LEFAUCHEUX

Paris, France, c. 1865. The use of revolvers by Lefaucheux in the Civil War has added to the appeal of these arms to the American collector. As pinfire cartridges became harder and harder to obtain, many of these revolvers became useless. A genuine C.S.A.-marked and/or pedigreed specimen will command a premium, sometimes several multiples of its value without such association. Another patron of Lefaucheux was the youthful Theodore Roosevelt—his first shotgun, a gift from his father, was a 12 gauge pinfire by this maker. The gun is part of the collection of the Sagamore Hill National Historic Site, Oyster Bay, New York. Of this piece TR would later recollect that it was "an excellent gun for a clumsy and often absent-minded boy."

HANDGUN, REVOLVER

	Fair	V. Good	Excellent
12mm Pinfire, Model 1863, Double Action, Finger Rest Trigger Guard, *Antique*	$200	$400	$450
9mm Pinfire, Double Action, Folding Trigger, Belgian, *Antique*	100	200	250
9mm Pinfire, Double Action, Paris, *Antique*	125	250	300

SHOTGUN, DOUBLE BARREL, SIDE-BY-SIDE

	Fair	V. Good	Excellent
Various Pinfire Gauges, Double Triggers, Hammers, *Antique*	75	125	150

LEFEVER SONS & CO.

Syracuse, N.Y. Nichols & Lefever, 1876–1878; D. M. Lefever, 1879–1889; Lefever Arms Co. 1889–1899; Lefever, Sons & Co. 1899–1926. Purchased by Ithaca Gun Co. 1926. Lefever marked guns manufactured until 1948. Once ranked among America's premier manufacturers of fine shotguns, Lefever continues to this day as a master restorer and finisher of quality sporting shotguns and other arms in Lee Center, New York.

SHOTGUN, DOUBLE BARREL, SIDE-BY-SIDE

	Fair	V. Good	Excellent
B, Various Gauges, Sidelock, Hammerless, Fancy Checkering, Fancy Engraving, Monte Carlo Stock, *Curio*	2200	5500	6500
BE, Various Gauges, Sidelock, Hammerless, Fancy Checkering, Fancy Engraving, Monte Carlo Stock, Automatic Ejector, *Curio*	4000	8500	9500
C, Various Gauges, Sidelock, Hammerless, Fancy Checkering, Fancy Engraving, Monte Carlo Stock, *Curio*	1600	3500	4000
CE, Various Gauges, Sidelock, Hammerless, Fancy Checkering, Fancy Engraving, Monte Carlo Stock, Automatic Ejector, *Curio*	2000	4500	5500
D, Various Gauges, Sidelock, Hammerless, Fancy Checkering, Engraved, Monte Carlo Stock, *Curio*	900	2500	2750
DE, Various Gauges, Sidelock, Hammerless, Fancy Checkering, Engraved, Monte Carlo Stock, Automatic Ejector, *Curio*	$900	$2750	$3000
DS, Various Gauges, Sidelock, Hammerless, Checkered Stock, *Curio*	400	850	1000
DSE, Various Gauges, Sidelock, Hammerless, Checkered Stock, Automatic Ejector, *Curio*	500	1250	1500
E, Various Gauges, Sidelock, Hammerless, Fancy Checkering, Engraved, *Curio*	600	1750	2000
EE, Various Gauges, Sidelock, Hammerless, Fancy Checkering, Engraved, *Curio*	900	2250	2500
F, Various Gauges, Sidelock, Hammerless, Checkered Stock, Engraved, *Curio*	450	1000	1250
FE, Various Gauges, Sidelock, Hammerless, Checkered Stock, Engraved, Automatic Ejector, *Curio*	550	1250	1500
G, Various Gauges, Sidelock, Hammerless, Checkered Stock, Light Engraving, *Curio*	550	1250	1500
GE, Various Gauges, Sidelock, Hammerless, Checkered Stock, Light Engraving, Automatic Ejector, *Curio*	700	1500	1750
H, Various Gauges, Sidelock, Hammerless, Checkered Stock, Light Engraving, *Curio*	450	1000	1250
HE, Various Gauges, Sidelock, Hammerless, Checkered Stock, Light Engraving, Automatic Ejector, *Curio*	600	1250	1500
Nitro Special, Various Gauges, Boxlock, Double Triggers, Checkered Stock, *Curio*	200	425	500
Nitro Special, Various Gauges, Boxlock, Single Triggers, Checkered Stock, *Curio*	250	500	575

SHOTGUN, SINGLESHOT

	Fair	V. Good	Excellent
A Grade Skeet, 12 Gauge, Hammerless, Vent Rib, Checkered Stock, Automatic Ejector, *Curio*	450	1000	1250
Long Range, Various Gauges, Field Grade, Hammerless, Checkered Stock, *Curio*	150	300	350
Trap Grade, 12 Gauge, Hammerless, Vent Rib, Checkered Stock, Automatic Ejector, *Curio*	250	500	550

LEFEVRE, PHILIP

Beaver Valley, Pa. 1731–1756. See Kentucky Rifles.

LEFEVRE, SAMUEL

Strasbourg, Pa. 1770–1771. See Kentucky Rifles.

LEIGH, HENRY

Belgium, c. 1890.

SHOTGUN, DOUBLE BARREL, SIDE-BY-SIDE

	Fair	*V. Good*	*Excellent*
Various Gauges, Outside Hammers, Damascus Barrel, *Curio*	$50	$100	$150

LEITNER, ADAM

York Co., Pa. See Kentucky Rifles and Pistols.

LENNARD

Lancaster, Pa. 1770–1772. See Kentucky Rifles and Pistols.

LEONHARDT

H. M. Gering & Co., Arnstadt, Germany, c. 1917.

HANDGUN, SEMI-AUTOMATIC

	Fair	*V. Good*	*Excellent*
Army, 7.65 ACP, Clip Fed, *Curio*	100	175	200
Gering, 7.65 ACP, Clip Fed, *Curio*	100	220	225

Leonhardt Gering

LEPCO

HANDGUN, SEMI-AUTOMATIC

	Fair	*V. Good*	*Excellent*
6.35mm, Clip Fed, Blue, *Modern*	50	100	125

Lepco

L.E.S.

Skokie, Ill.

HANDGUN, SEMI-AUTOMATIC

	Fair	*V. Good*	*Excellent*
P-18, 9mm Luger, Matte Stainless Steel, Clip Fed, Hammer, Double Action, *Modern*	$100	$225	$275
\P-18 Deluxe, 9mm Luger, Polished Stainless Steel, Clip Fed, Hammer, Double Action, *Modern*	125	250	325

LESCHER

Philadelphia, Pa., c. 1730. See Kentucky Rifles and Pistols.

LESCONNE, A.

French, c. 1650.

HANDGUN, FLINTLOCK

	Fair	*V. Good*	*Excellent*
Pair, Engraved, Silver Inlay, Long Screw Barrel, Rifled, Belt Hook, *Antique*	3000	8000	10000

LIBERTY

Made by Hood Firearms, 1880–1900.

HANDGUN, REVOLVER

	Fair	*V. Good*	*Excellent*
.22 Short R.F., 7 Shot, Spur Trigger, Solid Frame, Single Action, *Antique*	75	150	175
.32 Short R.F., 5 Shot, Spur Trigger, Solid Frame, Single Action, *Antique*	75	150	175

LIBERTY

Montrose, Calif.

HANDGUN, REVOLVER

	Fair	*V. Good*	*Excellent*
Mustang, .22 L.R.R.F., Single Action, Western Style, Adjustable Sights, *Modern*	25	50	75
Mustang, .22 LR/.22 WMR Combo, Single Action, Western Style, Adjustable Sights, *Modern*	25	50	75

LIBERTY

Retolaza Hermanos, Eibar, Spain, c. 1920.

HANDGUN, SEMI-AUTOMATIC

	Fair	*V. Good*	*Excellent*
M1924, 6.35mm, Clip Fed, *Curio*	50	125	150
Model 1914, 7.65mm, Clip Fed, Blue, *Curio*	75	150	175
Model 1914, 7.65mm, Clip Fed, Blue, Long Grip, *Curio*	75	150	175

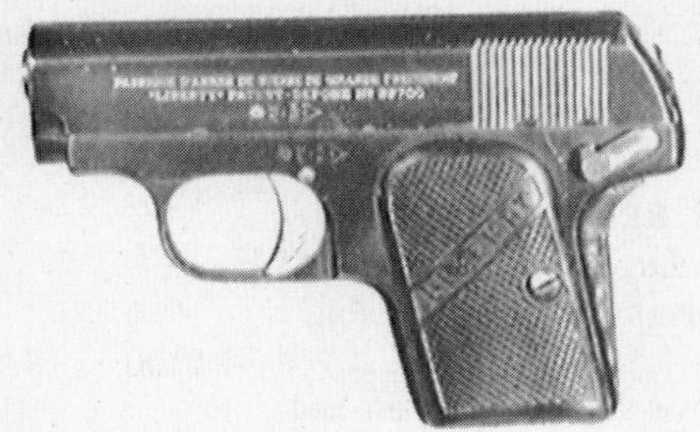

Liberty M1924

Liberty Long Grip

LIBERTY CHIEF

Miroku Firearms, Kochi, Japan.

HANDGUN, REVOLVER	*Fair*	*V. Good*	*Excellent*
Model 6, .38 Spec., Double Action, Blue, *Modern*	$50	$125	$150

LIBIA

Made by Beistegui Hermanos, c. 1920.

HANDGUN, SEMI-AUTOMATIC	*Fair*	*V. Good*	*Excellent*
6.35mm, Clip Fed, Blue, *Curio*	75	175	200
7.65mm, Clip Fed, Blue, *Curio*	100	200	225

LIEGEOISE D'ARMES A FEU

Robar et Cie., Liege, Belgium, c. 1920.

HANDGUN, SEMI-AUTOMATIC	*Fair*	*V. Good*	*Excellent*
New Model Melior, 6.35mm, Clip Fed, Blue, *Curio*	75	150	175
Spanish Copy, 6.35mm, Blue, Clip Fed, *Curio*	50	100	125
Spanish Copy, 7.65mm, Blue, Clip Fed, *Curio*	50	125	150

LIGHTNING

Echave y Arizmendi, Eibar, Spain, c. 1920.

HANDGUN, SEMI-AUTOMATIC	*Fair*	*V. Good*	*Excellent*
6.35mm, Clip Fed, Blue, *Curio*	$50	$125	$150

LIGNITZ, I. H.

Continental, c. 1650.

HANDGUN, WHEEL LOCK	*Fair*	*V. Good*	*Excellent*
Brass Barrel, Holster Pistol, Medium Ornamentation, *Antique*	2900	6500	7500

LIGNOSE

Successors to Theodor Bergmann, Suhl, Germany, c. 1925.

HANDGUN, SEMI-AUTOMATIC	*Fair*	*V. Good*	*Excellent*
For Original Wood Grips, Add 10%–15%			
Model 2, 6.35mm, Clip Fed, *Curio*	100	150	200
Model 2A, 6.35mm, Clip Fed, Einhand, Steel Cocking Piece, *Curio*	100	200	250

Lignose 2A

	Fair	*V. Good*	*Excellent*
Model 3A, 6.35mm, Clip Fed, Long Grip, Einhand, Brass Cocking Piece, *Curio*	100	200	250

LILIPUT

August Menz, Suhl, Germany, c. 1920.

HANDGUN, SEMI-AUTOMATIC	*Fair*	*V. Good*	*Excellent*
4.25mm Liliput, Clip Fed, Blue, *Curio*	200	400	450
6.35mm, Clip Fed, Blue, *Curio*	75	125	150

LION

Made by Johnson Bye & Co., c. 1870–1880. Sold by J. P. Lovell, Boston, Mass.

HANDGUN, REVOLVER	*Fair*	*V. Good*	*Excellent*
#1, .22 Short R.F., 7 Shot, Spur Trigger, Solid Frame, Single Action, *Antique*	75	150	175
#2, .32 Short R.F., 5 Shot, Spur Trigger, Solid Frame, Single Action, *Antique*	75	150	175

	Fair	V. Good	Excellent
#3, .38 Short R.F., 5 Shot, Spur Trigger, Solid Frame, Single Action, *Antique*	$75	$150	$175
#4, .41 Short R.F., 5 Shot, Spur Trigger, Solid Frame, Single Action, *Antique*	75	175	200

LITTLE GIANT

Made by Bacon Arms Co., c. 1880.

HANDGUN, REVOLVER

	Fair	V. Good	Excellent
.22 Short R.F., 7 Shot, Spur Trigger, Solid Frame, Single Action, *Antique*	75	150	175

LITTLE JOHN

Made by Hood Firearms, c. 1876.

HANDGUN, REVOLVER

	Fair	V. Good	Excellent
.22 Short R.F., 7 Shot, Spur Trigger, Solid Frame, Single Action, *Antique*	75	150	175

LITTLE JOKER

Made by John M. Marlin, New Haven, Conn. 1873–1875.

HANDGUN, REVOLVER

	Fair	V. Good	Excellent
.22 Short R.F., 7 Shot, Spur Trigger, Solid Frame, Single Action, *Antique*	75	175	200

LITTLE PET

Made by Stevens Arms.

SHOTGUN, SINGLESHOT

	Fair	V. Good	Excellent
Model 958, .410 Gauge, Automatic Ejector, Hammer, *Modern*	25	50	75
Model 958, 32 Gauge, Automatic Ejector, Hammer, *Modern*	25	50	75

LITTLE TOM

Alois Tomiska, Pilsen, Czechoslovakia, 1909–1918.

HANDGUN, SEMI-AUTOMATIC

	Fair	V. Good	Excellent
6.35mm, Clip Fed, Blue, Hammer, *Curio*	150	300	375
7.65mm, Clip Fed, Blue, Hammer, *Curio*	150	350	425

LITTLE TOM

Wiener Waffenfabrik, Vienna, Austria, 1918–1925.

HANDGUN, SEMI-AUTOMATIC

	Fair	V. Good	Excellent
6.35mm, Clip Fed, Blue, Hammer, *Curio*	$150	$275	$325

LJUTIC INDUSTRIES, INC.

Yakima, Wash. Shooters swear by their Ljutics, considered at the highest rank of trap shooting shotguns. The author remembers when these arms first came on the market; one of the early buyers and most vociferous endorsers of the Ljutic was Herb Glass, antique arms dealer and collector, who, with his wife Vi, shot trap for years. The only shortcomings for these guns were their ugly lines, compared to rivals like the Perazzi and Beretta. But performance on the trap field was what counted—and at that the Ljutic proved without peer.

SHOTGUN, DOUBLE BARREL, OVER-UNDER

	Fair	V. Good	Excellent
Bi-Gun Set, Various Calibers, Vent Rib, Skeet Grade, Checkered Stock, with 4 Sets of Barrels, *Modern*	4500	10000	12500
Bi-Gun, 12 Gauge, Vent Rib, Trap Grade, Checkered Stock, *Modern*	2900	6500	7500

SHOTGUN, SEMI-AUTOMATIC

	Fair	V. Good	Excellent
Bi Matic, 12 Gauge, Vent Rib, Trap Grade, Checkered Stock, *Modern*	800	1800	2000

SHOTGUN, SINGLESHOT

	Fair	V. Good	Excellent
Dyn-A-Trap, 12 Gauge, for Custom Stock Add $170.00-$300.00			
Dyn-A-Trap, 12 Gauge, Release Trigger, Add $150.00-$250.00			
Dyn-A-Trap, 12 Gauge, Trap Grade, Checkered Stock, Vent Rib, *Modern*	800	1800	2000
Mono-Gun, 12 Gauge, for Extra Barrel Add $565.00-$750.00			
Mono-Gun, 12 Gauge, Release Trigger Add $220.00-$300.00			
Mono-Gun, 12 Gauge, Trap Grade, Checkered Stock, Olympic Rib, *Modern*	1600	3500	4000
Mono-Gun, 12 Gauge, Trap Grade, Checkered Stock, Vent Rib, *Modern*	1400	3000	3500
X-73, 12 Gauge, Trap Grade, Checkered Stock, Vent Rib, *Modern*	900	2000	2500
X-73, 12 Gauge, for Extra Barrel Add $435.00-$600.00			
X-73, 12 Gauge, Release Trigger Add $220.00-$300.00			

LLAMA

Gabilondo y Cia., Elgoibar, Spain from 1930 to date. Imported by Stoeger Arms.

HANDGUN, REVOLVER

Chrome Plate, Add 20%–30%

	Fair	V. Good	Excellent
Commanche I, .22 L.R.R.F., Swing-Out Cylinder, Double Action, Blue, *Modern*	$100	$175	$200
Commanche II, .38 Special, Swing-Out Cylinder, Double Action, Blue, *Modern*	100	175	200
Commanche III, .357 Magnum, Swing-Out Cylinder, Double Action, Blue, *Modern*	100	200	225
Engraving, Add 25%–35%			
Gold Damascening, Add 300%-400%			
Martial, .38 Special, Swing-Out Cylinder, Double Action, Blue, *Modern*	75	150	175
Super Commanche IV, .44 Magnum, Swing-Out Cylinder, Double Action, Blue, *Modern*	100	250	275
Super Commanche V, .357 Magnum, Swing-Out Cylinder, Double Action, Blue, *Modern*	100	225	250

HANDGUN, SEMI-AUTOMATIC

	Fair	V. Good	Excellent
Chrome Plate, Add 20%-30%			
Engraving, Add 25%-35%			
Gold Damascening, Add 300%-400%			
Model I, .32 ACP. Clip Fed, Blue, *Modern*	100	175	200
Model II, .380 ACP. Clip Fed, Blue, *Modern*	100	200	225
Model III, .380 ACP. Clip Fed, Blue, *Modern*	100	175	200
Model IIIA, .380 ACP. Clip Fed, Grip Safety, Blue, *Modern*	100	200	225
Model IV, 9mm Bergmann, Clip Fed, Blue, *Modern*	100	175	200
Model V, .38 ACP. Clip Fed, Blue, *Modern*	100	175	200
Model VII, .38 ACP. Clip Fed, Blue, *Modern*	100	225	250
Model VIII, .38 ACP. Grip Safety, Blue, *Modern*	125	250	275
Model IX, .45 ACP. Clip Fed, Blue, *Modern*	125	275	300
Model IXA, .45 ACP. Clip Fed, Blue, *Modern*	125	275	300
Model X, .32 ACP. Clip Fed, Blue, *Modern*	100	175	200
Model XA, .32 ACP. Clip Fed, Grip Safety, Blue, *Modern*	100	200	225
Model XI, 9mm Luger, Clip Fed, Blue, *Modern*	125	275	300
Model XV, .22 L.R.R.F., Clip Fed, Grip Safety, Blue, *Modern*	125	225	250
Omni, 9mm Luger or .45 ACP, Clip Fed, Double Action, Blue, Military, *Antique*	150	350	375

LOBINGER, JOHANN

Vienna, Austria, c. 1780.

RIFLE, FLINTLOCK

	Fair	V. Good	Excellent
Yaeger, Smoothbore, Half-Octagon Barrel, Silver Furniture, Carved, *Antique*	$1400	$3500	$4000

LONG RANGE WONDER

Tradename used by Sears, Roebuck & Co.

SHOTGUN, SINGLESHOT

	Fair	V. Good	Excellent
12 Ga., Hammer, Break-Open, *Modern*	25	50	75

LONG TOM

Made by Stevens Arms.

SHOTGUN, SINGLESHOT

	Fair	V. Good	Excellent
Model 90, Various Gauges, Takedown, Automatic Ejector, Plain, Hammer, *Curio*	25	50	75
Model 95, 12 and 16 Gauges, Hammer, Automatic Ejector, *Curio*	25	50	75

LONGINES

Cooperative Orbea, Eibar, Spain, c. 1920.

HANDGUN, SEMI-AUTOMATIC

	Fair	V. Good	Excellent
7.65mm, Clip Fed, *Curio*	100	175	200

Longines

LOOKING GLASS

Domingo Acha and Acha Hermanos, Ermua, Spain, c. 1920.

HANDGUN, SEMI-AUTOMATIC

	Fair	V. Good	Excellent
6.35mm, Clip Fed, Hammer, *Curio*	75	125	150
6.35mm, Clip Fed, Hammerless, *Curio*	50	100	125
7.65mm, Clip Fed, Long Grip, Hammer, *Curio*	75	150	175
7.65mm, Clip Fed, Long Grip, Hammerless, *Curio*	75	125	150

LORD, J.

Orwigsburg, Pa. 1842–55. See Kentucky Rifles.

LOWELL ARMS CO.

Lowell, Mass. 1854–68.

HANDGUN, REVOLVER

	Fair	V. Good	Excellent
.22 Short R.F., 7 Shot, Spur Trigger, Tip-up, *Antique*	$150	$300	$350
.32 Long R.F., 6 Shot, Spur Trigger, Tip-up, Single Action			
.38 Long R.F., 6 Shot, Spur Trigger, Tip-up, Single Action, *Antique*	150	350	400

RIFLE, SINGLESHOT

	Fair	V. Good	Excellent
.38 Long R.F., *Antique*	150	350	375

LOWER, J. P.

Philadelphia, Pa., c. 1875.

HANDGUN, REVOLVER

	Fair	V. Good	Excellent
.22 Long R.F., 7 Shot, Single Action, Solid Frame, Spur Trigger, *Antique*	100	225	275
.32 Long R.F., 7 Shot, Single Action, Solid Frame, Spur Trigger, *Antique*	150	325	375

LUGER

Made by various companies for commercial and military use from 1900-45. Also see Mauser and German Military. The German Luger ranks among the world's great handguns, and was one of the first successful self-loading pistols. Its ingenious mechanism allows takedown simply by removal of the toggle on the left side of the receiver, above the trigger. These beautiful and functional arms have a substantial following of dedicated collectors. Although a careful study of these arms is important to the collector, to avoid being taken in by a fake or refinished example, the rewards of Luger collecting are many. These are one of the arms field's most consistent performers in terms of steady increase in value. Variations have been well established, several books on the subject are in print, and experts like Ralph Shattuck, Fred Datig, and the Simpsons (father and son) are keen to share their expertise with new and seasoned collectors alike. Note: The author is grateful to John R. Hansen, Jr., of Hansen & Co., Southport, Connecticut, for his assistance in establishing the values of the pistols listed in this section.

HANDGUN, SEMI-AUTOMATIC

	Fair	V. Good	Excellent
1900 Bulgarian, .30 Luger, *Curio*	3000	7000	8000
1900 Commercial, .30 Luger, *Curio*	900	2225	2500
1900 Eagle, .30 Luger, *Curio*	900	2000	2250
1900 Swiss Commercial, .30 Luger, *Curio*	900	2250	2500
1900 Swiss Military, .30 Luger, *Curio*	900	2250	2500
1900 Swiss Military, .30 Luger, Wide Trigger, *Curio*	900	2500	3000
1902 Commercial, 9mm Luger, *Curio*	$2200	$5500	$6500
1902 Eagle, 9mm Luger, *Curio*	2400	5000	5500
1902 Prototype, .30 Luger and 9mm Luger, *Curio*			Rare
1902 Test, .30 Luger and 9mm Luger, *Curio*	3000	6000	7000
1902, .30 Luger and mm Luger, Carbine, Blue, Curio Add 50% For Stock	2700	6500	9000
1902, 9mm Luger, Cartridge Counter, *Curio*	6000	12500	15000
1902-3 Presentation, .30 Luger, Carbine, *Curio*	3000	10000	12000
1903 Commercial, .30 Luger, *Curio*	3000	6500	8000
1904 Navy, 9mm Luger, *Curio*	4000	10000	12500
1906 Brazilian, .30 Luger, *Curio*	550	1200	1650
1906 Bulgarian, .30 Luger, *Curio*	1500	3750	4500
1906 Bulgarian, 9mm Luger, *Curio*	1400	3000	3500
1906 Commercial, .30 Luger, *Curio*	700	1500	1750

Luger 1906 Commercial

	Fair	V. Good	Excellent
1906 Commercial, 9mm Luger, *Curio*	800	1750	2100
1906 Dutch, 9mm Luger, *Curio*	700	1500	1950
1906 Eagle, .30 Luger, *Curio*	800	1500	2200
1906 Eagle, 9mm Luger, *Curio*	1100	2500	3000
1906 French, .30 Luger, *Curio*	1500	3000	3500
1906 Navy Commercial, 9mm Luger, *Curio*	1500	3000	4000
1906 Navy Military, 9mm Luger, *Curio*	1200	2500	3000

Luger 1906 Navy

	Fair	V. Good	Excellent
1906 Portuguese Army, .30 Luger, *Curio*	$600	$1250	$1500
1906 Portuguese Navy, .30 Luger, *Curio*	3000	6500	7000
1906 Portuguese Navy Crown, .30 Luger and 9mm Luger, *Curio*	3000	6500	7250
1906 Russian, 9mm Luger, *Curio*	3500	7500	9500
1906 Swiss Commercial, .30 Luger, *Curio*	900	2000	2350
1906 Swiss Military, .30 Luger, *Curio*	800	1900	2250
1906 Swiss Police, .30 Luger, *Curio*	900	2250	2500
1908 Bolivian, 9mm Luger, *Curio*	1500	3500	4000
1908 Bulgarian, 9mm Luger, *Curio*	900	2000	2500
1908 DWM Commercial, 9mm Luger, *Curio*	350	750	900
1908 Military, 9mm Luger, *Curio*	300	575	650
1908 Navy Commercial, .30 Luger, *Curio*	1500	3000	3500
1908 Navy Military, 9mm Luger, *Curio*	900	2250	2500
1913 Commercial, 9mm Luger, *Curio*	600	1400	1650
1914 Artillery, 9mm Luger, *Curio*	550	1250	1500
1914 Commercial, 9mm Luger, *Curio*	450	1000	1250
1914 Military, 9mm Luger, *Curio*	350	750	850
1914 Navy, 9mm Luger, *Curio*	1100	2450	2600
1918 Spandau, 9mm Luger, *Curio*			Rare
1920 Abercrombie & Fitch, .30 Luger and 9mm Luger, *Curio*	1900	4000	4500
1920 Artillery, 9mm Luger, *Curio*	450	1000	1300
1920 Commercial, .30 Luger and 9mm Luger, *Curio*	250	550	600
1920 Navy, 9mm Luger, *Curio*	700	1800	2000
1920 Simson, 9mm Luger, *Curio*	325	700	800
1920 Swiss Commercial, .30 Luger and 9mm Luger, *Curio*	550	1250	1500
1920 Swiss Rework, .30 Luger and 9mm Luger, *Curio*	550	1200	1550
1920-21, .30 Luger and 9mm Luger, *Curio*	250	500	650
1921 Krieghoff, .30 Luger, *Curio*	1100	2500	2800
1923 Commercial "Safe-Loaded," .30 Luger and 9mm Luger, *Curio*	450	1000	1250
1923 Commercial Krieghoff, 9mm Luger, *Curio*	550	1250	1500
1923 Commercial, .30 Luger and 9mm Luger, *Curio*	300	650	750
1923 Dutch, 9mm Luger, *Curio*	550	1200	1450
1923 Finnish Army, 9mm Luger, *Curio*	250	550	600
1923 Simson Commercial, 9mm Luger, *Curio*	800	1800	2000
1923 Simson Military, 9mm Luger, *Curio*	900	2000	2250
1923 Stoeger, .30 Luger and 9mm Luger, *Curio*	900	2250	2750

	Fair	V. Good	Excellent
1924 Bern, .30 Luger, *Curio*	$600	$1500	$2500
1924-7 Simson, 9mm Luger, Dated Chamber, *Curio*	1100	2500	3000
1929 Bern, .30 Luger and 9mm Luger, *Curio*	700	1750	2000
1930-33 Death Head, 9mm Luger, *Curio*	550	1250	1500
1933 K.I., 9mm Luger, *Curio*	400	850	1000
1933-35 Dutch, 9mm Luger, Royal Dutch Air Force, *Curio*	600	1450	1650
1933-35 Mauser Commercial, 9mm Luger, *Curio*	550	1250	1500
1934 P Commercial Krieghoff, .30 Luger and 9mm Luger, *Curio*	1100	2250	2500
1934 P Commercial, Krieghoff, 9mm Luger, *Curio*	900	2000	2250
1934 Sideframe, Krieghoff, 6" Barrel, 9mm Luger, *Curio*	1100	2500	3000
1935 Portuguese, "GNR,".30 Luger, *Curio*	800	1750	2000
1936 Persian, 9mm Luger, *Curio*	1400	3000	3500
1936-37, 9mm Luger, Krieghoff, *Curio*	800	1750	2250
1936-39, .30 Luger and 9mm Luger, 4" Barrel, *Curio*	350	750	900
1936-40 Dutch Banner, 9mm Luger, *Curio*	800	1500	1750
1936-9 S/42, 9mm Luger, *Curio*	325	750	875
1937-39 Banner Commercial, .30 Luger, 4" Barrel, *Curio*	700	1500	1750
1938, 9mm Luger, *Curio*	1200	2500	2650
1939-40 42, 9mm Luger, *Curio*	300	625	750
1940 42/44 byf, 9mm Luger, *Curio*	300	600	750
1940 Mauser Banner, .30 Luger and 9mm Luger, *Curio*	550	1250	1500
1940, 9mm Luger, Krieghoff, *Curio*	1000	2250	2500

Luger 1940-42 with Snail Drum

	Fair	V. Good	Excellent
1941-42 byf, 9mm Luger, *Curio*	350	750	900
1941-44, 9mm Luger, Krieghoff, *Curio*	1000	2250	2750
1945, 9mm Luger, Krieghoff, *Curio*	2500	5000	7500

Luger 1941-42 byf

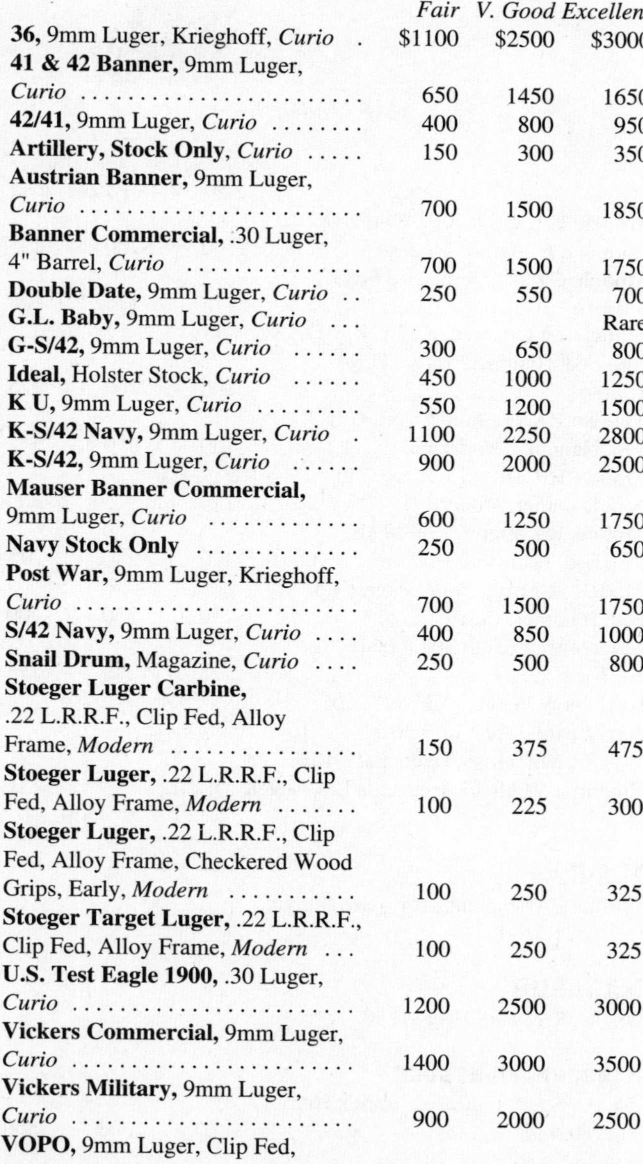

	Fair	V. Good	Excellent
36, 9mm Luger, Krieghoff, *Curio*	$1100	$2500	$3000
41 & 42 Banner, 9mm Luger, *Curio*	650	1450	1650
42/41, 9mm Luger, *Curio*	400	800	950
Artillery, Stock Only, *Curio*	150	300	350
Austrian Banner, 9mm Luger, *Curio*	700	1500	1850
Banner Commercial, .30 Luger, 4" Barrel, *Curio*	700	1500	1750
Double Date, 9mm Luger, *Curio*	250	550	700
G.L. Baby, 9mm Luger, *Curio*			Rare
G-S/42, 9mm Luger, *Curio*	300	650	800
Ideal, Holster Stock, *Curio*	450	1000	1250
K U, 9mm Luger, *Curio*	550	1200	1500
K-S/42 Navy, 9mm Luger, *Curio*	1100	2250	2800
K-S/42, 9mm Luger, *Curio*	900	2000	2500
Mauser Banner Commercial, 9mm Luger, *Curio*	600	1250	1750
Navy Stock Only	250	500	650
Post War, 9mm Luger, Krieghoff, *Curio*	700	1500	1750
S/42 Navy, 9mm Luger, *Curio*	400	850	1000
Snail Drum, Magazine, *Curio*	250	500	800
Stoeger Luger Carbine, .22 L.R.R.F., Clip Fed, Alloy Frame, *Modern*	150	375	475
Stoeger Luger, .22 L.R.R.F., Clip Fed, Alloy Frame, *Modern*	100	225	300
Stoeger Luger, .22 L.R.R.F., Clip Fed, Alloy Frame, Checkered Wood Grips, Early, *Modern*	100	250	325
Stoeger Target Luger, .22 L.R.R.F., Clip Fed, Alloy Frame, *Modern*	100	250	325
U.S. Test Eagle 1900, .30 Luger, *Curio*	1200	2500	3000
Vickers Commercial, 9mm Luger, *Curio*	1400	3000	3500
Vickers Military, 9mm Luger, *Curio*	900	2000	2500
VOPO, 9mm Luger, Clip Fed, *Modern*	600	1250	1450

Luger VOPO

LUR-PANZER

Echave y Arizmendi, Eibar, Spain.

HANDGUN, SEMI-AUTOMATIC

	Fair	V. Good	Excellent
Luger Type, .22 L.R.R.F., Toggle Action, Clip Fed, *Modern*	$75	$125	$150

LYMAN GUN SIGHT CORP.

Middlefield, Conn.

HANDGUN, PERCUSSION

	Fair	V. Good	Excellent
.36 1851 Navy, Color Case Hardened Frame, Engraved Cylinder, Reproduction	50	100	125
.36 New Model Navy, Brass Trigger Guard, Solid Frame, Reproduction	25	75	100
.44 1860 Army, Color Case Hardened Frame, Engraved Cylinder, Reproduction	50	100	125
.44 New Model Army, Brass Trigger Guard, Solid Frame, Reproduction	50	100	125

RIFLE, FLINTLOCK

	Fair	V. Good	Excellent
Plains Rifle, Various Calibers, Brass Furniture, Set Trigger, Reproduction	100	200	225

RIFLE, PERCUSSION

	Fair	V. Good	Excellent
Plains Rifle, Various Calibers, Brass Furniture, Set Trigger, Reproduction	75	150	175
Trade Rifle, Various Calibers, Brass Furniture, Set Trigger, Reproduction	50	125	150

RIFLE, SINGLESHOT

	Fair	V. Good	Excellent
Centennial, 45/70 Government, Ruger #1, Commemorative, Cased with Accessories, *Modern*	600	1200	1450

M

MAADI

RIFLE, SEMI-AUTOMATIC

	Fair	V. Good	Excellent
Paratrooper AKM, 7.62 × 39mm, Clip Fed, Assault Rifle, *Modern*	$350	$750	$1050
Standard AKM, 7.62 × 39mm, Clip Fed, Assault Rifle, *Modern*	350	750	950

MAB

Mre. d'Armes Automatiques Bayonne, Bayonne, France since 1921.

HANDGUN, SEMI-AUTOMATIC

	Fair	V. Good	Excellent
Modele A, 6.35mm, Clip Fed, *Modern*	75	150	175

MAB Modele A

	Fair	V. Good	Excellent
Modele B, 6.35mm, Clip Fed, *Modern*	100	225	250
Modele C, .380 ACP, Clip Fed, *Modern*	100	225	250
Modele C, 7.65mm, Clip Fed, *Modern*	100	200	225
Modele C/D, .380 ACP, Clip Fed, *Modern*	75	175	200
Modele C/D, 7.65mm, Clip Fed, *Modern*	75	150	175
Modele D, .380 ACP, Clip Fed, *Modern*	75	175	200
Modele D, 7.65mm, Clip Fed, *Modern*	75	150	175
Modele D, 7.65mm, Clip Fed, French Military, *Curio*	100	225	250
Modele E, 6.35mm, Clip Fed, Long Grip, *Modern*	100	200	225
Modele F, .22 L.R.R.F., Clip Fed, Hammer, 3" Barrel, *Modern*	75	175	200

MAB Modele E

	Fair	V. Good	Excellent
Modele F, .22 L.R.R.F., Clip Fed, Hammer, 5" Barrel, *Modern*	$100	$200	$225
Modele GZ, 7.65mm, Clip Fed, *Modern*	75	175	200
Modele Le Chasseur, .22 L.R.R.F., Clip Fed, Hammer, Target Grips, *Modern*	100	200	225
Modele PA-15, 9mm Luger, Clip Fed, Hammer, *Modern*	150	350	375
Modele R Court, 7.65mm, Clip Fed, Hammer, *Modern*	125	275	300
Modele R Longue, 7.65 MAS, Clip Fed, Hammer, *Modern*	125	250	275
Modele R Para, 9mm Luger, Clip Fed, Hammer, *Curio*	150	350	400
Modele R, 7.65mm, Clip Fed, *Modern*	125	250	275

Nazi Navy Proofs, Add 40%-50%
Nazi Proofs, Add 20%-30%
W.A.C. Markings, Deduct 5%-10%
(Importer Winfield Arms Co., Los Angeles, Calif.)

M.A.C.

(Military Armament Corp.) See Ingram.

MACLEOD

Doune, Scotland, 1711–1750.

HANDGUN, FLINTLOCK

	Fair	V. Good	Excellent
.54, All Steel, Engraved, Ram's Horn Butt, *Antique*	1400	3000	3500

MAGNUM RESEARCH INC.

Minneapolis, Minn. Also see Israeli Military.

	Fair	V. Good	Excellent
HANDGUN, SEMI-AUTOMATIC			
Desert Eagle, .357 Magnum, Clip Fed, Interchangeable Barrels, Gas Operated, Blue, *Modern*	$250	$500	$550

MAICHE, A.

France.

HANDGUN, FLINTLOCK			
.56, Brass Mountings, Holster Pistol, *Antique*	225	400	575

MALTBY-CURTIS

Agent for Norwich Pistol Co. 1875–1881.

HANDGUN, REVOLVER			
.22 Short R.F., 7 Shot, Spur Trigger, Solid Frame, Single Action, *Antique*	75	150	175
.32 Short R.F., 5 Shot, Spur Trigger, Solid Frame, Single Action, *Antique*	75	150	175

MALTY-HENLEY & CO.

New York City, 1878–1899. Made by Columbia Armory, Tenn.

HANDGUN, REVOLVER			
Spencer Safety Hammerless, .32 S & W, 5 Shot, Top Break, Hammerless, Double Action, *Curio*	100	200	275

MAMBA

Made by Relay Products in Johannesburg, South Africa, and Navy Arms in the U.S.

HANDGUN, SEMI-AUTOMATIC			
Navy Mamba, 9mm Luger, Stainless, Double Action, *Modern*	150	300	325
Relay Mamba, 9mm Luger, Stainless, Double Action, *Modern*	200	425	475
Rhodesian Mamba, 9mm Luger, Stainless, Double Action, *Modern*	700	1500	2000

MANHATTAN FIREARMS MFG. CO.

New York City & Newark, N.J. 1849–1864. Their closeness in appearance and quality to Colt Model 1849 Pocket and Model 1851 Navy and to early Smith & Wesson .22 rimfire revolvers have contributed to the demand for Manhattan firearms.

HANDGUN, PERCUSSION			
Bar Hammer, Double Action, Screw Barrel, Singleshot, *Antique*	150	300	350
Hero, Singleshot, Derringer, *Antique*	125	250	300
Pepperbox, .28, 3 Shot, Double Action, *Antique*	300	650	750

Manhattan Bar Hammer, .31 Caliber

	Fair	V. Good	Excellent
Pepperbox, .28, 6 Shot, Double Action, *Antique*	$250	$550	$650
Revolver, .31, Pocket Model, Single Action, *Antique*	200	400	475
Revolver, .36, Navy Model, Single Action, *Antique*	350	700	850
Revolver, Pocket, .22 Cal. Cartridge, *Antique*	175	375	425

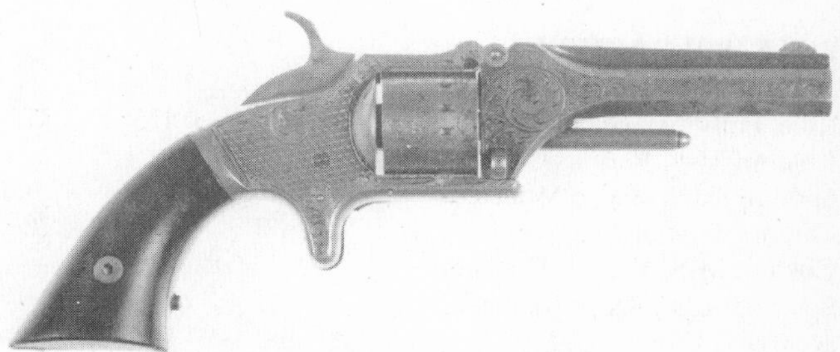

Manhattan Second Model, .22 Caliber

MANHURIN

Mre. de Machines du Haut-Rhin, Mulhouse-Bourtzwiller, France. Also see Walther.

HANDGUN, REVOLVER			
Model 73 Police, .357 Magnum, Double Action, Swing-Out Cylinder, *Modern*	400	900	1200
Model 73 Sport, .357 Magnum, Double Action, Swing-Out Cylinder, *Modern*	500	1000	1300

MANN

Fritz Mann Werkzeugfabrik, Suhl, Germany, 1919–1924.

HANDGUN, SEMI-AUTOMATIC			
.25 ACP, Clip Fed, *Curio*	150	300	325
Pocket, .32 ACP, Clip Fed, *Curio*	150	300	350
Pocket, .380 ACP, Clip Fed, *Curio*	150	325	375

MANN, MICHEL

Uhlenberg, Germany, c. 1630.

Mann Pocket

HANDGUN, WHEEL LOCK

	Fair	V. Good	Excellent
Miniature, All Metal, Gold Damascened, Ball Pommel, *Antique*	$1600	$3500	$4000

MANNLICHER-SCHOENAUER

Steyr-Daimler-Puch, Steyr, Austria.

RIFLE, BOLT ACTION

	Fair	V. Good	Excellent
Alpine, Various Calibers, Sporting Rifle, Full-Stocked, *Modern*	200	425	475
Custom M-S, Various Calibers, Sporting Rifle, Scope Mounted, Carbine, *Modern*	300	650	700
Custom M-S, Various Calibers, Sporting Rifle, Scope Mounted, *Modern*	300	675	725
High Velocity, Various Calibers, Sporting Rifle, Set Trigger, *Modern*	350	750	825
High Velocity, Various Calibers, Sporting Rifle, Takedown, Set Trigger, *Modern*	350	775	875
M-72 LM, Various Calibers, Sporting Rifle, Full-Stocked, *Modern*	350	750	800
M-72 S, Various Calibers, Sporting Rifle, *Modern*	350	775	850
M-72 T, Various Calibers, Sporting Rifle, *Modern*	400	800	875
Magnum M-S, Various Calibers, Sporting Rifle, Monte Carlo Stock, Set Trigger, *Modern*	400	825	875
MCA, Various Calibers, Sporting Rifle, Carbine, Monte Carlo Stock, *Modern*	425	875	950
MCA, Various Calibers, Sporting Rifle, Monte Carlo Stock, *Modern*	425	850	950
Model 1903, Various Calibers, Sporting Rifle, Carbine, Set Trigger, Full-Stocked, *Modern*	450	900	950
Model 1905, 9 × 56 M.S., Sporting Rifle, Carbine, Set Trigger, Full-Stocked, *Modern*	450	900	1200
Model 1908, Various Calibers, Sporting Rifle, Carbine, Set Trigger, Full-Stocked, *Modern*	450	925	975
Model 1910, 9.5 × 57 M.S., Sporting Rifle, Carbine, Set Trigger, Full-Stocked, *Modern*	$450	$950	$1025
Model 1924, .30-06 Springfield, Sporting Rifle, Carbine, Set Trigger, Full-Stocked, *Modern*	500	1000	1175
Model 1950, 6.5 × 54 M.S., Sporting Rifle, Carbine, Set Trigger, Full-Stocked, *Modern*	400	850	975
Model 1950, Various Calibers, Sporting Rifle, Carbine, Set Trigger, Full-Stocked, *Modern*	400	850	950
Model 1950, Various Calibers, Sporting Rifle, Set Trigger, *Modern*	350	750	825
Model 1952, 6.5 × 54 M.S., Sporting Rifle, Carbine, Set Trigger, Full-Stocked, *Modern*	400	900	1050
Model 1952, Various Calibers, Sporting Rifle, Carbine, Set Trigger, Full-Stocked, *Modern*	400	800	1000
Model 1952, Various Calibers, Sporting Rifle, Set Trigger, *Modern*	300	650	800
Model 1956, Various Calibers, Sporting Rifle, Carbine, Set Trigger, Full-Stocked, *Modern*	350	750	800
Model 1956, Various Calibers, Sporting Rifle, Set Trigger, *Modern*	350	725	800
Model L Varmint, Various Calibers, Checkered Stock, Set Trigger, *Modern*	225	475	525
Model M Professional, Various Calibers, Checkered Stock, Set Trigger, *Modern*	175	375	425
Model M, Various Calibers, Checkered Stock, Set Trigger, *Modern*	250	550	600
Model ML 79, Various Calibers, Checkered Stock, Set Trigger, *Modern*	350	700	750
Model S, Various Calibers, Checkered Stock, Set Trigger, *Modern*	300	625	675
Model S/T Magnum, Various Calibers, Checkered Stock, Set Trigger, *Modern*	300	650	675
Model SSG Match, .308 Win., Synthetic Target Stock, Set Triggers, Walther Peep Sights, *Modern*	250	575	650
Model SSG, .308 Win., Synthetic Target Stock, Set Triggers, *Modern*	200	450	500
Premier, Various Calibers, Sporting Rifle, Fancy Checkering, Engraved, *Modern*	250	575	650
Premier, Various Calibers, Sporting Rifle, Magnum Action, Fancy Checkering, Engraved, *Modern*	600	1250	1400

RIFLE, DOUBLE BARREL, SIDE-BY-SIDE

	Fair	V. Good	Excellent
Mustang, Various Calibers, Standard, Checkered Stock, Sidelock, *Modern*	2600	5000	6000

	Fair	V. Good	Excellent
Mustang, Various Calibers, Standard, Checkered Stock, Sidelock, Engraved, *Modern*	$2700	$5500	$6500

RIFLE, DOUBLE BARREL, OVER-UNDER

	Fair	V. Good	Excellent
Safari 72, .375 H & M Mag., Checkered Stock, Engraved, Double Trigger, *Modern*	1400	3000	3500
Safari 77, Various Calibers, Checkered Stock, Engraved, Double Trigger, Automatic Ejector, *Modern*	1900	4000	4500

SHOTGUN, DOUBLE BARREL, OVER-UNDER

	Fair	V. Good	Excellent
Edinbourgh, 12 Ga., Checkered Stock, Vent Rib, *Modern*	600	1250	1500

SHOTGUN, DOUBLE BARREL, SIDE-BY-SIDE

	Fair	V. Good	Excellent
Ambassador English, 12 and 20 Gauges, Checkered Stock, Sidelock, Automatic Ejectors, Engraved, *Modern*	3200	7000	7500
Ambassador Executive, 12 and 20 Gauges, Checkered Stock, Sidelock, Automatic Ejectors, Fancy Engraving, *Modern*	5500	12000	15000
Ambassador Extra, 12 and 20 Gauges, Checkered Stock, Sidelock, Automatic Ejectors, Engraved, *Modern*	3100	6500	7250
Ambassador Golden Black, 12 and 20 Gauges, Checkered Stock, Sidelock, Automatic Ejectors, Engraved, Gold Inlays, *Modern*	4100	8500	9500
London, 12 and 20 Gauges, Checkered Stock, Sidelock, Automatic Ejectors, Engraved, Cased, *Modern*	1100	2250	2500
Oxford Field, 12 and 20 Gauges, Checkered Stock, Automatic Ejectors, Engraved, *Modern*	450	1000	1300

MANTON J. & CO.

Belgium, c. 1900.

SHOTGUN, DOUBLE BARREL, SIDE-BY-SIDE

	Fair	V. Good	Excellent
Various Gauges, Hammerless, Damascus Barrel, *Modern*	75	150	300
Various Gauges, Hammerless, Steel Barrel, *Modern*	75	150	300
Various Gauges, Outside Hammers, Damascus Barrel, *Modern*	75	150	300
Various Gauges, Outside Hammers, Steel Barrel, *Modern*	75	150	300

SHOTGUN, SINGLESHOT

	Fair	V. Good	Excellent
Various Gauges, Hammer, Steel Barrel, *Modern*	25	50	75

MANTON, JOSEPH

London, England 1795–1835. One of the giants in the history of gunmaking, Joe Manton's reputation was such that he was considered a legend in his own lifetime. An exhaustively detailed and superbly illustrated Manton book, by David Back and Keith Neal, has been instrumental in the strength of the market of these guns. Among Joe Manton's distinctions were his development of the elevated barrel rib, the gravitating stop (prevented accidental firing during loading) and an improved patent breech.

HANDGUN, FLINTLOCK

	Fair	V. Good	Excellent
Pair, Octagon Barrel, Dueling Pistols, Gold Inlays, Light Engraving, Cased with Accessories, *Antique*	$3000	$6500	$7500

HANDGUN, PERCUSSION

	Fair	V. Good	Excellent
.55, Pair, Dueling Pistols, Octagon Barrel, Light Ornamentation, Cased with Accessories, *Antique*	1900	4000	5000

SHOTGUN, PERCUSSION

	Fair	V. Good	Excellent
12 Ga. Double Barrel, Side by Side, Damascus Barrels, Light Engraving, Gold Inlays, *Antique*	350	1000	1200

MANUFRANCE

Manufacture Francaise de Armes et Cycles de St. Etienne, St. Etienne, France. Also see Le Francaise. 1902-Date.

HANDGUN, SEMI-AUTOMATIC

	Fair	V. Good	Excellent
Model 1911 Astra-Manufacture, .32 ACP, Clip Fed, Blue, *Curio*	75	125	175

RIFLE, BOLT ACTION

	Fair	V. Good	Excellent
Buffalo Match, .22 L.R.R.F., Target Rifle, *Modern*	75	150	175
Club, .22 L.R.R.F., Singleshot, Carbine, *Modern*	50	75	100
Club, .22 L.R.R.F., Singleshot, Carbine, Checkered Stock, *Modern*	50	100	125
Mauser K98 Sporter, .270 Win., Sporterized, Checkered Stock, *Modern*	50	125	150
Mauser K98 Sporter, .270 Win., Sporterized, Plain, *Modern*	50	100	150
Rival, 375 H & H Mag., Checkered Stock, *Modern*	100	250	300

RIFLE, SEMI-AUTOMATIC

	Fair	V. Good	Excellent
Reina, .22 L.R.R.F., Carbine, Clip Fed, *Modern*	45	125	150
Sniper, .22 W.M.R., Carbine, Clip Fed, *Modern*	75	150	200

SHOTGUN, DOUBLE BARREL, OVER-UNDER

	Fair	V. Good	Excellent
Falcor Field, 12 Ga., Vent Rib, Automatic Ejector, Single Selective Trigger, Checkered Stock, *Modern*	250	575	650
Falcor Sport, 12 Ga., Vent Rib, Automatic Ejector, Single Selective Trigger, Checkered Stock, Extra Barrels, *Modern*	350	725	775

	Fair	V. Good	Excellent
Falcor Trap, 12 Ga., Vent Rib, Automatic Ejector, Single Selective Trigger, Checkered Stock, *Modern*	$300	$625	$675

SHOTGUN, DOUBLE BARREL, SIDE-BY-SIDE

	Fair	V. Good	Excellent
Ideal DeLuxe, 12 Ga. 3", Fancy Engraving, Checkered Stock, Double Triggers, *Modern*	800	1750	1950
Ideal Prestige, 12 Ga. 3", Fancy Engraving, Checkered Stock, Double Triggers, *Modern*	1100	2500	2750
Robust, 12 Ga. 3", Checkered Stock, Double Triggers, *Modern*	150	350	375
Robust Luxe, 12 Ga. 3", Engraved, Automatic Ejectors, Checkered Stock, Double Triggers, *Modern*	275	600	650

SHOTGUN, SEMI-AUTOMATIC

	Fair	V. Good	Excellent
Perfex Special, *Modern*	150	325	375
Perfex, 12 Ga., Checkered Stock, *Modern*	150	300	350

SHOTGUN, SINGLESHOT

	Fair	V. Good	Excellent
Simplex, 12 Gauge, Sling Swivels, *Modern*	75	125	150

SHOTGUN, SLIDE ACTION

	Fair	V. Good	Excellent
Rapid, 12 or 16 Gauges, Plain, *Modern*	75	150	175

MARK X

Made in Zestavia, Yugoslovia. Imported by Interarms.

RIFLE, BOLT ACTION

	Fair	V. Good	Excellent
Alaskan, Various Calibers, Magnum, Open Rear Sights, Checkered Stock, Sling Swivels, *Modern*	125	250	300
Cavalier, Various Calibers, Cheekpiece, Checkered Stock, Open Rear Sight, Sling Swivels, *Modern*	125	225	275
Mannlicher, Various Calibers, Carbine, Full-Stocked, Checkered Stock, Open Rear Sight, Sling Swivels, *Modern*	125	250	300
Marquis, Various Calibers, Carbine, Mauser Action, *Modern*	200	425	475
Standard, Various Calibers, Checkered Stock, Open Rear Sight, Sling Swivels, *Modern*	100	225	250
Viscount, Various Calibers, Plain, Open Rear Sight, Checkered Stock, Sling Swivels, *Modern*	75	175	200

MARKWELL ARMS CO.

Chicago, Ill.

HANDGUN, PERCUSSION

	Fair	V. Good	Excellent
.41 Derringer, Singleshot, Brass Furniture, Reproduction	$12	$25	$50
.44 C S A 1860, Revolver, 6 Shot, Brass Frame, Reproduction	25	50	75
.44 New Army, Revolver, 6 Shot, Brass Trigger Guard, Reproduction	25	50	75
.45 Colonial, Singleshot, Brass Furniture, Reproduction	15	25	50
.45 Kentucky, Singleshot, Brass Furniture, Reproduction	15	25	50
.45 Loyalist, Singleshot, Brass Furniture, Set Trigger, Adjustable Sights, Reproduction	25	50	75

RIFLE, PERCUSSION

	Fair	V. Good	Excellent
.45 Hawken, Brass Furniture, Reproduction	50	75	100
.45 Kentucky, Brass Furniture, Reproduction	25	50	75
.45 Super Kentucky, Brass Furniture, Set Trigger, Reproduction	75	100	125

MARLIN FIREARMS CO.

New Haven, Conn. J. M. Marlin, from 1870–1881. Marlin Firearms from 1881–1915. Marlin-Rockwell Corp. 1915–1926. From 1926 to date as Marlin Firearms Co., North Haven, Ct. Also see Ballard. Also see the Commemorative Section. John Mahlon Marlin was a former employee of Colt's Pt. F.A. Mfg. Co., who began his career as a gun manufacturer in 1863, with a singleshot derringer pistol. By the early 1880s his fledgling company was manufacturing lever-action rifles rivaling those of Winchester (both firms were neighbors, in New Haven, Connecticut). Marlin also built Ballard singleshot rifles and single- and double-action revolvers. First in his line of lever-action repeating rifles was the Model of 1881. Unlike O.F. Winchester, who was primarily an investor and businessman, John Marlin was an inventor and designer, and was issued several patents. The company's New Haven factory, an impressive brick building which still stands on Willow Street, was erected at the turn of the century. In 1901, on the death of John M. Marlin, the business assumed a new direction under his sons Mahlon H. and J. Howard. The sons sold the business in 1915, and Marlin became part of the Marlin-Rockwell Corporation. By the early 1920s the company, which had gone through various changes, was heavily in debt. Known by 1921 as the Marlin Firearms Corporation, the firm was sold in 1924 to Frank Kenna, Sr. The Marlin Firearms Company has remained under the sole ownership of the Kenna family ever since.

HANDGUN, REVOLVER

	Fair	V. Good	Excellent
Model 1887, .32 and.38, Double Action, Top Break, *Antique*	150	300	400
Standard 1875, .30 R.F., Tip Up, Spur Trigger, *Antique*	100	225	250
XX Standard 1873, .22 R.F., Tip Up, Spur Trigger, *Antique*	200	425	300
XX Standard 1873, .22 R.F., Tip Up, Spur Trigger, Octagon Barrel, *Antique*	150	375	300

	Fair	V. Good	Excellent
XXX Standard 1872, .30 R.F., Tip Up, Spur Trigger, *Antique*	$175	$375	$300
XXX Standard 1872, .30 R.F., Tip Up, Spur Trigger, Octagon Barrel, *Antique*	175	350	300

RIFLE, BOLT ACTION

	Fair	V. Good	Excellent
Glenfield M10, .22 L.R.R.F., Singleshot, *Modern*	15	25	50
Glenfield M20, .22 L.R.R.F., Clip Fed, *Modern*	25	50	75
Model 100, .22 L.R.R.F., Singleshot, Open Rear Sight, Takedown, *Modern*	15	25	50
Model 100-S, .22 L.R.R.F., Singleshot, Peep Sights, Takedown, *Modern*	50	75	100
Model 100-SB, .22 L.R.R.F., Singleshot, Smoothbore, Takedown, *Modern*	15	25	50
Model 101, .22 L.R.R.F., Singleshot, Open Rear Sight, Takedown, Beavertail Forend, *Modern*	25	50	75
Model 101-DL, .22 L.R.R.F., Singleshot, Takedown, Peep Sights, Beavertail Forend, *Modern*	25	50	75
Model 122, .22 L.R.R.F., Singleshot, Open Rear Sight, Monte Carlo Stock, *Modern*	25	50	75
Model 322 (Sako), .222 Rem., Clip Fed, Peep Sights, Checkered Stock, *Modern*	125	275	325
Model 455 (FN), Various Calibers, Peep Sights, Monte Carlo Stock, Checkered Stock, *Modern*	150	300	325
Model 65, .22 L.R.R.F., Singleshot, Open Rear Sight, *Modern*	25	50	75
Model 65E, .22 L.R.R.F., Singleshot, Peep Sights, *Modern*	25	50	75
Model 780, .22 L.R.R.F., Clip Fed, Open Rear Sight, *Modern*	50	75	100
Model 781, .22 L.R.R.F., Tube Feed, Open Rear Sight, *Modern*	50	75	100
Model 782, .22 WMR., Clip Fed, Open Rear Sight, *Modern*	50	75	100
Model 783, .22 WMR, Tube Feed, Open Rear Sight, *Modern*	50	100	125

Marlin 783 with 200 Scope

	Fair	V. Good	Excellent
Model 80, .22 L.R.R.F., Clip Fed, Open Rear Sight, Takedown, *Modern*	25	50	75
Model 80 DL, .22 L.R.R.F., Clip Fed, Beavertail Forend, Takedown, Peep Sights, *Modern*	$25	$50	$75
Model 80C, .22 L.R.R.F., Clip Fed, Beavertail Forend, Takedown, Open Rear Sight, *Modern*	25	50	75
Model 80E, .22 L.R.R.F., Clip Fed, Peep Sights, Takedown, *Modern*	25	50	75
Model 81, .22 L.R.R.F., Tube Feed, Takedown, Open Rear Sight, *Modern*	25	50	75
Model 81C, .22 L.R.R.F., Tube Feed, Takedown, Open Rear Sight, Beavertail Forend, *Modern*	25	50	75
Model 81DL, .22 L.R.R.F., Tube Feed, Takedown, Peep Sights, Beavertail Forend, *Modern*	25	50	75
Model 81E, .22 L.R.R.F., Tube Feed, Takedown, Peep Sights, *Modern*	25	50	75
Model 81G, .22 L.R.R.F., Tube Feed, Takedown, Open Rear Sight, Beavertail Forend, *Modern*	25	50	75
Model 980, .22 WMR, Clip Fed, Monte Carlo Stock, Open Rear Sight, *Modern*	50	75	100

RIFLE, LEVER ACTION

	Fair	V. Good	Excellent
Centennial Set 336-39 (1970), Fancy Checkering, Fancy Wood, Engraved, Brass Furniture, *Curio*	450	1000	1250

Marlin Cased Centennial Pair

	Fair	V. Good	Excellent
Glenfield M 30 A, .30-30 Win., Tube Feed, *Modern*	75	125	175
M1894 (Late), .357 Magnum, Tube Feed, Open Rear Sight, *Modern*	100	200	250
M1894 (Late), .41 Magnum, Tube Feed, Open Rear Sight, *Modern*	100	200	250
M1894 (Late), .44 Magnum, Tube Feed, Open Rear Sight, *Modern*	100	225	275
M1895 (Late), .45-70 Government, Tube Feed, Open Rear Sight, *Modern*	125	250	300
Model 1881 Standard, Various Calibers, Tube Feed, Open Rear Sight, *Antique*	500	1000	1250

	Fair	V. Good	Excellent
Model 1888, Various Calibers, Tube Feed, Open Rear Sight, *Antique*	$900	$2500	$3000
Model 1889 Standard, Various Calibers, Tube Feed, Open Rear Sight, *Antique*	300	650	800
Model 1891, .22 L.R.R.F., Tube Feed, Open Rear Sight, *Antique*	800	2000	2500
Model 1892 Over #177382, Various Calibers, Tube Feed, *Modern*	250	800	1000
Model 1892, Various Calibers, Tube Feed, Open Rear Sight, *Antique*	300	800	1000
Model 1893 over #177304, Various Calibers, Tube Feed, Solid Frame, Octagon Barrel, *Modern*	300	800	1000
Model 1893 over #177304, Various Calibers, Tube Feed, Solid Frame, Round Barrel, *Modern*	300	700	900
Model 1893 over #177304, Various Calibers, Tube Feed, Solid Frame, Round Barrel, Carbine, *Modern*	300	800	1000
Model 1893 over #177304, Various Calibers, Tube Feed, Takedown, Octagon Barrel, *Modern*	300	800	1200
Model 1893 over #177304, Various Calibers, Tube Feed, Takedown, Round Barrel, *Modern*	275	700	1000
Model 1893 over #177304, Various Calibers, Tube Feed, Sporting Carbine, 5 Shot, *Modern*	325	650	1000
Model 1893 over #177304, Various Calibers, Tube Feed, Sporting Carbine, Takedown, 5 Shot, *Modern*	400	800	1200
Model 1893 over #177304, Various Calibers, Tube Feed, Full-Stocked, with Bayonet, *Modern*	1500	4500	7000
Model 1893, Various Calibers, Tube Feed, Musket, with Bayonet, *Antique*	2000	5000	7000
Model 1893, Various Calibers, Tube Feed, Solid Frame, Octagon Barrel, *Antique*	500	1200	1500
Model 1893, Various Calibers, Tube Feed, Solid Frame, Round Barrel, *Antique*	400	1000	1200
Model 1893, Various Calibers, Tube Feed, Solid Frame, Round Barrel, Carbine, *Antique*	400	1000	1200
Model 1893, Various Calibers, Tube Feed, Sporting Carbine, 5 Shot, *Antique*	400	1000	1200
Model 1893, Various Calibers, Tube Feed, Sporting Light Weight Rifle Takedown, 5 Shot, *Antique*	550	1200	1500
Model 1893, Various Calibers, Tube Feed, Takedown, Octagon Barrel, *Antique*	700	1500	1750
Model 1893, Various Calibers, Tube Feed, Takedown, Round Barrel, *Antique*	600	1300	1500
Model 1894 over #175431, Various Calibers, Tube Feed, Takedown, Octagon Barrel, *Modern*	$500	$1000	$1200
Model 1894 over #175431, Various Calibers, Tube Feed, Takedown, Round Barrel, *Modern*	400	800	1000
Model 1894 over #175431, Various Calibers, Tube Feed, Solid Frame, Octagon Barrel, *Modern*	500	1000	1200
Model 1894 over #175431, Various Calibers, Tube Feed, Solid Frame, Round Barrel, *Modern*	400	800	1000
Model 1894, Various Calibers, Tube Feed, Solid Frame, Octagon Barrel, *Antique*	600	1200	1500
Model 1894, Various Calibers, Tube Feed, Solid Frame, Round Barrel, *Antique*	500	1000	1200
Model 1894, Various Calibers, Tube Feed, Takedown, Octagon Barrel, *Antique*	600	1200	1500
Model 1894, Various Calibers, Tube Feed, Takedown, Round Barrel, *Antique*	500	1000	1200
Model 1895 Carbine over #167531, Various Calibers, Tube Feed, Takedown, Octagon Barrel, *Modern*	2000	7000	10000
Model 1895 Carbine, Various Calibers, Tube Feed, Takedown, Octagon Barrel, *Antique*	3500	9000	12000
Model 1895 Lightweight over #167531, Various Calibers, Tube Feed, Solid Frame, Octagon Barrel, *Modern*	500	2000	2500
Model 1895 Lightweight, Various Calibers, Tube Feed, Solid Frame, *Antique*	900	2000	2500
Model 1895 Standard over #167531, Various Calibers, Tube Feed, Solid Frame, Round Barrel, *Modern*	700	1600	1800
Model 1895 Standard, Various Calibers, Tube Feed, Solid Frame, *Antique*	800	1800	2000
Model 1897 over #177197, .22 L.R.R.F., Tube Feed, Takedown, *Modern*	550	1200	1500
Model 1897, .22 L.R.R.F., Tube Feed, Takedown, *Antique*	550	1200	1500
Model 336 Marauder, Various Calibers, Tube Feed, Carbine, Open Rear Sight, Straight Grip, *Modern*	150	300	550
Model 336 Zane Grey, .30-.30 Win., Tube Feed, Octagon Barrel, Open Rear Sight, *Modern*	150	300	350
Model 336, .219 Zipper, Tube Feed, Sporting Carbine, Open Rear Sight, 5 Shot, *Modern*	250	600	900

	Fair	V. Good	Excellent
Model 336, Various Calibers, Tube Feed, Sporting Carbine, Open Rear Sight, 5 Shot, *Modern*	$175	$225	$275
Model 336A, Various Calibers, Tube Feed, Sporting Rifle, Open Rear Sight, 5 Shot, *Modern*	150	225	275

Marlin 336A

	Fair	V. Good	Excellent
Model 336A-DL, Various Calibers, Tube Feed, Sporting Rifle, Open Rear Sight, 5 Shot, Checkered Stock, *Modern*	125	175	225
Model 336C, Various Calibers, Tube Feed, Carbine, Open Rear Sight, *Modern*	125	175	225
Model 336T, .44 Magnum, Tube Feed, Carbine, Open Rear Sight, Straight Grip, *Modern*	125	175	225
Model 336T, Various Calibers, Tube Feed, Carbine, Open Rear Sight, Straight Grip, *Modern*	125	175	225
Model 36, Various Calibers, Tube Feed, Beavertail Forend, Open Rear Sight, Carbine, *Modern*	150	225	275
Model 36, Various Calibers, Tube Feed, Beavertail Forend, Open Rear Sight, Sporting Carbine, 5 Shot, *Modern*	150	250	300
Model 36A, Various Calibers, Tube Feed, Beavertail Forend, Open Rear Sight, 5 Shot, *Modern*	150	225	275
Model 36DL, Various Calibers, Tube Feed, Fancy Checkering, Open Rar Sight, 5 Shot, *Modern*	150	250	350
Model 39 Article II, .22 L.R.R.F., Takedown, Tube Feed, Hammer, Octagon Barrel, *Modern*	150	275	325
Model 39 Article II, .22 L.R.R.F., Takedown, Tube Feed, Hammer, Octagon Barrel, Carbine, *Modern*	150	325	350
Model 39 Century, .22 L.R.R.F., Takedown, Tube Feed, Hammer, Octagon Barrel, *Modern*	150	250	325

Marlin 39 Century Ltd.

	Fair	V. Good	Excellent
Model 39 M, .22 L.R.R.F., Takedown, Tube Feed, Hammer, Round Barrel, Carbine, *Modern*	$150	$250	$300
Model 39, .22 L.R.R.F., Takedown, Hammer, Octagon Barrel, *Modern*	200	650	1000
Model 39A Mountie, .22 L.R.R.F., Takedown, Tube Feed, Hammer, Round Barrel, *Modern*	150	200	300
Model 39A, .22 L.R.R.F., Takedown, Tube Feed, Hammer, Round Barrel, *Modern*	150	200	250

Marlin 39A

	Fair	V. Good	Excellent
Model 444, .444 Marlin, Tube Feed, Monte Carlo Stock, Open Rear Sight, Straight Grip, *Modern*	150	200	250
Model 56, .22 L.R.R.F., Clip Fed, Open Rear Sight, Monte Carlo Stock, *Modern*	100	125	150
Model 57, .22 L.R.R.F., Tube Feed, Open Rear Sight, Monte Carlo Stock, *Modern*	100	125	150
Model 57M, .22 WMR., Tube Feed, Open Rear Sight, Monte Carlo Stock, *Modern*	125	150	175
Model 62, Various Calibers, Clip Fed, Open Rear Sight, Monte Carlo Stock, *Modern*	175	200	225

RIFLE, SEMI-AUTOMATIC

	Fair	V. Good	Excellent
Glenfield M40, .22 L.R.R.F., Tube Feed, *Modern*	75	100	125
Glenfield M60, .22 L.R.R.F., Tube Feed, *Modern*	25	50	75
Model 49 DL, .22 L.R.R.F., Tube Feed, Open Rear Sight, *Modern*	50	75	100

Marlin Model 49 DL

	Fair	V. Good	Excellent
Model 50, .22 L.R.R.F., Clip Fed, Open Rear Sight, Takedown, *Modern*	50	75	100
Model 50E, .22 L.R.R.F., Clip Fed, Peep Sights, Takedown, *Modern*	50	75	100

	Fair	V. Good	Excellent
Model 88C, .22 L.R.R.F., Tube Feed, Takedown, Open Rear Sight, *Modern*	$50	$75	$100
Model 88DL, .22 L.R.R.F., Tube Feed, Takedown, Peep Sights, *Modern*	75	100	125
Model 89C, .22 L.R.R.F., Clip Fed, Takedown, Open Rear Sight, *Modern*	50	75	100
Model 89DL, .22 L.R.R.F., Clip Fed, Takedown, Peep Sights, *Modern*	75	100	125
Model 98, .22 L.R.R.F., Tube Feed, Solid Frame, Open Rear Sight, Monte Carlo Stock, *Modern*	50	75	100
Model 989 G, .22 L.R.R.F., Clip Fed, Open Rear Sight, Monte Carlo Stock, *Modern*	25	50	75
Model 989, .22 L.R.R.F., Clip Fed, Open Rear Sight, Monte Carlo Stock, *Modern*	25	50	75

Marlin Model 989 M-2

	Fair	V. Good	Excellent
Model 99 M-1, .22 L.R.R.F., Tube Feed, Open Rear Sight, Monte Carlo Stock, *Modern*	25	50	75

Marlin Model 99 M-1

	Fair	V. Good	Excellent
Model 99 M-2, .22 L.R.R.F., Clip Fed, Open Rear Sight, *Modern*	25	50	75
Model 99, .22 L.R.R.F., Tube Feed, Open Rear Sight, *Modern*	25	50	75
Model 990, .22 L.R.R.F., Tube Feed, Open Rear Sight, Monte Carlo Stock, *Modern*	25	50	75
Model 995, .22 L.R.R.F., Clip Fed, Open Rear Sight, *Modern*	25	50	75
Model 99C, .22 L.R.R.F., Tube Feed, Open Rear Sight, Monte Carlo Stock, *Modern*	25	50	75
Model 99DL, .22 L.R.R.F., Tube Feed, Open Rear Sight, Monte Carlo Stock, *Modern*	25	50	75
Model A-1, .22 L.R.R.F., Clip Fed, Takedown, Open Rear Sight, *Modern*	25	50	75
Model A-1E, .22 L.R.R.F., Clip Fed, Takedown, Peep Sights, *Modern*	$25	$50	$75

RIFLE, SLIDE ACTION

	Fair	V. Good	Excellent
Model 18, .22 L.R.R.F., Solid Frame, Tube Feed, Hammer, *Modern*	125	250	350
Model 20, .22 L.R.R.F., Takedown, Tube Feed, Hammer, Octagon Barrel, *Modern*	125	225	350
Model 25, .22 Short R.F., Takedown, Tube Feed, Hammer, *Modern*	125	250	400
Model 27, Various Calibers, Takedown, Tube Feed, Hammer, Octagon Barrel, *Modern*	100	200	350
Model 27-S, Various Calibers, Takedown, Tube Feed, Hammer, Round Barrel, *Modern*	100	200	350
Model 29, .22 L.R.R.F., Takedown, Tube Feed, Hammer, Round Barrel, *Modern*	115	225	350
Model 32, .22 L.R.R.F., Takedown, Tube Feed, Hammerless, Octagon Barrel, *Modern*	150	250	350
Model 38, .22 L.R.R.F., Takedown, Tube Feed, Hammerless, Octagon Barrel, *Modern*	150	250	350

SHOTGUN, BOLT ACTION

	Fair	V. Good	Excellent
Glenfield, 12 Ga. 3", Clip Fed, *Modern*	50	75	100
Model 55, 12 Ga. 3", Clip Fed, Adjustable Choke, *Modern*	75	100	125

Marlin Model 55 Slug Gun

	Fair	V. Good	Excellent
Model 55, Various Gauges, Clip Fed, *Modern*	50	75	100
Model 55, Various Gauges, Clip Fed, Adjustable Choke, *Modern*	75	100	125
Model 55 Goose Gun, 12 Ga. 3", Clip Fed, *Modern*	75	150	175
Model 55S, 12 Ga. 3", Clip Fed, *Modern*	75	125	150
Model Super Goose, 10 Ga. 3½", Clip Fed, *Modern*	100	175	200

SHOTGUN, DOUBLE BARREL, OVER-UNDER

	Fair	V. Good	Excellent
Model 90, 12 and 16 Gauges, Checkered, Double Triggers, *Modern*	150	350	400
Model 90, 12 and 16 Gauges, Checkered, Single Triggers, *Modern*	200	400	450

	Fair	V. Good	Excellent
Model 90, 20 and .410 Gauges, Checkered Stock, Double Triggers, *Modern*	$200	$425	$475
Model 90, 20 and .410 Gauges, Checkered Stock, Single Triggers, *Modern*	200	475	525

SHOTGUN, LEVER ACTION

	Fair	V. Good	Excellent
Four-Tenner, .410 Ga., Tube Feed, *Modern*	400	800	900

SHOTGUN, SLIDE ACTION

	Fair	V. Good	Excellent
Glenfield Model 778, 12 Ga., Hammerless, Tube Feed, *Modern*	100	175	225
Model 120, 12 Ga. 3", Hammerless, Tube Feed, *Modern*	125	250	300
Model 16 A, 12 Ga., Hammer, Tube Feed, *Modern*	125	250	275
Model 16 B, 12 Ga., Hammer, Tube Feed, Checkered Stock, *Modern*	150	350	400
Model 16 C, 12 Ga., Hammer, Tube Feed, Checkered Stock, Fancy Wood, Light Engraving, *Modern*	200	450	750
Model 16 D, 12 Ga., Hammer, Tube Feed, Checkered Stock, Fancy Wood, Engraved, *Modern*	400	850	1000
Model 17, 12 Ga., Hammer, Tube Feed, *Modern*	200	400	450
Model 1898 A, 12 Ga., Hammer, Tube Feed, *Modern*	150	325	375
Model 1898 B, 12 Ga., Hammer, Tube Feed, Checkered Stock, *Modern*	150	375	425
Model 1898 C, 12 Ga., Hammer, Tube Feed, Checkered Stock, Fancy Wood, Light Engraving, *Modern*	250	600	800
Model 1898 D, 12 Ga., Hammer, Tube Feed, Checkered Stock, Fancy Wood, Engraved, *Modern*	700	1500	1750
Model 19 A, 12 Ga., Hammer, Tube Feed, *Modern*	150	275	300
Model 19 B, 12 Ga., Hammer, Tube Feed, Checkered Stock, *Modern*	150	350	400
Model 19 C, 12 Ga., Hammer, Tube Feed, Checkered Stock, Fancy Wood, Light Engraving, *Modern*	225	600	750
Model 19 D, 12 Ga., Hammer, Tube Feed, Checkered Stock, Fancy Wood, Engraved, *Modern*	500	1200	1750
Model 21 B, 12 Ga., Hammer, Tube Feed, Checkered Stock, *Modern*	200	350	400
Model 21 C, 12 Ga., Hammer, Tube Feed, Checkered Stock, Fancy Wood, Light Engraving, *Modern*	250	500	700
Model 21 D, 12 Ga., Hammer, Tube Feed, Checkered Stock, Fancy Wood, Engraved, *Modern*	400	1200	1750

	Fair	V. Good	Excellent
Model 21 Field, 12 Ga., Hammer, Tube Feed, *Modern*	$150	$250	$275
Model 24 B, 12 Ga., Hammer, Tube Feed, Checkered Stock, *Modern*	200	350	400
Model 24 C, 12 Ga., Hammer, Tube Feed, Checkered Stock, Fancy Wood, Light Engraving, *Modern*	250	500	700
Model 24 D, 12 Ga., Hammer, Tube Feed, Checkered Stock, Fancy Wood, Engraved, *Modern*	600	1400	1750
Model 24 Field, 12 Ga., Hammer, Tube Feed, *Modern*	125	250	300
Model 26 Field, 12 Ga., Hammer, Tube Feed, *Modern*	175	225	275
Model 28 A, 12 Ga., Hammerless, Tube Feed, *Modern*	225	250	275
Model 28 B, 12 Ga., Hammerless, Tube Feed, Checkered Stock, *Modern*	200	350	400
Model 28 C, 12 Ga., Hammerless, Tube Feed, Checkered Stock, Fancy Wood, Light Engraving, *Modern*	200	425	500
Model 28 D, 12 Ga., Hammerless, Tube Feed, Checkered Stock, Fancy Wood, Engraved, *Modern*	400	850	1250
Model 28 Trap, 12 Ga., Hammerless, Tube Feed, *Modern*	150	275	400
Model 30 A, 12 Ga., Hammer, Tube Feed, *Modern*	200	275	300
Model 30 B, 12 Ga., Hammer, Tube Feed, Checkered Stock, *Modern*	200	350	400
Model 30 C, 12 Ga., Hammer, Tube Feed, Checkered Stock, Fancy Wood, Light Engraving, *Modern*	200	450	700
Model 30 D, 12 Ga., Hammer, Tube Feed, Checkered Stock, Fancy Wood, Engraved, *Modern*	350	1200	1750
Model 31 B, 12 Ga., Hammerless, Tube Feed, Checkered Stock, *Modern*	200	350	400
Model 31 D, 12 Ga., Hammerless, Tube Feed, Checkered Stock, Fancy Wood, Engraved, *Modern*	400	1200	1750
Model 31 Field, 12 Ga., Hammerless, Tube Feed, *Modern*	150	250	300
Model 31C, 12 Ga., Hammerless, Tube Feed, Checkered Stock, Fancy Wood, Light Engraving, *Modern*	300	450	800
Model 44 Field, 12 Ga., Hammerless, Tube Feed, *Modern*	150	350	375
Model 63 Field, 12 Ga., Hammerless, Tube Feed, *Modern*	150	325	350
Premier Mark I, 12 Ga., Hammerless, Tube Feed, *Modern*	150	200	225
Premier Mark II, 12 Ga., Hammerless, Tube Feed, *Modern*	150	225	250
Premier Mark IV, 12 Ga., Hammerless, Tube Feed, Vent Rib, *Modern*	150	250	300

MAROCCINI

Frabricca Fucili da Caccia di Luciano Maroccini, Gardone Val Trompia, Italy.

SHOTGUN, DOUBLE BARREL, OVER-UNDER

	Fair	V. Good	Excellent
Field Master Commander, 12 Gauge Magnum, Police Style, Detachable Buttstock, Double Triggers, Boxlock, *Modern*	$200	$425	$475
Field Master I, Various Gauges, Checkered Stock, Sling Swivels, Double Triggers, Boxlock, *Modern*	150	325	375
Field Master II, Various Gauges, Checkered Stock, Single Trigger, Boxlock, Automatic Ejectors, *Modern*	150	350	425

SHOTGUN, DOUBLE BARREL, SIDE-BY-SIDE

	Fair	V. Good	Excellent
Mondial, 12 Gauge, Checkered Stock, Sling Swivels, Double Triggers, Boxlock, *Modern*	50	100	150

MARQUIS OF LORNE

Made by Hood Arms Co. Norwich, Conn., c. 1880.

HANDGUN, REVOLVER

	Fair	V. Good	Excellent
.22 Short R.F., 7 Shot, Spur Trigger, Solid Frame, Single Action, *Antique*	75	150	175
.32 Short R.F., 5 Shot, Spur Trigger, Solid Frame, Single Action, *Antique*	100	175	200

MARS

Kohout & Spolecnost, Kydne, Czechoslovakia, c. 1925.

HANDGUN, SEMI-AUTOMATIC

	Fair	V. Good	Excellent
Mars, 6.35mm, Clip Fed, Blue, *Curio*	100	200	250
Mars, 7.65mm, Clip Fed, Blue, *Curio*	100	250	300

MARS

Spain, c. 1920.

HANDGUN, SEMI-AUTOMATIC

	Fair	V. Good	Excellent
Automat Pistole Mars, 6.35mm, Clip Fed, *Curio*	50	100	150

MARS AUTOMATIC PISTOL SYNDICATE

Distributors of the Gabbet Fairfax pistol made by Webley & Scott, Birmingham, England, 1902–1904.

HANDGUN, SEMI-AUTOMATIC

	Fair	V. Good	Excellent
.45 Long, Clip Fed, Blue, Hammer, *Curio*	5500	12000	15000
9mm, Clip Fed, Blue, Hammer, *Curio*	$3750	$8000	$10000

MARSHWOOD

Made by Stevens Arms.

SHOTGUN, DOUBLE BARREL, SIDE-BY-SIDE

	Fair	V. Good	Excellent
M 315, Various Gauges, Hammerless, Steel Barrel, *Modern*	100	150	175

MARSTON, STANHOPE

New York City, c. 1850s.

HANDGUN, PERCUSSION

	Fair	V. Good	Excellent
Swivel Breech, .31, Two Barrels, Ring Trigger, Bar Hammer, *Antique*	400	850	1000

MARSTON, WILLIAM W.

New York City, 1850–1875.

HANDGUN, PERCUSSION

	Fair	V. Good	Excellent
Breech Loader, .35, Half Octagon Barrel, Engraved, *Antique*	800	1800	2100
Pepperbox, .31, Double Action, 6 Shot, Bar Hammer, *Antique*	250	500	600
Pocket, .31, Bar Hammer, Double Action, Screw Barrel, *Antique*	150	300	375
Singleshot, .36, Bar Hammer, Single Action, Screw Barrel, *Antique*	150	350	425

MARTE

Erquiaga, Muguruzu y Cia, Eibar, Spain, c. 1920.

HANDGUN, SEMI-AUTOMATIC

	Fair	V. Good	Excellent
.25 ACP, Clip Fed, Blue, *Curio*	75	125	150

MARTIAN

Martin a Bascaran, Eibar, Spain, 1916–1927.

HANDGUN, SEMI-AUTOMATIC

	Fair	V. Good	Excellent
6.35mm, Clip Fed, Eibar Type, *Curio*	50	100	125
6.35mm, Clip Fed, Trigger Guard Takedown, *Curio*	100	200	225
7.65mm, Clip Fed, Eibar Type, *Curio*	75	125	150
7.65mm, Clip Fed, Trigger Guard Takedown, *Curio*	100	225	250

Martian

MARTIAN COMMERCIAL

Martin A Bascaran, Eibar, Spain 1919–1927.

HANDGUN, SEMI-AUTOMATIC

	Fair	V. Good	Excellent
6.35, Clip Fed, Eibar Type, *Curio*	$75	$125	$150
6.35, Clip Fed, Eibar Type, *Curio*	75	150	175

MARTIN, ALEXANDER

Glasglow & Aberdeen, Scotland, 1922–1928.

RIFLE, BOLT ACTION

	Fair	V. Good	Excellent
.303 British, Sporting Rifle, Express Sights, Engraved, Fancy Wood, Cased, *Curio*	400	950	1350

MASSACHUSETTS ARMS

Made by Stevens Arms.

SHOTGUN, DOUBLE BARREL, SIDE-BY-SIDE

	Fair	V. Good	Excellent
Model 311, Various Gauges, Hammerless, Steel Barrel, *Modern*	75	150	175

SHOTGUN, SINGLESHOT

	Fair	V. Good	Excellent
Model 90, Various Gauges, Takedown, Automatic Ejector, Plain, Hammer, *Modern*	25	50	75
Model 94, Various Gauges, Takedown, Automatic Ejector, Plain, Hammer, *Modern*	25	50	75

MASSACHUSETTS ARMS CO.

Chicopee Falls, Mass. 1850–1866. Also see Adams.

HANDGUN, PERCUSSION

	Fair	V. Good	Excellent
Maynard Belt Revolver, .31, 6 Shot, *Antique*	400	800	950
Maynard Pocket Revolver, .28, 6 Shot, *Antique*	300	600	750
Wesson & Leavitt Belt Revolver, .31, 6 Shot, *Antique*	450	1000	1200
Wesson & Leavitt Dragoon Revolver, .40, 6 Shot, *Antique*	$1500	$3000	$3500

MATADOR

Made in Spain for Firearms International, Washington, D.C.

SHOTGUN, DOUBLE BARREL, SIDE-BY-SIDE

	Fair	V. Good	Excellent
Matador II, 12 or 20 Gauges, Checkered Stock, Single Trigger, Selective Ejectors, *Modern*	100	200	250

MATCHLOCK ARMS EXAMPLES

RIFLE, MATCHLOCK

	Fair	V. Good	Excellent
.45, India mid-1600s, 4 Shot, Revolving Cylinder, Light Ornamentation, Brass Furniture, *Antique*	2100	4500	5000
.57, Japanese Full Stock Musket, Octagon Barrel, Silver Inlay, Brass Furniture, *Antique*	800	1800	2000

MAUSER

Germany Gebruder Mauser et Cie from 1854–1890. From 1890–1994 is known as Mauser-Werke. 1994 to Date Mauser-Werke Oberndorf Waff Ensysteme GmbH. Also see German Military, Luger.

HANDGUN, REVOLVER

	Fair	V. Good	Excellent
Colt Type, .38 Spec., Double Action, 6 Shot, 2" Barrel, *Curio*	75	125	175
M 78 Zig Zag, 10.6mm, Tip-Up, *Antique*	1500	3500	4500

Mauser M 78 Zig Zag

	Fair	V. Good	Excellent
M 78 Zig Zag, 7.6mm, Tip-Up, *Antique*	1250	3250	4000
M 78 Zig Zag, 9mm Mauser, Tip-Up, *Antique*	1250	3250	4000
M 78 Zig Zag, Tip-Up, Fancy Engraving, *Antique*	1750	4500	6000

HANDGUN, SEMI-AUTOMATIC

	Fair	V. Good	Excellent
Chinese Shansei, .45 ACP, with Shoulder Stock, *Curio*	$1900	$4000	$4500
HSc 1 of 5,000, .380 ACP, Blue, Post-War, Cased, *Modern*	100	200	300
HSc Army, .32 ACP., Nazi-Proofed, *Curio*	150	325	375
HSc Navy, .32 ACP., Nazi-Proofed, *Curio*	250	500	575
HSc NSDAP SA, .32 ACP., Nazi-Proofed, *Curio*	300	600	750
HSc Police, .32 ACP., Nazi-Proofed, *Curio*	150	300	375
HSc Swiss, .32 ACP., *Curio*	450	950	1200
HSc, .32 ACP, Nickel Plated, Post-War, *Modern*	150	275	300
HSc, .32 ACP, Post-War, Blue, *Modern*	125	250	275
HSc, .32 ACP. Pre-War, Nazi-Proofed, Commercial, *Curio*	200	425	500
HSc, .32 ACP. Pre-War, Prototype, Commercial, *Curio*	150	300	325
HSc, .380 ACP, Blue, Post-War, *Modern*	125	250	275
HSc, .380 ACP, Nickel Plated, Post-War, *Modern*	150	275	300
M 1896 (Early), 7.63 Mauser, Small Ring, *Curio*	1800	3000	3500
M 1896 (Italian), 7.63 Mauser, Slabside, *Curio*	1800	3000	3500
M 1896 Banner, 7.63 Mauser, *Curio*	900	2000	2250
M 1896 Bolo, 7.63 Mauser, Post-War, *Curio*	900	2000	2500
M 1896 French Police, 7.63 Mauser, *Curio*	800	1500	1750
M 1896 Persian, 7.63 Mauser, *Curio*	900	2000	2500
M 1896 Police, 7.63 Mauser, *Curio*	450	1050	1250
M 1896 System Mauser, 7.63 Mauser, With Conehammer, *Curio*	4000	9000	10500
M 1896 Turkish, 7.63 Mauser, Conehammer, *Curio*	1700	3500	4000
M 1896 WW I, 7.63 Mauser, Military, *Curio*	350	750	1000
M 1896 WW I, 9mm Luger, Military, *Curio*	$500	$1200	$1500
M 1896, 7.63 Mauser, 10 Shot, Conehammer, *Curio*	1100	2500	2750

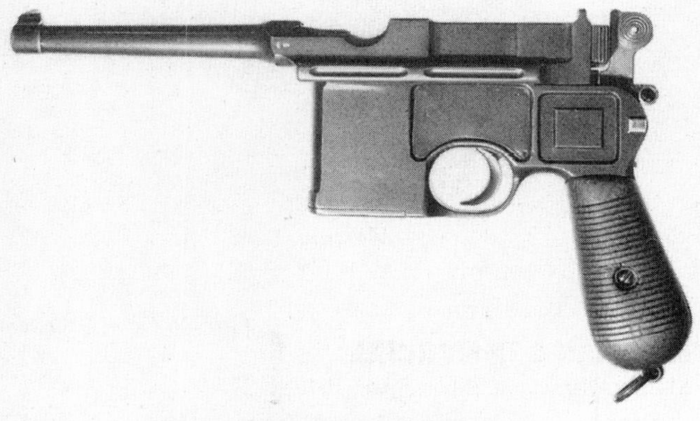

Mauser 1896 Conehammer

	Fair	V. Good	Excellent
M 1896, 7.63 Mauser, 10 Shot, Fixed Sight Conehammer, *Curio*	1200	2750	3000
M 1896, 7.63 Mauser, Conehammer with Shoulder Stock, *Curio*	1400	3250	3750
M 1896, 7.63 Mauser, Fixed Sight Conehammer with Shoulder Stock, *Curio*	1400	3750	4250
M 1896, 7.63 Mauser, Flatside, *Curio*	900	2000	2200
M 1896, 7.63 Mauser, Pre-War, Commercial, *Curio*	450	1000	1250
M 1896, 7.63 Mauser, Transitional, *Curio*	1000	2250	2500
M 1896, Factory Engraving Add 300%			
M 1896, Original Holster Stock Add 20%-35%			
M 1896, 20-Shot Model Add 50%-80%			
M 1896, 40-Shot Model Add 100%			
M 1896, 6-Shot Model Add 75%-100%			
M 1906/08, 7.63 Mauser, Clip Fed, *Curio*	9000	25000	30000
M 1910, .25 ACP, Clip Fed, *Curio*	150	300	350

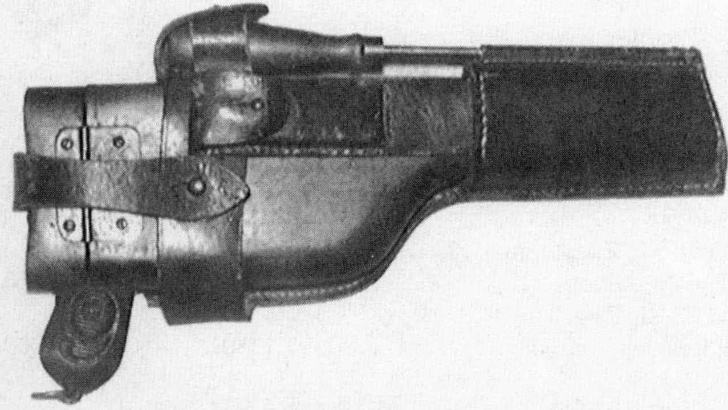

Mauser M 1896 WWI with Holster Stock

Mauser M 1910

	Fair	V. Good	Excellent
M 1912/14, 9mm Luger, Clip Fed, *Curio*	$7000	$17500	$20000
M 1914 Army, .32 ACP, Clip Fed, *Curio*	150	275	325

Mauser M 1914

	Fair	V. Good	Excellent
M 1914 Early, .32 ACP, Clip Fed, *Curio*	125	225	275
M 1914 Humpback, .32 ACP, Long Barrel, Clip Fed, *Curio*	1100	2500	2700
M 1914 Navy, .32 ACP, Clip Fed, *Curio*	150	300	350
M 1914 Post-War, .32 ACP, Clip Fed, *Modern*	100	175	225
M 1914 War Commercial, .32 ACP, Clip Fed, *Curio*	100	200	250
M 1934 Navy, .32 ACP, Clip Fed, *Curio*	250	500	600
M 1934 Police, .32 ACP, Clip Fed, *Curio*	150	300	350
M 1934, .32 ACP, Clip Fed, *Curio*	125	250	300
New Model Carbine, 9mm Luger, 12" Barrel, Grip Safety, *Modern*	2000	4500	5500
Parabellum Bulgarian, .30 Luger, Grip Safety, Commemorative, *Modern*	450	1000	1250
Parabellum Cartridge Counter, 9mm Luger, Grip Safety, Commemorative, *Modern*	900	2000	2500
Parabellum P.O8, .30 Luger, 6" Barrel, Grip Safety, *Modern*	200	450	500
Parabellum PO 8, .30 Luger, 4" Barrel, Grip Safety, *Modern*	250	575	625
Parabellum PO 8, 9mm Luger, Various Barrel Lengths, Grip Safety, *Modern*	250	500	600
Parabellum Russian, .30 Luger, Grip Safety, Commemorative, *Modern*	450	1000	1250
Parabellum Sport, .30 or 9mm Luger, Heavy Barrel, Target Sights, *Modern*	550	1200	1500
Parabellum Swiss, 7.65mm, 6" Barrel, Grip Safety, *Modern*	200	400	450

	Fair	V. Good	Excellent
Parabellum Swiss, 9mm Luger, 4" Barrel, Grip Safety, *Modern*	$225	$450	$550
W T P I, 6.35mm, Clip Fed, *Modern*	100	250	300
W T P II, 6.35mm, Clip Fed, *Modern*	200	450	500

RIFLE, BOLT ACTION

	Fair	V. Good	Excellent
Model 10 Varminter, .22-250 Post-War, Heavy Barrel, Monte Carlo Stock, Checkered Stock, *Modern*	600	1400	1550

Mauser W T P

	Fair	V. Good	Excellent
Model 2000, Various Calibers, Post-War, Monte Carlo Stock, Checkered Stock, *Modern*	150	300	350
Model 3000, Various Calibers, Post-War, Left-Hand, Magnum Action, Monte Carlo Stock, Checkered Stock, *Modern*	200	425	475
Model 3000, Various Calibers, Post-War, Left-Hand, Monte Carlo Stock, Checkered Stock, *Modern*	200	450	525
Model 3000, Various Calibers, Post-War, Magnum Action, Monte Carlo Stock, Checkered Stock, *Modern*	225	475	550
Model 3000, Various Calibers, Post-War, Monte Carlo Stock, *Modern*	200	400	475
Model 4000, Various Calibers, Varmint, Checkering, Flared, *Modern*	150	350	400
Model 66S, Various Calibers, Post-War, Takedown, Monte Carlo Stock, Checkered Stock, *Modern*	600	1250	1500
Model 66S Safari, Various Calibers, Post-War, Takedown, Monte Carlo Stock, Checkered Stock, Magnum, *Modern*	800	1750	2000
Model 98, Various Calibers, Sporting Rifle, Full-Stocked, Pre-WW2, Military, Commercial, *Modern*	150	325	375
Model A, Various Calibers, Sporting Rifle, Pre-WW2, Magnum Action, *Curio*	1400	3000	3500

	Fair	V. Good	Excellent
Model A, Various Calibers, Sporting Rifle, Pre-WW2, Short Action, *Curio*	$1500	$3250	$3500
Model A British, Various Calibers, Sporting Rifle, Express Sights, Pre-WW2, *Curio*	1400	3000	4000
Model A British, Various Calibers, Sporting Rifle, Peep Sights, Pre-WW2, Octagon Barrel, Set Trigger, *Curio*	1600	3500	4500
Model B, Various Calibers, Sporting Rifle, Pre-WW2, Octagon Barrel, Set Trigger, *Curio*	900	2000	2500
Model B, Various Calibers, Sporting Rifle, Pre-WW2, Set Trigger, Express Sights, *Curio*	900	2000	2250
Model DSM 34, .22 L.R.R.F., Pre-WW2, Singleshot, Tangent Sights, Military Style, Stock, *Curio*	150	275	325
Model EL 320, .22 L.R.R.F., Pre-WW2, Singleshot, Sporting Rifle, Adjustable Sights, *Curio*	100	225	275
Model EN 310, .22 L.R.R.F., Pre-WW2, Singleshot, Open Rear Sight, *Curio*	100	200	250
Model ES 340, .22 L.R.R.F., Pre-WW2, Singleshot, Tangent Sights, Sporting Rifle, *Curio*	115	250	300
Model ES 340B, .22 L.R.R.F., Pre-WW2, Singleshot, Tangent Sights, Sporting Rifle, *Curio*	115	250	300
Model ES 340B, .22 L.R.R.F., Pre-WW2, Singleshot, Target Sights, Target Stock, *Curio*	150	350	400
Model ES 350, .22 L.R.R.F., Pre-WW2, Singleshot, Target Sights, Target Stock, *Curio*	200	400	450
Model K, Various Calibers, Sporting Rifle, Pre-WW2, Short Action, *Curio*	200	425	500
Model KKW, .22 L.R.R.F., Pre-WW2, Singleshot, Tangent Sights, Military Style Stock, *Curio*	150	350	400
Model M, Various Calibers, Express Sights, Carbine, *Modern*	250	550	700
Model M, Various Calibers, Sporting Rifle, Pre-WW2, Full- Stocked, Tangent Sights, Carbine, *Curio*	200	450	500
Model MM 410, .22 L.R.R.F., Pre-WW2, 5 Shot Clip, Tangent Sights, Sporting Rifle, *Curio*	150	300	375
Model MM 410B, .22 L.R.R.F., Pre-WW2, 5 Shot Clip, Tangent Sights, Sporting Rifle, *Curio*	175	350	425
Model MS 350B, .22 L.R.R.F., Pre-WW2, 5 Shot Clip, Target Sights, Target Stock, *Curio*	200	425	500
Model MS 420, .22 L.R.R.F., Pre-WW2, 5 Shot Clip, Tangent Sights, Sporting Rifle, *Curio*	125	275	350
Model MS 420B, .22 L.R.R.F., Pre-WW2, 5 Shot Clip, Tangent Sights, Target Stock, *Curio*	$150	$350	$400
Model S, Various Calibers, Sporting Rifle, Pre-WW2, Full-Stocked, Set Trigger, Carbine, *Curio*	900	2000	2250
Standard, Various Calibers, Sporting Rifle, Set Trigger, Pre-WWI, *Curio*	1100	2500	2750
Various Calibers, Sporting Rifle, Pre-WWI, Military, Commercial, *Curio*	700	1500	1750
Various Calibers, Sporting Rifle, Set Trigger, Pre-WWI, Short Action, *Curio*	1100	2500	3250
Various Calibers, Sporting Rifle, Set Trigger, Pre-WWI, Carbine, Full-Stocked, *Curio*	800	1750	2250

RIFLE, SEMI-AUTOMATIC

	Fair	V. Good	Excellent
M 1896, 7.63 Mauser, Carbine, *Curio*	1900	4000	4500

RIFLE, DOUBLE BARREL, OVER-UNDER

	Fair	V. Good	Excellent
Model Aristocrat, .375 H & H Magnum, Fancy Checkering, Engraved, Open Rear Sight, Cheekpiece, Double Trigger, *Modern*	875	2500	3000
Model Aristocrat, Various Calibers, Fancy Checkering, Engraved, Open Rear Sight, Cheekpiece, Double Trigger, *Modern*	625	1800	2000

SHOTGUN, BOLT ACTION

	Fair	V. Good	Excellent
16 Gauge, *Modern*	75	100	125

SHOTGUN, DOUBLE BARREL, OVER-UNDER

	Fair	V. Good	Excellent
Model 610, 12 Gauge, Skeet Grade, with Conversion Kit, Vent Rib, Checkered Stock, *Modern*	800	1500	1600
Model 610, 12 Gauge, Trap Grade, Vent Rib, Checkered Stock, *Modern*	350	750	900
Model 620, 12 Gauge, Automatic Ejector, Double Trigger, Vent Rib, Fancy Wood, *Modern*	400	800	875
Model 620, 12 Gauge, Automatic Ejector, Single Selective Trigger, Vent Rib, Fancy Wood, *Modern*	400	850	1000
Model 620, 12 Gauge, Automatic Ejector, Single Trigger, Vent Rib, Fancy Wood, *Modern*	350	700	950
Model 71E, 12 Gauge, Field Grade, Double Trigger, Checkered Stock, *Modern*	150	325	375
Model 72E, 12 Gauge, Skeet Grade, Checkered Stock, Light Engraving, *Modern*	200	450	500

	Fair	V. Good	Excellent
Model 72E, 12 Gauge, Trap Grade, Checkered Stock, Light Engraving, *Modern*	$200	$450	$500

SHOTGUN, DOUBLE BARREL, SIDE-BY-SIDE

	Fair	V. Good	Excellent
Model 496, 12 Gauge, Trap Grade, Vent Rib, Single Trigger, Checkered Stock, Box Lock, *Modern*	225	500	575
Model 545, 12 and 20 Gauges, Single Trigger, Recoil Pad, Checkered Stock, Box Lock, *Modern*	200	450	500
Model 580, 12 Gauge, Engraved, Fancy Checkering, Fancy Wood, *Modern*	400	800	975

SHOTGUN, SINGLESHOT

	Fair	V. Good	Excellent
Model 496, 12 Gauge, Trap Grade, Engraved, Checkered Stock, *Modern*	250	500	550
Model 496 Competition, 12 Gauge, Trap Grade, Engraved, Fancy Wood, Fancy Checkering, *Modern*	300	650	725

MAYER & SOEHNE

Arnsberg, W. Germany.

HANDGUN, REVOLVER

	Fair	V. Good	Excellent
Target, .22 L.R.R.F., Break Top, 5 Shot, Target Sights, Double Action, *Modern*	50	100	125

MAYESCH

Lancaster, Pa. 1760–1770. See Kentucky Rifles and Pistols.

MAYOR, FRANCOIS

Lausanne, Switzerland.

HANDGUN, SEMI-AUTOMATIC

	Fair	V. Good	Excellent
Rochat, 6.35mm, Clip Fed, *Modern*	250	500	650

MBA

San Ramon, Calif., 1965–1975.

HANDGUN, POCKET PISTOL

	Fair	V. Good	Excellent
Gyrojet, For Nickel Plating, Add 10%-15%			
Gyrojet, For U.S. Property Stamping Add 75%-100%			
Gyrojet Mark I Model A, Clip Fed, *Modern*	250	550	650
Gyrojet Mark I Model A Exp., Clip Fed, *Modern*	400	800	950
Gyrojet Mark I Carbine Model B Exp., Clip Fed, *Modern*	450	1000	1250
Gyrojet Mark I Carbine Model B Snub, Clip Fed, *Modern*	450	950	1100
Gyrojet Mark I Carbine Model B, Clip Fed, *Modern*	$350	$750	$1000
Gyrojet Mark I Carbine Model C, Clip Fed, *Modern*	300	650	750
Gyrojet Mark I, Clip Fed, Presentation Cased with Accessories, *Modern*	700	1500	1850

MCCOY, ALEXANDER

Philadelphia, Pa. 1779. See Kentucky Rifles.

MCCOY, KESTER

Lancaster, Pa. See Kentucky Rifles and Pistols.

MCCULLOUGH, GEORGE

Lancaster, Pa. 1770–1773. See Kentucky Rifles.

MEIER, ADOLPHUS

St. Louis, Mo. 1845–1850.

RIFLE, PERCUSSION

	Fair	V. Good	Excellent
.58 Plains Type, Double Barrel, Side by Side, Half-Octagon Barrel, Rifled, Plain, *Antique*	900	2000	2500

MELIOR

Liege, Belgium, Made by Robar et Cie. 1900–1959.

HANDGUN, SEMI-AUTOMATIC

	Fair	V. Good	Excellent
New Model Pocket, .22 L.R.R.F., Clip Fed, *Modern*	75	150	175
New Model Pocket, .380 ACP, Clip Fed, *Modern*	75	150	175
New Model Pocket, 7.65mm, Clip Fed, *Modern*	50	125	150
New Model Vest Pocket, .22 Long R.F., Clip Fed, *Modern*	50	125	150
New Model Vest Pocket, 6.35mm, Clip Fed, *Modern*	75	150	175
Old Model Pocket, 7.65mm, Clip Fed, *Modern*	75	150	175
Old Model Vest Pocket, 6.35mm, Clip Fed, *Modern*	75	150	175
Target, .22 L.R.R.F., Clip Fed, Long Barrel, *Modern*	100	200	250

MENDOZA

Mexico City, Mexico.

HANDGUN, SINGLESHOT

	Fair	V. Good	Excellent
K-62, .22 L.R.R.F., *Modern*	50	100	125

RIFLE, BOLT ACTION

	Fair	V. Good	Excellent
Modelo Conejo, .22 L.R.R.F., 2 Shot, *Modern*	75	125	175

MENTA

Made by August Menz, Suhl, Germany, c. 1916.

HANDGUN, REVOLVER

	Fair	V. Good	Excellent
7.65mm, Clip Fed, Commercial, *Curio*	$100	$250	$300

Menta .32

	Fair	V. Good	Excellent
7.65mm, Clip Fed, Military, *Curio*	150	300	350

MENZ, AUGUST

Suhl, Germany 1912–1937. Also see Menta.

HANDGUN, SEMI-AUTOMATIC

	Fair	V. Good	Excellent
Lilliput, 6.35mm, Clip Fed, *Curio*	150	300	350
Model I, 7.65mm, Clip Fed, *Curio*	100	250	300

Menz Model I

	Fair	V. Good	Excellent
Model II, 7.65mm, Clip Fed, *Curio*	125	275	325
Model III, 7.65mm, Clip Fed, Hammer, *Curio*	150	350	425
P & B Special, .380 ACP, Clip Fed, Hammer, Double Action, *Curio*	300	725	825
P & B Special, 7.65mm, Clip Fed, Hammer, Double Action, *Curio*	250	500	575

MERCURY

Made by Robar et Cie., Liege, Belgium for Tradewinds.

RIFLE, SEMI-AUTOMATIC

	Fair	V. Good	Excellent
M 622 VP, .22 L.R.R.F., Clip Fed, *Modern*	50	100	300

SHOTGUN, DOUBLE BARREL, SIDE-BY-SIDE

	Fair	V. Good	Excellent
Mercury, 10 Gauge 3", Hammerless, Magnum, Checkered Stock, Double Trigger, *Modern*	$85	$170	$350
Mercury, 12 and 20 Gauges, Hammerless, Magnum, Checkered Stock, Double Trigger, *Modern*	80	160	325

MERIDEN FIRE ARMS CO.

Meriden, Conn. 1907–1909. Also made handguns marked with trade names as follows: Aubrey, Eastern Arms Co., Empire Arms, Empire State, Federal Arms, Howard Arms.

HANDGUN, REVOLVER

	Fair	V. Good	Excellent
.38 S & W, 5 Shot, Top Break, Hammerless, Double Action, *Modern*	50	100	200

RIFLE, SINGLESHOT

	Fair	V. Good	Excellent
Model 10, .22 L.R.R.F., *Modern*	25	50	100

RIFLE, SLIDE ACTION

	Fair	V. Good	Excellent
Model 15, .22 L.R.R.F., Tube Feed, *Modern*	100	200	225

MERKEL

Gebruder Merkel, Suhl, Germany, from 1920. After WWII, VEB Fahrzeug u. Jagdwaffenwerk Ernst Thalmann, Suhl, East Germany.

COMBINATION WEAPON, DRILLING

	Fair	V. Good	Excellent
Model 142, Various Calibers, Pre-WW2, Double Trigger, Engraved, Checkered Stock, *Curio*	1500	3500	4000
Model 142, Various Calibers, Pre-WW2, Double Trigger, Checkered Stock, *Curio*	1400	3000	3500
Model 145, Various Calibers, Pre-WW2, Double Trigger, Engraved, Checkered Stock, *Curio*	1200	2500	3000

COMBINATION WEAPON, OVER-UNDER

	Fair	V. Good	Excellent
Model 210, Various Calibers, Pre-WW2, Engraved, Checkered Stock, *Curio*	600	1750	2250
Model 211E, Various Calibers, Engraved, Checkered Stock, Automatic Ejector, *Modern*	1200	2500	3000
Model 213E, Various Calibers, Sidelock, Fancy Checkering, Fancy Engraving, Automatic Ejector, *Modern*	2500	6000	6500
Model 313E, Various Calibers, Sidelock, Fancy Checkering, Fancy Engraving, Automatic Ejector, *Modern*	3500	7500	8500

RIFLE, DOUBLE BARREL, OVER-UNDER

	Fair	V. Good	Excellent
Model 220E, Various Calibers, Pre-WW2, Checkered Stock, Engraved, *Curio*	$2200	$6000	$6500
Model 221E, Various Calibers, Engraved, Checkered Stock, Automatic Ejector, *Curio*	3000	6500	7500
Model 323E, Various Calibers, Sidelock, Fancy Checkering, Fancy Engraving, Automatic Ejector, *Modern*	7000	15000	17500

SHOTGUN, DOUBLE BARREL, OVER-UNDER

	Fair	V. Good	Excellent
Model 100, Various Gauges, Pre-WW2, Plain Barrel, Checkered Stock, *Curio*	400	850	1000
Model 100, Various Gauges, Pre-WW2, Raised Matted Rib, Checkered Stock, *Curio*	500	1000	1250
Model 101, Various Gauges, Pre-WW2, Raised Matted Rib, Checkered Stock, Light Engraving, *Curio*	500	1050	1250
Model 101E, Various Gauges, Pre-WW2, Raised Matted Rib, Checkered Stock, Light Engraving, Automatic Ejector, *Curio*	500	1100	1350
Model 200, Various Gauges, Pre-WW2, Raised Matted Rib, Checkered Stock, Light Engraving, *Curio*	450	950	1200
Model 201, Various Gauges, Pre-WW2, Raised Matted Rib, Checkered Stock, Engraved, *Curio*	550	1250	1500
Model 201E, Various Gauges, Pre-WW2, Raised Matted Rib, Checkered Stock, Engraved, Automatic Ejector, *Curio*	700	1500	1750
Model 202, Various Gauges, Pre-WW2, Raised Matted Rib, Fancy Checkering, Fancy Engraving, *Curio*	900	2000	2250
Model 202E, Various Gauges, Pre-WW2, Raised Matted Rib, Fancy Checkering, Fancy Engraving, Automatic Engraving, *Curio*	1000	2250	2500
Model 203E, Various Gauges, Sidelock, Fancy Checkering, Fancy Engraving, Automatic Ejector, *Modern*	1200	2650	3000
Model 204E, Various Gauges, Pre-WW2, Sidelock, Fancy Checkering, Fancy Engraving, Automatic Ejector, *Curio*	1900	4250	4700
Model 300, Various Gauges, Pre-WW2, Raised Matted Rib, Checkered Stock, Engraved, *Curio*	700	1750	2000
Model 300E, Various Gauges, Pre-WW2, Raised Matted Rib, Checkered Stock, Engraved, Automatic Ejector, *Curio*	800	1950	2200
Model 301, Various Gauges, Pre-WW2, Raised Matted Rib, Fancy Checkering, Engraved, *Curio*	$1500	$3500	$4000
Model 301E, Various Gauges, Pre-WW2, Raised Matted Rib, Fancy Checkering, Engraved, Automatic Ejector, *Curio*	2100	4500	5000
Model 302, Various Gauges, Pre-WW2, Raised Matted Rib, Fancy Checkering, Fancy Engraving, Automatic Ejector, *Curio*	3250	7250	7500
Model 303E, Various Gauges, Sidelock, Single Selective Trigger, Automatic Ejector, Fancy Engraving, Fancy Checkering, *Modern*	4500	9500	11000

SHOTGUN, DOUBLE BARREL, SIDE-BY-SIDE

	Fair	V. Good	Excellent
Model 127, Various Gauges, Pre-WW2, Sidelock, Fancy Engraving, Fancy Checkering, Automatic Ejector, *Curio*	7000	15000	17500
Model 130, Various Gauges, Pre-WW2, Fancy Engraving, Fancy Checkering, Automatic Ejector, *Curio*	3500	8500	10000
Model 147E, Various Gauges, Fancy Checkering, Fancy Engraving, *Modern*	600	1250	1400
Model 147E, Various Gauges, Fancy Checkering, Fancy Engraving, Single Selective Trigger, *Modern*	700	1450	1600
Model 147S, Various Gauges, Fancy Checkering, Fancy Engraving, Sidelock, *Modern*	1500	3250	3600
Model 147S, Various Gauges, Fancy Checkering, Fancy Engraving, Sidelock, Single Selective Trigger, *Modern*	1900	4000	4600
Model 47E, Various Gauges, Checkered Stock, Engraved, *Modern*	400	850	1000
Model 47E, Various Gauges, Single Selective Trigger, Checkered Stock, Engraved, *Modern*	450	950	1100
Model 47S, Various Gauges, Sidelock, Checkered Stock, Engraved, *Modern*	1200	2500	2800
Model 47S, Various Gauges, Sidelock, Single Selective Trigger, Checkered Stock, Engraved, *Modern*	1300	2750	3000

MERRILL CO.

Formerly in Rockwell City, Iowa, now in Fullerton, Calif.

HANDGUN, SINGLESHOT

Sportsman, For Extra 14" Barrel and Dies
Add $125.00-$185.00
Sportsman, For Extra Barrel
Add $75.00-$110.00

	Fair	V. Good	Excellent
Sportsman, Wrist Attachment Add $15.00-$25.00			
Sportsman, Various Calibers, Target Pistol, Top Break, Adjustable Sights, Vent Rib, *Modern*	$150	$300	$350

MERRIMAC ARMS & MFG. CO.

Newburyport, Mass. Absorbed by Brown Mfg. Co. Worcester, Mass. 1861–1866. Also see Ballard.

HANDGUN, SINGLESHOT

	Fair	V. Good	Excellent
Southerner, .41 Short R.F., Derringer, Iron Frame, Light Engraving, *Antique*	250	500	550

RIFLE, DOUBLE BARREL, SIDE-BY-SIDE

	Fair	V. Good	Excellent
Various Calibers, Octagon Barrel, *Antique*	450	950	1200

SHOTGUN, SINGLESHOT

	Fair	V. Good	Excellent
20 Gauge, Falling Block, *Antique*	125	250	300

MERVEILLEUX

Rouchouse, Paris, France.

HANDGUN, MANUAL REPEATER

	Fair	V. Good	Excellent
Palm Pistol, 6mm, Engraved, Nickel Plated, *Curio*	300	600	750

MERWIN & BRAY

Worcester, Mass. 1864–1868. Became Merwin & Simpkins in 1868 and also Merwin-Taylor & Simpkins the same year, also within the same year became Merwin, Hulbert & Co. Also see Ballard, Merwin, Hulbert & Co.

HANDGUN, REVOLVER

	Fair	V. Good	Excellent
"Navy," .32 Short R.F., 6 Shot, Single Action, Solid Frame, Finger-Rest Trigger Guard, *Antique*	200	400	475
"Navy," .38 Short R.F., 6 Shot, Single Action, Solid Frame, Finger-Rest Trigger Guard, *Antique*	200	475	550
"Original," .28 Cup Primed Cartridge, 6 Shot, Single Action, Spur Trigger, Tip-Up, *Antique*	300	600	675
"Original," .30 Cup Primed Cartridge, 6 Shot, Single Action, Spur Trigger, Tip-Up, *Antique*	300	650	725
"Original," .42 Cup Primed Cartridge, 6 Shot, Single Action, Spur Trigger, Tip-Up, *Antique*	350	700	775
"Original," Various Cup-Primed Calibers, Extra Cylinder, Percussion, Add $95.00-$160.00			
.22 Short R.F., 7 Shot, Single Action, Solid Frame, Spur Trigger, *Antique*	75	150	200
.28 Cup Primed Cartridge, 6 Shot, Single Action, Spur Trigger, Solid Frame, *Antique*	$75	$150	$200
.30 Cup Primed Cartridge, 6 Shot, Single Action, Spur Trigger, Solid Frame, *Antique*	125	175	225
.31 R.F., 6 Shot, Single Action, Solid Frame, Spur Trigger, *Antique*	75	125	175
.32 Short R.F., 6 Shot, Single Action, Solid Frame, Spur Trigger, *Antique*	75	125	175
.42 Cup Primed Cartridge, 6 Shot, Single Action, Spur Trigger, Solid Frame, *Antique*	100	200	250
.42 Cup Primed Cartridge, 6 Shot, Single Action, Spur Trigger, Solid Frame, 6" Barrel, *Antique*	150	375	425
Reynolds, .25 Short R.F., 5 Shot, Single Action, Spur Trigger, 3" Barrel, *Antique*	100	175	200

HANDGUN, SINGLESHOT

	Fair	V. Good	Excellent
.32 Short R.F., Side-Swing Barrel, Brass Frame, 3" Barrel, Spur Trigger, *Antique*	100	225	275

MERWIN, HULBERT & CO.

Successors to Merwin & Bray, et al. in 1868, and became Hulbert Bros. in 1892. Out of business in 1896. The author was introduced to the innovative and high-quality guns of Merwin & Hulbert by Stan Nelson, the gunsmith and gun dealer at the Stagecoach Museum, Shakopee, Minnesota. The innovative mechanisms, featuring a twist of the barrel to allow for ejection and then manual reloading, were unique in the arms trade, and required highly competent gunmakers for their construction.

HANDGUN, REVOLVER

	Fair	V. Good	Excellent
Army Model, "Safety Hammer," Add $65.00–$100.00			
Army Model, .44-40 WCF, Belt Pistol, 7" Barrel, Double Action, Round Butt, 6 Shot, *Antique*	500	1200	1500
Army Model, .44-40 WCF, Belt Pistol, 7" Barrel, Single Action, Square Butt, 6 Shot, *Antique*	700	1800	2000
Army Model, .44-40 WCF, Pocket Pistol, 3½" Barrel, Double Action, Round Butt, 6 Shot, *Antique*	500	1300	1500
Army Model, .44-40 WCF, Pocket Pistol, 3½" Barrel, Single Action, Square-Butt, 6 Shot, *Antique*	600	1300	1500
Army Model, Extra Barrel, Add $200.00–$300.00			
Pocket Model, .32 S & W, 5 Shot, Double Action, *Antique*	150	300	500
Target Model, .32 S & W, 7 Shot, Double Action, *Antique*	150	325	375

	Fair	V. Good	Excellent

MESSERSMITH, JACOB
Lancaster, Pa. 1779–1782. See Kentucky Rifles and Pistols.

METEOR
Made by Stevens Arms.

RIFLE, BOLT ACTION

	Fair	V. Good	Excellent
Model 52, .22 L.R.R.F., Singleshot, Takedown, *Modern*	$15	$25	$50

METROPOLITAN
Made by Crescent for Siegel Cooper Co., New York City, c. 1900. See Crescent Fire Arms Co., Shotgun, Double Barrel, Side-by-Side; Shotgun, Singleshot.

METROPOLITAN POLICE
Made by Norwich Falls Pistol Co., Norwich, Conn., c. 1885.

HANDGUN, REVOLVER

	Fair	V. Good	Excellent
.32 Short R.F., 5 Shot, Spur Trigger, Solid Frame, Single Action, *Antique*	75	125	175

METZGER, J.
Lancaster, Pa., c. 1728. See Kentucky Rifles.

MEUHIRTER, S.
See Kentucky Rifles.

MEXICAN MILITARY

HANDGUN, SEMI-AUTOMATIC

	Fair	V. Good	Excellent
Obregon, .45 ACP, Clip Fed, Military, *Modern*	800	1750	2000

RIFLE, BOLT ACTION

	Fair	V. Good	Excellent
M1902 Mauser, 7mm, Military, *Curio*	150	275	300
M1936 Mauser, 7mm, Military, *Curio*	150	250	275

RIFLE, SEMI-AUTOMATIC

	Fair	V. Good	Excellent
M1908 Mondragon, 7mm, Clip Fed, S.I.G., *Curio*	1100	2500	3000

MIDLAND
Imported from England by Jana International, c. 1973.

RIFLE, BOLT ACTION

	Fair	V. Good	Excellent
Midland, Various Calibers, Checkered Stock, Open Sights, *Modern*	100	225	275

MIIDA
Tradename of Marubeni America Corp. on Japanese shotguns.

SHOTGUN, DOUBLE BARREL, OVER-UNDER

	Fair	V. Good	Excellent
Model 612, 12 Gauge, Field Grade, Checkered Stock, Light Engraving, Single Selective Trigger, Vent Rib, *Modern*	$350	$700	$850
Model 2100, 12 Gauge, Skeet Grade, Checkered Stock, Engraved, Single Selective Trigger, Vent Rib, *Modern*	400	800	850
Model 2200 S, 12 Gauge, Skeet Grade, Checkered Stock, Engraved, Single Selective Trigger, Wide Vent Rib, *Modern*	400	900	1000
Model 2200 T, 12 Gauge, Trap Grade, Checkered Stock, Engraved, Single Selective Trigger, Wide Vent Rib, *Modern*	450	1000	1200
Model 2300 S, 12 Gauge, Skeet Grade, Fancy Wood, Engraved, Single Selective Trigger, Vent Rib, *Modern*	500	1100	1350
Model 2300 T, 12 Gauge, Trap Grade, Fancy Wood, Engraved, Single Selective Trigger, Vent Rib, *Modern*	700	1400	1650
Model Grandee, 12 Gauge, Fancy Engraving, Fancy Wood, Gold Inlays, Single Selective Trigger, Vent Rib, *Modern*	800	1750	2000

MIKROS
Tradename of Manufacture d'Armes Des Pyrenees, Hendaye, France, 1934–1939, 1958 to date.

HANDGUN, SEMI-AUTOMATIC

	Fair	V. Good	Excellent
6.35mm, Clip Fed, Magazine Disconnect, *Modern*	75	150	175
7.65mm, Clip Fed, Magazine Disconnect, *Modern*	75	150	175
KE, .22 Short R.F., Clip Fed, Hammer, Magazine Disconnect, 2" Barrel, *Modern*	75	125	150
KE, .22 Short R.F., Clip Fed, Hammer, Magazine Disconnect, 4" Barrel, *Modern*	75	125	150
KE, .22 Short R.F., Clip Fed, Hammer, Magazine Disconnect, 2" Barrel, Lightweight, *Modern*	50	100	125
KE, .22 Short R.F., Clip Fed, Hammer, Magazine Disconnect, 4" Barrel, Lightweight, *Modern*	50	100	125
KN, .25 ACP, Clip Fed, Hammer, Magazine Disconnect, 2" Barrel, *Modern*	50	100	125

	Fair	V. Good	Excellent
KN, .25 ACP, Clip Fed, Hammer, Magazine Disconnect, 2" Barrel, Lightweight, *Modern*	$50	$100	$125

MILITARY

Retolaza Hermanos, Eibar, Spain, c. 1915.

HANDGUN, SEMI-AUTOMATIC

	Fair	V. Good	Excellent
Model 1914, 7.65mm, Clip Fed, *Curio*	75	125	150

MILLER, MATHIAS

Easton, Pa. 1771–1788. See Kentucky Rifles.

MILLS, BENJAMIN

Charlottesville, N.C. 1784–1790, 1790–1814 at Harrodsburg, Ky. See Kentucky Rifles, U.S. Military.

MINNEAPOLIS FIREARMS CO.

Minneapolis, Minn., c. 1883.

HANDGUN, PALM PISTOL

	Fair	V. Good	Excellent
The Protector, .32 Extra Short R.F., Nickel Plated, *Antique*	500	1300	1500

MIQUELET-LOCK EXAMPLES

HANDGUN, MIQUELET-LOCK

	Fair	V. Good	Excellent
.52 Arabian, Holster Pistol, Tapered Round Barrel, Low Quality, *Antique*	150	300	350
.55, Russian Cossack Type, Tapered Round Barrel, Steel Furniture, Silver Furniture, *Antique*	350	700	850
Central Italian 1700s, Holster Pistol, Brass Furniture, Brass Overlay Stock, Medium Quality, *Antique*	900	2250	2500
Pair Cominazzo Early 1700s, Steel Inlay, Medium Quality, Holster Pistol, *Antique*	1400	3250	3500
Pair Late 1700s, Pocket Pistol, Medium Quality, Brass Furniture, Light Ornamentation, *Antique*	800	1750	2000
Pair Spanish Late 1600s, Belt Hook, Brass Overlay Stock, High Quality, *Antique*			Rare
Ripoll Type Late 1600s, Blunderbuss, Brass Inlay, *Antique*	1900	4250	4500
Ripoll Type Late 1600s, Blunderbuss, Silver Inlay, *Antique*	3100	7000	7500

RIFLE, MIQUELET—LOCK

	Fair	V. Good	Excellent
Mid-Eastern, Gold Inlays, Cannon Barrel, Front & Rear Bead Sights, Silver Overlay Stock, Silver Furniture, *Antique*	$1600	$3500	$3750
Mid-Eastern 1700s, Damascus Barrel, Gold Inlays, Many Semi-Precious Gem Inlays, Silver Furniture, Ornate, *Antique*	3100	6500	7500

MIROKU

Tokyo, Japan.

HANDGUN, REVOLVER

	Fair	V. Good	Excellent
Model 6, .38 Spec., Double Action, Swing-Out Cylinder, *Modern*	75	125	150

RIFLE, LEVER ACTION

	Fair	V. Good	Excellent
.22 L.R.R.F., Tube Feed, Plain, *Modern*	100	225	250

Miroku .22 Lever Action

	Fair	V. Good	Excellent
Center Fire, Various Calibers, Checkered Stock, Clip Fed, *Modern*	100	200	225

RIFLE, SEMI-AUTOMATIC

	Fair	V. Good	Excellent
.22 L.R.R.F., Takedown, Tube Feed Through Butt, *Modern*	100	175	200

Miroku .22 Auto

RIFLE, SINGLESHOT

	Fair	V. Good	Excellent
Model 78, Various Calibers, Checkered Stock, Falling Block, *Modern*	150	325	350

SHOTGUN, DOUBLE BARREL, OVER-UNDER

	Fair	V. Good	Excellent
Model 3800, 12 Ga., Checkered Stock, Vent Rib, *Modern*	200	425	475
Model H.S.W. DeLuxe, 12 Ga., Checkered Stock, Vent Rib, Engraved, *Modern*	400	800	950

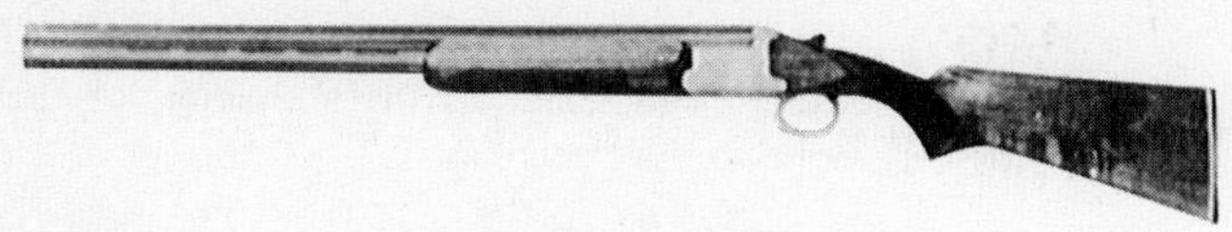

Miroku Model 3800

MISSISSIPPI VALLEY ARMS CO.

Made by Crescent for Shapleigh Hardware, St. Louis, Mo. See Crescent Fire Arms Co., Shotgun, Double Barrel, Side-by-Side; Shotgun, Singleshot.

MITCHELL ARMS

	Fair	V. Good	Excellent
HANDGUN, DOUBLE BARREL, OVER-UNDER			
Derringer, .357 Magnum, Spur Trigger, *Modern*	$75	$125	$150
HANDGUN, REVOLVER			
Army, Various Calibers, Single Action, Western Style, *Modern*	125	175	225

MITRAILLEUSE

Mre. de Armes et Cycles de St. Etienne, St. Etienne, France, c. 1893-1897.

	Fair	V. Good	Excellent
HANDGUN, PALM PISTOL			
Mitrailleuse, 8mm, Engraved, Nickel Plated, *Antique*	300	600	700

MOHAWK

Made by Crescent for Blish, Mize & Stillman, c. 1900. See Crescent Fire Arms Co., Shotgun, Double Barrel, Side-by-Side; Shotgun, Singleshot.

MOLL, DAVID

Hellerstown, Pa. 1814–1833. See Kentucky Rifles.

MOLL, JOHN

Hellerstown, Pa. 1770–1794. See Kentucky Rifles.

MOLL, JOHN JR.

Hellerstown, Pa. 1794–1824. See Kentucky Rifles.

MOLL, JOHN III

Hellerstown, Pa. 1824–1863. See Kentucky Rifles.

MOLL, PETER

Hellerstown, Pa. 1804–1833 with Brother John Moll Jr. Made some of the finest Kentucky Rifles in Pa. See Kentucky Rifles.

MONARCH

c. 1880.

	Fair	V. Good	Excellent
HANDGUN, REVOLVER			
.32 Short R.F., 5 Shot, Spur Trigger, Solid Frame, Single Action, *Antique*	$50	$100	$150

MONARCH

Made by Hopkins & Allen, c. 1880.

	Fair	V. Good	Excellent
HANDGUN, REVOLVER			
#1, .22 Short R.F., 7 Shot, Spur Trigger, Solid Frame, Single Action, *Antique*	50	100	150
#2, .32 Short R.F., 5 Shot, Spur Trigger, Solid Frame, Single Action, *Antique*	75	125	175
#3, .38 Short R.F., 5 Shot, Spur Trigger, Solid Frame, Single Action, *Antique*	75	125	175
#4, .41 Short R.F., 5 Shot, Spur Trigger, Solid Frame, Single Action, *Antique*	100	175	200

MONDIAL

Gaspar Arrizaga, Eibar, Spain.

	Fair	V. Good	Excellent
HANDGUN, SEMI-AUTOMATIC			
Model 1, 6.35mm, Clip Fed, Grip Safety, Magazine Disconnect, *Modern*	100	200	250
Model 2, 6.35mm, Clip Fed, Blue, *Modern*	75	150	200

Mondial Model 2

MONITOR

Made by Stevens Arms.

	Fair	V. Good	Excellent
SHOTGUN, DOUBLE BARREL, SIDE-BY-SIDE			
Model 311, Various Gauges, Hammerless, Steel Barrel, *Modern*	75	125	175
SHOTGUN, SINGLESHOT			
Model 90, Various Gauges, Takedown, Automatic Ejector, Plain, Hammer, *Modern*	25	50	75

Fair V. Good Excellent

MOORE PATENT FIREARMS CO.

Brooklyn, N.Y. 1863–1883. Since the teat-fire metallic cartridge had a relatively short presence on the gun market, Moore revolvers tend to be found in excellent condition. A standard feature was the presence of engraving, and sometimes of etched decoration (the latter on the cylinders, the former on the frames). Moore derringers were held in high regard, and the company was succeeded by the National, which in turn was bought out by the Colt Company (1870), which continued the production of its own First and Second Model derringer pistols. Moore firearms, therefore, have a direct association with the Colt Company, and some Colt enthusiasts include examples in their collections.

HANDGUN, REVOLVER

.32 T.F., Spur Trigger, Single Action, Brass Frame, No Extractor, *Antique* $150 $300 $450

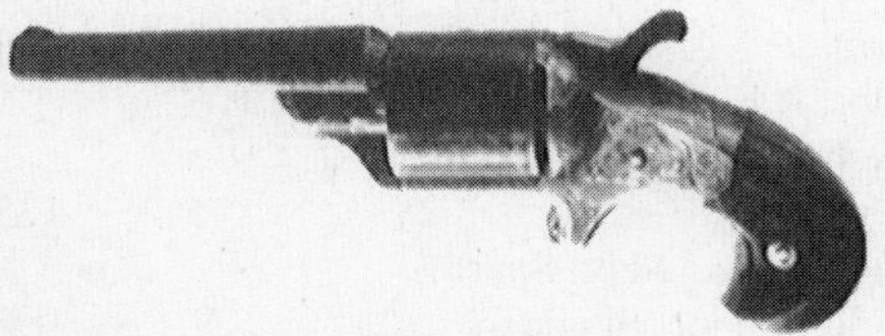

Moore .32 R.F

Williamson's Patent, .32 T.F., Brass Frame, Hook Extractor, *Antique* . . . 150 350 500

HANDGUN, SINGLESHOT

.41 Short R.F., Derringer, Brass Frame, *Antique* 300 700 850

MORRONE

Rhode Island Arms Co., Hope Valley, R.I., c. 1951.

SHOTGUN, DOUBLE BARREL, OVER-UNDER

Model 46, 12 Ga., Single Trigger, Plain Barrels, Checkered Stock, *Modern* 350 750 950

Model 46, 20 Ga., Single Trigger, Vent Rib, Checkered Stock, *Modern* 450 1050 1250

MORTIMER, H. W. & SON

London, England, 1800–1802.

HANDGUN, FLINTLOCK

.45, Barrel Duckfoot, Pocket Pistol, Steel Barrel and Frame, Plain, *Antique* 1900 4000 4500

MOSSBERG, O. F. & SONS

New Haven, Conn. 1919 to date. Fitchburg & Chicopee Falls, Mass, 1892–1919 as Oscar F. Mossberg. Interest in Mossberg firearms among collectors was given a boost by publication of *Mossberg—More Gun for the Money* by Victor and Cheryl Halvin.

Fair V. Good Excellent

The Halvins also were instrumental in the formation of the National Mossberg Collectors Association.

HANDGUN, MANUAL REPEATER

Brownie, .22 L.R.R.F., Top Break, Double Action, Rotating Firing Pin, 4 Barrels, 4 Shot, *Modern* $100 $160 $200

HANDGUN, REVOLVER

Abilene, .357 Mag., Single Action, Western Style, Adjustable Sights, Various Barrel Lengths, *Modern* . . 150 275 325

Abilene, .44 Mag., Single Action, Western Style, Adjustable Sights, Various Barrel Lengths, *Modern* . . 150 300 450

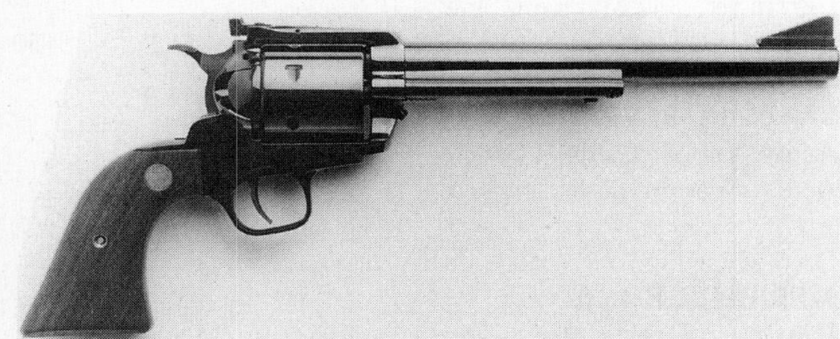

Mossberg Abilene, .44 Magnum

Abilene Silhouette, .357 Mag., Single Action, Western Style, Adjustable Sights, 10" Barrel, *Modern* 150 325 375

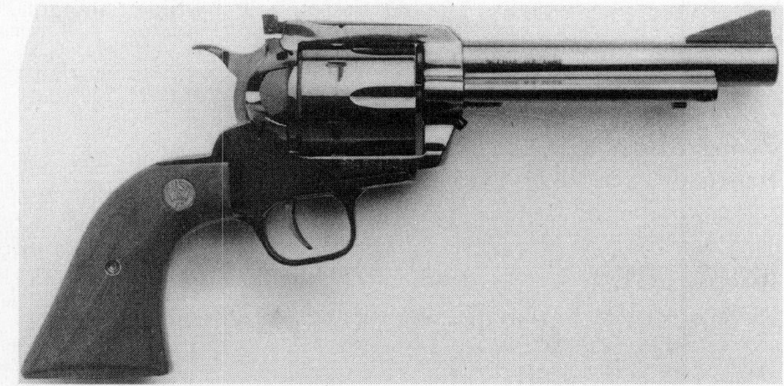

Mossberg Abilene, .357 Magnum

RIFLE, BOLT ACTION

Model 10, .22 L.R.R.F., Singleshot, Takedown, *Modern* 50 75 100

Model 14, .22 L.R.R.F., Singleshot, Takedown, Peep Sights, *Modern* . . 50 75 100

Model 140B, .22 L.R.R.F., Clip Fed, Peep Sights, Monte Carlo Stock, *Modern* 50 100 150

	Fair	V. Good	Excellent
Model 140K, .22 L.R.R.F., Clip Fed, Open Rear Sights, Monte Carlo Stock, *Modern*	$50	$75	$100
Model 142A, .22 L.R.R.F., Clip Fed, Carbine, Monte Carlo Stock, Peep Sights, *Modern*	75	125	150
Model 142A, .22 L.R.R.F., Clip Fed, Peep Sights, *Modern*	75	100	125
Model 142K, .22 L.R.R.F., Clip Fed, Carbine, Monte Carlo Stock, *Modern*	75	100	125
Model 142K, .22 L.R.R.F., Clip Fed, Open Rear Sights, *Modern*	50	75	100
Model 144, .22 L.R.R.F., Clip Fed, Heavy Barrel, Target Stock, Target Sights, *Modern*	75	150	175
Model 144LS, .22 L.R.R.F., Clip Fed, Heavy Barrel, Lyman Sights, Target Stock, *Modern*	125	175	225
Model 146B, .22 L.R.R.F., Takedown, Tube Feed, Monte Carlo Stock, Peep Sights, *Modern*	75	125	150
Model 20, .22 L.R.R.F., Singleshot, Takedown, *Modern*	50	75	100
Model 25, .22 L.R.R.F., Singleshot, Takedown, Peep Sights, *Modern*	50	75	100
Model 25A, .22 L.R.R.F., Singleshot, Takedown, Peep Sights, *Modern*	75	100	125
Model 26B, .22 L.R.R.F., Singleshot, Takedown, Peep Sights, *Modern*	50	75	100
Model 26C, .22 L.R.R.F., Singleshot, Takedown, Open Rear Sight, *Modern*	50	75	100
Model 30, .22 L.R.R.F., Singleshot, Takedown, Peep Sights, *Modern*	50	75	100
Model 320B, .22 L.R.R.F., Singleshot, Peep Sights, *Modern*	75	100	125
Model 320K, .22 L.R.R.F., Singleshot, Open Rear Sight, Monte Carlo Stock, *Modern*	50	75	100
Model 321K, .22 L.R.R.F., Singleshot, Open Rear Sight, *Modern*	50	75	100
Model 340B, .22 L.R.R.F., Clip Fed, Peep Sights, *Modern*	75	100	125
Model 340K, .22 L.R.R.F., Clip Fed, Open Rear Sight, *Modern*	50	75	100
Model 340M, .22 L.R.R.F., Clip Fed, Full-Stocked, Carbine, *Modern*	125	175	225
Model 341, .22 L.R.R.F., Clip Fed, Open Rear Sight, *Modern*	50	75	100
Model 342K, .22 L.R.R.F., Clip Fed, Open Rear Sight, *Modern*	50	75	100
Model 346B, .22 L.R.R.F., Tube Feed, Peep Sights, Monte Carlo Stock, *Modern*	75	100	125
Model 346K, .22 L.R.R.F., Tube Feed, Monte Carlo Stock, Open Rear Sight, *Modern*	75	100	125
Model 352K, .22 L.R.R.F., Clip Fed, Monte Carlo Stock, Open Rear Sight, Carbine, *Modern*	$50	$75	$100
Model 430, .22 L.R.R.F., Tube Feed, Monte Carlo Stock, Checkered Stock, Open Rear Sight, *Modern*	50	75	100
Model 432, .22 L.R.R.F., Tube Feed, Western Style, Carbine, *Modern*	50	75	100
Model 50, .22 L.R.R.F., Takedown, Tube Feed, Open Rear Sight, *Modern*	75	125	150
Model 51, .22 L.R.R.F., Takedown, Tube Feed, Peep Sight, *Modern*	75	125	150
Model 51M, .22 L.R.R.F., Takedown, Tube Feed, Peep Sight, Full-Stocked, *Modern*	75	125	150

RIFLE, LEVER ACTION

	Fair	V. Good	Excellent
Model 400, .22 L.R.R.F., Tube Feed, Open Rear Sight, *Modern*	100	150	175
Model 402, .22 L.R.R.F., Tube Feed, Open Rear Sight, Monte Carlo Stock, *Modern*	100	150	175
Model 472, Various Calibers, Pistol-Grip Stock, Tube Feed, Open Rear Sight, *Modern*	75	125	175
Model 472C, Various Calibers, Straight Grip, Tube Feed, Open Rear Sight, Carbine, *Modern*	75	125	150

RIFLE, SEMI-AUTOMATIC

	Fair	V. Good	Excellent
Model 151K, .22 L.R.R.F., Takedown, Tube Feed, Open Rear Sight, *Modern*	50	100	125
Model 151M, .22 L.R.R.F., Takedown, Tube Feed, Peep Sights, Full-Stocked, *Modern*	75	125	150
Model 152, .22 L.R.R.F., Clip Fed, Monte Carlo Stock, Peep Sights, Carbine, *Modern*	75	125	150
Model 152K, .22 L.R.R.F., Clip Fed, Monte Carlo Stock, Open Rear Sight, Carbine, *Modern*	50	100	125
Model 350K, .22 L.R.R.F., Clip Fed, Monte Carlo Stock, Open Rear Sight, *Modern*	25	50	75
Model 351C, .22 L.R.R.F., Tube Feed, Monte Carlo Stock, Open Rear Sight, Carbine, *Modern*	50	75	100
Model 351K, .22 L.R.R.F., Tube Feed, Monte Carlo Stock, Open Rear Sight, *Modern*	50	75	100
Model 35, .22 L.R.R.F., Singleshot, Target Stock, Target Sights, *Modern*	100	175	225
Model 35A, .22 L.R.R.F., Singleshot, Target Stock, Target Sights, *Modern*	100	200	225

	Fair	V. Good	Excellent
Model 35A-LS, .22 L.R.R.F., Singleshot, Target Stock, Lyman Sights, *Modern*	$100	$225	$250
Model 35B, .22 L.R.R.F., Singleshot, Target Sights, Heavy Barrel, Target Stock, *Modern*	100	225	250
Model 40, .22 L.R.R.F., Takedown, Tube Feed, Open Rear Sight, *Modern*	50	75	100
Model 42, .22 L.R.R.F., Takedown, Clip Fed, Open Rear Sight, *Modern*	50	75	100
Model 42A, .22 L.R.R.F., Takedown, Clip Fed, Peep Sights, *Modern*	50	75	100
Model 42B, .22 L.R.R.F., Takedown, 5 Shot Clip, Peep Sights, *Modern*	50	75	100
Model 42C, .22 L.R.R.F., Takedown, 5 Shot Clip, Open Rear Sight, *Modern*	50	75	100
Model 42M, .22 L.R.R.F., Takedown, Clip Fed, Full-Stocked, Peep Sights, *Modern*	75	125	150
Model 42 MB (British), .22 L.R.R.F., Takedown, Clip Fed, Full-Stocked, Peep Sights, *Modern*	75	150	175
Model 43, .22 L.R.R.F., Clip Fed, Heavy Barrel, Target Sights, Target Stock, *Modern*	75	200	225
Model 44 US, .22 L.R.R.F., Clip Fed, Target Sights, Target Stock, Heavy Barrel, *Modern*	125	250	275
Model 44B, .22 L.R.R.F., Target Stock, Clip Fed, Target Sights, *Modern*	100	200	225
Model 45, .22 L.R.R.F., Takedown, Tube Feed, Peep Sights, *Modern*	75	125	150
Model 45A, .22 L.R.R.F., Takedown, Tube Feed, Peep Sights, *Modern*	75	125	150
Model 46, .22 L.R.R.F., Takedown, Tube Feed, Peep Sights, *Modern*	75	125	150
Model 46-ALS, .22 L.R.R.F., Takedown, Tube Feed, Lyman Sights, *Modern*	100	175	200
Model 46B, .22 L.R.R.F., Takedown, Tube Feed, Peep Sights, *Modern*	50	100	125
Model 46M, .22 L.R.R.F., Takedown, Tube Feed, Full-Stocked, Peep Sights, *Modern*	50	100	125
Model 46M, .22 L.R.R.F., Takedown, Tube Feed, Open Rear Sight, *Modern*	75	125	150
Model 46T, .22 L.R.R.F., Takedown, Tube Feed, Heavy Barrel, Target Stock, Peep Sights, *Modern*	100	150	175
Model 83D, .410 Ga., Takedown, 3 Shot, *Modern*	75	150	175
Model 85D, .20 Ga., Takedown, 3 Shot, Adjustable Choke, *Modern*	50	75	100
Model L45A, .22 L.R.R.F., Takedown, Tube Feed, Open Rear Sight, *Modern*	75	150	175

	Fair	V. Good	Excellent
RIFLE, SINGLESHOT			
Model L, .22 L.R.R.F., Lever Action, Falling Block, Takedown, *Modern*	$150	$275	$325
RIFLE, SLIDE ACTION			
Model K, .22 L.R.R.F., Takedown, Tube Feed, Hammerless, *Modern*	100	175	200
Model M, .22 L.R.R.F., Takedown, Tube Feed, Hammerless, Octagon Barrel, *Modern*	100	175	225
SHOTGUN, BOLT ACTION			
Model 173, .410 Ga., Takedown, Singleshot, *Modern*	50	75	100
Model 173Y, .410 Ga., Clip Fed, Singleshot, *Modern*	50	75	100
Model 183D, .410 Ga., Takedown, 3 Shot, *Modern*	50	75	100
Model 183K, .410 Ga., Takedown, Adjustable Choke, Clip Fed, *Modern*	50	75	100
Model 183T, .410 Ga., Clip Fed, *Modern*	50	75	100
Model 185D, 20 Ga., Takedown, 3 Shot, *Modern*	50	75	100
Model 185K, 20 Ga., Takedown, 3 Shot, Adjustable Choke, *Modern*	50	75	100
Model 190D, 16 Ga., Takedown, Clip Fed, *Modern*	50	75	100
Model 190K, 16 Ga., Takedown, Adjustable Choke, Clip Fed, *Modern*	50	75	100
Model 195D, 12 Ga., Takedown, Clip Fed, *Modern*	50	75	100
Model 195K, 12 Ga., Takedown, Adjustable Choke, Clip Fed, *Modern*	50	75	100
Model 385K, 20 Ga., Clip Fed, Adjustable Choke, *Modern*	50	75	100
Model 385T, 12 Ga. Mag. 3", Clip Fed, Adjustable Choke, *Modern*	50	75	100
Model 390K, 16 Ga., Clip Fed, Adjustable Choke, *Modern*	50	75	100
Model 390T, 16 Ga., Clip Fed, *Modern*	50	75	100
Model 395K, 12 Ga. Mag. 3", Clip Fed, Adjustable Choke, *Modern*	50	75	100

Mossberg 395K, 12 Gauge

	Fair	V. Good	Excellent
Model 395S, 12 Ga. Mag. 3", Clip Fed, Open Rear Sight, *Modern*	50	75	100

	Fair	V. Good	Excellent
Model 395T, 12 Ga., Clip Fed, *Modern*	$50	$75	$100
Model 73, .410 Ga., Takedown, Singleshot, *Modern*	50	75	100
Model 800, Various Calibers, Open Rear Sight, Monte Carlo Stock, *Modern*	100	175	200
Model 800D, Various Calibers, Monte Carlo Stock, Checkpiece, Checkered Stock, Open Rear Sight, *Modern*	100	200	225
Model 800M, Various Calibers, Open Rear Sight, Full-Stocked, *Modern*	100	200	225
Model 800SM, Various Calibers, Scope Mounted, Monte Carlo Stock, *Modern*	100	225	250
Model 800V, Various Calibers, No Sights, Monte Carlo Stock, Heavy Barrel, *Modern*	100	200	225
Model 810, Various Calibers, Magnum Action, Open Rear Sight, Monte Carlo Stock, *Modern*	100	200	225
Model 810, Various Calibers, Open Rear Sight, Long Action, Monte Carlo Stock, *Modern*	100	200	225
Model B, .22 L.R.R.F., Singleshot, Takedown, *Modern*	25	50	75
Model L42A, .22 L.R.R.F., Takedown, Clip Fed, Peep Sights, Left-Hand, *Modern*	50	75	100
Model L43, .22 L.R.R.F., Clip Fed, Heavy Barrel, Target Sights, Target Stock, Left-Hand, *Modern*	50	125	150
Model L45A, .22 L.R.R.F., Takedown, Tube Feed, Peep Sights, *Modern*	50	100	125
Model L46A-LS, .22 L.R.R.F., Takedown, Tube Feed, Lyman Sights, Left-Hand, *Modern*	75	125	150
Model R, .22 L.R.R.F., Takedown, Tube Feed, Open Rear Sight, *Modern*	25	50	75

SHOTGUN, SLIDE ACTION

	Fair	V. Good	Excellent
Cruiser, 12 Ga., One-Hand Grip, Nickel Plated, *Modern*	75	150	175
Model 200D, 12 Ga., Clip Fed, Adjustable Choke, *Modern*	50	100	125
Model 200K, 12 Ga., Clip Fed, Adjustable Choke, *Modern*	50	100	125
Model 500 Super, Checkered Stock, Vent Rib, *Modern*	100	200	250
Model 500A, 12 Ga. Mag. 3", Field Grade, *Modern*	100	175	200
Model 500AA, 12 Ga. Mag. 3", Trap Grade, *Modern*	100	225	275
Model 500AHTD, Trap Grade, High Vent Rib, with Choke Tubes, *Modern*	150	350	425
Model 500AK, Field Grade, Adjustable Choke, *Modern*	$100	$200	$250
Model 500AKR, Field Grade, Adjustable Choke, Vent Rib, *Modern*	100	225	275
Model 500AM, Field Grade, Magnum, *Modern*	100	175	225
Model 500AMR, Field Grade, Magnum, Vent Rib, *Modern*	100	175	225
Model 500AR, Field Grade, Vent Rib, *Modern*	100	175	225
Model 500AS, Field Grade, Open Rear Sight, *Modern*	100	200	250
Model 500ATR, Trap Grade, Vent Rib, *Modern*	100	200	250
Model 500B, 16 Ga., Field Grade, *Modern*	100	200	250
Model 500BK, 16 Ga., Adjustable Choke, *Modern*	100	175	225
Model 500BS, 16 Ga., Open Rear Sight, *Modern*	100	175	225
Model 500C, 20 Ga., Field Grade, *Modern*	100	175	225
Model 500CK, 20 Ga., Field Grade, Adjustable Choke, *Modern*	100	175	225
Model 500CKR, 20 Ga., Field Grade, Vent Rib, Adjustable Choke, *Modern*	100	175	225
Model 500CR, 20 Ga., Field Grade, Vent Rib, *Modern*	100	175	225
Model 500CS, 20 Ga., Field Grade, Open Rear Sight, *Modern*	100	200	250
Model 500E, .410 Ga., Field Grade, *Modern*	100	175	225
Model 500EK, .410 Ga., Field Grade, Adjustable Choke, *Modern*	100	200	250
Model 500EKR, .410 Ga., Field Grade, Vent Rib, Adjustable Choke, *Modern*	100	175	225
Model 500ER, .410 Ga., Field Grade, Vent Rib, *Modern*	100	175	225

MOSTER, GEO.

Lancaster, Pa. 1771–1779. See Kentucky Rifles and Pistols.

MOUNTAIN EAGLE

Made by Hopkins & Allen, c. 1880.

HANDGUN, REVOLVER

	Fair	V. Good	Excellent
.32 Short R.F., 5 Shot, Spur Trigger, Solid Frame, Single Action, *Antique*	50	100	150

M.S.

Modesto Santos, Eibar, Spain, c. 1920.

	Fair	V. Good	Excellent
HANDGUN, SEMI-AUTOMATIC			
Action, 7.65mm, Clip Fed, Blue, *Curio*	$75	$125	$150
Model 1920, .25 ACP, Clip Fed, Blue, *Curio*	50	100	125

MT. VERNON ARMS

Belgium, c. 1900.

	Fair	V. Good	Excellent
SHOTGUN, DOUBLE BARREL, SIDE-BY-SIDE			
Various Gauges, Hammerless, Damascus Barrel, *Modern*	100	150	175
Various Gauges, Hammerless, Steel Barrel, *Modern*	100	175	200
Various Gauges, Outside Hammers, Damascus Barrel, *Curio*	100	150	175
Various Gauges, Outside Hammers, Steel Barrel, *Modern*	100	150	175
SHOTGUN, SINGLESHOT			
Various Gauges, Hammer, Steel Barrel, *Modern*	25	50	75

MUGICA

Jose Mugica, Eibar, Spain, tradename on Llama pistols. See Llama for equivalent models.

MUSGRAVE

South Africa.

	Fair	V. Good	Excellent
RIFLE, BOLT ACTION			
Mk. III, Various Calibers, Checkered Stock, *Modern*	150	275	325
Premier NR5, Various Calibers, Checkered Stock, *Modern*	150	300	350
Valiant NR6, Various Calibers, Checkered Stock, *Modern*	$150	$250	$300

MUSKETEER

Tradename used by Firearms International, Washington, D.C., c. 1968.

	Fair	V. Good	Excellent
RIFLE, BOLT ACTION			
Carbine, Various Calibers, Monte Carlo Stock, Checkered Stock, Sling Swivels, *Modern*	150	300	325
Deluxe, Various Calibers, Monte Carlo Stock, Checkered Stock, Sling Swivels, *Modern*	150	325	350
Mannlicher, Various Calibers, Full Stock, *Modern*	150	275	325
Sporter, Various Calibers, Monte Carlo Stock, Checkered Stock, Sling Swivels, *Modern*	150	275	300

MUTTI, GEROLIMO

Brescia, c. 1680.

	Fair	V. Good	Excellent
HANDGUN, SNAPHAUNCE			
Pair, Belt Pistol, Brass Mounts, Engraved, Ornate, *Antique*	5000	13000	15000

MUTTI, GIESU

Brescia, c. 1790.

	Fair	V. Good	Excellent
HANDGUN, SNAPHAUNCE			
Pair, Engraved, Belt Hook, Medium Ornamentation, *Antique*	4000	8500	10000

N

NAPOLEON

Made by Thomas Ryan, Jr., Pistol Mfg. Co., c. 1870–1876.

HANDGUN, REVOLVER

	Fair	V. Good	Excellent
.22 Short R.F., 7 Shot, Spur Trigger, Solid Frame, Single Action, *Antique*	$75	$125	$150
.32 Short R.F., 5 Shot, Spur Trigger, Solid Frame, Single Action, *Antique*	75	150	175

NATIONAL

Made by Norwich Falls Pistol Co., c. 1880.

HANDGUN, REVOLVER

	Fair	V. Good	Excellent
.32 Short R.F., 5 Shot, Spur Trigger, Solid Frame, Single Action, *Antique*	75	150	200
.38 Short R.F., 5 Shot, Spur Trigger, Solid Frame, Single Action, *Antique*	75	150	200

HANDGUN, SINGLESHOT

	Fair	V. Good	Excellent
.41 Short R.F., Derringer, All Metal, Light Engraving, *Antique*	100	225	600

NATIONAL ARMS CO.

Made by Crescent, c. 1900. See Crescent Fire Arms Co., Shotgun, Double Barrel, Side-by-Side; Shotgun, Singleshot.

NATIONAL ORDNANCE

South El Monte, Calif.

RIFLE, BOLT ACTION

	Fair	V. Good	Excellent
1903A3, .30-06 Springfield, *Modern*	75	125	150

RIFLE, SEMI-AUTOMATIC

	Fair	V. Good	Excellent
Garand, .30-06 Springfield, *Modern*	200	400	550
M-1 Carbine, .30 Carbine, Clip Fed, *Modern*	75	125	150
M-1 Carbine, .30 Carbine, Clip Fed, Folding Stock, Reweld, *Modern*	75	150	175
Tanker Garand, .308 Win., Reweld, Military, *Modern*	200	400	500

NAVY ARMS

Ridgefield, N.J. 1959-Date. Factory opened up in Martinsburg, W. Va. in early 1990s. A true pioneer in and unequivocal advocate of blackpowder shooting. Val Forgett deserves credit for much of the revival of muzzle-loaders in contemporary shooting and collecting. Just prior to the Civil War centennial, Forgett was confident that the shooting public would welcome accurately made replicas of bygone firearms. His Navy Arms Co. has been in the vanguard of this movement ever since. The extraordinary array of the company's product line can only be fully appreciated by visiting the company store, in Ridgefield, New Jersey, by carefully scrutinizing Navy Arms Co. color catalogs, or by visiting the Navy Arms and Gibbs Rifle factory site in Martinsburg, West Virginia. The Governor's Place, Williamsburg, Virginia, was outfitted with panoplies of flintlock pistols and muskets, and of swords, by Val Forgett and Navy Arms Co. The brilliant displays of these guns were instrumental in re-creating the original atmosphere and ambiance of one of colonial America's most striking public architectural landmarks.

HANDGUN, FLINTLOCK

	Fair	V. Good	Excellent
.44 "Kentucky," Belt Pistol. Brass Furniture, Brass Barrel, Reproduction	$100	$200	$250
.44 "Kentucky," Belt Pistol. Brass Furniture, Reproduction	100	200	250
.577 Scotch Black Watch, Military, Belt Pistol, all Metal, Reproduction	100	225	275
.69 M1763 Charleville, Military, Belt Pistol, Reproduction	150	375	450
.69 M1763 Charleville, Military, Belt Pistol, Reproduction	100	225	275
.69 M1777 Charleville, Military, Belt Pistol, Reproduction	100	225	275
.69 Tower, Military, Belt Pistol, Reproduction	50	100	125

A Engraving Pistol, Add $115.00-$225.00
A Engraving Rifle, Add $145.00-$300.00
B Engraving Pistol, Add $140.00-$300.00
B Engraving Rifle, Add $215.00-$450.00
C Engraving Pistol, Add $265.00-$500.00
C Engraving Rifle, Add $495.00-$1000.00
Presentation Case Only, Add $25.00-$50.00
Silver Plating, Add $95.00-$250.00
Tiffany Grips Only, Add $155.00-$350.00

HANDGUN, PERCUSSION

	Fair	V. Good	Excellent
.36 M1851 New Navy, Revolver, Brass Grip Frame, Reproduction	100	200	250
.36 M1851 New Navy, Revolver, Silver-Plated Grip Frame, Reproduction	100	200	250

	Fair	V. Good	Excellent
.36 M1853, Revolver, Pocket Pistol, 4½" Barrel, Reproduction	$100	$200	$250
.36 M1853, Revolver, Pocket Pistol, 5½" Barrel, Reproduction	100	200	250
.36 M1853, Revolver, Pocket Pistol, 6½" Barrel, Reproduction	100	200	250
.36 M1860 Reb, Revolver, Brass Frame, Reproduction	100	200	250
.36 M1860 Sheriff, Revolver, Brass Frame, Reproduction	100	200	250
.36 M1861 Navy, Revolver, Engraved Cylinder, Reproduction	100	200	250
.36 M1861 Navy, Revolver, Fluted Cylinder, Reproduction	100	200	250
.36 M1861, Revolver, Sheriff's Model, with Short Barrel, Reproduction	100	200	250
.36 M1862 Police, Revolver, 5 Shot, Brass Grip Frame, Cased with Accessories, Reproduction	100	250	300
.36 M1862 Police, Revolver, 5 Shot, Brass Grip Frame, 4½" Barrel, Reproduction	100	200	250
.36 M1862 Police, Revolver, 5 Shot, Brass Grip Frame, 5½" Barrel, Reproduction	100	200	250
.36 M1862 Police, Revolver, 5 Shot, Brass Grip Frame, 6½" Barrel, Reproduction	100	200	250
.36 M1862 Police, Revolver, Fancy Engraving, Silver Plated, Gold Plated, Reproduction	100	800	950
.36 M1863, Revolver, Sheriff's Model, with Short Barrel, Reproduction	100	200	250
.36 Remington, Revolver, Target Pistol, Adjustable Sights, Reproduction	100	225	275
.36 Spiller & Burr, Revolver, Solid Frame, Reproduction	100	175	225
.44 "Kentucky," Belt Pistol, Brass Furniture, Brass Barrel, Reproduction	100	225	275
.44 "Kentucky," Belt Pistol, Brass Furniture, Reproduction	100	175	225
.44 First Model Dragoon, Revolver, Brass Grip Frame, Reproduction	100	225	275
.44 M1847 Walker, Revolver, Brass Grip Frame, Engraved, Gold Inlays, Reproduction	200	450	550
.44 M1847 Walker, Revolver, Brass Grip Frame, Reproduction	100	250	300
.44 M1860 Army, Revolver, Engraved Cylinder, Reproduction	75	150	200
.44 M1860 Army, Revolver, Fluted Cylinder, Reproduction	75	150	200
.44 M1860 Reb, Revolver, Shoulder Stock Only, Reproduction	25	50	75
.44 M1860 Sheriff, Revolver, Brass Frame, Reproduction	100	125	150
.44 M1860, Revolver, Sheriff's Model, with Short Barrel, Reproduction	100	175	225

	Fair	V. Good	Excellent
.44 Remington Army, Revolver, Nickel Plated, Reproduction	$100	$225	$275
.44 Remington, Revolver, Solid Frame, Reproduction	100	150	175
.44 Remington, Revolver, Stainless Steel, Reproduction	100	225	275

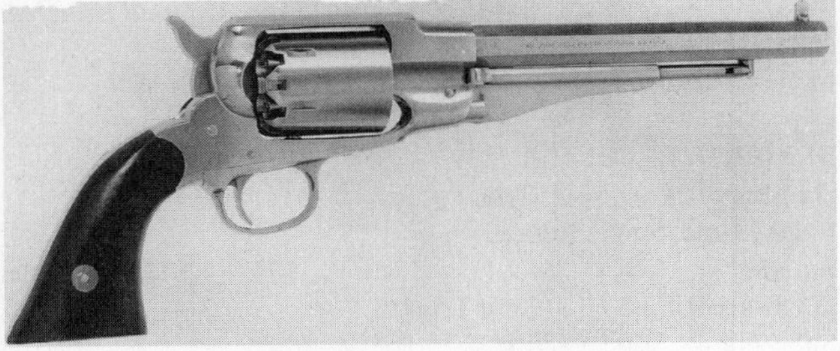

Navy Arms .44 Remington Stainless

	Fair	V. Good	Excellent
.44 Remington, Revolver, Target Pistol, Adjustable Sights, Reproduction	100	225	275
.44 Second Model, Dragoon, Revolver, Brass Grip Frame, Reproduction	150	300	375
.44 Third Model Dragoon, Revolver, Brass Grip Frame, with Detachable Shoulder Stock, Reproduction	150	350	425
.44 Third Model Dragoon, Revolver, Brass Grip Frame, Reproduction	150	325	375
.44 Third Model Dragoon, Revolver, Buntline, with Detachable Shoulder Stock, Reproduction	150	350	425
.58 M1806, Harper's Ferry, Brass Furniture, Military, Belt Pistol, Reproduction	75	150	175
.58 M1855, Harper's Ferry, Holster Pistol, Military, with Detachable Shoulder Stock, Reproduction	100	200	250

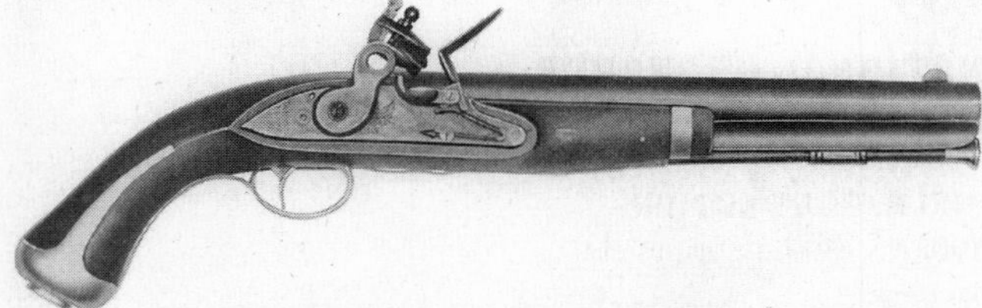

Navy Arms Harper's Ferry 1806

	Fair	V. Good	Excellent
.58 M1855, Harper's Ferry, Shoulder Stock Only	25	50	75

HANDGUN, REVOLVER

	Fair	V. Good	Excellent
Cattleman, Various Calibers, Color Case Hardened Frame, Single Action, Western Style, *Modern*	150	300	350

	Fair	V. Good	Excellent
Cattleman Buntline, .45 Colt, Color Case Hardened Frame, Single Action, Western Style, Adjustable Sights, with Detachable Shoulder Stock, *Modern*	$200	$425	$400
Cattleman Carbine, Various Calibers, Color Case Hardened Frame, Single Action, Western Style, Adjustable Sights, *Modern*	200	400	475
Cattleman Target, .357 Magnum, Color Case Hardened Frame, Single Action, Western Style, Adjustable Sights, with Detachable Shoulder Stock, *Modern*	150	325	375
M1875 Remington, .357 Magnum, Color Case Hardened Frame, Western Style, Single Action, *Modern*	125	250	300
M1875 Remington, .357 Magnum, Nickel Plated, Western Style, Single Action, *Modern*	150	300	350
M1875 Remington, .44-40 WCF, Color Case Hardened Frame, Western Style, Single Action, *Modern*	150	300	350
M1875 Remington, .44-40 WCF, Nickel Plated, Western Style, Single Action, *Modern*	150	325	400
M1875 Remington, .45 Colt, Color Case Hardened Frame, Western Style, Single Action, *Modern*	150	275	325
M1875 Remington, .45 Colt, Nickel Plated, Western Style, Single Action, *Modern*	150	300	350
M1875 Remington, .45 Colt, Stainless Steel, Western Style, Single Action, *Modern*	150	325	375

HANDGUN, SINGLESHOT

	Fair	V. Good	Excellent
Rolling Block, .22 Hornet, Half-Octagon Barrel, Color Case Hardened Frame, Adjustable Sights, *Modern*	100	250	300
Rolling Block, .22 L.R.R.F., Half-Octagon Barrel, Color Case Hardened Frame, Adjustable Sights, *Modern*	100	200	250
Rolling Block, .357 Magnum, Half-Octagon Barrel, Color Case Hardened Frame, Adjustable Sights, *Modern*	100	250	300

RIFLE, BOLT ACTION

	Fair	V. Good	Excellent
Mauser '98, .45-70 Government, Carbine, Checkered Stock, *Modern*	100	225	275
Mauser '98, .45-70 Government, Checkered Stock, *Modern*	100	225	275

RIFLE, LEVER ACTION

	Fair	V. Good	Excellent
M1873 1 of 1000, .44-40 WCF, Blue Tube, Octagon Barrel, Steel Buttplate, Engraved, *Modern*	300	675	750
M1873-".101," .22 L.R.R.F., Color Case Hardened Frame, Tube Feed, Round Barrel, Steel Buttplate, Carbine, *Modern*	250	500	600
M1873-".101," .44-40 WCF, Color Case Hardened Frame, Tube Feed, Octagon Barrel, Steel Buttplate, *Modern*	$250	$550	$650
M1873-".101," .44-40 WCF, Color Case Hardened Frame, Tube Feed, Round Barrel, Steel Buttplate, Carbine, *Modern*	300	600	700
M1873-".101," Trapper, .22 L.R.R.F., Color Case Hardened Frame, Tube Feed, Round Barrel, Steel Buttplate, *Modern*	250	450	550
M1873-".101," Trapper, .44-40 WCF, Color Case Hardened Frame, Tube Feed, Round Barrel, Steel Buttplate, *Modern*	200	425	500
Yellowboy Trapper, .22 L.R.R.F., Brass Frame, Tube Feed, Round Barrel, Brass Buttplate, *Modern*	300	650	750
Yellowboy Trapper, .38 Special, Brass Frame, Tube Feed, Round Barrel, Brass Buttplate, *Modern*	300	650	750
Yellowboy Trapper, .44-40 WCF, Brass Frame, Tube Feed, Round Barrel, Brass Buttplate, *Modern*	325	700	800
Yellowboy, .22 L.R.R.F., Brass Frame, Tube Feed, Round Barrel, Brass Buttplate, Saddle-Ring Carbine, *Modern*	250	525	625
Yellowboy, .38 Special, Brass Frame, Tube Feed, Octagon Barrel, Brass Buttplate, *Modern*	250	550	650
Yellowboy, .38 Special, Brass Frame, Tube Feed, Round Barrel, Brass Buttplate, Saddle-Ring Carbine, *Modern*	300	600	700
Yellowboy, .44-40 WCF, Brass Frame, Tube Feed, Octagon Barrel, Brass Buttplate, *Modern*	300	600	700
Yellowboy, .44-40 WCF, Brass Frame, Tube Feed, Round Barrel, Brass Buttplate, Saddle-Ring Carbine, *Modern*	300	600	700

RIFLE, FLINTLOCK

	Fair	V. Good	Excellent
.45 "Kentucky," Carbine, Brass Furniture, Reproduction	150	300	350
.45 "Kentucky," Long Rifle, Brass Furniture, Reproduction	150	300	350
.58 M1803, Harper's Ferry, Brass Furniture, Military, Reproduction	150	325	400

Navy Arms .58 1803 Harper's Ferry

	Fair	V. Good	Excellent
.69 M1795 Springfield, Musket, Modern Reproduction	200	400	475

	Fair	V. Good	Excellent
.69 M1809 Springfield, Musket, Modern Reproduction	$200	$400	$475
.75 Brown Bess (Jap), Musket, Modern Reproduction	200	400	475
.75 Brown Bess, Carbine, Modern Reproduction	250	500	575
.75 Brown Bess, Musket, Modern Reproduction	250	500	575

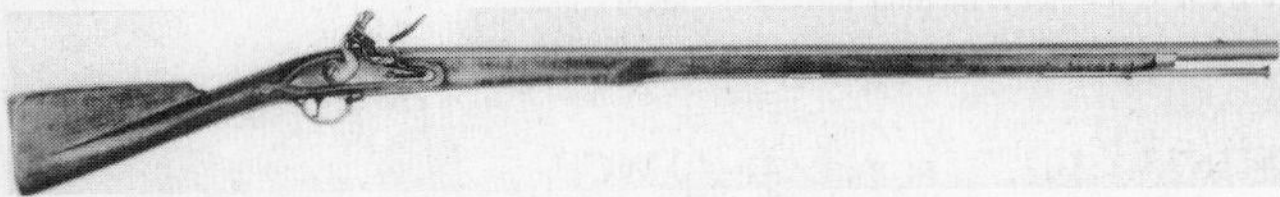

Navy Arms Brown Bess Rifle

RIFLE, PERCUSSION

	Fair	V. Good	Excellent
.44 Remington, Revolving, Carbine, Brass Furniture, Reproduction	125	200	275
.45 "Kentucky," Carbine, Brass Furniture, Reproduction	125	275	325
.45 "Kentucky," Carbine, Brass Furniture, Reproduction	125	275	325
.45 "Kentucky," Long Rifle, Brass Furniture, Reproduction	125	275	325
.45 Hawken Hurricane, Octagon Barrel, Brass Furniture, Reproduction	150	300	375
.45 Morse, Octagon Barrel, Brass Frame, Reproduction	100	200	250
.50 Hawken Hurricane, Octagon Barrel, Brass Furniture, Reproduction	150	325	375
.50 Morse, Octagon Barrel, Brass Frame, Reproduction	100	225	275
.54 Gallagher, Carbine, Military, Steel Furniture, Reproduction	150	300	375
.577 M1853 3-Band, Military, Musket, (Parker-Hale), Reproduction	150	375	450
.577 M1858 2-Band, Military, Rifled, (Parker-Hale), Reproduction	150	325	375
.577 M1861, Military, Musketoon, (Parker-Hale), Reproduction	150	325	375
.58 Buffalo Hunter, Round Barrel, Brass Furniture, Reproduction	150	300	350

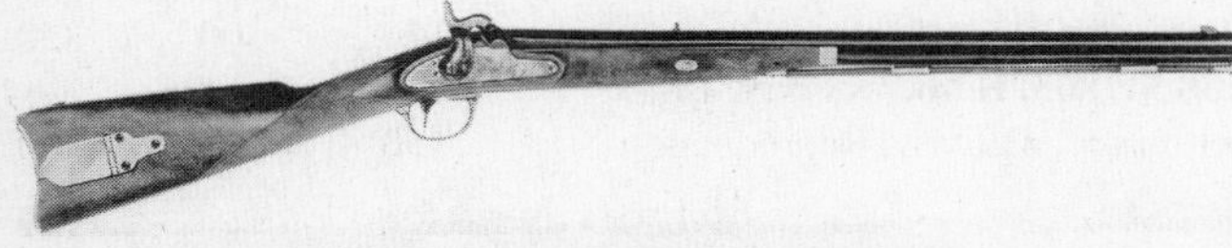

Navy Arms .58 Buffalo Hunter

	Fair	V. Good	Excellent
.58 Hawken Hunter, Octagon Barrel, Brass Furniture, Reproduction	150	325	375
.58 J.P. Murray Artillery Carbine, Brass Furniture, Military, Reproduction	$150	$300	$350
.58 M1841 Mississippi Rifle, Brass Furniture, Military, Reproduction	150	300	350
.58 M1863 Springfield, Military, Rifled, Musket, Reproduction	150	300	350

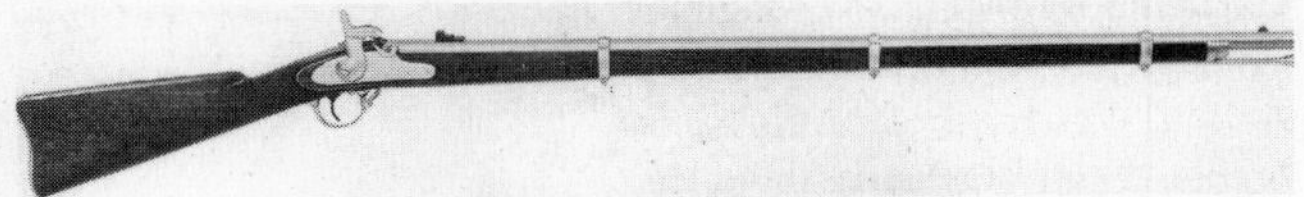

Navy Arms 1863 Springfield

	Fair	V. Good	Excellent
.58 M1864 Springfield, Military, Rifled, Musket, Reproduction	150	325	375
.58 Morse, Octagon Barrel, Brass Frame, Reproduction	150	275	325
.58 Zouave 1864, Military, Carbine, Brass Furniture, Reproduction	150	300	350
.58 Zouave, Military, Reproduction	150	300	350

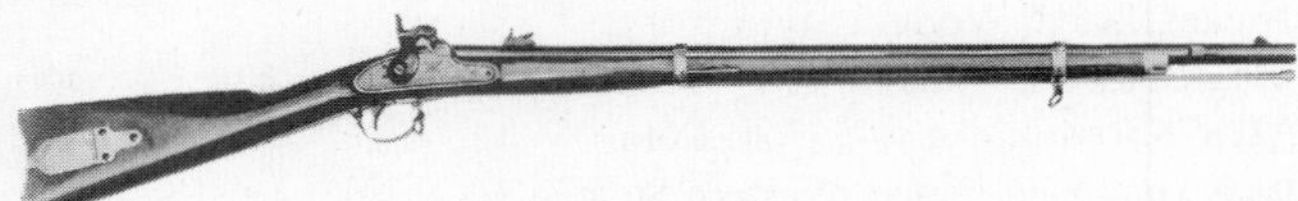

Navy Arms Zouave Rifle

RIFLE, SEMI-AUTOMATIC

	Fair	V. Good	Excellent
AP-74, .22 L.R.R.F., Clip Fed, Plastic Stock, *Modern*	75	150	175
AP-74, .22 L.R.R.F., Clip Fed, Wood Stock, *Modern*	100	175	200
AP-74, .32 ACP, Clip Fed, Plastic Stock, *Modern*	100	175	200
AP-74 Commando, .22 L.R.R.F., Clip Fed, Wood Stock, *Modern*	75	150	175

RIFLE, SINGLESHOT

	Fair	V. Good	Excellent
Buffalo, .45-70 Government, Rolling Block, Color Case Hardened Frame, Octagon Barrel, Open Rear Sights, Various Barrel Lengths, *Modern*	100	200	250
Buffalo, .45-70 Government, Rolling Block, Color Case Hardened Frame, Half-Octagon Barrel, Open Rear Sights, Various Barrel Lengths, *Modern*	100	200	250
Buffalo, .50 U.S. Carbine, Rolling Block, Color Case Hardened Frame, Octagon Barrel, Open Rear Sights, Various Barrel Lengths, *Modern*	100	200	250
Buffalo, .50 U.S. Carbine, Rolling Block, Color Case Hardened Frame, Half-Octagon Barrel, Open Rear Sights, Various Barrel Lengths, *Modern*	100	175	225

	Fair	V. Good	Excellent
Creedmore, .45-70 Government, Rolling Block, Color Case Hardened Frame, Octagon Barrel, Vernier Sights, 30" Barrel, *Modern*	$150	$350	$425
Creedmore, .45-70 Government, Rolling Block, Color Case Hardened Frame, Half-Octagon Barrel, Vernier Sights, 30" Barrel, *Modern*	150	325	375
Creedmore, .50 U.S. Carbine, Rolling Block, Color Case Hardened Frame, Octagon Barrel, Vernier Sights, 30" Barrel, *Modern*	150	325	375
Creedmore, .50 U.S. Carbine, Rolling Block, Color Case Hardened Frame, Half-Octagon Barrel, Vernier Sights, 30" Barrel, *Modern*	150	325	375
Creedmore, .50-140 Sharps, Rolling Block, Color Case Hardened Frame, Octagon Barrel, Vernier Sights, 30" Barrel, *Modern*	175	375	425
Martini, .45-70 Government, Color Case Hardened Frame, Half- Octagon Barrel, Open Rear Sight, Checkered Stock, *Modern*	200	400	450
Martini, .45-70 Government, Color Case Hardened Frame, Octagon Barrel, Open Rear Sight, Checkered Stock, *Modern*	200	400	450
Rolling Block, .22 Hornet, Carbine, Color Case Hardened Frame, Adjustable Sights, *Modern*	150	300	350
Rolling Block, .22 L.R.R.F., Carbine, Color Case Hardened Frame, Adjustable Sights, *Modern*	125	250	300
Rolling Block, .357 Magnum, Carbine, Color Case Hardened Frame, Adjustable Sights, *Modern*	125	250	300

SHOTGUN, PERCUSSION

	Fair	V. Good	Excellent
Magnum Deluxe, 12 Ga., Double Barrel, Side by Side, Outside Hammers, Checkered Stock, Reproduction	100	200	225
Morse/Navy, 12 Ga., Singleshot, Brass Frame, Reproduction	75	150	175

Navy Arms Morse Navy Shotgun

	Fair	V. Good	Excellent
Upland Deluxe, 12 Ga., Double Barrel, Side by Side, Outside Hammers, Checkered Stock, Reproduction	75	150	175
Zouave, 12 Ga., Brass Furniture, Reproduction	75	150	175

NEIHARD, PETER

Northhampton, Pa. 1785–1787. See Kentucky Rifles.

NERO

Made by Hopkins & Allen., c. 1880. Sold by C.L. Riker.

HANDGUN, REVOLVER

	Fair	V. Good	Excellent
.22 Short R.F., 7 Shot, Spur Trigger, Solid Frame, Single Action, *Antique*	$100	$200	$250
.32 Short R.F., 5 Shot, Spur Trigger, Solid Frame, Single Action, *Antique*	125	250	300

NERO

Made by J. Rupertus Arms Co., c. 1880. Sold by E. Tryon Co.

HANDGUN, REVOLVER

	Fair	V. Good	Excellent
.22 Short R.F., 7 Shot, Spur Trigger, Solid Frame, Single Action, *Antique*	125	250	275
.32 Short R.F., 5 Shot, Spur Trigger, Solid Frame, Single Action, *Antique*	150	300	325

NEW CHIEFTAIN

Made by Stevens Arms.

SHOTGUN, SINGLESHOT

	Fair	V. Good	Excellent
Model 94, Various Gauges, Takedown, Automatic Ejector, Plain, Hammer, *Modern*	25	50	75

NEW NAMBU

Shin Chuo Kogyo, Tokyo, Japan, c. 1960.

HANDGUN, REVOLVER

	Fair	V. Good	Excellent
Model 58, .38 Special, Swing-Out Cylinder, Double Action, *Modern*	75	100	125

HANDGUN, SEMI-AUTOMATIC

	Fair	V. Good	Excellent
Model 57A, 9mm Luger, Clip Fed, Blue, *Modern*	100	175	200
Model 57B, .32 ACP, Clip Fed, Blue, *Modern*	75	150	175

NEW RIVAL

Made by Crescent for Van Camp Hardware & Iron Co., Indianapolis, Ind. See Crescent Fire Arms Co., Shotgun, Double Barrel, Side-by-Side; Shotgun, Singleshot.

NEW YORK ARMS CO.

Made by Crescent for Garnet Carter Co. Tenn., c. 1900. See Crescent Fire Arms Co., Shotgun, Double Barrel, Side-by-Side; Shotgun, Singleshot.

NEW YORK PISTOL CO.

New York City, c. 1870.

HANDGUN, REVOLVER

	Fair	V. Good	Excellent
.22 Short R.F., 7 Shot, Spur Trigger, Solid Frame, Single Action, *Antique*	$75	$150	$175
.32 Short R.F., 5 Shot, Spur Trigger, Solid Frame, Single Action, *Antique*	75	125	150

NEWCOMER, JOHN

Lancaster, Pa. 1770–1772. See Kentucky Rifles.

NEWHARDT, JACOB

Allentown, Pa. 1770–1777. See Kentucky Rifles.

NEWPORT

Made by Stevens Arms.

SHOTGUN, DOUBLE BARREL, SIDE-BY-SIDE

	Fair	V. Good	Excellent
Model 311, Various Gauges, Hammerless, Steel Barrel, *Modern*	75	125	150

NEWTON ARMS CO.

Buffalo, N.Y. 1914–1918, reorganized 1918–1930 as Newton Rifle Corp.

RIFLE, BOLT ACTION

	Fair	V. Good	Excellent
1st Type, Various Calibers, Sporting Rifle, Set Trigger, Checkered Stock, Open Rear Sight, *Curio*	400	850	1000
2nd Type, Various Calibers, Sporting Rifle, Set Trigger, Checkered Stock, Open Rear Sight, *Curio*	350	750	850
Newton-Mauser, Various Calibers, Sporting Rifle, Set Trigger, Checkered Stock, Open Rear Sight, *Curio*	325	675	775

NICHOLS, JOHN

Oxford, England, 1730–1775.

HANDGUN, FLINTLOCK

	Fair	V. Good	Excellent
Holster Pistol, Engraved, Brass Furniture, High Quality, *Antique*	1300	3000	3500

NIKKO SPORTING FIREARMS

Japan. Imported by Kanematsu-Gosho U.S.A. Inc., Arlington Heights, Ill. 1958–1989. Sold in the U.S. as "Golden Eagle."

RIFLE, BOLT ACTION

	Fair	V. Good	Excellent
Model 7000, Various African Calibers, Grade 1, Checkered Stock, *Modern*	$150	$400	$575
Model 7000, Various Calibers, Grade 1, Checkered Stock, *Modern*	125	400	525

SHOTGUN, DOUBLE BARREL, OVER-UNDER

	Fair	V. Good	Excellent
Model 5000, 12 and 20 Gauge, Field Grade 2, Vent Rib, Checkered Stock, Light Engraving, Gold Overlay, *Modern*	350	775	850
Model 5000, 12 and 20 Gauge, Field Grade, Vent Rib, Checkered Stock, Light Engraving, Gold Overlay, *Modern*	300	675	750
Model 5000, 12 and 20 Gauge, Skeet Grade 2, Vent Rib, Checkered Stock, Light Engraving, Gold Overlay, *Modern*	350	800	875
Model 5000, 12 and 20 Gauge, Skeet Grade, Vent Rib, Checkered Stock, Light Engraving, Gold Overlay, *Modern*	325	700	775
Model 5000, 12 and 20 Gauge, Trap Grade 2, Vent Rib, Checkered Stock, Light Engraving, Gold Overlay, *Modern*	350	800	875
Model 5000, 12 and 20 Gauge, Trap Grade, Vent Rib, Checkered Stock, Light Engraving, Gold Overlay, *Modern*	325	700	775
Model 5000 Grandee, 12 and 20 Gauge, Field Grade 3, Vent Rib, Checkered Stock, Fancy Engraving, Gold Overlay, *Modern*	700	1750	2000
Model 5000 Grandee, 12 and 20 Gauge, Skeet Grade 3, Vent Rib, Checkered Stock, Fancy Engraving, Gold Overlay, *Modern*	800	2000	2250
Model 5000 Grandee, 12 and 20 Gauge, Trap Grade 3, Vent Rib, Checkered Stock, Fancy Engraving, Gold Overlay, *Modern*	800	2000	2250

NITRO PROOF

Made by Stevens Arms.

SHOTGUN, SINGLESHOT

	Fair	V. Good	Excellent
Model 115, Various Gauges, Hammer, Automatic Ejector, *Modern*	25	50	75

NIVA

Kohout & Spolecnost, Kydne, Czechoslovakia.

	Fair	V. Good	Excellent
HANDGUN, SEMI-AUTOMATIC			
Niva, 6.35mm, Clip Fed, Blue, *Modern*	$50	$125	$150

NOBLE

Haydenville, Mass. 1950–1971.

	Fair	V. Good	Excellent
RIFLE, BOLT ACTION			
.98 Mauser, .30-06 Springfield, Monte Carlo Stock, Open Rear Sight, *Modern*	50	100	125
Model 10, .22 L.R.R.F., Singleshot, *Modern*	15	25	50
Model 20, .22 L.R.R.F., Singleshot, *Modern*	15	25	50
Model 222, .22 L.R.R.F., Singleshot, *Modern*	25	50	75
RIFLE, LEVER ACTION			
Model 275, .22 L.R.R.F., Tube Feed, *Modern*	25	50	75
RIFLE, SEMI-AUTOMATIC			
Model 285, .22 L.R.R.F., Tube Feed, *Modern*	50	75	100
RIFLE, SLIDE ACTION			
Model 235, .22 L.R.R.F., Wood Stock, *Modern*	50	75	100
Model 33, .22 L.R.R.F., Plastic Stock, *Modern*	25	50	75
Model 33A, .22 L.R.R.F., Wood Stock, *Modern*	50	75	100
SHOTGUN, DOUBLE BARREL, SIDE-BY-SIDE			
Model 420, Various Gauges, Hammerless, Checkered Stock, Recoil Pad, *Modern*	50	125	150
Model 420EK, Various Gauges, Hammerless, Checkered Stock, Recoil Pad, Fancy Wood, *Modern*	75	150	175
Model 450E, Various Gauges, Hammerless, Checkered Stock, Recoil Pad, *Modern*	100	200	250
SHOTGUN, SEMI-AUTOMATIC			
Model 80, .410 Ga., *Modern*	50	100	150
SHOTGUN, SLIDE ACTION			
Model 160 Deergun, 12 and 20 Gauges, Peep Sights, *Modern*	25	75	125
Model 166L Deergun, 12 and 16 Gauges, Peep Sights, *Modern*	25	75	125
Model 166LP Deergun, 12 and 16 Gauges, Peep Sights, *Modern*	25	75	125
Model 200, 20 Ga., *Modern*	25	75	125
Model 200, 20 Ga., Adjustable Choke, *Modern*	25	75	125
Model 200, 20 Ga., Trap Grade, *Modern*	$25	$75	$125
Model 200, 20 Ga., Vent Rib, Adjustable Choke, *Modern*	25	75	125
Model 300, 12 Ga., *Modern*	25	75	125
Model 300, 12 Ga., Adjustable Choke, *Modern*	25	75	125
Model 300, 12 Ga., Trap Grade, *Modern*	50	100	150
Model 300, 12 Ga., Vent Rib, Adjustable Choke, *Modern*	50	125	150
Model 390, 12 Ga., Peep Sights, *Modern*	25	75	125
Model 40, 12 Ga., Hammerless, Solid Frame, Adjustable Choke, *Modern*	25	75	125
Model 400, .410 Ga., *Modern*	25	75	125
Model 400, .410 Ga., Adjustable Choke, *Modern*	25	75	125
Model 400, .410 Ga., Skeet Grade, *Modern*	25	75	125
Model 400, .410 Ga., Skeet Grade, Adjustable Choke, *Modern*	25	100	150
Model 50, 12 Ga., Hammerless, Solid Frame, *Modern*	25	50	100
Model 60, 12 and 16 Gauges, Hammerless, Solid Frame, Adjustable Choke, *Modern*	25	75	125
Model 60 RCLP, 12 and 16 Gauges, Hammerless, Solid Frame, Vent Rib, Adjustable Choke, Checkered Stock, *Modern*	25	75	125
Model 602, 20 Ga., *Modern*	25	75	125
Model 602CLP, 20 Ga., Adjustable Choke, *Modern*	25	75	125
Model 602RCLP, 20 Ga., Adjustable Choke, Vent Rib, *Modern*	25	100	150
Model 602RLP, 20 Ga., Vent Rib, *Modern*	25	75	125
Model 60ACP, 12 and 16 Gauges, Hammerless, Solid Frame, Adjustable Choke, Vent Rib, *Modern*	25	75	125
Model 60AF, 12 and 16 Gauges, Hammerless, Solid Frame, Vent Rib, Adjustable Choke, *Modern*	25	75	125
Model 65, 12 and 20 Gauges, Hammerless, Solid Frame, *Modern*	25	50	100
Model 662CR, 20 Ga., Vent Rib, *Modern*	25	75	125
Model 66CLP, 12 and 16 Gauges, Adjustable Choke, *Modern*	25	75	125
Model 66RCLP, 12 and 20 Gauges, Hammerless, Solid Frame, Adjustable Choke, Vent Rib, *Modern*	25	75	125
Model 66RLP, 12 and 20 Gauges, Hammerless, Solid Frame, Vent Rib, *Modern*	25	75	125
Model 66XLP, 12 and 20 Gauges, Hammerless, Solid Frame, *Modern*	25	75	125
Model 70, .410 Ga., *Modern*	25	50	100

	Fair	V. Good	Excellent
Model 70CLP, .410 Ga., Hammerless, Solid Frame, Adjustable Choke, *Modern*	$25	$75	$125
Model 70RL, .410 Ga., *Modern*	25	75	125
Model 70X, .410 Ga., *Modern*	25	50	100
Model 70XL, .410 Ga., *Modern*	25	50	100
Model 757, 20 Ga., Adjustable Choke, Lightweight, *Modern*	50	100	150

NOCK, HENRY

London & Birmingham, England 1760–1810.

RIFLE, FLINTLOCK

	Fair	V. Good	Excellent
.65, Ellett Carbine, Musket, Military, *Antique*	700	1750	2000

SHOTGUN, PERCUSSION

	Fair	V. Good	Excellent
Fowler, Converted from Flintlock, Patent Breech, *Antique*	400	800	1000

NONPAREIL

Made by Norwich Falls Pistols Co., c. 1880.

HANDGUN, REVOLVER

	Fair	V. Good	Excellent
.32 Short R.F., 5 Shot, Spur Trigger, Solid Frame, Single Action, *Antique*	75	150	175

NORTH AMERICAN ARMS, INC.

Provo, Ut.

HANDGUN, REVOLVER

	Fair	V. Good	Excellent
.450 Magnum, Single Action, Western Style, High Polish Finish, 5 Shot, *Modern*	350	800	950
Mini, .22 L.R.R.F., 5 Shot, Single Action, Spur Trigger, 1" Barrel, Derringer, *Modern*	50	100	125
Mini, .22 L.R.R.F., 5 Shot, Single Action, Spur Trigger, 1½" Barrel, Derringer, *Modern*	50	100	125
Mini, .22 Short, 5 Shot, Single Action, Spur Trigger, 1" Barrel, Derringer, *Modern*	50	75	100
Mini, .22 W.M.R., 5 Shot, Single Action, Spur Trigger, 1" Barrel, Derringer, *Modern*	50	125	150

NORTHWESTERNER

Made by Stevens Arms.

RIFLE, BOLT ACTION

	Fair	V. Good	Excellent
Model 52, .22 L.R.R.F., Single Action, Takedown, *Modern*	15	25	50

SHOTGUN, SINGLESHOT

	Fair	V. Good	Excellent
Model 94, Various Gauges, Takedown, Automatic Ejector, Plain, Hammer, *Modern*	$25	$50	$75

NORTON

See Budischowsky and Americam Arms & Ammunition Co.

NORWEGIAN MILITARY

HANDGUN, SEMI-AUTOMATIC

	Fair	V. Good	Excellent
Mauser Model 1914, 7.65mm, Blue, Clip Fed, *Curio*	225	275	300
Model 1914, 11.25mm, Military, Clip Fed, *Curio*	325	700	800
Model 1914, 11.25mm, Military, Clip Fed, Nazi-Proofed, *Curio*	600	1250	1500

RIFLE, BOLT ACTION

	Fair	V. Good	Excellent
Model 1894 Krag, 6.5 × 55mm, Military, *Curio*	300	650	750
Model 1925 Krag Sniper, 6.5 × 55mm, Military, *Curio*	350	800	950

NORWICH PISTOL CO.

Norwich, Conn. 1875–1881. Also made handguns marked with trade names as follows: America, Bull Dozer, Chieftain, Crescent, Crown Jewel, Defiance, Exelsior, Frontier, Hartford Arms Co., Maltby-Curtis, Metropolitan Police, National, Nonpareil, Norwich Pistol Co., Patriot, Penetrator, Pinafore, Prairie King, Protection, Scott Arms Co., Spy, True Blue, U.M.C. Co., Veteran, Winfield Arms Co.

HANDGUN, REVOLVER

	Fair	V. Good	Excellent
.22 Short R.F., 7 Shot, Spur Trigger, Solid Frame, Single Action, *Antique*	100	150	175
.32 Short R.F., 5 Shot, Spur Trigger, Solid Frame, Single Action, *Antique*	75	125	150

NOT-NAC MFG. CO.

Made by Crescent for Belknap Hardware Co., Louisville, Ky. See Crescent Fire Arms Co., Shotgun, Double Barrel, Side-by-Side; Shotgun, Singleshot.

NOVA

La France Specialties, San Diego, Calif.

HANDGUN, SEMI-AUTOMATIC

	Fair	V. Good	Excellent
Nova, 9mm Luger, Clip Fed, "Electrofilm" Finish, Reduced M1911 Style, *Modern*	200	400	450

NOYS, R.

Wiltshire, England 1800–1830.

HANDGUN, FLINTLOCK

	Fair	V. Good	Excellent
Pocket Pistol, Screw Barrel, Box Lock, Steel Barrel and Frame, Plain, *Antique*	$250	$550	$700

NUMRICH ARMS CO.

West Hurley, N.Y. Also see Auto Ordnance, Thompson, Hopkins & Allen.

HANDGUN, SEMI-AUTOMATIC

	Fair	V. Good	Excellent
M1911A1, .45 ACP, Clip Fed, Blue, Military Style, *Modern*	100	200	250
Model ZG-51, .45 ACP, Clip Fed, Finned Barrel, Adjustable Sights, with Compensator, (Numrich), *Modern*	100	225	275

RIFLE, SEMI-AUTOMATIC

	Fair	V. Good	Excellent
Model 27A1, .45 ACP, Clip Fed, without Compensator, *Modern*	$150	$375	$450
Model 27A1, .45 ACP, Clip Fed, without Compensator, Cased with Accessories, *Modern*	225	550	650
Model 27A1 Deluxe, .45 ACP, Clip Fed, Finned Barrel, Adjustable Sights, with Compensator, *Modern*	200	450	525
Model 27A3, .22 L.R.R.F., Clip Fed, Finned Barrel, Adjustable Sights, with Compensator, *Modern*	150	300	350

NUNNEMACHER, ABRAHAM

York, Pa. 1779–1783. See Kentucky Rifles.

O

OAK LEAF
Made by Stevens Arms.

SHOTGUN, SINGLESHOT

	Fair	V. Good	Excellent
Model 90, Various Gauges, Takedown, Automatic Ejector, Plain, Hammer, *Modern*	$12	$25	$50

OCCIDENTAL
Belgium, c. 1880.

SHOTGUN, DOUBLE BARREL, SIDE-BY-SIDE

	Fair	V. Good	Excellent
Various Gauges, Outside Hammers, Damascus Barrel, *Modern*	50	100	150

OLD TIMER
Made by Stevens Arms.

SHOTGUN, SINGLESHOT

	Fair	V. Good	Excellent
Model 94, Various Gauges, Takedown, Automatic Ejector, Plain, Hammer, *Modern*	15	25	50

OLYMPIC
Made by Stevens Arms.

SHOTGUN, DOUBLE BARREL, SIDE-BY-SIDE

	Fair	V. Good	Excellent
M 315, Various Gauges, Hammerless, Steel Barrel, *Modern*	125	150	175
Model 311, Various Gauges, Hammerless, Steel Barrel, *Modern*	125	150	175

SHOTGUN, SINGLESHOT

	Fair	V. Good	Excellent
Model 94, Various Gauges, Takedown, Automatic Ejector, Plain, Hammer, *Modern*	15	25	50

O.M.
Ojanguren y Marcaido, Eibar, Spain, c. 1920.

HANDGUN, REVOLVER

	Fair	V. Good	Excellent
S & W Type, Various Calibers, Double Action, Swing-Out Cylinder, Blue, *Curio*	50	75	100

OMEGA
Armero Especialistas Reunidas, Eibar, Spain, c. 1925.

HANDGUN, SEMI-AUTOMATIC

	Fair	V. Good	Excellent
6.35mm, Clip Fed, *Curio*	$75	$100	$125
7.65mm, Clip Fed, Grip Safety, *Curio*	100	125	150

OMEGA
Torrance, Calif. Made by Hi-Shear Corp. 1980s.

RIFLE, BOLT ACTION

	Fair	V. Good	Excellent
Omega III, Various Calibers, No Sights, Fancy Wood, Adjustable Trigger, *Modern*	325	375	425

ORBEA HERMANOS
Orbea Hermanos and Orbea y Cia., Eibar, Spain, c. 1860–1935.

HANDGUN, REVOLVER

	Fair	V. Good	Excellent
S & W Type, .44 Russian, Double Action, Top-Break, *Antique*	75	100	125

Orbea Hermanos .44

OREA
Orechowsky, Graz, Austria, c. 1930.

RIFLE, SINGLESHOT

	Fair	V. Good	Excellent
Heeren Rifle, Various Calibers, Checkered Stock, Engraved, Fancy Wood, *Modern*	750	1250	1750

ORTGIES

Germany, 1918–1921, 1921 Taken over by Deutsche-Werke, Erfurt, Germany.

HANDGUN, SEMI-AUTOMATIC

	Fair	*V. Good*	*Excellent*
D Pocket, .380 ACP, Clip Fed, *Curio*	$175	$225	$275

Ortgies D Pocket

	Fair	*V. Good*	*Excellent*
D Pocket, 7.65mm, Clip Fed, *Curio*	125	175	225
D Vest Pocket, 6.35mm, Clip Fed, *Curio*	125	175	225
H O Pocket, .380 ACP, Clip Fed, *Curio*	150	200	250
H O Vest Pocket, 6.35mm, Clip Fed, *Curio*	100	175	225

OSGOOD GUN WORKS

Norwich, Conn., c. 1880.

HANDGUN, REVOLVER

	Fair	*V. Good*	*Excellent*
Duplex, .22/.32 R.F., 8 Shot .22, Singleshot .32, Two Barrels, Spur Trigger, *Antique*	$300	$650	$750

OUR JAKE

HANDGUN, REVOLVER

	Fair	*V. Good*	*Excellent*
.32 R.F., Spur Trigger, Solid Frame, Hammer, *Antique*	75	125	150

OWA

Oesterreichische Werke Anstalt, Vienna, Austria, c. 1920–1925.

HANDGUN, SEMI-AUTOMATIC

	Fair	*V. Good*	*Excellent*
Model 1921 Standard, 6.35mm, Clip Fed, *Curio*	100	200	250

OXFORD ARMS

Made by Stevens Arms.

SHOTGUN, DOUBLE BARREL, SIDE-BY-SIDE

	Fair	*V. Good*	*Excellent*
Model 311, Various Gauges, Hammerless, Steel Barrel, *Modern*	75	150	175

OXFORD ARMS CO.

Made by Crescent for Belknap Hdw. Co., Louisville, Ky. See Crescent Fire Arms Co., Shotgun, Double Barrel, Side-by-Side; Shotgun, Singleshot.

P

P.A.F.

Pretoria Arms Factory, Pretoria, South Africa, c. 1955.

HANDGUN, SEMI-AUTOMATIC

	Fair	*V. Good*	*Excellent*
Junior, For Cocking Indicator Add 10%–15%			
Junior, 6.35mm, High Slide, Clip Fed, Blue, *Curio*	$100	$225	$275

P.A.F. Junior

	Fair	*V. Good*	*Excellent*
Junior, 6.35mm, Low Slide, Clip Fed, Blue, *Curio*	100	250	300
Junior, 6.35mm, Sight Rib, Clip Fed, Blue, *Curio*	125	275	325

PAGE, T.

Norwich, England, 1766–1776.

HANDGUN, FLINTLOCK

	Fair	*V. Good*	*Excellent*
.60, Queen Anne Style, Pocket Pistol, Screw Barrel, Box Lock, Brass Furniture, Engraved, *Antique*	600	1400	1600

PAGE-LEWIS ARMS CO.

See Stevens, J. Arms & Tool Co. for similar listings.

PALMER, THOMAS

Philadelphia, Pa. 1772–1776. See Kentucky Rifles and U.S. Military.

PALMETTO

Made by Stevens Arms.

SHOTGUN, SINGLESHOT

	Fair	*V. Good*	*Excellent*
Model 90, Various Gauges, Takedown, Automatic Ejector, Plain, Hammer, *Curio*	$15	$25	$50
Model 94, Various Gauges, Takedown, Automatic Ejector, Plain, Hammer, *Modern*	25	50	75

PANNABECKER, JEFFERSON

Lancaster, Pa. 1790–1810. See Kentucky Rifles.

PANNABECKER, JESSE

Lancaster, Pa. 1833–1860. See Kentucky Rifles.

PANTAX

Tradename used by E. Woerther, Buenos Aires, Argentina.

PANZER

G.M.F. Corp., Watertown, Ct.

HANDGUN, DOUBLE BARREL, OVER-UNDER

	Fair	*V. Good*	*Excellent*
Panzer, .22 L.R.R.F., Twist Barrel, Spur Trigger, *Modern*	25	50	75

PARAGON

Made by Stevens Arms.

SHOTGUN, DOUBLE BARREL, SIDE-BY-SIDE

	Fair	*V. Good*	*Excellent*
Model 311, Various Gauges, Hammerless, Steel Barrel, *Modern*	75	150	175

PARAGON

Possibly made by Hopkins & Allen, c. 1880.

HANDGUN, REVOLVER

	Fair	*V. Good*	*Excellent*
.32 Short R.F., 5 Shot, Spur Trigger, Solid Frame, Single Action, *Antique*	75	150	175

PARAMOUNT

Retolaza Hermanos, Eibar, Spain, c. 1920.

	Fair	V. Good	Excellent
HANDGUN, SEMI-AUTOMATIC			
7.65mm, Clip Fed, *Curio*	$50	$100	$125
M 1914, 7.65mm, Clip Fed, Long Grip, *Curio*	50	125	150
Vest Pocket, 6.35mm, Clip Fed, *Curio*	50	100	125

PARKER BROTHERS

Imported from Italy by Jana International.

	Fair	V. Good	Excellent
SHOTGUN, DOUBLE BARREL, OVER-UNDER			
California Trap Model, 12 Ga., Single Selective Trigger, Automatic Ejectors, Checkered Stock, Engraved, Double Vent Rib, *Modern*	200	475	550
Field Model, 12 Ga. 3", Single Selective Trigger, Automatic Ejectors, Checkered Stock, Engraved, Vent Rib, *Modern*	150	300	350
Field Model, 12 Ga., Single Selective Trigger, Automatic Ejectors, Checkered Stock, Engraved, Vent Rib, *Modern*	150	275	325
Monte Carlo Stock, 12 Ga., Single Selective Trigger, Automatic Ejectors, Checkered Stock, Engraved, Vent Rib, *Modern*	150	300	375
Skeet Model, 12 Ga., Single Selective Trigger, Automatic Ejectors, Checkered Stock, Engraved, Vent Rib, *Modern*	150	300	350

PARKER BROTHERS

Meriden, Conn. 1868–1934. In 1934 Parker Bros. was taken over by Remington Arms Co. Parkers occupy a key position and status among America's gunmaking legends; over 243,000 shotguns were made by that august firm from the late 1860s to 1942. The founder of the Parker enterprise was Charles (1809–1902), beginning with his patented coffee grinder. The first gun by Parker was a Model 1861 Springfield .58 caliber musket (marked Parker's Snow & Co.), built on private contract during the Civil War (total of 15,000). Still another Civil War product, the Triplett & Scott repeating carbine, was built by Parker with his partners William and George Miller, under the name Meriden Manufacturing Co. (5,000 made). From 1865 to 1867, Meriden Manufacturing also altered an unknown quantity of Model 1861 muskets, from percussion to metallic cartridge breechloaders. With his brothers, Wilbur and Dexter, Charles brought out the first double-barrel Parker shotgun in 1868. The company was known as Parker Brothers, and was established c. 1867–68. The first Parker catalog appeared in 1869, and the firm would remain in continuous operation in Meriden, until January 1934, at which time the new owners became the Remington Arms Co. However, the works were not moved to Ilion, New York, until 1938. The line was discontinued in 1942, when Remington was concentrating on wartime production. The complete line of Parker production is as follows: pre-1899—grades K, L, M, O, Q, and R; some of the following pre-date 1899, some were introduced post 1899—grades U, T, S, R, I, H, G, F, E, D, C, B, A, AA Pigeon Gun, the A1-Special and the Invincible. Nearly 100,000 Parkers were made before 1900. Hammer models were built as late as 1920, and some appear to have been available even after that late date. The so-called "lifter" action was the first locking system on Parkers; a protrusion on the bottom of the frame was pushed upwards to break open the breech. The lifter system remained in use until about 1900. The top-lever release system was adopted well before, and became the standard after the turn of the century. The Parker marque is of such fame and of such solid design that production was revived in the post–World War II period, by both the Remington Arms Co. and by "Parker Reproductions by Winchester"—the former made in the U.S., the latter made in Japan, beginning in 1983 with the DHE grade Parker. Pre-war Parkers were advertised with such legitimate claims as "The most discriminating gun users in America shoot guns made by Parker Bros." and "Makers of guns that satisfy." Parker Bros. were instrumental in introducing several innovations to American shotgun design: among them a hammerless lock mechanism, an automatic ejector, the first 28-gauge and the first ventilated rib. Parker's single barrel trap gun became a favorite of U.S. trapshooters. The ultimate grades of Parkers were the A-1 Special and the Invincible. Only about 320 A-1 Specials were built, and only a handful of the Invincibles. One of the latter, made for Czar Nicholas II of Russia, was never shipped, due to the 1917 Revolution. Parker Bros. described the Invincible as placing "before the discriminating shooting public of the world, a gun equaled by few and excelled by none."

	Fair	V. Good	Excellent
SHOTGUN, DOUBLE BARREL, SIDE-BY-SIDE			
A-1 Special, 12 Ga., Hammerless, Double Trigger, Automatic Ejector, *Modern*	$20000	$40000	$50000
A-1 Special, 16 Ga., Hammerless, Double Trigger, Automatic Ejector, *Modern*	20000	40000	50000
A-1 Special, 20 Ga., Hammerless, Double Trigger, Automatic Ejector, *Modern*	25000	50000	75000
A-1 Special, 28 Ga., Hammerless, Double Trigger, Automatic Ejector, *Modern*	30000	65000	75000
AAHE, 12 Ga., Hammerless, Double Trigger, Automatic Ejector, *Modern*	15000	30000	35000
AAHE, 16 Ga., Hammerless, Double Trigger, Automatic Ejector, *Modern*	15000	30000	35000
AAHE, 20 Ga., Hammerless, Double Trigger, Automatic Ejector, *Modern*	17000	40000	45000
AAHE, 28 Ga., Hammerless, Double Trigger, Automatic Ejector, *Modern*	20000	50000	55000
AHE, .410 Ga., Hammerless, Double Trigger, Automatic Ejector, *Modern*	30000	55000	65000
AHE, 10 Ga., Hammerless, Double Trigger, Automatic Ejector, *Modern*	9000	25000	30000
AHE, 12 Ga., Hammerless, Double Trigger, Automatic Ejector, *Modern*	7000	15000	20000

	Fair	V. Good	Excellent
AHE, 16 Ga., Hammerless, Double Trigger, Automatic Ejector, *Modern*	$6000	$15000	$20000
AHE, 20 Ga., Hammerless, Double Trigger, Automatic Ejector, *Modern*	9000	25000	30000
AHE, 28 Ga., Hammerless, Double Trigger, Automatic Ejector, *Modern*	12000	35000	40000
Beavertail Forend, for BHE through A-1 Add 20%			
Beavertail Forend, VHE through CHE Add $300.00–$500.00			
BH, .410 Ga., Hammerless, Double Trigger, Automatic Ejector, *Modern*	12000	30000	35000
BH, 10 Ga., Hammerless, Double Trigger, Automatic Ejector, *Modern*	3000	8000	10000
BH, 12 Ga., Hammerless, Double Trigger, Automatic Ejector, *Modern*	2500	6500	7500
BH, 16 Ga., Hammerless, Double Trigger, Automatic Ejector, *Modern*	2000	6000	8000
BH, 20 Ga., Hammerless, Double Trigger, Automatic Ejector, *Modern*	4000	12000	15000
BH, 28 Ga., Hammerless, Double Trigger, Automatic Ejector, *Modern*	8000	20000	25000
CH, .410 Ga., Hammerless, Double Trigger, Automatic Ejector, *Modern*	10000	20000	25000
CH, 10 Ga., Hammerless, Double Trigger, Automatic Ejector, *Modern*	2000	6500	7500
CH, 12 Ga., Hammerless, Double Trigger, Automatic Ejector, *Modern*	1750	4500	6000
CH, 16 Ga., Hammerless, Double Trigger, Automatic Ejector, *Modern*	1750	4500	6000
CH, 20 Ga., Hammerless, Double Trigger, Automatic Ejector, *Modern*	4000	10000	12000
CH, 28 Ga., Hammerless, Double Trigger, Automatic Ejector, *Modern*	4500	12500	15000
DH, .410 Ga., Hammerless, Double Trigger, Automatic Ejector, *Modern*	9000	25000	30000
DH, 10 Ga., Hammerless, Double Trigger, Automatic Ejector, *Modern*	1500	5000	6500
DH, 12 Ga., Hammerless, Double Trigger, Automatic Ejector, *Modern*	1000	3500	5000
DH, 16 Ga., Hammerless, Double Trigger, Automatic Ejector, *Modern*	1000	3500	5000
DH, 20 Ga., Hammerless, Double Trigger, Automatic Ejector, *Modern*	$2200	$5000	$6500
DH, 28 Ga., Hammerless, Double Trigger, Automatic Ejector, *Modern*	3000	7500	10000
Early Model, Various Gauges, Outside Hammers, Damascus Barrel, Under-Lever, *Antique*	700	1750	2500
Extra Barrel, Add 30%-40%			
For Damascus Barrel, Deduct 60%-75%			
For Ejectors, Add 50% (E)			
For Upgrades, Deduct 40%-60%			
GH, .410 Ga., Hammerless, Double Trigger, Automatic Ejector, *Modern*	5000	15000	20000
GH, 10 Ga. $3^1/_2$", Hammerless, Double Trigger, *Modern*	1500	3500	4500
GH, 10 Ga. $3^1/_2$", Hammerless, Double Trigger, Automatic Ejector, *Modern*	2000	4000	5000
GH, 12 Ga., Hammerless, Double Trigger, *Modern*	800	1750	2500
GH, 12 Ga., Hammerless, Double Trigger, Automatic Ejector, *Modern*	1000	2500	3000
GH, 16 Ga., Hammerless, Double Trigger, *Modern*	800	1750	2500
GH, 16 Ga., Hammerless, Double Trigger, Automatic Ejector, *Modern*	1000	2500	3000
GH, 20 Ga., Hammerless, Double Trigger, *Modern*	1000	3000	4000
GH, 20 Ga., Hammerless, Double Trigger, Automatic Ejector, *Modern*	1200	3500	4500
GH, 28 Ga., Hammerless, Double Trigger, *Modern*	1200	4000	6000
GH, 28 Ga., Hammerless, Double Trigger, Automatic Ejector, *Modern*	1500	6000	9000
Invincible, 12 Ga., Hammerless, Double Trigger, Automatic Ejector, *Modern*	30000	100000	125000
Invincible, 16 Ga., Hammerless, Double Trigger, Automatic Ejector, *Modern*	30000	100000	125000
Outside Hammers with Steel Barrels, Deduct 20%-30%			
Single Selective Trigger, Add 20%			
Skeet Grade, Add 15%-25%			
Trap Grade, Add 10%-15%			
Trojan, 12 and 16 Gauges, Hammerless, Double Trigger, *Modern*	600	1200	1500
Trojan, 20 Ga., Hammerless, Double Trigger, *Modern*	800	1500	2250
Vent Rib, 20%-50%			

	Fair	V. Good	Excellent
VH, .410 Ga., Hammerless, Double Trigger, Automatic Ejector, *Modern*	$4000	$8000	$10000
VH, 12 Ga., Hammerless, Double Trigger, Automatic Ejector, *Modern*	700	1800	2000
VH, 16 Ga., Hammerless, Double Trigger, Automatic Ejector, *Modern*	700	1800	2000
VH, 20 Ga., Hammerless, Double Trigger, Automatic Ejector, *Modern*	1000	2000	2500
VH, 28 Ga., Hammerless, Double Trigger, Automatic Ejector, *Modern*	2700	6000	6500

SHOTGUN, SINGLE BARREL TRAP

	Fair	V. Good	Excellent
S.A., 12 Ga., Hammerless, Vent Rib, Automatic Ejector, *Modern*	1200	4000	4500
S.A.-1 Special, 12 Ga., Hammerless, Vent Rib, Automatic Ejector, *Modern*	6000	17000	20000
S.A.A., 12 Ga., Hammerless, Vent Rib, Automatic Ejector, *Modern*	4000	15000	18000
S.B., 12 Ga., Hammerless, Vent Rib, Automatic Ejector, *Modern*	2000	6000	9000
S.C., 12 Ga., Hammerless, Vent Rib, Automatic Ejector, *Modern*	1000	2000	3000

PARKER SAFETY HAMMERLESS

Made by Columbia Armory, Tenn., c. 1890.

HANDGUN, REVOLVER

	Fair	V. Good	Excellent
.32 S & W, 5 Shot, Top Break, Hammerless, Double Action, *Curio*	50	75	100

PARKER, WILLIAM

London, England 1790–1840.

SHOTGUN, PERCUSSION

	Fair	V. Good	Excellent
14 Ga., Single Barrel, Smoothbore, High Quality, Cased with Accessories, *Antique*	600	1250	1500

SHOTGUN, FLINTLOCK

	Fair	V. Good	Excellent
16 Ga., Double Barrel, Side by Side, Engraved, High Quality, *Antique*	1700	3500	4000

PARKER-HALE LTD.

Birmingham, England. Purchased by Navy Arms in 1991.

HANDGUN, REVOLVER

	Fair	V. Good	Excellent
S & W Victory, .22 L.R.R.F., Conversion, Adjustable Sights, *Modern*	125	225	250

RIFLE, BOLT ACTION

	Fair	V. Good	Excellent
Model 1200, Various Calibers, Checkered Stock, Open Rear Sight, Monte Carlo Stock, *Modern*	$250	$500	$550
Model 1200M, Various Calibers, Magnum, Checkered Stock, Open Rear Sight, Monte Carlo Stock, *Modern*	250	550	600
Model 1200V, Various Calibers, Heavy Barrel, Checkered Stock, No Sights, Monte Carlo Stock, *Modern*	225	475	525

RIFLE, PERCUSSION

	Fair	V. Good	Excellent
.451, Whitworth Military Target Rifle, 3 Bands, Target Sights, Checkered Stock, Reproduction,	150	325	350
.54 Gallagher, Breech Loader, Carbine, Brass Furniture, Reproduction,	100	150	175
.58 M1853 Enfield Rifle, Rifled, Brass Funiture, Reproduction,	100	175	200
.58 M1853 Enfield, Musket, Rifled, 2 Bands, Brass Furniture, Reproduction,	100	175	200
.58 M1861 Enfield, Musketoon, Rifled, 2 Bands, Brass Furniture, Reproduction,	100	150	175

SHOTGUN, SEMI-AUTOMATIC

	Fair	V. Good	Excellent
Model 640A, 12 Ga., Checkered Stock, Vent Rib, *Modern*	200	475	550
Model 640M, 10 Ga. 3", Checkered Stock, Vent Rib, *Modern*	300	600	700

PARKHILL, ANDREW

Phila., Pa. 1778–1785. See Kentucky Rifles and Pistols.

PAROLE

Made by Hopkins & Allen, c. 1880.

HANDGUN, REVOLVER

	Fair	V. Good	Excellent
.22 Short R.F., 7 Shot, Spur Trigger, Solid Frame, Single Action, *Antique*	100	150	175

PARR, J.

Liverpool, England, c. 1810.

RIFLE, FLINTLOCK

	Fair	V. Good	Excellent
.75, 3rd Model Brown Bess, Musket, Military, *Antique*	700	1200	1500

PARSONS, HIRAM

Baltimore, Md., c. 1819. See Kentucky Rifles.

PATRIOT
Made by Norwich Falls Pistol Co., c. 1880.

HANDGUN, REVOLVER

	Fair	V. Good	Excellent
.32 Short R.F., 5 Shot, Spur Trigger, Solid Frame, Single Action, *Antique*	$75	$150	$175

PECK, ABIJAH
Hartford, Conn. See U.S. Military.

PEERLESS
Made by Crescent H. & D. Folsom, c. 1900. See Crescent Fire Arms Co., Shotgun, Double Barrel, Side-by-Side; Shotgun, Singleshot.

PEERLESS
Made by Stevens.

RIFLE, BOLT ACTION

	Fair	V. Good	Excellent
Model 056 Buckhorn, .22 L.R.R.F., 5 Shot Clip, Peep Sights, *Modern*	25	50	75
Model 066 Buckhorn, .22 L.R.R.F., Tube Feed, Peep Sights, *Modern*	25	50	75
Model 53, .22 L.R.R.F., Singleshot, Takedown, *Modern*	15	25	50

PENCE, JACOB
Lancaster, Pa. 1771. See Kentucky Rifles and Pistols.

PENETRATOR
Made by Norwich Falls Pistol Co., c. 1880.

HANDGUN, REVOLVER

	Fair	V. Good	Excellent
.32 Short R.F., 5 Shot, Spur Trigger, Solid Frame, Single Action, *Modern*	75	125	175

PENNYPACKER, DANIEL
Berks County, Pa. 1773–1808. See Kentucky Rifles and Pistols.

PENNYPACKER, WM.
Berks County, Pa. 1808–1858. See Kentucky Rifles and Pistols.

PERCUSSION EXAMPLES

HANDGUN, PERCUSSION

	Fair	V. Good	Excellent
.40 English, 6 Shot, Pepperbox, Pocket Pistol, Light Engraving, German Silver Frame, Steel Barrel, *Antique*	150	350	500
.45, Pair French, Target Pistol, Octagon Barrel, Single Set Trigger, Brass Furniture, Cased with Accessories, *Antique*	$1100	$2500	$3000
.70, French Sotiau, Belt Pistol, Steel Furniture, Rifled, Octagon Barrel, *Antique*	200	450	600
Boot Pistol, Bar Hammer, Screw Barrel, *Antique*	100	200	250
Boot Pistol, Boxlock, Screw Barrel, *Antique*	100	250	300
Boot Pistol, Sidelock, Derringer Style, *Antique*	100	200	250
Pair, Dueling Pistols, Octagon Barrel, Single Set Trigger, German Silver Furniture, Medium Quality, Cased with Accessories, *Antique*	900	2000	2500

HANDGUN, REVOLVER

	Fair	V. Good	Excellent
.36, Navy Colt Type, Belgian Make, Medium Quality, *Antique*	100	200	250
.45, Adams Type, Double Action, Octagon Barrel, Plain, Cased with Accessories, *Antique*	400	850	1000

RIFLE, PERCUSSION

	Fair	V. Good	Excellent
American Indian Trade Gun, Belgian, Converted from Flintlock, Brass Furniture, *Antique*	1100	2500	3500
Benchrest, Various Calibers, Heavy Barrel, Set Triggers, Target Sights, Light Decoration, *Antique*	350	700	850

Percussion Arms, Unknown Maker Benchrest Rifle

	Fair	V. Good	Excellent
Benchrest, Various Calibers, Heavy Barrel, Set Triggers, Target Sights, Medium Decoration, *Antique*	350	800	1000
German, Schutzen Rifle, Rifled, Ivory Inlays, Gold Inlays, Ornate, *Antique*	2200	5000	6000

SHOTGUN, PERCUSSION

	Fair	V. Good	Excellent
English, 12 Ga., Double Barrel, Side by Side, Light Ornamentation, Medium Quality, *Antique*	150	350	500
English, 12 Ga., Double Barrel, Side by Side, Light Ornamentation, High Quality, Cased with Accessories, *Antique*	325	700	950

	Fair	V. Good	Excellent

PERFECT
Made by Foehl & Weeks. Phila., Pa., c. 1890.

HANDGUN, REVOLVER

	Fair	V. Good	Excellent
.38 S & W, 5 Shot, Double Action, Top Break, *Modern*	$50	$75	$100

PERFECTION
Made by Crescent for H. & G. Lipscomb & Co., Nashville, Tenn. See Crescent Fire Arms Co., Shotgun, Double Barrel, Side-by-Side; Shotgun, Singleshot.

PERFECTION AUTOMATIC REVOLVER
Made by Forehand Arms Co.

HANDGUN, REVOLVER

	Fair	V. Good	Excellent
.32 S & W, 5 Shot, Double Action, Top Break, *Antique*	50	75	100
.32 S & W, 5 Shot, Double Action, Top Break, Hammerless, *Antique*	50	100	125

PERLA
Frantisek Dusek, Opocno, Czechoslovakia, c. 1935.

HANDGUN, SEMI-AUTOMATIC

	Fair	V. Good	Excellent
.25 ACP, Clip Fed, Blue, *Modern*	100	175	225

PETTIBONE, DANIEL
Philadelphia, Pa. 1799–1814. See Kentucky Rifles and Pistols.

PHILIPPINE MILITARY

SHOTGUN, SINGLESHOT

	Fair	V. Good	Excellent
WW2 Guerrilla Weapon, 12 Ga., *Modern*	50	125	150

PHOENIX
Spain, Tomas de Urizar y Cia., c. 1920.

HANDGUN, SEMI-AUTOMATIC

	Fair	V. Good	Excellent
Vest Pocket, 6.35mm, Clip Fed, *Curio*	50	125	150

PHOENIX ARMS CO.
Lowell Arms Co., Lowell, Mass., c. 1920.

HANDGUN, SEMI-AUTOMATIC

	Fair	V. Good	Excellent
Vest Pocket, .25 ACP, Clip Fed, *Curio*	200	425	475

PIC
Made in West Germany for Precise Imports Corp., Suffern, N.Y.

Phoenix Arms Co. .25

HANDGUN, REVOLVER

	Fair	V. Good	Excellent
.22 L.R.R.F., Double Action, Blue, *Modern*	$15	$50	$75

PIC .25

HANDGUN, SEMI-AUTOMATIC

	Fair	V. Good	Excellent
Vest Pocket, .22 Short R.F., Clip Fed, *Modern*	15	25	50
Vest Pocket, .25 ACP., Clip Fed, *Modern*	15	25	50

PICKFATT, HUMPHREY
London, England, 1714–1730.

HANDGUN, FLINTLOCK

	Fair	V. Good	Excellent
Pair, Holster Pistol, Engraved, Brass Furniture, High Quality, *Antique*	3500	8000	10000
Pair, Queen Anne Style, Box Lock, Pocket Pistol, Silver Furniture, *Antique*	1100	2500	3000

PIEDMONT
Made by Crescent for Piedmont Hdw. Danville, Pa. See Crescent Fire Arms Co., Shotgun, Double Barrel, Side-by-Side; Shotgun, Singleshot.

PIEPER
Henry Pieper, Harstal, Belgium 1859. Became Nicolas Pieper in 1898, and in 1905 became Anciens Etablissments Pieper.

	Fair	V. Good	Excellent
COMBINATION WEAPON, SIDE-BY-SIDE			
Various Calibers, Hammer, Open Rear Sight, Checkered Stock, Plain, *Curio*	$200	$375	$450
HANDGUN, SEMI-AUTOMATIC			
Bayard Model 1908 Pocket, .380 ACP, Blue, Clip Fed, *Curio*	75	150	175
Bayard Model 1908 Pocket, 6.35mm, Blue, Clip Fed, *Curio*	50	125	150
Bayard Model 1923 Pocket, 6.35mm, Blue, Clip Fed, *Curio*	75	150	175
Bayard Model 1923 Pocket, 7.65mm, Blue, Clip Fed, *Curio*	100	200	225
Bayard Model 1930 Pocket, 6.35mm, Blue, Clip Fed, *Curio*	100	200	225
Model A (Army), 7.65mm, Clip Fed, 7 Shot, *Curio*	75	150	175
Model B, 7.65mm, Clip Fed, 6 Shot, *Curio*	75	125	150
Model C, 6.35mm, Clip Fed, *Curio*	75	125	150
Model C, 6.35mm, Clip Fed, Long Grip, *Curio*	75	150	175
Model D (1920), 6.35mm, Clip Fed, Tip-Up, *Curio*	75	150	175

Pieper Model D

	Fair	V. Good	Excellent
Model Legia, 6.35mm, Clip Fed, *Curio*	75	125	150
Model Legia, 6.35mm, Clip Fed, Long Grip, *Curio*	75	150	175
Model N, 7.65mm, Clip Fed, Tip-Up, 7 Shot, *Curio*	75	125	150
Model O, 7.65mm, Clip Fed, Tip-Up, 6 Shot, *Curio*	75	125	150
Model P, 6.35mm, Clip Fed, Tip-Up, *Curio*	75	150	175
RIFLE, BOLT ACTION			
Singleshot, .22 L.R.R.F., Plain, *Curio*	25	50	75
RIFLE, SEMI-AUTOMATIC			
Pieper Carbine, .22 L.R.R.F., Checkered Stock, English Grip, *Curio*	50	100	125
Pieper Musket, .22 L.R.R.F., Military Style Stock, *Curio*	$50	$100	$125
Pieper Musket, .22 L.R.R.F., Military Style Stock, with Bayonet, *Curio*	75	125	150
Pieper/Bayard Carbine, .22 Long, Checkered Stock, Pistol Grip, *Curio*	50	100	125
Pieper/Bayard Carbine, .22 Short, Checkered Stock, Pistol Grip, *Curio*	50	75	100
SHOTGUN, DOUBLE BARREL, SIDE-BY-SIDE			
Bayard, Various Gauges, Hammerless, Boxlock, Light Engraving, Checkered Stock, *Modern*	100	175	200
Hammer Gun, Various Gauges, Light Engraving, Steel Barrels, *Modern*	75	150	200
Hammer Gun, Various Gauges, Plain, Damascus Barrels, *Modern*	75	125	150
Hammer Gun, Various Gauges, Plain, Steel Barrels, *Modern*	75	150	175

PIEPER, ABRAHAM

Lancaster, Pa. 1801–1803. See Kentucky Rifles and Pistols.

PIEPER, HENRY

Also see Pieper.

	Fair	V. Good	Excellent
COMBINATION WEAPON, SIDE-BY-SIDE			
Various Calibers, Double Trigger, Outside Hammers, Side Lever, *Antique*	150	375	450

PINAFORE

Made by Norwich Falls Pistol Co., c. 1880.

	Fair	V. Good	Excellent
HANDGUN, REVOLVER			
.22 Short R.F., 7 Shot, Spur Trigger, Solid Frame, Single Action, *Antique*	75	125	175

Pinafore

PINKERTON

Gaspar Arizaga, Eibar, Spain, c. 1930.

	Fair	V. Good	Excellent
HANDGUN, SEMI-AUTOMATIC			
Browning Type, 6.35mm, Clip Fed, Blue, *Curio*	$75	$125	$150
Mondial Type, 6.35mm, Clip Fed, Blue, *Curio*	100	175	200

PIONEER

c. 1880.

	Fair	V. Good	Excellent
HANDGUN, REVOLVER			
.38 Short R.F., 5 Shot, Spur Trigger, Solid Frame, Single Action, *Antique*	75	150	175

PIONEER

Made by Stevens Arms.

	Fair	V. Good	Excellent
RIFLE, SEMI-AUTOMATIC			
Model 87, .22 L.R.R.F., Tube Feed, Open Rear Sight, *Modern*	25	50	75

PIONEER ARMS CO.

Made by Crescent for Kruse Hardware Co. Cincinatti, Ohio. See Crescent Fire Arms Co., Shotgun, Double Barrel, Side-by-Side; Shotgun, Singleshot.

PIOTTI

Brescia, Italy. Currently Imported by Ventura Imports.

	Fair	V. Good	Excellent
SHOTGUN, DOUBLE BARREL, SIDE-BY-SIDE			
Monte Carlo, 12 and 20 Gauges, Sidelock, Automatic Ejector, Single Selective Trigger, Fancy Checkering, Fancy Engraving, *Modern*	3500	7500	8500
Westlake, 12 and 20 Gauges, Sidelock, Automatic Ejector, Double Trigger, Fancy Checkering, Fancy Engraving, *Modern*	2700	6000	7000

PJK

Bradbury, Calif. 1960s.

	Fair	V. Good	Excellent
RIFLE, SEMI-AUTOMATIC			
M-68, 9mm Luger, Clip Fed, Carbine, Flash Hider, *Modern*	75	150	200

PLAINFIELD MACHINE CO.

Dunellen, N.J., Also see Iver Johnson.

	Fair	V. Good	Excellent
HANDGUN, SEMI-AUTOMATIC			
Super Enforcer, .30 Carbine, Clip Fed, *Modern*	100	175	225
RIFLE, SEMI-AUTOMATIC			
M-1, .30 Carbine, Carbine, *Modern*	$75	$150	$200
M-1, .30 Carbine, Carbine, Sporting Rifle, *Modern*	75	150	175
M-1, 5.7mm Carbine, Carbine, *Modern*	75	125	175
M-1 Deluxe, .30 Carbine, Carbine, Sporting Rifle, Monte Carlo Stock, Checkered Stock, *Modern*	75	150	200
M-1 Paratrooper, .30 Carbine, Carbine, Folding Stock, *Modern*	100	200	225
M-1 Presentation, .30 Carbine, Carbine, Sporting Rifle, Monte Carlo Stock, Fancy Wood, *Modern*	100	200	225

PLAINFIELD ORDNANCE CO.

Middlesex, N.J.

	Fair	V. Good	Excellent
HANDGUN, SEMI-AUTOMATIC			
Model 71, .22 L.R.R.F. and 25 ACP, Clip Fed, Stainless Steel, with Conversion Kit, *Modern*	100	175	200
Model 71, .22 L.R.R.F., Clip Fed, Stainless Steel, *Modern*	75	125	150
Model 71, 25 ACP, Clip Fed, Stainless Steel, *Modern*	50	100	125
Model 72, .22 ACP, Clip Fed, Lightweight, *Modern*	75	125	150
Model 72, .22 L.R.R.F. and 25 ACP, Clip Fed, Lightweight with Conversion Kit, *Modern*	100	175	225
Model 72, .22 L.R.R.F., Clip Fed, Lightweight, *Modern*	75	150	175

PLANT'S MFG. CO.

New Haven, Conn. 1860–1866. Like the Moore teat-fire revolvers, Plants were extremely well made, and occasionally are found engraved and/or inscribed and sometimes handsomely cased. Engraved examples, which demand a premium, have been observed, decorated exactly in the same style as much of the Henry Rifle engraving—undoubtedly by the same hand.

	Fair	V. Good	Excellent
HANDGUN, REVOLVER			
Army, .42 Cup Primed Cartridge, 6 Shot, Single Action, Spur Trigger, 1st Model, *Antique*	600	1250	1500

Plant's .42 C.P.

	Fair	V. Good	Excellent
Army, .42 Cup Primed Cartridge, 6 Shot, Single Action, Spur Trigger, 2nd Model, *Antique*	$450	$1000	$1250
Army, .42 Cup Primed Cartridge, 6 Shot, Single Action, Spur Trigger, 3rd Model, *Antique*	500	1200	1400
Pocket, .30 Cup Primed Cartridge, 5 Shot, Single Action, Spur Trigger, Solid Frame, *Antique*	200	400	450

PLUS ULTRA

Gabilondo y Cia., Eibar, Spain, c. 1930.

HANDGUN, SEMI-AUTOMATIC

	Fair	V. Good	Excellent
7.65mm, Extra Long Grip, Military, *Curio*	200	425	500

POND, LUCIUS W.

Worcester, Mass., c. 1863–72.

HANDGUN, REVOLVER

	Fair	V. Good	Excellent
Front Loader, .22, 7 Shot, 3½" barrel., *Antique*	250	500	600

Lucius W. Pond Seven Shot Cartridge Revolver, .22 Caliber

	Fair	V. Good	Excellent
Front Loader, .32, 7 Shot, 3½" barrel., *Antique*	200	475	575

PORTER, PATRICK W.

New York City, c. 1851–54.

HANDGUN, PERCUSSION

	Fair	V. Good	Excellent
Patent Turret Pistol, .41, 9 Shot, *Antique*	5000	10000	12000

Patrick W. Porter Turret Pistol, .41 Caliber

PORTUGUESE MILITARY

RIFLE, BOLT ACTION

	Fair	V. Good	Excellent
Kropatchek M1886, 8mm, Tube Feed, *Antique*	$100	$200	$250
Mauser-Vergueiro, 6.5mm, Rifle, *Curio*	150	250	300

POUS, EUDAL

Spain, c. 1790.

HANDGUN, MIQUELET-LOCK

	Fair	V. Good	Excellent
Pair, Holster Pistol, Low Quality, Light Brass Furniture, *Antique*	1200	2750	3000

PRAGA

Zbrojovka Praga, Prague, Czechoslovakia, 1918–1926.

HANDGUN, SEMI-AUTOMATIC

	Fair	V. Good	Excellent
Model 1921, 6.35mm, Clip Fed, Folding Trigger, *Curio*	100	200	225
Vz 21, 7.65mm, Clip Fed, *Curio*	150	275	325

Praga Praha

PRAIRIE KING

Made by Norwich Falls Pistol Co., c. 1880.

HANDGUN, REVOLVER

	Fair	V. Good	Excellent
.22 Short R.F., 7 Shot, Spur Trigger, Solid Frame, Single Action, *Antique*	75	125	150

PREMIER

Brooklyn, N.Y.

SHOTGUN, DOUBLE BARREL, SIDE-BY-SIDE

	Fair	V. Good	Excellent
Ambassador, Various Calibers, Checkered Stock, Hammerless, Double Trigger, *Modern*	150	325	375
Brush King, 12 and 20 Gauges, Checkered Stock, Hammerless, Double Trigger, *Modern*	125	225	275

	Fair	V. Good	Excellent
Continental, Various Calibers, Checkered Stock, Outside Hammers, Double Trigger, *Modern*	$100	$200	$250
Monarch, Various Calibers, Hammerless, Double Trigger, Checkered Stock, Engraved, Adjustable Choke, *Modern*	150	375	450
Presentation, Various Calibers, Adjustable Choke, Double Trigger, Fancy Engraving, Fancy Checkering, Extra Shotgun Barrel, *Modern*	400	850	1000
Regent Magnum, 10 Ga. 3½", Checkered Stock, Hammerless, Double Trigger, *Modern*	150	275	350
Regent, Various Calibers, Checkered Stock, Hammerless, Double Trigger, *Modern*	125	225	325
Regent, Various Calibers, Checkered Stock, Hammerless, Double Trigger, Extra Shotgun Barrel, *Modern*	150	300	400

PREMIER

Made by Stevens Arms.

RIFLE, BOLT ACTION

	Fair	V. Good	Excellent
Model 52, .22 L.R.R.F., Singleshot, Takedown, *Modern*	15	25	50
Model 53, .22 L.R.R.F., Singleshot, Takedown, *Modern*	25	50	75
Model 66 Buckhorn, .22 L.R.R.F., Tube Feed, Open Rear Sight, *Modern*	25	50	75

RIFLE, SLIDE ACTION

	Fair	V. Good	Excellent
Model 75, .22 L.R.R.F., Tube Feed, Hammerless, *Modern*	75	125	175

PREMIER

Made by Thomas E. Ryan, Norwich, Conn., c. 1870–1876.

HANDGUN, REVOLVER

	Fair	V. Good	Excellent
.22 Short R.F., 7 Shot, Spur Trigger, Solid Frame, Single Action, *Antique*	75	125	175
.32 Long R.F., 6 Shot, Spur Trigger, Solid Frame, Single Action, *Antique*	75	125	175

PREMIER

Tomas de Urizar y Cia., Eibar, Spain, c. 1920.

HANDGUN, SEMI-AUTOMATIC

	Fair	V. Good	Excellent
6.35mm, Clip Fed, Blue, *Modern*	75	100	125

PREMIER TRAIL BLAZER

Made by Stevens Arms.

RIFLE, SLIDE ACTION

	Fair	V. Good	Excellent
Model 75, .22 L.R.R.F., Tube Feed, Hammerless, *Modern*	$75	$125	$175

PRESCOTT, E. A.

Worcester, Mass. 1860–1874.

HANDGUN, REVOLVER

	Fair	V. Good	Excellent
"Navy" .38 Short R.F., 6 Shot, Single Action, Solid Frame, Finger-Rest Trigger Guard, *Antique*	100	650	750
Belt .32 Short R.F., *Antique*	250	500	600
Pocket .22 Short R.F., 7 Shot, Spur Trigger, Solid Frame, Single Action, *Antique*	200	450	550
Pocket .31 Percussion, 6 Shot, Spur Trigger, Solid Frame, Single Action, *Antique*	300	600	750

PRICE, J. W.

Made by Stevens Arms.

SHOTGUN, SINGLESHOT

	Fair	V. Good	Excellent
Model 90, Various Gauges, Takedown, Automatic Ejector, Plain, Hammer, *Modern*	25	50	75

PRIMA

Mre. d'Armes des Pyrenees, Hendaye, France.

HANDGUN, SEMI-AUTOMATIC

	Fair	V. Good	Excellent
6.35mm, Clip Fed, *Curio*	75	125	150

Prima

PRINCEPS

Tomas de Urizar, Eibar, Spain, c. 1920.

HANDGUN, SEMI-AUTOMATIC

	Fair	V. Good	Excellent
6.35mm, Clip Fed, *Curio*	75	125	150

PRINCESS

c. 1880.

Princeps

	Fair	V. Good	Excellent
HANDGUN, REVOLVER			
.22 Short R.F., 7 Shot, Spur Trigger, Solid Frame, Single Action, *Antique*	$75	$150	$175

PROTECTION

Made by Norwich Falls Pistol Co., c. 1860.

	Fair	V. Good	Excellent
HANDGUN, REVOLVER			
Pocket .28 Percussion, 6 Shot, Spur Trigger, Solid Frame, Single Action, *Antique*	250	500	600

PROTECTOR ARMS CO.

Spain, c. 1900.

	Fair	V. Good	Excellent
HANDGUN, SEMI-AUTOMATIC			
M 1918, 6.35mm, Clip Fed, *Curio*	75	125	150

PURDEY, JAMES

	Fair	V. Good	Excellent
RIFLE, PERCUSSION			
.52, Double Barrel, Side by Side, Damascus Barrel, Engraved, Fancy Wood, Gold Inlays	2750	6500	7500
RIFLE, DOUBLE BARREL, SIDE-BY-SIDE			
.500 #2 Express, Damascus Barrel, Outside Hammers, Under-Lever, Engraved, Ornate, *Antique*	1800	4000	5000

PURDEY, JAS. & SONS

London, England, 1814 to Date.

	Fair	V. Good	Excellent
RIFLE, BOLT ACTION			
Sporting Rifle, Various Calibers, Fancy Wood, Checkered Stock, Express Sights, *Modern*	2200	5500	6000
RIFLE, DOUBLE BARREL, SIDE-BY-SIDE			
Various Calibers, Sidelock, Fancy Engraving, Fancy Checkering, Fancy Wood, *Modern*	9000	22000	25000
SHOTGUN, DOUBLE BARREL, OVER-UNDER			
12 Ga., Vent Rib, Single Selective Trigger, Pistol-Grip Stock, *Modern*	$11000	$25000	$30000
Purdy, Various Gauges, Sidelock, Automatic Ejector, Double Trigger, Fancy Engraving, Fancy Checkering, *Modern*	9000	20000	25000
Purdy, Various Gauges, Sidelock, Automatic Ejector, Single Trigger, Fancy Engraving, Fancy Checkering, *Modern*	9000	20000	25000
Various Gauges, Extra Barrels Only $3,000.00-$5,000.00			
Woodward, Various Gauges, Sidelock, Automatic Ejector, Double Trigger, Fancy Engraving, Fancy Checkering, *Modern*	8000	18000	20000
Woodward, Various Gauges, Sidelock, Automatic Ejector, Single Trigger, Fancy Engraving, Fancy Checkering, *Modern*	9000	25000	30000
SHOTGUN, DOUBLE BARREL, SIDE-BY-SIDE			
12 Ga., Extra Barrel, Vent Rib, Single Selective Trigger, Engraved, Cased with Accessories, *Modern*	9000	20000	25000
12 Ga., Extra Barrels, 10 Ga., Pistol-Grip Stock, Cased with Accesories, *Modern*	9000	20000	25000
Featherweight, Various Gauges, Sidelock, Automatic Ejector, Double Trigger, Fancy Engraving, Fancy Checkering, *Modern*	7000	18000	20000
Featherweight, Various Gauges, Sidelock, Automatic Ejector, Single Trigger, Fancy Engraving, Fancy Checkering, *Modern*	9000	20000	22500
Game Gun, Various Gauges, Sidelock, Automatic Ejector, Double Trigger, Fancy Engraving, Fancy Checkering, *Modern*	7000	18000	20000
Game Gun, Various Gauges, Sidelock, Automatic Ejector, Single Trigger, Fancy Engraving, Fancy Checkering, *Modern*	9000	20000	22750
Pigeon Gun, 12 Ga., Single Selective Trigger, Vent Rib, Cased Straight Grip, *Modern*	9000	20000	22750
Pigeon Gun, Various Gauges, Sidelock, Automatic Ejector, Double Trigger, Fancy Engraving, Fancy Checkering, *Modern*	7000	18000	20000
Pigeon Gun, Various Gauges, Sidelock, Automatic Ejector, Single Trigger, Fancy Engraving, Fancy Checkering, *Modern*	7000	18000	20000
Two-Inch, 12 Ga. 2", Sidelock, Automatic Ejector, Double Trigger, Fancy Engraving, Fancy Checkering, *Modern*	7000	15000	17000

	Fair	V. Good	Excellent
Two-Inch, 12 Ga. 2", Sidelock, Automatic Ejector, Single Trigger, Fancy Engraving, Fancy Checkering, *Modern*	$9000	$18000	$20000
Various Gauges, Extra Barrels Only $2,600.00–$3,750.00			

SHOTGUN, SINGLESHOT

	Fair	V. Good	Excellent
12 Ga., Vent Rig, Plain, Trap Grade, *Modern*	5000	13500	15000

PZK

Kohout & Spolecnost, Kydne, Czechoslovakia.

HANDGUN, SEMI-AUTOMATIC

	Fair	V. Good	Excellent
PZK, 6.35mm, Clip Fed, *Modern*	$75	$150	$175

Q

QUACKENBUSH

Herkimer, N.Y., c. 1880.

RIFLE, SINGLESHOT BOY'S RIFLE

	Fair	*V. Good*	*Excellent*
.22 R.F., Side Swing Breech, Nickel Plated, Takedown, *Curio*	$150	$300	$350

QUAIL

Made by Crescent, c. 1900. See Crescent Fire Arms Co., Shotgun, Double Barrel, Side-by-Side; Shotgun, Singleshot.

QUAIL'S FARGO

Tradename used by Dakin Gun Co. and Simmons Specialties.

SHOTGUN, DOUBLE BARREL, SIDE-BY-SIDE

	Fair	*V. Good*	*Excellent*
12 Ga., Checkered Stock, Plain, *Modern*	$75	$150	$175

QUEEN CITY

Made by Crescent for Elmira Arms Co., c. 1900. See Crescent Fire Arms Co., Shotgun, Double Barrel, Side-by-Side; Shotgun, Singleshot.

R

RADIUM
Gabilondo y Urresti, Guernica, Spain, c. 1910.

HANDGUN, SEMI-AUTOMATIC

	Fair	V. Good	Excellent
6.35mm, Fixed Magazine, Side Loading, Blue, *Curio*	$75	$150	$175

RADOM
Fabryka Broni w Radomu, Radom, Poland, c. 1930 through WWII.

HANDGUN, REVOLVER

	Fair	V. Good	Excellent
Ng 30, 7.62mm Nagant, Gas Seal, Double Action, *Curio*	150	300	325

HANDGUN, SEMI-AUTOMATIC

	Fair	V. Good	Excellent
VIS 1935, 9mm Luger, Clip Fed, Military, Nazi-Production, Early, *Curio*	200	400	450

Radom, Early Nazi

	Fair	V. Good	Excellent
VIS 1935, 9mm Luger, Clip Fed, Military, Nazi-Proofed, Early Type, *Curio*	700	1500	1750
VIS 1935 Navy, 9mm Luger, Clip Fed, Military, Nazi-Production, Late, *Curio*	450	1000	1250
VIS 1935 Polish, 9mm Luger, Clip Fed, Military, *Curio*	450	1000	1250

RANDALL
Randall Firearms Mfg. Corp., Sun Valley, Calif.

HANDGUN, SEMI-AUTOMATIC

	Fair	V. Good	Excellent
Compact Model, Various Calibers, Stainless Steel, M1911A1 Style, Herritt Grips, Adjustable Sights, *Modern*	$300	$600	$700
Service Model, Various Calibers, Stainless Steel, M1911A1 Style, Herritt Grips, Adjustable Sights, *Modern*	325	700	800
Target Model, Various Calibers, Stainless Steel, M1911A1 Style, Herritt Grips, Adjustable Sights with Rib, *Modern*	325	700	900

RANGER
Made by E.L. Dickinson, Springfield, Mass.

HANDGUN, REVOLVER

	Fair	V. Good	Excellent
#2, .32 Short R.F., 5 Shot, Spur Trigger, Solid Frame, Single Action, *Antique*	75	125	175

RANGER
Made by Hopkins & Allen, c. 1880.

HANDGUN, REVOLVER

	Fair	V. Good	Excellent
.22 Short R.F., 7 Shot, Spur Trigger, Solid Frame, Single Action, *Antique*	75	150	175
.32 Short R.F., 6 Shot, Spur Trigger, Solid Frame, Single Action, *Antique*	75	150	175

RANGER
Made by Stevens Arms.

RIFLE, SLIDE ACTION

	Fair	V. Good	Excellent
Model 70, .22 L.R.R.F., Solid Frame, Hammer, *Modern*	75	125	175
Model 75, .22 L.R.R.F., Tube Feed, Hammerless, *Modern*	75	150	175

SHOTGUN, DOUBLE BARREL, SIDE-BY-SIDE

	Fair	V. Good	Excellent
Model 215, 12 and 16 Gauges, Steel Barrels, Outside Hammers, *Modern*	75	125	175
Model 315, Various Gauges, Steel Barrels, Hammerless, *Modern*	75	150	175

SHOTGUN, SINGLESHOT

	Fair	V. Good	Excellent
Model 89 Dreadnaught, Various Gauges, Hammer, *Modern*	$25	$50	$75

RANGER ARMS, INC.

Gainesville, Tex., c. 1972.

RIFLE, BOLT ACTION

	Fair	V. Good	Excellent
Bench Rest/Varminter, Various Calibers, Singleshot, Target Rifle, Thumbhole Stock, Heavy Barrel, Recoil Pad, *Modern*	200	425	500
Governor Grade, Various Calibers, Sporting Rifle, Fancy Checkering, Fancy Wood, Recoil Pad, Sling Swivels, *Modern*	150	375	450
Governor Grade Magnum, Various Calibers, Sporting Rifle, Fancy Checkering, Fancy Wood, Recoil Pad, Sling Swivels, *Modern*	200	400	475
Senator Grade, Various Calibers, Sporting Rifle, Fancy Checkering, Recoil Pad, Sling Swivels, *Modern*	150	325	400
Senator Grade Magnum, Various Calibers, Sporting Rifle, Fancy Checkering, Recoil Pad, Sling Swivels, *Modern*	175	350	425
Statesman Grade, Various Calibers, Sporting Rifle, Checkered Stock, Recoil Pad, Sling Swivels, *Modern*	125	250	325
Statesman Grade Magnum, Various Calibers, Sporting Rifle, Checkered Stock, Recoil Pad, Sling Swivels, *Modern*	150	300	350

RASCH

Brunswick, Germany, 1790–1810.

RIFLE, FLINTLOCK

	Fair	V. Good	Excellent
Yaeger, Octagon Barrel, Brass Furniture, Engraved, Carved, Target Sights, *Antique*	1200	3000	3500

RATHFONG, GEORGE

Lancaster, Pa. 1774–1809. See U.S. Military, Kentucky Rifles.

RATHFONG, JACOB

Lancaster, Pa. 1810–1839. See Kentucky Rifles and Pistols.

RAVEN

Raven Arms, Industry, Calif. 1970–1991.

HANDGUN, SEMI-AUTOMATIC

	Fair	V. Good	Excellent
MP-25, .25 ACP, Clip Fed, Nickel, *Modern*	15	25	50
MP-25, .25 ACP, Clip Fed, Teflon, *Modern*	$15	$25	$50
MP-25, .25 ACP, Clip Fed, Teflon, *Modern*	15	25	50
P-25, .25 ACP, Clip Fed, Blue, *Modern*	15	25	50
P-25, .25 ACP, Clip Fed, Chrome, *Modern*	15	25	50
P-25, .25 ACP, Clip Fed, Nickel, *Modern*	15	25	50

REASOR, DAVID

Lancaster, Pa. 1749–1780. See Kentucky Rifles and Pistols.

RECK

Reck Sportwaffenfabrik, Arnsberg, West Germany.

HANDGUN, REVOLVER

	Fair	V. Good	Excellent
.22 L.R.R.F., Double Action, Blue, *Modern*	15	25	50

HANDGUN, SEMI-AUTOMATIC

	Fair	V. Good	Excellent
P-8, 6.35mm, Clip Fed, Blue, *Modern*	25	50	75

RED CLOUD

HANDGUN, REVOLVER

	Fair	V. Good	Excellent
.32 Long R.F., 5 Shot, Single Action, Solid Frame, Spur Trigger, *Antique*	75	150	175

RED JACKET

Made by Lee Arms, Wilkes-Barre, Pa., c. 1870.

HANDGUN, REVOLVER

	Fair	V. Good	Excellent
.22 Long R.F., 7 Shot, Single Action, Solid Frame, Spur Trigger, *Antique*	75	150	175
.32 Long R.F., 5 Shot, Single Action, Solid Frame, Spur Trigger, *Antique*	75	150	175

REED, JAMES

Lancaster, Pa. 1778–1780. See Kentucky Rifles.

REFORM

August Schueler, Suhl, Germany, 1900–1905.

HANDGUN, MANUAL REPEATER

	Fair	V. Good	Excellent
6mm R.F., 4 Barrel, Double Action, Hammer, *Curio*	250	550	650

REFORM

Spain, c. 1920.

	Fair	V. Good	Excellent
HANDGUN, SEMI-AUTOMATIC			
6.35mm, Clip Fed, Blue, *Curio* ...	$50	$100	$125

REGENT
Gregorio Bolumburu, Eibar, Spain, c. 1925.

HANDGUN, SEMI-AUTOMATIC			
6.35mm, Clip Fed, Blue, *Curio* ...	50	100	125

REGENT
Karl Burgsmuller, Kreiensen, Germany.

HANDGUN, REVOLVER			
.22 L.R.R.F., Double Action, Blue, *Modern*	25	50	75

REGINA
Gregorio Bolumburu, Eibar, Spain, c. 1920.

HANDGUN, SEMI-AUTOMATIC			
Pocket, 7.65mm, Clip Fed, Blue, *Curio*	75	125	150
Vest Pocket, 6.35mm, Clip Fed, Blue, *Curio*	50	100	125

Regina Vest Pocket

REGNUM
Tradename used by August Menz, Suhl, Germany.

HANDGUN, MANUAL REPEATER			
6.35mm, 4 Barrels, Spur Trigger, Hammer, *Curio*	200	400	450

REID PATENT REVOLVERS
Made by W. Irving for James Reid, N.Y., 1862–1884.

HANDGUN, REVOLVER			
Model 1.22 Short R.F., 7 Shot, Spur Trigger, Solid Frame, Single Action, *Antique*	450	1000	1200
Model 2.32 Short R.F., 7 Shot, Spur Trigger, Solid Frame, Single Action, *Antique*	400	800	1000

Regnum

	Fair	V. Good	Excellent
My Friend .41 Short R.F., .22 R.F., Knuckleduster, 7 Shot, *Antique* ...	$1500	$3500	$3750
My Friend, .22 R.F., Knuckleduster, 7 Shot, *Antique*	350	750	850
My Friend, .32 R.F., Knuckleduster, 7 Shot, *Antique*	400	850	950

REIMS
Azanza y Arrizabalaga, Eibar, Spain, c. 1914.

HANDGUN, SEMI-AUTOMATIC			
1914 Model, 6.35mm, Clip Fed, *Curio*	50	100	125
1914 Model, 7.65mm, Clip Fed, *Curio*	75	125	150

REINA
Mre. d'Armes des Pyrenees, Hendaye, France, c. 1930.

HANDGUN, SEMI-AUTOMATIC			
7.65mm, Clip Fed, Blue, *Curio* ...	50	125	150

REISING
Hartford, Conn. 1916–1924.

HANDGUN, SEMI-AUTOMATIC			
Target (Hartford), .22 L.R.R.F., Clip Fed, Hammer, *Curio*	250	525	575
Target (N.Y.), .22 L.R.R.F., Clip Fed, Hammer, *Curio*	300	600	650

REMINGTON ARMS CO.
Eliphalet Remington, Herkimer County, N.Y. 1816–1831. Ilion, N.Y. 1831 to Date. 1856, E. Remington & Sons; 1888, Remington Arms Co.; 1910, Remington Arms U.M.C. Co.; 1925 to Date Remington Arms Co., Ilion, N.Y. Also see the Commemorative Section. America's oldest gunmaker, Remington was founded by Connecticut-born Eliphalet Remington, in 1816, in central New York State. The site eventually came to be called Ilion; initial production was of gun barrels. An 1845 government contract was instrumental in expanding the operation for the quality manufacture of complete guns, beginning with the Jenks breechloading

rifle. As the line expanded, revolvers were added, their design—in some details—superior to the Colt, the exclusive patent for which had expired in 1857. During the Civil War, Remington was awarded substantial contracts, and the armory was expanded significantly. The founder was a skillful businessman, adept at hiring talented designers who created a solid line of firearms bearing the Remington name. The death of Eliphalet in 1861 left the business in the hands of his three sons. Philo, Eliphalet III and Samuel Remington all carried on the family enterprise. By the end of the 1860s the company offered a more broad-based line of firearms than any other American gunmaker—primarily revolvers and rifles, derringers, rolling block breechloading pistols and rifles, a cane gun, military rifles, a percussion shotgun, and singleshot target rifles. Financial problems in the 1880s led to the purchase by the New York firm Hartley & Graham, leading jobbers of the day. The same company had established the Union Metallic Cartridge Company, Bridgeport, Connecticut, in 1867. In 1912 Remington Arms merged with Union Metallic Cartridge Company, and the name was changed to Remington-UMC. In 1935, after another reorganization, the name was changed to Remington Arms Company, Inc. From 1933 to 1993 the Du Pont Corporation owned Remington; in 1993 Du Pont's interest was bought out by the New York investment banking group of Clayton, Dubilier, Rice. Remington's fame has undergone somewhat of a revival, with a much more proactive management, and the running of the Remington stock car, on the NASCAR circuit, beginning in the 1995–96 season.

HANDGUN, DOUBLE BARREL, OVER-UNDER

	Fair	V. Good	Excellent
"Over and Under" Derringer, 1st Model, .41 Short R.F., Spur Trigger, Tip-Up, No Extractor, Markings on Side of Barrel, E. Remington & Sons, *Antique*	$600	$1700	$2000
"Over and Under" Derringer, 2nd Model, .41 Short R.F., Spur Trigger, Tip-Up, No Extractor, Markings on Side of Barrel, E. Remington & Sons, *Antique*	600	1700	2000
"Over and Under" Derringer, 3rd Model, .41 Short R.F., Spur Trigger, Tip-Up, No Extractor, Markings on Top of Barrel, E. Remington & Sons, *Antique*	325	800	1000
"Over and Under" Derringer, 4th Model, .41 Short R.F., Spur Trigger, Tip-Up, No Extractor, Markings on Top of Barrel, Remington Arms Co., *Curio*	300	800	900
"Over and Under" Derringer, 5th Model, .41 Short R.F., Spur Trigger, Tip-Up, with Extractor, Markings on Top of Barrel, *Curio*	300	800	900
"Over and Under" Derringer, 6th Model, .41 Short R.F., Spur Trigger, Tip-Up, with Extractor, Remington Arms Co. #'s L75925-L99941, *Curio*	300	800	900

HANDGUN, MANUAL REPEATER

	Fair	V. Good	Excellent
Elliot Derringer, .22 Short R.F., 5 Shot, Double Action, Ring Trigger, Rotating Firing Block, *Antique*	$325	$850	$950
Elliot Derringer, .32 Short R.F., 5 Shot, Double Action, Ring Trigger, Rotating Firing Block, *Antique*	300	550	700
Rider Single Shot Derringer, .32 Extra Short R.F., Tube Feed, Spur Trigger, 5 Shot, *Antique*	600	1200	1400

HANDGUN, PERCUSSION

	Fair	V. Good	Excellent
.31, Beals #1, Revolver, Pocket Pistol, 5 Shot, Octagon Barrel, 3" Barrel, *Antique*	350	750	900
.31, Beals #2, Revolver, Pocket Pistol, 5 Shot, Octagon Barrel, 3" Barrel, Spur Trigger, *Antique*	1700	4000	4500
.31, Beals #3, Revolver, Octagon Barrel, 4" Barrel, Spur Trigger, with Loading Lever, *Antique*	600	1200	1500
.31, New Model Pocket, Revolver, Safety Notches on Cylinder, Spur Trigger, 5 Shot, Octagon Barrel, *Antique*	400	800	1000
.31, Rider Pocket, Revolver, Double Action, 5 Shot, Octagon Barrel, 3" Barrel, *Antique*	300	625	700
.36, Beals Navy, Revolver, Single Action, Octagon Barrel, 7½" Barrel, *Antique*	600	1800	2000
.36, Belt Model, Revolver, Safety Notches on Cylinder, Single Action, Octagon Barrel, 6½" Barrel, *Antique*	500	1000	1200
.36, Belt Model, Revolver, Safety Notches on Cylinder, Double Action, Octagon Barrel, 6½" Barrel, *Antique*	500	900	1000
.36, Model 1861 Navy, Revolver, Channeled Loading Lever, Single Action, Octagon Barrel, 7½" Barrel, *Antique*	700	1400	1600
.36, New Model Navy, Revolver, Safety Notches on Cylinder, Single Action, Octagon Barrel, 7½" Barrel, *Antique*	600	1300	1500
.36, Police Model, Revolver, Single Action, Octagon Barrel, Various Barrel Lengths, 5 Shot, *Antique*	450	900	1000
.44, Beals Army, Revolver, Single Action, Octagon Barrel, 8" Barrel, *Antique*	1200	2500	3000
.44, Model 1861 Army, Revolver, Channeled Loading Lever, Single Action, Octagon Barrel, 8" Barrel, *Antique*	1200	2500	3000

	Fair	V. Good	Excellent
.44, New Model Army, Revolver, Safety Notches on Cylinder, Single Action, Octagon Barrel, 7½" Barrel, *Antique*	$700	$2100	$2500

HANDGUN, REVOLVER

	Fair	V. Good	Excellent
Iroquois, .22 L.R.R.F., 7 Shot, Solid Frame, Spur Trigger, Single Action, Fluted Cylinder, *Antique*	200	400	450
Iroquois, .22 L.R.R.F., 7 Shot, Solid Frame, Spur Trigger, Single Action, Unfluted Cylinder, *Antique*	200	450	500
Model 1875, .44-40 WCF, Single Action, Western Style, Solid Frame, *Antique*	1600	3250	3750
Model 1875, .45 Colt, Single Action, Western Style, Solid Frame, *Antique*	1200	3000	3500
Model 1890, .44-40 WCF, Single Action, Western Style, Solid Frame, *Antique*	1700	4000	5000
Smoot #1, .30 Short R.F., 5 Shot, Solid Frame, Spur Trigger, Single Action, *Antique*	150	350	400
Smoot #2, .32 Short R.F., 5 Shot, Solid Frame, Spur Trigger, Single Action, *Antique*	150	325	375
Smoot #3, .38 Long R.F., 5 Shot, Solid Frame, Spur Trigger, Single Action, Birdhead Grip, *Antique*	175	400	450
Smoot #3, .38 Long R.F., 5 Shot, Solid Frame, Spur Trigger, Single Action, Saw Handle Grip, *Antique*	200	450	500
Smoot #4, .38 S & W, 5 Shot, Solid Frame, Spur Trigger, Single Action, No Ejector Housing, *Antique*	150	325	375
Smoot #4, .41 Short R.F., 5 Shot, Solid Frame, Spur Trigger, Single Action, No Ejector Housing, *Antique*	150	350	400
Zig-Zag Derringer, .22 Short R.F., Pepperbox, Double Action, 6 Shot, Ring Trigger, *Antique*	1400	3000	3250

HANDGUN, SEMI-AUTOMATIC

	Fair	V. Good	Excellent
Model 51, .32 ACP, Early, Clip Fed, Grip Safety, *Modern*	150	350	400
Model 51, .32 ACP, Late, Clip Fed, Grip Safety, *Modern*	150	325	375
Model 51, .380 ACP, Early, Clip Fed, Grip Safety, *Modern*	150	400	450
Model 51, .380 ACP, Late, Clip Fed, Grip Safety, *Modern*	150	375	425

HANDGUN, SINGLESHOT

	Fair	V. Good	Excellent
#1 Vest Pocket, .22 Short R.F., Iron Frame, No Breech Bolt, Spur Trigger, *Antique*	250	500	650
#2 Vest Pocket, .30 Short R.F., Iron Frame, "Split Breech" Model, Spur Trigger, *Antique*	$300	$775	$850
#2 Vest Pocket, .41 Short R.F., Iron Frame, "Split Breech" Model, Spur Trigger, *Antique*	400	850	1000
Elliot Derringer, .41 Short R.F., Iron Frame, Birdhand Grip, No Breech Bolt, *Antique*	500	1175	1400
Mark III, 10 Gauge, Signal Pistol, 9" Barrel, Spur Trigger, Brass Frame, *Curio*	150	300	350
Model 1865 Navy, .50 Rem. Navy R.F., Rolling Block, Sour Trigger, 8½" Barrel, *Antique*	900	2000	2500
Model 1867 Navy, .50 Rem. Rolling Block, 7" Barrel, *Antique*	500	1000	1250
Model 1871 Army, .50 Rem. Rolling Block, 8" Barrel, *Antique*	700	1500	1650
Model 1891 Target, .22 L.R.R.F., Rolling Block, 8" Barrel, Half-Octagon Barrel, Plain Barrel, *Antique*	800	1750	2000
Model 1891 Target, .25 Short R.F., Rolling Block, 8" Barrel, Half-Octagon Barrel, Plain Barrel, *Antique*	650	1250	1500
Model 1891 Target, .32 Long R.F., Rolling Block, 8" Barrel, Half-Octagon Barrel, Plain Barrel, *Antique*	650	1400	1600
Model 1891 Target, .32 S & W, Rolling Block, 8" Barrel, Half-Octagon Barrel, Plain Barrel, *Antique*	800	1650	2000
Model 1891 Target, .32–20 WCF, Rolling Block, 8" Barrel, Half-Octagon Barrel, Plain Barrel, *Antique*	900	2000	2500
Model 1891 Target, Rolling Block, 10" Barrel, Add 15%-20%			
Model 1891 Target, Rolling Block, 12" Barrel, Add 15%-20%			
Model 1901 Target, .22 L.R.R.F., Rolling Block, 10" Barrel, Checkered Stock, Half-Octagon Barrel, *Modern*	650	1450	1650
Model 1901 Target, .44 Russian, Rolling Block, 10" Barrel, Checkered Stock, Half-Octagon Barrel, *Modern*	700	1800	2500
XP-100 Silhouette, 7mm BR Rem., Bolt Action, Target Nylon Stock, 15" Barrel, Vent Rib, Open Sights, Cased, *Modern*	150	375	425
XP-100, .221 Rem. Fireball, Bolt Action, Target Nylon Stock, 10½" Barrel, Vent Rib, Open Sights, Cased, *Modern*	150	300	350

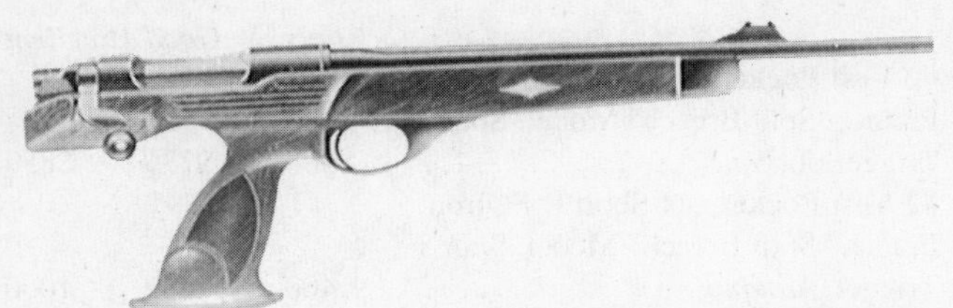

Remington XP-100

RIFLE, BOLT ACTION

	Fair	*V. Good*	*Excellent*
Enfield 1914, .303 British, Full-Stocked, Military, *Curio*	$125	$250	$300
International (1961), Various Calibers, Singleshot, Target Stock, No Sights, with Accessories, *Modern*	200	400	450
Model 1907/15 French, 8 × 50R Lebel, Carbine, Military, *Curio*	150	300	350
Model 1907/15 French, 8 × 50R Lebel, Military, *Curio*	150	325	375
Model 1917 U.S., .30-06 Springfield, Full-Stocked, Military, *Curio*	150	300	350
Model 30A, Various Calibers, Sporting Rifle, Plain, Open Rear Sight, *Modern*	150	375	425
Model 30F Premier, Various Calibers, Sporting Rifle, Fancy Checkering, Fancy Engraving, Fancy Wood, *Modern*	500	1200	1500
Model 30R, Various Calibers, Sporting Rifle, Plain, Carbine, Open Rear Sights, *Modern*	200	425	475
Model 30S, Various Calibers, Sporting Rifle, Checkered Stock, Peep Sights, *Modern*	225	600	750
Model 33A, *Modern*	50	75	100
Model 33A, .22 L.R.R.F., Plain, Singleshot, Peep Sights, *Modern*	50	75	100
Model 33NRA, .22 L.R.R.F., Plain, Singleshot, Peep Sights, Sling Swivels, *Modern*	75	100	125
Model 341A, .22 L.R.R.F., Tube Feed, Takedown, Open Rear Sight, *Modern*	50	100	275
Model 341P, .22 L.R.R.F., Tube Feed, Takedown, Peep Sights, *Modern*	75	150	175
Model 341SB, .22 L.R.R.F., Tube Feed, Takedown, Smoothbore, *Modern*	50	100	600
Model 34A, .22 L.R.R.F., Tube Feed, Takedown, Lyman Sights, *Modern*	75	100	125
Model 34A, .22 L.R.R.F., Tube Feed, Takedown, Open Rear Sight, *Modern*	75	100	125
Model 34NRA, .22 L.R.R.F., Tube Feed, Takedown, Lyman Sights, Target, *Modern*	65	125	275

	Fair	*V. Good*	*Excellent*
Model 37A, .22 L.R.R.F., 5 Shot Clip, Target Stock, Target Sights, Target Barrel, *Modern*	$150	$325	$400
Model 37A, .22 L.R.R.F., 5 Shot Clip, Target Stock, Target Sights, Target Barrel, Fancy Wood, *Modern*	150	375	425
Model 37AX, .22 L.R.R.F., 5 Shot Clip, Target Stock, No Sights, Target Barrel, *Modern*	150	325	375
Model 40-XB CF-H2, Various Calibers, Stainless Steel Barrel, Heavy Barrel, Target Stock, No Sights, *Modern*	450	1000	1100
Model 40-XB CF-S2, Various Calibers, Stainless Steel Barrel, Target Stock, No Sights, *Modern*	500	1150	1250
Model 40-XB RF-H2, .22 L.R.R.F., Heavy Barrel, Target Stock, No Sights, *Modern*	400	850	950
Model 40-XB RF-S2, .22 L.R.R.F., Target Stock, No Sights, *Modern*	350	700	800
Model 40-XB-BR, Various Calibers, Stainless Steel, Heavy Barrel, Target Stock, No Sights, *Modern*	625	1350	1500

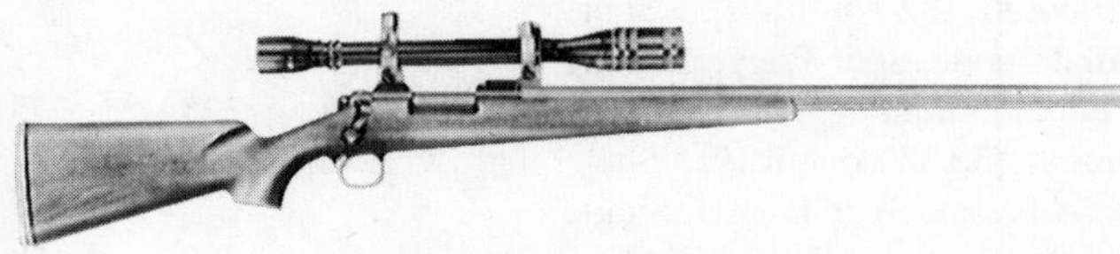

Remington 40-XB-BR

Model 40-XB-BR, For 2 oz. Trigger, Add $40.00–$65.00

Model 40-XB-CF, For Repeater, Add $25.00

	Fair	*V. Good*	*Excellent*
Model 40X-CFH2, Various Calibers, Singleshot, Target Stock, No Sights, Heavy Barrel, *Modern*	400	850	950
Model 40X-CFS2, Various Calibers, Singleshot, Target Stock, No Sights, *Modern*	400	800	900
Model 40X-H1, .22 L.R.R.F., Singleshot, Target Stock, Target Sights, Heavy Barrel, *Modern*	400	800	900
Model 40X-H2, .22 L.R.R.F., Singleshot, Target Stock, No Sights, Heavy Barrel, *Modern*	350	750	850
Model 40X-S1, .22 L.R.R.F., Singleshot, Target Stock, Target Sights, *Modern*	300	650	750
Model 40X-S2, .22 L.R.R.F., Singleshot, Target Stock, No Sights, *Modern*	300	600	700
Model 40XB Sporter, .22 L.R.R.F., *Modern*	500	1150	1250
Model 40XC National Match, .308 Winchester, Target Stock, Target Sights, *Modern*	700	1500	1750
Model 40XR Position, .22 L.R.R.F., Target Stock, no Sights, *Modern*	300	675	750

	Fair	V. Good	Excellent
Model 41A, .22 L.R.R.F., Takedown, Singleshot, Plain, Open Rear Sight, *Modern*	$25	$50	$75
Model 41AS, .22 WRF, Takedown, Singleshot, Plain, Open Rear Sight, *Modern*	75	125	150
Model 41P, .22 L.R.R.F., Takedown, Singleshot, Plain, Target Sights, *Modern*	25	50	75
Model 41SB, .22 L.R.R.F., Takedown, Singleshot, Plain, Smoothbore, *Modern*	75	150	175
Model 510A, .22 L.R.R.F., Singleshot, Open Rear Sight, Plain, Takedown, *Modern*	25	50	75
Model 510C, .22 L.R.R.F., Singleshot, Carbine, Plain, Takedown, *Modern*	25	50	75
Model 510P, .22 L.R.R.F., Singleshot, Peep Sights, Plain, Takedown, *Modern*	25	50	75
Model 510SB, .22 L.R.R.F., Singleshot, Smoothbore, Plain, Takedown, *Modern*	75	100	125
Model 510X, .22 L.R.R.F., Singleshot, Plain, *Modern*	50	75	100
Model 510X, .22 L.R.R.F., Singleshot, Plain, Smoothbore, *Modern*	50	75	100
Model 511A, .22 L.R.R.F., Clip Fed, Open Rear Sight, Plain, Takedown, *Modern*	50	75	100
Model 511P, .22 L.R.R.F., Clip Fed, Peep Sights, Plain, Takedown, *Modern*	50	75	100
Model 511SB, .22 L.R.R.F., Clip Fed, Smoothbore, Plain, Takedown, *Modern*	50	75	100
Model 511X, .22 L.R.R.F., Clip Fed, Plain, *Modern*	50	75	100
Model 512A, .22 L.R.R.F., Tube Feed, Plain, Open Rear Sight, *Modern*	50	75	100
Model 512P, .22 L.R.R.F., Tube Feed, Plain, Peep Sights, *Modern*	50	75	100
Model 512SB, .22 L.R.R.F., Tube Feed, Plain, Smoothbore, *Modern*	50	75	100
Model 512X, .22 L.R.R.F., Tube Feed, Plain, *Modern*	50	75	100
Model 513SA, .22 L.R.R.F., Clip Fed, Sporting Rifle, Open Rear Sight, Takedown, Checkered Stock, *Modern*	75	150	200
Model 513SP, .22 L.R.R.F., Clip Fed, Sporting Rifle, Peep Sights, Takedown, Checkered Stock, *Modern*	100	175	200
Model 513TR, .22 L.R.R.F., Clip Fed, Target Stock, Target Sights, Takedown, *Modern*	100	200	225
Model 513TX, .22 L.R.R.F., Clip Fed, Target Stock, No Sights, Takedown, *Modern*	75	125	175
Model 514, .22 L.R.R.F., Singleshot, Plain, Open Rear Sight, *Modern*	$25	$50	$75
Model 514BR (Youth), .22 L.R.R.F., Singleshot, Plain, Open Rear Sight, *Modern*	25	50	75
Model 514P, .22 L.R.R.F., Singleshot, Plain, Peep Sights, *Modern*	75	125	150
Model 521TL, .22 L.R.R.F., Takedown, Clip Fed, Target Stock, Lyman Sights, *Modern*	75	150	175
Model 540 XRJR Position, .22 L.R.R.F., Target Stock, No Sights, *Modern*	100	200	250
Model 540XR Position, .22 L.R.R.F., Target Stock, No Sights, *Modern*	100	225	275
Model 541-S, .22 L.R.R.F., Clip Fed, Checkered Stock, Fancy Wood, *Modern*	125	275	325
Model 580 BR (Youth), .22 L.R.R.F., Singleshot, Plain, *Modern*	50	75	100
Model 580 SB, .22 L.R.R.F., Singleshot, Plain, Smoothbore, *Modern*	25	50	75
Model 580, .22 L.R.R.F., Singleshot, Plain, *Modern*	50	75	100
Model 581, .22 L.R.R.F., Clip Fed, Plain, *Modern*	75	125	150
Model 581, .22 L.R.R.F., Clip Fed, Plain, Left-Hand, *Modern*	75	125	150
Model 582, .22 L.R.R.F., Tube Feed, Plain, *Modern*	75	125	150
Model 591, 5mm Rem. RFM, Clip Fed, Monte Carlo Stock, Plain, *Modern*	75	150	175
Model 592, 5mm Rem. RFM, Tube Feed, Monte Carlo Stock, Plain, *Modern*	100	250	300
Model 600 Montana Centennial, Trap Grade, Carbine, Checkered Stock, Commemorative, *Curio*	150	300	425
Model 600, Various Calibers, Vent Rib, Carbine, Checkered Stock, *Modern*	175	375	425
Model 600, Various Calibers, Vent Rib, Carbine, Magnum, Recoil Pad, Checkered Stock, *Modern*	200	400	450
Model 660, Various Calibers, Carbine, Checkered Stock, *Modern*	225	475	525
Model 660, Various Calibers, Carbine, Magnum, Recoil Pad, Checkered Stock, *Modern*	225	500	550
Model 700 Safari, Various Calibers, Magnum, Checkered Stock, Fancy Wood, *Modern*	300	675	750
Model 700ADL, Various Calibers, Checkered Stock, *Modern*	150	300	375
Model 700ADL, Various Calibers, Magnum, Checkered Stock, *Modern*	150	325	400
Model 700BDL, Various Calibers, Checkered Stock, Fancy Wood, *Modern*	175	350	400

	Fair	V. Good	Excellent
Model 700BDL, Various Calibers, Checkered Stock, Fancy Wood, Magnum, Left-Hand, *Modern*	$200	$400	$450
Model 700BDL, Various Calibers, Checkered Stock, Fancy Wood, Left-Hand, *Modern*	150	325	400
Model 700BDL, Various Calibers, Heavy Barrel, Varmint, Checkered Stock, Fancy Wood, *Modern*	200	400	450
Model 700BDL, Various Calibers, Magnum, Checkered Stock, Fancy Wood, *Modern*	175	375	425
Model 700C Custom, Various Calibers, Checkered Stock, Fancy Wood, *Modern*	350	775	850
Model 700D Peerless, Various Calibers, Fancy Checkering, Fancy Wood, Engraved, *Modern*	550	1175	1300
Model 700F Premier, Various Calibers, Fancy Checkering, Fancy Wood, Fancy Engraving, *Modern*	900	2000	2500
Model 720A, Various Calibers, Sporting Rifle, Open Rear Sight, *Modern*	450	950	1200
Model 720A, Various Calibers, Sporting Rifle, Target Sights, *Modern*	500	1050	1300
Model 720R, Various Calibers, Sporting Rifle, Open Rear Sight, Carbine, *Modern*	500	1000	1250
Model 720R, Various Calibers, Sporting Rifle, Target Sights, Carbine, *Modern*	500	1050	1300
Model 720S, Various Calibers, Sporting Rifle, Target Sights, *Modern*	500	1050	1300
Model 721 Peerless, Various Calibers, Long Action, Sporting Rifle, Fancy Wood, Engraved, Fancy Checkering, *Modern*	250	575	750
Model 721 Premier, Various Calibers, Long Action, Sporting Rifle, Fancy Wood, Fancy Engraving, Fancy Checkering, *Modern*	600	1250	1400
Model 721 Special, Various Calibers, Long Action, Sporting Rifle, Checkered Stock, Fancy Wood, *Modern*	100	200	250
Model 721, For .300 H & H Magnum, Add $20.00–$35.00			
Model 721A, Various Calibers, Long Action, Sporting Rifle, Plain, *Modern*	150	200	225
Model 721ADL, Various Calibers, Long Action, Sporting Rifle, Checkered Stock, *Modern*	150	300	350
Model 721BDL, Various Calibers, Long Action, Sporting Rifle, Monte Carlo Stock, Checkered Stock, Fancy Wood, *Modern*	175	375	450
Model 722, For .222 Rem. Add $25.00–$35.00			

	Fair	V. Good	Excellent
Model 722A, Various Calibers, Short Action, Sporting Rifle, Plain, *Modern*	$100	$200	$225
Model 722ADL, Various Calibers, Short Action, Sporting Rifle, Checkered Stock, *Modern*	150	300	350
Model 722BDL, Various Calibers, Short Action, Sporting Rifle, Checkered Stock, Fancy Wood, *Modern*	150	325	400
Model 722D Peerless, Various Calibers, Short Action, Sporting Rifle, Fancy Wood, Fancy Checkering, Engraved, *Modern*	450	950	1200
Model 722F Premier, Various Calibers, Short Action, Sporting Rifle, Fancy Wood, Fancy Engraving, Fancy Checkering, *Modern*	600	1250	1650
Model 725ADL, Various Calibers, Long Action, Magnum, Sporting Rifle, Checkered Stock, Fancy Wood, *Modern*	200	450	500
Model 725ADL, Various Calibers, Long Action, Sporting Rifle, Checkered Stock, Fancy Wood, *Modern*	150	350	400
Model 725D Peerless, Various Calibers, Long Action, Sporting Rifle, Engraved, Fancy Checkering, Fancy Wood, *Modern*	450	1000	1225
Model 725F Premier, Various Calibers, Long Action, Sporting Rifle, Fancy Engraving, Fancy Checkering, Fancy Wood, *Modern*	900	2150	2600
Model 788, Various Calibers, Clip Fed, Left-Hand, Plain, *Modern*	100	225	250
Model 788, Various Calibers, Clip Fed, Plain, *Modern*	100	200	225
Nylon 10, .22 L.R.R.F., Singleshot, Plastic Stock, *Modern*	25	50	75
Nylon 10-SB, .22 L.R.R.F., Singleshot, Plastic Stock, Smoothbore, *Modern*	100	200	225
Nylon 12, .22 L.R.R.F., Tube Feed, Plastic, *Modern*	50	75	100

RIFLE, LEVER ACTION

	Fair	V. Good	Excellent
Nylon 76, .22 L.R.R.F., Tube Feed, Plastic Stock, *Modern*	75	150	175

RIFLE, SEMI-AUTOMATIC

	Fair	V. Good	Excellent
Model Four, Various Calibers, Clip Fed, Sporting Rifle, Open Rear Sight, Checkered Stock, Fancy Wood, *Modern*	150	300	350
Model 10C Mohawk, .22 L.R.R.F., Clip Fed, Plastic Stock, *Modern*	50	75	100
Model 16, .22 Rem. Automatic R.F., Takedown, Tube Feed, *Modern*	125	175	225

	Fair	V. Good	Excellent
Model 16D, .22 Rem. Automatic R.F., Takedown, Tube Feed, Checkered Stock, Engraved, *Modern*	$800	$1700	$2000
Model 16F, .22 Rem. Automatic R.F., Takedown, Tube Feed, Fancy Checkering, Fancy Engraving, *Modern*	1100	2500	3000
Model 241A, .22 L.R.R.F., Tube Feed, Takedown, Open Rear Sight, *Modern*	100	225	275
Model 241A, .22 Short R.F., Tube Feed, Takedown, Open Rear Sight, *Modern*	100	200	350
Model 241D, .22 L.R.R.F., Tube Feed, Takedown, Fancy Checkering, Engraved, *Modern*	800	1700	2000
Model 241F, .22 L.R.R.F., Tube Feed, Takedown, Fancy Checkering, Fancy Engraving, *Modern*	1100	1700	3000
Model 24A, .22 L.R.R.F., Takedown, Plain, *Modern*	75	150	175
Model 24A, .22 Short R.F., Takedown, Plain, *Modern*	75	150	350
Model 24C, .22 L.R.R.F., Takedown, Checkered Stock, *Modern*	85	175	400
Model 24D Peerless, .22 L.R.R.F., Takedown, Fancy Checkering, Engraved, *Modern*	800	1700	2000
Model 24F Premier, .22 L.R.R.F., Takedown, Fancy Checkering, Fancy Engraving, *Modern*	1100	2700	3000
Model 550-2G, .22 Short R.F., Takedown, Open Rear Sight, Plain, *Modern*	50	125	150
Model 550A, .22 L.R.R.F., Takedown, Open Rear Sight, Plain, *Modern*	75	100	125
Model 550P, .22 L.R.R.F., Takedown, Peep Sights, Plain, *Modern*	75	100	125
Model 552A, .22 L.R.R.F., Tube Feed, Plain, *Modern*	75	100	125
Model 552BDL, .22 L.R.R.F., Tube Feed, Checkered Stock, *Modern*	75	125	150
Model 552C, .22 L.R.R.F., Tube Feed, Carbine, Plain, *Modern*	75	100	125
Model 552GS, .22 Short R.F., Tube Feed, Plain, *Modern*	75	125	150
Model 740 Peerless, Various Calibers, Clip Fed, Sporting Rifle, Open Rear Sight, Fancy Checkering, Engraved, *Modern*	900	1550	2100
Model 7400, Various Calibers, Clip Fed, Sporting Rifle, Open Rear Sight, Checkered Stock, *Modern*	150	325	350
Model 740A, Various Calibers, Clip Fed, Sporting Rifle, Open Rear Sight, Plain, *Modern*	100	200	250
Model 740ADL, Various Calibers, Clip Fed, Sporting Rifle, Open Rear Sight, Checkered Stock, *Modern*	125	225	275
Model 740BDL, Various Calibers, Clip Fed, Sporting Rifle, Open Rear Sight, Checkered Stock, Fancy Wood, *Modern*	150	275	325

	Fair	V. Good	Excellent
Model 740F Premier, Various Calibers, Clip Fed, Sporting Rifle, Open Rear Sight, Fancy Checkering, Fancy Engraving, *Modern*	$1400	$3000	$3500
Model 742 Canadian Centennial, Clip Fed, Sporting Rifle, Open Rear Sight, Checkered Stock, Commemorative, *Curio*	150	325	350
Model 742 Peerless, Various Calibers, Clip Fed, Sporting Rifle, Open Rear Sight, Fancy Checkering, Engraved, *Modern*	900	2000	2400
Model 742 Premier, Various Calibers, Clip Fed, Sporting Rifle, Open Rear Sight, Fancy Checkering, Engraved, *Modern*	1400	3500	4000
Model 742, .30-06 Springfield, Bicentennial, Clip Fed, *Modern*	150	300	325
Model 742, Various Calibers, Clip Fed, Sporting Rifle, Open Rear Sight, Checkered Stock, *Modern*	150	275	300
Model 742ADL, Various Calibers, Clip Fed, Sporting Rifle, Open Rear Sight, Checkered Stock, *Modern*	150	250	275
Model 742BDL, Various Calibers, Clip Fed, Sporting Rifle, Open Rear Sight, Checkered Stock, Fancy Wood, *Modern*	150	325	400
Model 742C, Various Calibers, Clip Fed, Sporting Rifle, Open Rear Sight, Carbine, Checkered Stock, *Modern*	125	250	300
Model 742CDL, Various Calibers, Clip Fed, Sporting Rifle, Open Rear Sight, Carbine, Fancy Wood, *Modern*	125	275	325
Model 77, .22 L.R.R.F., Clip Fed, Plastic Stock, *Modern*	50	75	100
Model 81A, Various Calibers, Takedown, Plain, *Modern*	150	275	325
Model 81D Peerless, Various Calibers, Takedown, Fancy Checkering, Engraved, *Modern*	800	1700	2000
Model 81F Premier, Various Calibers, Takedown, Fancy Checkering, Fancy Engraving, Fancy Wood, *Modern*	1700	3500	4500
Model 8A Standard, Various Calibers, Plain, *Modern*	150	275	325
Model 8C Special, Various Calibers, Checkered Stock, *Modern*	150	325	375
Model 8D Peerless, Various Calibers, Fancy Checkering, Light Engraving, *Modern*	300	800	1000
Model 8E Expert, Various Calibers, Fancy Checkering, Engraved, *Modern*	350	875	1000
Model 8F Premier, Various Calibers, Fancy Checkering, Fancy Engraving, Fancy Wood, *Modern*	2000	4500	5500
Nylon 11, .22 L.R.R.F., Clip Fed, Plastic Stock, *Modern*	25	50	75

	Fair	V. Good	Excellent
Nylon 66, .22 L.R.R.F., Tube Feed, Bicentennial, Plastic Stock, *Modern*	$75	$150	$175
Nylon 66, .22 L.R.R.F., Tube Feed, Plastic Stock, *Modern*	50	75	100
Nylon 66GS, .22 Short R.F., Tube Feed, Plastic Stock, *Modern*	75	100	125

RIFLE, SINGLESHOT

	Fair	V. Good	Excellent
1867 Cadet Navy, 50/45 C.F., Military, *Antique*	700	1450	1700
1867 Navy, 50/45 C.F., Military, Carbine, *Antique*	500	1150	1200
Beals, .32 R.F., Sliding Barrel, Plain, *Antique*	300	625	700
Hepburn #3, Various Calibers, Sporting Rifle, Checkered Stock, Hammer, *Curio*	900	2000	2500
Model 1, Various Calibers, Rolling Block, Sporting Rifle, Adjustable Sights, Plain Stock, *Curio*	500	1200	1500

Variations of Remington Rolling Blocks, from the top, *a mid-range target rifle,* center, *a .44-100 Target rifle with unusually heavy barrel (rifle weighs 15½ lbs.) and extreme styling to buttstock; at* bottom, *a Sporting or "buffalo" rifle, in 50/70 caliber with 30" octagonal heavyweight barrel.*

	Fair	V. Good	Excellent
Model 1, Various Calibers, Rolling Block, Target, Adjustable Sights, Checkered Stock, *Curio*	1200	3000	3500
Model 4, .22 L.R.R.F., Rolling Block, Takedown, *Modern*	200	425	450
Model 4S Boy Scout, .22 L.R.R.F., Rolling Block, Full-Stocked, *Curio*	250	725	600
Model 4S Boy Scout, .22 L.R.R.F., Rolling Block, Full-Stocked, with Bayonet, *Curio*	400	850	950
Model 5, Various Calibers, Rolling Block, Sporting Rifle, Adjustable Sights, Plain Stock, *Curio*	600	1200	1500
Model 6, .22 L.R.R.F., Rolling Block, Takedown, *Modern*	125	300	300
Model 6, .32 Long Rifle, Rolling Block, Takedown, *Modern*	$150	$325	$350
Model 7, Various Rimfires, Rolling Block, Target, Adjustable Sights, Checkered Stock, *Curio*	900	2100	2500
Model 7, Various Rimfires, Rolling Block, Target, Swiss Buttplate, Checkered Stock, Adjustable Sights, *Curio*	1200	2500	3000
Model 7, Various Rimfires, Rolling Block, Target, Swiss Buttplate, Checkered Stock, Peep Sights, *Curio*	1400	2750	3250
Split Breech, .46 R.F., Military, Carbine, *Antique*	700	1500	1750
Split Breech, .50 R.F., Military, Carbine, *Antique*	600	1200	1500

RIFLE, SLIDE ACTION

	Fair	V. Good	Excellent
Model Six, Various Calibers, Clip Fed, Sporting Rifle, Open Rear Sight, Monte Carlo Stock, Checkered Stock, *Modern*	150	350	375
Model 12A Standard, .22 L.R.R.F., Plain, Round Barrel, Tube Feed, *Modern*	200	450	600
Model 12B Gallery, .22 Short R.F., Plain, Round Barrel, Tube Feed, *Modern*	200	450	600
Model 12C, .22 L.R.R.F., Plain, Octagon Barrel, Tube Feed, Target, *Modern*	200	400	500
Model 12C-NRA, .22 L.R.R.F., Plain, Octagon Barrel, Tube Feed, Peep Sights, *Modern*	200	400	450
Model 12CS Special, .22 WRF, Plain, Octagon Barrel, Tube Feed, *Modern*	200	450	500
Model 12D Peerless, .22 L.R.R.F., Checkered Stock, Octagon Barrel, Tube Feed, Light Engraving, *Modern*	800	1800	2000
Model 12E Expert, .22 L.R.R.F., Fancy Checkering, Octagon Barrel, Tube Feed, Engraved, *Modern*	900	2000	2200
Model 12F Premier, .22 L.R.R.F., Fancy Checkering, Octagon Barrel, Tube Feed, Fancy Engraving, Fancy Wood, *Modern*	1400	3750	4500
Model 121A, .22 L.R.R.F., Takedown, Tube Feed, Plain, *Modern*	200	400	425
Model 121D Peerless, .22 L.R.R.F., Takedown, Tube Feed, Fancy Checkering, Engraved, *Modern*	800	1800	2000
Model 121F Premier, .22 L.R.R.F., Takedown, Tube Feed, Fancy Checkering, Fancy Engraving, *Modern*	1400	3750	4500
Model 121S, .22 WRF., Takedown, Tube Feed, Plain, *Modern*	300	625	700

	Fair	V. Good	Excellent
Model 121SB, .22 L.R.R.F., Takedown, Tube Feed, Plain, *Modern*	$250	$500	$600
Model 14, Various Calibers, Tube Feed, Plain, *Modern*	175	325	375
Model 14 A, Various Calibers, Tube Feed, Short Action, Plain, *Modern*	150	325	350
Model 14½, Various Calibers, Tube Feed, Short Action, Carbine, Plain Barrel, *Modern*	200	400	425
Model 141A, Various Calibers, Takedown, Tube Feed, Plain, *Modern*	175	375	400
Model 141D Peerless, Various Calibers, Takedown, Tube Feed, Fancy Checkering, Engraved, *Modern*	400	800	1000
Model 141F Premier, Various Calibers, Takedown, Tube Feed, Fancy Checkering, Fancy Engraving, *Modern*	1400	3750	4500
Model 141R, Various Calibers, Takedown, Tube Feed, Plain, Carbine, *Modern*	225	500	600
Model 14C Special, Various Calibers, Tube Feed, Checkered Stock, *Modern*	300	700	900
Model 14D Peerless, Various Calibers, Tube Feed, Fancy Checkering, Engraved, *Modern*	800	1800	2000
Model 14F Premier, Various Calibers, Tube Feed, Fancy Checkering, Fancy Wood, Fancy Engraving, *Modern*	1400	3750	4000
Model 14R, Various Calibers, Tube Feed, Carbine, Plain, *Modern*	250	500	600
Model 25A, Various Calibers, Takedown, Plain, *Modern*	200	450	500
Model 25D Peerless, Various Calibers, Takedown, Checkered Stock, Engraved, *Modern*	800	1800	2000
Model 25F Premier, Various Calibers, Takedown, Fancy Checkering, Fancy Engraving, *Modern*	1400	3750	4500
Model 25R, Various Calibers, Takedown, Plain, Carbine, *Modern*	300	600	800
Model 572, .22 L.R.R.F., Tube Feed, Open Rear Sight, Lightweight, Fancy Checkering, Chrome, *Modern*	75	150	175
Model 572A, .22 L.R.R.F., Tube Feed, Open Rear Sight, Plain, *Modern*	75	125	150
Model 572BDL, .22 L.R.R.F., Tube Feed, Open Rear Sight, Checkered Stock, *Modern*	75	150	175
Model 572SB, .22 L.R.R.F., Tube Feed, Plain, Smoothbore, *Modern*	50	125	150
Model 760, .30-06 Springfield, Bicentennial, Clip Fed, *Modern*	125	250	300

	Fair	V. Good	Excellent
Model 760A, Various Calibers, Clip Fed, Sporting Rifle, Open Rear Sight, Plain, *Modern*	$125	$225	$275
Model 760ADL, Various Calibers, Clip Fed, Sporting Rifle, Open Rear Sight, Monte Carlo Stock, Checkered Stock, *Modern*	150	275	325
Model 760BDL, Various Calibers, Clip Fed, Sporting Rifle, Open Rear Sight, Monte Carlo Stock, Checkered Stock, *Modern*	100	200	275
Model 760C, Various Calibers, Clip Fed, Sporting Rifle, Open Rear Sight, Carbine, Plain, *Modern*	125	250	325
Model 760CDL, Various Calibers, Clip Fed, Sporting Rifle, Open Rear Sight, Carbine, Checkered Stock, *Modern*	150	300	375
Model 760D Peerless, Various Calibers, Clip Fed, Sporting Rifle, Open Rear Sight, Fancy Checkering, Engraved, *Modern*	700	1500	1700
Model 760F Premier, Various Calibers, Clip Fed, Sporting Rifle, Open Rear Sight, Fancy Checkering, Fancy Engraving, *Modern*	1200	2750	3000
Model 7600, Various Calibers, Clip Fed, Sporting Rifle, Open Rear Sight, Monte Carlo Stock, Checkered Stock, *Modern*	150	300	375

SHOTGUN, DOUBLE BARREL, OVER-UNDER

	Fair	V. Good	Excellent
Model 32, Raised Solid Rib, Add $55.00–$150.00			
Model 32, for Vent Rib Add $95.00–$200.00			
Model 32, 12 Ga., Skeet Grade, Engraved, Fancy Checkering, *Modern*	800	2000	2500
Model 32A, 12 Ga., Double Trigger, Automatic Ejector, Plain Barrel, Engraved, Checkered Stock, *Modern*	600	1200	1500
Model 32A, 12 Ga., Single Selective Trigger, Automatic Ejector, Plain Barrel, Engraved, Checkered Stock, *Modern*	800	1500	1700
Model 32D, 12 Ga., Fancy Checkering, Fancy Wood, Fancy Engraving, *Modern*	900	2250	2500
Model 32E, 12 Ga., Fancy Checkering, Fancy Wood, Fancy Engraving, *Modern*	1400	3500	4000
Model 32F, 12 Ga., Fancy Checkering, Fancy Wood, Fancy Engraving, *Modern*	2500	5000	6000
Model 32TC, 12 Ga., Trap Grade, Single Selective Trigger, Engraved, Fancy Checkering, *Modern*	1200	2500	2750

	Fair	V. Good	Excellent
Model 3200, 12 Ga. Mag 3", Field Grade, Automatic Ejector, Single Selective Trigger, Vent Rib, Checkered Stock, *Modern*	$400	$800	$950
Model 3200, 12 Ga., Field Grade, Automatic Ejector, Single Selective Trigger, Vent Rib, Checkered Stock, *Modern*	350	775	850
Model 3200, 12 Ga., Skeet Grade, Automatic Ejector, Single Selective Trigger, Vent Rib, Checkered Stock, *Modern*	400	875	950
Model 3200, 12 Ga., Trap Grade, Automatic Ejector, Single Selective Trigger, Vent Rib, Checkered Stock, *Modern*	350	750	900
Model 3200 Competition, 12 Ga., Skeet Grade, Automatic Ejector, Single Selective Trigger, Vent Rib, Engraved, *Modern*	400	900	1000
Model 3200 Competition, 12 Ga., Skeet Grade, Automatic Ejector, Single Selective Trigger, Vent Rib, Engraved, Extra Barrels, *Modern*	1800	3750	4000
Model 3200 Competition, 12 Ga., Trap Grade, Automatic Ejector, Ejector, Single Selective Trigger, Vent Rib, Engraved, *Modern*	650	1050	1350

SHOTGUN, DOUBLE BARREL, SIDE-BY-SIDE

	Fair	V. Good	Excellent
Model 1882, Various Gauges, Hammer, Damascus Barrel, Checkered Stock, Double Trigger, *Antique*	400	900	1100
Model 1883, Various Gauges, Hammer, Damascus Barrel, Checkered Stock, Double Trigger, *Antique*	400	900	1100
Model 1883, Various Gauges, Hammer, Steel Barrel, Checkered Stock, Double Trigger, *Antique*	400	900	1100
Model 1894-A, Various Gauges, Hammerless, Damascus Barrel, Plain, Checkered Stock, Double Trigger, *Curio*	400	900	1100
Model 1894 AE, Various Gauges, Hammerless, Damascus Barrel, Automatic Ejector, Checkered Stock, Double Trigger, *Curio*	400	900	1100
Model 1894 AEO, Various Gauges, Hammerless, Steel Barrel, Automatic Ejector, Checkered Stock, Double Trigger, *Curio*	550	1000	1200
Model 1894 AO, Various Gauges, Hammerless, Steel Barrel, Plain, Checkered Stock, Double Trigger, *Curio*	400	900	1000
Model 1894 B, Various Gauges, Hammerless, Damascus Barrel, Light Engraving, Checkered Stock, Double Trigger, *Curio*	$400	$900	$1000
Model 1894 BE, Various Gauges, Hammerless, Damascus Barrel, Automatic Ejector, Light Engraving, Checkered Stock, *Curio*	450	900	1100
Model 1894 BEO, Various Gauges, Hammerless, Steel Barrel, Automatic Ejector, Light Engraving, Checkered Stock, *Curio*	450	900	1100
Model 1894 BO, Various Gauges, Hammerless, Steel Barrel, Light Engraving, Checkered Stock, Double Trigger, *Curio*	450	900	1000
Model 1894 C, Various Gauges, Hammerless, Damascus Barrel, Engraved, Checkered Stock, Double Trigger, *Curio*	500	1000	1200
Model 1894 CE, Various Gauges, Hammerless, Damascus Barrel, Automatic Ejector, Engraved, Checkered Stock, *Curio*	500	1200	1400
Model 1894 CEO, Various Gauges, Hammerless, Steel Barrel, Automatic Ejector, Engraved, Checkered Stock, *Curio*	550	1200	1400
Model 1894 CO, Various Gauges, Hammerless, Steel Barrel, Engraved, Checkered Stock, Double Trigger, *Curio*	550	1000	1200
Model 1894 D, Various Gauges, Hammerless, Damascus Barrel, Fancy Engraving, Fancy Checkering, Fancy Wood, *Curio*	750	1400	1600
Model 1894 DE, Various Gauges, Hammerless, Damascus Barrel, Automatic Ejector, Fancy Engraving, Fancy Checkering, *Curio*	800	1800	2000
Model 1894 DEO, Various Gauges, Hammerless, Steel Barrel, Automatic Ejector, Fancy Engraving, Fancy Checkering, *Curio*	800	1800	2000
Model 1894 DO, Various Gauges, Hammerless, Steel Barrel, Fancy Engraving, Fancy Checkering, Fancy Wood, *Curio*	600	1250	1450
Model 1894 E, Various Gauges, Hammerless, Damascus Barrel, Fancy Engraving, Fancy Checkering, Fancy Wood, *Curio*	700	1500	1800
Model 1894 EE, Various Gauges, Hammerless, Damascus Barrel, Automatic Ejector, Fancy Engraving, Fancy Checkering, *Curio*	1000	2200	2500
Model 1894 EEO, Various Gauges, Hammerless, Steel Barrel, Automatic Ejector, Fancy Engraving, Fancy Checkering, *Curio*	1200	2500	3000

	Fair	V. Good	Excellent
Model 1894 EO, Various Gauges, Hammerless, Steel Barrel, Fancy Engraving, Fancy Checkering, Fancy Wood, *Curio*	$900	$2000	$2250
Model 1894 Special, Various Gauges, Hammerless, Steel Barrel, Automatic Ejector, Fancy Engraving, Fancy Checkering, *Curio*	1400	3500	4000
Model 1900 K ED, 12 and 16 Gauges, Hammerless, Damascus Barrel, Automatic Ejector, Palm Rest, Checkered Stock, *Curio*	450	900	1000
Model 1900 K, 12 and 16 Gauges, Hammerless, Steel Barrel, Plain, Checkered Stock, *Curio*	350	700	800
Model 1900 KD, 12 and 16 Gauges, Hammerless, Damascus Barrel, Plain, Checkered Stock, *Curio*	350	700	800
Model 1900 KE, 12 and 16 Gauges, Hammerless, Steel Barrel, Automatic Ejector, Plain, Checkered Stock, *Curio*	400	800	1000
Model Parker AHE, 12 Ga., Double Trigger, Checkered Stock, *Modern*			

SHOTGUN, SEMI-AUTOMATIC

	Fair	V. Good	Excellent
Autoloading, 12 Ga., for Solid Rib, Add $35.00–$75.00			
Autoloading-0, 12 Ga., Takedown, Riot Gun, Plain, *Modern*	200	400	450
Autoloading-1, 12 Ga., Takedown, Plain, *Modern*	100	200	250
Autoloading-2, 12 Ga., Takedown, Checkered Stock, *Modern*	125	275	325
Autoloading-4, 12 Ga., Takedown, Fancy Checkering, Fancy Wood, Engraved, *Modern*	350	750	850
Autoloading-6, 12 Ga., Takedown, Fancy Checkering, Fancy Wood, Fancy Engraving, *Modern*	450	1000	1250
Model 11 Sportsman, Various Gauges, Skeet Grade, Vent Rib, Light Engraving, Checkered Stock, *Modern*	100	225	275
Model 11, for Vent Rib, Add $45.00–$100.00			
Model 11, Raised Solid Rib, Add $30.00–$50.00			
Model 11-48 R, 12 Ga., Riot Gun, Plain Barrel, *Modern*	250	500	550
Model 11-48A, Various Gauges, Plain Barrel, *Modern*	100	200	250
Model 11-48B, Various Gauges, Vent Rib, Checkered Stock, Fancy Wood, *Modern*	100	225	275
Model 11-48F Premier, Various Gauges, Vent Rib, Fancy Wood, Fancy Engraving, Fancy Checkering, *Modern*	800	1800	2000
Model 11-48 D Tournament, Various Gauges, Vent Rib, Fancy Wood, Fancy Engraving, Fancy Checkering, *Modern*	$325	$700	$1000
Model 11-48 RSS, 12 Ga., Open Rear Sight, Slug, Checkered Stock, *Modern*	125	225	275
Model 11-48 SA, Various Gauges, Skeet Grade, Vent Rib, Checkered Stock, *Modern*	125	250	325
Model 11-48 Special, Various Gauges, Vent Rib, Checkered Stock, *Modern*	150	375	425
Model 1100 Cutts, Various Gauges, Skeet Grade, Vent Rib, Checkered Stock, *Modern*	100	250	300
Model 1100 D Tournament, Various Gauges, Vent Rib, Fancy Checkering, Fancy Wood, Fancy Engraving, *Modern*	800	1800	2000
Model 1100 Deer Gun, Various Gauges, Open Rear Sight, Checkered Stock, *Modern*	125	250	325
Model 1100 Premier, Various Gauges, Vent Rib, Fancy Checkering, Fancy Wood, Fancy Engraving, *Modern*	1200	2700	3000
Model 1100 TA, 12 Ga., Bicentennial, Trap Grade, Vent Rib, Checkered Stock, *Modern*	150	275	325
Model 1100 TA, 12 Ga., Bicentennial, Trap Grade, Vent Rib, Monte Carlo Stock, Checkered Stock, *Modern*	150	300	350
Model 1100 TA, 12 Ga., Trap Grade, Vent Rib, Checkered Stock, *Modern*	150	250	300
Model 1100 TA, 12 Ga., Trap Grade, Vent Rib, Checkered Stock, Monte Carlo Stock, *Modern*	150	300	350
Model 1100, 12 Ga. Lightweight, Add $25.00–$50.00			
Model 1100, 12 Ga., Bicentennial, Skeet Grade, Vent Rib, Checkered Stock, *Modern*	150	350	325
Model 1100, for .28 Ga. or .410 Ga., Add $25.00–$50.00			
Model 1100, for Left Hand, Add $35.00–$75.00			
Model 1100, Various Gauges, Plain Barrel, Checkered Stock, *Modern*	125	250	225
Model 1100, Various Gauges, Plain Barrel, Magnum, Checkered Stock, *Modern*	150	300	325
Model 1100, Various Gauges, Skeet Grade, Vent Rib, Checkered Stock, *Modern*	175	300	425
Model 1100, Various Gauges, Vent Rib, Checkered Stock, *Modern*	150	275	325
Model 1100, Various Gauges, Vent Rib, Magnum, Checkered Stock, *Modern*	150	350	400

	Fair	V. Good	Excellent
Model 11A Sportsman, 12 Ga., Plain Barrel, Fancy Wood, Light Engraving, Checkered Stock, *Modern*	$100	$225	$275
Model 11A Sportsman, Various Gauges, Plain Barrel, Light Engraving, *Modern*	100	175	225
Model 11A, 12 Ga., Plain Barrel, *Modern*	100	175	250
Model 11A, 12 Ga., Plain Barrel, Fancy Wood, Checkered Stock, *Modern*	100	200	250
Model 11C, 12 Ga., Plain Barrel, Trap Grade, Fancy Checkering, Fancy Wood, *Modern*	150	325	375
Model 11D Sportsman, Various Gauges, Plain Barrel, Engraved, Fancy Checkering, *Modern*	300	650	800
Model 11D, 12 Ga., Plain Barrel, Fancy Checkering, Fancy Wood, Fancy Engraving, *Modern*	300	650	800
Model 11E Sportsman, Various Gauges, Plain Barrel, Fancy Checkering, Fancy Wood, Fancy Engraving, *Modern*	400	800	950
Model 11E, 12 Ga., Plain Barrel, Fancy Checkering, Fancy Wood, Fancy Engraving, *Modern*	350	750	900
Model 11F Sportsman, Various Gauges, Plain Barrel, Fancy Checkering, Fancy Wood, Fancy Engraving, *Modern*	800	1800	2000
Model 11F, 12 Ga., Plain Barrel, Fancy Checkering, Fancy Wood, Fancy Engraving, *Modern*	800	1800	2000
Model 11R, 12 Ga., Riot Gun, Commercial, *Modern*	200	400	450
Model 11R, 12 Ga., Riot Gun, Military, *Modern*	300	650	750
Model 48-D Sportsman, Various Gauges, Vent Rib, Fancy Checkering, Fancy Wood, Fancy Engraving, *Modern*	400	900	1000
Model 48-F Sportsman, Various Gauges, Vent Rib, Fancy Checkering, Fancy Wood, Fancy Engraving, *Modern*	700	1600	1800
Model 48-SA Sportsman, Various Gauges, Skeet Grade, Vent Rib, Rib, Checkered Stock, *Modern*	150	250	300
Model 48A Sportsman, Various Gauges, Plain Barrel, *Modern*	150	300	350
Model 48B Sportsman, Various Gauges, Vent Rib, Checkered Stock, *Modern*	175	300	350
Model 58 ADL, 12 and 20 Gauges, Vent Rib, Recoil Pad, Checkered Stock, Magnum, *Modern*	150	300	350
Model 58 ADL, Various Gauges, Plain Barrel, Checkered Stock, *Modern*	100	200	250
Model 58 ADL, Various Gauges, Vent Rib, Checkered Stock, *Modern*	$125	$250	$300
Model 58 ADX, Various Gauges, Vent Rib, Checkered Stock, Fancy Wood, *Modern*	100	200	250
Model 58 BDL, Various Gauges, Plain Barrel, Checkered Stock, Fancy Wood, *Modern*	125	250	300
Model 58 BDL, Various Gauges, Vent Rib, Checkered Stock, Fancy Wood, *Modern*	150	300	350
Model 58 D Tournament, Various Gauges,Vent Rib, Fancy Checkering, Fancy Wood, Fancy Engraving, *Modern*	300	800	1000
Model 58 F Premier, Various Gauges,Vent Rib, Fancy Checkering, Fancy Wood, Fancy Engraving, *Modern*	600	1350	1500
Model 58 RSS, 12 Ga. Slug, Open Rear Sight, Checkered Stock, *Modern*	100	200	250
Model 58 SA, Various Gauges, Skeet Grade, Vent Rib, Checkered Stock, *Modern*	125	275	325
Model 58 TB, 12 Ga., Trap Grade, Vent Rib, Checkered Stock, *Modern*	125	275	325
Model 878 A, 12 Ga., Plain Barrel, *Modern*	75	150	200
Model 878 A, 12 Ga., Vent Rib, *Modern*	100	175	225
Model 878 ADL, 12 Ga., Plain Barrel, Checkered Stock, *Modern*	100	175	225
Model 878 ADL, 12 Ga., Vent Rib, Checkered Stock, *Modern*	100	200	250
Model 878 D, 12 Ga., Vent Rib, Fancy Checkering, Fancy Wood, Fancy Engraving, *Modern*	350	700	800
Model 878 F, 12 Ga., Vent Rib, Fancy Checkering, Fancy Wood, Fancy Engraving, *Modern*	600	1200	1400
Model 878 SA, 12 Ga., Skeet Grade, Vent Rib, Checkered Stock, *Modern*	100	200	250

SHOTGUN, SINGLESHOT

	Fair	V. Good	Excellent
Model 3 (M1893), 12 Ga., 24 Ga., 28 Ga., Add $35.00			
Model 3 (M1893), Various Gauges, Takedown, Plain, *Curio*	75	125	150
Model 9 (M1902), Various Gauges, Automatic Ejector, Plain, *Curio*	50	100	150

SHOTGUN, SLIDE ACTION

	Fair	V. Good	Excellent
Model 10A, 12 Ga., Takedown, Plain, *Modern*	100	175	225
Model 10C, 12 Ga., Takedown, Fancy Wood, Checkered Stock, *Modern*	125	250	300

	Fair	V. Good	Excellent
Model 10D, 12 Ga., Takedown, Fancy Checkering, Fancy Wood, Engraved, *Modern*	$250	$550	$625
Model 10E, 12 Ga., Takedown, Fancy Checkering, Fancy Wood, Fancy Engraving, *Modern*	500	900	1000
Model 10F, 12 Ga., Takedown, Fancy Checkering, Fancy Engraving, Fancy Wood, *Modern*	600	1200	1500
Model 10R, 12 Ga., Takedown, Riot Gun, Plain, *Modern*	65	125	200
Model 10S, 12 Ga., Takedown, Trap Grade, Checkered Stock, *Modern*	100	200	250
Model 17, 20 Ga., for Solid Rib, Add $25.00–$40.00			
Model 17A, 20 Ga., Takedown, Plain, *Modern*	125	250	350
Model 17B, 20 Ga., Takedown, Checkered Stock, *Modern*	175	350	400
Model 17C, *Modern*	250	450	500
Model 17D, 20 Ga., Takedown, Fancy Wood, Fancy Checkering, Engraved, *Modern*	300	700	800
Model 17E, 20 Ga., Takedown, Fancy Wood, Fancy Checkering, Fancy Engraving, *Modern*	400	800	1000
Model 17F, 20 Ga., Takedown, Fancy Wood, Fancy Checkering, Fancy Engraving, *Modern*	800	1800	2000
Model 17R, 20 Ga., Takedown, Riot Gun, Plain, *Modern*	100	175	225
Model 1908-0, 12 Ga., Takedown, Riot Gun, Plain, *Modern*	100	175	225
Model 1908-1, 12 Ga., Takedown, Plain, *Modern*	100	175	225
Model 1908-3, 12 Ga., Takedown, Checkered Stock, Fancy Wood, *Modern*	100	225	275
Model 1908-4, 12 Ga., Takedown, Fancy Checkering, Fancy Wood, Engraved, *Modern*	400	900	1000
Model 1908-6, 12 Ga., Takedown, Fancy Checkering, Fancy Wood, Fancy Engraving, *Modern*	475	1350	1500
Model 29, for Solid Rib, Add $25.00–$35.00			
Model 29, for Vent Rib, Add $35.00–$55.00			
Model 29A Sportsman, 12 Ga., Plain Barrel, Takedown, *Modern*	100	175	225
Model 29B, 12 Ga., Checkered Stock, Takedown, *Modern*	100	175	225
Model 29C, 12 Ga., Trap Grade, Takedown, *Modern*	125	225	275
Model 29R, 12 Ga., Riot Gun, Plain Barrel, *Modern*	75	150	200
Model 29S, 12 Ga., Trap Grade, Plain Barrel, Checkered Stock, *Modern*	100	200	250
Model 29TA, 12 Ga., Trap Grade, Vent Rib, Checkered Stock, *Modern*	$150	$275	$325
Model 29TC, 12 Ga., Trap Grade, Vent Rib, Checkered Stock, Fancy Wood, *Modern*	150	300	375
Model 29TD, 12 Ga., Trap Grade, Vent Rib, Fancy Checkering, Fancy Wood, Engraved, *Modern*	300	700	800
Model 29TE, 12 Ga., Trap Grade, Vent Rib, Fancy Checkering, Fancy Wood, Fancy Engraving, *Modern*	600	1350	1500
Model 29TF, 12 Ga., Trap Grade, Vent Rib, Fancy Checkering, Fancy Wood, Fancy Engraving, *Modern*	700	1600	1800
Model 31, for Solid Rib, Add $15.00–$30.00			
Model 31, for Vent Rib, Add $45.00–$60.00			
Model 31, Various Gauges, Skeet Grade, Vent Rib, Checkered Stock, Fancy Wood, *Modern*	300	600	700
Model 31A, Various Gauges, Plain Barrel, *Modern*	250	450	500
Model 31B, Various Gauges, Plain Barrel, Checkered Stock, Fancy Wood, *Modern*	250	500	600
Model 31D Tournament, Various Gauges, Plain Barrel, Checkered Stock, Fancy Wood, Engraved, *Modern*	450	900	1000
Model 31E Expert, Various Gauges, Plain Barrel, Fancy Checkering, Fancy Wood, Fancy Engraving, *Modern*	550	1000	1200
Model 31F Premier, Various Gauges, Plain Barrel, Fancy Checkering, Fancy Wood, Fancy Engraving, *Modern*	900	2100	2500
Model 31H Hunter, Various Gauges, Checkered Stock, Fancy Wood, Plain, Barrel, *Modern*	150	300	375
Model 31R, 12 Ga., Plain Barrel, Riot Gun, *Modern*	125	250	300
Model 31S, 12 Ga., Raised Matted Rib, Checkered Stock, Fancy Wood, *Modern*	250	500	600
Model 31TC, 12 Ga., Trap Grade, Vent Rib, Recoil Pad, *Modern*	300	700	750
Model 870 All American, 12 Ga., Trap Grade, Vent Rib, Fancy Checkering, Engraved, *Modern*	300	600	675
Model 870 Brushmaster, 12 and 20 Gauges, Open Rear Sight, Recoil Pad, Checkered Stock, *Modern*	125	225	275
Model 870 Competition, 12 Ga., Trap Grade, Vent Rib, Checkered Stock, Singleshot, *Modern*	150	325	400
Model 870 D Tournament, Various Gauges, Vent Rib, Fancy Checkering, Fancy Wood, Fancy Engraving, *Modern*	600	1400	1500

	Fair	V. Good	Excellent
Model 870 Deergun, 12 Ga., Open Rear Sight, Checkered Stock, *Modern*	$175	$225	$275
Model 870 F Premier, Various Gauges, Vent Rib, Fancy Checkering, Fancy Wood, Fancy Engraving, *Modern*	900	2200	2500
Model 870 Police, 12 Ga., Open Rear Sight, *Modern*	150	200	250
Model 870 Police, 12 Ga., Plain Barrel, *Modern*	125	175	225
Model 870 SC, Various Gauges, Skeet Grade, Vent Rib, Checkered Stock, *Modern*	150	300	350
Model 870, for .28 Ga. or .410 Ga., Add $20.00–$25.00			
Model 870, for Left Hand, Add $10.00–$15.00			
Model 870, For Lightweight 20, Add $20.00–$25.00			
Model 870, Various Gauges, Plain Barrel, Checkered Stock, *Modern*	100	175	225
Model 870, Various Gauges, Plain Barrel, Magnum, Checkered Stock, *Modern*	100	200	250
Model 870, Various Gauges, Vent Rib, Checkered Stock, *Modern*	100	225	275
Model 870, Various Gauges, Vent Rib, Magnum, Checkered Stock, *Modern*	150	250	300
Model 870SA Cutts, Various Gauges, Skeet Grade, Vent Rib, Checkered Stock, *Modern*	125	225	250
Model 870SA, 12 Ga., Bicentennial, Skeet Grade, Vent Rib, Checkered Stock, *Modern*	125	250	300
Model 870SA, Various Gauges, Skeet Grade, Vent Rib, Checkered Stock, *Modern*	125	250	300
Model 870TB, 12 Ga., Bicentennial, Trap Grade, Vent Rib, Checkered Stock, *Modern*	125	250	300
Model 870TB, 12 Ga., Bicentennial, Trap Grade, Vent Rib, Checkered Stock, Monte Carlo Stock, *Modern*	125	250	300
Model 870TB, 12 Ga., Trap Grade, Vent Rib, Checkered Stock, *Modern*	100	225	275
Model 870TB, 12 Ga., Trap Grade, Vent Rib, Checkered Stock, Monte Carlo Stock, *Modern*	125	250	300
Model 870TC, 12 Ga., Trap Grade, Vent Rib, Checkered Stock, *Modern*	150	325	375
Model 870TC, 12 Ga., Trap Grade, Vent Rib, Checkered Stock, Monte Carlo Stock, *Modern*	150	350	400

REPUBLIC

Spain, unknown maker.

HANDGUN, SEMI-AUTOMATIC

	Fair	V. Good	Excellent
.32 ACP, Clip Fed, Long Grip, *Modern*	$75	$125	$150

RETRIEVER

Made by Thomas Ryan, Norwich, Conn. 1870–1876.

HANDGUN, REVOLVER

	Fair	V. Good	Excellent
.32 Short R.F., 5 Shot, Spur Trigger, Solid Frame, Single Action, *Antique*	75	150	175

REV-O-NOC

Made by Crescent for Hibbard-Spencer-Bartlett Co., Chicago. See Crescent Fire Arms Co., Shotgun, Double Barrel, Side-by-Side; Shotgun, Singleshot.

REVELATION

Trade name used by Western Auto.

RIFLE, BOLT ACTION

	Fair	V. Good	Excellent
Model 107, .22 WMR, Clip Fed, *Modern*	25	50	75
Model 210B, 7mm Rem. Mag., Checkered Stock, Monte Carlo Stock, *Modern*	75	150	175
Model 220A, .308 Win., Checkered Stock, Monte Carlo Stock, *Modern*	75	150	175
Model 220AD, .308 Win., Checkered Stock, Monte Carlo Stock, Fancy Wood, *Modern*	100	175	200
Model 220B, .243 Win., Checkered Stock, Monte Carlo Stock, *Modern*	75	150	175
Model 220BD, .243 Win., Checkered Stock, Monte Carlo Stock, Fancy Wood, *Modern*	75	150	200
Model 220C, .22-250, Checkered Stock, Monte Carlo Stock, *Modern*	75	150	175
Model 220CD, .22-250, Checkered Stock, Monte Carlo Stock, Fancy Wood, *Modern*	75	150	200

RIFLE, LEVER ACTION

	Fair	V. Good	Excellent
Model 117, .22 L.R.R.F., Tube Feed, *Modern*	25	50	75

RIFLE, SEMI-AUTOMATIC

	Fair	V. Good	Excellent
Model 125, .22 L.R.R.F., Clip Fed, *Modern*	15	25	50

RIFLE, SINGLESHOT

	Fair	V. Good	Excellent
Model 100, .22 L.R.R.F, *Modern*	15	25	50

SHOTGUN, BOLT ACTION

	Fair	V. Good	Excellent
Model 312B, 12 Ga., Clip Fed, *Modern*	15	25	50
Model 312BK, 12 Ga., Clip Fed, Adjustable Choke, *Modern*	25	50	75

	Fair	V. Good	Excellent
Model 316B, 16 Ga., Clip Fed, *Modern*	$15	$25	$50
Model 316BK, 16 Ga., Clip Fed, Adjustable Choke, *Modern*	15	25	50
Model 325B, 20 Ga., Clip Fed, *Modern*	15	25	50
Model 325BK, 20 Ga., Clip Fed, Adjustable Choke, *Modern*	15	25	50
Model 330, .410 Ga., Clip Fed, *Modern*	15	25	50

SHOTGUN, SLIDE ACTION

	Fair	V. Good	Excellent
Model 310, Various Gauges, Plain Barrel, Takedown, *Modern*	75	125	150
Model 310R, Various Gauges, Vent Rib, Takedown, *Modern*	75	125	150

REYNOLDS, PLANT & HOTCHKISS

Also see Plant's Mfg. Co.

HANDGUN, REVOLVER

	Fair	V. Good	Excellent
.25 Short R.F., 5 Shot, Single Action, Spur Trigger, 3" Barrel, *Antique*	75	150	200

R.G. INDUSTRIES

R.G. tradename belongs to Rohm GmbH, Sontheim/Brenz, West Germany, and after 1968 also made in Miami, Fla. for American consumption. Operations ceased in 1986.

HANDGUN, DOUBLE BARREL, OVER-UNDER

	Fair	V. Good	Excellent
RG-16, .22 WMR, 2 Shot, Derringer, *Modern*	25	50	75
RG-17, .38 Special, 2 Shot, Derringer, *Modern*	50	75	100

HANDGUN, REVOLVER

	Fair	V. Good	Excellent
Partner RG-40P, .38 Special, 6 Shot, Double Action, Swing-Out Cylinder, *Modern*	50	75	100
RG-14, .22 L.R.R.F., 6 Shot, Double Action, *Modern*	50	75	100
RG-23, .22 L.R.R.F., 6 Shot, Double Action, *Modern*	25	50	75
RG-30, .22 L.R.R.F., 6 Shot, Double Action, Swing-Out Cylinder, *Modern*	25	50	75
RG-30, .22 LR/.22 WMR Combo, 6 Shot, Double Action, Swing- Out Cylinder, *Modern*	50	75	100
RG-30, .22 WMR, 6 Shot, Double Action, Swing-Out Cylinder, *Modern*	25	50	75
RG-40, *Modern*	50	75	100
RG-57, .357 Magnum, 6 Shot, Double Action, Swing-Out Cylinder, *Modern*	50	100	125
RG-57, .44 Magnum, 6 Shot, Double Action, Swing-Out Cylinder, *Modern*	75	125	150
RG-63, .22 L.R.R.F., 6 Shot, Double Action, Western Style, *Modern*	$15	$25	$50
RG-63, .22 LR/.22 WMR Combo, 6 Shot, Single Action, Western Style, *Modern*	25	50	75
RG-66T, .22 LR/.22 WMR Combo, 6 Shot, Single Action, Western Style, Adjustable Sights, *Modern*	25	50	75
RG-74, .22 L.R.R.F., 6 Shot, Double Action, Swing-Out Cylinder, *Modern*	25	50	75
RG-88, .357 Magnum, 6 Shot, Double Action, Swing-Out Cylinder, *Modern*	50	75	100

HANDGUN, SEMI-AUTOMATIC

	Fair	V. Good	Excellent
RG-25, .25 ACP, *Modern*	25	50	75
RG-26, .25 ACP, *Modern*	25	50	75

RHEINMETALL

Rheinsche Metallwaren u. Maschinenfabrik, Sommerada, Germany, 1922–1927.

HANDGUN, SEMI-AUTOMATIC

	Fair	V. Good	Excellent
7.65mm, Clip Fed, Blue, *Curio*	100	250	300

Rheinmetall

RICHARDS, JOHN

London & Birmingham, England, 1745–1810.

SHOTGUN, FLINTLOCK

	Fair	V. Good	Excellent
Blunderbuss, Half-Octagon, Steel Barrel, Folding Bayonet, *Antique*	400	900	1000

RICHARDS, W.

Belgium, c. 1900.

SHOTGUN, DOUBLE BARREL, SIDE-BY-SIDE

	Fair	V. Good	Excellent
Various Gauges, Hammerless, Damascus Barrel, *Modern*	75	150	175
Various Gauges, Hammerless, Steel Barrel, *Modern*	75	150	175
Various Gauges, Outside Hammers, Damascus Barrel, *Modern*	75	150	175
Various Gauges, Outside Hammers, Steel Barrel, *Modern*	75	150	175

	Fair	V. Good	Excellent
SHOTGUN, SINGLESHOT			
Various Gauges, Hammer, Steel Barrel, *Modern*	$25	$50	$75

RICHARDSON INDUSTRIES

New Haven, Conn.

	Fair	V. Good	Excellent
SHOTGUN, SINGLESHOT			
Model R-5, 12 Ga., 24" Barrel, *Modern*	15	25	50

RICHLAND ARMS CO.

Importer. Bussfield, Mich.

	Fair	V. Good	Excellent
RIFLE, PERCUSSION			
Wesson Rifle, .50, Set Triggers, Target Sights, Reproduction, *Antique*	100	200	250
SHOTGUN, DOUBLE BARREL, OVER-UNDER			
Model 808, 12 Ga., Single Trigger, Checkered Stock, Vent Rib, *Modern*	150	375	425
Model 810, 10 Ga. 3½", Double Trigger, Checkered Stock, Vent Rib, *Modern*	200	450	525
Model 828, 28 Ga., Single Trigger, Checkered Stock, *Modern*	200	400	475
Model 844, 12 Ga., Single Trigger, Checkered Stock, *Modern*	125	275	350
SHOTGUN, DOUBLE BARREL, SIDE-BY-SIDE			
Model 200, Various Gauges, Double Trigger, Checkered Stock, *Modern*	125	275	300
Model 202, Various Gauges, Double Trigger, Extra Shotgun Barrel, *Modern*	125	250	275
Model 707 Deluxe, 12 and 20 Gauges, Double Trigger, *Modern*	125	275	300
Model 707 Deluxe, 12 and 20 Gauges, Double Trigger, Checkered Stock, Extra Shotgun Barrel, *Modern*	150	300	350
Model 711, 10 Ga. 3½", Double Trigger, *Modern*	125	275	325
Model 711, 12 Ga. Mag. 3", Double Trigger, *Modern*	150	300	350

RICHTER, CHARLES

Made by Crescent for New York Sporting Goods Co. c. 1900. See also Crescent Fire Arms Co., Shotgun, Double Barrel, Side-by-Side; Shotgun, Singleshot.

RICKARD ARMS

Made by Crescent for J.A. Rickard Co. Schenectady, N.Y. See Crescent Fire Arms Co., Shotgun, Double Barrel, Side-by-Side; Shotgun, Singleshot.

RIGARMI

Industria Galesi, Brescia, Italy.

	Fair	V. Good	Excellent
HANDGUN, SEMI-AUTOMATIC			
Militar, .22 L.R.R.F., Clip Fed, Hammer, Double Action, *Modern*	$75	$150	$175
Pocket, 7.65mm, Clip Fed, Hammer, Double Action, *Modern*	75	125	150
RG-217, .22 Long R.F., Clip Fed, *Modern*	50	75	100
RG-218, .22 L.R.R.F., Clip Fed, *Modern*	50	100	125
RG-219, 6.35mm, Clip Fed, *Modern*	50	75	100

RIGBY, JOHN & CO.

Dublin, Ireland & London, England from 1867. Founded in 1765, the history of J. Rigby & Co. places it securely within the traditions of Britian's best-quality gun trade, with its specialty primarily rifles for big game hunting, but also supplying side-by-side game guns of its own make and by Spanish manufacturers. In 1983 the firm was purchased by J. Roberts & Son.

	Fair	V. Good	Excellent
RIFLE, BOLT ACTION			
.275 Rigby, Sporting Rifle, Express Sights, Checkered Stock, *Modern*	3500	6500	8500
.275 Rigby, Sporting Rifle, Lightweight, Express Sights, Checkered Stock, *Modern*	4000	7000	8500
.350 Rigby, Sporting Rifle, Express Sights, Checkered Stock, *Modern*	4000	8500	9500
Big Game, .416 Rigby, Sporting Rifle, Express Sights, Checkered Stock, *Modern*	4500	10000	12000
RIFLE, DOUBLE BARREL, SIDE-BY-SIDE			
Best Grade, Various Calibers, Sidelock, Double Trigger, Express Sights, Fancy Engraving, Fancy Checkering, *Modern*	12000	27000	30000
Second Grade, Various Calibers, Box Lock, Double Trigger, Express Sights, Fancy Engraving, Fancy Checkering, *Modern*	3000	9000	10000
Third Grade, Various Calibers, Box Lock, Double Trigger, Express Sights, Engraved, Fancy Checkering, *Modern*	2700	7000	8000
SHOTGUN, DOUBLE BARREL, SIDE-BY-SIDE			
Chatsworth, Various Gauges, Box Lock, Automatic Ejector, Double Trigger, Fancy Engraving, Fancy Checkering, *Modern*	1400	3000	3500
Regal, Various Gauges, Sidelock, Automatic Ejector, Double Trigger, Fancy Engraving, Fancy Checkering, *Modern*	4000	10000	12000

	Fair	V. Good	Excellent
Sackville, Various Gauges, Box Lock, Automatic Ejector, Double Trigger, Fancy Engraving, Fancy Checkering, *Modern*	$2500	$4000	$5000
Sandringham, Various Gauges, Sidelock, Automatic Ejector, Double Trigger, Fancy Engraving, Fancy Checkering, *Modern*	3500	7500	8500

RINO GALESI

Industria Galesi, Brescia, Italy.

HANDGUN, SEMI-AUTOMATIC

	Fair	V. Good	Excellent
Model 9, 6.35mm, Clip Fed, Blue, *Modern*	75	100	125

RIOT

Made by Stevens Arms.

SHOTGUN, PUMP

	Fair	V. Good	Excellent
Model 520, 12 Ga., Takedown, *Modern*	75	125	150
Model 620, Various Gauges, Takedown, *Modern*	75	150	175

RIPOLI

HANDGUN, MIQUELET-LOCK

	Fair	V. Good	Excellent
Ball Butt, Brass Inlay, Light Ornamentation, *Antique*	900	2250	2500
Pair, Fluted Barrel, Pocket Pistol, Engraved, Silver Furniture, *Antique*	3000	7000	7500

RITTER, JACOB

Philadelphia, Pa. 1775–1783. See Kentucky Rifles and Pistols.

RIVERSIDE ARMS CO.

Made by Stevens Arms & Tool Co.

SHOTGUN, DOUBLE BARREL, SIDE-BY-SIDE

	Fair	V. Good	Excellent
Model 215, 12 and 16 Gauges, Outside Hammers, Steel Barrel, *Modern*	75	150	175

ROB ROY

Made by Hood Firearms, Norwich, Conn., c. 1880.

HANDGUN, REVOLVER

	Fair	V. Good	Excellent
.22 Short R.F., 7 Shot, Spur Trigger, Solid Frame, Single Action, *Antique*	75	150	175

ROBBINS & LAWRENCE

Robbins, Kendall & Lawrence, Windsor, Vt. 1844–1857. Became Robbins & Lawrence about 1846. Also see Sharps, U.S. Military.

HANDGUN, PERCUSSION

	Fair	V. Good	Excellent
Pepperbox, Various Calibers, Ring Trigger, *Antique*	$400	$850	$1000

ROBIN HOOD

Made by Hood Firearms, Norwich, Conn., c. 1875.

HANDGUN, REVOLVER

	Fair	V. Good	Excellent
.22 Short R.F., 7 Shot, Spur Trigger, Solid Frame, Single Action, *Antique*	100	125	150
.32 Short R.F., 5 Shot, Spur Trigger, Solid Frame, Single Action, *Antique*	100	150	175

ROESSER, PETER

Lancaster, Pa. 1741–1782. See Kentucky Rifles and Pistols.

ROGERS & SPENCER

Willowvale, N.Y., c. 1862.

HANDGUN, PERCUSSION

	Fair	V. Good	Excellent
.44 Army, Single Action, *Antique*	900	2000	2250

Rogers & Spencer

ROLAND

Francisco Arizmendi, Eibar, Spain, c. 1922.

HANDGUN, SEMI-AUTOMATIC

	Fair	V. Good	Excellent
6.35mm, Clip Fed, Blue, *Curio*	50	100	125
7.65mm, Clip Fed, Blue, *Curio*	75	125	150

ROME REVOLVER AND NOVELTY WORKS

Rome, N.Y., c. 1880.

HANDGUN, REVOLVER

	Fair	V. Good	Excellent
.32 Short R.F., 5 Shot, Spur Trigger, Solid Frame, Single Action, *Antique*	75	125	150

ROMER

Romerwerke AG, Suhl, Germany, 1924–1926.

HANDGUN, SEMI-AUTOMATIC

	Fair	V. Good	Excellent
.22 L.R.R.F., Clip Fed, 2½" and 6½" Barrels, Blue, *Curio*	$300	$600	$700
.22 L.R.R.F., Clip Fed, One Barrel, Blue, *Curio*	250	550	650

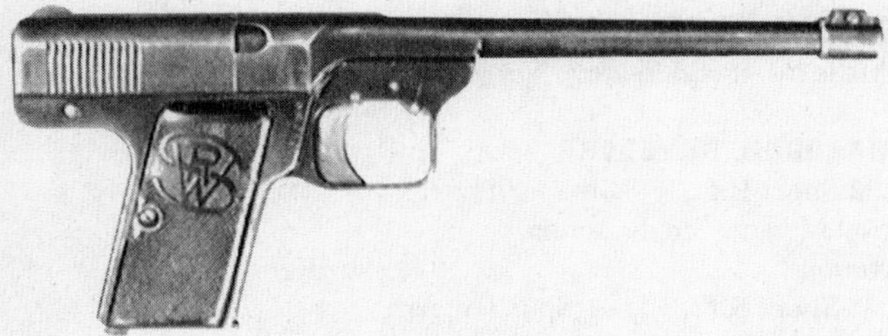

Romer

ROOP, JOHN

Allentown, Pa., c. 1775. See Kentucky Rifles.

ROSS RIFLE CO.

Quebec, Canada. Also see Canadian Military. 1896–1915.

RIFLE, BOLT ACTION

	Fair	V. Good	Excellent
Canadian Issue, .303 British, Military, *Modern*	150	300	350
Model 1903 MK I, .303 British, Sporting Rifle, Open Rear Sight, *Modern*	150	350	400
Model 1905 MK II, Various Calibers, Open Rear Sight, *Modern*	125	250	300
Model 1910 MK III, Various Calibers, Open Rear Sight, Checkered Stock, *Modern*	150	275	325

ROSSI

Amadeo Rossi S.A., Sao Leopoldo, Brazil. Also see Garrucha.

HANDGUN, REVOLVER

	Fair	V. Good	Excellent
Model 31, .38 Special, Solid Frame, Swing-Out Cylinder, 5 Shot, 4" Barrel, *Modern*	50	75	100
Model 51, .22 L.R.R.F., Solid Frame, Swing-Out Cylinder, Adjustable Sights, 5 Shot, 6" Barrel, *Modern*	50	75	100
Model 68, .38 Special, Solid Frame, Swing-Out Cylinder, Adjustable Sights, 5 Shot, 3" Barrel, *Modern*	75	100	125
Model 68/2, .38 Special, Solid Frame, Swing-Out Cylinder, Adjustable Sights, 5 Shot, 2" Barrel, *Modern*	75	125	150
Model 69, .32 S & W Long, Solid Frame, Swing-Out Cylinder, Adjustable Sights, 5 Shot, 3" Barrel, *Modern*	50	75	100

Rossi 68/2

	Fair	V. Good	Excellent
Model 70, .22 Short R.F., Solid Frame, Swing-Out Cylinder, Adjustable Sights, 5 Shot, 3" Barrel, *Modern*	$50	$75	$100
Model 88, .38 Special, Solid Frame, Swing-Out Cylinder, Adjustable Sights, Stainless Steel, 5 Shot, 3" Barrel, *Modern*	75	125	150
Model 89, The Stainless Lady, .38 Special, Stainless, 3" Barrel, *Modern*	75	150	175
Model 94, .38 Special, Medium Frame, Shrouded Ejector Rod, *Modern*	75	100	125

Rossi 94

HANDGUN, SINGLESHOT

	Fair	V. Good	Excellent
.22 Short R.F., Derringer, *Modern*	15	25	50

RIFLE, SLIDE ACTION

	Fair	V. Good	Excellent
Gallery, .22 L.R.R.F., Tube Feed, Takedown, Hammer, *Modern*	50	100	125

Rossi Gallery Rifle

	Fair	V. Good	Excellent
Gallery, .22 L.R.R.F., Tube Feed, Takedown, Hammer, Octagon Barrel, *Modern*	$75	$125	$150
Saddle Ring, .357 Mag., Tube Feed, Hammer, Carbine, *Modern*	75	125	175
Saddle Ring, .357 Mag., Tube Feed, Hammer, Carbine, Nickel, *Modern*	75	150	200

Rossi Saddle Ring Carbine Rifle

SHOTGUN, DOUBLE BARREL, SIDE-BY-SIDE

	Fair	V. Good	Excellent
12 Ga. Mag. 3", Checkered Stock, Hammerless, Double Trigger, *Modern*	125	175	225
12 Ga. Mag. 3", Hammerless, Double Trigger, *Modern*	125	175	200
Overland, 12 and 20 Gauges, Checkered Stock, Outside Hammers, Double Trigger, *Modern*	100	200	225

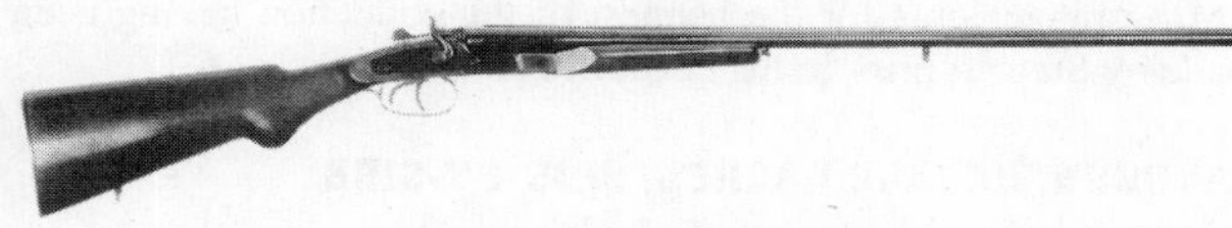

Rossi Overland Shotgun

	Fair	V. Good	Excellent
Overland, 12 and 20 Gauges, Outside Hammers, Double Trigger, *Modern*	100	200	225
Overland II, Various Gauges, Checkered Stock, Outside Hammers, Double Trigger, *Modern*	100	225	250
Squire Model 14, Various Gauges, Hammerless, Double Trigger, *Modern*	125	250	300

ROTTWEIL

Germany, Imported by Eastern Sports Milford, N.H.

RIFLE, DOUBLE BARREL, OVER-UNDER

	Fair	V. Good	Excellent
Standard Grade, Various Calibers, Engraved, Fancy Checkering, Open Rear Sight, *Modern*	900	2000	2150

SHOTGUN, DOUBLE BARREL, OVER-UNDER

	Fair	V. Good	Excellent
American, 12 Ga., Trap Grade, Single Selective Trigger, Automatic Ejector, Vent Rib, Engraved, *Modern*	800	1800	1950
Montreal, 12 Ga., Trap Grade, Vent Rib, Single Selective Trigger, Checkered Stock, *Modern*	650	1350	1600
Olympia, 12 Ga., Skeet Grade, Single Selective Trigger, Automatic Ejector, Vent Rib, Engraved, *Modern*	700	1500	1850
Olympia, 12 Ga., Trap Grade, Single Selective Trigger, Automatic Ejector, Vent Rib, Engraved, *Modern*	$700	$1500	$1850
Olympia 72, 12 Ga., Skeet Grade, Trap Grade, Single Selective Trigger, Checkered Stock, *Modern*	700	1450	1650
Supreme, 12 Ga., Field Grade, Single Selective Trigger, Automatic Ejector, Vent Rib, Engraved, *Modern*	700	1500	1950
Supreme, 12 Ga., Vent Rib, Single Selective Trigger, Checkered Stock, *Modern*	600	1200	1550

ROVIRO, ANTONIO

Iqualada, Spain, c. 1790.

HANDGUN, MIQUELET-LOCK

	Fair	V. Good	Excellent
Pair, Belt Pistol, Belt Hook, Engraved, Light Ornamentation, *Antique*	2200	4500	5500

ROYAL

M. Zulaika y Cia., Eibar, Spain.

HANDGUN, SEMI-AUTOMATIC

	Fair	V. Good	Excellent
12 Shot, 7.65mm, Clip Fed, Long Grip, *Modern*	100	225	250

Royal 12 Shot

	Fair	V. Good	Excellent
7.65mm, Clip Fed, Long Grip, *Modern*	100	175	200
Mauser M1896 Type, 7.63mm, Blue, *Modern*	125	325	375
Novelty, 6.35mm, Clip Fed, Blue, *Curio*	100	175	200
Novelty, 7.65mm, Clip Fed, Blue, *Curio*	100	200	225

ROYAL

Possibly Hopkins & Allen, c. 1880.

	Fair	V. Good	Excellent
HANDGUN, REVOLVER			
.22 Short R.F., 7 Shot, Spur Trigger, Solid Frame, Single Action, *Antique*	$75	$150	$175
.32 Short R.F., 5 Shot, Spur Trigger, Solid Frame, Single Action, *Antique*	75	150	175

Ruby .32

RUBY

Gabilondo y Cia., Vitoria, Spain.

	Fair	V. Good	Excellent
HANDGUN, REVOLVER			
Ruby Extra, For Chrome Plating Add $35.00-$75.00			
Ruby Extra, For Engraving Add $60.00-$100.00			
Ruby Extra Model 12, .38 Spec., Double Action, Blue, Swing-Out Cylinder, *Curio*	25	50	75
Ruby Extra Model 14, .22 L.R.R.F., Double Action, Blue, Swing-Out Cylinder, *Curio*	25	50	75
Ruby Extra Model 14, .32 S & W Long, Double Action, Blue, Swing-Out Cylinder, *Curio*	25	50	75
HANDGUN, SEMI-AUTOMATIC			
7.35mm, Clip Fed, Blue, *Curio*	75	150	175

Ruby .45

RUMMEL

Made by Crescent for A.J. Rummel Arms Co., Toledo, Ohio. See Crescent Fire Arms Co., Shotgun, Double Barrel, Side-by-Side; Shotgun, Singleshot.

RUPERTUS, JACOB

Philadelphia, Pa., 1858–1899. The gunmakers of Philadelphia included several luminaries, among them Sharps, E.K. Tryon, Henry Deringer, and Jacob Rupertus. For many years one of the leading authorities on antique arms was Henry M. Stewart, Jr., resident of Philadelphia, and truly one of the venerable "old timers" of gun collecting. Seeing the Stewart Collection, and visiting with this individual, was a treat for any collector. Had he not been preoccupied with business and other matters, and suffered from ill health in his later years, Henry Stewart could have authored a landmark book on the Philadelphia gun trade. This was a thriving arms making center with several talented gunsmiths and a few leading gun dealers—among them J.C. Grubb & Co., one of the foremost Colt jobbers, and the likely company involved in the manufacture of the unique Colt Van Syckel Dragoons—one of the most exquisite sets of Colt firearms ever made. Rupertus happened to be one of the local gunmakers represented rather substantially in the Stewart collection. Particularly in European arms, and some of the rare American pieces, the bulk of the material remains intact, at VMI, arrangements for the bequest of the collection having been made by Stewart prior to his death in 1988.

	Fair	V. Good	Excellent
HANDGUN, DOUBLE BARREL, SIDE-BY-SIDE			
.22 Short R.F., Derringer, Side-Swing Barrel, Iron Frame, Spur Trigger, *Antique*	$325	$800	$1000
HANDGUN, REVOLVER			
.22 Short R.F., 5 Shot, Spur Trigger, Solid Frame, Single Action, *Antique*	150	275	350
.22 Short R.F., Pepperbox, 8 Shot, Iron Frame, Spur Trigger, *Antique*	200	500	700
.25 Short R.F., 6 Shot, Spur Trigger, Solid Frame, Single Action, *Antique*	1400	3000	3500
.36 Patent Navy, Percussion, 6 Shot, *Antique*	2700	6000	7000

Jacob Rupertus Patent Navy Six Shot, .36 Caliber

	Fair	V. Good	Excellent
.44 Patent Army, 6 Shot, Solid Frame, Single Action, *Antique*	2700	6000	7000

	Fair	V. Good	Excellent
HANDGUN, SINGLESHOT			
.22 Short R.F., Derringer, Side-Swing Barrel, Iron Frame, Spur Trigger, *Antique*	$125	$250	$300
.32 Short R.F., Derringer, Side-Swing Barrel, Iron Frame, Spur Trigger, *Antique*	100	200	250
.38 Short R.F., Derringer, Side-Swing Barrel, Iron Frame, Spur Trigger, *Antique*	100	225	275
.41 Short R.F., 5 Shot, Spur Trigger, Solid Frame, Single Action, *Antique*	125	250	300

RUPP, HERMAN

Pa. 1784. See Kentucky Rifles.

RUPP, JOHN

Allentown, Pa. See U.S. Military, Kentucky Rifles and Pistols.

RUPPERT, WILLIAM

Lancaster. Pa., c. 1776. See U.S. Military, Kentucky Rifles and Pistols.

RUSH, JOHN

Philadelphia, Pa. 1740–1750. See Kentucky Rifles and Pistols.

RUSSIAN MILITARY

Czarist and Communist plants include: Tula, Izshevsky, and many others. Foreign manufacturers for Czarist Russia include: S.I.G. Neuhasen, Switzerland; St. Etienne, France; and Remington Arms U.S.A. Foreign manufacturers for Moisin-Nagant only. Tokarev and SKS Communist Russia produced. With the collapse of the Soviet regime, tremendous changes are now taking place in Russia. Mikhail Kalashnikov, renowned inventor of the AK-47 military rifle (estimated total production to date in excess of 35 million!), has visited in the United States, once under the aegis of William B. Ruger (1992). The study of Russian military arms received an impressive boost in scholarship with publication of *Guns for the Tsar, American Technology and the Small Arms Industry in Ninetenth-Century Russia,* authored by Joseph Bradley. Although dealing with the Czarist era of the 19th and 20th centuries, the impact of Samuel Colt, his products, and his machinery, as well as other gunmakers, on Russian industry provides a fascinating area of interest.

	Fair	V. Good	Excellent
HANDGUN, FREE PISTOL			
MC, .22 L.R.R.F., Clip Fed, *Modern*	$100	$200	$225
MCU, .22 Short, Clip Fed, *Modern*	100	225	275
Vostok M-TOZ-35, .22 L.R.R.F., *Modern*	250	500	575
Vostok M-TOZ-35, .22 L.R.R.F., Cased with Accessories, *Modern*	300	775	875

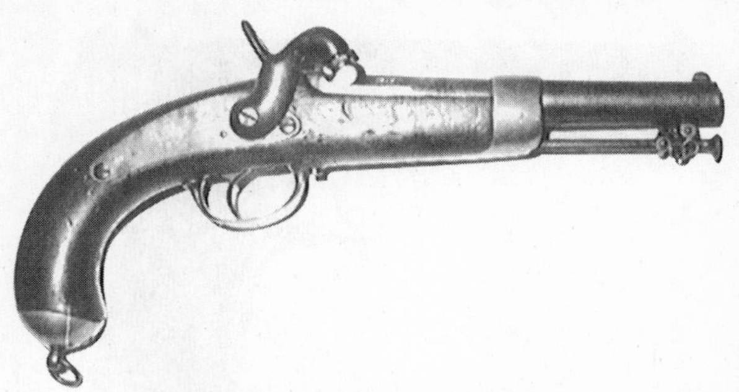

Russian Military Handgun Percussion

	Fair	V. Good	Excellent
HANDGUN, REVOLVER			
M1890, 7.62mm Nagant, Gas-Seal Cylinder, Communist, *Curio*	$100	$175	$200

Russian Military M1890 Communist

	Fair	V. Good	Excellent
M1890, 7.62mm Nagant, Gas-Seal Cylinder, Imperial, *Curio*	100	200	250
M1890, 7.62mm Nagant, Gas-Seal Cylinder, Police, *Curio*	100	175	225
HANDGUN, SEMI-AUTOMATIC			
Makarov, 9mm Makarov, Clip Fed, Double Action, *Modern*	300	750	900

Russian Military Makarov

	Fair	V. Good	Excellent
Tokarev TT-30, 7.62mm Tokarev, Clip Fed, *Modern*	100	250	300
Tokarev TT-33 Early, 7.62mm Tokarev, Clip Fed, *Modern*	100	200	250

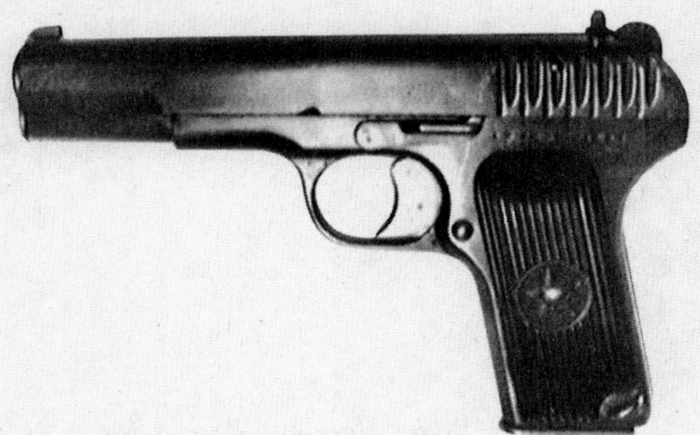

Russian Military Tokarev

RIFLE, BOLT ACTION

	Fair	V. Good	Excellent
1891 Moisin-Nagant, 7.62 Cal, 31-inch Barrel, Bolt Action. (The rear sight of these early rifles are graduated not in meters but in arshins. An arshin is eqivalent to .78 yards. After the Revolution, Russia adopted the metric system and the sights for the Model 1891/30 and later rifles and carbines are graduated in meters.)	$50	$75	$100
1891 Remington, Same as Russian Nagent, except made in U.S.A., by Remington for export to Czarist Russia. (Few were ever delivered. Much higher quality than Russian produced models)	75	125	150
1891/30 Sniper Rifle, Especially Selected for Accuracy, Bolt Handle turned down and fitted with either 4 × P.E. or 3.5 × P.U. Telescopic Sight (still in use in Russia.) Very Rare	250	575	650
1891/38 Carbine, 7.62.54 Cal., 20-inch Barrel, Hooded Front Sight, Rear Sight graduated from 100-1000 meters, no bayonet mounting	50	100	125
1938 Russian Tokarev, Semi-Automatic Gas Operated Rifle, Two Piece Stock, 10 Shot Magazine, Fitted with Muzzlebreak, Cleaning Rod on Right Side of Stock, First of Tokarev Series	$125	$275	$350
1940 Tokarev Model, 24-Inch Barrel, Semi-Automatic Gas Operated Rifle, (Similar to Model 1938 but much more rugged, was very successful action similar to that of Belgian FN Rifle.)	100	250	300
KK M, CM 2, .22 L.R.R.F., Match Rifle, Target Sights, *Modern*	150	300	375
M1919, 7.62 × 54R Russian, Military, Carbine, *Modern*	100	200	250
Russian SKS, 7.62.39M43 Cal., 20-Inch Barrel, (A Russian attempt to develop a gas operated carbine) 10 Shot Magazine, Folding Bayonet, Very Well Made	100	200	250

RWS

Rheinische-Westfalische Sperengstoff, since 1931. Now Dynamit Nobele AG, Troisdorf-Oberlar, West Germany.

RIFLE, BOLT ACTION

	Fair	V. Good	Excellent
Repeater, Various Calibers, Checkered Stock, Set Triggers, Open Sights, *Modern*	200	400	475

RYAN, THOMAS

Norwich, Conn., c. 1870.

HANDGUN, REVOLVER

	Fair	V. Good	Excellent
.22 Short R.F., 7 Shot, Spur Trigger, Solid Frame, Single Action, *Antique*	75	150	175
.32 Short R.F., 5 Shot, Spur Trigger, Solid Frame, Single Action, *Antique*	75	150	175

S

	Fair	V. Good	Excellent

S-M CORP.

Sydney Manson, Alexandria, Va., c. 1953.

HANDGUN, SEMI-AUTOMATIC

	Fair	V. Good	Excellent
Sporter, .22 L.R.R.F., Blowback, *Modern*	$50	$125	$150

SABLE

Belgium, Maker unknown.

HANDGUN, REVOLVER

	Fair	V. Good	Excellent
Baby Hammerless, .22 Short R.F., Folding Trigger, *Modern*	50	100	125

SAKO

O. Y. Sako AB, Riihmaki, Finland.

RIFLE, BOLT ACTION

	Fair	V. Good	Excellent
Deluxe (Garcia), Various Calibers, Sporting Rifle, Monte Carlo Stock, Fancy Checkering, Long Action, *Modern*	300	650	725
Deluxe (Garcia), Various Calibers, Sporting Rifle, Monte Carlo Stock, Fancy Checkering, Medium Action, *Modern*	300	650	725
Deluxe (Garcia), Various Calibers, Sporting Rifle, Monte Carlo Stock, Fancy Checkering, Short Action, *Modern*	300	650	725
Finnbear Carbine, Various Calibers, Sporting Rifle, Monte Carlo Stock, Checkered Stock, Long Action, Full-Stocked, *Modern*	300	675	750
Finnbear, Various Calibers, Sporting Rifle, Monte Carlo Stock, Checkered Stock, Long Action, *Modern*	300	625	700
Forester Carbine, Various Calibers, Sporting Rifle, Monte Carlo Stock, Checkered Stock, Medium Action, Full-Stocked, *Modern*	300	650	725
Forester, Various Calibers, Sporting Rifle, Monte Carlo Stock, Checkered Stock, Medium Action, *Modern*	300	600	675
Forester, Various Calibers, Sporting Rifle, Monte Carlo Stock, Checkered Stock, Medium Action, Heavy Barrel, *Modern*	300	600	675
Hi-Power Mauser (FN), Various Calibers, Sporting Rifle, Monte Carlo Stock, Checkered Stock, *Modern*	$200	$475	$550
Magnum Mauser (FN), Various Calibers, Sporting Rifle, Monte Carlo Stock, Checkered Stock, *Modern*	250	575	650
Model 74 (Garcia), Various Calibers, Sporting Rifle, Monte Carlo Stock, Checkered Stock, Long Action, *Modern*	200	400	475
Model 74 (Garcia), Various Calibers, Sporting Rifle, Monte Carlo Stock, Checkered Stock, Medium Action, *Modern*	200	400	475
Model 74 (Garcia), Various Calibers, Sporting Rifle, Monte Carlo Stock, Checkered Stock, Short Action, *Modern*	200	400	475
Model 74 (Garcia), Various Calibers, Sporting Rifle, Monte Carlo Stock, Checkered Stock, Heavy Barrel, Medium Action, *Modern*	200	425	500
Model 74 (Garcia), Various Calibers, Sporting Rifle, Monte Carlo Stock, Checkered Stock, Heavy Barrel, Short Action, *Modern*	200	425	500
Model 78 (Stoeger), .22 Hornet, Sporting Rifle, Monte Carlo Stock, Checkered Stock, *Modern*	150	300	375
Model 78 (Stoeger), .22 L.R.R.F., Sporting Rifle, Monte Carlo Stock, Checkered Stock, *Modern*	125	250	325
Model 78 (Stoeger), .22 L.R.R.F., Sporting Rifle, Monte Carlo Stock, Checkered Stock, Heavy Barrel, *Modern*	200	400	475
Model 78 (Stoeger), .22 W.M.R., Sporting Rifle, Monte Carlo Stock, Checkered Stock, *Modern*	150	375	450
Vixen Carbine, Various Calibers, Sporting Rifle, Monte Carlo Stock, Checkered Stock, Short Action, Full-Stocked, *Modern*	350	750	850
Vixen, Various Calibers, Sporting Rifle, Monte Carlo Stock, Checkered Stock, Short Action, *Modern*	300	650	750
Vixen, Various Calibers, Sporting Rifle, Monte Carlo Stock, Checkered Stock, Short Action, Heavy Barrel, *Modern*	325	700	800

	Fair	V. Good	Excellent
RIFLE, LEVER ACTION			
Finnwolf, Various Calibers, Sporting Rifle, Monte Carlo Stock, Checkered Stock, *Modern*	$250	$525	$600

SAMPLES, BETHUEL

Urbana, Ohio. See Kentucky Rifles and Pistols.

SANDERSON

Portage, Wisc.

	Fair	V. Good	Excellent
SHOTGUN, SINGLESHOT			
M200-S 1, Various Gauges, Checkered Stock, Automatic Ejectors, Engraved, *Modern*	150	350	425
Neumann, 10 Gauge Mag., Checkered Stock, Automatic Ejectors, Engraved, *Modern*	150	350	425
Neumann, Various Gauges, Checkered Stock, Automatic Ejectors, Engraved, *Modern*	100	225	275

SANTA BARBARA

Santa Barbara of America, Inc. of Irving, Tx. on Mauser actions made in La Caruna, Spain.

	Fair	V. Good	Excellent
RIFLE, BOLT ACTION			
Sporter, Various Calibers, Custom Made, High Quality, *Modern*	75	150	200
Sporter, Various Calibers, Custom Made, Medium Quality, *Modern*	75	125	150

SARASQUETA, FELIX

Eibar, Spain, imported by Sarasquetta of N.A., Coral Gables, Fla.

	Fair	V. Good	Excellent
SHOTGUN, DOUBLE BARREL, OVER-UNDER "MERKE"			
Model 500, 12 Gauge, Checkered Stock, Boxlock, Light Engraving, Double Triggers, *Modern*	85	175	275
Model 510, 20 Gauge, Checkered Stock, Boxlock with Sideplates, Light Engraving, Double Triggers, *Modern*	75	150	225

SARASQUETE, VICTOR

Victor Sarasqueta, Eibar, Spain from 1934.

	Fair	V. Good	Excellent
RIFLE, DOUBLE BARREL, SIDE-BY-SIDE			
Various Calibers, Sidelock, Automatic Ejector, Fancy Engraving, Fancy Checkering, *Modern*	3500	8000	8500
SHOTGUN, DOUBLE BARREL, SIDE-BY-SIDE			
#10E, Various Gauges, Sidelock, Fancy Checkering, Fancy Engraving, *Modern*	$700	$1500	$1650
#11E, Various Gauges, Sidelock, Fancy Checkering, Fancy Engraving, *Modern*	700	1600	1750
#12E, Various Gauges, Sidelock, Fancy Checkering, Fancy Engraving, *Modern*	750	1750	2000
#3, Various Gauges, Double Trigger, Checkered Stock, Light Engraving, *Modern*	250	500	600
#4, Various Gauges, Sidelock, Checkered Stock, Light Engraving, *Modern*	200	475	525
#4E, Various Gauges, Sidelock, Checkered Stock, Light Engraving, *Modern*	250	500	575
#6E, Various Gauges, Sidelock, Fancy Checkering, Engraved, *Modern*	300	650	750
#7E, Various Gauges, Sidelock, Fancy Checkering, Engraved, *Modern*	325	700	800
203, Various Gauges, Sidelock, Fancy Checkering, Fancy Engraving, *Modern*	250	525	600
203E, Various Gauges, Sidelock, Fancy Checkering, Fancy Engraving, *Modern*	300	600	700

SATA

Sabolti & Tantagiro Fabbrica o' Armi, Gardone, Val Trompia, Italy.

	Fair	V. Good	Excellent
HANDGUN, SEMI-AUTOMATIC			
.22 Short, Clip Fed, Blue, *Modern*	50	125	150
6.35mm, Clip Fed, Blue, *Modern*	75	150	175

SAUER, J. P. & SOHN

1855 to date, first in Suftt, now in Eckernforde, West Germany. Also see Hawes.

	Fair	V. Good	Excellent
COMBINATION WEAPON, DRILLING			
Model 3000E, Various Calibers, Double Trigger, Engraved, Checkered Stock, *Modern*	1400	3000	3500
Model 3000E Deluxe, Various Calibers, Double Trigger, Fancy Engraving, Fancy Checkering, *Modern*	1400	3000	3500
HANDGUN, MANUAL REPEATER			
Bar Pistole, 7mm, Double Barrel, 4 Shot, Folding Trigger, *Curio*	150	325	450
HANDGUN, SEMI-AUTOMATIC			
Behorden, .32 ACP, Clip Fed, *Modern*	100	200	250

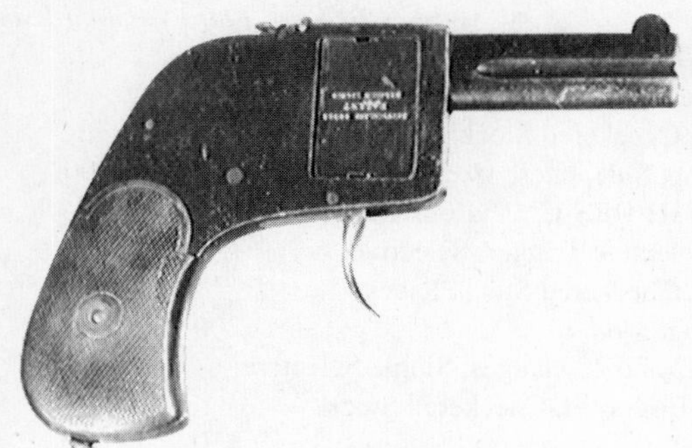
Sauer Bar Pistole

	Fair	V. Good	Excellent
Behorden, .32 ACP, Clip Fed, Lightweight, *Modern*	$150	$350	$400
Behorden 4mm, .32 ACP, Clip Fed, Extra Barrel, *Modern*	300	700	800
Behorden Dutch Navy, .32 ACP, Clip Fed, Military, *Modern*	150	350	400
Model 1913, .25 ACP, Clip Fed, *Modern*	100	225	275

Sauer Model 1913, .25

	Fair	V. Good	Excellent
Model 1913, .32 ACP, Clip Fed, *Modern*	100	225	275

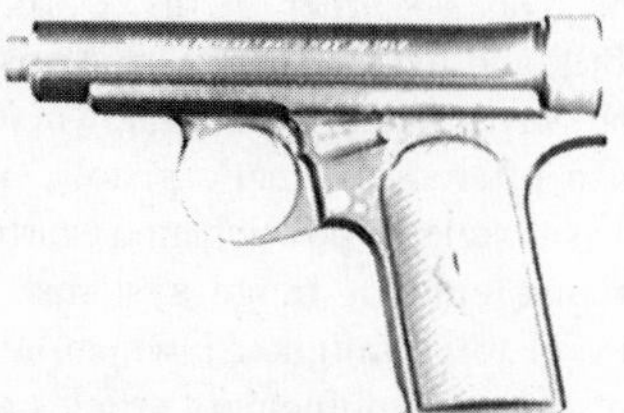
Sauer Model 1913, .32

	Fair	V. Good	Excellent
Model 28, .25 ACP, Clip Fed, *Modern*	125	250	300
Model 38H, .22 L.R., Double Action, Clip Fed, Hammer, *Curio*	700	1500	2000
Model 38H, .380 ACP, Double Action, Clip Fed, Hammer, *Modern*	500	1000	1200

Sauer Model 38H

	Fair	V. Good	Excellent
Model 38H, .380 ACP, Double Action, Clip Fed, Hammer, Commercial, *Modern*	$100	$225	$275
Model 38H, .380 ACP, Double Action, Clip Fed, Hammer, Nazi-Proofed, Military, *Modern*	100	225	325
Model 38H, .380 ACP, Double Action, Clip Fed, Hammer, Nazi-Proofed, No Safety, Military, *Modern*	125	275	325
Model 38H, .380 ACP, Double Action, Clip Fed, Hammer, Lightweight, *Modern*	200	475	500
Roth-Sauer, 8mm, Clip Fed, *Curio*	400	900	1200

Sauer Roth-Sauer

	Fair	V. Good	Excellent
W.T.M. 1922, .25 ACP, Clip Fed, *Modern*	150	300	350
W.T.M. 1928, .25 ACP, Clip Fed, *Modern*	125	275	325
W.T.M. 1928/2, .25 ACP, Clip Fed, *Modern*	100	225	275

RIFLE, BOLT ACTION

	Fair	V. Good	Excellent
Mauser Custom, Various Calibers, Set Trigger, Checkered Stock, Octagon Barrel, *Modern*	300	600	650

COMBINATION WEAPON, OVER-UNDER

	Fair	V. Good	Excellent
BBF, Various Calibers, Double Trigger, Set Trigger, Engraved, Checkered Stock, *Modern*	700	1700	1900

	Fair	V. Good	Excellent
BBF Deluxe, Various Calibers, Double Trigger, Set Trigger, Fancy Engraving, Fancy Checkering, *Modern*	$800	$1900	$2100

SHOTGUN, DOUBLE BARREL, OVER-UNDER

	Fair	V. Good	Excellent
Model 66 GR I, 12 Ga., Single Selective Trigger, Selective Ejector, Hammerless, Sidelock, Engraved, *Modern*	700	1650	1800
Model 66 GR I, 12 Ga., Skeet Grade, Selective Ejector, Hammerless, Sidelock, Engraved, *Modern*	600	1450	1600
Model 66 GR II, 12 Ga., Single Selective Trigger, Selective Ejector, Hammerless, Sidelock, Fancy Engraving, *Modern*	1100	2500	2800
Model 66 GR II, 12 Ga., Skeet Grade, Selective Ejector, Hammerless, Sidelock, Fancy Engraving, *Modern*	1100	2300	2550
Model 66 GR II, 12 Ga., Trap Grade, Selective Ejector, Hammerless, Sidelock, Fancy Engraving, *Modern*	1100	2350	2600
Model 66 GR III, 12 Ga., Single Selective Trigger, Selective Ejector, Hammerless, Sidelock, Fancy Engraving, *Modern*	1400	3000	3500
Model 66 GR III, 12 Ga., Skeet Grade, Selective Ejector, Hammerless, Sidelock, Fancy Engraving, *Modern*	1200	2500	3000
Model 66 GR III, 12 Ga., Trap Grade, Selective Ejector, Hammerless, Sidelock, Fancy Engraving, *Modern*	1200	2500	3000

SHOTGUN, DOUBLE BARREL, SIDE-BY-SIDE

	Fair	V. Good	Excellent
.410 Gauge, Double Trigger, Light Engraving, *Modern*	300	625	675
Artemis I, 12 Ga., Single Selective Trigger, Engraved, Checkered Stock, *Modern*	1600	3500	4500
Artemis II, 12 Ga., Single Selective Trigger, Fancy Engraving, Fancy Checkering, *Modern*	2100	4500	5500
Model Kim, Various Gauges, Double Triggers, Checkered Stock, Light Engraving, *Modern*	125	250	300
Model VIII, Various Gauges, Double Triggers, Checkered Stock, Light Engraving, *Modern*	125	250	300
Model VIII DES, Various Gauges, Single Selective Trigger, Selective Ejectors, Checkered Stock, Light Engraving, *Modern*	125	250	300
Model VIII DES-01, Various Gauges, Single Selective Trigger, Selective Ejectors, Checkered Stock, Engraved, *Modern*	150	325	375
Model VIII DES-05, Various Gauges, Single Selective Trigger, Selective Ejectors, Checkered Stock, Fancy Engraving, Sideplates, *Modern*	$300	$700	$800
Model VIII DES-07, Various Gauges, Single Selective Trigger, Selective Ejectors, Checkered Stock, Fancy Engraving, *Modern*	200	425	500
Royal, 12 and 20 Gauges, Single Selective Trigger, Engraved, Checkered Stock, *Modern*	450	1000	1250

SAVAGE ARMS CO.

Utica, N.Y. 1893–1899, renamed Savage Arms Co. 1899. J. Stevens Arms Co. Springfield Arms Co. and A. H. Fox are all part of Savage. Also see U.S. Military. Also see Commemorative section. One of America's oldest gunmakers, the Savage Repeating Arms Company was incorporated in West Virginia in 1894, founded by inventor/designer Arthur Savage. The first Savage rifle, the Model of 1895, was made on subcontract by the Marlin Fire Arms Company of New Haven, in a quantity of 5,000. It was that first effort which led to the Model 1899, an American gunmaking icon still in production and still one of the most popular lever-action rifles. The company was re-incorporated under New York State law as the Savage Arms Company. In 1915 the firm was acquired by the Driggs-Seabury Ordnance Co., of Sharon, Pennsylvania. In 1917 the gunmaker's name was changed again, this time to Savage Arms Corporation. In 1920 Savage acquired the widely known and respected J. Stevens Arms Co., of Chicopee Falls, and operated that firm as a subsidiary until 1936, when the two were merged. Savage production facilities remained in Utica, New York until 1926 when purchasing the Page-Lewis Co., of Chicopee Falls and moving the Savage part of the plant to the Stevens facility. From 1959 production has been at Westfield, Massachusetts. From the mid-1960s the firm was renamed the Savage Arms Division of American Hardware, late the Emhart Corporation. In 1981 the division was sold, becoming Savage Industries, and from 1989, Savage Arms, Inc. Among other corporate acquisitions by Savage were the A.H. Fox Gun Co. (Philadelphia, 1930), the Davis-Warner Arms Corporation (Norwich, Connecticut, 1930), and the Crescent Fire Arms Co. (also of Norwich, 1931). The Savage line is best known for rifles and shotguns, but has also offered automatic pistols, accessories, sights, reloading tools, smokeless powder and cartridges, and more recently, indoor and outdoor range systems. In promoting the Savage automatic pistol, gunfighter-lawman-buffalo hunter W.B. "Bat" Masterson wrote complimentary articles and memoirs about the Wild West, and how the pistol would have been welcomed by the old-time shootists. Savage's emergence as a force to be reckoned with in American gunmaking coincided with the introduction of smokeless powder, a critical point of transition in the firearms field. On the cutting edge of rifle and cartridge development, the firm evolved their own .22 High Power, .250/3000, .300 and .303 calibers. For years it maintained one of the best equipped ballistic research operations in the firearms field. And having acquired gun companies the likes of Stevens and Fox, Savage had become makers of one of the world's most prestigious lines of sporting firearms. Savage was a pioneer in the use of coiled wire springs in the manufacture of sporting rifles and handguns. It was the Model

Fair V. Good Excellent

99 which established Savage's reputation, more than any other product or innovation. A long-term Savage claim has been that the 99 is the strongest lever-action rifle in the world. To demonstrate the strength and safety of the Model 99 mechanism, the inventor fired the rifle as a single shot, with thirteen parts of the mechanism removed, representing nearly one half of the breech system. He also fired the rifle without the buttstock or forearm, to demonstrate the light recoil with the .303 cartridge. In 1995 Savage celebrated the centennial of the Model 99 with the "Centennial Edition," 1,000 rifles chambered for .300 Savage, marked with serial numbers AS0001 through AS1000. The classic Model 99 had added one more landmark in its immortality. The Model 1899 Savage Rifle Sporting Rifle, Early Model, with 26" octagon or half octagon barrel, sporting sights. Carbine, 20" barrel; short forend with barrel band; carbine buttplate and sights, left side of frame with saddle ring. Saddle Gun, as above, but without saddle ring, 22" barrel, and adaptations to barrel and stock, primarily to reduce weight. Military Rifle, .303 and .30-30 calibers, 30" barrel, full length forend, two barrel bands, bayonet lug on muzzle, fitted for saber or angular bayonet. Takedown Model, round barrel, available in rifle and Featherweight versions. Featherweight Model, reduced to about 6 pounds, solid frame or takedown; 20" barrel, straight stock, unusual style of forearm.

HANDGUN, SEMI-AUTOMATIC

	Fair	V. Good	Excellent
Military Model, .45 ACP. Clip Fed, Original, *Curio*	$4000	$9000	$10000
Military Model, .45 ACP. Clip Fed, Surplus, Reblue, *Curio*	3000	7000	8000
Model 1907 (1908), .32 ACP, Clip Fed, Burr Cocking Piece, (under #10,899), *Curio*	125	250	300
Model 1907 (1909), .32 ACP, Clip Fed, Burr Cocking Piece, (#'s 10900-70499), *Curio*	125	275	300
Model 1907 (1912), .32 ACP, Clip Fed, Burr Cocking Piece, (Higher # than 70500), *Curio*	125	250	300
Model 1907 (1913), .380 ACP, Clip Fed, Burr Cocking Piece, *Curio*	150	325	300
Model 1907 (1914), .32 ACP, Spur Cocking Piece, *Curio*	125	250	300
Model 1907 (1914), .380 ACP, Spur Cocking Piece, *Curio*	125	250	300
Model 1907 (1918), .308 ACP, Clip Fed, Burr Cocking Piece, (After #10000B), *Curio*	150	325	300
Model 1907 (1918), .32 ACP, Clip Fed, No Cartridge Indicator, Burr Cocking Piece, *Curio*	100	225	300
Model 1907 (1918), .380 ACP, Clip Fed, Spur Cocking Piece, (After # 195000), *Curio*	100	250	300
Model 1907 Military, .32 ACP, Clip Fed, Burr Cocking Piece, *Curio*	125	275	325
Model 1907 Military, .32 ACP, Clip Fed, Burr Cocking Piece, (Portuguese Contract), *Curio*	150	375	425
Model 1907, Factory Nickel, Add $50.00–$95.00			
Model 1907, Grade A Engraving (Light), Add $100.00–$150.00			
Model 1907, Grade C Engraving (Light), Add $325.00–$450.00			
Model 1915, .32 ACP, Clip Fed, Hammerless, Grip Safety, *Curio*	$125	$250	$300
Model 1915, .380 ACP, Clip Fed, Hammerless, Grip Safety, *Curio*	125	250	300
Model 1917, .32 ACP, Clip Fed, Spur Cocking Piece, Flared Grip, *Curio*	125	250	300
Model 1917, .380 ACP, Clip Fed, Spur Cocking Piece, Flared Grip, *Curio*	125	250	300

HANDGUN, SINGLESHOT

	Fair	V. Good	Excellent
Model 101, .22 L.R.R.F., Western Style, Single Action, Swing-Out Cylinder, *Modern*	25	50	75

RIFLE, BOLT ACTION

	Fair	V. Good	Excellent
Model 10, .22 L.R.R.F., Target Sights, (Anschutz), *Modern*	75	150	175
Model 110, Magnum Calibers, Add $35.00			
Model 110, Various Calibers, Open Rear Sight, Checkered Stock, *Modern*	100	175	200
Model 110-B, Various Calibers, Open Rear Sight, *Modern*	100	225	275
Model 110-BL, Various Calibers, Open Rear Sight, Left-Hand, *Modern*	125	250	300

Savage 110-BL

	Fair	V. Good	Excellent
Model 110-C, Various Calibers, Clip Fed, Open Rear Sight, *Modern*	100	200	250
Model 110-CL, Various Calibers, Clip Fed, Open Rear Sight, Left-Hand, *Modern*	100	225	275
Model 110-E, Various Calibers, Open Rear Sight, *Modern*	100	175	200
Model 110-EL, Various Calibers, Open Rear Sight, Left-Hand, *Modern*	100	175	225
Model 110-ES, Various Calibers, Internal Box Mag. Scope, *Modern*	125	250	300
Model 110-M, Various Calibers, Open Rear Sight, Monte Carlo Stock, Checkered Stock, Magnum Action, *Modern*	100	175	225
Model 110-MC, Various Calibers, Open Rear Sight, Monte Carlo Stock, Checkered Stock, *Modern*	75	150	175

	Fair	V. Good	Excellent
Model 110-MCL, Various Calibers, Open Rear Sight, Monte Carlo Stock, Checkered Stock, Left-Hand, *Modern*	$75	$150	$200
Model 110-ML, Various Calibers, Open Rear Sight, Monte Carlo Stock, Checkered Stock, Magnum Action, Left-Hand, *Modern*	100	175	225
Model 110-P, Various Calibers, Open Rear Sight, Fancy Wood, Monte Carlo Stock, Fancy Checkering, Sling Swivels, *Modern*	150	300	350
Model 110-PE, Various Calibers, Engraved, Fancy Checkering, Fancy Wood, Sling Swivels, *Modern*	225	550	600
Model 110-PEL, Various Calibers, Engraved, Fancy Checkering, Fancy Wood, Sling Swivels, Left-Hand, *Modern*	225	550	600
Model 110-PL, Various Calibers, Fancy Wood, Monte Carlo Stock, Fancy Checkering, Sling Swivels, Left-Hand, *Modern*	150	350	400
Model 110-S Silhouette Rifle, .308 Winchester and 7mm-08 Remington, Free Floating Barrel, Monte Carlo Stock, *Modern*	125	275	325
Model 110-V Varmint, Various Calibers, 26" Heavy Barrel, *Modern*	150	300	350
Model 111, Various Calibers, Clip Fed, Monte Carlo Stock, Checkered Stock, *Modern*	100	200	250
Model 112-V, Various Calibers, Singleshot, No Sights, *Modern*	125	250	300
Model 1407 "I.S.U.,", .22 L.R.R.F., Heavy Barrel, No Sights, (Anschutz), *Modern*	200	425	475

Savage Anschutz 1407

	Fair	V. Good	Excellent
Model 1407, Sights Only, Add $150.00			
Model 1407-L "I.S.U.," .22 L.R.R.F., Heavy Barrel, No Sights, Left-Hand, (Anschutz), *Modern*	200	450	500
Model 1408, .22 L.R.R.F., Heavy Barrel, No Sights, (Anschutz), *Modern*	150	350	400
Model 1408-ED, .22 L.R.R.F., Heavy Barrel, No Sights, (Anschutz), *Modern*	200	450	500

Savage Anschutz 1408-ED

	Fair	V. Good	Excellent
Model 1408-L, .22 L.R.R.F., Heavy Barrel, No Sights, Left-Hand, Anschutz), *Modern*	$150	$325	$375
Model 1411 "Prone," .22 L.R.R.F., Heavy Barrel, No Sights, (Anschutz), *Modern*	200	425	500

Savage Anschutz 1411

	Fair	V. Good	Excellent
Model 1411, Sights Only, Add $125.00			
Model 1411-L "Prone," .22 L.R.R.F., Heavy Barrel, No Sights, Left-Hand, (Anschutz), *Modern*	200	425	500
Model 1413 "Match," .22 L.R.R.F., Heavy Barrel, No Sights, (Anschutz), *Modern*	300	625	700
Model 1413, .22 L.R.R.F., Sights Only, Add $125.00			
Model 1413-L "Match," .22 L.R.R.F., Heavy Barrel, No Sights, Left-Hand, (Anschutz), *Modern*	300	675	750
Model 1418, .22 L.R.R.F., Clip Fed, Mannlicher, Fancy Checkering, (Anschutz), *Modern*	150	300	350
Model 1432, .22 Hornet, Sporting Rifle, Clip Fed, Fancy Checkering, (Anschutz), *Modern*	200	425	500
Model 1433, .22 Hornet, Mannlicher, Clip Fed, Fancy Checkering, (Anschutz), *Modern*	200	450	550
Model 1518, .22 WMR, Clip Fed, Mannlicher, Fancy Checkering, (Anschutz), *Modern*	150	300	375
Model 1533, .222 Rem., Mannlicher, Clip Fed, Fancy Checkering, (Anschutz), *Modern*	200	450	525
Model 164, .22 L.R.R.F., Sporting Rifle, Clip Fed, Checkered Stock, (Anschutz), *Modern*	100	225	275
Model 164-M, .22 WMR, Sporting Rifle, Clip Fed, Checkered Stock, (Anschutz), *Modern*	100	225	275
Model 19-H, .22 Hornet, 5 Shot Clip, Peep Sights, *Modern*	150	350	400

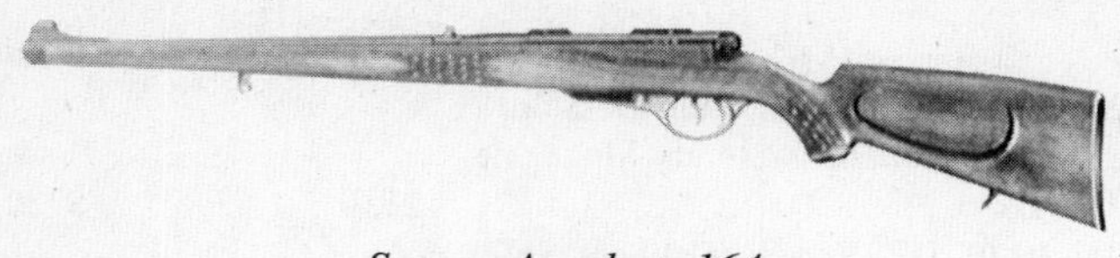

Savage Anschutz 164

Savage Anschutz 164-M

	Fair	V. Good	Excellent
Model 19-L, .22 L.R.R.F., 5 Shot Clip, Lyman Sights, *Modern*	$100	$225	$250
Model 19-M, .22 L.R.R.F., 5 Shot Clip, Heavy Barrel, *Modern*	100	225	275
Model 19-N.R.A., .22 L.R.R.F., 5 Shot Clip, Full-Stocked, Peep Sights, *Modern*	100	200	300
Model 19-Speed Lock, .22 L.R.R.F., 5 Shot Clip, Peep Sights, *Modern*	100	200	225
Model 1904, .22 L.R.R.F., Singleshot, Takedown, *Modern*	50	100	125
Model 1904-Special, .22 L.R.R.F., Singleshot, Takedown, Fancy Wood, *Modern*	65	125	200
Model 1905, .22 L.R.R.F., Target, Singleshot, Takedown, Swiss Buttplate, *Modern*	50	100	200
Model 1905-B, .22 L.R.R.F., *Modern*	65	125	150
Model 1905-Special, .22 L.R.R.F., Fancy Wood, *Modern*	75	150	200
Model 1911, .22 Short R.F., Target, Singleshot, Takedown, *Modern*	50	75	100
Model 20, Various Calibers, Open Rear Sight, *Modern*	100	250	300
Model 20, Various Calibers, Peep Sights, *Modern*	125	275	325
Model 23A, .22 L.R.R.F., 5 Shot Clip, Open Rear Sight, *Modern*	75	125	175
Model 23AA, .22 L.R.R.F., 5 Shot Clip, Open Rear Sight, Monte Carlo Stock, *Modern*	75	125	175
Model 23B, .25 WCF, 5 Shot Clip, Open Rear Sight, Monte Carlo Stock, *Modern*	75	150	250
Model 23C, .32-20 WCF, 5 Shot Clip, Open Rear Sight, Monte Carlo Stock, *Modern*	75	150	250
Model 23D, .22 Hornet, 5 Shot Clip, Open Rear Sight, Monte Carlo Stock, *Modern*	100	225	350
Model 3, .22 L.R.R.F., Singleshot, Takedown, Open Rear Sight, *Modern*	50	75	100

	Fair	V. Good	Excellent
Model 3-S, .22 L.R.R.F., Singleshot, Takedown, Peep Sights, *Modern*	$50	$75	$100
Model 3-ST, .22 L.R.R.F., Singleshot, Takedown, Peep Sights, Sling Swivels, *Modern*	50	75	100
Model 340, Various Calibers, Clip Fed, *Modern*	100	175	225
Model 340-C, Various Calibers, Clip Fed, Carbine, *Modern*	100	175	225
Model 340-S Deluxe, Various Calibers, Clip Fed, Peep Sights, *Modern*	125	225	275
Model 342, .22 Hornet, Clip Fed, *Modern*	100	200	250
Model 342-S, .22 Hornet, Clip Fed, Peep Sights, *Modern*	100	175	225
Model 35, .22 L.R.R.F., Clip Fed, *Modern*	50	75	100
Model 35-M, .22 W.M.R., Clip Fed, *Modern*	50	75	100
Model 36, .22 L.R.R.F., Singleshot, *Modern*	50	75	100
Model 4, .22 L.R.R.F., 5 Shot Clip, Takedown, *Modern*	50	100	125
Model 4-M, .22 WMR, 5 Shot Clip, Takedown, *Modern*	65	100	125
Model 4-S, .22 L.R.R.F., 5 Shot Clip, Takedown, Peep Sights, *Modern*	50	75	100
Model 40, Various Calibers, Open Rear Sights, *Modern*	125	275	325
Model 45 Super, Various Calibers, Peep Sights, Checkered Stock, *Modern*	150	300	375
Model 5, .22 L.R.R.F., Tube Feed, Takedown, Open Rear Sight, *Modern*	50	100	125
Model 5-S, .22 L.R.R.F., Tube Feed, Takedown, Peep Sights, *Modern*	50	100	125
Model 54, .22 L.R.R.F., Sporting Rifle, Clip Fed, Fancy Checkering, (Anschutz), *Modern*	150	350	400
Model 54-M, .22 WMR, Sporting Rifle, Clip Fed, Fancy Checkering, (Anschutz), *Modern*	175	375	425
Model 63, .22 L.R.R.F., Singleshot, Open Rear Sight, *Modern*	25	50	75
Model 63-K, .22 L.R.R.F., Singleshot, Open Rear Sight, *Modern*	25	50	75
Model 63-M, .22 WMR, Singleshot, Open Rear Sight, *Modern*	50	75	100
Model 64, .22 L.R.R.F., Heavy Barrel, No Sights, (Anschutz), *Modern*	100	200	250
Model 64, .22 L.R.R.F., Sights Only, Add $30.00-$55.00			
Model 64-CS, .22 L.R.R.F., Heavy Barrel, No Sights, Lightweight, (Anschutz), *Modern*	100	200	275
Model 64-CSL, .22 L.R.R.F., Heavy Barrel, No Sights, Left-Hand, Lightweight, (Anschutz), *Modern*	100	225	275

	Fair	V. Good	Excellent
Model 64-L, .22 L.R.R.F., Heavy Barrel, No Sights, Left-Hand, (Anschutz), *Modern*	$100	$200	$250
Model 64-S, .22 L.R.R.F., Heavy Barrel, No Sights, (Anschutz), *Modern*	100	225	275
Model 64-SL, .22 L.R.R.F., Heavy Barrel, No Sights, Left-Hand, (Anschutz), *Modern*	125	250	300
Model 65-M, .22 WMR, Clip Fed, Open Rear Sight, *Modern*	50	75	100
Model 73, .22 L.R.R.F., Singleshot, *Modern*	25	50	75
Model 73-Y Boys, .22 L.R.R.F., Singleshot, *Modern*	25	50	75

RIFLE, LEVER ACTION

	Fair	V. Good	Excellent
Model 1895, .303 Savage, Hammerless, Rotary Magazine, Open Rear Sight, *Antique*	600	1300	1500
Model 1899, .30-30 Win., Hammerless, Rotary Magazine, Full-Stocked Military, *Modern*	1200	2700	3000
Model 1899, Various Calibers, Hammerless, Rotary Magazine, Open Rear Sight, *Modern*	150	350	400
Model 89, .22 L.R.R.F., Singleshot, Open Rear Sight, *Modern*	25	50	75
Model 99, for Extra Barrel, Add $110.00-$150.00			
Model 99 E, Various Calibers, Solid Frame, Carbine, Hammerless, Rotary Magazine, *Modern*	150	300	400
Model 99-1895 Anniversary, .308 Win., Octagon Barrel, Hammerless, Rotary Magazine, *Modern*	150	325	375
Model 99-358, .358 Win., Solid Frame, Hammerless, Rotary Magazine, *Modern*	175	350	400
Model 99-A, Various Calibers, Solid Frame, Hammerless, Rotary Magazine, *Modern*	200	425	500
Model 99-B, Various Calibers, Takedown, Hammerless, Rotary Magazine, *Modern*	300	675	750
Model 99-C, Various Calibers, Clip Fed, Solid Frame, Featherweight, Hammerless, *Modern*	200	400	475

Savage Model 99-C

	Fair	V. Good	Excellent
Model 99-CD, Various Calibers, Hammerless, Clip Fed, Solid Frame, Monte Carlo Stock, *Modern*	175	375	425
Model 99-D, Various Calibers, Solid Frame, Hammerless, Rotary Magazine, *Modern*	$150	$275	$325
Model 99-DE, Various Calibers, Solid Frame, Monte Carlo Stock, Light Engraving, Hammerless, Rotary Magazine, *Modern*	250	550	650
Model 99-DL, Various Calibers, Solid Frame, Monte Carlo Stock, Hammerless, Rotary Magazine, *Modern*	125	250	300
Model 99-EG, Various Calibers, Takedown, Checkered Stock, Hammerless, Rotary Magazine, *Modern*	175	375	425
Model 99-F, Various Calibers, Featherweight, Takedown, Hammerless, Rotary Magazine, *Modern*	150	275	325
Model 99-F, Various Calibers, Solid Frame, Featherweight, Hammerless, Rotary Magazine, *Modern*	125	250	300
Model 99-G, Various Calibers, Takedown, Checkered Stock, Hammerless, Rotary Magazine, *Modern*	225	475	525
Model 99-H, Various Calibers, Carbine, Solid Frame, Hammerless, Rotary Magazine, *Modern*	125	250	325
Model 99-K, Various Calibers, Takedown, Light Engraving, Checkered Stock, Hammerless, Rotary Magazine, *Modern*	600	1200	1500
Model 99-PE, Various Calibers, Solid Frame, Monte Carlo Stock, Engraved, Hammerless, Rotary Magazine, *Modern*	600	1200	1500
Model 99-R, Various Calibers, Solid Frame, Checkered Stock, Pre-War, Hammerless, Rotary Magazine, *Modern*	200	400	450
Model 99-R, Various Calibers, Solid Frame, Checkered Stock, Hammerless, Rotary Magazine, *Modern*	125	250	300
Model 99-RS, Various Calibers, Solid Frame, Peep Sights, Pre-War, Hammerless, Rotary Magazine, *Modern*	225	475	525
Model 99-RS, Various Calibers, Solid Frame, Peep Sights, Hammerless, Rotary Magazine, *Modern*	150	275	325
Model 99-T, Various Calibers, Solid Frame, Featherweight, Hammerless, Rotary Magazine, *Modern*	150	275	325

COMBINATION WEAPON, OVER-UNDER

	Fair	V. Good	Excellent
Model 24, Various Calibers, Hammer, *Modern*	75	100	125

Savage Model 24

	Fair	V. Good	Excellent
Model 24-C, .22/20 Ga., Hammer, *Modern*	$75	$125	$150
Model 24-D, Various Calibers, Hammer, *Modern*	100	170	200
Model 24-V, Various Calibers, Checkered Stock, Hammer, *Modern*	100	225	250
Model 389, Various Calibers, Checkered Stock, Hammer, *Modern*	200	450	550

RIFLE, SEMI-AUTOMATIC

	Fair	V. Good	Excellent
Model 6, .22 L.R.R.F., Takedown, Tube Feed, Open Rear Sight, *Modern*	50	75	100
Model 6-S, .22 L.R.R.F., Takedown, Tube Feed, Peep Sights, *Modern*	75	100	125
Model 60, .22 L.R.R.F., Monte Carlo Stock, Checkered Stock, Tube Feed, *Modern*	50	75	100
Model 7, .22 L.R.R.F., 5 Shot Clip, Takedown, Open Rear Sight, *Modern*	50	75	100
Model 7-S, .22 L.R.R.F., 5 Shot Clip, Takedown, Open Rear Sight, *Modern*	75	100	125
Model 80, .22 L.R.R.F., Tube Feed, *Modern*	25	50	75
Model 88, .22 L.R.R.F., Tube Feed, *Modern*	25	50	75
Model 90, .22 L.R.R.F., Carbine, Tube Feed, *Modern*	50	75	100
Model 987 Stevens Rimfire, .22 Autoloader, Tubular Mag. 15 Rounds, Walnut Stock, *Modern*	75	100	125
Model 987-T Stevens Rimfire, .22 Autoloader, Tubular Mag. 15 Rounds, 4 × Scope and Mount, *Modern*	75	100	125

RIFLE, SINGLESHOT

	Fair	V. Good	Excellent
Model 219, Various Calibers, Hammerless, Top Break, Open Rear Sight, *Modern*	75	100	125
Model 219L, Various Calibers, Hammerless, Top Break, Open Rear Sight, Side Lever, *Modern*	50	75	100
Model 221, .30-30 Win., Hammerless, Top Break, Extra Shotgun Barrel, *Modern*	50	75	100
Model 222, .30-30 Win., Hammerless, Top Break, Extra Shotgun Barrel, *Modern*	$50	$75	$100
Model 223, .30-30 Win., Hammerless, Top Break, Extra Shotgun Barrel, *Modern*	50	75	100
Model 227, .30-30 Win., Hammerless, Top Break, Extra Shotgun Barrel, *Modern*	50	75	100
Model 228, .30-30 Win., Hammerless, Top Break, Extra Shotgun Barrel, *Modern*	50	75	100
Model 229, .30-30 Win., Hammerless, Top Break, Extra Shotgun Barrel, *Modern*	50	75	100
Model 71 Stevens Favorite, .22 L.R.R.F., Lever Action, Falling Block, Favorite, *Modern*	75	125	150
Model 72, .22 L.R.R.F., Lever Action, Falling Block, *Modern*	50	75	100
Model 89 Stevens Rimfire, .22 L.R.R.F., Lever Action, 18" Barrel, Sporting Sights, *Modern*	75	100	125

RIFLE, SLIDE ACTION

	Fair	V. Good	Excellent
Model 170, Various Calibers, Open Rear Sight, *Modern*	100	150	175

Savage 170

	Fair	V. Good	Excellent
Model 170-C, .30-30 Win., Carbine, Open Rear Sight, *Modern*	75	125	150
Model 1903, .22 L.R.R.F., Hammerless, Clip Fed, Octagon Barrel, *Modern*	100	175	200
Model 1903-EF, .22 L.R.R.F., Hammerless, Clip Fed, Octagon Barrel, Fancy Wood, Engraved, *Modern*	200	450	525
Model 1903-Expert, .22 L.R.R.F., Hammerless, Clip Fed, Octagon Barrel, Checkered Stock, Light Engraving, *Modern*	100	250	275
Model 1909, .22 L.R.R.F., Half-Octagon Barrel, Takedown, Clip Fed, *Modern*	75	125	150
Model 1914, .22 L.R.R.F., Half-Octagon Barrel, Takedown, Tube Feed, *Modern*	75	175	225
Model 1914-E.F., .22 L.R.R.F., Half-Octagon Barrel, Takedown, Tube Feed, Fancy Engraving, *Modern*	525	1000	1200

	Fair	V. Good	Excellent
Model 1914-Expert, .22 L.R.R.F., Half-Octagon Barrel, Takedown, Tube Feed, Fancy Engraving, *Modern*	$200	$425	$475
Model 1914-Gold Medal, .22 L.R.R.F., Half-Octagon Barrel, Takedown, Tube Feed, Checkered Stock, Light Engraving, *Modern*	200	700	800
Model 25, .22 L.R.R.F., Tube Feed, Octagon Barrel, Open Rear Sight, Monte Carlo Stock, *Modern*	100	200	250
Model 29, .22 L.R.R.F., Tube Feed, Octagon Barrel, Open Rear Sight, Monte Carlo Stock, *Modern*	100	175	225
Model 29, .22 L.R.R.F., Tube Feed, Round Barrel, Open Rear Sight, *Modern*	75	150	175
Model 29-G, .22 Short R.F., Tube Feed, *Modern*	75	150	175

SHOTGUN, BOLT ACTION

	Fair	V. Good	Excellent
Model 58, .410 Ga., Singleshot, *Modern*	25	50	75

SHOTGUN, DOUBLE BARREL, OVER-UNDER

	Fair	V. Good	Excellent
Model 242, .410 Ga., Hammer, Single Trigger, *Modern*	100	200	275
Model 330, 12 and 20 Gauges, Hammerless, Extra Shotgun Barrel, Cased, *Modern*	200	425	475
Model 330, 12 and 20 Gauges, Hammerless, Single Selective Trigger, *Modern*	150	350	400
Model 333, 12 and 20 Gauges, Hammerless, Vent Rib, Single Selective Trigger, *Modern*	150	350	400

Savage Model 333

	Fair	V. Good	Excellent
Model 333-T, 12 Ga., Hammerless, Vent Rib, Trap Grade, Single Selective Trigger, *Modern*	200	400	450
Model 420, Various Gauges, Hammerless, Takedown, Double Trigger, *Modern*	100	250	300
Model 420, Various Gauges, Hammerless, Takedown, Single Trigger, *Modern*	150	300	350
Model 430, Various Gauges, Hammerless, Takedown, Checkered Stock, Recoil Pad, Double Trigger, *Modern*	150	300	350
Model 430, Various Gauges, Hammerless, Takedown, Checkered Stock, Recoil Pad, Single Trigger, *Modern*	$175	$375	$425
Model 440, 12 Ga., Hammerless, Vent Rib, Single Selective Trigger, Checkered Stock, *Modern*	175	375	425
Model 440-T, 12 Ga., Hammerless, Vent Rib, Checkered Stock, *Modern*	200	400	450
Model 444, 12 Ga., Hammerless, Vent Rib, Single Selective Trigger, Checkered Stock, Selective Ejector, *Modern*	200	425	475

RIFLE/SHOTGUN COMBINATION

	Fair	V. Good	Excellent
Model 2400 Field Combo, .22 L.R. Top Barrel, 4 10 Bore or 20 Gauge Bottom Barrel, Walnut Stock, *Modern*	225	475	525
Model 2400-C Combo Gun Camper's Break Action, .22 L.R. Top Barrel, 20 Gauge Bottom Barrel, *Modern*	250	500	550
Model 2400-CS Camper /Survival Combo Gun, Break Action, .22 L.R. Top Barrel, 20 Gauge Bottom Barrel, Pistol Grip, Satin Nickel, *Modern*	250	550	600
Model 2400-D Combo Gun, .22 L.R., Top Barrel, 20 Gauge Bottom Barrel, Folding Rear Sight, *Modern*	250	550	600
Model 2400-V Combo Gun, Break Action, .22 Hornet, Top Barrel, 20 Gauge Bottom Barrel, Monte Carlo Stock, *Modern*	250	550	600
Model 2400-VS Camper/Survival Combo Gun, Break Action, .357 Magnum Top Barrel, 20 Gauge Bottom Barrel, Pistol Grip, Satin Nickel, *Modern*	275	575	625

SHOTGUN, DOUBLE BARREL, SIDE-BY-SIDE

	Fair	V. Good	Excellent
Model B Fox, Various Gauges, Hammerless, Vent Rib, Double Trigger, *Modern*	100	175	225

Savage Fox Model B

	Fair	V. Good	Excellent
Model B-SE Fox, Various Gauges, Hammerless, Vent Rib, Selective Ejector, Single Trigger, *Modern*	100	225	275

SHOTGUN, SEMI-AUTOMATIC

	Fair	V. Good	Excellent
Model 720, 12 Ga., Tube Feed, Checkered Stock, Plain Barrel, *Modern*	75	125	175
Model 720-P, 12 Ga., Checkered Stock, Adjustable Choke, *Modern*	75	125	175

	Fair	V. Good	Excellent
Model 720-R, 12 Ga., Riot Gun, *Modern*	$150	$300	$350
Model 721, 12 Ga., Tube Feed, Checkered Stock, Raised Matted Rib, *Modern*	75	150	200
Model 722, 12 Ga., Tube Feed, Checkered Stock, Vent Rib, *Modern*	75	150	200
Model 723, 16 Ga., Tube Feed, Checkered Stock, Plain Barrel, *Modern*	50	100	150
Model 724, 16 Ga., Tube Feed, Checkered Stock, Raised Matted Rib, *Modern*	75	125	175
Model 725, 16 Ga., Tube Feed, Checkered Stock, Vent Rib, *Modern*	75	125	175
Model 726, 12 and 16 Gauges, 3 Shot, Checkered Stock, Plain Barrel, *Modern*	75	125	175
Model 727, 12 and 16 Gauges, 3 Shot, Checkered Stock, Raised Matted Rib, *Modern*	75	125	175
Model 728, 12 and 16 Gauges, 3 Shot, Checkered Stock, Vent Rib, *Modern*	75	125	175
Model 740-C, 12 and 16 Gauges, Skeet Grade, *Modern*	100	175	225
Model 745, 12 Ga., Lightweight, *Modern*	75	150	200
Model 750, 12 Ga., *Modern*	100	175	225
Model 750-AC, 12 Ga., Adjustable Choke, *Modern*	100	175	225
Model 750-SC, 12 Ga., Adjustable Choke, *Modern*	100	175	225
Model 755, 12 and 16 Gauges, *Modern*	75	125	175
Model 755-SC, 12 and 16 Gauges, Adjustable Choke, *Modern*	75	150	200
Model 775, 12 and 16 Gauges, Lightweight, *Modern*	75	150	200
Model 775-SC, 12 and 16 Gauges, Adjustable Choke, Lightweight, *Modern*	75	150	200

SHOTGUN, SINGLESHOT

	Fair	V. Good	Excellent
Model 220, Various Gauges, Hammerless, Takedown, *Modern*	50	75	100
Model 220-AC, Various Gauges, Hammerless, Takedown, Adjustable Choke, *Modern*	25	50	75
Model 220-P, Various Gauges, Hammerless, Takedown, Adjustable Choke, *Modern*	25	50	75
Model 94, Various Gauges, Hammer, Takedown, *Modern*	75	100	125
Model 94-C, Various Gauges, Hammer, Takedown, *Modern*	50	75	100
Model 94-Y Youth, Various Gauges, Hammer, Takedown, *Modern*	25	50	75

Savage Model 94-Y

	Fair	V. Good	Excellent
Model 9478, Various Gauges, Hammer, Auto Ejection, 42" to 52" Overall, *Modern*	$75	$100	$125

SHOTGUN, SLIDE ACTION

	Fair	V. Good	Excellent
Model 21-A, 12 Ga., Hammerless, Takedown, *Modern*	75	125	175
Model 21-B, 12 Ga., Hammerless, Takedown, Raised Matted Rib, *Modern*	75	125	175
Model 21-C, 12 Ga., Hammerless, Takedown, Riot Gun, *Modern*	50	100	150
Model 21-D, 12 Ga., Hammerless, Takedown, Trap Grade, *Modern*	100	200	250
Model 21-E, 12 Ga., Hammerless, Takedown, Fancy Wood, Fancy Checkering, Vent Rib, *Modern*	125	250	300
Model 28-A, 12 Ga., Hammerless, Takedown, *Modern*	75	125	175
Model 28-B, 12 Ga., Hammerless, Takedown, Raised Matted Rib, *Modern*	75	125	175
Model 28-C, 12 Ga., Hammerless, Takedown, Riot Gun, *Modern*	50	100	150
Model 28-D, 12 Ga., Hammerless, Takedown, Trap Grade, *Modern*	100	200	250
Model 28-S, 12 Ga., Hammerless, Takedown, Fancy Checkering, *Modern*	100	200	250
Model 30, For Vent Rib, Add $15.00-$20.00			
Model 30, Various Gauges, Hammerless, Solid Frame, *Modern*	75	150	175

Savage Model 30

	Fair	V. Good	Excellent
Model 30-AC, Various Gauges, Hammerless, Solid Frame, Adjustable Choke, *Modern*	100	175	200
Model 30-ACL, Various Gauges, Hammerless, Solid Frame, Left-Hand, Adjustable Choke, *Modern*	100	175	200
Model 30-D, Various Gauges, Hammerless, Solid Frame, Light Engraving, Recoil Pad, *Modern*	75	125	175

	Fair	V. Good	Excellent
Model 30-L, Various Gauges, Hammerless, Solid Frame, Left-Hand, *Modern*	$75	$150	$175
Model 30-Slug, 12 Ga., Hammerless, Solid Frame, *Modern*	75	150	175

Savage Model 30-Slug

	Fair	V. Good	Excellent
Model 30-T, 12 Ga., Hammerless, Solid Frame, Monte Carlo Stock, Recoil Pad, Vent Rib, *Modern*	75	125	175
Model 67, 12 or 20 Gauge, Tubular Mag, Hammerless, Walnut Stock, *Modern*	75	150	200
Model 67-T Stevens, 12 or 20 Gauge, Three Choke Tubes, 28" Barrel, *Modern*	100	175	225
Model 67-VR Stevens, 12 Gauge, 4 Shot Tubular, Vent Ribs, *Modern*	100	175	225
Model 69-N Guard Gun, 12 Gauge, 7 Shot Tubular Mag., 18¼" Cylinder Bore, Nickel, *Modern*	100	225	275
Model 69-R Guard Gun, 12 Gauge, 5 Shot Tubular Mag., 20" Cylinder Bore, *Modern*	100	175	225
Model 69-RXL Guard Gun, 12 Gauge, 7 Shot Tubular Mag., 18¼" Cylinder Bore, *Modern*	25	175	225

SCHALL & CO.

Hartford, Conn.

HANDGUN, MANUAL REPEATER

	Fair	V. Good	Excellent
.22 L.R.R.F., Target Pistol, Clip Fed, *Curio*	150	350	425

SCHEANER, WM.

Reading, Pa. 1779–1790. See Kentucky Rifles.

SCHILLING, V. CHARLES

Suhl, Germany. Also see Bergmann, German Military.

RIFLE, BOLT ACTION

	Fair	V. Good	Excellent
Model 88 Sporter, Various Calibers, Checkered Stock, *Curio*	150	300	350

SCHMIDT & HABERMANN

Suhl, Germany, 1920–1940.

COMBINATION WEAPON, OVER-UNDER

	Fair	V. Good	Excellent
Various Calibers, Pre-WW2, Engraved, Checkered Stock, *Curio*	$300	$650	$750

SCHMIDT, ERNST

Suhl, Germany.

RIFLE, SINGLESHOT

	Fair	V. Good	Excellent
8mm Roth-Steyr, Schutzen Rifle, Engraved, Set Trigger, Takedown, Octagon Barrel, *Modern*	350	750	850

SCHMIDT, HERBERT

Ostheim/Rhon, Germany.

HANDGUN, REVOLVER

	Fair	V. Good	Excellent
Liberty 11, .22 L.R.R.F., Double Action, Swing-Out Cylinder, Blue, *Modern*	25	50	75
Texas Scout, .22 L.R.R.F., Western Style, Blue, *Modern*	25	50	75

SCHOUBOE

Dansk Rekylriffel Syndikat, Copenhagen, Denmark 1902–1917.

HANDGUN, SEMI-AUTOMATIC

	Fair	V. Good	Excellent
Model 1902/07, 11.35mm Sch., *Curio*	1900	4000	5000
Model 1902/10, 11.35mm Sch., *Curio*	1900	4000	5000
Model 1902/10, 11.35mm Sch., with Holster Stock, *Curio*	2500	5500	6500
Model 1903, 7.65mm, Clip Fed, Blue, *Curio*	1500	3250	4000

SCHULTZ & LARSEN

Otterup, Denmark.

HANDGUN, SINGLESHOT

	Fair	V. Good	Excellent
Free Pistol, .22 L.R.R.F., Bolt Action, Target Trigger, Target Sights, *Modern*	125	275	350

RIFLE, BOLT ACTION

	Fair	V. Good	Excellent
M54, Various Calibers, *Modern*	300	725	800
Model 47, .22 L.R.R.F., Target Rifle, Thumbhole Stock, Adjustable Trigger, Singleshot, *Modern*	250	550	650
Model 61, .22 L.R.R.F., Target Rifle, Thumbhole Stock, Adjustable Trigger, Singleshot, *Modern*	300	650	750
Model 62, Various Calibers, Target Rifle, Thumbhole Stock, Adjustable Trigger, Singleshot, *Modern*	400	800	950

	Fair	V. Good	Excellent
Model 65DL, Various Calibers, Sporting Rifle, Checkered Stock, Adjustable Trigger, No Sights, Repeater, *Modern*	$250	$575	$650
Model 68DL, .458 Win. Mag., Sporting Rifle, Checkered Stock, Adjustable Trigger, No Sights, Repeater, *Modern*	300	650	750
Model 68DL, Various Calibers, Sporting Rifle, Checkered Stock, Adjustable Trigger, No Sights, Repeater, *Modern*	275	575	650

SCHUTZEN RIFLE EXAMPLES

RIFLE, SINGLESHOT

	Fair	V. Good	Excellent
Aydt System, Various Calibers, Dropping Block, Fancy Tyrol Stock, Fancy Engraving, Target Sights, *Modern*	600	1300	1500
Aydt System, Various Calibers, Dropping Block, Plain Tyrol Stock, Light Engraving, Target Sights, *Modern*	400	1000	1100
Martini System, Various Calibers, Dropping Block, Fancy Tyrol Stock, Fancy Engraving, Target Sights, *Modern*	500	1000	1200

SCHWARZLOSE

Andreas W. Schwarlose, Berlin, Germany 1911–1927.

HANDGUN, SEMI-AUTOMATIC

	Fair	V. Good	Excellent
M 1908 Pocket, 7.65mm, Blow-Forward, Clip Fed, Grip Safety, *Curio*	200	400	475
M 1908 W.A.C. Pocket, 7.65mm, Blow-Forward, Clip Fed, Grip Safety, *Curio*	175	375	450

Schwarzlose M 1908 WAC

	Fair	V. Good	Excellent
M96 Standardt, 7.65mm Mauser, Clip Fed, Blue, *Curio*	1400	3000	3500

SCOTT ARMS CO.

Norwich Falls Pistol Co., c. 1880.

HANDGUN, REVOLVER

	Fair	V. Good	Excellent
.32 Short R.F., 5 Shot, Spur Trigger, Solid Frame, Single Action, *Antique*	$75	$150	$175

SCOTT REVOLVER-RIFLE

Hopkins & Allen, c. 1880.

HANDGUN, REVOLVER

	Fair	V. Good	Excellent
24½" Brass Barrel, .38 Short R.F., 5 Shot, Spur Trigger, Solid Frame, Single Action, *Antique*	100	225	275

SCOTT, D.

Edinburgh, Scotland, 1727–1745.

HANDGUN, FLINTLOCK

	Fair	V. Good	Excellent
Queen Anne Type, .59, Screw Barrel, Holster Pistol, Marked "Edinboro," *Antique*	750	1500	1750

SCOUT

Made by Hood Firearms for Frankfurt Hardware of Milwaukee, Wisc., c. 1870.

HANDGUN, REVOLVER

	Fair	V. Good	Excellent
.32 Short R.F., 5 Shot, Spur Trigger, Solid Frame, Single Action, *Antique*	100	150	175

SCOUT

Made by Stevens.

SHOTGUN, DOUBLE BARREL, SIDE-BY-SIDE

	Fair	V. Good	Excellent
Model 311, Various Gauges, Hammerless, Steel Barrel, *Modern*	100	175	200

S.E.A.M.

Fab. d'Armes de Soc. Espanola de Armas y Municiones, Eibar, Spain.

HANDGUN, SEMI-AUTOMATIC

	Fair	V. Good	Excellent
Eibar Type, 6.35mm, 11 Slide Grooves, Good Quality, Clip Fed, Blue, *Modern*	75	150	175
Eibar Type, 6.35mm, 13 Slide Grooves, Fair Quality, Clip Fed, Blue, *Modern*	50	100	125
Walther Type, 6.35mm, Clip Fed, Blue, *Modern*	100	175	225

SEARS

Sears, Roebuck & Co., Chicago, Ill. Also see Ted Williams.

RIFLE, BOLT ACTION

	Fair	V. Good	Excellent
Semi-Sporterized Mauser, 8mm Mauser, Converted Military, *Modern*	$50	$100	$125
Sporterized Mauser, 8mm Mauser, Converted Military, Recoil Pad, *Modern*	75	125	150

SHOTGUN, BOLT ACTION

	Fair	V. Good	Excellent
.410 Gauge, Clip Fed, Blue, Plain, *Modern*	15	25	50
.410 Gauge, Singleshot, Plain, *Modern*	15	25	50
12 or 20 Gauges, Clip Fed, Adjustable Choke, Blue, Plain, *Modern*	50	50	75

Sears 12 Ga. Bolt Action

	Fair	V. Good	Excellent
12 or 20 Gauges, Clip Fed, Blue, Plain, *Modern*	15	25	50

SHOTGUN, SINGLESHOT

	Fair	V. Good	Excellent
Various Gauges, Top Break, Plain, *Modern*	15	25	50
Youth, 20 or .410 Gauges, Plain, *Modern*	15	25	50

Sears Youth

SECRET SERVICE SPECIAL

Made for Fred Biffar, Chicago by Iver Johnson and Meriden.

HANDGUN, REVOLVER

	Fair	V. Good	Excellent
.32 S & W, 5 Shot, Top Break, Hammerless, Double Action, *Modern*	75	125	150
.38 S & W, 5 Shot, Top Break, Hammerless, Double Action, *Modern*	75	125	150

SECURITY INDUSTRIES OF AMERICA

Little Ferry, N.J.

HANDGUN, REVOLVER

	Fair	V. Good	Excellent
Police Pocket, .357 Magnum, Stainless Steel, 2" Barrel, Swing- Out Cylinder, Double Action, Spurless Hammer, *Modern*	$100	$175	$225
Security Undercover, .357 Magnum, Stainless Steel, 2" Barrel, Swing-Out Cylinder, Double Action, *Modern*	100	175	225

SEDGLEY, R.F., INC.

Philadelphia, Pa. 1911–1938. Successor to Henry Kolb.

HANDGUN, REVOLVER

	Fair	V. Good	Excellent
Baby Hammerless, .22 L.R.R.F., Double Action, Folding Trigger, *Modern*	75	125	150

RIFLE, BOLT ACTION

	Fair	V. Good	Excellent
Springfield, Carbine, Various Calibers, Sporting Rifle, Lyman Sights, Checkered Stock, Full-Stocked, *Modern*	450	1000	1250
Springfield, Various Calibers, Sporting Rifle, Lyman Sights, Checkered Stock, *Modern*	400	800	950
Springfield, Various Calibers, Sporting Rifle, Lyman Sights, Checkered Stock, Left-Hand, *Modern*	400	800	950

SELECTA

Echave y Arizmendi, Eibar, Spain.

HANDGUN, SEMI-AUTOMATIC

	Fair	V. Good	Excellent
Model 1918, 6.35mm, Double Safety, Clip Fed, *Modern*	75	125	150
Model 1918, 6.35mm, Triple Safety, Clip Fed, *Modern*	75	150	175
Model 1919, 7.65mm, Double Safety, Clip Fed, *Modern*	75	150	175

Selecta Model 1919

	Fair	V. Good	Excellent
Model 1919, 7.65mm, Triple Safety, Clip Fed, *Modern*	75	150	200

	Fair	V. Good	Excellent

SEMMERLING

Semmerling Corp., Newton, Mass. Currently manufactured by American Derringer Corp. Waco, Tex.

HANDGUN, MANUAL REPEATER

	Fair	V. Good	Excellent
LM-4, .45 ACP, Double Action, Clip Fed, *Modern*	$600	$1250	$1500

SHAKANOOSA ARMS MFG. CO.

1862–1864. See Confederate Military.

RIFLE, PERCUSSION

	Fair	V. Good	Excellent
.58, Military (C S A), *Antique*	5000	10000	12000
.58, Military, Carbine (C S A), *Antique*	4000	9000	10000

SHARPE

English, 1670–1680.

HANDGUN, FLINTLOCK

	Fair	V. Good	Excellent
Pair, Pocket Pistol, Screw Barrel, Octagon, High Quality, *Antique*	1400	3250	3500

SHARPS, CHRISTIAN

Mill Creek, Pa. 1848; moved to Hartford, Connecticut, in 1851 and became Sharps Rifle Mfg. Co., changing its name to Sharps Rifle Co. in 1874, continuing operations until 1881. In 1854 formed C. Sharps & Co. in Philadelphia, Pa., became Sharps & Hankins in 1862, C. Sharps & Co. again in 1866, and continued until 1880. Inventor and gun designer Christian Sharps, a native of New Jersey, was founder of the Sharps Rifle Manufacturing Company. After becoming a master machinist and gathering extensive experience in the gun trade, including at the Harpers Ferry Armory, Sharps launched his own company in Hartford, Connecticut in 1851. With Colt's Patent Fire Arms Mfg. Co. as a crosstown rival, the Sharps company concentrated on singleshot rifles with a falling block breech mechansim. However, in 1854 the inventor resigned from the firm, moving to Philadelphia. There he set up C. Sharps & Company, manufacturers of singleshot percussion pistols, followed by pepperbox-style four-barrel pistols. Sharps later joined forces with William Hankins, setting up Sharps & Hankins and adding a breech-loading carbine to the line. Sharps died in Vernon, Connecticut in 1874. The Sharps operations in Hartford, complete with a new factory built in 1853, came to be managed by Robbins & Lawrence of Windsor, Vermont. A broad line of falling block breechloading rifles made up the Sharps line, with the famed Civil War era "Beecher's Bibles" adding to the firm's notoriety. The percussion line was succeeded by metallic cartridge rifles, with similar falling block actions. Transition to the new models took place during and after the Civil War. Sales to the military and civilian trade brought substantial business to Sharps, whose buffalo rifles became part of the warp and woof of the Great American West. The "Old Reliable" trademark was stamped on the barrels of thousands of Sharps rifles, and is one of the best known of marketing slogans from nineteenth century gunmaking. The heavy-hitting, long range cartridges featured various .40, .44, .45, .50 calibers, accurate for hunting at ranges up to four and five hundred yards, and more. The true Sharps Buffalo Rifles were made in limited numbers only, with specific requirements for sights, barrel weight, and cartridges. Generally these arms were with octagonal barrels, with double set triggers, and weighed from approximately 10½ to as much as 20 pounds. Nearly coinciding with the demise of the great buffalo hunts, and in the face of stiff competition from repeating rifles, particularly the Winchester, the Sharps Rifle Company closed its doors in 1881. One of the legends of American gunmaking, the Sharps name lives on in modern firms, in the Shiloh Sharps and the Montana Armory companies, both of Big Timber, Montana. These firms, as well as Italian gunmakers, produce accurate, reliable and finely built reproductions based on the original Sharps singleshots of the nineteenth century.

HANDGUN, PERCUSSION

	Fair	V. Good	Excellent
Bryce Revolver, .25, Tip-Up, 6 Shot, Blue, Spur Trigger, Single Action, *Antique*	$800	$1600	$2000
Medium Frame Percussion Pistol, .31 & .34, *Antique*	900	2200	3000
Pistol Rifle Percussion Pistol, .31 & .38, *Antique*	1400	3000	4000
Revolver, .25, Tip-Up, 6 Shot, Blue, Spur Trigger, Single Action, *Antique*	800	1500	1800
Small Frame Percussion Pistol, .31 & .34, *Antique*	1100	2500	3200

HANDGUN, PERCUSSION REVOLVER

	Fair	V. Good	Excellent
Percussion Revolver, .25 caliber	760	1800	2000

HANDGUN, MULTI-BARREL

	Fair	V. Good	Excellent
.22 R.F., Model 1A, 4 Barreled Pistol, *Antique*	150	350	400
.22 R.F., Model 1B, 4 Barreled Pistol, *Antique*	150	350	400
.22 R.F., Model 1C, 4 Barreled Pistol, *Antique*	150	300	350
.22 R.F., Model 1D, 4 Barreled Pistol, *Antique*	200	450	550
.30 R.F., Model 2C, 4 Barreled Pistol			
.30 R.F., Model 2C, 4 Barreled Pistol, *Antique*	125	350	400
.30 R.F., Model 1E, 4 Barreled Pistol, *Antique*	500	1000	1200
.30 R.F., Model 2, 4 Barreled Pistol, *Antique*	100	250	350
.30 R.F., Model 2B, 4 Barreled Pistol, *Antique*	150	350	400
.32 R.F. Bulldog, Model 4, 4 Barreled Pistol, Pin on Side of Frame, *Antique*	200	425	475
.32 R.F. Bulldog, Model 4, 4 Barreled Pistol, Screw Under Frame, *Antique*	200	400	450
.32 R.F., Model 3, 4 Barreled Pistol, *Antique*	200	400	450
.32 R.F., Model 4, 4 Barreled Pistol, Bird Head Grip, *Antique*	200	450	550

	Fair	V. Good	Excellent
.32 R.F., Model 4, 4 Barreled Pistol, Mechanism on Hammer, *Antique*	$300	$750	$850

HANDGUN, SINGLESHOT

	Fair	V. Good	Excellent
Medium Frame, Various Calibers, Single Action, Dropping Block, Hammer, *Antique*	900	2250	2750
Small Frame, Various Calibers, Single Action, Dropping Block, Hammer, *Antique*	900	2000	2250

Christian Sharps Patent Single Shot, .36 Caliber

RIFLE, PERCUSSION

	Fair	V. Good	Excellent
1849 Rifle, .36 & .44, *Antique*	2200	5000	6000
1850 Rifle, .36 & .44, *Antique*	1900	4000	4500
1851 Carbine, .52, Maynard Primer, *Antique*	2200	5000	6000
1852 Carbine, .52, Pellet Primer, *Antique*	1000	2000	2500
1853 Carbine, .52, Pellet Primer, *Antique*	1000	2000	2500
1855 Carbine, .52, Maynard Primer, *Antique*	1600	3500	4000
1855 Rifle, .52, Maynard Primer, *Antique*	1600	3500	4000

Military rifled Musket by Spencer (at top) in .52 caliber; a military-style rifle by Triplett & Scott in .56-50 Spencer rimfire; and the New Model 1863 Rifled percussion Musket by Sharps in .50-70 caliber.

	Fair	V. Good	Excellent
1859 Carbine, .52, Pellet Primer, *Antique*	800	2000	2200
1863 Carbine, .52, Lawrence Cut-off, *Antique*	$700	$1500	$1750
1863 Rifle, .52, Lawrence Cut-off, *Antique*	900	1800	2000

RIFLE, SINGLESHOT

	Fair	V. Good	Excellent
1874 Hunting Rifle, Various Calibers, Open Sights, *Antique*	1900	4000	4500
1874 Long Range Rifle, Various Calibers, Target Sights, *Antique*	3000	6500	7500
1874 Sporting Rifle, Various Calibers, Set Trigger, Target Sights, *Antique*	3000	3750	4500

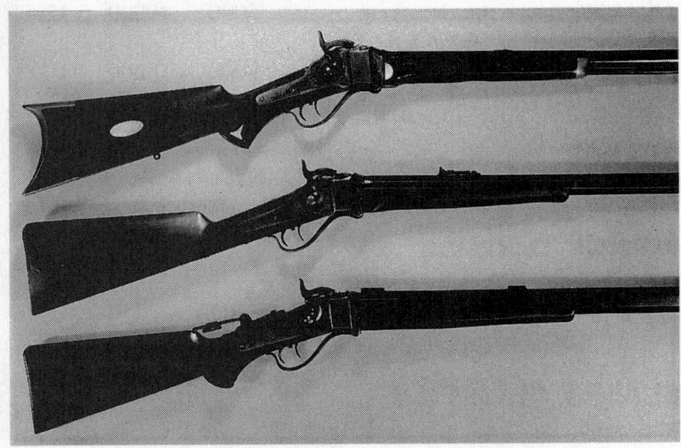

Sharps Model 1874 Sporting rifles, each with special features, including double-set triggers. The top rifle in .40-70 caliber custom built by H. Slotterbek, Los Angeles; note silver plaque inlaid on pistol grip stock, half-octagonal barrel with cleaning rod; center *in .45/100 caliber with Old Reliable barrel;* bottom *in .45 3¼" caliber with semi-pistol grip stock, tang peep sight, extra-heavy octagonal barrel, weighing 16¼ lbs.*

	Fair	V. Good	Excellent
1877 Target Rifle, .45 Caliber, *Antique*	7000	14000	15000
1878 Hunters Rifle, .40 & .45 Calibers, *Antique*	900	2200	2500
1878 Long Range Rifle, .40 & .45 Calibers, *Antique*	3000	6000	6500

SHARPSHOOTER

Hijos de Calixto Arrizabalaga, Eibar, Spain, c. 1920.

HANDGUN, SEMI-AUTOMATIC

	Fair	V. Good	Excellent
"Sharp-Shooter," .380 ACP, Clip Fed, Hammer, Hinged Barrel, Blue, *Curio*	125	250	275
"Sharp-Shooter," 6.35mm, Clip Fed, Hammer, Hinged Barrel, Blue, *Curio*	100	175	200
"Sharp-Shooter," 7.65mm, Clip Fed, Hammer, Hinged Barrel, Blue, *Curio*	100	200	225

SHATTUCK, C.S.

Hatfield, Mass. 1880–1890.

	Fair	V. Good	Excellent
HANDGUN, REVOLVER			
Lincoln/Garfield Grips, Hard Rubber, Add 20%-30%, *Antique*	$100	$200	$250
.22 R.F., Single Action, Spur Trigger, Swing-Out Cylinder, *Antique*	100	225	275
.38 R.F., Double Action, Spur Trigger, Swing-Out Cylinder, *Antique*	150	275	300
.41 R.F., Double Action, Spur Trigger, Swing-Out Cylinder, *Antique*	200	375	400

SHAW, JOHN

London, England, c. 1688.

	Fair	V. Good	Excellent
HANDGUN, FLINTLOCK			
Holster Pistol, Engraved, Steel Mounts, High Quality, *Antique*	1900	2000	2500

SHELL, JOHN

Leslie County, Ky. 1810–1880. See Kentucky Rifles.

SHERIDEN

Racine, Wisc. 1953–1960.

	Fair	V. Good	Excellent
HANDGUN, SINGLESHOT			
Knockabout, .22 L.R.R.F., Tip-Up Barrel, Single Action, Hammer, Blue, *Modern*	75	100	125

SHILEN

Ennis, Tex.

	Fair	V. Good	Excellent
RIFLE, BOLT ACTION			
DGA Benchrest, Various Calibers, Target Rifle, *Modern*	300	625	700
DGA Silhouette, Various Calibers, Target Rifle, *Modern*	225	550	600
DGA Sporter, Various Calibers, Blind Magazine, Plain Stock, *Modern*	250	550	600
DGA Varmint, Various Calibers, Heavy Barrel, *Modern*	250	550	600

SHILOH RIFLE MANUFACTURING CO.

Mfg. of Sharps Rifle Replicas, Big Timber, Mt.

	Fair	V. Good	Excellent
RIFLE, PERCUSSION			
Model 1859 New Model Cavalry Carbine, .54, Reproduction	150	325	400
Model 1862 Robinson Confederate Cavalry Carbine, .54, Reproduction	300	650	750
Model 1863 Cavalry Carbine, .54, Reproduction	250	500	600
Model 1863 New Model Military Rifle, .54, Reproduction	$300	$600	$700
Model 1863 Sporting Rifle #2, .54, Reproduction	200	450	550
Model 1863 Sporting Rifle #3, .54, Reproduction	200	400	500
RIFLE, SINGLESHOT			
Model 1874 Business Rifle, Various Calibers, Reproduction, *Modern*	600	1200	1500
Model 1874 Hunter's Rifle, Various Calibers, Reproduction, *Modern*	600	1200	1500
Model 1874 Military Carbine, Various Calibers, Reproduction, *Modern*	250	575	650
Model 1874 Military Rifle, Various Calibers, Reproduction, *Modern*	300	650	750
Model 1874 Sporting Rifle #2, Various Calibers, Reproduction, *Modern*	600	1200	1500
Model 1874 Sporting Rifle #3, Various Calibers, Reproduction, *Modern*	600	1200	1500

SHORER, ANDREW

Northhampton, Pa. 1775–1776. See Kentucky Rifles.

SICKEL'S ARMS CO.

Belgium for Robert Sickel's & Preston Co., Davenport, Iowa.

	Fair	V. Good	Excellent
SHOTGUN, DOUBLE BARREL, SIDE-BY-SIDE			
Various Gauges, Hammerless, Damascus Barrel, *Modern*	75	150	175
Various Gauges, Hammerless, Steel Barrel, *Modern*	100	175	200
Various Gauges, Outside Hammers, Damascus Barrel, *Modern*	75	150	175
Various Gauges, Outside Hammers, Steel Barrel, *Modern*	100	175	200
SHOTGUN, SINGLESHOT			
Various Gauges, Hammer, Steel Barrel, *Modern*	50	75	100

S.I.G.

Schweizerische Industrie Gesellschaft, Neuhausen, Switzerland since 1857.

	Fair	V. Good	Excellent
HANDGUN, SEMI-AUTOMATIC			
P210 Luxus, Various Calibers, Clip Fed, Fancy Engraving, Gold Inlay, High-Polish Blue Finish, Carved Wood Grips, *Modern*	1500	3000	3500
P210-1, .22 L.R.R.F., Clip Fed, Blue, High-Polish Finish, Wood Grips, *Modern*	600	1250	1450

	Fair	V. Good	Excellent
P210-1, .22 L.R.R.F., Conversion Unit Only, *Modern*	$250	$500	$550
P210-1, .30 Luger, Clip Fed, Blue, High-Polish Finish, Wood Grips, *Modern*	600	1350	1500
P210-1, .9mm Luger, Clip Fed, Blue, High-Polish Finish, Wood Grips, *Modern*	600	1400	1550
P210-1, Various Calibers, Clip Fed, Blue, High-Polish Finish, with 3 Caliber Conv. Units, Wood Grips, *Modern*	900	2000	2500
P210-2, .30 Luger, Clip Fed, Blue, Plastic Stock, *Modern*	450	950	1200
P210-2, .9mm Luger, Clip Fed, Blue, Plastic Stock, *Modern*	500	1000	1150
P210-5, .30 Luger, Clip Fed, Blue, Plastic Stock, Target Pistol, 6" Barrel, *Modern*	600	1200	1450
P210-5, .9mm Luger, Clip Fed, Blue, Plastic Stock, Target Pistol, 6" Barrel, *Modern*	600	1250	1400
P210-6, .30 Luger & 4mm, Clip Fed, Blue, Plastic Stock, Target Pistol, 4½" Barrel, *Modern*	500	1050	1250

S.I.G. P210-6

	Fair	V. Good	Excellent
P210-7, .9mm Luger, Clip Fed, Blue, Plastic Stock, Target Pistol, Long Barrel, *Modern*	900	2250	2500
P 220 SIG-Sauer, Various Calibers, Clip Fed, Double Action, Blue, *Modern*	250	550	650
P 225 SIG-Sauer, .9mm Luger, Clip Fed, Double Action, Blue, *Modern*	250	525	625
P 230 SIG-Sauer, Various Calibers, Clip Fed, Double Action, *Modern*	175	350	400
P 2305L SIG-Sauer, Various Calibers, Clip Fed, Double Action, Stainless, *Modern*	200	400	450
SP 47/8 (Pre-210), 9mm Luger, Clip Fed, German Border Patrol, *Modern*	700	1750	2000
SP 47/8 (Pre-210), 9mm Luger, Clip Fed, Swiss Military, *Modern*	1100	2500	3000

RIFLE, SEMI-AUTOMATIC

	Fair	V. Good	Excellent
SIG AMT, .308 Win., Clip Fed, Bipod, *Modern*	$700	$1750	$2000
SIG STG-57, 7.5 Swiss, Clip Fed, Bipod, *Modern*	1200	2500	2750

SILE

Imported by Sile Distributers, New York City.

HANDGUN, SEMI-AUTOMATIC

	Fair	V. Good	Excellent
Seecamp, .25 ACP, Double Action, Clip Fed, Stainless Steel, *Modern*	125	250	300

SIMPLEX

Made in Belgium. 1901-1906. Also see Bergmann.

HANDGUN, SEMI-AUTOMATIC

	Fair	V. Good	Excellent
Simplex, 8mm Bergmann, Blue, *Curio*	450	1000	1250

SIMSON & CO.

Waffenfabrik Simson & Co., Suhl, Germany 1910–1939. Also see Luger.

HANDGUN, SEMI-AUTOMATIC

	Fair	V. Good	Excellent
M1927 Vest Pocket, .25 ACP, Clip Fed, Blue, *Curio*	225	450	500

RIFLE, BOLT ACTION

	Fair	V. Good	Excellent
Model 1933, .22 Extra Long, Singleshot, Checkered Stock, Target Sights, *Curio*	50	100	125
Precision Carbine, 6mm Shot, Singleshot, Plain, *Curio*	75	125	150
Precision Carbine, 9mm Shot, Singleshot, Plain, *Curio*	75	125	150
Sportrifle #7, .22 Extra Long, Singleshot, Checkered Stock, Target Sights, *Curio*	50	75	100

SHOTGUN, DOUBLE BARREL, OVER-UNDER

	Fair	V. Good	Excellent
Trap Grade, 12 Ga., Automatic Ejectors, Checkered Stock, Engraved, Cocking Indicators, *Curio*	700	1500	1750

SHOTGUN, DOUBLE BARREL, SIDE-BY-SIDE

	Fair	V. Good	Excellent
Astora, Various Calibers, Checkered Stock, Plain, *Curio*	150	300	350
Magnum, 12 Ga. 3", Checkered Stock, Engraved, *Curio*	350	700	750
Monte Carlo, 12 Ga., Checkered Stock, Fancy Engraving, Automatic Ejectors, Sidelock, *Curio*	700	1500	1650

SINGER

Arizmendi y Geonaga, Eibar, Spain.

	Fair	V. Good	Excellent
HANDGUN, SEMI-AUTOMATIC			
6.35mm, Clip Fed, Blue, *Modern*	$50	$100	$125
7.65mm, Clip Fed, Blue, *Modern*	75	125	150

SINGER

Frantisek Dusek, Opocno, Czechoslovakia.

	Fair	V. Good	Excellent
HANDGUN, SEMI-AUTOMATIC			
Duo, 6.35mm, Clip Fed, Blue, *Modern*	50	100	125

SJOGREN

Sweden.

	Fair	V. Good	Excellent
SHOTGUN, SEMI-AUTOMATIC			
12 Ga., 5 Shot, Checkered Stock, Recoil Operated, *Curio*	200	400	450

SKB

Tokyo, Japan.

	Fair	V. Good	Excellent
SHOTGUN, DOUBLE BARREL, OVER-UNDER			
Model 500, 12 and 20 Gauges, Field Grade, Selective Ejector, Vent Rib, *Modern*	225	475	500
Model 500, 12 Ga. Mag. 3", Field Grade, Selective Ejector, Vent Rib, *Modern*	250	525	550
Model 600, .410 Gauges, Skeet Grade, Selective Ejector, Vent Rib, *Modern*	250	525	575
Model 600, 12 and 20 Gauges, Field Grade, Selective Ejector, Vent Rib, *Modern*	300	625	675
Model 600, 12 and 20 Gauges, Skeet Grade, Selective Ejector, Vent Rib, *Modern*	300	625	650
Model 600, 12 Ga., Trap Grade, Selective Ejector, Vent Rib, *Modern*	300	600	650
Model 600, 12 Ga., Trap Grade, Selective Ejector, Vent Rib, Monte Carlo Stock, *Modern*	275	575	625
Model 600 Combo Set, Various Gauges, Skeet Grade, Selective Ejector, Vent Rib, Cased, *Modern*	325	750	1000
Model 680 English, 12 and 20 Gauges, Field Grade, Selective Ejector, Vent Rib, *Modern*	350	700	750
Model 700, 12 and 20 Gauges, Skeet Grade, Selective Ejector, Vent Rib, *Modern*	400	825	875
Model 700, 12 Ga., Trap Grade, Selective Ejector, Vent Rib, *Modern*	400	800	900
Model 700, 12 Ga., Trap Grade, Selective Ejector, Vent Rib, Monte Carlo Stock, *Modern*	$400	$800	$850
Model 700 Combo Set, Various Gauges, Skeet Grade, Selective Ejector, Vent Rib, Cased, *Modern*	700	1500	1750
SHOTGUN, SEMI-AUTOMATIC			
XL 900, 12 and 20 Gauges, Skeet Grade, *Modern*	125	250	325
XL 900, 12 Ga., Trap Grade, Monte Carlo Stock, *Modern*	125	250	325
XL 900 MR, 12 and 20 Gauges, Vent Rib, *Modern*	125	225	275
XL 900 Slug, 12 and 20 Gauges, Open Rear Sight, *Modern*	125	250	300

SLOANS

Importers, New York City. Also see Charles Daly.

	Fair	V. Good	Excellent
SHOTGUN, DOUBLE BARREL, SIDE-BY-SIDE			
POS, .410 Ga., Checkered Stock, Hammerless, Double Trigger, *Modern*	75	150	175
POS, 10 Ga., 3½", Checkered Stock, Hammerless, Double Trigger, *Modern*	75	150	200
POS, 12 and 20 Gauges, Checkered Stock, Hammerless, Double Trigger, *Modern*	75	150	175
POS Coach Gun, 12 and 20 Gauges, Checkered Stock, Outside Hammers, Double Trigger, *Modern*	75	150	175

SMITH & WESSON

Started in Norwich, Connecticut, in 1855 as Volcanic Repeating Arms Co. Reorganized at Springfield, Mass. as Smith & Wesson in 1857 (Volcanic Repeating Arms moved to New Haven, Conn. in 1856 and was purchased in 1857 by what would become Winchester Repeating Arms Co.). Smith & Wesson at Springfield, Massachusetts to date. Also see U.S. Military and the Commemorative section. One of America's oldest gunmakers, Smith & Wesson shares its early years with the predecessor firms to the Winchester Repeating Arms Co. Seventeen years older than D. B. Wesson, Horace Smith had eighteen years of experience at the Springfield Armory, fine-tuning his expertise at factories in New Haven and Norwich, Connecticut, and at Worcester, Massachusetts. Wesson had worked with his older brothers, Edwin and Frank, themselves accomplished riflemakers, as well as with other Massachusetts gunmakers. Smith and Wesson had years of experience with Cortlandt Palmer in Norwich, building the patented magazine firearm known as the Volcanic. In 1855 the patent for that design was sold and the business relocated in New Haven, evolving eventually into the Winchester Repeating Arms Co. Smith and Wesson both served the New Haven factory as superintendents. Wesson's successor was none other than B. Tyler Henry, one of the most accomplished mechanics of his day, and the designer of both the Henry lever-action repeating rifle, and the

.44 cartridge that it fired. It was the development of what became the first successful repeating handgun for metallic self-contained cartridges that reunited Smith and Wesson, only months before Samuel Colt's master revolver patent would expire, in 1857. The partners had a windfall of $18,000, from sale of the Volcanic operation. They soon had a design for a revolver, in which the cylinder was bored end to end, permitting loading of the new .22 caliber rimfire cartridge, which they termed the No. 1—the revolver also came to be known as the Model 1. An April 3, 1855, patent of inventor Rollin White had secured rights to the manufacture of a bored through cylinder. Smith and Wesson arranged for White to license their use of that feature, for a flat fee of $500 and a royalty of 25 cents per revolver. However, the agreement shrewdly specified that White himself had to defend the exclusivity of his patent, a requirement which would consume much of his royalties over the years. Within a year Smith & Wesson had established itself, and by September 1858 extra-quality plated pistols were in the line, as well as such amenities as frames plated in gold or silver, ivory grips, and hand engraving. By the 1870s and 1880s the Smith & Wesson line had expanded to one of the most complete selections of metallic cartridge handguns in the world. Mechanisms ranged from single action to double action, and, in the twentieth century, automatic pistols were introduced. Revolver calibers, for both single and double actions, ranged from the .22 short on up to the .45 S & W. A 12-gauge side-by-side shotgun, designed by D.B. Wesson, was brought out in 1868. Only about 219 were made by the Wesson Fire Arms Co. Smith & Wesson's ownership in the twentieth century has changed over the years. Bangor Punta owned the company from 1965 to 1984; present ownership is Tompkins p.l.c., of Great Britain.

SHOTGUN, DOUBLE BARREL

	Fair	*V. Good*	*Excellent*
Shotgun, Double Barrel, Hammer, Damascus, 12 Gauge; Premium if Specially Decorated Beyond Standard	$800	$1500	$3500

HANDGUN, REVOLVER

	Fair	*V. Good*	*Excellent*
.32 Double Action, .32 S & W, 1st Model, Top Break, 5 Shot, Straight-Cut Sideplate, Rocker Cylinder Stop, *Antique*	1800	3500	4000
.32 Double Action, .32 S & W, 2nd Model, Top Break, 5 Shot, Irregularly Cut Sideplate, Rocker Cylinder Stop, *Antique*	150	300	400
.32 Double Action, .32 S & W, 3rd Model, Top Break, 5 Shot, Irregularly Cut Sideplate, *Antique*	150	300	400
.32 Double Action, .32 S & W, 4th Model, Round-Back Trigger Guard, Top Break, 5 Shot, Irregularly Cut Sideplate, *Curio*	150	275	400
.32 Double Action, .32 S & W, 5th Model, Round-Back Trigger Guard, Top Break, 5 Shot, Irregularly Cut Sideplate, Front Sight Forged on Barrel, *Curio*	150	300	400
.32 Hand Ejector 1903, .32 S & W Long, Solid Frame, Swing-Out Cylinder, 6 Shot, Double Action, *Curio*	$150	$300	$400
.32 Hand Ejector, (Bekeart), .32 S & W Long, Solid Frame, Swing-Out Cylinder, 6 Shot, Target Sights, Double Action, *Curio*	300	600	700
.32 Hand Ejector, .32 S & W Long, 1st Model, Solid Frame, Swing-Out Cylinder, Hammer Actuated Cylinder Stop, 6 Shot, *Curio*	300	700	800
.32 Regulation Police, .32 S & W Long, Solid Frame, Swing-Out Cylinder, 6 Shot, Double Action, *Curio*	150	225	300
.32 Safety Hammerless, .32 S & W Long, 1st Model, Double Action, Top Break, 5 Shot, Push-Button Latch, *Curio*	150	250	350
.32 Safety Hammerless, .32 S & W Long, 2nd Model, Double Action, Top Break, 5 Shot, T Latch, *Curio*	150	300	400
.32 Safety Hammerless, .32 S & W, 3rd Model, Double Action, Top Break, 5 Shot, Over #170,000, *Curio*	150	250	350
.32 Single Action, .32 S & W, 10" Barrel, Add 75%-100%			
.32 Single Action, .32 S & W, 6" or 8" Barrel, Add 50%-75%			
.32 Single Action, .32 S & W, Top Break, Spur Trigger, 5 Shot, *Antique*	100	250	350
.38 D A Perfected, .38 S & W, Made Without Side Latch, Hand-Ejector Action, Top Break, Double Action, *Curio*	150	300	500
.38 D A Perfected, .38 S & W, Trigger Guard, Thumbpiece Hand-Ejector Action, Top Break, Double Action, *Curio*	150	325	400
.38 Double Action, .38 S & W, 1st Model, Straight-Cut Sideplate, Rocker Cylinder Stop, Double Action, Top Break, 5 Shot, *Antique*	300	700	775
.38 Double Action, .38 S & W, 2nd Model, Irregularly Cut Sideplate, Rocker Cylinder Stop, Double Action, Top Break, 5 Shot, *Antique*	100	200	250
.38 Double Action, .38 S & W, 3rd Model, Irregularly Cut Sideplate, Double Action, Top Break, 5 Shot, *Antique*	100	200	250
.38 Double Action, .38 S & W, 4th Model, #'s 32701-539000, Double Action, Top Break, 5 Shot, *Curio*	100	200	250

	Fair	V. Good	Excellent
.38 Double Action, .38 S & W, 5th Model, #'s 539001-554077, Double Action, Top Break, 5 Shot, *Curio*	$100	$250	$300
.38 Hand Ejector 1902, .38 Special, Military and Police, Solid Frame, Swing-Out Cylinder, Double Action, *Curio*	100	250	300
.38 Hand Ejector 1902, .38 Special, Military and Police, Solid Frame, Swing-Out Cylinder, Double Action, Adjustable Sights, *Curio*	200	400	500
.38 Hand Ejector 1905, .38 Special, Military and Police, Solid Frame, Swing-Out Cylinder, Double Action, *Curio*	150	300	350
.38 Hand Ejector 1905, .38 Special, Military and Police, Solid Frame, Swing-Out Cylinder, Double Action, Adjustable Sights, *Curio*	200	400	500
.38 Hand Ejector, .38 Long Colt, 1st Model, Solid Frame, Swing-Out Cylinder, No Cylinder-Pin Front-Lock, U.S. Army Model, *Curio*	400	900	1000
.38 Hand Ejector, .38 Long Colt, 1st Model, Solid Frame, Swing-Out Cylinder, No Cylinder-Pin Front-Lock, U.S. Navy Model, *Curio*	700	1400	1500
.38 Hand Ejector, .38 Special, 1st Model, Solid Frame, Swing-Out Cylinder, No Cylinder-Pin Front-Lock, Adjustable Sights, *Curio*	250	500	600
.38 Hand Ejector, .38 Special, 2nd Model, Solid Frame, Swing-Out Cylinder, *Curio*	150	250	350
.38 Hand Ejector, .38 Special, 2nd Model, Solid Frame, Swing-Out Cylinder, Adjustable Sights, *Curio*	250	500	600
.38 Safety Hammerless, .38 S & W, 1st Model-Button Latch, Release on Left Topstrap, Top Break, Double Action, *Antique*	200	600	750
.38 Safety Hammerless, .38 S & W, 2nd Model-Button Latch, Release on Top of Frame, Top Break, Double Action, *Antique*	150	250	350
.38 Safety Hammerless, .38 S & W, 3rd Model-Button Latch, Release on Rear Topstrap, Top Break, Double Action, *Antique*	150	250	350
.38 Safety Hammerless, .38 S & W, 4th Model T-Shaped Latch, Top Break, Double Action, *Curio*	150	250	350
.38 Safety Hammerless, .38 S & W, 5th Model T-Shaped Latch, Top Break, Double Action, Front Sight Forged on Barrel, *Curio*	150	250	300

	Fair	V. Good	Excellent
.38 Single Action, .38 S & W, 1st Model, Baby Russian, Top Break, Spur Trigger, *Antique*	$200	$500	$600
.38 Single Action, .38 S & W, 2nd Model, Top Break, Spur Trigger, Short Ejector Housing, *Antique*	150	300	350
.38 Single Action, .38 S & W, 3rd Model, Top Break, with Trigger Guard, *Curio*	400	700	800
.38 Single Action, .38 S & W, 3rd Model, Top Break, with Trigger Guard, with Extra Singleshot Barrel, *Curio*	600	1300	1500
.38 Single Action, .38 S & W, Mexican Model, Top Break, Spur Trigger, 5 Shot, *Curio*	900	2000	2500
.38 Win. Double Action, .38-40 WCF, Top Break, *Curio*	1200	2700	3000
.44 Double Action Frontier, for Target Sights, Add 30%-50%			
.44 Double Action, .44 Russian, 1st Model, Top Break, 6 Shot, *Antique*	500	1000	1200
.44 Double Action, for Target Sights, Add 20%-30%			
.44 Double Action, Wesson Favorite, 6 Shot, Lightweight, Top Break, *Antique*	1100	2700	3000
.44 Hand Ejector, .44 Special, 1st Model, Triple-Lock, Solid Frame, Swing-Out Cylinder, New Century, *Curio*	400	725	800
.44 Hand Ejector, .44 Special, 2nd Model, Un-Shrouded Ejector Rod, Solid Frame, Swing-Out Cylinder, *Curio*	300	500	600
.44 Hand Ejector, .44 Special, 3rd Model, Shrouded Ejector Rod, Solid Frame, Swing-Out Cylinder, *Curio*	350	500	600
.44 Hand Ejector, 1st Model, for Target Sights, Add 20%-30%			
.44 Hand Ejector, 2nd Model, for Target Sights, Add 20%-30%			
.44 Hand Ejector, 3rd Model, for Target Sights, Add 20%-30%			
.44 Hand Ejector, Calibers other than .44 Spec., Add 15%-25%			
.44 Hand Ejector, Calibers other than .44 Spec., Add 15%-25%			
.44 New Model #3 Frontier, .44-40 WCF, Top Break, 6 Shot, *Antique*	900	2000	2500
.455 MK II Hand Ejector, Solid Frame, Swing-Out Cylinder, Double Action, Military, *Curio*	250	500	600
22/32 Bekeart Model, .22 L.R.R.F., #'s 138220-139275, Target Pistol, Double Action, Adjustable Sights, 6" Barrel, *Curio*	300	700	1000

	Fair	V. Good	Excellent
22/32 Kit Gun, .22 L.R.R.F., Early Model, Double Action Adjustable Sights, 4" Barrel, Pre-World War II, *Curio*	$300	$700	$900
32/20 Hand Ejector 1902, .32-20 WCF, 2nd Model, Solid Frame, Swing-Out Cylinder, 6 Shot, *Curio*	200	400	500
32/20 Hand Ejector 1902, .32-20 WCF, 2nd Model, Solid Frame, Swing-Out Cylinder, 6 Shot, Adjustable Sights, *Curio*	300	600	700
32/20 Hand Ejector 1905, .32-20 WCF, Solid Frame, Swing-Out Cylinder, 6 Shot, Adjustable Sights, *Curio*	225	600	700
32/20 Hand Ejector 1905, .32-20 WCF, Solid Frame, Swing-Out Cylinder, 6 Shot, Victory Model, *Curio*	150	250	350
32/20 Hand Ejector, .32-20 WCF, 1st Model, Solid Frame, Swing-Out Cylinder, 6 Shot, No Cylinder-Pin Front-Lock, *Curio*	225	475	525
38/200 British (Model 11), .38 S & W, Military & Police, Solid Frame, Swing-Out Cylinder, Double Action, Military, *Curio*	150	300	350
First Model Schofield, .45 S & W, Top Break, Single Action, Military, *Antique*	1700	3500	4500
First Model Schofield, .45 S & W, Top Break, Single Action, Commercial, *Antique*	2200	4500	5000
First Model Schofield, .45 S & W, Wells Fargo, Top Break, Single Action, *Antique*	1500	3000	3500
K-22 Masterpiece, .22 L.R.R.F., 2nd Model, K-22 Hand Ejector, Speed Lock Action, Double Action, Adjustable Sights, 6" Barrel, *Modern*	250	500	600
K-22 Outdoorsman, .22 L.R.R.F., 1st Model, Double Action, Adjustable Sights, 6" Barrel, *Modern*	300	600	700
K-32 Masterpiece, .32 S & W Long, 1st Model, Pre-War, 6 Shot Adjustable Sights, Target Pistol, only made 97, *Modern*	2200	4000	4500
K-32 Masterpiece, .32 S & W Long, 2nd Model, Post-War, 6 Shot, Adjustable Sights, Target Pistol, *Modern*	400	900	1200
Model "13," .357 Magnum, Double Action, Swing-Out Cylinder, *Modern*	300	500	575
Model #1, .22 Short R.F., 1st Issue, Tip-Up, Spur Trigger, 7 Shot, *Antique*	1200	3500	4500

	Fair	V. Good	Excellent
Model #1, .22 Short R.F., 2nd Issue, Tip-Up, Spur Trigger, 7 Shot, *Antique*	$150	$400	$500
Model #1, .22 Short R.F., 3rd Issue, Tip-Up, Spur Trigger, 7 Shot, *Antique*	100	300	400
Model #1 1/2, .32 Short R.F., 1st Issue, Tip-Up, Spur Trigger, 5 Shot, Non-Fluted Cylinder, *Antique*	150	350	450
Model #1 1/2, .32 Short R.F., 2nd Issue, Tip-Up, Spur Trigger, 5 Shot, Fluted Cylinder, *Antique*	150	350	450
Model #2 Old Army, .22 Short R.F., Tip-Up, Spur Trigger, 6 Shot, *Antique*	400	800	900
Model #3 American, .44 Henry, 1st Model, Single Action, Top Break, 6 Shot, *Antique*	3000	5500	6000
Model #3 American, .44 Henry, 2nd Model, #'s 8000-32800, Single Action, Top Break, 6 Shot, *Antique*	2500	5000	5500
Model #3 American, .44 S & W, 1st Model, Single Action, Top Break, 6 Shot, *Antique*	1600	3500	4000
Model #3 American, .44 S & W, 2nd Model, #'s 8000-32800, Single Action, Top Break, 6 Shot, *Antique*	1100	2700	3000
Model #3 Fronter, .38-40 WCF, Single Action, Top Break, 6 Shot, *Antique*	3500	6500	7000
Model #3 Fronter, .44-40 WCF, Single Action, Top Break, 6 Shot, *Antique*	1200	2700	3000
Model #3 New Model, .44 Russian, Argentine Model, Add 15%-25%			
Model #3 New Model, .44 Russian, Australian Police with Shoulder Stock, Add 50%-100%			
Model #3 New Model, .44 Russian, Japanese Navy Issue, Add 15%-25%			
Model #3 New Model, .44 Russian, Single Action, Top Break, 6 Shot, *Antique*	900	2200	2500
Model #3 New Model, .44 S & W, Turkish Model, Add 15%-25%			
Model #3 New Model, Calibers other than.44 Russian			
Model #3 New Model, Calibers, Calibers other than .44 Russian			
Model #3 Russian, .44 Russian, 1st Model, Single Action, Top Break, 6 Shot, Military, *Antique*	1100	2700	3000
Model #3 Russian, .44 Russian, 2nd Model, Finger-Rest Trigger Guard, Single Action, Top Break, 6 Shot, *Antique*	1000	2500	2750
Model #3 Russian, .44 Russian, 2nd Model, Finger-Rest Trigger Guard, Single Action, Top Break, with Shoulder Stock, *Antique*	1750	3500	4000

	Fair	V. Good	Excellent
Model #3 Russian, .44 Russian, 3rd Model, Front Sight Forged on Barrel, Single Action, Top Break, 6 Shot, *Antique*	$1100	$2500	$2750
Model #3 Target, .32-44 S & W, 38-44 S & W, New Model #3, Single Action, Top Break, *Curio*	900	2750	3500
Model 10, .38 Special, Double Action, Blue, Various Barrel Lengths, Swing-Out Cylinder, *Modern*	100	150	250
Model 10, .38 Special, Double Action, Swing-Out Cylinder, 4" Barrel, Heavy Barrel, Blue, *Modern*	125	175	275
Model 10, .38 Special, Double Action, Swing-Out Cylinder, 4" Barrel, Heavy Barrel, Nickel Plated, *Modern*	100	200	300
Model 10, .38 Special, Double Action, Swing-Out Cylinder, Various Barrel Lengths, Nickel Plated, *Modern*	100	200	275
Model 11 (.38/200), .38 S & W, Double Action, Swing-Out Cylinder, *Modern*	125	225	300
Model 12 (U.S.A.F. Model 13), .38 Special, Double Action, Swing-Out Cylinder, Lightweight, *Modern*	300	600	750
Model 12, .38 Special, Double Action, Swing-Out Cylinder, Various Barrel Lengths, Blue, *Modern*	125	300	400
Model 12, .38 Special, Double Action, Swing-Out Cylinder, Various Barrel Lengths, Nickel Plated, *Modern*	125	325	450
Model 14 SA, .38 Special, Single Action, Swing-Out Cylinder, 6" Barrel, Blue, Adjustable Sights, *Modern*	125	275	325
Model 14 SA, .38 Special, Single Action, Swing-Out Cylinder, 8³/₈" Barrel, Blue, Adjustable Sights, *Modern*	150	300	350
Model 14, .38 Special, Double Action, Swing-Out Cylinder, 6" Barrel, Blue, Adjustable Sights, *Modern*	125	225	275
Model 14, .38 Special, Double Action, Swing-Out Cylinder, 8³/₈" Barrel, Blue, Adjustable Sights, *Modern*	150	250	300
Model 15, .38 Special, Double Action, Swing-Out Cylinder, Various Barrel Lengths, Blue, Adjustable Sights, *Modern*	125	225	300
Model 15, .38 Special, Double Action, Swing-Out Cylinder, Various Barrel Lengths, Nickel Plated, Adjustable Sights, *Modern*	125	250	325
Model 16, .32 S & W Long, Double Action, Swing-Out Cylinder, Adjustable Sights, Target Pistol, *Modern*	125	650	950

S & W Model 15

	Fair	V. Good	Excellent
Model 17, .22 L.R.R.F., Double Action, Swing-Out Cylinder, 6" Barrel, Adjustable Sights, Blue, *Modern*	$125	$250	$300
Model 17, .22 L.R.R.F., Double Action, Swing-Out Cylinder, 8³/₈" Barrel, Adjustable Sights, Blue, *Modern*	150	275	325
Model 18, .22 L.R.R.F., Double Action, Swing-Out Cylinder, 4" Barrel, Adjustable Sights, Blue, *Modern*	125	250	300
Model 19, .357 Magnum, Double Action, Swing-Out Cylinder, Various Barrel Lengths, Adjustable Sights, Blue, *Modern*	150	300	350
Model 19, .357 Magnum, Double Action, Swing-Out Cylinder, Various Barrel Lengths, Adjustable Sights, Nickel Plated, *Modern*	150	275	325
Model 1917, .45 Auto-Rim, Double Action, Swing-Out Cylinder, Brazilian Contract, + 45 ACP, *Curio*	100	200	250
Model 1917, .45 Auto-Rim, Double Action, Swing-Out Cylinder, Military, + 45 ACP, *Modern*	200	450	650
Model 20, .38 Special, Double Action, Swing-Out Cylinder, *Modern*	125	300	450
Model 21 "1950 Military," .44 Special, Double Action, Swing-Out Cylinder, Various Barrel Lengths, *Modern*	150	400	500
Model 22 "1950. 45 Military," .45 Auto-Rim, Double Action, Swing-Out Cylinder, *Modern*	150	300	400
Model 23, .38 Special, Double Action, Swing-Out Cylinder, Adjustable Sights, Target Pistol, *Modern*	300	700	800
Model 24, .44 Special, Double Action, Swing-Out Cylinder, Various Barrel Lengths, Adjustable Sights, *Modern*	225	475	525
Model 25, .45 Auto-Rim, Double Action, Swing-Out Cylinder, Target Pistol, Blue, 125th Anniversary, Cased with Accessories, + 45 ACP, *Modern*	150	300	400

	Fair	V. Good	Excellent
Model 25, .45 Auto-Rim, Double Action, Swing-Out Cylinder, Target Pistol, Blue, *Modern*	$150	$300	$350
Model 26, .45 Auto-Rim, Double Action, Swing-Out Cylinder, *Modern*	300	600	700
Model 27 with Registration, .357 Magnum, Double Action, Swing-Out Cylinder, Pre-World War II, Adjustable Sights, *Curio*	800	1600	1750
Model 27, .357 Magnum, Double Action, 8³/₈" Barrel, Adjustable Sights, Cased with Accessories, Nickel Plated, *Modern*	150	300	350
Model 27, .357 Magnum, Double Action, 8³/₈" Barrel, Adjustable Sights, Cased with Accessories, Blue, *Modern*	150	300	350
Model 27, .357 Magnum, Double Action, Swing-Out Cylinder, Pre-War, Adjustable Sights, *Curio*	300	750	900
Model 27, .357 Magnum, Double Action, Swing-Out Cylinder, Various Barrel Lengths, Adjustable Sights, Blue, *Modern*	150	250	300
Model 27, .357 Magnum, Double Action, Swing-Out Cylinder, Nickel Plated, *Modern*	150	250	325
Model 27, .357 Magnum, Double Action, Swing-Out Cylinder, 8³/₈" Barrel, Blue, *Modern*	150	250	350
Model 27, .357 Magnum, Double Action, Swing-Out Cylinder, 8³/₈" Barrel, Nickel Plated, *Modern*	150	250	350
Model 27, .357 Magnum, Double Action, Various Barrel Lengths, Adjustable Sights, Cased with Accessories, Nickel Plated or blue, *Modern*	150	250	300
Model 28, .357 Magnum, Double Action, Various Barrel Lengths, Adjustable Sights, Blue, Highway Patrolman, *Modern*	100	200	250

S & W Model 28

	Fair	V. Good	Excellent
Model 29, .44 Magnum, Double Action, 8³/₈" Barrel, Adjustable Sights, Swing-Out Cylinder, Blue, *Modern*	200	250	350
Model 29, .44 Magnum, Double Action, 8³/₈" Barrel, Adjustable Sights, Swing-Out Cylinder, Nickel Plated, *Modern*	$200	$250	$350
Model 29, .44 Magnum, Double Action, 8³/₈" Barrel, Adjustable Adjustable Sights, Cased with Accessories, Blue, *Modern*	225	275	375
Model 29, .44 Magnum, Double Action, 8³/₈" Barrel, Adjustable Adjustable Sights, Cased with Accessories, Nickel Plated, *Modern*	225	275	375
Model 29, .44 Magnum, Double Action, Various Barrel Lengths, Adjustable Sights, Swing-Out Cylinder, Blue, *Modern*	150	250	350
Model 29, .44 Magnum, Double Action, Various Barrel Lengths, Adjustable Sights, Swing-Out Cylinder, Nickel Plated, *Modern*	150	250	350
Model 29, .44 Magnum, Double Action, Various Barrel Lengths, Adjustable Sights, Cased with Accessories, Blue, *Modern*	175	275	375
Model 29, .44 Magnum, Double Action, Various Barrel Lengths, Adjustable Sights, Cased with Accessories, Nickel Plated, *Modern*	175	275	375
Model 30, .32 S & W Long, Double Action, Swing-Out Cylinder, *Modern*	100	200	300
Model 31, .32 S & W Long, Double Action, Swing-Out Cylinder, Various Barrel Lengths, Nickel Plated, *Modern*	100	250	350
Model 31, .32 S & W Long, Double Action, Swing-Out Cylinder, Various Barrel Lengths, Blue, *Modern*	100	200	300
Model 32, .32 S & W, Double Action, Swing-Out Cylinder, 2" Barrel, *Modern*	100	200	325
Model 33, .32 S & W, Double Action, Swing-Out Cylinder, *Modern*	100	250	350
Model 34 "Kit Gun," .22 L.R.R.F., Double Action, Swing-Out Cylinder, Various Barrel Lengths, Adjustable Sights, Blue, *Modern*	150	250	325
Model 34 "Kit Gun," .22 L.R.R.F., Double Action, Swing-Out Cylinder, Various Barrel Lengths, Adjustable Sights, Nickel Plated, *Modern*	150	300	350
Model 35, .22 L.R.R.F., Double Action, Swing-Out Cylinder, Target Pistol, Adjustable Sights, *Modern*	150	325	425
Model 36, .38 Special, Double Action, Swing-Out Cylinder, Various Barrel Lengths, Blue, *Modern*	100	150	250
Model 36, .38 Special, Double Action, Swing-Out Cylinder, Various Barrel Lengths, Nickel Plated, *Modern*	100	200	300

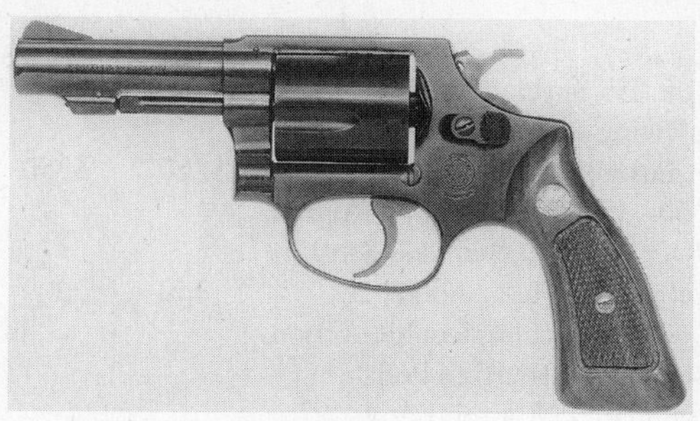

S & W Model 36

	Fair	V. Good	Excellent
Model 36, .38 Special, Double Action, Swing-Out Cylinder, 3" Barrel, Heavy Barrel, Blue, *Modern*	$100	$150	$250
Model 36, .38 Special, Double Action, Swing-Out Cylinder, 3" Barrel, Heavy Barrel, Nickel Plated, *Modern*	100	200	300
Model 37, .38 Special, Double Action, Swing-Out Cylinder, Various Barrel Lengths, Lightweight, Blue, *Modern*	150	250	350
Model 37, .38 Special, Double Action, Swing-Out Cylinder, Various Barrel Lengths, Lightweight, Nickel Plated, *Modern*	150	300	400
Model 38, .38 Special, Double Action, Swing-Out Cylinder, 2" Barrel, Hammer Shroud, Blue, *Modern*	125	225	325

S & W Model 38

	Fair	V. Good	Excellent
Model 38, .38 Special, Swing-Out Cylinder, 2" Barrel, Hammer Shroud, Nickel Plated, Double Action, *Modern*	225	275	325
Model 40, .38 Special, Double Action, Swing-Out Cylinder, Hammerless, *Modern*	200	400	500
Model 42, .38 Special, Double Action, Swing-Out Cylinder, Hammerless, Lightweight, *Modern*	150	275	400
Model 43, .22 L.R.R.F., Double Action, Swing-Out Cylinder, Adjustable Sights, Lightweight, *Modern*	200	300	400

	Fair	V. Good	Excellent
Model 45 USPO, .22 L.R.R.F., Double Action, Swing-Out Cylinder, *Modern*	$200	$300	$500
Model 45, .22 L.R.R.F., Double Action, Swing-Out Cylinder, Commercial, *Modern*	200	300	450
Model 48, .22 WMR, Double Action, Swing-Out Cylinder, Various Barrel Lengths, Blue, Adjustable Sights, *Modern*	150	250	400
Model 48, .22 WMR, Double Action, Swing-Out Cylinder, 8³/₈" Barrel, Blue, Adjustable Sights, *Modern*	150	300	425
Model 49, .38 Special, Double Action, Swing-Out Cylinder, 2" Barrel, Hammer Shroud, Nickel Plated, *Modern*	150	200	325
Model 49, .38 Special, Double Action, Swing-Out Cylinder, 2" Barrel, Hammer Shroud, Blue, *Modern*	150	200	300
Model 50, .38 Special, Double Action, Swing-Out Cylinder, Adjustable Sights, *Modern*	300	450	650
Model 51, .22 WMR Combo, Double Action, Swing-Out Cylinder Adjustable Sights, *Modern*	200	300	400
Model 51, .22LR/.22 WMR Combo, Double Action, Swing-Out Cylinder, Adjustable Sights, *Modern*	250	325	450
Model 53, .22 Rem. Jet, Double Action, Swing-Out Cylinder Adjustable Sights, *Modern*	300	500	650
Model 53, .22 Rem. Jet, Double Action, Swing-Out Cylinder Adjustable Sights, Extra Cylinder, *Modern*	325	550	700
Model 547, 9mm Luger, Double Action, Swing-Out Cylinder, Blue, *Modern*	150	200	250
Model 56, .38 Special, Double Action, Swing-Out Cylinder 2" Barrel, Adjustable Sights, *Modern*	650	700	750
Model 57, .41 Magnum, Double Action, Swing-Out Cylinder Various Barrel Lengths, Blue, Adjustable Sights, *Modern*	200	275	350
Model 57, .41 Magnum, Double Action, Swing-Out Cylinder Various Barrel Lengths, Nickel Plated, Adjustable Sights, *Modern*	200	300	375
Model 57, .41 Magnum, Double Action, Swing-Out Cylinder 8³/₈" Barrel, Blue, Adjustable Sights, *Modern*	200	300	350
Model 57, .41 Magnum, Double Action, Swing-Out Cylinder 8³/₈" Barrel, Nickel Plated, Adjustable Sights, *Modern*	200	325	400

	Fair	V. Good	Excellent
Model 57, .41 Magnum, Double Action, Swing-Out Cylinder Various Barrel Lengths, Blue, Cased with Accessories, *Modern*	$200	$300	$400
Model 57, .41 Magnum, Double Action, Swing-Out Cylinder Various Barrel Lengths, Nickel Plated, Cased with Accessories, *Modern*	200	325	400
Model 57, .41 Magnum, Double Action, Swing-Out Cylinder 8³/₈" Barrel, Blue, Cased with Accessories, *Modern*	250	325	400
Model 57, .41 Magnum, Double Action, Swing-Out Cylinder 8³/₈" Barrel, Blue, Cased with Accessories, *Modern*	250	325	400
Model 58, .41 Magnum, Double Action, Swing-Out Cylinder 4" Barrel, Blue, *Modern*	200	250	300
Model 58, .41 Magnum, Double Action, Swing-Out Cylinder 4" Barrel, Nickel Plated, *Modern*	200	250	300
Model 581, .357 Magnum, Double Action, Swing-Out Cylinder Blue, *Modern*	150	175	200
Model 581, .357 Magnum, Double Action, Swing-Out Cylinder Nickel, *Modern*	125	175	225
Model 586, .357 Magnum, Double Action, Swing-Out Cylinder Blue, Adjustable Sights, *Modern*	225	275	325

S & W Model 586

	Fair	V. Good	Excellent
Model 586, .357 Magnum, Double Action, Swing-Out Cylinder Nickel, Adjustable Sights, *Modern*	250	300	350

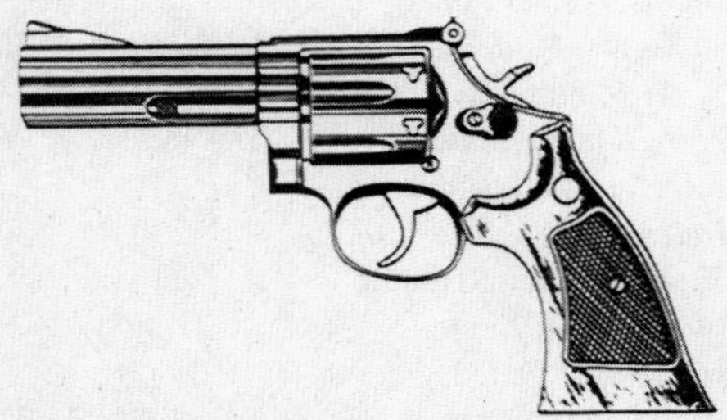

S & W Model 586 Stainless

	Fair	V. Good	Excellent
Model 60, .38 Special, Double Action, Swing-Out Cylinder Stainless Steel, Adjustable Sights, *Modern*	$250	$350	$450
Model 60, .38 Special, Double Action, Swing-Out Cylinder Stainless Steel, 2" Barrel, *Modern*	150	200	250
Model 60, .38 Special, Double Action, Swing-Out Cylinder High Polish Stainless Steel, 2" Barrel, Early model, *Modern*	200	300	400
Model 629, .44 Magnum, Double Action, Swing-Out Cylinder Stainless Steel, Adjustable Sights, *Modern*	250	300	400
Model 629, .44 Magnum, Double Action, Swing-Out Cylinder 8³/₈" Barrel, Stainless Steel, Adjustable Sights, *Modern*	300	400	450
Model 63, .22 L.R.R.F., Double Action, Swing-Out Cylinder, Stainless Steel, 4" Barrel, Adjustable Sights, *Modern*	200	250	300
Model 64, .38 Special, Double Action, Swing-Out Cylinder Stainless Steel, Various Barrel Lengths, *Modern*	125	225	275
Model 649 Bodyguard, .38 Special, J Frame, 5 Shot, Stainless Steel, *Modern*	150	200	300
Model 65, .357 Magnum, Double Action, Swing-Out Cylinder Stainless Steel, 4" Barrel, Heavy Barrel, *Modern*	125	225	200
Model 650, .22 W.M.R., Double Action, Swing-Out Cylinder, Stainless Steel, *Modern*	150	200	300
Model 651, .22 W.M.R., Double Action, Swing-Out Cylinder, Stainless Steel, Adjustable Sights, *Modern*	150	200	250
Model 66, .357 Magnum, Double Action, Swing-Out Cylinder Stainless Steel, 2¹/₂" Barrel, *Modern*	125	200	250
Model 66, .357 Magnum, Double Action, Swing-Out Cylinder Stainless Steel, Various Barrel Lengths, *Modern*	125	200	250
Model 67, .38 Special, Double Action, Swing-Out Cylinder Stainless Steel, 4" Barrel, *Modern*	125	200	250
Model 681, .357 Magnum, Double Action, Swing-Out Cylinder Stainless Steel, *Modern*	150	200	250
Model 686, .357 Magnum, Double Action, Swing-Out Cylinder Stainless Steel, Adjustable Sights, *Modern*	175	225	275
Model M Head Ejector, .22 Long R.F., 1st Model Ladysmith, Solid Frame, Swing-Out Cylinder, Double Action, *Curio*	400	800	1200

	Fair	V. Good	Excellent
Model M Head Ejector, .22 Long R.F., 2nd Model Ladysmith, Solid Frame, Swing-Out Cylinder, Double Action, *Curio*	$400	$800	$1200
Model M Head Ejector, .22 Long R.F., 3rd Model Ladysmith, Solid Frame, Swing-Out Cylinder, Double Action, *Curio*	400	800	1200
Model M Head Ejector, .22 Long R.F., 3rd Model Ladysmith, Solid Frame, Swing-Out Cylinder, Double Action, $2\frac{1}{4}$" & 6" Barrel, *Curio*	500	1250	2500
Second Model Schofield, .45 S & W, Knurled Latch, Top Break, Single Action, Military, *Antique*	1600	3500	4500
Second Model Schofield, .45 S & W, Knurled Latch, Top Break, Single Action, Commercial, *Antique*	2100	4250	4750
Second Model Schofield, .45 S & W, Wells Fargo, Knurled Latch, Top Break, Single Action, *Antique*	1200	2500	3000
Target Models, For Target Hammer, Target Trigger, Target Stocks, Add $40.00-$75.00			
Target Models, For Target Hammer, Target Trigger, Target Stocks, Stocks, Add $45.00-$75.00			
Victory, .38 Special Military & Police, Solid Frame, Swing-Out Cylinder, Double Action, Military, *Modern*	150	200	250

HANDGUN, SEMI-AUTOMATIC

	Fair	V. Good	Excellent
.32 ACP, Blue, *Curio*	1200	2500	2750
.35 S & W Automatic, Blue, *Curio*	250	525	600
.35 S & W Automatic, Early Model, *Curio*	250	550	700
Model 39, 9mm Luger, Double Action, Blue, *Modern*	150	275	325
Model 39, 9mm Luger, Double Action, Nickel Plated, *Curio*	150	275	350
Model 39, 9mm Luger, Double Action, Steel Frame, *Curio*	400	850	950

S & W Model 39

	Fair	V. Good	Excellent
Model 41, .22 L.R.R.F., Various Barrel Lengths, *Modern*	250	550	600
Model 41-1, .22 Short R.F., Various Barrel Lengths, *Modern*	250	525	575
Model 44, 9mm Luger, Single Action, *Modern*			
Model 46, .22 L.R.R.F., Various Barrel Lengths, *Modern*	$200	$425	$500
Model 52A, .38 Special, Blue, *Modern*	900	2250	2500
Model 59, 9mm Luger, Double Action, Blue, *Modern*	150	325	375
Model 59, 9mm Luger, Double Action, Nickel Plated, *Modern*	150	325	425
Model 61 Escort, .22 L.R.R.F., Clip Fed, Blue, *Modern*	100	225	275
Model 61 Escort, .22 L.R.R.F., Clip Fed, Nickel Plated, *Modern*	100	250	300

S & W Model 61

	Fair	V. Good	Excellent
Model 439, 9mm Luger, Double Action, Blue, *Modern*	150	300	325
Model 439, 9mm Luger, Double Action, Nickel Plated, *Modern*	150	300	350
Model 459, 9mm Luger, Double Action, Blue, *Modern*	150	325	375
Model 459, 9mm Luger, Double Action, Nickel Plated, *Modern*	150	350	400
Model 469, (12 Shot), 9mm Luger, Double Action, Blue, *Modern*	150	300	350
Model 539, 9mm Luger, Double Action, Blue, *Modern*	150	325	375
Model 539, 9mm Luger, Double Action, Nickel Plated, *Modern*	150	350	400
Model 639, 9mm Luger, Double Action, Stainless, *Modern*	150	300	350
Model 659, (12 Shot), 9mm Luger, Double Action, Stainless Steel, *Modern*	150	300	350
Model 659, 9mm Luger, Double Action, Stainless, *Modern*	150	325	375

HANDGUN, SINGLESHOT

	Fair	V. Good	Excellent
Model 1891 Set, Various Calibers, Extra Cylinder, Extra Barrel, Target Pistol, Single Action, 1st Model, *Antique*	200	400	600
Model 1891, .22 L.R.R.F., Target Pistol, Single Action, 1st Model, Various Barrel Lengths, *Antique*	200	400	650

	Fair	V. Good	Excellent
Model 1891, .22 L.R.R.F., Target Pistol, Single Action, 2nd Model, No Hand or Cylinder Stop, *Curio*	$200	$400	$600
Perfected Olympic, .22 L.R.R.F., Double Action, Top Break, Tight Bore and Chamber, Target Pistol, *Modern*	200	450	750
Perfected, .22 L.R.R.F., Double Action, Top Break, Target Pistol, *Modern*	150	375	600
Straight Line, .22 L.R.R.F., Cased, *Curio*	600	1100	1500

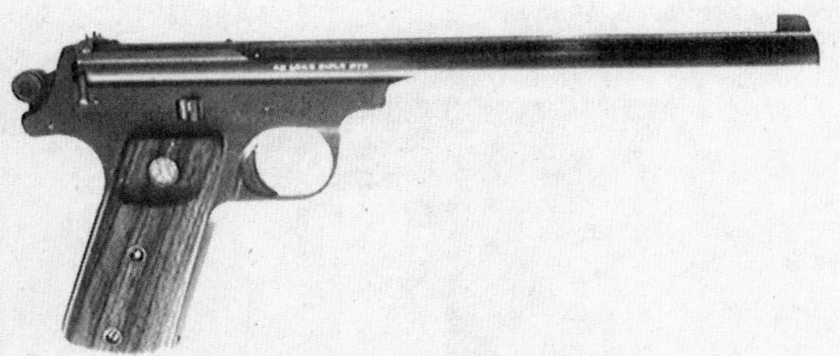

S & W Straight Line

RIFLE, BOLT ACTION

	Fair	V. Good	Excellent
Model 1500, Various Calibers, Monte Carlo Stock, Checkered Stock, *Modern*	150	200	250
Model 1500 Deluxe, Various Calibers, Monte Carlo Stock, Checkered Stock, *Modern*	150	225	275
Model 1500 Magnum, Various Calibers, Monte Carlo Stock, Checkered Stock, *Modern*	150	200	250
Model 1500 Varmint, Various Calibers, Monte Carlo Stock, Checkered Stock, Heavy Barrel, *Modern*	150	225	275
Model 1700 Classic, Various Calibers, Monte Carlo Stock, Checkered Stock, Clip Fed, *Modern*	150	275	325
Model A, Various Calibers, Monte Carlo Stock, Checkered Stock, *Modern*	150	275	325
Model B, Various Calibers, Monte Carlo Stock, Checkered Stock, *Modern*	150	225	275
Model C, Various Calibers, Sporting Rifle, Checkered Stock, *Modern*	125	225	275
Model D, Various Calibers, Mannlicher, Checkered Stock, *Modern*	150	325	375
Model E, Various Calibers, Monte Carlo Stock, Mannlicher, *Modern*	150	325	375

RIFLE, REVOLVER

	Fair	V. Good	Excellent
Model 320, .320 S & W Rifle, Single Action, Top Break, 6 Shot, Adjustable Sights, Cased with Accessories, *Antique*	4000	8000	9000

RIFLE, SEMI-AUTOMATIC

	Fair	V. Good	Excellent
Light Rifle, MK I, 9mm Luger, Clip Fed, Carbine, *Curio*	$600	$1250	$1500
Light Rifle, MK II, 9mm Luger, Clip Fed, Carbine, *Curio*	800	1750	2000

SHOTGUN, SEMI-AUTOMATIC

	Fair	V. Good	Excellent
Model 1000 Field, 12 Ga., Vent Rib, *Modern*	125	250	300

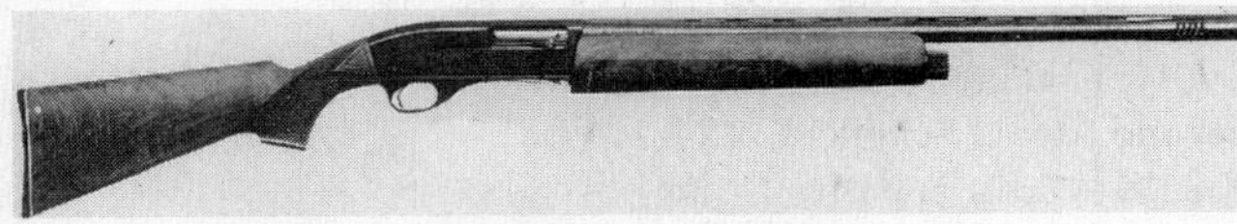

S & W Model 1000

	Fair	V. Good	Excellent
Model 1000 Skeet, 12 Ga., Vent Rib, *Modern*	150	300	350
Model 1000 Super 12, 12 Ga., Vent Rib, *Modern*	150	375	425
Model 1000 Trap, 12 Ga., Open Sights, *Modern*	200	450	500

SHOTGUN, SLIDE ACTION

	Fair	V. Good	Excellent
Model 916 Eastfield, Various Gauges, Plain Barrel, *Modern*	75	125	150
Model 916T Eastfield, Various Gauges, Plain Barrel, *Modern*	75	150	175
Model 3000 Field, 12 Ga. 3", Vent Rib, *Modern*	100	250	275
Model 3000 Police, 12 Ga., Open Sights, *Modern*	100	225	250
Model 3000 Police, 12 Ga., Open Sights, Folding Stock, *Modern*	125	250	300
Model 3000 Slug, 12 Ga. 3", Open Sights, *Modern*	125	250	300

SMITH, ANTHONY

Northampton, Pa. 1770–1779. See Kentucky Rifles and Pistols.

SMITH, L. C. GUN CO.

Syracuse, N.Y., 1877–1890. Manufactured after 1890 by Hunter Arms, and in 1948 became a division of Marlin.

SHOTGUN, DOUBLE BARREL, SIDE-BY-SIDE

	Fair	V. Good	Excellent
Crown Grade, Various Calibers, Sidelock, Double Trigger, Automatic Ejector, Fancy Engraving, Fancy Checkering, *Curio*	2100	4750	5250
Crown Grade, Various Calibers, Sidelock, Single Selective Trigger, Automatic Ejector, Fancy Engraving, Fancy Checkering, *Curio*	2200	5000	5500
Eagle Grade, 12 Ga., Double Trigger, Checkered Stock, Vent Rib, *Curio*	1700	3500	4000

L.C. Smith Field Grade

	Fair	V. Good	Excellent
Field Grade, Various Calibers, Sidelock, Double Trigger, Checkered Stock, Light Engraving, *Curio*	$250	$750	$900
Field Grade, Various Calibers, Sidelock, Double Trigger, Automatic Ejector, Checkered Stock, Light Engraving, *Curio*	450	1000	1200
Field Grade, Various Calibers, Sidelock, Single Trigger, Checkered Stock, Light Engraving, *Curio*	450	950	1100
Field Grade, Various Calibers, Sidelock, Single Trigger, Automatic Ejector, Checkered Stock, Light Engraving, *Curio*	550	1200	1350
Ideal Grade, Various Calibers, Sidelock, Double Trigger, Checkered Stock, Engraved, *Curio*	400	850	1000
Ideal Grade, Various Calibers, Sidelock, Double Trigger, Automatic Ejector, Checkered Stock, Engraved, *Curio*	550	1150	1300
Ideal Grade, Various Calibers, Sidelock, Single Selective Trigger, Checkered Stock, Engraved, *Curio*	450	1050	1200
Ideal Grade, Various Calibers, Sidelock, Single Selective Trigger, Automatic Ejector, Engraved, Checkered Stock, *Curio*	550	1300	1450
Monogram Grade, Various Calibers, Sidelock, Single Selective Trigger, Automatic Ejector, Engraved, Checkered Stock, *Curio*	3250	7500	8500
Skeet Grade, Various Calibers, Sidelock, Single Selective Trigger, Automatic Ejector, Engraved, Checkered Stock, *Curio*	1200	2500	2750
Skeet Grade, Various Calibers, Sidelock, Single Trigger, Automatic Ejector, Engraved, Checkered Stock, *Curio*	1200	2750	3000
Specialty Grade, Various Calibers, Sidelock, Double Trigger, Engraved, Checkered Stock, *Curio*	900	2250	2500
Specialty Grade, Various Calibers, Sidelock, Single Selective Trigger, Automatic Ejector, Engraved, Checkered Stock, *Curio*	1100	2500	2750
Trap Grade, 12 Ga., Sidelock, Single Selective Trigger, Automatic Ejector, Engraved, Checkered Stock, *Curio*	550	1250	1500

SHOTGUN, SINGLESHOT

	Fair	V. Good	Excellent
Crown Grade, 12 Ga., Trap Grade, Vent Rib, Automatic Ejector, Fancy Engraving, Fancy Checkering, *Curio*	$1200	$2500	$3000
Olympic Grade, 12 Ga., Trap Grade, Vent Rib, Automatic Ejector, Engraved, Fancy Checkering, *Curio*	600	1250	1500
Specialty Grade, 12 Ga., Trap Grade, Vent Rib, Automatic Ejector, Engraved, Fancy Checkering, *Curio*	600	1250	1500

SMITH, OTIS A.

Middlefield & Rockfall, Conn. 1873–1890.

HANDGUN, REVOLVER

	Fair	V. Good	Excellent
.22 Short R.F., 7 Shot, Spur Trigger, Solid Frame, Single Action, *Antique*	100	200	250
.32 S & W, 5 Shot, Single Action, Top Break, Spur Trigger, *Antique* .	100	175	225
.32 Short R.F., 5 Shot, Spur Trigger, Solid Frame, Single Action, *Antique*	100	200	250
.38 Short R.F., 5 Shot, Spur Trigger, Solid Frame, Single Action, *Antique*	100	200	250
.41 Short R.F., 5 Shot, Spur Trigger, Solid Frame, Single Action, *Antique*	100	225	275

SMITH, STOEFFEL

Pa. 1790–1800. See Kentucky Rifles and Pistols.

SMITH, THOMAS

London, England, c. 1850.

RIFLE, PERCUSSION

	Fair	V. Good	Excellent
16 Ga., Smoothbore, Anson-Deeley Lock, Octagon Barrel, Fancy Wood, Cased with Accessories, *Antique* ..	1100	2500	3250

SMITH, WM.

England.

HANDGUN, SEMI-AUTOMATIC

	Fair	V. Good	Excellent
Pocket, 6.35mm, Clip Fed, 1906 Browning Type, *Modern*	150	375	450

SMOKER

Made by Johnson Bye & Co. 1875–1884.

HANDGUN, REVOLVER

	Fair	V. Good	Excellent
#1, .22 Short R.F., 7 Shot, Spur Trigger, Solid Frame, Single Action, *Antique*	$75	$150	$175
#2, .32 Short R.F., 5 Shot, Spur Trigger, Solid Frame, Single Action, *Antique*	75	150	175
#3, .38 Short R.F., 5 Shot, Spur Trigger, Solid Frame, Single Action, *Antique*	75	150	175
#4, .41 Short R.F., 5 Shot, Spur Trigger, Solid Frame, Single Action, *Antique*	75	150	200

SNAPHAUNCE, EXAMPLE

HANDGUN, SNAPHAUNCE

	Fair	V. Good	Excellent
.45 Italian Early 1700s, Holster Pistol, Half-Octagon Barrel, Engraved, Carved, High Quality, Furniture, *Antique*	900	2000	2500
Early 1800s Small, Plain, *Antique*	500	900	1000
English Late 1500s, Ovoid Pommel, Engraved, Gold, Damascened, High Quality, *Antique*	6000	15000	20000
Italian 1700s, High Quality, Belt Pistol, Light Ornamentation, *Antique*	1100	2500	3000
Italian Early 1700s, Medium Quality, Brass Furniture, Plain, *Antique*	400	800	1000

RIFLE, SNAPHAUNCE

	Fair	V. Good	Excellent
Arabian, .59, Ornate, Inlaid with Silver, Ivory Buttstock Inlays, *Antique*	200	450	600
Italian Mid-1600s, Half-Octagon Barrel, Carved, Engraved, Silver Inlay, Steel Furniture, Ornate, *Antique*	4000	9000	10000

SODIA, FRANZ

Ferlach, Austria.

COMBINATION WEAPON, MULTI-BARREL

	Fair	V. Good	Excellent
Bochdrilling, Various Calibers, Fancy Wood, Fancy Checkering, Fancy Engraving, *Antique*	3000	5500	6500
Doppelbuchse, Various Calibers, Fancy Wood, Fancy Checkering, Fancy Engraving, *Antique*	1900	3750	4500
Over-Under Rifle, Various Calibers, Fancy Wood, Fancy Checkering, Fancy Engraving, *Antique*	1700	3500	4000

SOLER

Ripoll, Spain, c. 1625.

HANDGUN, WHEELOCK

	Fair	V. Good	Excellent
Enclosed Mid-1600's, Ball Pommel, Ornate, *Antique*	4500	10000	12500

SOUTHERN ARMS CO.

Made by Crescent for H. & D. Folsom, New York City. See Crescent Fire Arms Co., Shotgun, Double Barrel, Side-by-Side, Shotgun, Singleshot.

SPAARMAN, ANDREAS

Berlin, Germany, c. 1680.

RIFLE, FLINTLOCK

	Fair	V. Good	Excellent
.72, Jaeger, Octagon Barrel, Swamped, Rifled, Iron Mounts, Ornate, Set Trigger, *Antique*	$1800	$3500	$4000

SPANISH GUNMAKERS, FROM EIBAR

Most of the production of the Colt or FN type .25 caliber semi-automatic pistols, some of .32 autos, and some of double-action copies of Colt or S & W–type revolvers: Modesto Santos, Armero Especialistas Reunides, Gaspar Arizaga, Antonio Azpiri y Cia, Apaolozo Hermanos, Retolaza Hermanos, Arriola Hermanos, Orbea Hermanos Azanza y Arrizabalaga, Arrizabalaga Hilos De Calixto, Astra, Avion, Azanza y Arrizabalaga, Azul, Berasaluze Areitio-Arutena y Cia, Francisco Arizamendi, Echave y Arizmendi, Arizmendi Zulaika y Cia, Gregorio Bolumburu, Juan Esteban Bustindiu, Hijos de A Echevera, Tomas de Urizar y Cia, Antonio Azpiri y Cia, Fabbrique d'Arms de Guerre de Grand Precision (Etxezagarra & Abitua), Iraola Salaverria, Erquiaga Muguruzu y Cia, Echave y Arizmendi, Eulogio Arostegui, Anitua, Garate, Amas Garbi, Bonifacio Echeverra, Cooperative Orbea, San Martin y Cid, Martin a Bascaran, Gaspar Arrizaga, Jose Mugica, Ojanguren y Marcaido, Armero Especialistas Reunidas, Gabilondo y Cia, Gregorio Bolumburu, M. Zulaica y Cia, Felix Sarasqueta, S.E.A.M., Star, Stosel, Retolaza Hermanos, Charola y Anitua, Colon, T.A.C. (Trocaola, Aranzabal y Cia), Tomas de Urizair y Cia, Arizmendi y Geonaga, Ojanguran y Vidosa, Gaspar Arizaga, hijos de Calixto Arrizabalaga.

SPANISH MILITARY

Also see Astra, Star.

HANDGUN, SEMI-AUTOMATIC

	Fair	V. Good	Excellent
Jo-Lo-Ar, 9mm Bergmann, Clip Fed, Military, Hammer, *Curio*	250	550	650
M1913-16 Campo-Giro, 9mm Bergmann, Clip Fed, Military, *Curio*	200	425	500

RIFLE, BOLT ACTION

	Fair	V. Good	Excellent
Destroyer, 9mm Bayard Long, Clip Fed, Carbine, *Modern*	75	150	175
M98 La Caruna, 8mm Mauser, Military, *Curio*	75	150	175

RIFLE, SEMI-AUTOMATIC

	Fair	V. Good	Excellent
CETME Sport, .308 Win., Clip Fed, *Modern*	600	1250	1500

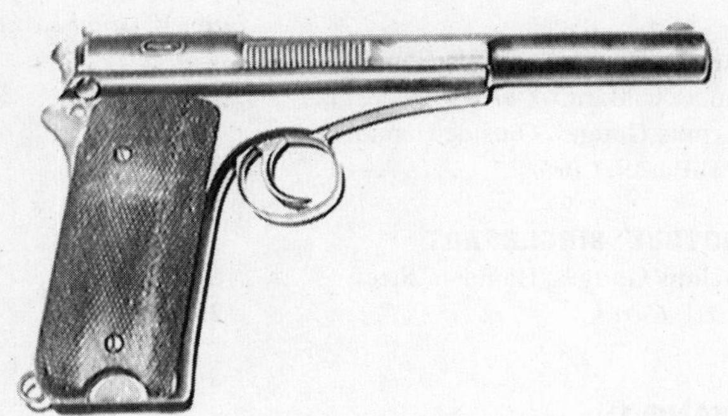

Spanish Military M1913-16

SPENCER ARMS CO.

Windsor, Conn., 1886–1888.

	Fair	V. Good	Excellent
SHOTGUN, SLIDE ACTION			
Spencer, Roper, 12 Ga., Tube Feed, *Antique*	$150	$350	$400

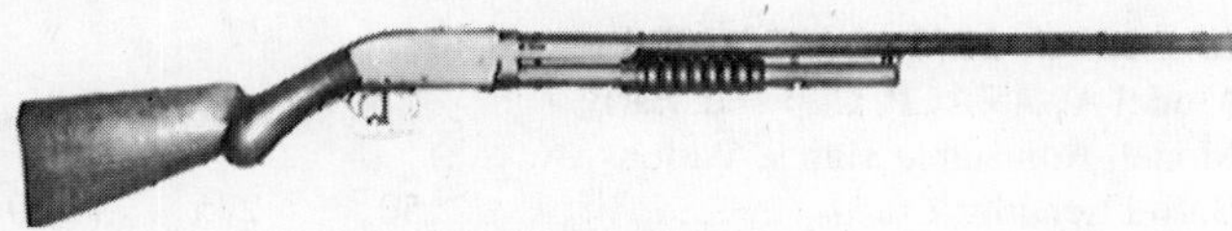

Spencer Roper

SPENCER GUN CO.

Made by Crescent for Hibbard & Spencer Bartlett, c. 1900. See Crescent Fire Arms Co., Shotgun, Double Barrel, Side-by-Side; Shotgun, Singleshot.

SPENCER SAFETY HAMMERLESS

Made by Columbia Armory, Tenn., c. 1892.

	Fair	V. Good	Excellent
HANDGUN, REVOLVER			
.38 S & W, 5 Shot, Top Break, Hammerless, Double Action, *Antique*	50	100	125

SPORTSMAN

Made by Crescent for W. Bingham Co. Cleveland, Ohio, c. 1900. See Crescent Fire Arms Co., Shotgun, Double Barrel, Side-by-Side; Shotgun, Singleshot.

SPORTSMAN

Made by Steven Arms.

	Fair	V. Good	Excellent
SHOTGUN, DOUBLE BARREL, SIDE-BY-SIDE			
M 315, Various Gauges, Hammerless, Steel Barrel, *Antique*	75	150	175
SHOTGUN, SINGLESHOT			
Model 90, Various Gauges, Takedown, Automatic Ejector, Plain, Hammer, *Antique*	$25	$50	$75

SPRINGFIELD ARMORY

Manufactured by Springfield, Inc., Geneseo, Ill.

	Fair	V. Good	Excellent
RIFLE, SEMI-AUTOMATIC			
M1A Match, .308 Win., Clip Fed, Version of M-14, *Modern*	450	1050	1250
M1A Standard, .308 Win., Clip Fed, Version of M-14, *Modern*	400	850	1000
M1A Standard, .308 Win., Clip Fed, Version of M-14, Folding Stock, *Modern*	425	950	1100
M1A Super Match, .308 Win., Clip Fed, Version of M-14, Heavy Barrel, *Modern*	550	1250	1500

SPRINGFIELD ARMS

Made by Crescent, c. 1900. See Crescent Fire Arms Co., Shotgun, Double Barrel; Shotgun, Singleshot.

SPY

Made by Norwich Falls Pistol Co., c. 1880.

	Fair	V. Good	Excellent
HANDGUN, REVOLVER			
.22 Short R.F., 7 Shot, Spur Trigger, Solid Frame, Single Action, *Antique*	75	150	175

SQUARE DEAL

Made by Crescent for Stratton-Warren Hdw. Co., Memphis, Tenn. See Crescent Fire Arms Co., Shotgun, Double Barrel, Side-by-Side; Shotgun, Singleshot.

SQUIBMAN

Made by Squires, Bingham, Makati, Philippines.

	Fair	V. Good	Excellent
HANDGUN, REVOLVER			
Model 100 D, .38 Spec., Double Action, Blue, Swing-Out Cylinder, Vent Rib, *Modern*	50	100	125
Model 100 DC, .38 Spec., Double Action, Blue, Swing-Out Cylinder, *Modern*	50	100	125
Thunder Chief, .38 Spec., Double Action, Blue, Swing-Out Cylinder, Vent Rib, Heavy Barrel, *Modern*	75	125	150
RIFLE, BOLT ACTION			
M 14D, .22 L.R.R.F., Clip Fed, Checkered Stock, *Modern*	15	25	50

	Fair	V. Good	Excellent
M 15, .22 WMR, Clip Fed, Checkered Stock, *Modern*	$25	$50	$75

RIFLE, SEMI-AUTOMATIC

	Fair	V. Good	Excellent
M-16, .22 L.R.R.F., Clip Fed, Flash Hider, *Modern*	25	50	75
M20D, .22 L.R.R.F., Clip Fed, Checkered Stock, *Modern*	25	50	75

SHOTGUN, SLIDE ACTION

	Fair	V. Good	Excellent
M 30/28, 12 Ga., Plain, *Modern*	50	75	100

ST. LOUIS ARMS CO.

Belgium for Shapleigh Hardware Co., c. 1900.

SHOTGUN, DOUBLE BARREL, SIDE-BY-SIDE

	Fair	V. Good	Excellent
Various Gauges, Hammerless, Damascus Barrel, *Modern*	75	150	175
Various Gauges, Hammerless, Steel Barrel, *Modern*	75	150	200
Various Gauges, Outside Hammers, Damascus Barrel, *Modern*	75	150	175
Various Gauges, Outside Hammers, Steel Barrel, *Modern*	75	125	175

SHOTGUN, SINGLESHOT

	Fair	V. Good	Excellent
Various Gauges, Hammer, Steel Barrel, *Modern*	25	50	75

STAGGS-BILT

Staggs Enterprises, Phoenix, Ariz., c. 1970.

COMBINATION WEAPON, OVER-UNDER

	Fair	V. Good	Excellent
20 Ga./.30-30, Top Break, Hammerless, Double Triggers, Top Break, *Modern*	75	100	125

STANDARD ARMS CO.

Wilmington, Del., 1909–1911.

RIFLE, SEMI-AUTOMATIC

	Fair	V. Good	Excellent
Model G, Various Calibers, Takedown, Tube Feed, Hammerless, *Curio*	200	400	450

RIFLE, SLIDE ACTION

	Fair	V. Good	Excellent
Model M, Various Calibers, Takedown, Tube Feed, Hammerless, *Curio*	150	275	325

STANLEY

Belgium, c. 1900.

SHOTGUN, DOUBLE BARREL, SIDE-BY-SIDE

	Fair	V. Good	Excellent
Various Gauges, Hammerless, Damascus Barrel, *Curio*	75	150	175
Various Gauges, Hammerless, Steel Barrel, *Curio*	75	175	200
Various Gauges, Outside Hammers, Damascus Barrel, *Curio*	$75	$150	$175
Various Gauges, Outside Hammers, Steel Barrel, *Curio*	75	175	200

SHOTGUN, SINGLESHOT

	Fair	V. Good	Excellent
Various Gauges, Hammer, Steel Barrel, *Curio*	25	50	75

STANTON

London, England, c. 1778.

HANDGUN, FLINTLOCK

	Fair	V. Good	Excellent
.55 Officers, Belt Pistol, Screw Barrel, Box Lock, Brass, *Antique*	800	1750	2000

STAR

Made by Bonifacio Echeverria, Eibar, Spain 1911 to date.

HANDGUN, SEMI-AUTOMATIC

	Fair	V. Good	Excellent
Model A, .45 ACP, Clip Fed, Early Model, Adjustable Sights, Various Barrel Lengths, *Curio*	150	275	300

Star Model A

	Fair	V. Good	Excellent
Model A, 7.63mm, Clip Fed, *Curio*	125	250	275
Model A, 9mm Bergmann, Clip Fed, Early Model, Adjustable Sights, Various Barrel Lengths, *Curio*	100	175	225
Model A, 9mm, Clip Fed, *Curio*	125	250	275
Model A, Carbine, 7.63 Mauser, Clip Fed, Early Model, Adjustable Sights, Various Barrel Lengths, Stock Lug, *Curio*	600	1250	1500
Model A, Various Calibers, Holster Stock, Add $250.00-$500.00			
Model AS, .38 Super, Clip Fed, *Curio*	100	200	250
Model B, 9mm Luger, Clip Fed, *Curio*	100	200	250
Model B, 9mm Luger, Clip Fed, German Military Marked, *Modern*	300	650	750
Model BKM, 9mm Luger, Clip Fed, Lightweight, *Curio*	100	225	275

	Fair	V. Good	Excellent
Model BKS-Starlight, 9mm Luger, Clip Fed, Lightweight, *Curio*	$100	$225	$250
Model BM, 9mm Luger, Clip Fed, Steel Frame, *Curio*	175	200	225
Model C, 9mm Browning Long, Clip Fed, 8 Shot, *Curio*	125	175	225
Model C O, 6.35mm, Clip Fed, *Curio*	100	150	200
Model C U, 6.35mm, Clip Fed, Lightweight, *Curio*	75	125	175
Model D, .380 ACP, Clip Fed, 15 Shot Clip, *Curio*	125	175	225
Model D, .380 ACP, Clip Fed, 6 Shot, *Curio*	100	150	200
Model DK, .380 ACP, Clip Fed, Lightweight, *Curio*	250	275	300
Model E Vest Pocket, .25 ACP, Clip Fed, *Curio*	100	150	200
Model F, .22 L.R.R.F., Clip Fed, *Curio*	75	125	175
Model F R S, .22 L.R.R.F., Clip Fed, Target Pistol, Adjustable Sights, *Curio*	100	175	200
Model F T B, .22 L.R.R.F., Clip Fed, Target Pistol, *Curio*	75	150	200
Model F-Olympic, .22 Short R.F., Clip Fed, Target Pistol, *Curio*	100	200	250
Model F-Sport, .22 L.R.R.F., Clip Fed, 6" Barrel, *Curio*	75	150	200
Model FR, .22 L.R.R.F., Clip Fed, *Curio*	75	125	175
Model H, 7.65mm, Clip Fed, 7 Shot, *Curio*	75	125	175
Model HF, .22 L.R.R.F., Clip Fed, *Curio*	75	150	200
Model HK Lancer, .22 L.R.R.F., Clip Fed, Lightweight, *Curio*	75	150	175
Model HN, .380 ACP, Clip Fed, *Curio*	75	150	175
Model I, 7.65mm, Clip Fed, 9 Shot, *Curio*	100	200	225

Star Model 1 .32

	Fair	V. Good	Excellent
Model IN, .380 ACP, Clip Fed, *Curio*	100	225	275
Model M, .38 ACP, Clip Fed, *Curio*	$75	$125	$175
Model Military, 9mm, Clip Fed, *Modern*	100	225	275
Model MMS, 7.63 Mauser, Clip Fed, Stock Lug, *Curio*	325	750	850
Model NZ, 6.35mm, Clip Fed, *Curio*	175	375	450
Model P, .45 ACP, Clip Fed, *Modern*	125	250	300
Model PD, .45 ACP, Clip Fed, *Modern*	125	250	300
Model S, .380 ACP, Clip Fed, *Modern*	100	175	200
Model S I, *Modern*	100	200	225
Model SM, .380 ACP, Clip Fed, *Modern*	100	200	250
Model Starfire, .380 ACP, Clip Fed, Lightweight, *Modern*	150	325	375
Model Starlet, 6.35mm, Clip Fed, Lightweight, *Modern*	100	225	250
Model Super A, .38 ACP, Clip Fed, *Modern*	100	225	250
Model Super B, 9mm Luger, Clip Fed, *Modern*	100	200	225
Model Super P, .45 ACP, Clip Fed, *Modern*	125	275	325
Model 28, 9mm Luger, Clip Fed, *Modern*	150	300	350

RIFLE, SINGLESHOT

	Fair	V. Good	Excellent
Rolling Block, Various Calibers, Carbine, *Modern*	75	125	175

STAR GAUGE

Spain, Imported by Interarms.

SHOTGUN, DOUBLE BARREL, SIDE-BY-SIDE

	Fair	V. Good	Excellent
12 and 20 Gauges, Checkered Stock, Adjustable Choke, Double Trigger, *Modern*	100	175	225

STARR ARMS CO.

Yonkers and Binghamton, N.Y. 1860–1868.

HANDGUN, PERCUSSION

	Fair	V. Good	Excellent
1858 Army, .44 Revolver, 6 Shot, 6" Barrel, Double Action, *Antique*	400	1000	1200
1858 Navy, .36 Revolver, 6 Shot, 6" Barrel, Double Action, *Antique*	600	1200	1500
1862 Army, .44 Revolver, 6 Shot, 6" Barrel, Double Action, *Antique*	400	1000	1200

RIFLE, PERCUSSION

	Fair	V. Good	Excellent
Carbine, .54, Underlever, *Antique*	350	1200	1500

RIFLE, SINGLESHOT

	Fair	V. Good	Excellent
Carbine, .52 R.F., Underlever, *Antique*	$450	$1200	$1500

STATE ARMS CO.

Made by Crescent for J.H. Lau & Co., c. 1900. See also Crescent Fire Arms Co., Shotgun, Double Barrel, Side-by-Side; Shotgun, Singleshot.

STEIGLEDER, ERNST

Suhl & Berlin, Germany 1921–1935.

RIFLE, DOUBLE BARREL, SIDE-BY-SIDE

	Fair	V. Good	Excellent
Various Calibers, Box Lock, Engraved, Checkered Stock, Color Case Hardened Frame, *Modern*	900	2250	2750

STENDA

Stenda Werke Waffenfabrik, Suhl, Germany, c. 1920.

HANDGUN, SEMI-AUTOMATIC

	Fair	V. Good	Excellent
7.65mm, Blue, Clip Fed, *Curio*	100	175	225

STERLING ARMS CO.

Gasport and Lockport, N.Y.

HANDGUN, SEMI-AUTOMATIC

	Fair	V. Good	Excellent
#283 Target 300, .22 L.R.R.F., Hammer, Adjustable Sights, Various Barrel Lengths, *Modern*	75	125	150
#284 Target 300, .22 L.R.R.F., Hammer, Adjustable Sights, Tapered Barrel, *Modern*	75	125	150
#285 Huskey, .22 L.R.R.F., Hammer, Heavy Barrel, *Modern*	50	100	125
#286 Trapper, .22 L.R.R.F., Hammer, Tapered Barrel, *Modern*	50	100	125
Model 300, .25 ACP, Blue, *Modern*	50	75	100
Model 300N, .25 ACP, Nickel Plated, *Modern*	50	75	100
Model 300S, .25 ACP, Stainless Steel, *Modern*	50	75	100
Model 302, .22 L.R.R.F., Blue, *Modern*	50	75	100
Model 302N, .22 L.R.R.F., Nickel Plated, *Modern*	50	75	100
Model 302S, .22 L.R.R.F., Stainless Steel, *Modern*	50	75	100
Model 400, .380 ACP, Blue, Clip Fed, *Modern*	100	200	225
Model 400N, .380 ACP, Nickel Plated, Clip Fed, *Modern*	100	225	250
Model 400S, .380 ACP, Stainless Steel, Clip Fed, *Modern*	125	250	275
Model 402, .22 L.R.R.F., Blue, Clip Fed, *Modern*	$75	$100	$125
Model 402, .22 L.R.R.F., Nickel Plated, Clip Fed, *Modern*	75	100	125
Model 402 MkII, .32 ACP, Blue, Clip Fed, *Modern*	75	125	150
Model 402 MkIIS, .32 ACP, Stainless Steel, Clip Fed, *Modern*	75	150	175
Model 450, .45 ACP, Clip Fed, Double Action, Adjustable Sights, Blue, *Modern*	125	275	300
Model PPL, .380 ACP, Short Barrel, Clip Fed, *Modern*	125	250	275

Sterling PPL

RIFLE, SINGLESHOT

	Fair	V. Good	Excellent
Backpacker, .22 L.R.R.F., Takedown, *Modern*	25	50	75

STERLING ARMS CORP.

Made by Crescent for H. & D. Folsom, c. 1900. See Crescent Fire Arms Co., Shotgun, Double Barrel, Side-by-Side; Shotgun, Singleshot.

STERLING REVOLVERS

c. 1880.

HANDGUN, REVOLVER

	Fair	V. Good	Excellent
.22 Short R.F., 7 Shot, Spur Trigger, Solid Frame, Single Action, *Antique*	75	150	175
.32 Short R.F., 5 Shot, Spur Trigger, Solid Frame, Single Action, *Antique*	75	150	175

STEVENS, J. ARMS & TOOL CO.

Chicopee Falls, Mass. 1864–1886. Became J. Stevens Arms & Tool Co. in 1886, absorbed Page-Lewis Arms Co., Davis-Warner Arms Co., and Crescent Firearms Co. in 1926. Became a subsidiary of Savage in 1920. Also see the Commemorative Section. Stevens received highly complimentary publicity from the use of its large frame target pistols by such famous shooters as Buffalo

Fair V. Good Excellent

Bill Cody and Annie Oakley. Following trade names marked by Stevens on various firearms: REVOLVERS, Acme Arms; SINGLE SHOT PISTOLS, Gem; DOUBLE BARREL SHOTGUNS, Aristocrat, Central, Continental, Eastern, Essex, Hercules, King Nitro, Knickerbocker, Massachusetts Arms, Monitor, Newport, Olympic, Oxford Arms, Paragon, Ranger, Riverside Arms Co., Scout, Triumph, Wittes Hardware Co., George Worthington; SINGLE BARREL SHOTGUNS, Central, Climas, Continental, Cruso, Delphian, Diamond, Eastern, Gibralter, Goose Gun, Hercules, Hermitage, Little Pet, Massachusetts Arms, Monitor, Nitro Proof, Northwesterner, Premier; SLIDE-ACTION RIFLES, Premier, Premier trail blazer, Ranger; and PUMP-ACTION SHOTGUN, Riot.

HANDGUN, SINGLESHOT

	Fair	V. Good	Excellent
1888 #1, Various Calibers, Tip-Up, Octagon Barrel, Open Rear Sight, *Antique*	$75	$150	$175
1888 #2 "Gallery," .22 L.R.R.F., Tip-Up, Octagon Barrel, Open Rear Sight, *Antique*	75	150	175
1888 #3 "Combined Sight," Various Calibers, Tip-Up, Octagon Barrel, *Antique*	75	150	175
1888 #4 "Combined Sight," .22 L.R.R.F., Tip-Up, Octagon Barrel, *Antique*	75	150	175
1888 #5 "Expert," Various Calibers, Tip-Up, Half Octagon Barrel, *Antique*	75	150	175
1894 "New Ideal," Various Calibers, Level Action, Falling Block, Vernier Sights, *Antique*	125	275	325
Model 10, .22 L.R.R.F., Tip-Up, Target, Various Barrel Lengths, *Modern*	75	150	250
Model 23 "Sure-Shot," .22 L.R.R.F., Side-Swing Barrel, Hammer, *Antique*	75	100	125
Model 34 "Hunters Pet," Various Rimfires, Tip-Up, Half-Octagon Barrel, with Shoulder Stock, Vernier Sights, *Curio*	200	450	500
Model 34 "Hunters Pet," Various Rimfires, Tip-Up, Octagon Barrel, with Shoulder Stock, *Curio*	200	400	450
Model 35 Target, .22 L.R.R.F., Tip-Up, Target, Ivory Grips, Various Barrel Lengths, *Modern*	150	400	500
Model 35 Target, .22 L.R.R.F., Tip-Up, Target, Various Barrel Lengths, *Modern*	125	275	350
Model 37 "Gould," Various Calibers, Tip-Up, *Modern*	200	400	500
Model 38 "Conlin," .22 L.R.R.F., Tip-Up, *Modern*	250	500	600
Model 40 New Model Pocket Rifle, Various Calibers, Tip-Up, with Shoulder Stock, *Curio*	200	400	450
Model 41, .22 L.R.R.F., Tip-Up, Pocket Pistol, *Modern*	100	275	300

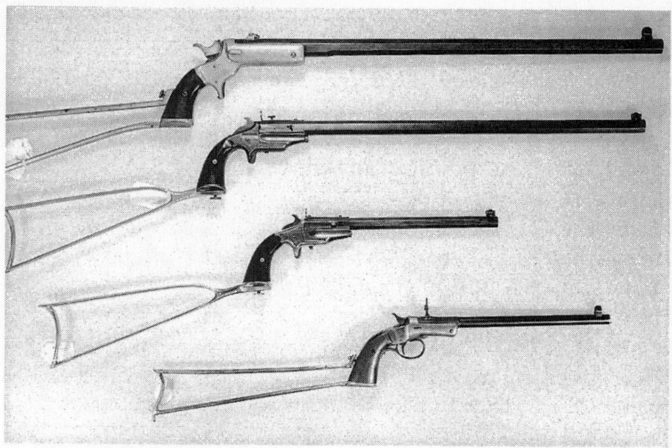

Variations of Stevens Pocket rifles, with attachable shoulder stocks. At top, The Hunter's Pet, so-called Buggy Model in .32 rimfire caliber, another in .22 rimfire (10" barrel), and bottom, *The Pocket rifle in .32 rimfire. Note differences in frame sizes, trigger types, sights, and barrels.*

	Fair	V. Good	Excellent
Model 42 Reliable Pocket Rifle, .22 L.R.R.F., Tip-Up, with Shoulder Stock, *Curio*	$150	$400	$500
Model 43 "Diamond," .22 L.R.R.F., Tip-Up, Spur Trigger, 6" Barrel, Octagon Barrel, *Modern*	100	175	200
Model 43 "Diamond," .22 L.R.R.F., Tip-Up, Spur Trigger, 10" Barrel, Octagon Barrel, *Modern*	100	200	225
Model 43 "Diamond," .22 L.R.R.F., Tip-Up, Spur Trigger, 6" Barrel, Globe Sights, *Modern*	100	200	225
Model 43 "Diamond," .22 L.R.R.F., Tip-Up, Spur Trigger, 10" Barrel, Globe Sights, *Modern*	100	225	275

RIFLE, BOLT ACTION

	Fair	V. Good	Excellent
Model 053 Buckhorn, Various Rimfires, Singleshot, Peep Sights, *Modern*	25	50	75
Model 056 Buckhorn, .22 L.R.R.F., 5 Shot Clip, Peep Sights, *Modern*	50	75	100
Model 066 Buckhorn, .22 L.R.R.F., Tube Feed, Peep Sights, *Modern*	50	75	100
Model 083, .22 L.R.R.F., Singleshot, Peep Sights, Takedown, *Modern*	25	50	75
Model 084, .22 L.R.R.F., 5 Shot Clip, Peep Sights, Takedown, *Modern*	25	50	75
Model 086, .22 L.R.R.F., Tube Feed, Takedown, Peep Sights, *Modern*	50	75	100
Model 15, .22 L.R.R.F., Singleshot, (Springfield), *Modern*	25	50	75
Model 15Y, .22 L.R.R.F., Singleshot, *Modern*	25	50	75
Model 322, .22 Hornet, Clip Fed, Carbine, Open Rear Sight, *Modern*	50	125	250

	Fair	V. Good	Excellent
Model 322-S, .22 Hornet, Clip Fed, Carbine, Peep Sights, *Modern*	$50	$125	$250
Model 325, .30-30 Win., Clip Fed, Carbine, Open Rear Sight, *Modern*	50	125	200
Model 325-S, .30-30 Win., Clip Fed, Carbine, Peep Sights, *Modern*	50	125	200
Model 416, .22 L.R.R.F., 5 Shot Clip, Peep Sights, Target Stock, *Modern*	100	200	225
Model 419, .22 L.R.R.F., Singleshot, Peep Sights, *Modern*	50	75	100
Model 48, .22 L.R.R.F., Singleshot, Takedown, *Modern*	25	50	100
Model 49, .22 L.R.R.F., Singleshot, Takedown, *Modern*	25	50	100
Model 50, .22 L.R.R.F., Singleshot, Takedown, *Modern*	25	50	100
Model 51, .22 L.R.R.F., Singleshot, Takedown, *Modern*	25	50	100
Model 52, .22 L.R.R.F., Singleshot, Takedown, *Modern*	25	50	100
Model 53, .22 L.R.R.F., Singleshot, Takedown, *Modern*	25	50	100
Model 56 Buckhorn, .22 L.R.R.F., 5 Shot Clip, Open Rear Sight, *Modern*	25	50	75
Model 65 "Little Krag," .22 L.R.R.F., Singleshot, Takedown, *Modern*	75	150	175
Model 66 Buckhorn, .22 L.R.R.F., Tube Feed, Open Rear Sight, *Modern*	25	50	75
Model 82, .22 L.R.R.F., Singleshot, Peep Sights, (Springfield), *Modern*	25	50	75
Model 83, .22 L.R.R.F., Singleshot, Open Rear Sight, Takedown, *Modern*	15	25	50
Model 84, .22 L.R.R.F., 5 Shot Clip, Open Rear Sight, Takedown, *Modern*	25	50	75
Model 86, .22 L.R.R.F., Tube Feed, Takedown, Open Rear Sight, *Modern*	25	50	75

RIFLE, LEVER ACTION

	Fair	V. Good	Excellent
Model 425, Various Calibers, Hammer, *Curio*	200	400	500
Model 430, Various Calibers, Hammer, Checkered Stock, *Curio*	300	600	700
Model 435, Various Calibers, Hammer, Light Engraving, Fancy Checkering, *Curio*	900	2000	2500
Model 440, Various Calibers, Hammer, Fancy Checkering, Fancy Engraving, Fancy Wood, *Curio*	1900	4000	5000

COMBINATION WEAPON, OVER-UNDER

	Fair	V. Good	Excellent
Model 22-410, .22-.410 Ga., Hammer, Plastic Stock, *Modern*	50	75	100
Model 22-410, .22-.410 Ga., Hammer, Wood Stock, *Modern*	50	100	125

RIFLE, SEMI-AUTOMATIC

	Fair	V. Good	Excellent
Model 057 Buckhorn, .22 L.R.R.F., 5 Shot Clip, Open Rear Sight, *Modern*	$50	$75	$100
Model 057 Buckhorn, .22 L.R.R.F., 5 Shot Clip, Peep Sights, *Modern*	50	75	100
Model 076 Buckhorn, .22 L.R.R.F., Peep Sights, Tube Feed, *Modern*	50	75	100
Model 085 Springfield, .22 L.R.R.F., 5 Shot Clip, Peep Sights, *Modern*	50	75	100
Model 76 Buckhorn, .22 L.R.R.F., Open Rear Sight, Tube Feed, *Modern*	50	75	100
Model 85 Springfield, .22 L.R.R.F., 5 Shot Clip, Open Rear Sight, *Modern*	50	75	100
Model 87, .22 L.R.R.F., Tube Feed, Open Rear Sight, *Modern*	50	75	100
Model 87-S, .22 L.R.R.F., Peep Sights, Tube Feed, *Modern*	50	75	100
Model 87K Scout, .22 L.R.R.F., Tube Feed, Open Rear Sight, Carbine, *Modern*	50	75	100

RIFLE, SINGLESHOT

	Fair	V. Good	Excellent
1888 #10 "Range," Various Calibers, Tip-Up, Half-Octagon Barrel, Fancy Wood, Vernier Sights, *Antique*	200	400	500
1888 #12 "Ladies," Various Calibers, Tip-Up, Half-Octagon Barrel, Open Rear Sight, Fancy Wood, *Antique*	300	600	700
1888 #13 "Ladies," Various Calibers, Tip-Up, Half-Octagon Barrel, Vernier Sights, *Antique*	200	400	500
1888 #14 "Ladies," Various Calibers, Tip-Up, Half-Octagon Barrel, Vernier Sights, Fancy Wood, *Antique*	300	600	700
1888 #15 "Crack Shot," Various Calibers, Tip-Up, Half-Octagon Barrel, Peep Sights, *Antique*	100	225	250
1888 #16 "Crack Shot," Various Calibers, Tip-Up, Half-Octagon Barrel, Peep Sights, Fancy Wood, *Antique*	150	300	350
1888 #22 "Ladies," Various Calibers, Tip-Up, Half-Octagon Barrel, Open Rear Sight, *Antique*	100	200	225
1888 #6 "Expert," Various Calibers, Tip-Up, Half-Octagon Barrel, Fancy Wood, *Antique*	100	200	225
1888 #7 "Premier," Various Calibers, Tip-Up, Half-Octagon Barrel, Globe Sights, *Antique*	100	175	225
1888 #8 "Premier," Various Calibers, Tip-Up, Half-Octagon Barrel, Fancy Wood, Globe Sights, *Antique*	100	225	275
1888 #9 "Range," Various Calibers, Tip-Up, Half-Octagon Barrel, Vernier Sights, *Antique*	100	175	225

	Fair	V. Good	Excellent
Model 101 Featherweight, .44-40 WCF, Lever Action, Tip-Up, Smoothbore, Takedown, Half-Octagon Barrel, *Modern*	$100	$150	$175
Model 101, with Extra 22 Barrel, .44-40 WCF, Lever Action, Tip- Up, Smoothbore, Takedown, Half-Octagon Barrel, *Modern*	100	225	250
Model 11 "Ladies," Various Rimfires, Tip-Up, Open Rear Sight, *Modern*	200	400	500
Model 12 "Marksman," Various Rimfires, Hammer, Lever Action, Tip-Up, *Modern*	75	150	175
Model 13 "Ladies," Various Rimfires, Tip-Up, Vernier Sights, *Modern*	200	400	500
Model 14 "Little Scout," .22 L.R.R.F., Hammer, Rolling Block, *Curio*	100	125	150
Model 14 1/2 "Little Scout," .22 L.R.R.F., Hammer, Rolling Block, *Modern*	75	125	150
Model 15 "Maynard Jr.," .22 L.R.R.F., Lever Action, Tip-Up, *Modern*	75	125	150
Model 15 1/2 "Maynard Jr.," .22 L.R.R.F., Lever Action, Tip-Up, *Modern*	75	125	150
Model 17, Various Rimfires, Lever Action, Takedown, Favorite, Open Rear Sight, *Modern*	75	150	175
Model 18, Various Rimfires, Lever Action, Takedown, Favorite, Vernier Sights, *Modern*	100	175	200
Model 19, Various Rimfires, Lever Action, Takedown, Favorite, Lyman Sights, *Modern*	75	150	175
Model 2, Various Rimfires, Tip-Up, Open Rear Sight, *Modern*	125	250	275
Model 20, Various Rimfires, Lever Action, Takedown, Favorite, Smoothbore, *Curio*	75	150	175
Model 26, Various Rimfires, Lever Action, Takedown, Open Rear Sight, *Curio*	75	150	175
Model 26 1/2, Various Rimfires, Lever Action, Takedown, Smoothbore, *Curio*	75	150	175
Model 27, Various Rimfires, Lever Action, Takedown, Favorite, Octagon Barrel, Open Rear Sight, *Modern*	75	175	200
Model 28, Various Rimfires, Lever Action, Takedown, Favorite, Octagon Barrel, Vernier Sights, *Modern*	100	175	200
Model 29, Various Rimfires, Lever Action, Takedown, Favorite, Octagon Barrel, Lyman Sights, *Modern*	100	175	200
Model 404, .22 L.R.R.F., Hammer, Falling Block, Target Sights, Full-Stocked, *Modern*	225	475	525
Model 414 "Armory," .22 L.R.R.F., Lever Action, Lyman Sights, *Modern*	150	325	450

	Fair	V. Good	Excellent
Model 417-0, Various Calibers, Lever Action, Walnut Hill, *Modern*	$200	$400	$450
Model 417-1, Various Calibers, Lever Action, Lyman Sights, Walnut Hill, *Modern*	200	400	550
Model 417-2, Various Calibers, Lever Action, Vernier Sights, Walnut Hill, *Modern*	200	450	550
Model 417-3, Various Calibers, Lever Action, No Sights, Walnut Hill, *Modern*	200	425	550
Model 417 1/2, Various Calibers, Lever Action, Walnut Hill, *Modern*	200	400	530
Model 418, .22 L.R.R.F., Lever Action, Takedown, Walnut Hill, *Modern*	200	400	550
Model 418 1/2, Various Rimfires, Lever Action, Takedown, Walnut Hill, *Modern*	200	450	550
Model 44 "Ideal," Various Calibers, Lever Action, Rolling Block, *Modern*	200	400	500
Model 44 1/2 "Ideal," Various Calibers, Lever Action, Falling Block, *Modern*	400	800	900
Model 49 "Ideal," Various Calibers, Walnut Hill, Lever Action, Falling Block, Engraved, Fancy Checkering, *Modern*	500	1100	1350
Model 5, Various Rimfires, Tip-Up, Vernier Sights, *Modern*	150	250	300
Model 51 "Pope," Various Calibers, Schutzen Rifle, Lever Action, Falling Block, Engraved, Fancy Checkering, *Modern*	1900	3500	4000

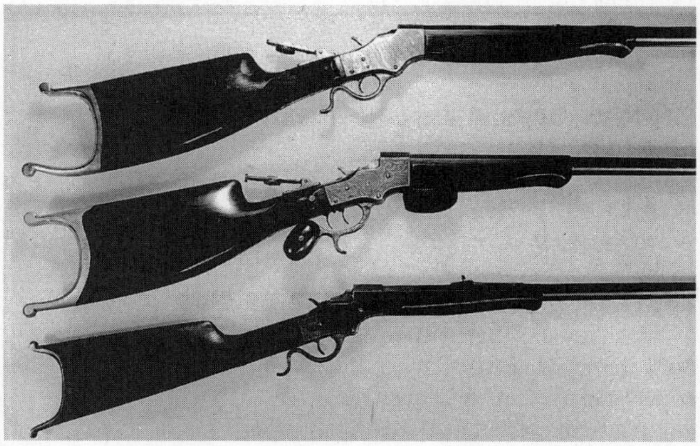

Three variations of Stevens singleshot rifles; each with Swiss butts: from the top, *deluxe off-hand model; benchrest Model 51 with scarce etched frame; and Ideal Sporting Model with No. 44 action, in .25/20 caliber.*

	Fair	V. Good	Excellent
Model 52 "Pope Jr.," Various Calibers, Schutzen Rifle, Lever Action, Falling Block, Engraved, Fancy Checkering, *Modern*	1900	3500	4000

	Fair	V. Good	Excellent
Model 54 "Pope," Various Calibers, Schutzen Rifle, Lever Action, Falling Block, Fancy Engraving, Fancy Checkering, *Modern*	$1900	$3500	$4000
Model 56 "Pope Ladies," Various Calibers, Schutzen Rifle, Lever Action, Falling Block, Fancy Checkering, *Modern*	900	1800	2000
Model 7 "Swiss Butt," Various Rimfires, Tip-Up, Vernier Sights, *Modern*	125	350	400

RIFLE, SLIDE ACTION

	Fair	V. Good	Excellent
Model 70, .22 L.R.R.F., Hammer, Solid Frame, *Modern*	100	175	200
Model 71, .22 L.R.R.F., Hammer, Solid Frame, *Modern*	100	200	225
Model 75, .22 L.R.R.F., Tube Feed, Hammerless, *Modern*	100	200	225
Model 80, Various Rimfires, Tube Feed, Takedown, *Modern*	75	150	175

SHOTGUN, BOLT ACTION

	Fair	V. Good	Excellent
Model 237, 20 Ga., Takedown, Singleshot, (Springfield), *Modern*	15	25	50
Model 258, 20 Ga., Takedown, Clip Fed, *Modern*	25	50	75
Model 37, .410 Ga., Takedown, Singleshot, (Springfield), *Modern*	25	50	75
Model 38, .410 Ga., Takedown, Clip Fed, (Springfield), *Modern*	25	50	75
Model 39, .410 Ga., Takedown, Tube Feed, (Springfield), *Modern*	25	50	75
Model 58, .410 Ga., Takedown, Clip Fed, *Modern*	25	50	75
Model 59, .410 Ga., Takedown, Tube Feed, *Modern*	25	50	75

SHOTGUN, DOUBLE BARREL, OVER-UNDER

	Fair	V. Good	Excellent
Model 240, .410 Ga., Hammer, Plastic Stock, *Modern*	100	175	200
Model 240, .410 Ga., Hammer, Wood Stock, *Modern*	100	200	225

SHOTGUN, DOUBLE BARREL, SIDE-BY-SIDE

	Fair	V. Good	Excellent
M 315, Various Gauges, Hammerless, Steel Barrel, *Modern*	100	175	200
Model 215, 12 and 16 Gauges, Outside Hammers, Steel Barrel, *Modern*	100	175	200
Model 235, Various Gauges, Outside Hammers, Checkered Stock, Steel Barrel, *Modern*	75	150	175
Model 250, Various Gauges, Outside Hammers, Checkered Stock, Steel Barrel, *Modern*	75	150	175
Model 255, 12 and 16 Gauges, Outside Hammers, Checkered Stock, Steel Barrel, *Modern*	75	150	175
Model 260 "Twist," Various Gauges, Outside Hammers, Checkered Stock, Damascus Barrel, *Modern*	$75	$150	$175
Model 265 "Krupp," 12 and 16 Gauges, Outside Hammers, Checkered Stock, Steel Barrel, *Modern*	100	175	200
Model 270 "Nitro," Various Gauges, Outside Hammers, Checkered Stock, Damascus Barrel, *Modern*	100	175	200
Model 311 ST, Various Gauges, Hammerless, Steel Barrel, Single Trigger, *Modern*	100	200	225
Model 311, Various Gauges, Hammerless, Steel Barrel, *Modern*	100	200	225
Model 311-R Guard Gun, 12 or 20 Gauge, Double Trigger, 18½" Bore, Solid Rib, *Modern*	125	250	300
Model 3151, Various Gauges, Hammerless, Recoil Pad, Front and Rear Bead Sights, *Modern*	100	200	225
Model 330, Various Gauges, Hammerless, Checkered Stock, *Modern*	100	175	200
Model 335, 12 and 16 Gauges, Hammerless, Steel Barrel, Checkered Stock, Double Trigger, *Modern*	100	175	200
Model 345, 20 Ga., Hammerless, Checkered Stock, Steel Barrel, Double Trigger, *Modern*	100	175	200
Model 355, 12 and 16 Gauges, Hammerless, Steel Barrel, Checkered Stock, Double Trigger, *Modern*	100	175	200
Model 365 "Krupp," 12 and 16 Gauges, Hammerless, Checkered Stock, Steel Barrel, Double Trigger, *Modern*	100	175	200
Model 375 "Krupp," 12 and 16 Gauges, Hammerless, Light Engraving, Fancy Checkering, Double Trigger, Steel Barrel, *Modern*	100	200	225
Model 385 "Krupp," 12 and 16 Gauges, Hammerless, Fancy Engraving, Fancy Checkering, Double Trigger, Steel Barrel, *Modern*	100	225	250
Model 515, Various Gauges, Hammerless, *Modern*	75	150	175
Model 5151, Various Gauges, Hammerless, Steel Barrel, *Modern*	100	175	200
Model 530 ST, Various Gauges, Hammerless, Steel Barrel, Single Trigger, *Modern*	100	200	225
Model 530, Various Gauges, Hammerless, Steel Barrel, Double Trigger, *Modern*	100	175	200

	Fair	V. Good	Excellent
Model 530M, Various Gauges, Hammerless, Plastic Stock, *Modern*	$75	$150	$175

SHOTGUN, PUMP

	Fair	V. Good	Excellent
Model 520, 12 Ga., Takedown, *Modern*	75	150	175
Model 620, Various Gauges, Takedown, *Modern*	75	150	175

SHOTGUN, SEMI-AUTOMATIC

	Fair	V. Good	Excellent
Model 124, 12 Ga., Plastic Stock, *Modern*	75	125	150

SHOTGUN, SINGLESHOT

	Fair	V. Good	Excellent
Various Gauges, Hammer, Automatic Ejector, *Modern*	25	50	75
Various Gauges, Hammer, Automatic Ejector, Raised Matted Rib, *Modern*	50	75	100
1888 "New Style," Various Gauges, Tip-Up, Hammer, Damascus Barrel, *Antique*	100	200	275
Model 100, Various Gauges, Selective Ejector, Hammer, *Modern*	25	50	75
Model 102, .410 Ga., Hammer, Featherweight, *Modern*	25	50	75
Model 102, 24, 28, and 32 Gauges, Hammer, Featherweight, *Modern*	25	50	75
Model 104, .410 Ga., Hammer, Featherweight, Automatic Ejector, *Modern*	25	50	75
Model 104, 24, 28, and 32 Gauges, Hammer, Automatic Ejector, Featherweight, *Modern*	25	50	150
Model 105, 20 Ga., Hammer, *Modern*	25	50	75
Model 105, 28 Ga., Hammer, *Modern*	25	50	100
Model 106, .32 Ga., Hammer, *Modern*	25	50	150
Model 106, .410 Ga. 2½", Hammer, *Modern*	25	50	75
Model 106, .44-40 WCF., Hammer, Smoothbore, *Modern*	25	50	100
Model 107, Various Gauges, Hammer, Automatic Ejector, *Modern*	25	50	75
Model 108, .32 Ga., Hammer, Automatic Ejector, *Modern*	25	50	150
Model 108, .410 Ga. 2½", Hammer, Automatic Ejector, *Modern*	25	50	75
Model 108, .44-40 WCF., Hammer, Automatic Ejector, Smoothbore, *Modern*	25	50	100
Model 110, Various Gauges, Selective Ejector, Checkered Stock, Hammer, *Modern*	25	50	100
Model 120, Various Gauges, Selective Ejector, Fancy Checkering, Hammer, *Modern*	25	50	150
Model 125 Ladies, .20 Ga., Automatic Ejector, Hammer, *Modern*	$25	$50	$75
Model 125 Ladies, .28 Ga., Automatic Ejector, Hammer, *Modern*	25	50	75
Model 140, Various Gauges, Selective Ejector, Hammerless, Checkered Stock, *Modern*	25	50	100
Model 160, Various Gauges, Hammer, *Modern*	25	50	75
Model 165, Various Gauges, Automatic Ejector, Hammer, *Modern*	25	50	75
Model 170, Various Gauges, Automatic Ejector, Hammer, Checkered Stock, *Modern*	25	50	75
Model 180, Various Gauges, Hammerless, Automatic Ejector, Checkered Stock, Round Barrel, *Modern*	50	75	100
Model 182, 12 Ga., Hammerless, Automatic Ejector, Light Engraving, Checkered Stock, Trap Grade, *Modern*	75	125	250
Model 185, 12 Ga., Hammerless, Automatic Ejector, Checkered Stock, Half-Octagon Barrel, *Modern*	75	125	150
Model 185, For 16 or 20 Gauge, Add 20%			
Model 185, For Damascus Barrel, Deduct 25%			
Model 190, 12 Ga., Hammerless, Automatic Ejector, Fancy Checkering, Light Engraving, Half-Octagon Barrel, *Modern*	100	175	200
Model 190, For 16 or 20 Gauge, Add 20%			
Model 190, For Damascus Barrel, Deduct 25%			
Model 195, 12 Ga., Hammerless, Automatic Ejector, Fancy Checkering, Fancy Engraving, Half-Octagon Barrel, *Modern*	150	300	325
Model 195, For 16 or 20 Gauge, Add 20%			
Model 195, For Damascus Barrel, Deduct 25%			
Model 89 Dreadnaught, Various Gauges, Hammer, *Modern*	25	50	75
Model 90, Various Gauges, Takedown, Automatic Ejector Plain, Hammer, *Modern*	25	50	75
Model 93, 12 and 16 Gauges, Hammer, *Modern*	25	50	75
Model 94, Various Gauges, Takedown, Automatic Ejector Plain, Hammer, *Modern*	25	50	75
Model 944, .410 Ga., Hammer, Automatic Ejector, (Springfield), *Modern*	25	50	75
Model 94A, Various Gauges, Hammer, Automatic Ejector, *Modern*	25	50	75

	Fair	V. Good	Excellent
Model 94C, Various Gauges, Hammer, Automatic Ejector, Modern, *Modern*	$25	$50	$75
Model 95, 12 and 16 Gauges, *Modern*	25	50	75
Model 958, .410 Ga., Automatic Ejector, Hammer, *Modern*	25	50	75
Model 958, 38 Ga., Automatic Ejector, Hammer, *Modern*	25	50	150
Model 97, 12 and 16 Gauges, Hammer, Automatic Ejector, *Modern*	15	25	50
Model 970, 12 Gauge, Hammer, Automatic Ejector, Checkered Stock, Half-Octagon Barrel, *Modern*	25	50	75

SHOTGUN, SLIDE ACTION

	Fair	V. Good	Excellent
Model 520, 12 Ga., Takedown, *Modern*	75	150	175
Model 522, 12 Ga., Trap Grade, Takedown, Raised Matted Rib, *Modern*	75	150	175
Model 620, Various Gauges, Takedown, *Modern*	100	250	275
Model 621, Various Gauges, Hammerless, Checkered Stock, Raised Matted Rib, Takedown, *Modern*	75	150	175
Model 67, Various Gauges, Hammerless, Solid Frame, (Springfield), *Modern*	75	150	175
Model 67-VR, Various Gauges, Hammerless, Solid Frame, Vent Rib, (Springfield), *Modern*	100	175	200
Model 77, 12 and 16 Gauges, Hammerless, Solid Frame, *Modern*	75	150	175
Model 77, For Vent Rib, Add $10.00-$15.00			
Model 77, Various Gauges, Hammerless, Solid Frame, *Modern*	75	150	175
Mode 77 S C, 12 and 16 Gauges, Hammerless, Solid Frame, Recoil Pad, Adjustable Choke, *Modern*	75	150	175
Model 77-AC, Various Gauges, Hammerless, Solid Frame, Adjustable Choke, *Modern*	75	125	150
Model 77-M, 12 Ga., Hammerless, Solid Frame, Adjustable Choke, *Modern*	75	125	150
Model 820, 12 Ga., Hammerless, Solid Frame, *Modern*	75	125	150

STEVENS, JAMES

SHOTGUN, PERCUSSION

	Fair	V. Good	Excellent
14 Ga., Double Barrel, Side by Side, Engraved, Light Ornamentation, *Antique*	200	450	550

STEYR

Since 1863 in Steyr, Austria as Werndl Co.; in 1869 became Oesterreichische Waffenfabrik Gesellschaft; after WWI became Steyr Werke; in 1934 became Steyr-Daimler-Puch. Also see German Military, Austrian Military, Mannlicher-Schoenauer.

HANDGUN, SEMI-AUTOMATIC

	Fair	V. Good	Excellent
Model 1901 Mannlicher, 7.63mm Mannlicher, Commercial, *Curio*	$350	$700	$750
Model 1905 Mannlicher, 7.63mm Mannlicher, Military, *Curio*	175	375	425
Model 1908, 7.65mm, Clip Fed, Tip-Up, *Modern*	100	225	250
Model 1909, 6.35mm, Clip Fed, Tip-Up, *Modern*	100	225	275
Model 1909, 7.65mm, Clip Fed, Tip-Up, *Modern*	125	250	300
Model 1911, 9mm Steyr, Commercial, *Curio*	150	350	400
Model 1912, 9mm Luger, Nazi-Proofed, Military, *Curio*	200	400	450
Model 1912, 9mm Steyr, Military, *Curio*	100	200	225
Model 1912 Roumanian, 9mm Steyr, Military, *Curio*	125	250	275
Model GB, 9mm Luger, Clip Fed, Double Action, *Modern*	200	400	450
Model SP, .32 ACP, Clip Fed, Double Action, *Modern*	250	525	575
Solohurn, .32 ACP, Clip Fed, *Modern*	100	200	225

STOCK, FRANZ

Franz Stock Maschinen u. Werkbaufabrik, Berlin Germany 1920–1940.

HANDGUN, SEMI-AUTOMATIC

	Fair	V. Good	Excellent
6.35mm, Clip Fed, *Modern*	150	300	325
7.65mm, Clip Fed, *Modern*	125	275	300

Franz Stock .25

STOCKMAN, HANS

Dresden, Germany 1590–1621.

	Fair	V. Good	Excellent
HANDGUN, WHEELOCK			
Pair, Holster Pistol, Pear Pommel, Horn Inlays, Light Ornamentation, *Antique*	$5000	$12500	$15000

STOEGER, A.F.

Stoeger Arms Corp., New York City, now in South Hackensack, N.J. Also see Luger.

	Fair	V. Good	Excellent
COMBINATION WEAPON, DRILLING			
Model 259, 3 Calibers, Side Barrel, Box Lock, Double Triggers, Checkered Stock, *Modern*	900	2000	2500
Model 297, Various Calibers, 2 Rifle Barrels, Box Lock, Double Triggers, Engraved, Checkered Stock, *Modern*	900	2000	2500
Model 300, Vierling, 4 Barrels, Box Lock, Double Triggers, Checkered Stock, *Modern*	1800	3500	4000
COMBINATION WEAPON, OVER-UNDER			
Model 290, Various Calibers, Blitz System, Box Lock, Double Triggers, Engraved, Checkered Stock, *Modern*	800	1800	2000
SHOTGUN, DOUBLE BARREL, SIDE-BY-SIDE			
Victor Special, 12 Ga., Checkered Stock, Double Triggers, *Modern*	100	175	200
SHOTGUN, SINGLESHOT			
Model 27 Trap, 12 Ga., Engraved, Vent Rib, Checkered Stock, Recoil Pad, *Modern*	325	700	750

STOSEL

Retolaza Hermanos, Eibar, Spain.

	Fair	V. Good	Excellent
HANDGUN, SEMI-AUTOMATIC			
Model 1913, 6.35mm, Clip Fed, *Modern*	75	125	150

STUART, JOHAN

Edinburgh, Scotland 1701–1750.

	Fair	V. Good	Excellent
HANDGUN, SNAPHAUNCE			
All Steel Highland, Engraved, Scroll Butt, Ball Trigger, *Antique*	4000	8500	10000

STURM, RUGER & CO

Southport, Conn. 1946 to Date. Also see Commemorative section. The Samuel Colt of modern times and an all-American original, William B. Ruger, with his partner, Alexander McCormick Sturm, founded their company in 1949, as underdogs: They were told "it can't be done." From the $50,000 investment that launched their first pistol—the .22 Standard—the company rose to occupy a leadership role in the firearms field. Now the largest American firearms manufacturer, Sturm, Ruger & Co. has produced over 15 million pistols, revolvers, rifles, and shotguns through 1997. WIlliam B. Ruger began designing firearms at the age of 17, while growing up in Brooklyn, New York. As a youth he learned about firearms history and technology by scouring the New York Public Library and visiting shops the likes of Griffin & Howe. Ruger was fascinated not only by firearms, but by machine tools and how they could carve and shape steel. In his early 20s he unsuccessfully sought employment with various American gunmakers. But in 1939, at the request of the Ordnance Department of the U.S. Army, he worked as an engineer and designer at the Springfield Armory. During World War II Ruger designed a Light Machine Gun for the Auto-Ordnance corporation. Still another project was a sighting device for aircraft machine guns. It was at Auto-Ordnance Corporation that Ruger first learned about the advantages of investment castings, an ancient process often termed "lost wax" due to the material's role in creating the final cast part. At war's end Ruger had an advanced knowledge of design and manufacturing, and was perfectly prepared for a career in gunmaking. However, it was not until the 1949 partnership with Alexander Sturm that Ruger's experience and ideas would begin to come to fruition. With his friend Sturm supplying the start-up capital, Sturm, Ruger & Company began production with the .22 Standard, a uniquely designed self-loading pistol. Alex Sturm prepared the first advertisements, and the company's first brochure. A gifted artist and published author, Sturm also designed the company's distinctive "red eagle" logo. The .22 Standard was billed as "the first overall improvement in automatic pistol design since the Browning patent of 1905." The initial series, of which over 1,250,000 pistols were produced, was succeeded in 1982 by the Mark II Standard and target models, of which over 1,500,000 were completed by the end of 1996; production continues at an impressive pace. The .22 Standard began a continuing series of firearms products—pistols, revolvers, rifles and shotguns—which now number approximately 50 models and over 250 variations. Founder, Chairman of the Board, and Chief Executive Officer William B. Ruger continues to develop new designs. He celebrated his eighty-first birthday on June 16, 1997. Note: The assistance of John R. Hansen, Jr., Executive Director, Ruger Collectors Association, in the preparation of these values is greatly appreciated. For more information on membership in this group contact the RCA at P.O. Box 240, Green Farms, Connecticut 06436.

	Fair	V. Good	Excellent
HANDGUN, PERCUSSION			
Old Army, .44, Single Action, Blue, Adjustable Sights, Reproduction, *Antique*	$100	$250	$300
Old Army, .44, Single Action, Stainless, Adjustable Sights, Reproduction, *Antique*	175	250	300
HANDGUN, REVOLVER			
.22 L.R.R.F., Western Style, Single Action, Blue, Lightweight, Early Model, *Modern*	100	200	250
Bearcat, .22 L.R.R.F., Western Style, Single Action, Blue, Brass Gripframe, *Modern*	100	200	250

Ruger Old Army

	Fair	V. Good	Excellent
Bearcat, .22 L.R.R.F., Western Style, Single Action, Blue, Aluminum Gripframe, Early Model, *Modern*	$100	$200	$250
Bisley Single Six, *Modern*	150	250	300
Bisley Single Six, .22 L.R., *Modern*	100	175	200
Blackhawk, .30 Carbine, Western Style, Single Action, Blue, New Model, *Modern*	150	350	400
Blackhawk, .30 Carbine, Western Style, Single Action, Blue, *Modern*	150	350	400
Blackhawk, .357 Magnum, *Modern*	100	225	250
Blackhawk, .357 Magnum, Western Style, Single Action, Blue, New Model, *Modern*	100	200	250
Blackhawk, .357 Magnum, Western Style, Single Action, Blue, *Modern*	125	275	325
Blackhawk, .357 Magnum, Western Style, Single Action, Blue, Flat-Top Frame, Early Model, *Modern*	150	325	375
Blackhawk, .357 Magnum, Western Style, Single Action, Blue, 10" Barrel, *Modern*	150	300	350
Blackhawk, .357 Magnum, Western Style, Single Action, Blue, New Model, *Modern*	150	300	325
Blackhawk, .357 Magnum, Western Style, Single Action, Stainless Steel, New Model, *Modern*	150	325	375
Blackhawk, .357 Magnum/9mm Combo, Western Style, Single Action, Blue, New Model, *Modern*	150	275	325
Blackhawk, .357 Magnum/9mm Combo, Western Style, Single Action, Blue, *Modern*	150	275	325
Blackhawk, .41 Magnum, *Modern*	150	225	250
Blackhawk, .41 Magnum, Western Style, Single Action, Blue, New Model, *Modern*	150	250	300
Blackhawk, .41 Magnum, Western Style, Single Action, Blue, *Modern*	150	275	325
Blackhawk, .44 Magnum, *Modern*	150	250	300
Blackhawk, .45 Colt, *Modern*	150	225	250
Blackhawk, .45 Colt, Western Style, Single Action, Blue, *Modern*	150	325	375

	Fair	V. Good	Excellent
Blackhawk, .45 Colt, Western Style, Single Action, Blue, New Model, *Modern*	$150	$275	$325
Blackhawk, .45 Colt/.45 ACP Combo, Western Style, Single Action, New Model, Blue, *Modern*	150	300	350
Blackhawk, .45 Colt/.45 ACP Combo, Western Style, Single Action, Blue, *Modern*	150	300	350
BP-7 Old Army Cap and Ball Revolver, .44 Black Powder, Blue Walnut Grip, Reproduction, *Antique*	100	200	250
Brass GripFrame, Add $20.00-$30.00			
KBP-7 Old Army Cap and Ball Revolver, .44 Black Powder, Stainless, Walnut Grip, Reproduction, *Antique*	100	200	250
KRH-35 Redhawk Double Action Revolver, .357 Magnum, Stainless, 7½" Barrel, *Modern*	125	250	300
KRH-355 Redhawk Double Action Revolver, .357 Magnum, Stainless, 5½" Barrel, *Modern*	125	250	300
KRH-41 Redhawk Double Action Revolver, .41 Magnum, Stainless, 7½" Barrel, *Modern*	125	250	300
KRH-415 Redhawk Double Action Revolver, .41 Magnum, Stainless, 5½" Barrel, *Modern*	125	250	300
Redhawk, .44 Magnum, Double Action, Stainless, Interchangeable Sights, Swing-Out Cylinder, *Modern*	125	250	300

Ruger Redhawk

	Fair	V. Good	Excellent
Security-Six, .357 Magnum, Double Action, Swing-Out Cylinder, Stainless Steel, Adjustable Sights, *Modern*	100	200	250
Security-Six, .357 Magnum, Double Action, Swing-Out Cylinder, Blue, Adjustable Sights, *Modern*	100	175	200
Service-Six, .357 Magnum, Double Action, Swing-Out Cylinder, Blue, *Modern*	100	175	200

	Fair	V. Good	Excellent
Service-Six, .357 Magnum, Double Action, Swing-Out Cylinder, Stainless Steel, *Modern*	$100	$150	$200
Service-Six, .38 Spec., Double Action, Swing-Out Cylinder, Blue, *Modern*	100	175	200
Service-Six, .38 Spec., Double Action, Swing-Out Cylinder, Stainless Steel, *Modern*	100	175	200
Service-Six, 9mm Luger, Double Action, Swing-Out Cylinder, Blue, *Modern*	100	175	200
Service-Six, 9mm Luger, Double Action, Swing-Out Cylinder, Stainless Steel, *Modern*	100	175	200
Single-Six, .22 L.R.R.F., Western Style, Single Action, Blue, Engraved, Cased, *Modern*	800	1500	2000
Single-Six, .22 L.R.R.F., Western Style, Single Action, Blue, Flat Loading Gate, Early Model, *Modern*	150	300	400
Speed-Six, .357 Magnum, Double Action, Swing-Out Cylinder, Blue, *Modern*	100	175	200
Speed-Six, .357 Magnum, Double Action, Swing-Out Cylinder, Stainless Steel, *Modern*	100	175	200
Speed-Six, .38 Spec., Double Action, Swing-Out Cylinder, Blue, *Modern*	100	175	200
Speed-Six, .38 Spec., Double Action, Swing-Out Cylinder, Blue, Stainless Steel, *Modern*	100	225	300
Speed-Six, 9mm Luger, Double Action, Swing-Out Cylinder, Blue, Blue, *Modern*	100	175	200
Super Blackhawk, .44 Magnum, Western Style, Single Action, Blue, New Model, 10$\frac{1}{2}$" Barrel, *Modern*	125	275	350
Super Blackhawk, .44 Magnum, Western Style, Single Action, Blue, New Model, *Modern*	125	275	350
Super Blackhawk, .44 Magnum, Western Style, Single Action, Stainless, New Model, *Modern*	150	325	450
Super Blackhawk, .44 Magnum, Western Style, Single Action, Stainless, New Model, 10$\frac{1}{2}$" Bull Barrel, *Modern*	150	350	500
Super Blackhawk, .44 Magnum, Western Style, Single Action, Stainless, 10$\frac{1}{2}$" Barrel, New Model, *Modern*	150	350	500
Super Blackhawk, .44 Magnum, Western Style, Single Action, Blue, *Modern*	150	300	400
Super Blackhawk, .44 Magnum, Western Style, Single Action, Blue, Flat-Top Frame, Early Model, *Modern*	300	600	700
Super Blackhawk, .44 Magnum, Western Style, Single Action, Blue, 10" Barrel, *Modern*	250	500	600

	Fair	V. Good	Excellent
Super Single Six, .22 LR/.22 WMR Combo, Western Style, Single Action, Blue, New Model, *Modern*	$100	$150	$200
Super Single Six, .22 LR/.22 WMR Combo, Western Style, Single Action, Blue, New Model, 9$\frac{1}{2}$" Barrel, *Modern*	100	150	200
Super Single Six, .22 LR/.22 WMR Combo, Western Style, Single Action, Blue, *Modern*	100	175	200
Super Single Six, .22 LR/.22 WMR Combo, Western Style, Single Action, Blue, 9$\frac{1}{2}$" Barrel, *Modern*	100	175	200
Super Single Six, .22 LR/.22 WMR Combo, Western Style, Single Action, Stainless Steel, New Model, *Modern*	100	175	200

HANDGUN, SEMI-AUTOMATIC

	Fair	V. Good	Excellent
MK I, .22 L.R.R.F., Clip Fed, Adjustable Sights, Target Pistol, *Modern*	75	125	250
MK I, .22 L.R.R.F., Clip Fed, Adjustable Sights, Target Pistol, Wood Grips, *Modern*	75	150	250
MK II, .22 L.R.R.F., Clip Fed, Adjustable Sights, Stainless, *Modern*	150	200	250
MK II, .22 L.R.R.F., Clip Fed, Adjustable Sights, Target Pistol, *Modern*	75	125	250
MK II, .22 L.R.R.F., Clip Fed, Adjustable Sights, Target Pistol, Bull Barrel, *Modern*	100	175	250

Ruger MK II Bull Barrel

	Fair	V. Good	Excellent
MK II, .22 L.R.R.F., Clip Fed, Adjustable Sights, Target Pistol, Bull Barrel, Stainless, *Modern*	175	225	275
MK II Standard, .22 L.R.R.F., Clip Fed, Fixed Sights, Stainless, *Modern*	150	200	250
Standard, .22 L.R.R.F., Clip Fed, *Modern*	100	125	150

Ruger MK II

	Fair	V. Good	Excellent
Standard (Under #25600), .22 L.R.R.F., Clip Fed, Early Model, Blue, *Modern*	$125	$250	$500
Standard MK II, .22 L.R.R.F., Clip Fed, *Modern*	100	125	150

HANDGUN, SINGLESHOT

	Fair	V. Good	Excellent
Hawkeye, .256 Win. Mag., Western Style, Single Action, Blue, *Modern*	700	1100	1200

RIFLE, BOLT ACTION

	Fair	V. Good	Excellent
M-77RSI, Various Calibers, Checkered Stock, Open Rear Sight, Mannlicher Stock, Scope Mounts, *Modern*	150	325	375
M-77, for.338 Win. Mag., Add $15.00-$35.00			
M-77, for.488 Win. Mag., Add $50.00-$75.00			
M-77/22R, .22 Caliber Rimfire, Detachable Ten Shot Magazine, Blue, *Modern*	150	300	350

Ruger .22 Rimfire

	Fair	V. Good	Excellent
M-77/22S, .22 Caliber Rimfire, Detachable Ten Shot Magazine, Blue, *Modern*	150	300	350
M-77R, Various Calibers, Checkered Stock, Scope Mounts, No Sights, *Modern*	125	275	325
M-77RL, Various Calibers, Checkered Stock, Scope Mounts, Ultra Light, No Sights, *Modern*	125	275	325
M-77RS Tropical, .458 Win. Mag., Checkered Stock, Open Rear Sight, Scope Mounts, *Modern*	200	400	500
M-77RS, Various Calibers, Checkered Stock, Open Rear Sight, Scope Mounts, *Modern*	150	300	350
M-77ST, Various Calibers, Checkered Stock, Open Rear Sight, *Modern*	$125	$275	$325
M-77V, Various Calibers, Heavy Barrel, Varmint, No Sights, Scope Mounts, Checkered Stock, *Modern*	125	350	400

Ruger Model 77V

RIFLE, SEMI-AUTOMATIC

	Fair	V. Good	Excellent
10/22, .22 L.R.R.F., Clip Fed, Plain, *Modern*	75	100	125
10/22 Deluxe, .22 L.R.R.F., Clip Fed, Checkered Stock, *Modern*	100	150	175
10/22 International, .22 L.R.R.F., Clip Fed, Full-Stocked, *Modern*	150	325	375
10/22 Sporter I, .22 L.R.R.F., Clip Fed, Monte Carlo Stock, *Modern*	75	125	150
10/22 Sporter II, .22 L.R.R.F., Clip Fed, Checkered Stock, *Modern*	75	125	150
K Mini-14/20 GB, .223 Rem., Clip Fed, Carbine, with Flash Hider and Bayonet Stud, Folding Stock, *Modern*	200	400	450
K Mini-14/20 GB-F, .223 Rem., Clip Fed, Carbine, Stainless, with Flash Hider and Bayonet Stud, Folding Stock, *Modern*	200	425	475
Mini-14, .223 Rem., Clip Fed, Carbine, *Modern*	150	300	350
Mini-14, .223 Rem., Clip Fed, Carbine, Stainless, *Modern*	150	325	375
Mini-14/20 GB, .223 Rem., Clip Fed, Carbine, with Flash Hider and Bayonet Stud, *Modern*	150	300	350
Mini-14/20 GB-F, .223 Rem., Clip Fed, Carbine, Stainless, with Flash Hider and Bayonet Stud, *Modern*	150	325	375
Model 44 Deluxe, .44 Magnum, Tube Feed, Plain, Peep Sights, Sling Swivels, *Modern*	150	350	400
Model 44 International, .44 Magnum, Tube Feed, Full-Stocked, *Modern*	225	500	550
Model 44 Sporter, .44 Magnum, Tube Feed, Monte Carlo Stock, *Modern*	150	300	350

Ruger 44 Magnum Rifle

	Fair	V. Good	Excellent
Model 44 Standard, .44 Magnum, Tube Feed, Plain, Open Rear Sight, *Modern*	$150	$275	$325
XGI, .308, *Modern*			Rare

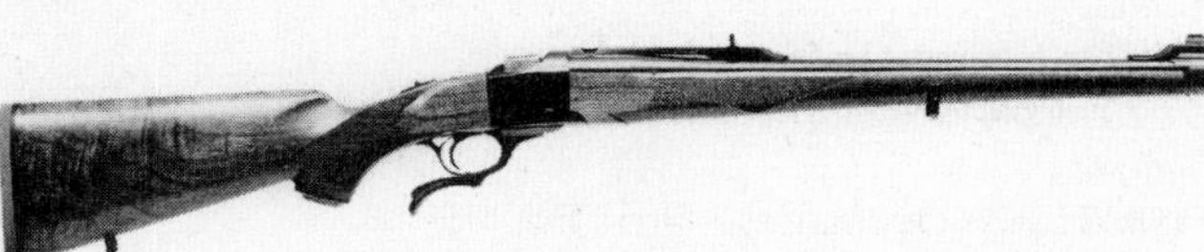

Ruger #1 International

RIFLE, SINGLESHOT

	Fair	V. Good	Excellent
#1 International, Various Calibers, Open Rear Sight, Checkered Mannlicher Stock, *Modern*	200	425	475
#1 Light Sporter, Various Caliber, Open Rear Sight, Checkered Stock, *Modern*	200	375	425
#1 Medium Sporter, Various Caliber, Open Rear Sight, Checkered Stock, *Modern*	150	300	400
#1 Standard Sport, Various Calibers, No Sights, Scope Mounts, Checkered Stock, *Modern*	150	300	400

Ruger #1 Sporter

	Fair	V. Good	Excellent
#1 Tropical, Various Calibers, Open Rear Sight, Checkered, *Modern*	150	350	400

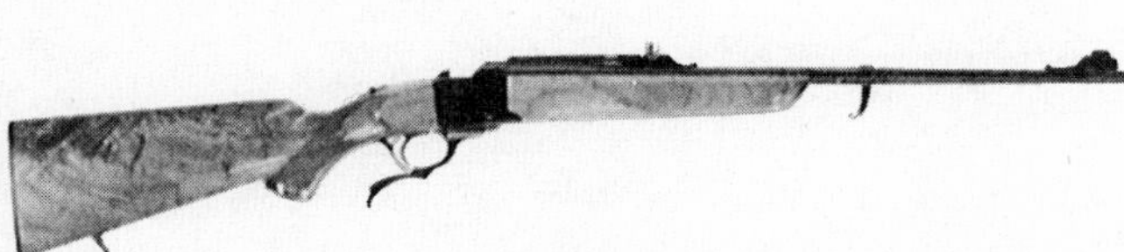

Ruger #1 Tropical

	Fair	V. Good	Excellent
#1 Varminter, Various Calibers, Heavy Barrel, No Sights, Checkered Stock, *Modern*	150	325	375
#3 Carbine, Various Calibers, Open Rear Sight, *Modern*	100	175	200

Ruger #3 Carbine

SHOTGUN, DOUBLE BARREL, OVER-UNDER

	Fair	V. Good	Excellent
Red Label, 12 or 20 Gauges, Checkered Stock, Single Trigger, *Modern*	$300	$600	$650

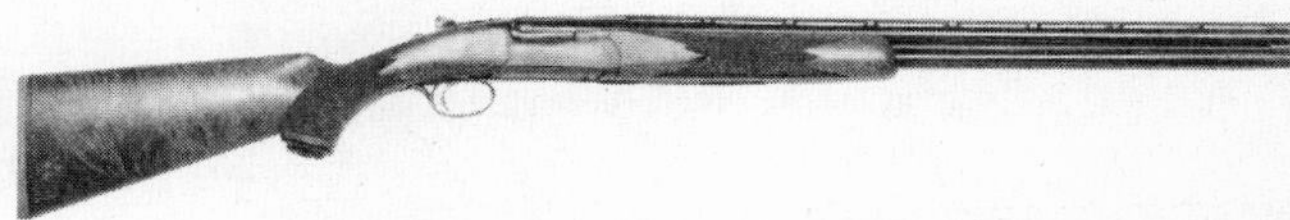

Ruger Red Label

SULLIVAN ARMS CO.

Made by Crescent for Sullivan Hardware, Anderson, S.C., c. 1900. See Crescent Fire Arms Co., Shotgun, Double Barrel, Side-by-Side; Shotgun, Singleshot.

SUPER DREADNAUGHT

Made by Stevens Arms.

SHOTGUN, SINGLESHOT

	Fair	V. Good	Excellent
Model 89 Dreadnaught, Various Gauges, Hammer, *Modern*	25	50	75

SUPER RANGE GOOSE

Made by Stevens Arms.

RIFLE, SEMI-AUTOMATIC

	Fair	V. Good	Excellent
Model 85 Springfield, .22 L.R.R.F., 5 Shot Clip, Open Rear Sight, *Modern*	25	50	75

SUTHERLAND, JAMES

Edinburgh, Scotland, c. 1790.

HANDGUN, FLINTLOCK

	Fair	V. Good	Excellent
.50, All Steel, Engraved, Ram's Horn Butt, *Antique*	1200	2500	2750

SUTHERLAND, RAMSEY

London and Birmingham, England, 1790–1827.

HANDGUN, FLINTLOCK

	Fair	V. Good	Excellent
.67, George III, Calvary Pistol, Military, Tapered Round Barrel, Brass Furniture, *Antique*	500	1000	1200

RIFLE, FLINTLOCK

	Fair	V. Good	Excellent
.75, 3rd Model Brown Bess, Musket, Military, *Antique*	600	1250	1500

SVENDSEN

E. Svendsen, Itasca, Ill., c. 1965.

	Fair	V. Good	Excellent
HANDGUN, MANUAL REPEATER			
Four Aces, .22 Short, Four Barrels, Derringer, Spur Trigger, *Modern*	$75	$100	$125

SWAMP ANGEL

Made by Forehand & Wadsworth, Worcester, Mass., c. 1871.

	Fair	V. Good	Excellent
HANDGUN, REVOLVER			
.41 Short, 5 Shot, Spur Trigger, Solid Frame, Single Action, *Antique*	100	175	200

SWEDISH MILITARY

	Fair	V. Good	Excellent
HANDGUN, REVOLVER			
M1887 Husqvarna, 7.5mm, Double Action, Blue, *Antique*	125	250	275
RIFLE, BOLT ACTION			
M1896 Mauser, 6.5 × 55mm, Gustav, *Curio*	100	200	225
RIFLE, SINGLESHOT			
M1867/89 Remington, 11.7mm, Full Stock, *Antique*	150	350	400

SWEITZER, DANIEL & CO.

Lancaster, Pa. 1808–1814. See Kentucky Rifles.

SWIFT

Made by Iver Johnson, Fitchburg, Mass. 1890–1900.

	Fair	V. Good	Excellent
HANDGUN, REVOLVER			
.38 S & W, 5 Shot, Double Action, Top Break, *Curio*	50	75	100
.38 S & W, 5 Shot, Top Break, Hammerless, Double Action, *Curio*	50	75	100

SWISS MILITARY

	Fair	V. Good	Excellent
HANDGUN, REVOLVER			
M1872 Swiss Ordnance, 10.4mm R.F., Double Action, Blue, Military, *Antique*	$400	$800	$850
M1872/78 Swiss Ordnance, 10.4mm C.F., Double Action, Blue, Military, *Antique*	200	400	475
M1882 Swiss Ordnance, 7.5mm, Double Action, Blue, Military, *Antique*	75	150	200
M1882 Swiss Ordnance, 7.5mm, Double Action, Blue, Military, with Holster Stock and All Leather, *Antique*	600	1250	1500
RIFLE, BOLT ACTION			
Vetterli, Bern 1878, .41 Swiss R.F., Tube Feed, Military, *Antique*	100	200	225
Vetterli, Bern 1878/81, .41 Swiss R.F., Tube Feed, Military, *Antique*	100	175	200
Vetterli, Carbine, .41 Swiss R.F., Tube Feed, Military, *Antique*	400	800	900
M1893, 7.5 × 55 Swiss, Military, *Curio*	200	400	450
M 1889/1900, 7.5 × 55 Swiss, Short Rifle, *Curio*	200	400	600
M1889, 7.5 × 55 Swiss, Military, *Modern*	100	175	200
M1911 Schmidt Rubin, 7.5 × 55 Swiss, Clip Fed, Carbine, Military, *Curio*	75	125	150
M1911 Schmidt Rubin, 7.5 × 55 Swiss, Clip Fed, Military, *Curio*	75	100	125
RIFLE, PERCUSSION			
Federal Rifle, .41 Caliber, Full Stocked, *Antique*	350	750	850

T

T.A.C.

Trocaola, Aranzabal y Cia., Eibar, Spain.

HANDGUN, REVOLVER

	Fair	V. Good	Excellent
Modelo Militar, .44 Spec., S & W Triple Lock Copy, Double Action, Blue, *Moden*	$100	$175	$225
OP No. 2 Mk I, .455 Eley, British, Double Action, Top Break, *Curio*	75	150	175
S & W Frontier Copy, .44 American, Double Action, Top Break, Blue, *Modern*	75	125	150
S & W M&P Copy, .38 Spec., Double Action, Blue, *Modern*	50	75	100

TALLARES

Tallares Armas Livianas Argentinas, Punta Alta, Argentina.

HANDGUN, SEMI-AUTOMATIC

	Fair	V. Good	Excellent
T.A.L.A., .22 L.R.R.F., Clip Fed, *Modern*	75	125	150

TANARMI

Made in Italy, Imported by Excam.

HANDGUN, REVOLVER

	Fair	V. Good	Excellent
E-15, For Chrome, Add $5.00			
E-15, .22 L.R.R.F, Single Action, Western Style, *Modern*	15	25	50
E-15, .22LR/.22 WMR Combo, Single Action, Western Style, *Modern*	15	25	50
TA-22, For Chrome, Add $5.00			
TA-22, .22 L.R.R.F, Single Action, Western Style, Brass Grip Frame, *Modern*	15	25	50
TA-22, .22LR/.22 WMR Combo, Single Action, Western Style, Brass Grip Frame, *Modern*	25	50	75
TA-76, For Chrome, Add $5.00			
TA-76, .22 L.R.R.F, Single Action, Western Style, *Modern*	15	25	50
TA-76, .22LR/.22 WMR Combo, Single Action, Western Style, *Modern*	15	25	50

TANKE

HANDGUN, SEMI-AUTOMATIC

	Fair	V. Good	Excellent
.25 ACP, Clip Fed, *Modern*	$50	$75	$100

TANNER

Andrae Tanner, Werkstatte fur Praszisionswaffen, Fulenbach, Switzerland.

RIFLE, BOLT ACTION

	Fair	V. Good	Excellent
300m Match, .308 Win., Offhand Target Rifle, Target Stock, Palm Rest, *Modern*	1900	3500	3750
50m Match, .22 L.R.R.F., Offhand Target Rifle, Target Stock, Palm Rest, *Modern*	1700	3250	3500
Hunting Match, Various Calibers, Checkered Monte Carlo Stock, Singleshot, *Modern*	1200	2500	2750
Standard UIT, .308 Win., Repeater, Target Rifle, Monte Carlo Target Stock, *Modern*	1900	3250	3500
Standard UIT, .308 Win., Singleshot, Target Rifle, Monte Carlo Target Stock, *Modern*	1900	3250	3500

TANQUE

Ojanguran y Vidosa, Eibar, Spain, c. 1930.

HANDGUN, SEMI-AUTOMATIC

	Fair	V. Good	Excellent
6.35mm, Clip Fed, *Modern*	75	150	175

TARGA

Guiseppi Tanfoglio, Gardone Val Trompia, Italy, imported by Excam.

HANDGUN, SEMI-AUTOMATIC

	Fair	V. Good	Excellent
Chrome Plating, For All Models, Add $5.00			
GT22B, .22 L.R.R.F., Clip Fed, Blue, *Modern*	50	75	100
GT27, .25 ACP, Clip Fed, Blue, *Modern*	15	25	50
GT32C, .22 L.R.R.F., Clip Fed, Blue, *Modern*	50	75	100
GT32XBE, .32 ACP, Clip Fed, *Modern*	75	125	150
GT380B, .380 ACP, Clip Fed, Blue, *Modern*	75	100	125

	Fair	V. Good	Excellent
GT380BE, .380 ACP, Clip Fed, Engraved, Blue, *Modern*	$50	$125	$150
GT380XE, .380 ACP, Clip Fed, *Modern*	50	125	150

T.A.R.N.

Swift Rifle Co., London, England, c. 1943.

HANDGUN, SEMI-AUTOMATIC

	Fair	V. Good	Excellent
Polish Air Force, 9mm Luger, Clip Fed, Blue, *Curio*	1800	3500	4000

TAURUS

Forjas Taurus S.A., Porto Alegre, Brazil.

HANDGUN, REVOLVER

	Fair	V. Good	Excellent
Model 65, .38 Special, Solid Frame, Swing-Out Cylinder, Double Action, *Modern*	100	175	225
Model 66, .38 Special, Solid Frame, Swing-Out Cylinder, Double Action, Adjustable Sights, *Modern*	100	200	250
Model 73, .32 S & W Long, Solid Frame, Swing-Out Cylinder, Double Action, Nickel Finish, *Modern*	75	150	200
Model 74, .32 S & W Long, Solid Frame, Swing-Out Cylinder, Double Action, Adjustable Sights, *Modern*	75	125	175
Model 80, .38 Special, Solid Frame, Swing-Out Cylinder, Double Action, *Modern*	75	125	175
Model 82, .38 Special, Solid Frame, Swing-Out Cylinder, Double Action, Heavy Barrel, *Modern*	75	150	175
Model 83, .38 Special, Solid Frame, Swing-Out Cylinder, Double Action, Adjustable Sights, *Modern*	75	150	175
Model 85, .38 Special, Solid Frame, Swing-Out Cylinder, Double Action, 3" Barrel, *Modern*	75	175	200
Model 86, .38 Special, Solid Frame, Swing-Out Cylinder, Double Action, Adjustable Sights, 6" Barrel, *Modern*	100	200	225
Model 94, .22 L.R.R.F., Solid Frame, Swing-Out Cylinder, Double Action, Adjustable Sights, *Modern*	75	150	175

HANDGUN, SEMI-AUTOMATIC

	Fair	V. Good	Excellent
PT-92, 9mm Luger, Clip Fed, Blue, Double Action, *Modern*	150	350	400
PT-99, 9mm Luger, Clip Fed, Blue, Double Action, *Modern*	175	375	425

T.D.E.

El Monte, Calif. Also see Auto-Mag.

HANDGUN, SEMI-AUTOMATIC

	Fair	V. Good	Excellent
Backup, .380 ACP, Stainless Steel, *Modern*	$100	$225	$250

TED WILLIAMS

Trade name of Sears, Roebuck, also see Sears.

RIFLE, BOLT ACTION

	Fair	V. Good	Excellent
Model 52703, .22 L.R.R.F., Singleshot, Plain, *Modern*	15	25	50
Model 52774, .22 L.R.R.F., Clip Fed, Plain, *Modern*	25	50	75
Model 53, Various Calibers, Checkered Stock, *Modern*	75	150	175

RIFLE, LEVER ACTION

	Fair	V. Good	Excellent
Model 120, .30/30 Win., Carbine, *Modern*	50	75	100

RIFLE, SEMI-AUTOMATIC

	Fair	V. Good	Excellent
Model 34, .22 L.R.R.F., *Modern*	25	50	75
Model 34, .22 L.R.R.F., Carbine, *Modern*	25	50	75
Model 3T, .22 L.R.R.F., Checkered Stock, *Modern*	50	75	100
Model 52811, .22 L.R.R.F., Plain, Tube Feed, Takedown, *Modern*	25	50	75
Model 52814, .22 L.R.R.F., Checkered Stock, Clip Fed, Takedown, *Modern*	75	100	125

SHOTGUN, BOLT ACTION

	Fair	V. Good	Excellent
Model 51106, 12 or 20 Gauges, Clip Fed, Adjustable Choke, *Modern*	25	50	75
Model 51142, .410 Gauge, Clip Fed, *Modern*	15	25	50

SHOTGUN, DOUBLE BARREL, OVER-UNDER

	Fair	V. Good	Excellent
Model Laurona, 12 Ga., Checkered Stock, Light Engraving, Double Trigger, Vent Rib, *Modern*	150	325	350
Model Zoli, 12 and 20 Gauges, Checkered Stock, Light Engraving, Double Trigger, Vent Rib, *Modern*	150	275	300
Model Zoli, 12 Ga., Checkered Stock, Light Engraving, Double Trigger, Vent Rib, Automatic Ejector, *Modern*	125	275	300

SHOTGUN, DOUBLE BARREL, SIDE-BY-SIDE

	Fair	V. Good	Excellent
Model 51226, 12 and 20 Gauges, Plain, Double Trigger, *Modern*	75	125	150
Model Laurona, 12 and 20 Gauges, Checkered Stock, Light Engraving, Hammerless, *Modern*	75	150	175

	Fair	V. Good	Excellent
SHOTGUN, SEMI-AUTOMATIC			
Model 300, 12 and 20 Gauges, Checkered Stock, Vent Rib, Adjustable Choke, *Modern*	$100	$175	$200
Model 300, 12 and 20 Gauges, Checkered Stock, Vent Rib, *Modern*	100	175	200
Model 300, 12 Ga., Plain, *Modern*	75	150	175
SHOTGUN, SINGLESHOT			
Model 5108, Various Gauges, Plain, *Modern*	15	25	50
SHOTGUN, SLIDE ACTION			
Model 200, 12 and 20 Gauges, Checkered Stock, Plain Barrel, *Modern*	75	125	150
Model 200, 12 and 20 Gauges, Checkered Stock, Vent Rib, Adjustable Choke, *Modern*	75	150	175
Model 200, 12 and 20 Gauges, Checkered Stock, Vent Rib, *Modern*	75	125	150
Model 200, 12 and 20 Gauges, Plain, *Modern*	50	100	125
Model 51454, .410 Ga., Plain, *Modern*	50	100	125

TEN STAR

Belgium, c. 1900.

	Fair	V. Good	Excellent
SHOTGUN, DOUBLE BARREL, SIDE-BY-SIDE			
Various Gauges, Hammerless, Damascus Barrel, *Modern*	100	150	175
Various Gauges, Hammerless, Steel Barrel, *Modern*	100	175	200
Various Gauges, Outside Hammers, Damascus Barrel, *Modern*	100	150	175
Various Gauges, Outside Hammers, Steel Barrel, *Modern*	100	175	200
SHOTGUN, SINGLESHOT			
Various Gauges, Hammer, Steel Barrel, *Modern*	50	75	100

TERRIBLE

Hijos de Calixto Arrizabalaga, Eibar, Spain, c. 1930.

	Fair	V. Good	Excellent
HANDGUN, SEMI-AUTOMATIC			
.25 ACP, Clip Fed, Blue, *Modern*	75	125	150

TERRIER

Made by J. Rupertus, Philadelphia, Pa. Sold by Tryon Bros., c. 1880.

	Fair	V. Good	Excellent
HANDGUN, REVOLVER			
.22 Short R.F., 7 Shot, Spur Trigger, Solid Frame, Single Action, *Antique*	$100	$150	$200
.32 Short R.F., 5 Shot, Spur Trigger, Solid Frame, Single Action, *Antique*	100	150	200
.38 Short R.F., 5 Shot, Spur Trigger, Solid Frame, Single Action, *Antique*	100	150	200
.41 Short R.F., 5 Shot, Spur Trigger, Solid Frame, Single Action, *Antique*	125	175	300

TERROR

Made by Forehand & Wadsworth, c. 1870.

	Fair	V. Good	Excellent
HANDGUN, REVOLVER			
.32 Short R.F., 5 or 6 Shot, Spur Trigger, Solid Frame, Single Action, *Antique*	75	150	175

TEUF-TEUF

Arizmendi y Goenaga, Eibar, Spain, c. 1912.

	Fair	V. Good	Excellent
HANDGUN, SEMI-AUTOMATIC			
.25 ACP, Clip Fed, Blue, *Curio*	75	125	150

TEUF-TEUF

Belgian maker, c. 1907.

	Fair	V. Good	Excellent
HANDGUN, SEMI-AUTOMATIC			
.25 ACP, Clip Fed, Blue, *Curio*	75	150	175

TEXAS RANGER

Made by Stevens Arms.

	Fair	V. Good	Excellent
SHOTGUN, SINGLESHOT			
Model 95, 12 and 16 Gauges, *Modern*	15	25	50

THAMES ARMS CO

Norwich, Conn., c. 1907.

	Fair	V. Good	Excellent
HANDGUN, REVOLVER			
.22 L.R.R.F., 7 Shot, Double Action, Top Break, *Curio*	75	150	175
.32 S & W, 5 Shot, Double Action, Top Break, *Curio*	50	100	125
.38 S & W, 5 Shot, Double Action, Top Break, *Curio*	75	125	150

THAYER, ROBERTSON & CARY

Norwich, Conn., c. 1907.

	Fair	V. Good	Excellent
HANDGUN, REVOLVER			
.32 S & W, 5 Shot, Double Action, Top Break, *Curio*	$50	$75	$100
.38 S & W, 5 Shot, Double Action, Top Break, *Curio*	50	75	100

THOMPSON

Developed by Auto-Ordnance, invented by Gen. John T. Thompson, made by various companies. Also see Numrich Arms.

	Fair	V. Good	Excellent
HANDGUN, SEMI-AUTOMATIC PISTOL/CARBINE			
Model 27A5, .45 ACP, Clip Fed, Finned Barrel, Adjustable Sights, with Compensator, (Numrich), *Modern*	200	450	500
RIFLE, SEMI-AUTOMATIC			
Model 27 A 1, .45 ACP, Clip Fed, without Compensator, (Numrich), *Modern*	225	550	600
Model 27 A 1, .45 ACP, Clip Fed, without Compensator,Cased with Accessories, (Numrich), *Modern*	250	550	650
Model 27 A 1 Deluxe, .45 ACP, Clip Fed, Finned Barrel, Adjustable Sights, with Compensator, (Numrich), *Modern*	300	675	750
Model 27 A 3, .22 L.R.R.F., Clip Fed, Finned Barrel, Adjustable Sights, with Compensator, (Numrich), *Modern*	150	300	350

THOMPSON, SAMUEL

Columbus, Ohio 1820–1822. See Kentucky Rifles.

THOMPSON/CENTER ARMS

Rochester, N.H. A relative newcomer to the family of American gunmakers, Thompson/Center was founded as a joint collaboration of inventor/designer Warren Center, and manufacturer Ken Thompson, president, K.W. Thompson Tool Co. Center had a novel firearms design, and Thompson was looking for a product to manufacture. The first Contender, the beginning of the firm's substantial line of singleshot closed breech pistols, came on the market in 1967. Since then over a million guns and over a million barrels have been made for a special dedicated clientele of handgun hunters and sihouette shooters. In 1970 the firm entered the blackpowder market by adding the Hawken singleshot muzzleloading rifle to the line, followed by the Renegade, Big Boar, Grey Hawk, Pennsylvania Hunter, White Mountain, and New Englander muzzle loaders and such innovations as the Fire Hawk and Thunder Hawk in-line ignition percussion rifles and carbines and the Scout in-line ignition rifle, carbine and pistol. With the in-line system, the percussion nipple is in a straight line with the barrel, and is struck directly from the rear by the firing pin. The design allows for fast ignition and high dependability, and the rifle resembles closely a conventional bolt-action rifle in pointability and balance. The Contender line was also expanded, by addition of a carbine design, which, like the pistols, offers the capability of interchangeable barrels. Additionally, Carbine Conversion Kits allowed adapting pistols into carbines, by changing the buttstock and forend and adding a 21" barrel. A full line of scopes and accessories rounds out the line. The New Hampshire–based firm is proud of its self-sufficiency, and is one of the few gunmakers in the world with its own investment casting foundry. The factory is equipped with state-of-the-art machinery. The company also boasts its own saw mill and kilns for walnut curing, in Perry, Kansas. Warren Center has been honored as Handgunner of the Year, a coveted trophy presented to such luminaries as William B. Ruger and Elmer Keith. The patented designs for the Contender pistol were intended to create a singleshot pistol versatile for a variety of hunting and shooting conditions and situations, with a wide choice of calibers and barrel lengths. The Contender has been made in as many as 19 centerfire pistol or rifle cartridges, and in .410 shotgun. Barrels are interchangeable in seconds: the forend is removed, the barrel pin pushed out, the new barrel installed, and the correct forend installed. The firing pin is designed with two strikers, alterable manually to rotate into position for rim or centerfire cartridges. The versatile firing pin system is designed to also serve as a safety. Still another feature is the automatic ejection system, found on selected barrels, in which the cartridge casing is totally ejected from the breech after firing. A total of over 500,000 Thompson/Center Contenders have been manufactured to date. Calibers have been: .22 L.R., .22 L.R. Match, .22 WMR, .17 Remington, .22 Hornet, .222 Remington, 7 mm T.C.U., 7-30 Waters, .30-30 Winchester, .32-20, .357 Magnum, .357 Remington Maximum, .35 Remington, .375 Winchester, 10 mm Auto, .44 Magnum, .445 Super Magnum, .45-70, .45 Colt and .410 shotgun. Barrel lengths have been: 10", 12", 14", 16", 16$^{1}/_{4}$", and 21" (carbine), standard round; octagonal for .22 Long Rifle only.

	Fair	V. Good	Excellent
HANDGUN, PERCUSSION			
.45 Patriot, Set Trigger, Octagon Barrel, Reproduction, *Antique*	$100	$200	$250
.45 Patriot, Set Trigger, Octagon Barrel, with Accessories, Reproduction, *Antique*	100	225	275
HANDGUN, SINGLESHOT			
Contender, Various Calibers, Adjustable Sights, *Modern*	150	325	350
Contender, Various Calibers, Adjustable Sights, Heavy Barrel, *Modern*	100	225	275
Contender, Various Calibers, Adjustable Sights, Super 14" Barrel, *Modern*	125	275	325
Contender, Various Calibers, Adjustable Sights, Vent Rib, *Modern*	150	350	375
Contender, Various Calibers, Heavy Barrel, No Sights, *Modern*	100	225	275
RIFLE, FLINTLOCK			
.45 Hawken, Set Trigger, Octagon Barrel, Reproduction, *Antique*	125	275	325

	Fair	V. Good	Excellent
.45 Hawken, Set Trigger, Octagon Barrel, with Accessories, Reproduction, *Antique*	$150	$300	$350
.50 Hawken, Set Trigger, Octagon Barrel, Reproduction, *Antique*	150	275	325
.50 Hawken, Set Trigger, Octagon Barrel, with Accessories, Reproduction, *Antique*	150	300	350
Hawken Cougar, .45 and .50 Caliber Caplock, Stainless Furniture, Reproduction, *Antique*	175	375	425

RIFLE, PERCUSSION

	Fair	V. Good	Excellent
Cherokee, .32 or .45 Caliber, Brass Furniture, 24" Barrel, *Modern*	150	300	350

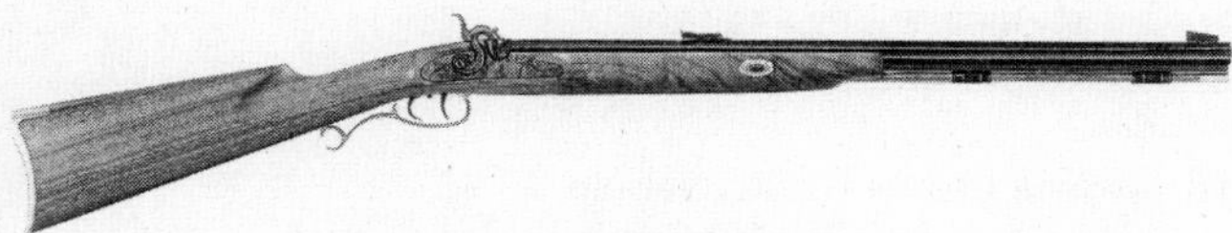

Thompson/Center Cherokee

	Fair	V. Good	Excellent
.36 Seneca, Set Trigger, Octagon Barrel, Reproduction, *Antique*	125	250	300
.36 Seneca, Set Trigger, Octagon Barrel, with Accessories, Reproduction, *Antique*	125	275	325
.45 Hawken, Set Trigger, Octagon Barrel, Reproduction, *Antique*	125	250	300
.45 Hawken, Set Trigger, Octagon Barrel, with Accessories, Reproduction, *Antique*	125	275	325
.45 Seneca, Set Trigger, Octagon Barrel, Reproduction, *Antique*	125	250	300
.45 Seneca, Set Trigger, Octagon Barrel, with Accessories, Reproduction, *Antique*	125	275	325
.50 Hawken, Set Trigger, Octagon Barrel, Reproduction, *Antique*	125	250	300
.50 Hawken, Set Trigger, Octagon Barrel, with Accessories, Reproduction, *Antique*	125	275	325
.54 Renegade, Set Trigger, Octagon Barrel, Reproduction, *Antique*	100	225	275
.54 Renegade, Set Trigger, Octagon Barrel, with Accessories, Reproduction, *Antique*	125	250	300

RIFLE, SINGLESHOT

	Fair	V. Good	Excellent
TCR83 Sports Rifle, Various Calibers, Interchangeable Barrels, Adjustable Double Set Triggers, *Modern*	250	500	550

THREE-BARREL GUN CO.

Moundsville, W. Va., 1906-1908, also at Wheeling, W. Va. as Royal Gun Co. and as Hollenbeck Gun Co.

COMBINATION WEAPON, DRILLING

	Fair	V. Good	Excellent
Various Calibers, Damascus barrel, *Antique*	$450	$1100	$1200

THUNDER

Martin Bascaran, Eibar, Spain, made for Alberdi, Teleria y Cia. 1912–1919.

HANDGUN, SEMI-AUTOMATIC

	Fair	V. Good	Excellent
M1919, .25 ACP, Clip Fed, *Curio*	75	100	125

TIGER

c. 1880.

HANDGUN, REVOLVER

	Fair	V. Good	Excellent
#2, .32 Short R.F., 5 Shot, Spur Trigger, Solid Frame, Single Action, *Antique*	75	150	175

TIGER

Made by Crescent for J.H. Hill Co. Nashville, Tenn., c. 1900. See Crescent Fire Arms Co., Shotgun, Double Barrel, Side-by-Side; Shotgun, Singleshot.

TIKKA

Oy Tikkakoski AB, Tikkakoski, Finland.

RIFLE, BOLT ACTION

	Fair	V. Good	Excellent
Model 55 Deluxe, Various Calibers, Clip Fed, Checkered Stock, *Modern*	225	475	550
Model 55 Sporter, Various Calibers, Clip Fed, Checkered Stock, Heavy Barrel, *Modern*	225	475	550
Model 55 Standard, Various Calibers, Clip Fed, Checkered Stock, *Modern*	225	450	525
Model 65 Deluxe, Various Calibers, Clip Fed, Checkered Stock, *Modern*	225	475	550
Model 65 Sporter, Various Calibers, Clip Fed, Checkered Stock, Target Rifle, Heavy Barrel, *Modern*	250	550	650
Model 65 Standard, Various Calibers, Clip Fed, Checkered Stock, *Modern*	225	450	525

TINDALL & DUTTON

London, England 1790–1820.

HANDGUN, FLINTLOCK

	Fair	V. Good	Excellent
Pocket Pistol, Various Calibers, Boxlock, *Antique*	150	350	450

TINGLE MFG. CO.

Shelbyville, Ind.

	Fair	V. Good	Excellent
HANDGUN, PERCUSSION			
Model 1960 Target, Octagon Barrel, Rifled, Reproduction, *Antique*	$75	$125	$150
RIFLE, PERCUSSION			
Model 1962 Target, Octagon Barrel, Brass Furniture, Rifled, Reproduction, *Antique*	100	175	200
SHOTGUN, PERCUSSION			
Model 1960, 10 or 12 gauges, Vent Rib, Double Barrel, Over-Under, Reproduction, *Antique*	100	200	225

TIPPING & LAWDEN

Birmingham, England, c. 1875.

	Fair	V. Good	Excellent
HANDGUN, MANUAL REPEATER			
Sharps Derringer, Various Calibers, 4 Barrels, Spur Trigger, Cased with Accessories, *Antique*	300	625	700
HANDGUN, REVOLVER			
Thomas Patent, .450, Solid Frame, Double Action, *Antique*	250	500	575

TITAN

Guiseppi Tanfoglio, Gardone, Val Trompia, Italy. Also see F.I.E.

	Fair	V. Good	Excellent
HANDGUN, SEMI-AUTOMATIC			
Pocket, .25 ACP, Clip Fed, Hammer, *Modern*	25	50	75

TITAN

Retolaza Hermanos, Eibar, Spain, c. 1900.

	Fair	V. Good	Excellent
HANDGUN, SEMI-AUTOMATIC			
M 1913, 6.35mm, Clip Fed, *Curio*	75	100	125

TITANIC

Retoloza Hermanos, Eibar, Spain, c. 1900.

	Fair	V. Good	Excellent
HANDGUN, SEMI-AUTOMATIC			
M 1913, 6.35mm, Clip Fed, *Curio*	75	100	125
M 1914, 7.65mm, Clip Fed, *Curio*	75	125	150

TOMPKINS

Varsity Mfg. Co., Springfield, Mass., c. 1947.

	Fair	V. Good	Excellent
HANDGUN, SINGLESHOT			
Target, .22 L.R.R.F., Full Stock, *Modern*	100	200	225

TOWER'S POLICE SAFETY

Made by Hopkins & Allen, Norwich, Conn. c. 1875.

	Fair	V. Good	Excellent
HANDGUN, REVOLVER			
.38 Short R.F., 5 Shot, Spur Trigger, Solid Frame, Single Action, *Antique*	$75	$150	$175

TRADEWINDS

Tacoma, Wash., Also see HVA.

	Fair	V. Good	Excellent
RIFLE, BOLT ACTION			
Husky (Early), Various Calibers, Checkered Stock, Monte Carlo Stock, *Modern*	100	225	375
Husky M-5000, Various Calibers, Checkered Stock, Clip Fed, *Modern*	125	275	325
Husqvarna Crown Grade, Various Calibers, Checkered Stock, Monte Carlo Stock, *Modern*	250	575	625
Husqvarna Imperial Custom, Various Calibers, Checkered Stock, Monte Carlo Stock, *Modern*	225	475	525
Husqvarna Imperial, Various Calibers, Checkered Stock, Monte Carlo Stock, Lightweight, *Modern*	225	500	550
Husqvarna Presentation, Various Calibers, Checkered Stock, Monte Carlo Stock, *Modern*	350	700	750
Husqvarna, Various Calibers, Checkered Stock, Monte Carlo Stock, Lightweight, *Modern*	225	525	575
Husqvarna, Various Calibers, Checkered Stock, Monte Carlo Stock, Lightweight, Full-Stocked, *Modern*	250	525	600
Model 1998, .222 Rem., No Sights, Heavy Barrel, Target Stock, *Modern*	225	475	525
Model 600K, Various Calibers, Clip Fed, No Sights, Heavy Barrel, Set Trigger, *Modern*	150	300	350
Model 600S, Various Calibers, Clip Fed, Heavy Barrel, Octagon Barrel, *Modern*	225	475	525
RIFLE, SEMI-AUTOMATIC			
Model 260A, .22 L.R.R.F., 5 Shot Clip, Checkered Stock, *Modern*	75	150	200
SHOTGUN, DOUBLE BARREL, OVER-UNDER			
Gold Shadow Indy, 12 Ga., Field Grade, Engraved, Fancy Checkering, Automatic Ejector, Vent Rib, *Modern*	600	1200	1550
Gold Shadow Indy, 12 Ga., Skeet Grade, Engraved, Fancy, Checkering, Automatic Ejector, Vent Rib, *Modern*	600	1250	1500

	Fair	V. Good	Excellent
Gold Shadow Indy, 12 Ga., Trap Grade, Engraved, Fancy, Checkering, Automatic Ejector, Vent Rib, *Modern*	$650	$1450	$1600
Shadow Indy, 12 Ga., Field Grade, Automatic Ejector, Vent Rib, Checkered Stock, *Modern*	225	475	525
Shadow Indy, 12 Ga., Skeet Grade, Automatic Ejector, Vent Rib, Checkered Stock, *Modern*	250	500	550
Shadow Indy, 12 Ga., Trap Grade, Automatic Ejector, Vent Rib, Checkered Stock, *Modern*	225	525	575
Shadow-7, 12 Ga., Field Grade, Automatic Ejector, Vent Rib, *Modern*	150	325	350
Shadow-7, 12 Ga., Skeet Grade, Automatic Ejector, Vent Rib, *Modern*	150	350	375
Shadow-7, 12 Ga., Trap Grade, Automatic Ejector, Vent Rib, *Modern*	175	375	400

SHOTGUN, DOUBLE BARREL, SIDE-BY-SIDE

Model G-1032, 10 Ga. 3 1/2", Checkered Stock, *Modern*	100	225	250
Model G-1228, 12 Ga. Mag. 3", Checkered Stock, *Modern*	100	250	275
Model G-2028, 20 Ga. Mag., Checkered Stock, *Modern*	125	250	275

SHOTGUN, SEMI-AUTOMATIC

Model D-200, 12 Ga., Field Grade, Vent Rib, Engraved, *Modern*	125	250	300
Model H-150, 12 Ga., Field Grade, *Modern*	100	200	225
Model H-170, 12 Ga., Field Grade, Vent Rib, *Modern*	100	225	275
Model T-220, 12 Ga., Trap Grade, Vent Rib, Engraved, *Modern*	125	250	300

SHOTGUN, SINGLESHOT

Model M50, 10 Ga., 3 1/2" Barrel, Checkered Stock, *Modern*	75	125	175

TRAMPS TERROR

Made by Hoods Firearms Co. Norwich, Conn., c. 1870.

HANDGUN, REVOLVER

.22 Short R.F., 7 Shot, Spur Trigger, Solid Frame, Single Action, *Antique*	75	150	175

TRIOMPH

Apaolozo Hermanos, Eibar, Spain.

HANDGUN, SEMI-AUTOMATIC

6.35mm, Clip Fed, Blue, *Modern*	50	100	125

TRIUMPH

Made by Stevens Arms.

SHOTGUN, DOUBLE BARREL, SIDE-BY-SIDE

	Fair	V. Good	Excellent
Model 311, Various Gauges, Hammerless, Steel Barrel, *Modern*	$75	$150	$175

TRUE BLUE

Made by Norwich Falls Pistols Co., c. 1880.

HANDGUN, REVOLVER

.32 Short R.F., 5 Shot, Spur Trigger, Solid Frame, Single Action, *Antique*	75	125	175

TRUST

Fab. d'Armes de Guerre de Grande Precision, Eibar, Spain.

HANDGUN, SEMI-AUTOMATIC

6.36mm, Clip Fed, Blue, *Modern*	50	100	125
7.65mm, Clip Fed, Blue, *Modern*	75	125	150

TRUST SUPRA

Fab. d'Armes de Guerre de Grande Precision, Eibar, Spain.

HANDGUN, SEMI-AUTOMATIC

6.35mm, Clip Fed, Blue, *Modern*	50	100	125

TUE-TUE

C. F. Galand, Liège, Belgium and Paris, France.

HANDGUN, REVOLVER

Velo Dog, Various Calibers, Double Action, Hammerless, *Curio*	75	125	150

TURBIAUX

J. E. Turbiaux, Paris, France, c. 1885.

HANDGUN, MANUAL REPEATER

Le Protector, Various Calibers, Palm Pistol, *Antique*	250	550	650

TURNER

Dublin, c. 1820.

HANDGUN, FLINTLOCK

.62, *Antique*	500	1200	1500

TURNER & ROSS

Made by Hood Firearms, Norwich, Conn., c. 1875.

	Fair	V. Good	Excellent
HANDGUN, REVOLVER			
.22 Short R.F., 7 Shot, Spur Trigger, Solid Frame, Single Action, *Antique*	$100	$150	$175

TWIGG

London, England 1760-1813.

	Fair	V. Good	Excellent
HANDGUN, FLINTLOCK			
.58, Pair, Belt Pistol, Flared, Octagon Barrel, Cased with Accessories, Plain, *Antique*	1500	3000	3500

TYCOON

Made by Johnson-Bye, Worcester, Mass. 1873–1887.

	Fair	V. Good	Excellent
HANDGUN, REVOLVER			
#1, .22 Short R.F., 7 Shot, Spur Trigger, Solid Frame, Single Action, *Antique*	75	150	175
#2, .32 Short R.F., 5 Shot, Spur Trigger, Solid Frame, Single Action, *Antique*	75	150	200
#3, .38 Short R.F., 5 Shot, Spur Trigger, Solid Frame, Single Action, *Antique*	$75	$150	$175
#4, .41 Short R.F., 5 Shot, Spur Trigger, Solid Frame, Single Action, *Antique*	75	125	150
#5, Short R.F., 5 Shot, Spur Trigger, Solid Frame, Single Action, *Antique*	100	200	250

TYROL

Made in Belgium for Tyrol Sport Arms, Englewood, Colo., c. 1963.

	Fair	V. Good	Excellent
RIFLE, BOLT ACTION			
Model DC, Various Calibers, Mannlicher Style, Checkered Stock, *Modern*	150	275	350
Model DCM, Various Calibers, Mannlicher Style, Checkered Stock, Recoil Pad, *Modern*	100	225	250
Model DM, Various Calibers, Checkered Stock, *Modern*	75	150	175

U

UBERTI, ALDO & CO.

Gardone, Val Trompia, Italy (est. 1959) and Lakeville, Connecticut (est. 1987). One of the foremost makers of replica muzzle-loading and cartridge firearms, and of miniatures, Aldo Uberti established his company at about the same time Val Forgett was setting up Navy Arms Co. The two have collaborated on many projects over the years, and can be credited, along with Turner Kirkland (founder-owner, Dixie Gun Works) with the launching of the replica firearms business as a major entity within the firearms industry. The most recent project of Uberti and Navy Arms was the Schofield S & W, a complex arm to manufacture, whether in the 1870s or the 1990s.

UHLINGER, W. L. & CO.

Philadelphia, Pa., c. 1880.

HANDGUN, REVOLVER

	Fair	*V. Good*	*Excellent*
.22 R.F., 7 Shot, Spur Trigger, Solid Frame, Single Action, *Antique*	$100	$225	$275
.32 Short R.F., 6 Shot, Spur Trigger, Solid Frame, Single Action, *Antique*	150	325	375

U.M.C. ARMS CO.

Probably Norwich Arms Co., c. 1880.

HANDGUN, REVOLVER

	Fair	*V. Good*	*Excellent*
.32 Short R.F., 5 Shot, Spur Trigger, Solid Frame, Single Action, *Antique*	75	150	175

UNION

Fab. Francaise.

HANDGUN, SEMI-AUTOMATIC

	Fair	*V. Good*	*Excellent*
7.65mm, Ruby Style, Clip Fed, *Modern*	100	225	275
7.65mm, Ruby Style, with Horseshoe Magazine, *Modern*	300	650	750

UNION

France, M. Seytres.

HANDGUN, SEMI-AUTOMATIC

	Fair	*V. Good*	*Excellent*
.25 ACP, Clip Fed, Long Grip, *Modern*	50	100	125
.32 ACP, Clip Fed, Long Grip, *Modern*	$75	$125	$150

UNION

Unceta y Cia., Guernica, Spain 1924-1931.

HANDGUN, SEMI-AUTOMATIC

	Fair	*V. Good*	*Excellent*
Model I, 6.35mm, Clip Fed, *Modern*	50	100	150
Model II, 6.35mm, Clip Fed, *Modern*	75	125	150
Model III, 7.65mm, Clip Fed, *Modern*	100	150	175
Model IV, 7.65mm, Clip Fed, *Modern*	75	150	175

UNION FIREARMS CO.

Toledo, Ohio, 1903–1913.

HANDGUN, SEMI-AUTOMATIC

	Fair	*V. Good*	*Excellent*
Lefever Patent Revolver, .32 Caliber, 6 Shot, Top Break, *Curio*	600	1200	1450
Reifgraber Patent Pistol, .32 S & W, 8 Shot, *Curio*	700	1400	1650

UNION JACK

Made by Hood Firearms Norwich, Conn., c. 1880.

HANDGUN, REVOLVER

	Fair	*V. Good*	*Excellent*
.22 Short R.F., 7 Shot, Spur Trigger, Solid Frame, Single Action, *Antique*	75	125	150
.32 Short R.F., 5 Shot, Spur Trigger, Solid Frame, Single Action, *Antique*	75	150	175

UNION REVOLVER

Maker unknown, c. 1880.

HANDGUN, REVOLVER

	Fair	*V. Good*	*Excellent*
.22 Short R.F., 7 Shot, Spur Trigger, Solid Frame, Single Action, *Antique*	75	125	150
.32 Short R.F., 5 Shot, Spur Trigger, Solid Frame, Single Action, *Antique*	75	150	175

UNIQUE

Made by C.S. Shattuck, 1880–1915.

HANDGUN, REPEATER

	Fair	V. Good	Excellent
Shattuck Palm Pistol, Various Calibers, 4 Shot, *Curio*	$250	$575	$1250

HANDGUN, REVOLVER

	Fair	V. Good	Excellent
.32 Short R.F., 5 Shot, Spur Trigger, Solid Frame, Single Action, *Antique*	75	150	200
.38 Short R.F., 5 Shot, Spur Trigger, Solid Frame, Single Action, *Antique*	75	150	200

UNIQUE

Mre. d'Armes de Pyrenees, Hendaye, France, 1923 to date.

HANDGUN, SEMI-AUTOMATIC

	Fair	V. Good	Excellent
Kreigsmodell, 7.65mm, Clip Fed, Magazine Disconnect, 9 Shot, Nazi-Proofed, Hammer, *Curio*	125	250	275
Model 10, 6.35mm, Clip Fed, Magazine Disconnect, *Modern*	75	150	200
Model 11, 6.35mm, Clip Fed, Magazine Disconnect, Safety, Cartridge Indicator, *Modern*	100	200	250
Model 12, 6.35mm, Clip Fed, Magazine Disconnect, Grip Safety, *Modern*	100	200	225
Model 13, 6.35mm, Clip Fed, Magazine Disconnect, Grip Safety, 7 Shot, *Modern*	100	200	225
Model 14, 6.35mm, Clip Fed, Magazine Disconnect, Grip Safety, 9 Shot, *Modern*	100	175	225
Model 15, 7.65mm, Clip Fed, Magazine Disconnect, 6 Shot, *Modern*	100	200	250
Model 16, 7.65mm, Clip Fed, Magazine Disconnect, 7 Shot, *Modern*	100	200	250
Model 17, 7.65mm, Clip Fed, Magazine Disconnect, 9 Shot, Nazi-Proofed, *Curio*	150	300	350
Model 17, 7.65mm, Clip Fed, Magazine Disconnect, 9 Shot, *Modern*	100	225	275
Model 18, 7.65mm, Clip Fed, Magazine Disconnect, 6 Shot, *Modern*	100	200	250
Model 19, 7.65mm, Clip Fed, Magazine Disconnect, 7 Shot, *Modern*	100	200	250
Model 20, 7.65mm, Clip Fed, Magazine Disconnect, 9 Shot, *Modern*	100	225	275
Model 21, .380 ACP, Clip Fed, Magazine Disconnect, 6 Shot, *Modern*	100	225	275
Model 51, .380 ACP, Clip Fed, Magazine Disconnect, 6 Shot, *Modern*	$100	$200	$250
Model 51, 7.65mm, Clip Fed, Magazine Disconnect, 9 Shot, *Modern*	100	200	250
Model 52, .22 L.R.R.F., Clip Fed, Hammer, Various Barrel Lengths, *Modern*	100	175	225
Model 540, 7.65mm, Clip Fed, Magazine Disconnect, 9 Shot, *Modern*	100	200	250
Model 550, *Modern*	100	200	250
Model C, 7.65mm, Clip Fed, 9 Shot, Hammer, *Modern*	100	200	250
Model D-1, .22 L.R.R.F., Clip Fed, Hammer, 3" Barrel, *Modern*	100	200	250
Model D-2, .22 L.R.R.F., Clip Fed, Hammer, Adjustable Sights, 4" Barrel, *Modern*	100	225	275
Model D-3, .22 L.R.R.F., Clip Fed, Hammer, Adjustable Sights, 8" Barrel, *Modern*	100	200	250
Model D-4, .22 L.R.R.F., Clip Fed, Hammer, Muzzle Brake, Adjustable Sights, 9½" Barrel, *Modern*	100	225	275
Model D-6, .22 L.R.R.F., Clip Fed, Hammer, Adjustable Sights, 6" Barrel, *Modern*	100	225	275
Model DES/69, .22 L.R.R.F., Clip Fed, Target Pistol, *Modern*	150	300	350
Model DES/VO 79, .22 L.R.R.F., Clip Fed, Rapid Fire Target Pistol, Gas Ports, *Modern*	300	650	750
Model DES/VO, .22 L.R.R.F., Clip Fed, Rapid Fire Target Pistol, *Modern*	250	525	600
Model E-1, .22 Short R.F., Clip Fed, Hammer, 3" Barrel, *Modern*	75	100	125
Model E-2, .22 Short R.F., Clip Fed, Hammer, Adjustable Sights, 4" Barrel, *Modern*	75	125	150
Model E-3, .22 Short R.F., Clip Fed, Hammer, Adjustable Sights, 8" Barrel, *Modern*	75	125	150
Model E-4, .22 Short R.F., Clip Fed, Hammer, Muzzle Brake, Adjustable Sights, 9½" Barrel, *Modern*	$75	$150	$200
Model F, .380 ACP, Clip Fed, 8 Shot, Hammer, *Modern*	100	225	275
Model L (Corsair), .22 L.R.R.F., Clip Fed, Hammer, *Modern*	100	175	225
Model L (Corsair), .22 L.R.R.F., Clip Fed, Hammer, Lightweight, *Modern*	100	175	225
Model L (Corsair), .32 ACP, Clip Fed, Hammer, *Modern*	75	125	150

	Fair	V. Good	Excellent
Model L (Corsair), .32 ACP, Clip Fed, Hammer, Lightweight, *Modern*	$75	$125	$150
Model L (Corsair), .380 ACP, Clip Fed, Hammer, *Modern*	75	150	175
Model L (Corsair), .380 ACP, Clip Fed, Hammer, Lightweight, *Modern*	75	125	150
Model Mikros, .25 ACP, Clip Fed, Magazine Disconnect, 6 Shot, *Modern*	75	150	175
Model RD (Ranger), .22 L.R.R.F., Clip Fed, Hammer, *Modern*	50	75	100
Model RD (Ranger), .22 L.R.R.F., Clip Fed, Muzzle Brake, Hammer, *Modern*	50	100	125

RIFLE, BOLT ACTION

	Fair	V. Good	Excellent
Audax, .22 L.R.R.F., Checkered Stock, Open Sights, *Modern*	75	150	175
Dioptra 3121, .22 L.R.R.F., Checkered Stock, Open Sights, *Modern*	200	450	500
Dioptra 3121, .22 L.R.R.F., Checkered Stock, Target Sights, *Modern*	250	575	650
Dioptra 4131, .22 WMR., Checkered Stock, Open Sights, *Modern*	250	575	650
Model T-66, .22 L.R.R.F., Target Stock, Target Sights, Singleshot, *Modern*	175	375	425

UNITED STATES ARMS

Riverhead, N.Y., distributed by Mossberg.

HANDGUN, REVOLVER

	Fair	V. Good	Excellent
Abilene, .44 Magnum, Single Action, Western Style, Adjustable Sights, *Modern*	150	300	450
Abilene, .44 Magnum, Stainless Steel, Single Action, Western Style, Adjustable Sights, *Modern*	150	325	450
Abilene, .44 Magnum, Stainless Steel, Single Action, Western Style, 10" Barrel, Adjustable Sights, *Modern*	175	350	400
Abilene, Various Calibers, Single Action, Western Style, Adjustable Sights, *Modern*	150	300	350
Abilene, Various Calibers, Single Action, Western Style, Adjustable Sights, Stainless Steel, *Modern*	150	325	375

UNIVERSAL

Hialeah, Fla., Now owned by Iver Johnson, Inc. Currently manufactured in Jacksonville, Arkansas.

HANDGUN, SEMI-AUTOMATIC

	Fair	V. Good	Excellent
Model 3000 Enforcer, .30 Carbine, Clip Fed, Blued, *Modern*	$100	$175	$200
Model 3000 Enforcer, .30 Carbine, Clip Fed, Nickel Plated, *Modern*	100	225	250
Model 3000 Enforcer, .30 Carbine, Clip Fed, Stainless, *Modern*	100	225	275

RIFLE, SEMI-AUTOMATIC

	Fair	V. Good	Excellent
Model 1001, .30 Carbine, Carbine, Clip Fed, *Modern*	75	150	200
Model 1002, .30 Carbine, Carbine, Clip Fed, Bayonet Lug, *Modern*	100	200	250
Model 1003, .30 Carbine, Carbine, Clip Fed, Walnut Stock, *Modern*	75	125	175
Model 1004, .30 Carbine, Carbine, Clip Fed, Scope Mounted, *Modern*	100	200	250
Model 1010, .30 Carbine, Carbine, Clip Fed, Nickel Plated, *Modern*	100	225	275
Model 1011 Deluxe, .30 Carbine, Carbine, Clip Fed, Nickel Plated, Monte Carlo Stock, *Modern*	125	250	300
Model 1015, .30 Carbine, Carbine, Clip Fed, Gold Plated, *Modern*	125	250	300
Model 1016 Deluxe, .30 Carbine, Carbine, Clip Fed, Gold Plated, Monte Carlo Stock, *Modern*	150	300	350
Model 1025 Ferret, .256 Win. Mag., Carbine, Clip Fed, Sporting Rifle, *Modern*	100	175	225
Model 1025 Ferret, .30 Carbine, Carbine, Clip Fed, Sporting Rifle, *Modern*	100	175	225
Model 1941 Field Commander, .30 Carbine, Carbine, Clip Fed, Fancy Wood, *Modern*	100	175	225

RIFLE, SLIDE ACTION

	Fair	V. Good	Excellent
Vulcan 440, .44 Magnum, Clip Fed, Sporting Rifle, Open Rear Sight, *Modern*	75	150	200

SHOTGUN, DOUBLE BARREL, OVER-UNDER

	Fair	V. Good	Excellent
Baikal 1J-27, 12 Ga., Double Trigger, Vent Rib, Engraved, Checkered Stock, *Modern*	100	200	250
Baikal 1J-27, 12 Ga., Double Trigger, Vent Rib, Engraved, Checkered Stock, Automatic Ejector, *Modern*	100	225	275

SHOTGUN, SINGLESHOT

	Fair	V. Good	Excellent
Model 1J18, 12 Ga., Hammerless, *Modern*	25	50	75
Model 7212, 12 Ga., Trap Grade, Vent Rib, Engraved, Checkered Stock, Monte Carlo Stock, *Modern*	400	850	950

UNIVERSAL

Made by Hopkins & Allen, Norwich, Conn., c. 1880.

HANDGUN, REVOLVER

	Fair	V. Good	Excellent
.32 S & W, 5 Shot, Double Action, Solid Frame, *Curio*	$50	$75	$100

UNWIN & ROGERS

Yorkshire, England, c. 1850.

HANDGUN, PERCUSSION

	Fair	V. Good	Excellent
Knife Pistol, with Ramrod and Mould, Cased with Accessories, *Antique*	450	1000	1250

U.S. ARMS CO.

Brooklyn, N.Y. 1874–1878.

HANDGUN, REVOLVER

	Fair	V. Good	Excellent
.22 Short R.F., 7 Shot, Spur Trigger, Solid Frame, Single Action, *Antique*	75	125	200
.32 Short R.F., 5 Shot, Spur Trigger, Solid Frame, Single Action, *Antique*	75	150	200
.38 Short R.F., 5 Shot, Spur Trigger, Solid Frame, Single Action, *Antique*	75	150	200
.41 Short R.F., 5 Shot, Spur Trigger, Solid Frame, Single Action, *Antique*	75	150	300

U.S. Arms Co., .41

U.S. ARMS CO.

Made by Crescent for H. & D. Folsom, c. 1900. See Crescent Fire Arms Co., Shotgun, Double Barrel, Side-by-Side; Shotgun, Singleshot.

U.S. MILITARY

HANDGUN, FLINTLOCK

	Fair	V. Good	Excellent
.54 M1805 (06), Singleshot, Smoothbore, Brass Mounts, Dated 1806, *Antique*	7000	18000	20000
.54 M1805 (06), Singleshot, Smoothbore, Brass Mounts, Dated 1807, *Antique*	6000	10000	12000
.54 M1805 (06), Singleshot, Smoothbore, Brass Mounts, Dated 1808, *Antique*	$6000	$13000	$15000
.54 M1807-8, Singleshot, Smoothbore, Brass Mounts, Various Contractors, *Antique*	3000	6500	7500
.54 M1816, Singleshot, Smoothbore, S North Army, Brass Furniture, *Antique*	700	1500	1750
.54 M1819, Singleshot, Smoothbore, S North Army, Iron Mounts, *Antique*	700	1500	1750
.54 M1826, Singleshot, Smoothbore, S North Army, Iron Mounts, *Antique*	2500	5250	5500
.54 M1836, Singleshot, Smoothbore, R Johnson Army, Iron Mounts, *Antique*	625	1750	2000
.64 M1808, Singleshot, Smoothbore, S North Army, Brass Furniture, *Antique*	5500	7000	8500
.69 M1799, Singleshot, North & Cheney, Brass Furniture, Brass Frame, *Antique*	12000	25000	30000
.69 M1811, Singleshot, Smoothbore, S North Army, Brass Furniture, *Antique*	2000	4500	5500
.69 M1817 (18), Singleshot, Smoothbore, Springfield, Iron Mounts, *Antique*	4000	8000	9500

HANDGUN, PERCUSSION

	Fair	V. Good	Excellent
.54 M1836, Singleshot, Smoothbore, U.S. Navy Conversion from Flintlock, Iron Mounts, *Antique*	600	1250	1500
.54 M1842 Aston, Singleshot, Smoothbore, Brass Mounts, *Antique*	600	1000	1200
.54 M1842 Johnson, Singleshot, Smoothbore, Brass Mounts, *Antique*	600	1250	1500
.54 M1843 Deringer Army, Singleshot, Rifled, Brass Mounts, *Antique*	900	2250	2500
.54 M1843 Deringer Army, Singleshot, Smoothbore, Brass Mounts, *Antique*	600	1250	1500
.54 M1843 Deringer Navy, Singleshot, Smoothbore, Brass Mounts, *Antique*	700	1500	1750

HANDGUN, SINGLESHOT

	Fair	V. Good	Excellent
Liberator, .45 ACP, Military, *Curio*	300	500	600

RIFLE, BOLT ACTION

	Fair	V. Good	Excellent
M1871 Ward-Burton, .50 C.F., Iron Mountings, Carbine, *Antique*	900	2000	2500
M1871 Ward-Burton, .50 C.F., Iron Mountings, Rifle, *Antique*	800	1750	2000
M1882 Chaffee-Reese, 45-70, Rifle, *Antique*	900	2000	2500
M1892/6 Krag, .30-40 Krag, Rifle, *Antique*	250	550	600
M1895 Lee Straight Pull, 6mm Lee Navy, Musket, *Antique*	450	1000	1250

	Fair	V. Good	Excellent
M1896 Krag, .30-40 Krag, Cadet, *Antique*	$8000	$20000	$25000
M1896 Krag, .30-40 Krag, Carbine, *Antique*	450	1000	1250
M1896 Krag, .30-40 Krag, Rifle, *Antique*	300	650	750
M1898 Krag, .30-40 Krag, Carbine, *Curio*	600	1250	1500
M1898 Krag, .30-40 Krag, Rifle, *Curio*	300	650	750
M1899 Krag, .30-40 Krag, Carbine, *Curio*	400	850	1000
M1903 MKI Pedersen, . .30-06 Springfield, *Curio*	7000	15000	17500
M1903 National Match, .30-06 Springfield, Target Rifle, *Curio*	1200	2500	2750
M1903 Sniper, .30-06 Springfield, Scope Mounts, *Curio*	1400	3000	3500
M1903, .30-06 Springfield, Machined Parts, *Modern*	6000	12500	15000
M1903/5, .30-03 Springfield, *Curio*	3000	6000	7500
M1903/5, .30-06 Springfield, *Curio*	1100	2250	2500
M1903/7, .30-06 Springfield, Early Receivers, *Curio*	700	1750	2000
M1903/Postwar, .30-06 Springfield, *Curio*	400	800	1000
M1903/WWI, .30-06 Springfield, *Curio*	800	2000	2250
M1903A1 National Match, .30-06 Springfield, Target Rifle, *Curio*	1200	2500	3000
M1903A1, .30-06 Springfield, Parkerized, Checkered Butt, Machined Parts, *Curio*	450	1000	1250
M1917 Eddystone, .30-06 Springfield, *Curio*	300	500	600
M1917 Remington, .30-06 Springfield, *Curio*	300	525	600
M1917 Winchester, .30-06 Springfield, *Curo*	400	650	700
M1922 Trainer, .22 L.R.R.F., Target Rifle, *Curio*	1200	2500	3000
M1922M2 Trainer, .22 L.R.R.F., Target Rifle, *Curio*	800	1800	2000

RIFLE, FLINTLOCK

	Fair	V. Good	Excellent
.52, M1819 Hall Whitney, Rifled, Breech Loader, 32½" Barrel, 3 Bands, *Antique*	1500	4000	5000
.52, M1819 Hall, Rifled, Breech Loader, 32½" Barrel, 3 Bands, *Antique*	1500	4000	5000
.54, M1807 Springfield, "Indian Carbine," 27¾" Barrel, *Antique*	7500	20000	22500
.54, M1814, Rifled, 36" Barrel, *Antique*	2000	4500	5000

RIFLE, PERCUSSION

	Fair	V. Good	Excellent
.45-70, M1873 U.S., "Trapdoor," Carbine, 22" Barrel, Single Band, *Antique*	600	1200	1500
.45-70, M1873 U.S., "Trapdoor," Rifle, 32⅝" Barrel, 2 Bands, *Antique*	$450	$1000	$1200
.45-70, M1888 U.S., "Trapdoor," Rifle, 32⅝" Barrel, 2 Bands, Ramrod-Bayonet, *Antique*	400	900	1000
.57, M1841 U.S. Cadet Musket, 40" Barrel, 2 Bands, *Antique*	4500	9000	10000
.57, M1851 U.S. Cadet Musket, Rifled, 40" Barrel, 2 Bands, *Antique*	600	1200	1500
.57, M1851 U.S. Cadet Musket, Smoothbore, 40" Barrel, 2 Bands, *Antique*	600	1200	1500
.58 Lindner, Breech Loader, Carbine, Rising Block, *Antique*	1250	3000	3750
.58, M1841 Contract, Rifled, 33" Barrel, 2 Bands, (Mississippi Rifle), *Antique*	900	2000	2500
.58, M1855 U.S., Carbine, Rifled, 22" Barrel, 1 Band, with Tape Priming System, *Antique*	4500	10000	12500
.58, M1855 U.S., Rifled, 40" Barrel, 3 Bands, with Tape Priming System, *Antique*	1250	3500	4000
.58, M1861 U.S., Rifled, 40" Round Barrel, 3 Bands, *Antique*	800	1800	2000
.58, M1863 U.S., Rifled, 40" Round Barrel, 3 Bands, *Antique*	800	1800	2000
.64, M1836 Hall-North, Rifled, Breech Loader, Carbine, 26⅛" Barrel, 2 Bands, *Antique*	1200	2500	3000
.69, M1842 U.S., Musket, 42" Barrel, 3 Bands, *Antique*	1100	2250	2500
.69, M1842 U.S., Rifled, Musket, 42" Barrel, 3 Bands, *Antique*	1100	2250	2500
.69, M1847 Artillery, Musketoon, 26" Barrel, 2 Bands, Steel Furniture, *Antique*	1400	3500	4000
.69, M1847 Cavalry, Musketoon, 26" Barrel, 2 Bands, Brass Furniture, *Antique*	1400	3000	3500
.69, M1847 Sappers, Musketoon, 26" Barrel, 2 Bands, Bayonet Stud on Right Side, *Antique*	1700	3500	4000
M1864 Training Rifle, Military, Wood Barrel, *Antique*	100	200	250

RIFLE, SEMI-AUTOMATIC

	Fair	V. Good	Excellent
M-1 Carbine IBM, .30 Carbine, Clip Fed, *Curio*	200	350	400
M-1 Carbine Inland, .30 Carbine, Clip Fed, *Curio*	200	350	400
M-1 Carbine Irwin-Pedersen, .30 Carbine, Clip Fed, *Curio*	300	700	800
M-1 Carbine Nat. Postal Meter, .30 Carbine, Clip Fed, *Curio*	300	700	800
M-1 Carbine Quality Hdw., .30 Carbine, Clip Fed, *Curio*	300	550	600

	Fair	V. Good	Excellent
M-1 Carbine Rockola, .30 Carbine, Clip Fed, *Curio*	$350	$750	$900
M-1 Carbine Underwood, .30 Carbine, Clip Fed, *Curio*	200	350	400
M-1 Carbine Winchester, .30 Carbine, Clip Fed, *Curio*	300	600	700
M-1 Garand National Match, .30-06 Springfield, Military, Target Sights, Target Trigger, Target Barrel, *Curio*	600	1200	1500
M-1 Garand Winchester, .30-06 Springfield, Pre WWII, *Curio*	500	1000	1200
M-1 Garand, .30-06 Springfield, Military, *Curio*	350	725	800
M-1A1 Carbine, .30 Carbine, Clip Fed, Folding Stock, *Modern*	375	750	800
M1941 Johnson, .30-06 Springfield, Military, *Curio*	500	1000	1200

U.S. REVOLVER CO.

MADE BY IVER JOHNSON

	Fair	V. Good	Excellent
.32 S & W, 5 Shot, Double Action, Solid Frame, *Modern*	$50	$75	$100
.32 S & W, 5 Shot, Top Break, Double Action, *Modern*	50	75	100
.32 S & W, 5 Shot, Top Break, Hammerless, Double Action, *Modern*	50	75	100
.32 Short R.F., 5 Shot, Spur Trigger, Solid Frame, Single Action, *Antique*	125	150	175
.38 S & W, 5 Shot, Double Action, Top Break, *Modern*	50	75	100
.38 S & W, 5 Shot, Double Action, Solid Frame, *Modern*	25	50	75
.38 S & W, 5 Shot, Top Break, Hammerless, Double Action, *Modern*	50	75	100

V

VALIANT

Made by Stevens Arms for Spear & Co., Pittsburgh, Pa.

RIFLE, BOLT ACTION

	Fair	V. Good	Excellent
Model 51, .22 L.R.R.F., Singleshot, Takedown, *Modern*	$12	$25	$50

VALMET

Valmet Oy, Tourula Works, Jyvaskyla, Finland.

RIFLE, SEMI-AUTOMATIC

	Fair	V. Good	Excellent
M-62S, 7.62 × 39 Russian, Clip Fed, AK-47 Type, Sporting Version of Military Rifle, *Modern*	500	1000	1250
M-71S, .223 Rem., Clip Fed, AK-47 Type, Sporting Version of Military Rifle, *Modern*	300	750	1000
M78 HV, .223 Rem., Clp Fed, Bipod, *Modern*	500	1000	1200
M78 Standard, .308 Win., Clip Fed, Bipod, *Modern*	500	1000	1200

VALOR ARMS

Importers, Miami, Fla.

HANDGUN, REVOLVER

	Fair	V. Good	Excellent
.22 L.R.R.F., Double Action, Lightweight, *Modern*	15	25	50
.32 S & W, Double Action, Lightweight, *Modern*	15	25	50

VANDERFRIFT, ISSAC AND JEREMIAH

Philadelphia, Pa. 1809–1815. See Kentucky Rifles and Pistols.

VEGA

Sacramento, Calif.

HANDGUN, SEMI-AUTOMATIC

	Fair	V. Good	Excellent
Vega 1911A1, .45 ACP, Stainless Steel, Clip Fed, *Modern*	150	300	350

VELO DOG

Various makers, c. 1900.

HANDGUN, REVOLVER

	Fair	V. Good	Excellent
5mm Velo Dog, Hammerless, Folding Trigger, *Curio*	$50	$100	$200
5mm Velo Dog, Hammerless, Folding Trigger, *Curio*	25	75	200
5mm Velo Dog, Hammerless, Trigger Guard, *Curio*	25	75	200
.25 ACP, Hammer, Folding Trigger, *Curio*	50	100	200
.25 ACP, Hammerless, Folding Trigger, *Curio*	50	100	200

VENCEDOR

San Martin y Cia., Eibar, Spain.

HANDGUN, SEMI-AUTOMATIC

	Fair	V. Good	Excellent
.25 ACP, Clip Fed, Blue, *Modern*	75	100	125
.35 ACP, Clip Fed, Blue, *Modern*	100	125	150

VENTURA IMPORTS (CONTENDO)

Seal Beach, Calif. Also see Bertuzzi and Piotti.

SHOTGUN, DOUBLE BARREL, OVER-UNDER

	Fair	V. Good	Excellent
MK-1 Contento, 12 Ga., Field Grade, Automatic Ejector, Single Selective Trigger, Engraved, Checkered Stock, *Modern*	400	850	1000
MK-2 Contento, 12 Ga., Field Grade, Automatic Ejector, Single Selective Trigger, Engraved, Checkered Stock, *Modern*	500	1100	1300
MK-2 Contento, 12 Ga., Trap Grade, with Extra Single Trap Barrel, Engraved, Checkered Stock, *Modern*	650	1400	1600
MK-2 Luxe Contento, 12 Ga., Field Grade, Automatic Ejector, Single Selective Trigger, Engraved, Checkered Stock, *Modern*	500	1000	1200
MK-2 Luxe Contento, 12 Ga., Trap Grade, with Extra Single Trap Barrel, Engraved, Checkered Stock, *Modern*	700	1500	1800
MK-3 Contento, 12 Ga., Field Grade, Automatic Ejector, Single Selective Trigger, Engraved, Checkered Stock, *Modern*	600	1250	1500

	Fair	V. Good	Excellent
MK-3 Contento, 12 Ga., Trap Grade, with Extra Single Trap Barrel, Engraved, Checkered Stock, *Modern*	$900	$2000	$2500
MK-3 Luxe Contento, 12 Ga., Field Grade, Automatic Ejector, Single Selective Trigger, Engraved, Checkered Stock, *Modern*	700	1500	1800
MK-3 Luxe Contento, 12 Ga., Trap Grade, with Extra Single Trap Barrel, Engraved, Checkered Stock, *Modern*	1100	2500	3000
Nettuno Contento, 12 Ga., Field Grade, Automatic Ejector, Single Selective Trigger, Engraved, Checkered Stock, *Modern*	200	400	450

SHOTGUN, DOUBLE BARREL, SIDE-BY-SIDE

Ventura Model 51, 12 and 20 Gauges, Boxlock, Checkered Stock, *Modern*	150	350	400
Ventura Model 62 Standard, 12 and 20 Gauges, Sidelock, Checkered Stock, Engraved, *Modern*	400	800	900
Ventura Model 64 Standard, 12 and 20 Gauges, Sidelock, Checkered Stock, Engraved, *Modern*	350	775	850

VENUS

Tomas de Urizar y Cia., Eibar, Spain.

HANDGUN, SEMI-AUTOMATIC

7.65mm, Clip Fed, *Modern*	50	100	150

VENUS

Venus Waffenwerk Oskar Will, Zella Mehils, Germany, c. 1912.

HANDGUN, SEMI-AUTOMATIC

7.65mm, Target Pistol, Hammerless, Blue, *Curio*	250	500	600

VERNEY-CARRON

St. Etienne, France.

HANDGUN, SEMI-AUTOMATIC

6.35mm, Clip Fed, Blue, *Modern*	75	150	175

SHOTGUN, DOUBLE BARREL, OVER-UNDER

Field Grade, 12 Ga., Automatic Ejectors, Checkered Stock, Engraved, *Modern*	400	800	950

VESTA

Hijos de A. Echevera, Eibar, Spain.

HANDGUN, SEMI-AUTOMATIC

Pocket, 7.65mm, Clip Fed, Long Grip, *Modern*	75	125	150

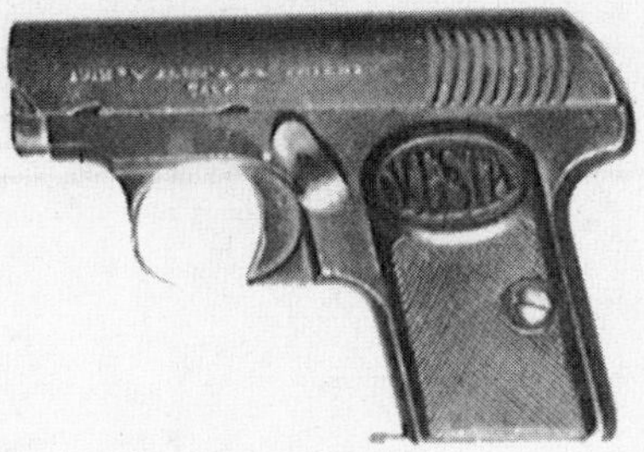

Vesta

	Fair	V. Good	Excellent
Vest Pocket, 6.35mm, Clip Fed, *Modern*	$75	$100	$125

VETERAN

Made by Norwich Falls Pistol Co., c. 1880.

HANDGUN, REVOLVER

.32 Short R.F., 5 Shot, Spur Trigger, Solid Frame, Single Action, *Antique*	75	125	175

VETO

c. 1880.

HANDGUN, REVOLVER

.32 Short R.F., 5 Shot, Spur Trigger, Solid Frame, Single Action, *Antique*	125	150	175

VICI

Belgian.

HANDGUN, SEMI-AUTOMATIC

7.65mm, Clip Fed, *Modern*	75	100	125

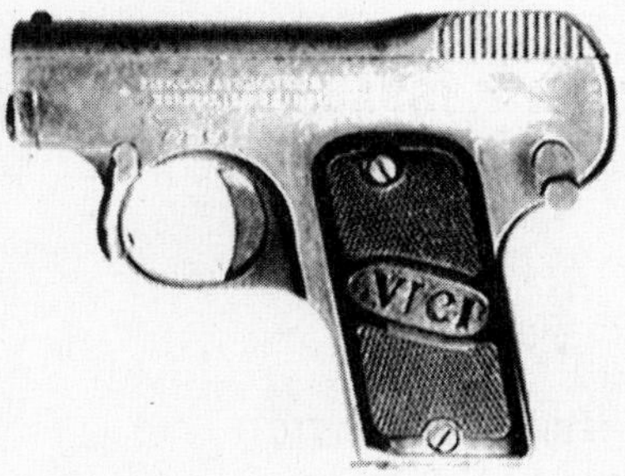

Vici

VICTOR

Francisco Arizmendi, Eibar, Spain, c. 1916.

HANDGUN, SEMI-AUTOMATIC

6.35mm, Clip Fed, Blue, *Curio*	75	100	125

	Fair	V. Good	Excellent
7.65mm, Clip Fed, Blue, *Curio*	$100	$125	$150

VICTOR

Made by Crescent, c. 1900. See Crescent Fire Arms Co., Shotgun, Double Barrel, Side-by-Side; Shotgun, Singleshot.

VICTOR # 1

Made by Harrington & Richardson, c. 1876.

HANDGUN, REVOLVER

	Fair	V. Good	Excellent
#1, .22 Short R.F., 7 Shot, Spur Trigger, Solid Frame, Single Action, *Antique*	125	150	175
#2, .32 Short R.F., 5 Shot, Spur Trigger, Solid Frame, Single Action, *Antique*	125	150	175
.32 S & W, 5 Shot, Single Action, Solid Frame, *Antique*	50	75	100

VICTOR SPECIAL

Made by Crescent for Hibbard-Spencer-Bartlett Co., c. 1900. See Crescent Fire Arms Co., Shotgun, Double Barrel, Side-by-Side; Shotgun, Singleshot.

VICTORIA

Made by Hood Firearms, c. 1875.

HANDGUN, REVOLVER

	Fair	V. Good	Excellent
.32 Short R.F., 5 Shot, Spur Trigger, Solid Frame, Single Action, *Antique*	125	150	175

VICTORIA

Spain, Esperanza y Unceta, c. 1900.

HANDGUN, SEMI-AUTOMATIC

	Fair	V. Good	Excellent
6.35mm, Clip Fed, *Modern*	75	100	125
M1911, .32 ACP, Clip Fed, *Modern*	100	125	150

Victoria

VICTORY

M. Zulaica y Cia., Eibar, Spain.

HANDGUN, SEMI-AUTOMATIC

	Fair	V. Good	Excellent
6.35mm, Clip Fed, *Modern*	$50	$100	$150

VILAR

Spain, 1920–1938.

HANDGUN, SEMI-AUTOMATIC

	Fair	V. Good	Excellent
Pocket, 7.65mm, Clip Fed, Long Grip, *Modern*	75	100	125

VINCITOR

M. Zulaica y Cia., Eibar, Spain.

HANDGUN, SEMI-AUTOMATIC

	Fair	V. Good	Excellent
Model 14 No. 2, 7.65mm, Clip Fed, Blue, *Curio*	125	150	175
Model 1914, 6.35mm, Clip Fed, Blue, *Curio*	100	125	150

VINDEX

Mre. d'Armes des Pyrenees, Hendaye, France.

HANDGUN, SEMI-AUTOMATIC

	Fair	V. Good	Excellent
7.65mm, Clip Fed, Blue, *Modern*	75	100	125

VIRGINIA ARMS CO.

Made by Crescent for Virginia-Caroline Co., c. 1900. See Crescent Fire Arms Co., Shotgun, Double Barrel, Side-by-Side; Shotgun, Singleshot.

VIRGINIAN

Imported and manufactured (1976–1984) by Interarms, Alexandria, Va.

HANDGUN, REVOLVER

	Fair	V. Good	Excellent
Dragoon, Buntline, Various Calibers, Single Action, Western Style, Target Sights, Blue, *Modern*	150	200	250
Dragoon, Deputy, Various Calibers, Single Action, Western Style, Fixed Sights, Blue, *Modern*	150	175	200
Dragoon, Deputy, Various Calibers, Single Action, Western Style, Fixed Sights, Stainless Steel, *Modern*	125	175	225
Dragoon, Engraved, Various Calibers, Single Action, Western Style, Target Sights, Blue, *Modern*	300	375	450
Dragoon, Engraved, Various Calibers, Single Action, Western Style, Target Sights, Presentation Case, *Modern*	275	400	525

	Fair	V. Good	Excellent
Dragoon, Silhouette, .44 Magnum, Single Action, Western Style, Target Sights, Stainless Steel, *Modern*	$175	$225	$275
Dragoon, Standard, Various Calibers, Single Action, Western Style, Target Sights, Blue, *Modern*	175	200	225
Dragoon, Standard, Various Calibers, Single Action, Western Style, Target Sights, Stainless Steel, *Modern*	150	200	250

VITE

Echave y Arizmendi, Eibar, Spain, c. 1913.

HANDGUN, SEMI-AUTOMATIC

	Fair	V. Good	Excellent
Model 1912, 6.35mm, Clip Fed, Blue, *Curio*	75	100	125
Model 1915, 7.65mm, Clip Fed, Blue, *Curio*	100	125	150

VOERE

Voere GmbH, Vohrenbach, West Germany. Owned by Mauser since 1987.

RIFLE, BOLT ACTION

	Fair	V. Good	Excellent
Model 2145, .308 Win., Match Rifle, Target Stock, *Modern*	350	700	800
Model 3145 DJV, .223 Rem., Match Rifle, Target Stock, *Modern*	250	500	550
Premier Mauser, Various Calibers, Sporting Rifle, Checkered Stock, Recoil Pad, Open Rear Sight, *Modern*	150	300	350
Shikar, Various Calibers, Sporting Rifle, Fancy Checkering, Fancy Wood, Recoil Pad, No Sights, *Modern*	$200	$450	$500
Titan-Menor, Various Calibers, Sporting Rifle, Checkered Stock, Recoil Pad, Open Rear Sight, *Modern*	150	350	400

VOERE

Voere Tiroler Jagd u. Sportwaffenfabrik, Kufstein, Austria.

RIFLE, BOLT ACTION

	Fair	V. Good	Excellent
Model 2155, Various Calibers, Sporting Rifle, Checkered Stock, Open Rear Sight, *Modern*	150	325	375
Model 2165/1, Various Calibers, Sporting Rifle, Checkered Stock, Recoil Pad, Open Rear Sight, *Modern*	200	475	525

VOLUNTEER

Made by Stevens Arms for Belknap Hardware Co., Louisville, Ky.

SHOTGUN, SINGLESHOT

	Fair	V. Good	Excellent
Model 94, Various Gauges, Takedown, Automatic Ejector, Plain, Hammer, *Modern*	25	50	75

VULCAN ARMS CO.

Made by Crescent, c. 1900. See Crescent Fire Arms Co., Shotgun, Double Barrel, Side-By-Side; Shotgun, Singleshot.

W

WAFFENFABRIK BERN

Eidgenossische Waffenfabrik, Bern, Switzerland. Also see Swiss Military.

RIFLE, BOLT ACTION

	Fair	V. Good	Excellent
Model 31, 7.5mm Swiss, Military Style, *Modern*	$250	$575	$650
Model 31 Target, 7.5mm Swiss, Military Style, Match Rifle, Target Sights, *Modern*	350	775	850

WALDMAN

Arizmendi Y Goenaga, Eibar, Spain.

HANDGUN, SEMI-AUTOMATIC

	Fair	V. Good	Excellent
6.35mm, Clip Fed, *Curio*	75	100	125
7.65mm, Clip Fed, *Curio*	75	125	150

WALMAN

F. Arizmendi Y Goenaga, Eibar, Spain.

HANDGUN, SEMI-AUTOMATIC

	Fair	V. Good	Excellent
.380 ACP, Clip Fed, *Curio*	100	175	225
6.35mm, Clip Fed, *Curio*	50	100	125
7.65mm, Clip Fed, *Curio*	75	125	150

WALSH FIREARMS CO.

New York City, c. 1860.

HANDGUN, PERCUSSION

	Fair	V. Good	Excellent
Navy, .36, Revolver, 12 Shot, Double-Charge Cylinder, *Antique*	1400	3000	3500
Pocket, .31, Revolver, 12 Shot, Double-Charge Cylinder, *Antique*	700	1500	1750

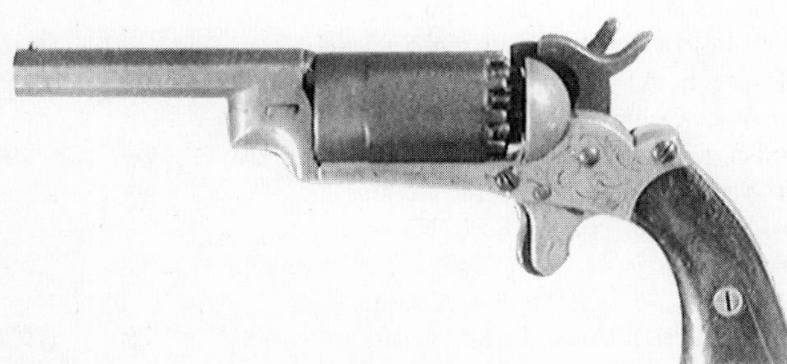

Walsh Pocket .31

WALSH, JAMES

Philadelphia, Pa. 1775–1779. See Kentucky Rifles and Pistols and U.S. Military.

WALTHER

First started in 1886 by Carl Walther in Zella Mehlis, Germany. After his death in 1915 the firm was operated by his sons Fritz, George, and Erich. Post WWII production in Ulm/Donau, West Germany. Also see German Military and Manurhin.

AIRGUNS

	Fair	V. Good	Excellent
Model CP-2 C02, .177 Caliber, Singleshot, Blue	$200	$500	$600
Model LGR Match, .177 Caliber, Singleshot, Blue	600	1250	1500
Model LGR Running Boar, .177 Caliber, Singleshot, Blue	500	1000	1250
Model LGR, .177 Caliber, Singleshot, Blue	400	800	1000
Model LP-3, .177 Caliber, Singleshot, Blue	150	375	475

TARGET PISTOLS

	Fair	V. Good	Excellent
Model GSP C, .22 Short, 5 Shot Clip, Target Pistol, *Modern*	500	1050	1100
Model GSP C, .22 Short, 5 Shot Clip, Target Pistol, with .22 L.R. Conversion Kit	350	750	1000
Model GSP, .22 L.R.R.F., 5 Shot Clip, Target Pistol, *Modern*	400	950	1200
Model OSP, .22 Short, Blue, Five Rounds Capacity, *Modern*	400	850	1100
Olympia Rapid Fire, .22 L.R.R.F., Target Pistol, *Modern*	350	750	900
Olympia Sport, .22 L.R.R.F., Target Pistol, *Modern*	350	600	850

HANDGUN, SEMI-AUTOMATIC—PRE 1945

	Fair	V. Good	Excellent
ac40 (40 added), 9mm, Double Action, *Curio*	450	1200	1500
Model 1, .25 ACP, Blue, *Curio*	200	400	450
Model 2, .25 ACP, Pop-Up Rear Sight, Blue, *Curio*	250	950	1350
Model 3, .32 ACP, Blue, *Curio*	500	1250	1500
Model 4, .32 ACP, Blue, *Curio*	150	350	400
Model 5, .25 ACP, Solid Rib, Blue, *Curio*	150	300	350
Model 6, 9mm Luger, Blue, *Curio*	2000	4500	5500
Model 7, .25 ACP, Blue, *Curio*	275	450	625
Model 8, .25 ACP, Blue, *Curio*	200	375	500

	Fair	V. Good	Excellent
Model 9, .25 ACP, Blue, *Curio*	$200	$400	$500
Model HP, .30 Luger, Single Action, *Curio*	2000	4000	5000
Model HP, .30 Luger, Single Action, Wood Grips, *Curio*	2500	4500	5500
Model HP, 9mm, H Prefix Serial Number, *Curio*	600	1200	1500
Model HP, 9mm, Hi-Gloss Blue, *Curio*	500	1000	1200
Model HP, 9mm, Military, Blue with Eagle/359 on Right Slide, *Curio*	500	1000	1200
Model HP, 9mm, Military, Blue, *Curio*	400	800	1000
Model HP, Commercial Finish, 9mm Luger, Double Action, Lightweight, *Curio*	1600	3500	4000
Model P38, 9mm, *Curio*	600	1200	1500
P-38 ac-45 Zero Series, 9mm, Double Action, Military, *Curio*	400	800	1000
P-38, "480," 9mm, Double Action, Military, *Curio*	600	1300	2000
P-38, 1st, Model Zero Series, 9mm, Double Action, *Curio*	1600	3500	4500
P-38, 2nd, Model Zero Series, 9mm, Double Action, Military, *Curio*	900	2200	3500
P-38, 3rd, Model Zero Series, 9mm, Double Action, Military, *Curio*	500	900	1200
P-38, ac No Date, 9mm, Double Action, Military, *Curio*	2200	5000	6000
P-38, ac-40, 9mm, Double Action, Military, *Curio*	450	1200	1500
P-38, ac-41 Military Finish, 9mm, Double Action, Military, *Curio*	250	500	650
P-38, ac-41, 9mm, Double Action, Military, *Curio*	400	800	1000
P-38, ac-42, 9mm, Double Action, Military, *Curio*	250	450	650
P-38, ac-43 Double Line, 9mm, Double Action, Military, *Curio*	200	400	500
P-38, ac-43 Police, 9mm, Double Action, Military, *Curio*	1000	2500	3000
P-38, ac-43 WaA 135, 9mm, Double Action, Military, *Curio*	450	900	1200
P-38, ac-43, Single Line, 9mm, Double Action, Military, *Curio*	225	500	700
P-38, ac-44 WaA140 Frame, 9mm, Double Action, Military, *Curio*	200	425	500
P-38, ac-44 Police, 9mm, Double Action, Military, *Curio*	1100	2500	3000
P-38, ac-44, 9mm, Double Action, Military, *Curio*	150	325	400
P-38, ac-45 Mismatch, 9mm, Double Action, Military, *Curio*	150	300	375
P-38, ac-45, 9mm, Double Action, Military, *Curio*	175	350	400
P-38, byf-42, 9mm, Double Action, Military, *Curio*	300	650	800
P-38, byf-43 Police, 9mm, Double Action, Military, *Curio*	500	1000	1500

	Fair	V. Good	Excellent
P-38, byf-43, 9mm, Double Action, Military, *Curio*	$300	$400	$500
P-38, byf-44 police F Dual T, 9mm, Double Action, Military, *Curio*	500	1000	1500
P-38, byf-44 Police L Dual T, 9mm, Double Action, Military, *Curio*	1100	1800	2500
P-38, byf-44 Police L, 9mm, Double Action, Military, *Curio*	500	1000	1500
P-38, byf-44, 9mm, Double Action, Military, *Curio*	300	400	500
P-38, crq Zero Series, 9mm, Double Action, Military, *Curio*	450	600	750
P-38, crq, 9mm, A or B Prefix, *Curio*	300	450	600
P-38, crq, 9mm, Double Action, Military, *Curio*	275	325	375
P-38, svw-45 French, 9mm, Double Action, Military, *Curio*	200	350	400
P-38, svw-45 Police, 9mm, Double Action, Military, *Curio*	1000	2500	3000
P-38, svw-45, 9mm, Double Action, Military, *Curio*	300	700	800
P-38, svw-46 French, 9mm, Double Action, Military, *Curio*	200	400	500
PP "A.F. Stoeger, Inc., New York," .32 ACP, Double Action, Pre-War, High-Polish Finish, *Curio*	500	1250	1500
PP "Chas A. Heyer & Co., Nairobi," .32 ACP, Double Action, Pre-War, High-Polish Finish, *Curio*			Rare
PP (Early) 90 Degree Safety, .32 ACP, Double Action, Pre-War, Commercial, High-Polish Finish, *Curio*	300	700	775
PP (Early) Bottom Magazine, .380 ACP, Double Action, Pre-War, Commercial, High-Polish Finish, *Curio*	400	800	900
PP AC Police F, .32 ACP, Double Action, Pre-War, Nazi-Proofed, *Curio*	300	700	775
PP AC Waffenamt, .32 ACP, Double Action, Pre-War, Nazi-Proofed, *Curio*	200	350	400
PP AC, .32 ACP, Double Action, Nazi-Proofed, *Curio*	125	275	300
PP Bottom Magazine Release, .32 ACP, Double Action, Pre-War, Commercial, High-Polish Finish, *Curio*	400	850	1000
PP Bottom Magazine Release, .32 ACP, Double Action, Pre-War, Commercial, High-Polish Finish, Lightweight, *Curio*			Rare
PP Czech, .32 ACP, Double Action, Pre-War, Commercial, High- Polish Finish, *Curio*	400	800	900
PP NSKK, .32 ACP, Double Action, Pre-War, High-Polish Finish, Nazi-Proofed, *Curio*	900	2000	2500
PP PDM, .32 ACP, Double Action, Pre-War, High-Polish Finish, *Curio*	300	750	900
PP Persian, .380 ACP, Double Action, Pre-War, Commercial, High-Polish Finish, *Curio*	900	1800	2000

	Fair	V. Good	Excellent
PP Police C, .32 ACP, Double Action, Pre-War, High-Polish Finish, Nazi-Proofed, *Curio*	$450	$900	$1150
PP Police C, .32 ACP, Double Action, Pre-War, Nazi-Proofed, *Curio*	350	725	800
PP Police F, .32 ACP, Double Action, Pre-War, Nazi-Proofed, *Curio*	300	600	650
PP RFV, .32 ACP, Double Action, Pre-War, High-Polish, *Curio*	300	600	650
PP RJ, .32 ACP, Double Action, Pre-War, High-Polish Finish, *Curio*	300	650	700
PP SA, .32 ACP, Double Action, Pre-War, High-Polish Finish, *Curio*	600	1250	1500
PP Verchromt, .32 ACP, Double Action, Pre-War, Commercial, *Curio*	600	1250	1500
PP Verchromt, .380 ACP, Double Action, Pre-War, Commercial, *Curio*	900	1800	2250
PP Waffenamt, .32 ACP, Double Action, Pre-War, High-Polish Finish, Nazi-Proofed, *Curio*	200	450	500
PP Waffenamt, .32 ACP, Double Action, Pre-War, Nazi-Proofed, *Curio*	200	400	450
PP Waffenamt, .380 ACP, Double Action, Pre-War, High-Polish Finish, Nazi-Proofed, *Curio*	400	850	1000
PP with Lanyard Loop, .32 ACP, Double Action, Pre-War, Commercial, High-Polish Finish, Nazi-Proofed, *Modern*	200	450	500
PP, .22 L.R.R.F., Double Action, Pre-War, Commercial, Nickel Plated, *Curio*			Rare
PP, .22 L.R.R.F., Double Action, Pre-War, Commercial, Nickel Plated, Nazi-Proofed, *Curio*			Rare
PP, .22 L.R.R.F., Double Action, Pre-War, Commercial, High-Polish Finish, *Curio*	300	750	900
PP, .22 L.R.R.F., Double Action, Pre-War, Commercial, High-Polish Finish, Nazi-Proofed, *Curio*	300	750	900
PP, .25 ACP, Double Action, Pre-War, Commercial, High-Polish Finish, *Curio*	1400	3000	3250
PP, .32 ACP, Double Action, Pre-War, Commercial, High-Polished Finish, *Curio*	200	400	450
PP, .32 ACP, Double Action, Pre-War, Commercial, High-Polished Finish, Nazi-Proofed, *Curio*	200	400	450
PP, .32 ACP, Double Action, Pre-War, Commercial, Lightweight, High-Polish Finish, *Curio*	300	600	675
PP, .32 ACP, Double Action, Pre-War, Commercial, Nazi-Proofed, *Curio*	150	325	375
PP, .32 ACP, Double Action, Pre-War, Commercial, Nickel Plated, Nazi-Proofed, *Curio*			Rare
PP, .32 ACP, Double Action, Pre-War, Commercial, Nickel Plated, *Curio*			Rare
PP, .32 ACP, Double Action, Pre-War, Nazi-Proofed, Lightweight, High-Polish Finish, *Curio*	$300	$600	$675
PP, .32 ACP, Double Action, Pre-War, Nazi-Proofed, Lightweight, *Curio*	200	400	450
PP, .380 ACP, Double Action, Pre-War, Commercial, High-Polish Finish, *Curio*	400	800	900
PP, .380 ACP, Double Action, Pre-War, Commercial, High-Polish Finish, Nazi-Proofed, *Curio*	400	800	900
PP, .380 ACP, Double Action, Pre-War, Commercial, Nickel Plated, *Curio*			Rare
PP, .380 ACP, Double Action, Pre-War, Commercial, Nickel Plated, Nazi-Proofed, *Curio*			Rare
PPK "Cas A. Heyer & Co., Nairobi," .32 ACP, Double Action, Pre- War, High-Polish Finish, *Curio*			Rare
PPK "Stoeger," .32 ACP, Double Action, Pre-War, High-Polish Finish, *Curio*			Rare
PPK (Early) 90 Degree Safety, .32 ACP, Double Action, Pre-War, Commercial, High-Polish Finish, *Curio*	250	550	600
PPK Czech, .32 ACP, Double Action, Pre-War, Commercial, High- Polish Finish, *Curio*	400	850	1000
PPK DRP, .32 ACP, Double Action, Pre-War, High-Polish Finish, *Curio*	400	850	900
PPK Party Leader, .32 ACP, Double Action, Pre-War, High-Polish Finish, *Curio*	900	2250	2500
PPK PDM, .32 ACP, Double Action, Pre-War, High-Polish Finish, Lightweight, *Curio*	600	1350	1500
PPK Police C, .32 ACP, Double Action, Pre-War, High-Polish Finish, Nazi-Proofed, *Curio*	300	675	750
PPK Police C, .32 ACP, Double Action, Pre-War, Nazi-Proofed, *Curio*	250	550	600
PPK Police F, .32 ACP, Double Action, Pre-War, Nazi-Proofed, *Curio*	400	800	900
PPK RFV, *Curio*	400	850	950
PPK RZM, .32 ACP, Double Action, Pre-War, High-Polish Finish, *Curio*	400	850	900
PPK Verchromt, .32 ACP, Double Action, Pre-War, Commercial, *Curio*	800	1800	2000

	Fair	V. Good	Excellent
PPK Verchromt, .380 ACP, Double Action, Pre-War, High-Polish Finish, *Curio*	$900	$2000	$2250
PPK Waffenamt, .32 ACP, Double Action, Pre-War, High-Polish Finish, Nazi-Proofed, *Curio*	400	875	1000
PPK Waffenamt, .32 ACP, Double Action, Pre-War, Nazi-Proofed, *Curio*	350	750	800
PPK, .22 L.R.R.F., Double Action, Pre-War, Commercial, High-Polish Finish, *Curio*	500	1000	1200
PPK, .22 L.R.R.F., Double Action, Pre-War, Commercial, High-Polish Finish, Nazi-Proofed, *Curio*	500	1000	1200
PPK, .25 ACP, Double Action, Pre-War, Commercial, High-Polish Finish, *Curio*	2500	4500	5500
PPK, .32 ACP, Double Action, Pre-War, Commercial, High-Polish Finish, *Curio*	225	475	525
PPK, .32 ACP, Double Action, Pre-War, Commercial, High-Polish Finish, Nazi-Proofed, *Curio*	225	475	525
PPK, .32 ACP, Double Action, Pre-War, Commercial, Lightweight, High-Polish Finish, *Curio*	300	650	700
PPK, .32 ACP, Double Action, Pre-War, Commercial, Nazi-Proofed, *Curio*	200	450	500
PPK, .32 ACP, Double Action, Pre-War, Nazi-Proofed, Lightweight, High-Polish Finish, *Curio*	300	650	700
PPK, .32 ACP, Double Action, Pre-War, Nazi-Proofed, Lightweight, *Curio*	250	550	600
PPK, .380 ACP, Double Action, Pre-War, Commercial, High-Polish Finish, *Curio*	900	1800	2000
PPK, .380 ACP, Double Action, Pre-War, Commercial, High-Polish Finish, Nazi-Proofed, *Curio*	900	1800	2000
PPK, .380 ACP, Double Action, Pre-War, Commercial, Nickel Plated, *Curio*			Rare
PPK, .380 ACP, Double Action, Pre-War, Commercial, Nickel Plated, Nazi-Proofed, *Curio*			Rare

HANDGUN, SEMI-AUTOMATIC—POSTWAR

	Fair	V. Good	Excellent
P-1, 9mm, Double Action, Alloy Frame, *Modern*	150	350	450
P-38, .22 L.R.R.F., Double Action, *Modern*	300	600	850
P-38, .30 Luger, Double Action, Blue, *Modern*	350	700	850
P-38, 9mm, Double Action, *Modern*	200	500	600
P-38-IV (P-4), 9mm, Double Action, *Modern*	200	450	500
P-38k, 9mm, Double Action, Short Barrel, *Modern*	$400	$700	$800
P-5, 9mm, Interarms, Double Action, Blue, *Modern*	250	550	700
PP Super, 9 × 18mm, Clip Fed, Blue, *Modern*	200	500	650
PP, .22 L.R.R.F., Double Action, *Modern*	250	500	650
PP, .32 ACP, Double Action, Blue, *Modern*	200	450	600
PP, .380 ACP, Double Action, Blue, *Modern*	250	500	650
PPK, .22 L.R.R.F., Double Action, Lightweight, Post-War, *Modern*	300	600	700
PPK, .22 L.R.R.F., Double Action, Post-War, *Modern*	300	650	750
PPK, .32 ACP, Double Action, Lightweight, Post-War, *Modern*	200	425	500
PPK, .32 ACP, Double Action, Post-War, *Modern*	200	450	525
PPK, .380 ACP, Double Action, *Modern*	300	600	700
PPK/S, .22 L.R.R.F., Double Action, *Modern*	250	575	650
PPK/S, .32 ACP, Double Action, Blue, *Modern*	200	425	475
PPK/S, .380 ACP, Double Action, Blue, *Modern*	250	525	600
PPK/S, .380 ACP, Double Action, Blue, Seven Rounds Capacity, *Modern*	200	400	500
PPK/S, .380 ACP, Double Action, Stainless Steel, Seven Rounds Capacity, *Modern*	200	400	500
TPH, .22 L.R.R.F., Double Action, Clip-Fed, *Modern*	250	500	650
TPH, .22 L.R.R.F., Double Action, Clip-Fed, German Manuf., *Modern*	200	400	575
TPH, .25 ACP, Double Action, Clip-Fed, *Modern*	175	350	450
TPH, .25 ACP, Double Action, Clip-Fed, German Manuf., *Modern*	175	375	600

HANDGUN, SEMI-AUTOMATIC—WALTHER MARK II

	Fair	V. Good	Excellent
PP Mark II "Manurhin," .22 L.R.R.F., Double Action, High-Polish Finish, Blue, *Curio*	150	350	425
PP Mark II "Manurhin," .32 ACP, Double Action, High-Polish Finish, Blue, *Curio*	150	300	375
PP Mark II "Manurhin," .380 ACP, Double Action, High-Polish Finish, Blue, *Curio*	150	300	400
PPK Mark II "Manurhin," .22 L.R.R.F., Double Action, High-Polish Finish, Blue, *Curio*	225	500	550
PPK Mark II "Manurhin," .22 L.R.R.F., Double Action, High-Polish Finish, Blue, Lightweight, *Curio*	225	500	550

	Fair	V. Good	Excellent
PPK Mark II "Manurhin," .32 ACP, Double Action, High-Polish Finish, Blue, *Curio*	$150	$375	$450
PPK Mark II "Manurhin," .32 ACP, Double Action, High-Polish Finish, Blue, Lightweight, *Curio*	200	450	500
PPK Mark II "Manurhin," .380 ACP, Double Action, High-Polish Finish, Blue, *Curio*	250	500	550

RIFLE, BOLT ACTION

	Fair	V. Good	Excellent
KKJ, .22 Hornet, 5 Shot Clip, Open Rear Sight, Checkered Stock, *Modern*	250	500	700
KKJ, .22 Hornet, 5 Shot Clip, Open Rear Sight, Checkered Stock, Set Trigger, *Modern*	300	650	850
KKJ, .22 L.R.R.F., 5 Shot Clip, Open Rear Sight, Checkered Stock, *Modern*	200	400	500
KKJ, .22 L.R.R.F., 5 Shot Clip, Open Rear Sight, Checkered Stock, Set Trigger, *Modern*	200	450	600
KKJ, .22 WMR, 5 Shot Clip, Open Rear Sight, Checkered Stock, *Modern*	250	500	700
KKJ, .22 WMR, 5 Shot Clip, Open Rear Sight, Checkered Stock, Set Trigger, *Modern*	300	650	850
KKM International Match, .22 L.R.R.F., Singleshot, Target Stock, with Accessories, *Modern*	300	600	800
KKM-S Silhouette, .22 L.R., Singleshot, Blue, *Modern*	300	650	850
Model B, Various Caliber, Checkered Stock, Mauser Action, Set Triggers, *Modern*	150	350	425
Model GX-1, .22 L.R., Singleshot, Blue, *Modern*	600	1200	1500
Model KKW, .22 L.R.R.F., Pre-WW2, Singleshot, Tangent Sights, Military Style Stock, *Modern*	150	350	500
Model V "Meisterbushe," Singleshot, Pistol-Grip Stock, Target Sights, *Modern*	150	350	450
Model V, Singleshot, Sporting Rifle, Open Rear Sight, *Modern*	150	300	375
Moving Target, .22 L.R.R.F., Singleshot, Target Stock, with Accessories, *Modern*	225	550	700
Olympic, .22 L.R.R.F., Singleshot, Target Stock, with Accessories, *Modern*	350	750	950
Prone "400," .22 L.R.R.F., Singleshot, Target Stock, with Accessories, *Modern*	225	550	650
Running Boar, .22 L.R., Singleshot, Blue, *Modern*	300	650	900
U.I.T.-E. Universal Match, .22 L.R., Singleshot, Blue, *Modern*	400	950	1200
UIT Match, .22 L.R.R.F., Singleshot, Target Stock, with Accessories, *Modern*	$350	$750	$1000
UIT Special, .22 L.R.R.F., Singleshot, Target Stock, with Accessories, *Modern*	450	900	1200

RIFLE, SEMI-AUTOMATIC

	Fair	V. Good	Excellent
Model 1, Clip Fed, Carbine, *Modern*	150	300	375
Model 2, .22 L.R.R.F., Clip Fed, *Modern*	175	375	475

SHOTGUN, DOUBLE BARREL, SIDE-BY-SIDE

	Fair	V. Good	Excellent
Model S.F., 12 or 16 Gauges, Checkered Stock, Cheekpiece, Double Triggers, Sling Swivels, *Modern*	175	375	475
Model S.F.D., 12 or 16 Gauges, Checkered Stock, Cheekpiece, Double Triggers, Sling Swivels, *Modern*	250	500	600

WAMO

Wamo Mfg. Co., San Gabriel, Calif.

HANDGUN, SINGLESHOT

	Fair	V. Good	Excellent
Powermaster, .22 L.R.R.F., Target Pistol, *Modern*	75	100	125

WARNANT

L. & J. Warnant Freres, Hognee, Belgium.

HANDGUN, REVOLVER

	Fair	V. Good	Excellent
.32 S & W, Double Action, Folding Trigger, Break Top, *Curio*	50	75	100
.38 S & W, Double Action, Folding Trigger, Break Top, *Curio*	75	100	125

HANDGUN, SEMI-AUTOMATIC

	Fair	V. Good	Excellent
6.35mm, Clip Fed, Blue, *Curio*	125	175	225

HANDGUN, SINGLESHOT

	Fair	V. Good	Excellent
Traff, 6mm R.F., Spur Trigger, Parlor Pistol, *Curio*	75	100	125
Traff, 9mm R.F., Spur Trigger, Parlor Pistol, *Curio*	75	100	125

RIFLE, SINGLESHOT

	Fair	V. Good	Excellent
Amelung, Various Rimfires, Checkered Stock, Set Triggers, Parlor Rifle, *Curio*	50	75	100
Amelung, Various Rimfires, Plain, Parlor Rifle, *Curio*	25	50	75

WARNER

Warner Arms Corp., Brooklyn, N.Y., formed about 1912, moved to Norwich, Conn. in 1913, and in 1917 merged and became Davis-Warner Arms Corp., Assonet, Mass., out of business about 1919. See also Schwarzlose.

SEMI-AUTOMATIC

	Fair	V. Good	Excellent
Infallable, .32 ACP, Clip Fed, *Modern*	$150	$275	$300
Revolver, .32 CAL., 5-Shot, *Modern*	75	125	150

WARREN ARMS CORP.

Belgium, c. 1900.

SHOTGUN, DOUBLE BARREL, SIDE-BY-SIDE

	Fair	V. Good	Excellent
Various Gauges, Hammerless, Damascus Barrel, *Modern*	75	150	175
Various Gauges, Hammerless, Steel Barrel, *Modern*	100	175	200
Various Gauges, Outside Hammers, Damascus Barrel, *Modern*	75	150	175
Various Gauges, Outside Hammers, Steel Barrel, *Modern*	100	175	200

SHOTGUN, SINGLESHOT

	Fair	V. Good	Excellent
Various Gauges, Hammer, Steel Barrel, *Modern*	50	75	100

WATSON BROS.

London, England 1885–1931.

RIFLE, BOLT ACTION

	Fair	V. Good	Excellent
.303 British, Express Sights, Sporting Rifle, Checkered Stock, *Modern*	300	625	700

RIFLE, DOUBLE BARREL, SIDE-BY-SIDE

	Fair	V. Good	Excellent
.450/.400 N.E. 3", Double Trigger, Recoil Pad, Plain, Cased, *Modern*	2000	4000	5000

WATTERS, JOHN

Carlisle, Pa. 1778–1785. See Kentucky Rifles.

WEATHERBY

South Gate, Calif. 1945 to date. Designer, sportsman, ballistician and gunmaker Roy E. Weatherby planted the seed for his future fame and fortune while experimenting with high performance cartridges of his own design in 1937. The company he founded in 1945 made its reputation from an exclusive series of hunting rifles and high velocity ammunition, built to demanding standards for the discriminating outdoorsman and adventurer. Weatherby's experiments were in the designs of cartridge cases, capacities of powders, and calibers of the projectiles. The theories of this dedicated rifleman and ballistician were based on bullet speed being more important to the sportsman than bullet size and weight. The "one shot kill" became his goal. Extensive testing and experimentation revealed that fast-traveling bullets follow a trajectory flatter and of greater power. When striking their prey, the projectiles create extraordinary hydrostatic shock. The first Weatherby magnum high velocity cartridge was available to the public in 1945, built on such actions as the Mauser, Springfield Model 1903, the Enfield, and the Winchester Model 70. Beginning in the 1950s Weatherbys were built on the FN action, but the designer's goal was to build rifles on actions of his own design. Accordingly in 1958 he introduced the Weatherby Mark V, described as "a truly innovative mechanical design with nine locking lugs instead of the usual two, a streamlined enclosed bolt sleeve and a counterbored bolt face to receive and totally enclose the cartridge case head." The new rifle offered several features: "a hammer-forged barrel, fluted bolt body with three gas escape ports, and a high-luster epoxy stock finish." Many experienced hunters regarded the new rifle as the finest available for its price in the world. Weatherby's Mark V is built in the following calibers of the inventor's own design: .224 W.M. Varmintmaster (with a scaled down action, having six locking lugs), .240 W.M., .257 W.M., .270 W.M., 7 mm W.M., .30-06 Mark V, .300 W.M. (one of the world's finest sporting rifle cartridges), .340 W.M., .378 W.M., and the .460 W.M. Weatherby later developed a sophisticated over-and-under shotgun, as well as a special series of rifle, known as the Vanguard. This bolt-action series features a construction described by the factory as "rugged," with the quality and several details of the Mark V series. The shotguns are the Athena and the Orion, available initially in 12 and 20 gauges, but soon offered in 28 and .410 as well. In the mid 1990s, Weatherby brought out a competitive shotgun—the Athena Master—for skeet shooting. Billed as the "most versatile, and beautiful shotgun ever made," the Athena Master is fitted with double sets of barrels in 12, 20, 28, and .410 gauges! Weatherby prides itself on the excellence of its stock wood, usually selected from blanks of Northern California walnut. These carefully selected, thoroughly seasoned, and finely built stocks are a hallmark of Weatherby rifles and shotguns. The company also rests its reputation on the "consistent performance, durability and value" of its products. In 1989 Weatherby added its first cartridge to the original list of nine: the .416 Weatherby. The .416 was developed to offer a further choice for big game hunters, between the .378 and the .460. The company also refined the Vanguard group of bolt-actions, and added the Classic II model, featuring traditional styling, and such detailing as oil-finished stocks. The Vanguard Classics' appearance combined English elegance with American strength and durability. The result was a rifle series in distinct contrast to the original California style of Weatherby bolt-actions. Among other details of the Vanguard Classics are the hammer-forged barrels, the matte blue finish, and individual inletting and hand-bedding to the barreled actions. Still another innovation was the firm's addition of the Mark XXII semi-automatic .22 long rifle repeater (with singleshot selector system), "Weatherguard" synthetic stocks, and the development of a line of accessories—cases, slings, caps, jewelry, loading dies, and the famous lucite cartridge display block.

HANDGUN, SINGLESHOT

	Fair	V. Good	Excellent
Mk. V. Silhouette, Various Calibers, Thumbhole Target Stock, Target Sights, *Modern*	$800	$1750	$2000

RIFLE, BOLT ACTION

	Fair	V. Good	Excellent
Deluxe, .378 Wby. Mag., Magnum, Checkered Stock, *Modern*	400	850	950

	Fair	V. Good	Excellent
Deluxe, Various Calibers, Checkered Stock, *Modern*	$400	$800	$900
Deluxe, Various Calibers, Magnum, Checkered Stock, *Modern*	400	825	925
For German Manufacture, Add 30%-50%			
Mark V Crown Custom, Various Calibers, 24" or 26" Barrel, Right Hand Only, *Modern*	1400	3000	3500
Mark V Fibermark, Various Calibers, Fiberglass, Right Hand Only, *Modern*	350	750	850
Mark V Lazermark, Various Calibers, Carved Stock (Carved with Laser Beam), *Modern*	425	850	1100
Mark V, .378 Wby. Mag., Checkered Stock, *Modern*	450	900	1100
Mark V, .460 Wby. Mag., Checkered Stock, *Modern*	500	1000	1250
Mark V, Various Calibers, Checkered Stock, *Modern*	325	650	750
Mark V, Various Calibers, Varmint, Checkered Stock, *Modern*	400	850	950

Weatherby Mark V

	Fair	V. Good	Excellent
Vanguard, Various Calibers, Checkered Stock, *Modern*	200	400	450

RIFLE, SEMI-AUTOMATIC

	Fair	V. Good	Excellent
Mark XXII, .22 L.R.R.F., Clip Fed, Checkered Stock, *Modern*	150	300	325
Mark XXII, .22 L.R.R.F., Tube Feed, Checkered Stock, *Modern*	150	325	350
Model M-82, Various Gauges, Gas Operated, Various Barrel Lengths, *Modern*	200	400	450

SHOTGUN, DOUBLE BARREL, OVER-UNDER

	Fair	V. Good	Excellent
Athena Skeet Grade, 12 Gauge, Single Selective Trigger, 26" Barrels, *Modern*	600	1250	1500

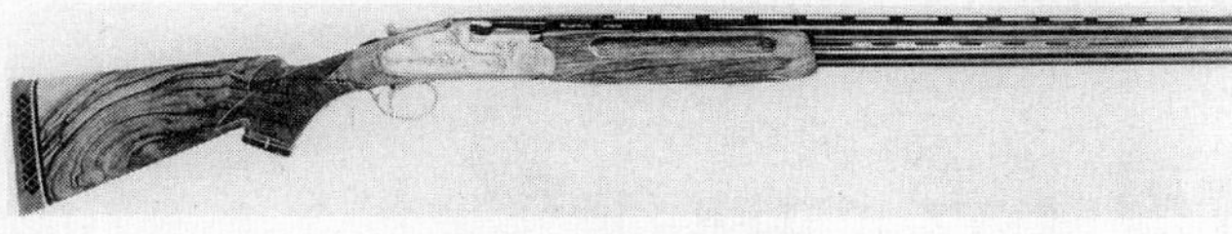

Weatherby Athena

	Fair	V. Good	Excellent
Athena Trap Grade, 12 Gauge, Single Selective Trigger, 30" Barrels, *Modern*	$500	$1000	$1250
Orion 20 Field Grade, 20 Gauge, Single Selective Trigger, 26" or 28" Barrel, *Modern*	350	775	850
Orion Field Grade, 12 Gauge, Single Selective Trigger, 26" or 28" Barrel, *Modern*	350	775	800
Orion Skeet Grade, 12 Gauge, Single Selective Trigger, 26" Barrels, *Modern*	350	750	825
Orion Trap Grade, 12 Gauge, Single Selective Trigger, 30" or 32" Barrel, *Modern*	350	750	825
Regency, 12 Gauge, Trap Grade, Vent Rib, Checkered Stock, Engraved, Single Selective Trigger, *Modern*	325	675	750
Regency, Field Grade, 12 and 20 Gauges, Vent Rib, Checkered Stock, Engraved, Single Selective Trigger, *Modern*	350	725	775

SHOTGUN, SEMI-AUTOMATIC

	Fair	V. Good	Excellent
Centurion, 12 Gauge, Field Grade, Vent Rib, Checkered Stock, *Modern*	100	225	275
Centurion, 12 Gauge, Trap Grade, Checkered Stock, Vent Rib, *Modern*	100	200	250
Centurion Deluxe, 12 Gauge, Checkered Stock, Vent Rib, Light Engraving, Fancy Wood, *Modern*	125	250	300

SHOTGUN, SLIDE ACTION

	Fair	V. Good	Excellent
Model M-92, 12 Gauge, Vent Rib, Three Sheel Mag., *Modern*	100	225	275
Patrician, 12 Gauge, Field Grade, Checkered Stock, Vent Rib, *Modern*	100	200	225
Patrician, 12 Gauge, Trap Grade, Checkered Stock, Vent Rib, *Modern*	100	225	250
Patrician, Deluxe, 12 Gauge, Checkered Stock, Light Engraving, Fancy Wood, Vent Rib, *Modern*	100	225	275

WEAVER, CRYPRET

Pa., c. 1818. See Kentucky Rifles.

WEBLEY & SCOTT LTD.

Located in Birmingham, England operating as P. Webley & Son, 1860–1897; Webley & Scott Revolver & Arms Co., 1898–1906; Webley & Scott 1906–1979.

HANDGUN, REVOLVER

	Fair	V. Good	Excellent
#1, .577 Eley, Solid Frame, Double Action, Blue, *Curio*	1500	3000	3500

	Fair	V. Good	Excellent
British Bulldog, Various Calibers, Solid Frame, Double Action, *Curio*	$100	$300	$350
Tower Bulldog, Various Calibers, Solid Frame, Double Action, *Curio*	100	275	325
Webley Kaufman, .45 Colt, Top Break, Square-Butt, Commercial, *Antique*	300	600	800
Webley MK 1, .455 Revolver Mk 1, Top Break, Round-Butt, Military, *Antique*	125	225	250
Webley MK 1*, .455 Revolver Mk 1, Top Break, Round-Butt, Military, *Antique*	100	200	225
Webley MK 1 Navy,** .455 Revolver Mk 1, Top Break, Round Butt, Military, *Modern*	100	200	225
Webley MK 2, .455 Revolver Mk 1, Top Break, Round Butt, Military, *Antique*	100	225	250
Webley MK 2*, .455 Revolver Mk 1, Top Break, Round Butt, Military, *Curio*	100	225	250
Webley MK 2,** .455 Revolver Mk 1, Top Break, Round Butt, Military, *Curio*	100	225	250
Webley MK 3, .455 Revolver Mk 1, Top Break, Round Butt, Military, *Curio*	100	250	275
Webley MK 4, .455 Revolver Mk 1, Top Break, Round Butt, Military, *Curio*	100	200	250
Webley MK 5, .455 Revolver Mk 1, Top Break, Round Butt, Military, *Curio*	100	225	275
Webley MK 6, .455 Revolver Mk 1, Top Break, Square-Butt, Military, *Curio*	150	300	350
Webley MK 6, Detachable Buttstock Only	150	300	350
Webley Mk III M & P, .38 S & W, Top Break, Square-Butt, Commercial, *Modern*	125	250	300
Webley Mk IV, .38 S & W, Top Break, Square-Butt, Military, *Curio*	100	225	275
Webley Mk VI, .22 L.R.R.F., Top Break, Square-Butt, Commercial, *Modern*	200	400	475
Webley R I C, .455 Revolver Mk 1, Solid Frame, Square-Butt, Commercial, *Antique*	100	225	250
Webley-Green, .455 Revolver Mk 1, Top Break, Square-Butt, Commercial, Target Pistol, *Antique*	200	425	475
Webley-Green, .476 Enfield Mk 3, Top Break, Square-Butt, Commercial, Target Pistol, *Antique*	250	500	600

HANDGUN, SEMI-AUTOMATIC

	Fair	V. Good	Excellent
Model 1904, .455 Webley Auto., Clip Fed, Grip Safety, Hammer, *Curio*	300	650	750
Model 1906, .25 ACP, Clip Fed, Hammer, *Modern*	$100	$225	$250
Model 1909 M & P, 9mm Browning Long, Clip Fed, Hammer, *Curio*	200	400	450
Model 1909 M & P, 9mm Browning Long, South African Police, Clip Fed, Hammer, *Curio*	250	500	550
Model 1909, .25 ACP, Clip Fed, Hammerless, *Modern*	100	225	250
Model 1909, 9mm, Clip Fed, Hammerless, *Modern*	200	400	450
Model 1911 Metro Police, .32 ACP, Clip Fed, Hammer, *Modern*	300	625	700
Model 1911 Metro Police, .380 ACP, Clip Fed, Hammer, *Modern*	350	700	800
Model 1912, .455 Caliber, Clip Fed, Hammerless, *Curio*	200	400	450
Model 1913 Mk 1 #2, .455 Webley Auto., Clip Fed, Grip Safety, Adjustable Sights, Hammer, *Curio*	400	950	1200
Model 1913 Mk 1, .455 Webley Auto., Clip Fed, Grip Safety, Military, Hammer, *Curio*	900	2000	2250
Model 1913, .38 ACP, Clip Fed, Hammerless, *Curio*	500	1000	1250

SHOTGUN, DOUBLE BARREL, SIDE-BY-SIDE

	Fair	V. Good	Excellent
Model 700, 12 and 20 Gauges, Box Lock, Hammerless, Checkered Stock, Light Engraving, Single Trigger, *Modern*	700	1450	1600
Model 701, 12 and 20 Gauges, Box Lock, Hammerless, Checkered Stock, Fancy Engraving, Double Trigger, *Modern*	900	2000	2500
Model 701, 12 and 20 Gauges, Box Lock, Hammerless, Checkered Stock, Fancy Engraving, Single Trigger, *Modern*	1000	2200	2600
Model 702, 12 and 20 Gauges, Box Lock, Hammerless, Checkered Stock, Engraved, Double Trigger, *Modern*	800	1750	2200
Model 702, 12 and 20 Gauges, Box Lock, Hammerless, Checkered Stock, Engraved, Single Trigger, *Modern*	800	1800	2250

WELSHANTZ, DAVID

York, Pa. 1780–1783. See Kentucky Rifles, U.S. Military.

WELSHANTZ, JACOB

York, Pa. 1777–1792. See Kentucky Rifles, U.S. Military.

WELSHANTZ, JOSEPH

York, Pa. 1779–1983. See Kentucky Rifles, U.S. Military.

WESSON & HARRINGTON

Worcester, Mass. 1871–1874. Succeeded by Harrington and Richardson.

HANDGUN, REVOLVER

	Fair	V. Good	Excellent
.22 Short R.F., 7 Shot, Spur Trigger, Solid Frame, Single Action, *Antique*	$75	$150	$175
.32 Short R.F., 5 Shot, Spur Trigger, Solid Frame, Single Action, *Antique*	75	150	175
.38 Short R.F., 5 Shot, Spur Trigger, Solid Frame, Single Action, *Antique*	75	175	200

WESSON, FRANK

Worcester, Mass. 1854 to 1865. 1865–1875 at Springfield, Mass. Also see U.S. Military, Wesson & Harrington, Harrington & Richardson.

HANDGUN, DOUBLE BARREL, OVER-UNDER

	Fair	V. Good	Excellent
Vest Pocket, .22 Short, Twist Barrel, Spur Trigger, *Antique*	350	700	1000
Vest Pocket, .32 Short, Twist Barrel, Spur Trigger, *Antique*	250	500	550
Vest Pocket, .41 Short, Twist Barrel, Spur Trigger, with Knife, *Antique*	500	1000	1250

HANDGUN, SINGLESHOT

	Fair	V. Good	Excellent
Model 1859, .22 Short, Tip-Up Barrel, Spur Trigger, *Antique*	200	400	500
Model 1859, .32 R.F., Tip-Up Barrel, Spur Trigger, *Antique*	200	450	600
Model 1859, .39 R.F., Tip-Up Barrel, Spur Trigger, *Antique*	200	450	600
Model 1862 Pocket Rifle, Various Calibers, Medium Frame, Spur Trigger, Target Sights, Detachable Stock, *Antique*	250	500	550
Model 1862, .22 Short, Tip-Up Barrel, Spur Trigger, *Antique*	100	250	300
Model 1862, .30 R.F., Tip-Up Barrel, Spur Trigger, *Antique*	200	450	600
Model 1862, .32 R.F., Tip-Up Barrel, Spur Trigger, *Antique*	200	450	600
Model 1870 Pocket Rifle, .22 Short, Small Frame, Spur Trigger, Target Sights, Detachable Stock, *Antique*	200	400	450
Model 1870 Pocket Rifle, Various Calibers, Large Frame, Spur Trigger, Target Sights, Detachable Stock, *Antique*	350	725	850
Model 1870 Pocket Rifle, Various Calibers, Medium Frame, Spur Trigger, Target Sights, Detachable Stock, *Antique*	200	400	500

RIFLE, SINGLESHOT

	Fair	V. Good	Excellent
.32 Long R.F., Two-Trigger, Tip-Up, *Antique*	$250	$500	$550

WESTERN ARMS CO.

HANDGUN, REVOLVER

	Fair	V. Good	Excellent
.32 Long.F., 5 Shot, Folding Trigger, Double Action, *Antique*	50	75	100

WESTERN FIELD

Trade name for Montgomery Ward.

RIFLE, BOLT ACTION

	Fair	V. Good	Excellent
Model 56 Buckhorn, .22 L.R.R.F., 5 Shot Clip, Open Rear Sight, *Modern*	25	50	75
Model 724, .30-06 Springfield, Checkered Stock, Full-Stocked, *Modern*	75	125	175
Model 732, .30-06 Springfield, Checkered Stock, Recoil Pad, *Modern*	75	125	175
Model 734, 7mm Rem. Mag., Checkered Stock, Recoil Pad, *Modern*	75	125	175
Model 765, .30-06 Springfield, Checkered Stock, *Modern*	50	100	150
Model 770, *Modern*	75	125	175
Model 78, Various Calibers, Checkered Stock, Sling Swivels, *Modern*	75	125	175
Model 780, Various Calibers, Checkered Stock, Sling Swivels, *Modern*	75	150	175
Model 815, .22 L.R.R.F., Singleshot, *Modern*	15	25	50
Model 822, .22 WMR, Clip Fed, *Modern*	15	25	50
Model 83, .22 L.R.R.F., Singleshot, Open Rear Sight, Takedown, *Modern*	15	25	50
Model 830, .22 L.R.R.F., Clip Fed, *Modern*	15	25	50
Model 832, .22 L.R.R.F., Clip Fed, Checkered Stock, *Modern*	15	25	50
Model 84, *Modern*	15	25	50
Model 840, .22 WMR, Clip Fed, *Modern*	25	50	75
Model 852, .22 L.R.R.F., Clip Fed, *Modern*	15	25	50
Model 86, .22 L.R.R.F., Tube Feed, Takedown, Open Rear Sight, *Modern*	15	25	50
Modl 842, .22 L.R.R.F., Tube Feed, *Modern*	15	25	50

	Fair	V. Good	Excellent
RIFLE, LEVER ACTION			
Model 72, .30-30 Win., Pistol Grip Stock, Plain, Tube Feed, *Modern*	$75	$100	$125
Model 72C, .30-30 Win., Straight Grip, Plain, Tube Feed, *Modern*	75	100	125
Model 79, .30-30 Win., Pistol Grip Stock, Plain, Tube Feed, *Modern*	75	100	125
Model 865, .22 L.R.R.F., Tube Feed, Sling Swivels, *Modern*	25	50	75
Model 895, .22 L.R.R.F., Tube Feed, Carbine, *Modern*	25	50	75
RIFLE, SEMI-AUTOMATIC			
Model 808, .22 L.R.R.F., Tube Feed, *Modern*	15	25	50
Model 828, .22 L.R.R.F., Clip Fed, Checkered Stock, *Modern*	25	50	75
Model 836, .22 L.R.R.F., Tube Feed, *Modern*	25	50	75
Model 846, .22 L.R.R.F., Tube Feed, *Modern*	25	50	75
Model 850, .22 L.R.R.F., Clip Fed, *Modern*	25	50	75
Model 880, .22 L.R.R.F., Tube Feed, *Modern*	50	50	50
Model M-1, .30 Carbine, Clip Fed, *Modern*	100	125	150
SHOTGUN, BOLT ACTION			
Model 150, .410 Ga., Clip Fed, *Modern*	15	25	50
Model 172-5, 12 and 20 Gauges, Magnum, Clip Fed, Adjustable Choke, *Modern*	25	50	75
SHOTGUN, DOUBLE BARREL, SIDE-BY-SIDE			
12 and 20 Gauges, Single Trigger, Hammerless, Checkered Stock, *Modern*	100	125	150
Long-Range, Various Gauges, Double Trigger, Hammerless, *Modern*	125	150	175
Long-Range, Various Gauges, Single Trigger, Hammerless, *Modern*	150	175	200
Model 330, Various Gauges, Hammerless, Checkered Stock, *Modern*	100	125	150
Model 5151, Various Gauges, Hammerless, Steel Barrel, *Modern*	100	125	150
Various Gauges, Hammerless, Plain, *Modern*	75	100	125
SHOTGUN, SEMI-AUTOMATIC			
Model 60, 12 Ga., Takedown, Plain Barrel, Checkered Stock, *Modern*	100	125	150
Model 600, 12 Ga., Takedown, Vent Rib, Checkered Stock, *Modern*	100	125	150

	Fair	V. Good	Excellent
SHOTGUN, SINGLESHOT			
Model 100, Various Gauges, Hammerless, Adjustable Choke, *Modern*	$15	$25	$50
Trap, 12 Ga., Hammer, Solid Rib, Checkered Stock, *Modern*	50	75	100
SHOTGUN, SLIDE ACTION			
Model 500, .410 Ga., Plain, Takedown, *Modern*	75	100	125
Model 502, .410 Ga., Checkered Stock, Light Engraving, Takedown, Vent Rib, *Modern*	75	100	125
Model 520, 12 Ga., Takedown, *Modern*	75	100	125
Model 550, 12 and 20 Gauges, Checkered Stock, Light Engraving, Vent Rib, Takedown, *Modern*	75	100	125
Model 550, 12 and 20 Gauges, Checkered Stock, Light Engraving, Vent Rib, Takedown, Adjustable Choke, *Modern*	100	125	150
Model 550, 12 and 20 Gauges, Plain, Takedown, *Modern*	75	100	125
Model 620, Various Gauges, Takedown, *Modern*	100	125	150

WESTLEY RICHARDS

Birmingham, England, Since 1812.

	Fair	V. Good	Excellent
RIFLE, BOLT ACTION			
Stalker, Various Calibers, Express Sights, Fancy Wood, Fancy Checkering, Repeater, *Modern*	4000	8000	9000
RIFLE, DOUBLE BARREL, SIDE-BY-SIDE			
Best Quality, Various Calibers, Sidelock, Double Trigger, Fancy Engraving, Fancy Checkering, Express Sights, *Modern*	12000	27000	30000
SHOTGUN, DOUBLE BARREL, OVER-UNDER			
Owundo, 12 Ga., Sidelock, Single Selective Trigger, Selective Ejector, Fancy Engraving, Fancy Checkering, *Modern*	4500	10000	12500
SHOTGUN, DOUBLE BARREL, SIDE-BY-SIDE			
10 Ga. Pinfire, Engraved, Carbine, *Antique*	400	850	950
Best, Pigeon, 12 Ga. Mag. 3", Sidelock, Hammerless, Fancy Engraving, Fancy Checkering, Double Trigger, *Modern*	7000	17500	20000
Best, Pigeon, 12 Ga. Mag. 3", Sidelock, Hammerless, Fancy Engraving, Fancy Checkering, Single Selective Trigger, *Modern*	8000	18500	21000

	Fair	V. Good	Excellent
Best Quality, Various Gauges, Box Lock, Hammerless, Fancy Engraving, Fancy Checkering, Single Selective Trigger, *Modern*	$3000	$7000	$8000
Best Quality, Various Gauges, Sidelock, Hammerless, Fancy Engraving, Fancy Checkering, Double Trigger, *Modern*	7000	17500	20000
Best Quality, Various Gauges, Sidelock, Hammerless, Fancy Engraving, Fancy Checkering, Single Selective Trigger, *Modern*	8000	20000	22500
Best Quality, Various Gauges, Sidelock, Hammerless, Fancy Engraving, Fancy Checkering, Double Trigger, *Modern*	4500	10000	12000
Deluxe Quality, Various Gauges, Box Lock, Hammerless, Fancy Engraving, Fancy Checkering, Double Trigger, *Modern*	3500	7000	8000
Deluxe Quality, Various Gauges, Box Lock, Hammerless, Fancy Engraving, Fancy Checkering, Single Selective Trigger, *Modern*	4000	8000	9000
Deluxe Quality, Various Gauges, Sidelock, Hammerless, Fancy Engraving, Fancy Checkering, Double Trigger, *Modern*	5500	12500	15000
Deluxe Quality, Various Gauges, Sidelock, Hammerless, Fancy Engraving, Fancy Checkering, Single Selective Trigger, *Modern*	6500	13500	16000
Model E, Various Gauges, Box Lock, Hammerless, Engraved, Double Trigger, Selective Ejector, *Modern*	2200	5000	5500
Model E, Various Gauges, Box Lock, Hammerless, Engraved, Double Trigger, *Modern*	1600	4000	4250
Model E Pigeon, 12 Ga. Mag. 3", Box Lock, Hammerless, Engraved, Double Trigger, Selective Ejector, *Modern*	1800	4000	4500
Model E Pigeon, 12 Ga. Mag. 3", Box Lock, Hammerless, Engraved, Double Trigger, *Modern*	1800	4250	4750

SHOTGUN, SINGLESHOT

	Fair	V. Good	Excellent
12 Ga., Trap Grade, Vent Rib, Fancy Engraving, Fancy Checkering, Hammerless, *Modern*	1200	4000	5000
12 Ga., Vent Rib, Plain, Monte Carlo Stock, Trap Grade, *Modern*	1200	2500	3000

WESTON, EDWARD

Sussex, England 1800–1835.

HANDGUN, FLINTLOCK

	Fair	V. Good	Excellent
.67, Pair, Dueling Pistols, Octagon Barrel, Silver Furniture, Plain, *Antique*	$1800	$4000	$4500

WHEEL LOCK EXAMPLES

COMBINATION WEAPON, PISTOL

	Fair	V. Good	Excellent
German, 1500s War-Hammer, All Metal, *Antique*	4500	12000	15000

HANDGUN, WHEEL LOCK

	Fair	V. Good	Excellent
Augsburg, Late 1500s, Ball Pommel, Engraved, Ornate, *Antique*	8000	18000	20000

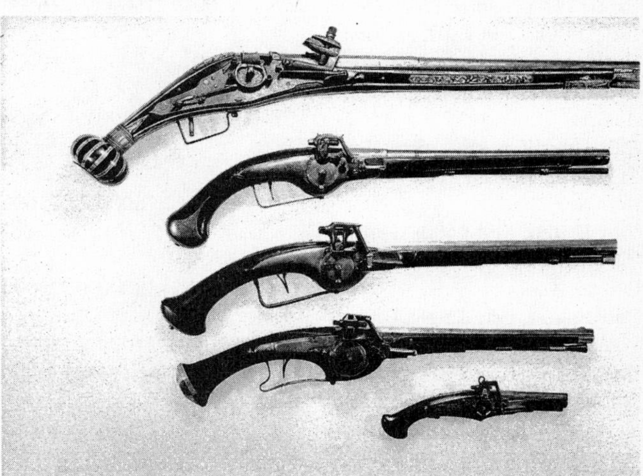

Wheel lock pistols, from the top, *German 16th-century ball-butt; military pistol with 14½" part round, part octagonal barrel; another military, perhaps English; French of c. 1700 with ebony stock and chased silver butt cap, ferrules, and forend mount; miniature-size pistol of only 9" overall length, one of smallest military wheel locks made.*

	Fair	V. Good	Excellent
Brescian, Mid-1600s, Military, Fish-Tail Butt, Plain, *Antique*	750	2000	2600
Embellished Original, Ornate, *Antique*	1450	2500	3550
Enclosed Lock German, Mid 1600s, Engraved, Holster Pistol, *Antique*	2200	3000	3800
Enclosed Lock, Late 1600s, Military, Plain, *Antique*	750	1500	2500
English, Mid 1600s, Military, Holster Pistol, Plain, *Antique*	750	1500	2500
English, Mid 1600s, Ornate, *Antique*	8000	18000	20000
Franch, Early 1600s, Military, Silver Inlays, *Antique*	1400	2500	3600
German Puffer, Late 1500s, Horn Inlays, Ball Pommel, *Antique*	3000	8000	10000

	Fair	V. Good	Excellent
German Style, Reproduction, Engraved, Inlays, High Quality, *Antique*	$800	$1400	$2000
German, 1600, Dagger-Handle Butt, Military, Plain, *Antique*	1200	2500	2800
German, Late 1500s, Carved, Horn Inlays, Ball Pommel, Flattened, *Antique*	7000	14500	18000
German, Mid-1500s, Horn Inlays, Dagger-Handle Butt, Gold and Silver Damascened, Ornate, *Antique*	9000	20000	22000
German, Mid-1600s, Military, Fish-Tail Butt, Plain, *Antique*	625	1250	2000
Italian, 1500s, Dagger-Handle, External Mechanism, *Antique*	4500	15000	16500
Late 1500s Odd Butt, all Metal, Engraved, Ornate, *Antique*	4000	9000	10000
Old Reproduction, High Quality, *Antique*	600	1200	1800
Pair Brescian, Mid-1600s, Inlays, Engraved, Ornate, Fish-Tail Butt, *Antique*	9000	18000	25000
Pair Dutch, Mid-1600s, Holster Pistol, Gold Damascened, Inlays, Ornate, *Antique*	9000	18000	25000
Pair Saxon, Late 1500s, Ball Pommel, Inlays, Engraved, *Antique*	12000	24000	30000
Pair Saxon, Late 1500s, Ball Pommel, Light Ornamentation, *Antique*	4500	12000	15000
Pair Saxon, Late 1500s, Ball Pommel, Medium Ornamentation, *Antique*	8000	18000	20000
Saxon, Dated 1579, Horn Inlays, Engraved, Ball Pommel, *Antique*	3000	7000	10000
Saxon, Double Barrel, Over-Under, Inlays, Ornate, Ball Pommel, *Antique*	11000	24000	30000
Saxon, Late 1500s, Ball Pommel, Checkered Stock, Military, Plain, *Antique*	2000	5000	6000

RIFLE, WHEEL LOCK

	Fair	V. Good	Excellent
Brandenburg 1620, Cavalry Rifle, Military, *Antique*	3000	7000	8000

WHIPPET

Made by Stevens Arms.

SHOTGUN, SINGLESHOT

	Fair	V. Good	Excellent
Model 94A, Various Gauges, Hammer, Automatic Ejector, *Modern*	25	50	75

WHITE POWDER WONDER

Made by Stevens Arms.

SHOTGUN, SINGLESHOT

	Fair	V. Good	Excellent
Model 90, Various Gauges, Takedown, Automatic Ejector, Plain, Hammer, *Modern*	$25	$50	$75

WHITE STAR

c. 1880.

HANDGUN, REVOLVER

	Fair	V. Good	Excellent
.32 Short R.F., 5 Shot, Spur Trigger, Solid Frame, Single Action, *Antique*	125	150	175

WHITE, ROLLIN ARMS CO.

Hartford, Conn. 1849–1858; Lowell, Mass. 1864–1892.

HANDGUN, REVOLVER

	Fair	V. Good	Excellent
.22 Short R.F., 7 Shot, Spur Trigger, Tip-Up, *Antique*	350	425	500

HANDGUN, SINGLESHOT

	Fair	V. Good	Excellent
SS Pocket, .32 Cal., no Trigger Guard, *Antique*	350	500	650

Rollin White Singleshot Pocket Pistol, .32 Caliber

WHITNEY ARMS CO.

New Haven, Conn. 1866–1876, also see U.S. Military.

HANDGUN, PERCUSSION

	Fair	V. Good	Excellent
Eagle Navy, .36, 6 Shot, Colt 1851 Type, *Antique*	700	1500	1750
Hooded Cylinder, .28, 6 Shot, Hammer, *Antique*	900	2000	2250
New Pocket Model, .28, 6 Shot, Single Action, *Antique*	300	625	700
Pocket Model, .31, 5 Shot, Single Action, *Antique*	300	675	750
Whitney Navy, .36, 6 Shot, *Antique*	350	750	1000
Whitney-Beals Walking Beam Pocket Revolver, .31 6 Shot, *Antique*	500	1000	1200
Whitney-Beals, .31, Ring Trigger, 7 Shot, *Antique*	1100	2500	3500

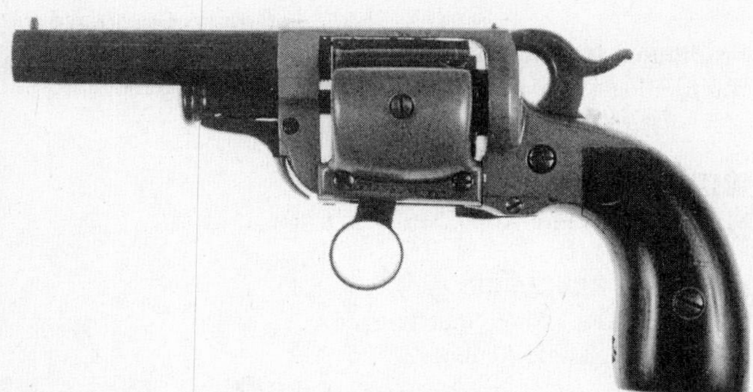

Whitney-Beals Walking Beam Pocket Revolver, .31 Caliber

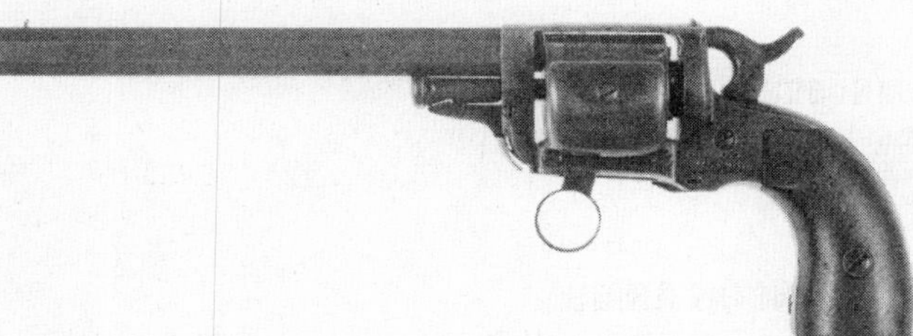

Whitney-Beals Standard Revolver, .31 Caliber

	Fair	V. Good	Excellent
HANDGUN, REVOLVER			
.22 Short R.F., 7 Shot, Spur Trigger, Solid Frame, Single Action, *Antique*	$150	275	325
.32 Short R.F., 5 or 6 Shots, Spur Trigger, Solid Frame, Single Action, *Antique*	150	225	275
.38 Short R.F., 5 Shot, Spur Trigger, Solid Frame, Single Action, *Antique*	150	275	325
RIFLE, LEVER ACTION			
Kennedy, Various Calibers, Tube Feed, Plain, *Antique*	600	1250	1500
Model 1886, Various Calibers, Tube Feed, Plain, *Antique*	700	1750	2000
RIFLE, SINGLESHOT			
Phoenix, Various Calibers, Carbine, Hammer, *Antique*	800	1750	2000
Phoenix, Various Calibers, Rifle, Hammer, *Antique*	900	2000	2250
Rolling Block, Various Calibers, Carbine, *Antique*	350	750	1000
Rolling Block, Various Calibers, Rifle, *Antique*	300	650	750
Whitney-Howard, .44 R.F., Carbine, Lever Action, *Antique*	500	1000	1250
Whitney-Howard, .44 R.F., Rifle, Lever Action, *Antique*	350	750	1000

	Fair	V. Good	Excellent
SHOTGUN, DOUBLE BARREL, SIDE-BY-SIDE			
12 Ga., Damascus Barrel, Outside Hammers, *Antique*	$250	$550	$650

WHITNEY FIREARMS CO.

Hartford, Conn. 1955–1962.

HANDGUN, SINGLESHOT			
Wolverine, .22 L.R.R.F., Blue, *Modern*	200	400	475

ELI WHITNEY

Whitneyville, Conn. Best known for creating the cotton gin, and for his role in the evolution of parts interchangeability and mass production, Eli Whitney (1765–1826) is one of the most renowned of all American inventors and entrepreneurs. Though the concept of parts interchangeability appears first to have come to America via Thomas Jefferson (while U.S. Ambassador to France), Whitney was a nearly, though not completely unsuccessful, practitioner. Whitney's first U.S government contract for muskets was in 1798, for a total of 10,000, at $13.40 each. However, problems in developing his programs for mass production meant that deliveries were not completed until 1809. The muskets were not fully interchangeable, but a significant beginning had been made toward what came to be known as the American System. Other makers, particularly Simeon North, Robbins & Lawrence, and Samuel Colt, carried on to pioneer a system which came to be copied, and admired, by enlightened manufacturers worldwide. Long before Henry Ford, the American firearms industry established true parts interchangeability and mass production, often with government support and with assistance from the national armories at Springfield and Harpers Ferry. Other federal contracts were awarded to Whitney, whose armory facilities were set up in a town, fittingly called Whitneyville. From 1812 to 1824, 33,000 more muskets were contracted from the Whitney Armory by the federal governments, and several thousand more from the states for militia units: the New York and Connecticut Contract Pre-1812 Muskets, U.S. and Massachusetts Contract 1812 Muskets, 1822 U.S. Contract Musket, South Carolina Contract 1816 Musket, Composite 1816 Musket, and the 1816 Massachusetts Percussion Conversion. Only military arms are believed to have been manufactured by the Whitney family, during the founder's lifetime. Following Whitney's death, January 8, 1826, the Armory carried on under direction of nephews Philos and Eli Whitney Blake, who in turn were succeeded by Eli Whitney, Jr. (1842). Among the firm's later production were 17,600 Model 1841 "Mississippi Rifles" (through 1855), 15,001 rifled-muskets, and approximately 11,214 revolvers in the Civil War period. A little known fact is that the Walker Colt revolvers were manufactured by the Whitney Armory, on contract for Samuel Colt. Many of the parts had been subcontracted, with final assembly at Whitneyville. Whitney and Colt had a profit-sharing agreement, and Colt retained ownership of machinery built or purchased for the Walker production. Unfortunately, Eli Whitney, Jr. lacked the inventive genius and business skills of his father. Attempts at re-servicing surplus firearms, buying out parts from such firms as the Robbins & Lawrence factory, and other schemes, proved largely unsuccessful. Following the Civil War Whitney greatly expanded the company's product line, even including rolling block and hinged-breech singleshot rifles, lever-action repeating rifles, and a double-barreled shotgun. Approximately 30,000 breechloading rimfire metallic cartridge revolvers were made, from 1871–79. Some of the longarm products were manufactured for other inventors. The firearms industry was highly competitive, especially following the Civil War, and Whitney, suffering business losses, began seeking a buyer for the Armory as early as 1883. In 1888 the Winchester Repeating Arms Co. bought the Whitney Armory, moving much of the machinery to New Haven, and selling out remaining stocks of firearms. Today the Whitney Armory site is occupied by the Eli Whitney Museum of Invention, founded by the late Merrill K. Lindsay. Among surviving buildings are the Whitney barn and employee dormitory, the water turbine–powered electric works, a blacksmith/foundry site, the reproduction Towne-patent covered bridge, and a factory building serving as museum offices, exhibit space (including the Anthony D. Darling Memorial Firearms Gallery), and workshops.

WHITNEYVILLE ARMORY

See Whitney Arms Co.

WHITWORTH

Made in England, imported by Interarms.

RIFLE, BOLT ACTION

	Fair	V. Good	Excellent
Express, Various Calibers, Checkered Stock, *Modern*	$250	$550	$650

WICHITA ARMS CO.

HANDGUN, SINGLESHOT

	Fair	V. Good	Excellent
Classic, Various Calibers, Singleshot, Target, *Modern*	900	2000	2250
Silhouette Pistol, Various Calibers, Bolt Action, *Modern*	350	750	850

RIFLE, BOLT ACTION

	Fair	V. Good	Excellent
Classic Magnum, Various Calibers, Repeater, *Modern*	450	1000	1250
Classic Silhouette, Various Calibers, Singleshot, Target, *Modern*	550	1250	1500
Classic Varmint, Various Calibers, Repeater, Target, *Modern*	600	1250	1500

WICKLIFFE

Triple-S Development, Wickliffe, Ohio. (Discontinued).

RIFLE, SINGLESHOT

	Fair	V. Good	Excellent
Deluxe, Various Calibers, Falling Block, *Modern*	150	350	400
Standard, Various Calibers, Falling Block, *Modern*	150	300	350
Stinger Deluxe, Various Calibers, Falling Block, *Modern*	150	350	400
Stinger Standard, Various Calibers, Falling Block, *Modern*	150	300	350
Traditional 1st, Various Calibers, Falling Block, *Modern*	$150	$300	$350

WIDE AWAKE

Made by Hood Fire Arms, Norwich, Conn., c. 1875.

HANDGUN, REVOLVER

	Fair	V. Good	Excellent
.32 Short R.F., 5 Shot, Spur Trigger, Solid Frame, Single Action, *Antique*	100	150	175

WILKINSON ARMS

Parma, Idaho.

HANDGUN, SEMI-AUTOMATIC

	Fair	V. Good	Excellent
Linda, 9mm Luger, Clip Fed, Blue, *Modern*	125	250	300

WILKINSON ARMS

South El Monte, Calif., c. 1976.

HANDGUN, SEMI-AUTOMATIC

	Fair	V. Good	Excellent
Diane, .25 ACP, Clip Fed, Blue, *Modern*	75	100	125

WILKINSON ARMS CO.

Made in Belgium for Richmond Hardware Co. Richmond, Va., c. 1900.

SHOTGUN, DOUBLE BARREL, SIDE-BY-SIDE

	Fair	V. Good	Excellent
Various Gauges, Hammerless, Damascus Barrel, *Modern*	75	150	175
Various Gauges, Outside Hammers, Steel Barrel, *Modern*	100	175	200
Various Gauges, Hammerless, Steel Barrel, *Modern*	100	175	200
Various Gauges, Outside Hammers, Damascus Barrel, *Modern*	75	150	175

SHOTGUN, SINGLESHOT

	Fair	V. Good	Excellent
Various Gauges, Hammer, Steel Barrel, *Modern*	50	75	100

WILLIAMS, FREDERICK

Birmingham, England, 1893–1929.

SHOTGUN, DOUBLE BARREL, SIDE-BY-SIDE

	Fair	V. Good	Excellent
Gga., Damascus Barrel, Outside Hammers, Checkered Stock, Engraved, *Antique*	200	400	450

WILLIAMSON, DAVID

Brooklyn, N.Y. and Greenville, N.J. 1864–1874. Also see Moore's Patent Firearms, Co.

	Fair	V. Good	Excellent
HANDGUN, SINGLESHOT			
.41 Short R.F., Derringer, Nickel Plated, *Antique*	$200	$400	$450

WILLIS, RICHARD

Lancaster, Pa., c. 1776. See Kentucky Rifles and Pistols.

WILMONT ARMS CO.

Belgium, c. 1900.

	Fair	V. Good	Excellent
SHOTGUN, DOUBLE BARREL, SIDE-BY-SIDE			
Various Gauges, Hammerless, Damascus Barrel, *Modern*	75	150	175
Various Gauges, Outside Hammer, Steel Barrel, *Modern*	100	175	200
Various Gauges, Hammerless, Steel Barrel, *Modern*	100	175	200
Various Gauges, Outside Hammer, Damascus Barrel, *Modern*	75	150	175
SHOTGUN, SINGLESHOT			
Various Gauges, Hammer, Steel Barrel, *Modern*	50	75	100

WILSON, R.

London, England 1720–1750.

	Fair	V. Good	Excellent
SHOTGUN, FLINTLOCK			
Fowling, 9 Ga., Queen Anne Style, Half-Stock, *Antique*	600	1250	1500

WILTSHIRE ARMS CO.

Belgium, c. 1900.

	Fair	V. Good	Excellent
SHOTGUN, DOUBLE BARREL, SIDE-BY-SIDE			
Various Gauges, Hammerless, Damascus barrel, *Modern*	75	150	175
Various Gauges, Outside Hammers, Steel Barrel, *Modern*	100	175	200
Various Gauges, Hammerless, Steel Barrel, *Modern*	100	175	200
Various Gauges, Outside Hammers, Damascus Barrel, *Modern*	100	150	175
SHOTGUN, SINGLESHOT			
Various Gauges, Hammer, Steel Barrel, *Modern*	50	75	100

WINCHESTER REPEATING ARMS CO.

New Haven, Conn. 1866 to date. In 1857 Oliver Winchester re-organized the Volcanic Repeating Arms Co. into the New Haven Arms Co., and it became Winchester Repeating Arms Co. in 1866. In 1869 Winchester absorbed Fogerty Repeating Rifle Co., and the American Rifle Co. In 1870 it acquired The Spencer Repeating Arms Co., and Adirondack Arms Co. in 1874. In 1981 the U.S. Repeating Arms Co. took over manufacture, under license from Olin Corporation. Also see U.S. Military and the Commemorative section. The company's complex history began with the Jennings Rifle and has continued with numerous upward and downward movements up through today's split identity: the Winchester Division of Olin (makers of ammunition only) and the U.S. Repeating Arms Co. (established 1981; makers of firearms). At its peak during World War II, Winchester was the largest gun and cartridge maker in the world—with over 61,000 employees (including Western Cartridge Co.) In ammunition alone, Winchester remains the world's largest. The mark is recognized as one of history's most famous brand names. Successor to the Henry was the Model 1866, the first Winchester to bear the name of the major stockholder and company president, O.F. Winchester himself. This was the arm known to Native Americans as "the yellow boy," due to its brass frame. Oliver F. Winchester, a New Haven shirtmaker and skilled businessman, had gradually increased his investments in the Volcanic operation. That struggling company evolved slowly for a few years, accumulating debt. But with the perfection of both a rimfire cartridge and a lever-action firearm, the reception given the Henry Rifle finally rewarded Winchester's entrepreneurial courage. Henry sales were followed quickly thereafter by the Model 1866—which reached over 170,000 by 1898. Even more popular was the Model 1873, with a total production run of over 720,000. The Winchester Model 1873 was first offered in the new .44-40 cartridge and was built in carbine, rifle and musket configurations. This model played a vital role in Winchester's emergence as the predominant maker of longarms and ammunition in America. A feature of the new rifle was a reloading tool, a design patented by the major stockholder's son. Most glamorous and appealing of variations of the Model 1873 was the 1 of 1000 and 1 of 100 series. These special rifles helped capture for Winchester an image of prestige, quality and performance. Only 133 Model 1873 One of One Thousands were made, and only eight One of One Hundreds. Each had a specially selected barrel, tested for extreme accuracy. The barrel breeches were engraved with the designations 1 of 1000 or 1 of 100, in numerals or spelled out in script letters. A similar series was built in the Model 1876, totaling 51 One of One Thousands and seven One of One Hundreds. Manufacture was from 1873 to 1919, sales from inventory continued through c. 1925; the total made was in excess 720,610. Calibers were .44-40, .38-40, .32 -20, with a special variation (lacking loading gate aperture on the sideplate) in .22 rimfire. Variations: Early First Model—from serial 1 to about 28000; dust cover (an innovation of the Model 1873) with guide grooves at front of frame; separately secured oval thumbrest motif on dust cover; two screws located above trigger on frame. Late First Model—serial range of about 28000 to 31000; similar-type dust cover with oval thumbrest; trigger pin under two frame screws, over trigger. Second Model—serial range of about 31000 to 90000; center rail mount for dust cover at rear of frame; checkered oval thumbrest panel later replaced by serrated style edges. Third Model—serial range of about 90000 to end of production; dust cover rail mounting now integral with frame; two frame screws and pin near trigger no longer present. Thanks to the long-time association between John Browning and Winchester, a string of rifle and shotgun designs were developed, entering into manufacture such recognizable rifle models as the 1879 singleshot and lever-action 1886, 1892, 1894, and 1895, plus miscellaneous pump-action rifles and a lever-action shotgun. With a production run over a century, and a total made in

Fair V. Good Excellent

excess of six million, the Model 1894 holds the record as the most popular lever-action rifle ever made, and the most popular arms design sold to Winchester by Browning. Inspired by the adoption of smokeless powder late in the nineteenth century, John Browning created the Model 1894 soon after his design of the Model 1892. The profile of the 1894 was strikingly similar to the 1892, which used a vertical bolt locking system. A flat plate which pivots at the bottom of the breech is the most visible distinguishing feature of the Model 94 from the Model 92. In the long production run of the Model 1894 no major design changes have been made, other than the introduction of side ejection (1983), the hammer block system (1984), the cross-bolt hammer stop (1992), as well as adoption of the .22 rimfire Model 9422 (1972) and of the .375 Winchester Big Bore Model 94 (1979). The .22 and .375 rifles have their own serial number ranges. Although initially marketed in the blackpowder cartridges of .32-40 and .38-55, the Model 1894 was the first lever-action repeating rifle to be made and marketed specifically for ammunition using smokeless powder. The new chamberings were .25-35 Winchester and .30-30 Winchester. The latter became the all-time classic of deer hunting cartridges, as did the rifle which to this day utilizes that cartridge more than any other: the equally classic deer rifle, the Model 94. Two other variations of the Model 1894 were the Models 55 and 64. The Model 55 was built from 1924 through 1932, with a total of more than 20,500. The Model 64 was marketed from 1933 to 1957, and over 66,700 were made. At the same time the 94 remained in production, in the carbine version only. These offspring were outlived by the venerable 94, whose immortality seems assured. Production of the Model 1894 continued from 1894 to date; with total production exceeding six million by 1997. Variations (basic types, numerous variants over the years): Rifle, 26" octagonal barrel, case hardened hammer, lever, trigger, buttplate. Rifle, blued finish. Rifle, blued finish, with round barrel. Extra Light Weight Rifle, barrel lengths from 22 to 26 inches; rapid taper round barrel, shotgun buttplate on straight buttstock. Takedown Model Rifle, dismantling system mounted at muzzle end of magazine tube. Carbine, 20" round barrel; made with or without saddle ring on left side of frame through 1925; carbine sights; shotgun buttplate. Trapper's Model Carbine; barrels at lengths of 14, 16, and 18 inches; saddle ring may not be present. Numerous variations in markings and finishes in a number of commemorative configurations based on the Model 94 (see Commemorative listing).

RIFLE, BOLT ACTION

	Fair	V. Good	Excellent
Hotchkiss 1st Model Fancy, .45-70 Gov't, Sporting Rifle, *Antique*	$600	$1200	$1500
Hotchkiss 1st Model, .40-65 Win., Sporting Rifle, *Antique*	500	900	1000
Hotchkiss 1st Model, .45-70 Government, Carbine, *Antique*	500	900	1000
Hotchkiss 1st Model, .45-70 Government, Military, Carbine, *Antique*	500	900	1000
Hotchkiss 1st Model, .45-70 Government, Military, Rifle, *Antique*	900	2200	2500
Hotchkiss 2nd Model, .45-70 Government, Military, Rifle, *Antique*	$400	$900	$1000
Hotchkiss 2nd Model, .45-70 Government, Navy Rifle, *Antique*	500	900	1000
Hotchkiss 2nd Model, .45-70 Government, Sporting Rifle, *Antique*	450	900	1000
Hotchkiss 3rd Model, .45-70 Government, Military, Carbine, *Antique*	400	900	1000
Hotchkiss 3rd Model, .45-70 Government, Military, Rifle, *Antique*	600	900	1000
Lee Straight-Pull, 6mm Lee Navy, Musket, *Antique*	300	800	900
Lee Straight-Pull, 6mm Lee Navy, Sporting Rifle, *Antique*	350	700	800
M121 Deluxe, .22 L.R.R.F., Singleshot, *Modern*	50	100	150
M121, .22 L.R.R.F., Singleshot, *Modern*	75	100	125
M121-Y, .22 L.R.R.F., Singleshot, *Modern*	75	100	125
M131, .22 L.R.R.F., Clip Fed, Open Rear Sight, *Modern*	50	100	150
M135, .22 WMR, Clip Fed, *Modern*	75	100	125
M141, .22 WMR, Tube Feed, *Modern*	100	125	150
M145, .22 WMR, Tube Feed, *Modern*	100	125	150
M1900, .22 Long R.F., Singleshot, *Modern*	200	300	400
M1902, Various Rimfires, Singleshot, *Curio*	150	200	250
M1904, Various Rimfires, Singleshot, *Curio*	100	175	250
M43 Special Grade, Various Calibers, *Modern*	250	525	600
M43, Various Calibers, Sporting Rifle, *Modern*	200	475	550
M47, .22 L.R.R.F., Singleshot, *Modern*	100	200	250
M52 International Prone, .22 L.R.R.F., *Modern*	300	600	650
M52 International, .22 L.R.R.F., *Modern*	300	625	700
M52 Slow-Lock, .22 L.R.R.F., *Modern*	200	450	500
M52 Speed-Lock, .22 L.R.R.F., *Modern*	200	400	450
M52 Sporting, .22 L.R.R.F., Rifle, *Modern*	900	1500	1800
M52, .22 L.R.R.F., Heavy Barrel, *Modern*	250	525	575
M52-B, .22 L.R.R.F., *Modern*	225	450	525
M52-B, .22 L.R.R.F., Bull Gun, *Modern*	250	575	625

	Fair	V. Good	Excellent
M52-B, .22 L.R.R.F., Heavy Barrel, *Modern*	$225	$550	$600
M52-B, .22 L.R.R.F., Sporting Rifle, *Modern*	550	1350	1600
M52-C, .22 L.R.R.F., *Modern*	250	550	600
M52-C, .22 L.R.R.F., Bull Gun, *Modern*	250	575	650
M52-C, .22 L.R.R.F., Standard Target, *Modern*	250	550	600
M52-D, .22 L.R.R.F., *Modern*	225	475	525
M54, Various Calibers, Sporting Rifle, *Modern*	250	500	700
M54 Match, Various Calibers, Sniper Rifle, *Modern*	300	675	750
M54 National Match, Various Calibers, *Modern*	350	750	850
M54 Super Grade, Various Calibers, *Modern*	400	900	1200
M54 Target, Various Calibers, *Modern*	250	550	600
M54, .270 Win., Carbine, *Curio*	300	600	750
M54, .30-06 Springfield, Sniper Rifle, *Modern*	350	750	850
M54, Various Calibers, Carbine, *Modern*	300	650	750
M56, .22 L.R.R.F., Sporting Rifle, *Modern*	200	450	500
M57, Various Rimfires, Target, *Modern*	225	450	500
M58, .22 L.R.R.F., Singleshot, *Modern*	125	250	275
M59, .22 L.R.R.F., Singleshot, *Modern*	150	375	425
M60, .22 L.R.R.F., Singleshot, *Modern*	100	200	250
M60-A, .22 L.R.R.F., Target, Singleshot, *Modern*	125	325	400
M67 Boy's Rifle, Various Rimfires, Singleshot, *Modern*	75	150	250
M67, Various Rimfires, Singleshot, *Modern*	50	100	150
M68, Various Rimfires, Singleshot, *Modern*	75	125	150
M69 Match, .22 L.R.R.F., Clip Fed, *Modern*	75	150	250
M69 Target, .22 L.R.R.F., Clip Fed, *Modern*	50	125	250
M69, .22 L.R.R.F., Clip Fed, *Modern*	75	150	250
M70 Action Only, Various Calibers, Pre '64, *Modern*	150	300	350
M70 African, .458 Win. Mag., Pre '64, *Modern*	1200	2500	3000
M70 Alaskan, Various Calibers, Pre '64, Checkered Stock, *Modern*	800	1500	1700
M70 Barreled Action Only, Various Calibers, Pre '64, Checkered Stock, *Modern*	250	475	550
M70 Bull Gun, Various Calibers, Pre '64, Checkered Stock, *Modern*	600	1250	1500

	Fair	V. Good	Excellent
M70 Carbine, Various Calibers, Pre '64, Checkered Stock, *Modern*	$600	$1250	$1500
M70 Featherweight Sporter Grade, Various Calibers, Pre '64, Checkered Stock, *Modern*	700	1500	1750
M70 Featherweight, Various Calibers, Pre '64, Checkered Stock, *Modern*	400	775	850
M70 National Match, .30-06 Springfield, Pre '64, *Modern*	450	900	1000
M70 Target, Various Calibers, Pre '64, Checkered Stock, *Modern*	500	900	1000
M70 Varmint, Various Calibers, Pre '64, Checkered Stock, *Modern*	400	900	1000
M70 Westerner, Various Calibers, Pre '64, Checkered Stock, *Modern*	350	650	800
M70, For Mint Unfired, Pre '64, Add 50%-100%			
M70, for Pre-War, Add 25%-50%			
M72, .22 L.R.R.F., Tube Feed, *Modern*	100	225	275
M75 Target, .22 L.R.R.F., Clip Fed, *Modern*	200	450	500
M75, .22 L.R.R.F., Sporting Rifle, Clip Fed, *Modern*	300	625	700
M99 Thumb Trigger, Various Rimfires, Singleshot, *Modern*	450	1000	1250
Model 52 I.M. Kenyon, .22 L.R.R.F., Post '64, Heavy Barrel, Target Stock, *Modern*	200	450	500
Model 52 I.M., .22 L.R.R.F., Post '64, Heavy Barrel, Target Stock, *Modern*	200	425	475
Model 52 I.M.I.S.U., .22 L.R.R.F., Post '64, Heavy Barrel, Target Stock, *Modern*	250	525	575
Model 52 International Prone, .22 L.R.R.F., Post '64, Heavy Barrel, Target Stock, *Modern*	200	425	475
Model 52D, .22 L.R.R.F., Post '64, Heavy Barrel, Target Stock, *Modern*	250	500	550
Model 677, Various Calibers, Post '64, Scope Mounted, *Modern*	500	1000	1250
Model 70 African, .458 Win. Mag., Post '64, Checkered Stock, Open Rear Sight, Magnum Action, *Modern*	300	600	675
Model 70 International Match, .308 Win., Post '64, Checkered Stock, Target Stock, *Modern*	250	575	650
Model 70 Standard, Various Calibers, Post '64, Checkered Stock, Open Rear Sight, *Modern*	150	275	325
Model 70 Target, Various Calibers, Post '64, Checkered Stock, Target Stock, *Modern*	200	475	525
Model 70 Varmint, Various Calibers, Post '64, Checkered Stock, Heavy Barrel, *Modern*	150	300	350

	Fair	V. Good	Excellent
Model 70, Various Calibers, Pre '64, Checkered Stock, Open Rear Sight, Magnum Action, *Modern*	$100	$250	$300
Model 70A Police, Various Calibers, Post '64, *Modern*	125	250	300
Model 70A Standard, Various Calibers, Post '64, *Modern*	100	225	275
Model 70A, Various Calibers, Post '64, Magnum Action, *Modern*	150	300	350
Model 70XTR Featherweight, Various Calibers, No Sights, *Modern*	175	350	400
Model 70XTR Featherweight, Various Calibers, with Sights, *Modern*	200	400	450
Model 70XTR Super Express Magnum, .375 H&H, *Modern*	250	500	575
Model 70XTR Super Express Magnum, .458 Win., *Modern*	250	525	600
Model XTR Ranger, Various Calibers, No Scope, *Modern*	150	275	325
Model XTR Sporter, Various Calibers, *Modern*	150	325	375
Model XTR Varmint, Various Calibers, *Modern*	150	325	375
Thumb Trigger, .22 L.R.R.F., Singleshot, *Curio*	200	450	500

RIFLE, LEVER ACTION

	Fair	V. Good	Excellent
Henry, .44 Henry, Brass Frame, Military, Rifle, *Antique*	9000	40000	60000
Henry, .44 Henry, Brass Frame, Rifle, *Antique*	7000	30000	50000
Henry, .44 Henry, Iron Frame, Rifle, *Antique*	20000	60000	75000
M1866 Improved Henry, .44 Henry, Carbine, *Antique*	4000	12000	15000
M1866 Improved Henry, .44 Henry, Rifle, *Antique*	3500	12000	15000
M1866, .44 Henry, Rifle, *Antique*	6000	17500	25000

Winchester M1866

	Fair	V. Good	Excellent
M1873 1 of 1,000, Various Calibers, Rifle, *Antique*	25000	100000	125000
M1873, For Deluxe, Add $500.00-$750.00			
M1873, For Extra Fancy Deluxe, Add $5000.00-$7500.00			
M1873, under #525,299, Various Calibers, Carbine, *Antique*	1250	4000	5000
M1873, under #525,299, Various Calibers, Musket, *Antique*	1000	1750	2500
M1873, under #525,299, Various Calibers, Rifle, *Antique*	1000	3000	4000

Winchester M1873

	Fair	V. Good	Excellent
M1873, Various Calibers, Carbine, *Curio*	$3500	$4000	$5000
M1873, Various Calibers, Musket, *Curio*	1500	4000	5000
M1873, Various Calibers, Rifle, *Curio*	875	4000	5000
M1876 RCMP, Various Calibers, Carbine, *Antique*	3000	8000	9000
M1876, For Deluxe, Add $550.00-$750.00			
M1876, For Extra Fancy Deluxe, Add $2000.00-$5000.00			
M1876, Various Calibers, Carbine, *Antique*	2000	5000	7000
M1876, Various Calibers, Musket, *Antique*	4000	9000	10000
M1876, Various Calibers, Octagon Barrel, Rifle, *Antique*	2000	7000	8000
M1876, Various Calibers, Round Barrel, Rifle, *Antique*	2000	6000	7000
M1886, For Deluxe, Add $400.00-$750.00			
M1886, For Extra Fancy Deluxe, Add $3500.00-$5000.00			
M1886, under #118,433, Various Calibers, Carbine, *Antique*	3500	10000	12000
M1886, under #118,433, Various Calibers, Musket, *Antique*	6000	12000	15000
M1886, under #118,433, Various Calibers, Rifle, *Antique*	1500	4000	5000
M1886, Various Calibers, Carbine, *Curio*	4000	8000	9000
M1886, Various Calibers, Musket, *Curio*	5000	9000	10000
M1886, Various Calibers, Rifle, *Curio*	1500	4000	5000
M250 Deluxe, .22 L.R.R.F., Tube Feed, *Modern*	75	100	125
M250, .22 L.R.R.F., Tube Feed, *Modern*	50	75	100
M255 Deluxe, .22 WMR, Tube Feed, *Modern*	100	125	150
M255, .22 WMR, Tube Feed, *Modern*	75	100	125
M53, Various Calibers, *Modern*	900	2000	2500
M55, Various Calibers, *Modern*	450	1000	1250
M64 Deer Rifle, Various Calibers, Pre '64, *Modern*	700	1200	1500
M64, .219 Zipper, Pre '64, *Modern*	600	1750	2000
M64, .30-30 Win., Late Model, *Modern*	150	300	350

	Fair	V. Good	Excellent
M64, Various Calibers, Pre '64, *Modern*	$600	$900	$1200
M65, .218 Bee, *Modern*	1200	2500	3000
M65, Various Calibers, *Modern*	1200	2000	2500
M71 Special, .348 Win., Tube Feed, *Modern*	550	750	950
M71, .348 Win., Tube Feed, *Modern*	400	725	800
M92, For Takedown, Add $150.00-$275.00			
M92, under #103316, Various Calibers, Carbine, *Antique*	800	1750	2000
M92, under #103316, Various Calibers, Musket, *Antique*	4000	8500	9500
M92, under #103316, Various Calibers, Rifle, *Antique*	700	1800	2000
M92, Various Calibers, Carbine, *Curio*	800	2000	2200
M92, Various Calibers, Musket, *Curio*	3500	7500	8500
M92, Various Calibers, Rifle, *Curio*	750	1800	2000
M94 Standard, .30-30 Win., *Modern*	100	175	250

Winchester M94XTR Big Bore

	Fair	V. Good	Excellent
M94 Trapper, .30-30 Win., Pre '64, *Curio*	1000	2000	3500
M94, .30-30 Win., Carbine, Late Model, *Modern*	100	200	250
M94, .44 Magnum, Carbine, *Modern*	100	225	275
M94, under #50,000 Various Calibers, Carbine, *Antique*	900	2500	3000
M94, under #50,000 Various Calibers, Rifle, *Antique*	800	2000	2500
M94, Various Calibers, Carbine, Pre '64, *Modern*	600	1250	1500
M94, Various Calibers, Carbine, Pre-War, *Curio*	800	1800	2000
M94, Various Calibers, Rifle, Pre-War, *Curio*	900	2500	2000
M94, Various Calibers, Rifle, Take-down, Pre-War, *Curio*	800	2000	2250
M94XTR Big Bore, .375 Win., *Modern*	125	200	275
M94XTR, .30-30 Win., *Modern*	100	175	250
M95, For Takedown, Add $100.00-$200.00			
M95, under #19,477, Various Calibers, Carbine, *Antique*	700	1500	2000

	Fair	V. Good	Excellent
M95, under #19,477, Various Calibers, Rifle, *Antique*	$900	$2000	$2500
M95, Various Calibers, Carbine, *Curio*	800	2000	2500
M95, Various Calibers, Musket, *Curio*	500	1200	1500
M95, Various Calibers, Rifle, *Curio*	800	1800	2000
Model 9422, .22 L.R.R.F., Tube Feed, *Modern*	150	200	250
Model 9422M, .22 WMR, Tube Feed, *Modern*	225	250	275
Model 9422MXTR, .22 WMR, Tube Feed, *Modern*	275	300	325
Model 9422XTR, .22 L.R.R.F., Tube Feed, *Modern*	250	275	300

RIFLE, SEMI-AUTOMATIC

	Fair	V. Good	Excellent
M100, Various Calibers, Clip Fed, *Modern*	200	400	450
M100, Various Calibers, Clip Fed, Carbine, *Modern*	250	500	550
M190, .22 L.R.R.F., Tube Feed, *Modern*	75	100	125
M1903, .22 Win. Auto R.F., Tube Feed, *Curio*	150	275	400
M1905, Various Calibers, Clip Fed, *Curio*	200	500	550
M1907 Police, .351 Win. Self-Loading, Clip Fed, *Curio*	200	400	450
M1907, .351 Win. Self-Loading, Clip Fed, *Curio*	175	350	400
M1910, .401 Win. Self-Loading, Clip Fed, *Curio*	225	475	650
M290 Deluxe, .22 L.R.R.F., Tube Feed, *Modern*	75	125	150
M490 Deluxe, .22 L.R.R.F., Clip Fed, Monte Carlo Stock, *Modern*	100	200	225
M55 Automatic, .22 L.R.R.F., *Modern*	75	125	150
M63, .22 L.R.R.F., Tube Feed, *Modern*	200	400	550
M74, .22 L.R.R.F., Clip Fed, *Modern*	75	150	175
M77, .22 L.R.R.F., Clip Fed, *Modern*	75	125	150
M77, .22 L.R.R.F., Tube Feed, *Modern*	75	150	175

RIFLE, SINGLESHOT

	Fair	V. Good	Excellent
High-Wall, Various Calibers, Musket, *Curio*	900	2000	2500
High-Wall, Various Calibers, Schutzen Rifle, *Curio*	2250	7000	7500
High-Wall, Various Calibers, Schutzen Style Rifle, *Curio*	2500	7000	7500
High-Wall, Various Calibers, Sporting Rifle, *Curio*	900	2000	2500
Low-Wall, .22 Long R.F., Carbine, *Curio*	2000	4500	5000

	Fair	V. Good	Excellent
Low-Wall, Various Calibers, Sporting Rifle, *Curio*	$900	$2000	$2500
Model 310, .22 L.R.R.F., Bolt Action, *Modern*	125	150	175
Winder, .22 Long R.F., Musket, *Curio*	600	700	800

RIFLE, SLIDE ACTION

	Fair	V. Good	Excellent
M1890, under #64,521, Various Rimfires, Case Hardened, *Antique*	900	3000	3500
M1890, Various Rimfires, *Curio*	300	700	750
M1906, .22 L.R.R.F., Tube Feed, Hammer, *Modern*	250	600	650
M270, .22 L.R.R.F., Tube Feed, *Modern*	50	75	100
M270 Deluxe, .22 L.R.R.F., Tube Feed, *Modern*	75	100	125
M275, .22 WMR, Tube Feed, *Modern*	75	100	125
M275 Deluxe, .22 WMR, Tube Feed, *Modern*	100	125	150
M61, .22 L.R.R.F., Tube Feed, *Modern*	200	425	475
M61, Various Rimfires, Tube Feed, Octagon Barrel, *Modern*	300	850	1000
M61 Magnum, .22 WMR, Tube Feed, *Modern*	400	550	600
M62, .22 L.R.R.F., Tube Feed, Hammer, *Modern*	200	400	450
M62 Gallery, .22 Short R.F., Tube Feed, Hammer, *Modern*	200	500	600

SHOTGUN, BOLT ACTION

	Fair	V. Good	Excellent
Model 36, 9mm Shotshell, Takedown, Singleshot, *Curio*	200	425	475
Model 41, .410 Ga., Takedown, Singleshot, *Modern*	150	300	350
Model 41, .410 Ga., Takedown, Singleshot, Checkered Stock, *Modern*	175	325	375

SHOTGUN, DOUBLE BARREL, OVER-UNDER

	Fair	V. Good	Excellent
Model 101 Pigeon 3 Barrel Set, Various Gauges, Skeet Grade, Single Trigger, Automatic Ejector, Checkered Stock, Engraved, *Modern*	900	2500	3000
Model 101 Magnum, 12 Ga. 3", Single Trigger, Automatic Ejector, Engraved, *Modern*	350	700	800
Model 101 Pigeon, 12 and 20 Gauges, Skeet Grade, Checkered Stock, Single Trigger, Automatic Ejector, Engraved, *Modern*	500	1000	1200
Model 101 Pigeon, 12 Ga., Trap Grade, Monte Carlo Stock, Single Trigger, Automatic Ejector, Engraved, *Modern*	600	1350	1600
Model 101 Pigeon, 12 Ga., Trap Grade, Single Trigger, Automatic Ejector, Engraved, *Modern*	$600	$1250	$1500
Model 101, 12 Ga. Mag. 3", Trap Grade, Single Trigger, Automatic Ejector, Checkered Stock, Engraved, *Modern*	300	675	750
Model 101, 12 Ga., Field Grade, Single Trigger, Automatic Ejector, Engraved, *Modern*	400	800	900
Model 101, 12 Ga., Trap Grade, Monte Carlo Stock, Single Trigger, Automatic Ejector, Engraved, *Modern*	400	850	1000
Model 101, 12 Ga., Trap Grade, Single Trigger, Automatic Ejector, Checkered Stock, Engraved, *Modern*	400	800	950
Model 101, Various Gauges, Featherweight, Single Trigger, Automatic Ejector, Checkered Stock, Engraved, *Modern*	400	850	950
Model 101, Various Gauges, Skeet Grade, Single Trigger, Automatic Ejector, Checkered Stock, Engraved, *Modern*	350	700	800
Model 96, 12 and 20 Gauges, Field Grade, Checkered Stock, Vent Rib, *Modern*	250	575	625
Model 96, 12 and 20 Gauges, Skeet Grade, Checkered Stock, Vent Rib, *Modern*	300	600	650
Model 96, 12 Ga., Trap Grade, Checkered Stock, Vent Rib, *Modern*	250	500	550
Model 96, 12 Ga., Trap Grade, Monte Carlo Stock, Vent Rib, *Modern*	250	550	600

SHOTGUN, DOUBLE BARREL, SIDE-BY-SIDE

	Fair	V. Good	Excellent
Model 21 Custom, 12 Ga., Hammerless, Single Selective Trigger, Selective Ejector, Fancy Engraving, Fancy Checkering, *Modern*	4000	6750	7500
Model 21 Custom, 20 Ga., Hammerless, Single Selective Trigger, Selective Ejector, Fancy Checkering, Fancy Engraving, *Modern*	4500	7500	8500
Model 21 Duck, 12 Ga. Mag. 3", Hammerless, Single Selective Trigger, Selective Ejector, Raised Matted Rib, *Modern*	1200	2500	3000
Model 21 Duck, 12 Ga. Mag. 3", Hammerless, Single Selective Trigger, Selective Ejector, Vent Rib, *Modern*	1500	3000	3500

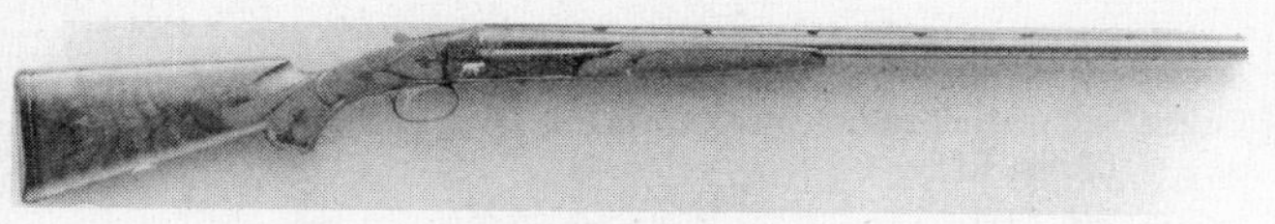

Winchester Model 21 Grand American

	Fair	V. Good	Excellent
Model 21 Grand American, 12 Ga., Hammerless, Single Selective Trigger, Selective Ejector, Fancy Engraving, Fancy Checkering, *Modern*	$6500	$10500	$12500
Model 21 Grand American, 20 Ga., Hammerless, Single Selective Trigger, Selective Ejector, Fancy Checkering, Fancy Engraving, *Modern*	8000	12500	15000
Model 21 Pigeon, 12 Ga., Hammerless, Single Selective Trigger, Selective Ejector, Fancy Engraving, Fancy Checkering, *Modern*	4000	8000	9000
Model 21 Pigeon, 20 Ga., Hammerless, Single Selective Trigger, Selective Ejector, Fancy Engraving, Fancy Checkering, *Modern*	7000	10000	12000
Model 21, .410 Ga., Checkered Stock, Fancy Wood, *Modern*	12000	20000	25000
Model 21, 12 and 16 Gauges, Field Grade, Double Trigger, Automatic Ejector, Hammerless, *Modern*	800	1800	2000
Model 21, 12 and 16 Gauges, Field Grade, Single Selective Trigger, Automatic Ejector, Hammerless, *Modern*	1200	3250	3500
Model 21, 12 and 16 Gauges, Skeet Grade, Hammerless, Single Selective Trigger, Selective Ejector, Vent Rib, *Modern*	1500	3000	3500
Model 21, 12 Ga., Trap Grade, Hammerless, Single Selective Trigger, Selective Ejector, Raised Matted Rib, *Modern*	1200	2750	3000
Model 21, 20 Ga., Field Grade, Double Trigger, Automatic Ejector, Hammerless, *Modern*	1500	2250	2500
Model 21, 20 Ga., Field Grade, Single Selective Trigger, Automatic Ejector, Hammerless, *Modern*	2200	3750	4250
Model 21, 20 Ga., Skeet Grade, Hammerless, Single Selective Trigger, Selective Ejector, Vent Rib, *Modern*	2500	4500	4750
Model 21, 20 Ga., Skeet Grade, Hammerless, Single Selective Trigger, Selective Ejector, Raised Matted Rib, *Modern*	2500	4250	4500

Model 21, For Extra Barrels, Add 25%-30%

Model 21, For Vent Rib, Add $400.00-$600.00

	Fair	V. Good	Excellent
Model 23 English, 12 or 20 Gauges, Hammerless, Single Trigger, Selective Ejector, Fancy Checkering, Engraved, *Modern*	$400	$850	$1000
Model 23 Grand European, 12 Ga., Hammerless, Single Selective Trigger, Selective Ejector, Fancy Engraving, Fancy Checkering, *Modern*	600	1250	1450
Model 23 Pigeon, 12 or 20 Gauges, Hammerless, Single Trigger, Selective Ejector, Engraved, Fancy Checkering, *Modern*	400	900	1050

Winchester Model 23 Pigeon

Model 24, Various Gauges, Double Trigger, Automatic Ejector, *Modern*	200	450	500

SHOTGUN, LEVER ACTION

1901, 10 Ga., 2 1/8", Tube Feed, Plain, *Curio*	500	1000	1250
M 1887, 10 Ga., 2 1/8", Tube Feed, Plain, *Curio*	700	1650	1850
M 1887, Deluxe Grade, 10 Ga., 27/8", Tube Feed, Checkered Stock, Damascus barrel, *Curio*	900	2500	2750
M 1887, Deluxe Grade, Various Gauges, *Antique*	900	2250	2500
M 1887, Various Gauges, *Antique*	700	1500	1750

SHOTGUN, SEMI-AUTOMATIC

Model 1400 Deer, 12 Ga., Open Sights, Slug Gun, *Modern*	125	225	250
Model 1400 Field, 12 and 20 Gauges, Winchoke, *Modern*	100	225	275
Model 1400 Field, 12 and 20 Gauges, Winchoke, Vent Rib, *Modern*	125	250	300

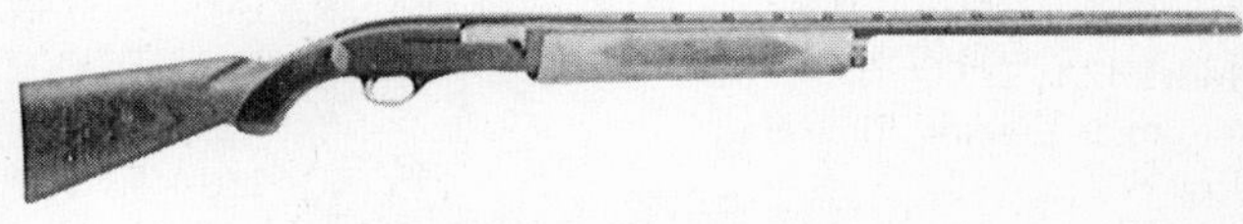

Winchester Model 1400

Model 1400 Skeet, 12 and 20 Gauges, Vent Rib, *Modern*	150	300	350
Model 1400 Trap, 12 Ga., Monte Carlo Stock, Vent Rib, *Modern*	150	325	375
Model 1400 Trap, 12 Ga., Vent Rib, *Modern*	150	300	350

	Fair	V. Good	Excellent
Model 1400 Trap, 12 Ga., Vent Rib, Recoil Reducer, *Modern*	$175	$375	$425
Model 1500, 12 or 20 Gauges, Field Grade, Plain, *Modern*	100	225	275
Model 1500, 12 or 20 Gauges, Field Grade, Vent Rib, *Modern*	125	250	300
Model 1911, 12 Ga., Takedown, Checkered Stock, *Modern*	175	375	425
Model 1911, 12 Ga., Takedown, Plain, *Modern*	150	350	400
Model 40, 12 Ga., Takedown, Field Grade, *Modern*	175	375	425
Model 40, 12 Ga., Takedown, Skeet Grade, Adjustable Choke, *Modern*	200	425	475
Model 50, 12 and 20 Gauges, Field Grade, Plain Barrel, Checkered Stock, *Modern*	150	300	350
Model 50, 12 and 20 Gauges, Field Grade, Vent Rib, Checkered Stock, *Modern*	175	350	400
Model 50, 12 and 20 Gauges, Skeet Grade, Vent Rib, Checkered Stock, *Modern*	250	500	600
Model 50, 12 Ga., Trap Grade, Vent Rib, Monte Carlo Stock, *Modern*	200	400	500

SHOTGUN, SINGLESHOT

	Fair	V. Good	Excellent
Model 101, 12 Ga., Trap Grade, Vent Rib, *Modern*	400	850	1000
Model 20, .410 Ga., 2 1/8", Takedown, Hammer, Checkered Stock, *Modern*	150	325	400
Model 37A, For Red Letter, Add 25%-40%			
Model 37A, .410 Ga., Takedown, Automatic Ejector, Plain Barrel, *Modern*	100	175	250
Model 37A, 12 Ga., Takedown, Automatic Ejector, Plain Barrel, *Modern*	100	125	150
Model 37A, 16 Ga., Takedown, Automatic Ejector, Plain Barrel, *Modern*	100	125	150
Model 37A, 20 Ga., Takedown, Automatic Ejector, Plain Barrel, *Modern*	100	125	150
Model 37A, 28 Ga., Takedown, Automatic Ejector, Plain Barrel, *Modern*	75	150	250

SHOTGUN, SLIDE ACTION

	Fair	V. Good	Excellent
Model 12, 12 Ga., Post '64, Trap Grade, Checkered Stock, *Modern*	250	550	600
Model 12, 12 Ga., Post '64, Trap Gun, Monte Carlo Stock, *Modern*	250	575	625
Model 12, 12 Ga., Pre '64, Takedown, Trap Grade, Raised Matted Rib, *Modern*	300	675	900
Model 12, 12 Ga., Pre '64, Takedown, Trap Grade, Vent Rib, *Modern*	300	725	1200

	Fair	V. Good	Excellent
Model 12, 12 Ga., Pre '64, Takedown, Trap Grade, Vent Rib, Monte Carlo Stock, *Modern*	$350	$775	$1200
Model 12, 12 Ga., Pre-War, Takedown, Riot Gun, *Curio*	400	800	900
Model 12, 12 Ga., Pre-War, Takedown, Vent Rib, *Curio*	300	700	900
Model 12, Featherweight, Various Gauges, Pre '64, Takedown, *Modern*	250	400	550
Model 12, Heavy Duck, 12 Ga. Mag. 3", Pre '64, Takedown, Vent Rib, *Modern*	225	450	700
Model 12, Heavy Duck, 12 Ga. Mag. 3", Pre '64, Takedown, Raised Matted Rib, *Modern*	300	475	650
Model 12, Pigeon Grade, 12 Ga., Pre '64, Takedown, Trap Grade, Vent Rib, *Modern*	800	1500	1750
Model 12, Pigeon Grade, 12 Ga., Pre '64, Takedown, Trap Grade, Raised Matted Rib, *Modern*	800	1450	1650
Model 12, Pigeon Grade, 12 Ga., Various Gauges, Pre '64, Takedown, Skeet Choke, Raised Matted Rib, *Modern*	800	1400	1550
Model 12, Pigeon Grade, Various Gauges, Pre '64, Takedown, Skeet Choke, Vent Rib, *Modern*	700	1400	1600
Model 12, Pigeon Grade, Various Gauges, Pre '64, Takedown, Skeet Choke, Plain Barrel, Adjustable Choke, *Modern*	400	800	900
Model 12, Pigeon Grade, Various Gauges, Pre '64, Takedown, Plain Barrel, *Modern*	400	1000	1500
Model 12, Pigeon Grade, Various Gauges, Pre '64, Takedown, Vent Rib, *Modern*	700	1550	1900
Model 12, Standard, Various Gauges, Pre '64, Takedown, *Modern*	300	600	700
Model 12, Super Pigeon, 12 Ga., Post '64, Takedown, Vent Rib, Engraved, Checkered Stock, *Modern*	800	2000	2500
Model 12, Various Gauges, Pre '64, Takedown, Raised Matted Rib, *Modern*	225	450	800
Model 12, Various Gauges, Pre '64, Takedown, Skeet Grade, Raised Matted Rib, *Modern*	350	1000	1200
Model 12, Various Gauges, Pre '64, Takedown, Skeet Grade, Vent Rib, *Modern*	375	750	1600
Model 12, Various Gauges, Pre '64, Takedown, Skeet Grade, Plain Barrel, *Modern*	300	675	900
Model 12, Various Gauges, Pre '64, Takedown, Skeet Grade, Plain Barrel, Adjustable Choke, *Modern*	350	700	775

	Fair	V. Good	Excellent
Model 1200, For Recoil Reducer, Add $50.00-$75.00			
Model 1200 Deer, 12 Ga., Open Sights, *Modern*	$100	$150	$200
Model 1200 Defender, 12 Ga., *Modern*	75	125	250
Model 1200 Field, 12 and 20 Gauges, *Modern*	100	150	200
Model 1200 Field, 12 and 20 Gauges, Adjustable Choke, *Modern*	150	200	250
Model 1200 Field, 12 and 20 Gauges, Adjustable Choke, Vent Rib, *Modern*	175	225	275
Model 1200 Field, 12 and 20 Gauges, Vent Rib, *Modern*	125	175	225
Model 1200 Field, 12 Ga. Mag. 3", *Modern*	150	175	200
Model 1200 Field, 12 Ga. Mag. 3", Vent Rib, *Modern*	125	175	225
Model 1200 Police Stainless, 12 Ga., *Modern*	150	200	250
Model 1300, 12 or 20 Gauges, Plain Barrel, *Modern*	200	250	300
Model 1300, 12 or 20 Gauges, Plain Barrel, Winchoke, *Modern*	250	300	350
Model 1300, 12 or 20 Gauges, Vent Rib, *Modern*	225	275	325
Model 1300, 12 or 20 Gauges, Vent Rib, Winchoke, *Modern*	275	325	375
Model 1300 Deer, 12 Ga., Open Sights, *Modern*	225	275	325
Model 25, 12 Ga., Solid Frame, Plain Barrel, *Modern*	150	300	500
Model 42, .410 Ga., Field Grade, Takedown, *Modern*	400	750	850
Model 42, .410 Ga., Field Grade, Takedown, Raised Matted Rib, *Modern*	500	800	1000
Model 42, .420 Ga., Skeet Grade, Takedown, Raised Matted Rib, *Modern*	800	1500	1750
Model 42 Deluxe, .410 Ga., Takedown, Vent Rib, Fancy Checkering, Fancy Wood, *Modern*	900	2000	2500
Model 97, 12 Ga., Solid Frame, Plain, *Modern*	250	500	550
Model 97, 12 Ga., Solid Frame, Riot Gun, *Modern*	250	500	600
Model 97, 12 Ga., Takedown, Plain, *Modern*	250	550	600
Model 97, 12 Ga., Takedown, Riot Gun, *Modern*	300	600	700
Model 97, 16 Ga., Solid Frame, Plain, *Modern*	250	550	600
Model 97, 16 Ga., Takedown, Plain, *Modern*	300	600	650
Model 97 Pigeon, 12 Ga., Takedown, Checkered, *Modern*	900	2000	2500
Model 97 Tournament, 12 Ga., Takedown, Checkered Stock, *Modern*	$600	$1200	$1500
Model 97 Trap, 12 Ga., Takedown, Checkered Stock, *Modern*	500	1000	1200
Model 97 Trench, 12 Ga., Solid Frame, Riot Gun, Military, *Curio*	700	1500	1750
Model 97 Trench, 12 Ga., Solid Frame, Riot Gun, Military, with Bayonet, *Curio*	800	1600	1850

WINFIELD ARMS CO.

Made by Crescent, c. 1900. See Crescent Fire Arms Co., Shotgun, Double Barrel, Side-by-Side; Shotgun, Singleshot.

WINFIELD ARMS CO.

Made by Norwich Falls Pistol Co., c. 1880.

HANDGUN, REVOLVER

	Fair	V. Good	Excellent
.32 Short R.F., 5 Shot, Spur Trigger, Solid Frame, Single Action, *Antique*	100	150	175

WINGERT, RICHARD

Lancaster, Pa. 1775–1777. See Kentucky Rifles, U.S. Military.

WINOCA ARMS CO.

Made by Crescent for Jacobi Hardware Co., Philadelphia, Pa. See Crescent Fire Arms Co., Shotgun, Double Barrel, Side-by-Side; Shotgun, Singleshot.

WINSLOW ARMS CO.

Established in Venice, Fla. in 1962, moved to Osprey, Fla. in 1976, and is now in Camden, S.C.

RIFLE, BOLT ACTION

	Fair	V. Good	Excellent
For Left-Hand Act, Add $70.00–$100.00			
Commander, Various Calibers, Fancy Checkering, Inlays, *Modern*	250	500	550
Crown, Various Gauges, Carved, Fancy Wood, Inlays, *Modern*	500	1250	1500
Emperor, Various Gauges, Carved, Fancy Engraving, Ornate, Fancy Wood, Inlays, *Modern*	3000	6000	6500
Imperial, Various Gauges, Carved, Engraved, Fancy Wood, Inlays, *Modern*	2200	3500	3750
Regal, Various Calibers, Fancy Checkering, Inlays, *Modern*	300	600	650
Regent, Various Calibers, Inlays, Carved, Fancy Wood, *Modern*	350	725	775
Regimental, Various Calibers, Carved, Inlays, *Modern*	400	850	1000
Royal, Various Calibers, Carved, Fancy Wood, Inlays, *Modern*	700	1500	1750

WITHERS, MICHAEL
Lancaster, Pa. 1774–1805. See Kentucky Rifles, U.S. Military.

WITTES HDW. CO.
Made by Stevens Arms.

SHOTGUN, DOUBLE BARREL, SIDE-BY-SIDE

	Fair	V. Good	Excellent
Model 311, Various Gauges, Hammerless, Steel Barrel, *Modern*	$75	$150	$175

SHOTGUN, SINGLESHOT

	Fair	V. Good	Excellent
Model 90, Various Gauges, Takedown, Automatic Ejector, Plain, Hammer, *Modern*	25	50	75
Model 94, Various Gauges, Takedown, Automatic Ejector, Plain, Hammer, *Modern*	25	50	75

WOGDON
London, England & Dublin, Ireland, 1760–1797.

HANDGUN, FLINTLOCK

	Fair	V. Good	Excellent
.56, Officers, Holster Pistol, Flared, Octagon Barrel, Steel Furniture, Engraved, High Quality, *Antique*	900	2500	3000

WOLF
Spain, c. 1900.

HANDGUN, SEMI-AUTOMATIC

	Fair	V. Good	Excellent
7.65mm, Clip Fed, *Modern*	100	125	150

WOLF, A. W.
Suhl, Germany, c. 1930.

SHOTGUN, DOUBLE BARREL, SIDE-BY-SIDE

	Fair	V. Good	Excellent
12 Ga., Engraved, Platinium Inlays, Ivory Inlays, Ornate, Cased, *Modern*	3000	6000	7000

WOLFHEIMER, PHILIP
Lancaster, Pa., c. 1774. See Kentucky Rifles.

WOLVERINE ARMS CO.
Made by Crescent for Fletcher Hardware Co., c. 1900. See Crescent Fire Arms Co., Shotgun, Double Barrel, Side-by-Side; Shotgun, Singleshot.

WOODWARD, JAMES & SONS
London, England.

SHOTGUN, DOUBLE BARREL, OVER-UNDER

	Fair	V. Good	Excellent
Best Quality, Various Gauges, Sidelock, Automatic Ejector, Double Trigger, Fancy Engraving, Fancy Checkering, *Modern*	$8000	$20000	$25000
Best Quality, Various Gauges, Sidelock, Automatic Ejector, Single Trigger, Fancy Engraving, Fancy Checkering, *Modern*	9000	22000	27000

SHOTGUN, DOUBLE BARREL, SIDE-BY-SIDE

	Fair	V. Good	Excellent
Best Quality, Various Gauges, Sidelock, Automatic Ejector, Double Trigger, Fancy Engraving, Fancy Checkering, *Modern*	8000	15000	20000
Best Quality, Various Gauges, Sidelock, Automatic Ejector, Single Trigger, Fancy Engraving, Fancy Checkering, *Modern*	8500	17000	22000

SHOTGUN, SINGLESHOT

	Fair	V. Good	Excellent
12 Ga., Trap Grade, Vent Rib, Hammerless, Fancy Engraving, Fancy Checkering, *Modern*	3000	7000	9500

WORTHINGTON ARMS
Made by Stevens Arms.

SHOTGUN, DOUBLE BARREL, SIDE-BY-SIDE

	Fair	V. Good	Excellent
M 315, Various Gauges, Hammerless, Steel Barrel, *Modern*	100	150	175
Model 215, 12 and 16 Gauges, Outside Hammers, Steel Barrel, *Modern*	100	150	175

WORTHINGTON ARMS CO.
Made by Crescent for Geo. Worthington Co., Cleveland, Ohio. See Crescent Fire Arms Co., Shotgun, Double Barrel, Side-by-Side; Shotgun, Singleshot.

WORTHINGTON, GEORGE
Made by Stevens Arms.

SHOTGUN, DOUBLE BARREL, SIDE-BY-SIDE

	Fair	V. Good	Excellent
M 315, Various Gauges, Hammerless, Steel Barrel, *Modern*	100	150	175
Model 215, 12 and 16 Gauges, Outside Hammers, Steel Barrel, *Modern*	75	125	150
Model 311, Various Gauges, Hammerless, Steel Barrel, *Modern*	100	150	175

WUETHRICH
W. Wuethrich, Werkzeugbau, Lutzelfluh, Switzerland.

	Fair	V. Good	Excellent
RIFLE, SINGLESHOT			
Falling Block, Various Calibers, Engraved, Fancy Wood, Scope Mounted, *Modern*	$500	$1000	$1250

Y

YATO

Hamada Arsenal, Japan.

HANDGUN, SEMI-AUTOMATIC

	Fair	*V. Good*	*Excellent*
Yato, .32 ACP, Clip Fed, Military, *Curio*	$900	$2000	$2200
Yato, .32 ACP, Clip Fed, Pre-War, *Curio*	1100	2500	3000

YDEAL

Made by Francisco Arizmendi, Eibar, Spain.

HANDGUN, SEMI-AUTOMATIC

	Fair	*V. Good*	*Excellent*
6.35mm, Clip Fed, Blue, *Curio*	75	100	125
7.65mm, Clip Fed, Blue, *Curio*	100	125	150

YOU BET

Made by Hopkins & Allen, c. 1880.

HANDGUN, REVOLVER

	Fair	*V. Good*	*Excellent*
.22 Short R.F., 7 Shot, Spur Trigger, Solid Frame, Single Action, *Antique*	$125	$150	$175

YOUNG AMERICA

See Harrington & Richardson Arms Co.

YOUNG, HENRY

Easton, Pa. 1774–1780. See Kentucky Rifles.

YOUNG, JOHN

Easton, Pa. 1775–1788. See Kentucky Rifles, U.S. Military.

Z

Z

Ceska Zbrojovka, Prague, Czechoslovakia.

HANDGUN, SEMI-AUTOMATIC

	Fair	V. Good	Excellent
Vest Pocket, 6.35mm, Clip Fed, *Modern*	$75	$100	$125

ZABALA

Zabala Hermanos, Eibar, Spain.

SHOTGUN, DOUBLE BARREL, SIDE-BY-SIDE

	Fair	V. Good	Excellent
12 Ga., Boxlock, Checkered Stock, Double Triggers, *Modern*	75	150	175

ZANOTTI

Brescia, Italy. 1625–Date.

HANDGUN, FLINTLOCK

	Fair	V. Good	Excellent
Brescia Style, .50, Carved Stock, Engraved, Reproduction, *Antique*	75	125	150

ZARAGOZA

Zaragoza, Mexico.

HANDGUN, SEMI-AUTOMATIC

	Fair	V. Good	Excellent
Corla, Type 1, .22 L.R.R.F., Colt System, Clip Fed, Blue, *Modern*	250	575	650
Corla Type 2, .22 L.R.R.F., Colt System, Blue, *Modern*	200	400	450

ZASTAVA ARMS

Zavodi Crvena Zastava, Kragujevac, Yugoslavia. Also see Mark X.

HANDGUN, SEMI-AUTOMATIC

	Fair	V. Good	Excellent
Model 65, 9mm Luger, Clip Fed, Blue, *Modern*	150	325	375
Model 67, .32 ACP, Clip Fed, Blue, *Modern*	125	225	275

ZEHNA

Made by E. Zehner Waffenfabrik, Suhl, Germany 1919–1928.

HANDGUN, SEMI-AUTOMATIC

	Fair	V. Good	Excellent
Vest Pocket, 6.35mm, Clip Fed, Blue, *Curio*	150	300	350
Vest Pocket, 6.35mm, Under #5,000, Clip Fed, Blue, *Curio*	$125	$250	$300

ZEPHYR

Tradename of A. F. Stoeger.

SHOTGUN, DOUBLE BARREL, SIDE-BY-SIDE

	Fair	V. Good	Excellent
Sterlingworth II, Various Gauges, Checkered Stock, Sidelock, Double Triggers, Light Engraving, *Modern*	250	575	650
Woodlander II, Various Gauges, Checkered Stock, Boxlock, Double Triggers, Light Engraving, *Modern*	200	425	475

ZOLI, ANGELO

Brescia, Italy.

RIFLE, PERCUSSION

	Fair	V. Good	Excellent
.50 Hawkin, Brass Furniture, Reproduction, *Antique*	100	150	175

SHOTGUN, DOUBLE BARREL, OVER-UNDER

	Fair	V. Good	Excellent
Angel, 12 and 20 Gauges, Field Grade, Single Selective Trigger, Engraved, Checkered Stock, *Modern*	300	675	750
Angel, 12 Ga., Trap Grade, Single Selective Trigger, Engraved, Checkered Stock, *Modern*	350	700	775
Condor, 12 and 20 Gauges, Single Selective Trigger, Field Grade, Checkered Stock, Engraved, *Modern*	300	600	675
Condor, 12 Ga., Trap Grade, Single Selective Trigger, Engraved, Checkered Stock, *Modern*	300	625	700
Monte Carlo, 12 and 20 Gauges, Field Grade, Single Selective Trigger, Engraved, Checkered Stock, *Modern*	350	750	850
Monte Carlo, 12 Ga., Trap Grade, Single Selective Trigger, Engraved, Checkered Stock, *Modern*	350	775	875

ZOLI, ANTONIO

Gardone, V.T., Italy.

SHOTGUN, DOUBLE BARREL, OVER-UNDER

	Fair	V. Good	Excellent
Golden Snipe, 12 and 20 Gauges, Skeet Grade, Single Trigger, Automatic Ejector, Engraved, Checkered Stock, *Modern*	$200	$450	$550
Golden Snipe, 12 and 20 Gauges, Vent Rib, Single Trigger, Automatic Ejector, Engraved, Checkered Stock, *Modern*	150	350	450
Golden Snipe, 12 Ga., Trap Grade, Single Trigger, Automatic Ejector, Engraved, Checkered Stock, *Modern*	200	450	550
Silver Snipe, 12 and 20 Gauges, Skeet Grade, Single Trigger, Vent Rib, Engraved, Checkered Stock, *Modern*	200	450	500
Silver Snipe, 12 and 20 Gauges, Vent Rib, Single Trigger, Engraved, Checkered Stock, *Modern*	200	425	475
Silver Snipe, 12 Ga., Trap Grade, Single Trigger, Vent Rib, Engraved, Checkered Stock, *Modern*	200	450	500

SHOTGUN, DOUBLE BARREL, SIDE-BY-SIDE

	Fair	V. Good	Excellent
Silver Hawk, 12 and 20 Gauges, Double Trigger, Engraved, Checkered Stock, *Modern*	$200	$400	$450

ZONDA

Hispano Argentina Fab. de Automiviles, Buenos Aires, Argentina.

HANDGUN, SINGLESHOT

	Fair	V. Good	Excellent
.22 L.R.R.F., Blue, *Modern*	100	225	275

ZULAICA

M. Zulaica y Cia., Eibar, Spain.

HANDGUN, SEMI-AUTOMATIC

	Fair	V. Good	Excellent
Royal, .32 ACP, Clip Fed, Blue, Military, *Curio*	100	150	175

AUTOMATIC, REVOLVER

	Fair	V. Good	Excellent
.22 L.R.R.F., Zig-Zag Cylinder, Blue, *Curio*	300	650	750

Appendix I: Bibliography

The organization of this listing of important reference works has been devised to allow the formation of a master library for the ultimate arms-collecting enthusiast. Rather than place these titles in various sections of the *Price Guide* under specific categories (e.g., Colt, Remington, S&W, Winchester), the author felt that organizing the listing by broader categories would be more useful. Further, it allows for xeroxing these pages and carrying them along to gun shows. A number of books are available at these shows, and dealers are usually comfortable with trading or discounts, though generally only for quantity purchases. One of the great pleasures of collecting is building a strong reference library, an unending and vital process.

The hundreds, and sometimes thousands, of books, magazines, and catalogues and other source materials that one can collect are a constant source of pleasure, and necessary in attempting to master the extraordinary world of firearms. For reference value alone, a library is the cheapest, most useful and important component of a collector or dealer's repertoire. This writer would be lost without his library—even though a great deal of my work requires original research with previously unpublished sources.

While this book was being written, the author's friend Peter Buxtun invited him to go through his own reference files, featuring a collection of articles removed from thousands of magazines and other sources over more than thirty-five years of collecting. The amount of material unearthed through this impressive collection was quite substantial—consider the fact that in the firearms world alone there must be over 150 publications on the subject worldwide. Even Poland and Russia now have firearms magazines, and enthusiasts of guns in Russia, judging just from subscribers to the leading magazine, are at least 100,000 strong!

One can never have too many books, or subscribe to too many firearms magazines, or accumulate too many articles, auction catalogues, or other records on the subjects of your collecting and/or dealing interests.

And if space is a consideration, there are many ways to lick the problem. Any good bookstore will have source works on how to effectively turn space into the most efficient storage imaginable. In the author's West Coast apartment he has very little space, but has adapted book shelving, a desk and computer complex, and closets to the extent that his bare-bones library still has space for more books and more reference materials as he toils on manuscripts like this one into the wee hours of every morning he is on site.

GENERAL TITLES

Antal, Laslo. *Competitive Pistol Shooting.* 1989.

Gates, Elgin T. *The Gun Digest Book of Metallic Silhouette Shooting.* 1988.

Hounshell, David A. *From the American System to Mass Production, 1800–1932.* 1984.

Mace, Boyd. *The Accurate Varmint Rifle.* 1991.

Matunas, Edward A. *Shooting.* 1986.

Meadows, Edward Scott. *U.S. Military Automatic Pistols 1894–1920.* 1993.

Mullen, John. *The Gun Report Subject Index June, 1955–May, 1990.* 1993.

Ota, Mitchell A. *Pin Shooting: A Complete Guide.* 1992.

Simpson, Layne. *The Custom Government Model Pistol.* 1992.

Stone, George Cameron. *A Glossary of the Construction, Decoration and Use of Arms and Armor in All Countries and in All Times.* 1934.

Taylerson, A.W.F. *Revolving Arms.* 1967.

———. *The Revolver 1865–1888.* 1966.

———. *The Revolver 1899–1914.* 1970.

———. and R.A.N. Andrews, J. Firth. *The Revolver 1818–1865.* 1968.

Wilson, R. K., and Ian V. Hogg. *Textbook of Automatic Pistols.* 1975.

Yuryev, A. A. *Competitive Shooting.* 1985.

Air Rifles and Pistols

Galan, J. I. *Air Gun Digest.* Various editions.

Allen, Ethan, Allen & Thurber, Allen & Wheelock (et al.)

Thomas, H. H. *The Story of Allen & Wheelock Firearms.* 1965.

Blackpowder

Adler, Dennis. *Collector and Shooter's Guide to Colt Blackpowder Reproductions.* Work in progress, for publication fall 1998.

Brockway, William R. *Recreating the Double Barrel Muzzle-Loading Shotgun.* 1985.

Buchele, William, et al. *Recreating the American Longrifle.* 1983.

Cline, Walter M. *The Muzzle-Loading Rifle, Then and Now.* 1991. Reprint.

Fadala, Sam. *The Complete Black Powder Handbook.* 1990.

——— and Dale Storey. *Black Powder Hobby Gunsmithing.* 1994.

Catalogues

In addition to original catalogues and numerous reprints on the market, two books of special interest are:

Saterlee, L.D. *Fourteen Old Gun Catalogues for the Collector, Volume 2.* 1962.

———. *Ten Old Gun Catalogues, Volume 1.* 1962.

Civil War

GENERAL

Coates, Earl J. and Dean S. Thomas. *An Introduction to Civil War Small Arms.* 1990.

Coggins, Jack. *Arms & Equipment of the Civil War.* 1983.

Edwards, William B. *Civil War Guns.* 1962.

Lord, Francis. *Civil War Collector's Encyclopedia.* 1963.

CONFEDERATE

Albaugh, William A., III and Edward N. Simmons. *Confederate Arms.* 1993.

——— and Hugh Benet. *Confederate Handguns.* 1993.

Albaugh, William A. *The Original Confederate Colt.* 1993.

———. *The Confederate Brass-Framed Colt and Whitney.* 1993.

———. *Tyler, Texas C.S.A.* 1958.

Forgett, Valmore J., and Alain and Marie-Antoinette Serpette. *LeMat: The Man, the Gun.* 1996.

Fuller, Claud E. and Richard Steuart. *Firearms of the Confederacy.*

Gary, William A. *Confederate Revolvers.* 1987.

Hill, Richard Taylor, and William Edward Anthony. *Confederate Long-arms and Pistols: A Pictorial Study.* 1978.

Murphy, Dr. J. *Confederate Carbines and Musketoons.* 1986.

———. *Confederate Rifles and Muskets.* 1995.

Wiggins, Gary. *Dance & Brothers: Texas Gunmakers of the Confederacy.* 1986.

UNION

Marcot, Roy M. *Civil War Chief of Sharpshooters Hiram Berdan, Military Commander and Firearms Inventor.* 1990.

See also numerous titles on gunmakers, e.g., Colt, Remington, Spencer, Sharps, Smith & Wesson, and others commonly used by Union forces.

Colonial, Revolutionary War, and War of 1812

Moore, Warren. *Weapons of the American Revolution and Accouterments.* 1967.

Neumann, George C. and Frank Kravic. *Collector's Illustrated Encyclopedia of the American Revolution.* 1989.

Peterson, Harold L. *Arms and Armor in Colonial America 1526–1783.* 1956.

Colt

Bady, Donald B. *Colt Automatic Pistols.* 1974.

Beinfeld, Wallace, ed. *Armsmear.* Reprint of 1866 edition; the first Colt book.

Brunner, Dr. John W. *Colt Pocket Hammerless Pistols.* Williamstown, New Jersey: Phillips Publications, 1997.

Clawson, Charles W. *Colt 45 Service Pistol Models of 1911 and 1911A1: Complete Military History, Development and Production, 1900 Through 1945.* 1993.

Cochran, Keith. *Colt Peacemaker Encyclopedia.* 1986. Vol. II, 1992.

Condry, Ken and Larry Jones. *The Colt Commemoratives 1961–1986.* 1989.

Edwards, William B. *The Story of Colt's Revolver: The Biography of Col. Samuel Colt.* 1957.

Ezell, Edward C. and R. Blake Stevens. *The Black Rifle, M16 Retrospective.* 1987.

Garton, George. *Colt's S.A.A. Post War Models.* 1987.

Goddard, William H. D. *The Government Models: The Development of the Colt Model of 1911.* 1988.

Graham, Ron, John A. Kopec, and C. Kenneth Moore. *A Study of the Colt Single Action Army Revolver.* 1976; revised edition, 1979.

Grant, Ellsworth. *The Colt Armory: A History of Colt's Manufacturing Company.* 1995.

Greeley, Horace IV. *The Colt U.S. General Officers' Pistols.* 1990.

Haven, Charles T., and Frank A Belden. *A History of the Colt Revolver.* 1940.

Houze, Herbert G. *Colt Rifles & Muskets from 1847 to 1870.* 1996.

Hughes, David R. *The History and Development of the M16 Rifle and Its Cartridge.* 1990.

Kopec, John A. *Colt Cavalry and Artillery Revolvers: A Continuing Study.* 1994.

Maxwell, Samuel L., Sr. *The Colt-Burgess Magazine Rifle.* 1985.

Moore, C. Kenneth. *Colt Revolvers and the U.S. Navy 1865–1889.* 1987.

———. *Colt Single Action Army Revolvers and the London Agency.* 1990.

Parsons, John E. *The Peacemaker and Its Rivals.* 1950.

———. *Sam Colt's Own Record 1847.* 1992. Reprint.

Rapley, Robin J. *Colt Percussion Accouterments 1834–1873.* 1994.

Rosa, Joseph G. *Colonel Colt London.* London: Arms and Armour Press, 1976.

Sellers, Frank. *Colts from the William M. Locke Collection.* 1996.

Serven, James E. *Colt Firearms from 1836.* Various editions since 1954.

Shelden, Douglas C. *A Collector's Guide to Colt's .38 Automatic Pistols,* 1987.

Shumaker, P. L. *Colt's Variations of the Old Model Pocket Pistol 1848–1872.* 1957.

———. *Colt Revolvers and the Tower of London.* 1988.

Swayze, Nathan L. *'51 Colt Navies.* 1993.

Ulrich, Arthur A. *A Century of Achievement.* Originally published 1936; reprint edition from Wolfe Publishing Co., 1992, under title: *Colt's 100th Anniversary Firearms Manual 1836–1936: A Century of Achievement.*

Whittington, Lt. Col. Robert D. *The Colt Whitneyville-Walker Pistol.* 1984.

Wilkerson, Don. *The Post-War Colt Single-Action Revolver.* 1980.

———. *Colt's Single Action Army Revolver Pre-War Post-War Model.* 1991.

Wilson, R. L. *Colt: An American Legend.* 1985. Official history of Colt firearms with detailed serial-number tables. *The Colt Heritage* (1979), a smaller edition by approximately 84 pages.

———. *The Book of Colt Firearms.* Considered the standard reference in the Colt field. 1971 and 1993.

———. *The Arms Collection of Colonel Colt.* 1963.

———. *Colt's Dates of Manufacture 1837–1978.* Detailed serial numbers by year; tables for all models of Colt handguns and long arms. 1985.

———. *Colt Commemorative Firearms.* 1969 and 1974 editions.

———. *Evolution of the Colt.* 1967.

———. *The Book of Colt Engraving* (1972), *Colt Engraving* (1982), *The Colt Engraving Book* (1997).

———. *The Colt Heritage.* 1979.

———. *Samuel Colt Presents.* Hartford, Connecticut: Wadsworth Atheneum, 1961.

———, and R. E. Hable. *Colt Pistols.* 1976.

———, and Philip R. Phillips. *Paterson Colt Pistol Variations.* Dallas. 1979.

———, and Janet Zapata. *The Arms of Tiffany.* Work in progress.

Videos

Son of a Gun or How Sam Colt Changed America. Hour-long video by BBC-TV, presenting history of Colonel Colt and the influence of Colt firearms on history.

Colt Firearms Legends. Narrated by Mel Torme, script by R. L. Wilson. Hour-long video done as companion to *Son of a Gun.*

Combat Handguns

Karwan, Chuck. *Combat Handgunnery.* Various editions, annual.

Taylor, Chuck. *The Complete Book of Combat Handgunning.* 1982.

Thompson, Leroy and Rene Smeets. *Great Combat Handguns.* 1993.

Custom Rifle Makers

Simmons, Dick. *Custom Built Rifles, Their Design & Production.*

Warner, Ken, ed. *The Gun Digest Review of Custom Guns.* 1980.

Derringers

Kirkland, Turner. *Southern Derringers of the Mississippi Valley.* 1971.

Parsons, John E. *Henry Deringer's Pocket Pistol.* 1952.

Wilson, R. L. and L. D. Eberhart. *The Deringer in America. Volume I: The Percussion Period.* 1985. *Volume II: The Cartridge Period.* 1993.

Engraving, Stockmaking, and Fine Guns

Abbiatico, Mario. *Modern Firearms Engraving.* 1980.

———. *Incisione delle Armi Sportive.* 1982.

Bleile, C. Roger. *American Engravers.* 1980. Study of contemporary engravers.

———, Gianoberto Lupi, and Franco Vaccari. *Grandi Incisioni su Armi d'Oggi.* 1977.

Grancsay, Stephen V. *Master French Gunsmiths' Designs of the Mid-Seventeenth Century.* 1950.

———. *Master French Gunsmiths' Designs.* 1970.

Gusler, Wallace B. and James D. Lavin. *Decorated Firearms 1540–1870.* 1977.

Harris, Dr. Fredric A. *Firearms Engraving as Decorative Art.* 1989.
Kennedy, Monte. *Checkering and Carving of Gun Stocks.* 1962.
Meek, James B. *The Art of Engraving.* 1973.
Nobili, Marco E. *Il Grande Libro Delle Incisioni.* 1989. Preface by Firmo Fracassi.
Prudhomme, E. C. *Gun Engraving Review.* 1961.
Wesbrook, Dave. *Professional Stockmaking.* 1994.
Wilson, R. L. *Steel Canvas: The Art of American Arms.* 1995. Decorative arms from the 1500s to modern times, primarily American, but including decorated European arms as well.
———. *L. D. Nimschke: Firearms Engraver.* 1965. Original engraver's record book and several pictured firearms of one of the 19th century's leading arms engravers.

Gatling Gun

Berk, Joseph. *The Gatling Gun: 19th Century Machine Gun to 21st Century Vulcan.* 1991.
Stephenson, E. Frank, Jr. *Gatling: A Photographic Remembrance.* 1994.
Toppel, Donald R. and Paul Wahl. *The Gatling Gun.* 1965.

Griffin & Howe

Howe, James Virgil. *The Modern Gunsmith.* 1934–41. (Deals with a number of makers, including Griffin & Howe.)

Handguns

GENERAL

Arnold A. *Shoot a Handgun.* 1993.
Baker, William Clyde, III. *The American Pocket Pistol 1848–1898.* 1970.
Comus, Steve. *The Gun Digest Book of 9mm Handguns.* 1993.
Cumming, Robert. *Christie's Guide to Collecting: Up-to-Date Information and Practical Advice on Becoming a Collector, Looking After a Collection, Buying and Selling.* 1984.
Gould, A. C. *Modern American Pistols and Revolvers.* 1988.
Konig, Klaus-Peter, and Martin Hugo. *9mm Parabellums: The History & Development of the World's 9mm Pistols & Ammunition.* 1993.
Leatherdale, Frank and Paul. *Successful Pistol Shooting.* 1988.
McGivern, Ed. *Fast and Fancy Revolver Shooting.* 1984.
Morrison, Gregory Boyce. *The Modern Technique of the Pistol.* 1991.
Shaw, John. *Shoot to Win.* 1985.
Swiggett, Hal. *Handguns '95.* 1995 and later editions, with identification by year.

AUTOMATICS

Bruch, Gordon. *Webley & Scott Automatic Pistols.* 1992.
Grennell, Dean A. *The Gun Digest Book of the .45.* 1989.
Hoffschmidt, E. J. *Know Your .45 Auto Pistols—Models 1911 & A1.* 1974.
Kasler, Peter Alan. *Glock: The New Wave in Combat Handguns.* 1993.
Ramos, J. M. *.45 ACP Super Guns.* 1991.
Wilson, R. K. *Textbook of Automatic Pistols.* 1990.

Revolvers

GENERAL

Keith, Elmer. *Sixguns.* 1992.
Numerous other titles under makers' names.

PERCUSSION

Smith, Samuel E., and Frank Sellers. *American Percussion Revolvers.* 1971.
Winant, Lewis. *Early Percussion Firearms.* 1959.

METALLIC CARTRIDGES

Brown, Taylor. *James Reid and His Catskill Knuckledusters.* 1990.
Phelps, Art. *The Story of Merwin, Hulbert & Co. Firearms.* 1991.
Sell, DeWitt, Ph.D. *Handguns Americana.* 1972.
Numerous other titles under makers' names.

"SATURDAY NIGHT SPECIALS"

Goforth, W. E. "Bill." *Iver Johnson's Arms & Cycle Works Handguns, 1871–1964.* 1991.
Webster, Donald B., Jr. *Suicide Specials.* 1958.

High Standard

Dance, Tom. *High Standard: A Collector's Guide to the Hamden & Hartford Target Pistols.* 1991.
Petty, Charles E. *High Standard Automatic Pistols 1932–1950.* 1989.

Holsters

Bianchi, John. *Blue Steel and Gunleather.* 1978.
Rattenbury, Richard. *Packing Iron.* 1993.

Kentucky Rifles and Pistols

Chandler, Roy F., and James B. Whisker, *Behold the Longrifle.* 1993.
Dillin, Captain John G. W. *The Kentucky Rifle.* 1993 (reprint).
Dresslar, Jim (David Wesbrook, photography). *Folk Art of Early America: The Engraved Powder Horn.* 1996.
Guthman, William H. *Drums A'beating Trumpets Sounding.* 1993.
Kauffmann, Henry. *The Pennsylvania-Kentucky Rifle.* 1960.
Kentucky Rifle Association. *Kentucky Rifles and Pistols 1756–1850.* 1976.
Kindig, Joe, Jr. *Thoughts on the Kentucky Rifle in Its Golden Age.* 1984.
Shumway, George. *Rifles of Colonial America, Vols. 1 and II.* 1980.

REGIONAL MAKERS

Bivens, John. *Longrifles of North Carolina.* 1988.
Harriger, Russell H. *Longrifles of Pennsylvania, Volume 1, Jefferson, Clarion & Elk Counties.* 1984.
Hartzler, Daniel D. *Arms Makers of Maryland.* 1975.
Hutslar, Donald A. *Gunsmiths of Ohio—18th & 19th Centuries: Volume 1, Biographical Data.* 1973.
Lewis, Michael H. *The Gunsmiths of Manhattan, 1625–1900: A Checklist of Tradesmen.* 1991.
Shumway, George. *George Schreyer, Sr. and Jr., Gunmakers of Hanover, Pennsylvania.* 1990.
———. *Pennsylvania Longrifles of Note.* 1977.

Lever-Action Rifles

Jamieson, G. Scott. *Bullard Arms.* Ontario, Canada: The Boston Mills Press, 1989.
Maxwell, Samuel L., Sr. *Lever-Action Magazine Rifles Derived from the Patents of Andrew Burgess.* 1976.
See also under manufacturers, e.g., Winchester, Marlin, Remington.

Machine Guns

Chinn, Colonel George M. *The Machine Gun.* Four volumes: Vol. 1 (1951), Vol. II (1952), Vol. III (1953), Vol. IV (1955).
Helmer, William J. *The Gun That Made the Twenties Roar.* 1977. (The Thompson submachine gun.)
Hill, Tracie L. *Thompson: The American Legend: The First Submachine Gun.* 1996.
Truby, J. David. *The Lewis Gun.* 1988.
Wardman, Wayne. *The Owen Gun.* 1991.

Manhattan

Nutter, Waldo E. *Manhattan Firearms.* 1958.
Wilson, R. L. *The Guns of Manhattan.* Work in progress.

Marlin

Brophy, Lt. Col. William S., USAR, Ret. *Marlin Firearms: A History of the Guns and the Company That Made Them.* 1989.

Military

MUZZLE-LOADING

Bazelon, and McGuinn. *A Directory of American Military Goods Dealers and Makers 1785–1915.* 1990.
Brophy, William S. *Krag Rifles.* 1980.
Dorsey, R. Stephen. *Indian War Cartridge Pouches, Boxes and Carbine Boots.* 1993.
Gluckman, Arcaidi. *United States Martial Pistols and Revolvers.* 1956.
———. *Identifying United States Muskets, Rifles and Carbines.* 1965.
Hicks, James. *U.S. Firearms 1776–1956, Notes on U.S. Ordnance, Vol. I.* 1957.
———. *Ordnance Correspondence, Vol. II.* 1940.
Huntington, R. T. *Hall's Breechloaders.*
Jordan, John W. *The Eagle on U.S. Firearms.* 1992.
Lewis, Berkeley R. *Small Arms and Ammunition in the United States Service.* 1956.
Lewis, Jack. *The Gun Digest Book of Assault Rifles.* Various editions; annual.
Madis, George. *U.S. Military Arms Dates of Manufacture from 1795.* 1989.
Moller, George D. *American Military Shoulder Arms: Volume I, Colonial and Revolutionary War Arms.* 1993.
———. *American Military Shoulder Arms: Volume 2, From the 1790s to the End of the Flintlock Period.* 1994.
———. *Massachusetts Military Shoulder Arms 1784–1877.* 1989.
North, S. and R. North. *Simeon North: First Official Pistol Maker of the United States.* 1972.
Pitman, Brigadier General John. *The Pitman Notes on U.S. Martial Small Arms and Ammunition, 1776–1933, Volume 2, Revolvers and Automatic Pistols.* 1990.
———. *U.S. Breech-Loading Rifles and Carbines, Cal. 45.* 1992. (Trapdoor rifles, muskets, carbines.)
Reilly, Robert M. *United States Martial Flintlocks.* 1986.
———. *U.S. Military Small Arms 1816–1865.* 1983.
Smith, Samuel E. and Edwin W. Bitter. *Historic Pistols: The American Martial Flintlock 1760–1845.* 1986.

METALLIC CARTRIDGE

Canfield, Bruce N. *A Collector's Guide to the M1 Garand and the M1 Carbine.*
———. *A Collector's Guide to the '03 Springfield,* 1989.
———. *A Collector's Guide to U.S. Combat Shotguns.* 1992.
Crossman, Captain E. C. *Military and Sporting Rifle Shooting.* 1988. Reprint.
Duff, Scott A. *The M1 Garand: World War 2.* 1990.
———. *The M1 Garand: Post World War.* 1993.
Gander, Terry. *Guerrilla Warfare Weapons.* 1990.
Hatcher, Major-General J. S. *The Book of the Garand.* 1977.
Ramos, J. M. *World's Deadliest Rimfire Battleguns.* 1990.
Russell, A. L. *Illustrated Handbook of Rifle Shooting.* 1992.
Ruth, Larry. *M1 Carbine.* 1987.
———. *War Baby!: The U.S. Caliber 30 Carbine, Volume I.* 1992.
———. *War Baby Comes Home: The U.S. Caliber 30 Carbine, Volume 2.* 1993.
Stevens, R. Blake. *U.S. Rifle M14—From John Garand to the M21.* 1991.
Swearengen, Thomas F. *The World's Fighting Shotguns.* 1979.

NAVAL

Gilkerson, William. *Boarders Away, Volume II: Firearms of the Age of Fighting Sail.* 1993.
Winter, Frederick R. *U.S. Naval Handguns, 1808–1911.* 1990.

New England

Achtermeier, William O. *Rhode Island Arms Makers & Gunsmiths 1643–1883.* 1980.
Deyrup, Felicia Johnson. *Arms Makers of the Connecticut Valley.* 1948.
Lindsay, Merrill K. *The New England Gun.* 1975.
Logan, Herschel C. *Underhammer Guns.* 1965.

Oddities

Frost, H. Gorden. *Blades and Barrels.* 1972.
Winans, Lewis. *Firearms Curiosa.* 1955.

Patents

British Patent Office. *Patents for Inventions, Class 119 (Small Arms), 1855–1930.* 1993. Seven volumes.
Stockbridge, V. D. *Digest of U.S. Patents Relating to Breech Loading and Magazine Small Arms, 1836–1873.* Reprint.

Pepperbox Firearms

Dunlap, Jack. *American British & Continental Pepperbox Firearms.* 1964.
Winant, Lewis. *Pepperbox Firearms.* 1952.

Plains Rifles

Baird, John D. *Fifteen Years in the Hawken Lode.* 1976.
———. *Hawken Rifles, The Mountain Man's Choice.* 1976.
Hanson, Charles E., Jr. *The Hawken Rifle: Its Place in History.* 1979.
———. *The Northwest Gun.* 1976.
———. *The Plains Rifle.* 1989.
Roberts, Ned H. *The Muzzle-Loading Cap Lock Rifle.* 1991.
Russell, Carl P. *Firearms, Traps, & Tools of the Mountain Men.* 1967.
———. *Guns of the Early Frontiers.* 1957.

Remington

Karr, Charles Lee, Jr. and Caroll Robbins Karr. *Remington Handguns.* 1956.
Lacy, John F. *The Remington 700.* 1990.
Layman, George. *The Military Remington Rolling Block Rifle.* 1992.
Marcot, Roy M. *It Never Failed Me.* 1997.
Peterson, Harold L. *The Remington Historical Treasury of American Guns.* 1966.

Ruger (Sturm, Ruger & Co., Inc.)

Dougan, John C. *Compliments of Col. Ruger: A Study of Factory Engraved Single Action Revolvers.* 1992.
———. *Know Your Ruger Single-Action Revolvers 1953–63.* 1981.
———. *Know Your Ruger Single-Actions: The Second Decade 1963–73.* 1989.
Hiddleson, Chad. *Encyclopedia of Ruger Rimfire Semi-Automatic Pistols: 1949–1992.* 1993.
Long, Duncan. *The Ruger "P" Models.* 1993.
———. *The Ruger .22 Automatic Pistol, Standard/Mark I/Mark II Series.* 1989.
Lueders, Hugo A., ed. by Don Findley. *Ruger Automatic Pistols and Single Action Revolvers.* 1993.
Roberts, Joseph Jr. *Ruger.* 1991 (Compilation of miscellaneous articles in

The American Rifleman, regarding Ruger firearms and William B. Ruger.)
Wilson, R. L. *Ruger & His Guns.* New York: Simon & Schuster, Inc., 1996.

Sharps

Bailey, DeWitt. *The Model 1874 Sharps.*
Hopkins, Richard E. *Military Sharps Rifles & Carbines, Vol. I.* 1967.
Sellers, Frank. *Sharps Firearms.* 1982.
Smith, Winston O. *The Sharps Rifle.* 1965.

Shotguns

GENERAL

Barnes, Mike. *The Complete Clay Shot.* 1993.
Brister, Bob. *Shotgunning: The Art and the Science.* 1976.
Butler, David F. *The American Shotgun.* 1973.
Conley, Frank F. *The American Single Barrel Trap Gun.* 1989.
Croft, Peter. *Clay Shooting.* 1990.
Davies, Ken. *The Better Shot.* 1992.
Hinman, Bob. *The Golden Age of Shotgunning.* 1982.
McIntosh, Michael. *Best Guns.* 1989.
Meyer, Jerry. *Clay Target Handbook.* 1993.
Wallack, L. R. *American Shotgun Design and Performance.* 1977.
Zutz, Don. *The Double Shotgun.* 1985.
———. *Shotgunning Trends in Transition.* 1990.

BROWNING

Browning, V. *A History of Browning Guns from 1831.* 1986.
Desert Publications. *Browning Hi-Power Pistols.* 1982.

FOX

McIntosh, Michael. *A. H. Fox: The Finest Gun in the World.* 1994.

ITHACA

Snyder, Walter Claude. *The Ithaca Gun Company from the Beginning.* 1991.

L. C. SMITH

Brophy, Lt. Col. William S. *L. C. Smith Shotguns.* 1979.

LEFEVER

Elliot, Robert W., and Jim Cobb. *Lefever: Guns of Lasting Fame.* 1986.

PARKER & BROS.

Baer, Larry L. *The Parker Gun.* 1980.

Single-Shot Rifles

Cleveland, H. W. S. *Hints to Riflemen.* 1864.
deHaas, Frank. *A Potpourri of Single Shot Rifles & Actions.* 1993.
———. *More Single Shot Rifles and Actions.* 1989.
Delisse, Frank and Mark. *Single-Shot Actions, Their Design and Construction.* 1991.
Grant, James J. *Single Shot Rifles.* 1947.
———. *Boy's Single Shot Rifles.* 1967.
———. *More Single Shot Rifles.* 1959.
———. *Single Shot Rifle Finale.* 1992.
Kelver, Gerald O. *Reloading Tools, Sights and Telescopes for Single Shot Rifles.* 1982.
Layman, George J. *A Guide to the Maynard Breechloader.* 1993.

Smith & Wesson

Jinks, Roy G. *Artistry in Arms.* 1991. Book accompanying worldwide tour of S&W firearms.
———. *The History of Smith & Wesson: No Thing of Importance Will Come Without Effort.* 1977. Revised 1988.
———, and Robert J. Neal. *Smith & Wesson 1857–1945.* 1975.
Parsons, John E. *Smith & Wesson Revolvers.* 1957.

Spencer

Marcot, Roy M. *Spencer Repeating Firearms.* 1983.

Sporting Rifles

deHaas, Frank. *Bolt Action Rifles.* 1984.
Fadala, Sam. *Legendary Sporting Rifles.* 1992.
———. *Rifle Guide.* 1993.
Fremantle, T. F. *The Book of the Rifle.* 1988. Reprint.
Keith, Elmer. *Big Game Rifles and Cartridges.* 1984. Reprint.
———. *Keith's Rifles for Large Game.* 1986.
McIntosh, Michael. *The Big-Bore Rifle.* 1990.
O'Connor, Jack. *The Big Game Rifle.* 1994. Reprint.
Truesdell, S. R. *The Rifle: Its Development for Big-Game Hunting.* 1992.

Springfield Armory

Brophy, Lt. Colonel William S. *The Springfield 1903 Rifles.* 1985.
———. *Arsenal of Freedom, The Springfield Armory, 1890–1948: A Year-by-Year Account Drawn from Official Records.* 1991.
Crossman, Edward C. and Roy F. Dunlap. *The Book of the Springfield.* 1990.
Fuller, Claude. *Springfield Shoulder Arms 1795–1865.* 1986.
Poyer, Joe and Craig Riesch. *The .45–70 Springfield.* 1991.
Waite, M. D. and B. D. Ernst. *The Trapdoor Springfield.* 1983.

Stevens Arms & Tool Co.

Cope, Kenneth L. *Stevens Pistols and Pocket Rifles.* 1992.

Target Rifles and Handguns

Fadala, Sam. *The Book of the Twenty-Two: The All American Caliber.* 1989.
Johnson, Rick. *Rifleman's Handbook: A Shooter's Guide to Rifles, Reloading & Results.* 1990. An NRA publication.
Parish, David. *Successful Rifle Shooting.* 1993.
Smith, Roy M. *The Story of Pope's Barrels.* 1993.

Underhammer Guns

Logan, Herschel C. *Underhammer Guns.* 1965.

Weatherby

Gresham, Grits and Tom. *Weatherby: The Man, The Gun, The Legend.* 1992.

Whitney

Fuller, Claud E. *The Whitney Firearms.* 1946.

Winchester Repeating Arms Co., Its Predecessors and Successors

Butler, David F. *Winchester Model 1873.*

Campbell, John. *The Winchester Single-Shot: A History and Analysis.* 1995.
Canfield, Bruce. *A Collector's Guide to Winchester in the Service.* 1991.
Fadala, Sam. *Winchester's .30–30, Model 94.* 1986.
Henshaw, Thomas E. *The History of Winchester Firearms 1866–1992.* Sixth edition. 1993.
Houze, Herbert G. *Winchester Repeating Arms Company: Its History & Development from 1865 to 1981.* 1995.
———. *To the Dreams of Youth: The .22 Caliber Single Shot Winchester Rifle.* 1993.
Madis, George. *The Winchester Book.* Various editions since 1961.
———. *Winchester Dates of Manufacture 1849–1984.* 1984.
———. *The Winchester Handbook.* 1981.
———. *The Winchester Model Twelve.* 1982.
McDowell, R. Bruce. *Evolution of the Winchester from the 1847 Hunt, the Jennings, Smith-Jennings, Smith & Wesson, "Volcanic," Henry Rifle, and Beyond.* 1985.
Parsons, John E. *The First Winchester.* 1955.
Poyer, Joseph. *U.S. Winchester Trench and Riot Guns and Other U.S. Military Combat Shotguns.* 1992.
Renneberg, Robert C. *The Winchester Model 94: The First 100 Years.* 1991.
Rule, Roger C. *A Catalogue Collection of 20th Century Winchester Repeating Arms Co.* 1984.
Schwing, Ned. *Winchester Slide-Action Rifles, Volume 1: Model 1890 & 1906.* 1992.
———. *Winchester Slide-Action Rifles, Volume 2: Model 61 & Model 62.* 1993.
———. *The Winchester Model 42.* 1990.
———. *Winchester's Finest, The Model 21.* 1990.
Stadt, Ronald W. *Winchester Shotguns and Shotshells.* 1984.
Watrous, George. *A History of Winchester Firearms, 1866–1966.*
Williamson, Clyde "Snooky." *Winchester Lever Legacy.* 1988.
Williamson, Harold F. *Winchester: The Gun That Won the West.* 1961.
Wilson, R. L. *Winchester: An American Legend.* 1991.
———. *Winchester Engraving.* 1991.
———. *Winchester: The Golden Age of American Gunmaking and the Winchester 1 of 1000.* 1983.

GENERAL SUBJECTS

Ammunition

Barnes, Frank. *Cartridges of the World.* Various editions.
Erlmeier, Hans A. and Jakob H. Brandt. *Manual of Pistol and Revolver Cartridges, Vol. 2, Centerfire U.S. and British Calibers.* 1981.
Hatcher, Julian. *Hatcher's Notebook.* 1992.
Hoyen, George A. *The History and Development of Small Arms Ammunition, Volumes 1 and 2.* 1991. (Volume 1 deals with military longarms and early machine guns and their ammunition, period of the 18th and 19th centuries.)
———. *The History and Development of Small Arms Ammunition (British Sporting Rifle) Volume 3.* 1991.
Huon, Jean. *Military Rifle & Machine Gun Cartridges.* 1990.
Iverson, Dick. *Encyclopedia and Price Guide of American Paper Shotshells.* 1991.
———. *The Shotshell in the United States.* 1988.
Keith, Elmer. *Sixgun Cartridges and Loads.* 1984.
Kent, Daniel W. *German 7.9mm Military Ammunition.* 1991.
Matthews, Paul A. *Loading the Black Powder Rifle Cartridge.* 1993.
Suydam, Charles R. *The American Cartridge.* 1986.
Wolfe Publishing Co. *Big Bore Rifles and Cartridges.* 1991.
Various authors. *Wildcat Cartridges, Volume I.* 1992. By writers for *Handloader* and *Rifle* magazines.
Various authors. *Wildcat Cartridges, Volume II.* 1992. By writers for *Handloader* and *Rifle* magazines.

HAND-LOADING

Bell, Bob. *Handloader's Digest.* Various editions, annual.
Grennell, Dean A. *The Gun Digest Book of Handgun Reloading.* 1987.
Sharpe, Philip B. *Complete Guide to Handloading.*
Whelen, Colonel Townshend. *Why Not Load Your Own?* 1957.

Children

Lindsay, Merrill. *The Lure of Antique Arms.* 1976.
Rees, Clair F. *Beginner's Guide to Guns and Shooting.* 1988.

Encyclopedic Volumes

Amber, John T. *Gun Digest.* Various editions. See also later editions, edited by Ken Warner.
Brownell, Bob. *The Encyclopedia of Modern Firearms, Volume 1.* 1959.
Grennell, Dean A. *Handgun Digest.* Various editions.
Murtz, Harold A. *The Gun Digest Book of Exploded Long Gun Drawings.*
———. *The Gun Digest Book of Exploded Handgun Drawings.* 1992.
National Rifle Association. *Firearms Assembly 3: The NRA Guide to Rifles and Shotguns.* 1980.
———. *Firearms Assembly 4: The NRA Guide to Pistols and Revolvers.* 1980.
Peterson, Harold L. *Encyclopedia of Firearms.* 1964.
Petzal, David E. *The Encyclopedia of Sporting Firearms.* 1992.
Rice, F. Philip. *Outdoor Life Gun Data Book.* 1987.
Steindler, R. A. *Steindler's New Firearms Dictionary.* 1985.
Warner, *Gun Digest.* Various editions, annual (see also *Gun Digest* published under editorship of John T. Amber).
Wood, J. B. *Firearms Assembly/Disassembly, Part I: Automatic Pistols.* 1990.
———. *Firearms Assembly/Disassembly, Part I: Revolvers.* 1990.
———. *Firearms Assembly/Disassembly, Part I: Rimfire Rifles.* 1994.
———. *Firearms Assembly/Disassembly, Part I: Centerfire Rifles.* 1991.
———. *Firearms Assembly/Disassembly, Part I: Shotguns.* 1992.
———. *Firearms Assembly/Disassembly, Part I: Law Enforcement Weapons.* 1981.

Fakes

Edgerly, Harold. *The Revolving-Cylinder Colt Pistol Story from 1839 to 1847.*
Peterson, Harold L. *How Do You Know It's Old?* 1975.

Gun Legislation and Gun Laws

Bureau of Alcohol, Tobacco and Firearms. Book of regulations; available free of charge from any BATF office, and occasionally obtainable from displays by BATF agents at firearms shows.
Gottlieb, Alan. *The Gun Grabbers.* 1988.
Greenwood, Colin. *Firearms Control: A Study of Armed Crime and Firearms Control in England and Wales.* 1972.
Halbrook, Stephen P. *A Right to Bear Arms.* 1989.
———. *That Every Man Be Armed: The Evolution of a Constitutional Right.* 1984.
Kates, Don, ed. *Restricting Handguns: The Liberal Skeptics Speak Out.* 1979.
———, ed. *Firearms and Violence.* 1984.
———, ed. *The Great American Gun Debate.* 1997.
Kukla, Robert J. *Gun Control: A Written Record of Efforts to Eliminate the Private Possession of Firearms in America.* 1973.
Quigley, Paxton. *Armed and Female.* 1989. Various editions.
Sturm, Ruger & Co., Inc. *Firearms Ownership in America—Our Responsibility for the Future.* 1995.
Wright, James D., Peter H. Rossi, Kathleen Daly. *Under the Gun: Weapons, Crime and Violence in America.* 1983.

Gunmaker Lists

Sellers, Frank. *American Gunsmiths.* 1983.

Gunsmithing, Gunmaking

Angier, R. H. *Firearms Bluing and Browning.*
Brownell, Bob. *Gunsmith Kinks.* 1969.
———. *Gunsmith Kinks 2.* 1983.
Brownell, Frank. *Gunsmith Kinks 3.* 1993.
Dunlap, Foy F. *Gunsmithing.* 1990.
Handloader and *Rifle* magazines, editors of. *Gunsmithing Tips and Projects.* 1992.
Matunas, Edward A. *Practical Gunsmithing.* 1989.
Mitchell, Jack. *The Gun Digest Book of Pistolsmithing.* 1980.
———. *The Gun Digest Book of Riflesmithing.* 1982.
Nonte, George C., Jr. *Pistolsmithing.* 1974.
Raynor, Ken and Brad Fenton. *The NRA Gunsmithing Guide—Updated.* 1984.
Stelle, J. P. and William B. Harrison. *The Gunsmith's Manual.* 1982.
Traister, John E. *First Book of Gunsmithing.* 1981.
———. *Gunsmithing at Home.* 1985.
Walker, Ralph. *The Gun Digest Book of Shotgun Gunsmithing.* 1983.

Guns of the West

Cunningham, Eugene. *Triggernometry.* 1970.
duMont, John S. *Custer Battle Guns.* 1988.
Garavaglia, Louis A. and Charles G. Worman. *Firearms of the American West 1803–1865.* 1984.
———. *Firearms of the American West 1866–1894.* 1985.
Markham, George. *Guns of the Wild West.* 1993.
Rattenbury, Richard and Thomas E. Hall. *Sights West: Selections from the Winchester Museum Collection.* 1981.
Rosa, Joseph G. *The West from Lewis and Clark to Wounded Knee: The Turbulent Story of the Settling of Frontier America.* 1994.
———. *The Gunfighter, Man or Myth?* 1969.
———, and Robin May. *Buffalo Bill and the Wild West.* 1992.
Schreiner, Charles III, et al. *A Pictorial History of the Texas Rangers.* 1969.
Serven, James E. *Conquering the Frontiers: Stories of American Pioneers and the Guns Which Helped Them Establish a New Life.* 1974.
Wilson, R. L. *The Peacemakers: Arms and Adventure in the American West.* 1992.

Video

A & E Network. *The Guns That Tamed the West.* 1995.

Hunting

Aitken, Russell Barnett. *Great Game Animals of the World.* 1974.
Atwater, Sally and Judith Schnell. *Ruffed Grouse.* 1989.
Batten, John H. *The Formidable Game.* 1983.
Bell, W.D.M. *Karamojo Bell.* 1990.
———. *The Wanderings of an Elephant Hunter.* 1990.
Bland, Dwain. *Turkey Hunter's Digest.* 1986.
Boddington, Craig. *Campfires and Game Trails: Hunting North American Big Game.* 1985.
———. *Safari Rifles: Double Magazine Rifles and Cartridges for African Hunting.* 1990.
Boone & Crockett Club. *Records of Hunting North American Big Game.* Various editions.
Buckingham, Nash. *"Mr. Buck": The Autobiography of Nash Buckingham.* 1990.
Bull, Bartle. *Safari: A Chronicle of Adventure.* 1989.
Cadieux, Charles L. *Pronghorn, North America's Unique Antelope.* 1986.
Capstick, Peter. *Death in the Long Grass.* 1977. (One of several books of African safari adventure by a former Wall Street banker who became a professional hunter in Africa.)
Corbett, Jim. *The Jim Corbett Collection.* 1991.
Elliott, Brook. *The Complete Smoothbore Hunter.* 1986.
Elman, Robert. *1001 Hunting Tips.* 1983.
———, and George Peper. *Hunting America's Game Animals and Birds.* 1975.
Fergus, Jim. *A Hunter's Road.* 1992.
Fish, Chet, ed. *The Outdoor Life Bear Book.* 1983.
Foster, William Harnden. *New England Grouse Shooting.* 1983.
Gassett, Jose Ortega y. *Meditations on Hunting.* 1985.
Gates, Elgin T. *Trophy Hunter in Asia.* 1982.
Grinnell, George Bird. *American Duck Shooting.* 1991 (reprint).
Halls, Lowell K. *White-Tailed Deer: Ecology and Management.* 1984.
Hemingway, Ernest. *Green Hills of Africa.* (First published 1935; reflects Hemingway's fascination with safari hunting.)
Huggler, Tom. *Quail Hunting in America.* 1987.
Karsnitz, Jim and Vivian. *Sporting Collectibles.* 1992.
Laycock, George. *The Hunters and the Hunted.* 1990.
Levinson, John M. and Somers G. Headley. *Shorebirds: The Birds, The Hunters, The Decoys.* 1991.
Madsen, John, et al. *The Outdoor Life Deer Hunter's Encyclopedia.* 1985.
Mellon, James. *African Hunter.* 1988. (The definitive book on African hunting.)
Morris, David. *Hunting Trophy Whitetails.* 1993.
National Muzzle Loading Rifle Association. *The North American Big Game Muzzleloading Record Book.* 1992.
O'Connor, Jack. *Sheep and Sheep Hunting.* 1992.
Patterson, J. H. *Man-Eaters of Tsavo.* 1986.
Reiger, George. *The Wildfowler's Quest.* 1989.
———. *The Wings of Dawn.* 1989. (Waterfowl hunting, including history thereof.)
Rikhoff, Jim. *Fair Chase.* 1984.
Roosevelt, Theodore. *Ranch Life and the Hunting Trail.*
———, and George Bird Grinnell, et al. *Hunting in Many Lands.*
Ruark, Robert. *The Old Man and the Boy and The Old Man Grows Older.* 1989. Reprint.
———. *Horn of the Hunter.* 1987. Reprint.
———. *Use Enough Gun.* 1992. Reprint.
Rue, Leonard Lee, III. *Whitetails.* 1991.
Sheehan, Laurence. *The Sporting Life: A Passion for Hunting and Fishing.* 1992.
Smith, Steven. *Hunting Ducks and Geese.* 1984.
———. *Hunting Upland Game Birds.* 1987.
van Zwoll, Wayne. *Elk Rifles, Cartridges and Hunting Tactics.* 1992.
Waterman, Charles F. *The Hunter's World.* 1983.
Wegner, Dr. Robert. *Deer and Deer Hunting: The Serious Hunter's Guide.* 1984. Followed by *Deer and Deer Hunting Book 2* and *Deer and Deer Hunting Book 3.*
———. *Wegner's Bibliography on Deer and Deer Hunting.* 1993.
Wildlife Management Institute. *Big Game of North America, Ecology and Management.* 1983.
Wilson, R. L. *Theodore Roosevelt Outdoorsman.* 1971 and 1994.
Woolner, Frank. *Timberdoodle.* 1987. (A woodcock hunting classic.)
Wooters, John. *Hunting Trophy Deer.* 1983.
Vettier, Jacques. *Big Game Hunting in Asia, Africa, and Elsewhere.* 1993.
Zumbo, Jim and Robert Elman, ed. *All-American Deer Hunter's Guide.* 1983.

Video

In the Blood. Feature film documents two African safaris: the first led by President Roosevelt in 1909, the second by his grandson nearly 80 years later. Proof of the key role of hunting in the conservation of wildlife.

HUNTING WITH HANDGUNS

Boothroyd, Geoffrey. *The Handgun.* 1989.

Kelly, Larry and J. D. Jones. *Hunting for Handgunners.* 1990.

Identification and/or Values

Fjestad, Steven. *Blue Book of Gun Values.* 18th edition. 1997.

Flayderman, Norm. *Flayderman's Guide to Antique American Firearms and Their Values.* Various editions.

Herr, Eugene. *Der Neue Stockel.* International listing of gunmakers from 1400 through 1900; in three volumes: 1978, 1979, 1982.

Quertermous, Russell and Steve. *Modern Guns: Identification & Values.* 1992.

Schroeder, Joe. *The Gun Digest Book of Modern Gun Values.* Various editions, annual.

Schwing, Ned and Herbert Houze. *Standard Catalog of Firearms.* Various editions, annual.

Law Enforcement

Askins, Charles, Jr. *Unrepentant Sinner.* 1985.

Ferguson, Tom. *Modern Law Enforcement Weapons & Tactics.* 1991.

FitzGerald, J. H. *Shooting.* 1993.

Jordan, William H. *No Second Place Winner.* 1962.

Keith, Elmer. *Hell, I Was There!* 1979.

Military

George, Lieutenant Colonel John. *Shots Fired in Anger.* 1991.

Hesketh-Prichard, Major H. *Sniping in France.* 1993.

Hogg, Ian V. *Military Small Arms of the 20th Century, 6th Edition.* 1991.

———. *Small Arms: Pistols and Rifles.* 1994.

———. *Pistols of the World.* 1992. Various editions.

Hunnicutt, Robert W., ed. *Semi-Auto Rifles: Data and Comment.* 1988.

McBride, H.W. *A Rifleman Went to War.* 1987.

Stevens, R. Blake and Edward C. Ezell. *The SPIW: Deadliest Weapon That Never Was.* 1985.

Walter, John. *Rifles of the World.* 1993.

Weeks, John. *World War 2 Small Arms.* 1989.

Articles from *The American Rifleman.*

Miniatures

Keeble, K. Corey. *From the Kingdom of Lilliput: The Miniature Firearms of David Kucer* combined with *The Making of Miniatures*, by David Kucer. 1994.

Lindsay, Merrill. *Miniature Firearms.*

Auction-House and Dealer Catalogues

Bourne, Richard A., Co. *The Remington Collection of Karl F. Moldenhauer.* October 20, 1980.

Dexter, F. Theodore. *Thirty-Five Years Scrap Book of Antique Arms.* Vols. 1 and 2.

Francis Bannerman Sons. Eightieth-anniversary hardbound catalogue.

Martin, Greg. *The Estate of Richard C. Marohn, M.D.* San Francisco: Butterfield & Butterfield, October 16, 1996. (Catalogue of the Marohn Collection, including artifacts, documents and memorabilia of L. D. Nimschke, and of the Young family of engravers.)

———. Miscellaneous auction catalogues including the John R. Woods Collection (October 22, 1991), the Warren Anderson Collection (March 23 and July 14, 1992), the Press Collection (various dates), the Lowenstein Collection (July 24, 1996), and the George R. Repaire Collection (April 14, 1997).

U.S. Cartridge Co. *Illustrated Catalogue of United States Cartridge Company's Collection of Firearms.* c. 1905.

Wilson, R. L., Peter Hawkins, Christopher Brunker. *Colt/Christie's Auction of Fine and Rare Firearms.* October 7, 1981.

GENERAL REFERENCE

Amber, John T. (ed.). *Gun Digest.* Annual first appeared in 1947. (Amber was succeeded by Ken Warner, c. 1979.)

Fjestad, Steven. *Blue Book of Gun Values,* various editions (18 as of 1997).

Flayderman, Norm. *Flayderman's Guide to Antique American Firearms . . . and Their Values.* Various editions, annual.

———, ed. *Illustrated Catalogue of Arms and Military Goods.* New Milford, Conn.: N. Flayderman & Co., 1961. Reprint edition of the 1864 Schuyler, Hartley & Graham company catalogue.

Hand, R. A. *A Bookman's Guide to Hunting, Shooting, Angling and Related Subjects.* 1991.

Hayward, John F. *The Art of the Gunmaker.* 1962–63. Two volumes.

———. *One Hundred Great Guns.* 1967.

Held, Robert. *The Age of Firearms.* Various editions since 1957.

Houze, Herbert G. *The Sumptuous Flaske.* 1989.

Logan, Herschel C. *From Hand Cannon to Automatic.* 1944.

Murtz, Harold A. *Gun Digest Treasury.* Various editions. (Earlier editions edited by John T. Amber.)

———. *Guns Illustrated.* Various editions, annual.

O'Connor, Jack. *Complete Book of Shooting: Rifles and Shotguns, Handguns.* 1983.

Peterson, Harold L. *Treasury of the Gun.* 1962.

———, and Robert Elman. *The Great Guns.* 1971.

Pollard, H.B.C., ed. by Claude Blair. *A History of Firearms.* 1983.

Pope, Dudley. *Guns: An Illustrated History of Artillery.* 1971.

Rattenbury, Richard. *Packing Iron: A Survey of Military and Civilian Gunleather on the Western Frontier.* 1993.

Riling, Ray. *The Powder Flask Book.* 1953.

———. *Guns and Shooting, A Selected Bibliography.* 1982.

Schroeder, Joseph J. *Gun Collector's Digest.* Various editions, annual.

Sellers, Frank. *American Gunsmiths.* 1983.

———. *The William M. Locke Collection.* 1973.

Sheldon, Lawrence P. *California Gunsmiths 1846–1900.* 1977.

Stoeger. *Shooter's Bible.* Various editions, annual.

———. *Gun Trader's Guide.* Various editions.

Tanner, Hans. *Guns of the World.* 1977.

Tappan, Mel. *Survival Guns.* 1993.

Tarassuk, Leonid. *Antique European and American Firearms at the Hermitage Museum.* 1971.

Traister, John. *How to Buy and Sell Used Guns.* 1984.

van Zwoll, Wayne. *America's Great Gunmakers.* 1992.

Warner, Ken, ed. *Gun Digest.* Various editions, annual.

Weil, Robert. *Contemporary Makers of Muzzle Loading Firearms.* 1980.

Wilkerson, Frederick. *Small Arms.* 1966.

OTHER COUNTRIES

General

Walter, John. *Guns of the First World War, Rifles, Handguns and Ammunition from the Text Book of Small Arms, 1909.* 1991.

Britain

Blackmore, Howard L. *Gunmakers of London 1350–1850.* 1986.

Bruce, Gordon and Christien Reinhart. *Webley Revolvers.* 1988.

George, J. N. *English Pistols and Revolvers.* 1979; first published 1938.

Glendenning, *British Pistols and Guns 1640–1840.*

Grancsay, Stephen V. and Clay P. Bedford. *Early Firearms of Great Britain and Ireland from the Collection of Clay P. Bedford.* 1971.

Jackson, H. J. and C. E. Whitelaw. *European Hand Firearms of the Sixteenth, Seventeenth, and Eighteenth Centuries.* 1923.
Markham, George. *Guns of the Empire.* 1991.
———. *Guns of the Elite.* 1987. (Special Forces arms, from 1940.)
Munson, H. Lee. *Mortimer, The Gunmakers, 1753–1923.* 1992.

GAME GUNS

Akehurst, Richard. *Game Guns & Rifles: Percussion to Hammerless Ejector in Britain.* 1993.
Baxter, D. R. *Blunderbusses.* 1970.
Rogers, H.C.B. *Weapons of the British Soldier.* 1972.
Shore, Captain C. *With British Snipers to the Reich.* 1988.

REVOLVERS

Chamberlain, W.H.J. and A.W.F. Taylerson. *Revolvers of the British Services 1854–1954.* 1982.
———. *Adams' Revolvers.* 1976.
Wilkinson, Frederick. *The Illustrated Book of Pistols.* 1979.

SPORTING ARMS

Back, D.H.L. *Great British Gunmakers: The Mantons 1782–1878.* 1994.
———. *Great Irish Gunmakers: Messrs. Rigby 1760–1869.* 1993.
Baker, *Baker's Remarks on the Rifle.* Reprint.
Beaumont, Richard. *Purdey's, The Guns and the Family.* 1984.
Boothroyd, Geoffrey. *Gun Collecting.* 1989. Rather complete listing of British gunmakers of the 19th century.
Cradock, Chris. *Cradock on Shotguns.* 1989.
———. *A Manual of Clayshooting.* 1983.
Crudington, I. M. and D. J. Baker. *The British Shotgun, Volume I, 1850–1870.* 1979.
———. *The British Shotgun, Volume 2, 1870–1890.* 1989.
Dallas, Donald. *Boss & Co. Builders of Best Guns Only.* 1995.
King, Peter. *The Shooting Field with Holland & Holland.* 1990.
Kirton, Jonathan. *The British Falling Block Breechloading Rifle from 1865.* 1997.
McIntosh, Michael. *Best Guns.* 1989.
Taylerson, A.W.F. *Revolving Arms.*
Taylor, John. *African Rifles and Cartridges.* 1977. (Reprint)
———. *Big Game and Big Game Rifles.* 1993. (Reprint)

Scotland

Kelvin, Martin. *The Scottish Pistol: Its History, Manufacture and Design.* 1996.
Whitelaw, C. E., ed. by S. Barter-Bailey. *Scottish Arms Makers.* 1977.

Belgium

Gaier, Claude. *Liege Firearms.* 1985.
Stevens, R. Blake. *UK and Commonwealth FALS.* 1987.

Canada

Phillips, Roger F., and Donald J. Klancher. *Arms and Accouterments of the Mounted Police 1873–1973.* 1982.

Czechoslovakia

Ramos, J. M. *The CZ-75 Family: The Ultimate Combat Handgun.* 1990.
Berger, R. J. *Know Your Czechoslovakian Pistols.* 1989.

Denmark

Hoff, A. *The Rasmussen Revolving Gun.*

France

Hicks, Major James E. *French Military Weapons, 1717–1938.* 1973.
Medlin, Eugene and Jean Huon. *Military Handguns of France 1858–1958.* 1993.

Germany

Datig, Fred A. *German Military Pistols 1904–1930.* 1990.
Dugelby, Thomas B. and R. Blake Stevens. *Death from Above: The German FG42 Paratrooper Rifle.* 1990.
Gotz, Hans Dieter. *German Military Rifles and Machine Pistols, 1871–1945.* 1990.
Markham, George. *Guns of the Reich.* 1989.
Quarrie, Bruce. *Weapons of the Waffen-SS.* 1991.
Whittington, Robert. *German Pistols and Holsters 1934–1945, Vol. 2.* 1990.
———. *German Pistols and Holsters, 1934–1945, Volume 4.* 1991.

LUGERS

Bender, Eugene J. *Luger Holsters and Accessories of the 20th Century.* 1993.
Datig, Fred A. *The Luger Pistol: Its History & Development from 1893 to 1947; Monograph IV: The Swiss Variations 1897–1947.* 1992.
Gibson, Randall. *The Krieghoff Parabellum.* 1988.
Gortz, Joachim and John Walter. *The Navy Luger.* 1988.
Jones, Harry E. *Luger Variations.* 1975.
Kenyon, Charles, Jr. *Lugers at Random.* 1990.
———. *Luger: The Multi-National Pistol.* 1991.
McFarland, David J. *The P-08 Parabellum Luger Automatic Pistol.* 1982.

MAUSER

Belford & Dunlap. *The Mauser Self-Loading Pistol.*
Berger, R. J. *Know Your Broomhandle Mausers.* 1985.
Kuhnhausen, Jerry. *The Mauser M91 Through M98 Bolt Actions: A Shop Manual.* 1991.
Law, Richard D. *The German K98k Rifle, 1934–1945: The Backbone of the Wehrmacht.* 1993.
Olsen, Ludwig. *Mauser Bolt Rifles.* 1976.
Smith, Walter H. B. *Mauser Rifles and Pistols.* 1990.

WALTHER

Gangarosa, Gene, Jr. *P-38 Automatic Pistol.* 1993.
Hoffschmidt, E. J. *Know Your Walther P-38 Pistols.* 1974.
———. *Know Your Walther PP & PPK Pistols.* 1975.
Kersten, Manfred. *Walther Eine Deutsche Legende.* 1997. (In German, with English translation planned for 1998–99.)
Long, Duncan. *Powerhouse Pistols—The Colt 1911 and Browning Hi-Power Source.* 1989.
Nonte, Major George C. *Walther P-38 Pistol.* 1982.
———. *Pistol & Revolver Guide.* 1975.
———. *Pistol Guide.* 1991.
———. *Revolver Guide.* 1991.
Rankin, James L. *Walther Models PP and PPK, 1929–1945.* 1974.
———. *Walther, Volume II, Engraved, Presentation and Standard Models.* 1977.
———. *Walther, Volume III, 1908–1980.* 1981.

Holland

Kist, J. B. *Dutch Muskets and Pistols.* 1974.
Visser, Hank. Five-volume series on Dutch guns. 1996.

Italy

Held, Robert and Marco Morin. *Beretta: The World's Oldest Industrial Dynasty.* 1980.
Wood, J. B. *Beretta Automatic Pistols.* 1985.

Japan

Honeycutt, Fred L. Jr. *Military Pistols of Japan.* 1991.
———. *Military Rifles of Japan, 4th Edition.* 1989.
Leithe, Frederick E. *Japanese Handguns.* 1985.

Russia

Datig, Fred A. *Soviet Russian Postwar Military Pistols and Cartridges.* 1988.
———. *Soviet Russian Tokarev "TT" Pistols and Cartridges 1929–1953.* 1993.
Ezell, Edward, Ph.D. *The AK47 Story.* 1988.
Remling, John. *A Collector's Guide to Tokarev Pistols.* 1984.

Spain and Portugal

Antaris, Leonardo M. *Astra Automatic Pistols.* 1989.
Lavin, James. *Spanish Firearms.*

Sweden

Wennberg, Kaa. *European Firearms in Swedish Castles.* 1986.

Appendix 2: Booksellers*

Dan Antrim, Bookseller
PO Box 675
Devon PA 19333

Blacksmith Corp.
830 N. Road No. 1 E.
PO Box 1752
Chino Valley AZ 85323

Blacktail Mountain Books
42 First Ave. W.
Kalispell MT 59901

Blue Book Publications
3009 34th Ave. S., #175
Minneapolis MN 55425

Braverman Arms Co.
912 Penn Ave.
Pittsburgh PA 15221

Brownell's Inc.
200 S. Front St.
Montezuma IA 50171

Cape Outfitters
599 County Rd. 206
Cape Girardeau MO 63701

Clark's Brothers
Rte. 5, Box 100
Warrenton VA 22186

Dick's Gun Room
3010 State Rd.
Cuyahoga Falls OH 44223

Dixie Gun Works
PO Box 130
Union City TN 38261

Bert Garber (BSG Books)
305 Bent Tree Court
Covington, LA 70433

Golden Age Arms Co.
115 E. High St.
Ashley OH 43003

Gullivers, Inc.
2918 Vine St., #270
Hays KS 67601

Guncraft Books
10737 Dutchtown Rd.
Knoxville TN 37932

Gunnerman Books
PO Box 214292
Auburn Hills MI 48321

Heritage/VSP Gun Books
PO Box 887
McCall ID 83638

Hungry Horse Books
4605 Hwy. 93 S.
Whitefish MT 59937

I.D.S.A. Books
PO Box 1457
Piqua OH 45356

Intersports
Royal Publications, Inc.
790 W. Tennessee Ave.
Denver CO 80223

Jaqua's Fine Guns
900 E. Bigelow Ave.
Findlay OH 45840

Little John's Antique Arms, Inc.
1740 W. LaVeta
Orange CA 92668

Little Professor Book Center
22174 Michigan Ave.
Dearborn MI 48124

Little Professor Book Center
101 Boardman-Canfield Rd.
Boardman OH 44512

J. Martin Bookseller
PO Drawer AP
Beckley WV 25802

J. Millet & Co.
PO Box 6506
Santa Ana CA 92706

Navy Arms Co., Inc.
689 Bergen Blvd.
Ridgefield NJ 07657

Old Western Scrounger, Inc.
12924 Hwy. A-12
Montague CA 96064

Old West Gun Room
3509 Carlson Blvd.
El Cerrito CA 94530

Outdoorsman's Bookstore
Llangorse
Brecon
Powys
LD3 7UE England

Gerald Pettinger Books
Rte. 2, Box 125
Russell IA 50238

Pioneer Guns
5228 Montgomery Rd.
Cincinnati OH 45212

Potomac Arms Corp.
PO Box 35
Alexandria VA 22313

R & R Books
4447 East Lake Rd.
Livonia NY 14487

Rettig's Frontier Ohio
16 N. 3rd St., PO Box 122
Waterville OH 43566–1411

Martin B. Retting, Inc.
11029 Washington Blvd.
Culver City CA 90230

Rich's Cigar Store, Inc.
801 SW Alder St.
Portland OR 97205

Ray Riling Arms Books
6844 Gorsten St, PO Box 18925
Philadelphia PA 19119

Rutgers Book Center
127 Raritan Ave.
Highland Park NJ 08904

S & S Firearms
74–11 Myrtle Ave.
Glendale NY 11385

San Francisco Gun Exchange
124 Second St.
San Francisco CA 94105

Shooting Gallery Books
53 Blue Spruce Lane
Ballston Lake NY 12019

George Shumway
3900 Deep Run Lane
York PA 17402

*Should this list have any omissions, booksellers are invited to contact the author for inclusion.

Stoeger Industries
5 Mansard Court
Wayne NJ 07470

Ken Trotman Arms Books
135 Ditton Walk
Unit 11
Cambridge England CB5 8PY

M.C. Wiest
10737 Dutchtown Rd.
Knoxville TN 37932

Appendix 3: Auction Houses

Butterfield & Butterfield, Inc.
220 San Bruno Ave.
San Francisco CA 94103

Christie's
8 King St.
London England

David Condon, Inc.
109 E. Washington St.
Middleburg VA 22117

Pete de Coux (Ammunition and Related Items)
235 Oak St., Box 8
Butler PA 16001

J.C. Devine, Inc.
PO Box 413
20 South St.
Milford NH 03055

Dunnings
755 Church Rd.
Elgin IL 60123

Faintich Auction Services, Inc.
10902 St. Charles Rock Rd.
St. Louis MO 63074

Fischer Galleries
Haldenstrasse 19
Lucerne Switzerland 6006

Wm. "Pete" Harvey
1270 Rte. 28A
PO Box 280
Cataumet MA 02534

James D. Julia, Inc.
Rt. 201, Skowhegan Rd.
PO Box 830
Fairfield ME 04937

Little John's Auction Service, Inc.
1740 W. La Veta
Orange CA 92868

Rock Island Auction Co. (Richard S. Ellis, Consultant)
1050 36th Ave.
Moline IL 61265

Sotheby's
1334 York Ave.
New York NY 10021

Supica's Old Town Station, Ltd.
PO Box 15351
Lenexa KS 66285

Wallis & Wallis
West Street Auction Galleries
Lewes, Sussex BN7 2NJ
England

Weller & Dufty
141 Bromsgrove St.
Birmingham
W. Midlands B5 GRQ
England

Witherell's Americana Auctions
3620 West Island Court
Elk Grove CA 95758

Appendix 4: Arms Dealers

PROFESSIONAL ANTIQUE-ARMS DEALERS

Ackerman & Co.
16 Cortez St.
Westfield MA 01085

Ahlman Guns
Rte. 1, Box 20
Morristown MN 55052

Mike D'Ambria
PO Box 177107
San Diego CA 92177

American Heritage Investment, Inc.
1574 Pennwood Circle N.
Clearwater FL 34616

American Ordnance Preservation Association, Ltd.
311 Millbank Rd.
Bryn Mawr PA 19010

Dale C. Anderson
4 W. Confederate Ave.
Gettysburg PA 17325

Antique Arms Co.
1110 Cleveland Ave.
Monett MO 65708

Antique & Modern Firearms, Inc.
2263 Nicholasville Rd.
Lexington KY 40503

James O. Aplan Antiques & Art
HC 80
Box 793-25
Piedmont SD 57769

The Armoury, Inc.
Rte. 202, Box 2340
New Preston CT 06777

Knox Baldwin
PO Box 262
Brentwood TN 37024

Bedlan's
1318 E. St. Box 244
Fairbury NE 68352

Bell Consulting, Inc.
PO Box 579
Lady Lake FL 32158-0579

Bellinger's Military Antiques
Box 76371
Atlanta GA 30358

Robert B. Berryman
PO Box 143
Mt. Home TX 78058

William Boggs
1816 Riverside Drive Circle
Columbus OH 43212

Andrew Bottomley
The Coach House
Huddersfield Rd.
Holmfirth
W. Yorkshire England HD7 2TT

Bernard Braverman
1183 St. Vincent
Monroeville PA 15046

British Antiques
PO Box 7
Latham NY 12110

Buckskin Machine Works
3235 S. 358th St.
Auburn WA 98001

David Buehn
16881 Bolero Lane
Huntington Beach CA 92649

Buffalo Arms
123 S. Third, Suite 6
Sandpoint ID 83864

Cannon's Guns
Box 1036
320 Main St.
Polson MT 59860

Douglas R. Carlson
PO Box 71035
Des Moines IA 50325

Larry Carpenter (Old West Catalogue)
Box 1173
Kingsport TN 37662

Jim Chambers Flintlocks Ltd.
Rte. 1, Box 513-A
Candler NC 28715

Cherry's
3402-A W. Wendover Ave.
Greensboro NC 27435-0307

Chuck's Gun Shop
PO Box 597
Waldo FL 32694

Cole's Gun Works
Old Bank Building
Rte. 4, Box 250
Moyock NC 27958

Collector's Firearms
Mike Clark
3301 Fondren
Houston TX 77042

Richard Cowles
Box 1629
Silver City NM 88062

D & D Gunsmiths, Ltd.
363 E. Elmwood
Troy MI 48083

David's Firearms, Ltd.
PO Box 6039
Falmouth ME 04105

Delhi Gun House
1374 Kashmere Gate
Delhi India

Dixie Gun Works, Inc.
PO Box 130
Gun Powder Lane
Union City TN 38261

Dixon Muzzleloading Shop, Inc.
RD 1, Box 175
Kempton PA 19529

Charles E. Duffy
Williams Lane
West Hurley NY 12491

Peter Dyson & Son Ltd.
29–31 Church St.
Honley Huddersfield
W. Yorkshire England HD7 2AH

Ed's Gun House
Rt. 1, Box 62
Minnesota City MN 55959

Richard S. Ellis
1000 36th Ave.
Moline IL 61265

Elmira Arms Co., Inc.
1128 Broadway
Elmira NY 14904

Enguix Import-Export
Alpujarras 58
Alzira
Valencia Spain 46600

Erickson's Frontier & Western Antiques
PO Box 9483
Fargo ND 58106

Floyd Everhart
PO Box 129
New Paris OH 45347

William Fagan
22952 15 Mile Rd.
Clinton Township MI 48035

Jeff Faintich
10902 St. Charles Rock Rd.
St. Louis MO 63074

Peter Finer, Ltd.
The Old Rectory
Ilmington, Shipston-on-Stour
Warwickshire England CV 36 4JQ

Jack First, Inc.
1201 Turbine Dr.
Rapid City SD 57701

Marshall F. Fish
Rte. 22 North, PO Box 2439
Westport NY 12993

N. Flayderman & Co., Inc.
PO Box 2446
Ft. Lauderdale FL 33303

Val Forgett (Navy Arms Co.)
689 Bergen Blvd.
Ridgefield NJ 07657

Chet Fulmer's Antique Firearms
PO Box 792, Rte. 2
Buffalo Lake
Detroit Lakes MN 56501

Herb Glass, Sr., and Jr.
Bullville NY 10915

James Goergen
Rte. 2, Box 182
Austin MN 55912

Golden Age Arms Co.
115 E. High St.
Ashley OH 43003

Will Gorges
Civil War Antiques
2100 Trent Blvd.
New Bern NC 28560

Great Northern Guns, Inc.
Joseph Andreis
2920 Tudor Rd.
Anchorage AL 99507

Leon E. "Bud" Greenwald
2553 S. Quitman St.
Denver CO 80219

The Gun Room
1121 Burlington
Muncie IN 47302

The Gun Room
127 Raritan Ave.
Highland Park NJ 08904

The Gun Works
247 South 2nd
Springfield OR 97477

Guncraft Sports, Inc.
10737 Dutchtown Rd.
Knoxville TN 37932

Guthman Americana
PO Box 392
Westport CT 06881

Thomas Haas
Guns Unlimited
RR 2, Ponderosa Ranch
Spencer IN 47460

Hansen & Co.
244 Old Post Rd.
Southport CT 06490

Wm. "Pete" Harvey
1270 Rte. 28A
PO Box 280
Cataumet MA 02534

Historical Investors Group
60 Harvest Moon Rd.
Easton CT 06612

The Horse Soldier
PO Box 184
Cashtown PA 17310

Investment Arms
PO Box 40253
Molrose Station
Nashville TN 37204

Jeb Klitzke
Main St.
Ransom KS 67572

Martin Lane Historical Americana, Inc.
205 W. Houston St.
New York NY 10010

Larry's Gun Room
105 N. 8th St.
Beresford SD 57004
Tom Lewis
PO Box 1748
Evergreen CO 80439

Liberty Antique Gunworks
19 Key St. PO Box 183
Eastport ME 04631

Little John's Antique Arms, Inc.
1740 W. La Veta
Orange CA 92868

Lock's Philadelphia Gun Exchange
6700 Rowland Ave.
Philadelphia PA 19149

Log Cabin Sport Shop
8010 Lafayette Rd.
Lodi OH 44254

Mitch Luksich
PO Box 1527
Sonoma CA 95476

Jack Malloy
PO Box 276
Wye Mills MD 21679

R.J. Maroni & Son, Inc.
Box 43325
Upper Montclair NJ 07043

Greg Martin
PO Box 330011
San Francisco CA 94133

Martin's Gun Shop
937 S. Sheridan Blvd.
Lakewood CO 80226

George E. Mathews & Son, Inc.
10224 S. Paramount Blvd.
Downey CA 90241

Ray Meibaum
Box 524
Florissant MO 63033

John A. Mendez
PO Box 620984
Orlando FL 32862

LeRoy Merz
Rt. 1—Nirschl Addition #2
Fergus Falls MN 56537

Damon Mills
718 Spring Valley Rd.
Montgomery AL 36116

Model Investments, Inc.
1032 26th St.
West Palm Beach FL 33407

Montana Outfitters (Lewis E. Yearout)
308 Riverview Dr. E.
Great Falls MT 59404

Mountain Bear Rifle Works, Inc.
100 B Ruritan Rd.
Sterling VA 20164

Museum of Historical Arms
2750 Coral Way, Suite 204
Miami FL 33145

Muzzleloaders, Etcetera, Inc.
9901 Lyndale Ave. S.
Bloomington MN 55420

N.C. Ordnance Co.
PO Box 3254
Wilson NC 27895

Ogan Antiques Ltd.
PO Box 14381
North Palm Beach FL 33408-0831

Pioneer Guns
5228 Montgomery Rd.
Norwood OH 45212

Pony Express Sport Shop, Inc.
16606 Schoenbom St.
North Hills CA 91343

W.R. Powell
PO Box 186
Roanoke TX 76262

Brian Radcliffe
229 N. Main St.
Cheboygan MI 49721

Rare Arms Co.
PO Box 6107
Plymouth MI 48170

Martin B. Retting, Inc.
11029 Washington
Culver City CA 90232

Dick Reyes
PO Box 3296
Carson City NV 89702

Tommy Rholes
PO Box 638
Van TX 75790

Steve Rogers (Civil War)
PO Box 6595
Ithaca NY 14851

S & S Firearms
74-11 Myrtle Ave.
Glendale NY 11385

Frank Sellers
Crane Brook Rd.
Alstead NH 03602

Charles Semmer
7885 Cyd Dr.
Denver CO 80221

Ralph E. Shattuck (specializing in German Lugers)
19044 N. 98th Lane
Peoria AZ 85382

Simmons Gun Company
PO Box 495
Leichhardt
NSW 2040 Australia

Simpson Ltd. (Lugers)
140 S. Seminary St.
Galesburg IL 61401

C.W. Slagle
PO Box 4185
Scottsdale AZ 85261

Paul Sorrell
PO Box 7918
Beaumont TX 77726

Steve's House of Guns
Rte. 1
Minnesota City MN 55959

Stott's Creek Armory
RR 1, Box 70
Morgantown IN 46160

Victor W. Strawbridge
6 Pineview Dr.
Dover NH 03820

Jim Supica
Old Town Station
PO Box 15351
Lenexa KS 66285

Sweeney's Emporium
PO Box 936
Shawnee Mission KS 66201

David W. Taylor (Civil War)
Box 87
Sylvania OH 43560

Vintage Arms, Inc.
6003 Saddle Horse
Fairfax VA 22030

Mike Wamsher
17732 W. 67th St.
Shawnee KS 66217

Paul Weisberg
Rt. 30, PO Box 581
Schoharie NY 12157

Tom Wibberley
11001 Lincoln Ave.
Hagerstown MD 21740

M.C. Wiest
10737 Dutchtown Rd.
Knoxville TN 37932

Dean Williams
1304 140th St.
Spirit Lake IA 51360

The Winchester Sutler, Inc.
270 Shadow Brook Lane
Winchester VA 22603

Michael Zomber Co.
11050 Washington Blvd.
Culver City CA 90232

DEALERS PRIMARILY IN HIGH-GRADE MODERN AND VINTAGE SPORTING ARMS, SOME OF WHOM ALSO HANDLE ANTIQUE ARMS*

Albemarle Arms Co.
Mahlon G. Kelly/Thierry Duguet
Box 288, Rt. 250 West
Ivy VA 22945

Bill Birkbeck
Route 112 Box 7
Conway NH 03818

Thomas Bland & Sons
PO Box 363
Benton PA 17814

Cabela's
812–13th Ave.
Sidney NE 69160

Cape Outfitters
599 County Rd. 206
Cape Girardeau MO 63701

Herschel Chadick
Chadick's Ltd.
PO Box 100
Terrell TX 75160

Champlin Firearms, Inc.
PO Box 3191
Woodring Airport
Enid OK 73701

*There is an association of collectors and arms dealers, organized for membership of professionals and active collectors; membership is by application and invitation: Collector Arms Dealers Association (CADA), PO Box 427, Thomson IL 61285.

Classic Guns, Inc.
Frank S. Wood
3230 Medlock Bridge Rd., Suite 110
Norcross GA 30092

Colonial Gun Shop
143 Boone Square St.
Hillsborough NC 27278

Lewis Drake & Associates
305 South 8th St.
Murray KY 42071

Tony Galazan
PO Box 1692
New Britain CT 06051

Griffin & Howe, Inc.
36 W. 44th St., Suite 1011
New York NY 10036

Hallowell & Co.
340 W. Putnam Ave.
Greenwich CT 06830

Gary Herman
Safari Outfitters
Rte. 44, Washington Hollow Plaza
R.D. 1, Box 2
Salt Point NY 12578

Holland & Holland, Ltd.
50 E. 57th St.
New York NY 10022

Imperial Russian Armory, Inc. (Miniatures)
Joel Morrow
10547 South Post Oak
Houston TX 77035
Jacqua's Fine Guns
900 E. Bigelow Ave.
Findlay OH 45840

Lefever Arms Co., Inc.
6234 Stokes
Lee Center Rd.
Lee Center NY 13363

William Larkin Moore & Co.
8727 E. Via de Commencio, Suite A
Scottsdale AZ 85258

New England Arms Co.
Box 278
Lawrence Lane
Kittery Point ME 03905

The Orvis Co.
Rt. 7
Manchester VT 05254

Allen B. Postel
Postel Gun Sales
214 S.E. 2nd
Ames IA 50010

Quality Arms
PO Box 19477
Houston TX 77224

Thad Scott Fine Guns, Inc.
PO Box 412
Indianola MS 38751

Specialty Firearms
Brian Radcliffe
229 N. Main St.
Cheboygan MI 49721

Wingshooting Adventures
0-1845 West Leonard
Grand Rapids MI 49544

Appendix 5: Arms Collectors' Organizations

NATIONAL ORGANIZATIONS

BY MAKE AND TYPE

Automatic Pistol Collectors Association, National
PO Box 15738
Tower Grove Station
St. Louis MO 63163

Bayonet Collectors, The Society of
PO Box 234
East Islip NY 11730

Browning Collectors Association
PO Box 526
Aurora NE 68818

Cartridge Collectors Association, International
PO Box 5297
Ormond Beach FL 32174

Colt Collectors Association
3200 Westminster
Dallas TX 75205

Deringer Collectors, National Association
PO Box 20572
San Jose CA 95160

Deringer Collectors Association
500 East Old 66
Shamrock TX 79079

Garand Collectors Association
PO Box 181
Richmond KY 40475

Golden Eagle Collectors Association
11144 State Creek Road
Grass Valley CA 95945

Harrington & Richardson Gun Collectors Association
330 S.W. 27th Ave., Suite 603
Miami FL 33135

Hopkins & Allen Arms and Memorabilia Society
1309 Pamela Circle
Delphos OH 45833

Mannlicher Collectors Association
PO Box 7144
Salem OR 97303

Marlin Firearms Collectors Association
407 Lincoln Building
44 Main St.
Champaign IL 61820

Miniature Arms Collectors/Makers Society, Ltd.
4910 Kilburn Ave.
Rockford IL 61101

M1 Carbine Collectors Association
PO Box 4895
Stateline NV 89449

Mossberg Collectors Association
PO Box 22156
St. Louis MO 63116

Muzzle Loading Rifle Association, National
PO Box 67
Friendship IN 47021

Remington Society of America
8268 Lone Feather Lane
Las Vegas NV 89123

Ruger Collectors Association
PO Box 240
Greens Farms CT 06436

Sako Collectors Association
1725 Woodhill Lane
Bedford TX 76021

Scheutzen Society, Southern California
34657 Ave. E
Yucaipa CA 92399

Single Shot Rifle Association, American
709 Carolyn Dr.
Delphos OH 45833

Smith & Wesson Arms Collectors Association
2711 Miami St.
St. Louis MO 63118

Thompson/Center Association
PO Box 792
Northboro MA 01532

Weatherby Collectors Association
PO Box 128
Moira NY 12957

The Winchester Arms Collectors Association
PO Box 6754
Great Falls MT 59406

The Winchester Club of America
3070 South Wyandot
Englewood CO 80110

NATIONAL ORGANIZATIONS OTHER THAN BY MANUFACTURER OR TYPE

American Custom Gunmakers Guild
PO Box 812
Burlington IA 52601

American Pistolsmiths Guild
PO Box 67
Louisville TN 37777

American Shooting Sports Council
10 Perimeter Way #B-250
Atlanta GA 30339

American Society of Arms Collectors
PO Box 2567
Waxahachie TX 75165

Benchrest Shooters Association, Englishtown
64 Cooke Ave.
Carteret NJ 07008

Blackpowder Hunting Association, International
PO Box 1180
Glenrock WY 82637

Boone & Crockett Club
250 Station Dr.
Missoula MT 59801

Buckskinners, National Association of
1981 E. 94th Ave.
Thornton CO 80229

Citizens Committee for the Right to Keep and Bear Arms
Liberty Park
12500 NE Tenth Place
Bellevue WA 98005

Collector Arms Dealer Association (CADA)
PO Box 427
Thomson IL 61285

Ducks Unlimited, Inc.
One Waterfowl Way
Memphis TN 38120

Federally Licensed Firearms Dealers, National Association of
2455 E. Sunrise
Ft. Lauderdale FL 33304

Fifty Caliber Shooters Association
11469 Olive Street Rd.
Suite 50
St. Louis MO 63141

Firearms Coalition
PO Box 6537
Silver Spring MD 20906

Firearms Engravers Guild of America
332 Vine St.
Oregon City OR 97045

Foundation for North American Wild Sheep
720 Allen Ave.
Cody WY 82414

Gun Owners Civil Rights Alliance
PO Box 131254
St. Paul MN 55113

Gun Owners of America
8001 Forbes Place, Suite 102
Springfield VA 22151

Handgun Hunters International
PO Box 357 MAG
Bloomingdale OH 43910

Handgun Metallic Silhouette Association, International (IHMSA)
PO Box 5038
Meriden CT 06450

Handloading Association, International
6471 Airpark Dr.
Prescott AZ 86301

Hunter Education Association
PO Box 525
Draper UT 84020

Jews for the Preservation of Firearms Ownership
2872 South Wentworth Ave.
Milwaukee WI 53207

Mule Deer Foundation
1005 Terminal Way, Ste. 110
Reno NV 89502

National Alliance of Stocking Gun Dealers
PO Box 187
Havelock NC 28532

National Association to Keep and Bear Arms
PO Box 78336
Seattle WA 98178

National Firearms Association
PO Box 160038
Austin TX 78716

National Foundation for Firearms Education
Mark K. Benenson, President
185 Madison Ave.
New York NY 10016

National Rifle Association of America
11250 Waples Mill Rd.
Fairfax VA 22030

National Shooting Sports Foundation
Flintlock Ridge Office Center
11 Mile Hill Rd.
Newtown CT 06470

National Skeet Shooting Association
PO Box 680007
San Antonio TX 78268

National Sporting Clays Association
PO Box 680007
San Antonio TX 78268

National Wild Turkey Federation
PO Box 530
Edgefield SC 29824

North American Hunting Club
PO Box 3401
Minnetonka MN 55343

North-South Skirmish Association
204 W. Holly Ave.
Sterling VA 20164

Quail Unlimited
Rte. No. 3, PO Box 29B
Edgefield SC 29824

Rocky Mountain Elk Foundation
PO Box 8249
Missoula MT 59807

Safari Club International
4800 West Gates Pass Rd.
Tucson AZ 85745

Second Amendment Foundation
James Madison Building
12500 N.E. 10th Place
Bellevue WA 98005

Sporting Arms and Ammunition Institute
Flintlock Ridge Office Center
11 Mile Hill Rd.
Newton CT 06470

Sporting Clays of America
9 Mott Ave., Suite 103
Norwalk CT 06850

U.S. Practical Shooting Association (IPSC)
PO Box 811
Sedro Woolley WA 98284

U.S. Revolver Association
40 Larchmont Ave.
Taunton MA 02780

The Varmint Hunters Association
PO Box 759
Pierre SD 57501

The Wildcatters
PO Box 170
Greenville WI 54942

The Women's Shooting Sports Foundation
1505 Highway 6 South
Suite 101
Houston TX 77077

ORGANIZATIONS BY STATE

Alabama

Alabama Gun Collectors Association
PO Box 70965
Tuscaloosa AL 35407

Alaska

Alaska Gun Collectors Association
5240 Little Tree
Anchorage AK 99507

Arizona

Arizona Arms Association
4837 Bryce Ave.
Glendale AZ 85301

California

California Rifle & Pistol Association
12062 Valley View St., Suite 107
Garden Grove CA 92645

California Waterfowl Association
4630 Northgate Blvd., #150
Sacramento CA 95834

Greater California Arms & Collectors Association
8291 Carburton St.
Long Beach CA 90808

Los Angeles Gun and Cartridge Collectors Association
20810 Amie Ave., Apartment No. 9
Torrance CA 90503

San Bernardino Valley Arms Collectors
18710 Cajon Blvd.
San Bernardino CA 92407

Santa Barbara Historical Arms Collectors Association
PO Box 6291
Santa Barbara CA 93160

San Fernando Valley Arms Collectors Association
PO Box 65
North Hollywood CA 91603

Colorado

Colorado Gun Collectors Association
2553 South Quitman St.
Denver CO 80219

Connecticut

Ye Connecticut Gun Guild
PO Box 425
Windsor CT 06095

Delaware

Delaware Weapons Association
97 Johnson Rd.
Bangor PA 18013

Florida

Florida Gun Collectors Association
1621 South Dr.
Sarasota FL 34239

Palm Beach Gun Collector's Association
c/o Lake Worth Police F.O.P. Club House
Avenue A
Lake Worth FL

Tampa Bay Arms Collectors Association
2461-67th Ave. S.
St. Petersburg FL 33712

United Sportsmen of Florida
PO Box 6565
Tallahassee FL 32314

Georgia

Georgia Arms Collectors Association
PO Box 277
Alpharetta GA 30239

Hawaii

Hawaii Historic Arms Association
PO Box 1733
Honolulu HI 96806

Illinois

Central Illinois Gun Collectors Association
PO Box 875
Jacksonville IL 62651

Illinois Gun Collectors Association
PO Box 971
Kankakee IL 60901

Illinois State Rifle Association
PO Box 637
Chatsworth IL 60921

Mississippi Valley Gun and Cartridge Collectors Association
PO Box 61
Port Byron IL 61275

Sauk Trail Gun Collectors
PO Box 1113
Milan IL 61264

Wabash Valley Gun Collectors Association
2601 Willow Rd.
Urbana IL 61801

Indiana

Indiana State Rifle and Pistol Association
PO Box 552
Chesterton IN 46304

Southern Indiana Gun Collectors Association
309 W. Monroe St.
Boonville IN 47601

Iowa

Beaver Creek Plainsmen
PO Box 298
Bondurant IA 50035

Central States Gun Collectors Association
1104 S. First Ave.
Marshtown IA 50158

Kansas

Chisholm Trail Antique Gun Association
1906 Richmond
Wichita KS 67203

Kansas Cartridge Collectors Association
Box 84
Plainville KS 67663

Kentucky

Kentuckiana Arms Collectors Association
PO Box 1776
Louisville KY 40201

Kentucky Gun Collectors Association
PO Box 64
Owensboro KY 42302

Louisiana

Ark-La-Tex Gun Collectors
9601 Blom Blvd.
Shreveport LA 71118

Bayou Gun Club
PO Box 73402
Metairie LA 70033

Pelican Arms Collectors Association
PO Box 747
Clinton LA 70722

Washitaw River Renegades
PO Box 256
Main St.
Grayson LA 71435

Maryland

Baltimore Antique Arms Association
1034 Main St.
Darlington MD 21304

Maryland Arms Collectors Association
33 S. Main St.
PO Box 206
Loganville PA 17342

Potomac Arms Collectors Association
PO Box 2676
Laurel MD 20811

Massachusetts

Bay Colony Weapons Collectors
PO Box 111
Hingham MA 02043

Massachusetts Arms Collectors
PO Box 31
North Carver MA 02355

Michigan

Boardman Valley Collectors Guild
County Rd. 600
Manton MI 49663

Minnesota

Minnesota Rifle and Revolver Association
10 Pheasant Lane
North Oaks MN 55127

Minnesota Weapons Collectors Association
PO Box 662
Hopkins MN 55343

Zumbro Valley Arms Collectors
PO Box 6621
Rochester MN 55901

Mississippi

Mississippi Gun Collectors Association
PO Box 16323
Hattiesburg MS 39402

Missouri

Mineral Belt Gun Collectors Association
1110 Cleveland Ave.
Monett MO 65708

Missouri Valley Arms Collectors Association
PO Box 33033
Kansas City MO 64114

Montana

Montana Arms Collectors Association
308 Riverview Dr. E.
Great Falls MT 59404

Northwest Montana Arms Collectors Association
PO Box 653
Kalispell MT 59901

Weapons Collectors Society of Montana
3100 Bancroft
Missoula MT 59801

New Hampshire

New Hampshire Arms Collectors
Route 28, PO Box 44
Windham NH 03087

New Jersey

Civil War Round Table of North New Jersey
124 Conover Lane
Red Bank NJ 07701

Jersey Shore Antique Arms Collectors
PO Box 100
Bayville NJ 08721

New Jersey Arms Collectors Club
230 Valley Rd.
Montclair NJ 07042

New York

Iroquois Arms Collectors Association
PO Box 142
Ransomville NY 14131

Long Island Antique Gun Collectors Association
35 Beach St.
Farmingdale, Long Island NY 11735

Mid-State Arms Collectors and Shooters Club
24 S. Mountain Terrace
Binghamton NY 13903

North Eastern Arms Collectors Association
PO Box 185
Amityville NY 11701

North Carolina

North Carolina Gun Collectors Association
3231-7th Street Northeast
Hickory NC 28601

Ohio

Ohio Gun Collectors Association
PO Box 24170
Cincinnati OH 45224

The Stark Gun Collectors
5666 Waynesburg Dr.
Waynesburg OH 44688

Tri-State Gun Collectors
PO Box 1201
Lima OH

Oklahoma

Indian Territory Gun Collectors Association
PO Box 4491
Tulsa OK 74159

Oregon

Oregon Arms Collectors Association
PO Box 13000
Portland OR 97213

Oregon Cartridge Collectors Association
52 Northwest 2nd
Gresham OR 97030

Williamette Valley Arms Collectors Association
PO Box 5191
Eugene OR 97405

Pennsylvania

Central Penn Antique Arms Association
978 Thistle Rd.
Elizabethtown PA 17022

Lancaster Muzzle Loading Rifle Association
779 Prospect Rd.
Columbia PA 17512

Pennsylvania Antique Arms Collectors Association
PO Box 63
Media PA 19063

Pennsylvania Antique Gun Collectors Association
28 Fulmer Ave.
Havertown PA 19083

Presque Isle Gun Collectors Association
156 East 37th St.
Erie PA 16504

South Carolina

195 Phillips Dr.
Belton SC 29627

South Carolina Shooting Association
PO Box 12658
Columbia SC 29211

South Dakota

Dakota Territory Gun Collectors Association
Castlewood SD 57223

Tennessee

Memphis Antique Weapons Association
108 Clark Place
Memphis TN 38104

Smoky Mountain Gun Collectors Association
PO Box 23225
Knoxville TN 37933

Tennessee Gun Collectors Association
3556 Pleasant Valley Rd.
Nashville TN 37204

Texas

Austin Gun Collectors Association
c/o McBride's Guns
2915 San Gabriel
Austin TX

Houston Gun Collectors Association
PO Box 741429
Houston TX 77274

Texas Cartridge Collectors Association
14738 C Perthshire Rd.
Houston TX 77079

Texas Gun Collectors Association
PO Box 253
Manvel TX 77578

Texas State Rifle Association
PO Drawer 710549
Dallas TX 75371

Virginia

Virginia Arms Collectors Association
c/o American Historical Foundation
1142 W. Grace St.
Richmond VA 23220

Virginia Arms Collectors Association
c/o NRA Headquarters
11250 Waples Mill Rd.
Fairfax VA 22030
(contact: 540 882 3543)

Washington

Washington Arms Collectors
PO Box 7335
Woodridge Lane
Waukesha WI 53188

Wisconsin

Great Lakes Arms Collectors Association
2913 Woodridge Lane
Waukesha WI 53188

Indianhead Firearms Association
RR #9 Box 186
Chippewa Falls WI 54729

Wisconsin Gun Collectors Association
PO Box 181
Sussex WI 53089

Wyoming

Wyoming Weapons Collectors
PO Box 284
Laramie WY 82070

INTERNATIONAL

Australia

Sporting Shooters Association of Australia
PO Box 2066
Kent Town, SA 5071
Australia

Canada

Canadian Historical Arms Society
PO Box 901
Edmonton, Alberta, Canada T5J 2L8

National Firearms Association
PO Box 1779
Edmonton, Alberta, Canada T5J 2PI

Tri-County Antique Arms Fair
PO Box 122
RR No. 1
North Lancaster, Ontario, Canada KOC 120

England

Arms and Armour Society
E.J.B. Greenwood
Field House
Upper Dicker
Halisham, East Sussex BN27 3PY
England

Historical Breechloading Smallarms Association
D. J. Penn M.A.
Imperial War Museum
Lambeth Road
London SE 1 6HZ
England

National Rifle Association
Bisley Camp
Brookwood, Woking
Surrey GU24 OPB
England

France

Syndicat National de l'Arquebue serie du Commerce de l'Arme Historique
B.P. No. 3
78110 Le Vesinet
France

Germany

Bund Deutscher Sportschutzen e.v. (BDS)
Borsigallee 10, 53125
Bonn 1
Germany

New Zealand

New Zealand Deerstalkers Association
Michael Watt
PO Box 6514
Wellington, New Zealand

South Africa

Historical Firearms Society of South Africa
PO Box 145
5 Newlands
Republic of South Africa

SAGA (S.A. Gunowners' Association)
PO Box 35204
Northway 4065
Republic of South Africa

Index

ABOUT THE AUTHOR

R. L. WILSON is a freelance consultant and author in the broad fields of firearms and engraving. His career began with intern positions at the Royal Armouries, H.M. Tower of London, and the Corcoran Gallery of Art, as well as at the Wadsworth Atheneum, where he was appointed Curator of Firearms at the age of twenty-three. He has served on advisory boards or as consultant on arms-related subjects to the Metropolitan Museum of Art, the U.S. Marshals Service, Colt's Mfg. Co., Inc., the Winchester Museum (now known as Cody Firearms Museum), Buffalo Bill Historical Center, the U.S. Historical Society, the U.S. Society of Arms and Armour, Tiffany & Co., and the Autry Museum of Western Heritage. He is consultant on American arms to Christie's, for whom he was active in organizing the Colt/Christie's sale of October 7, 1981, and the Metropolitan Museum of Art Arms and Armor Department's benefit auction of October 8, 1985, as well as auctions of May 1987 and January 1991, which set record prices for American firearms—four milestones in the history of arms collecting, which launched the current popularity of public firearms auctions.

Wilson was born in Minnesota, the son, nephew, and grandson of Presbyterian ministers, and studied history and art as a scholarship student at Carleton College. A resident of Connecticut, he is author of approximately thirty books and more than 200 articles on firearms and engraving subjects. Publishers of his works include Random House, Simon & Schuster, Abbeville Press, the Buffalo Bill Historical Center, the Wadsworth Atheneum, and *Audubon* magazine. He has been the subject of (or noted in) articles in a variety of newspapers and magazines, including *The New York Times*, *The Washington Post*, *The Wall Street Journal*, *M*, *The Chicago Tribune*, *Newsday*, *Business Week*, *The Houston Chronicle*, *Art & Antiques*, *Esquire*, *Robb Report*, and *Town & Country*. He is Editor Emeritus and a regular columnist of *Gun Journal* (one of the leading periodicals in the firearms field), and Official Historian of the Colt Cowboy Association and its publication, *Frontier*.

Appearing frequently on radio and television nationally and internationally, he has taken part in the following: A&E's *The Story of Guns* and *The Guns That Tamed the West*, Discovery Channel's *Gunpower*, CNN's *Business Day* and *Pinnacle*, and a two-minute profile shown in 1994/95, the milestone documentary "Gunfight USA" on PBS's *Frontline*, *Good Morning Australia*, Japan Broadcasting TV, *The Barry Gray Show* on WMCA and WOR, New York, Channel 4 in London, and BBC-TV documentaries *The Gun Industry in America* and *Son of a Gun or How Sam Colt Changed America*.

Additionally, Wilson was scriptwriter for the Sony video presentation *Colt Firearms Legends* (narrated by Mel Torme), and is president of Castle View Productions, engaged in producing *Winchester Firearms Legends* and *Millie Miglia: The Most Beautiful Race in the World* (1995).

Wilson's book *The Colt Heritage* is the only firearms-related work ever nominated for the American Book Awards (1979). *Colt: An American Legend* (the official history of Colt firearms) was hailed by author-publisher Michael Korda as "a classic . . . the most beautiful book on firearms ever published and a milestone in modern book design and production." In promotion of that title, Abbeville Press organized a two-week, seven-city author's tour, during which Wilson made more than thirty-five interview appearances on TV and radio, and with newspapers and at bookstores. Over 170,000 copies of these Colt titles are in print. *Winchester: An American Legend* appeared in June 1991 (50,000 copies first edition) and is the official history of Winchester firearms and ammunition. *The Peacemakers: Arms and Adventure in the American West* appeared in 1992, and was honored with a Wrangler Award from the National Cowboy Hall of Fame. *Colt*, *Winchester*, and *The Peacemakers* are also in Italian, French, and German editions. Still another Random House book, *Steel Canvas: The Art of American Arms* (fall 1995), is a fifth title in this unique set of firearms books (with its foreword by William R. Chaney, chairman of the board, Tiffany & Co.) and appeared in foreign-language editions in 1996. Spanish translations are planned. These titles will be joined by *Buffalo Bill's Wild West*, to be published by Random House in fall 1998, which will be accompanied by an exhibition drawn from the book, opening at the Royal Armouries Museum, Leeds, in the summer of 1999.

Wilson is a member of the Appraisers Association of America, and clients of his appraisal services have included Gene Autry, Mel Torme, and numerous other distinguished private collectors, as well as such institutions as the Autry Museum of Western Heritage, Sagamore Hill Historic Site, Theodore Roosevelt National Park, the Art Institute of Chicago (Wielgus Collection), the Buffalo Bill Museum, the National Cowboy Hall of Fame, Wadsworth Atheneum, the Texas Ranger Museum, and members of the Lilly, Ford, Mellon, Phillips, and Deering families. He was a consultant to the Wadsworth Atheneum on a lavish Colt exhibition, "Sam and Elizabeth Colt: Legend and Legacy of Colt's Empire," in 1996.

In collaboration directly with George A. Strichman, then chairman of the board of Colt Industries, Wilson organized the Colt Industries Museum Collection (1972–85), as well as Mr. Strichman's own 165-piece Colt collection, both now featured exhibits at the Autry Museum.

A keen sportsman, Wilson has been on nine African safaris, as well as game shooting in England, Scotland, France, Spain, Belgium, Australia, India, Alaska, Canada, Argentina and Mexico, and at various sites in the continental United States. An active conservationist, he is a member of the historic Camp Fire Club of America (1897) and the Hammonassett Fishing Association (founded 1888). He is also a member of a number of other firearms and conservation organizations, as well as a life member of the National Rifle Association. From 1989 to 1995 he was president of the Armor and Arms Club of New York, and he is currently an honorary director of the Texas Gun Collectors Association. He has spoken on fine guns before the Boone & Crockett Club, the Mzuri-Safari Club, the Connecticut Historical Society, the Australian Arms Collectors Society, the Museum of Fine Arts, Houston, and other groups.

With the expressed interest of the Royal Armouries, Tower of London, Wilson is currently working on a major international museum loan exhibition, "The Art of American Arms," likely to be accompanied by a book and video. He appears in and is co-executive producer of a feature-length theatrical and video film on conservation, hunting, and the African safari, entitled *In the Blood*. Still another project is an exhibition and video, "The Arms of Tiffany & Co.," in collaboration with former Tiffany & Co. archivist Janet Zapata. Additionally, he has a dozen firearms books in progress, including *Beretta: An International Legend* and *The Guns of Manhattan*.

A devoted student of automobile racing, Wilson has attended numerous Formula 1, Indianapolis, and endurance events (including the LeMans 24 Hours, the Grand Prix of Monaco, and the Indianapolis 500), has seen several museum and private automobile collections throughout Europe and North America, and has participated in such competitions as Italy's Mille Miglia (1993, '94, '95, and '97), the Tour de France (1996, '97), and the U.S. Express (known popularly as the "Cannonball"). Wilson is also a graduate of the three-day single-seater race-car course and the two-day advanced single-seater course of the Jim Russell Driving School (at Laguna Seca, near Monterey, California), and a graduate of the three-day single-seater course of the Skip Barber School (at Bridgehampton, New York). He has been researching a lavishly illustrated book on the North

American Racing Team and on the celebrated race driver and Ferrari importer Luigi Chinetti and his son, race driver and automobile designer-Ferrari importer Luigi Chinetti Jr.

"Larry Wilson's contributions to the study, collecting, and appreciation of Colt firearms and history have no parallel."—George A. Strichman, Chairman Emeritus, Colt Industries.

"R. L. Wilson has examined, handled and written about more fine and historical guns than anyone in the entire history of firearms."—Mel Torme

Books by the Author Which Can Be Ordered Directly from R. L. WILSON BOOKS

PO BOX 430, HADLYME, CONNECTICUT 06439 U.S.A.
FAX: 860 526 9514
E-MAIL: WILSONBOOK @ AOL.COM
WEB SITE: WILSONBOOKS.COM

R. L. WILSON THE OFFICIAL PRICE GUIDE TO GUN COLLECTING. The most comprehensive book ever published on gun collecting, with in-depth commentary on the entire world of arms collecting, and featuring a history of the "world's greatest hobby" and virtually everything anyone would want or need to know about this most captivating field. Over 600 illustrations, covering the entire spectrum of arms collecting, and including over 35,000 gun value figures, a listing of museums displaying firearms, selected reference books, the world of gun shows, cataloguing, buying, selling, trading, and much, much more. **$19.95.** First edition.

THE COLT ENGRAVING BOOK. This third edition from the original texts of 1974 and 1982 has been fine-tuned, and is by far the most complete and illuminating. Oblong format, part of the author's "History of American Firearms" series. Over 700 illustrations, more than two-thirds in color. 500 pages. Work in progress.

RUGER & HIS GUNS: A HISTORY OF THE MAN, THE COMPANY AND THEIR FIREARMS. The story of the Sam Colt of our time, and his dedication to firearms. Official history, profusely illustrated, and including Colts, Winchesters, Remington, S&W, fine U.S. and British singleshot rifles, double rifles, and more. Fifth in the author's oblong-format "History of American Firearms" books. 368 pages; over 2,000 illustrations, several created by Peter Beard, and photographed by Allan Brown. **$65.00.** *Author's own numbered limited edition of 500 copies* **$85.00**

COLT, AN AMERICAN LEGEND. Over 400 color plates, over 110 B&W. Official history of Colt firearms with detailed serial-number tables. All-time best-selling book on Colt firearms. Standard edition. **$40.00.** *Numbered limited edition of 500 copies* **$65.00**

STEEL CANVAS: THE ART OF AMERICAN ARMS. For the first time, a comprehensive, panoramic tribute to fine American arms, their European predecessors and contemporary arms of the finest quality. Featured are leading gunmakers from the Kentucky rifle to Colt, Winchester, Remington, Sharps, Marlin, Deringer and many, many more. This extraordinary compilation of fine guns from the 1700s to modern times includes richly decorated European arms as well. Over 325 color plates and 165 B&W. Random House. 1995. **$65.00.** *Special limited edition of 500 copies, numbered and signed by the author.* **$85.00**

THE PEACEMAKERS: ARMS AND ADVENTURE IN THE AMERICAN WEST. A unique pictorial celebration of the West, lavishly illustrated and unsurpassed in its authenticity: a collector's item for anyone interested in America's colorful past. From the Lewis & Clark Expedition to today's Western films and videos, the arms and adventurers who made the Colt, the Winchester, and many other marquees into American gun legends. Over 325 color plates, and over 225 B&W. Standard reference. Random House, 1992. **$65.00.** *Special limited edition of 500 copies, numbered and signed by the author* **$85.00**

THE BOOK OF COLT FIREARMS. 1993 re-edition of the 1971 work, considered the standard reference in the Colt field. Improvements and changes made over the original work, including introduction detailing how the book was created. **$150.00.** *Special limited edition of 500 copies, numbered and signed by the author* **$175.00**

COLT PISTOLS, R. E. Hable & R. L. Wilson. Lavish presentation of the Hable Collection of Colt firearms. This is the most elaborate book on Colt handguns ever published, and covers production from the 1830s to the late 1970s. Profuse color illus., limited edition, with slipcase. Out of print. **$150.00**

COLT'S DATES OF MANUFACTURE 1836-1978. Detailed serial numbers by year. Tables for all models of Colt handguns and long arms. **$10.00**

L.D. NIMSCHKE: FIREARMS ENGRAVER. Large format. Unique pictorial record of engraving impressions and gun photographs revealing the work of one of America's foremost arms engravers; active 1850–1904. Numerous prints and photographs of deluxe guns of Lt. Col. George Armstrong Custer, cowboys and ranchers, kings and queens, and more. 2nd edition. **$100.00**

THE RUSSIAN COLTS, Dr. Leonid Tarassuk and R. L. Wilson. Published on occasion of a loan exhibition of presentation Colt revolvers by the Hermitage Museum, St. Petersburg, to the Metropolitan Museum of Art. With details on all other known gold-inlaid percussion Colts. Profusely illustrated. 32 pages. **$25.00**

WINCHESTER: AN AMERICAN LEGEND. Official history of Winchester arms and ammunition, issued in conjunction with Winchester's 125th anniversary. Companion book to **COLT: AN AMERICAN LEGEND.** Featuring color photography by Allan Brown. Detailed appendix tables. Random House, 1991. Over 300 color plates, over 160 B&W. *Special limited edition of 500 copies, numbered and signed by the author* **$85.00.** Standard edition **$65.00**

WINCHESTER ENGRAVING. Only book devoted to Winchester arms embellishment, from the Jennings, Volcanic and Henry on up to modern times. Over 500 pages, 100 color plates and 700 B&W. **$115.00**

WINCHESTER: THE GOLDEN AGE OF AMERICAN GUNMAKING AND THE WINCHESTER 1 OF 1000, R. L. Wilson. Published by the Winchester Museum. Lavishly illus., with considerable text on the keen interest of famed hunters and shooters, e.g., Buffalo Bill Cody and George A. Custer in fine Colt, Winchester and other firearms, c. 1850–1900. *Deluxe numbered edition only available* **$125.00**

THE DERINGER IN AMERICA, Vol. 1 (Percussion period), L. D. Eberhart & R. L. Wilson. Standard reference on the derringer, c. 1830–1870, with exhaustive detail on all known makers. 28 color plates and over 400 B&W plates. 8½" × 11" format. **$65.00.** *Serial numbered edition, signed and limited to 500 copies* **$95.00**

DERINGER IN AMERICA, Vol. 2 (Cartridge period), L. D. Eberhart & R. L. Wilson. Standard reference on the derringer, c. 1860–early 20th century. Covers over 75 makers of cartridge pistols, as well as an updating of percussion derringers missed in volume 1. Like vol. 1, presents voluminous information not found in any other book. Same 8½" × 11" format, special color section and over 500 B&W illus. Colt, Remington, Sharps, and much, much more. **$65.00.** *Serial numbered edition, signed and limited to 500 copies* **$95.00**

THE COLT HERITAGE poster with cover and eight dramatic color shots from **THE COLT HERITAGE** book, published in 1979. Rare memento of classic Colt book. **$15.00**

THEODORE ROOSEVELT OUTDOORSMAN. 1994 edition. TR as hunter, conservationist and arms collector. Foreword by son Archibald and preface by great-grandson Tweed. Details over 50 Winchesters, Colts and other guns owned by the president. Over 175 B&W illus. and 350 pages. Inspiring example of the world's foremost conservationist/sportsman-hunter. **$85.00**

PATERSON COLT PISTOL VARIATIONS, P. R. Phillips & R. L. Wilson. Only publication on the rarest of all Colt arms. Over 100 B&W and color illus., with detailed text. 232 pp. 8 1/2" × 11". **$45.00**

VIDEOS:

SON OF A GUN or How Sam Colt Changed America, Hour-long video by BBC-TV, presenting history of Colonel Colt and the influence of Colt firearms on history. Appearances by Mel Torme, Greg Martin and R. L. Wilson. **$30.00**

COLT FIREARMS LEGENDS, narrated by Mel Torme, script by R. L. Wilson. Hour-long video done as companion to **SON OF A GUN.** Shows over $25,000,000 worth of fine and rare Colt firearms. Rated best collector-oriented gun video done to date. **$30.00**

THE GUNS THAT TAMED THE WEST, A&E production from *The Real West*, narrated by Kenny Rogers. Program inspired by ***The Peacemakers*** book, and considered the best video on guns of the West produced to date. **$30.00**

IN THE BLOOD. Feature film by the director of *Pumping Iron.* Starring Robin Hurt, Tyssen Butler, President Theodore Roosevelt, R. L. Wilson. Gripping tale of hunter and hunted. Documents two African safaris: the first led by President Roosevelt in 1909, the second by his grandson nearly 80 years later. Features TR's Holland & Holland rifle. Intense, powerful, provocative, breathtaking; and proof of the key role of hunting in the conservation of wildlife. **$39.95**

NOTE: The author has a total of more than 20 books in various stages of completion. **THE ARMS OF TIFFANY, BUFFALO BILL'S WILD WEST** and **THE GUNS OF MANHATTAN** are but three of the titles. He is collecting photographs and information on arms subjects continually and appreciates hearing from collectors and other sources for his ever-expanding pictorial archives on arms and armor.

NOTE: Books, articles, or videos ordered from this list will be sent via UPS or parcel post insured. Please add $4 per title for postage and handling in the U.S. Please add $10 per title for international orders. Check or money order, or Mastercard/Visa. Should you wish books by RLW inscribed, please so indicate on order.